THE BLUE GUIDES

Albania
Austria
Belgium and Luxembourg
China
Cyprus
Czechoslovakia
Denmark
Egypt

FRANCE
France
Paris and Versailles
Burgundy
Loire Valley
Midi-Pyrénées
Normandy
South West France
Corsica

GERMANY
Berlin and Eastern Germany
Western Germany

GREECE
Greece
Athens and environs
Crete

HOLLAND
Holland
Amsterdam

Hungary
Ireland

ITALY
Northern Italy
Southern Italy
Florence
Rome and environs
Venice
Tuscany
Umbria
Sicily

Malta and Gozo
Mexico
Morocco
Moscow and Leningrad
Portugal

SPAIN
Spain
Barcelona
Madrid

Sweden
Switzerland

TURKEY
Turkey
Istanbul

UK
England
Scotland
Wales
London
Museums and Galleries
  of London
Oxford and Cambridge
Country Houses of England
Gardens of England
Literary Britain and Ireland
Victorian Architecture in
  Britain
Churches and Chapels
  of Northern England
Churches and Chapels
  of Southern England
Channel Islands

USA
New York
Boston and Cambridge

Head of Antiochus I at Nemrut Dağı, Adıyaman

The publishers and the author welcome comments, suggestions and corrections for the next edition of Blue Guide Turkey. Writers of the most informative letters will be awarded a free Blue Guide of their choice.

BLUE GUIDE

Turkey

Bernard Mc Donagh

Atlas, maps and plans by John Flower

A&C Black
London

WW Norton
New York

Second edition 1995
First edition published as Blue Guide Turkey:
the Aegean and Mediterranean Coasts, 1989

Published by A & C Black (Publishers) Ltd
35 Bedford Row, London WC1R 4JH

A CIP catalogue record of this book is available from the British Library.

ISBN   0–7136–3829–X

Published in the United States of America by
WW Norton and Company, Inc
500 Fifth Avenue, New York, NY 10110

Published simultaneously in Canada by
Penguin Books Canada Limited
10 Alcorn Avenue, Toronto, Ontario M4V 3BE

ISBN   0–393–31195–3   USA

The author and the publishers have done their best to ensure the accuracy of all the
information in Blue Guide Turkey; however, they can accept no responsibility for any
loss, injury or inconvenience sustained by any traveller as a result of information or
advice contained in the guide.

Photographs by the author.

Lecturer, author, broadcaster, and fomer civil servant, **Bernard Mc Donagh** has two
consuming passions—travelling and writing. His official duties took him to Kinshasa
where he was awarded the Order of Zaire, to Hamburg and Stuttgart where he was
British Consul, and to Brussels where he represented the UK on several EC committees.
In addition to writing the first and second editions of Blue Guide Turkey, he is the
author of Blue Guide Belgium and Luxembourg and a book for children, Turkish
Village. The first edition of Blue Guide Turkey was awarded the Thomas Cook Prize
for the best guidebook in the English language in 1990. In 1992 he was given an award
by the Turkish Government for his work in making Turkey better known and appreciated abroad. He is currently working on a new edition of Blue Guide Cyprus and on
an archaeological guide to Tunisia.

Dr M. Naim Turfan teaches Politics at the School of Oriental and African Studies,
University of London.

Printed by Bath Press

PREFACE

This new edition of the Blue Guide covers the whole of Turkey. All of the cities, principal towns, archaeological and historical sites between Edirne in the west and Kars in the east are described in detail. In many cases the descriptions are complemented by specially drawn site plans and recent photographs. There are town plans, regional maps and an atlas section covering the whole country. Background information includes a chronology of Turkish history, and glossaries of architectural terms and mythological figures and of those Turkish words and phrases which visitors are most likely to encounter. There is a large section of practical information. This covers topics as diverse as travelling in Turkey, Turkish food and drink, customs and behaviour. The list of some of the books which I consulted while writing the Blue Guide may help readers to investigate further topics raised in the text. There is a historical introduction to Turkey by Dr M. Naim Turkey.

No guide book of this size and complexity could have been written without a great deal of help, advice and informed comment. The kindness of some of the friends who have helped me is acknowledged below, but there are many others, some who wish to remain anonymous or were *mes amis du voyage*.

Turkey is a country of great beauty, infinite variety and, sometimes, startling contrasts. Each time I start out from İstanbul, 'Anatolia takes me by the throat'! Every journey which I make there is preceded by a period of feverish excitement. What will the next turn in the road reveal? Turkey is a palimpsest. Examine it carefully and you will find traces of the many peoples who have lived within its borders. It has been my good fortune to see and study the monuments which they have left to posterity. At Ephesus, Nemrut Dağı, Aspendus, Troy, Assos, Van, Konya, Ani, Sivas, Perge, Bursa and other ancient cities and sites the buildings, statuary, carvings, frescoes and mosaics are potent reminders of past glories. I have had the good luck to travel in a land 'where dwell many diverse folks... of diverse manners and laws' and to have made a number of them my friends. I hope readers of this Blue Guide will find it a satisfactory *vade mecum*, one that will help them to enjoy their visits to Turkey as much as I have enjoyed mine. *İyi yolculuklar*.

London, January 1995   **Bernard Mc Donagh**

This book is for John, Elizabeth and Anthony Mc Donagh

Acknowledgements

Grateful thanks to Abdülkadir Ateş, former Turkish Minister for Tourism, Candemir Önhon, Turkish Ambassador in London, and Lady Daunt for their help and encouragement; to Mustafa Türkmen, Director of the Turkish Tourist Office in London, and to his colleagues, especially Anna-Maria Allmark, Simru Önhon, Mina Belcher, Hüseyin Gökşan and Döne Çay, who always had time to answer my questions; to Zehra Sulupınar and her staff at the Ministry for Tourism in Ankara who helped me to organise my itineraries; to Ahmet Ersoy, former Press Counsellor, Turkish Embassy,

London, who was generous with his advice and time; to the directors and staffs of the regional Tourist Information Offices in Turkey who facilitated my visits to the ancient sites and places of interest in their areas; to my friends at the British Institute of Archaeology at Ankara who were unstinting in their advice, assistance and hospitality; to Stephen Mitchell, who read the section on Pisidia and made valuable comments on the text; to Ender Varınlıoğlu for recent information on Stratoniceia; to Caroline Russell Lawrence, Riet van Bremen, Dominique Collon, Edip Özgür, Pınar Aydemir and Tolga Kirkoyun, who provided information about a number of sites; to the many friends, especially Robert Moore, Dennis and Ann Franklin, Ralph Broughton, Mike Grisdale and Marjorie Grimes, who sustained and encouraged me during the long months of writing; to Gemma Davies, my editor, who brought order to a lengthy and complicated manuscript; to John Flower who produced the excellent maps and site plans that illuminate the text; to John Desmond who solved my computer problems; and to the staffs of the British Library, the London Library, the Joint Library of the Hellenic and Roman Societies, and Banstead Library for producing many of the books I needed when I needed them. Finally, I would like to thank my many friends in Turkey. This book is a small expression of my gratitude for the welcome and hospitality which they extended to me over the years and a memoir of the many pleasant hours which we spent together.

How to use the Guide

The way this guide is organised will be familiar to readers of previous editions or other Blue Guides. It divides Turkey into routes which are journeys between major points on the map. These have been devised so that they can be followed by public transport as well as by car. The route system has the merit of grouping places which are close to each other on the map close to each other on the page. The comprehensive index encourages readers to follow their own plan. Bold type is used to indicate points of interest and bold caps for places of particular significance. The smaller type is used for historical background, detours off the beaten track and for practical information sections at the beginning of town descriptions.

Abbreviations
In addition to generally accepted and self-explanatory abbreviations, the following appear in the guide:

Bulv. *Bulvar* (Boulevard)
c *circa* (about, concerning a date)
C Century
Cad. *Cadde* (*Caddesi* in certain circumstances for grammatical purposes) (road in built up area, street)
m metres
Meyd. *Meydan* (Square)
Rte Route
Sok. *Sokak* (Street)

Note on Spelling
Throughout the main text Greek proper nouns and place names are written, as a rule, in the familiar English or Latin forms, e.g. Cnidus rather than Knidos, Dionysus rather than Dionysos, odeum rather than odeion.

CONTENTS

Maps and Plans

Map of Turkey at the back of the book

Turkey: the Building of a Modern State

What haven't we done for this country!
Some of us died;
Some of us gave speeches.
Orhan Veli Kanık, *Vatan İçin*.

by **M. NAİM TURFAN**

Prologue

To anyone visiting Turkey attributes of unity-in-diversity immediately become apparent. One could argue that this stems from the amalgamation of drastically varying physical geography with an almost too profuse history. The resulting overall affinity is more with Asia and less with Europe; even the territory of present-day Turkey strengthens this assertion in that it combines a portion of European Thrace with the whole of Asian Anatolia. The name Turkey (since the 12C Turkia, Turquia or Turchia) evokes a political entity embodying an unbroken chain of past and present, corporeal and spiritual, man and his culture. Yet while expressing universal recognition of the long dominance of the Turks there, it does not preclude other peoples' as well as their own sense of permanence nor lasting contribution to the many distinct civilisations in that homeland—reaching back for the last known 9000 years*. The permanency has consequently been imbued with an achieved social order, a whole way of life, so that each civilisation has left its trace upon the terrain of Turkey; each has contributed to developments in world history in terms of highly-evolved urban order and economy. Turkey is thus the setting for many of those momentous occasions in human history that have shaped our times and coloured our perceptions.

It is true that history is one field of study in which one cannot begin at the beginning. But it is equally true that one can begin within the confines of a land which has had physical reality and significance in every given age. For the mainspring of all historical knowledge is awareness that the past was once a living reality. And we, now, are certainly aware that the huge 13-hectare Neolithic settlement of Çatalhöyük near Konya, dating from the 7th millennium BC, provided one of the earliest patterns of urbanisation. With its elaborate wall-paintings, its sophisticated jewellery and weapons, its extensive agriculture and stock-breeding and its identification of property-ownership by use of seals, Çatalhöyük is striking as representing the first of a sequence of at least nine major civilisations.

Between 2000 and 1200 BC, the civilisation of the incoming Hittites, as they came to be known, was caught up in the dominant culture of the indigenous peoples—Hattis, Hurrians and Luwians—and assumed in time a character and significance of its own. Moreover, the Hittite civilisation directly affected its own successors—the late Hittite principalities, Urartians, Hellenes and Etruscans. After all, since civilisations are the creation of societies not races, their characters are passed on by social traditions not blood ties; so, for example, the ancient Greek mythology and religion in one direction, no less than Urartian in the other, show marked Hittite influence. Then, the peoples of Turkey did not form a single society. There were numerous local societies with different material, spiritual and linguistic conventions; each built up its own tradition, preserved and then trans-

*Covered in my *Note on the Anatolian Civilisations*, pp 13–107, Blue Guide Turkey: the Aegean and Mediterranean Coasts, 1st edition, 1989.

mitted it. Thus, at the time of the Hittite imperium, when over 20 languages (inflective or agglutinative) were in use, intercourse among peoples had already begun to draw them into a larger human mosaic. This produced a social pattern, both geographically and historically, in which traditions were blended, discoveries and inventions passed on and, most important, customs and habits diffused. For instance, myths and epics borrowed by the Hittites from outside, particularly Babylon, travelled extensively through other cultures of the ancient world, from the Sumerian of the fourth and third millennia BC in Mesopotamia as far in time and space as the Hellenistic period (323–27 BC) of western Turkey and the Aegean. The centrality of the latter to epic and myth is witnessed in Homer's 'Iliad' and 'Odyssey' based around Troy (Hisarlık) and the return of Odysseus after the Trojan War, together with the fabled Midas (725–696? BC) and Croesus (560–547/6 BC), kings of Phrygia and Lydia.

And the passage of time was marked by the development of language into something far more complex than a mere vehicle for the transmission of tradition and experience. Its utilisation for the expression of ideas and concepts saw the emergence of western Turkey by the 6C BC as the home also of philosophy. Thales, Anaximander and Anaximenes, all natives of Miletus (Balat), established the area as the cultural heart of the world's landscape. The mid-4C BC heralded the thrust of the accumulated civilisation of the classical period throughout the surrounding regions of the so-called Near East and the Mediterranean, until blocked by the rise of Rome some two centuries later. For the eastward conquest of Alexander of Macedon (336–323 BC) prompted the mutual accommodation of the cultures of Asia and Europe, and the development of the earliest urban centres of the Hellenistic age—the coastal cities of Pergamum (Bergama), Ephesus (Selçuk), Priene (Güllübahçe), Miletus and Didyma (Yenihisar). The cultural equals of Rome in its heyday, these cities with their flourishing art had a direct and important influence on the civilisation of the Roman Empire and no less on its Eastern Roman successor right up to the Byzantine zenith in the 10C AD.

Subsequently, as the region came to be dominated by the Selçuks in the 11C, their particular mastery in, for example, the building of *medreses* (Islamic institutes of higher education), hospitals, observatories, bridges and *kervansarays* (caravansarais)—as well as in carpet-weaving and other crafts—made its own distinctive contribution. Then, from the 13–20C, one of the world's most durable imperial dynasties, the Ottoman, impressed its own seal on the culture of Turkey and created a vast territorial empire, based on the strength and integrity of this cultural resource-base.

And so we come to modern Turkey, a society moulded through the ages by a diversity of peoples, cultures and influences into a unique form—supplemented, preserved and handed on by its custodians of the last millennium, the western Muslim Turks.

History

I

The Ottoman period in the history of Turkey closed effectively with the ending of the First World War. The Central Powers, to which the Empire had attached its last hopes of political survival, crumbled in late 1918. The Ottoman Empire was forced to sign an armistice of surrender; an Allied Armada with discretionary powers formally occupied İstanbul, the capital, and threw the Turks into a temper of despair. Not even the earlier successes against the Entente, notably the epic defence of Gallipoli (Gelibolu), could compensate for the magnitude of defeat. Worse still, recovery from this latest disaster since the Ottoman retreat from the gates of Vienna in 1683 seemed unlikely because it completed a long disintegration. Since the days when the Empire had overawed its rivals in Europe, Ottoman rulers had seen a progressive deterioration in most aspects of state and society. The Empire had failed to prevent its Christian subjects from breaking off into independent states under the auspices of the powers of Christendom. The most recent loss, of the Arab provinces, to Britain and France had left only the Anatolian heartland and an enclave in Thrace. It appeared to most contemporaries that this battered and broken remnant of a world empire could only survive as the protectorate of some European power—those powers who did not even bother to respect the terms of the October 1918 Armistice; some demoralised Turkish intellectuals went so far as to support the idea of an American mandate.

Anatolia had become, by most criteria, with Arabia the most 'backward' part of the Empire. The bulk of the population, unlike its religious minorities, consisted of illiterate peasants and provincial notables with, at the centre, an élite of men educated on the western European model—itself a palliative measure to curb the all too evident decline of the Empire. The efforts of such men at reform and reconstruction— including, most recently, the Young Turks—seemed to many to have provoked final ruin.

This background is important because it helps to explain the presumptuous attitude of the victors in the War, the Allied Powers. The Ottoman Empire appeared to them irretrievably decadent, so that the last thing any thinking observer expected was a Turkish revival. Allied statesmen were wary of sympathy towards the Turks among their own, oppressed, Muslim subjects and anxious lest the new vogue, communism, might spread to the disillusioned Turkey; but that the Turks would attempt what the defeated Germans had not—that is, to resist Allied demands—was entirely unexpected. Moreover, disunity in Anatolia made Allied statesmen hopeful of utilising some of the populace towards the partition of what little territories remained: Greek subjects dreamed of uniting with Greece, Armenians had their own separatist aims, even the loyalty of some Muslim Kurdish chiefs was in doubt. The Turks thus had to face the long-meditated territorial designs of western Europe, to culminate in the imposition by the Paris Peace Conference of the Treaty of Sèvres in August 1920: Turkey was to be divested of its wealthiest and most productive regions, and the Turkish majority populations in them, and reduced to a portion of central Anatolia attached to a demilitarised coastal zone containing a trapped and helpless İstanbul. In effect, a combination of motives brought into play from the date of the Armistice onward—chiefly by means of military occupation by British, French and Italian troops directly or by their Greek and Armenian proxies—was intended to demolish Turkey and subdue the bulk of its Turkish people.

Meanwhile, the Sultan-Caliph and successive Imperial Governments in İstanbul had seemed willing, even eager, to cooperate with the occupying authorities—sometimes as a means of attacking existing political opponents, parties and individuals alike—and efficiently put into effect the disarming of the Ottoman armed forces. There were no mutinies as had occurred in Germany and elsewhere but, partly influenced by Allied propaganda, large-scale desertions were taking place, amounting almost to a silent mutiny. And the population at large, desolated by an almost continuous war effort since at least the beginning of the Balkan War in 1912, was profoundly depressed, bewildered and disaffected. But, as the harshness of the occupation bit deeper, there appeared across the hinterland signs of a more violent resistance by the 'Defence of Rights' associations than their earlier protests and regional self-help networks against the intended partition of the homeland amongst former subject peoples; spontaneous if haphazard outbreaks by local National Forces occurred, notably against the French and Armenians in the south and east, the Greeks in the north and west and the British all over but especially in and around the capital. The immediate effect was to add to the breakdown of order and rise in general banditry as armed deserters often joined forces with these guerrilla armies, rendering the uprisings disorganised, uncontrolled and liable to alienate the local population by their casual brutality. And with the emergence of counter-guerrilla groups, organised by the İstanbul Governments and financed by the Allies as destabilising agents, a situation akin to civil war ensued in which the Nationalists were denounced as 'traitors to Islam' and 'irreligious Bolsheviks'.

The event required to initiate the drawing-in of a regular, nationalist armed force—clearly necessary if any large-scale, coherent and genuinely popular resistance were to be established, let alone succeed—took place in May 1919. The İstanbul Government, at the behest of the occupying authorities, was seeking to quell the unrest which had reached disturbing proportions in parts of the north and east by the appointment of an emissary with wide-ranging powers to appraise the situation and take appropriate action. The man chosen was an Ottoman officer, one of the most distinguished commanders produced by the War, Brigadier-General Mustafa Kemal (Atatürk) *Paşa* (1881–1938)—known for his opposition to Turkey's untimely entry as a German ally and his lack of accord with those who had instigated it. And the British authorities in İstanbul, supposing that this implied an anti-German and therefore pro-British stance, approved his appointment as Inspector-General of the 9th Army.

Mustafa Kemal's covert aim, however—no doubt with the connivance of some Government officials—was, once away from the frustrating and dangerous constrictions of the capital, to coordinate and organise Turkish defence. In fact, he planned a national movement which would establish a new, independent, Turkish state, even though limited roughly to Anatolia and eastern Thrace. With his reputation as a brilliant, successful and popular commander combined, initially at least, with his present authority, Mustafa Kemal was perhaps the only man with the prestige and ability to transform the burgeoning resistance movements into a national movement. But the final impetus was provided by the decision of the Supreme Allied Council, in their internal bickering over the spoils, to authorise the occupation of İzmir and its environs by, of all people, a 'despised subject race'—the Greeks—towards planting what the British hoped would be a client state in the eastern Mediterranean. It so happened that the Greek forces landed on 15 May 1919, the day before Mustafa Kemal left İstanbul, and rapidly initiated a particularly vicious and destructive eastward and northward invasion which shocked the still largely numbed populace into reaction. Thus, the national movement became an ever more acceptable counterpoise to the İstanbul Governments as the latter collaborated, naively, with the occupying Allies against the Nationalists, leaving themselves vulnerable to portrayal as being imprisoned within an occupied seat of government.

The legitimacy of the armed resistance was in due course provided by a revolutionary Assembly sitting in Ankara from April 1920, after Parliament had prorogued itself in protest at the further occupation of İstanbul by the Allies and mass arrests of Nationalist sympathisers, including many Deputies. The Grand National Assembly, with its broad-based representation, thus formed a focal point for more and more adherents to the cause of national independence. And such a tendency was particularly accentuated by this most recent, high-handed ostentation of, mainly, the British with their intent to intimidate not only Turkish but also colonial nationalists. Yet intrinsic Allied territorial rivalries and disagreements, at first controlled, became a serious problem as the Nationalists, though hard-pressed financially, showed themselves to be a formidable force—militarily, diplomatically and through attracting popular allegiance. The long and bitter war on various fronts continued for over two more years of indescribable hardship before Britain was reduced, after the decisive expulsion of the Greeks in September 1922, to seeking a settlement by negotiation; the French and Italians had long recognised the likely futility of their ambitions, made their own arrangements with the fledgling Ankara Government and withdrawn their troops. Against all odds, the country which had in 1918 seemed to be dying, if not already dead, defied the world's most powerful states in its National Struggle and, too, won almost everything it claimed at the negotiating table.

II

The Treaty of Lausanne (July 1923), the only treaty negotiated on equal terms between the participants in the First World War, ratified the Turkish victory over the Allies and recognised the independent state of Turkey. Yet the country faced immense problems.

The trauma which loss of Empire might have produced was swept away by the exhilaration of victory. Nevertheless, victory involved a sharp break with the past—a break that meant far more than did, for example, the loss of its colonial empire for the British. While British overseas expansions were additions to a long-existing state from which they could be relinquished without serious internal political repercussions, in Ottoman Turkey the empire was the state; not only had every institution been geared to imperial needs but the Turks' world-view was based on their self-awareness as a ruling race at least as far back as their Central Asian Göktürk Empire of the 6–9C. The Ottoman Empire had been in retreat for over two centuries, with the loss of major provinces in Europe, Africa and Arabia. And these losses allowed the new Turkey to escape the complications of an extensive multi-ethnic and multi-religious state that had so beset the Empire during its decline. Turkey did inherit, however, almost all the other problems that had contributed to the wrecking of that Empire. The inherent poverty had been rendered worse, not only by Allied occupations and invasions and local uprisings but also by the conscription and further conscription of every able-bodied man into the forces for the last decade or more that the Ottomans had been fighting around the Empire. The country had officers and bureaucrats in plenty but a dearth of businessmen, doctors, teachers, engineers, even agricultural labourers. Imperial institutions, even where their activities were suited to modern conditions, had declined from their original efficiency. If the state were to endure, still more if it were to provide tolerable conditions, it would have to be reconstructed from its foundations. So much was plain. What was not so plain was what those foundations were to be. The choice lay mainly in the hands of the now Field-Marshal Mustafa Kemal *Paşa*, although neither his supporters nor his opponents may have realised it at the time.

After the victory, Mustafa Kemal's ability to impose his own ideas was facilitated by his critics' lack of any definite programme. His was a vision of social order fashioned out of long reflection on the disorder he lived through. He knew what was; he deduced what ought to be. And to the people, Mustafa Kemal was the unequivocal hero, as is known from reports of his reception wherever he visited and from the folk poems of travelling minstrels. His hold on popular imagination as well as his grip on the administration increased as time passed and his domination meant that the national revolution had both the inspiration and the limitation of a single personality. His acts sprang, contrary to prevalent belief, from a doctrine of policy; they were not merely the response of a military genius to the challenge of political events. So Atatürk the soldier-turned-statesman, long before his retirement from the army in 1927, began to build the state as a Republic for which he aimed to create, especially through education, an appropriate citizenry with its own bourgeoisie.

Atatürk introduced no wholly novel ideas; the originality of his political thinking lay rather in the interpretation of familiar concepts to form a viable method of tackling an actual situation. He sought to establish an inherently capitalist nation-state based upon the principle of popular sovereignty, whose moral substance would be a conscious synthesis of native and universal elements. His vision of social order assumed a modern state inclining toward social democracy in which ideas that had taken root in Reformation Europe would be grafted on to the liberated Turkey through the complementary concepts of contemporaneity and nationalism.

He considered contemporaneity to derive from the rationalist essence of civilisation, contemporary civilisation being equivalent to but not identical with civilisation in western Europe. And while the acquisition of contemporary civilisation has long been called 'Westernisation' by wishful thinkers in the 'West' and ill-informed supporters and critics alike of Atatürk in Turkey, it was not so named nor regarded by its progenitor. Rather, it was inspired by the desire not to ape the so-called 'West' (itself at best a conceptually nebulous term) but to appropriate to the Turks the western European perception, since the Enlightenment, of reason as the ultimate authority in society. Despite, however, his awareness of the distinction between the two concepts, Atatürk never wholly succeeded in clarifying that distinction, at times casually conflating the terms himself. Succeeding generations of Turks have continued, therefore, to treat contemporaneity as identical with the 'West'—although, through disappointment and disillusionment with the 'Western' behaviour and attitude, use of 'Westernisation' to mean 'contemporanisation' seems now to have been abandoned. Yet generally the concept misformation still occasions even opponents of the 'West' to fall into the trap of attacking their adversary by using that adversary's own term.

Central to the whole idea of contemporaneity was that of the dynamism, from age to age, of world civilisation in which every nation might participate and no peoples were debarred even if they had declined from past achievements. Indeed, Atatürk acknowledged the major contribution of medieval Islamic civilisation, as the contemporary civilisation of a previous age, towards the construction of the modern form, centred this time in western Europe; and the notion of the unity of civilisation, to which he constantly referred in his speeches, involved recognition of the multiplicity of its origins. He thus linked civilisation with the idea of progress as technological development and economic growth compounded with continuous moral improvement. Towards this, Atatürk was determined to cultivate the principle of rational enquiry in the society he sought to mould. This he thought would open the path towards gaining individual self-awareness and thence national unity.

Starting from this premiss, Atatürk's own 'idealist' social philosophy emphasised mentality as the determining force in history. It was on this ground that he held the current state of the Islamic world to be lamentable; over the centuries Muslims' gradual retreat from rationalism to blind acquiescence in theology had rendered them defenceless and submissive in all aspects of society. The turning towards western Europe that contemporaneity necessitated was thus influenced by a consideration of the historical problem of why Islam, once the inspiration of a world civilisation, had allowed the Muslim world to fall so far behind Christendom, and why in particular the Ottoman Empire, which up to the 16C had appeared so superior to its rival European states, had failed to respond to the challenge posed by intellectual and technical developments of the Renaissance and Reformation in some of them. Atatürk blamed, *inter alia*, the ignorance and, more importantly, contempt first promoted then enforced by the Ottoman religious hierarchy. His low esteem for Muslim intellectual history in recent centuries strengthened his conviction that the weight of rigid orthodoxy must be lifted from Turkish society not merely for the sake of the people but for that of Islam itself. For he considered that Islam needed cleansing of its irrational and inflexible accretions so as to recover its essence as a belief in which knowledge preponderates and according to which man seeks the divine through his intellect not, as in Christianity, by making a blind leap of faith. He therefore envisaged a contemporary secular society wherein the existence of Islam depended upon the voluntary adherence of the individual Muslim—a state for Muslims rather than a Muslim state. The mental emancipation of the Turks so achieved was vital for the secularising institutional reforms he planned.

The process of adjusting conditions to the requirements of contemporaneity served admirably to separate Turkey from its Ottoman past. But the separation itself might undermine the bonds holding society together. In the Ottoman Empire loyalty had focused on the Sultan-Caliph, for Muslims the Shadow of God on Earth and for non-Muslims the personification of the state whose tolerance protected them and preserved their faiths. For the Muslim masses any sentiment of nationalism had been so intermingled with allegiance to Islam as to be long submerged. Now the struggle to establish the new state and the Sultan's antagonism towards it meant that for most of those involved in the National Struggle, loyalty to country had already begun to supersede loyalty to Sultan-Caliph, opening the way for Atatürk to elicit a Turkish nationalism almost mystical in its intensity. The creed expounded by Atatürk was a kind of patriotism, the will to maintain and defend what is one's own and cherished. In this sense, nationalism would be the rediscovery and reassertion by Turkey's Turks of their Turkishness. For this, Atatürk postulated a nationhood founded upon the prerequisites of common polity, vocabulary, territory, ancestry, history and morality, the sum of which exactly fitted the Turks. Yet the exclusivity of this definition for general use moved him to concede that any citizen was a Turk who considered himself such and who shared a distinctively Turkish outlook 'without distinction of, or reference to, race or religion'—a definition enshrined in the Republic's 1924 Constitution.

Since the establishment of a unitary state was deemed to conform with the tradition of centralism, and since this involved constitutional admittance of the unrestricted powers of central government, it is axiomatic that assimilation through absorption of those who might consider themselves non-Turks, such as some Kurds, was stressed. Educational and other policies aimed at ethnic coherence in terms more of culture than biology—which, in any case, was largely negated by at least a millennium of intermixing. The positive side of assimilation has been the absence of discrimination since the foundation of Turkey, as in the Ottoman and indeed the Anatolian Selçuk states. For example, there have normally been Kurdish personnel up to the highest level of state administration—generals, ambassadors and senior judges, to include only the three key political institutions of state. The cost of assimilation, however, has been the non-recognition of separate legal identity. The more appropriate choice for an established democracy might have been to define, say, the Kurds as a minority and then integrate them. Yet recognition of minorities and their, often cosmetic, integration in democracies has everywhere involved the corollary of discrimination, whether overtly or covertly; only those individuals who effectively discard their minority affiliation and join the majority will hope to enter the ranks of the ruling élite. Turkey was, for long, no democracy; moreover, in order to pursue a coordinated, centralised attack on the problems facing the country, a homogeneous nation within a nation-state was judged essential, at the cost of not recognising any Muslim minority. The term 'minority' has only been used in Turkey in official connection with non-Muslims. That said, the increasingly virulent assertion in recent years, through rural and urban terrorism, of a separatist Kurdish identity has surely nullified the potential for assimilation; it will almost certainly underpin a new policy of integration with, inevitably, the closing of positions in the political institutions of state to adherents of the Kurdish cause. And the Kurds will further be undermined by acting as pawns in the international power-games of the new world 'disorder'.

To recap, Atatürk's clear perception of nationhood and the place of the nation within its contemporary civilisation led him to the idea of the complementary relationship between contemporaneity and nationalism, in the sense of unity-in-diversity. Despite the break with the past required by contemporaneity, in all revolutions some continuity must be preserved, and openly so, lest the concealed continuity which no revolutionary effort can dissolve foster the worst attributes of the past. Nationalism would serve as the counterbalance, providing a visible continuity. The application of these two concepts formed the basis of Atatürk's entire, and drastic, reform programme and explain much of his policy. For with his belief in the efficacy of psychological change and the power of ideas, it was Atatürk's *dirigiste* conviction that without first changing the individual true development of society would be impossible.

III

The secularisation of the state, involving the question of the form of government, had to precede the proposed secularisation of society. The country was legally, until the abolition of the Sultanate in November 1922, a constitutional monarchy although real power and authority lay with the Grand National Assembly in Ankara—symbolising, as capital from 1923, all that was fresh and different about the new Turkey. This revolutionary Assembly, with its hybrid presidential and parliamentary executive, had already opted for democracy by declaring, in its 1921 revision of the existing Ottoman Constitution, that 'Sovereignty belongs unconditionally to the people'. While partly resting upon the acknowledgement that the authority claimed by the Assembly had no legal validity and that the only basis on which a rebel Government could hope to legitimise itself was the will of the people, it also represented an aspiration—an aspiration further confirmed in 1923 when Atatürk both organised his own political party, the People's Party, and was elected the first President of the Republic of Turkey.

The Sultan, by taking refuge with the British and fleeing the country, had in effect abdicated; but this had not solved the problem of the nominal continuance of the Sultanate and Caliphate. The abolition of the Sultanate presented more difficulties than that of European monarchies. The institution itself and the Ottoman dynasty (1299–1922) were more closely interwoven with the history of the Turkish people than were the German or Austrian monarchies with their national stories, and far more closely than the makeshift kings, say, of Greece and the Balkans. And there was the added complication of the position of the Sultan as Caliph, the leader of Muslims.

Nationalism might have suggested the retention of the Sultanate; nor did the principle of contemporaneity necessarily prohibit it. The arguments for constitutional monarchy made Nationalist leaders, themselves mostly distinguished former Ottoman military officers, as well as conservative intellectuals believe the preservation of a modified Sultanate to be in the best interest of the country and to conform with their own affection and residual personal loyalty. The sincerity of these men, especially those still under oath to the sovereign, is unquestionable. But they also probably regarded it as a potential counterweight to the growing power, authority and influence of Atatürk—a consideration which would naturally have intensified the determination of the latter, who also recognised this possibility, to resist. He would after all have been only too aware of the inevitability of any Sultan becoming a rallying-point for reaction.

More important, however, was Atatürk's conviction that representative democracy, in the shape of a majority government elected by universal suffrage, was the best political arrangement. Yet it need not immediately or suddenly be introduced in full into a country which had known only traditional and hereditary autocracy and an all-too-brief period of constitutional monarchy, and which was thus inclined to regard governmental tolerance of opposing views as a sign of weakness. Authoritarian government for the sake of stability and longevity was therefore a consequence of prevailing political thinking. Meanwhile, if the purpose of the state was to produce conditions which would allow each individual to develop his full potential, the first step in reform had to be to remove laws and customs that would impede or prevent this process. In the case of secularisation, for example, the liberal course should have been to rely on persuasion. But before the development of radio and television, the outcome of any such approach would have been a confrontation between Government, armed only with poorly-fashioned weapons of persuasion and propaganda, and the *hocas* (Islamic religious teachers) with their close contact and hold over the rural populace; even if eventually won by Government, a long period of discussion and dispute, and probably major alteration in policy, would have been unavoidable.

There is no doubt of Atatürk's certainty that as the leader of the National Struggle and, in effect, the founder of the state, he had the moral right to mould it as he pleased. He chose the instrument of the one-party system, the mechanism associated with totalitarianism, together with the tools of censorship and, for a time, special Independence Tribunals for trying political offences. Yet what was chosen did not bear the hallmark of totalitarianism, nor could it have done so given the limited technology at the state's disposal. Moreover, the animating spirit was quite different. Those who disobeyed the laws, whether relating to wearing the fez or spreading communist ideas, were prosecuted and the penalties could be harsh; but there were no undefined offences such as existed in Nazi Germany, Fascist Italy or Socialist Russia, no concentration camps and no sustained persecution of defeated political opponents. Political quarrels there were in plenty, such as an assassination attempt against Atatürk in 1926. Of the alleged conspirators, some were hanged and others imprisoned or exiled; more were tried and acquitted. Significant among insurrections was that, in 1925, of Şeyh (Sheikh) Said, a wealthy religious figure from a prominent Kurdish family—an uprising that, while including a Kurdish separatist element, was couched and propagated in religious terms as a reaction to the new secularism: the rebels made no demands for independence but proclaimed their intention of restoring the Şeriat (body of Islamic law) under a new Sultan-Caliph. Armed with emergency powers, the Government succeeded in crushing all opposition over the next two years—including the closure of the Republic's first true opposition party, the so-called Progressive Republican Party.

The situation created by the uprising included three of the classic problems of democracy? Is it possible to make revolutionary reforms by democratic methods? Do democratic principles insist that people should be allowed unwittingly to injure themselves? Does the principle of freedom of expression, without which democracy is meaningless, demand that parties rejecting these principles be allowed to exist?

The argument that revolution cannot be carried out by democratic methods has been used to justify every kind of oppression, including the elimination of opposition and stifling of criticism. Yet it is not possible to effect a rapid social and, particularly, political transformation, which will inevitably provoke reaction, and at the same time retain full rights of opposition and free discussion, especially in a volatile geopolitical setting. And in Turkey, the dissolution of the Empire and the total disruption of life as a result of prolonged warfare had produced a unique opportunity for making revolutionary changes. Moreover, in the early 1920s Turkey faced further imperialist designs, while there continued to exist at home reserves of both religious zealotism and sheer inertia that might easily be exploited to frustrate reform, harm social groups and damage the polity. There was also the added complication of whether or not the activities of anti-democratic parties and pressure-groups should be permitted. For Turkey between the two World Wars, a greater threat than political agitation by communist or fascist groups was perceived to be that of reactionary Muslims, whose victory against a secular structure would have denied freedom of expression, ironically the only principle on which the die-hard religious groups could claim a right to articulate their views. The establishment of a one-party system must have seemed the only solution, for it avoided too wide-ranging discussion and criticism of fundamental principles and policies—upon which, even in a multi-party democracy, some general agreement is necessary. In Turkey at that time no such agreement existed, nor could it easily have been created.

Yet Atatürk from the earliest days hankered after a 'loyal opposition' which, accepting the given structure and functions of the state, could criticise details and offer alternatives on policy while informing public opinion about their aims and actions. On the formation of the Free Republican Party in 1930, however, opposition of this limited kind was found to be intolerable. Party leaders, themselves sincere if critical supporters of the regime, were unable to cope with the upsurge of popular discontent—demonstrations and strikes—which shocked the Government into withdrawing from the experiment by dissolving the opposition party. Shortly afterwards, the brutal killing of a young reserve officer by a mob of religious fanatics in the western town of Menemen disturbed and infuriated the Government and convinced it that the period of political tutelage must continue and the introduction of genuine democracy wait until a new generation, educated in democratic values, had grown up. Nevertheless, the newspapers' vehement opposition to the abolition of the Sultanate and Caliphate and criticism of the hasty proclamation of the Republic reveal substantial freedom of the press, even after the Şeyh Said incident. While outright criticism of republicanism or democracy and public support of communism, fascism or religious acitivism was prohibited, serious discussion and criticism of, for example, the cultural crisis in Turkey in connection with the neglect of Islam, was publishable. Mention should be made here of the radical journal, '*Kadro*', founded in 1932 in response to Atatürk's call for intellectuals to formulate a revolutionary ideology for the Republic; its blend of nationalist, Marxist and corporatist thinking on economic and broader social problems was at first supported, but '*Kadro*' later clashed with the programme of the Republican People's Party and closed in 1934.

Dictatorial though Atatürk may have been (and as only a popular hero such as he could become), in the sense that he consistently provided the impetus behind the Government and decisively intervened at moments of crisis, his relations with the people tended towards the patriarchal. He toured the provinces discussing and arguing with local residents, in a policy of explanation that was wholly novel and came to be formalised as *halkçılık* (loosely, populism), one of the principles on which his Republican People's Party was based. In essence, *halkçılık*, a corollary of republicanism, comprised communication with the people and explaining political decisions in a way that the people understood—in the sense of government ruling solely for the benefit of the people. In the more oppressive European atmosphere of the 1930s, however, it became distorted into a means both of rendering potential class conflict nugatory and of entrenching the position as trustees of the ruling élite—all in the name of harmony and order. Yet *halkçılık* originally developed out of Atatürk's concern lest the people be alienated from his republicanism through ignorance, and awareness that any form of government depends for its proper functioning on being understood; though it seems he was not wholly successful in this endeavour. Scenes following his death in 1938 revealed that Atatürk was not only popular but genuinely loved. But he was revered as the saviour of Turkey and father of his country rather than as a party leader with a programme, so that it was possible to support him wholeheartedly and yet be less than enthusiastic about his policies. And the disorderly protests following his attempt to organise an opposition party revealed widespread incomprehension and dissatisfaction with the Government for, probably, a variety of reasons that had previously found no channel for expression.

IV

The establishment of the one-party system, by blocking effective opposition, enabled Atatürk to put his ideas into practice without risking embittered and potentially debilitating political conflict. Contemporaneity and nationalism were both present and one or other dominant in almost all his reforms. Contemporaneity was more readily apparent in, for example, the secularisation of the polity, law and education (and all this entailed for religion), the substitution of the Roman for the Arabic alphabet and the encouragement of occidental, or *Allafranga*, music in lieu of classical Ottoman, or *Allaturca*. Yet the emphasis on suitability for the Turkish nation, as in law and language, and on Turkish themes, as in music and the other arts, involved a high level of conscious nationalism rather than mere national consciousness.

The abolition of the Sultanate had not automatically included that of the Caliphate, long borne by the Ottoman Sultans, because while the former was an essentially secular Turkish institution the latter held authority over Muslims everywhere. By the 20C, however, such authority was largely technical as apart from the centuries-old division of the Muslim world into separate states, not all recognising the same Caliph, many Muslim peoples were ruled by the powers of Christendom and hence in no position to recognise or to obey Caliphal authority. In a complete departure from Islamic tradition, Atatürk detached from the Caliphate the monarchical power of the Sultan's office. Yet the expedient of the Grand National Assembly endowing a member of the Ottoman dynasty with the title of Caliph and confining him virtually to ceremonial functions required a massive change in perception, by the Caliph himself and by the people. Even if personally compliant, the Caliph would inevitably become a focus for conservative opposition, or for foreign attempts to destabilise or even overthrow the regime; and the newly-appointed Caliph, Abdülmecid *Efendi*, was willing to play the role of sovereign in Turkey and figure-head for opposition movements. It was also argued that Islam possessed no purely spiritual office like that to which the Caliph had been reduced, as he was simply the head of the Islamic community. Clearly the compromise was unworkable; it was, moreover, fundamentally inconsistent with the concept of a secular state. The abolition of the Caliphate in 1924, even without the interference of foreign Muslims and by implication their Christian masters, was inevitable.

With this concluded, probably the most important advance towards secularisation was in the domain of law, particularly civil. Ottoman law had involved a complex application of a number of legal codes, both secular and religious. The Şeriat had over the centuries been superseded in many respects by secular administrative, penal and commercial law, often of foreign derivation, until it covered family and inheritance law only. Apart from the secular and Islamic courts, there existed separate codes and courts dealing with the religious minorities. Legal activity, then, was confused, cumbersome and complicated. The time had come for the introduction of a single, secular code of law applicable to all citizens. Given what appeared to be insuperable problems in drafting a new unified code that would satisfy all, in 1926 the Government adopted the Swiss civil code, Italian penal code and a commercial code based on the German and Italian models.

The changes in the laws relating to family affairs are of particular interest, as they were to Atatürk. Long determined to raise the status of women, he had admired their dedication and selfless contribution during the National Struggle and resolved that the new state register its appreciation in tangible form. The abolition of polygamy, introduction of civil rather than religious marriage, rights to and protection against divorce, equal share in inheritance and full participation in the life of the country through employment and, in due course, franchise—in short, equal rights and the emancipation of women, were targeted through these and later legal reforms and his own unflagging support. Yet aware as the Government was of the power of conservative opinion, especially in the rural areas, they would not abolish the veil as they did the fez, the men's headgear, in possibly the most symbolic application of contemporaneity.

Other reforms, ranging from the introduction of surnames (e.g., Atatürk) to the abolition of imperial honours and titles, all helped to settle Turkey firmly within contemporary civilisation. The Gregorian calendar was adopted in place of the Ottoman lunar and solar variants and Sunday, instead of the traditional Friday, made the weekly holiday. With the legal reform, the religious functionaries lost their role in both civil procedure and the administration of law. With the closure of the Şeriat courts came also the closing of the mystical orders, the tombs and shrines of saints and, as attention was fixed on education, the Islamic schools. Yet for all his emphasis on secularisation, Atatürk strove for religious enlightenment in Turkey; he was instrumental in changing the language of worship from classical Arabic to Turkish and persistently attempted to provide an authorised Turkish version of the Kur'an for public use, that the people might read and understand rather than learn by rote.

Perhaps the most powerful instrument for social transformation is education, and Atatürk was determined to use it to inculcate the values of contemporaneity and nationalism. He came more and more to believe that only a new generation, bred in the national schools on the new principles, could create the kind of society he wished to see. Major educational reforms were, along with the abolition of the religious schools already mentioned, the improvement of the existing state schools and universities, including provision at the tertiary level for religious instruction, and the extension of free state education to all. The single most important step in accelerating the process of literacy and education was that of finally abandoning almost overnight, in 1928, the Arabic script, in use since the Turks' adoption of Islam though unsuitable for the Turkish language. And the choice of the much simpler Roman alphabet, whose phonetic structure was flexible enough to accommodate all the Turkish vowels and consonants, further aligned the Republic with contemporary civilisation.

As for the content of the new education, independence of mind and judgement was considered paramount. The major problem was, however, and has continued to be, the recruitment and training of good teachers, even though a large proportion of the Republic's meagre financial resources was devoted to education and foreign scholars of repute attracted to Turkish universities whenever possible; for example, oppressed Jewish and other intellectuals forced to leave Nazi Germany during the 1930s were welcomed in Turkey. The problem of inducing urban teachers to work in villages lacking basic amenities and often dominated by religious reactionaries and entrenched landlords, was eventually solved by establishing, in 1940, Village Institutes to create a revolutionary vanguard in the countryside. These taught, at a regional level, a practical curriculum that the peasants could take home to their own villages and demonstrate. Though short-lived in their original conception, for they gradually succumbed to suspicious conservative opposition, the Village Institutes made a substantial and novel contribution to rural education. A similar project for adult education had comprised the setting up, from 1932, of a network of People's Houses and People's Rooms by the Republican People's Party. While these urban community centres disseminated party ideology they also offered courses, provided library facilities and organised a variety of cultural activities. Being associated with the single-party, however, they fell into desuetude once that system was superseded in 1950.

V

What epitomises perhaps most clearly the convergence of Atatürk's principles of contemporaneity and nationalism was his search for the basis of the nation's self-identification in a national language and a national history.

The Empire had, in essence, two languages—the speech of illiterate Anatolia, substantially the unaltered language of the Turks' Central Asian forebears, and the Ottoman Turkish of the educated élite which, while retaining the grammatical structure of Turkish, was so interlaced with alien Arabic and Persian words and expressions as to be incomprehensible to the average Turk, even if he were to master the script. Moreover, the latter had developed over the centuries a style of extreme elaboration that was a prerequisite in all official documents and literary composition as well as in the spoken discourse of the élite—a sign of imperial grandeur. As a result, the gap between the educated few and the multitude was immense and apparently unbridgable. Yet if the new state wished to become more than simply an artificial political entity, it needed to impose some sense of cultural unity, induce in the different sections of the population some consciousness of belonging to a nation—and this before the process of government or economic progress could be given any real direction. And homogeneity of language could provide the expression of a community of interest and cultural cohesion. Further, if democracy were to be achieved, it was clearly necessary that newspapers and political information in general—quite apart from the cultural medium of literature, the discourse of science and technology and the language of religious practice—be written and spoken in a language that the people could understand.

Attempts at simplification had been made before but without success; these had been movements by intellectuals only and frustrated by a desire not to jeopardise the Islamic heritage through cutting all links with Arabic or by an unwillingness to risk losing the Ottoman Turks' own literary patrimony through changes so drastic that Ottoman Turkish would no longer be read with ease. Atatürk, however, in his zeal to unify and educate the citizens of the Republic, had no qualms about severing such links. The language reform that became the official policy of Turkey was a return to the unadulterated speech of Anatolia. Yet to build upon this form of Turkish, make it a vehicle for modern ideas and then persuade everyone to use it, was a formidable task compared with the mere change in script.

The Turkish Language Society, still in existence today, was established in 1932 at Atatürk's suggestion and from his personal funds, and in the same year he convened the first Language Conference. The Society's dual aim was the collection and publication of Turkish words in the language of Anatolia and in ancient Turkish scripts, and to create new words, or neologisms, from Turkish roots for both modern technical terms and the loan-words used in written Turkish. The collection of words from common parlance, folk-songs and proverbs was undertaken along with an intensive study of works in old Turkish—ancient inscriptions, popular and mystical poetry and prose commentaries on the Kur'an; words were also adopted from the living Turkish dialects of other countries, from the Balkans (itself a Turkish word) across Central Asia to Eastern Turkistan (now Xinjiang in China). The words thus collected or created replaced the Arabic and Persian loans being expurgated, so as to produce a purer and clearer Turkish language of and for the people.

The high degree of success of the language reform can be measured in the sense both that Turkey's Turkish has been transformed and that it has been perhaps the most popular of all the reforms. Yet ineptitude by the Society, the backlash—as well as methodological problems—caused by over-fervent purification, and carelessness, even pretentiousness, in common usage have distorted the reform and resulted in an influx of, now, mainly English technical terms rather than automatic creation and use of acceptable Turkish neologisms. These setbacks notwithstanding, the language currently provides a standard for the dialects of the newly independent but previously isolated Turkish republics of the ex-Soviet Union in their work towards a common alphabet and unified written language as a means of cultural integration. As for literature and scholarship in Turkey, the excision of foreign words and substitution of popular for élitist forms might, and in some countries would, have had an adverse effect. In Turkey, on the contrary, it has liberated writers in both style and vocabulary and opened up the language to the people. Yet the appropriation by intellectuals of specific sets of words—Ottoman Turkish, more recent foreign loans or revived pure Turkish—to display their personal political stance is a somewhat disturbing phenomenon. For it cramps the language and hence inhibits thinking; nor does it aid the development of the language's national unity within Turkey, let alone beyond its borders.

In the realisation of Atatürk's efforts through revolution to change fundamentally the society's cultural and intellectual fabric, the reform of language was only the second vehicle, the recovery of history being the principal. It is possible to create a sentiment of cultural unity and nationality within a language shared by other nations, witness the English-speaking lands of Australasia and North America or the Spanish-speaking countries of Central and South America. But a knowledge of the shared past, whether imagined or proven, is vital to the idea of a nation. Nothing can be said about the past that does not have some bearing on the present, and those dealing with the present cannot help but employ material provided by legend and tradition or mainstream research. The politics of the past is not simply an academic pursuit; it is integral to every people's search for a heritage essential to national autonomy and identity. Yet the history taught in schools is paramount in shaping the way in which people view the world.

In pre-Republican historiography, the history of the Turks had been submerged in that of Islam and restricted to the political, and especially dynastic, history of the Ottoman Empire. Against this background, Atatürk sought to revitalise the self-respect of the Turks who had not only just lost their most recent empire but had long suffered the kind of negative image that goes with a slow decline. While the Muslim Turks had been portrayed as the Christians' deepest foe from the 11C Crusades, it was in the 16C that the Ottoman Empire specifically was both hated as the enemy of Christendom and yet feared and respected for its overwhelming superiority and military might. Since then, a gradual shift had occurred in the relative positions of the two camps. Consequently, the image had come to be created, particularly by the French, of western European political and economic advance, combined with the Christian faith, as the counterpoint of all the negative attributes they sought to abandon—characteristics attributed to the still hated but now no longer revered Ottoman Turks. Intuitively aware of all this, Atatürk strove to detach the Turks from overt memories of the Empire, while encouraging them to take pride in their racial history. As the concepts of nationality and national sovereignty were placed among the fundamentals of the new political order, the Republic, Atatürk made it his business to seek for the tools of the nation's self-assertion at the intellectual level—and he found them in national history even more than in national language. In reality, neither history nor language needed to be 'nationalised'. Alongside the Turkish language existed the long history of the Turks; like the language, Turkish history had, through the centuries, been overlaid with a variety of imperial, and concomitantly racial and religious, varnishes. For Atatürk, the task was to scrape off the varnishes and reveal the Turkish past beneath.

The obligation of the Turk was to find himself within his own history which provided, with his language, the mainstay of his cultural continuity—the nationalist facet of Atatürk's political thinking. The recovery of the nation's history, like its language, through scholarship, represents the facet of contemporaneity, for it postulates the use of methods belonging to contemporary civilisation. To Atatürk, it was essential that the nation 'know itself'. For unless the inherited cultural tradition of a nation is sought and then attached in its proper historical setting, it allows the development of dogma without thought. Hence, inspired by Atatürk, a society was formed for the study of Turkish history. It held its first Congress in 1932 and a second, international, one five years later—and it continues today. The Turkish Historical Society, despite the lack of all resources, gave great impetus to historical research in Turkey, and its investigations especially into ancient Turkish history opened new paths and new perspectives. The question has been less one of giving a new interpretation to a past already known, rather of stimulating interest in a hitherto unknown and more distant past.

Republican historians and others looked to the ancient civilisations of Anatolia and Mesopotamia whose relics had started to come to light with the archaeological discoveries and deciphering of scripts in the late 19C and early 20C. A school of history developed that sought to establish a direct link between the Sumerians, Hittites and Turks and, by implication, between the Turks and the establishment of civilisation in Europe. Dismissed as effrontery by the bulk of 'Western' scholars, whose own assumed cultural and racial derivations were threatened by such assertions, it is now recognised that there is a basis to these claims that cannot be evaded. For example, the late renowned Sumerologist, Samuel Kramer, wrote in 1990 of

> "... a people, the Sumerians, that, it is not <u>impossible</u>, or even <u>improbable</u>, spoke a <u>Turkic</u>-like agglutinative tongue, and that may have come into Southern Mesopotamia some six to seven thousand years ago from somewhere in Central Asia—the idea current in Ataturk's day that the Sumerians were a Turkic-related people, may well prove to be not so far from the <u>truth</u>." (Emphasis his)

Speculative though this may still seem to the sceptic, the linguist Osman Nedim Tuna has recently proved that Sumerian, the earliest-known literary language of mankind, contained at least 350 Turkish loan-words. This, relying on extant Sumerian inscriptions, shows not only that Turkish may be the oldest living written language, but also that the Turkish race, under whatever local name, existed in Mesopotamia if not further north—in eastern Anatolia—as long ago as 3500 BC. Moreover, of the known modern languages of Asia, Turkish is the closest in structure to Sumerian and located geographically the nearest.

Republican historians also concentrated on the much more clear-cut claim that the ancestors of the Ottoman Turks had founded empires in Central Asia which both challenged China, Persia and India and furnished them with dynasties. The decipherment of the famous Orhon, Turfan and other inscriptions and the uncovering of the material culture of the Central Asian Turks—showing them to have been far more sophisticated and advanced than previously credited and, indeed, to have constituted a civilisation in their own right—was incorporated into the national curriculum.

The revision of Asian and ancient Near Eastern history necessitated by all these discoveries was naturally gratifying to the Turks, but Atatürk's interest lay neither in a simplistic glorification of the present nor a nostalgic dwelling on vanished achievements. He seems to have encouraged rather the use of history for Turkish regeneration—to link Turkey with the contemporary world, with a racial past that crossed Asia and with a homeland in Anatolia that spanned the centuries and dated back several millennia before Islam. This also provided a counterweight to the iconoclasm of his modernising zeal by making it easier for the Turks to accept both the toning-down of more recent memories and the drastic changes required by social revolution. Nonetheless, there never developed in Turkey the kind of official history produced by the totalitarian regimes of Europe—not least because of a lack of the requisite organisation, finance, knowledge and techniques. Nor even, in those early days of enthusiastic conjecture, did a national scholarly synthesis emerge on Turkish history and historiography. In fact, Turkish historians have yet to agree on a workable methodology for continuity in Turkish history—a continuity that would involve a fusion of the Turkish, trans-Asian and Islamic pasts.

VI

The radical reforms in so many aspects of life from the 1920s altered the face and indeed the heart of Turkey, but for all his keen interest in politics, law, language and history, Atatürk never forgot the underlying importance of the economy. He placed the Republic firmly within the capitalist camp, rejecting, with the individualist slant of his political thinking, the socialist system and corresponding lack of opportunity for personal initiative. The Republic's economic policies were, however, interventionist, as they needed to be in the circumstances of a new state ravaged by years of warfare, overwhelmingly agricultural and underpopulated, shouldering the burden of a massive Ottoman Public Debt and lacking much of the infrastructure required by a modern industrial state. Not surprisingly, the early economic programme was unambitious, aiming for a balanced budget, stable currency and elimination of the deficit on foreign trade. The basis of the economic, as of all other, policies was a balance of nationalism and contemporaneity; while developing to fit into the world capitalist economy, economic advantage would always be sacrificed to economic independence. The fundamental purpose of Turkey's economic strategy was to avoid foreign domination of the national economy. Yet attraction of foreign investment was seen as part of the solution to the difficulties caused by shortage of capital, even though past experience prompted caution. Investment had historically often been undertaken as much for political as for economic reasons and often, therefore, proved unprofitable for the country, and the import of western European manufactures had in many cases ruined native handicraft industries such as silk and cotton textiles. And resentment aroused by the Capitulations, the agreements (heavily abused) by which foreigners in the Empire were not subject to Ottoman law but possessed all kinds of privileges, gave further impetus to the determination to emphasise national capital and create a national bourgeoisie, especially as the Turkish delegates to the 1923 Lausanne Conference were forced to make substantial economic concessions in terms of tariffs to the Allies before the latter would agree to the abolition of the lucrative Capitulations.

By 1923 what little cash remained in the country tended to be in the hands of the minorities who owned most of the few industrial enterprises and virtually monopolised commerce. The population exchange with Greece had included much of the Greek Orthodox Anatolians' moveable assets while the İstanbul and İzmir Armenians, largely untouched by the bungled relocation in 1915 that had led to the deaths of several hundred thousand from the wartorn eastern provinces, had been ruined financially by the privations of the National Struggle. The weakness of the industrial sector was aggravated by the economy being thoroughly uncoordinated, with no sense of a national market. From the beginning, when public money was desperately short, Turkey encouraged private capital and joint ventures with foreign investment yet consistently failed to attract foreign technology. A 1927 law encouraged industrialisation in the private sector through the provision of state incentives, which worked all too profitably for private businesses but proved disastrous for the national economy and coincided with the onset of the world depression.

Largely in response to the economic circumstances that unfolded in 1929, including the withdrawal of foreign capital, a move was made towards statism, by which the state played a major role in production and investment, taking the initiative on behalf of the private sector through the establishment of state industries as models for private entrepreneurs or as ventures that the private sector was too weak or poor to carry out itself. In addition, the state was able to create a nationwide industrial base through its railway (and later road) policies and by spreading projects throughout Turkey rather than concentrate on the more accessible and profitable areas of the north-west. Despite these major accomplishments, the standard of living declined and workers' conditions were harsh, a situation that led, for the duration of the single-party period, to the prohibition of unions, strikes and lock-outs and of non-state monopolies. Yet these actions, and still more the explanations given for them, were very much in line with the authoritarian paternalism implicit in statism: social harmony, along with national unity, was to be maintained at all costs and the notion of class conflict between workers and employers, producers and consumers, should not be allowed to develop.

Land reform also conformed closely with the principle of statism. The division of the relatively few large estates and their distribution among peasants was always part of the Republican People's Party programme and was emphasised by Atatürk. The inefficiency of the land registry, however, on the legal change to an entirely new form of land tenure, provided immense opportunity for cheating, injustice and dispute. Added to this, the land-owning provincial notables formed a powerful pressure group, well represented in the Grand National Assembly, who possessed the means of influencing successive Governments, for instance, that retention of their holdings was in the best interest of their tenantry as well as themselves. Moreover, the creation of more peasant holdings was not a pressing economic need, given the small population. Primitive methods of cultivation, shortage of labour and lack of integrated road and rail facilities were initially just as damaging to profitable agricultural production. Probably as urgent and useful to the small-holders was the abolition of tithes in 1925, undertaken partly in order to lift a burden from the farmers' shoulders and partly as a necessary preliminary to land reform; it was an economic symbol of the Government's good faith with regard to the peasantry, whose acquiescence was held to be vital for the continuance of the Republican regime.

Disrupted in its development by the Second World War, Turkey's economy subsequently fluctuated between boom and depression as Governments grappled with shifting international conditions and a succession of short-term programmes promoting rapid industrialisation. The ideological and political turmoil of the 1960s and 1970s at both governmental and street level, coupled with the severe effects of the 1973 and 1979 oil crises, prompted IMF-led structural adjustment; experiments in financial liberalisation and economic stabilisation since 1980, under the guidance of the late Turgut Özal (soon to become Prime Minister and later President), have resulted in growth, for example an unprecedented export and consumer boom. The gradual transformation from a protective and traditionally statist to a privatised, free-market economy seems reasonably successful. And it is ironical that overall concern, as in so many democracies, has been to maintain and even strengthen political centralisation in order effectively to decentralise the economy.

Epilogue

Compared with those theories that promise the fulfillment of every human aspiration as well as the solution to the perennial problems of government, the ideas upon which the Republic's policies were based and to which successive Governments in Turkey, not altogether consciously or willingly, have tended to adhere, may now seem prosaic, limited and even jejune. It must be admitted that the Turkish Revolution did not follow any broad scheme of revolutionary development; it lacked the element of popular excitement, of the expectation of a different and better world such as inspired the masses in the French Revolution. In short, it was not a response to popular demand. Nor did it conform with the facile definition which makes the essence of every revolutionary movement the dislodgement from power of one dominant class by another. If anything, it was the reassertion of the dominance of the Ottoman military institution, now imbued with Turkish nationalism; for armed struggle against foreign militaries was the only means of preserving independent existence and creating a new state. And comprehensive victory on the battlefield over the enemies of Turkey was the most significant cause of the military's preponderance in the new state with its awesome obligation, legally enshrined in 1935, 'to look after and protect...the Turkish Republic'. Moreover, it would have been, and was indeed perceived by Atatürk, illogical and unsound strategy to emphasise, in the midst of a defensive war, the division of the so-called classes and thus collapse under external pressure into the class struggle. After all, the overriding problem was quite different, the result of the dissolution of the institutional and ideological framework which had held society together. So the choice Atatürk made was for a nationalist revolution following a national struggle, involving a change in perception as its most important element. He realised many of the developments he hoped to bring about must await the psychological transformation and seems to have thought of his own task as being primarily to remove the mental obstacles in the way of participation in progress while reviving the Turkish identity that had been constant throughout a long history. For this, too, he sought to harness culture and aesthetics as a social force for national advancement, combining modern techniques and forms of expression in literature, the performing and the visual arts with indigenous sources of inspiration; the conjunction of contemporaneity and nationalism should prevail, from opera to painting; from ballet to architecture.

So how successful were the policies he originated in achieving these aims? He is arguably the only 'dictator' whose character was not assailed and policies intentionally reversed immediately after his death. This was perhaps because of the continuance of authoritarian government under his closest collaborator and successor, President İsmet İnönü. But in the multi-party system that İnönü initiated in 1945, dissent, then allowed free play, succeeded in making both apparently minor changes such as the reversion to Arabic of the call to prayer and, more significant and far-reaching, the introduction of religious instruction in state schools (nowadays compulsory) and the reintroduction of religious schools—undermining the very principle of secularism. Reactionary opinion was not wholly appeased, however, and under the Democrat Party Governments of 1950–60 the most extreme proposals were put forward, such as for the restoration of the Sultanate and the compulsory veiling of women, during an elective dictatorship that imposed a run of repressive legislation. Leaders of all parties readily wooed this kind of opinion in their trawl for mass votes, although how far they were really prepared to reintroduce discarded institutions is questionable. They did not openly attack Atatürk or his general policies but concentrated on the reinterpretation of specific aspects, such as language reform which they did their best to discourage. This kind of modification has continued, for example by the Justice Party who, on coming to power in 1965 almost as a successor to the now banned Democrat Party, forbade the use of certain new words in official communications—in circulars couched in new Turkish, like the protests of writers against the excision of Arabic and Persian terms.

Universal reverence for Atatürk's memory has persisted, at times amounting to a personality cult in which almost anyone has felt the need to justify his political allegiance, however extreme, by using Atatürk's name. Likewise, political leaders have tended to cling to his maxims, whatever the circumstances. More damagingly, they build up Atatürkism into a rigid dogma as a substitute for less acceptable ideologies, rather than maintain it as a framework within which the fittest contemporary ideologies might flourish. Atatürk's influence, therefore, on the collective mind remains strong. Turkey is secular and democratic because he declared that it must be so. But with 99 per cent of its population Muslim, it is a Muslim society. And indeed, the reassertion of an instinctive Islam has become apparent in recent years, remarkably perhaps, in terms of a yearning by learned and unlearned alike in their increasingly defensive reaction against the perceived hostility of the non-Muslim and non-Turkish world—a yearning that finds satisfaction in the 'Turkish-Islamic synthesis', the conjunction of Turkish nationalism and Muslim internationalism that is now widespread. For the ideology is gaining ground through the ballot-box, as it touches a receptive chord among the economically-distressed urban lower classes, including the migrant population that is swelling the cities and overloading public services.

The reflex nature of, especially, the Islamic element of this reaction may in part be explained by the fact that Atatürk felt obliged to abandon, in the absence of religious scholars of sufficiently revolutionary calibre, his earlier feeling that a secular state should necessarily make some kind of provision for the regulation and instruction of Islam so that individual Muslims might develop their belief. His consequent withdrawal during the 1930s to the thesis that the Government of such a state has no role in the people's religious development, and to the legal implementation of this, was, I would argue, misconceived. For it created, over a long period, the paradox of the unlettered *hoca*, lacking adequate state-led education yet blamed for perpetuating ignorance and bigotry among the faithful. And the mistake was further compounded by the subsequent compromising of secularist principles through the backsliding of opportunist politicians and unimaginative Governments towards the present massive increase in religious instruction and its full incorporation into the state educational system—conceived in part as an ideological antidote to the pervasive socialist activism of the 1970s. The state should from its inception have provided the infrastructure for both the autonomous administration of religious affairs and for solid, regulated, religious instruction alongside but not within secular state education. It would thus have avoided the growth of a religious opposition which was ill-founded and incoherent, and thence the subsequent extreme counter-measures deemed necessary to neutralise that opposition.

The same strategy should have underpinned, for example, the Republic's constitution and laws, so as to stimulate the sentiment of temporal political obligation to a secular authority—the Turkish state and its constitution—while still facilitating the spiritual religious obligation of individuals to Islam. For a Muslim society, the basic constitutional norm inherent in the supremacy of a secular constitution and a unified secular legal code would have been far more fitting, far more secure if generally not inimical to the ethical precepts of the Kur'an rather than, as outlined earlier, a simple validation *en bloc* of foreign legal codes with inherently Christian ethical precepts. And the reason for this was, and is still, the ignorance of the intellectuals of Turkey and their consequent inability successfully to create new and contemporary structures imbued with the spirit of their own traditions and history. In addition, the need to use ex-Ottoman bureaucrats with their lingering imperial psychology and administrative methods, given the shortage of educated and experienced manpower with the correct revolutionary credentials, helped to solidify the fluid state yet, far more significantly, aggravated the stultification of the Revolution. But the necessary thinking, the motive power required to push through the diversity of reforms to their logical conclusions, was lacking from the start; ignorance bred inadequacy, inadequacy led to intolerance and intolerance stifled thought. In particular, the weakness of the young and insecure political institutions, notably the bureaucracy and the judiciary, led, despite the traditional aspiration towards the strong state (subsuming an orderly civil society), to discouragement of any serious consideration of the nature of state and society, as may be seen from the end of the 1930s. Hence, the original ideas of Atatürk became blurred and ultimately lost in the quagmire of intellectual deficiency and conformity. And this paternal liberalism, this desire for order, infected almost all aspects of society, becoming one of the dominant impulses of the Republican era. A representative example is Turkey's dependent foreign policy with its lack of a reasoned egoistic basis; its practitioners have generally sought to advance the country's interest by being conciliatory rather than confrontational, reactive not proactive—even under extreme provocation, as when some 60 Turkish diplomats at embassies and consulates around the world were killed or injured in a series of assassination attacks between 1973 and 1985.

Central to the Revolution was Atatürk's endorsement of the value of democracy and the democratic idea—important, given the history of modern Turkey, in that it is above all the armed forces who, cherishing Atatürk's memory, consider the Republic sacrosanct and themselves the guardians of the public interest. In view of the three military interventions since the multi-party system was established, this part of his legacy may seem of doubtful value. But, at the cost of constricting the natural development of a pluralist system able effectively to regulate itself, it has protected the country from too entrenched, authoritarian, civilian governance—let alone communist- or fascist-party totalitarianism. Witness the 1960 intervention against the dictatorial Government of the Democrat Party and the disabling of autocratic executive control of society by the 1961 Constitution so that new life and freer forms of expression than in any previous period of the Republic sprang into existence. Yet constitutionally untrammelled, even irresponsible, abuse of this freedom permitted little, if any, defence by the still feeble political institutions against the domestic crises and world traumas of the later 1960s and 1970s, exemplified by the student movements of 1968. It eventually required an almost complete reversal in the Constitution that followed upon the military's 1980 intervention to prevent the society from tearing itself apart. For without the controls that fully-fledged, industrialised democracies were able to bring to bear, the events of those years had a massive impact and spread sharp shock-waves through Turkey, already weakened by chronic economic mismanagement and unavoidably huge defence expenditure since its foundation. Unable to remain aloof from the terrorist phenomenon sweeping Europe and elsewhere in the 1970s, the state could not, with its existing civilian organs, contain the political polarisation, violence and breakdown of law and order into virtual civil war, not least because of a weak economy's lack of finance for the organisation of effective counter-measures.

None of this, however, absolves the elected politicians of responsibility for the governmental paralysis of the period. To be sure, it reveals the mediocrity of successive, unstable and indisciplined coalition Governments, comprising uneasy partnerships between highly incompatible factions in a plethora of large and small, centrist and extreme parties. But, at a deeper level, it also implicates the intellectually-constrained intelligentsia in general and even society at large; their narrow and ill-informed regard for 'Western' models, opinions and methods laid, and continues to lay, them wide open to the ills of contemporary democracy without its protective structures—including that of a sound economy. Nor has any more profound understanding of 'Eastern' models been evident among the spectrum of opponents of 'capitalist democracy'. All in all, in the retrospect of the Republic's history, it has become only too clear that successive aberrations and failures in the modernisation process have been due, in the main, to the lack of political sagacity of its institutions and their general inability to comprehend the nature of contemporary political systems; keen to emulate, they could only imitate. Consequently, Turkey has provided little intellectual challenge to its rival contemporary democracies. These days, awareness of this inadequacy provokes an intermittent self-assertion which reflects both the will to power and its obverse, a sense of inferiority—with all the confused and confusing problems of political identity that this entails.

To conclude, a revolution which has achieved its aim sometimes appears as no revolution at all. The Turkish Revolution began some 70 years ago and is still going on. But difficult as it may be to discern its ultimate consequences, there is no doubt that the Revolution has already achieved its initial aim, that of orienting Turkey towards a modern, national, secular democracy. Its founding father would, perhaps, not be too surprised to learn that this state has met with many difficulties along the way, some due to events beyond its control and some to its own weaknesses. But Atatürk never supposed that his revolution would solve every problem, nor did he hold out any such prospect to the people of Turkey. Rather, he sought to create the conditions, mentally and materially, for the citizens to build their own state within contemporary civilisation. He showed the way, with his emphasis on the paired concepts of contemporaneity and nationalism, towards a balance of Turkey's identity and the requirements of today's world—to be achieved by his Janus-like Turks through the cultivation of rational enquiry and thence a social philosophy, without which no society can successfully be constructed. Atatürk was the architect; Turkey is still in the hands of its builders.

Chronological table

BC

c 10,500–7000	Cave dwellings at Karain; primitive stone implements and weapons
c 7000	First settlement at Hacılar; earliest evidence of agriculture in Anatolia
c 6500–5500	Çatalhöyük becomes first cultural centre; earliest known religious shrines, pottery, frescoes and statuettes in Anatolia
c 5500	Sophisticated painted pottery and figurines at Hacılar and Çatalhöyük
c 5000–3000	First settlements at Alacahöyük, Alişar, Canhasan and Beycesultan
c 3000	First settlement at Troy
c 2500–2000	Period of Hattian culture
c 1950	Assyrian merchant-colony at Kanesh (Kültepe), first written records in Anatolia
c 1900	Founding of Hattusa by Hittites
c 1700–1450	Old Hittite Kingdom
c 1450–1200	Hittite Empire
c 1260	Fall of Troy
c 1180	Destruction of Hattusa
c 12–1100	Foundation of Neo-Hittite states at Carchemish, Karatepe and Zincirli
c 1100–1000	Migration of Greeks to Aegean coaast of Anatolia
c 900	Rise of Urartian culture in eastern Anatolia
c 900–800	Rise of Phrygian, Lydian, Carian and Lycian cultures in western Anatolia
c 800	Foundation of Panionic League and rise of Greek culture in western Anatolia
c 756	Foundation of Cyzicus by Miletus
c 750	Foundation of Greek trading post at Al Mina
717	Carchemish and Neo-Hittite states captured by Assyria
c 700	Cimmerians ravage cities in W Anatolia
c 700	Homer born at Smyrna
c 660	Foundation of Byzantium by Megara
c 654	Foundation of Lampsacus by Phocaea
c 640	First use of coinage in Asia Minor
c 650–600	Miletus founds colonies at Amisus and Trebizond
600–500	Beginning of Greek science and philosophy in Ionia
c 610	Thrasybulus tyrant of Miletus
c 600	Foundation of Massilia (Marseilles) by Phocaea
585	Battle between Cyaxares of Media and Alyattes of Lydia
561–546	Croesus ruler of Lydia
546	Cyrus of Persia defeats Croesus, Ionia comes under Persian rule
539	Phocaea defeated by Etruscan and Carthagenian navies at Alalia (Corsica)
c 535	Phocaians found Elea (Magna Graecia)
522	Darius king of Persia
512	Darius captures Byzantium
499	Ionians revolt against Persian rule begins

498	Ionians capture and burn Sardis
494	Ionian revolt against Persian rule begins
490	Persians defeated at Marathon
486	Death of Darius
481	Xerxes at Sardis
480	Xerxes invades Greece, battles of Thermopylae and Salamis
479	Persians suffer further defeats at Plataea and Mycale. Ionian cities regain their freedom
478	Ionian cities become members of the Delian League
467	Athenians defeat the Persians at the battle of Eurymedon
431	Beginning of the Peloponnesian War
410	Athens victorious at Cyzicus
409	Foundation of the city of Rhodes
408	Athens recaptures Byzantium
404	End of the Peloponnesian War
401	Xenophon and the Ten Thousand begin their expedition to Persia
400	Thibron's campaign in Asia Minor
399	Socrates put to death in Athens
395	Agesilaus lays siege to Sardis
394	Battle of Cnidus
386	King's peace. Ionia once more under Persian rule
356	Birth of Alexander the Great
336	Assassination of Philip of Macedon. Accession of Alexander
334	Alexander crosses into Asia Minor and defeats the Persians at the battle of the Granicus. Ionian cities liberated. Alexander lays siege to Miletus and Halicarnassus
334–33	Alexander conquers Lycia, Pamphylia and W Pisidia
333	Alexander conquers Cilicia. Inflicts second defeat on the Persians at the battle of Issus. Darius routed
323	Alexander dies at Babylon on 10 June at the age of 32. Outbreak of war between the Diadochi, Alexander's successors
318–17	Antigonus master of Asia Minor
305	Demetrius besieges Rhodes
301	Battle of Ipsus. Antigonus defeated and killed. Lysimachus rules Anatolia and Seleucus controls N Syria
300	Foundation of Antioch
295	Seleucus occupies Cilicia and Lysimachus Ionia
281	Battle of Corupedium. Seleucus defeats Lysimachus and becomes master of Anatolia. Death of Seleucus
278–77	Celts come to Anatolia and are defeated by Antiochus
263–41	Rise of the Attalid kings of Pergamum. Reign of Eumenes I
230	Rome and Pergamum become allies. Pergamum defeats the Celts
204	Baitylos of Pessinus taken to Rome
188	Treaty of Apamea. End of Seleucid rule in Anatolia
186	Prusias I of Bithynia attacks Pergamum
133	Death of Attalus III, last king of Pergamum. He bequeaths his kingdom to Rome

130	Roman province of Asia established. Aristonicus defeated
100	Mithridates VI Eupator becomes king of Pontus
88	Mithridates VI Eupator overruns Asia Minor; Roman citizens massacred
83	End of Seleucid Empire
80	Commagene kingdom founded
78	P. Servilius campaigns against pirates in Isauria, Lycia and Pamphylia
74	Nicomedes IV of Bithynia dies and leaves his kingdom to Rome
66	Mithridatic wars end. Rome in control of most of Asia Minor, including Cilicia
41	Antony meets Cleopatra at Tarsus
40	Antony and Cleopatra marry at Antioch
33–32	Antony and Cleopatra at Antioch
31	Antony defeated at Actium by Octavian
30	Antony and Cleopatra commit suicide. Octavian makes triumphant visit to Antioch

AD

14	Death of Augustus and accession of Tiberius
18	Germanicus in Asia Minor
19	Death of Germanicus at Antioch
40–56	Journeys of St Paul. First Christian community established at Antioch
43	Lycia becomes an imperial province
111	Pliny the Younger governor of Bithynia
117	Death of Trajan at Selinus, Cilicia
124	Hadrian visits Asia Minor
129	Galen born at Pergamum
165	Plague in Asia Minor
215	Caracalla in Antioch
303	Persecution of Christians in Nicomedia
325	Council of Nicaea
381	Coucil of Constantinople
392	Christianity made state religion by Theodosius the Great
395	Division of the Roman Empire
431	Council of Ephesus
527–65	Reign of Justinian the Great. Byzantine power reaches its zenith
626	Avars and Slavs besiege Constantinople
726–80	First Iconoclastic Period
923	Bulgars take Adrianople and besiege Constantinople
963–69	Nicephorus Phocas victorious over Arabs and regains Cilicia and Cyprus
1054	Schism between Greek and Roman churches
1071	Byzantines defeated by Selçuks at Manzikert. Turks overrun Anatolia
1071–1283	The Sultanate of Rum; Selçuks dominant power in Anatolia
1096	Beginning of First Crusade. Latin armies enter Anatolia for first time
1176	Selçuks annihilate Greeks at Myriocephalon; Byzantium loses last chance to expel the Turks from Anatolia

1203	Beginning of Fourth Crusade; Latins attack Constantinople
1204	Latins sack Constantinople; dismemberment of Byzantine Empire. Lascarids set up Byzantine capital in Nicaea. Comneni found Empire of Trebizond
1240	Ottoman Turks make first appearance in western Anatolia. Mongols invade eastern Anatolia
1242	Mongols defeat Selçuks at Kosedag and destroy their power in Anatolia
1261	Michael VIII Palaeologus retakes Constantinople and restores Byzantine Empire
1324	Death of Osman Gazi, founder of Ottoman dynasty
1326	Ottomans under Sultan Orhan take Prusa and establish their first capital there
1389	Turks defeat Serbians at Kossovo
1396	Beyazit I defeats Crusader army at Nicopolis
1397	First Turkish siege of Constantinople
1402	Tamerlane defeats Turks at Ankara and captures Beyazit I; Mongols overrun Anatolia
1422	Second Turkish siege of Constantinople
1439	Council of Florence. Last attempt to unite Roman Catholic and E Orthodox churches
1444	Turks crush Crusader army at Varna
1448	Turks defeat Hungarians at second battle of Kossovo
1453	Turks under Mehmet II conquer Constantinople; Constantine XI, last emperor of Byzantium, dies in battle. Istanbul becomes capital of Ottoman Empire, which now comprises most of Greece, the southern Balkans and western Anatolia
	1517 Selim I captures Cairo and assumes the title of Caliph. The Ottoman Empire has by now expanded into southern Europe, eastern Anatolia, Syria, Palestine, Egypt and Algeria
1520–66	Reign of Süleyman the Magnificent. Zenith of Ottoman power
1571	Turks conquer Cyprus. Christian powers defeat Turkish fleet at battle of Lepanto
1578–1666	'The Rule of the Women'. Ineffective sultans give up control of the empire to their women and Grand Vezirs
1666–1812	Period of intermittent wars between Turks and European powers. Ottoman Empire loses much territory in southern Europe
1821	Greek War of Independence begins
1826	Mahmut II destroys Janisssary Corps
1832	Greece achieves independence. Ibrahim Paşa of Egypt invades Anatolia
1839–76	The Tanzimat Period. Programme of reform in the Ottoman Empire
1877	Establishment of first Turkish parliament. Dissolved the following year by Sultan Abdul Hamit II
1908	Constitutional rule and parliament restored
1909	Abdul Hamit II deposed
1912–13	Balkan Wars; Turks lose Macedonia and part of Thrace
1914	Turkey enters World War I as ally of Germany
1915	Turks repel Allied landings on Gallipoli peninsula

1918	Turks surrender to Allies. İstanbul occupied by Anglo-French army
1919	Sivas Congress. Atatürk leads Turkish Nationalists in beginning of struggle for national sovereignty. Greek army lands at Smyrna
1920	Establishment of Grand National Assembly of Turkey with Atatuürk as President. Greek army advances into Asia Minor
1922	Turks defeat Greeks and drive them out of Asia Minor; Sultanate abolished
1923	Treaty of Lausanne establishes sovereignty of modern Turkey, defines its frontiers and arranges for exchange of minority populations between Greece and Turkey. Establishment of the Turkish Republic with Atatürk as first President
1924	Abolition of Caliphate
1925–38	Atatuürk's programme of reforms to modernise Turkey
1938	Death of Atatürk
1945	Turkey enters World War II on side of Allies
1946	Turkey becomes charter member of the United Nations
1950	Turkey enters Korean War as part of United Nations force
1973	Bosphorus Bridge built between Europe and Asia; opened on 50th anniversary of the founding of the Turkish Republic

Chronology of Kings and Emperors

The Ptolemies of Egpyt

Ptolemy I Soter 305–282
Ptolemy II Philadelphus 282–246
Ptolemy III Euergetes I 246–222
Ptolemy IV Philopator 222–205
Ptolemy V Epiphanes 204–180
Ptolemy VI Philometor 180–145
Ptolemy VII Neos Philopator 145
Ptolemy VIII Euergetes II 146–116

Ptolemy IX Soter II 116–107; 88–80
Ptolemy X 107–88
Ptolemy XI 80
Ptolemy XII Auletes 80–58; 55–51
Ptolemy XIII 51–47
Ptolemy XIV47–44
Ptolemy XV (Caesarion) 44–30

The Kings of Pontus

Mithridates I c 302–265
Ariobarzanes c 265–255
Mithridates II c 255–220
Mithridates III c 220–185
Pharnaces I c 185–169

Mithridates IV Philopator
   Philadelphus 169–150
Mithridates V Euergetes c 150–120
Mithridates VI Eupator 120–63
Pharnaces (King of Bosporus) 63–47

The Seleucids of Syria

Seleucus I Nicator 321–280
Antiochus I Soter 280–261
Antiochus II Theos 261–246
Seleucus II Callinicus 246–226
Seleucus III Soter 226–223
Antiochus III the Great 223–187
Seleucus IV Philopator 187–175
Antiochus IV Epiphanes 175–164

Antiochus V Eupator 164–162
Demetrius I Soter 162–150
Alexander Balas 150–146
Demetrius II Nicator 146–140
   129–125
(usurper Tryphon 142–139)
Antiochus VI Epiphanes 145–142
Antiochus VII Sidetes 139–129

Seleucus V 125
Antiochus VIII Grypus 121–96

Antiochus IX Cyzicenus 115–95

Attalids of Pergamum
Philetaerus 282–263
Eumenes I 263–241
Attalus I Soter 241–197
Eumenes II Soter 197–160

Attalus II 160–138
Attalus III 138–133
(Eumenes III = Aristonicus
    133–129)

The Kings of Bithynia
Zipoetes c 297–279
Nicomedes I c 279–255
Ziaelas c 255–228
Prusias I 228–185
Prusias II 185–149

Nicomedes II
    Epiphanes 149–128
Nicomedes III Euergetes 128–94
Nicomedes IV Philopator 94–74

Ephiphanes = god made manifest; noble,distinguished. *Soter* = Saviour.
Philopator = devoted to one's father. *Eupator* = born of a noble father.
Euergetes = Well-doer, Benefactor.

The Kings of Commagene
Ptolemaeus c 163/3–c 130
Samus II Theosebes Dikaios
    c 130–c 100
Mithridates I Callinicus c 100–c 70
Antiochus I Theos Dikaios
    Epiphanes Philoromaios
    Philhellen c 70– c 35

Mithridates II c 31
(Antiochus II did not reign, died 29)
Mithridates III c 20
Antiochus III died AD 17
    (After his death, Commagene was
    annexed by Rome)
Antiochus IV 38–72

Roman Emperors
Augustus 27 BC–AD 14
Tiberius 14–37
Caligula 37–41
Claudius 41–54
Nero 54–68
Galba June 68–Jan. 69
Otho Jan–April 69
Vitellius Jan.–Dec. 69
Vespasian 69–70
Titus 79–81
Domitian 81–96
Nerva 96–98
Trajan 98–117
Hadrian 117–38
Antoninus Pius 138–61
Marcus Aurelius 161–80
L. Verus 161–69
Commodus 180–92
Pertinax Jan.–March 193
Didius Julianus March–June 193
Septimius Severus 193–211

Caracalla 211–17
Geta 211–12
Macrinus 217–18
Elagabalus 218–22
Alexander Severus 222–35
Maximinus 235–38
Gordian I 238
Gordian II 238
Pupienus 238
Balbinus 238
Gordian III 238–44
Philip I 244–49
Decius 249–51
Trebonianus Gallus 251–53
Aemilian 253
Valerian 253–60
Gallienus 253–68
Claudius II 268–70
Quintillus 270
Aurelian 270–75
Tacitus 275–76

Florian 276
Probus 276–82
Carus 282–83
Carinus 282–85
Numerian 283–84
Diocletian 285–305
Maximian 286–305
Licinius 308–24
Constantine the Great 306–37

Byzantine Emperors
Arcadius 395–408
Theodosius II 408–50
Marcian 450–57
Leo I 457–74
Leo II 474
Zeno 474–91
Anastasius 491–518
Justin I 518–27
Justinian the Great 527–65
Justin II 565–78
Tiberius II 578–82
Maurice 582–602
Phocas 602–10
Heraclius 610–41
Constantine II 641
Heracleonas 641
Constantine III 641–68
Constantine IV 668–85
Justinian II 685–95
Leontius 695–98
Tiberius III 698–705
Justinian II (second reign) 705–11
Philippicus Bardanes 711–13
Anastasius II 713–15
Theodosius III 715–17
Leo III 717–41
Constantine V 741–75
Leo IV 775–80
Constantine VI 780–97
Eirene 797–802
Nicephorus I 802–11
Stauracius 811
Michael I 811–13
Leo V 813–20
Michael II 820–29
Theophilus 829–42
Michael III 842–67

Constantine II 337–40
Julian 361–63
Jovian 363–64
Valentinian I 364–75
Valens 364–78
Gratian 367–83
Valentinian II 375–92
Theodosius I 378–95

Basil I 867–86
Leo VI 886–912
Alexander 912–13
Constantine VII 913–59
Romanus I (co-emperor) 914–44
Romanus II 959–63
Nicephorus II Phocas 963–69
John I Tzimisces 969–76
Basil II 976–1025
Constantine VIII 1025–28
Romanus III Argyrus 1028–34
Michael IV 1034–41
Michael V 1041–42
Theodora and Zoe 1042
Constantine IX 1042–55
Theodora (second reign) 1055–56
Michael VI 1056–57
Isaac Commenus 1057–59
Constantine X Ducas 1059–67
Romanus IV Diogenes 1067–71
Michael VII Ducas 1071–78
Nicephorus III 1078–81
Alexius I Comnenus 1081–1118
John II Comnenus 1118–43
Manuel I Comnenus 1143–80
Alexius II Comnenus 1180–83
Andronicus I Comnenus 1183–85
Isaac II Angelus 1185–95
Alexius III Angelus 1195–1203
Isaac Angelus (second reign)
  1203–04
Alexius IV Angelus (co-emperor)
  1203–04
Alexius V Ducas 1204
*Theodore I Lascaris 1204–22
*John III 1222–54
*Theodore II Lascaris 1254–58
*John IV 1258–61

Alexius V Ducas 1204
*Theodore I Lascaris 1204–22
*John III 1222–54
*Theodore II Lascaris 1254–58
*John IV 1258–61
Michael VIII Palaeologus 1261–82
Andronicus II Palaeologus 1282–1328
John V Palaeologus 1341–91

John VI Cantacuzenus
  (co-emperor) 1341–54
Andronicus (IV) (co-emperor) 1376–79
John (VII) (co-emperor) 1390
Manuel II Palaeologus 1391–1425
John VIII Palaeologus 1425–48
Constantine XI Dragases 1449–53

Ottoman Sultans

Orhan Gazi 1324–59
Murat I 1359–89
Beyazit I 1389–1403
(Interregnum 1403–13)
Mehmet I 1413–21
Murat II 1421–51
Mehmet II, the Conqueror 1451–81
Beyazit II 1481–1512
Selim I, the Grim 1512–20
Süleyman I, the Magnificent 1520–66
Selim II 1566–74
Murat III 1574–95
Mehmet III 1595–1603
Ahmet I 1603–17
Mustafa I 1617–18
Osman II 1618–22
Mustafa I (second reign) 1622–23
Murat IV 1623–40
İbrahim 1640–48

Mehmet IV 1648–87
Süleyman II 1687–91
Ahmet II 1691–95
Mustafa II 1695–1703
Ahmet III 1703–30
Mahmut I 1730–54
Osman III 1754–57
Mustafa III 1757–74
Abdül Hamit I 1774–89
Selim III 1789–1807
Mustafa IV 1807–08
Mahmut II 1808–39
Abdül Mecit I 1839–61
Abdül Aziz 1861–76
Murat V 1876
Abdül Hamit II 1876–1909
Mehmet V 1909–18
Mehmet VI 1918–22
Abdül Mecit (II) (Caliph only) 1922–24

Glossary

ABACUS. The upper member of a capital

ACROPOLIS. Fortified hilltop. Citadel of a city

ACROTERION (ACROTERIUM). Statues or ornaments at the apex and inner corners of a pediment

ADYTON. Inner sanctuary of a temple

AEGIS. Cuirass or shield with Gorgon's head and ring of snakes

AGORA. Public square or market-place

ALYTARCH. An official charged with producing games in honour of the emperor

AMAZONOMACHIA. Combat between Greeks and Amazons

AMBO. Pulpit in a Christian basilica; facing pulpits in a church from which the epistle and gospel were read

AMPHITHEATRE. An elliptical or circular space surrounded by seats arranged in tiers; used by the Romans for gladiatorial contests

AMPHORA. Two-handled container for wine or water.

ANALEMMA. Supporting wall at the side of a theatre

ANASTYLOSIS. Reconstruction

ANDRON. Mens' apartment, banqueting hall

ANTA. Projecting pilasters ending the lateral walls of the cella of a Greek temple

ANTEFIX. Ornament on the eave or cornice of a building; a feature used to hide the end of the tiles

ANTHEMION. Flower ornament

APOTROPAION. A protective symbol to turn away evil

APSE. A semicircular recess in a wall, especially in a church or in a Roman law-court

ARCHITRAVE (EPISTYLE). A lintel or main beam resting on columns. The lowest member of the entablature

ARCOSOLIUM. Burial niche

ASHLAR (MASONRY). Square cut stones and masonry constructed of these

ASTRAGAL. A moulding at the top or base of a column

ATLANTES. Columns in the form of male figures; cf. Caryatid

ATRIUM. The court of a Roman house, roofed at the sides, but exposed to the sky in the centre or the entrance to a Byzantine church

BALLISTA. War machine which catapulted large stones; used to break down defensive walls

BAS-RELIEF. Low relief sculpture on a marble or stone slab

BASILICA. A Roman public hall; a building with a central hall and side halls which were lower in height; a Christian church of this type

BEMA. Rostrum or a raised section of the chancel of a Byzantine church

BOULE. City council.

BOULEUTERION. Meeting place of the Boule, the legislative council of a city. The city hall

BUCHRANIUM. Sculptured ox skull usually garlanded

CADUCEUS. The wand carried by Mercury, usually represented with two snakes twined around it

CAIQUE. Small wooden trading vessel frequently found in Greek and E Mediterranean waters

CAPITAL. The topmost part of column

CARYATID. Column in the form of a female figure; cf. Atlantes

CAVEA. The auditorium of a theatre; name derived from the fact that originally it was dug out of a hill

CELLA. The great hall of a temple which contained the cult statue

CHITON. A tunic worn short by men and long by women

CHLAMYS. Light cloak worn by ephebes

CHTHONIC. Dwelling in or under the ground

CIPPUS. A small column, sometimes without base or capital, bearing an inscription. Used as a landmark or funeral monument

CLEPSYDRA. A water-clock

COLONNADE (see also STOA and PORTICO. A row of columns which supports an entablature

COLUMNAE CAELATAE. Sculptured columns

COMPOSITE CAPTIAL. Corinthian capital with Ionic volutes, which are slightly reduced in size

CONVENTUS. Provincial court of justice

CORNICE. The upper member of the entablature

CREPIDOMA. The stepped platform on which a temple stood

CUNEIFORM. Wedge-shaped characters of ancient Persian and Assyrian inscriptions

CUNEUS. Wedge-shaped division in the cavea of a theatre

CYCLOPEAN MASONRY. Masonry composed of large, irregular shaped blocks laid out without mortar and not in courses

DEISIS. Reproduction of Christ flanked by the Blessed Virgin and St John

DEME. A village

DEMOS. The people of a land or city

DEXIOSIS SCENE. Offering of the right hand, eg a Commagene king and Hercules at Nemrut Dağı

DIADOCHOS (pl. -OI). Successor of Alexander the Great.

DIAZOMA. A horizontal passage in the cavea of a theatre (διάζωμα, girdle)

DIPTEROS. A temple surrounded by two rows of columns

DORMITION. Scene showing the death of the Virgin

DROMOS. A long narrow entrance to a building, sometimes lined with columns or statues. Passage giving access to a tholos or beehive tomb

EGG AND TONGUE or EGG AND DART. A moulding of alternate eggs and arrowheads

ENGAGED COLUMN. Partly detached column

ENTABLATURE. The stonework resting on a row of columns, including architrave, frieze and cornice

EPHEBUS. Greek youth of 18 or over, usually undergoing training either in the army or at a university

EPISTYLE (Greek). The architrave

EROTES. Figures of Eros, the god of love

EXEDRA. Semicircular recess, usually with a seat, in a Classical or Byzantine building

EXONARTHEX. In a Byzantine church a transverse vestibule preceding the façade

FIBULA. A clasp, buckle or brooch

FLUTES. The vertical channels cut into the sides of columns

FORUM. Roman market place

FRIEZE. The middle member of the entablature

GEISON (Greek). Cornice

GIGANTOMACHIA. War of or with the giants

GYMNASIARCH. Superintendent of the palaestrae who paid the trainers etc

HERM. Quadrangular pillar usually adorned with an erect pahllus and surmounted by a bust

HEROON. Shrine or temple dedicated to a demigod of deified hero

HIERON. Temple or sacred enclosure

HIEROTHESION. A funerary sanctuary

HIMATION. An oblong cloak thrown over the left shoulder and fastened over or under the right

HIPPODROME. A place for horse or chariot races

HOPLITE. Heavily-armed foot-soldier

HYDRA. Jar for carrying water.

HYPAETHRAL. Open to the sky

HYPOGEUM. Underground room or vault

ICONOSTASIS. Screen bearing icons in a Greek Orthodox church

IMPLUVIUM. Basin in the centre of the atrium of a Roman house which was filled with water from the roof

IN ANTIS. With columns between the antae

INSULA. Detached house or block of houses

ISODOMIC. A term applied to masonry laid in courses of equal height

KANTHARUS. Wine cup with two large curving handles, usually associated with Dionysus

KARUM. Assyrian trading colony

KATHOLIKOS. Patriarch of Armenia

KLINE. Couch, bed or bier

KOMAST. A reveller; often depicted

singing or dancing at or following a symposium

KORE. Maiden. Archaic female figure

KOUROS. Boy. Archaic male figure

KYLIX. Shallow wine cup

LABRYS. A double-axe; religious symbol of great antiquity

MACELLUM. Provision market where flesh, fish and vegetables were sold

MAENAD. Bacchante. A 'raver'. A female follower of Dionysus. (From the Greek Μανιάς, raving, frantic)

MANDORLA. Almond-shaped aureole which signifies divinity

MARTYRION. Shrine of a martyr

MEGABYXUS. Chief priest of the temple of Artemis at Ephesus

MEGALE METER. Cybele, the Mother Goddess of Asia Minor

MEGARON. Large hall of a palace or house

METOPE. Plain rectangular panel in a Doric frieze, which was replaced in the Classical period by a sculptrued relief

NAISKOS. Cella of modest proportions in a Greek temple

NAOS (Greek). A temple or sometimes the cella of a temple

NARTHEX. Narrow vestibule along the W side of a church

NAUMACHIA. A mock naval battle staged in a flooded amphitheatre

NEOCORUS. Title borne by a city which possessed a temple dedicated to the imperial cult

NIKE. The personification of victory

NYMPHAEUM. Lit. Temple of the Nymphs, an ornamental fountain with statues

ODEUM/ODEION. Small building with semicircular seating used for concerts and meetings

OIKOS. A house

OINOCHOE. Wine jug

OMPHALOS. A sacred stone commemorating the centre of the earth where the eagles of Zeus met

OPISTHODOMUS. The porch at the rear of a temple which was sometimes used to store valuables

ORCHESTRA. Large circular space occupied by the chorus and actors in Greek theatres

ORTHOSTATS. Upright slabs at the base of a wall

OSTOTHEK. Funerary urn

PALAESTRA. Training area for wrestlers, boxers, etc.

PANCRATION. Athletic contest involving wrestling and boxing; everything except biting or gouging of eyes was permitted

PARODOS. Space between the cavea and the stage of a theatre

PEDIMENT. A low-pitched gable above a portico

PELIKE. Amphora with a wide mouth and pear-shaped outline

PEPLOS. A mantle in one piece worn draped by women

PERIBLOS. A precinct or the circuit around it

PERIPTEROS. A temple surrounded by a row of columns

PERISTASIS. A row of columns surrounding a temple

PERISTYLE. A row or rows of columns surrounding a building or open court

PETASUS. Broad-brimmed hat worn by an ephebe

PHIALE. Saucer or bowl

PILASTER. Shallow pier or column projecting from a wall

PITHOS. Large earthenware jar used for storing oil, grain, etc.

PLINTH. A square block forming the base of a column

PODIUM. A platform, also a low wall or continuous pedestal carrying a colonnade

POLOS. Stiff high hat

PORTICO. A stoa or colonnade

PORTOLANO. Sailing directions

PROHEDRIA. Special seat in a theatre reserved for an important person

PRONAOS. The porch in front of a temple

PROPYLON (pl. Propylaia). Entrance gate to a temenos

PROSKENION. A raised platform in front of the stage-building used by the actors in a Roman theatre

PROSTYLOS. A building with free-standing columns in a row

PROTHESIS. Laying out of a corpse

PRUTANEIS. Member of the executive committee of the Boule

PRYTANEION or PRYTANAEUM. The administrative building in a city. This contained an altar dedicated to Hestia, on which burned a perpetual flame

PSEUDO-DIPTEROS. A dipteral temple without the inner row of columns

PTERON (Greek). A row of columns surrounding a Greek temple

PULPITUM. A platform of boards, a stage

QUADRIGA. Four-horsed chariot

RHYTON. A one-handled cup shaped like an animal's head

SATYR. Follower of Dionysus, usually depicted as half-animal, half-human with tail, hooves and permanently erect phallus

SCAENAE FRONS. Elaborately ornamented front of the scene building in a theatre

SKENE. The stage-building of a Roman theatre

SHAFT. The body of a column between the base and capital

SILENUS. An old satyr, the son of Pan or Hermes and a nymph, who reared Dionysus. Ususally depicted as a grotesque, fat drunken old man precariously balanced on the back of a donkey

SIMA. The gutter of a building

SOCLE. Projecting part of a base or pedestal

SOFFIT. The lower surface of an architectural element

SPINA. Barrier in the centre of a Roman amphitheatre.

STADIUM. Long building in which foot-races and other athletic contests were held

STATHMOS. Quarters for travellers or soldiers

STELE. Narrow stone slab set upright bearing writing or a decoration. Often used as a grave stone or marker

STOA (See also COLONNADE and PORTICO). A porch or portico not attached to a larger building

STRATEGOS. Commander of an army, a general

STYLOBATE. The top step of a crepidoma

SYMPOLITY. A federal union of cities or states, a confederation

SYNOECISM. The union of several cities or towns under one capital city

SYNTHRONON. Semicircular bench or benches for the clergy in the apse or in rows on either side of the Bema

TABULA ANSTATA. Decorative panel

TEMENOS. A sacred enclosure

TEMPLE-IN-ANTIS. Simple building in which the side walls were extended to form a porch. This had two columns between the antae

TETRASTOON. A square surrounded by four colonnades

THEATRON. At first applied to the section of the theatre occupied by the audience, later extended to the whole building. (From the Greek θεατρον, the see-ing place; cf. AUDITORIUM (Latin) the hearing place)

THEME (Byzantine). A province

THERIOMORPHIC. Resembling mythical or real animals

THOLOS. A circular building. Term sometimes applied to an under-ground beehive tomb

THYRSUS. Staff, wreathed with vine leaves and ivy and surmounted with a pine-cone, carried by Dionysus and his followers

TORUS. A large convex moulding, e.g. at the base of a column

TRICONCHOS. A building composed of three 'conches', i.e. of three semicircular niches surmounted by half-domes

TRIGLYPH. Part of Doric frieze bearing three vertical grooves, which alternated with the metopes

TRISKELES. Three legs radiating from a common centre

TYMPANON or TYMPANUM. The area enclosed by the mouldings of a pediment

TRIREME. Greek galley rowed by three banks of oars

VELUM. Canvas used to protect spectators in the auditorium of a Roman theatre from the sun

VOMITORIUM. Covered exit in a Roman theatre

XOANON. A primitive wooden cult statue or idol, frequently believed to have fallen from heaven

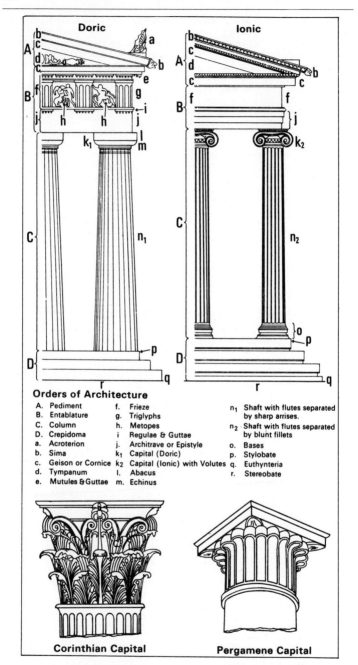

Orders of Architecture

A. Pediment	f. Frieze	n_1 Shaft with flutes separated by sharp arrises.
B. Entablature	g. Triglyphs	
C. Column	h. Metopes	n_2 Shaft with flutes separated by blunt fillets
D. Crepidoma	i. Regulae & Guttae	
a. Acroterion	j. Architrave or Epistyle	
b. Sima	k_1 Capital (Doric)	o. Bases
c. Geison or Cornice	k_2 Capital (Ionic) with Volutes	p. Stylobate
d. Tympanum	l. Abacus	q. Euthynteria
e. Mutules & Guttae	m. Echinus	r. Stereobate

Corinthian Capital

Pergamene Capital

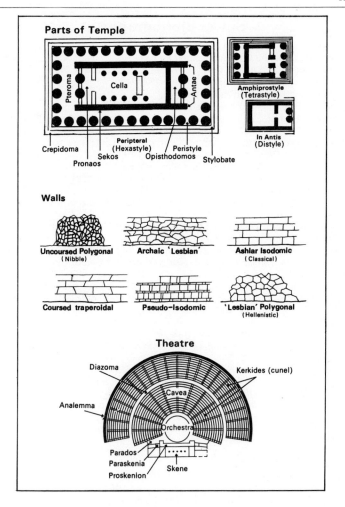

Parts of Temple

Pteroma

Cella

Antae

Amphiprostyle
(Tetrastyle)

In Antis
(Distyle)

Crepidoma

Sekos

Pronaos

Peripteral
(Hexastyle)

Opisthodomos

Peristyle

Stylobate

Walls

Uncoursed Polygonal
(Nibble)

Archaic 'Lesbian'

Ashlar Isodomic
(Classical)

Coursed traperoidal

Pseudo-Isodomic

'Lesbian' Polygonal
(Hellenistic)

Theatre

Diazoma

Kerkides (cunel)

Cavea

Analemma

Orchestra

Parados

Paraskenia

Skene

Proskenion

Select Bibliography

Akurgal, E. *Ancient Civilisations and Ruins of Turkey*, İstanbul, 6thed.1985.

Arrian, *Life of Alexander*, trans. A. de Selincourt, London 1958.

Baldick, Julian *Mystical Islam*, London 1989.

Bayburtluoğlu, C. *Lycie*, n.d. Ankara.

Beaufort, F. *Karamania*, London 1817.

Bieber, Margaret. *The History of the Greek and Roman Theater*, Princeton 1971.

Blake, Evrett and Edmonds, Anne G. *Biblical Sites in Turkey*, Istanbul 1972.

Boardman, J. *The Greeks Overseas*, London 1980.

Boase, T.S.R. ed. *The Cilician Kingdom of Armenia*, Edinburgh 1978.

Braund, David, *Rome and the Friendly King*, London 1984.

Brownrigg, Ronald, *Pauline Places*, London 1989.

Burkert, W. *Greek Religion*, Oxford 1985. *Homo Necans*, trans. P. Bing, Berkeley 1983.

Charlemont Lord. *The Travels of Lord Charlemont in Greece and Turkey*, 1749, ed W.B. Stanford and E.J. Finopoulos, London 1984.

Casson, L. *Ships and Seamanship in the Ancient World*, Princeton 1986.

Çelebi, Evliya, *Travels in Europe, Asia and Africa*, trans. J. von Hammer 1834–1850.

Chandler, R. *Travels in Asia Minor and Greece*, 3rd edition London 1817; with Revett, N. and Pars, W. *Ionian Antiquities*, Soc. of Dilettanti 1769.

Chuvin, Pierre, *Chronicles of the Last Pagans*, Harvard 1990.

Cumont, Franz. *Oriental Religions in Roman Paganism*, New York 1956. *The Mysteries of Mithra*, New York 1956.

Davis, Norman & Kraay, Colin, M. *The Hellenistic Kingdoms, Portrait Coins and History*, London 1973.

Emlyn-Jones, C.J., *The Ionians and Hellenism*, London 1980.

Erim, Kenan T. *Aphrodisias, City of Venus Aphrodite*, London 1986.

Erzen, Alif, *Çavuştepe I*, Ankara 1978

Fellows, C. *Asia Minor*, London 1839. *Lycia*, London 1840.

Ferguson, J. *The Religions of the Roman Empire*, London 1970.

Fontenrose, Joseph, *Didyma, Apollo's Oracle, Cult and Companions*, Berkeley 1988

Fox, Robin Lane. *Alexander the Great*, London 1973. *Pagans and Christians*, London 1986.

Freely, John, *Classical Turkey*, London 1990.

Garland, R. *The Greek Way of Death*, London 1985.

Gibbon, E. *The Decline and Fall of the Roman Empire*, London 1910.

Gilles, Pierre, *The Antiquities of Constantinople*, London 1729

Glazebrook, Philip, *Journey to Kars*, London 1984

Goodwin, Godfrey. *Ottoman Turkey*, London 1977. *A History of Ottoman Architecture*, London 1987.

Guest, John S., *The Yezidis*, London 1987.

Hägg, Tomas, *The Novel in Antiquity*, Oxford 1983.

Haynes, Sybille, *Land of the Chimaera*, London 1974.

Hamilton, W.J. *Researches in Asia Minor*, London 1842.

Haroutunian, Arto der. *A Turkish Cookbook*, London 1987.

Herodotus. *The Histories* trans. Aubrey de Selincourt, London 1955.

Hill, Henry, *Light from the East*, Toronto 1988.

Hornblower, Simon, *Mausolus*, Oxford 1992.

Ibn Battuta. *Travels in Asia and Africa 1325–1354*, London 1983. *Voyages. II. De la Mecque aux steppes russes*, trans. Paris 1932.

Inalcik, Halil, *The Ottoman Empire, the Classical Age 1300–1600*, London 1973.
Inan, Jale *Roman Sculpture in Side*, Ankara 1975.
Jones, A.H.M. *The Later Roman Empire. 284–602* 2 vols, Oxford 1986.
Kinross, Patrick, *Atatürk, the Rebirth of a Nation*, London 1964.
The Ottoman Centuries, London 1977.
Kostof, Spiro, *Caves of God. Cappadocia and its Churches*, Oxford 1989.
Lloyd, Seton, *Early Anatolia*, London 1956. *Ancient Turkey*, London 1989.
Macaulay, Rose, *Towers of Trebizond*, London 1956.
Macqueen, J.G., *The Hittites and their contemporaries in Asia Minor*, London 1986.
MacMullen, R. *Paganism in the Roman Empire*, Yale 1981.
Mango, Cyril, *Byzantium, the Empire of the New Rome*, London 1980.
Matthews, John, *The Roman Empire of Ammianus*, London 1989.
Metzger, H. *Anatolia II*, Geneva 1969.
Mitchell, Stephen, *Anatolia, Land, Men and Gods in Asia Minor*, (two vols) Oxford 1993.
Newton, C.T. *Travels and Discoveries in the Levant*, London 1865.
Nicol, Donald M., *The Immortal Emperor*, Cambridge 1992.
Norwich, John Julius, *Byzantium, the Early Centuries*, London 1988.
Byzantium, the Apogee, London 1991.
Oberleitner, W., Gschwantler, K., Bernhard-Walcher, A., Bammer, A. *Funde aus Ephesos und Samothrake*, Vienna 1978.
Ovid. *Metamorphoses* trans. Mary M. Innes. London 1986.
Özgür, Edip, *Aspendus*, Antalya 1984; *Perge*, İstanbul 1988
Palmer, Andrew, *Monk and Mason on the Tigris Frontier*, Cambridge 1990.
Parks, W. *Oracles of Apollo in Asia Minor*, Beckenham 1985.
Pausanias. *Guide to Greece* trans. Peter Levi, 2 vols, London 1984.
Pekman, Adnan. *Perge Tarihi. (History of Perge)*, Ankara 1973.
Pereira, Michael, *East of Trebizond*, London 1971.
Poliakoff, Michael B. *Combat Sports in the Ancient World*, Yale 1987.
Price, S.R.F. *Rituals and Power*, Cambridge 1986.
Ramsay, W.M. *Letters to the Seven Churches*, 2nd ed. 1906.
Reynolds, J.M. *Aphrodisias and Rome*, London 1982. With Tannenbaum, R., *Jews and Godfathers at Aphrodisias*, Cambridge 1987.
Rosenbaum, E. Huber, G. Onurkan, S. *A Survey of Coastal Cities in Western Cilicia*, Ankara 1967.
Runciman, Steven, *The Fall of Constantinople*, Cambridge 1965. *The Great Church in Captivity*, Cambridge 1968.
Sansone, D. *Greek Athletics and the Genesis of Sport*, Berkeley 1988.
Segal, J.B., *Edessa, the Blessed City*, Oxford 1970.
Slatter, Enid *Xanthus, Travels and Discoveries in Turkey*, London 1994.
Spratt, T.A.B. and Forbes, E. *Travels in Lycia*, London 1847.
Stark, Freya. *Ionia: a Quest*, London 1954. *The Lycian Shore*, London 1956. *Alexander's Path*, London 1958.
Stoneman, R. *Land of the Lost Gods*, London 1987. *Across the Hellespont*, London 1987. *The Traveller's History of Turkey*, Adlestrop, Moreton-in-Marsh 1993.
Strabo. *The Geography*, vols V and VI, London 1970 and 1928.
Sullivan, Richard D., *Near Eastern Royalty and Rome*, Toronto 1990.
Texier, Charles. *Asie Minor*, Paris 1862.
Vermaseren, Maarten, *Cybele and Attis, the Myth and the Cult*, London 1977.
Williams, Gwyn, *Eastern Turkey*, London 1972.

PRACTICAL INFORMATION

This part of the Blue Guide has been prepared with two objects in mind. It is hoped that it will assist travellers to prepare for their journey to Turkey and that, when read in conjunction with the chapters on the various routes, it will help them to have a problem-free and enjoyable visit.

Based on recent first-hand experience of living and travelling in Turkey, it has been compiled with the assistance of the London office of the Turkish Ministry of Tourism. It is as comprehensive as the scope of the guide permits. Readers seeking additional information are advised to consult the specialist sources listed under the different subject-headings.

Turkey's tourist industry continues to expand and alterations are taking place all the time. The author and the publishers would be pleased to hear from readers about changes which they have come across in the course of their visits to Turkey.

Sources of Information

General information on Turkey may be obtained from the overseas offices of the *Ministry of Tourism*. In Great Britain enquiries should be addressed to the Turkish Tourist Office at 170–173 Piccadilly, London, W1V 9DD, tel. 0171 355 4207, fax. 0171 491 0773 and in the United States to 821 United Nations Plaza, New York, NY 10017, tel. (212) 687 2194, fax. (212) 599 7568 or to 1717 Massachusetts Avenue, NW Suite 306, Washington DC 20036, tel. (202) 429 9844, fax. (202) 429 5649.

The Ministry produces a number of informative publications which are available free of charge from its overseas offices. These include *Turkey, A Travel Guide*, illustrated pamphlets on various regions of Turkey, a folding map, the *Youth Travel Guide*, and a booklet listing some of the operators who offer holidays in, and flights to Turkey. The offices can also supply brochures produced by some of the travel companies. In addition, the Ministry's experienced staff can advise on a wide range of subjects—anything from the resort most likely to suit an individual enquirer to the best time of the year to visit a particular part of the country.

The books listed in the bibliography on page 46–7 provide useful background information on the country and its history and additional details of the various archaeological sites.

Among the most useful maps are: Turkey by Kümmerly and Frey 1:1000000, and Western Asia and Turkey-East published by Roger Lascelles, 47, York Road, Brentford, Middlesex, TW8 OQP. The first covers Thrace and Asiatic Turkey as far east as Samsun and Antakya on a scale of 1:800,000. On the reverse it shows Turkey in relation to its neighbours on a scale of 1:2,500,000. The second map covers central and eastern Anatolia on the same scale. The whole country is shown on two sheets produced by Freytag & Berndt on a scale of 1:2,000,000. All of these maps may be obtained from shops like Edward Stanford Ltd, 12–14 Long Acre, London WC2, or ordered through booksellers. A useful road map showing western Anatolia from İzmit to Antalya on a scale of 1:800,000 and the whole country on a scale of 1:2,000,000 is produced by Ada Kitabevi, Kibris Caddesi No. 10, Kuşadası, but this is available only in Turkey.

When to visit Turkey

The best seasons to visit places on the Marmara, Aegean and Mediterranean coasts, and in Thrace and western Anatolia, are spring and autumn. Around the middle of March the weather begins to improve dramatically. The countryside, which lay dormant during the long months of winter rain, burgeons forth in a dazzling display of colour. Farmers, busily ploughing their fields for summer's harvest, are stalked by lines of solemn storks. At Kuş Cenneti and other sanctuaries, noisy flocks of migrant birds fill the air with their cries. In the ruins of Troy, Pergamum and Ephesus lizards, warmed by the growing power of the sun, crawl sluggishly over ancient walls. Carpets of anemones, which range in colour from a red so intense that it is almost black to palest white, cover every inch of soil in sites like Xanthus, Tlos and Pinara. Deep in the pine woods near Fethiye asphodel, that flower of the Elysian Fields and pallid reminder of the shades of ancient · Telmessian heroes, nods its ghostly head.

There are fewer tourists at those times of year, so accommodation, particularly in the small resorts, is cheap and easy to find. Buses and trains are not crowded with foreign visitors, so reservations may be made without difficulty and journeys completed in reasonable comfort. Visits to the ancient cities and sites and to the museums are more pleasant in the absence of the crowds that fill them later.

During the months of June, July and August a different situation prevails. Many resorts are full to bursting point and prices are at their highest. Travelling in crowded buses and trains in day-temperatures of up to 30°C can be an ordeal. Mid-summer is really for the seasoned sun worshipper.

From the middle of September to early December the days are warm and sunny, the nights fine but cool. The debilitating heat of summer has passed and with it have gone the crowds. Although the verdant hues of spring have disappeared from the countryside, the mosaic of brown and umber which has replaced them, has its own beauty. As at the beginning of the year prices are lower and it is not usually necessary to book accommodation in advance. Autumn days in Marmaris, Fethiye, or Bodrum have a particular quiet charm, as many discerning travellers will attest.

The situation on the Mediterranean coast is broadly the same. Spring and autumn in this part of Turkey are delightful. However, summers are even hotter and more exhausting than on the Aegean coast. In August a day-temperature of 40°C is not uncommon in Mersin, Adana and Antakya.

Spring comes late to central and eastern Anatolia. The best time for visits is between the end of April and the end of October. On the eastern Black Sea coast the summer months are often cloudy with high temperatures and high humidity. From Giresun westward there is a marked increase in the number of hours of sunshine per day.

Formalities

Passports and Visas. It is necessary to be in possession of a valid passport to enter Turkey. Citizens of the United Kingdom, the Republic of Ireland, Austria, Italy and Spain require a visa. This may be obtained at the point of entry. At the time of writing the visa costs £5 or its equivalent in foreign currency. Citizens of the United States, Australia, New Zealand, Canada and other countries in Western Europe do not require a visa. Nationals of all these countries may stay up to three months. Nationals of other countries should ask the nearest Turkish Consulate for information about the regulations which apply to them.

A foreigner who wishes to stay in Turkey for longer than three months should apply for a residence permit. The authorities normally require an applicant to prove that he or she has adequate financial means, e.g. income from a source outside the country or has legal employment in Turkey. Some long-term residents, who do not wish to involve themselves in the complications of applying for a permit, leave the country before the end of each three-month period. After a few days' absence abroad, they return and begin a further three months' stay. This practice appears to be acceptable to the Turkish authorities.

Customs Regulations. Apart from the occasional spot-check, visitors to Turkey are not asked, as a rule, to open their baggage on arrival in the country. They are allowed to bring in personal effects and other items, e,g. one camera and five rolls of film, a transistor radio, sports equipment, 200 cigarettes, 50 cigars, 1.5kg of coffee, 1.5kg of instant coffee and 5 (100cc) or 7 (70cc) bottles of wines and/or spirits. There is a full list in *Turkey, A Travel Guide* (see above). Any valuable items, including antiques, should be noted on the visitor's passport to facilitate customs control on departure.

Sharp instruments (including camping knives) and weapons, may not be brought in without special permission.

Turkey prohibits the import, use of, and trade in narcotics including marijuana. Offences against this law are punished by severe penalties.

Currency Regulations. Not more than $5000 worth of Turkish currency may be brought into or taken out of the country. There is no limit on the amount of foreign currency which may be brought in. Keep all receipts obtained for the exchange of foreign currency into Turkish lira. You may have to show these when converting unused Turkish lira back into foreign currency or when taking goods purchased in Turkey out of the country.

Health Regulations. No vaccinations are required by the Turkish authorities, but see the suggestions in the section on 'Health' below.

Travellers wishing to bring in domestic animals, including hunting dogs, must have a Certificate of Origin which gives the health record of the animal and a Certificate of Health which has been issued not more than 15 days before the animal is brought into the country. This must show that the animal is in good health and has been vaccinated against rabies.

Motoring. Motorists are advised to consult their motoring organisation before travelling to Turkey. On arrival at the frontier they must be in possession of the following: a valid passport, an international driving licence, car registration papers, an international green card and (for those who intend to go on to countries in the Middle East) a 'Carnet de Passage'.

Accidents, whether they involve injuries to persons or not, must be reported to the police. That report has to be certified by the nearest local authority. The owner should apply to the customs authority with his passport and the report.

If the vehicle can be repaired, it is necessary to inform the customs authority first and then take the vehicle to a garage. If the vehicle cannot be repaired and the owner wishes to leave the country without it, he has to deliver it to the nearest customs office and have the registration of the vehicle on his passport cancelled. The owner can not leave the country until this cancellation has been made.

Private Yachts. Yacht owners in possession of a Transit Log may keep their boats in Turkish waters for up to two years for wintering or maintenance. Certain marinas are licenced for the storage of yachts for a period of two to five years. Details may be obtained from the marinas concerned.

On arrival in Turkish waters the yacht owner should proceed to the nearest port of entry: Botaş (Adana), Antalya, Kemer, Alanya, Kaş, Finike, Kuşadası, Didim, Akçay, Ayvalık, Bandırma, Çanakkale, İskenderun, Mersin (İçel), Taşucu (Silifke), Anamur, İstanbul, Dikili, Çeşme, Derince, Marmaris, Güllük, Bodrum, Datça, Fethiye, Ordu, Samsun, Tekirdağ, Trabzon, Hopa, Zonguldak, Giresun, Rize, or Sinop, so that the log may be controlled.

Owners should acquaint themselves with the various regulations which apply to those sailing in Turkish waters. Details may be obtained from Turkish Embassies or the relevant yachting associations. In particular the following should be noted: International navigation rules should be followed at all times. The Turkish courtesy flag should be flown between 08.00 and sunset. Zig-zagging between Turkish and Greek waters should be avoided. Yachtsmen should not take archaeological objects from Turkish coastal waters. The penalty for doing so is confiscation of the yacht. Yachts should not be moored in the forbidden zones. Further information about these zones may be obtained from any Turkish Embassy or Consulate.

Getting there

Air. There are frequent flights by Turkish Airlines (THY) from many of the capitals and cities of the world to İstanbul and Ankara with onward connections to all the principal cities of Turkey. There are also some direct flights to İzmir, Antalya and Dalaman. British Airways flies from London to İstanbul. From the United States of America there are connecting flights to destinations in Turkey via London, or via Amsterdam with KLM.

THY offers substantial reductions to students, sports groups and families. When planning a holiday, budget-conscious travellers should note that the air fare constituent in the price of a package tour is usually much less than the cost of a flight-only ticket.

Companies which specialise in inclusive tours include Prospect Music and Art (tel. 0181-995 2151), Martin Randall Tours (0181-995 3642), Special Tours (tel. 0171-730 2297), Page and Moy (tel. 01533 542000), Regent Holidays (tel. 01272 211711, President Holidays (also flight only; tel. 0171-249 9836).

Students and those who wish to limit their expenditure will be attracted by the cheap charter flights which operate from London during the holiday season. Some of these restrict the visitor to a maximum stay of two weeks.

Details of charter flights to Turkey operated by companies like Regent Holidays, Shanklin, Isle of Wight are given in the brochure published by the Turkish Ministry of Tourism (see above.) They are also frequently advertised in the holiday sections of the *The Times, Sunday Times, The Observer, The Guardian*, and other daily and weekly papers.

Flights to Dalaman in SW Turkey bring Bodrum, Marmaris, Fethiye and the small, beautiful resorts of the Lycian coast within the reach of travellers who have a limited amount of time at their disposal. The tour companies usually have special coaches to take their clients from the airport to their destinations. Individual travellers should take a taxi or dolmuş to Dalaman village, where they can pick up one of the regular bus or dolmuş services.

There are bus services, for which a small charge is made, from all Turkish airports, except Dalaman, to the city terminals. Taxis are also available.

By Sea. The Turkish Maritime Line operates a service from Venice to a number of ports in Turkey. For details of prices and schedules, and to make bookings, contact Sunquest Holidays, 9 Grand Parade, Green Lanes, London N4 1JX, tel. 0181 800 8030.

There are sailings from Famagusta (Gazimağusa) and Kyrenia (Girne) in the Turkish Republic of North Cyprus to Mersin and Silifke respectively. For details apply to Sunquest Holidays. There are frequent services between the Greek islands of Lesbos, Chios, Samos, Cos and Rhodes and the Turkish mainland during the holiday season. Information about times and fares may be obtained from local travel agents.

By Rail. While it is possible to travel by rail from London to İstanbul, the rigours of this journey, which can take three days, are such that it will commend itself only to the most hardy travellers. The trains, which are popular with immigrant workers returning to Greece and Turkey from Western Europe, are usually very crowded and the condition of the carriages and the toilets tends to deteriorate as the journey progresses.

The trains are slow, subject to delays and are frequently late in arriving at their destination. Any illusions about the luxury enjoyed by the characters in Agatha Christie's celebrated crime novel vanish after a few hours in the noisy, smoke-filled compartments.

The 'İstanbul Express' provides a daily service from Munich, Vienna and Athens. There are weekly departures, with sleeping cars, to İstanbul from Budapest, Bucharest and Moscow. Discounts are available to minors and students under the age of 26.

By Road. It is approximately 3000km from London to İstanbul. Any driver willing to tackle this distance must be prepared to do battle with the convoys of TIR lorries which carry goods to Turkey and beyond. Although most of the roads *en route* are well surfaced and well-maintained, some sections are very busy. An additional disincentive is provided by the checks at the various international borders, which are often long-winded and time-consuming. Information about car insurance, the international driving licence, etc., may be obtained from the AA (tel. 01256 20123) or the RAC (tel. freephone 0800 678000, or 01345 333222). Both organisations can also provide their members with detailed route maps and town plans.

Two routes are suggested: the northern route by Belgium, Germany, Austria, Hungary, Romania and Bulgaria and the southern route by Belgium, Germany, Austria and Italy and thence by ferry to Turkey.

By Coach. There are express coach services from Paris (with a connecting bus from London), Strasbourg, Munich and Vienna to İstanbul. Enquiries in England should be made to Eurolines, tel. 01582 404511 or any National Express booking agent. The operating companies give a number of reductions. Refer to Eurolines for details. Travellers who dislike flying may find that the coaches, which are faster, cleaner, and more comfortable than the trains, offer a suitable alternative.

Travel in Turkey

By Air. Passengers arriving at the international airports of Ankara, İstanbul, İzmir and Antalya will find connecting flights, operated by THY and some other companies, to the principal cities in Turkey. There is a free bus service between the international and domestic terminals at İstanbul airport.

Turkish Airlines offers reductions on internal flights to students, families and sports groups of five or more. Details may be obtained from THY.

By Sea. For information about local boat and ferry services in İstanbul see Route 1. Turkish Maritime Lines operate passenger services to Trabzon and to İzmir from İstanbul. There are discounts available to children, students, journalists and groups.

By Rail. During recent years the Turkish Government has spent a considerable amount of money improving the rolling stock and equipment of the country's 10,000km rail-network. This operates mainly in central, eastern and south-eastern Anatolia. Several trains are faster and as comfortable as the best of the long-distance coaches on the same routes. Frequent services, including an excellent night train with sleeping berths and reclining seats, link İstanbul and Ankara. Turkish Railways gives reductions to groups of 24 or more, to students and to purchasers of return tickets.

By Long-Distance Bus. In Turkey most long-distance journeys are made by bus. The country is covered with a network of services, operated by private companies, which compete vigorously with each other for passengers. Most of the buses in use are modern vehicles of German manufacture; Mercedes and MAN predominate. The buses are clean and well-maintained. Ticket prices are very low.

A number of buses have air-conditioning installed, but this may not always function. Even if it is in working order, it is not unusual for some passengers, who claim to be sensitive to draughts, to ask to have it turned off and the roof vents closed.

Some operators provide services at certain times of the day which do not permit smoking. Enquire about these when making a reservation. Varan, Ulusoy and one or two other companies use double-decker coaches which confine smokers to the upper floor. Journeys on these may cost a little more, but the additional comfort which they offer and the provision of light refreshments during the journey, more than justify the additional expense. In Ankara, Ulusoy and Varan have their own clean, comfortable terminals on the outskirts of the city.

Throughout Turkey, long-distance services start from the *otogar*, which is usually located on the outskirts of the town. There is often a courtesy minibus which will take passengers from the company's town office and, in some cases from the principal hotels, to the *otogar*. Ask your hotel receptionist about this service.

If you wish to avoid the frantic activity of the *otogar*, plan your bus journeys well in advance, particularly if long distances are involved. Having decided on the time you wish to travel, find out which companies operate suitable services. On main routes you will generally have a choice of four or five services. Select the most expensive—the additional cost will be negligible—as those buses are likely to be newer, more comfortable and may have a non-smoking section. If you are travelling in daytime during the summer months, take the direction of your journey into account and ensure that you are seated on the shaded side of the bus. Do not rely on claims that the bus is air-conditioned (see above). If travelling at night, make sure that you have reserved accommodation at your destination—particularly if your bus arrives during the middle of the night or early in the morning.

At present travel by bus at night in eastern or south-eastern Turkey is not recommended.

All seats on long distance buses are numbered and, providing you make your reservation sufficiently far in advance, you should be able to choose where you want to sit. The best seats are 1 to 4. These are located just behind the driver and near the front entrance.

If you are a non-smoker, and smokers are not segregated (see above), it is particularly important to book the front seats. Despite vigorous Government propaganda, the average Turkish male continues to be a chain-smoker, so proving the Italian expression *'Fumare come un Turco'*. Fresh air from the window near the driver and from the front door, when it is opened, will help to keep the air reasonably clear of cigarette-smoke. The front seats also give the best views of the countryside.

Turkish bus music—sometimes called arabesque music—is definitely an acquired taste. Not even all Turks enjoy it! If you think that you are likely to find it distracting, bring a personal stereo and a supply of tapes. Talking books are an excellent choice for long journeys.

There is a high incidence of travel-sickness among passengers on some routes. You can get proprietary medicines without prescription, which help to combat travel sickness, from Turkish chemists shops (*eczahane*). To keep the air fresh near you take a small bottle of eau-de-Cologne.

Long-distance buses stop about every two hours for approximately 30 minutes at a *kahve* or *lokanta*. On a night-journey from the Aegean or Mediterranean coast to the interior, take some warm clothing, as even during the summer months the temperature on the Anatolian plateau drops sharply after dark.

The Turks are a gregarious and friendly people and your fellow passengers will almost certainly attempt to engage you in conversation. It is not unusual for them to offer tea or other refreshments at one of the stops. As the offer springs from the hospitality which the Turks are accustomed to display towards visitors to their country, it would be discourteous to refuse.

Long-distance bus journeys provide an opportunity to see Turkey and to experience an aspect of Turkish life which is denied to those travellers who stick to organised tours. The journeys are amusing and exasperating by turn. Though often tiring, they are always vastly rewarding and should on no account be missed by anyone who takes more than a superficial interest in the country.

By Dolmuş. The dolmuş or shared taxi is a colourful feature of Turkish life. Vehicles carry a yellow band. Like a bus, it operates over a specified route, which is stated on a notice fixed to the windscreen or announced by the shrill cries of a small boy who hangs precariously out of the front passenger door. In cities and towns the dolmuş may be a large, much-repaired American car. In country areas it will probably be a mini-bus. It does not operate to a timetable but leaves when it is full. Dolmuş means 'stuffed' or 'filled' in Turkish and as more and more people pile in, you will begin to appreciate the apt choice of name.

By Taxi. Taxis in Turkey, which are easily distinguished by their yellow colour, operate from ranks but will also pick up fares while cruising. All should have meters in working order. For long journeys try to agree on the fare before starting. Your hotel receptionist will give you an idea of how much to pay. He may also intervene in any dispute with the taxi driver.

By Private Transport. Turkey has an excellent network of approximately 50,000km well-maintained main roads. The crossing of the Bosphorus at İstanbul has been speeded up by the completion of a bypass and two toll bridges which lead to the İstanbul–İzmir and Gerede–Ankara express roads. 'E' indicates European Road Network, 'A' Asian Road Network and 'M' Middle East Road Network.

Side roads to villages are usually asphalted, but are often very narrow. Be on the look-out for slow-moving tractors which can take up most of the road. Access to the remoter archaeological sites is sometimes by rough tracks which may be impassable during bad weather.

Road signs conform to international standards. Look out for the following warnings: DUR = Stop; DIKKAT = Caution. Archaeological and historical sites are indicated by distinctive yellow signs.

In the countryside, where it is possible to travel for long distances without seeing another vehicle, avoid being lulled into a false sense of security. Around the next corner there may be a slow-moving farm vehicle or a procession of overloaded lorries crawling along in low gear. Keep a sharp look out also for herds of sheep and goats which graze the verges and sometimes stray across the road.

Garages undertaking repairs are usually grouped in one or more areas of a city or town. There are some also on the main routes. Spare parts for most cars are available and mechanics are trained to repair both Turkish and foreign makes. Visitors may obtain assistance from the Turkish Touring Automobile Club.

Petrol, which is slightly cheaper in Turkey than in most European countries, may be bought from Petrol Ofisi, Türk Petrol, BP, Mobil or Shell. Super grade is widely available, though it may be difficult to obtain in some of the remoter areas. Unleaded petrol is sold at most stations; the price may vary. On the main roads filling stations often have adjoining service facilities, 24 hour restaurants and sometimes small motels, e.g. the attractive Karan Motel near Anamur.

There are **car-rental** offices in Ankara, İstanbul, İzmir and in most large towns and cities and in the popular holiday resorts. In addition to Hertz, Avis, and Europcar there are many local companies. A list may be obtained from Tourist Information Offices or from travel agencies.

In Turkey traffic circulates on the right. The speed limit is 50km in towns, 90km outside. To avoid problems with the traffic police, stick to these limits.

In many tourist resorts motorcycles and mopeds are available for hire. Crash helmets are not usually provided, so bring your own protective headgear. Bicycles may be hired in some places.

Accommodation

Hotels and pensions. In Turkey these range from establishments like the Hilton and Sheraton in İstanbul and Ankara, the Büyük Efes in İzmir, the Talya in Antalya and the Büyük Sürmeli in Adana to family-run concerns in the cities, towns and holiday resorts of Thrace and Anatolia.

Accommodation is still very reasonably priced. A stay in a 5-star hotel, which provides every comfort and offers meals guaranteed to tempt the most jaded appetite, may cost less than in a medium-class hotel in many European countries. Travellers on a limited budget can stay in small pensions or private houses for a very modest outlay, even during the holiday season. During March and April, October, November and December the cost will be even less.

The Ministry of Tourism publishes a booklet which lists the hotels and pensions registered with it. They have agreed to abide by certain regulations and standards of facilities. A copy of the booklet, which gives the star ratings but not the prices charged, may be obtained from Ministry of Tourism offices abroad and in Turkey. Hotels registered with the municpal authorities, have also agreed to maintain certain standards.

Hotels registered with the Ministry are obliged to keep a book in which complaints and suggestions may be made by guests. This book is examined regularly by inspectors. Complaints, if sustained, may result in certain sanctions being taken against them. Complaints may also be made direct to the Ministry.

Turkey has a relatively high rate of inflation, which, inevitably, is reflected in the cost of accommodation. For this reason hotel and pension prices are not given in the Blue Guide. On arriving at their destination visitors making their own holiday arrangements are advised to contact the Tourist Information Office which can provide details of the prices charged by the local hotels and pensions. The address of this office appears at the beginning of the description of each city, principal town and resort.

In some hotels the prices, though payable in Turkish lira, will be quoted in US $ or German Marks. As a result the cost of accommodation may vary slightly from day to day in line with fluctuations in the rate of exchange.

Prices are reviewed annually by the Ministry of Tourism and any increases sanctioned come into effect on 1 January. This unfortunate arrangement does little to encourage visitors to come to Turkey during the 'low' season.

Most hotels accept payment by credit card (see the section on credit cards) or travellers' cheques. Turkish and foreign currency is always welcome.

Breakfast and some other meals may be served in your room. There is usually an additional charge for this service. In the smaller, simpler establishments breakfast may not be provided at all.

While the standards of service and cleanliness in the hotels registered with the Ministry of Tourism are generally excellent, shortcomings are found from time to time.

Many establishments rely on solar panels to heat water for baths and showers. There should be a back-up heating system of some kind, but this may not always work or the management may be reluctant to use it for reasons of cost. As a result at the beginning and end of the year, when sunshine can vary both in duration and intensity, there may be no hot water supply to the rooms or it may be available during certain hours only. Remedy: badger the management, make a note in the complaints book and report your dissatisfaction to the local Tourist Information Office.

The baths in some of the smaller hotels do not have plugs. Remedy: complain as outlined above, or to avoid endless arguments, which may spoil your holiday, be prepared, take a bath plug with you. ·

Motels. While a number of establishments calling themselves motels have separate chalets in a landscaped garden and some located near the sea have their own private stretch of beach, many are indistinguishable from ordinary hotels. Their prices are as high or often higher than hotels offering equivalent facilities. Motels registered with the Ministry are listed in the publication mentioned above.

Holiday Villages. Along the Marmara, Black Sea, Aegean and Mediterranean coasts there are a number of holiday villages. These vary widely in style and in the services and facilities which they offer. Some are expensive and cater almost exclusively for visitors from abroad. Others are patronised by Turkish and foreign guests. In general they attract holidaymakers who like all their recreations and amusements to be in one location.

Private Rooms. In many places it is possible to get a room in a private house. Inevitably, these vary a great deal. The best are very good and are on a par with rooms in the smaller pensions. Look out for signs, usually in German or English, outside those houses where rooms are available. Alternatively, make enquiries at the *otogar*. Families offering this kind of accommodation often meet incoming buses.

The cost of staying in a private house is usually very modest. Single rooms are often difficult to get and you should be prepared to share with one or more guests. (Turkish propriety will ensure that only members of the same sex are involved in this arrangement.) Breakfast is often included in the cost of accommodation. If you have a bath or shower, there is usually a small extra charge.

Camp Sites. There are camp sites approved by the Ministry of Tourism in various parts of Turkey. These are listed in the publication *Turkey Travel Guide* which may be obtained from Tourist Information Offices in Turkey or abroad.

Sites are clearly signposted. Some have their own restaurants and private beaches. Camping outside the registered sites is possible, but is not recommended by the authorities.

Young People. Facilities available to students and young people are listed in the publication *Youth Travel Guide Book* which may be obtained from any office of the Ministry of Tourism. This gives information about dormitories, forest camps etc in places all over Turkey. It also lists private establishments which offer discounts to young people. Prices vary, but in general are quite low.

Food and Drink

Turkish cuisine has always been highly praised by visitors. Even the French have been obliged, grudgingly, to acknowledge its merits. Based on the use of best-quality meat, fresh fish and vegetables, carefully prepared and served, it eschews the elaborate sauces used by cooks of other nationalities to disguise the shortcomings of their less-successful offerings. Because of the uncomplicated nature of Turkish cooking even the most unpretentious establishments often provide satisfying meals. For a list of the most popular dishes, see the reference section below.

In cities the more expensive restaurants usually open for lunch and dinner only. However, smaller establishments start to serve meals early in the morning and do not close until late at night. Even if you arrive in the middle of the afternoon, a time when you would be sent packing by European restaurateurs, you should be able to obtain a cooked meal. Service, although it may not always be very quick, is accompanied by a smile.

Restaurants in the cities and larger towns usually add a service charge to the bill. You may wish to give a small additional amount to show your appreciation. If a service charge is not shown, 10 per cent is acceptable as a gratuity.

While lapses do occur from time to time, disappointing experiences reported by foreign visitors are, almost always, due to misunderstandings arising from language difficulties or to a lack of knowledge of Turkish customs by the diner. The following comments may help readers to avoid some of these.

Eating out in Turkey is a serious business, so be prepared to allow plenty of time for your meal. Begin by asking for a selection of *meze*, hors d'oeuvres, and over these consider your choice of main course and pudding. If, in the European fashion, you order all the courses at the beginning of the meal, they will probably all arrive at the same time—*meze* or soup, main dish, vegetables and dessert. You will then have to chose which of the rapidly-cooling dishes to eat first!

In Turkey hot dishes are not usually served at the same temperature as is customary in Europe. This is particularly the case in the *Hazır Yemek* (fast food) restaurants, where the dishes are prepared early in the day and kept warm in *bains-maries*. It also happens in south and south-eastern Turkey where restaurateurs are strongly influenced by the customs of their Arab neighbours.

To avoid problems say to the waiter, when you are ordering the meal, '*hepsi çok sıcak olsun*', let everything be very hot. This should ensure that your nice, freshly-cooked steak does not arrive with a garnish of tepid vegetables and tired, flaccid chips.

Breakfast (*Kahvaltı*). Hotel and pension breakfasts usually consist of tea, fresh bread, butter, jam, sheep's cheese, olives and sometimes a boiled egg. In Marmaris and other places in SW Turkey instead of jam you will almost certainly be offered a portion of the delicious *Çam Balı*, pine honey, for which that region is famous. In Artvin and the surrounding area another delicious locally-produced honey graces the breakfast table.

If you tire of hotel fare, try breakfasting in a pastry-shop. Ask for *Su böreği*. This looks like *mille feuille*, but contains soft white cheese sprinkled with herbs. Accompanied by a large glass of sweet, milkless tea, it makes a tasty and sustaining breakfast.

Many Turks like to begin the day with a bowl of chicken soup. If you are weary after an overnight journey by bus, try this as a restorative. During the winter months, *Salep*, a hot, sweetened milk drink made from the pounded dried tubers of certain orchidaceous plants is an excellent, if slightly exotic alternative.

As a rule coffee is not offered for breakfast in Turkey. Sachets of imported Nescafé are usually available, but they may add a sizeable amount to your bill. If you are unable to start the day without coffee, take a jar of your favourite brand with you. Only in the expensive hotels is this practice frowned upon.

Lunch and Dinner (*Öğle yemeği* and *Akşam Yemeği*). Meze, hors d'oeuvres, play an important part in lunch and dinner. They are so delicious and satisfying that many diners skip the main course altogether. In addition to *börek*, pastry filled with cheese and herbs, you will probably be offered *dolma*, stuffed vine leaves, Russian salad, soft white cheese, olives, excellent Turkish Rocquefort cheese, *cacık*, yogurt flavoured with cucumber and garlic, taramasalata, and various spicy dips. Not to be missed on any account is *İmam bayıldı*. The name of this dish, which consists of aubergines stuffed with onions and tomatoes, means 'the Imam fainted'. Presumably his syncope resulted from the dish's delicious taste, though some say it was because it is so costly to prepare.

For the main course there is a wide choice of fish, beef, poultry and lamb cooked in a variety of ways. As the majority of Turks belong to the Islamic faith, they do not eat pork and it rarely appears on restaurant menus. However, haunches of wild boar are sometimes on sale at yacht marinas.

Fish (*Balık*). Some of the fish on the menu are native to the eastern Mediterranean and may be unfamiliar to you. They are usually displayed in refrigerated cabinets in the restaurant. Fish-lovers recommend *lüfer*, blue-fish, *levrek*, sea bass, *palamut*, tuna, *kalkan*, turbot and *kılıç balığı*, sword-fish. Fish is usually grilled, *ızgara* or fried *tava*.

In İstanbul near the Galata Bridge try the *Hamsi*, anchovies, *Uskumru*, mackerel, or *Sardalya*, sardines. Freshly grilled and pressed into sandwiches, they are delicious.

Meat (*Et*). In addition to *bonfile*, a small fillet steak, there is the ubiquitous *kebab*, some varieties of which are named after the places where they were first prepared—Bursa, Adana and Urfa. Rivalling the *kebab* in popularity are *köfte*, especially *İnegöl köftesi*. These meatballs of minced lamb served with raw onion rings are named after a town near Bursa.

Offal, particularly *kara ciğer*, liver and *işkembe*, tripe, often appears on the menu. Try *Arnavut ciğeri*, Albanian-style liver fried with a spicy mixture of onions, or *işkembe çorbasi*, tripe soup. Adventurous spirits may like to sample *koç yumurtası*, lambs' testicles. Esteemed by the Turks as a nourishing delicacy, they are often served in a mixed grill.

Vegetables (*Sebze*). A walk through the weekly market in any Anatolian town is one of the pleasures of a visit to Turkey. There you will find great piles of the vegetables produced in the surrounding area—potatoes, onions, beans, cauliflowers, aubergines, cucumbers, tomatoes—all of which are used with great skill by Turkish cooks. Sample them when dining in one of the local restaurants.

Dessert (*Tatlı*). Turkish meals are usually brought to a close with *baklava*, pastry filled with almonds and pistachio nuts and soaked in syrup. This is one of the many very sweet desserts which are popular with Turkish diners. If you are not tempted by the erotic *kadın göbeği*, 'Lady's navel', try *sütlaç*, cold, creamy rice pudding or end your meal with some of the excellent locally-produced fresh fruit.

Coffee (*Kahve*). Although it is possible to order Nescafé or an equivalent in most restaurants, they are poor substitutes for Turkish coffee, which provides the perfect end to a Turkish meal. As sugar is added to Turkish coffee while it is being prepared, remember to tell the waiter whether you want it *sade*, without sugar, *az şekerli*, with a little sugar, *orta*, with a moderate quantity of sugar, or *çok şekerli*, with a lot of sugar.

Do not empty the cup. If you do so, you will get a mouthful of grounds! A little cold water added to the coffee before you begin to drink will cause the grounds to settle in the bottom of the cup.

If you have been invited by a Turkish family to dine in their home, you will be offered, and it is polite to accept, more than one cup of coffee.

Fast Food. For a quick snack go to a *büfe*. There you can have *börek* (see above), toasted sandwiches or *lahmacun*, a wafer-thin pizza coated with a spicy mixture of chopped lamb and onion in a creamy tomato sauce. An excellent accompaniment to *lahmacun* is *ayran*, a chilled drink made from yogurt diluted with water. One of the best places for *lahmacun* in Turkey is the *Büfe* near a flight of steps at the right-hand side of the main entrance to İstanbul's Sirkeçi railway station.

A more familiar type of pizza may be obtained in *pide* restaurants. *Pide* is a thick dough base covered with either *et*, meat, *yumurta*, eggs or *peynir*, cheese. As in the case of *lahmacun*, *ayran* goes very well with *pide*.

In many Turkish cities there are restaurants which serve hamburgers and European-style pizzas. Unfortunately, the pizzas are often rather poor imitations of the genuine article. In İstanbul and Ankara McDonalds have opened hamburger restaurants.

Alcohol. There is no ban on the sale of alcohol in Turkey and many Turks drink beer, wine or *rakı*, an aniseed-flavoured spirit of considerable potency. Popularly known as *aslan sütü*, 'lion's milk', this is a type of grape-brandy which resembles the Arab *arrack* or the Greek *ouzo*. As an accompaniment to a meal it is customary to mix a quantity of *rakı* with an equal quantity of cold water.

In addition to the beer made by *Tekel*, there are light and dark beers produced by *Efes Pilsen*. *Tuborg* is also brewed under licence in Turkey. Most towns have at least one pub, where beer only is sold.

In Anatolia, to avoid offending those who follow the strict rule of Islam which forbids the drinking of alcohol, pubs are usually tucked away in side streets. Patrons sit at small tables, where their drinks, often accompanied by appetising snacks, are brought to them. The atmosphere is decorous and relaxed.

In İstanbul, Ankara and some of the larger cities, pubs are more like their European counterparts. They are often noisy, smoke-filled places with sawdust on the floor. In resorts on the Marmara, Black Sea, Aegean and Mediterranean coasts, pubs are usually found in the areas frequented by foreign visitors. Their ambience generally reflects the mixed Turkish and foreign clientèle.

In recent years Turkish wines have become much better known. As demand has increased, greater care is being taken in their production and, as a result, the quality of the top brands is good. Wine is still very inexpensive in Turkey.

Recommended are *Villa Doluca* red (*kırmızı*) or white (*beyaz*), and *Kavaklıdere Çankaya*. Somewhat less expensive are *Buzbağ*, *Dikmen* and *Lal*.

In addition to the supermarkets, the *Tekel* (state monopoly) shops sell a range of Turkish wines, spirits and beers. Imported gin, whisky, vodka and cognac are usually available, at a price, in the larger cities.

Soft Drinks and Mineral Water. While water is safe to drink in most places in Turkey, many visitors quickly develop a liking for pleasant tasting, locally-produced mineral water (*maden suyu*). Children and adults who do not drink alcohol quench their thirst with Coca-Cola, Pepsi-Cola, *Yedigün* (a fizzy, lemon-flavoured drink) or any of a number of excellent fruit juices. *Ayran* (see above) is a refreshing drink at meal-time. It goes particularly well with highly spiced food.

If you are visiting Turkey during the winter months, try *salep* (see above). In summer *boza*, a thick, pleasantly flavoured drink made from fermented millet, is popular. According to the 17C traveller, Evliya Çelebi, *boza* was so appreciated by the inhabitants of Bursa that the city had no fewer than 97 boza-houses! Some etymologists believe that the English word 'booze' is derived, by way of Low German and Dutch, from *boza*.

The Menu

As Turkish cooks are ingenious and inventive, they produce a wide range of dishes, many of which you will encounter on your travels. Those listed in the Menu below and mentioned in the text of the Blue Guide are just a few of the many culinary delights that await the travelling gourmet.

Meze (Hors d'oeuvres)
Arnavut ciğeri, Spiced liver
Beyaz peynir, White goat cheese
Börek, Pastry filled with soft, white cheese and herbs (sometimes deep-fried)
Cacık, Yogurt flavoured with grated cucumber, garlic and olive oil
Fava, Bean paste
İmam bayıldı, Stuffed aubergine
Pilaki, White beans and onion with vinegar
Sardalya, Sardines
Tarama, A paste of red caviar, yogurt, garlic and olive oil
Yaprak dolması, Stuffed vine leaves

Çorba (Soup)
Domates çorbası, Tomato soup
Et suyu, Consommé
Sebse çorbası, Vegetable soup
Tavuk suyu, Chicken soup
Yayla çorbası, Mutton soup with yogurt

Salata (Salads)
Amerikan salatası, Mixed Russian salad with carrots and peas in mayonnaise
Beyin salatası, Sheep's brain salad on lettuce
Çoban salatası, Mixed chopped salad of tomatoes, cucumbers, peppers, etc.
Karışık salata, Mixed salad
Patlican salatası, Cooked aubergines with yogurt
Yeşil salata, Green salad

Balık (Fish)
Alabalık, Trout
Barbunya, Red mullet
İstakoz, Lobster
Kalkan, Turbot
Kefal, Grey mullet
Kılıč, Swordfish
Mercan, Bream
Mersin, Sturgeon
Midye, Mussels
Palamud, Tuna

Et (Meat)
Bonfile, Filet steak
Döner kebab, Slices of lamb roasted on a vertical spit
İzmir koftesi, Croquettes of lamb in gravy
Pirzola, Lamb chops
Sebzeli rosbif, Roast beef served with vegetables
Şiş kebab, Charcoal-grilled chunks of lamb and tomatoes
Şiş köfte, Grilled croquettes of lamb

Sebze (Vegetables)
Bamya, Okra
Bezelye, Peas
Biber, Green sharp peppers
Domates, Tomatoes
Havuç, Carrots
Kabak, Marrow or pumpkin
Lahana, Cabbage
Patates, Potatoes
Taze fasulye, French beans

Tatlı (Puddings)
Bülbül Yuvası, Pastry with pistachio and walnut purée and ice cream
Dondurma, Ice cream
Kabak tatlısı, Pumpkin served with nuts and syrup

Mevya (Fruit)
Çilek, Strawberry
Elma, Apple
Erik, Plum
İncir, Fig
Kiraz, Cherries
Kavun, Yellow melon
Karpuz, Water melon
Muz, Banana
Portakal, Orange
Şeftali, Peach
Üzüm, Grapes

Language

According to a United Nations survey, Turkish is one of the world's most widely-used languages. In its various forms it is spoken by c 150 million people in an area that stretches from the centre of former Yugoslavia to the province of Sinkiang in China. A member of the Ural-Altaic group, its closest European relatives are Finnish and Hungarian.

Since it was adopted on 4 May 1278 by the Karamanoğlu ruler of Konya, Mehmet Bey, it has been the official language of the Turkish people. One of the SW group of Turkic languages, it was heavily influenced by Persian and Arabic during the period of Ottoman greatness. At that time Persian was the language of courtly literature, particularly of poetry, while Arabic, the language of science and religion, was widely used and known throughout the empire.

In effect, modern Turkish is the language of the Ottoman period purged of the vocabulary and idioms which it had acquired from Arabic and Persian. This cleansing operation took place in 1932 under the direction of Atatürk, the founder of modern Turkey, a short time after he had organised the changeover from the Arabic to the Roman alphabet.

There are 29 letters in the Turkish alphabet. Atatürk and his reforming committee omitted q, w and x and added six additional letters: ç, ğ, ı, ö, ş and ü. Each letter has a fixed sound, a factor which makes the language easy to read and to pronounce.

Turkish is an agglutinative language—changes are made to the endings of nouns to indicate different meanings e.g. *-a* or *-e* = to, *-dan* or *-den* = from. There are no genders and no articles. To meet the requirements of modern life, its vocabulary has been expanded with borrowings from many European languages e.g. *otogar, kamion, tren, istasyon, gazete, banka.*

With a little application it is possible to acquire a basic knowledge of Turkish in a comparatively short time. Although at first sight the grammar may seem difficult, it is soon mastered. *Colloquial Turkish,* by Yusuf Mardin, is published by Kegan Paul, and *Teach Yourself Turkish,* by G.L. Lewis, by Hodder and Stoughton. Available in Turkey only is *Türkçe Öğreniyoruz,* a series of books and cassettes designed for students who wish to acquire a good working knowledge of the language. Less ambitious travellers will find 'Tourist Turkish' a useful aid during their visits to Turkey.

Ideal for dealing with recurring situations like booking a room or ordering a meal, 'Tourist Turkish' needs only an English/Turkish dictionary and the use of four key-words: *Var* (there is); *Yok* (there is not); the interrogative particle *Mı*; and *Lütfen* (please). (A good, inexpensive English/Turkish, Turkish/English dictionary published by the Redhouse Press, İstanbul is on sale all over Turkey.)

Look up the Turkish word for the object or service which you require e.g. a room, (*Oda*), and say, *'Lütfen, oda var mı'.* If the hotel receptionist replies *'Var'*, you have a room. If he replies *'Yok'*, you try the next hotel. As you become more proficient, you can increase the range of your questions by the use of words like *Nerede* (Where), *Ne* (What), and *Ne zaman* (When), plus the appropriate noun e.g. *'Otogar nerede?'*, Where is the bus station?

Even a smattering of Turkish will greatly increase the pleasure which you derive from your stay in the country. However, to communicate properly with everyone it is essential to be able to speak the language.

Turks, young and old, will be pleased and flattered, if you take the trouble to master even a few of the Turkish words and phrases in everyday use— *Merhaba,* Hello; *Nasılsınız,* How are you? *Lütfen,* Please; *Günaydın,* Good Morning—will evoke beaming smiles from those you encounter.

Glossary of Turkish words

Ada, Island

Ahi, Member of a semi-religious fraternity or of a trade guild.

Alem, Crescent and star frequently found on top of the dome of a mosque or on a minaret

Arasta, Street in a bazaar devoted to one trade

Avlu, Courtyard or area.

Bedesten, Domed building in a market or bazaar where luxury goods are sold and stored.

Bekçi, Watchman, guardian

Belediye, Municipality.

Beylik, Domain of a minor ruler or vassal

Bulvar, Boulevard

Cami, Mosque

Caravanserai/Kervansaray, Inn; usually on trade route (see also *Han*)

Cariye, Female slave, concubine

Çarşı, Market

Çaybahçe, Tea garden

Çesme, Fountain

Dağ, Mountain

Darülkura, School for learning the Koran.

Deniz, Sea

Dere, River

Dershane, Lecture hall, and on occasions study-hall

Devşirme Levy of Christian boys for the Janissaries or state service made during the Ottoman period.

Divan, Ottoman Council of State and justice

Eczane or *Eczahane*, Pharmacy

Eski, Old

Eyvan, Domed or vaulted recess, which is open on one side

Geçid, Mountain pass

Göl, Lake

Hamam, Turkish bath

Han, Inn, usually in a town (see also *Caravanserai/Kervansaray*.

Harem, Women's part of the house

Hisar, A fort or castle

Hoca, Teacher

Horon/Horan, Folk dance from the Black Sea area

Hüyük/Höyük, Mound or tell

İç oğlanları, Royal pages

İlwan, Portal which is higher than the level of the roof

İmam, Islamic cleric who presides over the public prayer in the mosque

İmaret, Soup kitchen which provided food for students and the needy

Irmak, Large river

İskele, Quay

Kadi, District judge

Kafes, Cage where Ottoman princes were confined

Kahve, Coffee, coffee house.

Kale, A fort or castle

Kapı, Gate or door

Kaplıca, Thermal spring with swimming pool

Karakucak, Type of wrestling practised at Artvin

Kaymakam, Governor of a kaza (administrative district)

Kıble, Direction of Mecca

Kilim, Carpet without pile, woven matting

Kilise, Church

Köşk, Pavilion or summerhouse

Köy, Village

Konak, Mansion or official residence

Külliye, Charitable and educational buildings which surrounded a mosque

Kümbet, Conical-roofed tomb

Kütüphane, Library

Liman, Harbour

Lokanta, Restaurant

Mangal, Brazier

Medrese, College of Islamic theology

Mescid, Small mosque

Meydan, Square

Mihrab, Niche in a mosque which gives the direction of Mecca

Mimar, Architect

Mimber/Minber, Pulpit in a mosque

Misafirhane, House for guests

Müezzin, Islamic cleric who gives the call to prayer

Namazgah, Open-air mescid or mosque

Nehir, River

Oda, Room

Ova, Grassy plain or meadow

Padişah, Sultan

Pazar, Bazaar or market

Peştamal Large bath towel or women's head covering in Black Sea area.

Şadırvan, Fountain for ritual ablutions before prayer

Şalvar Baggy Turkish trousers

Saray, Palace

Sebil, Public fountain

Şehir, Town

Selamlık, Men's part of the house

Sema, Dervishes' dance

Semahane, Hall in dervish convent used for ritual dances

Şerefe, Balcony on a minaret

Sıbyan Mekteb, Koranic school for boys

Sıcakluk, Hot room in a hamam

Soğukluk, Cool room in a hamam

Su, Water

Sünnet, Ritual circumcision

Tabhane, Hospice in a külliye

Tavla, Backgammon

Tekke, Dervish convent

Tımarhane Lunatic asylum

Tıp Medrese Medical school

Tuğra, Sultan's monogram, imperial cipher

Türbe, Mausoleum or tomb

Vali, Provincial governor

Vilayet, Province governed by a Vali

Yalı, House built near the Bosphorus

Yayla, Summer camping-place or pasture in the mountains

Yeni, New

Yol, Road, street or path

Yürük, Nomad (lit. fast, fleet)

Yurt, Home or native land

Zaviye, Lodging frequently used by dervishes

Customs and Behaviour

Some differences between the customs and behaviour current in N America and Europe and those in Turkey have been touched on already. A good deal of the formality, which developed during the Ottoman period, is still retained in Turkish society, particularly in Anatolia. For example, when you visit the home of a Turkish friend he will greet you as follows, '*Hoş Geldiniz*', Welcome, to which the correct reply is '*Hoş Bulduk*', I am pleased to be here. He will then ask how you are—'*Nasılsınız*', to which you reply '*Iyiyim, teşekkür ederim*', I am very well thank you. No matter how often you meet, this formula is almost always used before a conversation gets under way.

Before entering a Turkish house—especially in Anatolia—it is customary for visitors to take off their shoes and leave them by the door. As a rule they will be given a pair of slippers by the host. Apart from houses in the larger towns and cities, which are generally furnished in European style, Turkish houses follow a traditional pattern. The living-room will have a large divan along one or more walls. Sit cross-legged on this, but be careful not to show the soles of your feet to those present. Similarly do not point your finger at anyone. You will be offered tea. It is polite to drink at least three of the small glasses. Avoid blowing your nose in public. If possible leave the room or at least turn your head away and try to carry the operation out as unobtrusively as possible. This is particularly important in public places like restaurants. Displays of affection in public, like kissing and embracing, are often frowned on.

If a lady goes to the toilet in a public place, e.g. a restaurant, it is not unusual for her escort to accompany her as far as the door, to wait for her there and then conduct her back to the table.

Always ask permission before taking photographs of people, particularly if the subject is female. If the lady's husband or a male relative is present, make sure that you get his permission also.

When visiting a mosque, leave your shoes at the door. Dress as you would for a visit to a church. Do not wear shorts or jeans or give a general impression of slovenliness. Do not take photographs using a flash or walk in front of worshippers. Non-Muslims should avoid visiting mosques during the daily prayer periods which take place in the early morning, at midday, mid-afternoon, early evening and at nightfall. This is particularly important on Friday, the Muslim holy day. During the month of Ramazan, when many Muslims fast during the daylight hours, avoid ostentatious displays of eating, drinking or smoking in public.

In Anatolia you may encounter behaviour which would be considered unusual and bordering on the impolite in western society. A man may be asked his age, whether he is married, how much he earns and other personal questions by casual acquaintances or strangers. This is not considered impolite and you should not be offended. You may be stared at a good deal, particularly when you eat in restaurants, in the smaller Anatolian towns.

Do not wear shorts in central, eastern and south-eastern Anatolia. This may give offence or at the very least provoke ribald comments. If it is very hot, invest in a pair of *şalvar*, the baggy Turkish trousers, which are cool and comfortable when the temperature soars.

Health

Inoculation. Unless you arrive from an area where diseases like cholera or typhoid are rife, you will not need proof that you have been inoculated. Some visitors from Europe and N America, particularly if they are going to spend some time in the country or intend to travel to the remoter areas, have prophylactic inoculations or treatment against cholera, tetanus, typhoid, polio, rabies and hepatitis. If in doubt, consult your doctor.

Insurance. Take out a health-insurance policy which will cover you for the duration of your stay in Turkey and the time spent travelling to and from the country. Make sure that the policy covers both Asiatic and European Turkey.

Malaria. According to the authorities, malaria has been eradicated in Turkey but, unfortunately, the anopheles mosquito ignores international boundaries. If you are going to travel in the S or SE of the country, it is sensible to take all reasonable steps against infection. Some malarial parasites have now become resistant to certain drugs, so consult your doctor or one of the specialist bodies like the London School of Hygiene and Tropical Medicine, Keppel St, London, WC1E 7HT (tel. 0171 636 8636), the Hospital for Tropical Diseases, 3, St Pancras Way, London, NW1 OPE (tel. 0171 387 4411) or the clinic at Thomas Cook, 45 Berkeley St, London W1A 1EB, well in advance of your departure date.

Take one of the recommended anti-mosquito sprays and a mosquito repellent cream with you. Wear clothes that cover your arms and ankles during the evening. Use the spray in your room before going to sleep. There are various anti-mosquito devices on sale in Europe and in Turkey.

Stomach Problems. For stomach problems take Lomotil or one of the recommended remedies which may be obtained from your doctor before departure or purchased, usually without prescription, from a chemist, *Eczane*, in Turkey. Do not overindulge in oily and highly-spiced dishes. It is advisable to wash and peel fruit before eating it.

Disposable Needles. Increasingly, travellers are taking disposable needles with them, in case they fall ill and need an injection while abroad. These may be purchased from Thomas Cook, 45 Berkeley St, London W1A 1EB, any British Airways Travel Clinic (tel 071-831 5333) or Trailfinders, 194 Kensington High St, London W8 7RG before departure. To avoid problems, if your baggage is opened on arrival, take a letter from your doctor which explains clearly why you have the needles in your possession. This should prevent you from falling foul of Turkey's very tough anti-drug legislation.

Chemists (*Eczane*). Chemists in Turkey carry out many of the functions performed by doctors in other countries. They provide simple first aid, give injections and are able to advise on the treatment of many minor ailments. They carry a wide range of drugs, some of which are made under licence in Turkey, while others are imported from Germany, Britain and the USA.

Doctors and Hospitals. Apart from the nationals of a few countries, which have reciprocal arrangements with Turkey, visitors have to pay for drugs, treatment by private doctors and hospital fees. However, the cost of treatment is low. Visitors wishing to claim against insurance, when they return home, should get receipts for both medicines and treatment. There are foreign hospitals in İstanbul and Ankara.

İstanbul. American Hospital, Nisantasi, Güzelbahçe 20. French Hospital, Taşkışla Cad. 3. Taksim. Italian Hospital, Tophane, Defterdar Yokuşu, 37. German Hospital, Taksim, Sıraselviler Cad., 119. Austrian Hospital, Bereketzade Medresesi, Sok. 5/7 Karaköy.

Ankara. American Hospital, Balgat Amerikan Tes.

Rabies. As in many European countries, some foxes and other wild animals in certain parts of Turkey carry the rabies virus. They are believed to pass this on from time to time to domestic animals. For this reason it is inadvisable to pat or fondle any animal which you may meet on your travels. If you are bitten or scratched by a wild animal, a dog or a cat, particularly if it is behaving in an uncharacteristic fashion, get immediate medical attention.

Toilets. As a rule there are toilets, with separate sections for men and women, near mosques. A small fee is usually charged for their use. Although vast improvements have been made in recent years to the cleanliness of toilets in places like bus stations, some are still basic and rather odorous. Usually consisting of a hole in the floor and a place for your feet, they are, theoretically at least, more hygienic than European-style toilets. However, it takes some practice to be able to use them without embarrassment—or worse. Hazards that await the unwary include overbalancing and falling on the floor or having to recover the contents of pockets from the same insalubrious surface! For this reason keep valuable possessions like money and passports in a purse, wallet or buttoned pocket.

Toilet paper is rarely provided in public toilets.

General Information

Post. Turkey's postal services are well-organised and efficiently-run. Letters between Turkey and the United Kingdom take about five working days. All post offices bear the distinctive yellow PTT sign. The larger offices are open from 08.00–24.00 from Monday to Saturday and from 09.00–19.00 on Sunday.

If you wish to the use the 'Poste Restante' system, ask to have your letters addressed as follows: Name, Poste Restante, Merkez Posthanesi, Town/city, Turkey.

To collect mail from the Poste Restante, you will have to produce your passport and pay a small fee. Note that letters are sometimes filed under the addressee's first name and not his or her surname. For this reason ask your correspondents to put your surname first on the envelope, e.g. Smith, John/Jane rather than John/Jane Smith.

Telephone. Turkish cities are linked by an efficient direct dialling system. To use the telephone you will need to purchase jetons (tokens) or a telephone card. Jetons come in two sizes. Small jetons are used for local calls. The larger ones, which are more expensive, are needed for long-distance calls. Yellow telephone cards have varying numbers of units: 30, 60 and 100. They can be used for internal and international calls. Cards are sold at most post offices. They are also on sale in hotels, but at a higher price. During the holiday season telephone cards are sometimes in short supply and, mysteriously, are only available from non-official sources. There have been whispers about an incipient racket!

The Turks are enthusiastic users of the telephone and you may have to wait some time, particularly in the evening, to find a vacant booth. Telephone calls made from hotels are almost always subject to an additional charge imposed by the management.

Important Telephone Numbers: 155 Police; 112 Emergency; 110 Fire; 118 Information (900 447 090 in Ankara only).

Money. The unit of currency is the Turkish Lira (TL). There are coins of 50, 100, 500, 1000, 2500 TL and bank notes of 5000, 10000, 50,000, 100,000 and 250,000 TL. The rate of exchange for the major currencies is displayed prominently in the banks and given in the daily papers. **Note: it is a criminal offence carrying heavy penalties to deface Turkish currency.**

Cheques. Eurocheques and most travellers' cheques may be cashed in banks on production of your passport. They are also accepted in payment by many hotels, restaurants and shops.

Credit Transfers. It is possible to transfer money from your home account to a bank in Turkey, but, as this can take time, it is not recommended to those making a short stay in the country.

Credit Cards. Credit cards are accepted by most shops, restaurants and hotels in the principal cities and towns. If you use them to purchase goods, you may be asked to pay an additional amount to cover the commission charged by the card company. This applies particularly to bazaars or to shops where you have bargained over a purchase.

Occasionally the display of a credit card symbol does not mean that establishment in question is either willing or capable of accepting payment by that method. The symbol is just decoration. If you discover any misuse of a credit card symbol, do not hesitate to report it to the local Tourist Office and to the credit card company concerned when you return home.

Banks. Banks are usually open between 08.30 and 12.00 and between 13.30 and 17.00 on weekdays. They are closed on Saturdays and Sundays. Special arrangements operate in holiday resorts. When purchasing your travellers' cheques, ask for the name of the corresponding Turkish bank. Unfortunately, not all Turkish banks accept all travellers' cheques.

Time. Local time in Turkey is equal to GMT plus 2 hours during the summer months. For the USA it is seven hours in advance of EST.

Electricity Electricity has been standarised on 220v all over Turkey. Visitors from Britain should bring an adaptor, as sockets are designed to accept the round two-pin European plugs. Adaptors for the American flat-pin plugs are available from many of the electrical shops in the cities and large towns.

Newspapers. The chatty and informative *Turkish Daily News*, published in Ankara, is on sale in all cities, holiday resorts and most large towns. It covers both Turkish and international news in considerable detail and gives TV and radio programmes. There is a useful weekend supplement which has articles on various aspects of Turkish life, entertainment, sport etc.

Foreign papers are available in Turkey the day after publication. Some foreign magazines like *Time, Paris Match* and *Der Spiegel* are sold in the cities and holiday resorts.

Radio. Short-wave radios will pick up the BBC World Service and Voice of America programmes. Details of frequencies and times of broadcasts in English for the eastern Mediterranean area may be obtained from either organisations.

TRT, Turkish Radio and Television Service has daily broadcasts in English, French and German on Radio 3 FM at 09.00, 12.00, 14.00, 19.00 and 22.00.

Tourism Radio also broadcasts news in English, French and German daily at 08.30–10.30, 12.30–18.30 and 21.30. In addition, Tourism Radio broadcasts information about Turkey of interest to foreigners, music programmes and features. Its transmitters and frequencies, which are on the air daily from 07.30 to 12.45 and from 18.30 to 22.00 local time are: İzmir 100.5MHz; Antalya 100.6MHz; Nevşehir 103.0MHz; Kuşadasi 101.9MHz; Pamukkale 101.0MHz; Bodrum 97.4MHz; Çeşme 99.1MHz; İstanbul 101.6MHz; Marmaris 101.0MHz; Kakan 105.9MHz.

Television. At 22.00 each day TRT TV2 broadcasts news in English. Many hotels now receive CNN and BBC TV programmes by satellite.

Public and Religious Holidays. The official public holidays are: 1 January, New Year's Day; 23 April, National Independence and Children's Day; 19 May, Atatürk Commemoration and Youth and Sports Day; 30 August, Victory Day (War of Independence 1922); 29 October, Republic Day.

Approximately 99 per cent of Turks subscribe to the Muslim faith. During the two great Islamic festivals, *Şeker Bayramı*, which marks the end of Ramazan, and *Kurban Bayramı*, which follows sometime later, the festivities last for three and four days respectively. Shops and bazaars are closed on the first day of both festivals. Note: the time of Ramazan changes each year.

Festivals. In practically every month there is a festival or fair somewhere in Turkey. Here are some of the most interesting. A full list may be obtained from any office of the Ministry of Tourism.

January	Camel-wrestling Festival, Selçuk
March	İstanbul International Film Festival
April	International Children's Day, Ankara
April/May	Ephesus Festival of Culture, Selçuk
May	International Music and Folklore Festival, Silifke
May	Ankara International Arts Festival
May	Yunus Emre Culture and Art Week, Eskişehir
May	International Yachting Festival, Marmaris
June	Marmaris Festival
June	Bergama Festival
June	Kafkasör Culture and Art Festival, Artvin
June	Architectural Treasures and Folklore Week, Safranbolu
June/July	International Culture and Art Festival, İstanbul
June/July	International İzmir Festival
June/July	Kırkpınar Wrestling, Edirne
July	International Culture and Art Festival, Bursa
July	International Folk Dance Festival, Samsun
August	Troy Festival, Çanakkale
Ausust/September	İzmir International Fair
September	International Grape Festival, Ürgüp
September/October	International Mediterranean Song Contest, Antalya
November	International Yacht Race, Marmaris
December	International St Nicholas' Symposium, Demre
December	Mevlana Commemoration Ceremony, Konya

Consulates and Embassies. Visitors staying in Turkey for any length of time are advised to register with their national embassy in Ankara or their nearest consulate.

Embassies: British Embassy, Şehit Ersan Cad. 46A, Çankaya, Ankara (tel. 0-312 427 4310/15). **American Embassy**, Atatürk Bulvarı 110, Kavklıdere, Ankara (tel. 0-312 426 5470). **Australian Embassy**, Nenehatun Cad. 83, Gaziosmanpaşa, Ankara (tel. 0-312 436 1240/45). **Canadian Embassy**, Nenehatun Cad. 75, Gaziosmanpaşa, Ankara (tel. 0-312 436 1275/79).

Consulates: United Kingdom, İstanbul. British Consulate-General, Meşrutiyet Cad. 34, Beyoğlu/Tepebaşı, İstanbul (tel. 0-212 244 7540). İzmir. British Consulate, 1442 Sokak 49, P.K. 300 Alsancak, İzmir (tel. 0-232 421 1795). Antalya. British Honorary Consul, Kazım Özalp, Cad. 149A, Antalya. (tel. 0-242 241 1815).

United States of America, İstanbul. American Consulate, Meşrutiyet Cad. 104–108, Tepebaşı, İstanbul (tel. 0-212 251 3602). İzmir. Alsancak, Atatürk Cad. No. 92 (tel. 0-232 484 9426). Adana. American Consulate, Atatürk Cad., Vali Yolu, (tel. 0-322 234 2145).

Australia, İstanbul. Australian Consulate, Etiler, Tepecik Yolu Üzeri, 58, (tel. 0-212 257 7050.

Canada, İstanbul. Canadian Consulate, Gayrettepe, Büyükdere Cad. 107, Bengun Han, Kat. 3 (tel. 0-212 272 517 4.

Summer Opening Times. In the Aegean and Mediterranean areas government offices and some other establishments are closed in the afternoon during the summer months. Check with the local Tourist Information Office, as the arrangements may vary from province to province.

Laundry and Dry Cleaning. In Turkey these services are fast, cheap and efficient. Most hotels will arrange for guests' clothes to be valeted, but visitors who wish to make their own arrangements will find laundry and dry-cleaning establishments in all cities, towns and resorts.

Shops. Shops are usually open between 09.30 and 13.00 and 14.00 and 19.00. They are normally closed on Sunday. However, during the holiday season shops in resorts are open daily and during the evenings. Often they do not close for lunch. (See also summer opening hours above.)

Turkey is a treasure-house of hand-made products. These range from carpets and kilims to gold and silver jewellery, embroidery, ceramics from Kütahya, leather and suede clothing, meerschaum pipes, ornaments fashioned from alabaster, copper and bronze, pans and vessels. Many happy— and relatively inexpensive—hours may be spent bargaining for these in the bazaars of the cities and in the many speciality shops in the coastal resorts.

Resist the temptation to buy antiques. There are many skilfully-produced fakes on sale and the export of genuine antiques is forbidden. Infractions are punished by severe penalties, which may include imprisonment. (See also Antiquities below.)

Museums and Palaces. Most Turkish museums and palaces are open every day from Tuesday to Sunday between 08.30 and 12.30 and between 13.30 and 17.30. Admission charges are very modest, but an additional fee must be paid by those wishing to take photographs or make amateur films or videos. Professional film-makers require a special permit which must be obtained in advance from the General Directorate of Antiquities and Museums, Ankara.

Topkapı Sarayı in İstanbul is closed on Tuesday. In Ankara most museums are closed on the first day of religious holidays.

In a few museums not all the objects on display are labelled. In a number they are labelled in Turkish only, in others in Turkish and English or Turkish and German. Although most museums sell postcards and replicas of the most important exhibits, few publish guide-books. Detailed information about the exhibits in all the principal museums is given in the Blue Guide.

Some museums provide light refreshments: soft drinks, tea, and coffee, often in pleasant, relaxing surroundings. The pergola annex to the café in Antalya's Archaeological Museum, where visitors refresh themselves surrounded by 2C AD Roman statuary, is particularly attractive.

Points to Note

Theft and Crime. There is very little crime in Turkey. In Anatolia a foreign visitor is still regarded as a '*misafir*', a guest, and is accorded the traditional protection given to strangers. The safety of his person and property are regarded as being the personal responsibility of his host. However, it is still advisable to take normal, sensible precautions to protect your property, particularly your money and your passport. Most hotels will keep guests' valuables for them in the hotel safe.

If you are unlucky enough to lose any property during your stay in Turkey, report the matter as soon as possible to the nearest police-station. Ask for a copy of the statement, which you make to the authorities, as your insurance company will require you to produce this, if, subsequently, you make a claim.

In shops it is unlikely that you will be overcharged and even more unlikely that you will be shortchanged. This is also the case in the bazaars in İstanbul and in the cities and larger towns, where bargaining is an accepted practice. Once a price has been agreed, that is all you will have to pay.

Security Areas. Photography is not permitted in certain places e.g. docks, airports, military establishments, and frontier areas. It is also forbidden to photograph military personnel. If you are in doubt about where or when to take pictures, take the advice of the local Tourist Information Office.

Drugs. The illegal possession, sale or use of drugs like hashish, heroin and cocaine is strictly forbidden by Turkish law. Any transgression is likely to result in serious trouble and the offender will, almost certainly, end up in prison.

Antiquities. Amateur digging of ancient sites is forbidden by Turkish law and visitors should not indulge in this activity. It would be inadvisable to bring a metal-detector to Turkey.

Visitors to Ephesus, Pamukkale, Perge, Aspendus and other sites in Turkey are sometimes approached by persistent small boys or furtive-looking adults who offer to sell them 'genuine' ancient coins or small antiquities. Often the vendors claim that the objects were found in a tomb nearby. In most cases these are modern copies and the only loser is the purchaser who parts with a substantial sum of money for something of little value.

However, from time to time genuine antiquities, the product of illegal excavation, are offered for sale. Under no circumstances should these be purchased. The sale, purchase and possession of antiquities is strictly controlled by Turkish law and any transgressions are punished severely. For example, the owner of a yacht, who removes or permits any member of his ship's company to remove ancient objects from the seas adjoining the Turkish coast, may have his yacht confiscated and, in addition, he and any others involved may be sent to prison.

Unfortunately, the illegal digging of ancient sites is all too common. This not only robs the country of its patrimony but it also denies archaeologists vital evidence, which would enable them to increase our knowledge of the past. Every illegal purchase encourages the seller to make another illegal dig. Visitors should not become involved in this sordid process.

Sport and Entertainment

Turkey has much to offer visitors who are interested in watching or taking part in sport. Most cities and towns have football stadia, where enthusiasts shout themselves hoarse every Sunday afternoon, encouraging their national or local heroes to greater efforts.

Violence at football matches is rare in Turkey, so it is not uncommon to find a mix of family groups and exuberant youngsters in the stands.

Look out for the festivals of traditional Turkish sports, which take place in various centres throughout the year, e.g. Turkish wrestling at Edirne and in the great Roman theatre of Aspendus.

Underwater Diving. Underwater swimming and diving for leisure purposes with amateur equipment is permitted in Turkey in certain areas. The sport is controlled by the local authorities. More information may be obtained from the Tourist Information Office at the resort. (See the note above about illegal diving for antiquities.)

Fishing. Visitors may fish for sport in non-prohibited areas without a licence. Only amateur equipment and noncommercial, multi-hooked lines are permitted. Nets should not weigh more than 5kg. Full information about the regulations covering the sport may be obtained from the Department of Fisheries, Ministry of Agriculture, Forestry and Rural Affairs, Tarım, Orman ve Köyişleri Bakanlığı, Su Ürünleri Daire Başkanlığı, Ankara.

Commercial fishing by foreigners is an offence carrying severe penalties.

If you just like to laze around in boats, you will certainly be attracted to the *Mavi Yolculuk*, the Blue Voyage itinerary which extends from Çeşme on the Aegean Coast to Antalya on the Mediterranean. Yachts sail from Kuşadaşı, Bodrum, Datça, Marmaris, Fethiye, Kaş, Kemer and Antalya. The Blue Voyages are arranged by various companies and private individuals like Hanna Desjardins, 22 Blenheim Tce, St John's Wood, London NW8 0EB and Cağa Tour, Fethiye, for groups of 8–12 persons.

Hunting. Visitors may only take part in hunts organised by travel agencies which have been specially authorised by the Ministry of Agriculture, Forestry and Rural Affairs. Information about the regulations applying to hunting in Turkey may be obtained from the Union of Travel Agencies (TURKSAB), Esentepe, Gazeteciler Sitesi, Haberler Sok., 15, İstanbul.

Skiing. Skiing has become increasingly popular in Turkey during recent years. The principal resorts are at Bursa—Uludağ, Antalya—Saklıkent, Bolu—Köroğlu, Erzurum—Palandöken, Kars—Sarıkamış, Kayseri—Erciyes, Ankara—Elmadağ, İlgaz Dağ and Zigana—Gümüşhane. Further information may be obtained from any office of the Ministry of Tourism.

Mountaineering. There are interesting climbs to be made in the Beydağları to the W of Antalya, Büyük Ağrı Dağı, Turkey's highest mountain, Cilo-Sat Dağları, in SE Turkey near Hakkari, Kaçkar Mountains, between Rize and

Hopa on the Black Sea coast, Erciyes Dağı, an extinct volcano S of Kayseri, Aladağlar Mountains, S of Niğde, Süphan Dağ, near Adilcevaz, Bolkar Mountains, in the middle of the Toros Group, Mercan Mountain, between Tunceli and Erzincan, and Hasandağı, near the Ihlara valley.

Advice and assistance may be obtained from Tourist Information Offices and from the Turkish Mountaineering Club. It is advisable to contact the club before starting out on a climb, so that the authorities are forewarned and may be able to render assistance, should this be required.

Foreign mountaineering groups must obtain special permission to climb Büyük Ağrı Dağı and the Cilo-Sat range. Apply to the Ministry of Foreign Affairs, Ankara, tel. (9-4) 212 51 25.

Rafting and Canoeing. Hardy spirits will find plenty of challenges in Turkey's rivers. Rafting and canoeing are practiced on the Çoruh, Barhal, Berta, Fırtına Denizi, Solakı, Köprüçay, Manavgat, Dragon, Göksü (Silifke), Zamantı, Göksü-Feke and Kızılırmak rivers.

Wind Sports. There are instruction courses for ten or more people, who speak the same language, at a number of places in Turkey. If you are interested in plane gliding, hang gliding, parachuting or single engine flying, contact Türk Hava Kumru Genel Başkanlığı Havacılık Müdürlüğü, Atatürk Bul. 33, Opera-Ankara.

Plateau Hiking. The meadows of the high uplands are a nature lover's paradise. For an unique and wonderful experience visit the Tekir and Bürücek plateaux or the meadows of Artvin-Kafkasör, Rize-Ayder, Trabzon-Kadırga and Giresun-Kümbet in the Black Sea area.

Evening Entertainment. In Ankara, İstanbul and İzmir the State Symphony Orchestra, the State Opera and Ballet perform works by Turkish and foreign composers under the direction and batons of famous Turkish and foreign conductors. From time to time theatrical companies from abroad bring their productions to those cities.

There are nightclubs in all the large cities and discotheques everwhere for those who wish to dance the night away. Some cinemas in Ankara and İstanbul show foreign films with the original soundtrack and Turkish subtitles. For details of these see the *Turkish Daily News.*

In the principal cities and tourist centres there are licensed casinos where visitors may try their luck. Ask the hotel receptionist for further information. You will be asked to show your passport at the entrance to the casino.

Wild Life

In the national parks and in the more remote parts of Turkey wildlife is varied, abundant, and sometimes dangerous. Bears, wolves, foxes, jackals, wild boar, red and roe deer, water buffalo, lynx, wild goats, snakes, scorpions and spiders of various kinds exist, but are not often seen by visitors. During the course of his extensive travels, which covered the whole country and took place over fourteen years, the author's experience of Turkey's more unusual fauna has been limited to two sightings of snakes and one interesting encounter with a spectacular jumping-spider.

Camels, singly and in trains, may be seen almost anywhere in Turkey. At the Letoön in Lycia somnolent tortoises sunbathe on the ancient stones, while frogs, the descendants, if legend is to be believed, of the shepherds, who mocked Leto, fill the air with their raucous calls. In spring the fields and hillsides on Turkey's SE and E coasts are home to hosts of brilliantly-coloured butterflies. Along the Aegean and Mediterranean coasts, the butterflies give way in summer to yellow and black striped hornets and other less attractive insects, while the ubiquitous female mosquito fills the evening air with her monotonous, menacing whine.

Give a wide berth to the guard-dogs which protect the encampments of the *Yürük* people and keep predators away from the sheep and goats which sometimes graze the sparse roadside vegetation.

In summer, visitors who stray from the main paths at ancient sites like Ephesus, Xanthus, Sardis and Ani, or who poke among the stones or crevices in ancient buildings, should keep a sharp look-out for snakes and scorpions. It is unlikely that they will be troubled, as these creatures, sensitive to vibration, usually avoid contact with humans, but it is wise to take precautions. If bitten or stung seek medical attention immediately.

National Parks. Turkey has a number of large and well-maintained national parks. These include:

Uludağ the ancient Mt Olympus (2554m), near Bursa.

Kuşcenneti, in the province of Balıkesir, an ornithological reserve, which is home to more than 200 species of birds.

Sipil Dağ, in Manisa province.

Dilek Yarımadası, where Samsundağ towers over the sea near Kuşadası.

Kovada Gölü forests and lakes near İsparta.

Güllük Dağı, at the site of ancient Termessus, near Antalya.

Beydağları-Olympus, W of Antalya.

Karatepe-Aslantaş, in Adana province. Hittite and Roman remains in a picturesque setting in the Ceyhan river valley.

Köprülü Kanyon, NE of Antalya. Roman bridge and remains of ancient Selge.

Kızıl Dağ, beautiful park of cedar trees near İparta.

Munzur Vadisi, trout streams near Tunceli.

Gelibolu Yarımadası, dedicated to the soldiers—Turkish and foreign— who died during the Gallipoli campaign.

Yedigöller, seven lakes to the N of Bolu.

Altındere, near Trabzon; it includes the monastery of Sumela.

Göreme. Near Nevşehir. Famous for its rock churches and strange land scape.

Boğazkale-Alacahöyük, magnificent flora and fauna and Hittite monu ments.

Nemrut Dağı. Near Kahta, the sacred mountain of the Commagene kings.

Thermal Resorts. There are more than 1000 thermal resorts and spas in Turkey and for centuries people have flocked to them for relief and treatment for a wide range of medical conditions. They include:

Bursa. Waters contain bicarbonate, sulphate, sodium, calcium and magnesium and are suitable for drinking and bathing. Treatment offered for rheumatism, gynaecological and dermatological problems.

Yalova. Waters contain sulphate, sodium and calcium. Treatment for rheumatism, urinary and nervous complaints.

Oylat. Located in a picturesque, rural setting near İnegöl. Restful and unpretentious.

Gönen. Province of Balıkesir. Waters contain sulphate, sodium, hydrocarbon and carbon dioxide. Treatment for dermatological, urinary and nervous complaints.

Çeşme. In the Bay of İlıca and Şifne to the W of İzmir. Waters contain chloride, sodium, magnesium, fluoride and are suitable for drinking and bathing. Treatment for dermatological and gynaecological and urinary complaints.

Pamukkale and Karahayıt. NW of Denizli. Waters contain hydrocarbon, sulphate, calcium and carbon dioxide. Suitable for bathing and drinking. Treatment for heart and circulatory complaints and rheumatism, digestive and kidney diseases.

Balçova. W of İzmir. Water suitable for drinking and bathing. Treatment for sciatica, gynaecological and nervous disorders and urinary and intestinal problems.

Harlek. Near İzmir. The water suitable for drinking and bathing is used to treat sciatica, gynaecological and nervous disorders and urinary and intestinal problems.

Bolu. Waters contain calcium, magnesium and sulphur and are used to treat patients suffering from rheumatism, sciatica, gynaecological problems, liver and kidney diseases.

Balıklı-Yılanlı Çermik. 12km NE of Kangal in the province of Sivas, the waters (35° C) contain calcium and magnesium. The small fish, which live in the pools, play an important part in the cure of psoriasis. They nibble at the infected areas. The waters also benefit patients suffering from rheumatism, arteriosclerosis, and gynaecological complaints.

Further information about Turkey's thermal resorts may be obtained from any office of the Ministry of Tourism.

Turkish Baths. No stay in Turkey would be complete without a visit to a *hamam*. Most towns of any size will have one or more of these establishments. Some are reserved for men, others for women. Where there is only one *hamam* in a town, different days or times are allocated to each sex.

In keeping with a tradition that dates back to Roman times the Turkish *hamam* is generally a clean and well-run establishment. It is also very inexpensive.

Haghia Sophia, İstanbul

1

İstanbul

Among the great cities of the world İstanbul is unique. Built partly in Europe, partly in Asia and filled with striking reminders of two great civilisations and the débris of a long history, this ancient coquette on the shores of the Bosphorus captures the hearts of all who visit her.

The largest city in Turkey, İstanbul has, according to the official census, a population of ten million. Unofficial estimates put the figure much higher and sometimes it would seem that all the İstanbulers have decided to travel on the buses, trams and dolmuşes of their city at the same time!

Route 1 provides an outline history of the city and describes its sights and monuments. There are detailed descriptions of Haghia Sophia, the Blue Mosque, Topkapı Sarayı, and the Suleymaniye and other important buildings. There is advice on where to stay, where to eat, and where to shop. 'It stands in Europe but looks out over Asia', wrote a 16C Hapsburg ambassador. Enjoy this city of two continents. Once you have succumbed to her charms, you will want to return to savour them again and again.

History. 'Almighty God, have mercy', cried the terrified inhabitants of Constantinople, as the victorious Turkish soldiers poured into the city. On Tuesday 29 May 1453 the fighting had lasted from dawn until the ninth hour and the slaughter was very great. When at last it was over, 'the dead bodies both of Christians and Turks were thrown into the Hellespont, and they were carried along the current like melons in the canals'. (Kritovoulos, *De rebus gestis Mechmetis II*). Two days later Mehmet II entered the palace of the Byzantine emperor and, saddened by the devastation which he saw around him, murmured an elegiac distich by a Persian poet,

'The spider has wove his web in the Imperial palace,
And the owl hath sung her watch-song on the towers of Afrasiab'.
(Gibbon, Vol VIII. Ch.68)

This turning-point in the history of the city was preceded by a portent observed by both Christians and Muslims. According to Niccolò Barbaro, a Venetian ship's doctor, the moon should have been full when it rose on 22 May, but it looked as though it were three days old. It kept that appearance for about four hours. As there was a prophecy that the city would fall when the full moon assumed an unusual shape, the Turks rejoiced at the phenomenon. It filled the Byzantines with fear.

Mehmet II was 23 years old when he captured Constantinople. On the morning of the assault he addressed his soldiers and, according to Kritovoulos, promised them rich spoils from the palaces, churches and great houses of the city. They would take many slaves, young and comely women, 'virgins lovely for marriage...and boys, too, very many and beautiful and of noble families...Fight bravely', he exhorted them, 'I will lead the attack and be by your side'.

It happened as Mehmet had promised. Seeking the corpse of Constantine XI among the slain, he questioned Grand Admiral Notaras who was next in precedence to the emperor. Was Constantine in one of the Genoese ships which had escaped during the battle, he asked? Notaras was unable to satisfy his curiosity, as he had been fighting in another part of the city. Later, Mehmet heard two Janissaries boasting that they had killed Constantine and he ordered the head of the emperor to be brought to him.

Initially, the conqueror showed great favour towards Notaras and his family and rewarded them with gold, but when he ordered the admiral to hand over his youngest son, the horrified Notaras refused. As a result he and the older children were beheaded. The 14-year-old boy was then brought to his apartments.

Byzantium, Constantinople, İstanbul, the names change but the city remains. The earliest settlement on the W side of the Bosphorus dates from the 13C BC and there has been a city here since the eponymous founder, Byzas of Megara, landed at the head of a band of Athenian and Megarian colonists in 667 BC. It was ruled by the Persians from 512 until 478 BC when it was captured by a Greek force led by the Spartan general Pausanias. During the 5C and 4C the city was under the control of Athens and Sparta at different times.

Xenophon and the remnants of his Ten Thousand caused consternation when they arrived in Byzantium c 399 BC at the end of their long march across Anatolia. The *harmost*, the Spartan governor, and many of the citizens thought that their uninvited guests were about to seize the city. In a panic some of them took refuge in their houses and others launched ships to escape. Because of help received from the goddess Hecate, when Byzantium was besieged by Philip II of Macedon in 340–339 BC, Byzantine coins began to carry her symbols, the crescent moon and the star. (These were adopted by the Turks after they captured the city in 1453.) During the 3C Byzantium suffered greatly from attacks by the Celts and its rulers paid the invaders large sums of money which were recovered later from taxes imposed on shipping using the Bosphorus.

By the 3C BC Byzantium had acquired a certain reputation for debauchery and louche behaviour. In *Auletris, The Flute Girl*, Menander (342–292 BC) portrays its merchants as drunken sots. 'I booze all night', boasts one of the characters, 'and on waking after the dose, I fancy I have no less than four hundred heads upon my shoulders'. Some modern visitors to Istanbul might add, 'and all of them ache'.

The city, chosen by Constantine I the Great to be his capital in AD 330, became known in the West as Constantinople. In the 5C Constantinople was made the capital of the Eastern Roman Empire. In 1054 there was a break between the Roman and the Eastern Orthodox churches and Pope Leo IX excommunicated the patriarch Michael Cerularius. The papal bull, which was laid on the altar of Haghia Sophia on 16 July of that year, listed the grounds for excommunication. 'Simoniacs sell the gifts of God. Valerii castrate their guests and not only make them priests, but even bishops. The Manichaeans say among much other nonsense that whatever is fermented has a soul, the Nazarenes…deny baptism to babies dying within eight days of birth…(and) forbid the sacraments to menstruating women… For all these reasons…our most reverend pope has excommunicated Michael and his successors, unless they come to their senses'. Apart from a brief period in the 15C the division between the two Churches continued. The excommunication was not lifted until 1965, when there was a meeting between Pope Paul VI and the Ecumenical Patriarch Athenagoras.

The Byzantine Empire suffered a series of attacks by Christian armies. Constantinople was seized and looted by the Latins on Monday 12 April 1204 during the Fourth Crusade. According to the Chronicle of Novgorod they tore down the doors of Haghia Sophia and cut them into pieces. They broke the silver- cased pulpit, they took gospels, crosses, silver lamps, priceless icons and 40 barrels of pure gold. A prostitute sat on the patriarch's chair and the tombs of the emperors were looted. They also stripped the Church of the Holy Mother of God in the palace of Blachernae and they stole countless treasures and relics from other churches.

The four great gilded bronze horses of Lysippus, which for centuries stood over the main door of the Basilica of St Mark in Venice, were taken by the Venetians from the Hippodrome where they had been since the days of Constantine. They also stole the miraculous icon of the Virgin, the Nicopoeia, the Bringer of Victory, which preceded Byzantine armies into battle. Much of the loot, the candlesticks, crosses, crystal lamps and agate cups, is in the treasury of St Mark's basilica. According to a French knight, Robert of Clari, the Crusaders found a number of sacred relics in the chapel of the Bucoleon, the imperial palace. One of these was 'a crystal phial which contained a good quantity of his (Christ's) blood'. This is probably the relic which is preserved in the Heilig Bloedbasiliek in Bruges, Belgium.

The city remained under Latin rule until 1261. However, it never quite recovered from the ordeal inflicted on it by fellow Christians…'depleted of its inhabitants, Constantinople became but a shadow of its former self'. (Mango, *Byzantium*.) In 1403 the Spanish ambassador reported that within the walls there were just a few hamlets, some gardens and fields. At the time of its capture by the Turks the population was less than 50,000. It was a place of decay and dreams where

'…such a form Grecian goldsmiths make
Of hammered gold and gold enamelling

> To keep a drowsy Emperor awake;
> Or set upon a golden bough to sing
> To lords and ladies of Byzantium
> Of what is past, or passing, or to come'.

W. B. Yeats. *Sailing to Byzantium.*

In 1452 the breach with Rome was healed temporarily and on 12 December of that year the Latin Mass was celebrated by Cardinal Isidore in Haghia Sophia in the presence of the emperor. There were many opponents to the reconciliation, led by the Patriarch Gennadius, who was under house arrest, and by Grand Admiral Lucas Notaras, who said he would prefer to see the turban of the Turk in Constantinople to the hat of a cardinal. Notaras had his wish fulfilled, but it cost him his head.

The city is a palimpsest on which many hands have left their mark. The works of its Greek, Roman, Byzantine and Ottoman rulers are sometimes superimposed one on another. According to the philosopher Heracleitus of Ephesus, '*panta rhei*', all things flow, all things are in a state of flux, and so it was in Constantinople. The glorious churches of the Byzantines were replaced by the great mosques of Islam.

After the conquest new buildings arose. According to Kritovoulos, Mehmet ordered the great palace, later known as Topkapı Sarayı, to be built on the promontory where the ancient city projected into the sea. In addition to granaries, inns, markets, mosques, shrines and shipyards, many fine houses were constructed. Mehmet's successors followed his example. In the mid 16C Süleyman the Magnificent ordered Sinan to build him an imperial mosque, which would match the glory of his achievements, and the Süleymaniye was created. In 1616 the slender minarets of Sultan Ahmet Camii pierced İstanbul's skyline and successive sultans continued to enlarge and adorn Topkapı Sarayı, that beautiful palace redolent of beauty, sensuality and cruelty which had been started by the conqueror.

The Ottoman city was a place of parades, pageantry and street entertainment. The 16C French traveller Philippe du Fresne-Canaye watched Selim II go to Friday prayers in Beyazit Camii. He has left a rather disrespectful account of the procession. The sultan was preceded by Janissaries, then by troop leaders whose bonnets, decorated with egret feathers, looked like 'feather dusters from Ferrara'. Then came some splendidly caparisoned horses and the sultan's intimate servants whose tall bonnets were shaped like chamber pots. The sultan was mounted on a horse which had been lifted by a harness into the air the previous night and denied his oats to ensure that Selim's progress would be slow and dignified.

According to Evliya Çelebi, there were 1001 guilds in the city in the 17C. Listed in a census ordered by Murad IV, they included perfumers, snow and ice merchants, sellers of rose water, flower merchants, firework makers, clowns and jugglers and executioners. There was also a troupe of Jewish boys, tumblers, fire-eaters and ball-players, who disliked gipsies. They sometimes performed a play in which a Jewish boy is discovered in a compromising position with a gipsy girl. Then, much to the delight of the spectators, the girl was paraded through the streets wearing a crown of putrid intestines. The executioners, who prepared the condemned for death, read the *fatwa*, comforted them, directed their gaze to Mecca and cut off their heads with a two-handed sword, wore the instruments of torture—borers, nails, matches, blinding powders, razors, clubs and hatchets—on their belts.

Panta Rhei. İstanbul has continued to change. Haghia Sophia, once the greatest church in Christendom and then a mosque for 500 years, has become a museum where the gold mosaics of Byzantium glow like jewels in delicate counterpoint to the more sober monuments of Islam. Modern technology has flung two great bridges across the Bosphorus to join Europe with Asia. Yet, in spite of all the changes İstanbul continues its vital, chaotic, frenetic life. Modern travellers will be amazed by this great city which can, in turn, impress, baffle and exasperate. 'That is no country for old men', Yeats sang, but 'monuments of unageing intellect'.

Transport. Atatürk Airport is c 30km from the city centre. There are frequent flights by THY and foreign airlines and charter companies. A half-hourly bus service links the airport with the THY terminal in Şişhane. By request, passengers may alight at Aksaray in the old part of the city.

Visitors taking a taxi should agree the fare before leaving the airport. At the time of writing, it costs c £10 to most places in the European part of the city, but this is likely to increase because of Turkey's high rate of inflation. Passengers travelling to destinations in the Asian part of İstanbul must pay the bridge toll in addition to the cab fare. The main **bus station** for long-distance services is **Topkapı Otogarı**. Located at the end of Millet Cad. just outside the city walls, it should not be confused with Topkapı Sarayı in Eminönü. As the *otogar* is a confused and confusing place, travellers are advised to buy their tickets at a travel agency or in one of the town offices of the many bus companies. Those travelling to destinations in Anatolia may pick up the bus at **Harem Otogarı** in Üsküdar. This is located near the ferry terminal. Buses starting at Topkapı call at Harem, but may be full when they arrive there.

City buses start from from Taksim Square in Beyoğlu, Eminönü near Sirkeci railway station, and Beyazit near the Kapalı Çarşı. They run from c 06.00 to midnight. Passengers must be in possession of a ticket before boarding the bus. Tickets may be bought from kiosks or from street vendors who charge a small premium.

A new **tram service** runs between Sirkeci and Aksaray. At present this is free and, consequently, is always crowded. Getting on and getting off can be quite an adventure. An ancient subway called **Tünel** will take you from Galata Bridge to İstiklal Cad. and there is a delightful antique **tram service** from Tünel to Taksim Square.

Taxis in İstanbul are clean, comfortable and relatively cheap. All should be, and most are, metered. Some of the drivers are moonlighting and consequently their knowledge of the city may be sketchy. Drivers expect a tip.

In addition to the services mentioned above there is the ubiquitous **dolmuş** where you pay for the distance travelled. *Dolmuş* means 'filled' or 'stuffed' in Turkish and the ancient cars and newer minibuses are usually crowded to bursting point. No rush-hour in İstanbul would be complete without the strident voices of the dolmuş boys touting for business and calling out their destinations.

İstanbul has two railway stations. **Sirkeci Station**, near the Golden Horn, is the terminus for trains from Europe and Thrace. **Haydarpaşa Station** in Üsküdar is the starting point for train services to central and southern Anatolia and countries to the E of Turkey.

One of İstanbul's delights is a trip on one of the **ferry boats**. Many start from **Eminönü Vapur İsk**. There are frequent services to Harem on the Asian side—surely the world's shortest and cheapest intercontinental crossing—and regular trips up the Bosphorus as far as Anadolu Kavağı, to the Princes Islands and to various destinations on the Haliç, the Golden Horn. İstanbul is linked with İzmir and ports on the Black Sea by the Turkish Maritime Lines. From Eminönü and Kabataş there are services to Yalova and Mudanya which shorten the journey to Bursa considerably. You must buy jetons or tokens for trips across the Bosphorus and tickets for longer journeys before travelling.

Tourist Information. The Ministry of Tourism has information offices at Sultanahmet, Karaköy Maritime Terminal, in the Hilton Hotel and in the international terminal of Atatürk Airport. They provide pamphlets, information on current events in the city and a very useful map of İstanbul and its environs.

Accommodation. There is a very wide range of accommodation in İstanbul. More than 150 hotels, which have been inspected by the Ministry of Tourism, are listed in a guide available free of charge from Turkish National Tourism offices abroad. (See Introduction.)

The *Renaissance Hotel* is conveniently located near the airport. In the old city, the friendly three-star *Erboy Oteli*, Ebussuut Cad., No. 32, Sirkeci, and the new three-star *Pierre Loti Hotel*, Divan Yolu are recommended. The Erboy is within easy walking distance of the Archaeological Museum, Haghia Sophia and Topkapı Sarayı. Pierre Loti is near Sultan Ahmet Camii and the Kapalı Çarşı, the Grand Bazaar.

In Taksim there are the *Divan Oteli, Hilton Oteli, Sheraton Oteli* and *Hyatt Regency*. All have five stars. A little farther out is the splendid five-star *Çırağan Sarayı* which has excited favourable comment. The four-star *Perapalas Oteli*, Meşrutiyet Cad., No. 98, is İstanbul's oldest luxury hotel. Among the famous who have stayed here are Atatürk, Edward VIII of England, Carol of Romania, Zog of Albania, Tito, Pierre Loti, Ernest Hemingway, Agatha Christie, Graham Greene and Alfred Hitchcock.

The two-star *Bebek Oteli*, Cevdetpaşa Cad. No. 113, is right on the Bosphorus. The fine views of the international waterway which it offers, more than compensate for the half-hour taxi journey from the city centre.

On the Asian side the three-star *Harem Oteli*, Ambar Sok., No. 2, Selimiye-Üsküdar, is quiet and has a pleasant garden overlooking the Bosphorus. Easily reached by ferry boat from Eminönü, it is not far from the Selimiye Barracks, where Florence Nightingale nursed the wounded during the Crimean War. Her quarters have been converted into a museum by the Turkish Nursing Association.

For an unusual experience try the *Ayasofya Pansiyonlar* which are located at the back of Haghia Sophia in cobblestoned Soğukçeşme Sokak. The rooms in these renovated Ottoman houses have period furniture and rugs. Guests may eat in the nearby *Sarnıç Restaurant* which has been created from a 9C Byzantine cistern.

Restaurants. Eating out in İstanbul is always interesting and there are restaurants with prices to suit all pockets. Those in the big hotels, the Çırağan Sarayı, Hilton, Ramada, Sheraton, Marmara and Divan, offer excellent meals at very reasonable prices. The restaurant in the Divan Oteli has been much praised.

Undoubtedly one of the very best places to dine in İstanbul is *Dört Mevsim,* the Four Seasons Restaurant, in İstiklal Cad., not far from the entrance to the Tünel. Presided over by Musa Hiçdönmez and his English wife Gaye, it offers beautifully prepared food in quiet, intimate surroundings. The puddings are irresistible.

Other restaurants which have been commented on favourably are *Pandelis* above the entrance to the Mısır Çarşısı, *Konyalı* opposite Sirkeci railway station, *Liman Lokantası* over the boat terminal at Karaköy, *S* near Bebek's yacht marina, *Ziya* also in Bebek, *Tarabya* to the N of Bebek, *Abdullah Lokantası* in Emirğan, *Karaca* and the *Han,* both at Rumeli Hisari, *Kale* opposite Rumeli Hisarı on the Asian shore and *Körfez* which is also on the Asian side of the Bosphorus.

For an unforgettable gourmet experience in an exotic setting visit the **Darrüziyafe** which is housed in the 500-year-old *imaret* of the Süleymaniye complex. In a fine vaulted chamber youths in Ottoman costume bring a variety of dishes prepared from old Turkish recipes. Recommended are *Sultan Gözdesi*, Süleymaniye soup of red lentils, and chicken stuffed with spiced rice, meat and pistachio nuts. For dessert there is a mouthwatering milk pudding flavoured with chopped almonds, pistachios, hazelnuts and coconut. The food is excellent, the service impeccable and the cost modest. Because of its proximity to the mosque, no alcohol is served, but creamy, chilled *ayran* complements the food perfectly. The Darrüziyafe has that atmosphere of authenticity so often lacking in other so called Ottoman restaurants which reek of manufactured antiquity. It is open for lunch and dinner throughout the year.

Useful Addresses. The **British Consulate** occupies a splendid building in Meşrutiyet Cad., 34, Tepebaş. The **American Consulate** is also in Meşrutiyet Cad., at Nos 104–8. The **Canadian Consulate** is at Büyükdere Cad., Gayrettepe. The **Australian Consulate** is at Tepecik Yolu Üzeri 58, Etiler. The Dutch, French, Russian and Swedish consulates are all in İstiklal Cad.

İstanbul's **principal post office** is in Yeni Postahane Cad. in Sirkeci. The office of the **Touring and Automobile Club of Turkey (TTOK)** is located in Şişli at Halaskargazi Cad., 364.

Religious Services. The **Greek Orthodox Patriarchate Church of St George** is in Sadrazam Ali Paşa Cad. in Fener. Other Greek Orthodox churches are **Aghia Triada**, off Taksim Square and the **Panaghia Mouchliotissa** in Fener.

Some of the **Roman Catholic churches** are St Antoine, Istiklal Cad. (Assyrian Catholics hold services in the crypt), **St Louis des Français** in the grounds of the French Consulate, **St Esprit**, Cumhuriyet Cad. near the Hilton Hotel, and **SS Peter and Paul**, which serves the Maltese community, near the Galata Tower. For centuries, **St Benoît** in Kemeraltı Cad. was a place of pilgrimage for Hungarians, as the tomb of Francis II Rakocski was here. He died in exile in 1735 (see also Tekirdağ).

Anglican services are held in the **Church of St Helena** in the grounds of the British Consulate. **Protestants** worship in the **Dutch Chapel** which is behind the Dutch Consulate.

One of İstanbul's 35 Armenian churches, **Surp (St) Reşdagabet**, is near Balat Kapısı. Another, **Surp Kirkor Lusavoriç** (St. Gregory the Illuminator), is in Kemeraltı Cad. İstanbul's **Bulgarian Christian community** worships in the church of **St. Stephen of the Bulgars** in Fener.

The **Beth Israel Synagogue** is in Şişli Square, the **Neve Shalom Synagogue** in Büyük Hendek Cad. near the Galata Tower.

Essential Istanbul

Spring is the best time of the year to visit İstanbul. Then the hills along the Bosphorus are green with new growth and the flowers of the judas trees dance in the sunlight. Fresh breezes from the Black Sea blow away the last traces of winter's smogs. In summer it can be very hot, especially when the *lodos*, a SW wind from the Marmara, blows. Keep cool then with a glass of *boza*, a fermented drink made from millet. In winter there are frequent fogs whose baleful influence is aggravated by smoke from the coal and oil fires used for domestic heating. Snow comes rarely to İstanbul and never lasts very long, but the winter winds from the Bosphorus can be very cold. At that time of year fight the chill with *salep*, an exotic mixture of hot milk and pounded orchid roots.

'*Per Roma non basta una vita*', For Rome one life is not long enough. The same could be said about İstanbul. However, there are certain places and buildings like Haghia Sophia, the Blue Mosque and the Covered Bazaar, which no visitor to the city should miss. These are described below.

There is no better place to begin your visit than in the Byzantine Hippodrome which is in the centre of the old city. Behind you is the massive bulk of Haghia Sophia, former church and mosque, to the E the domes and minarets of the Blue Mosque blot out the sky, while not far away to the N are the courts and kiosks of Topkapı Sarayı, where Ottoman sultans dallied during long, perfumed days and nights with their favourite odalisques.

The **Byzantine Hippodrome** was not only concerned with chariot racing and circuses, it was also the place where great civic events took place. Generals celebrated their triumphs here, heretics were burned here, emperors received the approbation of their subjects here and, on occasions, the bodies of fallen rulers were exposed to the derision and ridicule of the mob in this great open space.

Plus ça change... The Hippodrome is now called **At Meydanı**, the Square of the Horses.

The Hippodrome was 480m long by 117.5m wide and it had an estimated capacity of 100,000. Originally constructed by the emperor Septimius Severus c AD 200 to pacify the Byzantines whose city he had captured and sacked in 196, it was rebuilt and enlarged in the 4C AD by Constantine when he made Byzantium his capital. The *spina*, which ran down the centre, was marked by statues, obelisks and columns. On the top of the outer wall there was an arcade of columns with a classical architrave. Charioteers, performers and the public entered at the N side. The semicircular S end of the Hippodrome is now covered by buildings. The emperor's box, the *kathisma*, which was surmounted by the gilded horses of Lysippus, was on the E side. It was connected by a private colonnade to the Daphne palace so that the emperor could make good his escape, if the crowd became threatening.

The spectators, who flocked to the Hippodrome, were originally divided into four factions closely associated with the trade guilds of the city. They were the Blues, Greens, Whites and Reds, colours linked with the four elements, water, earth, air and fire. In time the Whites and Reds were absorbed by the other two factions. Both the Blues and the Greens drew members from all classes of society but the leaders of the Blues came mainly from the great landowners and the Senate, while the Greens chose their leaders from trade and industry and from courtiers from the eastern part of the empire. In religion the Blues supported Orthodox Christianity, while the Greens favoured Monophysitism and other heresies.

In January 532 rioting broke out between the two factions in the Hippodrome. The emperor Justinian I acted promptly and had seven of the ringleaders arrested, tried and executed. Five of them died, but two, a Blue and a Green, were found to be alive when they were cut down, and were spirited across the Bosphorus to the monastery of St Lawrence. The authorities decided to starve them to death and posted a guard before the gate. When Justinian took his place in the *kathisma* the next day, he was greeted with boos and shouts of '*Nika, Nika*' 'Win, Win' from both factions which had combined to show their anger and resentment. The races were started, but had to be abandoned when the mob left the circus and rampaged through the city. They released the prisoners from the palace of the City Prefect and burned it to the ground. Many other civic buildings and churches were destroyed. The next day the mob returned to the Hippodrome and proposed that a man called Probus be elected emperor. Justinian took decisive action. Two groups of Scandinavian mercenaries were despatched to the Hippodrome. In a short time they killed more than 30,000 of the rioters so bringing the Nika revolt to a bloody end.

In 1118 the heresiarch, Basil, was burned at the stake in the Hippodrome. He belonged to the Bogomils, an amalgam of the Manichaeans or Paulicians and the Massalians, who believed that Satan had created the world and mankind and who rejected, among other things, marriage, the eating of meat and the real presence of Christ in the Eucharist (see also Divriği). Rejecting all the arguments of the emperor and the Holy Synod, Basil refused to recant. 'He was ready to undergo fire and scourgings, to die a thousand deaths'. (The Alexiad of Anna Comnena.)

An enormous trench was dug in the Hippodrome and it was filled with huge tree trunks which were set alight. A cross was placed at one side, so that, if he wished, the heretic could recant at the last moment. In the great crowd, which had gathered to watch, there was a large number of Bogomils. At first Basil laughed and said that angels would pluck him from the flames. Then 'he was plainly troubled. Like a man at his wit's end he darted his eyes now here, now there, struck his hands together and beat his thighs...he stood, despicable, helpless before every threat, every terror, gaping now at the pyre, now at the spectators' (*Alexiad*). Then the executioners, fearful of the demons which Basil might conjure up, and of the effect that delay would have on the spectators, picked up his cloak and threw it into the flames. Basil cried out, 'Look, my cloak flies up to the sky', and the executioners, seeing that this was the decisive moment, threw him, clothes, shoes and all on to the pyre. There was no odour, just one smoky line in the centre of the fire.

After the Ottoman conquest the Hippodrome, now the At Meydanı, continued to be used for feasts and spectacles. The Seigneur Michael Baudier (1589–1645) has left a vivid account of the celebrations and ceremonies enacted there for the circumcision of one of the sultan's sons. After the presentation of gifts, there were mock battles between soldiers dressed as Muslims and Christians, a re-enactment of the siege of Famagusta, and displays by tumblers, mountebanks and performing animals. Then, the young prince for whom all this had been arranged 'was brought into his Father's Chamber, where he was circumcised by one of the great Men of the Court in the presence of all the Bashas. His wound being cured within a few dayes, hee goes to take his last leave of the Sultana his Mother, whom she shall see no more untill hee comes to take possession of the Empire, after the death of his Father, if hee be the eldest, or to end his life with a halter if hee be a younger brother, when his elder shall Raigne'.

Perhaps the last great event to take place in the At Meydanı was the revolt of the Janissaries in 1826.

Sultan Mahmut II wished to incorporate a quarter of the Janissaries in the new corps of infantry which he had formed. They refused. After assembling here, they sent a unit to attack the palace of the Agha of the Janissaries, Hussein Paşa, who supported the sultan's order. Fortunately for him they did not find him. He was in the toilet. So they had to be content with breaking the doors and the windows and attempting to set fire to his palace. Early the next day the Janissaries brought their famous kettles, which they were accustomed to beat when disaffected, to the circus and they sought the support of idle persons. Bands of malcontents, led by Mustafa the Fruiterer and Mustafa the Drunkard, set off to ransack and loot the houses of the Janissaries' enemies. The sultan, with the support of the political and religious establishment, sealed off the At Meydanı. The Janissaries refused to listen to reason and the great door of their barracks was blown down and 4000 of them were slain. Many more were rounded up in the capital and in the provinces. All were executed. The power of the Janissaries was broken forever.

Many of the columns of the Hippodrome were reused in Ottoman buildings. The last part of the structure was destroyed in 1609 to make room for Sultan Ahmet Camii. Excavations carried out about 30 years ago have revealed sections of the NE section. Unfortunately, no attempt has been made to preserve these remains and they have suffered considerable damage from weathering and vandalism. Traces of the stairs and the supporting arches, and a few of the seats are still visible.

The **obelisk**, the **Dikili Taş**, in the centre of the amphitheatre was erected by Thutmose III (1549–1503 BC) at Deir el Bahri in Upper Egypt. Its top was capped with gold, so that it shone in the sunlight and on it was written 'Thutmose, who crossed the great river of Nahrain (Euphrates) as a mighty conqueror at the head of his army'. It was brought to Constantinople sometime in the 4C and lay on the Marmara shore until 390, when it was erected in its present position by Theodosius I. Originally it was 60m tall, but only the upper third survived the journey. London and Washington also have obelisks of Thutmose III from Deir el Bahri.

The obelisk is supported by four bronze blocks which rest on a marble base. On this base there are reliefs which show Theodosius supervising the erection of the obelisk (N side), watching a chariot race with his family (S side), standing between his sons Arcadius and Honorius (later rulers of the Eastern and Western Roman empires, respectively) and holding a laurel crown for the victor (E side) and, with his nephew Valentinian II ruler of the Western Roman Empire, receiving homage from kneeling captives (W side). The emperors are flanked by Arcadius and Honorius. In the eastern relief note the faces of the spectators below the *kathisma*. The base is on the original level of the Hippodrome.

Next is the damaged **Serpentine Column**, the **Yılanlı Sütun**. Originally, the three intertwined serpents supported a victory trophy which stood in the temple of Apollo at Delphi. The trophy was formed from the shields carried by Persian soldiers commanded by Mardonius at the battle of Plataea in Boeotia in 479 BC. The Persians were defeated by a coalition of Greek states led by Pausanias of Sparta and Aristeides of Athens.

Pierre Gilles saw the monument in the 16C. According to him the heads of the serpents were, 'in a triangular pattern and rise very high upon the shaft of the pillar'. It is alleged that they were lopped off by a drunken Polish diplomat after a carouse one night in April 1700. One of the heads has been found and is now in the Archaeological Museum. On the base of the column are the names of the 31 Greek cities which had sent contingents to Plataea.

At the S end of the Hippodrome there is a **Stone Pillar**, the **Örmetaş**, which has been dated variously to the reigns of Constantine the Great (324–37) and Theodosius I (379–95). According to an inscription, it was restored during the reign of Constantine VII Porphyrogenitus (913–957) when its limestone blocks were covered with gilt bronze sheets. These disappeared a long time ago, probably during the rape of Constantinople by the Latins in the early 13C (see above).

Sultan Ahmet Camii or the **Blue Mosque** as it is sometimes called, is built partly on the site of the Hippodrome and partly on the area once occupied by the Byzantine imperial palace. All that remains of the palace are some mosaics from a colonnaded court which probably led from the private apartments of the imperial family to the *kathisma*. The mosaics are believed to date from c 500 and may be seen in the **Mosaic Museum** which is on a lower level to the E of the mosque.

The courtyard of Sultan Ahmet Camii, the Blue Mosque, İstanbul

A **monumental portal** leads to a huge rectangular **courtyard** which offers a magnificent view of the façade of the mosque with its enormous central dome and flanking semidomes. The courtyard is bordered by **colonnades** which are covered by 30 small domes. In the centre there is a fine octagonal **şadırvan**. The mosque has six fluted **minarets**. Those on the corners have three *şerefes*. The others have two each. Religious tracts and souvenirs are sold in the colonnades.

Visitors enter from a door on the E side. If possible, they should avoid the five times of daily prayers and should always be modestly dressed and behave correctly. Photography is not allowed inside the mosque. During the summer there are *son-et-lumière* displays each evening. They begin at 20.00 and the commentaries are in Turkish, English, French and German on successive evenings. Seating is in the square to the E of the mosque.

It took seven years to build Sultan Ahmet Camii and its associated buildings: a *medrese*, a hospital, a *han*, a primary school, a market, an *imaret* and the *türbe* of the founder. The hospital, the *han* and the market were pulled down in the 19C, but the market has been restored. The *imaret* now forms part of Marmara University. Sultan Ahmet was only 19 years old when he commissioned the architect Mehmet Ağa to build his mosque. So anxious was he to see it completed that he often helped with the construction work. In the 17C apparently only the mosque at Mecca had six minarets and, to avoid problems with the religious establishment, Ahmet sent his architect there to construct a seventh.

Inside, the mosque measures 53m by 51m. The central dome is supported by four huge, free standing pillars, which continue above the roof level in the form of octagonal towers. The dome is 23.5m in a diameter and the distance from the floor to its centre is 43m. The *mihrab* and the *mimber* are elaborately carved from white Proconnesian marble. In the *mihrab*, which is flanked by two fine candelabra, there is a small piece of the stone of the Kaaba from Mecca. The announcement of the dissolution of the Janissaries was made from the *mimber* in 1826 (see above). The roof of the **Sultan's loge** is beautifully decorated with painted floral and arabesque designs.

The great glory of Sultan Ahmet Camii is the decoration of the lower section of the walls of the prayer hall and of the galleries with 20,000 tiles. The best of these were produced in İznik, some of them before 1585. They were the work of Persian and Turkish ceramists. The remainder, which are cruder and heavier in design, were made in Kütahya. The İznik tiles depict carnations, lilies, tulips, roses and cypresses and other trees. They are in the galleries, which are not usually open to the public, and on the N wall above the main entrance. It is said that each of the İznik tiles cost the sultan 18 *akçes*. An *akçe* was one third of a *para*. (By way of comparison a teacher in the palace school received about three *paras* a day).

Two hundred and sixty windows fill the mosque with a soft gentle light. They were once set with beautiful 17C stained glass. Unfortunately, this has disappeared and has been replaced with inferior copies. Before leaving the mosque note the elaborate decoration of the **window shutters** and the fine **bronze doors** in the courtyard.

On the W side of the At Meydanı is the **Museum of Turkish and İslamic Art**. This occupies the former **Palace of İbrahim Paşa**, the Grand Vizier of Süleyman the Magnificent. Used for a time as a barracks and a prison, it has been lovingly restored in recent years.

This palace proved to be the undoing of İbrahim. Roxelana, who had always been jealous of his friendship with her husband, persuaded Süleyman that his Grand Vizier had ambitions to replace him on the throne and that these ambitions were made manifest by his grand new palace. As a result of her scheming, Ibrahim was executed and his possessions, including the palace, were confiscated.

The museum has a splendid collection of ceramics, miniatures, calligraphy, objects of wood and metal, manuscripts, kilims, glassware and folk art. Note especially the fascinating display in the ethnographic section of exhibits concerning the *Yürük* people.

'The mind rises sublime to commune with God, feeling that He cannot be far off, but must especially love to dwell in the place which he has chosen'. Thus wrote the 6C historian Procopius about **Haghia Sophia**. For Paul the Silentiary Justinian's great church resembled a beacon in the darkness, 'not only does it guide the merchant at night, like the rays of the Pharos on the coast of Africa, but it shows the way to the living God'.

Haghia Sophia was built by Justinian to replace the earlier Theodosian church which was destroyed during the Nika riots in 532 (see above). It was the third church to occupy this site. The first, erected during the reign of Constantius, was burned down in 404 during the riots which marked the second banishment of the patriarch, St John Chrysostom, by the emperor Arcadius. Its replacement was consecrated on 10 October 415 during the reign of Theodosius II (408–50).

Unusually, Justinian chose mathematicians, Anthemius of Tralles and Isidorus of Miletus, to design and build his church. Anthemius died shortly after work had begun on the building and it was completed by Isidorus in five years. It was consecrated to Haghia Sophia, the Divine Wisdom of Christ, on the feast of the Protomartyr St Stephen, 26 December 537, in the presence of Justinian and the empress Theodora. According to the late and largely legendary *Narratio* Justinian is said to have exclaimed on entering the building, 'Glory to God who has thought me worthy to finish this work. Solomon, I have outdone you'.

Damaged by an earthquake, it was rebuilt by Isidorus the Younger, the nephew of Isidorus of Miletus who had died, and was reconsecrated on Christmas Eve 563. Justinian, who was 81 years old, attended the ceremony alone. Theodora had died 25 years before. Apart from the period of the Latin Occupation of Constantinople between 1204 and 1261, it was the principal church of Greek Orthodox Christians until the capture of the city by Mehmet II in 1453. Mehmet had a minaret added to the SE corner and converted it into a mosque and so it remained until 1932. It was re-opened in 1934 as a museum.

Many great religious and imperial ceremonies took place in Haghia Sophia during the centuries of Byzantine rule. According to the Primary Russian Chronicle the emissaries of Prince Vladimir of Kiev (972–1015) were so overcome when they attended a service there that they knew not whether they were in heaven or on earth. 'For on earth there is no such splendour or such beauty, and we are at a loss how to describe it. We only know that God dwells there among men, and their service is fairer than the ceremonies of other nations. For we cannot forget that beauty'.

Haghia Sophia was sacked by the Latins in 1204 and many of its treasures carried away to the West (see above). It suffered another violent change after the fall of Constantinople to the Turks in 1453. According to Evliya Çelebi Mehmet II:

> caused this ancient place of worship to be cleared of its idolatrous impurities and purified from the blood of the slain, and having refreshed the brain of the victorious Muslims by fumigating it with amber and lign-aloes, converted it that very hour into a cami, by erecting a contracted mihrab, mimber, mahfil, and menareh, in that place which might rival Paradise. On the following Friday the faithful were summoned to prayer by the muezzins, who proclaimed with a loud voice this text (Kor. XXXIII. 56): 'Verily, God and his angels bless the Prophet'.
>
> Then Mehmet had a turban placed on his head and a naked sword in his hand, and ascending the mimber, cried out in a loud voice 'Praise be to God the Lord of all the worlds' (Kor.i.i.) and all the victorious Muslims lifted their hands and gave a great shout of joy.

Grave stelae, columns and architectural fragments, which were found in various parts of the city during recent years, are displayed in the garden of Haghia Sophia. Note the reconstructed ambo from Beyazit Basilica A.

Just in front of the exonarthex are the remains of the Theodosian church. An idea of its size may be gained from the massive fragments scattered on the ground nearby. Apparently, this was a basilica with a wide nave and four side aisles. Look for the helpful plan and reconstruction near the ruins.

Justinian's Haghia Sophia is a rectangular building measuring c 70m by 75m. On the W side there are an **exonarthex** and a **narthex** and on E a semicircular **apse**. Above the central area is the **dome**. This is flanked on the E and W sides by **semidomes** and **conches**. There are galleries over the side aisles and the narthex.

Later additions to the building include the buttresses on all four sides, which were intended mainly to counteract earthquake damage, the four minarets, which were added after the church was converted into a mosque, the **baptistery**, the **şadırvan** and the **Ottoman tombs** on the S side. All of the mosaics in Haghia Sophia were covered with plaster and whitewash by the Muslims. They were cleaned and restored by members of the Byzantine Institute between 1932 and 1964.

In the narthex, above the **Imperial Gate**, as the great door into the nave was called, there is a mosaic of an enthroned Christ. The Greek text on the open book, which he holds in his left hand, states, 'Peace be with you, I am the Light of the World'. His right hand is raised in blessing. In two roundels there are representations of the Blessed Virgin and of a angel holding a wand. This mosaic has been dated to the reign of Leo VI the Wise (886–912). The prostrate figure on the left is believed to be that of the emperor.

Mosaics from Justinian's church may be seen on the vaults of the narthex and of the side aisles. They have architectural forms and multicoloured geometrical and floral designs surrounded by large areas of plain gold. It is not known with certainty whether any of the mosaics in his church depicted the human form; such images would not have survived the excesses of the Iconoclastic period (730–843).

The central section of the great **nave** is delimited by four massive pillars. Above it is the **dome**, 31m in diameter and, at its highest point, 55m from the marble floor. According to Procopius this wonderful structure 'does not appear to rest upon a solid foundation, but to cover the place beneath as though it were suspended from heaven by the fabled golden chain'.

The two huge **urns** of Proconnesian marble on either side of the great door were a gift of Murat III (1574–95). With a capacity each of 1250 litres, they were filled with water which was used by the worshippers to quench their thirst and for lustral rites. The structure to the right of the apse was for the cantors during the Ottoman period. A mosaic circle on the floor is believed to mark the position of the Byzantine emperor's throne during the coronation ceremony.

The **mihrab** in the apse, the carved **mimber**, and the eight painted wooden disks, date from the period when the building was used as a mosque. The 17C disks, which bear the names of God, Muhammad, two of the caliphs and two of the grandsons of the Prophet, were taken down after the building became a museum. Too large to pass through the doors and too valuable to cut up they were replaced in their original positions.

In the conch of the apse there is a very fine mid 9C mosaic of the **Mother of God and the Christ Child**. Note the massive figure of the Archangel Gabriel at the bottom of the arch which surrounds the apse. Only fragments of the matching figure of the Archangel Michael on the other side remain. On the N tympanum wall there are mosaic portraits of three important saints of the Catholic and Orthodox Churches: the 9C Ignatius of Constantinople (on the right), the 5C John Chrysostom (in the centre) and the 2C Ignatius of Antioch, surnamed Theophoros, the Bearer of God (on the left). John Chrysostom and Ignatius were patriarchs of the city.

The only figurative mosaics to remain uncovered during the Ottoman period were those of the angels on the E pendentives. They date from the mid 14C. Those on the W pendentives are 19C copies. In the S gallery there a mosaic of the Empress Zoe and her third husband Constantine IX (1042–55) kneeling on either side of an enthroned Christ.

Zoe was singularly unlucky in love. At the age of 23 she was engaged to the Holy Roman Emperor Otto III, but he died of a fever and Zoe spent the next 20 years confined to the women's quarters of the palace. Her father Constantine VIII had no son to succeed him, so a marriage was arranged in haste between Zoe and the sexagenarian senator Romanus Argyrus. As she was well beyond the age of childbearing, Zoe and Romanus resorted to all kinds of charms, ointments and potions in an effort to make her pregnant. They had no success and Romanus, tiring of the game, came to hate his wife.

Zoe became infatuated with a low-born Paphlagonian boy, Michael, the brother of a eunuch, John the Orphanotrophus, who held an important position in the court. Zoe seduced the boy and after Romanus conveniently died, possibly of hellebore poisoning, married Michael in 1034. She was 56, he was 16. Michael had never loved Zoe and soon after their marriage, refused to have any physical contact with her. She was banished again to the women's quarters. Michael IV had always suffered from epilepsy and the attacks became more frequent and prolonged. He began to deteriorate physically. He lost his good looks completely and become gross and bloated. Before he died in 1041, Zoe was brought to the court and induced to adopt a nephew of John the Orphanotrophus, called Michael Calaphates (Calaphates means 'caulker', the trade of Michael's father).

Michael V Calaphates (1041–42) had always hated Zoe and about a year after his coronation he accused her of attempted regicide. His soldiers dragged her from the women's quarters and she was shut up in a convent in Prinkipo (Büyük Ada). It is said that Michael gloated over her shaven tresses as she was taken away from Constantinople. However, Zoe was to have her revenge. She and her sister Theodora were much loved by the people who called them familiarly in Greek, 'Mamai', the 'Mums'. Zoe was brought back from exile and after a period of terrible rioting in the city, on the evening of 20 April 1042 Michael V was deposed, blinded and exiled to the monastery of Eleimon on Chios.

In 1042 Zoe ruled the Byzantine Empire with her sister Theodora. This period of joint rule was not successful and at the age of 64 Zoe married again. Her third husband was Constantine IX Monomachus. He had a mistress, Sclerina, and it would appear that Zoe shared her husband with Sclerina in a happy *ménage à trois* until her death at the age of 72 in 1050. The head on this mosaic is that of Constantine IX. It replaced those of her first and second husbands, Romanus III Argyrus (1028–34) and Michael IV (1034–41).

Also in the S gallery there is a fine fragmentary late 13C mosaic of the Deisis. Christ is flanked by St John on the right and Mary on the left. The artist has produced a powerful representation of their pleas for the salvation of mankind.

Opposite this mosaic is the lid of the sarcophagus of Enrico Dandolo, the Doge of Venice, who died on 1 June 1205. Dandolo was 90 years old when he led the Crusaders and the Venetian soldiers against Constantinople in 1204 (see above). According to the historian Andrea Dandolo, the Doge was arrested and partially blinded on the orders of Manuel I Comnenus (1143–80), when he came to Constantinople in 1171 as one of the Venetian peace emissaries. At any rate he hated, and perhaps envied, the Byzantines. It is said that after the capture of the city by the Turks in 1453 Dandolo's tomb was broken open and his bones fed to the dogs.

The third mosaic in the gallery is to the right of the window. This shows John II Comnenus (1118–43 and his wife Eirene presenting gifts to the Virgin and the Christ Child. The 17-year-old prince depicted on the side wall is their eldest son, Alexius, who died in 1122 shortly after the mosaic was finished. His pale, lined face already shows signs of the illness which was to carry him away. John Comnenus was probably the greatest of the Comneni emperors, prudent, energetic and upright. He put an end to the invasions of the Patzinaks, warlike nomads from southern Russia, established his sovereignty over the Serbs, gained important victories against the Danishmendid Turks and the Armenians and captured Antioch.

In the NW corner of the northern gallery there is a mosaic of Alexander (912–13) wearing the magnificent dress of a Byzantine emperor. An inscription in four roundels says, 'Lord help thy servant, the orthodox and faithful Emperor Alexander'. Neither orthodox nor faithful, Alexander was one of the worst emperors ever to occupy the throne of Byzantium. Mad, bad and cruel, he proposed to castrate his six-year-old nephew, Constantine, so as to make him ineligible for the succession. Fortunately his reign was short. After 13 months he died, worn out by constant dissipation. Boorish and drunken, Alexander was also credulous. Believing that the bronze boar in the Hippodrome was his *alter idem*, he had it fitted with new teeth and genitalia in the hope that this would revive his own exhausted parts.

To the left of the entrance, in the N aisle, is the so called sweating pillar. This is associated with St Gregory Thaumaturgus, St Gregory the Wonder-worker (c 213–70). A native of Pontus and a disciple of Origen, Gregory became bishop of Neocaesarea in 240. There was a popular belief that the saint had appeared in the church shortly after its completion and placed healing powers in the stone of this pillar. It was considered to be particularly efficacious for eye diseases and infertility problems and the church authorities had to encase the stone with brass to protect it from the hands of sufferers. However, they managed to pierce the brass and people still place their fingers in the hole to catch some drops of the precious healing liquid.

Leave Haghia Sophia by the Vestibule of the Warriors at the S end of the narthex. During the Byzantine period the imperial guard waited here while the emperors attended church services. In the lunette above the door leading from the vestibule to the narthex there is a beautiful mosaic of the Blessed Virgin and the Christ Child flanked by two figures. On the right Constantine the Great offers a miniature city, Constantinople, while on the left Justinian I offers a model of Haghia Sophia. This mosaic is believed to date from the reign of Basil II Bulgaroctonus, the Bulgar-Slayer (976–1025).

The domed building to the left of the exit was the Byzantine **baptistery**. The Ottomans used it first as a lamp store and then as a mausoleum.

Two sultans are buried here. Both of them were mad. Mustafa I (1617–18 and 1622–23) came straight from the *Kafes*, knowing only what he had learned from women and eunuchs. Acting frequently on whim, he made two of his favourite pages governors of Damascus and Cairo. Incompetent and constantly in fear of execution, he was soon deposed and replaced by the able Osman II (1618–22). Mustafa returned to the throne, however, after Osman had fallen to the wrath of the Janissaries, and his second term in office was even more disastrous than his first. He was declared insane and removed.

Sultan İbrahim (1640–56) came from a similar background. He was 24 years old when he acceded and had been in the *Kafes* from the age of two. Without education or experience, he depended on cliques of competing courtiers and family members for advice. At the time of his accession he was the only living descendent of Osman and so was encouraged to father children. However, he was subject to bouts of impotence and turned for help to a quack named Cinci Hoca (lit. the Witch Doctor Teacher). Apparently Cinci's potions worked and he was loaded with gifts, but when Ibrahim was deposed, Cinci Hoca and his friend Pezevenk (lit. the Pimp) were torn to piece by a mob in the At Meydanı.

A year after coming to the throne, it was reported that 24 concubines pleasured İbrahim in the course of a single day. He made one, an enormously fat Armenian, governor of Damascus. Called Şeker Parça (Piece of Sugar), it is said she weighed more than 136kg.

There are many bizarre stories told about İbrahim and his concubines. One, perhaps apocryphal, concerns a girl who was caught *in flagrante*. Informed secretly of this slight to his honour, İbrahim tried to discover the name of the offender. His efforts proved unsuccessful and he had all 280 concubines drowned in batches. A diver, who went down to examine a wreck in the Bosphorus, found a great number of sacks, each with a dead woman inside, swaying and bobbing in the current. Only one managed to escape. She was taken aboard a boat bound for France and told her rescuers about the ghastly vengeance of the sultan.

İbrahim had a passion for furs, especially sables, and covered the walls of Topkapı with rare specimens. He devoted most of his time and energy to his concubines and his extravagant ways drained the treasury. Towards the end of his reign he was known to his subjects as Deli İbrahim, Crazy İbrahim. Deposed, he was strangled on the strength of a *fatwa* issued by the chief jurisconsult.

On the W shore of the Bosphorus, not far from Sirkeci station where for many years Orient Express passengers alighted, there is a a more pleasant reminder of İbrahim's reign. The **Sepetçiler Köşkü** takes its name from the *sepetçiler* or basket weavers who built this pavilion for him in 1647. From here İbrahim and his successors were accustomed to embark on one of the royal barges for a day's excursion on the Bosphorus or the Golden Horn. The pavilion was restored recently and it is now the **International Press Centre**.

The Turkish rococo **şadırvan** in the centre of the courtyard was the gift of Mahmut I (1730–54). The small domed building to the left of the exit to the street was the **muvakkitane**, the clock room of the mosque timekeeper. Look for his sundial on the SW corner of Haghia Sophia.

There are several imperial Ottoman tombs in this part of the garden of Haghia Sophia. The small **Türbe of the Princes** contains the bodies of five infant sons of Murat IV (1622–40). They were the victims of one of the many epidemics that raged through the Harem from time to time.

In the adjoining, larger *türbe* are buried Murat III (1574–95), his favourite wife, Safiye, four of his concubines, 23 of his sons and 25 of his daughters. He had 40 concubines in all and fathered about 130 sons and countless daughters. (According to Evliya Çelebi he had a total of 326 children.) To ensure the succession of her son, Mehmet, Safiye ordered the execution of 19 of Murat's sons and 20 of his daughters on the day of his death. One was torn from its mother's breast and, mewing and crying, was speedily despatched. Mehmet III summoned his brothers to his presence and told them that they need have no fear. The time had come for their circumcisions. The oldest was eleven and they were 'very fair and pretty boys'. The surgeons were in the next room and the cutting was done quickly. Then the children were taken to the adjoining room where the deaf mutes were waiting with their silken cords. One young boy was eating chestnuts when the executioner approached him. 'Let me eat my chestnuts', the child begged, 'and strangle me afterwards'. His request was refused.

This was the last time the Ottoman practice of killing possible contenders to the throne was carried out. Thereafter the younger brothers of the new sultan were confined in the *kafes*, in Topkapı where nothing was denied them but their freedom.

The hexagonal *türbe* was constructed by the architect Davut Ağa in 1599. Note the very fine İznik tiles on its walls.

The next *türbe* is that of **Selim II** (1566–74), sometimes known as Selim the Sot. The dome of this square building rests on the outer walls which are covered, outside and inside, with the finest İznik tiles. It was built by Sinan, architect to Süleyman the Magnificent, in 1577. In addition to Selim, Nur Banu his first wife, five of his sons who were murdered by Nur Banu to ensure the succession of her son Murat, three of his daughters and 32 of his grandchildren, the children of Murat III, are buried here.

The last *türbe*, an octagonal structure, houses the remains of **Mehmet III** (1595–1603) who was succeeded by his oldest surviving son, Ahmet I.

In 1599 Mehmet received the gift of an organ from Elizabeth I of England. Hoping to curry favour with him and to gain his support for her struggle against Spain, she cited the hatred of the Protestants and the Muslims for 'worshippers of images'. The organ was brought to Constantinople by one Thomas Dallam and set up in a beautifully decorated kiosk which Dallam believed had been specially constructed for the strangling of members of the sultan's family. 'I stood there', he wrote, 'playinge suche things as I could until the cloke strouke'. Rewarded by the sultan, who was very pleased by the recital, Dallam was taken on a tour of the palace and allowed a glimpse of members of the harem playing ball in a garden. If caught, the penalty for this act of voyeurism would have been death, probably preceded by lengthy torture.

After the conquest of Constantinople Mehmet II lived in a new palace which he had constructed on the Third Hill. Later known as Eski Saray, this has disappeared completely. Most of the site is now occupied by the buildings of the University of İstanbul. Later Mehmet commenced the building of **Topkapı Sarayı**, the **Palace of the Cannon-Gate** on the site of the old Byzantine acropolis.

Its name was derived from two cannon which pointed towards Saray Burnu and the stretch of water beyond. Mehmet's successors added to the palace and, at the height of its glory, more than 3000 persons lived there. In 1853 Abdül Mecit I (1839–61) moved his court to the newly-built Dolmabaçe Palace on the Bosphorus. Until 1909, when the

Harem was disbanded, the wives and concubines of former sultans continued to live in Topkapı. In its last, sad days it was the refuge of a few servants and eunuchs. They remained there until the palace was turned into a museum in 1924. In recent years many of the buildings have been repaired and restored and parts of the Harem have been opened to the public for the first time.

The palace was divided into four courts. In the first court there were the royal bakeries, a hospital for the pages, the imperial mint, part of the treasury and servants' accommodation. The second court was the Court of the Divan, the Imperial Council. In addition to the Council Chamber it had a mosque, the records' office, the palace kitchen, the stables and the inner treasury. One of the entrances to the Harem was located here. The third court was occupied mainly by buildings for the training of the *iç oğlanları*, the royal pages. Only members of the sultan's household and high officials could enter this part of the palace. The fourth court contained the residential quarters of the sultan and the royal princes, the Harem and a number of pavilions in a large enclosed garden.

Entrance to the **First Court** is by the **Bab-i Hümayun**, the Imperial Gate or the Gate of Felicity. This was built by Mehmet II. The niches on either side were often used to display the heads of executed criminals or rebels. In addition to Mehmet's *tuğra* there are inscriptions recording the building of the gate and its reconstruction in the 19C by Abdul Aziz, and some verses from the Koran. The First Court was sometimes known as the Court of the Janissaries, as they assemble here when on guard duty at the palace. Unfortunately, **Haghia Eirene**, the church of Divine Peace, located to the left of the gate, is often closed.

From the earliest times there was a church on this site. Rebuilt by Constantine the Great or his son Constantius, Haghia Eirene was the scene of some of the religious disputations between the heretical Arians and the orthodox majority which accepted the Nicene Creed. The Second Ecumenical Council, which upheld the Creed and condemned the Arians, was held here in 381. Haghia Eirene was burned down during the Nika riots in 532 (see above) and rebuilt c 537. Thereafter, both it and Haghia Sophia were served by the same clergy. The building was badly damaged by fire in 564 and restored by Justinian. It suffered further damage from an earthquake in 740 and was repaired by Leo III or his son Constantine V. Some minor additions were made during the Ottoman period when the church was used as an arsenal by the Janissaries.

Entrance is by a porch on the W side erected during the Turkish period. A ramp leads down to the aisle—the floor of the building is c 5m lower than the level of the ground outside. The original approach was by way of an atrium and narthex on the NW side. The church, which measures c 42m by 36.7m, has an apse at the SE end. The central area is covered by a dome supported by a high drum. On the conch of the apse there is a mosaic cross on a gold background. The Greek inscription above is a rather inaccurate rendering of Psalm 65, vs. 4 and 5. It reads, 'Happy is the man of thy choice, whom thou dost bring to dwell in thy courts; let us enjoy the blessing of thy house, thy holy temple'. The inscription above the bema arch is from Amos ix. 6. The rather plain sarcophagi in the atrium are believed to contain the bones of early Byzantine emperors.

Concerts of classical music are given in Haghia Eirene during İstanbul's annual International Festival.

The Ottoman imperial mint and outer treasury were housed in buildings to the N of Haghia Eirene. The *iç oğlanları* were treated in the infirmary in the first court. While ill, rules were relaxed and they were allowed to drink wine which was lowered over the wall by the palace gardeners. After performing his morning duties the Chief Executioner, who was also the Head Gardener, washed his hands and sword in the **Cellad Çeşmesi** the Executioner's Fountain. This is in the NE corner of the court. The short pillars on either side of the fountain were called the 'Example Stones', as decapitated heads were placed on them *pour encourager les autres*.

The **Bab-üs Selam**, the Gate of Salutations leads into the **Second Court**. Sometimes known as the **Orta Kapı**, the Middle Gate, it is much more ornate than the Imperial Gate. The outer door bears the date 1524–25 and above it is the *tuğra* of Süleyman the Magnificent. Only authorised visitors were allowed through this gate and then only on foot. One of the small rooms to the right was reserved for visiting ambassadors and other callers of note. On the left there was a tiny room for the principal executioner and a cell where condemned prisoners were held while awaiting decapitation. It was in these rooms that Lord Byron and the British Ambassador were detained, when they came for an audience with Mahmut II in 1809. Much to his lordship's disgust they had to wait for a very long time, in darkness, until the Janissaries, who numbered about 4000, had 'run for their pilau, which is placed in innumerable little pewter dishes and, at a given signal, scrambled for and seized upon by the soldiery'.

On the S side of the court are the ten **Royal kitchens**. Here, in the great period of Ottoman power, the cooks prepared food for more than 4000 people every day. The Janissaries came to the palace three times in the year for their pay and were each given a loaf of bread. All the loaves had to be the same weight. From time to time one was chosen at random and weighed. If found to be too light or too heavy, the baker who had made it could have his right hand chopped off. The palace's fine collection of porcelain is now displayed in the kitchens. The distinctive chimneys were added by Sinan after the fire of 1574.

On the NW side are the **Stables** which are not open to the public. To the right of this complex is the entrance to the **Harem**. A separate ticket is needed for this part of the palace. During the holiday period visitors may have to wait several hours before being able to join a tour of the Harem. Accordingly, buy your ticket immediately after entering the second court.

The domed building next to Harem entrance is the **Divan**. The room on the left was the Council Chamber. The low couch around three sides of the room is the divan which gave its name to the Council. The Grand Vizier sat in the centre with the other viziers on either side in order of seniority. The small window, covered by a grille, on the wall above the Grand Vizier's head was called the Eye of the Sultan, as this allowed the ruler to see and hear the discussions of the Council without being seen himself. The Council Chamber has been restored to the state it was in after the repairs of Murat III in the 16C. Note the fine İznik tiles on the lower part of the walls and the rather faded painted decoration on the upper section and on the dome.

The next room was the **Records' Office**. It now houses the palace's collection of clocks which includes one made in London in 1740 and another, the gift of Napoleon, ornamented with rubies and emeralds. The third room was the **Office of the Grand Vizier**. Next to the Divan is the **Inner Treasury** where there is a splendid collection of arms and armour.

The **Bab-ü Saadet**, the **Gate of Felicity**, led to the private part of the palace. This dates from the reign of Mehmet II, but was reconstructed in the 16C and redecorated two centuries later. On religious holidays and at the time of his accession the sultan sat before this gate to receive pledges of loyalty from his subjects. Immediately beyond the gate is the **Arz Odası**, the Audience Chamber. Here the sultan received ambassadors and the Grand Viziers who reported to him on the proceedings of the Divan and here he gave the royal assent to those proposals of the Council which he accepted. The foundations of the chamber date from the time of the Conqueror, but it has been restored several times. The canopy over the throne and the chimney piece are the only furnishings to survive a disastrous fire in the mid 19C. The circular red stone near the entrance marks the spot where the body of the reforming sultan Selim III rested after his cowardly assassination by his nephew Mustafa IV.

The rooms to the right and the left of the gate were the introductory schools for the *iç oğlanları*, the royal pages, and the living quarters of the White Eunuchs and their Ağa who were responsible for the discipline and education of the boys.

Just behind the Audience Chamber is the early 18C **Library of Ahmet III** which is not open to the public. It contains about 3000 valuable books and manuscripts including a number in Arabic and Greek.

The **Costume Museum** houses about 3000 costumes, some of them dating from the time of the Conqueror. Note the blood-stained kaftan of the youthful and able Osman II (1618–22) who was deposed and then murdered by the Janissaries. His assassination set a fearful precedent which was to be followed all too often in later years.

The **Treasury** occupies the suite of rooms used by Mehmet II and some of successors as a *selamlık*. Among the many valuable objects exhibited here are the emerald-encrusted **Topkapı Dagger**, the **Throne of Shah Ismail**, and the 86 karat **Kaşıkçı Elması** the **Spoonmaker's Diamond**.

Topkapı's collection of about 13,000 **miniatures** is, perhaps, its greatest treasure. Look especially for the three *Albums of Mehmet II* which contain miniatures depicting scenes of the Turkish homeland in Central Asia, these are believed to date from the 13C to the middle of the 15C; the *Description of Süleyman's Campaign in the Two Iraqs* by Matrakci Nasuh; and the *Hünername*, the *Shahanshahname*, and *Surname*, the books of accomplishments, of the king of kings and of festivals, which were commissioned by Murat III.

On the W side of the court are the **Ağalar Camii**, the Pavilion of the Holy Mantle and the **Has Oda**. Teachers and pupils worshipped in the Ağalar Camii. In the Pavilion of the Holy Mantle are the relics of the Prophet which Selim I brought from Egypt in 1517. In addition to the **Holy Mantle**, a plain black camel hair cloak, there are hairs from the beard of the Prophet, one of his teeth, his seal and his footprint. The **Holy Standard**, which preceded Ottoman sultans into battle from the 16C onwards, is also kept here.

The pages were drawn mainly from the boys produced by the periodic *devşirme* levies of Christian children. The most comely and talented, who attended on the sultan, were trained in the **Has Oda**, where they learned to read and write Persian, Arabic and Ottoman Turkish. They were instructed in religion, practised calligraphy and became proficient in the use of arms. There was a considerable emphasis on sport, particularly wrestling, weight-lifting, archery and riding. The discipline was strict. Great care was taken over their physical appearance. A page had to bathe each day and shave twice a week. He had a weekly manicure and pedicure and a haircut once each month. He was subjected to a body search each day for spices, which were believed to inflame the passions, and for love letters written, presumably, by his companions, as pages were allowed no contact with girls. At the beginning of the reign of the youthful Mehmet IV (1648–87), his Grand Vizier Sofu Mehmet ended the *devşirme* system and dismissed most of the pages, 'who traditionally had served the sultans and satisfied their pleasures' (Stanford J. Shaw). The highest offices in the land were open to graduates of the Has Oda and many served in important government posts, contributing substantially to the stability and strength of the Ottoman Empire. According to the Venetian ambassador Morosini, they proudly claimed to be the slaves of their lord, the sultan, as they knew that the government was composed of slaves whom they commanded.

The Has Oda now houses a collection of manuscripts which display fine calligraphy from all periods.

The **Rivan Köşkü** commemorates the capture of Erivan in Armenia by Murat IV in 1636. The **Sünnet Odası** was built by the mad Sultan İbrahim (see above) in 1641. It was used for the circumcision ceremonies of Ottoman princes until the 18C. Note the beautiful tiles on the exterior and interior walls.

In the **Fourth Court** there are several structures set in a pleasant garden overlooking the Sea of Marmara. These include the **Baghdad Köşkü**, which commemorates Murat IV's capture of Baghdad in 1638, and a delightful small balcony covered with a domed canopy. Here Ibrahim the Mad was accustomed to break his fast after sunset during the month of Ramazan. There is a fine view westward from the balcony towards the Golden Horn and the buildings which crowd the skyline above it. Nearby is the large marble fountain into which İbrahim was accustomed to throw his lady friends during his frequent wild orgies.

In the lower garden Ahmet III (1673–1736) celebrated some of his famous Tulip Festivals. Interest in tulips was so intense at this time that it became known as the *Lale Devri*, the Tulip Period. Rare strains of the flower were grown and their possession often led the owner to high office. At night parties and festivals were celebrated in beautifully laid out gardens in the palace and in other parts of the city. Dancers, musicians and singing birds entertained the guests while illumination was provided by candles carried on the backs of tortoises. Trousers and gowns became all the rage and sofas and chairs replaced the traditional divans.

The **Sofa Köşkü** in the lower garden was probably used by Ahmet for discreet rendezvous. The tower to the S was known variously as the **Başlala Kulesi**, the Head Tutor's Tower, and the **Hekimbaşı Odası**, the Room of the Sultan's Chief Physician. The **Mecidiye Köşkü** was built at the behest of Abdul Mecit I in 1840, 13 years before he moved with his court to the new palace of Dolmabaçe on the Bosphorus. The pavilion now houses the **Konyalı Restaurant**, a delightful place where visitors may relax and refresh themselves before going on to explore the Harem. There are fine views of the Bosphorus and the Sea of Marmara from the restaurant terrace.

There are about 300 rooms in the **Harem**, but only about 20 are visited during the course of the guided tour. The *cariyeler*, the concubines, were brought to the palace when they were between 12 and 14 years old. Some were captives, others were simply kidnapped, while a number were bought from their poverty-stricken parents. They had to be intelligent and had to conform to the standards of beauty prevailing at the time. They were paid a small wage and taught to read and write. They learned embroidery, cooking, dancing and how to play musical instruments. Foreign girls had to learn Turkish. The ambition of each concubine was to catch the eye of the sultan, be bedded by him and produce a male child. A *cariye* whose son succeeded to the throne became the *Valide Sultan*, the Queen Mother, a position of great power not only in the Harem but also in the state. The first concubine to reside in Topkapı was Roxelana (see below).

The *cariyeler* were supervised by the sinister Black Eunuchs who were chosen for their ugliness so that they would not arouse unwelcome passions in the breasts of their charges. Exercising almost unlimited power, the eunuchs carried in their turbans, almost as a badge of office, the silver tube which permitted them to urinate. The tour will take you to the **Courtyard of the Black Eunuchs**, then through the *Cümle Kapısı*, the principal door to the Harem, and on to the *Altın Yol*, the **Golden Passageway**. This leads to the **Courtyard of the Valide Sultan**.

One of the finest rooms in the Harem is the **Salon of Murat III**. Note the beautiful İznik tiles, the bronze chimney piece and the fountain of carved polychrome marble. Other notable rooms are the 17C **Library of Ahmet I** and the **Dining Room of Ahmet III** with its characteristic Tulip Period decoration (see above). A delightful touch is provided by the representation of a duck and her brood of downy yellow ducklings.

When the Ottomans abandoned the practice of killing all the male relatives of a new sultan, they were confined to the *kafes* or **cage** in the Harem (see above). This was probably located over the strangely named **Cinlerin Meşveret Yeri**, the **Council Place of the Djinns**. The schoolroom of the princes was above the quarters of the Ağa of the Black Eunuchs. The royal children were allowed to exercise in the grounds of the palace, taught to ride and fight and learned a skill. After puberty they had access to *cariyeler*, but were forbidden to father children. Their concubines were either sterilised or obliged to use pessaries made of a mixture of amber, aloes, cardamon, musk, cloves, ginger and pepper. Any concubine found to be pregnant was drowned immediately.

A narrow street near Haghia Eirene leads down to three of the most important museums in İstanbul: the Archaeological Museum, the Museum of the Ancient Orient and the Çinli Köşkü. The sarcophagi, capitals, columns and architectural fragments, which line the sides of this street, are part of the Archaeological Museum's vast collection. There are more in the museum's garden, near the Çinli Köşkü and on either side of the entrance to the main building. Note particularly the 4C and 5C porphyry sarcophagi which once housed the bones of Byzantine emperors and empresses.

There is a pleasant *çaybahçesi* set around with ancient statues in the museum complex where one may relax over a glass of tea or a soft drink.

This area once formed part of the **Fifth Court** of Topkapı Sarayı. Mehmet II had the Çinli Köşkü built in 1472 as a refuge from the Court and a place from which he could watch the princes and the pages play *cirit*, a rumbustious game which originated in Central Asia. The contestants, mounted on horseback, tried to catch and return the javelins which they threw at each other. The pavilion continued to be used until the sultan moved to Dolmabahçe in 1856. Refurbished and restored to its original form, it now houses a wonderful collection of rare tiles and ceramics from the Selçuk and Ottoman periods. Of special interest are an early 16C **Blue and White İznik Mosque Lamp**, a late 16C İznik **Polychrome Tile Panel**, and an İznik **Mosque Lamp** from Sokollu Mehmet Paşa Camii in İstanbul.

The **Museum of the Ancient Orient** has a representative collection of ancient Egyptian, Sumerian, Akkadian, Babylonian, Hittite, Urartian, Aramaic and Assyrian objects. These are arranged in a series of attractive and informative displays. Among the museum's treasures are a 9C BC **late Hittite guardian lion** from Zincirli, the statue of a **deified king** from Babylon which dates to the beginning of the second millennium BC, 6C BC, **lion and bull reliefs** from the Ishtar Gate in Babylon, **cuneifrom tablets**, dated to 1900 BC, from Kanesh, a 9C BC Late Hittite **grave stele** from Maraş, an 8C BC Late Hittite **column base with a double sphinx** from Zincirli, and a copy of the mid 13C BC **Kadesh Treaty** which was found at Boğazköy (see below).

The **Archaeological Museum** was established in the late 19C largely through the zeal, application and hard work of its first director, Hamdi Bey. It houses some 45,000 artefacts and, although two new galleries were opened recently, it is possible to display only a limited number at one time. Among the museum's finest exhibits are the sarcophagi discovered in 1887 in the necropolis of Sidon in the Lebanon. The **Alexander Sarcophagus**, so called because of its representation of Alexander the Great at peace and at war, is the finest of these. Apart from the loss of the metal ornamentation and the head of one of the figures, the sarcophagus, which was fashioned from Pentelic marble, probably in Sidon, is in a very fine condition. Traces of the paints used on the hair, eyes, eyelashes, lips and clothes of the figures—yellow, violet, burnt sienna, blue, red, and purple—are still visible. Note particularly the head of Alexander. The sarcophagus, which is be-lieved to date from 311 BC, was probably intended for Abdalonymous, the last king of Sidon, who was appointed by Alexander in 332. The battle scene is almost certainly that of Issus, where Alexander defeated a Persian army led by Darius III, and the hunting scene probably represents an entertainment arranged by Abdalonymous for Alexander and the Compan-ions in the royal hunting park.

The other sarcophagi found at Sidon are: the **Sarcophagus of Mourning Women**; the **Satrap Sarcophagus**; the **Lycian Sarcophagus**, the **Anthropoid Sarcophagus of a Woman** and the **Tabnit Sarcophagus**. The Anthropoid Sarcophagus, which dates from c 460 BC, displays an interesting fusion of Greek and Egyptian styles. The diorite Sarcophagus of Tabnit dates from the 6C BC and, according to the inscription, was originally made for an Egyptian commander named Penephtah. A second inscription states that it was reused later at Tabnit. The archaeologists also found painted funeral stelae from the Hellenistic period at Sidon. Two of these bear the names of the deceased, Salmamodes(?) and Balboura.

The museum has the oldest Hebrew inscription known to scholars. This is the **Gezer Calendar** which was discovered near Jerusalem. Written on a tablet of limestone, it is believed to be an agricultural calendar listing the months for sowing and harvesting.

From Pergamum there is a 2C BC idealised **head of Alexander the Great** and from Magnesia-ad-Sipylum (Manisa) a larger than life statue of Alex-ander which had an accompanying inscription, 'Menas of Pergamum, son of Aias, made (it)'. The sensitively sculpted **statue of an Ephebe** found at Tralles, modern Aydın, is believed to date from the late 1C BC or early 1C AD. This masterly representation of a boy aged about 12, shows him leaning against a pillar wrapped in a cloak, presumably just after exercises. The pose and the cloak draw attention to the boy's head. 'The large eyes, and the childish charming face with its air of mystery are often encountered among Mediterranean people. This head is unequalled by any other head of antiquity so far discovered' (Alpay Pasinli).

On no account miss a visit to the galleries in the new wing. Two of the galleries are open, two more are in preparation.

On the second floor there is a chronological display of finds from **Troy**, on one side of the room, and from a number of other sites in **Anatolia** on the opposite side. The third floor has a dazzling arrangement of artefacts from Cyprus, Syria and Palestine. These include a fine collection of **Palmyran funerary portrait sculptures** near the entrance to the room, a strange **terracotta incense burner** from Palestine and, in the cabinet devoted to Cyprus, statues of obese, grinning **child temple prostitutes**.

The first floor gallery will trace the history of İstanbul through objects from the prehistoric, Roman, Byzantine and Ottoman periods, while on the ground floor there will be a display of classical sculpture from Anatolia. This will include a full-size reproduction of the temple of Athena at Assos (Behramkale) (see below).

'The people had not the least suspicion of it, although they daily drew their water out of the wells that were sunk into it'. 'It' was the **Imperial Cistern** which the French antiquary and traveller, Pierre Gilles, rediscovered in the mid 16C. The cistern had been constructed by Justinian in 532 following the Nika disturbances, to store water for the Imperial Palace. It served the same purpose for Topkapı Sarayı after the Turkish conquest, but its existence appears to have been forgotten until the persistence and curiosity of Pierre Gilles located it once more.

Now called **Yerebatan Saray**, the **Underground Palace**, it is a short distance to the W of Haghia Sophia. Gilles explored the cistern by torchlight from a small boat which was rowed between the 336 marble columns supporting the roof. His latter day Charon profited from the visit by spearing some of the fish which abounded in the stygian depths. In 1826 the remnants of the Janissaries put up a last, desperate resistance to the troops of Mahmut II (see above) here. Splashing and floundering in the dark they fought and died in water incarnadined by their blood.

Walkways have been constructed in the cistern, which measures 138m by 64.6m, and, to the accompaniment of changing, coloured lights and classical music, you make your way to the far end where two of the columns rest on Classical bases carved in the form of Medusa heads. Whether the music and the illumination add anything to the visitor's appreciation of this wonderful structure is questionable.

Stop for a few minutes in the shop and gallery near the exit from the cistern. This sells books, postcards and original cartoons by Turkish artists.

Another interesting place is the **Sahaflar Çarşısı**, the Market of the Second-Hand Book Sellers, which is reached from the SE corner of Beyazit Square. Books were first sold here during the Byzantine period when it was called the Chartoprateia. In recent years some shops have taken to selling Turkish miniatures of doubtful authenticity at inflated prices.

After you have made your purchases in the Sahaflar Çarşısı, pause for a glass of tea under the huge plane tree near the **Beyazit Camii**, one of the most charming mosques in İstanbul.

From Beyazit Camii it is just a few minutes' walk to the **Kapalı Çarşı,** the **Grand Bazaar**. The first covered market was established here by Mehmet II in the 15C. Destroyed by fire several times, it has more than 4000 shops, nearly 500 stalls, 18 fountains, a large mosque and 12 *mescits*, a primary school, a *türbe*, two banks, a public toilet, five or six restaurants, a police station, a post office, several restaurants and an information centre.

Similar products are grouped together, so there are streets lined with goldsmiths, silversmiths, sellers of leather goods, shoes, clothes, copperware, carved alabaster, pots and pans. Some of the more valuable objects are kept in the **Bedesten** which is in the centre of the bazaar.

Whether you intend to buy or not, it is worth spending a few hours in the Kapalı Çarşı to experience the vivacity, exuberance and persuasiveness of the vendors and the determination with which they pursue a sale. The bazaar is lively, exciting and colourful. Bargaining is accepted, indeed welcomed, except in the jewellery shops, and is usually a lengthy business conducted over many glasses of tea. Browsing is not always easy, as some traders are pushy and intrusive. Once a price has been agreed, it is very unlikely that a foreigner would be cheated or shortchanged. The goldsmiths, Şale Kuyumcusu at Kalpakçilar Cad. 183–85 are among the many shopkeepers who extend a warm welcome to visitors from abroad.

A short distance to the N of the University of İstanbul is the **Süleymaniye**. Occupying a magnificent site, high up on the Third Hill, it consists of a

A brush shop in Aksaray, İstanbul

mosque, *medreses*, a *hamam*, a library, a junior school, an *imaret*, a hospital and mental asylum, and several *türbes*. It was designed and built by Süleyman's great architect Sinan. The mosque was completed between 1550 and 1550. The other buildings were finished a few years later.

The approach to the **mosque** is by Tıryaki Çarşısı, the Market of the Addicts. During the Ottoman period the coffee-houses here served opium, coffee and tobacco, all of which were forbidden or frowned on at different times. Süleyman permitted coffee, even though a contemporary called it 'the black enemy of sleep and copulation'.

The mosque is preceded by a great rectangular courtyard surrounded by porticoes whose columns are shaped from the finest porphyry, granite and marble. The four minarets and the ten *şerifes* are said to commemorate the fact that Süleyman was the fourth sultan to rule in İstanbul and the tenth of the Ottoman line. The inscription over the entrance implores, 'O God who opens all doors, open the door of felicity'. The interior of the mosque measures c 58.5m by 57.5m. The diameter of the dome is 27.5m and its centre is 47m above the floor.

The mosque has always excited feelings of admiration, and not only among Muslims. Eyliya Çelebi relates how ten 'Frankish infidels skillful in geometry and architecture' reacted to it. They gazed around them, then each raised his right hand, laid his forefinger across his open mouth and tossed his hat in the air, crying out in astonishment, 'Mother of God'!

There were *medreses* on the N, NW and SW sides of the mosque. The hospital, caravanserai and *imaret* were on the W. Süleyman is buried in the garden in a *türbe* designed by Sinan. With him lie Mihrimah his daughter, and two of his successors, Süleyman II (1687–91) and Ahmet II (1691–95). Nearby is the smaller tomb of **Haseki Hürrem**, better known as **Roxelana**, the sultan's favourite wife. Sinan himself is buried in a triangular garden on the NW side of the mosque.

After a visit to the Süleymaniye, lunch or dine in the wonderful **Darrüziyafe** which now occupies the former *imaret* of the complex.

İstanbul has more wonders and delights than it has been possible to describe here. There can be few greater pleasures than a leisurely day trip by steamer on the Bosphorus to the little village of **Anadolu Kavağı** or a visit to the largest of the **Princes Islands**, **Büyük Ada**, where motor vehicles are not allowed and visitors view the scenery from horse-drawn phaetons. For the less energetic, lunch on the terrace of the **Malta Köşkü**, once the discreet rendezvous of the sultans, may be followed by a lazy afternoon watching the ships that pass up and down the Bosphorus. Information about these and many more of İstanbul's attractions are to be found in John Freely's *Blue Guide Istanbul.*

2

İstanbul to Gallipoli

Total distance 471km. İstanbul—77km Silivri—(58km Tekirdağ)—44km Çorlu—46km Lüleburgaz—14km Babaeski—28km Havsa—27km Edirne—63km Uzunköprü—45km Keşan—54km Bolayır—15km Gelibolu—c 13km Aegospotami—c 17km Sestus—6km Eceabat—c 4km Kilitbahir—c 25km Alçıtepe—c 5km İlyasbaba Burnu—2km Elaeus.

Thrace, the birthplace of Orpheus, is a land of bare, windswept hills and melancholy, marshy plains. Bordering on Greece and Bulgaria, it has been blessed or cursed with a long and eventful history. When the Romans formed the Province of Asia, they constructed the Via Egnatia the main route from Rome to the east. Today the sound of marching legionary feet has been replaced by the thunder of heavy lorries on the E5, Turkey's main road link with Europe, which follows the line of its Roman predecessor.

According to Herodotus the Thracians would have been invincible, if only they could have agreed among themselves! Xenophon said that like the men who made them, the images of the Thracian gods had blue eyes, red hair and freckles. Some Thracians, he added, lived on the plunder which they took from ships wrecked on sandbanks in the Euxine (the Black Sea). He comments wryly on the fierce Thracian winter when the countryside lay under a blanket of snow and the dinner wine and water came frozen to the table. Some of the Greeks lost noses and ears from frostbite, but the Thracians were prepared for the cold. They wore fox skins around their heads and ears and covered their bodies in long tunics. When riding they had cloaks that reached down to their feet. According to Strabo 'those who devoted their attention to the music of early times are called Thracians', and he gives as examples Orpheus, Musaeus and Thamyris. By all accounts Thracian women were to be feared rather than loved. Aphrodite filled them with lust for Orpheus, but as no woman would allow another to possess him, they tore the unfortunate demigod to pieces.

During the Byzantine period the so called **Long Wall** was built c 64km to the W of Constantinople to protect the capital from barbarian attacks. The wall, which was c 45km long, 5m high and 3m wide ran from the Sea of Marmara to the Black Sea coast. It was strengthened during the reign of the emperor Anastasius (AD 491–518).

There are frequent express bus services from İstanbul's Topkapı *otogarı* to Edirne. Motorists leave İstanbul by the Londra Asfalt and then follow the signs for Silivri, Çorlu, Lüleburgaz and Edirne. Traffic on this road is very heavy and delays are frequent. The road as far as Büyükçekmece is dull and uninteresting. At Kümbergaz, a weekend refuge for İstanbulers, there are a few breaks in the dreary urban sprawl and an occasional, fleeting glimpse of the Sea of Marmara.

At the approaches to **Silivri**, the ancient Selymbria or Selybria, look on the left for a graceful Ottoman bridge. This is one of a chain of bridges built by Sinan over lagoons where Süleyman liked to hunt. The sultan was almost drowned here by a flash flood on 20 September 1563. He had to scramble on to the roof of a pavilion to avoid the rapidly rising waters.

Selymbria was founded in 677 BC by colonists from Megara, a district in Greece between the Corinthian and Saronic gulfs. In the 3C BC it was absorbed by its more powerful sister colony, Byzantium, which had also been established by Megarians. In addition to the few late Roman and Byzantine architectural fragments in the Kale Park, you can see the fine early 16C **Piri Mehmet Paşa Camii**.

For Tekirdağ take the signposted left-hand fork on to the E25 c 15km to the W of Silivri. After 15km a turning on the left brings you to the picturesque fishing village of **Marmaraereğlisi**. Here there are ruined fortifications, an acropolis, ancient harbour, theatre and stadium of the Samian colony of Perinthus Heracleia. Do not miss the 16C **Ayaz Paşa Camii** and the open air museum in the amphitheatre. There is a small beach.

Tekirdağ is a port and seaside resort favoured by Turkish holidaymakers. Its old houses have an air of decayed gentility which lends the town an attractive faded charm. The fish restaurants on the sea front are famous.

Information and Accommodation. Tekirdağ has a single hotel, the one-star *Yat Oteli*, Yalı Cad. No. 8, the *Sözer Pansiyon*, Yalı Cad.; No. 107 and a motel, the *Miltur Tur. Tesisleri*, Kumbağ Köyü on the Ministry of Tourism list. The **Tourist Information Office** is at Atatürk Bulv., İskele Yanı, No. 65.

History. Originally a Thracian settlement, Tekirdağ was known as **Bisanthe** after the establishment of a Samian colony on the site. Its name was changed to Rhaedestus when it became the capital of Pezos the king of Thrace. Subsequently it was called Rodosto, Rodosçuk and, romantically, Tekfurdağ, the Mountain of the Byzantine Prince. It was captured by the Ottoman Turks in 1357.

Visit the 16C **Rüstem Paşa Camii** and the **Bedesten** both designed by Sinan. The **Archaeological and the Ethnographic Museum**, housed in the ornate Naval Club, has a collection of plant and animal fossils, prehistoric artefacts and pottery, architectural fragments, inscriptions, grave stelae, statues, terracotta figurines, amphorae, glass and coins from the Greek, Roman and Byzantine periods. In the ethnographic section there are Ottoman inscriptions, embroidery, weaving, jewellery, copper utensils, and costumes.

A **house** in Tekirdağ, once occupied by Prince Ferenc II Rakoczi (1676–1735), the Hungarian patriot who led an unsuccessful revolt against Austria, was converted into a museum by the Hungarian government in 1932. Among the Rakoczi memorabilia are Hungarian weapons, documents, paintings and his flag. The prince's last years were spent as a Carmelite friar first in France and later in Tekirdağ where he died.

Leaving Tekirdağ, you have two choices—return to Silivri and continue the journey as described below to Edirne via Çorlu or go first to Gallipoli and follow this route in reverse order. At the time of writing, the coastal road to Gallipoli had a very uneven surface. It passes many vineyards and frequent views of the Sea of Marmara. For a description of Gallipoli, see below.

At **Çorlu**, the ancient Cenuporio, the emperor Aurelian (AD 270–75) was murdered by his generals while campaigning against the Persians. The town fell into the hands of the Ottomans in 1359. On 25 April 1512 the Janissaries forced **Beyazit II** to abdicate and put his son **Selim I** (1512–20) on the throne. The next day Beyazit left İstanbul for his birthplace, Demotica, but died at Çorlu, ostensibly from natural causes but probably from poison administered by his doctor on Selim's orders. Just outside the town there are the ruins of a **Roman bridge** which carried the Via Egnatia over a small river. No trace remains of the *kulliye* which Sinan built for Süleyman in Çorlu.

Lüleburgaz, ancient name Bergula, was a staging post on the Thracian road from Perinthus Heracleia (see above). Its name was changed in the late 4C AD to Arcadiopolis in honour of the emperor Arcadius (395–408). A fine 2C AD Roman copy of a Greek statute of Apollo found in Lüleburgaz is in the Edirne's Archaeological Museum. The **Sokollu Mehmet Paşa Külliye**, built by Sinan in 1569–71 for Süleyman's grand vizier, merits a visit. In addition to the mosque, the *medrese, hamam*, a *türbe* and a market still stand. However, only the portal of the caravanserai remains. **Sokollu Mehmet** (1505–79) was a Christian boy from Bosnia who was selected under the *devşirme* system and brought to İstanbul. He rose to a position of power in the administration during the latter part of the 16C.

Traces of Bronze Age occupation have been discovered in **Babaeski**, 19km W of Lüleburgaz. The only building of interest is the **Semiz Ali Paşa Camii** which was built by Sinan. At **Havsa** the **Kasim Paşa Camii** of 1576 is also the work of Sinan. It commemorates the son of Sokollu Mehmet Paşa.

The approach to Edirne is charmless: the road passes through a dank bogland where sedge-rimmed pools reflect a pallid sky. In the early evening, you may be rewarded by the sight of a livid, apocalyptic sunset like those found in the canvases of some medieval German painters.

Edirne, like many border towns, has a frenetic air. The streets are full of foreign voices and crowded with off-duty soldiers—a reminder of its proximity to Turkey's borders with Bulgaria and Greece. Since its foundation at the confluence of the Meriç and Tunca rivers, the ancient Hebrus and Tonsus, this town has been fought over, captured, sacked, burned and rebuilt. For a time it was the capital of the Ottoman Empire. At the beginning of the 20C it was just a minor halt for the Orient Express. Edirne is vibrant, exciting, sensual, hard, European and Oriental at the same time, frequently exasperating, but seldom boring.

Information and Accommodation. It is not well provided with good hotels. On the Ministry of Tourism list there are two with two stars, three with one star. The *Rustempaşa Kervansaray Oteli*, which occupies an inn built by Sinan, a grade two motel and a pension are also listed. The **Tourist Information Office**, which has a rather relaxed attitude to its duty towards visitors, is at Hürriyet Meydanı No. 17. There are frequent bus services to İstanbul. Long-distance coaches to various European destinations pass through Edirne and it is still served by the successor to the Orient Express.

History. According to Strabo, the territory of a tribe called the Odrysae stretched along the Hebrus river as far as Odessus (Varna). It is believed that they established a settlement here called Odrysia sometime in the 7C BC. Later the Orestae, an Epeirote tribe, settled in the area and founded a town called Orestia. Both places maintained their separate identities until AD 125, when they were combined and named Hadri-anopolis (Adrianople) in honour of the emperor. Hadrian made it a garrison town and set up an armaments industry. During the reign of Diocletian (284–305) Adrianople was one of 15 places in the Eastern Empire which had *fabricae* for the production of shields and arms. The *fabricences* were organised into trade guilds and exercised considerable influence on the city's affairs. Diocletian divided Thrace into four prov-inces and made Adrianople the capital of one of them.

In AD 343 a dissident council of bishops met in Adrianople. This condemned Athanasius and the clergy, who supported him, and promulgated a new creed which differed from that formulated at Nicaea. The bishops and their conclusions were not popular with the town's people. The *fabricenses* played a leading part in demonstra-tions against this Arian council.

Licinius, emperor of the east, a Dacian peasant who had been made Augustus by Galerius, was defeated by Constantine I the Great in 324 at Adrianople. Thirty-four thousand men were slain in this battle. Licinius was later captured and, according to Gibbon, asked pardon for his offences. He 'laid himself and his purple at the feet of his master, was raised from the ground with insulting pity, was admitted the same day to the imperial banquet, and soon after sent away to Thessalonica…His confinement was soon terminated by death'. On 9 August 378 the eastern emperor Valens (364–378) was defeated by the Goths in a battle waged near Adrianople. The emperor and many of his officers and soldiers perished in the slaughter.

The city and the area around it was besieged many times and held by many foreign armies. During the Second Crusade (1147–49) members of the German contingent burned a monastery and murdered all the monks because one of their band had been killed by robbers. In 1188 Frederick Barbarossa wintered here.

Adrianople was taken by the Ottomans in 1362. It replaced Bursa as the seat of government and was renamed Edirne. Cannon forged in Edirne helped Mehmet II to take Constantinople. During the years of Ottoman rule the city was adorned with many fine buildings by Murat II, Süleyman the Magnificent and other sultans. Süleyman liked to hunt game in the countryside around Edirne with dogs and falcons, only returning to Constantinople when the croaking of the frogs became unbearable!

During the last years of the Ottoman Empire the fortunes of Edirne declined. Its possession by Turkey was disputed by the Bulgarians and the Russians. The treaty of Adrianople of 1829 recognised the independence of Greece and of a number of Danubian principalities. The city was occupied by the Russians in 1829 and 1878, by the Bulgarians in 1913 and by the Greeks from 1919–23. It was returned to Turkish rule by the 1923 treaty of Lausanne.

It is said that Edirne had nearly 300 mosques when it was the second city of the Ottoman empire. The oldest extant mosque, **Eski Cami**, was built of cut stone and brick in 1402–14. According to an inscription over the door the architect was Hacı Alaettin of Konya and the builder Ömer ibn Ibrahim. Work was commenced by Süleyman Çelebi, son of Beyazit I, following his father's defeat by Tamerlane at the battle of Ankara. It was completed by his brother Mehmet, after he overcame and killed Süleyman and another brother Musa in the course of a dynastic struggle. The mosque, which resembles Bursa's Ulu Cami in style, is a square structure divided into nine sections, each covered by a dome. Damaged by fire and by an earthquake in the 18C, it was restored by Mahmut I. Further restoration was carried out in 1924–34. Note the fine white marble portal and the decorative calligraphy on the interior walls and pillars and on the *mimber*.

The restored **Rüstem Paşa Keravansaray** nearby has been converted into a hotel. Built by Sinan between 1560 and 1561, the caravanserai is in two parts. One was reserved for the merchants of Edirne, the other for travellers. In summer the beautiful central courtyard, which is shaded by a plane tree, is filled with the heady scent of flowers. The hotel is a popular place for weddings and the family celebrations which follow *sünnet* ceremonies. These are often noisy and continue late into the night.

Edirne's **bedesten**, with its 14 domes, is not far from Eski Cami. It was built by Mehmet I shortly after the completion of the mosque. Like all bedestens it was used by merchants as a secure place to display and store their valuable goods.

The **Semiz Ali Paşa Arasta** is also the work of Sinan. Completed in 1589, it is a long tunnel-like building with shops on both sides. Here you may buy one of Edirne's specialities, soap shaped like fruit or vegetables. Many of the shops sell new and second-hand books.

The 12C **Kule Kapısı** is all that remains of the tower which once protected the principal gate of the citadel. It was rebuilt by John Comnenus II (1118–43) as part of his repair of the Hadrianic defensive system.

At the time of writing the **Üç Şerefeli Camii** was closed for necessary restoration. Its name is derived from the three balconies, *üç şerefe*, on the SE minaret. Each balcony is reached by a separate stairway. The decorative tile designs on the minarets are all different. The mosque of Burgaz limestone was completed in 1447 during the reign of Murat II. It too was damaged by fire and earthquake in the 18C and restored by Mahmut I (1730–54). In the centre of the colonnaded courtyard there is a fine *şadırvan*. The prayer hall is covered by a dome c 23m in diameter. The largest Ottoman dome constructed up to that time, it is supported on the N and S by the walls and on the other sides by two enormous hexagonal pillars. This design allows most worshippers to have an unrestricted view of the interior.

Üç Şerefeli, according to Goodwin, 'is dark and mystical and its mood strange for an Ottoman building', and, he affirms, its dome 'was the most important development in the structure of the mosque in the fifteenth century'.

At the back of the mosque there are some picturesque **Ottoman houses** which are still inhabited. A few have been restored.

Across the road from the mosque is the **Sokollu Mehmet Paşa Hamamı** which was built by Sinan in 1568–69. The fine dome and plasterwork of the disrobing room are noteworthy, but the İznik tiles have disappeared. The hamam is open to men only.

Edirne's crowning glory, the **Selimiye**, was built for Selim II the Sot (1566–74) by Sinan who was *Darüs-saadet*, Architect of the Abode of Felicity, for 50 years. It was the masterpiece of Sinan's old age. He was 79 when it was completed in 1575. It is said that he regarded the Şehzade Mosque in İstanbul as apprentice work, the Süleymaniye as journeyman work and the Selimiye as his *chef d'oeuvre*.

It is built on a high terrace, the Kavak Meydanı, the Square of the Poplar, on the site of a 14C palace built by Beyazit I. In addition to the mosque and the *avlu* there are in the *külliye* a *medrese*, a cemetery, a *darül-kurra*, and the *Kavaflar Arasta*.

Flights of steps lead up through formal gardens to the Selimiye which is built of red and honey-coloured stone. There are four fluted minarets on the corners. Each minaret is almost 71m high and has three *şerefes*. The pavement of the rectangular courtyard and the façade of the area where latecomers pray are of Marmara marble. The great door is believed to come from Birgi's Ulu Cami. The marble *mihrab* is placed in a deep apse, the lower part of which is covered with İznik tiles. Note the exquisite openwork carving of the *mimber* which is also of marble. The *müezzins'* tribune, supported by 12 low arches, is under the centre of the dome. There is a small fountain underneath. The great dome has a diameter of 31.28m and its centre is 43.5m above the floor. It rests on eight massive piers which are fluted below, plain above. The sultan's loge is in the NE corner. Its balustrade, surmounted by a 17C lattice, is joined to that of the E gallery.

The **Kavaflar Arasta**, the Cobblers' Market, is the work of Sinan's student and successor Davut Ağa. Added during the reign of Murat III (1574–95) its purpose was to bring revenue to the *külliye* and to attract worshippers from old Edirne which was some distance away from the mosque. The shops now sell religious objects, cheap souvenirs and ornaments made of onyx.

The **medrese** at the back of the mosque on the SE side of the *kıble* wall is now the **Museum of Turkish and Islamic Art**. In the entrance there are Ottoman stone inscriptions from mosques, caravanserais, fountains and hamams which no longer exist, and Ottoman period tiles, manuscript copies of the Koran, embroidery, weapons and glass. In the large hall there is an embroidered satin tent in which Ottoman viziers conducted their state business. In the side rooms there are examples of carved furniture and wood work from Edirne including the doors from the *külliye* of Beyazit II. A separate section is devoted to objects from a dervish *tekke*. These include inscriptions, healing cups and medallions. One room has photographs, pictures and records of the Turkish wrestling matches which are held each year in Edirne. In the central garden there is a collection of tombstones dating from the 15C to the end of the Ottoman period. One marked the grave of Sitti Şah Sultan, the wife of Mehmet Fatih.

The Edirne **Archaeological and Ethnographic Museum** is a few minutes' walk away. Opened in 1971, it has a fine collection of objects from Thrace and Anatolia dating from the Prehistoric Age to the Islamic period. There are Thracian ceramics, bronze fibulae and capitals with a spiral design, marble portrait busts, pottery, jewellery, reliefs, glass, statuettes and terra-cottas from the Greek and Roman periods. Note the displays of Greek, Roman and Byzantine gold, silver and bronze coins and the fine 2C AD Roman copy of a Greek statute of Apollo found in Lüleburgaz. The ethno-graphic section has Thracian and Anatolian carpets, kilims, prayer mats and saddle bags, embroidered costumes, swords, scimitars, axes, bows, arrows, shields, maces and guns inlaid with mother of pearl, gold and silver.

In the garden there are funerary stelae and architectural fragments. The sarcophagus by the entrance has some interesting carving on the lid.

What do the Turks think of the Selimiye? A perceptive analysis of the building, by Professor Doğan Kuban, concludes:

'…the symmetrical design strongly emphasised by the four minarets and the soaring rise of the central dome is not far removed from the composition of a Leonardo, and testifies to the classical spirit of the Mediterranean. Thus Selimiye may be regarded as the symbol of a layer of the Ottoman culture in the 16C which had unconsciously participated in the development of western culture. Finally, like all the other great mosques, Selimiye is the affirmation of the power of the Ottoman Empire, its religious foundation and its sovereignty over vast territories of Europe'.

In the gardens of the Selimiye there are groups of off-duty soldiers, itinerant photographers, pedlars, families taking the air and playing chil-dren, while in its isolated, sheltered bowers amorous couples explore their own private worlds. Stop for refreshment in the coffee house by the entrance to the gardens before continuing your exploration of Edirne.

Take a taxi to three of Edirne's outstanding monuments. The **Muradiye** of Murat II (1421–51, on a hill to the NE of Edirne, was built in 1435 as a *zaviye* for the Melevi order of dervishes. Later the *zaviye* was converted into a mosque and the dervishes were accommodated in a *tekke* in the garden. Note the fine early 15C İznik tiles in and around the *mihrab*.

To reach the **Beyazit Külliyesi** cross the shallow waters of the Tunca by the **Bridge of Mehmet Fatih** which was completed in 1453. The *Beyazit külliye* is the largest in Edirne. In addition to the mosque, the complex had an *imaret*, a *tımarhane*, a *tıp medresesi* and a provisions store. The *tıp medresesi* was famous for the skill of its surgeons. In the octagonal, domed *tımarhane* the insane were treated by musical therapy. The thrice weekly concerts were designed to relieve melancholy and give the patients spiritual nourishment. They were also offered flowers as their scent was supposed to restore their sanity. As in Bedlam, there were organised visits to the *tımarhane*. According to Evliya Çelebi it was an excursion much favoured by the gilded youth of Edirne.

The University of Thrace now holds art classes in part of the *medrese*.

To the W of the Beyazit *külliye*, in a meadow called **Sarayiçi**, the contests of *Kırkpınar yağlı güreş*, Turkish wrestling, are held each year in the middle of June. The wrestlers, who wear stout leather trousers and cover themselves with diluted olive oil, have a huge following in Turkey. Crowds of up to 100,000 attend the matches and for a week Edirne is *en fête*. It is believed that the contests started in the mid 14C, when the Turks first came to Thrace. The games derived the name *Kırkpınar*, Forty Springs, from an old legend. When the 40 heroes, who were the first to practise the sport, died in battle, a spring gushed forth from the place where they fell.

In the 17C Evliya Çelebi wrote the following account of the sport.

'Young men from Rumeli (Thrace) gather here (in the House of the Wrestlers) every Friday. 70 or 80 pairs of stalwarts, all rubbed down with grease, meet to wrestle with each other. After the hug and hand kiss they catch each other around the neck and thus the fight starts... With bare legs and naked chests they often fight for hours, using all kinds of tricks, but not being able to have the referee and the spectators draw a conclusion. Finally one or the other manages to detect the weak point of his opponent and to revenge himself by trapping him'.

In the House of the Wrestlers the equipment of former wrestlers was kept—iron bows, truncheons, unusual bows and arrows and greasy trousers made of buffalo hide, each weighing 40 to 50 *okkas* (i.e. 51kg to 63kg).

Tickets for the contests may be purchased in Edirne's *belediye*, town hall, which is located near the gardens of the Selimiye.

The name of the wrestling field, *Sarayiçi*, refers to the *saray* or palace which once stood here. Started by Murat II and completed by Mehmet II (1451–81), it was burned to the ground during the occupation of Edirne by the Russians in 1878.

To the SW of Beyazit *külliye* is **Murat I Camii**. Built on a ruined Greek church, this is in a poor state of repair.

Leave Edirne by the E5 and at Havsa turn right on to the E24. The town of **Uzunköprü** gets its name from the long bridge built during the reign of Murat II. The bridge, which crosses the Ergene Nehri, has 174 arches and is more than a kilometre long.

Shortly after (45km) Keşan the road climbs the pine-clad slopes of Kuru Dağı before descending to the plain at the head of the Saroz Körfezi. At **Bolayır**, where the Gallipoli peninsula is at its narrowest, it is possible to see the Saros gulf and the Dardanelles at the same time. In 1358 Süleyman Paşa, the son of Orhan Gazi, had a fatal accident here while engaged in his favourite sport of falconry. His tomb outside the village is shaded by cypress trees. Nearby is the grave of the poet and reformer Namık Kemal (1840–88). He longed to revive the heroic virtues of the early Ottoman period so clearly displayed by Süleyman and asked to be buried near him.

GELIBOLU or **GALLIPOLI** is the principal town at the northern end of the Dardanelles. Many visitors come here each year to visit the battlefields of the ill-fated Gallipoli campaign.

Information. There is only one hotel in the area on the Ministry of Tourism list, the three-star *Boncuk Oteli* in Sütlüce Köyü a few kilometres to the S of Gelibolu. However, there is ample accommodation across the strait in Çanakkale.

To visit the battlefields you will need either your own transport, hire a taxi, or take one of the organised tours. Tours are arranged by the Troy-Anzac and Ana-Tur agencies in Çanakkale. By prior arrangement these can be joined at Eceabat. A local supervisor in the War Graves Commission in Çanakkale looks after the upkeep of the cemeteries and the memorials. The Commission produces a useful information sheet about the Gallipoli Peninsula which may be obtained from the supervisor's office.

For further information about Çanakkale, the Dardanelles and places on the eastern side of the strait, see Route 6.

History. Gelibolu is a corruption of the town's Greek name, Callipolis, which means the beautiful city. The fortress established here by Justinian in the mid 6C was restored and enlarged by Philippicus Bardanes a century and a half later. From the earliest times Callipolis was an important embarkation point on the European side of the strait. On his way to the Third Crusade (1189–92) Frederick Barbarossa, worried about transporting his army over the Hellespont, wrote to his son Henry, 'the crossing…is impossible unless we obtain from the emperor of Constantinople the most important hostages'. For Villehardouin, chronicler of the Fourth Crusade (1202–04), the passage was a colourful event… 'the Hellespont to eastward, with the full array of warships, galleys and transports, seemed as if it were in flower. It was, indeed, a marvellous experience to see so lovely a sight'.

In the early 14C a wild band of Catalan mercenaries, who had been recruited by the Byzantines to fight the Turks, captured and held the fortress. From here they pillaged the towns and cities of Thrace and for seven years resisted all attempts to dislodge them. The Turks gained their first foothold in Thrace in 1354, when they were given the castle of Tzympe by the Byzantine Grand Chancellor, Cantacuzenus, as a reward for services rendered to the emperor Andronicus III. Tzympe was not far from Callipolis and when shortly afterwards the walls of Callipolis were destroyed by a great earthquake, they occupied it. The Byzantines, believing that the earthquake was a manifestation of the will of God, offered no resistance. Apart from brief periods Callipolis remained in Turkish hands thereafter and was developed as a naval base.

The ruined **Byzantine castle** in the inner harbour was used as a prison during the Ottoman period. Incarcerated here for six months in 1666 was **Sabbatai Zvi**, the False Messiah. The son of a Jewish poulterer from Smyrna (İzmir), he was born on the Ninth of Av, an auspicious day in the Jewish calendar. Hailed from infancy as the long awaited Messiah, Sabbatai proclaimed his divine status in 1666 and many Jews in the Ottoman empire and in other countries accepted his claims. His activities soon came to the notice of the authorities and he was brought before Mehmet IV in Edirne. Accused of treason and of deceiving the people, he was told that the penalty for these crimes was a slow and painful death. He would be dragged naked behind a spirited horse until he expired. In the face of this threat Sabbatai's resolve crumbled. He renounced his claims, apostasied and, accepting the turban, became a Muslim.

Gelibolu's modest free-standing **bedesten** has six domes in two rows. The fine 15C **namazgah** dates from 1407. Note the use of ancient marble in the structure and the two *mimbers* which flank the *mihrab*. A number of famous Turkish sailors were buried in Gelibolu. Among them was Piri Reis (1465–1554), the swashbuckling Mediterranean pirate who helped Selim I in his Egyptian campaign and wrote the great Ottoman geographical compendium, the *Kitab-ı-Bahriye* or Book of the Sea. He is commemorated in Gelibolu by a statue on the sea front and a small museum.

In 405 BC the final and decisive battle of the Peloponnesian War took place at the Cumalı Çayı, the **Aegospotami** or Goat's River of the Greeks, c 13km SW of Gelibolu. The Athenians camped here. Lysander and the Spartans were at Lampsacus on the other side of the strait. For five days the Athenians sailed to Lampsacus and challenged the Spartans to fight. Each day the challenge was ignored. After the Athenians had returned to Aegospotami on the fifth day and started their daily search of the countryside for food, Lysander attacked. There was little resistance, as most of the Athenians were away from their camp. The Spartans captured 170 triremes and cold-bloodedly massacred about 3000 Athenians found on them.

The theory of the 5C BC philosopher Anaxagoras of Clazomenae that the heavenly bodies were made of stone wrenched from the earth and made incandescent by their motion may have been influenced by the fall of a meteorite in the neighbourhood of Aegospotami in 467.

All that remains on the site of ancient **Sestus**, an Aeolian colony established in the 7C BC, are the ruined medieval walls and castle. Sestus has associations with the ill-fated lovers Hero and Leander, with Xerxes, with Alexander the Great and with Lord Byron. (See Abydus in Route 6.)

On 25 April 1915 the first Allied troops landed on the Gallipoli peninsula. From the beginning things went badly. A signals failure sent the ANZAC contingent to the wrong beach where they were pinned down by enemy fire. The Anglo-French landing fared little better. It met fierce resistance and suffered heavy losses. During the eight months of the campaign the Allies were able to make little progress inland. Their Turkish opponents were commanded brilliantly by Lieutenant-Colonel Mustafa Kemal (Atatürk) who told his soldiers, 'I am not ordering you to attack, I am ordering you to die'.

During the campaign acts of great bravery were performed by the soldiers of both sides. On the day of the first landings Australian troops were led ashore by teenage British midshipmen, two of whom were in their first term at Dartmouth Naval College.

The cemeteries are in two groups, one to the NW of Eceabat, the other near the tip of the Thracian Chersonese. To visit the first group, look out for a signposted turning on the right by Kilye Bay just to the N of Eceabat. This will bring you to **Anzac Cove**. En route you pass the **Kabate Museum** where there are displays of photographs, maps, weapons and militaria found in the area. Shortly after reaching the coast, the road turns N and runs parallel with the sea. Here above the quiet, peaceful cove more than 3000 soldiers are buried in nine cemeteries. Their names, Shell Green, Shrapnel Valley, Beach, Plugge's Plateau, Arı Burnu, Canterbury, No. 2 Outpost, N.Z. No. 2 Outpost and Embarkation Pier, are poignant reminders of the dreadful and tragic events which took place here in 1915.

To the N of the beach, near the Salt Lake, there are four cemeteries, Azmak, Hill 10, Green Hill, and Lala Baba, with about 5000 graves. To the SE of the lake is Hill 60 Cemetery and a New Zealand memorial where 900 of the fallen are commemorated.

From Anzac Cove a rough track leads up to a further group of cemeteries, to the Lone Pine memorial and a second New Zealand memorial. In the Lone Pine, Johnston's Jolly, 4th Battalion Parade Ground, Courtney's and Steel's Post, Quinn's Post, Walker's Ridge, the Nek, Baby, and Çunuk Bair cemeteries a further 3700 young men are buried. More than 5700 more are listed on the two memorials.

The Turkish dead are remembered on Çonkbayiri Hill. Five great stones, like the fingers of a dead man's hand, rise from the ground in silent protest to God for the waste of human life which took place during this campaign.

To reach the cemeteries near the tip of the Thracian Chersonese return to the main road and continue S to Eceabat.

At **Eceabat**, the 7C BC Aeolian foundation known as Madytus, there are frequent ferry boat services to Çanakkale. The promontory to the S of Eceabat was known as **Cynos-Sema**, where it was said Hecuba was buried (Strabo 13.1.28). The name Cynos-Sema, which means the Grave of the Bitch, was explained in an ancient legend. According to this, when Hecuba was stoned to death for killing Polymestor, king of the Chersonese, her murderers found not a human corpse beneath the stones, but a bitch with eyes of fire. Another legend says that Hecuba was transformed into a bitch, as she was being chased by the companions of her slain son Polydorus.

Towards the end of 411 BC the Athenians defeated the Spartan fleet, which was under the command of the inept Mindarus, near Cynos-Sema.

About 4km to the S is **Kilitbahir** whose name, the Lock of the Sea, is derived from a fortress built here by Mehmet II before he began his attack on Constantinople in 1453. It was linked with a similar castle, known as Kalei Sultaniye (now Çanakkale), on the Asian side of the straits. The Allies lost three battleships and almost 3000 sailors in a failed attempt to take the castles in 1915.

The road follows the coast for a short distance to the S of Kilitbahir then turns inland to Alçıtepe where it divides. The right fork will take you to Twelve Tree Copse cemetery, where there are 3660 burials and a New Zealand memorial. At Pink Farm cemetery there are 610 graves.

The **İlyasbaba Burnu**, the ancient Mastusia Promontory, is the westernmost point of the Thracian Chersonese. Near the tip are the Lancashire Landing and V Beach cemeteries, where more than 1900 rest. From the cliff top Turkish gunners mowed down Allied soldiers as they attempted to make a landing here in 1915. The slaughter was so great that the sea was red with blood for a great distance from the shore.

The **Helles Memorial**, an obelisk more than 30m high, which commemorates those whose graves are unknown or who were lost or buried at sea, stands at the tip of the peninsula, where it may be seen by passing ships.

To the E of the memorial is Morto Bay. Here in the French cemetery 10,000 French troops, who fell in the Gallipoli campaign, are remembered. To the NE of the bay is the **Çanakkale Martyrs Memorial** erected in memory of the Turkish dead. This is sometimes known as the **Mehmetcik Anıtı**, the Mehmetcik Memorial. '*Mehmetcik*' is an affectionate term sometimes applied to the Turkish private soldier.

The site of ancient **Elaeus**, a colony founded in the 6C BC by settlers from Athens, which was near the tip of the peninsula, was almost completely destroyed during the Gallipoli campaign. Schliemann excavated it and the putative tomb of Protesilaus, the first Achaian to be killed in the Trojan War. He was struck down by Hector as he leapt from his ship on to the Asian shore. Strabo says that there was a temple at Elaeus dedicated to Protesilaus. Alexander the Great sacrificed at the tomb before crossing the straits to ensure that he had better luck. According to Arrian, Alexander probably crossed the straits from Elaeus 'at the helm of the admiral's ship…half way over he slaughtered a bull as an offering to Poseidon and poured wine from a golden cup into the sea to propitiate the Nereids'.

It is estimated that 160,000 Allied soldiers and about 90,000 Turkish soldiers died on the killing fields of Gallipoli. Only 30,000 of the Allied dead are in known graves. Many of the fallen came from Australia and New Zealand and Anzac Cove is now a place of pilgrimage for people from both countries. They come here in search of the graves of relatives or just to see where so many of their countrymen, in many cases no older than themselves, died in the course of the ill-fated Gallipoli adventure. Sometimes groups of these travellers make fires on the beach and pass the night away singing ballads and drinking companionably. Then in the cold light of dawn they visit the graves of those who died too soon and pay their own homage in their own way. Perhaps they derive comfort from Atatürk's epitaph for the Allied fallen which is engraved on one of the memorials: 'There is no difference between the Mehmetciks and the Johnnies to us where they lie side by side here in this country of ours. You the mothers … wipe away your tears. Your sons are now lying in our bosom and are at peace. Having lost their lives on this land they have become our sons as well'.

Return to Eceabat where you must choose between going back to İstanbul via Tekirdağ or crossing over to Çanakkale and joining Route 7.

3

İstanbul to Bursa

Total distance (by the coastal road) 234km. İstanbul—55km Gebze—Hisar—Libyssa—78km Hereke—105km İzmit—66km Yalova—35km Gemlik—28km Bursa.

Between İstanbul and İzmit, motorists must choose between the fast new toll road and the coastal highway. On the motorway there is only the occasional glimpse of the İzmit Gölü to relieve the monotony. Gebze, Libyssa and Hereke are on or near the coast road where traffic is heavy and there are often long delays. Almost all long-distance coaches go by the motorway. Some local buses from İstanbul go to places on the coast road.

In **Gebze**, the ancient Dakybiza, is the Byzantine fortress of **Eskihisar** which was part of a defensive system protecting the eastern approach to Constantinople. In the house of the late 19C artist, Osman Hamdi Bey, there is a collection of his paintings. The area has mooring facilities and yards where boats may be wintered. The early 16C **Orhan Gazi Camii** and the later **Çoban Mustafa Paşa Camii** merit a visit.

The Carthaginian general **Hannibal**, wearied by years of warfare, retired to nearby **Libyssa** in his sixty-fourth year. However, he was not allowed to end his days in peace. In 183 BC Quinctius Flamininus demanded that Prusias I of Bithynia deliver his former friend and ally to Rome. Craven Prusias agreed to this demand. Warned by a noise of the stealthy approach of his would-be captors, Hannibal decided not to be taken alive and took poison. According to Plutarch, in his final agony he cried out, 'Let us ease the Romans of their continual dread and care, who think it long and tedious to await the death of a hated old man'.

A signpost points to the putative site of his tomb, on a windy height above the İzmit Gölü in a large grassy clearing surrounded by cypress trees. A single marble shaft c 2m long is all that remains of the funerary monument.

At noon on Whitsunday, 22 May 337 **Constantine the Great** died in the castle of Ankyrion at **Hereke**. Nothing remains of this building where, newly baptised by Bishop Eusebius of Nicomedia, and dressed in white he quietly awaited his end. **Mehmet II the Conqueror** died in the nearby village of **Hünkür Çayre**. Famous in Ottoman times for the quality of the fine silk fabric produced there, it is still a centre for the sale of silk carpets.

For a description of the places between İzmit and Bursa, see Route 4C.

4

Bursa

BURSA (614,133 inhab.), the capital of ancient Bithynia, sprawls across the verdant slopes of Mysian Olympus. Surrounded by gardens and orchards, it is often called Yeşil Bursa, Green Bursa. A spa since antiquity, it has become an important manufacturing centre, in particular of silk and cotton textiles.

Information and Accommodation. The **Tourist Information Office** is in the centre of the city near Ulu Cami. It can supply a list of Bursa's hotels, pensions, and restaurants and information about museums and interesting excursions.

Some of the best, and most expensive, hotels are in the suburb of Çekirge, a 10-minute drive from the city centre. Most of Çekirge's hotels have their own mineral water baths.

Post office and banks. The principal post office is in Atatürk Cad., near Ulu Cami. Branches of the main Turkish banks are located nearby.

Transport. Bursa is an important communications centre, linked by good roads to Ankara, İstanbul and İzmir. Frequent long-distance coach services to the principal Turkish cities depart from the *otogar*, which is in the lower part of the city near the junction of Ulu Yol Cad. and Road 200. There is a ferry-boat service from 55km Yalova to İstanbul. A faster link is provided by coach and hydrofoil via 24km Mudanya. Details of services from Bursa's airport may be obtained from the THY office in Çakır Hamam Temiz Cad., 16B or from the Tourist Information Office. Bursa is not on the rail network.

Museums. The Archaeological Museum is in the Kültürpark; the Atatürk Museum in Çekirge Cad.; the Museum of Turkish Art near Yeşil Cami and the Murat Evi in Muradiye.

Specialities. Among the silk and cotton goods produced in Bursa are table-cloths, serviettes, towels and dressing gowns. Collectors of the antique and curious will enjoy browsing in the speciality shops in the bazaar. Bursa is famous for its peaches, *Bursa Şeftalı*, and candied fruits, especially chestnuts. *İskender Kebab* and *İnegöl Köftesi* are among its other food specialities.

Baths. In addition to the baths in Çekirge's hotels there are several public baths: *Yeni Kaplıca* and *Eski Kaplıca* in Çekirge Cad., *Kaynarca* and *Kükürtlü*, which is valued for the high sulphur content of the water.

History. Bursa was originally called Prusa after its founder Prusias I (228–185 BC), king of Bithynia. According to legend, Hannibal, the great Carthagenian general and enemy of Rome, helped him to choose the site (see Libyssa above).

Herodotus states that the Bithynians came from Thrace. He describes them as being a cruel and savage race who fought clothed in fox skins with dirk and javelin. Their territory stretched from Pergamum and the Sea of Marmara on the W, to Pontus on the E, and the Black Sea on the N. Freed from Persian domination by Alexander, they formed an independent kingdom with its capital at Nicomedia, modern İzmit.

Prusias the grandson of Nicomedes I, the creator of the kingdom of Bithynia, was an ambitious and intelligent man, who extended the boundaries of his realm. He incorporated the Greek cities on the Propontis (the Sea of Marmara) and encouraged the development of an overland trade route with Armenia. In founding Prusa and giving it his own name, he was following a fashion popular among Hellenistic kings.

When Nicomedes IV of Bithynia (94–74 BC), a weak and vicious man, was driven from his kingdom by invading Pontians, he fled to Rome. Restored c 85 BC to his kingdom by the Romans, he ruled as their vassal in all but name until his death. Nicomedes had no legitimate male heir so, following the example of Attalus III of Pergamum, he willed his realm to Rome. His bequest was accepted and Bithynia came under direct Roman rule in 74 BC.

Prosperous under the Romans and the early Byzantines, Bursa suffered a decline in its fortunes during the Arab raids in the 7C and 8C. Captured by the Selçuk Turks in 1075, it was taken by Christian forces in 1097 during the First Crusade. In the next two centuries it changed hands frequently, sometimes being occupied by the Selçuks sometimes by the Byzantines. Finally, after a protracted siege it was taken in 1326 by Orhan Gazi who made it the capital of the new Ottoman Empire.

Although the Turks moved their capital first to Edirne and later to Constantinople, Bursa retained its status. The founder of the Ottoman dynasty, Osman Gazi, and five of his successors were buried here. Bursa was also an important commercial centre on the trade route between İstanbul and the principal cities of the Ottoman Empire. Its mineral springs, known to the Romans and Byzantines, were also appreciated by the Ottomans who built a number of luxurious baths here.

According to that redoubtable 17C traveller, Evliya Çelebi, Bursa was an earthly paradise: 'The inhabitants being fair, the air good, the water full of holiness, contribute altogether, to render Brússa one of the most delicious spots on earth'. The city had 9000 shops where everything could be bought. Full of poets, storytellers and entertainers, it was a city of pleasure:

> 'All coffee-houses, and particularly those near the great mosque, abound with men skilled in a thousand arts [*Hezár-fenn*] dancing and pleasure continue the whole night, and in the morning everybody goes to the mosque…There are also no less than 97 Búza-houses, which are not to be equalled in the world; they are wainscoted with fayence, painted, each capable of accommodating one thousand men. In summer the Búza is cooled with ice, like sherbet; the principal men of the town are not ashamed to enter these Búza houses, although abundance of youths, dancers and singers, girt with Brússa girdles, here entice, their lovers to ruin'.

Occupied by Greek troops in 1920, Bursa was recaptured by the Turkish army in 1922. Since then the city has expanded considerably.

Most of Bursa's principal monuments are located on or near streets which start at Yeşil Cad. in the NE, continue along the lower slopes of Ulu Dağ and pass through the centre of the city to Çekirge Cad. in the NW. As the distance is considerable, it is advisable to take a bus or dolmuş between the different groups of monuments.

From Cumhuriyet Alanı (Heykel), go to Yeşil Cad. In this street are two of the most interesting early Ottoman buildings in Bursa, Yeşil Cami and Yeşil Türbe. Originally they formed part of a complex which included, in addition to the mosque and tomb, an *imaret*, a *medrese* and a *hamam*.

Yeşil Cami, the Green Mosque, was built during the reign of Mehmet I (1413–21). The son of Yıldırım Beyazit, who died a captive in the hands of Tamerlane, Mehmet did much to restore the fortunes of the Ottomans.

The Green Mosque was never completed, as in accordance with Ottoman custom work ceased at the time of Mehmet's death. However, it remains one of the finest examples of Ottoman architecture. An inscription over the N door makes the proud claim that 'here is a building such as no nation has been presented with since the sky began to turn'. The mosque got its name from the wonderful green tiles which at one time covered the dome and the tops of the minarets. Evliya Çelebi compared them to emeralds sparkling in the sunlight. The simplicity of its plan—two rectangular chambers in the form of an inverted T surmounted by domes—accentuates the richness of its interior decoration. The sultan's loge, which is over the entrance, is flanked by screened balconies reserved for members of the imperial family. In the centre of an interior court is a *şadirvan*, which reflects the glowing colours of the windows, tiles and mosaics. Note the fine *mihrab*, which is raised slightly above floor level. The outside of the mosque is clad in pale white Proconessian marble.

Damaged by an earthquake in 1855, the Green Mosque was restored at the command of the Vali, Ahmet Vefik Paşa, by Léon Parvillée.

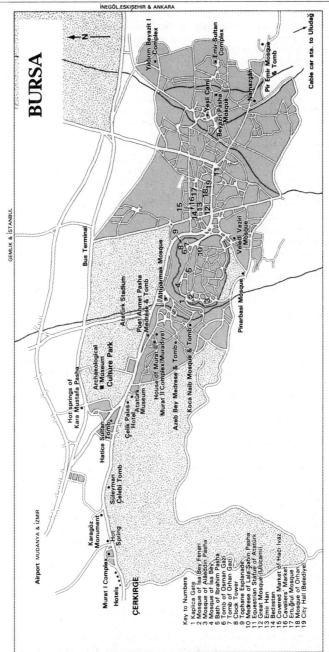

INEGÖL, ESKISEHIR & ANKARA

GEMLIK & İSTANBUL

BURSA

Airport MUDANYA & İZMIR

ÇERKIRGE

Cable car sta. to Uludağ

Key to Numbers

1 Kaplıca Gate
2 Mosque of Isa Bey Fenari
3 Mosque of Alâeddin Pasha
4 Mosque of Isa Bey
5 Bath of İbrahim Pasha
6 Tomb of Osman Gazi
7 Tomb of Orhan Gazi
8 Clock Tower
9 Tophane Esplanade
10 Medrese of Lala Sahin Pasha
11 Equestrian Statue of Atatürk
12 Great Mosque (Ulucami)
13 Emir Han
14 Bedastan
15 Covered Market of Hacı İvaz
16 Cavaliers' Market
17 Ertuğrul Mosque
18 Mosque of Orhan
19 City Hall (Belediye)

Nearby is the *medrese* which now houses a collection of Turkish and Islamic art including examples of fine calligraphy, books and Korans, jewellery, household goods, arms and armaments from the Ottoman period.

On the other side of the street at the top of a slight eminence stands **Yeşil Türbe**, the tomb of Mehmet I (died 1421). Its perfect proportions, position between cypress trees at the top of a short flight of steps, decoration inside and out combine to make it one of the most beautiful buildings in Turkey.

A simple octagon, its single chamber, surmounted by a dome, houses the elaborately decorated sarcophagus of the sultan. This is raised above floor level on a tiled dais. Nearby are the tombs of some members of his family and court. The sarcophagi are empty, as in accordance with Islamic law, Mehmet and the others were buried in the earth in vaults underneath the chamber. An examination of these vaults, which were entered from the E side of the building, revealed only a few sad bones that had been disturbed by rats. The walls of the tomb, decorated with a revetment of tiles and painted calligraphy, are pierced by small windows filled with richly coloured glass. Note the splendid *mihrab* and the door and window shutters, with their intricate, interlaced carved patterns.

Like the Green Mosque, Yeşil Türbe was damaged by the earthquake of 1855. Modern tiles from Kütahya were used by the restorers to replace those that had been lost or destroyed. To the left of Yeşil Cami there is a coffee-house with a fine view over the lower part of the city.

A short distance to the right is **Emir Sultan Camii**, which was reconstructed at the beginning of the 19C in an elaborate, overpowering style popular at that time. Its melancholy, cypress-shaded cemetery overlooks Bursa and the plain beyond.

Also in this part of Bursa is the **Yıldırım Beyazit complex**. Yıldırım (1389–1403), the father of Mehmet I, acquired his sobriquet, which means thunderbolt, from the speed with which he moved his armies. The complex, which had a mosque, an *imaret*, two *medreses*, a hospital, a palace and a *türbe*, has suffered much damage and has been restored twice. Today only the mosque, the *türbe* and one *medrese* remain.

Built in the familiar inverted T form, the mosque has an elaborate niche under the arch which divides the outer court from the prayer hall. This is the first known use of the so-called Bursa arch. Beyazit's emblem appears frequently in the decoration. The *medrese* has been heavily restored; originally the arches in the interior court were not glazed. Note the use of alternate lines of stone and brick in the construction of the building. This was an economy measure copied from the work of Byzantine architects.

On returning to Heykel walk in a SW direction along Atatürk Cad. **Ulu Cami**, the Great Mosque, is on the right-hand side of the street. Constructed of golden-hued limestone from Mt Olympus, it measures 56m by 68m and was the first congregational mosque erected by the Ottomans.

Before the battle of Nicopolis in 1396, according to tradition, Yıldırım Beyazit promised that, if God gave him victory, he would build 20 mosques. He defeated a mixed force of Crusaders from France, England, Flanders, Savoy, Lombardy, Scotland, and Germany allied with Hungarians under Sigismund, and slaughtered more than 10,000 prisoners after the battle. Then, interpreting his promise rather liberally, he used some of the booty to build Ulu Cami, instructing his architect to give it 20 domes. They are in four groups of five and are supported by 12 great pillars decorated with huge inscriptions from the Koran in stylised calligraphy. Under the central dome in the second rank on the N side is the *şadirvan*, which takes the form of a pool with a fountain in the centre. The oculus has been glazed. Note the beautiful walnut *mimber*, which is carved with representations of the heavenly bodies. The N entrance is believed to have been built by Tamerlane after he had captured Beyazit and occupied Bursa c 1402.

At first Ulu Cami had one minaret only, erected in the usual position on the NW side. A second minaret was added by Mehmet I who made it clear that only an imperial mosque could have more than one.

A short distance along Atatürk Cad. is **Orhan Gazi Camii**. Begun in 1339 this is the oldest of Bursa's royal mosques. Much restored, it has a *zaviye*.

Behind Ulu Cami lies Bursa's **market**. Destroyed by fire in 1955, it has been completely rebuilt. It has everything from jewellery and the finest silks to household goods and on most days is filled with shoppers bargaining excitedly over their purchases. The **Koza Hanı**, the silk cocoon *han*, which dates from 1451, was imaginatively restored recently. In its shops, built around a central courtyard, rolls of beautiful silk and brocade cascade temptingly over the counters in a display designed to tempt passersby.

Gold and silver jewellery and the most expensive products are sold in the **bedesten**, while the **Sipahilar Çarşısı** (the covered market of the cavalry soldiers), built during the reign of Mehmet I, has goods of every kind. Visitors leaving the market on the E side cannot miss the ornate façade of the **belediye**.

On returning to Atatürk Cad., continue past Ulu Camii to where the roads divide. To visit the **citadel** take Yiğitler Cad. on the left. This climbs steeply under the citadel's walls constructed during the Hellenistic period but much restored by the Byzantines and the Ottomans.

In the citadel are the **tombs of Osman Gazi and Orhan Gazi**. Osman Gazi (1288–1324), the founder of the Ottoman dynasty, was buried here in 1326, two years after the capture of the city by his son Orhan Gazi. His tomb was in the baptistery of a church dedicated to the Prophet Elias, which had been converted into a mosque. Orhan Gazi (1324–59) was buried in the nave of this former church. The buildings sheltering the tombs were destroyed and reconstructed several times, but a few fragments of mosaic from the church floor may be seen near Orhan's sarcophagus. From the terrace behind the tombs there is an excellent view of the lower part of the city.

In the narrow winding streets of the citadel are some fine old Turkish houses. Many have a projecting first floor which allows the occupants to see what is happening in the street below. At one time these old houses were destroyed in large numbers and replaced by characterless apartment blocks. However, in recent years their historical value has been recognised and they are being carefully restored with the assistance of the authorities.

The **Muradiye complex**, built during the reign of Murat II (1421–51), is reached by following Kaplıca Cad. from the citadel. It comprised a mosque, a *medrese*, an *imaret* and Murat's *türbe*. The mosque, decorated with floral and geometrical mosaics, is designed on the same plan as Orhan Gazi Camii. It also has two *zaviyes*, one on each side of the entrance.

The sultan's *türbe* is in a garden filled with roses and flowering shrubs and shaded by cypresses and plane trees. Although Bursa was no longer the capital of the Ottoman Empire, Murat was brought from Edirne to rest here. A strong and vigorous ruler, according to Gibbon, 'he seldom engaged in war till he was justified by a previous and adequate provocation. In the observance of treaties his word was inviolate and sacred'.

Murat's sarcophagus is under the oculus of a dome supported by antique columns. Nearby are the tombs of four of his sons. In other parts of the garden a dozen *türbes* shelter the remains of members of the imperial family who died in the following century.

Just outside the Muradiye is a restored 18C **Ottoman town house**. Sometimes called the Murat House, because it occupies the site of a building which belonged to Murat II, it has a number of rooms furnished in typical Ottoman style.

Descend from the Muradiye by Kaplıca Cad. to its junction with Çekirge Cad. On the left-hand side of Çekirge Cad. is the house where Atatürk stayed during the 13 visits he made to Bursa between 1922 and 1938. Now the **Atatürk Museum**, it was first opened to the public in 1973 on the 50th anniversary of the Turkish Republic.

On the right-hand side of the road is Bursa's **Kültürpark**. In addition to formal gardens, this has an exhibition area, fun-fair, boating lake, small zoo, several restaurants and coffee-houses. Bursa's Archaeological Museum is within its grounds and the city's football stadium is on its eastern edge.

Bursa's **Archaeological Museum** has four exhibition halls, a laboratory and a library, and contains exhibits from the provinces of Bursa, Balıkesir and Bilecik. Many objects are labelled in Turkish and English, but provenance and dates are not always given.

In **Room 1** are artefacts from the prehistoric period found in and near Bursa. There are also several stone fragments from the Roman period, including a headless statue of Tyche and part of a sarcophagus. In **Room 2** there are statues, busts and architectural pieces from the Archaic, Hellenistic, Roman and Byzantine periods including several representations of Cybele and members of the Olympian pantheon, a reclining Hercules and some Roman portrait busts. In the right-hand corner there are two columns, provenance and date not stated, surrounded by coiled, headless snakes. In a linking corridor some geometric pattern mosaics and a number of amphorae, which appear to have been recovered from the sea, are displayed. **Room 3** contains metal, glass and ceramic artefacts from the Hellenistic and Roman periods including terracottas, jewellery, ceramics, small bronzes and glass objects. In a case in the centre of the room there is a bronze statue of a youth whose inlaid eyes give him a lifelike, animated expression. A small gallery has a display of Roman jewellery and, from the Byzantine period, pottery and metal artefacts, religious objects, including crosses, and ceramics. **Room 4**, to the left of the mosaic corridor, contains a well-displayed coin collection. In addition to specimens from Bithynia, including some from Prusa, Nicaea and Nicomedia, there are coins from Mysia, the Troad, Myrina, Phrygia, Lycia, and Pergamum. There is also a representative selection of Roman and Byzantine coins. On the walls illustrations explain how coins were made in antiquity and outline the history of money.

On the terrace, in the garden, to the side and at the rear of the building there are stelae, architectural fragments, statues and reliefs.

Across the road from the Kültürpark is the oldest, most luxurious and best-known of Bursa's hotels, the **Çelik Palas**.

One of the earliest recorded visitors to Bursa to take the waters was the Byzantine Empress Theodora who came with a retinue of 4000 courtiers. The restorative and curative properties of its mineral springs were known to the Ottomans who constructed elaborate baths which still stand. The best-known of these are the **Yeni** and **Eski Kaplıca**. As a spa, Bursa reached its apogee in the 19C and early 20C, when minor European royalty and artists and writers such as Pierre Loti flocked here to take the cure.

On the right-hand side of the road, a short distance from the Çelik Palas hotel, are the **Yeni Kaplıca bath**s. Built in 1522 by Rüstem Paşa, the Grand Vizier of Süleyman the Magnificent, on the site of a Byzantine baths complex dating from the reign of Justinian, they are reserved for men.

The oldest of Bursa's hamams, the **Eski Kaplıca**, is at the foot of the hill just before Çekirge. It is likely that there were baths on this site in Roman and Byzantine times. According to İbn Battuta, who visited the city in 1333, an earlier building provided free accommodation, as custom required, for three days. According to Evliya Çelebi, the present structure was constructed during the reign of Murat I (1359–89). The architectural evidence appears to support this dating.

At the top of the hill are the **Mosque and Türbe of Murat I** (1359–89).

Known as Hüdavendigar, Creator of the Universe, Murat spent most of his reign at war. He extended the boundaries of the Ottoman Empire into Europe, adding Thrace and its principal city, Edirne, Macedonia and Bulgaria to his possessions. He founded the Corps of Janissaries which was to play such an important part in Turkish history. The Janissaries were chosen from the strongest of the Christian youths who were taken from their families by the *devşirme* and converted to Islam. For many centuries this highly-disciplined regiment was to form the backbone of the Ottoman army.

Aged 70 Murat had to quell a revolt of his Serbian subjects, who with the assistance of the Bosnians, Bulgarians, Albanians and Hungarians sought to regain their independence. He defeated the combined forces, led by King Lazarus of Serbia, at Kossovo on 27 August 1389. In the last moments of the battle Murat was fatally wounded by a Serbian noble, Milosch Kobilovitch, who had come to the Turkish camp in the guise of a deserter. Murat lived long enough to order the execution of Milosch and Lazarus.

On the day of Murat's victory and death, his son Beyazit I, who succeeded to the throne, had his brother Yacoub murdered in the presence of the body of their father. Yacoub, a brave and honourable soldier, had fought many battles to defend the Ottoman Empire. His murder was considered necessary because it was feared he might contest the succession, and it was justified by a verse from the Koran, which states that 'rebellion is worse than execution'. Beyazit's action initiated a practice that continued for many centuries. The sultan executed all his male relatives on the day of his accession, to ensure a trouble-free take over of power.

The mosque, although based on the conventional inverted T plan, has a number of unusual features. These are sometimes explained by a tradition that it was designed by a captured Italian architect. The ground floor combines a mosque with a *zaviye*. On the first floor there was a *medrese*.

Across the road on a commanding site on the cliff edge is Murat's *türbe*. In a chamber 17m sq the sultan's sarcophagus is set between eight columns which support the dome. Damaged by the earthquake of 1855, the *türbe* was restored on the orders of Abdül Hamit II.

Originally the complex also included an *imaret*, but this no longer exists. However, the well-appointed toilet is still in use. This domed chamber has two washrooms, a central fountain and five small cubicles.

Excursion to Uludağ. Uludağ (2554m), the ancient Mt Olympus of Mysia, may be reached from Bursa by a road which winds up the slope for 36km or by a cable-car which makes the ascent in c 30 minutes. Take a dolmuş at the bus station for the road journey or from Heykel for Teleferik, the cable-car terminal. The cable-car stops twice, at Kadıyayla and at Sarıalan. **Note**: in bad weather the cable car service is suspended.

If you use your own transport, leave the city centre by Çekirge Cad. and after c 4km take the turning signposted Uludağ.

According to the geographer Strabo, Mt Olympus was the haunt of brigands and vagabonds at the beginning of the Christian era. During the Byzantine period it became the home of monks and mystics. After the Arab conquest the Christians were replaced by Islamic dervishes who took over the abandoned monasteries. Today the mountain is one of Turkey's best-known and most popular national parks.

Uludağ National Park has an area of c 11,400 hectares. A paradise for naturalists and bird-watchers, its slopes are clothed in bay and olive, chestnut, elm, oak, plane and beach, pine, juniper and aspen, above 2000m, dwarf junipers and alpine flora.

Hotels have been built on Uludağ to serve the needs of summer ramblers and winter-sports enthusiasts. These are relatively expensive.

The walk to the summit from the hotel area takes about two hours and is not difficult. Uludağ is snow-covered to an average depth of 2–3m from December to May. Facilities for skiers are good. Rooms are in great demand during the winter and reservations should be made as far in advance as possible.

A. Bursa to İnegöl and Oylat

Total distance c 58km. Bursa—38km İnegöl—20km Oylat.

Allow one day for this excursion if travelling by public transport. In addition to local services, all long-distance coaches to Ankara stop at İnegöl's *otogar*. There is a dolmuş service to Oylat from İnegöl.

Hotels and restaurants. There are small hotels in İnegöl and Oylat offering basic accommodation. Rooms may be difficult to obtain in Oylat during Turkish holidays like Kurban Bayramı. Ask at Bursa's Tourist Information Office about availability, etc.

Most restaurants in İnegöl serve *köfte* and kebabs. For something more elaborate, try the *Şehir Lokantası* near the central square. Oylat has several small restaurants, and there are pleasant picnic places in the woods surrounding the spa.

Leave Bursa by Road 200 in the direction of Ankara. This crosses a fertile plain dotted with orchards, then climbs steadily, passing Bursa Gölü on the left. From the crest the road descends to İnegöl in a series of gentle bends which offer good views of Ulu Dağ on the right. In the hilly country to the left of the road vines are cultivated and in some villages between there and İznik a palatable white wine is produced on a non-commercial basis.

İnegöl (38km) is a pleasant market town famous for its *köfte*, its fruit and the manufacture of furniture. Throughout Turkey *İnegöl köftesi*, meatballs made from lamb and served with raw onion rings, are known and enjoyed. The town's residents, with a pardonable degree of campanilismo, claim that the genuine article is only obtainable here. Good quality traditional-style furniture is produced in factories on the outskirts of the town. This is sold not only in Turkey but throughout the Middle East.

Thursday is market day in İnegöl. The crowded streets present an animated spectacle, as villagers from the surrounding countryside sell their produce and make their purchases. Stalls covered with tempting displays of fruit and vegetables fill the market area and overflow on to the lanes nearby.

İnegöl shared a common history with Bursa, İznik,and other towns in NW Bithynia. Fought over by the Byzantines, Arabs, Selçuks and Crusaders, it came under Ottoman control at the beginning of the 14C. The only visible relic of the past is the **İshak Paşa complex** which consisted of a mosque, *medrese*, *dershane* and *tabhane*. This was built in 1482 by İshak Paşa, chief vizier to Mehmet II. He was dismissed from the court and exiled to İnegöl, his home town, by Mehmet's successor, Beyazit II. The main interest of the complex is in the positioning of the *medrese* and the mosque. They face each other across a courtyard, which has a *şadirvan* in the centre. Only the vaulted bays of the *medrese* remain. The walls of the mosque, with their mixture of brick and stone, give the building a charming rustic appearance.

A part of İnegöl's population is made up of the descendants of an Islamic minority that came to Turkey in the 19C from Georgia in southern Russia. A strikingly handsome people, many of them tall and fair-haired, they have retained some of their Georgian traditions. They are well-known for the exuberant, athletic dancing which they perform with great zest at weddings, family feasts and folklore festivals.

Oylat is c 20km from İnegöl. Continue on Road 200 in the direction of Ankara for c 10km, then turn right and after 5km right again on to a narrow track that climbs steeply to the ridge on which the village is built.

Of the many spas in the vicinity of Bursa, Oylat is probably the least well-known and is certainly the most beautifully sited. Its single small street ascends picturesquely under a beech hanger to the *hammam*.

This does not follow the usual *hamam* design. Apart from an enclosed trough-like area at one end, Oylat's **Yeni Hamam** is a conventional swimming pool. Each minute thousands of gallons of naturally hot mineral water pour into the trough and from there overflow into the pool. There are no masseurs in Oylat's bath; instead, great jets of hot water, which cascade over the bathers, provide a rough, stimulating massage.

The admission charge is low. Although towels may be hired, most bathers bring their own. Separate periods are allocated to men and women.

A few days at Oylat provide a healthy and restful break. There is no organised entertainment. Visitors spend idle days bathing, exploring the beech woods, playing *tavla* in the coffee-houses or enjoying the village's calm and peaceful atmosphere.

B. Bursa to İznik

Total distance c 76km. Bursa—c 28km Gemlik—c 48km İznik.

One day is needed for this excursion. That will allow sufficient time for the journey by public transport, for a visit to the principal monuments, including the museum, and for lunch or a picnic by İznik Gölu.

There are regular bus and frequent dolmuş services from Bursa's *otogar* to **İZNIK**. The journey takes c 1 hour.

Leave Bursa by Road 575 in the direction of Yalova. Shortly after passing through 28km Gemlik (see Route C below), take a signposted right-hand turn on to the minor road that skirts İznik Gölü, the ancient Lake Ascanius.

Accommodation and restaurants. Accommodation in İznik is limited. There is one small motel. Advance enquiries may be made to the **Tourist Information Office**, Belediye Pasajı 130/131 or to the information office in Bursa. There are several unpretentious restaurants. Some near the lake-shore, which specialise in fish, are open only during the summer season. There are many places where it is possible to picnic.

History. Founded in 316 BC by Antigonus I Monophthalmos (382–301), it was named Antigonia in his honour. After Lysimachus defeated Antigonus at Ipsus in 301 BC he renamed the city **Nicaea**, after his deceased wife, and made it the capital of Bithynia. Nicaea retained this position until 264 BC, when Nicomedes I (279–253 BC) made the new city of Nicomedia (İzmit) his capital. The last king of Bithynia, the weak and vicious Nicomedes IV Philopator (94–74 BC), willed his kingdom to Rome. Nicaea prospered,becoming one of the most important cities in the Roman province of Asia.

It attracted artists and writers. The 1C BC grammarian and poet, Parthenius of Nicaea, the author of *Metamorphoses*, introduced the Callimachean elegy to the Romans. He edited, from various Greek sources, the book of *Sorrowful Love-Stories* and is also credited with having taught Greek to Virgil.

Pliny the Younger (born AD 61) was governor of Bithynia from 111 to 113. During his term of office he resided at Nicaea and effected many improvements, including the reconstruction of the city's theatre and gymnasium.

Concerned about the activities of the Christians in his province, he wrote to the emperor for advice. Trajan counselled him not to hunt them down. Those accused and convicted should be punished, but those who repented and made sacrifice to the gods should be pardoned.

Destroyed by an earthquake in AD 123, the city was restored by Hadrian. During the Persian invasions in the mid 3C AD, Nicaea was razed to the ground. Rebuilt, it later welcomed Diocletian, Constantine and Justinian. After the triumph of Christianity, it became an important missionary centre. At the First Council of Nicaea in 325 the Arian heresy, which denied the divinity of Christ, was condemned and the Nicaean Creed, which sets out the criteria of Christian orthodoxy, was formulated. The first steps were also taken to establish formal co-operation between church and state.

For a short period during the reign of Julian the Apostate (360–363) pagan worship was resumed in Nicaea. In the 6C Justinian (527–565) ornamented the city with many splendid buildings including a basilica and a palace. Nicaea fended off several fierce attacks by the Arabs in the 8C. In 787 the Empress Irene, widow of Leo IV and regent for her son, Constantine VI, summoned the Seventh Ecumenical Council which took place in Nicaea's church of St Sophia. This settled the controversy about icons. Reverence (Gr. *proskynesis*), but not adoration (Gr. *latreia*), could be accorded to them.

During the centuries that followed, Nicaea was invested at different times by Persians, Mongols and Turks. In 1081 it was captured by the Selçuks, who renamed it İznik and made it the capital of the Sultanate of Rum. Restored to Christian hands in 1097, it was for a short period in the 13C the principal city of the Byzantine Lascarid dynasty. In 1331 İznik was taken by Orhan Gazi, the first Ottoman ruler. However, its trials were not over. It was captured and sacked by Tamerlane (1335–1405) in 1402.

After the Mongol army had retreated from Anatolia, the city, once more under the Ottomans, entered a period of great artistic development. Large deposits of kaolin, feldspar and silicon, needed for the production of ceramics, were found near Bursa and İznik. Mehmet Çelebi brought skilled craftsmen from Iran and under their tutelage the celebrated ceramic industry was created. In the early 16C there were 300 workshops in the city producing tiles which were used to decorate the Mosque of Omar at Jerusalem and other great Ottoman palaces and religious buildings.

Towards the end of the 16C war broke out between Persia and Turkey and the Persian artists in İznik were exiled to Rhodes. Without their skills the quality of the ceramics declined. Part of the city was burned down c 1605 and many of the remaining craftsmen left İznik and settled in Kütahya. According to Evliya Çelebi, who visited İznik towards the end of the 17C, only nine workshops were in operation.

During the following centuries, İznik continued to decline, until it became little more than a hamlet dwarfed by its ancient walls. In 1922, during the war with Greece, it suffered great damage. Many of its ancient buildings were destroyed and it became what it is today—the melancholy shadow of a once great city.

Coming from Bursa you enter İznik by the **Yenişehir Kapısı**. According to an inscription this was built by the Emperor Claudius II Gothicus (268–270) in 268. Repaired and strengthened by the Lascarids in the 13C, the second entrance is set at an angle to the first to facilitate its defence. The scene of fierce attacks by the Selçuks and the Ottomans, it is now in a ruinous condition.

Nicaea was defended by two lines of fortifications separated by a fosse. The older wall, which dates from the 3C, is c 5km in length. The Lascarids restored this and built a second wall which was protected by more than 100 towers. The city had four gates, three of which remain.

Nicaea was laid out in the form of a grid. The modern Atatürk Cad., which links Yenişehir Kapısı in the S with İstanbul Kapısı in the N, follows the line of one of the ancient streets. The E/W axis is marked by Mazharbey Cad., which runs from the Göl Kapısı to Lefke Kapısı.

A turning left from Atatürk Cad. leads to Nicaea's ruined **theatre** (Eski Saray). Built by Pliny the Younger, while he was governor of Bithynia between 111 and 113, it had a seating capacity of c 15,000. Excavations under way have revealed that, as in the case of the theatre at Side, the seats were supported by vaults. Archaeologists have uncovered the scaenium, proscaenium, cavea, vomitorium, diazoma and orchestra. Traces of a 13C three-aisled church and an extensive cemetery have been found on top of the cavea. In the scaenium they have discovered architectural fragments,

including a relief of Roman charioteers. Large quantities of Roman, Byzantine, Selçuk and Ottoman pottery have also been uncovered.

Turn left from the theatre and cross Atatürk Cad. On the right is the **Zaviye of Yacoub Çelebi**. After fighting bravely at the battle of Kossovo (1389), Yacoub was summarily executed by his brother Beyazit I on the battlefield in the presence of their father's corpse (see p 117).

Return to Atatürk Cad. and, crossing Sığır Meydanı, visit the site of **Koïmesis Kilisesi**, the church of the Dormition of the Virgin. Built in the 8C, it was restored several times before being completely destroyed in 1922 during the Greek-Turkish war. All that remains are a few pieces of marble sculpture and traces of the mosaic floor. The Lascarid emperor, Theodore I (1204–22), was buried here.

Walk up Istiklal Cad. and take the first turning on the left. On the right-hand side is **Süleyman Paşa Medresesi**, built by the brother of Orhan I on the site of a former monastery in the early 14C. Study-rooms and cells for the students lined the sides of a porticoed courtyard.

Return to Atatürk Cad. and turn right. The ruins of **Haghia Sophia**, the most important Byzantine building in İznik, are at the junction with Mazharbey Cad. Excavations made in 1935 revealed traces of a church constructed on this site by Justinian in the 6C. These include a 7C fresco in the nave representing the Deisis and parts of the mosaic pavements. Justinian's church was destroyed by an earthquake in 1065 and replaced by a new building on a higher level. This had a narthex and a central nave which was separated from the choir by a chancel.

After the conquest of Nicaea by Orhan Gazi in 1331 this church was converted into a mosque. A *mihrab* was placed in the chancel and a minaret added later. During the occupation of İznik by Tamerlane's army in 1402 the mosque was badly damaged and it suffered again from fire in the 16C. Süleyman I the Magnificent (1520–66) had it restored by his architect Sinan, but as İznik began to decline in importance, the mosque fell into disrepair and eventually was no longer used. The destruction of the building was completed in 1922 during the hostilities between Greece and Turkey.

On leaving Haghia Sophia continue along Mazharbey Cad. in the direction of Lefke Kapısı. At the fourth intersection on the left is **Haci Özbek Camii**. Built in 1333, this small building is the earliest Ottoman mosque whose date can be fixed accurately by an inscription. Its walls are constructed of stone blocks separated by a brick on either side and with a layer of three bricks above and below. Originally the mosque had a portico, but this was removed in 1939 to allow the street to be widened.

The third turning on the left, Teke Sok., leads to Yeşil Cami and Nilüfer Hatun İmareti. **Yeşil Cami** was built between 1378 and 1391 by Çandarlı Kara Halil Paşa. The architect, Hacı bin Musa, produced a pleasingly harmonious design by ensuring that the area of the portico and vestibule equalled the area of the prayer hall. The mosque got its name from the fine İznik tiles which covered the minaret. Unfortunately, these were destroyed and have been replaced by poor quality substitutes from Kütahya.

Nilüfer Hatun İmareti was built in 1388 by Murat I (1359–89) and named after his mother, a Greek princess, daughter of the Emperor John VI Catacuzenos. In 1346 Theodora or Nilüfer Hatun, as she became known, married Orhan Gazi, then aged 62, for reasons of state. She was allowed to remain a Christian. A powerful personality, she often acted as regent when Orhan was away on one of his many campaigns. At the *imaret* food was provided for students and lodgings for itinerant dervishes.

The *imaret*, which has been restored, is constructed of stone blocks separated by brick. An open vaulted colonnade leads to a large chamber under a central dome. This is flanked by smaller domed side chambers and it has an exedra at the rear. Now İznik's **museum**, the *imaret* houses artefacts found in and near the town and an ethnographical collection.

In the garden are sarcophagi, capitals, stelae, reliefs and inscriptions and a representative display of Islamic gravestones. The central chamber is devoted to objects from the Hellenistic and Roman periods. Note the fine Roman sarcophagus, decorated with garlands and representations of Medusa, the collection of Roman glass and the many portrait busts. The exedra has some excellent examples of İznik tiles, plates and bowls.

In the ethnographical collection there are flintlock pistols, dishes, censers, Korans, coins, writing instruments and embroidered cloths. The key to a Roman tomb outside the İstanbul Kapısı is kept in the museum.

From the museum return to Mazharbey Cad. and turn left to the **Lefke Kapısı**. This was a double gate. According to an inscription on the outer part it was dedicated to Hadrian in AD 123 by the proconsul Plancius Varus.

Return to Atatürk Cad. and continue in a N direction to the **İstanbul Kapısı**, the best preserved of all İznik's ancient gates. A double structure, this pierces both the 3C Roman wall and the 13C Lascarid fortification.

From the İstanbul Kapısı it is a pleasant walk along the tree-lined shore of İznik Gölü to the Göl Kapısı and thence to the town centre.

If you have your own transport you may like to return to Bursa by a different route. There are two possibilities: along the N shore of the lake to Orhangazi and from there to Gemlik; or over the soft rolling Bithynian hills to Yenişehir and İnegöl. The second is very picturesque. The road climbs in gentle curves past vineyards and descends into poplar-lined valleys. A fertile land, it is easy to see why so many invaders were attracted to it and decided to settle here.

C. Bursa to Yalova

Total distance 63km. Bursa—28km Gemlik—35km Yalova—(66km İzmit).

This is a half-day excursion. There are many local bus and dolmuş services to Gemlik and Yalova and long-distance coaches to İstanbul via İzmit may have some free seats.

Gemlik is a popular seaside resort and Yalova is both a spa and the terminal for a ferry service with İstanbul.

Leave Bursa by Road 575. After passing the industrial suburbs this climbs steadily for c 10km, then descends to the gulf on which 28km **Gemlik** is built.

History. Gemlik was known in antiquity as Cius, after one of the Argonauts who, according to a legend, founded it after his return from Colchis.

This area has associations with Hercules. While the Argo was sailing along the coast of the Propontis, Hercules broke his oar and, accompanied by his lover, Hylas, and Polyphemus of Larissa, went ashore to find a replacement. Hylas was sent to the spring of Pegae for a pitcher of water. When he leaned over the pool, a water-nymph, overcome by his beauty, pulled him down beneath the surface. Polyphemus hearing Hylas cry out for help, rushed to the boy's aid, but was too late. He and Hercules, who was distraught with grief, searched everywhere for the missing youth. Meanwhile, a favourable breeze blew up and the crew of the Argo sailed away, leaving Hercules and Polyphemus to their fruitless quest.

Traditionally the spring of Pegae was located on a strip of marshy ground between Cyzicus and Cius, modern Bandırma and Gemlik. Acccording to Strabo: 'still to this day a kind of festival is celebrated among the Prusians, a mountain-ranging festival, in which they march in procession and call Hylas, as though making their exodus to the forests in quest of him'.

First colonised by the Milesians, who used it as a staging post on their trading voyages to the Black Sea, Cius fell into the hands of the Antigonids of Macedon. In return for help received during the First Macedonian War, Philip V (221–179) of Macedon gave Cius to Prusias I (228–185) of Bithynia. He first sacked the city and enslaved its inhabitants, later rebuilding it and renaming it Prusias-ad-Marem.

Orhan Gazi (1324–59) established a shipbuilding yard here, hence the town's name (in Turkish *Gemi* means 'ship').

Gemlik is popular with holiday-makers from İstanbul. Its hotels and pensions are usually full during the season. Recent reports suggest that the waters of its beautiful gulf are not always free from pollution, so check before bathing here.

Apart from a 4C BC tomb, found near the town, and its shipbuilding industry, Gemlik has few links with its past.

From Gemlik continue to the village of 10km **Orhangazi**, where a turning to the right leads to İznik. From Orhangazi the road descends on the flanks of soft, rounded hillsides to the sea.

From earliest times, 35km **Yalova** has been a spa. Its waters offer relief from a number of maladies, including rheumatism and skin diseases.

Patronised by Roman and Byzantine emperors, it became popular once more in the 19C and early 20C during the last period of Ottoman rule. Like Gemlik visible signs of its past are few—the outline of a palace erected by Justin II (565–578) and a number of Hellenistic and Roman stelae in the town centre.

If you are not in a hurry, continue to 66km İzmit. This modern, heavily-industrialised and utterly charmless town occupies the site of ancient Nicomedia. Made capital of Bithynia by Nicomedes I (c 279–255 BC), it was a city of considerable splendour. Destroyed by the Goths, it was completely restored during the reign of Diocletian (284–305). Under the late Roman and early Byzantine emperors the city continued to flourish and at one time rivalled Alexandria in importance.

There are few reminders of İzmit's past grandeur. There is a small museum, and, above the town, the remains of a Byzantine fortress.

D. Bursa to Kütahya

Total distance (excluding deviations) 164km. Bursa—38km İnegöl—80km Tavşanlı—(15km Diliktaş)—46km Kütahya—(57km Çavdarhisar—Aizanoi)—(80km Eskişehir).

For the first part of this journey, Bursa to İnegöl, see Route 4A.

About 9km to the E of İnegöl turn right on to Road 595. Continue through a pleasant stretch of countryside to the towns of Domaniç, Tunçbilek and **Tavşanlı**. The most interesting of picturesque Tavşanlı's many mosques is the 12C **Kavalık Camii**. About 15km to W, just off the Balıkesir road and near the the village of Diliktaş, there is a **Phrygian rock tomb** with a façade ornamented with geometric designs.

Leave Tavşanlı by Road 230, signposted Kütahya. Shortly after the town of Köprüören you pass the Enne Dam and lake.

KÜTAHYA has been producing ceramic tiles at least since the beginning of the 17C. The industry still flourishes and its products are to be seen everywhere in the town. Even the pillars in the *otogar* are sheathed in tiles!

Information and Accommodation. There are six hotels in Kütahya on the Ministry of Tourism's list. The *Erbaylar Oteli*, Afyon Cad., has three-stars; the *Gönen Oteli*, Menderes Cad., the *Gülpalas* in Belediye Medyanı and three others have one-star each. The **Tourist Information Offices** are at Azarbeycan Parkı içi and in the Hükümet Komağı, Kat. 1.

Kütahya has good connections by long-distance buses to the principal cities in Turkey and to Ankara and İstanbul by train.

History. In ancient times Kütahya was known as Cotyaeum or Kotiaion. In the late 5C AD a great battle was fought near the city between the army of the newly appointed Emperor Anastasius (491–518) and a force of dissident Isaurians.

The church in Cotyaeum had some unusual rulers. Cyrus, a former praetorian prefect of the East and of Constantinople, was made bishop of the city when he fell from power. It was not uncommon in Byzantium for an influential subject to be relegated to a position where he could do no harm. Another bishop of Cotyaeum supported the Novatian heresy which rejected the reconciliation of Christians who had been excommunicated for sacrificing to the pagan gods during the Decian persecutions.

During the Byzantine period Cotyaeum was a staging post on the busy road which linked Constantinople and Attaleia (Antalya).

In 1182 the city was sacked by Kılıç Arslan II. The powerful Germiyanid Turks established a dynasty here in 1286. Because of their opposition to the Mongols, they attracted a large following among the Turcoman tribes. The Germiyanid did not have a good reputation. Ibn Battuta, the 14C Arab traveller, was given an escort by the ruler of Gül Hisar to protect him from 'Kermian brigands' who 'possess a town called Kütahiya'! Occupied briefly by the Mongols, it later returned to Germiyanid rule.

Towards the end of the 14C a *Beylerbeyi*, a 'bey of beys', was appointed for Anatolia. Kütahya was his capital. In a dynastic union, Orhan's grandson, the future Beyazit I (1389–1403), married the daughter of the Germiyanid ruler and acquired Kütahya and half of the principality as her dowry. In recognition of the assistance which he had received from the Germiyanid ruler during the Interregnum, Memet I (1413–21) contented himself with annexing Afyon Karahisar and Kütahya. When he died in 1428, he bequeathed the remainder of the principality to the Ottomans.

Prince Beyazit, the son of Süleyman the Magnificent, who had been falsely accused of treason and condemned to death, was saved by the intervention of Hürrem Sultan and appointed governor of Kütahya in 1555. During the course of one of his first journeys the youthful Evliya Çelebi visited the city in 1639.

The great Ottoman poet Şehi (d. 1429) was born in Kütahya. Trained as a physician, he became a member of the court of Mehmet I before retiring to write poetry in solitude. In his lyrical poems he played down the importance of ritual in religion and claimed that union with God could only be achieved by drinking the symbolic wine. He also composed satirical poems, the *Harname* or Book of the Donkey, in which conniving courtiers are represented by animals.

Ceramics were probably produced here in the 15C or even earlier, but this cannot be established with certainty as the records of the workshops in Kütahya were destroyed by fire in 1700. The clay of Kütahya is whiter than that of İznik and the temper is harder. Ceramic stalactites in blue, green and white, are characteristic of Kütahayan work. In Kütahya tiles of the 16C look for repeated small medallions, a small cup with a few stiff flowers and palm leaf designs. Enquire at the Tourist Information Office about visting one of the workships.

Kütahya's **museum** is in the restored **Vacidiye Medrese** which was built in 1314 during the Germiyanid period. A portal leads to a domed vestibule and thence to the courtyard which was covered with a dome during modern restorations. In an arched exedra is the tomb of Abdulvacid, a teacher at the *medrese*. The domed rooms at the sides of the courtyard were used to house the students.

The museum's archaeological collection is in two sections. The first contains statues, grave stelae and capitals from the Hellenistic, Roman and Byzantine periods. In the second are stone tools and pottery from the Prehistoric Period, Hittite and Phrygian pottery and ceramics and lamps, statuettes and coins from the Roman and Byzantine periods.

In the courtyard there are grave stelae and architectural monuments.

The **Kurşunlu Cami**, built in 1372 by Ahi Şeyh Mehmet, has a dome supported by triangular-shaped pendentives. The early 15C *külliye* of Yakub Bey II has a *medrese, mescit, imaret* and the domed *türbe* of the founder. The *imaret* was designed in the form of an inverted T with a *zaviye* and flanking rooms. Yakub Bey was ruler of the *beylik* from 1390–1409.

Other buildings of interest are the **Ulu Cami** which was commenced by by Beyazit I and finished by Mehmet II, the early 15C **İşak Fatih Camii**, and the nearby *medrese*.

It is a strenuous climb to the well preserved **Citadel** but the splendid view from the battlements is ample reward for the effort. The best approach is through the old quarter behind Ulu Cami. The citadel, built by the Byzantines, was enlarged and strengthened by later rulers. There are the ruins of a Byzantine church inside the fortifications. A café offers refreshments.

Leave Kütahya by Road 650, signposted Afyon. After c 10km take the right fork on to Road 240 and continue in the direction of Gediz. At first this picturesque road to Çavdarhisar and Aizanoi follows the course of the Porsuk Çayı.

At **Çavdarhisar** village take the Emet road and cross the bridge over the Kocasu, the ancient Rhyndacus. The ruins of **AIZANOI** are on the left. In addition to a magnificent temple there are substantial remains of two agoras, a macellum, a combined baths and gymnasium, bridges and quays on the Rhyndacus, a theatre and a stadium. Spring is, perhaps, the best season to visit Aizanoi. Then the site is carpeted with wild flowers and the lush new grass sets off the warm red of the temple perfectly. Geese, feeding greedily around the temenos, provide a classic touch. They give a noisy greeting to strangers, like their sisters who long ago warned Rome of approaching Celtic invaders.

As the remains of the city are spread over a large area, allow at least two hours for your visit. Çavdarhisar has no restaurants, but there are plenty of places on the site where a picnic lunch may be enjoyed.

Terracotta figurines found on the site suggest that there was a settlement at Aizanoi in the 1C BC. An ancient sanctuary dedicated to the Meter Steunene existed in the neighbourhood. All the visible remains date from the Roman period and testify to the city's importance in the 2C AD. In Byzantine times Aizanoi was an episcopal see. The temple of Zeus was converted into a church.

The **Temple of Zeus** was built during the reign of Hadrian (AD 117–138). Until it was damaged by an earthquake in 1970, it was the best preserved ancient temple in Turkey. The fallen columns have been re-erected. Constructed of marble, the temple stands on a high, stepped podium which measures c 33m by 37m. The naos is preceded by a porch, which has four composite columns. (Composite columns have both the Ionic volute and the Corinthian acanthus and are characteristic of Roman buildings of the period.) The shallow opisthodomos has two composite columns in antis. In this respect it hearkens back to the 2C BC temple of Zeus Sosipolis at Magnesia on the Maeander, which was probably designed by Hermogenes of Priene. The peristasis, of pseudodipteral arrangement, has 15 Ionic columns on the long sides and eight on the short. An inscription on one of the walls states that the temple was dedicated to Zeus, but the statue of the god, which stood in the naos, disappeared a long time ago. However, a statuette of an eagle, which was sacred to Zeus, was found in the precinct and coins of Aizanoi show a standing figure of the god holding a spear in his left hand and with an eagle perched on his right.

It has been suggested that Zeus shared the temple with Cybele, the Anatolian Mother Goddess. The long association of Aizanoi with the Meter Steunene, the acroterion from the pediment above the opisthodomus which shows a female bust, the discovery of terracotta figurines of Cybele in the vault under the temple, and the alignment of the building which opened on the W side, as do all Anatolian temples dedicated to Cybele, suggest that this hypothesis is correct. However, dissenting voices cite Dio LXIX 4 who mentions the use of temple cellars for storage purposes. Access to the barrel vaulted substructure is by a modern iron staircase at the rear of the temple. If it is locked, ask for the *bekçi* who has the key.

The **large agora** was between the temple and the river. There are the ruins of a **heroon** at the E side. Nearby is one of the four **Roman bridges** which spanned the Rhyndacus. From here follow the river in a SW direction to the site of the **macellum**. On the wall of a round building in the centre of the macellum there is an almost complete copy of the Edictum de Pretiis which Diocletian issued in AD 301. This early attempt at a prices and wages freeze set out, in great detail, the maximum prices and wages which could be paid. Offenders who charged more or withheld their goods were liable to the death penalty. Despite this threat of draconian punishment, the measure failed. Goods disappeared from the shops and markets, gold and silver coins were treated as bullion and changed hands at more than their face value. The edict was allowed to fall into desuetude.

By the macellum are two more **Roman bridges** and a **Roman quay**. Down river there are a further three quays and another bridge. The quays, evidence of the importance of Aizanoi as a river port in imperial times, are now used to control flooding. Diagonally across the river from the macellum is the site of the **Doric agora**. The ruins of the **gymnasium and baths**, where there is an interesting mosaic, are to the NW of the temple.

The **palaestra**, which was surrounded on three sides by colonnades, adjoined this complex. Farther to the N are the scant remains of Aizanoi's **stadium** and relatively well-preserved **theatre**. The stage building has collapsed, but could be reconstructed without much difficulty as most of the pieces still exist. Several rows of seats remain in position in the cavea.

Return to Kütahya from Çavdarhisar and follow Road 650 in a northerly direction. After c 41km turn right on to Road 230 and continue to Eskişehir.

ESKİŞEHİR, literally the Old City, does not quite live up to its name. Badly damaged during the fighting with the Greeks in 1921, it has kept very few of its ancient buildings. However, it has a long and interesting history. There has been a settlement of some kind in this area from early times.

Information and Accommodation. The **Tourist Information Office** is in Vilayet Binası, Kat. 1. Eight hotels appear on the Ministry of Tourism list. These include the three-star *Büyük Otel*, 27 Mayıs Cad., No. 40; four two-star, and three one-star hotels. Both the two-star *Has Termal Oteli*, Hamam Yolu Cad., No. 7 and the *Sultan Termal Oteli*, Suleyman Çakır Cad., No. 1 have thermal baths.

History. There was probably a Phrygian settlement here early in the first millennium BC. Evidence of an Ionian Greek presence or influence in the late 6C BC may be adduced from the discovery here of a marble stele now in the İstanbul Archaeological Museum. On one side there is a winged goddess, who wears a high tiara and holds a lion cub in her left hand, the Mistress of the Animals, and on the other side two groups, one of a horseman and groom, the second of a charioteer in a two-horse chariot.

The site of **Dorylaeum**, the historic predecessor of Eskişehir, has been placed variously at Sarıhöyük, c 3km to the NE and Karacahisar, 6km to the SW. The city owed its importance to its location on the edge of the Anatolian plateau and the fact that it was on a busy trade route linking Nicaea and Amorium. It was surrounded by a fertile plain watered by the Tembris and Bathys rivers which teemed with fish. The historian Cinnamus described it as 'one of the great cities of Asia and very noteworthy'.

In 1071 the ill-fated Romanus IV Diogenes (1067–1071) stopped at Dorylaeum on his way to Manzikert. Twenty-six years later the Turks were forced to retreat from a large part of Anatolia, including Dorylaeum, by Alexius I Comnenus (1081–1118).

On 30 June 1097 Crusaders led by Bohemund of Taranto and Raymond of Toulouse defeated a superior Turkish force commanded by Kılıç Arslan in a valley near Dorylaeum. Victory was clinched by the timely arrival of a small detachment led by Adhemar, the redoubtable Bishop of Le Puy. The anonymous author of the *Gesta Francorum* relates what happened after the battle:

'the Turks, Arabas, Saracens, and all the barbarians sped away in flight through the mountain passes across the plains. Altogether, the pagans numbered three hundred and sixty thousand, not counting the Arabs, whose numbers no one knows but God alone. They fled very quickly to their camp, but even there they could not stay for long. Again they took flight, and we followed them, killing as we went, for a whole day. We seized much booty, gold, silver, horses and asses, camels, sheep, oxen and many other things which we did not recognise'.

The remnants of the Turkish force retreated to Iconium (Konya), pursuing a scorched earth policy as they went, sacking the houses and churches of the Greek towns and destroying anything they could not carry away. They also took the male Greek children from the towns between Dorylaeum and Konya.

In the 12C, after its destruction by the Turks who razed it to the ground, the population was reduced to 2000 tent-living Turcomen. Because of attacks on his army by Turcomen tribes in the neighbourhood of Dorylaeum, Manuel I Comnenus (1143–80) drove out large numbers of the nomads. He rebuilt Dorylaeum and fortified it between 1175–76. However, after the disastrous defeat of the Byzantines at the battle of Myriocephalon later in that year, Kılıç Arslan demanded the destruction of the fortress of Dorylaeum, a demand which Manuel refused. The battle of Myriocephalon, the most significant since Manzikert, marked the end of attempts by the Byzantines to recapture Anatolia. Large numbers were slain on both sides. According to the 12C historian Nicetas Choniates, the Turks cut off the heads,and genitals of many of their dead to conceal their losses from the retreating Byzantine army.

Towards the end of the 13C Dorylaeum was taken by Osman. Thereafter it remained under Ottoman rule.

The **Archaeological Museum** has collections of plant and animal fossils from the region, prehistoric earthenware, statuettes, stone and bone objects from the Chalcolithic Age to the Hittite period, dishes, figurines, stelae, statues, objects of metal and glass from the Hittite to the Byzantine period. There are some fine late Roman mosaics from Dorylaeum and Greek, Roman, Byzantine and Turkish coins. In the courtyard there are Roman and Byzantine inscriptions, stelae, sarcophagi, capitals and other architectural fragments. Note the Phrygian relief of a peacock.

The Eskişehir **Ethnographic Museum** is housed in the 19C Yeşil Efendi Konağı which has some beautifully carved ceilings and cupboards.

The 13C **Alaeddin Camii** and the 16C **Kurşunlu complex** merit a visit. Meerschaum (hydrous silicate of magnesium), found locally, is carved into pipes, stick handles and ornaments. Widely sold in Turkey and abroad, meerschaum products contribute handsomely to the town's prosperity.

Eskişehir is a good centre for excursions to the interesting towns and historical sites in NW Turkey. Those in Phrygia are described in Route 56.

5

Bursa to Erdek

Total distance c 112km. Bursa—34km Gölyazı—2km Apollonia—58km Karacabey—(c 8km Hara)—(3km Manyas/Kuşcenneti)—35km Bandırma—c 8km Cyzicus—19km Erdek.

Buses for Erdek, via Bandırma, leave from the *otogar*. The journey takes about $2\frac{1}{2}$ hours.

The busy E90 bisects a featureless plain, whose monotony is relieved only by the gleaming waters at c 30km of **Uluabat Gölü** on the left. In this shallow lake there are perch, pike, sturgeon and crayfish and in the surrounding countryside pheasant, heron, crane and woodcock.

The site of the ancient city of **Apollonia**, near the village of **Gölyazı**, may be reached by a minor road on the left, 34km W of Bursa. Apart from a number of tombs in the necropolis near the peninsula, which links Gölyazı to the mainland, few traces of Apollonia remain. Today most visitors are attracted by the beauty of the site rather than by its historical associations. There is a daily bus service between Bursa and Gölyazı.

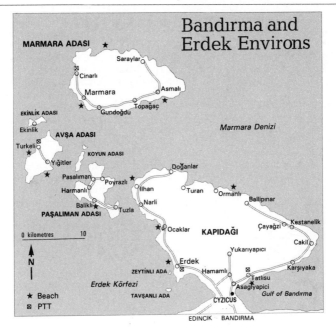

Just beyond the western confines of the lake at c 58km is the market-town of **Karacabey**. This was named after a relative of Murat II, who died in 1455. Karaca Bey's elaborate marble **tomb** stands under the five-arched portico of a mosque on the NE side of the town. His wife and daughter are believed to have been buried in the domed building nearby.

A short distance to the S from Karacabey on Road 220 is c 8km **Hara**. Also known as Karacabey Harası, this ancient foundation dates back to the time of Orhan Gazi (1324–59). A royal farm during the Ottoman period, it is now a stud (*hara*), and an agricultural station which specialises in the improvement of livestock and plants. Cattle, horses, fowl, cereals and grasses produced here are used by farmers all over Turkey. The station also offers advice on how to improve cultivation methods. A small pension and restaurant at Hara provide accommodation and refreshment.

Not surprisingly, the countryside around Karacabey has a reputation for producing excellent vegetables, especially fine-flavoured onions.

For **KUŞCENNETI NATIONAL PARK** leave the E90 c 12km before Bandırma where it joins Road 565 to Balıkesir. After 2km a track to the right leads to the car park and a small museum. Facilities in the park are limited to an observation tower, toilet, and drinking water. There is no accommodation or restaurant, and picnicking is not allowed.

A hydrobiological research station is maintained at Kuşcenneti by the University of İstanbul. The park's flora and fauna are strictly protected and visitors must comply with the regulations laid down by the authorities. It occupies c 52 hectares of woods and marshland on the shores of Lake Kuş, formerly Lake Manyas. As its name, Kuşcenneti, 'Bird Paradise', suggests, it is an important resting and breeding place for migratory and wintering species. Birds, which have spent the winter in the S, come to Kuşcenneti in the spring to lay their eggs and rear their young. The nestlings, nourished by the rich food supply, grow to maturity in the park's safe environment.

Between two and three million birds visit Kuşcenneti each year. Among the 239 recorded species are herons, cormorants, pelicans, geese, spoonbills, ibises, ducks and reed warblers. The lake, shaded by willow, alder and ash, swarms with fish. Pike, catfish, carp, grey mullet, and crayfish abound, while the bullrushes resound to the harsh croaking of a myriad frogs.

In the SE corner of Kuş Gölü are the ruins of the garrison city of **Dascylium**. According to Herodotus and Thucydides Pharnabazus, the Persian satrap ruled Hellespontine Phrygia from here. After Alexander's victory at Granicus, Dascylium was invested by a force under the command of Parmenion.

The scanty remains of the city are likely to interest specialists and students only. Reliefs found here and now in the İstanbul Archaeological Museum reveal strong Iranian thematic influences. They depict a bull and a ram being sacrificed in the Persian manner and a stately procession of mounted figures. A recent survey of the site by Turkish archaeologists produced a Graeco-Achaemenid funeral stele and a number of bullae with inscriptions in Aramaic. The stele is in the İstanbul Museum and the bullae are in the Archaeological Institute of Ankara University.

Bandırma is a dusty, uninspiring place. Linked to İstanbul by car-ferry, it is a convenient disembarkation point for visitors to Erdek and the other small resorts on Kapıdağ peninsula.

A winding road leads across the windswept isthmus that links Kapıdağ, ancient Arctonesus (Bear Island), with the mainland. The hillside monument to the left is to Turks who died during the 1919–22 war with Greece.

Conservationists, nature-lovers and local farmers are greatly concerned about the industrial development which has taken place on the isthmus during recent years. In this formerly unspoiled area there are now several chemical installations and a petrol storage depot. As a result the sea has been so polluted that bathing is no longer possible.

About 8km from Bandırma are the sparse remains of the city of **Cyzicus**. These are on the right-hand side of the road to Erdek towards the southeastern end of the isthmus. The site of Cyzicus, which has been excavated by Turkish archaeologists under the direction of Professor Akurgal, is very overgrown and is not easy to explore.

The remains of the city's **amphitheatre** lie in a ravine near the village of Hammamlı. Sections of the aqueducts that brought water from Mt Dindymus, and the hollow occupied by the theatre are still visible. In the SE corner there is a substantial section of the city walls.

The vaults, which supported the base of the great Temple of Hadrian, are known locally as the *bedesten* or *mağarlar*. According to Hasluck, who visited Cyzicus at the beginning of the century, these gloomy structures were shunned as they were believed to be inhabited by demons.

History. According to legend, Jason and the Argonauts were warmly received at Arctonesus by Cyzicus, king of the Doliones. While Cyzicus was entertaining them, monsters with six arms attacked Argo, but they were killed by Hercules.

After being provisioned and supplied with directions for the next stage of their voyage, the Argonauts put out to sea. During the night the wind rose and they were obliged to run for shelter. They beached the vessel in the dark and almost immediately were attacked by unknown men. In the morning they discovered to their horror that the attackers were the Doliones, who had thought that their territory was being invaded. Cyzicus was among the slain. Overcome by grief, his wife Clite hanged herself. Jason and his companions mourned their dead friend and joined in the funeral games arranged in his honour.

When they tried to resume their voyage, contrary winds blew the Argonauts back to the shore. They were told that they had angered Phrygian Cybele, Meter Oreie, the Mother of the Mountains, who under the title Meter Dindymene was worshipped on Mt Dindymus. To obtain forgiveness, Jason and his crew went in procession to her shrine and, imitating the Corybantes, danced around the statue of the goddess, while banging their swords on their shields. Cybele, placated by their action, allowed the Argonauts to continue their journey.

Excavations suggest that the city of Cyzicus was a Milesian colony and trading post founded towards the beginning of the 7C BC.

Strabo, writing in the 1C AD, describes Cyzicus as an island linked to the mainland by two bridges. A city of the same name built near the bridges rivalled 'the foremost of the cities of Asia in size, in beauty, and in its excellent administration of affairs both in peace and in war. And its adornment appears to be of a type similar to that of Rhodes and Massalia and ancient Carthage'.

In 334 BC Cyzicus supported Alexander the Great, closing its gates to the armies of the Persian satrap. This action embarrassed the Persians in a number of ways. As they did not mint their own coins, they relied on Cyzician currency, one of the most widely-used in antiquity, to pay their hired mercenaries. They were also unable to send their annual tribute to Persepolis.

The Romans made Cyzicus a free city and awarded it a substantial grant of territory in northern Mysia because of its resistance to Mithridates in 74 BC. The temple, begun during the reign of Hadrian and dedicated to him, was completed by Marcus Aurelius (AD 167). Regarded as one of the wonders of the ancient world, it was damaged by an earthquake in the 6C AD. That indefatigable traveller, Cyriac of Ancona, claimed to have seen the whole of the upper section of the building in 1431.

Objects discovered in Cyzicus are to be found in Erdek, İstanbul and Paris. Part of a column decorated with bunches of grapes is in the open-air museum at Erdek. In the İstanbul Archaeological Museum there are reliefs, coins and architectural fragments which combine Greek and Oriental elements in what may be described as a Propontine style. These include a circular base ornamented in high relief with the representation of a girl dancing between two youths, a kouros, and a relief showing a galloping chariot. Some fine 5C BC electrum staters show Poseidon riding a sea-horse, Silenus filling a cantharus and a delicately-executed female head.

A relief in the Louvre, dated to 46 BC, was dedicated to Cybele by one Soterides Gallos. The Great Mother told him in a dream that his friend, Marcus Stlaccius, who had disappeared during a battle, had been prisoner-of-war, but had been released at her intercession. On the upper portion of the relief, under a representation of the enthroned goddess, the preparations for a sacrifice are shown.

The approach to **Erdek** is through an avenue of olive groves, orchards and vineyards. A small resort, popular with Turkish visitors, it has simple, comfortable hotels and some good restaurants. Information about accommodation may be obtained from the **Tourist Information Office**. The small open-air museum is in the town centre near the Belediye.

Erdek is a good centre for visits to Kapıdağ, Marmara Adası, the ancient Proconnesus, and the neighbouring islands. Marmara Adası was famed for its fine white marble which has a pronounced blue streak. During the reign of Hadrian fashionable Roman society imported statues carved by Asiatic craftsmen from Proconnesian marble. Later, under Valens, a number of Egyptian monks were condemned to hard labour in the marble quarries.

Proconnesus was the birth place of Aristeas, a 7C BC geographer and traveller, who was roundly denounced by Strabo as a charlatan. Aristeas composed an epic poem, the Arimaspeia, about his journeys which took him as far afield as Magna Graecia and the Black Sea. Fragments believed to be from the poem survive. Aristeas claimed to possess magic powers which allowed him to leave his body and return to it at will.

Marmara Adası is now a popular holiday centre which offers fishing, swimming, climbing and other outdoor pursuits. It has a number of hotels and motels which cater for c 150,000 summer visitors. There is a daily ferry service to İstanbul and boat connections with Tekirdağ and Erdek.

6

Erdek to Çanakkale

Total distance 206km. Erdek—54km Gönen—56km Biga—(19km Karabiga/Priapus)—56km Lapseki—40km Çanakkale.

Shortly after Erdek Road 200 turns inland and passes through an austere landscape, where rocks protruding through the thin soil resemble the bones of ancient dinosaurs. Slow-moving flocks of sheep crop the sparse herbage under the watchful gaze of their youthful guardians. **Gönen** is a small market-town and spa, visited by sufferers from dermatological, urinary and nervous complaints. They bathe in, and drink, the waters which contain chloride, sodium, magnesium and fluoride.

Between Gönen and 56km Biga the road returns briefly to the sea at Denizkent, and then crosses a broad plain watered by the Koca Çayı, the ancient Granicus. Today a pastoral calm reigns over the small villages that dot the plain, each with its threshing floor and decoration of untidy storks' nests. In autumn clouds of pungent smoke from the burning stubble drift across the small river, that 'little trickle of water' as Alexander the Great called the Granicus contemptuously, where in 334 BC he inflicted his first great defeat on the Persians.

When they heard that Alexander had landed in Asia, the Persians under the command of Arsites, the satrap of Hellespontine Phrygia, left their lakeside fortress of Dascylium (see above) and regrouped their forces, believed to number 35,000 against the Macedonians' 50,000, at the town of Zeleia on the slopes of Mt Ida. Alexander, short of money and supplies, was anxious to engage the enemy in battle as quickly as possible. Ignoring the Greek city of Lampsacus, which closed its gates, he marched E to the Granicus. There, on a late afternoon in May, he found the Persians drawn up on the opposite bank. According to Arrian and Plutarch, writing in the 1C and 2C AD, Alexander disregarded the advice of the elderly general Parmenion, who suggested that the crossing be made under the cover of darkness. Instead he led the Mounted Scouts and Companions in a dramatic charge across the river and up the steep bank on the other side, opening the way for the Macedonian infantry to follow.

Diodorus Siculus (fl. 30 BC) gives a different account. According to him Alexander, leaving his camp fires burning to deceive the Persian scouts, quietly marched his army downstream during the night and crossed the river by a ford. The Persians awoke to find the Macedonians, drawn up in battle-order, facing them. All the historians agree that a desperate struggle followed. Alexander, conspicuous in the armour he had taken from the temple of Athena at Ilium, was the target for many attacks. Dazed by a blow that cut through his helmet and opened his scalp, he was saved by 'Black' Cleitus, his nurse's brother. He collapsed as the battle raged around him.

The Macedonians' strong cornel-wood thrusting-lances broke the Persian infantry line and the Companions and Parmenion's Thessalian cavalry completed the rout. The Greek mercenaries under the command of Memnon, withdrew to a hill and asked for quarters. Alexander, enraged by their action of 'fighting with Orientals against Greeks', refused. Memnon escaped, but of an estimated 20,000 mercenaries only 2000 survived the massacre that followed. They were sent in chains to work as slaves in the Macedonian mines. Casualties amongst the Persians were heavy. Many of their leaders were killed. The Macedonians lost 25 Companions and c 120 cavalry. The battle of the Granicus was the first of many successful military actions that led to the foundation of the greatest empire ever seen in Asia and took Alexander and his army through Syria, Egypt and Afghanistan to the gates of India.

Shortly after leaving **Biga**, with its narrow cobbled streets, a turning to the right leads to 19km **Karabiga**, a small town on the coast. This occupies the site of the ancient city of **Priapus**. According to Strabo, this was probably colonised by the Milesians at the time they established their settlements at Abydos and on Proconnesus.

As its name suggests, the city was sacred to that lusty Phrygian god of procreation and fertility, Priapus, who, in the words of the poet came and cried 'Why peak and pine, unhappy wight, when thou mightest bed a bride?' (Theocritus I 81).

The son of Aphrodite and Dionysus or Aphrodite and Hermes, Priapus was abandoned by his mother, because of his grotesque appearance. A popular god, his ithyphallic statues, decked with garlands, were placed in gardens and vineyards to protect the crops from the evil eye and to encourage growth. Donkeys were sacrificed in his honour, perhaps because of their reputation for unbridled lust or because a donkey awoke the sleeping nymph Lotis before Priapus could ravish her.

Strabo suggests that Priapus was honoured by the inhabitants of this part of the Propontis, because his father was Dionysus and, because 'their country is abundantly supplied with the vine'. According to another legend, he was born in Lampsacus, but was exiled by his fellow-citizens because of his ugliness. The gods took pity on him and made him the symbol of fertility and the protector of all growing things.

From Biga Road 200 ascends the NE slopes of Dede Dağı before descending to the sea near Şevketiye. It then follows the coastline to 56km **Lapseki**, the ancient Lampsacus, which was also associated with Priapus.

After his fall from power and flight to Persia, Themistocles (c 525–449 BC) was awarded Lampsacus, Magnesia and Myus by Artaxerxes. Just over 100 years later Alexander, bribed by the philosopher Anaximenes at the behest of the council, bypassed the city on his march to the Granicus. Lampsacus was described by Strabo (c 64 BC–c AD 24) as 'a notable city with a good harbour, and still flourishing, like Abydus'. It was famous for its wines which, its inhabitants claimed, were worthy of the gods.

From Lapseki Road 200 follows the coast before turning inland and passing through a flat, uninteresting stretch of countryside to reach Çanakkale.

ÇANAKKALE, an important communications centre, occupies a strategic position on the Asian side of the Dardanelles, which at this point are a little more than 1km wide. There are frequent services by car-ferry to Eceabat on the European shore.

Information and Accommodation. Because of its proximity to the battlefields of the Gallipoli campaign, and to Troy, Çanakkale's hotels are often full. The four-star *Akol Oteli* and the modest *Anzak Oteli* are recommended. The pleasant, comfortable three-star *Tusan Hotel* at Güzelyale S of Çanakkale is conveniently close to Troy. If possible, reservations should be made well in advance. The **Tourist Information Office** near the ferry terminal can advise on excursions to the battlefields and to Troy. The hotels and restaurants along the sea-front serve good, plain food.

Transport. Çanakkale's busy *otogar* is c 500m inland from the sea-front. There are frequent services via Bursa and Thrace to İstanbul and, via Edremit, to İzmir and by dolmuş to Troy.

The **Archaeological Museum** is c 1.5km from the town centre on the road to Troy. The Askeri Müze, is in the military area S of the ferry-terminal.

History. The legendary Helle and her brother Phrixus fled on the back of a winged ram from their evil stepmother Ino who planned to sacrifice them to Zeus Laphystius. Phrixus succeeded in reaching Colchis safely, but Helle fell from the ram's back and drowned in the strait which thereafter bore her name.

Because of its strategic situation it is probable that settlers were attracted to the Hellespont from very early times. According to Strabo, Abydus, which was a short distance to the N of Çanakkale, was founded by Milesian colonists, 'by permission of Gyges, king of the Lydians'.

According to another legend, the youth Leander swam each night from Abydus to visit the priestess Hero who lived in a high tower in Sestus on the European side of the Hellespont. One stormy night the light, placed by Hero to guide him, was extinguished by the wind and Leander drowned. In the morning Hero saw her lover's body at the base of the tower and, throwing herself down, was united with him in death.

In 480 BC the Persian Xerxes (?519–465 BC) set out from Asia Minor to subdue the Greeks. So that his army could across the Hellespont, he built a great pontoon bridge that stretched from Abydus to Sestus.

In May 334 BC Alexander the Great left Parmenion to supervise the crossing of the main body of the army from Sestus to Abydus and went south to Elaeus at the tip of the Thracian Chersonese. There, at the tomb of the ill-fated Protesilaus who was struck down by Hector as he leaped ashore at Troy, Alexander offered sacrifice to the hero's shade. Midway on the crossing to the Asian shore he offered a bull to Poseidon and poured wine from a gold cup into the sea to propitiate the Nereids. As the royal barge grounded in the shallows of the harbour of the Achaeans at Troy, emulating Protesilaus, Alexander cast his spear ashore to make his claim on the Persian empire.

In 1810 Lord Byron, imitating Leander, swam across the Hellespont from the European to the Asian side. In a letter to his friend Henry Drury he wrote:

'Salsette frigate, May 3d 1810 in the Dardanelles off Abydos. This morning I swam from Sestos to Abydos, the immediate distance is not above a mile but the current renders it hazardous, so much so, that I doubt whether Leander's conjugal powers must not have been exhausted in his passage to Paradise'.

In the military zone to the S of the quay is the **Kalei Sultaniye fortress**, now known as the Çimenlik Kale. This was built by Mehmet II Fatih (1451–81) in 1454 and enlarged during the reign of Abdül Aziz (1861–76). Still a military establishment, the top of the walls is out of bounds.

There is a reconstruction of the Turkish minelayer *Nusrat*, which played an important part in the Gallipoli campaign and an interesting collection of old French, English and German guns, the relics of many wars. A small museum houses exhibits connected with Atatürk and World War I.

The **Archaeological Museum** is a 20-minute walk from the town centre on the main road S towards Troy, past the market-place and a bridge. The museum is on the left-hand side of the road.

The collection, though small, is well displayed. Most exhibits are labelled, many in English. A large mural in the entrance hall shows the location of the principal sites in the Troad. There is no guide-book.

In the garden and on the terrace there are stelae, sarcophagi and funerary urns, from the Troad. Hellenistic and Roman stelae, one with the figures outlined against a red background, are exhibited in the entrance hall. Inside are fossils, prehistoric remains, a kouros from Lampsacus, various finds from Beşiğetepe, and a selection of artefacts dating from the archaic to the classical periods found at Anafartalar.

Among the exhibits from Troy are a crystal lion head and crystal amulet (Troy II); cycladic-type idols and a cover in the form of a female head (Troy III); stemmed goblets and a headless female statue (Troy VI); terracottas and statuettes, including some from the Calvert collection (Troy VIII). In addition to Roman, Byzantine and Ottoman coins there is a collection of electron ornaments and coins from the Troad.

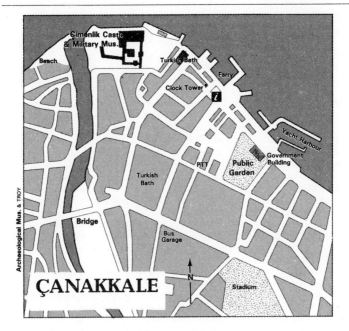

The **Dardanos tumulus**, 11km S of Çanakkale, which was excavated in 1974, was used for burials from the 4C to the 1C BC. Exhibits from the tumulus include bronze utensils, household goods, cinerary urns, remains of wooden objects, shoes, combs, boxes, diadems, gold and ivory ornaments and terracottas. Note the particularly fine Eros and the figure with a lyre.

Excavations in 1961 in the necropolis on **Bozcaada** (Tenedos) produced grave goods from the 7C to the 1C BC. In the museum are magnificent gold ornaments, fibulae, a ring with a representation of Artemis, three seated figures of Cybele, and a skyphos with a youth and sphinxes.

7

Çanakkale to Troy

Total distance 32km.

There is a dolmuş service, frequent during the summer, from Çanakkale's *otogar* to Troy. For the return journey you may have to hire a taxi, as the last dolmuş often leaves Troy in the mid afternoon, well before the site closes; the alternative is a 5km walk to the main road, where is it is usually possible to pick up a bus.

During the holiday season there are organised tours from Çanakkale to Troy and other places in the Troad. The time allowed at Troy on these tours, though limited, is usually sufficient for the non-specialist visitor. If you have your own transport you may like to use the three-star *Tusan Hotel* in Güzelyalı as a base for the exploration of Troy and the northern Troad.

From Çanakkale Road 550/E24 follows the coastline for c 14km before turning inland.

A turning to the right leads to the **Dardanus Tumulus** (see Çanakkale Archaeological Museum). The tumulus is not open to visitors.

The road curves upwards through a pine wood, passing memorials to the Turkish dead of World War I. From the crest, at the village of Intepe, there is a good view of Homer's 'wind-swept' Plain of Ilium.

After crossing the Dümrek Su, the ancient river Simois, a road to the right winds over bare, rounded hills to the village of **Truva** and the site of Troy.

In Truva there are souvenir shops, a few restaurants and coffee-houses. There is a washroom/toilet at the entrance to the site.

TROY is screened from the road by a clump of trees which provides welcome shade in summer. Entrance is through a small garden, which has a collection of architectural fragments. Note the marble pedestal of a statue of the Roman tribune Lucius Vinuleius Pataecius which was erected in his honour by the Boule and the people. The Greek inscription states that Lucius served as a cavalry commander in Africa, Asia and Thrace during the reign of Vespasian (AD 69–79). Nothing further is known about him.

Nearby there is an incongruous, modern reconstruction of the wooden horse. Many of the objects found at Troy are in the Çanakkale museum and in one of the new galleries of the İstanbul Archaeological Museum.

According to the 3C AD writer Philostratus, Troy was haunted by the ghosts of the great heroes who had lived, fought and died there. When Julian the Apostate (361–363) visited Troy, he was astonished to find that offerings were being made by Pegasios, the bishop of Ilium Novum, as the city was known in Roman times, at the tomb believed to shelter the bones of Hector, and in the temple of Athena. This association of the site with the Trojan War continued down through the ages and it may have been one of the factors that led Schliemann and the other 19C investigators to it.

Whatever credence one places in the story of the abduction of Helen by Paris and of the expedition mounted by her husband, Menelaus, to recover her and avenge the wrong done to him, it is certain that Troy existed at, and indeed long before, the time ascribed to these alleged events.

Excavations have unearthed 46 levels of occupation and nine cities or settlements, dating from 3000–2500 BC to AD 400, have been identified.

Troy I (3000–2500 BC) was a small fortification, probably occupied by a community that made its living from fishing. There has been considerable change in the geological structure of the area and it is almost certain that the sea was much nearer to the site than it is at present. Containers of bronze and of pottery which depict the human face were important finds here. The settlement was protected by walls in which comparatively small stones were laid in a herring-bone pattern. Troy I was destroyed by a conflagration.

Troy II (2500–2200 BC) is one of the first cities in western Asia Minor to show evidence of town-planning. Although the diameter of the area enclosed by its walls was only 110m, it contained a large megaron for the ruler and several smaller megara which were aligned to make a continuous frontage. As in Troy I, the principal gate was on the S side. There were several other entrances. On the SW there was a large paved ramp, 21m long and 7.5m wide, that sloped inwards as it rose. Schliemann believed that this had been used by the Trojans to bring the wooden horse inside the walls. However, the city of the Trojan War, if such a conflict ever took place, was either Troy VI or Troy VIIA and was c 1000 years later.

Schliemann was mistaken about the cache of gold and jewellery which he discovered in a section of wall to the left of the ramp and which he described as the 'treasure of Priam'. This also belonged to the period of Troy

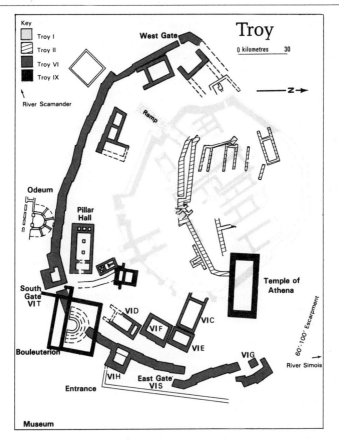

II. All that remains of this treasure are a gold bracelet and gold earrings, which are in the İstanbul Archaeological Museum. The bulk of the find, which Schliemann removed from Turkey without the permission of the government, was kept in a Berlin museum from where it disappeared during World War II. There is a suggestion that it may be in Moscow.

Troy II may have gained some of its wealth and importance from its strategic location. Some authorities believe that for the first time in its history it levied taxes on ships passing through the Hellespont and on goods carried overland through Trojan territory to avoid the difficult sea passage. Troy II was destroyed by fire, probably as the result of an attack by Indo-European invaders.

Troy III to Troy V (2300–1800 BC) were settlements of minor importance, apparently occupied by the descendants of those who survived the destruction of Troy II. There is no evidence that the invaders, who had taken the city, settled there. The houses were mean and small and, at least during Troy IV, the city was not fortified. The population probably supported itself by farming and fishing.

Troy VI (1800–1275 BC) marks a return to greatness. This city, built by newcomers to the site, was enclosed by well-constructed walls which ran in straight courses turning at an angle where a change of direction was needed. Substantial stretches remain and there is a good example of one of the city's defensive towers at the NW corner of the mound.

The roof of one of the houses in Troy VI was supported by large square pillars. Note the recesses in the walls which may have served as cupboards or shrines for cult-statues. Most of the pottery found at this level is grey Minyan, but there are also some examples of imported Mycenaean ware and there are many built-in storage pithoi.

Turkish archaeologists believe that this was the city of Priam which for ten years resisted the Greeks and which was finally destroyed by an earthquake. The most recent discoveries tend to support this hypothesis.

Troy VIIA (1275–1240 BC). Troy VIIA is believed by the American archaeologists to be the city of the Trojan War. They argue as follows. After the earthquake the walls were hastily and poorly repaired. There is evidence that many people were crowded into the small area inside the defensive system. Large quantities of food and other supplies were stored in pithoi under the floors of the houses. Trade with Mycenaean Greece ceased and, most tellingly, the city was destroyed by human action. According to Professor Blegen, Troy VIIA 'was ruthlessly laid waste by the hand of man who completed his work of destruction by fire'.

However, a number of historians do not accept that there was a war fought at Troy by a combination of Greeks or Mycenaeans against the Trojans and their allies. Professor Finley pointed out 'that the archaeologists had found no trace of war at Troy other than a single bronze arrowhead, and certainly no trace of a coalition, let alone a Mycenaean coalition'. A colloquium on the Trojan War held some years ago reached the same conclusion, stating that 'on present evidence there is neither room nor reason for Mycenaean hostilities against Troy'.

Finley suggested that the destruction of Troy in the 13C BC may be laid at the door of the mysterious Sea People, whose activities brought about the downfall of so many civilisations in the Eastern Mediterranean at that time. It appears unlikely that the contentious matter of the Trojan War will ever be settled conclusively.

Sometime after its destruction, the site was re-occupied by newcomers who brought with them a distinctive knobbed ware, previously found in sites in the Balkans. This phase lasted until c 1100 BC. Profesor Akurgal suggested that Troy may have been colonised by immigrants from the Aegean, who later took part in the destruction of Hattusa c 1180 BC and fought the Assyrian Tiglath-Pileser I c 1165 and Ramesses III (1198–76) of Egypt. Perhaps these invaders are the same as Finley's Sea People.

No remains have been found at Troy from 1100 for a period of c 400 years. The site was occupied by immigrants from Lesbos c 700 BC and the new settlement, Troy VIII, appears to have been a small market town. Captured by the Persians in the 6C, it remained under their control until the arrival of Alexander the Great in 334 BC (see above).

Troy IX (350 BC–AD 400) was the Hellenistic and Roman city. Before marching against the Persians, Alexander made a pilgrimage to Troy. He sacrificed at the temple of Athena, leaving his armour as an offering and taking in exchange weapons that were believed to date from the time of the Trojan War. Having made a propitiatory offering to the spirit of Priam, he received gold crowns from Menoetius, his sailing-master and from Chares, a citizen of Sigeum, the place where Menelaus and his Greek allies had beached their ships. Then, having anointed his body with oil, he ran naked to the place where Achilles was buried. He honoured the dead hero by placing a wreath on the tomb, while his friend Hephaestion performed the same service at the tomb of Achilles' companion Patroclus.

Alexander accorded a number of privileges to Troy and promised to build a new temple in honour of Athene. This promise was kept by his friend and successor, Lysimachus.

Destroyed c 82 BC during the Mithridatic Wars, Troy was rebuilt after a visit to the city by Julius Caesar in 48 BC. As the birthplace of Aeneas, the mythical founder of Rome, it was accorded special treatment by several Roman emperors. The reconstructed temple of Athena, promised by Julius Caesar, was completed during the reign of Augustus, and later an odeum, a theatre and other buildings were erected in the city.

Somewhat overshadowed by the newly-established city of Alexandria Troas in the southern Troad, the township of Ilium Novum, as Troy had become known, was an episcopal see in the 4C. It appears to have entered a period of gradual decline, perhaps because of the silting up of its harbour, but excavations show that it was occupied during the reign of Justinian in the 6C.

Coins and pottery testify to some kind of settlement here as late as the 12C, when the Troad was ruled by the Selçuks. Under the Ottoman Turks the site of the ancient city appears to have been abandoned, but there were several small villages in the surrounding plain.

Abandoned perhaps, but not forgotten. Troy continued to attract visitors during the centuries that followed. In 1444 that indefatigable traveller Cyriac of Ancona visited the Troad. He was followed almost 20 years later by Mehmet II. According to the historian Critoboulos of İmbros, after he had:

'inspected the ruins...(and was) shown the tombs of the heroes Achilles, Hector and Ajax, (he said) It is to me that Allah has given to avenge this city and its people.... Indeed it was the Greeks who before devastated this city, and it is their descendants who after so many years have paid me the debt which their boundless pride had contracted...towards us, the peoples of Asia'.

In the early 17C the Scottish traveller William Lithgow cast a sceptical eye over the remains of the ancient city:

'when we landed,' he wrote, 'we saw here and there many relics of old walls and many tombs, which were mighty ruinous. Our Greek [interpreter] pointed us particularly to the tombs of Hector, Ajax, Achilles, Troilus and many other valiant champions—well, I wot I saw infinite old sepulchres, but for their particular names and nomination of them I suspend; neither could I believe my interpreter, sith it is more than three thousand odd years ago that Troy was destroyed!'

Byron visited in May 1810. In a letter to Henry Drury he wrote:

'The Troad is a fine field for conjecture and Snipe-shooting, and a good sportsman and an ingenious scholar may exercise their feet and faculties upon the spot, or if they prefer riding lose their way (as I did) in a cursed quagmire of the Scamander who wriggles about as if the Dardan virgins still offered their wonted tribute. The only vestige of Troy, or her destroyers, are the barrows supposed to contain the carcases of Achilles, Antilochus, Ajax but Mt Ida is still in high feather, though the Shepherds are nowadays not much like Ganymede'.

In the 19C Frank Calvert explored many of the ancient sites in the Troad and he passed on some of his ideas, and his enthusiasm, to Schliemann.

Heinrich Schliemann (1822–90) was born in Mecklenburg in N Germany, the son of poor parents. Interested from an early age in the Greek myths, his ambition was to find Troy. He taught himself ancient Greek and several modern languages, became a successful business man, and amassed a considerable fortune. Then at the age of 46 he abandoned his commercial career and, Homer in hand, set out to find the city of Priam.

Schliemann made a number of remarkable discoveries, including the so-called 'Treasure of Priam'. His work was continued by Wilhelm Dörpfeld and later by Professor Blegen and archaeologists from the University of Cincinnati. Their combined efforts have revealed the nine cities described above, one of which may have been the 'well-walled city with lofty gates' of the *Iliad*.

Although visitors from William Lithgow and Lord Byron onwards have been disappointed by Troy, the sudden dramatic revelation of the mound beyond the trees seldom fails to produce a frisson of surprise. Allowed to decay for centuries and raped by treasure-hunters and archaeologists, it is 'an over-grown maze of superimposed ruins of many ages, a jumble of gullies and ditches choked with bushes and ruins', yet there is a sense that here is a place of great historical importance.

Archaeologists may argue about its physical remains and scholars debate the historicity of the Trojan War, nevertheless for many visitors Troy has a numinous appeal and imagination helps to conjure up the city of Homer from the chaotic muddle of stones and tangled vegetation.

In front of the excavated area there is a large plan, which shows the location of the various cities. There are also small descriptive notices in English on the site. Arrows indicate the route to be followed.

The visitor's attention is seized by a substantial section, c 90m long and 6m high, of the wall of cities VI and VII. This was reinforced by a tower (VIH on plan). Entrance to the site is by a gate (VIS on plan) on the E side of the mound. To the right there was a **look-out tower** (VIG on plan), which contained a large cistern.

Turning towards the centre the route passes on the left the ruins of four large **houses** (VIF, VIE, VIC and VID on plan). Note the storage *pithoi* in one.

At this point it is worth pausing to admire the fine view over the Plain of Troy. Two lines of willows mark the present courses of the rivers Simois (to the N) and Scamander (to the SW). These have probably changed their courses several times. To the N near Cape Sigeum is the **harbour of the Achaeans**, where the Greeks beached their ships. Not far from the harbour are the mounds that, according to tradition, mark the graves of Achilles and Ajax. If the weather is clear, Samothrace, from where Poseidon surveyed the events at Troy, may be glimpsed towering over nearer Imbros. To the SE is Mt Ida, where Zeus sat enthroned during the conflict.

On the right the site of the **Temple of Athena** is marked by a large hole, produced by various excavators. It was here that Xerxes sacrificed before starting out on his invasion of Greece. According to Herodotus,

> 'Xerxes had a strong desire to see Troy, the ancient city of Priam. Accordingly he went up into the citadel, and when he had seen what he wanted to see and heard the story of the place from the people there, he sacrificed a thousand oxen to the Trojan Athene, and the Magi made libations of wine to the spirits of the great men of old'.

Some fragments from the Doric temple constructed by Lysimachus, which covers part of Troy II's fortifications, may be seen in the excavation.

After passing some of the oldest remains on the site, fortifications and houses from Troy I, the route reaches the **large ramp** (see Troy II above), where Schliemann found the treasure. It then goes outside the fortified area, where there Hellenistic and Roman remains. These include a **baths complex** with mosaic pavements, the **odeum** and the **bouleuterion**.

To the left of the bouleuterion the S gate (VIT) provides access to the so-called **pillar-house** (see Troy VI above).

Excavations continue at Troy. The partly-collapsed tower R of Troy I fortifications has been restored and the E part of the trench made by Schliemann cleared.

8

Troy to Assos

Total distance 64km. Troy—24km Ezine—(c 16km Neandria) (c 21km Alexandria Troas—c 20km Bozcaada)—22km Ayvacık—18km Behramkale (Assos) (26km—Apollo Smintheus).

According to Strabo, writing in the 1C AD, the Troad, an area of rich farmland and forest, attracted many colonists both Greek and barbarian. Stretching S from Troy, the regular pattern of its fields of wheat and maize is pleasantly broken by groves of cypress, tamarisk and valonia oak. Vines and olives are cultivated extensively and the slopes of Mt Ida, which dominates the SE section, are covered with forests.

Transport. A good bus service links Çanakkale with Ezine and Ayvacık. There are infrequent dolmuş services from Ezine to Odun İskelesi (Alexandria Troas) and from Ayvacık to Behramkale.

If you do not have your own transport you will need to rent a car or take a taxi to visit Neandria and Apollo Smintheus.

Accommodation and restaurants. There are a few pensions and restaurants around Odun İskelesi and Behramkale has several small hotels, pensions and restaurants in the lower village. The *Hotel Behram* in Behramkale is recommended. Many of the hotels and pensions are open only during the holiday season.

To visit **Neandria** take the road from Ezine to Geyikli and Odun İskelesi. After c 6km, take the signposted turning on the left to the site. Neandria was built on an outcrop of Mt Çığrı sometime in the 7C BC. The city, which occupied an area c 1.5km long by 500m wide, is enclosed by a well-preserved wall. In the centre there are the remains of a small temple of simple construction. Elaborately ornamented Aeolic capitals from seven columns in the centre of the cella are now in the İstanbul Archaeological Museum.

Return to the main road continue for c 5km towards Odun İskelesi. The ruins of **Alexandria Troas** are scattered over a wide area and are not easy to explore. Eric Newby remarks ruefully in *On the Shores of the Mediterranean*, 'although the city was said to have walls six miles long and itself covered 1000 acres it was perfectly possible ... to walk into it through one of the now enormous gaps in the walls and walk out through a similar gap on the far side, without ... seeing much of Alexandria Troas at all'.

History. After the death of Alexander the Great in 323 BC, his empire was dismembered by his generals. Antigonus I Monophthalmus acquired Greater Phrygia, Lycia and Pamphylia. About 300 BC he founded a city, which he named Antigonia after himself and to which he brought the inhabitants of Neandria and other settlements in the Troad. In 301 Antigonus, then aged 81, and his son Demetrius were slain at the battle of Ipsus in Phrygia. The victor Lysimachus, king of Macedonia, took over their territories and renamed Antigonia Alexandria Troas, in honour of Alexander the Great.

Although the city had only an artificial harbour, it became a major trading centre. Its strategic location enabled it to take over the control, previously exercised by Troy, of the sea and land-traffic between the Aegean and the Propontis (Sea of Marmara).

During both the Hellenistic and Roman periods, Alexandria Troas prospered, acquiring wealth and status. A city of rich and beautiful buildings, both Julius Caesar and Constantine considered establishing their capitals there.

Alexandria Troas was visited twice by St Paul. With Timothy he had intended to go to Bithynia, but during the night he had a vision in Alexandria Troas: 'A certain Macedonian stood by him in entreaty, and said, Come over into Macedonia, and help us. So we put out from Troas, making a straight course for Samothrace, and next day to Neapolis (Kavala)'. (Acts 16, 9–12.) On the second occasion Paul continued preaching long after midnight and a young man named Eutychus, overcome by sleep, fell from a third-storey window. 'Paul went down, bent over him, and embraced him; then he said, Do not disturb yourselves; his life is yet in him'. (Acts 20,10.) Later he wrote to Timothy and asked him to bring 'the cloak which I left in Carpus' hands in Troas; the books, too, and above all the rolls of parchment'. (II Timothy, 4,13.)

As Constantinople increased in importance so Alexandria Troas declined. During the Ottoman period, when the city was known as Eski Stamboul, it was plundered for building material. Stone and marble taken from here were used to construct a number of buildings, including Sultan Ahmet Camii (the Blue Mosque).

Richard Chandler, who visited the city in the summer of 1764, saw the considerable remains of the city's fortifications, which had square towers at regular intervals. He also found the foundations of a large building, which he believed to have been a temple. He was told that bandits hid there, presumably to rob any passing travellers. However, the only living creatures he saw were large bats, which, disturbed by his party, eventually returned to settle on the roof. He also found a number of inscriptions and examined the baths, which he wrongly identified as a gymnasium.

Apart from the ruins of the **baths**, which the magnate Herodes Atticus donated to the city c AD 135, very little is visible of Alexandria Troas. The baths, located on the right-hand side of the road at the approach to the site, had several large vaulted chambers.

Most of the city is now covered by fields, over whose surface a vast quantity of pottery sherds is scattered. Clumps of valonia oak crown small eminences and outline the boundaries. Unidentified architectural fragments covered by undergrowth are encountered from time to time. Down by the harbour there are parts of a few columns, presumably abandoned by those who carried away the stone and marble to İstanbul.

Around the harbour and on the road S to Tavakli İskele there are several small restaurants. A ferry from Odun İskelesi goes to **Bozcaada**, ancient Tenedos. Here Achilles slew Tenes, the son of Apollo, and it was to Tenedos that the Greeks withdrew their ships, when they wished to make the Trojans believe that they had abandoned the siege of Troy. Xerxes used the island as a naval base. Later it supported Athens during the Peloponnesian War. Re-occupied by the Persians, it was liberated by Alexander the Great. Today Bozcaada is best known for its light white wine which is much appreciated by habitués of certain restaurants in İstanbul and İzmir.

By making a slight detour at Gülpınar, you can visit the site of the 2C BC **Temple of Apollo Smintheus** at ancient Chryse.

Well-signposted, this is reached by following a narrow lane for c 250m from the centre of the village. Shaded by pomegranate trees, the temple, a pseudo-dipteros of the Ionic order with 8 by 14 columns, is currently being excavated. The stylobate, which measures 24m by 43m, has been exposed and is surrounded by fragments of sculpture, inscriptions and a number of Turkish tombstones. The site was visited by Spratt in the middle of the 19C.

The legendary Teucer, a hero born on Mt Ida in Crete, left with his father, Scamander, and a group of followers during a period of famine and came to the Troad. Before their departure they were told by a seer that they should settle at the place where they were attacked by 'the sons of the earth'. On waking one morning they found that their armour and equipment had been partly eaten by mice. Deciding that this must be the place meant by the oracle, they made a settlement and built a temple in honour of Apollo Smintheus, i.e. Apollo Lord of the Mice. According to Aelian there was a representation of a mouse in the temple. Teucer became the first king of Troy and for that reason the Trojans were sometimes called Teucri.

About 100m down the lane there are the remains of some other buildings which so far have not been excavated.

From Gülpınar, continue to 26km Behramkale.

Leave Ezine on Road 550 for 22km Ayvacik. A minor road winds high above a deep valley, then crosses a bare plateau before reaching the village of **Behramkale** (ancient **ASSOS**). A short distance from the village, the old road is carried on the graceful pointed arches of a 14C Turkish **bridge** over the Tuzla brook, the ancient Satnioeis. Behramkale occupies a picturesque site on the crest of a ridge that descends steeply, on the S side, to the sea.

Accommodation and Restaurants. Clustered around the harbour at the bottom of the ridge are several hotels, pensions, and restaurants which are usually open only during the season. Öcal Elmacioğlu presides over the well-run *Hotel Behram* whose dining room is a just few metres from the sea. Behramkale, still largely the preserve of the cognoscenti, is a most attractive and restful place where one may spend delightful days exploring the ruins of Assos or gazing idly at mist-shrouded Lesbos which floats, an insubstantial wraith, on the distant horizon.

History. Assos was founded by immigrants from Methymna in Lesbos early in the first millennium BC. In the 6C BC it was ruled by Lydia and later, as part of the province of Phrygia, it came under Persian dominion. The governor of Assos, Ariobarzanes, revolted against Persian rule in 365 BC, but he was defeated by Artaxerxes.

Its period of greatest glory in the 4C BC, when with the Troad and Lesbos, it was ruled by the eunuch Hermeias. A former student of Plato, Hermeias welcomed a number of philosophers and scientists to the city. Aristotle and Theophrastus lived here during the years 348–345 and carried out some important studies in the natural sciences. Aristotle became a close friend of Hermeias and eventually married his niece, Pythia. Later, the philosopher moved to Lesbos and then to Pella, where he became tutor to the young Alexander. Hermeias had an unhappy end. He was captured by the Persians and tortured to death.

Cleanthes, the Stoic philosopher, who studied under Zeno, was born in Assos c 331 BC. In Athens he aroused suspicion because he had no visible means of support. When it was discovered that he worked all night drawing water and studied all day, the Areopagus awarded him a small pension. Zeno forbade him to take it.

Cleanthes stressed disinterestedness. To do good to others with a view to one's own benefit was no different from feeding cattle in order to eat their flesh.

Like Troy, Assos was overshadowed by Alexandria Troas, and declined in importance during the Hellenistic period. From 241–133 BC it was ruled by the kings of Pergamum.

St Paul, walking overland from Alexandria Troas, came to Assos during his third missionary journey. He met Luke and other companions in the city and together they sailed to Lesbos. During the Byzantine period Assos declined in importance and was little more than a hamlet. This situation continued after its conquest by Orhan in 1330.

Interest in Assos was revived in the 19C as a result of research by an American archaeological team. The site is currently being excavated by Turkish archaeologists.

You approach the upper part of ancient Assos through the narrow lanes of the modern village. Here children proffer hand-knitted and crocheted garments to visitors. On the left, at the top of the hill, beyond the Byzantine fortifications, there is a **mosque**, now secularised, which is believed to date from the reign of Murat I Hüdavendigar (1359–89). Constructed with materials from a 6C church, it has two marble columns, each surmounted by a different type of capital, at its entrance. Over the door a marble slab with a cross and Chi-Rho symbol carries an inscription in Greek which states that the church was built by one Cornelius for the forgiveness of his sins. Surmounted by a dome 11m in diameter, the building has traces of decoration on its interior walls. Note the interesting lozenge design over the second window from the entrance gate to the enclosure. There is a fine view over the village and N towards the 14C Turkish bridge from the terrace.

A short climb will bring you to a plateau, 238m above sea-level, on which the **Temple of Athena** stood. Like many of the buildings at Assos, this was constructed of andesite, an igneous rock often found in volcanic areas. Dating from c 530 BC, it was a mixture of the Doric and Ionic styles, with a decorative frieze on the architrave. A temple in antis with 13 by 6 columns, its stylobate measures 14m by 30m. The temenos, which is currently being excavated by Turkish archaeologists, is covered with scattered columns and capitals. Some of the columns have been re-erected. A number of the reliefs from the temple are in İstanbul's Archaeological Museum.

In summer the view from the temple is one of the most beautiful in W Turkey. Across the calm waters of the Bay of Edremit, Lesbos, homeland of the first settlers in Assos, is clothed in a purple haze. Far below lies the little harbour, from which St Paul sailed on his missionary journeys, while on terraces cut into the steep slope of the hill the ruins of the ancient city protrude like sun-dried bones through the maquis.

A goat track leads down from the plateau to the **agora**, whose buildings of andesite date for the most part from the 3C and 2C BC. At the W end are the barely-distinguishable ruins of the 2C BC **agora temple**, which appears to have been modified when it was used for Christian worship. On the N side of the agora there was a two-storey Doric **colonnade**, which measured 111m by 12.5m. Note the holes in the rear wall which held the timber supports of the upper floor.

On the S this was complemented by a three-storey **stoa** of unusual construction. The top floor, which was on the same level as the first floor of the N colonnade, was completely open. Overlooking both the agora and the sea, it was a pleasant promenade for the citizens of Assos. The lower and basement floors, which were closed on the N side, housed 13 shops, a bathing establishment and cisterns. An air gap of 20cm between the middle floor and the rock-wall served to insulate it, ensuring that it was free from humidity and had the same temperature throughout the year.

At the E end of the agora at right angles to the **Hellenistic bouleuterion** stood a **bema**, from which politicians, philosophers and others could address the public. The 3C BC Greek-style **theatre** of Assos, of which practically nothing remains, was built on a terrace below the E end of the agora.

An arched gateway to the W of the agora temple leads to the site of a 2C BC **gymnasium**, which contained a paved courtyard surrounded by colonnades. During the Byzantine period a church was constructed on the NE side of this courtyard. Today little remains of either structure.

Assos was protected by a magnificent **wall** of carefully cut and fitted stone blocks. This is one of the most impressive ancient fortifications in Anatolia. Built during the 4C BC, it stretched for more than 3km and was strengthened by towers that had slits and openings from which missiles and stones could be hurled at the enemy. The best preserved section, which reaches a height of 14m, is to the W of the gymnasium. The **principal gate** of the city was here. This was flanked by two towers, one of which (on the E side) is almost complete. There were several other gates, all of which differed in style. One, very well-preserved, is a short distance to the NE.

The necropolis of Assos, which is being excavated, was on a hillside to the W of the city. Here there is a confusion of Hellenistic and Roman sarcophagi, lying in the sad disorder created by ancient tomb-robbers. The sarcophagi of Assos were famous during antiquity and were exported widely. According to Pliny the stone from which they were made contained a caustic substance which consumed the flesh of bodies placed in them within 40 days. 'Sarcophagus', which means 'carnivorous' or 'flesh-eater', is derived from that property.

The stretch of wall to the left of the modern road shows an interesting join between the regular courses laid down by the 4C BC builders and an older polygonal fortification. Note also, on the right-hand side of the road, the remains of a paved street which descended towards the harbour area.

9

Assos to Pergamum

Total distance c 182km. Assos—18km Ayvacık—59km Edremit/Akçay—
46km Ayvalık—30km Dikili—24km Bergama/Pergamum.

From Assos you have the choice of returning to Ayvacık or taking the picturesque coastal road to Küçükkuyu. Continue to Edremit. Long distance buses stop here, but some by-pass Ayvalık, dropping passengers off on the main road c 5km from the town. A number make the detour to Bergama. There are also bus and dolmuş services from Ayvalık.

There are several hotels on the road to Edremit, notably the three-star *Güneş Hotel* at Altınoluk. In the town there is the two-star *Bilgiçler Hotel*, Menderes Bul. 63, and a number of one-star hotels. The **Tourist Information Office** is at Edremit Cad, 20. Edremit.

Ayvalık is a popular seaside resort and has a wide range of accommodation. In addition to the five-star *Grand Hotel Temizel* at Sahilboyu Mevkii Sarımsaklı, there are seven three-star and many two- and one-star hotels in the town and at Sarımsaklı Plaj, a pleasant suburb to the S. The **Tourist Information Office** is in Yat Limanı Karşısı.

In Bergama there is one two-star hotel, *Bergama İskender Oteli*, İzmir Cad., and a number of more modest establishments. The comfortable M2 *Tusan Bergama Moteli* is 8km outside the town at the junction of 550/E24 with the 240 to Bergama.

From Ayvacık you climb through sharp bends over a spur of Kaz Dağı (1710m), the ancient Mt Ida where Paris gave the golden apple to Aphrodite and set in train the events that ended with the destruction of Troy.

Road 550/E24 descends through a deep cleft, reaching the sea at Küçük-kuyu. It passes some fine sandy beaches, each with its complement of holiday villas. The coastline of the Gulf of Edremit, sheltered by Mt Ida, enjoys a warmer, more temperate climate than the Troad. Its green, fertile landscape is dotted with tiny villages set in a sea of fruit trees and olive groves.

Both Edremit and Akçay have associations with the Trojan War. **Edremit** (64km), which preserves the form of its ancient name, Adramyttium, was the home of Achilles' beautiful captive, Chryseis, and it was from Antan-dros near Akçay that Aeneas, his father Anchises and their Trojan followers set sail for Rome. Today **Akçay** is one of many small, popular seaside resorts in the north Aegean.

After Akçay the road turns away from the sea and does not return to the coastline again, until it reaches 46km **Ayvalık**. It has some good restaurants both in the centre and on Ali Bey Adası which is linked by a causeway to the mainland. Magnificent sunsets and a panoramic view of Ayvalık's island-studded bay provide an agreeable accompaniment to dinner in the restaurant at Şeytan Sofrası, the 'Devil's Dinnertable', a plateau to the SW of the town.

Between May and September there is a daily ferry-boat service from Ayvalık to the Greek island of **Lesbos (Mytileni)**. Out of season there is usually one boat a week. For the current schedule, fares and formalities apply to the Tourist Information Office.

From Ayvalık the road crosses a narrow fertile plain to 42km Dikili. Here it turns inland to Bergama. **Dikili**, a former fishing village, is a port-of-call for cruise ships, whose passengers disembark here for Pergamum.

Towards 1100 BC mainland Greeks displaced by the Dorian invasions colonised the W shore of Asia Minor. Those who settled in the area known as Aeolia between the Troad and the River Hermus married with the local people and founded 11 cities. According to Herodotus, although Ionia to the S had a better climate, Aeolia was more fertile. Its people appear to have lived quiet, pastoral lives and little is known about their history. Today the scanty remains of their settlements, which for the most part were scattered along the coastline, are likely to be of interest mainly to the specialist.

About 16km from Dikili turn left to 8km **Bergama**, the town which occupies part of the site of ancient **PERGAMUM**.

History. The first settlement at Pergamum was probably made by Aeolic Greeks in the 8C BC. However, possibly because of its distance from the coast, the city appears to have taken little or no part in the affairs of Aeolia.

One of the earliest references to Pergamum is to be found in Xenophon's *Anabasis* (VII.8). In 399 BC, at the end of their long march from Cunaxa near Babylon, Xenophon and his companions reached Pergamum, where they well received by Hellas, the wife of Gongylus of Eretria.

Pergamum came into prominence after the death of Alexander the Great in 323 BC, when it became part of the territory ruled by Lysimachus, one of the Diadochoi. He amassed great wealth from his possessions in Asia Minor and left a substantial part of this, about 9000 talents, in the care of one of his officers, Philetaerus, in the treasury at Pergamum. When Lysimachus, who earlier had murdered his son Agathocles, was slain at the battle of Corupedion in 281 BC by Seleucus I Nicator of Syria, the money and the city remained in the control of Philetaerus. He used it to consolidate his position as *de facto* ruler and to ornament the city with fine public buildings.

Philetaerus was unmarried—it was rumoured that a childhood injury had unmanned him—and he adopted his nephew Eumenes as heir. Though neither man called himself king, Eumenes I (263–241 BC) is usually regarded as the founder of the Pergamene royal dynasty. He soon obtained his independence from Seleucid rule by defeating Antiochus I at the battle of Sardis in 262 BC. His reign was troubled by the incursions of a marauding Celtic tribe which had come from central Europe c 278 BC and settled in Galatia, the area around Ankara. To keep them at bay Eumenes paid bribes and built fortified cities at Philetaeria in the Troad and at Attalia on the Hermus river to the S. Under his rule agriculture and industry prospered. To increase trade he developed the port of Elaea at the mouth of the river Caicus. An inscription records the gratitude of his subjects, who accorded him divine status.

Eumenes was followed by his adopted son, Attalus I (241–197 BC). Perhaps the greatest achievement of his long reign was the defeat of the Celts, for which he was given the title of Soter (Saviour). Less successful in his encounters with the Seleucids and the Macedonians, he sought the assistance of the Romans. It is suggested that he obtained their help by procuring for them from Pessinus in SW Galatia the bethel, a sacred stone, which was believed to represent Cybele the Magna Mater.

During the reign of his successor, Eumenes II (197–160 BC), Pergamum reached its apogee. Eumenes allied himself with Rome against the Seleucids and their combined armies defeated Antiochus the Great at the battle of Magnesia in 190 BC. Pergamum was given a large part of the lands formerly ruled by the Seleucids. This enlarged its territory, extending it from the Propontis to the Maeander and as far into Anatolia as the modern city of Konya.

From being the ruler of a comparatively small city state, Eumenes suddenly found himself in control of a population of c 5 million. His kingdom was fertile and well-endowed with industries. Like his predecessors, he used his resources wisely. Agriculture in all its forms was encouraged and, by the extensive employment of slave-labour, manufactured products like pottery and textiles were made in quantity. One of the most important industrial and cultural developments was the large-scale production of *pergamena*, the writing material made from treated animal skins later known as parchment. This enabled Pergamum to establish and develop a library, which rivalled in scope and size the great library of Alexandria.

Eumenes extended the area of the city and built a new wall to protect it. Terraces were made on the steep hillside and on these magnificent structures like the Great Altar of Zeus and Athena, the theatre, a gymnasium and a new agora were erected.

His generosity was not limited to Pergamum. In Athens he had a two-tiered stoa constructed in the agora. The arts were encouraged and a distinctive Pergamene style, exemplified by works like the frieze depicting the conflict of the Gods and Giants on the Great Altar and the statue of the Dying Celt or Gaul, was developed.

During Eumenes' long reign his kingdom was frequently under attack by the Celts and by predatory and jealous neighbours like the rulers of Pontus and Bithynia. He died, worn out by illness and labour, in 160 BC.

Eumenes was succeeded by his 60-year-old brother, Attalus II (160–138 BC). Apart from a brief period, when he suppported his brother-in-law Ariarathes V in his claim to rule Cappadocia, Attalus maintained good relations with the Romans. He sought their assistance in his struggle with Bithynia and later sent his army to help them in Greece. Anxious to have direct access to the Mediterranean trade, Attalus founded the city of Attaleia (modern Antalya), which he named after himself.

Attalus III (138–133), the last king of Pergamum, was very unlike his predecessors. Remote and aloof, he was disliked by his subjects and had a sinister reputation. A student of medicine and zoology, it was said he experimented in the production of new poisons which he tested on criminals. His treatise on agriculture was frequently mentioned by later writers and there is some evidence of military success.

After a short reign, Attalus died in 133 BC, apparently unloved and unlamented. Eccentric to the end, his final act was to bequeath the kingdom of Pergamum to Rome.

Attalus's bequest was contested by Aristonicus, who claimed to be the illegitimate son of Eumenes II. He was supported by some sections of the population, and it was a number of years before the Romans were able to suppress the revolt and establish their unquestioned rule over the kingdom.

During the last years of the Pergamene monarchy, Roman influence in Asia Minor had been increasing steadily. If Attalus had not left his kingdom to them, it is likely they would have annexed it under one pretext or another. From the western part— Caria, Lydia, Ionia, Mysia and a section of Phrygia—they constructed the Roman province of Asia. The remainder was attached to various principalities and provinces in Anatolia. Under Roman rule Pergamum was, nominally, a free city.

That the change of rulers was accepted unwillingly is evidenced by the support given to Mithridates, king of Pontus, when in 88 BC he attempted to free the Aegean cities from Roman rule. Pergamum was occupied by him for some time and its inhabitants joined in, enthusiastically, in the slaughter of the Romans and Italians living in the city.

After the defeat of Mithridates, Pergamum entered a more stable phase. Under the Pax Romana, an important centre of entrepôt trading, it enjoyed a period of commercial expansion. Many new buildings were constructed and its inhabitants were noted for their liberal support of the arts. Among its most celebrated citizens were the rhetorician Apollodorus and the physician Galen. The author of several medical treatises, Galen (129–c 200) practised at Pergamum in the Asclepieum and in Rome, where the Emperors Marcus Aurelius and Lucius Verus were among his patients.

The city entered a period of decline at the end of the 1C and in the early part of the 2C AD. Competition from trading centres farther E and the damage caused by an earthquake contributed substantially to its decay.

Pergamum is one of the Seven Churches of the Revelation. 'The place where Satan has his altar' (Revelation 2,13) is believed to refer to the Great altar of Zeus. After the adoption of Christianity the city became an important missionary centre. It was an episcopal see during the Byzantine period.

Subjected to frequent attack by marauding Arabs, the city was sacked by them in 717. Later it passed through many hands. Byzantines, Crusaders, the Lascarid dynasty of Nicaea, the Selçuks—all ruled Pergamum before it fell to Orhan in 1336.

The uninteresting approach road to Bergama follows the valley of the Caicus, the modern Bakır Çayı. It is not until the outskirts of the town are reached that the theatre and acropolis are seen, suspended like a painted back-cloth above the roofs.

About 2km from the town turn right to a tumulus known as **Maltepe**. You will need a torch to explore the tumulus which has three burial chambers where the remains of sarcophagi were found. The names of those buried here are not known, but it is believed to date from the 2C or 3C AD.

The ruins of Pergamum are extensive and widely separated. To see them all and to visit the museum would require a minimum of one and a half days. If time permits, it is advisable to see them in this order: first the acropolis, then the Kızıl Avlu (the Red Hall), next the museum and the Islamic antiquities, followed by the Asclepieum, and finally the ruins in the surrounding countryside. If you do not have your own transport take a taxi to the acropolis, as the ascent is long and steep.

In the car-park there are kiosks selling postcards, souvenirs and soft drinks at prices appreciably higher than in the town.

The German Archaeological Institute, which has excavated at Pergamum since 1878, has placed a number of explanatory notices at various points on the site. These are particularly helpful in drawing attention to the most important and, in some cases, the most recent discoveries.

Left of the car-park are the ruins of the **heroon** where the kings of Pergamum, particularly Attalus I and Eumenes II, were honoured. This had an antechamber and cult-room on the E side of a peristyle court. Originally constructed during the Hellenistic period, the heroon was restored by the Romans. Across the street are the remains of storerooms or shops, believed to be Hellenistic.

The **great altar** dedicated to Zeus and Athena, was erected during the reign of Eumenes II to commemorate Pergamum's victory over the Celts by Attalus I. Centred in a square, which was entered from the E, it rested on a 6m-high podium. This was enclosed on three sides by a wall ornamented with a frieze. In a colonnade, which rested on the wall, statues were placed. Access to the altar stone, where sacrifice was offered, was by a magnificent marble stairway c 20m wide on the W side of the structure.

The frieze, which depicted the battle between the giants and the gods, was intended to symbolise the triumph of order over chaos. There were representations of the Olympian deities, including Leto, Artemis, Apollo, Helios, Poseidon, Amphitrite, Zeus and Athena.

The altar was carefully aligned with the earlier temple of Athena which was on a terrace c 25m higher up. This ensured that both buildings seen from a distance made a harmonious whole. As all that remains in situ is the podium, it requires a considerable effort to visualise the splendour of the altar, considered to be one of the finest examples of Hellenistic art.

At some point the altar was dismantled and the stone blocks of the principal frieze were incorporated in a wall. Rediscovered by German archaeologists in the 19C and taken to Germany, they are displayed in a reconstruction of the altar in the Pergamon Museum, Bodestrasse 1/3, Berlin. There is a model of the altar in Bergama's museum.

Pergamum's **upper agora** was immediately to the S of the altar at a slightly lower level. Surrounded by Doric colonnades, it had the usual mixture of shops and storerooms. A small temple, fronted by sacrificial altars, was probably dedicated to Hermes, the god of commerce, wealth and luck. With the exception of the structure in the NW corner, marked by a semicircular recess, which was modified during the Roman period, all of the buildings in the agora were Hellenistic.

From the agora a ramp led upwards to the main entrance to the city. To the left of this is the temenos of the 4C BC **Temple of Athena** The two-storeyed **propylon** at the entrance to the temenos bore an inscription recording its dedication by 'King Eumenes to Athena the bearer of victories'. It has been reconstructed in the Pergamon Museum in Berlin from fragments recovered on the site. The temple was a peripteros of 6 by 10 columns built of andesite in the Doric style. Of this, the oldest surviving temple in Pergamum, only part of the crepidoma remains.

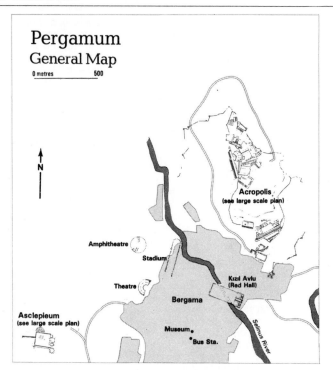

Pergamum
General Map

0 metres   500

N

Acropolis
(see large scale plan)

Amphitheatre

Stadium

Theatre

Kızıl Avlu
(Red Hall)

Bergama

Selinus River

Asclepieum
(see large scale plan)

Museum

Bus Sta.

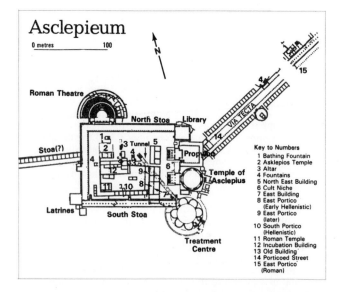

Asclepieum

0 metres   100

N

Roman Theatre

North Stoa   Library

VIA TECTA

4

15

Stoa(?)

14

Propylon

Tunnel   5

Temple of
Asclepius

Latrines

South Stoa

Treatment
Centre

Key to Numbers

1 Bathing Fountain
2 Asklepios Temple
3 Altar
4 Fountains
5 North East Building
6 Cult Niche
7 East Building
8 East Portico
  (Early Hellenistic)
9 East Portico
  (later)
10 South Portico
   (Hellenistic)
11 Roman Temple
12 Incubation Building
13 Old Building
14 Porticoed Street
15 East Portico
   (Roman)

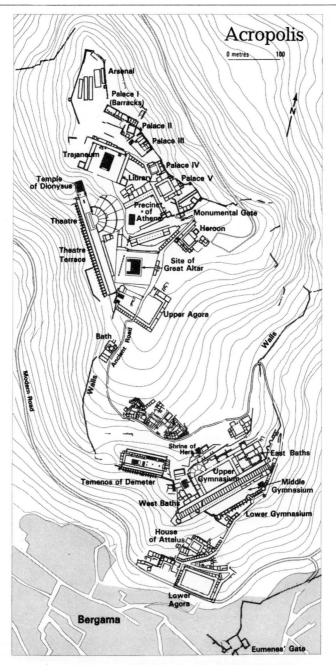

Acropolis

0 metres   100

Arsenal

Palace I
(Barracks)

Palace II

Palace III

Trajaneum

Palace IV

Library   Palace V

Temple
of Dionysus

Precinct
of Athena

Monumental Gate

Theatre   Heroon

Theatre
Terrace

Site of
Great Altar

Upper Agora

Bath

Ancient Road

Walls

Modern Road

Walls

Shrine of
Hera

East Baths

Temenos of Demeter

Upper
Gymnasium

Middle
Gymnasium

West Baths

Lower Gymnasium

House
of Attalus

Lower
Agora

Bergama

Eumenes' Gate

The kings of Pergamum were passionate collectors of books and at one time were reputed have c 200,000 volumes in their possession. As Athena was the goddess of wisdom and of the intellect, it was not inappropriate for Eumenes II to construct a library, on the N side of the temenos of her temple. Approached through the upper storey of the roofed colonnade, this library was believed to have a capacity of 17,000 volumes, so presumably the remainder of the royal collection was kept elsewhere.

There are substantial remains of the reading room on the E side of the building. Librarians handed books to the readers, who were prevented by a low stone bench from reaching the wooden shelves on which the volumes were stored. The bench was widened on the N side of the room to support a copy of the statue of Athena by Pheidias in the Parthenon. The Pergamene copy is now in Berlin. An air space between the wall and the shelves helped to preserve the precious volumes from damage by damp.

When the Egyptians, jealous of the growing size of Pergamum's library, prohibited the export of papyrus, the Attalids began to use parchment, an Ionian discovery. This in turn led to the production of paged books which have so many advantages that in time they replaced scrolls.

The library of Pergamum survived to Roman times, when it was given by Antony to Cleopatra. She had it transported to Alexandria, where it remained more or less intact until the 7C AD. Unfortunately it was destroyed after the capture of Alexandria in AD 640 by the Arabs on the orders of the fanatical Caliph Omar. He ruled that if the books in the library were in accord with the Koran, there was no need for them. If they contained matter which disagreed with the Koran, they should be destroyed. The books from Pergamum were used to feed the fires of Alexandria's 4000 public baths.

The temenos also housed the royal art collection, which included a number of bronze statues commemorating Pergamene victories over the Celts. A Roman copy in marble of one of these statues—a young Celtic warrior about to commit suicide after killing his wife—is in the Museo delle Terme in Rome.

The residences of the Pergamene kings were on the eastern edge of the escarpment. In the most southerly and the largest, dated to the reign of Eumenes II (197–160 BC), there was a private altar and a fine mosaic in one of the rooms on the NW side. Like the other palaces, which are attributed on the basis of material discovered in them and by examination of the structures to Attalus I, Attalus II and Philetaerus, it had a large cistern. All the palaces have the same design of a colonnaded court surrounded by rooms. The last and the most northerly building was converted at some stage into barracks for the garrison. A considerable section of the ashlar masonry of this building is still standing.

At the highest and safest point of the acropolis there were **storerooms**. Five narrow rectangular buildings held the city's reserve food supplies, weapons, and armour. A quantity of stone 'cannon balls', which were projected by *ballistae*, found nearby are now in the lower agora.

From here there is a fine view over the deep valley of the Caicus. To the W the ruins of the Roman amphitheatre are clearly visible and the Asclepieum may be glimpsed to the SW. The remains of the **Roman aqueduct**, which brought water 70km from Soma, are also visible. This supplemented the supply system installed by the Pergamene kings, whose aqueducts ran from the source at Madra Dağ, 45km to the N, to the city.

To the S of the storerooms is the **Trajaneum**, one of the most magnificent buildings in Pergamum. It was constructed during the Roman period on a terrace, partly cut from the mountain side, partly supported by arched vaults. The terrace, which measured c 60m by 70m, was surrounded by roofed colonnades on three sides. On the fourth there was a 23m-high supporting wall pierced by windows. Dedicated to Trajan (98–117), and to his distant relative and heir Hadrian (117–138), it was a peripteros of white marble with six by nine columns in the Corinthian style. It is currently being restored by German archaeologists. When this work is completed, perhaps the colossal marble heads of the emperors, which were found on the site and are now in Berlin, will be returned to Pergamum.

To the SW of the Trajaneum is one of the glories of Pergamum, the **Hellenistic theatre**. As a rule the cavea of a Greek theatre was greater than a semicircle. However, limitations of space at Pergamum made it impossible to respect this convention, so it was extended vertically. It has 80 rows of seats, divided by two diazomata, with seven cunei in the lower section and six in the middle and upper sections. With the exception of the marble royal box in the lower section, the seats were constructed of andesite. It had an estimated capacity of 10,000. Entrance was normally from the great terrace that extended from the upper agora to the temple of Dionysus. There was no permanent stage-building. The holes for posts supporting the scaenae frons and the proscenium are still visible in the pavement. The stone bema, which faces the theatre, dates from the Roman period.

At the northern end of the theatre terrace are the ruins of an **Ionic temple**, which, in view of its position, is believed to have been dedicated to Dionysus. Standing on a high base, the original andesite structure dated from the 2C BC. There was a sacrificial altar in front of the elaborate stairway which led to the cella. Fragments of an inscription, recording the temple's rededication, after it had been rebuilt in marble, to Caracalla (211–217), 'the new Dionysus', have been found on the site.

From the temple a **promenade** extended S to the upper agora. This was c 246 cm long and flanked by Doric stoas of andesite. At the southern end there was a twin-arched gateway. The visit to the upper part of the city finishes here.

To the W of the path from the upper agora to a residential area are the ruins of a **baths complex** constructed during the Roman Imperial period. Part of the tepidarium, marked by a large alcove, remains.

Excavations to the left of the path have revealed a number of buildings, most of which were erected or restored during the Roman period. The most important are a bath-gymnasium, an odeum and a heroon, the so-called 'marble hall'. These interconnected structures formed a multi-discipline complex believed to have been linked to a cult or association devoted to the development of the minds and bodies of young men. It was founded in honour of Diodorus Pasparos who was deified during his lifetime. The portrait head of this Pergamene citizen of the late 1C BC, who was well-known for his generous gifts to the city, is in the Bergama Museum.

The **Roman bath-gymnasium** had a large courtyard, which doubled as a palaestra, and the usual layout of caldarium, tepidarium, etc. To the W, on the other side of the street, was a latrine, which was connected to the main sewer. The **odeum**, which may have been used for meetings as well as performances, adjoined the **heroon**. Copies of 18 reliefs found in the heroon decorate the walls. (The originals are in the Bergama Museum.) They depict the Dioscuri, a fighting cock, armour, weapons etc. A relief showing an erect phallus, symbol of good luck and prosperity, found in the complex has been built into the wall of the modern shelter erected by the archaeologists.

To the E of the heroon are the ruins of a small restaurant and a shop. The restaurant had a dining room which opened on to the street. Cooking was done in an area which was partly excavated from the rock. At the back of the dining room there was another chamber whose walls were covered with paintings. Behind the shop counter, pithoi used for the storage of wine or oil were set into the rock face.

A **hall** measuring 24m by 10m, which appears to have been used for the worship of Dionysus between the 2C and the 4C AD, has been discovered to the NE of these buildings. While sharing a ritual meal, the worshippers reclined on a bench or platform 1m high by 2m wide which ran parallel to the walls. Facing the entrance was an altar and behind it a recess which probably contained the cult image. Outside the hall there was a fountain and a deep rock-cut pit which presumably received the blood of sacrifices.

The austerity and lack of hope which characterised conventional religion turned an increasing number of people to oriental mystery cults which promised a happier after-life to their followers. During the 1C and 2C AD these cults attracted many adherents, particularly from the poor and middle classes of the Roman Empire. In view of its location and date it is probable that the cult, which used the hall, drew its members from the merchants and small traders, who lived in this part of the city.

On the right of the road is the last group of buildings on the hillside. The most important of these are the temple of Demeter, three gymnasia, the temple of Hera, the house of the Consul Attalus and the lower agora.

The temenos of the **Temple of Demeter** occupied a terrace c 100m long by 50m wide. Inscriptions on the altar and in the temple state that it was erected by Philetaerus (282–263 BC) and his brother Eumenes in memory of their mother, Boa. It was enlarged and extended by his successors and again during the Roman period.

Demeter was the goddess of fertility and rebirth and was associated particularly with corn and the fruits of the earth. It was therefore appropriate that Philetaerus chose to erect her shrine in a rural setting outside the city walls. To the W of the temenos there is a deep stone-lined pit which received the blood of piglets sacrificed in the goddess's honour. Nearby are the remains of a fountain, where the worshippers were ritually purified.

Access to the temenos was by a **propylon** on the W side which was donated by Apollonis, the wife of Attalus I (241–197). Two of the unusual columns of this structure have been re-erected. Made of andesite in the Doric style they had Aeolic capitals with a design of palm leaves. Usually found in archaic structures in Aeolia, the presence of these columns in Pergamum may be due, perhaps, to the fact that Apollonis came from Cyzicus.

From the propylon a flight of steps led down into the temenos. This was surrounded on three sides by **stoas**. The stoa on the S, also the gift of Apollonis, was supported by a massive buttressed wall. On the N side the stoa was higher and fronted for half its length by ten rows of seats. Between 800 and 1000 postulants and initiates sat in this theatre to see and participate in the mysteries celebrated in honour of the goddess.

Demeter, the daughter of Cronus and Rhea, was worshipped in the ancient world wherever corn was grown. According to a myth, Persephone, Demeter's daughter by Zeus, was abducted by Hades and taken to his gloomy underworld kingdom. Demeter, distraught with grief, wandered the earth, torch in hand, looking for her lost child. She abandoned her divine duties and the land became barren and mankind was threatened with starvation. To avoid a catastrophe Hades was persuaded to re-unite mother and daughter. Unfortunately, while in the underworld Persephone had eaten a pomegranate seed, and so was obliged to spend a part of each year with her chthonic raptor.

Because of the kindness of King Celeus of Eleusis, when she was looking for her daughter, Demeter entrusted his son, Triptolemus, with a divine mission. He was to travel through the world teaching mankind how to grow and harvest corn.

The legend of Demeter and Persephone, is generally taken to refer to the sowing of corn in the dark earth in autumn, its apparent death during winter and its magical rebirth in the spring. The very ancient cult, which grew up around the myth, promised those who had been initiated into its mysteries a happier afterlife than that offered by official religion. Men and women, freemen and slaves were admitted to the cult. Postulants had to have 'a soul conscious of no evil and have lived well and justly'. Only those who had sinned grievously and were cursed or defiled were excluded.

Many of the ceremonies were held under cover of darkness and in secret, and little is known about their form or content. Severe punishments were invoked against initiates who broke the oath of secrecy that bound them. Aeschylus went in fear of death, because he was suspected of giving information about the mysteries in one of his plays.

Between the principal altar and the temple, which were sited slightly off-centre towards the W end of the temenos, there were several subsidiary altars. The **main altar**, constructed of andesite and adorned with marble volutes, stood in front of the 3C BC **Ionic temple in antis**. This measured c 7m by 13m and was also constructed of andesite. During the Roman period marble columns and a marble pediment were added, changing it into a Corinthian prostyle. At that time the temple was rededicated to Demeter Karpophoros, Demeter the Fruitful, and her daughter Kore, Persephone.

To the W of the temenos of Demeter is the **Shrine of Hera**, the wife of Zeus, and the gymnasia, which made up the largest building complex in Pergamum. The shrine, which comprised a temple and an altar, was built on two levels on the hillside above the gymnasia.

The **temple**, reached by a flight of steps, was a four-columned prostyle in the Doric order. Measuring c 7m by 12m, it was, according to an inscription, constructed during the reign of Attalus II (160–138). Built partly of andesite and partly of marble, it was flanked on the W by an exedra and on the E by a small stoa. The altar was on a lower terrace. Authorities disagree as to whether the headless marble statue of a male figure, found in the sanctuary represented Attalus or Zeus. This is now in the İstanbul Archaeological Museum. No trace of the cult statue of Hera has been found.

The **gymnasia** at Pergamum were designed to deal with all aspects of the intellectual and physical development of the boys and young men of the city. The complex was divided into three separate and distinct parts. The upper gymnasium was devoted to the young men, the central gymnasium to adolescents and the lower gymnasium to the youngest boys.

The **upper gymnasium** occupied a terrace which measured c 200m by 45m. Constructed of andesite during the Hellenistic period, it was modified extensively by the Romans. Their use of marble and mortar simplifies the work of distinguishing between the earlier buildings and later additions and alterations. The principal feature of the upper gymnasium was a large court, surrounded by colonnades, used for training sessions. To the NW of the court was an auditorium with a capacity of 1000, where the students assembled for lectures and cultural activities. To the W of this was a small Ionic prostyle temple dedicated to Asclepius, while on the N a room richly decorated with marble and marked by a double apse was, according to an inscription, reserved for use by the emperor. Between the emperor's room and the auditorium was the *ephebeion*, where important ceremonies concerned with the training and education of the young men took place. To the S, in the so-called **basement stadium**, athletic matches were held. The upper gymnasium was flanked on the E and W by baths which were used by the athletes after matches and training.

The **central gymnasium**, built on the next terrace down, was reached by a narrow staircase. Surrounded by walls, it had a long stoa on the N. One of the rooms on the E side of the stoa was dedicated to the emperor and to Hercules and Hermes, gods associated with physical fitness. The central area of the gymnasium was used for exercises and track events. Traces of a small prostyle **Corinthian temple**, measuring 7m by 12m, have been been found on the E side of the terrace. On its walls were lists of youths dating from the Hellenistic to the Roman periods. Note the large Hellenistic fountain nearby. Its rim is marked by the jugs and pots of those who once drew water from it.

A well-preserved covered stairs leads to the **young boys' gymnasium**. Constructed during the reign of Eumenes II, a substantial section of the gymnasium's N wall, which was strengthened by strong buttresses, remains intact. Niches in this wall had inscribed tablets listing the names of prizewinners, and statues of the most outstanding boys. A stele found here gave the names of the boys for 147 BC. The towers on the N wall date from the Byzantine period.

One of the most evocative reminders of Pergamum's past is the **ancient street** of large andesite blocks which leads down from the gymnasia to a group of shops and houses in the SW. About 5m wide, it shows many signs of wear and tear. There are deep ruts from chariots and carts and in a number of places the stones have been polished by the countless feet that passed over them. Signs of repair carried out in antiquity, particularly to the drainage system, are still clearly visible.

Where the street turns W there are the ruins of a 2C BC **peristyle house** which was modified during the Roman period. According to an inscription found on the base of a herm, it belonged to the Consul Attalus. Cheerfully, he invites his guests to enjoy with him the good things of life. The lower storey of the stoa, built around a central court measuring c 20m by 13.5m, was of andesite in the Doric style, the upper storey was of marble in the Ionic. Traces of wall paintings and of well-preserved mosaics have been given a protective cover. There were several cisterns, one of which, dating from the Hellenistic period, supplied water to a fountain in the lower agora.

The **lower agora**, which was devoted to commerce, is to the left of the ancient street. Rectangular in shape it measured c 64m by 34m and dates from the reign of Eumenes II (197–160). The paved central courtyard was surrounded by a two-storey Doric stoa which had shops at the rear. The fountain in the centre received its water supply from a cistern in the house of Attalus. Stone missiles, found near the arsenal on the summit of the acropolis, are stored here.

One of the finest existing examples of Hellenistic art, the head of Alexander the Great, now in the İstanbul Archaeological Museum, was discovered in the NW corner of the agora. No trace of the torso has been found. A number of inscriptions setting out the laws governing public works, such as drains, fountains, roads and houses, were displayed in the agora. They are now in Bergama's Museum.

The modern buildings are the headquarters and store of the German archaeologists who are working in Pergamum.

During the reign of Eumenes II the city walls were extended and reached a length of c 4km. Part of these fortifications are to the E of the S gate. All the buildings on the hillside, including the sanctuary of Demeter and the gymnasia, were enclosed and areas vulnerable to attack were protected by the new defensive system.

The main entrance to Pergamum was by the **S gate** which was a short distance below the lower agora. Precautions were taken to prevent invaders from getting into the city. Having passed through a fortified entrance on the W side, visitors found themselves in an open courtyard. This measured 20m by 20m and was protected by two towers on the S side, both of which were manned by soldiers. The booths of the money changers, scribes and small traders were in a colonnade by the E wall of this courtyard. It was necessary to make a sharp U-turn through a second gate on the W side of the courtyard to get inside the city. This gate was overlooked by a tower in the corner of the city wall which was also manned by soldiers.

The gateway of Eumenes II is the last monument in the upper area of the ancient city. Now return to the modern town of Bergama.

The 2C AD red-brick Kızıl Avlu at Pergamum

Clearly visible from the road is the **Kızıl Avlu**, the Red Hall, so called because of the colour of the brick from which it was built. Archaeologists believe that this huge structure, which dates from the first half of the 2C AD, was probably dedicated to the Egyptian gods, Serapis, Isis and Harpocrates. There are, however, dissentient voices. Mortimer Wheeler thought that it could have housed the famous library during the Roman period or even served as a university.

The complex, the largest in the ancient city, was made up of a courtyard measuring c 200m by 100m, the greater part of which is covered by modern houses, a building with a nave and a reversed apse, and two circular tower-structures fronted by courts. The river Selinus, the Bergama Çayı, is carried through the arched channels of a double tunnel that passes under the courtyard at an angle.

The **bulding**, which measures 60m by 26m, has walls that still stand to a height of 19m. A monumental entrance 7m wide and 14m high admitted to the nave, paved with marble, the western part of which was lit by windows in the side walls. The 10m image of the deity on a large podium dominated the tenebrous E section. A tunnel under its base allowed priests to enter the hollow statue, from where they delivered oracular pronouncements which the faithful believed were made by the god. In front of the podium there was a shallow marble basin containing water. Two staircases near the E wall led to a balcony resting on pillars, which encircled the structure. Some of the coloured marble decoration, which covered the whole surface of the brick walls, is still in position.

Sometime after the adoption of Christianity a church dedicated to St John the Evangelist was built inside the building. Part of the ruined walls of this building and its conventionally oriented apse remain.

The **circular tower buildings**, which flanked the basilica, were approached through courts surrounded by colonnades. Fragments of two of the curiously-shaped supports of these colonnades were found near the S tower. They were carved on one side as atlantes and on the other as caryatids. Both were in the Egyptian style. Hot and cold water was piped to a long, narrow pool in the centre of each of the courts. A warren of rooms underneath the towers may have been used for ritual purposes.

The orientation of the temple complex, which faces W, suggested it was dedicated to Serapis, and to Isis and Harpocrates, deities with which he was often linked. Worship of Serapis, a syncretic god of the underworld, was introduced to the Egyptians by Ptolemy I (305–282 BC), and it spread widely through the Roman Empire during the first centuries of the Christian era. A temple dedicated to him was found in York and a fine head of the god was discovered in 1954 under the temple of Mithras at Walbrook in London. Characteristic features of Egyptian religion found in the complex, like the pools for ritual bathing, the underground river thought to symbolise the Nile and the enormous courtyard eminently suited to processions and assemblies, together with the presence of the Egyptian-style ornamentation tend to support the archaeologists' theory.

Inside the modern wall on the W side of the courtyard there are architectural fragments and a number of stones bearing inscriptions in Hebrew. The stones appear to be late-19C Jewish gravemarkers. One is inscribed to 'the Widow of Mordechai Veervan' and is dated 5462 (AD 1882).

Between the Kızıl Avlu and the Archaeological Museum there are several interesting Islamic monuments including the minaret of a 14C Selçuk mosque and the small, but exquisite, **Parmaklı Camii**. Also worth a visit is **Ulu Cami**, which dates from the reign of Beyazit I (1389–1403). This is on the Kozak road near a bridge, Ulu Cami Köprüsü, which crosses the upper waters of the Selinus.

Near the Archaeological Museum there are several restaurants which serve adequate meals. The post office and *otogar* are in this part of the town. Branches of the principal banks are in a square 100m to the N. The **Tourist Information Office** is at the southern end of Bergama near the turning to the Asclepieum.

Bergama's **Archaeological Museum**, which opened in 1936, was the first museum in Turkey to concentrate on exhibiting finds from local excavations. Many of them are labelled in English. There is no guidebook.

In the garden there are architectural fragments, including stelae and Islamic tombstones. In the courtyard, immediately inside the entrance, there is a fine sarcophagus decorated with reliefs of garlands, a Medusa head and a horseman. This is flanked by two Hellenistic Aeolic capitals from the sanctuary of Demeter.

In the colonnade there are part of the sima and dentils from the sanctuary of Athena, a section of the Hellenistic frieze and architrave from the Athena propylon, part of the architrave from the altar of Zeus, a Corinthian and a

Composite capital from the Asclepieum, part of the frieze from the Roman temple of Dionysus, a section of a frieze depicting Cerberus, the three-headed dog which guarded the entrance to Hades, a hermaphroditic herm from the valley of the Caicus, and a horse from the altar of Zeus. There are several Hellenistic statues, all headless, a number of Hellenistic stelae, Roman statues, including an Artemis from the Trajaneum, Roman altars and inscriptions, and Hellenistic and Roman inscriptions honouring ephebes from the gymnasia. Note the small model of the altar of Zeus in the left-hand colonnade and the acroteria from the propylon of the Asclepieum, which are displayed in the centre area.

By the door there is a fine archaic *kouros* dated to 525 BC from Pitane, modern Çandarlı. A wall-case in the room to the right contains some exquisite terracottas. These include a youth with a goose, Silenus and Dionysus, Venus, and a youth hiding objects in his bunched-up toga. Among the Roman sculptures are a 3C AD head of Caracalla, a colossal **statue of Hadrian** from the Asclepieum, the goddess Fortuna, a head of Vespasian, and a bust of Euripides. Note the Roman Medusa mosaic from the acropolis.

A glass case by the back wall contains Hellenistic and Roman terracotta penes (votive objects?), and erotic lamps. There are also moulds for the production of these objects. Other wall cases contain Roman glass, including tear vases, small bronzes, Hellenistic, Roman and Byzantine coins, pottery and lamps, bronze strigils and tiny models of animals. Of particular interest are the offerings made by patients at the Asclepieum. These include representations of fingers, hands and feet, a bronze snake, and a head of Asclepius. Among the many small statues there are several of Cybele, pottery from the archaic and Byzantine periods, jewellery and ornaments of carved ivory and a number of very well-preserved 2C and 1C BC terracottas from Myrina.

The Asclepieum occupies a large area c 1km to the W of Bergama. Look out for a signpost to the right of the Tourist Information Office.

During the Hellenistic and Roman periods the **Asclepieum** of Pergamum was famous. It was a great medical centre that came to rival, and almost overshadow, Epidaurus in Greece. To judge by ancient accounts, it functioned very much like a fashionable spa in the 18C or 19C. While many came here in search of a cure, others frequented it to take the waters, to enjoy the performances in the theatre, to indulge in philosphical discussion or simply to be diverted by watching the more bizarre courses of treatment that were prescribed by the priests and doctors.

Although badly damaged by an earthquake in the 3C AD, the Asclepieum continued to function as a medical centre for some time after the arrival of Christianity in Pergamum. During the Byzantine era a church was constructed on the site of the temple of Asclepius.

According to the legends, Asclepius, the son of Apollo, having been abandoned by his mother, was educated by the centaur Chiron who taught him medicine. Rapidly acquiring great skill, he discovered how to bring the dead to life by using the Gorgon's blood which had been given to him by Athena. Zeus, fearing that this practice would upset the natural order, struck him dead with a thunderbolt. In compensation, Asclepius was placed among the stars.

As snakes were believed to have the power to renew themselves, they were sacred to Asclepius. Twined around a post, they formed his symbol, the caduceus which was also carried by Hermes. Patients, who had been cured at one of the shrines of Asclepius, offered a cock to the god, a fact that underlines the irony and pathos of Socrates' last words, 'Crito, we owe a cock to Asclepius. Make sure that it is paid'.

Asclepius was not deified until the 5C BC. To Homer he was 'the blameless physician', whose sons, Machaon and Podalirius, served as doctors to the Greek army at Troy. Among his five daughters were Panacea and Hygieia.

The worship of Asclepius was centred initially on Epidaurus in Greece and from there it was brought to Pergamum in the 4C BC. Archaeological evidence suggests that there was a shrine honouring a female deity at this site as early as the Bronze Age and that it also may have been connected with healing.

A substantial stretch of the ancient **paved street**, the *Via Tecta*, which began at the city theatre and linked Pergamum with the Asclepieum, has been cleared. The last section of c 150m before the propylon at the entrance to the sanctuary, was flanked by colonnades. On the right-hand side there are the remains of a late fountain and on the left of a large circular tomb which dates from the first years of the Christian era.

According to an inscription on the pediment, the **propylon** was the gift of a Pergamene citizen named Claudius Charax. Like most of the visible remains of the Asclepieum it dates from 2C AD, when, thanks to the generosity of Hadrian, Antoninus Pius and Marcus Aurelius and of local magnates, much building took place. The propylon was composed of two parts: an area surrounded on three sides by a colonnade in the Corinthian order and, on the W, a façade with four Corinthian columns which fronted a flight of steps leading down into the Asclepieum courtyard. Acroteria from the pediment of the propylon are in the Bergama Museum.

The **courtyard**, which measured 110m by 130m, had buildings on the E and stoas on the other three sides. Immediately to the right of the propylon are the remains of a niche which may have held a cult statue. The square building in the NE corner was the **library**. This was sometimes called the emperor's room, as the monumental statue of Hadrian, now in the Bergama Museum, stood in a recess in the E wall. According to an inscription on the base of the statue, it was the gift of Flavia Melitine. This lady may also have paid for the construction of the library.

While it probably housed a collection of medical texts, the library almost certainly had copies of the classics for the entertainment of the patients, who could spend as long as a year at the sanctuary. Light came from windows above the recesses in which the manuscripts were stored.

There are substantial remains of the **N stoa**, which was originally in the Ionic style. After the devastation caused by the earthquake of AD 175, ten new columns in the Composite style were erected on the E side of the colonnade.

At the W end of the stoa is the much-restored **Roman theatre**. It has a single diazoma and is divided into five cunei. The three rows below the diazoma were reserved for the most distinguished spectators. The 1m high stage was backed by a three-storey stage-building. Dedicated to Asclepius and Athena Hygieia, the theatre had a capacity of 3500.

The Ionic colonnade on the W side has disappeared. It fronted a stoa, behind which there was another building, outside the sanctuary courtyard, whose purpose has not been determined. At the SW corner there were two open-plan latrines, built over a channel carrying a constant flow of water. The larger, reserved for men, had 40 marble seats and was ventilated and lit by openings in a ceiling resting on four Corinthian columns. The ladies' room, which had 17 seats, was less lavishly furnished.

Because of the slope, the **S stoa** was constructed over a basement, which supported it. This stoa, too, has disappeared.

Accounts of treatment at the Asclepieum are provided by inscriptions found on the site and by the writings of Aelius Aristides, 2C AD orator and hypochondriac, who claimed to have spent 13 years here. Drinking and bathing in the water from the springs in the centre of the courtyard, mud-baths, herbal remedies, massage, dieting, exercise (especially running barefoot in the winter), and colonic-irrigation were among the methods favoured. In addition, patients suffering from psychosomatic illnesses had their dreams analysed by the priests of Asclepius in a way that anticipated Freud.

Doctors were also employed at the sanctuary, among them Galen (AD 129–c 200), one of the greatest physicians of antiquity. Born and educated in Pergamum and initially doctor to the city's gladiators, he became a consultant to the emperors.

Treatment was provided in the centre of the courtyard. Immediately to the S of the theatre there was a **Roman fountain**, where patients bathed and drank the water. Towards the centre of the W stoa there was a rock-cut pool, where patients also bathed and coated themselves with mud from the surrounding area. A third source, dated by the archaeologists to the Hellenistic period, was found near the exit from the tunnel that stretches to the large building in the SE corner. Once protected from the elements by a roof, but now open to the sky, this spring still offers its water to modern visitors. Aristides claimed that drinking it was an effective specific for asthma, chest infections and foot problems.

S of the springs was the **Hellenistic temenos of Asclepius** which was enclosed on three sides by a colonnade. On the N side of the temenos were the incubation and sleeping rooms, where the patients hoped to be cured by an encounter, in their dreams, with the god. An inscription stated that they had to sacrifice a white sheep decked with olive boughs and had to wear white robes. They were forbidden to wear a girdle or rings. Patients not cured had their dreams interpreted by the priests, who with the doctors made a diagnosis and prescribed a course of treatment.

Between the temenos and the theatre were temples dedicated to Apollo Kalliteknos, Apollo with fair children, Hygieia and Asclepius. According to Aristides, Telesphorus, a youthful deity associated with Asclepius, had a shrine in this area. Today only the barest traces of the temples remain.

From the centre of the courtyard a **Roman tunnel**, 80m long, led to a large **late Roman circular building** which projected from the SE corner of the complex. The tunnel had openings in the vaulted roof to admit light and air. Sometimes incorrectly described as the temple of Telesphorus, the circular building had two storeys. Only the lower storey, which is in a good state of preservation, remains. The structure, which had a diameter of 26.5m, was divided into six apsidal sections. Opinions are divided about its purpose, but the presence of recesses for washing and a sun-terrace on the lower floor and its link by the tunnel with the springs suggest that it was used in some way for treating the sick.

To the N of the round building are the ruins of the **Temple of Asclepius**. Modelled on the Pantheon in Rome, this was constructed with the care and skill for which Pergamene craftsmen were famous. Perhaps the most beautiful structure in the Asclepieum, it was the gift of the consul Lucius Rufinus and dates from c AD 150. It was a circular domed building fronted by a colonnaded entrance. A flight of steps led up from the central court to the temple. The dome, which had an oculus to admit light and air, measured c 24m in diameter. The walls and floor of the andesite structure were covered with marble mosaics. At intervals there were alternate round and rectangular recesses which held statues of the deities associated with healing. In the central recess, which faced the entrance, there was a huge statue of Asclepius. The temple, with the nearby propylon of Charax, formed a harmonious group of buildings on the E side of the Asclepieum.

At the E end of the Via Tecta, beyond the scanty remains of the **town theatre**, which had a capacity of 30,000, are the ruins of the **Roman** amphitheatre and the site of the **stadium**. Of the amphitheatre, which was built over a stream, only the ruins of a few of the huge arches, which supported the seats, remain.

The approach to these ruins from the Asclepieum passes near a restricted area. If you wish to visit and photograph them, seek the advice of the Tourist Information Office.

10

Pergamum to İzmir

This route includes diversions to the ancient sites at Pitane, Myrina, Yeni Foça, Buruncuk and Yanık, Neanteichos and Larisa.

Total distance c 38km. Bergama/Pergamum—(25km Çandarlı/Pitane)—(2km Elaea)—6km Gryneum—(5km Myrina)—(6km Cyme)—(15km Yeni Foça)—(27km Eski Foça Phocaea)—8km Buruncuk/Larisa—(2km Yanık Köy)—c 24km İzmir.

From Bergama (see Route 9) return to the junction with Road 550/E24 and continue towards İzmir. This route passes the sites of some of the ancient cities of Aeolia. In most cases only scant traces remain, they appeal mainly to specialists and are often difficult to reach by public transport.

At first the road follows the course of the Bakır Çay. After c 15km a turning to the right leads to 10km **Çandarlı**, ancient **Pitane**, the most northern of the Aeolian cities. Traces of a settlement dating back to the third millennium BC have been found here. A minor member of the Delian League, Pitane at first received help from Pergamum and later was absorbed by its powerful neighbour.

The city was sited at the end of a long, finger-shaped peninsula. There are traces of the ancient fortifications, the remains of a mole on the W side, and a medieval fortress built by the Venetians to guard the landward approaches. An archaic kouros, now in the Bergama Museum, was found in 1958 near the neck of the peninsula.

About 2km farther on the E87/550 a minor road leads to the site of **Elaea**. According to an ancient tradition this was founded at about the time of the Trojan War by settlers from Athens. Never a member of the Aeolian League, it prospered under the Attalids, who developed it as a base for their commercial and naval vessels. A section of the harbour wall and small stretches of the fortifications near the main road remain.

Gryneum, is c 6km to the S of Elaea near the village of **Yenişakran** on the narrow peninsula of Temaşalık Burnu. This city was a member of the Delian League. Occupied by the Persians in the early 5C BC, it was wrested from them in 335 BC by Parmenion who enslaved the inhabitants. Later ruled by Myrina, it had, according to Strabo and Pausanias, a famous oracle of Apollo who lived in a sacred grove of fruit-bearing and fragrant trees.

Some believe that the small mound surrounded by broken columns towards the end of the peninsula marks the site of the temple of Apollo. Others assert that the ruins are later, possibly Byzantine. The fruit trees and flowering shrubs that surround the sanctuary offer welcome shade and in spring their blossoms fill the air with a heady scent.

Myrina was c 5km to the S of Gryneum near the mouth of the Güzelhisar Cayı, the ancient Pythicus. According to Strabo it was named Myrina 'from the Amazon who lies in the Trojan plain [below Batieia] which verily men call Batieia, but the immortals the tomb of much-bounding Myrina'.

The city had a troubled history. Destroyed twice by earthquakes, it was rebuilt with assistance from the Emperor Tiberius. In gratitude Myrina changed its name to Sebastopolis, the City of the Emperor.

It was built on two hills, now called Birki Tepe and Öteki Tepe, which are c 2km from the road. Excavations at Birki Tepe have revealed the remains of an early polygonal wall and part of a Byzantine defensive system. The whole area is heavily overgrown and difficult to explore.

Towards the end of the 19C c 5000 graves, most undisturbed by robbers, were discovered in a **necropolis** to the N of Birki Tepe. A large quantity of Hellenistic terracotta figures and masks which date from the 2C and 1C BC were found in the graves. Terracottas were frequently buried with the dead for use in the after-life or because they had been favourite possessions of the deceased. Most touching are the articulated toys, many of which show evidence of wear at the hands of their young owners.

Echoing the style of Tanagra in Greece, the terracottas of Myrina cover a wide range of subjects—draped female figures, children, animals, Erotes, Victories, sirens, actors and various deities including Aphrodite and Dionysus were made in an expressive, lively style. Garments were sometimes reproduced in a series of daring patterns that made little or no attempt to suggest reality. Produced from a fine clay, which ranged in colour from orange to dark red, the pieces usually bear the artist's signature. There are representative collections of terracottas from Myrina in museums in İstanbul, London, Paris, Athens and Boston.

Shortly after passing the modern village of **Aliağa**, a turning to the right leads to the site (6km) of ancient **Cyme**. Named, like Myrina, after an Amazon, Cyme was, perhaps, the most important of the Aeolian cities. Under Persian rule at the end of the 5C and the beginning of the 4C BC, it provided naval suppport for Darius and Xerxes in their campaigns against Greece. An indication of its wealth and importance at a later period is provided by the size of its annual payment to the Delian League which exceeded the amount levied on any other city in Aeolia or Ionia.

Considered slow and stupid by their contemporaries, the people of Cyme appear to have led quiet, placid lives. Perhaps their proudest boast was that the father of Hesiod, the greatest Greek poet after Homer, was born in their city. According to Strabo, Ephorus, the city's historian, unable to find any important deeds in his list of Cymes's achievements, and yet unwilling not to mention it, wrote: 'At about the same time the Cymaeans were at peace'.

The remains are few: on a hilltop a small temple in the Ionic style consecrated to Isis; the remains of large building of indeterminate purpose in the valley near the road; and, under water, parts of the ancient harbour-works. The site is overgrown and any detailed exploration difficult.

About 16km S of the road for Cyme, a turning to the right leads to the seaside resorts of 15km **Yeni Foça** and 27km **Eski Foça**. Eski Foça, the ancient **Phocaea**, attracts many Turkish holidaymakers each year, while foreigners flock to the nearby Club Mediterranée. There are several small hotels, some open all the year round, and a number of good fish restaurants. The best beaches are to the S of the modern harbour.

Look for a remarkable 8C BC **rock-tomb**, known locally as Taş Kule, the Rock Tower. This is a stone cube 8.5m long by 5.8m wide and 6m high, surmounted on the E by a second cube resting on four steps. According to Bean, the top of the structure, which was damaged in antiquity, may have been crowned by a stone phallus. Entrance to the burial chamber, which contained a rectangular grave in the floor, is through an antechamber on the N side. Akurgal has drawn attention to the number of influences in the structure: Lycian—two storeys with a sarcophagus shaped cube on top, Persian—the stepped base under the cube, and Lydian—the decorative pattern near the entrance. It is believed to be the burial chamber of a local princeling or minor king.

Nearer Foça there is another rock-cut tomb called Şeytan Hamamı, the Devil's Bath which has been dated to the 4C BC.

History. Phocaea is believed to have been founded by colonists from the Ionian cities of Erythrae and Teos in the 8C BC. Its name was probably derived from the small hump-backed islands that lie offshore. To the imaginative these looked like seals—*Phoce* in Greek—animals which appear frequently on the city's coinage.

Because of its excellent harbour, Phocaea developed rapidly, becoming an important trading port. Its adventurous citizens roamed widely in the Mediterranean in large ships capable of carrying as many as 500 passengers and substantial quantities of cargo. They founded colonies in France at Massalia (modern Marseilles), in Spain at Tartessus (near Cadiz), in Corsica at Alalıa, and in Italy at Elea (Velia).

Liberated from Persian rule by Alexander, the Phocaeans sided with the Seleucids against the Romans and, as a consequence, their city was besieged, captured and looted in 190 BC. They were in conflict with Rome again c 133 BC, when they supported the claim of Aristonicus to the throne of Pergamum (see above). On that occasion they were saved from Roman wrath by the intercession of their colony, Massalia.

During the Byzantine period Phocaea was an episcopal see. Later, during the Middle Ages, it was occupied by the Genoese, who shipped alum and other products from its port. The city was captured by the Ottomans in 1455.

Pottery sherds and architectural fragments discovered by French archaeologists in the early 20C established that ancient Phocaea lies under the modern town of Eski Foça. Traces of a mid 6C BC temple, which is believed to have been dedicated to Athena, were found near the site of the modern secondary school. The Genoese occupation is recalled by the 13C fortress on the peninsula overlooking the southern harbour.

About 8km from the junction for Eski Foça are the villages of **Buruncuk** and **Yanık Köy**. On a hill rising 91m above Buruncuk is the site of a city believed to be that of ancient **Larisa**.

History. Homer mentions the 'warlike Pelasgians who dwelt around fertile Larisa', and the site near Buruncuk may be that of the city mentioned in the *Iliad*. Allies of the Trojans, their leader, Hippothous, was slain during the siege. Some time after their arrival from Greece, the Aeolian invaders built a fortress near Larisa, which they called Neonteichos. From here they harassed the Pelasgians, until eventually they conquered them. In 546 BC, after Cyrus had overrun Lydia, he moved the Egyptian troops, who had assisted Croesus, to Larisa and the city was sometimes referred to as 'Egyptian Larisa' from then onwards. During the Hellenistic period the fortunes of Larisa declined and by the 1C AD it appears to have been little more than a hamlet.

A stretch of ancient paved road leads up to the acropolis which was protected by substantial walls, a section of which remains on the NE side. Inside are the ruins of two temples and a structure which has been dubbed 'the palace' by the archaeologists. The necropolis was on the E slope of the hill and in a valley below. There are the remains of a number of tumuli.

A site at **Yanik Köy**, on a hill above the village, has not been excavated. Apart from the remains of defensive walls on the summit and on the side there is little see.

Shortly after Buruncuk Road 550/E24 passes through the small town of **Menemen**, whose vineyards produce grapes for İzmir's wines. On the left the bare, brown sides of Yamanlar Daği dominate the approach to the city.

Soon the crowded hillside suburbs come into view. Then the road follows the magnificent curve of İzmir Körfezi to the city centre.

11

İzmir

With a population of 2.7 million, İzmir is the third largest city in Turkey. After İstanbul the second busiest port, it is an important road and rail junction and is linked to Turkey's principal cities and many European capitals by frequent direct flights from Adnan Menderes Airport.

Each year İzmir stages an important International Fair where Turkish and foreign exhibitors display a wide range of products.

The city's splendid setting on the steep, umber-coloured hills that surround İzmir Körfezi, the wide palm-lined boulevards, the smart shops, hotels and restaurants, and the bustle of a busy port combine with the simplicity and exoticism of the old quarter in an attractive, unusual and elegant amalgam. İzmir has a pleasant climate. In summer the temperature, which can be oppressively hot in the Aegean, is tempered by the *İmbat*, that refreshing breeze from the sea.

İzmir is an excellent centre for visiting Pergamum, Sardis, Ephesus, Priene, Miletus and Didyma, all of which are within easy driving distance. There are frequent bus services to Bergama for Pergamum, to Sartmustafa for Sardis, and to Selçuk and Kuşadası for Ephesus. In addition, there are special tours bookable through local travel agencies to these places, and to Priene, Miletus and Didyma. Visits to Teos, Clazomenae, Çesme, Colophon, Claros and Notium may be made by dolmuş and local buses. However, these services are slow and in some cases relatively infrequent, so journeys need careful planning.

Information and Accommodation. The **Tourist Information Office** is located centrally at Gaziosmanpaşa Bulv. 1/D near the THY town-terminal and Büyük Efes hotel.

Accommodation in İzmir ranges from the excellent five-star *Grand Hotel Plaza* in the Teleferik district to small pensions which provide basic facilities. Near Basmane railway station there are some good, medium-priced hotels such as the *Billur Oteli* and the *Hisar Oteli* which has a good restaurant.

During the period of the İzmir International Fair (August–September) and when other specialised exhibitions are being held, it can be very difficult to get accommodation of any kind. Book as far in advance as possible.

Food in Izmir's premier hotels is excellent. In addition, some of the finest Turkish cuisine may be enjoyed in the restaurants by the sea on Atatürk Cad. (sometimes called Birinci Kordon). A pleasant evening may be spent at Karşıyaka on the N side of the bay, where restaurants line the waterfront. There are frequent ferryboats from Konak. A romantic journey across the bay under the stars is an added incentive to dine there.

Post Office and Banks. İzmir's principal post office is at Cumhuriyet Meydanı (see city plan). Branches of the main Turkish banks are in various parts of the city.

Consulates. İzmir is a major port, and more than 20 foreign countries are represented in the city. The British Consulate is at 1442 Sok. 49, P.K. 300 Alsancak and the United States Consulate at Atatürk Cad. 92, Alsancak.

Transport. Long-distance buses arrive at the *otogar* which is on the NE outskirts of the city. Most companies have a free courtesy-service minibus to the city centre. This operates infrequently and any traveller with luggage is advised to take a taxi. If you are on a strict budget, there are dolmuş taxis, but these are usually packed to bursting point and and may refuse to take large backpacks.

Most bus and dolmuş services operating in the city and in the surrounding area start and end at Konak (see city plan).

Rail travellers arrive at Basmane railway station in the city centre near the Kültür Parkı. It is a regular stop on many bus and dolmuş routes.

There are service buses to and from Adnan Menderes Airport which is 18km S of the city. They bring passengers to the THY town terminal.

Visitors arriving by sea disembark at Yeni Limanı in Alsancak. From there it is an easy journey by taxi, bus or dolmuş to the centre.

If you travel by car, you may have some difficulty in finding a parking place in İzmir.

Churches. In addition to the Cathedral of St John the Evangelist, Şehit Nevnes Bul. 29, there are two more Catholic churches in İzmir, St Polycarp in 2354 Sok. 41, and St Rosaire in 1461 Sok. 8.

İzmir's Anglican church, which has a resident chaplain, is in Alsancak on the corner of Atatürk Cad. and Mahmut Esat Bozkurt Cad.

Museums. As well as İzmir's excellent Archaeological Museum at Konak, there is the Atatürk Museum on Atatürk Bulv. The Ethnographical Museum occupies an old Turkish house near the Archaeological Museum.

Shopping. İzmir has excellent shops ranging from the smart boutiques on Atatürk Cad. and in Alsancak to the myriad small businesses in the Bazaar. All of the usual products—carpets, kilims, jewellery, brassware, clothing—are sold. There are also good fruit markets, where İzmir's famous fresh figs are available in season.

Getting Around. The best way to explore İzmir is on foot. However, the distances from Alsancak in the N to Konak in the S and Kadifekale, the ancient Mt Pagus, in the SE are considerable, and to be enjoyable any such exploration should not be hurried.

History. Traditionally the birthplace of Homer, who was honoured here in Classical times in the Homereium, İzmir, formerly **Smyrna**, has a long history. Traces of occupation from the third millennium BC were found at Bayraklı on the northern edge of the city. This site was excavated first by a team from Ankara University in collaboration with the British School at Athens and later by Turkish archaeologists under the direction of Professor Akurgal.

During the second millennium BC the settlement is believed to have come under Hittite influence. George Bean has linked this hypothesis with a legend that the city was founded by the Amazons—on Egyptian monuments Hittite warriors are generally depicted wearing skirt-like garments which gives them a feminine look.

Archaeology has confirmed the story in Herodotus that Smyrna came under the control of some Ionian Greeks from Colophon who were exiled from their native city in the 9C BC. They sought refuge in Smyrna. Then one day, while the Smyrnaeans were celebrating the feast of Dionysus outside the walls, their ungrateful guests closed the gates and seized the city. After a period of considerable prosperity, the settlement was subjected to sustained attacks by the Lydians and eventually was reduced to a state of impoverishment and decay.

It was refounded by Alexander the Great. Resting on Mt Pagus after a hunt, he was told in a dream by the tutelary Nemeseis to establish a new city here. The oracle of Apollo at Claros was consulted and gave the following advice:

'Three and four times happy shall those men be hereafter
Who shall dwell on Pagus beyond the sacred Meles'.

Encouraged, Alexander entrusted the building of the new city to two of his generals, Antigonus and Lysimachus. During the Hellenistic period Smyrna vacillated in its loyalty, sometimes supporting the Seleucids, sometimes the Attalids. Displaying the same diplomatic skill—and inconstancy—in its dealing with Rome, it continued to prosper and, like a number of other cities in the Roman province of Asia, was ornamented with many beautiful buildings. Favoured by several emperors including Hadrian and Caracalla, Smyrna was reconstructed in AD 178 with the help of generous donations from Marcus Aurelius after it had suffered severe damage from an earthquake.

Smyrna played an important part in the development of the Christian Church. The words of St John to the first Christians, 'Only be faithful till death, and I will give you the crown of life' (Revelation 2:10,11) must have been recalled by those who witnessed the martyrdom of St Polycarp, Bishop of Smyrna. In 156 he was betrayed to the authorities and brought to the arena where a pagan festival was taking place. Ordered by the proconsul Statius Quadratus to deny his faith, Polycarp refused saying, 'Eighty and six years I have served Him and He has done me no ill; how then can I blaspheme my King who hath served me?' The enraged crowd in the arena responded by shouting, 'This is the teacher of Asia; this is the destroyer of our gods; this is the father of the Christians'. Polycarp was thrown on a pyre and burned to death.

Until the Arab raids in the 7C Smyrna was a prosperous trading centre. Towards the end of the 11C the Selçuk Turks advanced to the Aegean coast for the first time and captured the city. It remained in their hands until the Byzantines regained it in 1097. From then until 1415, when it was taken by Mehmet I, Byzantines, Crusaders, Genoese and Turks contested its possession.

In the middle of the 18C the Society of Dilettanti made it their headquarters in Asia Minor. John Cleland (1709–89), the author of *Fanny Hill* and other erotic novels, was British Consul here for a short time. Though ravaged by earthquakes, the city maintained its commercial importance. Traders from Britain, the Netherlands and France came here and an Anglican church was built for the growing British community. According to Kinglake it was called '*Giaour Izmir*', Infidel Smyrna, by the Turks, because of the large number of foreigners who lived and worked here.

In the last days of the war between Greece and Turkey in 1921–22 much of the city was burned to the ground. Many fine old buildings were destroyed and others damaged beyond repair. The İzmir which rose from the ashes of that conflagration is the city visible today.

If you are not in a hurry, make the city your headquarters and intersperse expeditions to Pergamum, Ephesus and other sites in the surrounding countryside with visits to the Archaeological and Ethnographical Museums, the bazaar, Kadifekale, the Agora and Old Smyrna.

The **Kültür Parkı** is a good place to begin your visit. The pavilions of the İzmir International Fair line a network of cool, shaded alleyways surrounded by well-tended gardens. Restaurants and refreshment kiosks are scattered through the park.

The cornerstone of the **Cathedral of St John the Evangelist**, Şehit Nevres Bulv. 29, was laid in 1862 and the building was completed in 1874. Donations were received from many sources. The Catholics of Lyons in France, which had been converted to Christianity in the 2C by missionaries from Smyrna, were particularly generous in their contributions. So also was Sultan Abdül Aziz (1861–76), who made a gift of 11,000 gold Turkish Lira to help provide this splendid church for his Christian subjects.

The interior of the cathedral is richly decorated. In the sanctuary, in addition to a fine painting of St John the Evangelist, by A. von Hammer, there are pictures of St Augustine, St Andrew, St Athanasius, St John Chrysostom and of Smyrna's own martyr St Polycarp. Also commemorated in the cathedral is St Vincent de Paul, founder of the Vincentians or Lazarists, the order which has served the Christian community in Smyrna for many centuries.

Since 1965, by permission of the Archbishop of İzmir, Catholic and Protestant members of the NATO forces and their dependants stationed in İzmir worship regularly in the cathedral.

The monument of Archbishop Vincent Spaccapierra, Apostolic Delegate to Asia Minor and to the Kingdom of Greece and Archbishop of Smyrna, who dedicated the cathedral on 14 June 1874, is in the N side of the cathedral grounds.

The gardens at **Konak** are in one of the liveliest parts of the city. From the late Ottoman **clock-tower**, described by Goodwin as a 'mauresque bibelot',

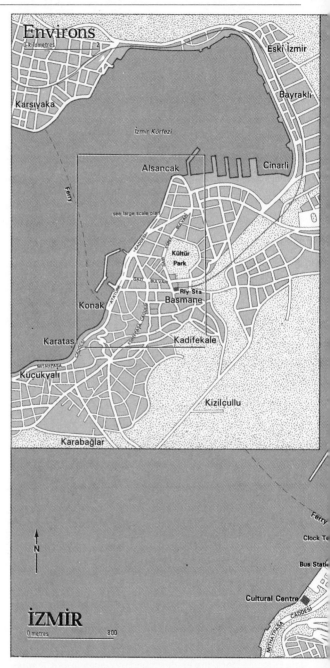

Environs

0 kilometres 2

Eski İzmir

Bayraklı

Karşıyaka

İzmir Körfezi

Alsancak

Cinarli

see large scale plan

Kültür Park

GAZI BULVARI

Rly Sta

Basmane

Konak

Karataş

Kadifekale

Kücükyalı

Kizilçullu

Karabağlar

Ferry

Clock T

Bus Stati

Cultural Centre

N

İZMİR

0 metres 800

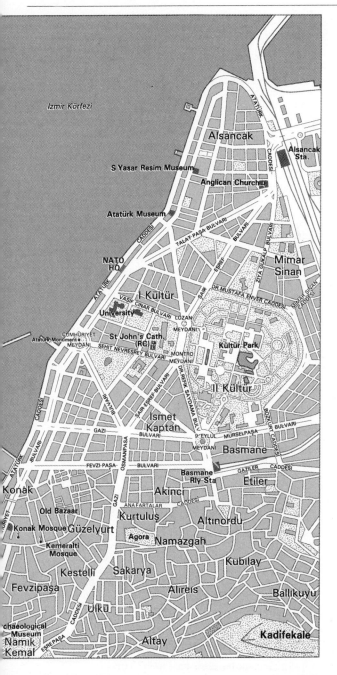

İzmir Körfezi

Alsancak

Alsancak Sta.

S Yasar Resim Museum

Anglican Church

Atatürk Museum

NATO HQ

Mimar Sinan

I Kültür

VASIF ÇINAR BULVARI

University

LOZAN MEYDANI

Atatürk Monument
CÜMHÜRIYET MEYDANI

St John's Cath. (RC)

SEHIT NEVRESBEY BULVARI

MONTRO MEYDANI

Kültür Park

II Kültür

Ismet Kaptan

ŞAIR EŞREF BULVARI

GAZI BULVARI

9 EYLÜL MEYDANI

MÜRSELPAŞA BULVARI

Basmane

FEVZI PAŞA BULVARI

Basmane Rly Sta

GAZILER CADDESI

Etiler

Konak

Old Bazaar

ANAFARTALAR CADDESI

Akıncı

Altınordu

Konak Mosque

Güzelyurt

Agora

Namazgah

Kemeralti Mosque

Kubilay

Kestelli

Sakarya

Fevzipaşa

Alireis

Ballıkuyu

Ülkü

Archaeological Museum

Namık Kemal

Altay

Kadifekale

TALAT PAŞA BULVARI

DR MUSTAFA ENVER CADDESI

DR REFIK SAYDAMA BULV

ATATÜRK CADDESI

ZIYA GÖKALP BULVARI

BOZKURT CADDESI

to the open-air city bus terminal strollers enjoying the *İmbat*, mingle with passengers waiting for bus or dolmuş or a ferry-boat to Karşıyaka.

A few metres away in a warren of twisting lanes and narrow courts, are the shops of Izmir's **Bazaar**. Here a bewildering range of goods—everything from flowers to antiques—is on offer at bargain prices.

From Konak it is only a few minutes walk to İzmir's **Archaeological and Ethnographical Museums**.

The Archaeological Museum houses a rich collection of finds from ancient Smyrna and from a number of other sites in the Aegean. Most of the exhibits are labelled in Turkish and English and there is additional information on wall panels. There is no guide-book.

Postcards, transparencies and booklets are sold in the **entrance hall** where there are toilets. Refreshments are usually available at a small bar.

The exhibits in the entrance hall are changed periodically. At the time of writing a number of **Roman portrait heads**, including two female heads from Pergamum, one from the Antonine period (2C AD), the other from 1C AD; a 4C male head also from Pergamum, and an Antiochus-type head from Metropolis (Torbalı) are exhibited.

From a circular opening in the centre of the entrance hall floor there is an excellent overhead view of a late **Roman mosaic** discovered near Kadifekale which is in the basement gallery. By the door that leads to the gallery on the right-hand side there is a small sculpture of a headless **Dionysus** and a **satyr**. Dating from the 2C AD, this was found at Ephesus.

The **Basement Gallery** is devoted mainly to large sculptures and sarcophagi. These include: the head and forearm of a colossal statue of Domitian from the temple dedicated to him at Ephesus; several sarcophagi; the 1C AD head of youthful, Julio-Claudian prince from Stratoniceia; the lid of a Roman 3C AD **sarcophagus** showing a reclining couple; a funeral stele with books, another with theatre masks; a reconstructed **Early Bronze Age tomb** (3000–2500 BC) with skeleton from Iasus; two archaic **statues of lions**, one from İzmir, the other from Bayındır; a 2C AD sarcophagus from Laodiceia decorated with portrait heads, erotes, medusa heads and garlands; a late Hellenistic **funeral stele** from Tralles; three decorated **terracotta sarcophagi**, one from Mordoğan, one from Clazomenae and one from Smyrna, and two 2C AD portrait statues from Ephesus, one of a sophist, the other of the magnate Flavius Damianus.

The **Basement Long Gallery** contains Roman statues of **Poseidon** and **Demeter** from an altar in the Agora at Smyrna; sculptures and a **relief** from the 3C BC Belevi tomb, and 4C and 5C BC capitals and pillar from Claros and Didyma.

In the **Long Gallery** on the right-hand side of the entrance hall are exhibited statues and reliefs from the Archaic, Classical and Roman periods. These include an **archaic statue** of a woman from Erythrae; a Classical statue of a seated man from Claros; small statues and reliefs of Cybele dating from 30 BC to AD 395 from various sites in western Anatolia; the **bust of a priestess** of Isis from Mylasa; the Hellenistic statue of a young woman from Magnesia; the late Hellenistic statue of **female 'twins'** from Metropolis; statuettes and heads of various figures—Zeus, Apollo, a satyr, etc.—from western Anatolia dating from 30 BC to AD 395; the 2C AD Roman copy of a late Hellenistic bronze statue of a runner, found in the sea off Cyme; a 2C AD Roman copy of a 5C BC head of Aspasa from Ephesus; statuettes of Aphrodite 30 BC to AD 395 from western Anatolia; an early Roman male head from Miletus; the Hellenistic bust of a woman from Stratoniceia; a late Hellenistic funeral stele from İzmir; the archaic head of a young man, and an archaic headless *kore* from Claros.

In the end alcove: a 2C AD chubby, **sleeping Eros** from Ephesus; a Roman head of Hermes from Pergamum; a late Hellenistic head of Athena from Cyme and various female heads from Pergamum and Ephesus.

In the **Parallel Gallery** there are statuettes of gods and goddesses from western Anatolia 30 BC to AD 395; a headless 2C AD statue of Aphrodite from Claros; a 2C AD **statue of Antinous as Androclus**, or, as Akurgal claims, of a hunter, from the Vedius Gymnasium, Ephesus; a late Hellenistic head of Hercules from Pergamum; a 2C AD **herm** of a bearded Hermes from Ephesus; and heads of Dionysus, Pan, etc., from western Anatolia 30 BC to AD 395; a Roman statue of a priest from Halicarnassus; a Roman statue of a sophist from Ephesus, and 2C AD statues of Athena and Tyche from Ephesus.

In the anteroom on the **First Floor** note the **Roman mosaic** from Smyrna showing a sleeping Aphrodite and Eros. Nearby are two Roman reliefs from Ephesus, one depicting Dionysus and nymphs, the other **Dionysus visiting the Athenian actor Ikarios**. (Compare the latter with a similar relief in the Townley Collection in the British Museum.)

The **Right-Hand Gallery** contains objects found during the excavation of a number of sites in Aeolia and Ionia. From Iasus there are vases and terracottas from the Archaic to the Roman periods (700 BC–AD 395). From Miletus Mycenaean, Protogeometric and archaic pottery (1400–300 BC). From Pitane black-figure vases, terracottas, small bronzes, and knuckle-bones from the Archaic and Orientalising periods (625–480 BC). From Smyrna pottery from the Early Bronze Age to the Archaic period (3000–700 BC), black-figure and red-figure vases and small heads and statuettes from the Archaic to the Classical period (700–300 BC). From Pitane pottery of the Orientalising period (625–480 BC). From Foça lamps and black-figure vases from the Archaic to the Roman period (700 BC–AD 395). From Iasus pottery from the Bronze Age (3000–2000 BC). From Erythrae Archaic pottery (700–450 BC), terracottas, bronze arrowheads, a **bronze decorated penis**. Hellenistic terracottas from Myrina dated to 190 BC, including a head ornamented with fruit and flowers and delicately executed erotes. From Pitane amphorae from the Orientalising period (625–480 BC). From the temple of Athena, Bayraklı Smyrna, a damaged **head of a female deity**, which is believed to have come from Cyprus, and a decorated capital.

In the **Left-Hand Gallery** there are Early Bronze Age (3000–2500 BC) pitchers with beaked spouts, Mycenaean pottery (1600–1200 BC) and Classical period (450–300) red-figure pottery all from western Anatolia; Roman pottery (30 BC–AD 395) including a number of inscribed, decorated flasks; terracottas from the Archaic, Classical and Hellenistic periods (700–30 BC), some bearing traces of colour, from various sites in western Anatolia; lamps from the Archaic, Classical, Hellenistic, Roman and Byzantine periods (700 BC–AD 453), some with erotic scenes.

There is a display of carved seals with magnified, colour illustrations of the designs in the **End Gallery**.

In wall cases there are bronze artefacts from the Archaic to the Byzantine era (700 BC–AD 1453), including lamps, balances, daggers, short swords and spear heads; Roman terracottas from western Anatolia; Byzantine pottery (AD 395–1453); Hellenistic pottery (300–30 BC); Archaic period (700–450 BC) black figure vases from western Anatolia; Early Bronze Age (3000–2500 BC) pottery from western Anatolia; Chalcolitic Age (5500–3000 BC) and Archaic and Orientalising period (700–480 BC) pottery from western Anatolia; two early Hellenistic (300–250 BC) hydrias, black with decoration on rim; Hellenistic and Roman glass (300 BC–AD 395) from western Anatolia.

If the **Museum Treasury** is locked, ask to have it opened. It has a fine collection of Roman, Byzantine and Venetian coins. Particularly interesting is a hoard found at Tralles, with specimens from the reigns of Trajan, Antoninus Pius, Caracalla, Elaqabalus, Julia Domna, Geta and Gallienus.

There are several small bronze votive offerings from various periods, also ornaments and jewellery from the 5C BC to the 15C AD. Note the beautiful 4C BC **head of Demeter** found in the sea near Bodrum.

In the garden at the rear of the museum there is a large collection of architectural fragments and sarcophagi from various sites.

The **Ethnographical Museum** occupies an old Ottoman house by the side of the Archaeological Museum. Appropriately, it concentrates on 19C Smyrna. The life of a typical couple is shown in tableaux that take them from marriage to the birth of their first child. Next to the infant in the cradle is a boy wearing the traditional *sünnet* (circumcision) costume. Among other exhibits are a camel decked out in the highly decorative harness worn for the sport of camel wrestling, (see Selçuk below), glassworkers making blue beads which are believed to protect the wearer against the evil eye and a potter at his wheel.

Take a dolmuş from Konak to **Kadifekale** (c 15 minutes), the ancient Mt Pagus. No certain trace has been found of the Hellenistic and Roman fortifications. The imposing ruins visible today date from the Middle Ages.

From Kadifekale there is an excellent view across the harbour to Karşıyaka. To the W you can see the shape of the arena where St Polycarp was martyred. The agora at the foot of the hill is clearly visible. Photographers will enjoy trying to capture the spectacular sunsets.

The area inside the fortifications is a popular playground for local children. Shouting with excitement, they clamber over the ancient walls or conduct stealthy games of hide and seek in the cavernous vaults. Visitors are in no danger from cannonballs, but on occasions may be forced to retreat from flying footballs to the small café which serves tea and soft drinks.

For the agora, return to Konak and ask for Anafartalar Cad. This street is only a few minutes' walk to the site which is called **Namazgah** in Turkish. Alternatively, you may stroll in about 20 minutes from Kadifekale through winding streets to the agora.

Occupying an area of c 120m by 80m, the **agora** was excavated by German and Turkish archaeologists between 1932 and 1941. Surrounded on the W and N by porticoes it had a large altar dedicated to Zeus in the centre. Statues of Poseidon and of Demeter, believed to come from this altar, are in now in the basement gallery of the Archaeological Museum.

The northern stoa was on two levels and rested on a substantial basement. The vaults are still visible. Law cases were heard in an exedra towards the western end of the stoa. A substantial part of the colonnade on the W side of the agora is still standing. Note the **portrait head of Faustina**, the wife of Marcus Aurelius, on an arch in the colonnade. This may commemorate the handsome contribution made by the emperor towards the reconstruction of Smyrna after the earthquake of AD 178.

In the eastern part of the agora there are several architectural fragments bearing **medieval coats of arms**. There is also a stone slab marked out with rectangles which may have been used as a **gaming board**.

Apart from traces of the **Roman theatre** among modern houses near Basmane railway station, the only other remains of Smyrna's past are the **Roman aqueducts** on the road to Ephesus, the so-called 'Baths of Diana', and the site of the first settlement at Bayraklı.

According to Strabo there was a **Homereium**, 'a quadrangular portico containing a shrine and wooden statue' of the poet in this city which, traditionally, was thought to be his birthplace. Homer was associated with the river Meles which has been identified with the modern Halka Pınar, a small river to the N of Alsancak. This forms a large pool popularly called the 'Baths of Diana', although no very firm connection has been made between it and the goddess. (A statue found nearby is believed to represent Artemis.) The pool, which covers the foundations of an ancient building and is surrounded by architectural fragments, is in the grounds of the İzmir Water Company.

In remote antiquity the area occupied by the modern suburb of Bornova was under the sea. Here the first settlement was established in the middle of the third millennium BC on a peninsula that projected into the northern part of the bay. The river Hermus, before it was diverted, brought down large deposits of soil which extended the land. As a result the site is now some distance inland on a hill in Bayraklı, known as Tepekule.

Tepekule, which is rather overgrown, is likely to appeal mainly to specialists. Substantial finds of Protogeometric pottery at the site suggest that the first Greek colonists arrived in the 10C BC. About 600 BC King Alyattes of Lydia laid siege to Smyrna and captured it. A large heap of soil discovered at the W side of the site is believed to have been used by the Lydians as an assault ramp. Although it was later reoccupied, the site remained of minor importance and was abandoned completely sometime in the 4C BC.

Houses dating from the 9C to the 7C BC were found by the archaeologists at Tepekule. The most important discovery, however, was of a temple dedicated to Athena. This, the oldest East Greek temple or shrine discovered in Asia Minor, was constructed towards the end of the 7C BC. It was altered and enlarged on several occasions, notably after its destruction by the Lydians. Capitals and column bases found here are remarkable for the beauty of their design and delicacy of their execution. Some are exhibited in İzmir's Archaeological Museum.

12

Excursions from İzmir

From İzmir (see Route 11) you may visit not only Sardis and Ephesus (see Routes 13 and 14) but a number of less well-known sites in the surrounding area. By private transport, these excursions are easily made. The distances are comparatively short, so the route depends largely on the number of sites which you wish to see in a day. If you use dolmuş or bus you must plan carefully. Buses do not always leave or arrive on time and a dolmuş leaves when it is full. To avoid being stranded, check the time of the last bus or dolmuş back to İzmir.

Some refreshments are available, even in the smallest villages, but there are many places on these routes where you can enjoy a pleasant picnic.

A.   The Baths of Agamemnon, Clazomenae, Erythrae and Çeşme

Total distance c 81km. İzmir—c 11km Baths of Agamemnon—25km Urla—
(c 8km Clazomenae)—(35km Mordoğan—18km Karaburun)—c 37km
Ilica—c 15km İldır/Erythrae—8km Çeşme.

This excursion covers sites and resorts on the N coast of the peninsula to
the W of İzmir. Take Road 300 from city in the direction of Çeşme. For some
distance this follows the coastline. After c 10km a turning to the left leads
1km to the **Baths of Agamemnon**. According to a legend, Agamemnon was
advised by an oracle to bring soldiers, who had been wounded at Troy, to
this place. The baths were used in Roman times but there are no visible
remains of any great antiquity. When Chandler visited the site in the
summer of 1765, he saw coagulated sheep blood on the pavement, which,
he was told, was often used instead of shaving soap.

Springs deliver water with an average temperature of 71°C and a high
sulphur content which is believed to be an excellent specific for rheumatism, skin diseases and sciatica. Sufferers, not only from İzmir but from all
over Turkey, come here in search of a cure.

After c 25km along Road 300, a turning on the right just before **Urla** leads
to ancient **Clazomenae**. Today there is a quarantine station and a hospital
on the peninsula for persons suffering from bone disease.

Very little of the ancient city remains. Like many settlements on the
Aegean coast its stone was transported to İstanbul for the construction of
new buildings. Clazomenae is mainly of interest to specialists.

Clazomenae was famous for the production of beautifully decorated
terracotta sarcophagi. More than 200 dating from the 6C BC were discovered in a small sheltered valley to the SW of Urla İskelesi. The technique
used to decorate vases was employed to ornament the sides and lids with
elaborate scenes of warfare and mythical beasts in heraldic poses. Because
of their relative fragility and weight—the lid of one in the British Museum
weighs 900kg—they were not carried far from the city.

Unfortunately, a large number of Clazomenae sarcophagi were destroyed
in the 1920s towards the end of the Greek-Turkish war. One from nearby
Mordoğan is in the basement gallery of the İzmir Archaeological Museum.
There are others in İstanbul and in various European museums.

History. 'Fretted by the incessant gales from the mouth of the gulf', according to
Professor Cook, 'the people of Clazomenae grew up restless and volatile'. Strabo states
that the city, a member of the Panionic League, was founded by Paralus, an Athenian
hero credited with having invented warships. The official Athenian trireme was called
the Paralos in his honour. Archaeologists believe that the first Greek settlers arrived
here in the 10C BC. The original site appears to have been on the mainland, but,
possibly because of fear of the Persians, the inhabitants moved to an island in the 5C
BC. There they remained until the defeat of Darius by Alexander released them from
danger. Then, possibly as a result of direct orders from Alexander, a causeway was
constructed which linked the island with the mainland. Traces of this structure, which
was 700m long by 9m wide, may be seen by the side of its modern counterpart. In the
mid 18C Chandler had an exciting ride across the ancient structure, 'we were ten
minutes', he wrote, 'in passing over it, the waves, which were impelled by a strong
inbat (sic), breaking over in a very formidable manner, as high as the bellies of our
horses'.

The Clazomenians' support for the Romans against Antiochus of Syria guaranteed
continued prosperity. However, as Smyrna increased in importance, so Clazomenae

declined. At the time of the arrival of the Ottomans on the Aegean coast in the 15C, it was little more than a village.

Clazomenae was the birthplace of two philosophers, Anaxagoras (c 500–428 BC) and Scopelianus (fl. c AD 90). At about the age of 20 Anaxagoras went to Athens. Counting Pericles and Euripides among his friends and pupils, he became a well-known and controversial philosopher. He taught that the universe was composed of an unlimited number of substances. These, under the guidance of an independent intelligence, which he called Nous (Mind), combined to produce all identifiable substances. Considered heretical, he was saved from prosecution, and possibly death, by Pericles. From Athens, he went to Lampsacus, where he died in 428 BC.

In the field of astronomy, Anaxagoras was the first to explain the working of solar eclipses. Portions of his treatise, *On Nature*, still exist.

Scopelianus made a successful plea to Domitian in AD 92 against a harsh imperial decree which would have required the destruction of all the vineyards in Ionia. For this he was greatly honoured by the citizens of Smyrna.

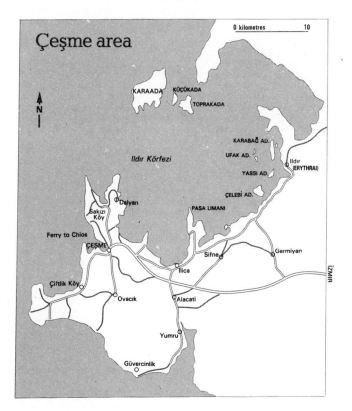

On the W side of the peninsula a short distance from the causeway there is a **cave** containing a sacred well. Beyond the quarantine station are the remains of an ancient harbour wall. Part of the city wall and of a quay may be seen on the NW extremity of the peninsula. On the hill nearby the outline of the **theatre**, which is mentioned by Chandler, is visible and there are traces of a building which may have been a temple.

From Urla continue in the direction of Çeşme for c 12km. A minor road to the right leads to the village of 35km **Mordoğan**, where protogeometric pottery and a terracotta sarcophagus of the Clazomenae-type were found. From Mordoğan continue to 18km **Karaburun**. Fine views over the sea compensate for some difficult driving.

On the main road continue towards Çeşme. About 15km after Uzunkuyu is **İlica**, a small summer resort much favoured by the people of İzmir. Here a turning right leads to the small village of 15km **İldır** which covers part of the ancient city of **Erythrae**.

History. According to Pausanias Erythrae got its name from Erythrus the 'Red', son of Rhadamanthys, who came here with a band of settlers from Crete. Later, immigrants from Lycia, Caria and Pamphylia and other parts of Ionia were added to this nucleus and the city was ruled by descendants of King Codrus of Athens. Erythrae became a member of the Panionic League and, making full use of its excellent harbour, which was sheltered and protected by the islands known as the Hippoi, the Horses, it expanded its trade and prospered.

Under Lydian domination c 560 BC, it became subject to the Persians in 545 BC. Later it sometimes supported Athens, sometimes Sparta. Towards the middle of the 4C BC Erythrae cultivated good relations with Mausolus, the ruler of Caria (377–353 BC). At about the same time it concluded a treaty of mutual assistance with Assos.

Liberated by Alexander, it came under the influence of the Attalids of Pergamum. The Romans made it a free city attached to the province of Asia. Like Clazomenae it was later overshadowed by Smyrna.

Under the Ottomans Erythrae was a village and was largely forgotten. When Chandler visited the site in the middle of the 18C, the area had acquired a reputation for banditry. Taking no chances, he slept guarded by an armed attendant, while other armed servants protected the periphery of the camp and the enclosure where the horses were hobbled.

Erythrae was also plundered of its stone. A large stretch of the late 4C BC **wall**, which guarded the landward approaches to the city, remains. Strengthened by towers and pierced at intervals by gates, this is between 4m and 5m thick and in places still stands to a considerable height. Small sections of the fortifications that protected the acropolis remain. Of the **theatre**, excavated by Turkish archaeologists in 1963, only the stairs are relatively intact. Most of the seating has disappeared and there is no trace of the stage-building.

Between the theatre and the N wall there is a fine **mosaic floor**. The **aqueduct** to the S of the site dates from the Byzantine era. During earlier periods the city received its water through terracotta pipes, as the stream which flows inside the fortified area is not suitable for drinking. This may be the river Aleon, which, according to Pliny, had the unusual property of encouraging the growth of body-hair.

Erythrae had a famous Sibyl, who was surpassed in importance only by the Sibyl of Cumae. According to Pausanias she was called Herophile and was 'born from a nymph and a shepherd of the district called Theodorus'. Greatly respected in Roman times, over 1000 of her prophetic verses were taken to Rome in 83 BC after the temple of Captoline Jupiter had been destroyed by fire. Towards the end of the 19C a certain M. Fontrier claimed to have discovered her cave. Unfortunately, its location has been forgotten.

No trace has been found of the temple of Hercules at Erythrae. According to Pausanias, a statue of the god arrived in the city under miraculous circumstances. Placed on a raft in Tyre (Phoenicia), it sailed through the

Ionian sea to Chios. Both the Erythraians and Chians attempted to capture it, but were unable to do so. A blind Erythraian fisherman named Phormion dreamt that it could be brought ashore if the women of his city made a rope from their hair and fastened it to the raft. The Erythraian women refused to make the sacrifice, but a number of Thracian female slaves gave up their long tresses. The statue was landed and placed in a temple dedicated to Hercules. As a reward only Thracian women were allowed to enter the Herakleion, where the rope was preserved. Phormion's sight was restored by the god. The Erythraians were so proud of their statue that it and the Herakleion appeared on their coinage.

Excavations by Professors Akurgal and Bayburtluoğlu have revealed the site of the Erythraian **temple** dedicated to Athena Polias which is also mentioned by Pausanias. In trenches on top of the acropolis, they found a large quantity of pottery and bronze and ivory offerings. An inscription on a bowl stated that the offerings were the property of the temple. They are now exhibited in a first floor gallery in İzmir's Archaeological Museum.

Return to Road 300 and continue to c 8km **Çeşme**. Overlooking a wind-swept bay, this slightly raffish resort is set in an unexciting landscape.

Accommodation and restaurants. In Çeşme and its environs there are many hotels. These include the four-star hotel *Turban Çeşme Oteli*, four three-star hotels, two two-star hotels, a number of pensions and the *Altin Yunus* (Golden Dolphin) complex. Reasonably-priced restaurants serve Turkish and international food. The *Sahil* and *Körgez*, which usually have fresh fish in the menu, are recommended.

Information. The **Tourist Information Office** near the harbour at İskele Meydanı 8 can provide information about hotels and visits to the Greek island of Chios.

Near the harbour area there is a well-preserved 14C **Genoese fortress**. Captured by Beyazit I c 1400, it was enlarged and strengthened by the Ottomans to protect the approaches to İzmir from attack by Christian forces. It houses a small museum of coins and terracotta figurines found in the area. Near the fortress are the ruins of a late Ottoman (18C) *caravanserai*.

The harbour of Çeşme, quiet now except for visiting yachts and the ferry-boat to (10km) Chios, was the scene of an attack by the Russian Navy on 5 July 1770. This resulted in the destruction of the Ottoman fleet.

Çeşme and the villages around it attract many Turkish and foreign visitors. There are good beaches but, even in summer, the sea can be chilly.

B.   Colophon, Claros and Notium

Total distance to Notium c 95km. İzmir—22km Güzelbahçe—18km Seferi-hisar—(c 6km Sığacık/Teos)—(19km Doğanbey—4km Myonnesus)—8km Lebedus—25km Bulgurla—5km Değirmendere—1.5km Colophon—c13km Claros—2km Notium.

Return journey either via 17km Selçuk or 20km Cileme—5km Bulgurla—12km Cumaovası.

This circular route will take you through interesting countryside to ancient sites and pleasant beaches S of İzmir. The roads are of variable quality and may require careful driving. It is possible to complete the circuit in one day by private transport. By bus or dolmuş divide the route into two parts: İzmir to Teos and Teos to Claros.

It is possible to go to Claros, Notium and Colophon from Selçuk. This road traverses a marsh and flooding has been reported in bad weather.

Leave İzmir by Road 300 and continue to 22km Güzelbahçe. Here turn left just outside the village for 18km Seferihisar and take a road on the right c 6km **Sığacık**, the nearest modern settlement to the site of ancient **Teos**.

Sığacık crouches under the shadow of a medieval Genoese fortress. A short distance away at **Akkum** there are some small hotels, camping places and good bathing from clean, sandy beaches. A recently-built holiday village on the road to Teos offers comfortable accommodation.

From Sığacık you may go to Myonnesus and Lebedus by boat or visit these places en route to Claros. For Myonnesus a 4km scramble from Doğanbey over a rough track not suitable for vehicles is required.

History. According to Pausanias Teos was founded at the beginning of the first millennium BC by Minyans from Orchomenus in Boeotia under the leadership of Athamas. Later they were joined by contingents from Ionia and Athens.

The inhabitants took full advantage of the city's excellent position between two good harbours and developed strong trading interests over a wide area of the Eastern Mediterranean. Early in the 7C BC Teos was sufficiently important to be proposed by Thales of Miletus as the political centre of the Panionic League. After the Persian conquest of Ionia in 546 BC the Teians temporarily abandoned their city and settled at Abdera in Thrace. However, some or all of them must have returned shortly afterwards, as Teos is recorded as having supplied 17 ships to the Ionian fleet which was defeated by the Persians at the battle of Lade in 494 BC. The city was liberated by Alexander the Great, who considered constructing a canal from Teos to İzmir Körfezi. Later the city came under the control of Antigonus and then of Lysimachus, who moved some of its inhabitants to the new foundation which he had created at Ephesus.

Teos had a large and famous temple dedicated to Dionysus, the god of wine and of the creative and artistic powers of nature. As he was the tutelary genius of drama, it is not surprising that towards the end of the 3C BC Teos was chosen to be the centre in Asia of the Guild of the Artists of Dionysus. These were professional actors and musicians, who performed at the festivals which were held then in all major centres. At first honoured by their presence, the Teians soon found the artists insufferably arrogant and difficult. After many quarrels between the citizens and members of the guild, the actors and musicians were obliged to move to Ephesus. Faring no better there, they were sent to the small settlement of Myonnesus, near Teos, and from there to Lebedus, where they appear to have to have found a permanent home.

Teos seems to have prospered at first under the Romans, but suffered a gradual decline. Like other Ionian cities it probably could not compete with the growing power and influence of Smyrna. During the Middle Ages and after the Ottoman conquest the population was concentrated in the village of Sığacık.

Richard Chandler, who visited Teos in the middle of the 18C, discovered a wilderness of abandoned ruins. He writes:

> 'We found this city almost as desolate as Erythrae and Clazomene. The walls, of which traces were extant, were, as we guessed, about five miles in circuit; the masonry handsome. Without them, by the way, are vaults of sepulchres stripped of their marble, as it were forerunners of more indistinct ruin. Instead of the stately piles, which once impressed ideas of opulence and grandeur, we saw a marsh, a field of barley in ear, buffaloes ploughing heavily by defaced heaps and prostrate edifices, high trees supporting aged vines, and fences of stones and rubbish, with illegible inscriptions,and time-worn fragments. It was with difficulty we discovered the temples of Bacchus; but a theatre in the side of the hill is more conspicuous. The vault only, on which the seats ranged, remains, with two broken pedestals in the area'.

Anacreon (c 570–485), often described as the last great lyric poet of East Greece, was undoubtedly the most famous Teian. With his fellows he moved to Abdera to escape the Persians. Later he went to Samos as an honoured guest at the court of the tyrant Polycrates and then to Athens at the invitation of Hipparchus.

A bon viveur and a hedonist, he was renowned for his glorification of of the arts, of music and of love. These he celebrated in poems like *To a Thracian Filly* or in the lines he addressed to his drinking companions:

'Come, let us not think of another Scythian drinking-bout with noise
and shouts, but let us drink gently with beautiful songs'.

Anacreon lived a life full of pleasure to the end. At the age of 85 he choked to death on a grape pip.

The site of Teos is c 1km to the S of the village of Sığacık. The small acropolis is on a low hill between the N and S harbours. There are the remains of an archaic polygonal wall on the W side. A structure to the NE of the acropolis has been identified by an inscription as a gymnasium. To the S of the acropolis are the ruins of the **theatre**. The cavea has been largely destroyed, but there are substantial remains of the stage-building. Originally con structed in the 2C BC, it was modified during the Roman period.

The main area of the city lies between the S boundary of the acropolis and the S harbour. Enclosed by a 3C BC Hellenistic wall is a large rectangular area that was extended on the E side to include a quay. A short stretch of the W wall remains visible. SE of the theatre are the well-preserved ruins of the odeum. Two statue bases found here have inscriptions honouring Teian citizens of the Roman period.

W of the odeum the excavators have laid bare part of an ancient street and some private houses. SW of this area are the substantial ruins of the **Temple of Dionysus**. Dating from c 130 BC, this was an Ionic peripteros with 6 by 11 columns resting on a stylobate which measured 18.5 by 35m. Consisting of an unusually large pronaos, a cella and a small opisthodomos, it was enclosed by a trapezoidal-shaped temenos. Believed to be the early work of Hermogenes of Priene, the temple was restored during the reign of Hadrian.

First excavated by members of the Society of Dilettanti in the 18C, further work was done on the temple by French archaeologists in the early 19C and by a Turkish team in the mid 1960s. A certain amount of restoration has been carried out on the structure. Fragments of an acroterion and of a frieze with reliefs from the temple are now in İzmir's Archaeological Museum. Before leaving this part of the site note the small stretch of an ancient street, with a central water channel, which lies between the temenos and the W wall of the city.

The small S harbour of Teos has been reduced considerably since ancient times by material brought down by the stream that flows in from the NE. Note the large mooring stones that are partly covered by the sea.

To visit Myonnesus, return to Seferihisar and continue S in the direction of Lebedus. After a very short distance a minor road on the right leads c 19km to **Doğanbey**, and from there it is a c 4km walk to Myonnesus.

Myonnesus, a rocky islet c 60m high, was joined to the mainland in ancient times by a causeway which may still be used by hardy souls. Normally the water reaches no higher than the waist. The overhanging cliffs provided ships with shelter from the elements and on at least one celebrated occasion from attack by enemies. However, the islet is too steep and too small to have supported a community of any size. Although no trace of buildings has been found on the mainland—not even of the theatre used by the Artists of Dionysus—the settlement must have been located somewhere on the flat ground near the end of the causeway. On the island there are the remains of an early cyclopean wall and the ruins of some buildings and cisterns, which date from more recent times.

Return to the junction just after Seferihisar and take the minor road to the left. The site of **Lebedus** is c 8km along the coast. The city, which occupied a small peninsula, was one of the poorest in the Panionic League. Surrounded on the landward side by the territory of its neighbours, it had an indifferent harbour and was never a commercial centre of any importance.

History. According to Strabo, Lebedus was founded by Andropompus, according to Pausanias by Andraemon, one of the many sons of Codrus, the last king of Athens. Andraemon is credited with having driven out the Carians, who occupied the site.

Later, part of its population was transferred to Ephesus by Lysimachus. However, the city continued to exist. In 266 BC it was under the rule of the Ptolemies and for a time it was the home of the Artists of Dionysus. Coins were isssued as late as the 2C AD. During the Byzantine era Lebedus was an episcopal see.

Lebedus has not been excavated and the visible remains are meagre. There are traces of fortification on the SE side of the acropolis and on the plain to the E the ruins of some unidentified buildings. On the peninsula there are the substantial remains of a Hellenistic ashlar wall which was strengthened by towers. In the E corner of this area are the ruins of a Byzantine church. According to Pausanias, 'The baths in the soil of Lebedus are as useful as they are wonderful to mankind'. Chandler visited them in the 18C and describes steam rising from 'a small tepid brook, called Elijah' which was hidden in a deep cleft. The water, as disagreeable as in most spas, tasted, he said, of copperas. A bath between Seferihisar and Ürkmez still attracts visitors in search of a cure for rheumatism and related complaints.

Continue to Colophon, Claros and Notium by a minor road via c 30m Değirmendere which skirts the edge of Karacadağ.

Colophon, which means summit or culmination (hence the frequent use of the word to describe the tail-piece of a book), was excavated by archaeologists from Harvard and the American School of Classical Studies in Athens in 1922. The site, which is on the summit of a hill, is reached by a narrow path from the end of the village of **Değirmendere** (c 1.5km).

History. Legend states that Colophon, originally occupied by Carians, was taken over by Greek settlers from Pylos, led by the hero Neleus.

The city was renowned for the skill of its cavalry and for using trained dogs to assist its soldiers. Dogs were also sacrificed to the gods at Colophon, particularly to Hecate, that mysterious and threatening goddess of the underworld, whose customary oblation was a black bitch offered under cover of darkness.

A member of the Panionic League, Colophon was at first vigorous in warfare and active in trade and commerce. Possibly because of the stratagem used by some Colophonians to capture Smyrna (see above) its people had a reputation for guile and cunning. Wealth from trading and revenue from the pilgrims, who came to the shrine of Apollo at Claros, produced ostentation, effeminacy and political and military weakness. Many of its citizens were accustomed to go into the agora dressed in costly purple robes and smothered in rare perfumes. As in the case of Sybaris in Magna Graecia, which was destroyed by the Crotonians, the profligate ways of the people of Colphon brought about their downfall. Captured first by Gyges, king of Lydia, the city later fell to the Persians. Even after its liberation by Alexander the Great Colophon's troubles were not over. The city supported Antigonus in his struggle against Lysimachus. The latter was victorious and c 300 BC, as a punishment, he forced many of the Colophonians to move to Ephesus to swell the population of his new foundation.

Colophon does not appear to have recovered from this blow. During the Hellenistic and Roman periods it was joined to Notium and was known simply as the Old Town. Overshadowed by nearby Ephesus, Colophon-Notium managed to exist on the dues of visitors, who came to consult the oracle at Claros. Its great days of wealth and power ended and it declined into poverty and obscurity.

The philosopher, poet and traveller Xenophanes was born in Colophon c 570 BC. He lived for some time in Elea (Velia), Magna Graecia, and was regarded as the originator of the Eleatic doctrine of the oneness of the universe.

Apart from sections of a Hellenistic wall there is little to see at the site. The archaeologists found parts of a stoa, a baths complex and sections of paved streets. However, the site is overgrown and these remains are no longer easy to find. Only the very keen will make the steep climb to the summit.

Claros is c 13km to the S of Colophon. Arrows point down a rough path on the left-hand side of the road to the site. The ruins of the sanctuary and oracle of Apollo are in a depression. This was the river valley of the Halys or Halesus, which, according to Pausanias, is the coldest river in Asia Minor. In the mid 18C Chandler identified the site by this peculiarity. It was excavated by a French expedition in 1970. Flooding in subsequent years has covered much of their discoveries. The temple and its associated buildings lie below the level of the water-table and, as at Letoön in Lycia, constant pumping would be needed to keep them clear of water and silt.

History. According to legend Claros was founded by settlers from Crete and Thebes. Among the Thebans was the prophetess Manto. She married the leader of the Cretans and in due course produced Mopsus, who became an oracle famed for the accuracy of his prophecies.

The first reference to the sanctuary is in the 7C BC Homeric hymn to Apollo. There is no mention of the oracle until the beginning of the Hellenistic period. One of the earliest known prophecies relates to the construction of the new city of Smyrna by Lysimachus in the 4C BC (see Route 11). During the late Hellenistic period the oracle of Claros appears to have been neglected. This may have been due to rivalry and some competition from nearby Didyma and the continuing effect of Colophon's unfortunate support of Antigonus in his struggle with Lysimachus.

The Roman period saw a revival in Claros. In AD 18, Germanicus, adopted son of Tiberius, was told by the oracle that his death was imminent. The prophecy was fulfilled within a year. He succumbed in Antioch to poison, which many believed was administered, if not at the behest, certainly with the knowledge of the emperor.

Hadrian contributed handsomely to the reconstruction and rededication of the temple and people from all over the Roman world flocked to Claros to consult the god. On the steps on the E side of the temple and on the inside walls of the propylon some of their names and homelands are recorded—Pisidia, Pontus, Caria and Phrygia, Corinth, Crete and Thrace. Inscriptions recording the advice of the oracle have been found as far away as Algeria, Dalmatia, Rome and Britain on subjects as diverse as love and the prospects for a good harvest.

Consultations took place at night. On the E side of the temple an underground passage led by a tortuous route to the adyton. Clients were not admitted here. They were obliged to wait in the pronaos. The adyton consisted of two chambers sited directly under the cella, which contained a giant statue of Apollo. In the inner chamber the prophet, who held office for a year, inspired by a draught of sacred water delivered the prophecy to the thespiode, who turned it into verse. The thespiode and the priest, who were appointed for life, waited in the outer chamber. In this room a portion of a large egg-shaped marble stone was found. This was the omphalos, the navel-stone of the world, which, originally associated with the worship of the god at Delphi in Greece, in the course of time came to be regarded as one of his most important symbols.

Entrance to the temenos from the S was by a propylon which rested on a three step crepidoma. On the N side of the columns of the propylon were inscribed the names of some of the clients who had consulted the oracle. To the right of the propylon there was an exedra and on the left a stoa. The sacred way, which was lined with statues of Roman notables, led to the **Hellenistic temple**. This, a 4C BC Doric peripteros measuring 46m by 26m with 11 by 6 columns, rested on a five step crepidoma. The peripteros was completed during the reign of Hadrian. In the cella there was a giant statue of the god estimated to be c 8m high. To judge by the coins of Claros, Apollo was seated, holding a lyre in his left hand and a wreath of bay leaves in his right. Artemis, his sister, stood on the right side of the god, Leto, his mother, on the left. Parts of the statue of Apollo found during the course of the excavations remain on the site.

A large marble **altar**, measuring 18.5m by 9m, dedicated to Apollo and Dionysus was found c 30m E of the temple. Nearby there was a Hellenistic sundial. To the S of the temple of Apollo was a small temple, believed to date to the 6C BC, dedicated to Clarian Artemis. Coins of the city suggest that the statue of the goddess was very similar to that of Artemis of Ephesus.

Some of the finds from Claros, including a splendid archaic statue of a man carrying a calf to sacrifice, are in the İzmir Archaeological Museum.

About 2km to the SW of Claros is the site of **Notium**. This occupies an area c 1km long by 500m wide on a hill above the sea. The splendid views S to Samos and SE to Ephesus and Kuşadası from the acropolis are some compensation for the paucity of visible remains.

History. Little is known about Notium. According to Herodotus an Aeolian foundation, it was never a member of the Panionic League. In the 5C BC some of its citizens allied themselves with Colophon which at that time supported the Persians against the Athenians. A wall was raised, which divided the city into two parts and separated the warring factions. However, the Athenians intervened and brought Notium once more under their control.

After Lysimachus removed a substantial part of the population of Colophon to Ephesus (see above), Notium increased in importance and became known as Neocolophon or Colophon-by-Sea. In time, however, as Ephesus prospered, it declined and with Colophon it decreased in size and importance.

Visiting the site, which is overgrown in parts, involves a climb up a fairly steep slope. The city was enclosed by a Hellenistic wall constructed of large, regular stone blocks. This structure, substantial sections of which remain, was c 4km in length. It was strengthened by towers at intervals and had a number of gates. Those on the W and N are still visible. On the W of the site there are the remains of a small Hadrianic Corinthian temple in antis dedicated to Athena Polias. On the E side of this there was an altar measuring c 5m by 8m. The temenos was surrounded by a Doric stoa. A few large blocks of stone in a flat area further to the E marks the site of one of the agoras. Just beyond the agora was the *bouleuterion*. A small Hellenistic **theatre** with 27 rows of seats, which was modified during Roman times, is at the top of the E hill. The **necropolis** was NW of the city. Burial was in low walled sepulchres or in tombs cut horizontally into the rock.

Nearby there is a sandy beach with plenty of places to enjoy an alfresco meal or a barbecue and restaurants which offer simple meals.

The return journey from Notium to İzmir may be made via Değirmendere and Cumaovası or Selçuk and the 550/E87.

13

İzmir to Sardis, Manisa, and Afyon

Total distance c 99km. İzmir—39km Manisa/Magnesia ad Sipylum—30km
Turgutlu—30km Sartmustafa/Sardis. Then 10km Salihli—47km Kula—
56km Uşak (—c 35km Sivaslı)—(Cabeira, Kainon Chorion)—(Sincarlı).

İzmir (see Route 11) is linked to Manisa and Sartmustafa (Sardis) by fast motor roads
(565 and E96/300). Road 250 from Manisa joins the E23/300 c 5km W of Turgutlu, so
a round trip is a feasible proposition. However, as there is a good deal to see in both
Manisa and Sardis, if you are not in a hurry, make separate journeys to each place.

There are frequent direct services from İzmir's otogar to Manisa and to Sartmustafa.
In both cases the journey takes about one hour. Again the round trip İzmir, Manisa,
Sartmustafa, İzmir is possible by public transport, but services from Manisa to
Sartmustafa are relatively infrequent so time could be lost waiting for a connection.

There are also guided tours from İzmir to Sardis. The remains of the ancient city are
scattered over a wide area and transport reduces the amount of physical effort required.
However, the time allowed at the site on organised tours is often limited.

The 14C Arab traveller Ibn Battuta described Manisa as 'a large and
beautiful city built on a mountain slope, in whose territory there are many
rivers, springs and fruitful orchards'. Today **Manisa** is a pleasant town of
c 130,000 inhabitants, somewhat overshadowed by İzmir but retaining
much of its ancient charm.

Accommodation and Information. Manisa has one two-star hotel, *Arma Oteli*, Doğu
Cad. 14, on the Ministry of Tourism list. However, as it is so close to İzmir most visitors
stay there. The **Tourist Information Office** is in Yarhasanlar Mah. Doğu Cad., No. 14/3.
The *Turistik Lokanta*, 5 Eylül Cad., offers meals and refreshments at reasonable prices.

History. According to legend, Manisa, the ancient **Magnesia ad Sipylum**, was founded
by Thessalians returning from Troy c 1190 BC. Captured by Croesus (561–546 BC), the
last Lydian king, it fell into the hands of the Persians in 546 BC, when they subjugated
Ionia. The city was liberated by Alexander the Great in 334 BC after his victory over
the Persian army at the battle of the Granicus. To maintain control of the area he settled
a number of Macedonian veterans in the city.
    After the death of Alexander, possession of Magnesia ad Sipylum was disputed by
the Diadochoi. It came under the control of Pergamum in 190 BC after the defeat of
Antiochus III by a combined Roman and Pergamene force.
    Magnesia enjoyed a period of prosperity under the Attalids and this continued under
Roman rule. Suffering extensive damage from the earthquake of AD 17, it received
financial assistance from Tiberius for the restoration of the public buildings.
    The city remained a centre of some importance under the Byzantines. In the early
13C, when Constantinople was occupied by the Crusaders, the emperor John III
(1222–54) built a citadel in Magnesia. He was buried here.
    After the return of the Byzantines to Constantinople in 1261, Magnesia declined in
importance. The Crusaders and the Selçuk Turks contested its possession. Captured
by the emir Surhan in 1313, it remained in Turkish hands thereafter.
    Ibn Battuta has left a moving and somewhat macabre account of the obsequies of
the son of Surhan. After his arrival in the city, he went to visit the ruler. He found him
in the burial chamber of the young prince who had died some months earlier. In the
company of the youth's mother, the emir had spent the night of the Feast of the Sacrifice
and part of the following day by his son's corpse. The body had been embalmed and
placed in a wooden coffin covered with a tin-plated iron lid and had been raised up
in the middle of the roofless chamber, so that the unpleasant odours of decay might
escape through the opening. Later the roof of the burial chamber was closed by a dome

and the coffin, draped with the mourning cerements of the youth, lowered to the ground. It seems likely that this procedure continued an ancient custom of the Turks, who, when they were still nomads, placed the body of a recently-dead member of the clan high in the branches of a tree until it had dried out and become partly mummified.

Surhan and his successors gave Manisa many fine buildings. After the capture of the city by Mehmet Çelebi, son of Bayezit I, in 1405, a further phase of construction was started by the Ottomans. As a result Manisa has a rich heritage of Islamic buildings.

For some time in the 18C the city came under the control of a semi-autonomous local dynasty. Chandler visited the town in the mid 18C. It was 'still populous and has a great trade. The mosques are numerous; and the Greeks have a large and handsome church, and also a monastery'. Many of Manisa's buildings were damaged during the fighting between the Greek and Turkish armies in the 1920s.

The buildings of greatest interest are in the centre of the town. The **Muradiye Camii**, which dates from 1586, adjoins the museum. Note the elaborate *mihrab* with its fine faïence decoration. The painting on the cupola and pendentives is comparatively recent, dating from the early 19C.

Ulu Camii was built in 1366 during the reign of Işak Bey on the foundations of a Byzantine fortress. Much ancient material was used in its construction. The columns of the portico before the prayer hall are crowned with Roman and Byzantine capitals. The tomb of Işak Bey is nearby.

In 1522 the **Valide complex** with its twin minarets was built by Süleyman the Magnificent in honour of his mother, Hafıse Hatun. A number of ancient columns were also used in the construction of the portico of this mosque. In the area surrounding the complex, the feast of Mesir Bayrami is celebrated with great enthusiasm on the last Sunday in April. The people of Manisa flock here to obtain the sweetmeat made locally since the 16C.

Off Atatürk Bulv. in a public park is the **Halk Evi**, the House of the People. In this building are incorporated the walls of an ancient library, where the youthful Mehmet II, the Conqueror, pursued his studies.

Manisa's **Archaeological and Ethnographical Museums** opened in 1935. The collections were reorganised, when they moved to their present site near Muradiye Camii in 1972.

The archaeological items are housed in a former *imaret*. In rooms around a central court are artefacts from the Prehistoric era, Hellenistic, Roman and Byzantine periods. Of particular interest are the objects found at Sardis, a site which has been excavated by American archaeologists since 1958. The finds are arranged by period and include some fine mosaics, ceramics, statues, terracottas, bronzes and inscriptions. There are also some artefacts from the town and the surrounding countryside. Note particularly the fine 2C AD statue of a child which was discovered in Manisa.

The ethnographical collection is in a *medrese*. The exhibits include weapons, wood carvings, ceramic tiles, embroidered garments, kilims and carpets. One room has been furnished in typical Turkish style.

Around the sides and on the summit of **Sandık Tepesi** are the remains of fortifications dating from the foundation of Magnesia to the 13C AD. Modern terracing makes the ascent of the hill difficult and only the view justifies the effort. The ruins are rather disappointing. The first two walls are completely Byzantine, the lower dating from the period of occupation by John III (see above) in the 13C. The wall on the summit was built during the middle Byzantine period c 8C on the foundations of a much earlier fortification, believed to date from the first foundation of the city.

In the countryside around Manisa there are some interesting curiosities. On the SW edge of the town to the right of the İzmir–Manisa road there is an natural rock formation that has been remarked on since antiquity. This is the so-called **Niobe rock** described by Pausanias. 'I myself have seen Niobe when I was climbing up the mountains to

Sipylos. Niobe from close up is a rock and a stream, and nothing like a woman either grieving or otherwise; but if you go further off you seem to see a woman downcast and in tears'. Niobe, the daughter of Tantalus, bore Amphion seven sons and seven daughters. Proud of her achievement she boasted that she was superior to Leto, who had only two children. However, these were the divinities Apollo and Artemis and, to avenge the insult to their mother, they slew all the children of Niobe.

At **Akpınar** c 7km E of Manisa on Road 250 there is a very weathered representation of a seated woman. The carving, believed to be Hittite, has been identified as a representation of the Anatolian Mother Goddess. She is depicted in full-face, seated in a recess with her arms across her breast. Her feet rest on two footstools. Outside the niche there is an illegible hieroglyphic inscription. The carving, which is sometimes called *Taş Suret*, the stone figure, is to the right of the main road. It is easily reached by a scramble across the scree and a short climb.

The village of **Sartmustafa**, whose name echoes its famous predecessor, is 60km from Manisa via (30km) Turgutlu. It occupies part of the site of ancient **SARDIS**, but the resemblance goes no further than the name. Described by Spon towards the end of the 17C as *'un pauvre village'*, it has changed little since then.

Sartmustafa, with its two coffee-houses, school and a scattering of cottages, is bisected by the E96/300. This busy road also divides the site. Despite the number of visitors to Sardis, the hospitality of the villagers is in the best Turkish tradition. They are friendly and courteous hosts and willing guides.

The ruins of Sardis are extensive and widely spread. In view of the time required for the journey from İzmir or Manisa, allow at least a day, if you wish to see them all.

Only tea and soft drinks are sold in the village and, as the nearest restaurants are in Salihli c 8km to the E, bring a picnic lunch which can be enjoyed in a pleasant meadow by the side of the tree-shaded Pactolus.

History. There is a reference in Homer to the Maeonians. According to Herodotus the Maeonians changed their name and called themselves Lydians. Modern research suggests, however, that the Lydians were invaders, who conquered and dispossessed the Maeonians at some time in the remote past. The Lydian language, which belongs to the Indo-Germanic group, has affinities with Lycian, Phrygian, Etruscan and, according to some authorities, Hittite. Although the Lydians borrowed the Greek alphabet and were influenced by Greek culture, they were not of Greek origin. They were, however, well known to the Greeks. Homer mentions landmarks like 'eddying' Hermus and 'snowy' Tmolus. Euripides set the birthplace of Dionysus on Tmolus, and Ovid suggested that the gold found in the Pactolus was carried downstream from Phrygia because Midas had once bathed in its upper reaches.

Sometime in the 8C BC a new line of kings, the Mermnadae, came into being in Lydia. According to Herodotus, Candaules, the last ruler of the Heraclid dynasty, was so besotted by his wife's beauty that he invited a courtier named Gyges to look on her naked body. Despite Candaules's assurance that this could be done without his wife's knowledge, Gyges was seen by the queen. Angered by what had happened, she summoned him to her presence and told him that he must kill the king and take his place or die himself. Gyges murdered Candaules, married the queen and proclaimed himself king. He was not accepted by all the Lydians and, to prevent civil strife, he agreed to submit the matter to the judgment of the oracle of Apollo at Delphi. The oracle found in Gyges's favour, but declared that the Heraclids would be revenged in the fifth generation. Gyges and his successors ignored this part of the prophecy which was fulfilled during the reign of Croesus. Gyges rewarded the oracle handsomely, sending gifts of gold and silver, including six golden mixing-bowls which weighed nearly 1134kg and which were kept in the Corinthian treasury at Delphi.

Gyges (680–652 BC) and his Mermnadae successors were vigorous rulers who extended their kingdom towards the coast and into Anatolia. They resisted the attacks of the Cimmerians, a barbarous people who, forced by invaders to move from their lands on the N shore of the Black Sea, had conquered Phrygia and advanced into Lydia sacking Sardis. Ardys (651–625) finally destroyed their power and the Cimmerians disappeared from the pages of ancient historians. Ardys then turned his attention to the Greek cities on the coast, capturing Priene. Alyattes (609–560) took Smyrna.

Croesus (560–546), the last of the Mermnadae, controlled all the cities on the Aegean except Miletus. The Lydians, having overrun Phrygia, had a common frontier on the river Halys, the Kızılırmak, with the Persian Empire. Croesus consulted the oracle of Apollo and was told that if he attacked the Persians he would destroy a great empire. He interpreted this ambiguous advice wrongly and was defeated by Cyrus. Croesus did indeed destroy a great empire, his own.

Croesus took refuge in Sardis, which was besieged by the Persians. Herodotus describes how the city, considered to be impregnable, was taken. One of the defenders accidentally dropped his helmet from the fortifications on the S side and clambered down to recover it. His action was witnessed by a besieger. Next day, with a group from his unit, he followed the same route and gained entrance to the city.

While his soldiers were sacking Sardis, Cyrus had Croesus bound and placed on a pyre. As the flames began to reach him, Croesus called on Apollo for help. The god answered his prayer and from a clear sky sent a downpour which extinguished the flames. Cyrus, awed by this manifestation of divine intervention, had Croesus freed from his bonds and placed the former king on a throne near him. Observing Persian activity in the city, Croesus asked his conqueror what was happening. Cyrus replied that his soldiers were sacking Sardis and carrying away Croesus's wealth. 'Not mine any longer', retorted Croesus. 'Nothing there belongs to me now. It is your city they are destroying and your treasure they are taking away'.

The Lydians claimed to have invented games like knucklebones and dice which they passed on to their Greek neighbours and through them to the rest of the ancient world. Perhaps their greatest contribution was the introduction and popularisation of coined money and the concept of retail trading. They produced the first coins whose value was guaranteed by the state. These bore no inscription but a representation of the emblem of Sardis, a lion's head. At first made from electrum, a mixture of gold and silver, pure gold and pure silver coins were introduced by Croesus. Among the customs that distinguished the Lydians from the Greeks, Herodotus mentions the fact that women were permitted to chose their own husbands and that working-class girls in Lydia prostituted themselves before marriage to acquire enough money for their dowries.

The Persians turned Lydia into a satrapy and, governed by their nominee, it enjoyed a limited degree of freedom. Angered by the revolt of a Lydian named Pactyes, the Persians forced his fellow countrymen to abandon all warlike pursuits and to devote themselves to trade and to the arts. The same measures were taken against the neighbouring Phrygians. One of the results of this policy was the development of the Phrygian and Lydian musical modes. The Phrygian mode was stimulating and exciting, the Lydian calm, reflective and somewhat effeminate in character.

Alexander the Great liberated Lydia from the Persian yoke. After his death, its possession was contested by the Diadochoi. During the reign of Antiochus III, Sardis was captured in circumstances reminiscent of those that occurred when the city was invested by Cyrus. Achaeus, a pretender to the throne, took refuge there and the city was besieged by Antiochus. One of his soldiers noticed that vultures and other birds of prey perched for long periods on a section of the city wall above a pit into which refuse including dead animals was thrown by the defenders. Concluding that this part of the fortifications was poorly defended, Antiochus mounted an attack there and captured the city.

After the defeat of Antiochus by a combined Roman and Pergamene force at the battle of Magnesia ad Sipylum (Manisa) in 190 BC, Sardis came under the rule of Pergamum. Prospering under the Attalids, it passed to the Romans in 133 BC, when the last king of Pergamum, the paranoiac Attalus III, willed his kingdom to them. Sardis continued to expand and develop under the Romans who made it an administrative centre and ornamented it with many beautiful buildings. After the great earthquake in AD 17 Tiberius gave large sums of money for restoration and rebuilding.

Christianity found converts at an early date in Sardis. It was one of the Seven Churches of Asia addressed by St John in the Book of Revelation. Even though the new faith appears to have made rapid progress there, John was not convinced that all

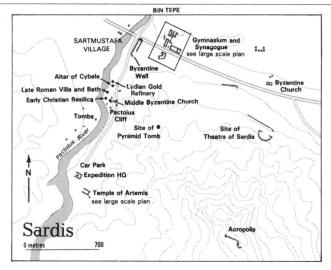

BIN TEPE

SARTMUSTAFA VILLAGE

Gymnasium and Synagogue
see large scale plan

Byzantine Wall

Altar of Cybele

Late Roman Villa and Bath

Early Christian Basilica

Lydian Gold Refinery

Byzantine Church

Middle Byzantine Church

Tombs

Pactolus Cliff

Site of Pyramid Tomb

Site of Theatre of Sardis

Pactolus River

N

Car Park

Expedition HQ

Temple of Artemis
see large scale plan

Sardis

Acropolis

0 metres   700

was well. He admonished the Christians of Sardis: 'though you have a name for being alive, you are dead. For I have not found any work of yours completed in the eyes of my God'. (Revelation 3:1–2.)

Sardis was an episcopal see during the Byzantine era. Its later history was marked by decline and decay which was accelerated by attacks from hostile forces. Captured by the Sassanids in the 7C, it fell into the hands of the Turks in the 11C. In 1401 it was taken by Tamerlane who razed it to the ground. Sardis never recovered and during the centuries of Ottoman rule it was a place of little importance.

Among the first travellers from the W to visit Sardis were Spon, who came here towards the end of the 17C, and Chandler, who explored its remains 100 years later. During the course of centuries the friable rock on the surrounding hills had collapsed and the detritus together with silt brought down by the Pactolus covered many of the ruins, causing Chandler to note that 'the site of this once noble city was now green and flowery'. The first attempts to explore Sardis scientifically were made at the beginning of this century. Since 1958 a team of American archaeologists from Harvard and Cornell Universities under the direction of Professor M.A. Hanfmann has been systematically unearthing and restoring the city's ancient buildings.

The principal ruins of Sardis are spread over four large and widely separated areas. The first is to the left of the E96 just after the crossroads in the centre of the village. From the large car-park a rough path leads to a section of the city's ancient street. Paved with marble slabs, this was lined on both sides with colonnades and shops. The southern colonnade and associated buildings now lie under the modern road.

The 29 buildings on the N side are Byzantine and have been dated to the 4C AD. They were probably occupied until the capture of the city by the Persians in the 7C. The first was a public toilet. Most of the rest were devoted to commerce. Note particularly **W8**, where there is a large basin marked with crosses which may have been used as a baptismal font. **E2** was a restaurant. Nearby, five columns of the colonnade, some crowned with Ionic some with Corinthian capitals, are still standing. **E7** was Jacob's paint shop. **E10** was a hardware shop. **E13**, the shop of Sabbatios, had a small private toilet. **E14** was the shop of Jacob, an elder of the synagogue.

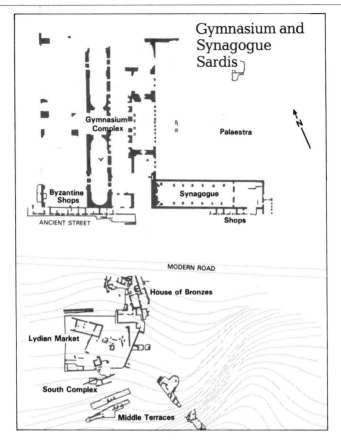

At the side entrance to the synagogue there is an area of decorated pavement. Note the inscribed slab on the ground nearby which refers to Germanicus, the nephew of Tiberius, who died under mysterious circumstances in Antioch in AD 19 (see Claros above). The Greek text is believed to date from either AD 17 or AD 43.

The **Gymnasium complex** to the N of the colonnaded street had two large halls, one on the N and one on S side. After various alterations and changes the southern hall was converted into a synagogue sometime in the 3C AD. An inscription in Hebrew found here suggests that the building may have been given by the Emperor Lucius Verus (161–169) to the local Jewish community. There is some evidence that Jews had settled in Sardis as early as 547 BC. Some authorities believe that Sardis, *Sfard* in Lydian, may be the city of the Sepharad who are mentioned in Obadiah 20.

Restored extensively, the synagogue has an atrium, which had a large marble basin surrounded by columns in its centre, and a long narrow assembly hall divided into seven sections. Three doors led to the hall from the atrium. Inside these doors there were two shrines. The southern shrine probably housed the Torah. This unusual arrangement was dictated by the

Temple of Artemis
Sardis

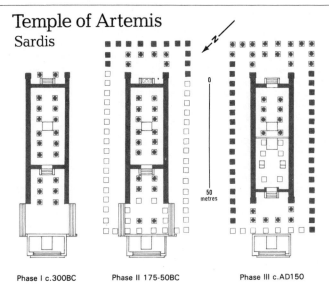

Phase I c.300BC   Phase II 175-50BC   Phase III c.AD150

fact that the building had not been designed as a synagogue and the shrines were placed here, the Jerusalem-facing part of the hall.

There appears to have been no separate section for women in the synagogue. They either worshipped with the men or were not permitted to enter the hall. There is no trace of any permanent seating for the congregation. They may have sat on the floor or on temporary wooden seats brought in for the services. At the W end of the main hall there was a semicircular apse, which had three rows of marble benches for the elders. In front of the apse stood a large marble table. This had eagles with open wings on the left and right sides and was flanked by double lions that faced backwards and forwards. Much of the floor area was covered by mosaics.

Access to the **gymnasium complex** was from the colonnades on the N, S and E sides. A substantial part of the W side of this imposing structure, which was completed in AD 211, has been restored to a height of c 18m. According to an inscription on the façade it was dedicated by the citizens of Sardis to Geta and Caracalla, the sons of Septimius Severus, and to their mother, Julia Domna. Beyond the W colonnade there was a large court surrounded by walls which were flanked by a forest of richly decorated soaring columns. This dazzlingly theatrical structure, which was roofed, had floors of patterned marble and walls lined with marble slabs. An arched doorway on the W side, surmounted by a niche, which probably housed a statue of the emperor, led to a large swimming pool.

In the area to the E of the gymnasium are the scant remains of a Byzantine church and of Roman and Byzantine baths. On the S side of the main road in the fields near the base of the acropolis a line of vaults marks the site of the city's stadium. Nearby are the remains of the **theatre** which, restored after the earthquake of AD 17, had an estimated seating capacity of 20,000.

On the way back to the village are the most recent excavations. One of the buildings is a few metres from the highway. The so-called **House of the**

Bronzes, which has been dated to c AD 550, is in this area. A number of bronze liturgical objects and a structure which has been identified as an altar were discovered in the basement of the house. Jars containing sulphur and mortars for crushing olives were also found here. It has believed that the house was occupied by a Christian dignitary, perhaps a bishop.

To the SW of the house of the bronzes rough walls mark the remains of the Lydian **market place** which functioned from c 1000 to 550 BC. In the large trench made by the archaeologists quantities of pottery were found.

From the centre of the modern village, take the road S. This follows the course of the Pactolus river. A short distance along on the right-hand side is the area which has been designated Pactolus North by the archaeologists. By the side of the road are the ruins of an **early Christian basilica** and its associated buildings. This appears to have been abandoned in the 7C, perhaps as a result of the Sassanid invasion. In the 13C during the occupation of Manisa by the Byzantine Lascarids (see above) a smaller **church** with five domes was built on the site of the basilica. A substantial part of this building, including one of the fallen domes, has been uncovered. Beyond the churches are the ruins of a large **Roman villa**, which had its own baths complex. This dates from c AD 350. Some fine mosaics found in the villa are now in the museum at Manisa.

The most interesting discoveries are in the centre of the site. In a number of small buildings, gold found in the Pactolus was melted down by the cupellation process and then refined in furnaces. This activity was presided over by Cybele, the ancient Anatolian Mother Goddess. Facing E is an altar, flanked by crouching lions, which was dedicated to her. These structures, which have been partially restored, date from the late 7C or mid 6C BC, when Alyattes and his son Croesus ruled in Lydia.

Continue S over a small stream. Here a path leads to the remains of the so-called **pyramid tomb** which was c 400m up on the S slope of the valley. Almost completely buried by landslips, it is not easy to find. Only the base remains, the burial chamber has disappeared completely. According to a popular tradition, based on an account in Xenophon, it was the tomb of the Persian Abradates who was killed in battle. Overcome by grief his wife committed suicide and on the orders of Cyrus was buried with her husband in a magnificent tomb overlooking the Pactolus.

Just before the site of the temple of Artemis, on the left of the road, is the house occupied by the excavation team. To the right an open stretch of ground provides ample space for parking. The area by the river, under the shade of the trees, is a favourite place for visitors to rest and enjoy a picnic.

Work on the **Temple of Artemis** was started c 334 BC, shortly after the city had been liberated from the Persians by Alexander the Great and at a time when it had begun to be profoundly affected by Greek influence. It is possible that money for the project was provided at a later time by the Seleucid kings of Syria. Probably conceived as a dipteros measuring 23m by 67m, only the pronaos, cella and opisthodomus were constructed during this phase. The entrance to the temple was on the W side, an unusual arrangement dictated by the nature of the site. Also on the W was an **altar** dedicated to Artemis which was considerably older than the temple. During the Hellenistic period this was incorporated into the large stepped platform which still exists.

Possibly because of the decline of Seleucid influence and patronage in Lydia during the late Hellenistic period, work on the temple appears to have been abandoned and was not resumed until c 175 BC. The plan was then altered and the temple was redesigned as a pseudo-dipteros. Again only part of the project was completed.

The Temple of Artemis, Sardis

Although it seems likely that the temple was damaged by the earthquake in AD 17, the third phase of construction did not commence until c AD 150. During the reign of Antoninus Pius (AD 138–161) Sardis was given neocorate status. This required the city to maintain a temple dedicated to the worship of the emperor and of his family. It was probably then that the cella was divided into two parts and an image of Faustina, the wife of Antoninus, was placed in the E section. There is some evidence that Artemis shared her temple with Zeus Polieus during the late Hellenistic period. However, this would not have required the division of the structure. The normal practice would be to place the images side by side in the cella.

The third construction phase left the temple unfinished—the fluting of the columns and the decoration of their bases was not completed. Possibly because of the spread of Christianity, the building was finally abandoned sometime during the 4C AD. It was then used as a source of building material for the construction of a new residential quarter that sprang up in the area. Gradually it disappeared under landslips and debris from the steep slopes behind it, so that when the American archaeologists began work the E section of the temple was buried to a depth of more than 9m.

To the NE of the temple there is a small church which is believed to date from the 4C. To the N a pedestal carries a Greek inscription honouring a '*kauein*', the Lydian word for a priestess. On the hillside to the NE there is a statue base, which bears a dedication in Lydian and Greek. According to Bean, the Lydian, which is written backwards, may be transliterated, '*Nannas Bakivalis Artimul*'. In Greek this is given as 'Nannas, son of Dionysicles, to Artemis'. Bakivalis appears to be derived from Bacchus, the name by which Dionysus was sometimes known.

The city's **necropolis**, on the hillsides above the valley of the Pactolus and on the slopes of Mt Tmolus, was in use from the 6C BC to Roman times. Burial was in horizontal stone-lined cists, chamber tombs cut from the rock or, sometimes, in elaborate tumuli. Shallow depressions on a hillside W of the Pactolus at a point opposite the temple of Artemis mark the site of a number of graves. Also on the W side of the river c 3km to the S of the temple there are five rock-cut tombs in the cliff face to the right of the road. Although many of the tombs were robbed in antiquity, the archaeologists found some grave goods. These include ornaments, figurines, lamps, plates and goblets of metal and pottery. Because of the friable nature of the rock at Sardis many of the tombs examined by the American archaeologists at the beginning of the century are no longer visible. They have been covered by landslides or have been washed way by the winter rains.

The ascent to the **acropolis** of Sardis is arduous and will tempt only the dedicated. The summit is reached after an exhausting trek through thorny undergrowth and tiring scrambles up steep, slippery scree. Wear stout shoes and allow one hour for the ascent. In the summer months look out for snakes which, the villagers assert, like to bask on the sunnier slopes.

Only the view over the site and the surrounding countryside justifies the effort. The ruins are nearly all from the Byzantine period and are not very impressive. On the S side there are some well-preserved early Byzantine fortifications. A large rock-cut chamber near the summit is believed to have been a chapel. There are some mysterious tunnels, whose function and date of excavation have not been established.

If you have your own transport, visit the so-called 'royal cemetery' of Sardis is at **Bin Tepe**, c 10km to the the N of Sartmustafa. Take the road by the side of the baths complex and continue in a northerly direction.

Some of the tumuli, which are similar to those at Larisa, Hierapolis and İzmir, were probably crowned by giant phalloi. One, the so-called Tumulus of Alyattes, has a diameter of 355m, a circumference of more than 1km and a height of 69m. According to Herodotus it was raised by tradesmen, craftsmen and prostitutes working together. Stone inscriptions placed on top of the tumulus recorded the labours of each group. The prostitutes were the best workers! The central burial chamber was examined in 1853 and 1962. Recently the American archaeologists investigated the tomb of Gyges and several of the larger tumuli. Almost all had suffered from the depredations of grave robbers. Some of the damage is recent.

To the N of the royal necropolis is **Lake Gygaea**, now called Marmara Gölü. According to Chandler, this lake abounded in fish and the air above it was full of birds and swarms of gnats. He recalled Strabo's story (VI.13.4.5) about the temple of Diana Coloene built on the side of Lake Gygaea where baskets danced of their own volition on festivals of the goddess.

From Sartmustafa continue to (10km) **Salihli** where the N/S road from Balıkesir and Akhisar meets the E/W highway E96 which links İzmir with Ankara and Konya. Soon after Salihli the road abandons the valley of the Gediz Nehri and begins to climb over the southern flank of Uysal Dağı. Here you enter the strange, desolate stretch of country which was known to the ancients as Katakekaumene, the Burned Land. The little town of **Kula** is surrounded by the petrified evidence of ancient volcanic activity. Legends associate the area with Typhon, a monster produced from eggs which Chronus coated with his own semen and gave to Hera. Typhon battled with Zeus and defeated him for a time, forcing the gods to take refuge in Egypt. He fathered a number of monsters including the dog Orthrus, the Hydra of Lerna and the Chimaera (see also Cennet Deresi).

Not far to the E of Kula the road enters a more gentle country which is watered by the Gediz Çayı and its tributaries. Continue to (56km) **Uşak** which is near the site of ancient Temenothyrae. Later renamed Flaviopolis, it was a neocorate. Today the town is famed for its excellent carpets which are produced in a variety of colours.

About 35km to the SE of Uşak near Sivaslı are the ruins of **Cabeira** where Mithridates built a palace, a water mill and zoological gardens. At **Kainon Chorion** nearby he kept his most precious treasures. After his defeat, these were seized by Pompey and placed in the Capitol in Rome. Queen Pythodoris of Cabeira adorned the city with many splendid buildings and changed its name to **Sebaste** in honour of Augustus. A temple of Men, the Anatolian moon god, was founded here by Pharnaces II, son of Mithridates and king of Bosphorus (Strabo, *Geography*, 12. 3. 30–31).

Artefacts from the Chalcolithic and Bronze Ages have been found nearby and a number of funeral chambers in Lydian type tumuli have been excavated. Sebaste was an episcopal see during the Byzantine period and there are the ruins of several churches and mortuary chapels. A Byzantine statue of a nude man, a 6C sculptured ambo, some architectural fragments and a number of small objects from ancient Sebaste and the surrounding area are kept in a store on the site.

Return to Uşak and continue towards Afyon. At c 102km a turning right leads to (5km) **Sincanlı** which boasts a *medrese* and an *eyvan*-type *türbe*, both 13C, and the Ottoman Sinan Paşa Camii and *külliye* of 1527.

For a description of Afyon and the surrounding area see Route 56.

14

İzmir to Ephesus (Efes)

Total distance c 79km. İzmir—(c 5km Buca)—(c 3km Belevi)—c 75km
Selçuk—c 4km Ephesus.

Road 550/E24 to Ephesus leaves İzmir (see Route 11) in a series of wide,
lazy bends, which offer a magnificent panoramic view of the city, from the
curve of its great bay to the crowded slopes of the surrounding hills.
Descending into a gorge, it soon passes an **aqueduct** which brought fresh
water during the Roman, Byzantine and Ottoman periods.

After c 5km a road on the left leads to **Buca**, a residential suburb favoured
by the foreign merchants who settled in İzmir during the 18C and 19C.

Beyond the straggling suburbs is a pleasant stretch of countryside which
bears the marks of intensive cultivation. Silver-green olive trees and sombre maritime pines contrast sharply with the vivid hues of the growing
crops. The highway, flanked by slender birches, leads eventually to a
verdant plain watered by the Küçük Menderes, the ancient river Cayster.

On the N edge of this plain, shortly before Belevi, look for the ruins of a
Byzantine castle high up on a jagged ridge to the right of the road. This is
Keçikalesi (Goat Castle), which can be reached, with some difficulty, by
way of a rough track. There are the remains of fortifications and a number
of cisterns and vaulted chambers constructed by the Byzantines, which
were later refurbished by the Ottomans.

A petrol station c 55km from İzmir marks the turning to c 3km **Belevi**.
Continue in the direction of Tire. About 2km from Belevi, above the road
on the right-hand side there is a **tumulus** which has been dated tentatively
to the 4C BC. Surrounded by a wall of ashlar masonry, it has two rectangular
burial chambers. No sarcophagi have been found. Presumably they were
removed by grave-robbers. Shaped stone blocks on top indicate that the
tumulus was originally surmounted by a monument of some kind.

The access tunnel, c 18m long, is blocked with the spoil produced by
illegal excavations. Although no inscription has been discovered at the
tumulus, its size and situation suggest that it was erected for the burial of
somebody important, possibly a local notable.

The **Mausoleum of Belevi** is a short distance farther on, near the right-
hand side of the road. It has been described as the most important funeral
monument in Asia Minor after the Mausoleum at Halicarnassus. Resting
on a base c 30 m sq, it consists of a cube-shaped central core c 11m high,
which was cut from the solid rock. The surface of the cube was covered
with large stone blocks. These were not only decorative, they also concealed the entrance to the burial-chamber, which had been hollowed out
of the S side of the rock-cube. The monument had a Doric peristasis, with
eight columns on each side of the three-step crepidoma. The lion-griffins
which stood on the roof are now in the museums of Selçuk and İzmir. The
ceiling coffers, which are decorated with representations of funeral games
and battles with centaurs, are in the İzmir museum.

The sarcophagus from the mausoleum, which is in the Selçuk Museum,
has a representation of the deceased on the lid. He is depicted lying on a
couch, resting comfortably on one elbow. The finely-carved sides of the
sarcophagus were decorated with a relief showing sirens.

There is much conjecture about who was buried in the mausoleum. Some authorities suggest that it was that feckless Seleucid king, Antiochus II Theos (261–246 BC), who is believed to have been poisoned by his estranged first wife, Laodice, while trying to effect a reconciliation with her at Ephesus. Others find Persian influences in the depiction of the lion-griffins, particularly in the presence of a stylised representation of the full and crescent moon on the animals' haunches. A similar carving has been found on lion-griffins in Susa. If the second theory is correct, it would date the burial to the early 4C BC, when the Persians occupied Ionia. It would also suggest that, like the nearby tumulus, the mausoleum was constructed for a local worthy. The matter remains, and seems likely to remain, unresolved.

SELÇUK is signalled by the outline of the fortress which crowns the hill of Ayasuluk on the right of the road. During recent years the number of visitors to nearby Ephesus has increased enormously and as a result Selçuk has experienced an explosion of growth, which has not been entirely beneficial. The town now has too many shops selling cheap souvenirs and not enough good restaurants and hotels.

Information and Accommodation. The **Tourist Information Office** is in a garden near the museum in the town centre.

There are several small hotels and many pensions in and around Selçuk. The *Tusan Efes Moteli*, is less than 1km from the site of the ancient city. The modestly-priced *Kale Han Moteli* is in the town centre. In the spring and autumn, when the evenings and nights are often chilly, the large open fire in the Kale Han's lounge is a welcome amenity.

Transport. Selçuk is well served by the long-distance buses which link İzmir and Kuşadası, Aydın and Denizli, Bodrum, Marmaris and the small resorts in Lycia. There is no *otogar*. Buses stop on the main road near the dolmuş garage (see below).

A slower but more comfortable mode of transport is provided by trains on the İzmir/Denizli line.

Dolmuş taxis serve the surrounding villages and with nearby towns like Kuşadası. They leave from the dolmuş open-air garage near the Archaeological Museum. There is no direct dolmuş service to Ephesus. Take a Kuşadası dolmuş to the Tusan Efes Moteli. From there it is an easy 15 minutes' walk to the site.

Taxis are parked near the dolmuş garage. There are fixed tariffs, which are displayed, for journeys to Kuşadası, Ephesus, Meryemana, etc.

Selçuk's **Ephesus Museum**, one of the best regional museums in Turkey, houses a large collection of objects found at Ephesus and in the surrounding countryside. They are displayed clearly and imaginatively in several rooms and in a large inner courtyard, and most are labelled in English. Postcards, slides and replicas are on sale and there is a small bar which offers light refreshments. Allow at least half a day for the visit to the museum which is an essential complement to a tour of the ancient city.

Room 1 contains mosaics, frescoes, statues, and bronzes from Ephesus. Note particularly the fine fresco of Socrates from one of the private houses on the slopes of Mt Coressus; the beautiful head of Eros, a Roman copy of a work by Lysippus; the small bronze statue of a boy, perhaps a youthful Arion or an Eros, on a dolphin; the statue of an Egyptian priest, evidence of links between Ephesus and Egypt; the triumphantly ithyphallic Bes and Priapus; and the mosaics depicting Medusa and Dionysus.

Room 2 is devoted to large sculpture and figures from various fountains. Note the Roman 1C head of Zeus, conceived in the Classical style; the statue of a warrior in repose, which fronted a fountain; the Polyphemus group originally from the temple of Augustus, but later placed around the fountain of Pollio; from the fountain of Trajan a particularly fine statue of a youthful Dionysus, and statues of members of the emperor's family; the statues of

Triton and nymphs from the fountain of Laecanius Bassus; and a number of idealised portrait heads, including the Roman copy of a 5C BC head of a warrior.

Room 3 contains a rich collection of small finds. These include bronze crosses, glazed bowls, panels painted with representations of the Blessed Virgin and the saints, part of a soapstone statuette and a number of medallions, all objects dating from the 10C to 12C; coins bearing representations of Artemis and of a bee, the symbol of Ephesus; a 1C AD glass tray; terracotta drinking cups from the 6C to the 2C BC; lamps and moulds for their production; two statues of Eros; a bust of Marcus Aurelius; terracotta theatre masks; and an ivory frieze from a private house in Ephesus depicting a conflict between Trajan and barbarians.

The **Courtyard** contains large sculptures. These include a fine sarcophagus decorated with representations of the Muses; a 1C AD inscription from the reign of Nero dealing with customs duties which was later incoporated in an ambon found in the basilica of St John on Ayasuluk; a reconstruction of the pediment from the fountain of Pollio; a 3C AD Roman sun dial; decorated capitals dating from the 7C BC; Hellenistic and Roman grave stelae; and the lion-griffins and sarcophagus from the Belevi mausoleum.

Room 4 is devoted to objects found in tombs in and around Ephesus. They include decorated Mycenaean pottery from Ayasuluk; a fine Archaic terracotta sarcophagus of the Clazomenae-type from the Agora at Ephesus; glassware of the archaic and Hellenistic periods; stelae showing the development of the worship of Cybele from the 5C BC; the 2C BC stele of Olympia, daughter of Diocles; and a variety of small objects found in early Christian graves near the Cave of the Seven Sleepers.

Room 5 is concerned with the worship of Artemis. The oldest object is a small 7C BC gold statuette of the goddess from the Artemision. Others are ivory statuettes including one of a Megabyxus; part of a quadriga from the archaic altar of Artemis; the head of a youth from one of the columnae caelatae; architectural fragments; and two statues of Artemis. One from the 1C AD is 2.92m high, the other is 1.74m high and dates from the 2C AD. Both were found in the Prytaneion at Ephesus.

Room 6 is the so-called Hall of the Imperial Cults and Statues. The most interesting objects are the frieze from the temple of Hadrian; the 6C AD statue of the Consul Stephanus; part of the altar from the temple of Domitian; and a number of Roman portrait statues from the 2C and 3C AD.

From the centre of Selçuk a street climbs steeply to Ayasuluk. Access is by the **Gate of Persecution**, so named because of a relief which once decorated it. This depicted Achilles in combat and was misinterpreted in Byzantine times, when it was believed to show a Christian martyrdom. The misunderstanding may have arisen from the place where the relief was found— the amphitheatre at Ephesus, where the Romans had organised gladiatorial games and where some of the early Christians had been killed for their religion. Taken from there and placed over the gate during the Byzantine period, it was later brought to England. A part is now in Woburn Abbey.

Re-used material was employed in the construction of the gate and its flanking towers which were built in the 7C and 8C during the period of the Arab invasions. At that time the basilica was incorporated in the defensive system of the fortress. Note the architectural fragments over the central arch and the column sections built into the right-hand tower. When these fortifications were being constructed the size of the interior courtyard was deliberately restricted so that any invaders who succeeded in forcing their

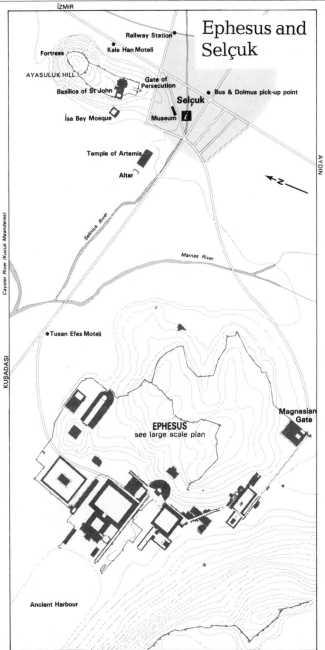

İZMIR

Ephesus and Selçuk

Railway Station

Kale Han Moteli

Fortress

AYASULUK HILL

Gate of
Persecution

Basilica of St John

Selçuk

Bus & Dolmus pick-up point

İsa Bey Mosque

Museum

Temple of Artemis

Altar

AYDIN

N

Selinius River

Marnas River

Cayster River (Kucuk Meanderes)

Tusan Efes Moteli

KUŞADASI

EPHESUS
see large scale plan

**Magnesian
Gate**

Ancient Harbour

way through the gate could be surrounded by the defenders and despatched quickly.

The principal building on Ayasuluk is the **Basilica of St John**. According to an ancient tradition, the Apostle, accompanied by the Blessed Virgin, came to Ephesus c 40. After his death c 100, he was buried in a small church on the hilltop which was replaced by a wooden-roofed basilica in the 4C. In the 6C the Emperor Justinian (527–565) built the magnificent structure whose remains are being studied and restored at present.

As early as the 2C the tomb of St John had begun to attract pilgrims and their numbers increased substantially during the centuries that followed. From the saint's name, St John Theologos, the town began to be called Ayio Theologo, which was modified in the course of time to become Ayasuluk. Justinian's basilica was a worthy setting for the veneration of St John, which continued, with some interruptions, until the late Byzantine period. After the Turkish conquest, the building was in such a dilapidated state that it required considerable repairs before it could be used as a mosque. Ibn Battuta, describes it as being 'built of finely hewn stones each measuring ten or more cubits in length. The cathedral mosque, which was formerly a church greatly venerated by the Greeks, is one of the most beautiful in the world'. After the construction of the İsa Bey mosque in the 14C, the basilica was neglected and fell into disrepair. Shortly afterwards it was severely damaged by an earthquake and abandoned.

The basilica was 110m long and 60m wide. Constructed in the form of a Latin cross, it was surmounted by six domes. The pillars, which supported the domes, may still be seen. Access was from an atrium on the W side, which measured 34m by 47m and was surrounded by a colonnade. This led by way of an exonarthex and a narthex to the nave, which was flanked by two side aisles covered by galleries. The nave was separated from the aisles by blue-veined marble pillars, which bore on their capitals the monograms of Justinian and of his wife, Theodora. The richly decorated interior of the basilica, whose walls were lined with marble facings, must have been an impressive sight. The **Tomb of St John**, raised on two steps and covered with mosaics, was under the central dome. Its position is now marked by a marble slab. Beyond the transept there was a synthronon.

The basilica's **treasury** was attached to the N transept. This was converted into a chapel in the 10C. The baptistery, which antedates the basilica, was on the N side of the nave. It was an octagonal chamber, with a narrow hall on one side. Steps led down to the baptismal pool which, flanked by a colonnade, was in the centre of the chamber.

From the ramparts of the **fortress**, erected by the Byzantines, and improved and enlarged by the Turks, which lies to the N of the basilica, there is a fine view across the plain to the sea. Inside the building, part of which is not open to the public, there are a number of cisterns, one of which occupies the site of a Byzantine church, and a ruined mosque.

Below Ayasuluk, to the SW, is the Selçuk **Mosque of İsa Bey**, which has been restored. If the building is locked, enquire about access at the museum. An inscription in Arabic above the main entrance states that the mosque was constructed in 1375 by the architect Ali ibn el Dımışki on the orders of İsa Bey, the son of the emir of Aydın. At that time the area around Selçuk formed part of the territory of the Aydın emirate. The mosque has suffered many changes of fortune and, unfortunately, the fabric has not escaped damage. The şadırvan has disappeared, the cap of the SW minaret is missing and only the base of the NE minaret remains. Stylistically interesting, it marks an intermediate phase between the Selçuk and Ottoman styles. According to Akurgal it is the oldest known Turkish mosque to possess an entry court and the earliest Anatolian columned mosque with a transept. It was built on a terrace measuring 51m by 57m, which was raised artificially on the W. The large court, which was formerly surrounded by a covered colonnade, occupies two thirds of the terrace.

Access to the prayer hall is through a triple arcade from the court. The hall is covered by two domes which rest on arches supported by four marble columns taken from a Roman building in Ephesus. Much ancient material was used. Note the traces of paint and gilding, which remain on the *mihrab*. The İsa Bey mosque is noted for the quality of its ornamentation, especially the finely-carved stalactite decoration over the main entrance and the beautiful faience mosaic in the S dome.

The last and, perhaps the most important, site in Selçuk is that of the great **Temple of Artemis**, one of the Seven Wonders of the Ancient World. Not far from the town, the site is a few metres from the right-hand side of the road to Ephesus and Kuşadası. The scanty remains, which are frequently covered with water, are not impressive. Of the temple only one incomplete column, which has been reconstructed, and the foundations of the Hellenistic altar survive. It requires a great effort of the imagination to picture the building, which so impressed Pliny and other ancient commentators.

From a remote period Cybele, the Anatolian Mother Goddess, was worshipped at Ephesus. Sometime after 1000 BC, when Greek colonists first settled in the area, Cybele was assimilated with Artemis. She managed, however, to make the change without losing either her ancient appearance or many of her attributes.

British archaeologists established that before the construction of the archaic temple of Artemis in the middle of the 6C BC there were three earlier structures on the site. The first, an altar, has been dated to c 700 BC, the second and third, which according to Akurgal comprised a naiskos, were built during the following 150 years.

The archaic temple of Artemis, an Ionic dipteros of c 560/50 BC, measured 55m by 115m. It was the first structure of that size to be built entirely of marble and the largest building ever produced by Greek architects. It was designed by Chersiphron and his son Metagenes, of Crete, and Theodorus of Samos. The Cretans were probably familiar with some of the massive buildings erected by the Egyptians and may have been influenced by them when preparing their plans.

Pliny, writing about the Hellenistic temple which later occupied the same site, describes the forest of columns, 127 in all, which supported the earlier building. The lower part of 36 of the archaic columns, each of which was 19m high, bore a decorative relief. One of these, the so-called *columnae caelatae*, is in the British Museum.

In the long narrow cella, behind the deep pronaos, the statue of the goddess stood in a naiskos. Greek temples as a rule faced E and, although the site did not require it, the archaic temple of Artemis at Ephesus, like the temples of Sardis and Magnesia on the Maeander, faced W. This supports the view that the deity worshipped here was of Anatolian, and not of Greek, origin. Further proof is provided by the names of the temple hierarchy, which are quite unlike those found in Greek temples. The principal priest was known as the *Megabyxus*. This is a Persian word, which means 'set free by God'. He was assisted by a group of virgins and by an order of minor priests, known as the *Essenes*. Other members of the temple staff were the *Curetes* and the *Acrobatae*, or 'walkers on tip-toe'.

According to tradition the archaic temple was destroyed by fire in 356 BC, the year Alexander the Great was born. The fire was started by Herostratus, a madman who believed that he would immortalise his name by this action. When Alexander came to Ephesus in 334 BC, he sacrificed to the goddess in the ruined sanctuary and offered to rebuild it. The Ephesians politely refused his proposal on the grounds that it would be inappropriate for one divinity to erect a temple in honour of another.

The new temple was built on the foundations of the old. Some of the foremost sculptors of the age, including Scopas and Praxiteles, contributed works for its decoration. To prevent the building from being flooded, it was raised c 3m above the ground on a 13-stepped crepidoma. The statue of Artemis, which stood in the same place in the cella, is believed to have resembled the Roman statues of the goddess now in the Selçuk museum. As in the earlier building, the lower part of some of the columns bore a decorative relief. One of these *columnae caelatae*, which shows Hermes, Thanatos (Death) and possibly Iphigenia, is in the British Museum.

The foundations of a horseshoe-shaped altar, which was erected at the same time as the Hellenistic temple, have been uncovered by the Austrian archaeologists who are working on the site.

During the Roman period the temple was stripped of many of its treasures, which were carried off to Italy. It suffered further damage at the hands of the Goths in AD 263 and, with the rise of Christianity, was allowed to decay. After the suppression of paganism by Theodosius, towards the end of the 4C, it appears to have been abandoned completely. During the Byzantine and Ottoman periods the temple was a convenient source of cut and shaped stone which was used to construct churches and mosques.

In time, the site was covered with silt brought down by the river Cayster and its existence was forgotten. The story of the rediscovery of the Artemision by John Turtle Wood in the middle of the 19C is one of the great detective stories of archaeology. Undeterred by troubles of many kinds, disease, the collapse of a trench, appalling lodgings, a broken collar-bone, an attempted assassination and murder, he continued his search. An inscription found in the theatre provided the clue that led him to the site. This stated that at the time of a performance certain holy images were brought from the temple along the sacred way through the Magnesian Gate to the theatre. Wood located the sacred way which he found to be very well preserved, and followed it to the temenos of the temple. Wood's researches, on which he had spent much of his considerable private fortune, were continued by Hogarth, who discovered a rich foundation treasure in 1904, and more recently by teams of Austrian archaeologists.

Near the single standing **column** are the foundations of the archaic temple, surmounted by the 3m-high **crepidoma** of its Hellenistic successor. To the right is the base of the 12th of the outer row of columns. A short distance to the W are the ruins of an **ancient sanctuary** whose axis was at right angles to the main temple.

At the western extremity of the site are the remains of the **great altar** of the Artemision. Here animal, and sometimes human, sacrifices were made to the goddess. The altar, which was surrounded by a colonnade, stood in a paved marble court entered from the W. To the left is a spring which may have had some ceremonial significance or which may have been used for the ritual purification of those taking part in the sacrifices.

At least one day is needed for **EPHESUS (Efes)**, as the ruins are extensive and widely scattered. During the holiday season thousands of visitors come from İzmir, from the nearby resorts and from the cruise ships which dock at Kuşadası. They congregate in the popular areas, restricting access and extending the time required to make a complete tour.

Dolmuş services between Selçuk and Kuşadası pass the site. Ask to be set down at the *Tusan Efes Moteli*. It is an easy walk from Selçuk to Ephesus, but the road is busy and the narrow verges offer little protection from traffic.

If you wish to see just the most important parts of the ancient city in the maximum comfort and with the minimum of effort, go to Ephesus in the early morning. Take the Aydın road to the Magnesian Gate on the SW side of the site. From here walk downhill to the principal ruins.

In summer the temperature at Ephesus can be uncomfortably high and, apart from the area near the theatre, there is little shade. There is a restaurant at the northern entrance near the Vedius Gymnasium. However, during the holiday season this is usually very crowded. Bring a picnic lunch. The authorities have no objection to visitors taking alfresco meals on the site, providing they do not impede other visitors and leave no litter.

Near the restaurant there are kiosks and boutiques selling souvenirs and bric-à-brac. Here or on the site itself you may be approached by touts offering 'ancient coins' and other 'antiquities'. These are almost certainly modern fakes of no value. If they are genuine, both the purchaser and the vendor are breaking Turkish law and could incur very severe penalties, including imprisonment. It is illegal to possess antiquities or to purchase them from anyone but a licensed dealer who has obtained the necessary permit for their sale and possible export.

History. Ephesus appears to have attracted settlers from the earliest times. It had a sheltered harbour on a river mouth, it was at the end of a traditional trade route that linked the great cities of the Middle East with the Aegean, and it had long associations with the worship of Cybele, the great Mother Goddess of Anatolia.

According to Pausanias, Strabo and Athenaeus, Ephesus was founded by Androclus, one of the sons of the legendary Codrus, king of Athens. He and his followers had been told by an oracle to settle in a place which would be indicated to them by a fish and a wild boar. On arriving at Ephesus the Greeks found some of the local people roasting fish near the sea-shore. One of the fish fell from the fire and, as it had pieces of burning wood attached to it, set a nearby thicket ablaze. This disturbed a wild boar which was chased and slain by Androclus.

This sequence of events, which is depicted on a frieze on the temple of Hadrian (see below), was taken to fulfil the prophecy and Androclus and his companions settled at Ephesus. They found Carians and Lydians in the neighbourhood and married with them, adopted some of their customs and practices and harmonised their religious beliefs, identifying Cybele with the Greek Artemis.

Some authorities suggest that Ephesus was the city which the Hittites called Apasas and which is believed to have existed on the Aegean coast c 1400 BC. The earliest archaeological evidence found in the area comes from a Mycenaean tomb of Ayasuluk. The first Greek settlement was made c 1000 BC, probably when the sea came much farther inland, on the harbour c 1km to the W of the Artemision.

Towards the middle of the 7C Ephesus was taken by the Cimmerians. A century later it came under the rule of the Lydians. Croesus appears to have treated the Ephesians well, donating several of the *columnae caelatae* to the archaic temple of Artemis. After the defeat of Croesus by Cyrus, Ephesus, with the rest of Ionia, fell into the hands of the Persians. Later it was for a time a member of the Delian League. Then it came under Persian control again and this continued until Alexander defeated the Persian army at the battle of the Granicus river. His visit to the city is described above.

After the death of Alexander Ephesus was ruled by Lysimachus, one of the Diado-choi. Much against the wishes of the inhabitants, he decided to move the city to a new location. This is the area occupied by the ruins visible today. He overcame the reluctance of the Ephesians to his plan by resorting to a stratagem. After a period of torrential rain, he blocked the drains of the old city, with the result that all the houses were flooded. Lysimachus also brought in people from Colophon and Lebedus to swell the numbers of his new settlement. He surrounded it with a massive defensive wall 10m high and c 9.65km long. Parts of this may still be seen on the summit of Mt Coressus and on the NE side of Mt Pion.

During the wars that followed the death of Lysimachus, Ephesus changed sides frequently. At first it supported the Seleucids, then dallied with the Ptolemies. It passed finally into the hands of the Attalids of Pergamum after the defeat of Antiochus III at the battle of Magnesia ad Sipylum in 190 BC (see Manisa above). When Attalus III bequeathed his kingdom to the Romans in 133 BC, Ephesus became one of the most important cities in the new province.

Under Roman rule Ephesus displayed traces of its old volatility. It supported the Roman cause against Aristonicus, the pretender to the Pergamene throne, contributing handsomely to his defeat. However, when Mithridates VI Eupator, king of Pontus, led a revolt against Rome in 88 BC, the Ephesians joined him and slaughtered a large number of the Romans in their city.

Fortunately Ephesus did not suffer as a result of its treachery. It became the seat of the Roman governor and the largest and most important trading centre on the Aegean coast. In early imperial times its population was estimated to be 250,000. The city was given favourable treatment by several emperors, who allowed centres for imperial worship to be set up, thus permitting the Ephesians to boast that their city had received the title of Neocorus on four separate occasions. Nero and Hadrian addressed themselves to the problem of the silting up of the harbour and several emperors ornamented the city with buildings whose remains may still be seen.

Among the many famous citizens of Ephesus were the philosopher Heracleitus, who taught that all things are in a state of flux, *panta rhei*; the poet Hipponax, who is credited with the invention of parody, and the painter Parrhasius. The fragments of Hipponax's work which remain display a mordant wit and are in an earthy Greek full of colloquialisms. His enemies went in fear of his biting tongue. The sculptor Bupalus, who had made an offensive representation of the poet, hanged himself when Hipponax attacked him in vigorous, acid verses.

Christianity came early to Ephesus. On his second missionary journey St Paul, accompanied by Aquila and Priscilla, taught in the synagogue for some time before leaving for Caesarea, in Phoenicia, and Jerusalem. The celebrated outcry of the silversmiths of Ephesus took place during the apostle's third journey, when he spent about two years in the city, preaching daily in the synagogue and in a lecture hall. After his caustic remark that gods fashioned by human hands are not gods at all, the sale of images of Ephesian Artemis plummeted. Demetrius, the leader of the city's silversmiths, fearful for his livelihood, put it about that if Paul were allowed to continue preaching and teaching disaster would overtake Ephesus. Cleverly he appealed to the religious feelings of the people saying: 'the sanctuary of the great goddess Diana (Artemis) will cease to command respect; and then it will not be long before she who is worshipped by all Asia and the civilised world is brought down from her divine pre-eminence' (Acts 19:27). His words produced a riot. The Ephesians rushed through the streets to the theatre where they held a protest meeting, crying loudly: 'Great is Diana of the Ephesians'. Eventually the mob was dispersed by calming words from the city officials, but Paul found it advisable to leave Ephesus for Macedonia.

Some believe that the apostle was imprisoned in Ephesus and base their argument on texts like II Corinthians 1:8: 'how serious was the trouble that came upon us in the province of Asia. The burthen of it was far too heavy for us to bear, so heavy that we even despaired of life'. Traditionally, a building c 1km to the W of the city, in the harbour area, is known as St Paul's prison.

It is believed that St John came to Ephesus from Patmos and that he took care of the Blessed Virgin here during the last years of her life. His tomb was enshrined in the basilica on Ayasuluk (see above). The house where it is said Mary lived is at Meryemana, c 8km from Ephesus.

Two of the great Councils of the early Church were held in Ephesus. In 431 Cyril of Alexandria presided over a gathering of bishops, convoked by Theodosius II and held in the presence of papal legates. At this council a heresy promulgated by Nestorius, patriarch of Constantinople, was condemned. The Nestorians taught that Jesus was two separate persons, one human and one divine, and that Mary was the mother of the human person only and, consequently, could not be called the Mother of God.

Theodosius called another council at Ephesus in 449. This was the so-called 'robber council', which deposed Flavian, the Patriarch of Constantinople, and restored the heretical Eutyches as priest and archimandrite.

The silting of the harbour, which proceeded unchecked, the abandonment of the Artemision after the adoption of Christianity as the state religion, and the increasingly ferocious attacks by the Arabs contributed to the decline of Ephesus. Sometime in the 6C the remaining inhabitants appear to have moved to the more easily defended acropolis at Ayasuluk. There was a brief revival under the rule of the emirs of Aydın, but after the conquest of the area by the Turks, Ephesus became a forgotten backwater.

During the centuries of Ottoman rule travellers from Western Europe had a variety of experiences in Ephesus and consequently left differing accounts in their writings. In 1611 Ephesus was visited by William Lithgow. He found the ruined city 'somewhat inhabited with Greeks, Jews and a few Turks, but no way answerable to its former glory and magnificence. Nevertheless it is pleasantly adorned with gardens, fair fields and green woods of olive trees, which on the sea do yield a delectable prospect'. Richard Chandler came to Ayasuluk and Ephesus in 1764–65 and discovered a sad, tumbled collection of ruined buildings, whose melancholy was accentuated by the call of the shrill-owl and of a jackal, which cried mournfully, 'as if foresaken by his companions, on the mountain'. J.T. Wood, who survived cholera, physical injury, appalling weather conditions and the malice of criminal workmen, laboured there in the mid 19C and discovered the site of the Artemision. In 1936 the ancient city was remote enough for

The great Graeco-Roman Theatre at Ephesus

H.G. Morton to describe it as a place with 'no sign of life but a goatherd leaning on a broken sarcophagus or a lonely peasant outlined againt a mournful sunset'. Three years later the road from İzmir was in such a poor condition that the vehicle in which George Bean was travelling ended up in a cornfield.

Today Ephesus is one of the most popular sites in Anatolia, attracting thousands of visitors each year. Concern has been expressed about the wear and tear on its ancient streets and structures and some would limit the number of visitors.

At the Tusan Efes Moteli the road to Ephesus is clearly signposted. It ascends a gentle slope by fields that in the summer are full of nodding sunflowers and tall rustling golden stalks of maize. Through the trees there are occasional glimpses of Ayasuluk with its fortress and ruined basilica.

Just before you pass through the Byzantine walls look for a track to the left which circles Mt Pion. If you are not in a hurry, follow this to the **Cave of the Seven Sleepers**. Take great care in the area around the cave, as many of the vaults and walls are in a dangerous condition.

According to a pious tradition, seven Christian youths, who lived in Ephesus during the reign of Decius (249–251), refused to offer sacrifice in the temple of the emperor and took refuge in a cave on the N slopes of Mt Pion where they fell into a deep sleep. When they awoke, one of them went into the city to purchase bread. His strange appearance, clothes of antique cut and ancient money provoked much comment. On making discreet enquiries, he discovered to his astonishment that he and his companions had been asleep, not for one night, but for 112 years. A Christian emperor, Theodosius II, was on the throne and Christianity was the state religion.

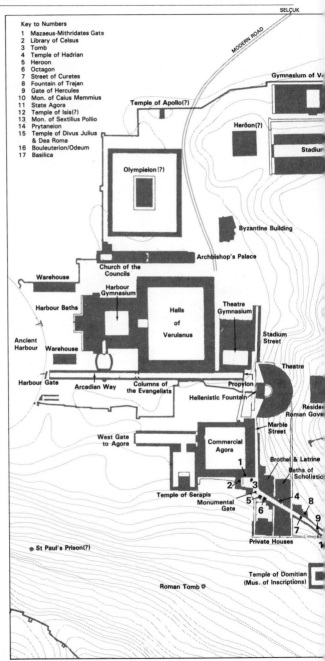

Key to Numbers

1 Mazaeus-Mithridates Gate
2 Library of Celsus
3 Tomb
4 Temple of Hadrian
5 Heroon
6 Octagon
7 Street of Curetes
8 Fountain of Trajan
9 Gate of Hercules
10 Mon. of Caius Memmius
11 State Agora
12 Temple of Isis(?)
13 Mon. of Sextilius Pollio
14 Prytaneion
15 Temple of Divus Julius
   & Dea Roma
16 Bouleuterion/Odeum
17 Basilica

SELÇUK

MODERN ROAD

Gymnasium of V

Temple of Apollo(?)

Heröon(?)

Stadiu

Olympieion(?)

Byzantine Building

Archbishop's Palace

Church of the
Councils

Warehouse

Harbour
Gymnasium

Halls
of
Verulanus

Theatre
Gymnasium

Harbour Baths

Stadium
Street

Ancient
Harbour

Warehouse

Theatre

Harbour Gate

Arcadian Way

Columns of
the Evangelists

Propylon

Reside
Roman Gove

Hellenistic Fountain

Marble
Street

West Gate
to Agora

Commercial
Agora

Brothel & Latrine

Baths of
Scholistic

1

Temple of Serapis

2   3

4   8

Monumental
Gate

5

6

9

7

St Paul's Prison(?)

Private Houses

Temple of Domitian
(Mus. of Inscriptions)

Roman Tomb

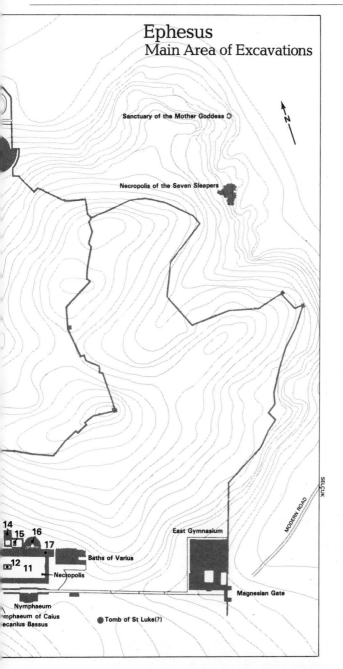

Ephesus
Main Area of Excavations

Sanctuary of the Mother Goddess ○

N

Necropolis of the Seven Sleepers

14

15 16

17

Baths of Varius

East Gymnasium

12 11

Necropolis

Nymphaeum

mphaeum of Caius
ecanius Bassus

● Tomb of St Luke(?)

Magnesian Gate

SELÇUK

MODERN ROAD

The Sleepers were buried in the cave and a church was built over their graves.

In religious iconography the Seven Sleepers are named and depicted as follows: SS John, Maximian and Constantine (symbol a club), SS Mortian and Malchus (symbol an axe), St Serapion (symbol a torch) and St Dionysus (symbol a large nail).

The archaeologists discovered the ruins of a small church above a gallery which was cut into the rock. This contains a number of burial chambers, on whose walls are written prayers and invocations to the Seven Sleepers. Offerings, including terracotta lamps, have been found in the graves of later Christians who were buried around the church and gallery. Clearly considered a holy place, the site was used up to the late Byzantine period. Graffiti dating from the time of the Crusades have been found here.

From the Cave of the Seven Sleepers, return to the N entrance to the site. The partially excavated structure on the left is the **gymnasium of Vedius**. Dedicated to Artemis and Antoninus Pius, it was constructed in AD 150 by Publius Vedius Antoninus, a protégé of the emperor.

Entrance was at the E side through a palaestra which had an elaborate propylon in its S wall. To the left of the propylon there was a well-furnished lavatory. The long narrow room on the W side of the palaestra was probably used for the worship of the emperor and for various formal ceremonies connected with the gymnasium. The statue, which once stood in the alcove in the W wall, was almost certainly a representation of the emperor. The large room beyond, which extended across the width of the gymnasium, was probably used for indoor athletics and practice sessions during bad weather. The swimming pool was on the W side. The remainder of the building was a baths complex. Among the statues found in the gymnasium are those of a sophist and a striking representation of Antinous as Androclus. These are now in the İzmir Archaeological Museum.

To the S of the gymnasium of Vedius are the ruins of the **stadium** which has been dated by an inscription to the reign of Nero (AD 54–68). It seems likely that this replaced an earlier structure built, when Lysimachus ruled the city. Shaped like a horseshoe, its principal entrance was through a well-preserved monumental gate on its W side. Measuring c 229m by 28m, the stadium was used for athletics, gladiatorial contests, fights with wild beasts and chariot racing. It narrowed in the centre, so that the eastern section could be turned into an arena for the more gory spectacles. Wild animals were kept in small rooms nearby. On the S side the spectators seats were cut from the side of Mt Pion, while those on the N rested on vaults. During the middle Byzantine period the stadium suffered a great deal of damage, when stone was taken from for the fortifications on Ayasuluk.

Across the road are the remains of a **Byzantine fountain**. Note the three niches, which held statues, and the remains of a watering trough.

Nearby are the scanty remains of a building whose function has not been established. Some believe it was a heroon, others that it was a macellum.

A short distance to the S are the ruins of a large building which some believe was a baths complex, others the private house of a wealthy Ephesian. It dates from the 6C AD.

Behind this building are the remains of a paved street which connected the stadium with the theatre. Excavations by Turkish archaeologists have brought to light a number of interesting finds from the ruins of the small shops which lined it.

The principal entrance to the site is at the end of a short road which is devoted entirely to commerce and the exploitation of visitors. In addition to a restaurant and shops there is a parking area.

Immediately inside the entrance to the site there are toilets with washing facilities. There is also a tap which claims to provide drinking water. Visitors are advised to stick to the bottled variety.

A path to the right of the toilets leads to the extensive ruins of the **Church of the Councils**. This curiously elongated building, which measures 260m by 30m, was erected in the early part of 2C AD. It had the typical basilical form of a central nave flanked by two side aisles. There was an exedra at each of the narrow ends, where, it is said, court business was transacted. Akurgal disagrees. In his opinion the building was probably used as a corn exchange, grain being displayed and sold in the nave, while bankers and brokers conducted their business in the small rooms that lined the side aisles. To support his theory he points out that the building was conveniently close to the harbour.

Another view is that the structure was a *museion*, a centre devoted to higher education, in particular to medicine and the sciences. Those who favour this theory offer as evidence an inscription found near the building. This states that the doctors and professors, who staffed the Ephesus *museion*, were to be exempted from taxes.

The building was abandoned sometime in the 3C AD, when the fortunes of the city were in decline because of the effects of the great plague, which raged through the Roman Empire, and the incursions of the Goths, who raided as far S as Ephesus between 258 and 262.

A **church** was built in the W part of the basilica at the beginning of the 4C. Entrance was through a large paved atrium and a narthex. The atrium was decorated with marble slabs brought from various buildings in the city, while the narthex had a floor-mosaic of geometric design.

The well-preserved baptistery on the N side of the church had a central pool in which catechumens were baptised. The walls of this cylindrical structure were decorated with crosses and metal rosettes.

Further extensions and alterations, which involved the construction of one and possibly two other churches and a chapel, were made to the original design. These included a small domed building erected in the 6C during the reign of Justinian. There is a plan near the church which helps to explain its very complicated development.

Appropriately, it was in the first church to be dedicated to Mary the mother of Jesus, that the Councils of Ephesus were held (see above). When Pope Paul VI came here in 1967, he commemorated these events by praying with a large congregation within these walls which had witnessed so many important events in the history of the early Christian Church.

A short distance to the right are the ruins of the largest structure in Ephesus. This complex, made up of the **halls of Verulanus**, the **harbour gymnasium** and the **harbour baths**, was completed during the reign of Domitian (AD 81–96). Only a part of the extensive area covered by these structures, which measure c 356m by 240m, has been excavated. Exploration is hampered by the thick undergrowth and the marshy ground.

An entrance from the Arcadian Way led to the halls of Verulanus which surrounded a tiled court, used as a palaestra, measuring 200m by 240m. The walls of the court were lined with 13 different coloured marble slabs, the gift of Claudius Verulanus, chief priest of the Roman Province of Asia during the reign of Hadrian (AD 117–138).

To the W lay a smaller palaestra and beyond that the baths. The hall to the N of the small palaestra was devoted to the worship of the emperor, while a similar room on the S was used for lectures and discussions.

During the 1896 season of excavations the archaeologists unearthed in the lecture room a broken bronze statue, 1.92m high, of a youth cleaning his body with a strigil. Painstakingly reconstructed from 234 separate fragments, this is a Roman copy of a 4C BC original. They also discovered a 2C BC Hellenistic bronze candlelabrum, 50cm high, which shows Hercules battling with a centaur, and a delightful group, 62cm high, of a child playing with a goose. The latter is a 2C AD Roman copy of a 3C BC original. All are now in the Ephesus Museum in Vienna.

To the E of the halls of Verulanus lie the remains of the 2C AD **theatre gymnasium**. This consisted of a palaestra, which measured 30m by 70m, surrounded on three sides by colonnades. On the N there were rows of seats for spectators. This allowed the gymnasium to be used as a miniature stadium. So far, only the palaestra has been uncovered. The baths, which completed the complex, await excavation.

Few visitors to Ephesus can fail to be impressed by the **Arcadian Way**, the great marble street that stretches from the theatre to the middle harbour gate. This was constructed during the reign of the Emperor Arcadius (AD 395–408), the unintelligent and ineffective elder son of Theodosius the Great who ruled the Eastern Roman Empire.

The Arcadian Way was a colonnaded street 11m wide and 600m long. On each side it had 5m-wide covered footpaths which were paved with mosaics and lined with shops. These walkways, protected from the excessive heat of summer and the cold rains of winter, must have been a favourite meeting place for the Ephesians. Refreshed by cool breezes from the harbour, they could hear the latest news from abroad, as they strolled among the crews of ships from Alexandria, from Ostia and other Mediterranean ports.

The mid-point was marked with statues of the four Evangelists on Corinthian columns. These were erected during the reign of Justinian (AD 527–565). Today only the shafts remain.

This harbour street was lit at night. An inscription found in the city claimed that the 'Arcadiane contains in its two stoas, as far as the wild boar, fifty lamps'. (The wild boar in question must have been a statue of the animal, which is mentioned in the foundation myth of the city). Ephesus was one of the three cities in the Roman Empire which had street-lighting. The other two were Rome and Antioch.

The ends of the Arcadian Way were marked with elaborately decorated propylaia. The propylon at the harbour end probably antedated the street. It is believed to have been constructed during the early Roman period.

At the E end of the Arcadian Way is the great Graeco-Roman **Theatre of Ephesus**, where St Paul fulminated against false gods, particularly against Artemis. This has been restored substantially in recent years—a process which has not pleased everyone and has provoked some controversy.

Constructed during the Hellenistic period, the theatre was enlarged and enriched with lavish decoration during the reigns of Claudius and Trajan. The elaborately ornamented skene, started c AD 54 in the reign of Nero, was completed towards the middle of the 2C AD. Thus, the building visible today is almost completely Roman. Sections of the Hellenistic skene, discovered in the Roman stage, have provided some useful information about the earlier structure.

The theatre is 145m wide and 30m high and had an estimated capacity of 24,000. There are two diazomata, 12 stairs, 11 cunei below the second diazoma and 22 above, and two parodoi. The colonnade at the top helped to improve the acoustics. Part of the cavea was covered with an awning which gave the spectators some protection from the weather.

In the Hellenistic theatre the actors performed without scenery. The Roman skene, when completed in the mid 2C AD, was 18m high. The

The statue of Arete (Goodness) which decorates the Library of Celsus at Ephesus

ground floor had a long corridor with eight rooms opening off it. This part of the structure is well preserved.

It is worth making the stiff climb to the top of the theatre for the fine view over the harbour area. Note how the slope increases as you ascend. This architectural device ensured that the spectators in the upper rows had a clear view of the stage.

Behind the theatre on the slopes of Mt Pion are the substantial ruins of a Roman building which has not been identified. Some believe it was the residence of the governor of the city. There are also the remains of a street that ran from the theatre to the baths of Scholasticia and the street of the Curetes.

Before leaving the theatre square note the fine late 3C or early 2C **Hellenistic fountain** set between two slender Ionic columns which has been built into the terrace wall. Water was delivered from three marble lion heads into the bowl.

On the side wall of an archway, which separated the theatre square from the marble street, there is a Greek inscription which reads, 'Long live the Christian emperors and the Greens'. The Greens were one of the four great circus factions in Roman and Byzantine times. The **marble street**, which led to the library of Celsus, was paved with large marble slabs in the 5C AD, the gift of a man named Eutropius. One of the main arteries of Ephesus, it formed part of the Sacred Way, which, encircling Mt Pion, linked the Artemision with the city centre.

Deep ruts in the street's surface testify to the frequent passage of wheeled vehicles. Pedestrians used a Doric colonnade on the W side which was erected in the time of Nero (AD 54–68). There were steps at each end of the colonnade which raised c 1.70m above the level of the street.

The colonnade was ornamented with reliefs of gladiatorial combats. Manholes placed at intervals in the centre provided access to one of the city's main drains. Note the graffiti showing the head of a woman, a heart and a foot, which may refer to the brothel behind the baths of Scholasticia.

Undoubtedly the best-known monument in Ephesus is the **Library of Celsus** which has been extensively restored. Reproduction on posters promoting tourism and in books, magazine and pamphlets has made it a symbol, not only of Ephesus, but of Turkey's archaeological heritage. Some purists regret the changes resulting from the restoration.

An inscription in Latin and Greek on the side of the front steps states that the library was erected by the Consul Gaius Julius Aquila in AD 110 as a memorial to his father, Gaius Julius Celsus Polemaeanus, governor of the Roman Province of Asia c AD 105–107. He was buried in a marble sarcophagus decorated with erotes, garlands, rosettes and representations of Nike. This was placed in a vault under the W apsidal wall of the building. In 1904 the archaeologists discovered the undisturbed tomb during the course of their restoration work. The body was in a lead coffin which had been placed in the sarcophagus. It has been replaced in the vault where it was found.

The library contained 12,000 scrolls which were kept in rows of niches in the walls of the inner chamber. This measured c 11m by 16.70m. Galleries, rather like those found in modern libraries, provided access to the niches on the upper levels. Between the inner and outer walls there was an air-gap of 1m which helped to prevent the scrolls being damaged by humidity or sudden variations in temperature. As at Pergamum, a librarian handed the scrolls to the readers. A sum of 25,000 denarii was left by Gaius Julia Aquila for the maintenance of the library and the purchase of new works.

Architectural devices were used to give the library, which was constructed between existing buildings, an impression of greater width. The façade was placed on a convex podium reached by nine steps and the columns and capitals on the sides were smaller than those in the centre.

On the lower of the two storeys of the façade, pairs of Corinthian columns flank the three entrances to the inner chamber. Niches in the outer wall contain reproductions of statues representing the four virtues: Sophia (Wisdom), Arete (Goodness), Ennoia (Thought) and Episteme (Knowledge). The originals are in the Ephesus Museum in Vienna.

In the middle of the 3C AD the library was badly damaged when the city was attacked by the Goths. A century later it was partly restored and a fountain was placed in front of the façade. This was surrounded with reliefs of the Parthian wars of the mid 2C AD which probably came from a monument erected in honour of Marcus Aurelius and Lucius Verus. The reliefs are now in the Ephesus Museum in Vienna. Sometime in the 10C the building suffered further grave damage from an earthquake and it remained in a ruinous condition, until the Austrian archaeologists began their work on it. Plaques provide information in Turkish and German about the methods used to construct the library and to restore it.

Note the remains of a circular **Hellenistic building** near the street. The 2C AD **sarcophagus** nearby was discovered in 1968. It belonged to Tiberius Claudius Flavianus Dionysius and had been robbed in antiquity.

To the right of the library is the commercial agora of Ephesus. This is reached by the **Gate of Mazaeus and Mithridates** which has been restored. Mazaeus and Mithridates were wealthy freedmen who built this three-arched gateway in 4 or 3 BC in honour of Augustus, his wife Livia and his son-in-law Agrippa. Only the sockets for the gold-plated bronze letters of the inscription, which was in Latin and Greek, remain.

There is an unusual **graffito** on the left wall and an **admonitory scribble** in a niche on the opposite side which threatens that 'whoever relieves himself here shall suffer the wrath of Hecate'. Inside the gate a 3C AD **inscription** states that the price of a 14oz loaf of fine bread was four obols and of a 10oz loaf of inferior bread two obols.

The first commercial agora was constructed during the Hellenistic period. It was altered extensively by the Romans, particularly during the reigns of Augustus, Nero and Caracalla. In the 4C AD, when further restoration work was undertaken to repair earthquake damage, columns of different architectural styles were used.

Surrounded by stoas, the agora measures 110m by 110m. The two storeyed Doric colonnade on the E side, the upper part of which flanked the marble street, dates from the reign of Nero. In addition to the gate of Mazeus and Mithridates there were entrances on the W and N sides. The ramp on the W side suggests that the agora was used sometimes as a cattle market. In the centre there was a ὡρολόγιον, a combined sundial and clepsydra (water-clock). Only the foundations remain. Inscriptions on extant bases show that the agora was ornamented with statues of philosophers, rhetoricians, heroes, athletes and public officials. The shops in the colonnades sold food and manufactured goods. In view of the agora's proximity to the harbour it is probable that much of the produce was imported.

Rioters who opposed Nestorius, the heretic bishop of Constantinople, filled the agora and welcomed enthusiastically the announcement of his deposition and banishment by the bishops of the Third Ecumenical Council which was held at Ephesus in AD 431.

A flight of steps in the SW corner leads to the ruins of a **massive building** dating from the 2C AD. Archaeologists believe that this was devoted to the cult of Serapis. Fragments of an Egyptian granite statue and a number of inscriptions concerning his worship have been found here. Serapis was a popular god in Imperial Rome and temples dedicated to him, sometimes in association with Isis, have been found in the capital and in many parts of the empire, especially in the cities of Asia Minor.

He is often portrayed with a *modius*, a grain measure, on his head. Egypt was one of the granaries of the Roman world and there is evidence of commercial links between Alexandria and Ephesus. When Hadrian visited the city in AD 129 the Ephesians obtained his permission to import Egyptian grain. Again, in the 2C AD an unknown Roman emperor wrote to Ephesus, 'If, as we pray, the Nile provides us with a flood of the customary level and a bountiful harvest of wheat is produced among the Egyptians, then you will be among the first after the homeland [to benefit from it]'. (Garnsey, Famine and Food Supply in the Graeco-roman World). It seems there was a colony of Egyptian traders in Ephesus and they could be expected to promote the worship of a deity favoured by business people and officials. A number of objects of Egyptian provenance, including the fine statue of a priest which is now in the Selçuk museum, have been found in the city.

Originally the temple was reached by a stoa 160m long and 24m wide which extended from the W gate of the Agora. A flight of steps led to the forecourt which was surrounded by colonnades on three sides. On the fourth side a wide staircase led to the porch where eight massive Corinthian columns supported an architrave, frieze and pediment. The monolithic columns, which were 14m high and had a lower diameter of 1.5m, weighed c 57 tons. Note the traces of the red colour with which they and other parts of the temple were painted. Heavy doors, studded with iron, moved on wheels to admit to the 30m-wide cella, which was covered by a stone vault. The grooves in which the doors moved are still visible.

The temple continued to be used into the 4C AD, but after the victory of Christianity, it was converted into a church. Pillars bearing the monogram **IOANNOY** suggest that it was dedicated to St John. Traces of the baptistery, which was added to the temple, are in the E part of the structure.

Clearly visible from the temple of Serapis are the well-preserved Hellenistic walls on Mt Coressus with which Lysimachus enclosed his new city. If you are not pressed for time, you may like to explore this part of the site. Allow a full day for the expedition. Wear boots and thorn-proof clothes. Take refreshments and be prepared for a fairly stiff climb—the summit of Mt Coressus is c 358m above sea-level. You will be rewarded by a splendid view of the city and the surrounding countryside and have the opportunity to explore a part of Ephesus rarely seen by visitors.

The so-called **Prison of St Paul** may be glimpsed from the temple. This lies on the SW slope of Mt Coressus above the marshy area which marks the site of the ancient harbour.

Where the marble street joins the Curetes Street (known as the Embolos during the Byzantine period), note the ruins on the right of a monumental arch. Archaeologists believe that this resembled the arch of Hadrian in Athens and so have dated it to the 2C AD. An anastylosis is planned.

Across the street are a brothel and public latrine, both dated to the 1C AD, and the early 5C AD **Baths of Scholasticia**. The downstairs rooms of the brothel, which had entrances in both streets, were built around a small atrium. The floor of the main reception room was covered with a mosaic of the four seasons. The figures of winter, whose head is covered, and of autumn, who is garlanded with flowers, are well-preserved. There is a stone bed in one of the rooms. Cubicles used by the girls to entertain their clients were on the first floor. The ithyphallic figurine of Priapus, now in the Selçuk museum, was found in a well on the side of the brothel near the street of the Curetes. This well is still in use.

The latrine was constructed over a channel which had an uninterrupted flow of water. The toilet seats, which were ranged around the walls, were roofed over. The rest of the large room, which had an *impluvium* in the centre, was open to the sky. The floor was covered with mosaics.

At the beginning of the 5C AD the complex was renovated by a wealthy lady named Scholasticia. It was enlarged and improved with material taken from other structures. Some of the columns in the entrance hall were brought from the temple of Hestia Boulaea (see below). They bear lists of the members of the Curetes, an order of priests, which served in the temple of Artemis (see above).

The baths of Scholasticia had a large hall which patrons used as a club-room and meeting place where they conducted business and exchanged gossip. The remainder of the building was taken up with the usual arrangement of hot and cold rooms. A headless statue, believed to be of Scholasticia, has been re-erected near the entrance.

On the right-hand side of the street are the remains of three **tombs**. The largest, known as the octagon because of its shape, was surrounded by Corinthian columns and had a pyramid-shaped roof. It was ornamented with a design of palm, lotus and acanthus leaves. Entrance to the burial chamber is by way of a passageway under the house at the rear. Archaeologists found the skeleton of a girl aged between 18 and 20 in an andesite sarcophagus. The tomb has been dated to the end of the 1C BC.

A **Byzantine fountain** was erected on the site of a heroon dating from the reign of Augustus. Nearby are a number of **imperial decrees** relating to the reconstruction of the city after the earthquake in the 4C AD.

The small temple in the street of the Curetes, which is generally known as the **Temple of Hadrian**, was in fact dedicated c AD 118 by one Publius Quintilius to Hadrian, Artemis and the people of Ephesus. After the library of Celsus probably the best-known monument in Ephesus, this simple structure consists of a pronaos and a cella. The pronaos has two pillars and two columns in the Corinthian style. They supported a pediment (now disappeared) and an architrave and decorated frieze which curve into an arch. In the centre of the arch there is a representation of the head of Tyche.

In the pronaos there are copies of reliefs (the originals are in the museum in Selçuk), most of which were taken from a 3C building and placed here at the time of its reconstruction in the 4C. The borrowed reliefs show: Androclus slaying the boar; the fight between Hercules and Theseus; and Amazons with various deities. The fourth section, which was made at the time of the 4C reconstruction, is most interesting. In it are the Emperor Theodosius I, that implacable enemy of paganism and his family in the company of a group of gods including Athena and Artemis of Ephesus. This illustrates the power which pagan deities, and particularly Artemis, continued to exercise in Ephesus after the triumph of Christianity.

In the arched tympanum over the entrance to the cella there is the semi-nude figure of a girl surrounded with a decoration of acanthus leaves. The cult statue of Hadrian stood on a low podium at the end wall.

In front of the temple there are bases on which rested statues of four Roman Emperors: Galerius, Maximian, Diocletian and Constantius Chlorus. Somewhere in the city there was a temple dedicated to the worship of Hadrian. So far, this has not been found.

Across the street there are ten small shops fronted by a 1C AD **colonnade** which is paved with a delightful geometric mosaic. This mosaic, which dates from the 5C AD, was commissioned by an unknown alytarch. Two of the shops had staircases, which led to small first-floor rooms, probably the living quarters of the owners or the sales staff. Behind the shops on the slopes of Mt Coressus are the well-preserved remains of a number of luxurious private houses.

Two of the **private houses**, which were occupied from the 1C to the 7C AD, are open to the public. In line with current practice, objects found during the course of the excavations have not been taken away to museums. They have been left in the places where they were found.

The decor and furnishings of the houses have provided some interesting information about the life style of the Ephesian élite during the Roman and early Byzantine periods. Inevitably, the houses have been compared with similar buildings found in other parts of the Roman Empire, particularly with the 1C villas of Pompeii and Herculaneum. The consensus is that the Ephesians' houses are in no way inferior to these.

The houses may be reached from the Curetes Street by a flight of steep steps. **Room A1** of the **first house** has a fine black and white mosaic. In the centre of the marble floor of **A2**, the atrium, there are the remains of a fountain. The walls of **A10** and **A11** are decorated with frescoes.

Undoubtedly, the most interesting room in the house is **A3**. This, the so-called 'theatre room', may offer a clue to the profession of one of the owners of the house. It was given its name by the archaeologists because of the frescoes of theatrical subjects with which it is decorated. On the right-hand wall there is a scene from Menander's comedy, *Perikeiromene,* or *The Girl Who Gets her Hair Cut*, and on the left from the *Orestes* of Euripides. There is also a fine representation of a mythological subject, the battle between Hercules and the river god, Achelous, for the hand of Deianeira. Achelous, who had the ability to transform himself into any shape he wished, assumed the form of a dragon and of a bull during the conflict. Only when Hercules tore off one of his horns did he accept defeat.

The **second house**, which is larger, was built in the 1C AD, altered and extended on a number of occasions and finally abandoned sometime in the 6C. Many of its rooms are decorated with mosaics and frescoes. Note the frescoes of the muses in **B9** and **B10**. It has two atria, the larger of which has a number of fine Corinthian columns. These border a passageway ornamented with a beautiful floor mosaic of a triton and a sea- nymph.

The great treasure of the second house is the delicate and unusual 5C **glass mosaic** in a niche in the atrium. In this niche, which is flanked by a decorative fresco of erotes supporting a garland, the heads of Dionysus and Ariadne, refulgent against a background of luxuriant foliage are surrounded by a glittering array of animals and birds. As the light in the atrium changes, the glass tesserae sparkle and glow, so that the figures in the mosaic appear to move, as though momentarily endowed with life.

It would seem that the houses gradually fell into decay. After they had been abandoned for some time a number became filled with soil from landslips. This helped to preserve them and their contents.

Farther up the Curetes Street on the left are the remains of the **fountain of Trajan**. According to an inscription this was erected in AD 114 by Tiberius Claudius Aristion in honour of Trajan (AD 98–117).

A colossal statue of the emperor towered over a rectangular pool which was surrounded on three sides by a two-storey colonnade. The columns in the upper storey were Corinthian, those in the lower storey Composite. Statues in the niches between the columns included representations of Aphrodite, Dionysus, a reclining satyr and members of the imperial family. They are now in the Ephesus Museum in Selçuk.

A partial anastylosis of the fountain has been made. Only the feet of the statue of Trajan and a large globe, on which it rested, remain.

The upper boundary of the Curetes Street is marked by the so-called **Gate of Hercules** which is believed to date from the beginning of the 4C AD. This two-storey structure had a large arched central opening. The pillars had representations of Hercules, clothed in the skin of the Nemean Lion, and there were winged victories on the upper corners of the archway.

In the Curetes Street there are the bases of several monuments erected by the Ephesians in honour of local worthies. They include the plinth which supported the statue of the consul Stephanus which is now in the Ephesus Museum, Selçuk (see above).

The large structure with four columns beyond the gate of Hercules is the **hydreion**. When this rectangular fountain was reconstructed in the 3C AD, statues of Diocletian, Maximian, Constantius Chlorus and Galerian, emperors also honoured at the temple of Hadrian, were placed in front.

The **Monument of Caius Memmius** which rested on a square base, had pillars decorated with dancing female figures. The pillars flanked arched niches, above which there were reliefs depicting Memmius, his father, and his grandfather, the dictator Sulla. It dates from the 1C AD. This is a somewhat surprising monument, as Sulla can hardly have been a popular figure in Ephesus. He sacked the city in 84 BC as punishment for its support of Mithridates and for the murder here of many Romans citizens during the revolt against Rome (see above).

The **circular monument** nearby was brought from another place in the city and erected here in the 4C. The relief of the winged victory came from the gate of Hercules (see above).

After the Ephesians had constructed the temple of Domitian towards the end of the 1C AD, the city was given the title of Neocorus or Temple-Warden for the first time. Few traces of the building which was sited on a terrace measuring c 100m by 50m, remain. It was a small prostyle of 8 by 13 columns with 4 columns in front. The stylobate, which rested on an eight-stepped crepidoma, measured c 24m by 34m. The cella containing the cult-statue was 9m by 17m. The head and forearm of the huge statue of the emperor are in the İzmir Archaeological Museum.

In the last years of his reign Domitian, the self-proclaimed 'Dominus et Deus', was tormented by doubts and suspicions. He set in motion a campaign of terror against members of the senate and prominent Romans, whom he accused of plotting against him. Eventually, frightened by his excesses, his wife, Domitia, induced the praetorian guard to assassinate him. When the news of the death of Domitian reached Ephesus, an exultant mob demolished the statue of the hated tyrant.

Underneath the terrace, on which the temple of Domitian rested, there were shops and storerooms. These rooms, which are well-preserved, now house some of the more important inscriptions found in the city. Unfortunately, the guardian of this **Museum of Inscriptions** keeps eccentric opening hours. To ensure admission, apply in advance to the museum in Selçuk.

Amongst the inscriptions, the earliest of which has been dated to the 7C BC, there are some relating to property and to the criminal law eg a request for the death penalty for a number of persons who had mistreated ambassadors and stolen temple gifts. Others include a commendation of a good tutor from Attalus II of Pergamum, and a tablet erected to commemorate the visit of Hadrian to Ephesus in 128.

Facing the square of Domitian was a two-storey **terrace**, part of which has been restored. The lower storey was an unfussy structure in the Doric style. The upper storey was more flamboyant. The pillars which supported it bore representations of some of the more exotic eastern gods.

Backing on to the state agora are the ruins of a **monument** erected by Caius Ofillus Proculus c AD 8 in honour of Caius Sextilius Pollio, who constructed the Marnas aqueduct. A statue of Pollio stood in the central arched niche. The structure was later embellished with sculpture, the so-called Polyphemus group now in the Ephesus Museum, Selçuk, which was brought from the Temple of Isis. It was joined to the Domitian fountain sometime after AD 93.

The **Nymphaeum of Caius Laecanius Bassus**, erected c AD 80, was functional as well as decorative. It supplied water to buildings in the neighbourhood. An elaborate façade, whose pediment reached a height of c 9m, was ornamented with statues of some of the minor deities, nereids, river-gods, and tritons associated with water. From delicately-chased conch shells and bowls on the structure water flowed into a large central basin.

Between the temple of Domitian and the state agora there are **two statue bases** or pillars from a gate, now demolished. One of the bases has a relief of a naked, youthful **Hermes**, who can be identified by his caduceus, leading a ram. The other shows a **youth**, who is gripping a goat. Both animals may be on their way to the sacrificial altar. Note also the depiction of an omphalos and a tripod. The authorities are divided about the significance of these objects.

The **prytaneion** was one of the most important civic structures in Ephesus. Dedicated to the goddess Hestia (Vesta), it contained the sacred flame of the city which was never allowed to go out. Hestia, the sister of Zeus and Hera, had charge of the hearth, the centre of domestic worship, and so was honoured not only in the temples but in every home. The cult of Hestia Boulaea was abandoned in the 4C.

The prytaneion was also the place where official guests were received by the religious and civil dignitaries of the city. Although a building must have existed on the site from the time of the refoundation of Ephesus by Lysimachus in the 3C BC, the structure, whose remains are visible today, dates from the reign of Augustus (27 BC–AD 14).

A Doric courtyard surrounded on three sides by a colonnade fronted a large temple-like hall. The courtyard was decorated with a mosaic, on which were depicted the shields of Amazons against an ornamental background. In the hall there are the remains of a basalt altar. Note the names of the Curetes (see above) on two of the pillars which have been re-erected. It was from the prytaneion that Scholasticia took columns and other material for the refurbishment of her baths at the bottom of the Curetes Street.

Archaeologists found two statues of Ephesian Artemis, now in the museum at Selçuk, in the prytaneion. The larger statue, which dates from the end of the 1C AD, was in the hall. The other, which was made about half a century later, had ben buried carefully in a small room in the sanctuary.

Next to the prytaneion is the site of the double **Temple of Divus Julius and Dea Roma**, erected on the instructions of Octavian in AD 29 in honour of Julius Caesar and of Rome.

The **odeum** was built c AD 150 by Publius Vedius Antoninus. It had a single diazoma and two parodoi covered with a wooden roof. The odeum had a seating capacity of 1400 and was probably used for lectures and musical performances as well as for matters concerning the government of the city. (It was not uncommon for an odeum to function also as a bouleuterion, i.e. council chamber. The proximity of the odeum to the state agora suggests this was the case in Ephesus.)

The state **agora**, an area c 56m by 160m, had colonnades on the N and S sides. It covered part of the city's ancient necropolis. On the W side there are the foundations of a small temple on a raised platform. Objects discovered here suggest that the temple was dedicated to Isis. The head of a colossal statue, which some identify as a representation of Mark Antony, was found nearby. In view of Antony's links with Egypt it has been suggested that he may have been connected with the temple in some way.

The Ionic colonnade on the N side, which dates from the early part of the 1C AD, was divided by two rows of columns into a central nave and two side aisles. Additional Corinthian columns were added later. Referred to in an inscription as the basilica, this structure was probably the city's law courts and administrative centre. Part of the colonnade has been excavated. Note the bulls' heads which adorn some of the Ionic capitals. Traces of a Hellenistic stoa have been found underneath the Roman structure.

The well-preserved remains to the E of the odeum are the so-called **Baths of Varius**. Erected towards the end of the 2C AD by Flavius Damianus they comprised a bathhouse and palaestra. Flavius Damianus, a sophist, lived in Ephesus c AD 200. His statue is in the İzmir Archaeological Museum.

To the S of the the state agora there was a large **nymphaeum** which distributed water from the Marnas river to various parts of the city. It was supplied by a conduit erected by Caius Sextilius Pollio (see above). An aqueduct on the Aydın road c 5km E of Ephesus formed part of the system.

The last major building in this part of the city is the **east gymnasium**. The discovery here of a statue of Flavius Damianus (see above) suggests that this building was also constructed by him c AD 200.

The ruins of the **small circular building** to the right, which at some time was turned into a church, is believed to mark the site of the tomb of St Luke. However, there is no substantial evidence to support this belief.

An insignificant jumble of stones is all that remains of the **Magnesian Gate**. So called because it marked the beginning of the road to Magnesia on the Maeander, it was erected during the reign of Vespasian (AD 69–79).

A modern road leads from the Magnesian Gate to c 8km **Meryemana** or Panaya Kapulu as it is sometimes called. According to an ancient tradition this was the house occupied by the Blessed Virgin during the last years of her life. Confided by Christ to the care of St John, it is believed that he brought her to Ephesus sometime between AD 37–48.

Catherine Emmerich (1775–1824), an invalid German nun, who had never visited Ephesus, described in great detail the house and its situation which she had seen in a vision. Towards the end of the 19C the Lazarist Fathers from İzmir instigated a search and discovered a building which fitted the description provided by the mystic. This had long been a place of pilgrimage for Orthodox Christians from the surrounding area. Each year crowds of Catholic, Orthodox amd Muslim pilgrims come here on 15 August to celebrate the Feast of the Assumption of Mary into Heaven.

Archaeologists, who have examined the small T-shaped building, believe that it dates from the 6C or 7C, but that the foundations are much older—probably from the 1C. The room on the right was the bedroom, that on the left the kitchen. The shrine is still in the care of the Lazarist Fathers. It is claimed that a number of miraculous cures have taken place here.

Inevitably there has been some commercial development. A small restaurant caters for pilgrims and there are shops selling religious souvenirs. However, the site has not been spoiled, and, irrespective of one's religious beliefs, a visit to Meryemana is interesting, enjoyable and thought-provoking.

15

Ephesus to Kuşadası, Priene, Miletus and Didyma

Total distance c 104km. Ephesus—17km Kuşadası—(20km Panionium)—
37km Priene/Prien—16km Miletus/Milet—20km Didyma/Didim—14km
Altınkum.

The road from Ephesus (see Route 14) to 17km Kuşadası, though narrow in
parts, is well-surfaced. It is very busy during the holiday season, when
coaches carry visitors between the resort and Ephesus, Selçuk and İzmir.

Across the delta of the Cayster river, the Küçük Menderes, the road skirts
the W edge of the Durmuş Dağı. Then it descends to Kuşadası through a
series of bends which offer some fine views over the sea.

Kuşadası has become increasingly popular with European holidaymakers
and its attractions fill the tour-operators' brochures. As a result, there has
been a proliferation of smart boutiques and specialist shops which cater
almost exclusively for tourists. However, this pretty Aegean town has not
been spoiled entirely. Enough remains to touch the heart—and the senses—
of even the most blasé visitor.

Information and Accommodation. Information about hotels, pensions, restaurants,
transport, excursions, etc is available from the **Tourist Information Office**, Liman Cad.

There is a very wide range of accommodation. According to the Ministry of Tourism
list there are four five-star hotels, one four-star hotel, 15 three-star hotels, 18 two-star
hotels, four one-star hotels, one special category hotel, the *Mehmetpaşa Kervansarayı*,
three motels, and 11 pensions in or near the resort.

Restaurants near the harbour offer a range of Turkish dishes in a very agreeable
setting at reasonable prices. The fish in Kuşadası is particularly good.

Transport. There are frequent bus services to İzmir, Aydın, Denizli, Muğla, Fethiye
and other towns in SW Turkey. Buses may be joined at the the companies' offices, at
the *otogar* or at points along the route. Purchase tickets in advance, particularly during
the holiday season.

Dolmuş taxis and minibuses leave from the town-centre. There are frequent departures in the morning to Selçuk which pass near Ephesus.

During the holiday season travel agencies organise visits by coach to Ephesus,
Pamukkale, Aphrodisias, Priene, Miletus, and Didyma, and by boat to Samos and the
Dilek Yarımadası National Park.

Marina. Kuşadası has an excellent marina which has a variety of facilities including a
restaurant and shop.

Recreations. Fishing, sailing, horse riding, windsurfing and swimming may be enjoyed
in Kuşadası. The cleanest beaches are some distance outside the town. Nature lovers
and bird watchers will wish to visit the Dilek Yarımadası National Park. Open from
April to December, it is one of the finest in Turkey. It may be reached by road (28km
from Kuşadası) or by boat.

Occupying an area of c 10,985 hectares, the park boasts a variety of wild life which
is said to include leopards, foxes, wild boar, lynxes, badgers, bears, jackals, striped
hyenas, hares, martens and porcupines. The vegetation ranges from Mediterranean
maquis on the N slopes to red and Austrian pine on the S. There are also carob trees,
cypresses, oriental planes, sweet bay, judas trees, and the poisonous, evil-smelling
bean trefoil. In spring look out for the blue *Anemone blanda* and *Anemone hortensis*.
There are orchids, *Ophrys lutea* and *Orchis anatolica*, and delicate cyclamens in the
shade. Butterflies flit through the glades: orangetips, eastern festoons and large

tortoiseshells. There are also large yellow and black striped hornets which, fortunately, do not usually sting. The highest point is Dilek Tepesi, 1237m.

There are facilities for picnics and barbecues, but the park has no restaurants or accommodation. Bathing is from clean, sandy or pebble beaches.

Visitors are required to respect the laws concerning the flora and fauna which are protected, and to observe all safety precautions, particularly with regard to fires. Contraventions of the regulations may result in severe penalties.

Kuşadası is believed to occupy the site of ancient Neapolis. However, no trace of this city has been found so far. During the Byzantine era the town was known as Ania. Later, when the Genoese and Venetians were trading on this part of the Turkish coast, they renamed the small port Scala Nuova.

A short distance to the N of Kuşadası near the beach at **Pamucak** there are Byzantine remains dating from the 13C. Some believe that these were built over the ruins of ancient Pygela, which Strabo said was here.

The site of the **Panionium**, the common sanctuary of the confederacy known as the Panionic League, a religious and cultural organisation which loosely united the 12 principal Ionian cities, is c 20km from Kuşadası.

According to tradition the confederacy was founded c 800, when a number of the cities in Ionia combined to bring the people of a small settlement called Melia to heel. They took over the Melian sanctuary and, dedicating it to Poseidon Heliconius, made it the cult-centre of the new league.

In addition to meetings of the league, a festival known as the Panionia was held here at regular intervals. On a medallion issued by Colophon during the reign of Gallus (AD 251–253) there is a representation of the sacrifice made by the delegates from the member cities. Thirteen figures, their right hands raised in blessing or intercession, stand around an altar at which a bull is about to be offered. Strabo says that it was a good omen if the animal bellowed during the ceremony.

The members of the league were Miletus, Myus, Priene, Samos, Ephesus, Colophon, Lebedus, Teos, Erythrae, Chios, Clazomenae and Phocaea. It is said that after dissidents from Colophon seized Smyrna, an Aeolian foundation, that city also applied for membership and was eventually admitted. But Strabo asserts that Smyrna was 'induced by the Ephesians to join the Ionian League; for the Ephesians were fellow-inhabitants of the Smyrnaeans in ancient times, when Ephesus was also called Smyrna'.

Members of the Panionic League retained complete freedom of action and all attempts to turn it into a political organisation failed. About 600 BC Thales of Miletus suggested that the Ionian cities form an assembly in Teos, so that they could work out a common foreign and domestic policy. That advice, like the proposal made by the Prienian philosopher Bias after the Persian conquest of Ionia that members of the League abandon their cities and found new settlements in Sardinia, was ignored. After a period of inactivity during the Persian occupation, the league was revived by Alexander and his successors and the Panionia continued to be celebrated, albeit in a reduced fashion, into Roman times.

As the Panionium was in Prienian territory, the priest was chosen from that city. To facilitate communication there was a road over Mt Mycale which joined Priene with the sanctuary. When Freya Stark visited Ionia in 1952, she glimpsed a track high up on the mountain side which, she thought, might be the remains of that ancient highway. The broken pavement, which Chandler and his companions followed in the spring of 1765 on their journey over the shoulder of Mycale from the site of the Panionium to the cities in the S, may have been part of the same route.

Through its dedication to Poseidon Heliconius, the Panionium was linked to the Greek city of Helice, one of the principal centres of the worship of Poseidon. Helice was named after the wife of Ion, the legendary ancestor of the Ionians. An interesting reference to the Panionia occurs in a letter dated to c 303 BC from Antigonus to the people of Teos regarding a proposal to unite that city with Lebedus in a synoecism. The letter ordains that whoever attends the Panionia should carry out the 'common rites for the same period of time, that he should pitch (a) tent, take part in the festival together with (your envoys) and be called a Tean'.

The remains of the Panionium are overgrown and difficult to explore. They lie on the N slopes of Mt Mycale (Samsun Dağı). The site is reached by taking a secondary road from Kuşadası first to Davutlar and then to Güzelçamlı.

On top of a small hill, formerly named after St Elias and now known as Otomatik Tepe, there are the ruins of the temenos wall. German archaeologists found traces of an ancient stone altar measuring c 17.5m by 4.25m in the centre of the temenos. At the foot of the hill are the ruins of a structure which is believed to have been the meeting-place of the league. This had 11 rows of seats facing a levelled rock which presumably served as a rostrum for delegates addressing the assembly.

A one day **excursion** from Kuşadası to the sites of Priene, Miletus and Didyma may be rounded off by a late afternoon swim at **Altınkum**. A round trip of c 176km through a varied and interesting landscape is involved and for this you will need your own transport. It would be difficult, if not impossible, to visit all three places in one day by public transport.

Refreshments are obtainable at or near all three sites, but it is more enjoyable and will save time if you take a picnic lunch.

Leave Kuşadası by the Söke road. This passes through a wooded valley which shelters small, neat villages. At 24km **Söke** take Road 525 in the direction of Milas. After c 5km a turning to the right leads to 8km **Güllü-bahçe**, the nearest village to Priene.

The road from the car park climbs steeply to the site of the ancient city. As it ascends, it offers fine views over the lower reaches of the Maeander, now the Büyükmenderes. The ruins of Priene's neighbour, Miletus, are sometimes visible through the haze. They lie across the river, away to the S. Entry to the site of **PRIENE** is through a breach in the ancient walls. The city occupied a series of terraces on the side of Mt Mycale, Samsun Dağı.

History. According to legend, Priene was founded by a group of adventurers led by Aepytus, grandson of Codrus, last king of Athens. They were joined sometime later by a band of Thebans under the command of an adventurer named Philotas. Perhaps there is some truth in the myth, as the inhabitants of Priene always felt that they had special ties with Athens.

Apart from a single coin, no trace of the first settlement at Priene has been found. It is probably buried under the silt brought down by the Maeander. The action of the river has been pushing the sea back for thousands of years. Visible proof of this is provided by the position of the former island of Lade, where in 494 BC the Ionian cities were defeated by the Persians in a naval battle. This is now marked by a small hill to the W of the theatre of Miletus and is about 6km from the present coastline. Strabo, writing towards the beginning of the 1C AD, placed Priene c 6.5km from the sea.

Priene was a leading member of the Panionic League whose sanctuary was in its territory on Mt Mycale (see Panionium above). The Prienians had the right to appoint the official who presided over the meetings of the League, and one of their number was priest at its sanctuary dedicated to Poseidon Heliconius.

When Alexander the Great came to Priene in 334 BC, the inhabitants were building their new city on the side of Mt Mycale. It is believed that they chose this site because it was near the harbour at Naulochus which had served the first settlement. Alexander offered to defray the cost of their temple dedicated to Athena, a part of which had been constructed. The people of Priene, less proud than the Ephesians (see above), accepted his offer. An inscription, which commemorates Alexander's generosity, is now in the basement architectural gallery of the British Museum.

After the death of Alexander, Priene came under the rule of the Attalids of Pergamum and from them it passed to Rome. Unlike Ephesus and some of its other neighbours, it received few gifts from its new masters. Apart from some minor alterations to the theatre and some of the other public buildings, the Hellenistic city was left untouched by the Romans. So the perceptive comment of von Wilamowitz-Moellendorff, which places the present day visitor firmly in the 2C BC, '*Da ist ja das characteristische, das der heutige Besucher in Priene im 2. Jahrhundert v. Chr. wandelt...*'.

Perhaps the silting of its new harbour, which appears to have become unusable, hardship resulting from the Mithridatic wars and the exactions of greedy Roman tax collectors, led Priene into decline. During the Byzantine era a bishop's see, it sank into obscurity under the Ottomans and was largely forgotten.

After the publication of the site by the Society of Dilettanti, excavations were carried out by the German archaeologists Carl Humann and Theodore Wiegand towards the end of the 19C. Most of the important finds were taken to Germany.

The city was surrounded by a wall which dates from the middle of the 4C BC. Constructed of a local stone, this reached an average height of c 6m. At intervals sections projected in a saw-tooth pattern which allowed the defenders to engage enemy attackers on the flank. The principal gate was on the NE side. There were other gates on the E and W.

Priene was constructed in accordance with the grid-iron plan popularised by Hippodamos of Miletus (fl. c 450 BC). Philosopher, town-planner, and political scientist, Hippodamos was the friend and confidant of Pericles. Notable use of his town-planning theories was made at Rhodes, Miletus, Ephesus and Piraeus.

In Priene, the main streets, which ran E–W, were intersected at right-angles by lanes or alleyways, many of which had flights of steps to accommodate the slope. As a rule there were four private houses in each insula formed by the grid-iron, while public and religious buildings occupied one insula or more.

The **temenos of the Egyptian Gods** was in the fourth insula to the SW of the main gate. Entrance was through a propylon on the NW side. It had an altar measuring 7.30m by 14.60m by 1.70m. An inscribed altar stone found here was dedicated to Serapis, Isis and Anubis. Other inscriptions set out in detail the rituals to be followed by the worshippers and prescribed penalties for any contraventions of the rubric.

Two insulae to the W is partly-excavated **upper gymnasium** which dates from the middle of the 4C BC. This consisted of a peristyle and courtyard. During the Roman Imperial period a bath and small temple dedicated to the worship of the emperor were added.

In the next insula to the W there are the partly-uncovered remains of a **Byzantine basilica**. The pulpit and the foundations of the altar are visible.

The whole of the insula to the N of the basilica is occupied by the **theatre** which, in its earliest form, is believed to date from the second half of the 4C BC. The presence of a clepsydra at the SW end of the passage behind the prohedria (see below), which could have been used to regulate the length of speeches, suggests that public meetings as well as theatrical performances were held in the building.

The cavea is greater than a semicircle. It was supported at each end by retaining walls and had an estimated capacity of 5000. Spectators entered the theatre through two unroofed parodoi and ascended to their seats by six narrow stairs. Only part of the seating has been uncovered.

The orchestra was separated from the cavea by a 4C BC *prohedria* which took the form of a semicircular bench with a high back. The prohedria incorporated five marble chairs separated from each other, which have been dated tentatively to the beginning of the 2C BC. Reserved for the principal religious and civil dignitaries, they were the gift, according to an inscription, of one Nysios. In the centre of the prohedria there was a 2C BC altar dedicated to Dionysus. Sacrifices were offered here before the performances. The space behind the prohedria had a double function: it provided access to the cavea and also allowed rain-water to drain away.

A substantial part of the proskenion and skene, which have been dated to the beginning of the 2C BC, remains. The proskenion is a narrow building

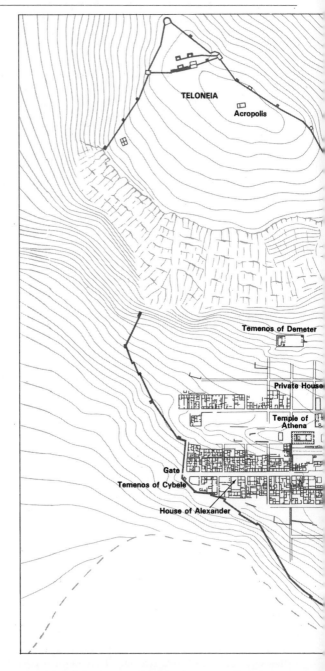

TELONEIA

Acropolis

Temenos of Demeter

Private House

Temple of
Athena

Gate

Temenos of Cybele

House of Alexander

Theatre

Necropolis

Gate

Temple of Egyptian Gods

Prytaneion

Bouleuterion

Temple of Zeus

gora

Gate

Aqueduct

Stadium

asium

N

Priene

0 metres   100

21m long and 2.75m wide, through which the performers passed into the orchestra. Stairs on the left provided access to the roof. When, towards the middle of the 2C BC, performances were moved from the orchestra to the roof of the proskenion, a new prohedria was built in the centre of the cavea in the fifth row of seats.

The original skene was a two-storey construction 18.5m by c 6m. Only the lower storey remains. It was modified considerably in the 2C AD during the period of Roman rule to give the actors more room. The existing structure on the upper storey was removed and was replaced by a new construction, which, resting on arches, was placed 2m farther back. This increased the width of the area over the proskenion from 2.75m to 4.75m.

Some of the most important buildings in Priene were to the S of the upper gymnasium. One insula was occupied by the bouleuterion and the prytaneion. These buildings were flanked by the sacred stoa, while across the principal street were the agora and the temple of Zeus.

The **bouleuterion**, which is in an excellent state of preservation, measured 20m by 21m. It is believed to date from the middle of the 2C BC. Rows of seats on three sides enclosed a small area which contained a marble altar decorated with bulls heads, garlands and representations of the gods. On the S side there was a large recess where speakers stood to address the elected councillors who composed the boule. The structure had a wooden roof which was supported at first by the walls and by pillars at the ends of the upper rows of seats. Later, further pillars were added to provide additional strength. The bouleuterion could seat about 640 persons.

Next door was the **prytaneion**, the administrative headquarters of the city. Part of this building contained the sacred fire of the city. The remainder was used by the prutaneis, the members of the boule. Their dining room, which was maintained out of official funds, was here.

To the N of the agora was the **sacred stoa**. This 116m-long structure is believed to date from the second half of the 2C BC. It was a gift to the city from Ariarathes VI of Cappadocia. Six steps led up from the street to a 6.5m-wide promenade. Like the Arcadian Way in Ephesus this must have been a popular meeting place for the Prienians. Here they could enjoy the refreshing breeze from the sea, exchange gossip and conduct business. Behind the promenade lay the stoa, its façade decorated with 49 Doric columns. The interior was divided into two equal sections by 24 Ionic columns which supported the roof. The structure was completed by 15 rooms at the back which were reserved for the use of the principal officials of the city. During the Roman period the room towards the centre, which contains a seat, was devoted to the imperial cult. The walls of the stoa were covered with inscriptions which provide information about Priene.

The **agora**, which measured 75m by 35m, occupied two insulae. Dating from the 3C BC, it was surrounded on three sides by Doric porticoes. Because of the slope the S portico was supported by a basement. There were shops in the W portico and on the W and E sides of the S portico. The centre of the S portico, which was protected by a wall from the cold N winds, formed another promenade. This offered excellent views over the lower gymnasium, the stadium and, in the distance, the harbour.

An **altar** dedicated to Hermes occupied a central position. To the E of the altar there was a **double dais** covered by an awning. This was probably reserved for the dignitaries, civil and religious, who presided over the many functions held here. Only the bases and foundations of the many statues, which once ornamented the agora, remain.

The insula to the E of the agora contained the 3C BC **Temple of Zeus Olympios**, an Ionic prostyle on a stylobate 13.5m by 8.5m. Only the foundations of the temple and of the altar, which faced the entrance, remain on the site. A number of finds by the German archaeologists were taken to Berlin. The temenos, which could be reached from the agora through the E portico, was bounded on the N by a colonnade. During the Byzantine period a castle was erected over the E part of the temenos.

In the insula to the W of the agora there was a **market** for foodstuffs, clothing and household goods.

Four insulae to the W is the so called **House of Alexander the Great** which may have been occupied by him in 334 BC, when he spent some time in Priene during the siege of Miletus. An inscription on the door-post states that only the pure, clothed in symbolic white garments, were permitted to enter the sanctuary. In a room to the N of the interior courtyard the archaeologists found a number of terracotta and marble figurines on a stone bench. In front of the bench a marble altar-table had been placed over a natural fissure in the floor. The discovery in the house of the head and upper part of the torso of a small marble statue which bears a strong resemblance to Alexander, led to the belief that this was the Alexandrium mentioned in an inscription found in the city. An alternative view, supported by the presence of the altar over the fissure, is that it was dedicated to the chthonic gods. The inscription and the statuettes are in Berlin.

To the W of the house of Alexander and close to the city wall is the **temenos of Cybele**, the ancient Mother Goddess of Anatolia, who had shrines in many Ionian cities. She is frequently associated with Attis and the hermaphrodite Agdistis. Attis was a handsome youth who is portrayed sometimes as her son, sometimes as her lover. During a fit of jealous rage, Cybele struck Attis with madness and he castrated himself. He then became the beloved of Agdistis. This myth has been used to explain the orgiastic rites which accompanied the worship of Cybele.

The goddess is usually shown wearing a turreted crown and seated on a throne between two lions. Her priests were known as Galli. Despite the disapproval of conservative elements, the cult of Cybele spread widely through the Roman Empire, attracting many followers. It became extinct only after Christianity was adopted as the state religion.

Today there is nothing to see in the temenos except the sacrificial pit. A small headless statue of Cybele found here is now in the İstanbul Archaeological Museum.

Four insulae to the E of the temenos of Cybele a stairway leads up to the **Temple of Athena Polias**. The most ancient and most prominent ruin in Priene, a partial anastylosis was made in 1964.

The temple, which was entered from the E side, was an Ionic peripteros of 11 by 6 columns. It was erected between the 4C and 2C BC. Constructed of marble from Mt Mycale, it had a large pronaos, a cella and an opisthodomus resting on a stylobate 37m by 19.5m. The entrance to the pronaos was flanked by two columns. The cult statue of Athena stood on a pedestal at the W end of the cella. There is some evidence that there was a grille or enclosure between the side-walls and the columns in front of the opisthodomus, which suggests that the temple's treasure was kept here. Traces of red and blue paint have been found on the ornamented parts of the building.

The Carian architect, Pytheos (fl. 353–334), who had worked on the Mausoleum at Halicarnassus, designed the temple of Athena Polias. It became the model for Ionic architecture. Pytheos wrote a treatise which dealt not only with the construction of the temple and the merits of its design but also touched on the training of architects. According to Vitruvius this work was still used as an instruction manual two centuries later.

The temple benefited from the generosity of a number of royal patrons. Alexander's contribution is recorded in an inscription now in the British Museum. This reads, 'King Alexander presented this temple to Athena Polias'. The cult statue of Athena is believed to have been a copy of the famous statue by Pheidias in the Parthenon in Athens. It was the gift of a Cappadocian prince, Orophernes, who appears to have spent part of his youth in Priene. Some fragments of a small Nike held by Athena were recovered by British archaeologists during their excavations in 1868–69.

The altar, which stood to the E of the temple, was a small-scale version of the great altar of Zeus at Pergamum. Only the foundation remains on the site. Reliefs of a gigantomachy, which decorated its base, are in the İstanbul Archaeological Museum.

During the 2C BC a **stoa** was constructed to the S of the temple. This was 78.5m long and had a single row of Doric columns. Like the sacred stoa and the portico to the S of the agora, it was another pleasant rendezvous for the citizens of Priene. Still visible are the steps and part of the wall of a **propylon** which was erected at the E end of the temenos of the temple of Athena Polias in the 1C AD. At this time the temple was rededicated. Athena was obliged to share her sanctuary with Augustus. Part of the inscription on the architrave, which recorded this event, lies on the stylobate.

The **private houses** of Priene have provided much information about life in the city. Although many are overgrown, their rooms filled with pine saplings and scrub, they merit an examination. These 3C and 4C BC houses have been compared with the 1C AD houses discovered at Pompeii and Herculaneum. They have many features in common. Both the Hellenistic and Roman builders used a design which proved itself effective all over the Mediterranean. Their houses were built so as to protect the occupants from the fierce heat of the summer sun and from the cold of winter.

The entrance, which was not always on the main street, led through a vestibule to a large courtyard which admitted light and air. To the N of the courtyard was an open-fronted antechamber which provided access to the dining and living rooms. The remains of stairs in some of the houses indicate the existence of an upper floor. As in Athens during the Classical period, this may have been reserved for the women of the household.

To ensure that they were cool and airy during the summer the ground floor rooms had high ceilings. Windows were near the top for privacy. As in many Turkish village houses the rooms were heated with portable stoves. Decoration was simple, usually geometric patterns, though some of the walls had stucco which imitated marble panels.

A variety of stone, bronze and terracotta objects have been discovered in the private houses. These include coins, mostly from the 3C BC, lamps, cooking utensils, bedsteads, statuettes and figurines. Surprisingly, only one small bathroom has been found. This measured 1.8m by 1m and contained a basin in which the occupant could place his feet. A few of the houses had toilets. Again this is surprising as there appear to have been no public latrines in Priene.

One of the largest of the private houses is in the fourth insula to the W of the theatre. This had 26 rooms, including separate women's quarters, an indication that it belonged to someone of wealth and importance. Many objects of value and an altar dedicated to Zeus Olympios were found here.

A short scramble up the slope leads to the **temenos of Demeter and Kore**. The temenos, which dates from the 4C BC, measures 45m by 17.75m. Facing the entrance, which was on the E side of the sacred enclosure, are pedestals on which statues of two of the priestesses, Timonassa and Nikeso, stood. The marble statue of Nikeso is now in Berlin. To the S of the temenos were the modest quarters of the priestesses.

Demeter was the goddess of growth and fruitfulness, particularly of life-sustaining corn. This belief was recorded on the early coins of Priene which bore a representation of a corn sheaf.

The goddesses were credited with bringing the gift of corn to mankind. When Demeter was looking for Kore, she was befriended by the king of Eleusis. To reward his kindness, she gave some sheaves of corn to his son, Triptolemus, and charged him with the task of spreading knowledge of its use and benefits throughout the world. A 5C relief found at Eleusis, now in the Archaeological Museum in Athens, shows a nude youth, Triptolemus, receiving a sheaf of corn from Demeter under the benevolent gaze of Kore (see also p 154).

Both goddesses were honoured with the celebration of mysteries, the most famous of which took place at Eleusis in Greece. According to Burkert they were linked with reports of perverse sexual practices. It was said that Demeter coupled with Poseidon, who came to her in the form of a stallion.

Just inside the temenos, on the right side, are the remains of a **Roman altar**. Between the entrance and the temple there is a large open space which presumably accommodated the participants in the mysteries. There is, however, no trace of the seating which was often provided (see Pergamum above). The temple, which occupies the W end of the temenos, is of a most unusual design. A slender passageway separated it from the N, W and S walls of the temenos. Entrance was through a narrow doorway which had three Doric columns in the side walls. Beyond this pronaos was the cella which had a N–S orientation. On the W side of the cella there was a high shelf or podium where votive offerings were placed.

Outside, on the S side of the temple, there was a **sacrificial pit** where sows were offered to the goddesses. It is believed that this square, stone-lined structure was covered with boards through which the blood of the sacrificial animals was allowed to flow.

If you have time, do not suffer from vertigo and are sure-footed, visit the **acropolis** on the summit of Mt Mycale. Allow c 90 minutes for the ascent and examination of the site which was known in antiquity as **Teloneia**.

Take the path at the back of the theatre which climbs diagonally across the slope towards the E fortifications. At the point where the aqueduct entered the city there are three **Hellenistic cisterns** which were repaired by the Byzantines. Water was distributed from these through terracotta pipes to various parts of Priene.

Paint marks on the rocks indicate the route to be followed. Note the small **Hellenistic shrine** with some reliefs and niches for statues cut into the cliff-face. Little remains of the fortifications which date from the 4C BC. There is, however, a splendid view of the city and of the green valley of the Maeander, with Miletus and the sea in the far distance. Chandler was very impressed by this 'most abrupt and formidable precipice'. The path down 'soon became difficult and dangerous', he writes, 'and frequently [was] not wider than the body, and so steep as scarcely to allow footing. Avoiding as much as possible the frightful view of the abyss beneath us, and shrinking from the brink, we were astonished at what we had done'.

The stadium and lower gymnasium are near the S wall, c 60m below the city centre, and are reached by a stairway which descends from the insula to the SW of the agora.

The **gymnasium**, the gift of a local magnate named Moschion, has been dated by an inscription found in the city to c 130 BC. Entered from the W through a Doric propylon, it consisted of a central palaestra which served as an exercise area. This was surrounded by four Doric stoas. Rooms for study and lecture lay behind the N and W stoas.

In the centre of the N stoa there was an **ephebeion** where young men of the city aged between 18 and 20 studied. Like students everywhere they have left a record of their presence in the form of **graffiti**. The walls of the ephebeion are covered with inscriptions which consist of the word for place (ο τοπος) followed by the name of the student, and sometimes that of his father, in the genitive case. Examples quoted by Bean are: 'Phileas, son of Metrodorus, his place', and 'Epicurus, son of Pausanias, his place'.

The other rooms in the ephebeion were used by the athletes to prepare themselves for exercise or for the games. In one the boxers pounded a punchbag; in another the wrestlers covered themselves with fine sand to provide a firm grip; while in a third contestants lubricated their bodies with olive oil. Olive oil was used to reduce the incidence of minor skin injuries caused by falls or scrapes and to keep the pores free from dirt. Its importance may be judged by the fact that the early names for a trainer were ἀθλήτς (Oiler) and παιδοτρίβης (Boy Rubber). The oil was very expensive and it was the duty of the gymnasiarch, the elected or wealthy voluntary official who superintended activities in the palaestra, to pay for it out of his own pocket. Such large quantities were used that this involved a considerable expenditure of private funds.

After exercise or a contest the athletes used a strigil to scrape the film of oil and dirt from their bodies. In the upper gymnasium, during the Roman period, there was a bath house with the usual complement of hot room, sweat room and cold plunge. Contestants in the lower gymnasium followed a simpler and more spartan regime. They used cold water. The wash basins, from whose lion-head spouts a constant stream of water poured, are still there. So, also, are the stone foot-baths.

To the right of the gymnasium was the **stadium** which measured 190m by 18m. Dating from the 2C BC, it replaced an earlier structure. On the N side there was a raised open **terrace**, where citizens could take the air and watch the contests. Behind the terrace there was a Doric stoa where instruction was given to the athletes and training took place during bad weather. Below the terrace there were rows of seats for the spectators. Only the centre seats were made of stone, the remainder were of wood.

Races were run from W to E. Two sets of **starting blocks** may be seen on the W side of stadium. The eight square stones in front, which have holes in them, date from the Hellenistic period. The ten stones behind are Roman. There are various theories about how the starting blocks were used. It has been suggested that in Roman times some kind of mechanism was employed to ensure that all runners started at the same time. A number of literary references indicate that mechanical means were not used during the Classical and Hellenistic periods.

In addition to foot-races, other contests were held in the stadium—boxing, wrestling, the pentathlon and the pancration. The pentathlon included running, wrestling, jumping, throwing the discus and the javelin. The pancration, which means 'complete victory', was like all-in wrestling without the rules. Only biting and gouging were prohibited. Kicking, boxing, wrestling and the application of pressure-locks and strangleholds were all permitted. In this contest, designed to determine the ability of one individual to establish physical mastery over another, there was no set number of rounds. Victory was declared when one of the participants was no longer able or willing to continue.

If you are not in a hurry and wish to avoid the long, steep climb back to the agora, follow the line of the walls round to either the SE or the W gate.

You will be able to have a close look at the fortifications and see how the Prienians used natural features to strengthen the defences of their city.

To reach Miletus from Priene you may either return to the main İzmir–Bodrum road and follow the signposts or cross the marsh in the valley of the Maeander by the new road.

MILETUS is not one of the most attractive sites in SW Turkey. During late autumn, winter, and early spring much of the area is an unpleasant morass. In summer this becomes a drab brown wilderness covered with low thorny scrub. A sense of profound melancholy broods over the ancient city, a feeling of abandonment and decay that is accentuated by a monotonous landscape little relieved by the occasional tall clump of reeds or the jagged stump of a ruined building.

To picture the city as it was in ancient times requires a considerable effort of imagination. Then it stood on a promontory at the head of the gulf of Latmus. Now the sea is far away, thanks to the unceasing labour of the Maeander, the Büyükmenderes, that river so aptly described by Herodotus as 'the worker'. The Classical and Hellenistic cities of Miletus disappeared a long time ago, and the Roman city that replaced them has neither the majesty of Pergamum nor the splendour of Ephesus. Indeed, after Priene on its dramatic mountain site, many visitors find Miletus a considerable anti-climax.

Near the large parking by the theatre there are kiosks which offer light refreshments, and there are restaurants at Didyma and in nearby Altınkum. As the ruins are scattered over a wide area, allow two to three hours for your visit to Miletus. The interesting collection of finds in the museum merit at least a further half hour of your time.

History. Excavations by German archaeologists on the acropolis at Kalabak Tepe to the SW of the site have shown that there was a Mycenaean colony there as early as 1500 BC. They found traces of fortifications and some houses as well as Minoan pottery. Miletus is mentioned by Homer who says that the city was occupied by barbarous Carians who fought on the side of the Trojans.

It seems the first Greek colonists arrived at Miletus as early as the 10C BC. Perhaps because it had poor land communications and was farther away than Priene and Myus from the great inland trade route that terminated at Ephesus, Miletus concentrated on sea-borne commerce. The Milesians are credited with the establishment of no fewer than 90 colonies in places as far apart as Naucratis in Egypt, Cyzicus on the Sea of Marmora and Sinope on the shores of the Black Sea.

According to Strabo, Miletus was founded by Neleus, son of Codrus, king of Athens. He joined forces with some Messenians who had been dispossessed by the Heraclids. The newcomers ousted the native Carians, taking their land and all their possessions. Herodotus has a curious story about the Athenians who settled in Miletus. Soon after their arrival they killed all the men and took their women to wife. He then relates the piquant result of this slaughter. 'The fact that these women were forced into marriage after the murder of their fathers, husbands, and sons was the origin of the law, established by oath and passed down to their female descendants, forbidding them to sit at table with their husbands or to address them by name'. Herodotus does not say how long this law was observed.

As a result of its extensive trading activities and of commerce generated by its proximity to the oracle of Apollo at Didyma, Miletus soon became one of the wealthiest cities in the Aegean. In the 7C and 6C BC this prosperity produced a climate that favoured remarkable developments in philosophy and science. Miletus was the home of Thales (636–546 BC), of Anaximander (610–c 546 BC) and Anaximenes (fl. c 544 BC), Hippodamus (fl. c 450 BC) and Hecataeus (fl. 500 BC).

Thales, who is counted as one of the Seven Sages was, perhaps, the first man to postulate a common base for all physical phenomena. This he suggested was water. Among experiments credited to him is one in which he calculated the height of the

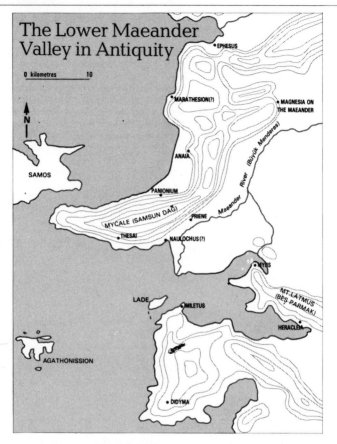

The Lower Maeander Valley in Antiquity

pyramids by measuring their shadows at the time of day when a man's shadow equalled his height. He is credited with predicting an eclipse of the sun, which took place during a battle between Alyattes of Lydia and Cyaxares the Mede in 585 BC, although the level of knowledge existing at the time makes this highly unlikely. He formulated 'Thales Theorem' which describes the inscription of a right-angled triangle in a circle. His dictum, 'Know thyself' was considered sufficiently important to be inscribed on a herm in the temple of Apollo at Delphi. The natural philosophers, Anaximander and Anaximenes, also propounded theories on the nature of the universe, while the architect, Hippodamus, is credited with promoting a grid-iron plan for towns. This was used in his native Miletus, in Priene and in many other cities of the ancient world. Hecataeus was a traveller and geographer whose work was greatly esteemed by his contemporaries and successors.

'The place of well-born married women, like their unmarried counterparts, was inside the home, secluded from the gaze of all but the immediate family.' (Garland.) In Athens a woman had no political rights, her marriage was arranged by her father or nearest male relative, she could not inherit or hold property, her freedom of action was severely limited by the law. This, perhaps, explains Thales's statement that he was glad to be a human being rather than an animal, a man rather than a woman, a Greek rather than a barbarian.

However, women of wit and intelligence made their mark on society. One of the best known and most successful was the courtesan, Aspasia (fl. 440 BC) who was born in

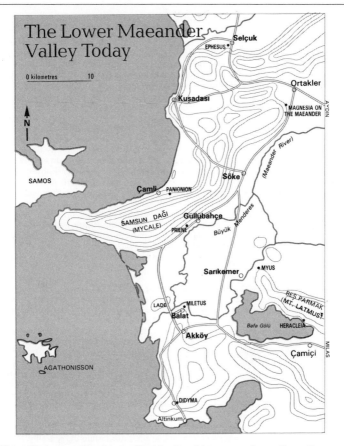

The Lower Maeander Valley Today

0 kilometres 10

N

EPHESUS Selçuk

Ortakler

Kuşadası

MAGNESIA ON THE MAEANDER

(Maeander River)

SAMOS

Çamlı PANIONION Söke

SAMSUN DAĞI (MYCALE) Güllübahçe

PRIENE Büyük Menderes

Sarıkemer MYUS

BEŞ PARMAK (MT. LATMUS)

LADE MILETUS Bafa Gölü HERACLEIA

Balat

Akköy Çamiçi

MILAS

AGATHONISSON

DIDYMA

Altınkum

Miletus. She became the mistress of Pericles, bore him a son, and according to Socrates, taught him oratory. She attracted the best literary and philosophical society in Athens and numbered Socrates among her friends.

Perhaps the greatest Milesian contribution to Greek civilisation was the Ionian alphabet, which, adopted by decree for legal documents in Athens in 403–402 BC, eventually superseded other versions, and has continued to be used ever since. The Greeks are believed to have learned the alphabet from the Phoenicians—they called letters Φοιγίκεια, Phoenician things—possibly as the result of trading contacts between Miletus and Phoenicia (but see also Al Mina below).

In the 6C BC all the Greek cities on the Aegean, except Miletus, came under the rule of Lydia. The Milesians, led by the tyrant Thrasybulus, successfully repulsed the attacks of Gyges, Alyattes and Croesus. After the defeat of Croesus and the capture of Sardis by Cyrus in 546 BC, the Persians went on to take the Ionian cities one by one. The Panionic League, of which Miletus was a leading member, proved quite unable to organise a united resistance. However, the Milesians were successful in securing special terms from the Persians who allowed them a considerable measure of freedom.

With the assistance of Athens, then a growing power, Miletus took part in the abortive revolt of the Ionian cities against Persian rule in the period between 500 BC and 494 BC. The city sent 80 ships to fight at the battle of Lade in 494 BC. After the revolt was crushed by the Persians, Miletus was occupied for the first time in its history. Most of the men were killed. Those spared were sent as prisoners to Susa. The women and children were enslaved. The temple of Apollo at Didyma was plundered and burned. Persians expropriated property in the city and the surrounding countryside.

In Athens the news of these events was received with consternation. When a dramatist named Phrynichus put on a play called *The Capture of Miletus*, Herodotus describes what happened: 'the audience in the theatre burst into tears, and the author was fined a thousand drachmae for reminding them of a disaster which touched them so closely. A law was subsequently passed forbidding anybody to put the play on the stage again'.

After the defeat of Darius by the Athenians and their allies at Marathon (490 BC) and the failure of Xerxes at Salamis and Platea ten years later, the Ionian cities regained their freedom. The Delian League was formed to unite the Greeks under the leadership of Athens so that they could resist any further expansionist moves by the Persians. Miletus was rebuilt and quickly regained much of its status and prosperity. Its recovery may be judged by the fact that in the mid 5C BC its annual contribution to the Delian League was assessed at five talents, almost as much as that levied on Ephesus.

In 404 BC the Peloponnesian War ended with the defeat of Athens and the Delian League came under the leadership of the Spartans. Unfortunately, they lacked the necessary organisational and diplomatic skills to run the League successfully and the Persians had litle difficulty in re-establishing control over the Ionian cities. However, even after their rule was formally acknowledged by the King's Peace of 387 BC, undercurrents of revolt against them continued in Ionia. These are evidenced by the close relations which Miletus appears to have established with neighbouring Caria. Milesian coins were issued bearing the names of Hecatomnos, the Carian ruler, and of his better-known son, Mausolus.

However, the Persians were in control of Miletus once more when Alexander the Great came to Ionia in 334 BC. The commander of the city's garrison, Hegesistratus, refused to surrender to him. Alexander occupied the outer suburbs, but the Persians retreated to the citadel and, closing the gates, prepared for a siege. Alexander anchored his fleet of 160 ships at the island of Lade and landed a contingent of troops to secure his position there. Then, undeterred by the presence of a much larger Persian fleet of 400 ships, crewed by experienced Cypriots and Phoenicians, which had anchored near Mt Mycale, he brought up siege engines and stormed the citadel.

After the death of Alexander in 323 BC his kingdom was divided among the Diadochoi. Miletus, with the other Ionian cities, was ruled first by Antigonus, then by Lysimachus. For a time it was under the control of the Seleucids of Syria, then under the Ptolemies until it finally passed into the hands of the Attalids. Attalus III, the last king of Pergamum, bequeathed his kingdom to Rome in 133 BC, and Miletus became one of the most important cities of the new Roman province of Asia.

Classed as a free city, it continued to flourish and its citizens continued to prosper. It received many benefits from its new rulers, as the ruins visible today testify. During the reigns of Claudius, Trajan and Hadrian local magnates vied with their imperial masters and with one another in their efforts to adorn the city with fine buildings.

Miletus had early connections with Christianity. St Paul made a brief visit here c AD 57 at the end of his third missionary journey. Though hurrying to Jerusalem to celebrate Pentecost with the brethren, he wished to address the bishops and elders of the church in Ephesus before leaving Asia. To save time he summoned them to meet him in Miletus. Having reminded them of their duties to guard the infant church, which had been placed in their care, he told the assembled Ephesians that he would see them no more. Then, having knelt and prayed with the apostle, the bishops, weeping profusely, accompanied him to the ship. This took Paul, by way of Cos and Rhodes, to Tyre in Syria and thence to Jerusalem.

During the late Roman period it became more and more difficult to use the harbour of Miletus because of the increasing quantities of silt brought down by the Maeander. By the 4C AD the area around the promontory had become a swampy marsh and the island of Lade had been abandoned by the sea. The inevitable decline in trade which resulted brought about a reduction of the city's wealth and in time of its population. For the few families left in the city life was miserable. The marshes were a breeding ground for mosquitoes which spread fever and other diseases among them. Later the impoverished settlement changed its name and became known as Balat. This is a corruption of Palatia, the fortress, which the Byzantines built on the hill that towers over the ruins of the theatre.

During the Ottoman period the site of ancient Miletus became 'the very mean place' which Chandler visited between September and October 1764. A little more than a century later the first excavations were carried out there by German archaeologists and their work, interrupted only by two world wars, has continued ever since.

The archaeologists have established that, after its destruction by the Persians in 494 BC, the city of Miletus was rebuilt in accordance with the grid-iron plan promoted by the Milesian architect, Hippodamus (fl. c 450 BC). He did not originate this, older cities in Mesopotamia like Babylon had streets that crossed each other at right-angles. Traces of the plan may still be observed in the ruins.

On the level ground in front of the theatre are the ruins of a 15C **caravanserai**, erected when this part of western Turkey was ruled by a Turcoman clan, the Menteşe. It measures 30m by 24m and had two storeys and a central courtyard 10.5m by 16m. The ground floor was taken up by stabling and the upper floor had rooms for the travellers who stayed here.

Undoubtedly the most striking ruin in Miletus is the **Graeco-Roman theatre**. The first building on this site was constructed in the 4C BC. It had an estimated seating capacity of just over 5000. During the Roman period this Hellenistic theatre was reconstructed and its capacity increased to 15,000. Alterations were also made to the division between the cavea and orchestra to allow the building to be used for gladiatorial shows and wild animal fights. This is the structure visible today.

In accordance with the usual Roman design the cavea, which has a diameter of 140m, is semicircular. Constructed on the S side of a small hill, the theatre faced one of the city's ancient harbours. The seating up to the first diazoma is well-preserved and there are substantial remains of the stage-building which resembles that of the great theatre of Ephesus. Some of the reliefs which decorated it may be seen on the SW side. In the centre of the front row of seats there are two of the four pillars which once supported the baldacchino that stretched over the imperial loge. The vaulted passages of the vomitoria are in an excellent state of repair. On the third row of seats there is an **inscription** which says that this was the 'place of the goldsmiths of the Blues'. The Blues were one of the factions which played such an important part in Byzantine history (see also İstanbul).

Towards the W of the upper diazoma there is an unusual **inscription** recording a dispute between workers and management during the construction of the theatre which was settled by the oracle of Apollo at Didyma.

On the hill behind the theatre there is a section of a **defensive wall** and the ruins of a **castle**, both from the Byzantine period. The outline of the promontory occupied by the ancient city is clearly visible from here.

Partly buried in the marsh to the NE are the **apotropaic lion statues** dating from the Hellenistic period. These marked the approach to the principal harbour and gave it its name. In times of danger the harbour of the lions could be closed by a chain stretched across the entrance.

Descending the SE slope of the hill you pass the remains of a **heroon**. This Hellenistic structure was made up of a courtyard with a circular tomb in its centre and rooms on its E and W sides. Nearby are traces of private houses and of a **synagogue** constructed on a basilical plan. Apart from this building, evidence for the existence of an important Jewish community in Miletus is provided by an **inscription** in the theatre which marks the 'place of the Jews also called the God-fearing'.

By the harbour of the lions are the remains of a Roman **monument** which commemorated the victory of Octavian and Agrippa over Antony and Cleopatra at the battle of Actium on 2 September 31 BC. On a stepped base a plinth supported a structure which was ornamented with reliefs of tritons and shaped at each end like the prow of a trireme. Above this there was a decorated slab bearing an inscription. The monument was surmounted by a cauldron 7.5m high which rested on the backs of lions. A partial restoration has been made by the archaeologists.

Nearby was a smaller **monument** which is believed to date from the reign of Vespasian (69–79). According to an inscription it was erected at the behest of a Roman citizen named Grattius. On the NE side of the harbour are the extensive remains of Roman **baths** which were constructed towards the end of the 1C AD. The complex had a palaestra surrounded by a stoa on the S and, on the N, a large vestibule and the usual complement of apodyterium, frigidarium, tepidarium and caldarium.

The harbour was surrounded on three sides by a quay paved with marble which was constructed during the Roman period. On the S side there were shops conveniently sited both to serve the needs of travellers and to supply the Milesians with imported products. The shops were fronted by a Doric stoa 160m long which dated from the Hellenistic period. No doubt this sheltered many departing voyagers when they took leave of their friends. St Paul may have parted from the Ephesian bishops here.

To the E of the stoa was the **Delphinion**, the oldest shrine in Miletus dedicated to Apollo. The very ancient personification of the god, as Apollo Delphinius, was explained by a legend which connected him with dolphins (Greek δελφίς, a dolphin). The delphinion consisted of a temenos, measuring 60m by 50m, surrounded by a Doric stoa (changed to Corinthian by the Romans). The archaeologists have found three separate levels of construction, the earliest dating from the 6C BC. The remains extant are of the original Hellenistic structure with its Roman modifications. In the central courtyard there were a Hellenistic heroon, an altar and two exedrae. According to Bean almost 200 inscriptions were found in the delphinion. These have provided much useful information about the history of Miletus.

A monumental gateway, dated to the 1C AD, provided access to the city centre. This marked the N boundary of a magnificent Roman street, the so-called processional way, which measured 100m by 28m and had pavements 5.75m wide. It was bounded on the E side by an **Ionic portico** which was constructed during the middle of the 1C AD. This is being restored.

The portico provided access to the enormous **Capito baths**. According to an inscription, the baths were built by Cornelius Vergilius Capito, Procurator of the Roman province of Asia towards the middle of 1C AD. They had a large palaestra which led through a vestibule to the customary arrangement of changing room, cold room etc.

To the S of the Capito baths are the scant remains of a **Hellenistic gymnasium** dating from the 2C BC. A propylon led into a palaestra surrounded by stoas. Behind the N stoa there was an **ephebeion** flanked by study and practice rooms reminiscent of the lower gymnasium at Priene.

The N agora was to the W of the processional way. A peristyle surrounded by shops, it was constructed during the late 5C and early 4C BC and was altered during the Hellenistic and Roman eras. To the NW there was a small market-place which had a similar history of reconstruction and alteration.

A short distance W of the N agora are the remains of the **Church of St Michael**. This 6C AD Byzantine basilica was constructed over a temple dedicated to Dionysus. An atrium provided access to the nave and side aisles. The base of the altar is in the apse at the E end. Otherwise little more than the outline of various parts of the structure is visible today. Adjoining the church was an **episcopal palace**. Part of the mosaic floor of this building remains. It has been roofed over to preserve it from the elements.

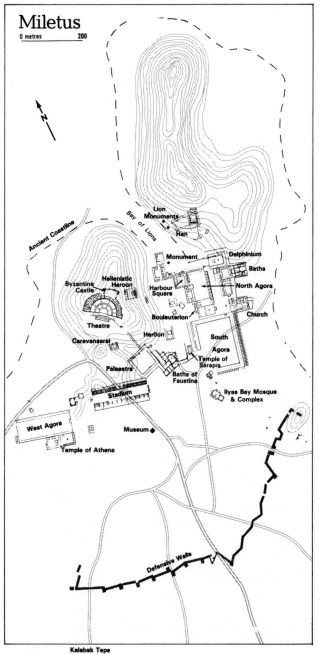

Miletus

0 metres   200

N

Ancient Coastline

Bay of Lions

Lion Monuments

Han

Monument

Delphinium

Baths

Byzantine Castle

Hellenistic Heroon

Harbour Square

North Agora

Theatre

Bouleuterion

Church

Caravanserai

Heroön

South Agora

Palaestra

Temple of Serapis

Stadium

Baths of Faustina

Ilyas Bey Mosque & Complex

West Agora

Museum

Temple of Athena

Defensive Walls

Kalabak Tepe

Nearby are the ruins of the **Mosque of Forty Steps**. This dates from the 14C and derives its name from the stairs in the NE angle of the building which served as a minaret.

S of the N agora are two ruins which have been tentatively identified as **temples** dedicated to Asclepius and to the cult of the emperors. They adjoin the well-preserved ruins of the **bouleuterion**. This was built during the reign of the Seleucid king Antiochus IV Epiphanes (175–164 BC) by Timarchus and Herakleides. A Corinthian propylon with three arched entrances provided access to a courtyard measuring c 25.5m by 23.75m. This was surrounded on three sides by Doric porticoes. In the centre of the courtyard there are the remains of a Roman tomb. The hall where the boule of Miletus met was on the W side of the courtyard. Four doors led into the chamber which could seat 1500 persons. Some rows of seats remain. The wooden roof of the bouleuterion rested on the walls and on four Ionic columns.

Facing the bouleuterion was the magnificent Roman **nymphaeum**, constructed during the 2C AD. Water brought by aqueducts from 6km to the SE filled two reservoirs at the back. From there part of the supply went to a large central decorative basin, while the remainder was distributed through a network of pipes and channels throughout the city. The basin was backed by a three-storey façade flanked by a double-storey colonnade. The façade was ornamented with vaulted niches, columns and statues of deities and nymphs. Some of the statues are in the İstanbul Archaeological Museum; others are in the Pergamon Museum in Berlin. The three lower niches, which have lost their marble covering, and a number of architectural fragments are all that remain of this splendid structure.

SE of the nymphaeum are the ruins of a large 6C **church**. Not easy to explore, this Byzantine building had a central nave, two aisles and an apse at the E end. Entrance from the street was through an atrium. The building to the N of the atrium was probably a baptistery while the circular structure S of the apse was a martyrion. The four-columned propylon which admitted to the church was taken from 3C AD building in another part of the city.

A monumental 2C AD propylon to the SE of the bouleuterion provided access to the enormous **Hellenistic S agora**. German archaeologists recovered the substantial remains of this gateway in 1908. It has been re-erected in the Pergamon Museum in Berlin. Only a part of the agora, which measured 164m by 194m, has been excavated. The remainder is covered with rough pasture. However, enough has been laid bare to establish its general plan. Rows of shops and storerooms stood behind the Doric stoas which surrounded all four sides. To the W there was a storage building c 163.5m by 13.5m, which dated from the Hellenistic period.

Adjoining the S part of the store are the ruins of the **Temple of Serapis**. This basilica dates from the 3C AD. A tetrastyle propylon in the Corinthian manner on a platform approached by six steps provided access. The roof of the propylon was ornamented with reliefs of the Egyptian gods while the pediment, still extant, bears a splendid representation of Serapis Helios. Most of the structure is concealed by the dense undergrowth.

A short distance to the NW of the temple of Serapis are the scant remains of a **Roman heroon** which took the form of a temple in antis.

A substantial section of the **fortifications** constructed during the reign of Justinian 27–565) lie between the temple of Serapis and the **Baths of Faustina**. This baths complex, which is in an excellent state of preservation, is named after the wife of Marcus Aurelius (161–180). It does not fit in to the grid-iron pattern of Hippodamus.

On the W side of the complex there is a **palaestra** which measured c 77.5m by 79.5m. This was surrounded by Corinthian colonnades. Bathers entered the apodyterium from the E side of the palaestra. This was a long narrow room which had cubicles for undressing. The discovery of statues of Apollo and of the muses at the N end suggests that it may have been used sometimes for lectures. In the frigidarium there was a large pool. Fountains in the form of a lion and of a reclining river god, the Maeander, have been left in their original positions. From the frigidarium the bathers went to the caldarium in the SE. From here they passed to the tepidarium on the W side and then back to the apodyterium where they dressed.

The statues of Apollo, Telesphorus ('he that brings to an end' a famulus of Asclepius), Asclepius, Aphrodite and other deities and the muses found in this richly-ornamented structure are now in the İstanbul Archaeological Museum and the Pergamon Museum in Berlin.

A survey and partial excavation has established some facts about the **stadium** of Miletus which was W of the baths of Faustina. This Hellenistic structure was built c 150 BC and enlarged by the Romans during the 3C AD. It had a capacity of 15,000 and measured 191m by 29.5m. As it was constructed on level ground, the spectators' seats were supported on vaults. At the W end of the stadium there was a Hellenistic gateway. During the late Roman period this was matched at the E end by an elaborate propylon which had seven arched entrances flanked by eight pairs of Corinthian columns.

To the NW of the stadium there are traces of the city's Roman W baths. The **Hellenistic W agora** was located between them and the city wall. Soundings by the archaeologists have established that the agora measured c 191 by 79m. A part is now covered by an Ottoman cemetery.

A stone podium to the S of the W agora marks the site of the 5C BC **Temple of Athena**. This measured 18m by 30m. Finds suggest that the temple had a peristasis of 6 by 10 Ionic columns and that the cella took the form of a temple in antis.

The discovery, near the temple of Athena, of **houses** containing Minoan and Mycenaean pottery dating from 1500 BC to 1100 BC shows that this part of the city was occupied from the earliest times. Protogeometric and geometric pottery from 900 BC to 700 BC, also found here, suggests that the first Hellenic settlements in Miletus were located in this area.

Before going on to Didyma, spend a little time in the small site museum and in the well-preserved 15C **mosque**. Partially hidden by clumps of reeds, this exquisite little building is a short distance to the left of the main road. Built c 1404 by İlyas Bey, emir of the Menteşe, it covers an area of 18.3 sq m and is surmounted by a dome. It has lost its minaret.

Much of the material used in the construction was taken from the ancient city. This includes the marble panels which cover the walls and form the pavement of the courtyard. The *medrese* and *imaret*, which were in the courtyard, have disappeared, the fine şadirvan remains. Note the doorway which is surmounted by an arch ornamented with carved stalactites, and, inside the building, the beautifully decorated *mihrab*.

The **museum** of Miletus, which houses finds from the ancient city and the surrounding countryside, is a short distance S of the mosque on the right side of the main road.

In the first hall small objects from the Mycenaean, Archaic, Classical, Hellenistic and Roman periods are arranged in chronological order. These include statues, amphorae, architectural fragments, protogeometric, geometric, black, and red figure vases, terracotta figures and coins. In the large hall there are mosaics, statues and stelae. Outside are larger sculptures, inscribed slabs and architectural details from Myus as well as from Miletus. These date from the earliest period to the Byzantine era. Note especially the lion statues and reliefs from the temple of Serapis.

After leaving the museum look out for the site of **Sacred Gate** which marked the starting point of the **Sacred Way**. This paved road linked the Delphinion with the temple of Apollo at Didyma. The gate, which dates from c 5C BC and which was restored during the reign of Trajan (98–117), was flanked by fortified towers. Its position today is marked by a depression in the ground which is waterlogged in the winter and covered with dense vegetation during the rest of the year.

The road from Miletus to 20km **DIDYMA** passes through a nondescript landscape which latterly has has been disfigured by advertising hoardings. The occasional coach full of tourists serves as a reminder that ahead lie the ruins of one of the most popular monuments of antiquity. To the right of the modern road a distant gleam of water signals the site of the port of **Panormus**, where during the Classical, Hellenistic and Roman periods nobles and commoners disembarked from the ships that had brought them to the shrine of Apollo.

They were joined by those who had travelled by the Sacred Way from Miletus to Didyma. The end of their journey was signalled by the stiff, imposing statues of priests and priestesses which lined the approach to the temple until Newton carried them away to the British Museum a century ago. The modern traveller comes suddenly, dramatically on this shrine of Apollo. It crowns a gentle rise, the columns of its ruined façade outlined against the sky.

The best time to visit the temple is just after sunset. Most of the tourists have departed and only a few silent figures linger among the giant columns. The walls, glimmering in the ghostly afterglow or pallid under a gibbous moon, are home to flocks of rooks which settle, rise and circle above the empty shrine. Only their harsh calls are heard. The oracle is silent.

Information. Restaurants in Didyma serve good, inexpensive meals. You can stay overnight at one of the hotels or camp-sites at 4km Altınkum. This resort has been developed, overdeveloped in the opinion of some. About the best thing that can be said about Altinkum is that it offers good bathing from its sandy beach.

History. Pausanias wrote, 'The sanctuary of Apollo at Didymoi and the oracle there are more ancient than the Ionian settlement'. All the available evidence supports him. It would seem that when the Greeks arrived in Ionia, they found an oracular shrine linked to a spring and a sacred grove already established at Didyma and that, as at Ephesus and in other places in Asia Minor, they took the shrine into their own religious beliefs and practices. A counter view proposed a Greek source for the cult drawing attention to the resemblance between 'Didyma' and the Greek word for twins δίδυμοι, and pointing out that Artemis, the twin sister of Apollo, was also worshipped here. However, this is now generally rejected and it is agreed that the name of the shrine is not derived from the Greek but, like Sidyma and Idyma, is Anatolian in origin.

Didyma was not a town. It was part of the territory of Miletus. Only the priests and the servants of the temple lived within the temenos described by Strabo. The geographer mentions the sacred grove which played a part in the ceremonies.

During the early period the priests were called Branchidae, as they claimed descent from Branchus, the son of Smicrus, a native of Delphi who had settled in Miletus. Branchus, a handsome youth, was a shepherd. One day, while guarding his father's flocks in the mountain pastures, he was seen by Apollo, who became infatuated with him and seduced him. Branchus, grateful for the god's affection, dedicated an altar to Apollo the Friendly and received from him the gift of divination. He then established the first oracular shrine at Didyma.

The giant Medusa head from the Temple of Apollo at Didyma

The earliest structures at Didyma appear to date from the end of the 8C BC. German archaeologists have found traces of a temenos wall, a well and altar from that period. A century later the fame of the oracle had spread as far as Egypt. Herodotus states that after Necho, the Egyptian king, (609–593 BC) defeated the Syrians at Magdolus, he made a gift of the armour he was wearing at the moment of victory to Apollo Branchidae. The most ancient statue of the god, the work of Canachos of Sicyon, has been dated to 500 BC. Apollo Philesis, Apollo the Affectionate, took the form of a nude youth holding a bow in his right hand and grasping a stag with his left.

It is believed that the archaic Didymaion was completed c 560 BC. Herodotus mentions a gift to the shrine about that time from Croesus, king of Lydia. He sent bowls and sprinklers of gold and silver and other costly offerings to the oracles of Apollo at Didyma and Delphi.

The archaic temple was an Ionic dipteros which measured c 85m by 38.5m. The peristasis had a total of 104 columns. The walls of the cella, which was unroofed, were c 18m high. In the cella were the sacred spring and laurel tree, and the ancient temenos, within which there was a small naiskos to house the statue of Apollo Philesis. The temple was built of tufa, but the capitals and columns were of marble and much of the visible structure was covered in marble slabs. Eight columns supported the roof of the pronaos. The lower sections of these columns bore reliefs similar to those which decorated the temple of Artemis at Ephesus.

In front of the temple there was a circular altar. Water from the sacred well to the right of the altar was probably used by clients to purify themselves before they presented their questions to the priests. The E side of the temenos was enclosed by a wall 3.5m high. Five sets of steps led up to a terrace on which there were two stoas and a number of statues.

After the defeat of the Ionian cities by the Persians at the Battle of Lade in 494 BC, the archaic Didymaion was destroyed and its treasures, including the statue of Apollo, were carried away. Either at that time or after the battle of Plataea in 479 BC, the

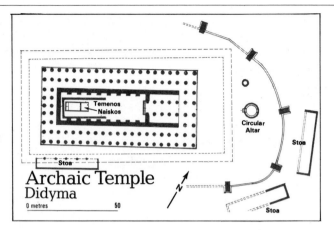

Archaic Temple
Didyma
0 metres   50

ancient historians disagree in their accounts of the events, the Branchidae behaved in a cowardly fashion, handing over the property of the temple to their conquerors. Then, fearing the wrath of the Milesians, they begged the Persian king to take them with him. He did so and settled them in a colony in Sogdiana.

The descendants of the traitorous priests were discovered by Alexander the Great a century and a half later. On the advice of his Milesian allies, he razed the settlement to the ground. The statue of Apollo finally came home to Didyma towards the end of the 4C. One of the Diadochoi, Seleucus Nicator, founder of the Seleucid Syrian dynasty, brought it from Ecbatana to the shrine.

Following its destruction by the Persians, the oracle of Apollo at Didyma went into a period of decline. This lasted for almost 150 years, until Alexander arrived in Ionia, an event marked by supernatural portents at the sanctuary. The sacred spring in the cella, which had long been dry, began to gush forth water once more and the oracle predicted Alexander's victory at the Battle of Gaugamela.

Alexander ordered the construction of a new temple at Didyma, and Seleucus Nicator commissioned the architects Paionios and Daphnis to design the building. This is the structure visible today. Plundered by marauding Celts in 278 BC and raided by pirates in the 1C BC, work on the great building continued for almost 500 years.

When Ionia became part of the Roman province of Asia, Didyma benefited from the generosity of its new masters. Julius Caesar extended the boundary of its sanctuary by 3km and c AD 100 Trajan paid for the paving of the Sacred Way from Miletus. Until the middle of 3C AD, when the shrine came under attack once again, this time from the Goths, the oracle continued to function and to receive enquirers.

However, a new and more formidable opponent appeared. Christianity was bitterly opposed to oracles which were categorised as works of the devil and forbidden to the faithful. The authority and power of Didyma declined. During the reign of Julian the Apostate (AD 361–363) this trend was reversed for a short time. On his orders a number of shrines dedicated to the Christian martyrs were removed from the vicinity of the sanctuary. However, the end came in AD 385 with the edict of Theodosius. This administered the *coup de grâce* to Didyma. It prohibited haruspicy and the consultation of oracles and provided severe penalties for those who disobeyed its provisions.

The temple, which after nearly 500 years of work remained incomplete, fell into disrepair and eventually a Christian church was erected in the cella. Little is known about the history of Didyma during the Byzantine and Ottoman periods. It appears to have continued to decline in parallel with its parent city, Miletus.

The visit of Richard Chandler in 1764 and the plates published by the Society of Dilettanti did much to revive interest in Didyma and other sites in Ionia. Chandler was captivated by what he found here. In *Travels in Asia Minor*, he writes:

'The memory of the pleasure which this spot afforded me will not be soon or easily erased. The columns yet entire are so exquisitely fine, the marble mass so vast and

Hellenistic Temple
Didyma

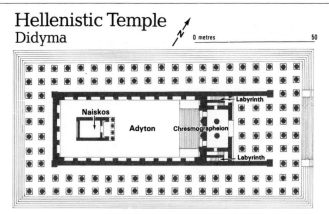

0 metres _____ 50

noble, that it is impossible perhaps to conceive greater beauty and majesty in ruin. At evening, a flock of goats, returning to the fold, their bells tinkling, spread over the heap, climbing to browse on the shrubs and trees growing between the huge stones. The whole mass was illuminated by the declining sun with a variety of rich tints, and cast a very strong shade. The sea, at a distance was smooth and shining, bordered by a mountainous coast, with a rocky island. The picture was as delicious as striking'.

Excavations conducted by the German Archaeological Institute during recent years have provided much information about the temple and the buildings which surrounded it. The material remains are sufficient to ensure a substantial restoration of the structure sometime in the future.

The **Hellenistic Didymaion** was built around the site of the archaic temple. Substantially larger than its predecessor, the stylobate of the new temple measured c 109m by 51m. An Ionic dipteros, it had 108 columns in the double peristasis; 21 on the longer and 10 on the shorter sides. There were a further 12 columns in the pronaos. Apart from those at the corners, which had representation of bulls' heads and of Zeus, Apollo, Artemis and Leto, the columns in the peristasis were in the Ionic style. Two from the inner row, complete with capitals and architrave, have been re-erected on the N side of the temple. Note the decorated bases of eight of the columns on the E section of the outer peristasis. These are believed to date from c AD 37.

The majesty of the structure was accentuated by the 3.5m-high crepidoma on which it stood. This was divided into seven levels but, as these were much too steep to be used as steps, there was a monumental stairs with 14 steps in the centre of the E side of the crepidoma. This led to the pronaos where those who had come to consult the oracle presented their questions. Behind the pronaos, and c 1.5m higher, was the 3C BC chresmographeion, the room where the oracular answers were written out and delivered by the priest. Two Corinthian half-columns flanked the entrance to the chresmographeion and there were two more full columns inside.

As in the archaic temple, the cella of the Hellenistic Didymaion, which measured c 53.5m by 21.5m, was open to the sky. It was reached from the chresmographeion by a broad flight of steps or by way of two vaulted passages which still exist. These passages, whose floors are worn and slippery, were probably used in ceremonies connected with the cult. Inside the cella note the fragments of the 2C BC frieze of griffins, scrolls and lyres, symbols of Apollo which ornamented the top of the wall.

Today only the foundations of the naiskos, which sheltered the cult statue and the sacred spring, remain. Resting on a three-stepped crepidoma, it took the form of a small Ionic prostyle with four columns across the front which measured c 14.25m by 8.25m. According to Akurgal it was the first Hellenistic structure in Asia Minor to show influence of the Attic style.

E of the temple is the **lustral well** and the circular **altar** on which sacrifices were offered by those who had come to consult the oracle. The giant **Medusa head** lying on the ground nearby came from the 2C AD frieze which ornamented the architrave over the outer row of columns. Akurgal suggests that this frieze and the decorated capitals are probably the work of sculptors from Aphrodisias. A staircase led from the temenos to a terrace which marked the end of the Sacred Way linking Didyma and Miletus.

Clients purified themselves with water from the well in front of the temple. Then they offered sacrifice—the victim was usually a goat—to determine if the god were present. From the altar they went to the pronaos to give their question to the priest.

Predictions at Didyma were made by a prophetess who had fasted and purified herself. According to a late account (4C AD) by the Neoplatonist philosopher Iamblichus, who was interested in mysteries and magic, she placed her feet in the sacred spring in the naiskos or inhaled vapour rising from it. Her words, uttered in a state of delirium, were noted by the priest and turned into hexameter verse by him or by his assistant. The priest of Apollo was a high-ranking Milesian official who lived during his year of office at Didyma.

Prophecies were recorded and kept in the chresmographeion. Most authorities now agree that this was the room behind the pronaos. However, some opine that it was located somewhere else in the temenos and attest as evidence the discovery of a number of stone slabs scattered around the temple which bear the names of prophets.

The earliest recorded prophecies date from the 6C BC. While many are on personal matters, e.g. should the enquirer get married, start a business, make a journey or embark on piracy; some are concerned with affairs of state. The oracle foretold Alexander's victory at Gaugamela and warned Seleucus I Nicator (321–280 BC) against crossing to Europe. Seleucus disregarded the advice and was assassinated by Ptolemy Ceraunus, the son of his old friend and ally.

People came to Didyma not only to consult the oracle, but also to attend the Great Didymeia. Celebrated every fourth year, the festival had competitions involving the arts—music, oratory and drama—as well as athletic events. The drama festival was held in the temenos and the athletic events in the stadium which lies to the S. Spectators sat on the steps of the sanctuary. Many carved their names there.

On the E side of the temple a section of the **Sacred Way**, which linked Didyma and Miletus, has been uncovered. Nearby are the ruins of a **Roman baths complex** which has a number of black-and-white floor mosiacs. The Sacred Way passes through a small depression which some authorities believe may mark the site of the sacred grove mentioned by Strabo.

16

Kuşadası to Bodrum

Total distance c 171km. Kuşadası—40km Ortaklar—4km Magnesia on the Maeander—(47km Myus)—(28km Heracleia under Latmus)—60km Euromus—(19km Iasus)—(c 23km Labraynda)–18km Milas—(c 15km Peçin Kale)—(c 18km Güllük)—(c 40km Ören/Ceramus)—55km Bodrum.

Some of the places on this route, in particular Myus, Heracleia and Iasus, are not easy to visit without private transport or taxis. They can be reached by a combination of dolmuş taxis, buses and walking, but the excursions will need careful planning and the expenditure of much time and a considerable amount of energy. In the case of Myus there is so little to see at the site that it is likely to interest specialists only. Finally, as refreshment facilities are very limited before Lake Bafa, bring picnic meals.

From Kuşadası (Route 15), you have a choice of two routes to the site of Magnesia on the Maeander: via Söke or via Ortaklar.

From Altınkum, return to Akköy, turn right and continue for c 7km to the junction with Road 525. Here turn left and proceed through Söke to the site.

Apart from the ruins of the temple of Artemis, there are few visible remains of **MAGNESIA ON THE MAEANDER** which proudly described itself on its coinage as the seventh most important city in the Roman province of Asia. Buildings laid bare in 1891–93 by the German archaeologist, Carl Humann, have disappeared once more under silt deposited by the river Lethaeus or are covered by an almost impenetrable tangle of vegetation. As a result, Magnesia is little visited. Those unaware of its chequered history spare it no more than a cursory glance as they speed by to more spectacular ruins. However, it is well worth spending an hour here in the remains of this once great city.

History. The first settlers are believed to have been Aeolians, whose original home was Magnesia in northern Greece. Preserving its links with Aeolia, Magnesia on the Maeander never became a member of the Panionic League. Originally the city was located at the point where the Lethaeus and Maeander met. It was moved c 400 BC to its present position.

In the 7C BC, when Magnesia was occupied by the Lydians, it received particularly harsh treatment from Gyges because of its rough handling of the poet, Magnes, one of the Lydian king's favourites. Magnes had abused the hospitality of the Magnesians by seducing the wives of some of the city's prominent citizens.

According to Strabo, Magnesia was razed to the ground by the Treres, a Cimmerian tribe and later occupied by its Ionian neighbours from Miletus. Despite these reverses, the Magnesians were not without success in warfare. On more than one occasion they conducted skilful campaigns against the Ephesians. The Magnesian cavalry earned itself a considerable reputation and, as in Colophon, specially-trained dogs formed part of the city's formidable battle-force.

About 530 BC Magnesia came under Persian rule. In 464 BC Themistocles, who had defeated the Persians at Salamis, came to live in the city. Exiled by the Athenians, he sought refuge with his former enemies and was warmly received by them. Artaxerxes, the king of Persia, awarded him the revenues of three cities: Lampsacus was to provide him with wine, Myus with ὄψον (anything eaten with bread to give it a flavour, e.g. meat, fish), and Magnesia with his daily bread.

Themistocles appears to have enjoyed part at least of his brief period of exile in Magnesia. His daughter Mnesiptolema, or perhaps his wife, as Strabo suggests, served as priestess at a temple which he dedicated to the Phrygian Mother Goddess, Cybele Dindymene. When c 462 he was ordered by the king's messenger to take the field against Greece, he decided to end his life. Plutarch describes what happened: 'Having, therefore, sacrificed to the gods, assembled his friends, and taken his last leave, he drank bull's blood or, as some relate it, he took a quick poison, and ended his days at Magnesia, having lived sixty-five years, most of which he spent in civil or military employment'. Themistocles was not forgotten in death. The Magnesians erected a fine funerary monument in the agora in his honour.

During the 5C BC the city was moved to its present site, probably to escape from the seasonal flooding by the rivers which had plagued it. The Spartans, who controlled Magnesia at that time, may also have felt that its proximity to the shrine of Artemis Leucophryene (the White-Browed) might afford the city some protection from Persian attack. Unfortunately, this did not prove to be the case and the city was re-occupied by the Persians and it remained under their rule until Alexander's arrival in Ionia.

According to Arrian, representatives of Magnesia and Tralles (Aydın) came to Ephesus to submit to Alexander in 334 BC. He received them well and sent a force of cavalry and foot-soldiers under Parmenion to secure both cities. Magnesia played no great part in the struggles of his successors. Its citizens appear to have accepted the rule of the Seleucids and the Attalids without protest and to have spent their time quietly increasing their wealth.

Magnesia was in a fertile area which produced an abundance of agricultural produce. It was famous in antiquity for the figs and olives which with wheatmeal and soft cheese formed the standard diet of its athletes. The city lay at the crossroads of the routes from the Gulf of Latmus E to Cilicia and N to Byzantium. Tolls exacted from traders made Magnesia rich.

The city was also a meeting place of many cultures and, according to Strabo, suffered as a consequence. With indignation he lists the cultural lapses of some Magnesians.

'Hegesias the orator initiated the Asiatic style whereby he corrupted the established Attic custom. Simus the melic poet corrupted the style handed down by the earlier melic poets and introduced the Simoedia [an obscene kind of song] just as that style was corrupted still more by Cleomachus the pugilist, who, having fallen in love with a certain cinaedus [sodomite] and with a young female slave who was kept as a prostitute by the cinaedus, imitated the style of dialects and mannerisms that was in vogue among the cinaedi'.

When Attalus III of Pergamum bequeathed his kingdom to Rome in 133 BC, Magnesia became part of the new province of Asia. It supported the Romans against Mithridates VI Eupator, king of Pontus, in 88 BC and was rewarded for its loyalty. Declared a free city, it became an important administrative and judicial centre.

Under Roman rule Magnesia continued to produce unusual people. Anaxenor the Citharoede (one who accompanied himself on the Cithara, a kind of lyre), a protégé of Mark Antony, was one of the bright young men who decorated the triumvir's eastern court. Strabo retails a juicy piece of gossip about Anaxenor's rise to fame and its unwelcome consequences for the city of his birth:

'Antony exalted him all he possibly could, since he even appointed him exactor of tribute from four cities, giving him a body-guard of soldiers. Further, his native land greatly increased his honours, having clad him in purple as consecrated to Zeus Sosipolis, as is plainly indicated in his painted image in the market-place. And there is also a bronze statue of him in the theatre, with the inscription, 'Surely this is a beautiful thing, to listen to a singer such as this man is, like unto the gods in voice''.

Unfortunately, Strabo continues, the Magnesians' gesture misfired, earning them not fame, but a reputation for being ignorant and ill-read. The sculptor left out the last letter (an iota) of the last word in the second verse of the quotation from the Odyssey and so changed a dative into a nominative. As a result, the Magnesians became the laughing-stock of their neighbours.

There is an interesting sequel to Strabo's story. Towards the end of the 19C German archaeologists found this statue base in the theatre. According to Bean they reported that there was just sufficient space at the edge of the stone for the insertion of a narrow letter. There was a mark in that space on the base, but whether it was a badly formed iota, scratched in by a Magnesian tired of jokes about his city or the result of damage and weathering is impossible to say. The stone is now in Berlin.

After the triumph of Christianity, Magnesia was an important bishopric. During the Byzantine era it continued to be a relatively prosperous trading and market centre for the surrounding countryside. However, in the troubled period between the 11C and 14C it began to decline and this trend continued until it was finally abandoned.

Magnesia was visited by Richard Chandler in 1765. He found some architectural fragments in the Corinthian and Ionic styles on the site, but was unable to discover the place which Pausanias called the tunnels. According to Pausanias, there was a grotto dedicated to Apollo, 'not very marvellous for size, but the statue of Apollo is extremely ancient and gives you physical powers of every kind; men consecrated to this statue leap from precipitous cliffs and high rocks, they pull up giant trees by the roots, and travel with loads on the narrowest footpaths'. Modern archaeologists have been equally unlucky in their search for the grotto.

Road 525 cuts through the Byzantine defences—the ancient city was unwalled, relying for protection on the temple of Artemis—and divides the site into two unequal parts. The large structure to the E of the road is believed to have been a **Roman bath**.

The **Temple of Artemis** was to the W of the modern road. The temple, which was designed by Hermogenes, dates from c 130 BC. It replaced an earlier structure which may have been dedicated to Cybele.

Hermogenes was a native of Priene. In addition to the temple of Artemis Leucophryene at Magnesia, he also designed the temple of Dionysus on Teos. Both structures exemplify his strong preference for the Ionic style, which he praised in his teaching and writings.

The temple, an Ionic pseudo-dipteros with 15 by 8 columns, rested on a stylobate measuring 41m by 67m. Facing W, it stood on a nine-stepped crepidoma. Entering through the large pronaos, one passes into the cella where the base of the cult statue may still be seen. Behind the cella there was a spacious opisthodomus. The wall separating the two sections of the structure has disappeared. The large pronaos overlooked an altar which was modelled on the altar of Zeus at Pergamum. During the Roman period the temenos was surrounded by a Doric stoa. There are sculptures from the temple's frieze in the Archaeological Museum in İstanbul, the Pergamon Museum in Berlin and in the Louvre in Paris.

According to Strabo the temple of Artemis at Magnesia 'in the size of its shrine and in the number of its votive offerings is inferior to the temple of Ephesus, but in the harmony and skill shown in the structure of the sacred enclosure is far superior to it. And in size it surpasses all the sacred enclosures in Asia except two, that at Ephesus and that at Didymi'.

The use of the pseudodipteral style produced a pleasing contrast between the brightly lit and the shaded parts of the temple and greatly enhanced its appearance, while the space freed by the employment of a single row of columns formed a pleasant promenade sheltered from the elements. The success of this design, which was taken up by the Augustan architect Vitruvius, had a profound effect on architecture and has been copied in countless buildings from the Renaissance to the present day.

Inscriptions found in the temple area provide information about the festival of Artemis Leucophryene.

A propylon on the W side of the temenos opened on to the agora, in the centre of which stood the **Temple of Zeus Sosipolis** (Saviour of the City). This temple, a small Ionic prostyle from the middle of the 2C BC, and all the other structures in this area have been covered by alluvial deposits.

Nearby are the remains of a small **theatre** which had an estimated capacity of 3000. Only one row of seats and parts of the stage-building are visible. A tunnel, which connected the stage-building with the centre of the orchestra, was probably used by actors to make spectacular entrances. When Bean saw it in 1939, the tunnel had lost its roof and was a deep, masonry-lined trench choked with brambles. Since then it has been filled in, presumably to prevent accidents. To the S of the theatre there was an **odeum** and beyond that a **stadium** and a **gymnasium**. All date from the Roman period. The dense undergrowth which covers much of the site makes any detailed exploration of these structures very difficult.

Leave Magnesia and continue S across the plain of the Maeander for c 25km to a turning on the left which leads c 7km to Myus. Here *Glycyrrhiza glabra*, a hardy shrub, grows wild in the Maeander valley and on the slopes of the surrounding hills. Liquorice is made from its roots. Lake Bafa is signalled by the dramatic outline of Mt Latmus which, because of the rocky peaks that crown it, is called by the Turks Beş Parmak (Five Fingers).

A reasonably good minor road leads from Road 525 to Sarıkemer. From here there is a rough track to the hamlet of Avşar. The sparse ruins of **Myus** are on a hillside to the NW, near the river. Today the site of this ancient settlement, one of the least successful in Ionia, has a desolate, forgotten air which is in keeping with its sombre history.

History. According to Strabo, Myus was founded by Cydrelus, bastard son of Codrus, king of Athens. It was built on a promontory c 15km to the NE of Miletus. As the silt brought down by the Maeander pushed the shoreline farther and farther to the S, the fortunes of the city declined. In 499 BC 200 warships, under the command of the Persian Megabates, anchored here. Five years later Myus was able to contribute only three vessels to the Ionian squadron at the battle of Lade. Not only was the economy of the city weakened by a loss of trade caused by the disappearance of its harbour but the health of its citizens was undermined by the mosquitoes which bred in increasing numbers in the new marshlands.

In 464 BC Myus was one of three cities presented by the Persian king, Artaxerxes to Themistocles, who had abandoned the Greek cause (see Magnesia). About 250 years later, Myus suffered the humiliation of being given away again. Philip V of Macedon awarded the city to the Magnesians who had supplied his hungry troops with figs.

Impoverished by the decline in their trade, harrassed by their Milesian neighbours, who claimed part of their territory, weakened by malaria-carrying mosquitoes and demoralised by being awarded as a prize by foreign tyrants, the people of Myus eventually admitted defeat. Pausanias (fl. c AD 150) describes how, taking all their movable goods and the statues of their gods, they left their city and moved to Miletus. The abandoned buildings proved a useful quarry for the Milesians, who carried away any re-usable stone or marble. When Pausanias visited Myus he found 'nothing there but a white marble temple of Dionysus'. The German archaeologists at Miletus have verified this ancient account. They discovered architectural fragments bearing inscriptions which refer to Myus in the temple of Athena and in the theatre of Miletus.

Chandler visited the Maeander valley in 1764, but confused Heracleia with Myus. The site was excavated for the first time by Wiegand in 1908. A number of architectural fragments and some reliefs depicting chariot-races were sent by him to Berlin. Further excavations, made by a German team between 1964 and 1966, have established the identity of the few ruins that have survived centuries of spoliation and neglect.

The most prominent building on the site is **Avşar Kale**, a Byzantine castle that crowns a small rise near the river. The city occupied the area SE of this hill on whose sides cisterns, rock-cut tombs and houses have been found.

Buildings stood on two terraces below the hill. On the upper terrace were the remains of an **archaic Ionic temple** which is believed to have been dedicated to Apollo Terebintheus, Lord of the turpentine tree. The lower terrace had a 6C BC **Ionic peripteros** with 6 by 10 columns, which rested on a stylobate measuring c 17.25m by 29.75m. The reliefs of the chariot-races found by Wiegand came from a frieze which is believed to have decorated the cella of this building. The discovery of the base of a single marble column has suggested that this may have been the temple of Dionysus, described by Pausanias. However, Akurgal argues convincingly that, as it opened on to the W, it was probably been dedicated to an

*Lake Bafa, with the Byzantine ruins of Heracleia under Latmus
in the distance*

Anatolian deity who in time became identified with a member of the Greek
pantheon, perhaps Artemis. (See also Sardis, Ephesus and Magnesia on
the Maeander.)

Leave the remains of unsuccessful, unhappy Myus and return to Road
525. Continuing S in the direction of Milas, you soon reach **Lake Bafa** (Bafa
Gölü). The view from the road, which runs parallel to the lake for c 20km,
is undoubtedly one of the most beautiful in Turkey.

On the left the blue waters of Bafa Gölü, dotted with tiny islands, mirror
the barren, arid peaks of Mt Latmus. Overhead, flocks of waterfowl,
disturbed by passing cars, protest noisily as they wheel and circle before
returning to the lake to resume their feeding. By the roadside herds of goats
snatch greedily at every edible scrap of vegetation while cheerful *yürük*
children guide the animals towards their encampment, patiently rounding
up the strays that have wandered on to the road.

The shores of Lake Bafa are an agreeable setting for a picnic or for a meal
in one of the small roadside restaurants. Their fish dishes, especially the
grey mullet, are excellent. Near the restaurants is the Çerinin camp-site
which offers rather basic facilities for a pittance.

If you have time, cross the lake by boat to the village of **Kapıkırı** which
occupies the site of **HERACLEIA UNDER LATMUS**. A less romantic and
less comfortable route is from the village of Çamiçi on the eastern side of
the lake. This passes though a strange landscape of tortured, convoluted
peaks and huge granite boulders—ancient rockfalls from the mountain.

At the entrance to Kapıkırı the road divides. The lower branch goes to some small lakeside restaurants which are open during the holiday season, while the upper branch leads to the village and the ruins of Heracleia.

Heracleia under Latmus was never a place of much importance. Miletus at the entrance to the gulf captured most the seaborne trade and the settlement was too far to the S to gain from the caravans that passed through Magnesia on their way to and from Ephesus. Although geographically in Ionia, Heracleia was a Carian city in character and its history was shaped by events in Caria. One of the earliest references to the area is unflattering. Among the supporters of the Trojan cause Homer (*Iliad* 2. 868) counts those 'who dwell around Miletus and Phtheiron' (the mountain of lice). According to Strabo the Milesian sage and geographer Hecataeus (c 550–490 BC) believed that Phtheiron was Mt Latmus.

History. The first inhabitants lived in a settlement called Latmus which was to the E of the modern village. They were Anatolian people. Although certainly influenced by their Aeolian and Ionian neighbours, their Hellenisation was probably not completed until the end of the 4C BC, when Alexander removed the Persians from Asia Minor.

In the 5C BC, when the annual contribution from Miletus and Ephesus to the Delian League was assessed at between six or seven talents, Heracleia contributed only one talent. In the 4C BC Mausolus of Halicarnassus used a stratagem to capture Latmus which he then fortified. Shortly afterwards the inhabitants moved to the new settlement of Heracleia on the W. This was later surrounded by a massive defensive wall.

Although it had many fine buildings during the Hellenistic and Roman periods, from about the end of the 1C BC the prosperity of Heracleia, like that of Miletus, began to decline. The change in fortune was due to the loss of trade caused by the closing of Heracleia's link with the sea. Silt brought down by the Maeander gradually turned the Gulf of Latmus into the large brackish lake that exists today.

Heracleia has always been linked with the legend of Endymion, the handsome shepherd who was seduced by Selene the moon goddess. Loved also by Zeus and, perhaps by Hera, the youth escaped death and old-age by begging Zeus to let him sleep for ever in a cave on Mt Latmus. Selene saw him there and was overcome by his beauty. She laid with him at night. Endymion, without waking once from his magic slumbers, gave her 50 daughters.

In Christian times the story was given a more decorous turn. Endymion, it was said, was a mystic who, after years of studying the moon, learned the secret name of God. Once a year the priests opened his tomb and, in an attempt to pass on his secret to men, his bones emitted a strange humming noise.

The story of Endymion has captured the imagination of artists and poets from many ages and cultures. One of the best-known ancient representation of the legend is a relief in the Capitoline Museum in Rome. The sleeping youth is shown half-reclining on a marble bench, while his abandoned dog bays at the moon. Many English poets were captivated by the legend. Arnold, Drayton, Hood, Keats, Shakespeare, Shelley, Spenser, Swift, Tennyson, Vaughan and Wordsmith, all wrote about Endymion. In the *Merchant of Venice*, Act 5, Shakespeare reminds us that,

'the moon sleeps with Endymion,
And would not be awaked !',

while Keats avows,

'tis with full happiness that I
Will trace the story of Endymion'.

and Edmund Spenser in 'Epithalamion' wrote of the

'...fleece of woll, which privily
The Latmian shepherd once unto thee brought,
His pleasures with thee wrought...'.

Sometime in the 7C AD anchorites and monks, who had fled from Arabia, settled in caves on Mt Latmus and in small communities around Lake Bafa and on the islands. Surviving repeated attacks by the Saracens, they produced saints like Arsenius,

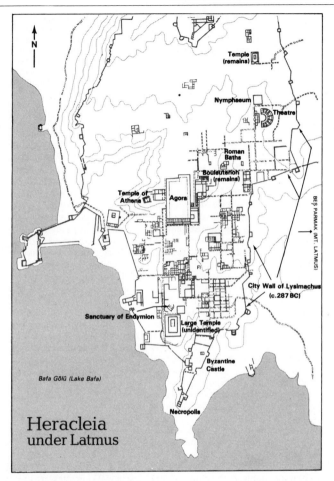

Heracleia
under Latmus

Acacius and Paul Junior, whose fame spread through Christendom and attracted pilgrims from as far away as Rome.

St Paul Junior, who wished to be a stylite, settled eventually for life in a cave in one of the most inaccesible parts of the mountain. Despite the inconvenience of frequent earthquakes he stayed there for many years, living frugally on a diet of acorns. Eventually his reputation for holiness made him so popular that he fled to Samos in search of solitude.

In the middle of the 11C the monks were obliged to leave the area around Mt Latmus because of attacks by the advancing Turks. They returned after the Crusaders' victory at Dorylaeum on 29 June 1097 and remained at Heracleia until the beginning of the 14C, when western Anatolia came under Turkish rule.

Heracleia was visited by Chandler in 1765. He described the site, which he confused with Myus, as being 'as romantic as its fortune was extraordinary'. He located the theatre, which even at that time had lost its marble seats, the agora and the temple of Athena. He was impressed by the city walls and noted their similarity with the Lysimachean fortifications at Ephesus. He found the necropolis down by the lake and a funerary inscription commemorating the untimely death of a youth named Seleucus.

Chandler was taken up the mountain by the villagers to examine an anchorite's shelter and chapel. 'We came', he writes, 'in about an hour to a large rock, which was scooped out, and had the inside painted with the history of Christ in compartments, and with heads of bishops and saints. It is in one of the most wild and retired recesses imaginable. Before the picture of the crucifixion was a heap of stones piled as an altar, and scraps of charcoal, which had been used in burning incense'.

Commenting that Latmus had become 'a holy retreat, when monkery, spreading from Egypt, toward the end of the fourth century, overran the Greek and Latin empires', he concluded that the existence of a lake abounding in large fish, which 'afforded an article of diet not unimportant under a ritual which enjoined frequent abstinence from flesh', must have been an important factor in influencing the choice of the holy men.

Heracleia's attraction springs more from the beauty of its situation than from the quality or variety of its ancient remains. Apart from the Hellenistic fortifications, which are a spectacular construction achievement, the ruins are not very impressive. The city was built on the grid-plan popularised by Hippodamus of Miletus, but it is difficult to see evidence of this now. An hour should be sufficient for an examination of the principal sites, but if you intend to explore the fortifications on the mountain allow a further two to three hours. There is a pleasant beach where swimming may be enjoyed, providing you avoid the stretches covered with reeds or weed.

The anchorites' cells on the mountain, one of which was visited by Chandler, are difficult to locate. If you wish to see them, take a guide.

The schoolhouse and playground in the centre of the village occupy the site of the **Hellenistic agora**. At the S end there are the well-preserved remains of a **market building** which was divided into separate shops. Across the street, at the rear of some houses, are the scanty remains of the 2C BC **bouleuterion**. This resembled the council chamber in Priene. Only a few rows of seats and part of the supporting wall remain.

A short distance to the E, picturesquely situated in an olive grove, are the scanty ruins of the **Roman theatre**. There are traces of the seating and stage-building. To the left are the remains of a **nymphaeum** and of a structure identified as a **temple**.

The **Hellenistic city walls**, which extend for 6.5km and rise to a height of c 488m, are in a remarkable state of preservation. They were probably built by Lysimachus c 287 BC. 'Grey like the mountain', writes Freya Stark, 'they climb through the chaos of boulders high up the mountain shoulder; they lose themselves and reappear among rocks like a swimmer in waves'. There are towers, stairs, gates and sally-ports in plenty to explore. In places, where the wall has disappeared, the niches, which held the missing stones, look like giant hand-holds. A stout pair of shoes and a walking stick are essential equipment for a walk on Mt Latmus.

Prominent on a spur below the agora is the **Hellenistic Temple of Athena**. This building, identified by an inscription, was a temple in antis with a pronaos and cella which were approximately the same size.

The small island across from the landing stage was fortified during the Byzantine period. It was formerly joined to the mainland by a wall which has been submerged by the rising waters of the lake.

The lower track out of the village passes the ruins of one of the most unusual buildings in Heracleia. This is believed to have been a **sanctuary** dedicated to Endymion. It took the form of a prostyle with a small pronaos and a cella. The pronaos has a structural oddity which can scarcely have facilitated access. It was fronted by an uneven number of columns—five— with pilasters at each end. The semicircular cella incorporated sections of unworked natural rock. These were joined by a wall of shaped stone which originally extended above them. The sanctuary faced W, as is customary in buildings erected in honour of heroes or demi-gods.

A short distance to the E on a promontory overlooking the lake are the remains of a **Byzantine castle**. There was an ancient **necropolis** below this building. The tombs, which are all of the Carian type, were cut out of the rock and covered with shaped stone lids. Some now lie under water. All were robbed of their grave-goods in antiquity.

About 1km to the E of the promontory is the site of the original foundation of Latmus. This lies 500m to the N of the road leading to Çamiçi. Surrounded by a wall, constructed by Mausolus, the site was occupied from c 6C BC. The buildings, both public and private, have provided useful information about pre-Greek settlements in Caria. The site was abandoned in the 4C BC, when the inhabitants moved W to the new settlement of Heracleia. Rather touchingly, however, they continued to bury their dead in Latmus. The site was re-occupied during the late Byzantine period, possibly because it was more easily defended. Evidence of this occupation is provided by the ruins of two churches and of a number of private houses.

The road from Çamiçi climbs steadily, passing through a pleasantly-wooded landscape which gives way gradually to a chequered pattern of cultivated fields and pastures grazed by flocks of black-haired goats. About 4km beyond the village of Selimiye is the site of the ancient city of **EUROMUS**. Here, half-hidden in a grove of olive trees, are the remains of one of the best-preserved temples in Turkey.

The city began to be called Euromus sometime towards the end of the 4C BC, when Caria came under Greek influence. A century earlier it was known as Kyromus or Hyromus, both non-Greek names. A place of some size and prosperity, it ranked next in importance to Mylasa, with which it was joined uneasily for some time in a sympolity. Euromus seems to have prospered during the Hellenistic and Roman periods, issuing its own coinage from the 2C BC to the 2C AD.

From the main road a short, bumpy track leads to the site. By the side of the track, half-hidden by the vegetation, are some interesting **Carian tombs**. Partly cut from the living rock, partly excavated, they were covered with huge stone lids. Unfortunately, all were opened and robbed a long time ago.

During the course of a survey and partial excavation of the **Temple of Zeus**, which was begun in 1969 by Turkish archaeologists, some interesting discoveries were made. The archaeologists found a number of archaic terracotta slabs, ornamented with chariots, birds and floral motifs which suggests that a shrine existed at the site as early as the 6C BC. An inscription from the Hellenistic period mentions Zeus Lepsynus to whom the sanctuary was dedicated at that time. Lepsynus is a non-Greek word which would suggest that some kind of synthesis had taken place between a native Carian deity and Zeus.

The existing building is a peripteros in the Corinthian style with 6 by 11 columns which rests on a stylobate measuring c 14.5m by 26.8m. It is believed to date from the reign of Hadrian (AD 117–138). The fact that some of the columns are unfluted suggests that the temple was never completed.

Inscriptions on a number of the columns record their donation by prominent citizens of Euromus. Menecrates, a state physician and magistrate gave five, while Leo Quintus, a magistrate, paid for seven.

Entrance to the temple was on the E side through a double row of columns. Steps led from the pronaos to the cella, where the cult-statue rested in a niche inside a naiskos. There was a small opisthodomos with two columns in antis. To the E of the temple are the remains of a marble altar, dating from the Hellenistic period.

Chandler came to Euromus in 1764. An examination of the remains led him to believe mistakenly that he had found Labraynda. He was horrified to discover a number of furnaces near the temple of Zeus. In these the peasants burned marble to produce lime which they used as fertiliser and to decorate their houses. How much of the ancient building was lost by this infamous practice will never be known.

Today 16 of the temple's columns are still standing. They support a part of the architrave. Note the decorative **lion head** on the S cornice which served to carry rain water away from the roof.

The temple was built outside the confines of the city which was a short distance to the N. This area has not been excavated and is very overgrown. Euromus was enclosed by substantial fortifications, which date from the early Hellenistic period. A **defensive tower** and part of the **city wall** crown a slight eminence to the N of the temple. Buildings identified in the city include the **theatre**, of which some seats and a part of the stage-building remain, a **Roman baths complex** and the **agora** which was surrounded by colonnades.

The temple at Euromus attracts few visitors. Apart from the track, which provides access, the site remains much as it was when Chandler visited it in the middle of the 18C. This graceful building, set among silver-green olive trees, is a place where one may rest quietly savouring the atmosphere and pondering on the impermanence of man's works.

About 4km from Euromus turn right by an isolated *kahve* to 19km **IASUS**. The road is narrow, but has a reasonably good surface. Passing through pine woods it emerges eventually on the crest of a hill which overlooks a stretch of marshy ground in the vicinity of Güllük. Shortly after decending to the plain it divides. Take the left-hand turning for Iasus.

The modern village of **Kuren**, which covers part of the site, is built around a south-facing harbour. At the water's edge there are several small restaurants which serve simple, inexpensive and very palatable meals. In line with ancient tradition the fish-dishes of Iasus are particularly good.

Like Euromus, Iasus does not attract many visitors. During the holiday season a certain number cross over by boat from the small resort of Güllük. However, for much of the year only the village people and the archaeologists are seen among the ruins of the ancient city. Since 1960 the site has been surveyed and excavated by an Italian team of archaeologists under the direction of Professor Doro Levi. The most important finds are in the İzmir Archaeological Museum. A number of objects are kept in an antiquarium housed in a Roman mausoleum at the entrance to the village.

History. Iasus was a very ancient foundation. The excellence of its harbours, the richness of its fishing-grounds, and the presence of quarries producing a fine red-tinted marble must have been among the factors which attracted colonists. Legendary accounts state that it was founded by Greeks from Argos who were assisted by the inhabitants of nearby Miletus. The first Greek settlers are believed to have arrived sometime in the 9C BC. However, the archaeologists have found evidence which shows that the site was occupied long before their arrival. It would appear that it was inhabited from the beginning of the second millennium BC. Minoan pottery (dating from c 2000–1550 BC) and the remains of Minoan houses point to a strong link between Iasus and Crete, while quantities of Mycenaean pottery, discovered at higher levels, indicate contact with the Greek mainland at a very early period.

In the 5C BC Iasus was a member of the Delian League and was assessed for an annual payment of one talent, the same amount as Mylasa. A supporter of Athens, Iasus was sacked by the Spartans, who were allied with the Persians, in 412 BC. It was invested again eight years later by a Spartan army under the command of Lysander. The male inhabitants were slaughtered and the women and children sold into slavery.

Shortly after Sparta's influence in the Aegean was destroyed by Conon's victory off Cnidus in 394 BC, Iasus joined a league of Aegean states which wished to rid the area of all foreign influence. The league, which included powerful cities like Ephesus, Rhodes and Byzantium, was not very successful. After the settlement known as the King's Peace in 386 BC, which recognised the suzerainty of the Persians over the Greek cities in Asia, Iasus came once more under foreign domination.

Apart from a brief period, when Mausolus of Halicarnassus endeavoured to establish an independent state, Iasus and its neighbours continued to be ruled by Persia until the arrival of Alexander the Great in 334 BC. After the confusion and disorder following his death had been resolved, Iasus came under the rule first of the Ptolemies of Egypt, then of the Seleucids. Following the intervention of the Romans, Iasus passed under the control of the Rhodians c 190 BC. The city supported Mithridates VI Eupator, king of Pontus, in 88 BC in his revolt against the Rome and, after his defeat, suffered for their bad judgment. Freebooters, allies of Rome, were permitted to sack the city.

During the Imperial period Iasus prospered. It had a number of fine buildings, the gifts of Hadrian, Commodus and some local magnates. As the surrounding countryside is not very fertile, most of the city's wealth must have come from its fishing fleet. Strabo tells a story about a visiting musician who held an Iasian audience enthralled until the bell that announced the opening of the fish market was rung. Then, apart from one man who was somewhat deaf, the audience rose and departed. Surprised and displeased, the musician approached this man and, not knowing that he was deaf, complemented him on his good manners and good taste in staying to hear the music after the bell had been rung. On hearing that the fish market was open the man hastily excused himself, wished the musician good day, and rushed after his fellow citizens.

Another story about Iasus involves a boy and a dolphin. After his daily exercise in the gymnasium this boy was accustomed to swim in a bay near the city. A dolphin, enamoured with the boy, would wait for him and carry him out to sea, and later return him safely back to shore. When Alexander the Great heard about this unusual occurrence, he sent for the boy and appointed him priest of Poseidon. The people of Iasus, proudly commemorated the event on their coinage. This showed the boy swimming near the dolphin and resting one arm on its back.

Iasus continued to issue its own coins until the 3C AD. The discovery of the ruins of several churches and of extensive fortifications testify to the city's importance during the Byzantine era. It was an episcopal see subject to the metropolitan of Aphrodisias. During the Middle Ages a castle was built by the Knights of Rhodes on the summit of the small hill in the centre of the peninsula.

Little is known of the history of Iasus after the Turkish conquest. It appears to have declined in importance and most of its inhabitants probably moved away. Like Alexandria Troas and a number of other ancient sites on the Aegean, it was plundered of its cut and shaped stone. This was used for building purposes in İstanbul.

When Chandler came to Iasus in the autumn of 1764, he found it almost deserted. Pinks and jonquils grew among the mastic bushes and there were large numbers of partridges feeding on the berries. He received a mixed reception from the few people, many of them Greeks, who lived among the ruins. Initially, he was refused entrance to the site by a Greek who lived in a sepulchre near the isthmus. Only when he returned armed with a permit from the ağa of Melasso, in whose jurisdiction Iasus lay, was he able to complete his examination of the site.

Even then a rude and ignorant Greek priest tried to prevent him from copying an inscription which mentioned the theatre, the prytaneum and some other public buildings. He identified the theatre and discovered the substantial remains of the fortifications. Among the inscriptions which he found was one recording the victory of a Iasian at Olympia and at the Capitoline games in Rome. He and his companions lodged in the sepulchre for some time, sharing the limited floor-space with the Greek and his family. In his journal he recorded that they were guarded by two fierce dogs which 'were continually in motion round about, barking furiously at the jackals and then looking in on us with an attention as remarkable as friendly and agreeable'.

The **necropolis** of Iasus was outside the city. Tombs dating from the third millennium BC to the Roman period are on the right-hand side of the road to the modern village. Some are of the Carian type with a recess for the body cut from a horizontal slab of rock which was closed by a stone slab.

The most striking is a magnificent **mausoleum**, dated to the Roman period, which is near the remains of the aqueduct. At one time this was thought to be the fish-market mentioned by Strabo or a gymnasium. It is a temple-tomb in the Syrian style. The burial chamber is surmounted by a beautiful little **Corinthian temple in antis** which rested on a ten-stepped crepidoma. Several skeletons were discovered in the burial chamber, but there was no inscription to indicate either their names or rank. The mausoleum was surrounded by stoas which now house some of the artefacts discovered by the archaeologists. These include fragments of sculpture, inscriptions and pottery from the Mycenaean to the Byzantine eras.

To the right of the road and behind the village are the extensive remains of a defensive wall dated to the 4C BC. It surrounded a large area, roughly rectangular in shape, which some believe to have been occupied by the garrison defending the city. The area may also have provided a place of refuge for the inhabitants in times of danger. Limited excavations have revealed a number of buildings, some of which have been dated to c 400 BC. Dense scrub makes any detailed exploration very difficult.

A muddy path leads across the isthmus which links the village with the site of Iasus. The principal remains lie to the N of a little hill covered with olive trees. Traces of the fortifications, which permitted the Iasians to close the S harbour by means of a chain, may still be seen. These, and the wall around the peninsula, were repaired during the Byzantine period.

A **dipylon** led to the **agora** which has been partly excavated. The remains to the left of the entrance belong to a **Byzantine fort** which awaits exploration. A number of graves found in the agora containing protogeometric and geometric pottery suggest that it was used as a cemetery at a time when the inhabitants occupied the fortified area on the mainland. The stylobate of three of the gates to the agora and the colonnade, which surrounded it, have been exposed and partly restored by the archaeologists.

To the S of the agora are the well-preserved remains of the **bouleuterion** which dates from the Imperial period. Four stairs divide the rows of seats, behind which there is a covered corridor. On either side steps lead to the interior through vaulted entrances.

On the E side of the agora are the ruins of a rectangular hall which measured 13m by 17m. This has been identified as a **Caesareum**. Artemis Astias, Zeus Megistos (the most powerful) and Apollo were the most important deities worshipped at Iasus. The remains of the **stoa of Artemis Astias** lay to the S of the agora. According to an inscription this was erected during the reign of Commodus (AD 180–192). It would appear that the cult statue of the goddess stood in an unroofed cella.

The scanty ruins of the **theatre** are on the E slope of the hill. Only the retaining walls of the cavea and a part of the Roman stage-building remain. There is a 2C BC inscription on the N wall which records the dedication of a section of the cavea and the stage to Dionysus and the people of Iasus.

Near the fortifications, which overlook the E harbour, there are the ruins of an **early Christian basilica**. This is believed to cover the site of the temple of Zeus Megistos, the temenos of which extended to the NE gate.

If you have time, follow the line of the city wall to its most southerly point. This will take you near the extensive remains of a **Roman villa** which has a number of fine mosaics and traces of wall-paintings. (The mosaics are covered with sand to protect them from the elements.) At the S end of peninsula there are the ruins of a **shrine** dedicated to Demeter and Kore. This was approached from the sea by a magnificent stepped propylon.

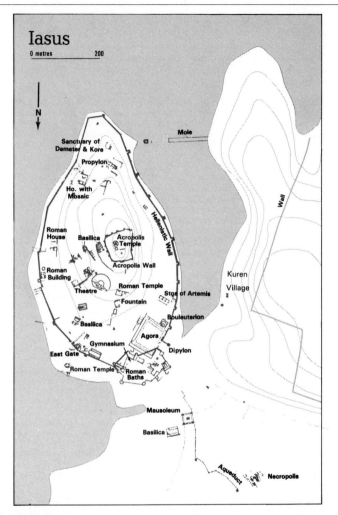

Traces of occupation dating to the end of the third millennium BC were found on the summit of the small hill which dominates the peninsula. Inside the walls of the **fortress** built by the Knights of Rhodes are the remains of a **small temple** of unknown dedication. The modern building at the NE end houses the Italian archaeologists.

Return to Road 525 and continue in the direction of Milas. A short distance before the town look for a signpost on the left to 13km **LABRAYNDA**, one of the most interesting sites in Caria. The rough track from the main road demands both a four-wheel drive vehicle and iron nerves. Because of the risk of damage to their vehicles, local taxi-drivers are not always willing to go to Labraynda. There are plans to improve the access road.

If you make the difficult journey to the site you will be rewarded with fine views over the plain of Milas. In springtime the roadside banks and the clearings between the trees are covered with wild flowers. Together with the blossoms of the many shrubs that grow on the mountainside, they provide a rich harvest for the bees of the local villagers. Their blue hives are to be seen in almost every sunlit glade.

History. Excavations conducted at Labraynda by Swedish archaeologists since 1948 have not produced any finds earlier than the end of the 7C BC. In initiating the excavations Professor Axel Persson of Uppsala University had hoped to discover material which would have assisted him in his work on Minoan and Mycenaean scripts. A few fragmentary Carian inscriptions were turned up, but the majority of the artefacts dated from the Greek and Roman periods.

Labraynda was never a city. It was an important religious centre linked with Mylasa by a Sacred Way. It was also a place of safety in times of danger and a pleasant refuge from the heat of the plains during the summer months. About 600m above sea-level, it was built on terraces cut from the steep hillside. Herodotus (484–420 BC), who was born in Halicarnassus, presumably knew the area well. He does not mention a temple, but says that there was a grove of sacred plane-trees, known as the precinct of Zeus Stratius, Zeus the Warlike, at the site. Strabo, writing c 400 years later, refers to an ancient shrine and a statue of the god in his *Geography*.

During the 4C BC the Hecatomnid dynasty of Mylasa (Milas) encouraged the worship of Zeus Stratius or Zeus Labrayndus, as the deity was sometimes called. On their coinage he is shown carrying a spear in his left hand and resting a labrys, a double axe, on his right shoulder. (According to Plutarch, Labrys is a Lydian word for double-headed axe.) The ancient cult statue pictured on some coins had a curious androgynous appearance. Bound in a tightly-fitting garment, the god was crowned with a polos and looked not unlike Artemis of Ephesus. This suggests that at some time in the remote past Zeus took over the shrine from a female deity whose attributes and, to some extent, appearance he adopted.

After the death of Alexander, possession of Caria was contested by the Seleucids and the Ptolemies. It was also controlled for a period by the Chrysaoric League which was based at Stratoniceia. The priests of the shrine at Labraynda had a certain amount of autonomy which they guarded jealously, frequently disputing the hegemony of neighbouring Milas. Apart from the fact that they erected two baths and an andron here, little is known of the effect of Roman rule on Labraynda. The site continued to be occupied into the Byzantine era. Evidence of this is provided by a large church which was built from materials salvaged from other buildings. Labraynda was finally abandoned in the 11C when the Selçuk Turks occupied western Turkey.

Labraynda is built on a series of artificial terraces on a steep mountain slope, so exploring the site involves a certain amount of scrambling and climbing. The Sacred Way, which stretched for a distance of c 13km from Mylasa, terminated at the **S and E propylaia**. It is probable that one of these imposing entrances to the temenos was a replacement for a gateway destroyed or damaged by an earthquake. To the E of the southern propylaia are the remains of the **Doric house**, so called because it was fronted by four Doric columns. During the Roman period part of this building was incorporated in a **baths complex**, the ruins of which lie to the right. At the extreme E of the terrace are the remains of a **Byzantine church**. A short distance to the SE is a building which the Swedish archaeologists describe as an **ablutions chamber**. Others suggest that the fish decorated with gold jewellery, which are mentioned by a number of ancient writers, may have been kept here. These fish functioned as an oracle like those at Sura.

A magnificent staircase, c 12m wide, leads from the area near the S propylaia to the level that contains the remains of a **stoa** and of **andron C** which dates from the Roman period. The andron, one of three at Labraynda, was used for sacred banquets, given in connection with ceremonies at the shrine. Nearby is the more solidly constructed **andron B** which was built

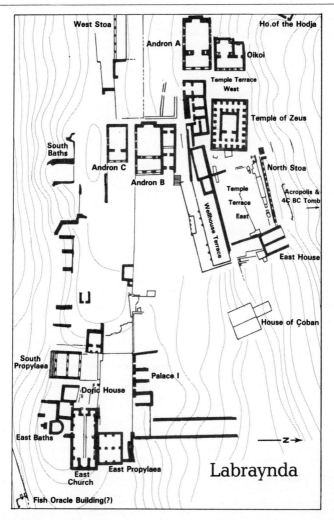

by Mausolus (fl. 377 BC). Larger and better preserved is **andron A** which is located to the SW of the temple of Zeus. Dedicated by Idrieus, the brother of Mausolus, andron A is a large rectangular structure which only lacks its roof. It was well lit by a number of large, deep windows which were fitted with shutters for protection against the elements. Both andrones A and B had rectangular recesses at the W end which may have contained statues.

A **sanctuary** dedicated to Zeus was built sometime in the 5C BC. This was incorporated in the structure dedicated by Idrieus a century later. The earlier building, a temple in antis, consisted of a rectangular cella and a pronaos. The pronaos had two columns between the antae. Idrieus added a small opisthodomus on the W side and surrounded the new building with an Ionic colonnade. To the W is a structure known as the ὅικοι, preceded by a small porch and four Doric columns. An inscription states that they were houses dedicated by Idrieus to Zeus Lambrayndus. They may have been used as stores for the temple's records or a residence for the priests. Pontus Hellström suggests that they were the priest's banqueting room.

A path leads up to the ruined **acropolis**. This may have been the fortress called Petra which is mentioned in a number of inscriptions. The view from the summit makes the effort worthwhile. A short distance from the path is a fine **tomb** from the 4C BC. This has a large forecourt and two burial chambers, one behind the other. The outer chamber contains fragments of two sarcophagi. In the inner chamber there are three well-preserved sarcophagi. Overhead is a roofed chamber which has a window-like opening on to the forecourt. The sanctuary of Labraynda is surrounded by Carian tombs, particularly along the Sacred Way, but this, the largest and most splendid of them all, clearly belonged to someone of importance. Perhaps, as some assert, Idrieus is buried here.

MILAS, c 18km from Euromus on Road 525, is a pleasant market town which has served as commercial and administrative centre for this part of Caria for centuries. Today its narrow, winding streets exemplify aspects of ancient and modern Turkey. Large diesel buses and farm tractors compete for the limited space with horse-drawn carts which differ little in design from those on ancient reliefs. The plaintive cries of sheep or goats being brought to market add their sad contribution to the mildly anarchical, but not unattractive uproar, which marks the town-centre.

Down by the canal the sagging façades of dilapidated Ottoman mansions are a melancholy reminder of the Milas's past glories. It may have been these houses that Chandler had in mind when he wrote, rather scathingly, about his visit in the autumn of 1764. The buildings, largely constructed of plaster, were he claimed, infested with scorpions. These unpleasant animals entered through the doors and windows and lingered in the rooms.

History. It seems likely that **Mylasa**, the predecessor of Milas, was sited originally on the more easily defensible Peçin Kale (see below) which is c 5km outside the town on the road to Muğla. The ancient city was probably moved in the 4C BC during the rule of the Hecatomnids to its present site.

The earliest reference to the city dates from the 7C BC, when Arselis of Mylasa assisted Gyges in his struggle to seize the kingdom of Lydia. The people of Caria were well-known for their interest in soldiering and appear to have served frequently as mercenaries. As a consequence the epithet 'Carian' was applied to military equipment like helmet crests, shield-holders and shield-emblems. Strabo quotes Anacreon, who wrote: 'Come, put thine arm through the shield-holder, work of the Carians', and Alcaeus, who spoke of 'shaking the Carian crest'.

By the mid 6C BC nominees of the Persians had replaced the Lydians as rulers of Mylasa and the other Carian cities. When, in 500 BC, the Carians and Ionians revolted against Persian rule, Mylasa joined in the struggle for freedom. Unfortunately, this was unsuccessful. The Persians defeated the allied forces at Miletus in 494 BC and then moved S into Caria where they re-established their control.

Following the Greek victories at Salamis and Plataea in 480–479 BC, Mylasa joined the Delian league which was controlled by Athens. The city was assessed for an annual contribution of one talent. The Delian league was disbanded after the defeat of Athens by Sparta in 404 BC and under the terms of the King's Peace in 387 BC the cities of Asia Minor came once more under Persian control.

The enormous Persian Empire was ruled by satraps who enjoyed a considerable degree of autonomy. Caria was placed under the control of a citizen of Mylasa named Hyssaldomus. He was succeeded by his son Hecatomnus who gave his name to the dynasty which continued in power for the next half century. Perhaps the best-known of the Hecatomnids was Mausolus who was satrap in 377–c 353 BC. A wise and capable ruler, he did much to consolidate his own position and reinforce the authority of his

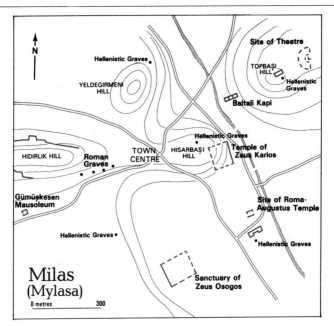

Milas
(Mylasa)
0 metres   300

family. He managed to increase his independence and remain on good terms with the Persians. An admirer of Greek culture, according to Hornblower he actively hellenised his satrapy. It is probable that the capital of Caria was moved during the rule of Mausolus from Peçin Kale to Milas. Later, recognising the superiority of the site at Halicarnassus, modern Bodrum, he made that his principal city.

After his untimely death, Mausolus was succeeded by his sister-wife Artemisia. Grief-stricken for her husband-brother, she constructed the splendid monument named after him which became one of the Seven Wonders of the Ancient World. After her death, her older brother Idrieus married his younger sister Ada and became dynast. After the death of Idrieus, Ada was exiled to Alinda by a younger brother, Pixodarus. There she remained until Alexander the Great restored her possessions in 334 BC.

Mylasa appears to have suffered little from the move of the administration to Halicarnassus. Fortunate in being sited near a quarry, which produced a marble of excellent quality, it was soon ornamented with splendid civic and religious buildings. An amusing story was told about the celebrated musician and wit, Stratonicus, who instead of the usual prefatory words Ἀκούετε, Λαοί, Hear, O people, introduced his performance in Mylasa with Ἀκούετε, Νάοι, Hear, O temples.

Because of its proximity to Labraynda, the great Carian religious centre which was linked by a Sacred Way c 13km long to the city, Mylasa continued to exercise a strong influence in the region during the Hellenistic period. Following the death of Alexander, it shared the fate of the rest of Caria. Its possession was disputed by the Diadochoi. However, despite the protests and intrigues of the priests of Zeus Labrayndus, it managed to retain control of the shrine at Labraynda and had its protective status confirmed by both its Seleucid and Macedonian rulers.

During the reign of Ptolemy II Philadelphus (282–246 BC) Mylasa was dominated to some extent by the Chrysaoric League, a grouping of Carian cities based at neighbouring Stratoniceia. Later it was given a limited degree of freedom by the Syrian, Seleucus II Callinicus (246–226 BC). After the defeat of Antiochus III (223–187 BC) by a combined Roman and Pergamene force, Caria, including Mylasa, came under the control of Rhodes. This situation was bitterly resented by the Mylasians and they freed themselves eventually from the rule of the hated Rhodians. Later, Mylasa endeavoured to consolidate and improve its position in Caria by forcing a number of its smaller neighbours to join with it in a sympolity. These included Euromus and Labrayanda.

Mylasa was a conventus, a judicial centre, and an administrative city in the Roman Province of Asia. According to Strabo (64 BC–AD 25), Mylasa, Alabanda and Stratoniceia were the three most important cities of inland Caria. About 40 BC the city was invested by the rebel Labienus at the head of a Parthian army and suffered considerable damage which was not quickly repaired. Calm was restored during the Imperial period and, despite a number of financial difficulties, the city enjoyed a moderate degree of prosperity, continuing to issue its own coinage until the 3C AD.

Apart from the fact that it was an episcopal see subject to the Metropolitan of Aphrodisias, little is known about the history of Milas during the Byzantine period. The city enjoyed a renaissance in the 14C when the Menteşe, a Turcoman tribe which preceded the Ottomans in SW Turkey, made it their capital. During the rule of the Menteşe a number of fine mosques and other buildings were erected in Milas and on Peçin Kale (see below). Their domination was ended by Murat II in 1425 when the city was taken into the Ottoman Empire.

The most important of the surviving remains in Milas is **Gümüşkesen** (the Silver Purse). This is a tomb, which, for lack of evidence, has not been dated precisely. It is believed to have been built sometime between the 2C and 1C BC. Because of its shape and the proximity of Milas to Halicarnassus, its design may have been influenced by the great mausoleum.

Located on the lower slopes of Hıdırlık hill to the W of the town, it consists of a burial chamber of cut and shaped stone which rests on a substantial base. Above the burial chamber is a platform surmounted by a shallow pyramid which has suffered some damage. The platform, which is supported by four pillars in the burial chamber, is enclosed by a Corinthian-style colonnade. This has square pilasters in each corner with two columns in between. The roof of the upper storey, which bears traces of colour, is decorated with an elaborate pattern of foliage, squares, circles and lozenges. A hole in the floor permitted mourners to pour libations of wine and honey into the burial chamber below. There is no inscription and no remains were found in the tomb which was desecrated and robbed of its grave goods long ago. Chandler states that the interior was painted blue; some traces of paint remain on the stonework.

After centuries of neglect and misuse—when Freely visited it, the tomb was being used as a cow-shed—the inside of the burial chamber has been cleaned and the surrounding area cleared of rubbish. A small garden has been planted and a guardian appointed to look after the monument. A ladder has been provided for the rather precarious ascent to the upper storey which any detailed examination of the delicate carving on the roof and of the colonnade requires.

On the side of Hisarbaşı hill, near the post office in the town centre, are the scant remains of a **temple** which has been dated to the middle of the 1C BC. The one slender Corinthian column that remains supports an untidy stork's nest. The temple, which rested on a podium 3.5m high, was enclosed by a temenos wall of fine masonry. Part of this, on the E side, is still standing. As the site is surrounded by houses, any detailed examination is difficult. It is believed that the temple was dedicated to Zeus Carius or Zeus Stratius.

A short distance away, across the canal, is **Baltalı Kapı**, the Gate of the Axe. Dated to the 2C AD, it gets its Turkish name from the carving of a labrys on the keystone on the N side. A watercolour by William Pars, who was commissioned in 1764 by the Society of Dilettanti to accompany Richard Chandler's expedition, shows the considerable remains of ancient structures at the side of the gate. These have largely disappeared.

The site of the **Temple of Zeus Osogos**, a Carian deity with marine associations who with Zeus Stratius played a tutelary role in Mylasa, lies to the SW of the town. Only part of the polygonal temenos wall survives. The shape of Mylasa's **theatre** may be discerned on the slope of Topbaşı hill to the E of the town. There are the remains of a protective wall, which encircled the acropolis, on Hıdırlık hill. The site of the **temple** dedicated to Rome and Augustus has been identified near the *Orta Okul* which is to the left of the road from Milas to Bodrum. Around Mylasa and in the surrounding countryside are a number of **Hellenistic and Roman tombs**. Perhaps the most interesting of these is the rock-tomb known as **Berber Yatağı**.

The Menteşe period is marked by a number of fine mosques. Of particular interest is **Firuz Bey Camii** which was built in 1394 with material taken from Hellenistic and Roman structures. Also noteworthy are **Ulu Cami** (1398) and **Salaheddin Camii** which was built by Orhan Bey in 1330.

About 5km from Milas on the Muğla road there is a remarkable flat-topped hill, **Peçin Kale** (height 213m). This was fortified by the Menteşe Turks in the 14C. If you have not eaten in Milas, picnic here under the trees.

The site is approached by a paved road(Turkish) on the W side of the hill. This leads to the ruins which are scattered through wooded glades watered by rivulets. The beauty of the setting and the tranquil atmosphere make Peçin Kale one of the most attractive sites in this part of Turkey.

The first city of Mylasa may have been located on this hill. Certainly the site was occupied from very early times. Bean witnessed the discovery of an obsidian blade-core which dated from the Early Bronze Age, c 2000 BC. Sherds from the 7C BC to the beginning of the 4C BC, including proto-geometric and geometric pottery of Carian manufacture, have also been found. The absence of Hellenistic and Roman remains tends to support the view that the city was moved from the hill to its present position by one of the Hecatomnids, probably Mausolus, in the 4C BC.

On the slope under the **Turkish castle** there is a short section of a shaped stone wall and inside on the right-hand side six marble steps which are believed to have come from a temple dedicated to Zeus Carius. It has not been possible to date these remains with certainty.

In addition to the castle, there are the ruins of a two-storey **medrese**. This is flanked by an **eyvan** which also served as a *türbe*. In the *eyvan* are four barrel-vaulted cells and the **tomb of Ahmet Bey** which has become the object of Sufi mysticism. Also on the site are the ruins of a *hamam*, a *mescit* and a *han* of unusual design which had two floors.

From Peçin Kale return to Road 330 and continue in the direction of c 75km Bodrum. The small domed structures visible at intervals in the fields or by the roadside are cisterns which store rainwater for irrigation purposes.

Accommodation in Milas is limited. However, the small seaside village of **Güllük**, which has a couple of two-star hotels and one pension on the Ministry of Tourism list, may be used for visiting this part of Caria.

To reach 20km Güllük from Milas, take Road 330 for c 14km, then turn right and continue for a further 6km. From Güllük you may make boat-trips to Iasus and **Bargylia**, a site which may also be approached, though with some difficulty, from Road 330. Refreshments are not available at Bargylia, but there are many possible picnic places en route.

History. According to an ancient legend Bargylia was named after Bargylus, the friend of Bellerophon, who was killed by an accidental blow from the hoof of the winged-horse Pegasus. However, there is no record of Greek colonisation here and the name is almost certainly of Anatolian origin. Bargylia appears to have come into prominence under the Hecatomnids.

After the death of Alexander, Bargylia suffered the same fate as its neighbours. It was occupied by the Seleucids, Macedonians and Rhodians, amongst others, at different times. The city declared itself against Aristonicus, the rebel who contested the bequest by Attalus III of his kingdom to Rome (see Pergamum above). Its principal deity was Artemis Cindyas, whom it appropriated from neighbouring Cindya. Representations of the goddess on Bargylian coins, which were issued from the beginning of the 2C BC to early in the 3C AD, suggest that she was of Carian origin.

Bargylia continued to be occupied during the Byzantine era. It was probably abandoned sometime after the conquest of Caria by the Menteşe Turks.

Today the site of the ancient city is surrounded by windswept marshes and disused salt-pans. The most prominent monuments are Byzantine: a castle, a church and part of a defensive wall. Among the many architectural fragments scattered throughout the area is a shattered **altar** which bears representations of Artemis Cindyas and Apollo and of a cloaked figure, who may be Bargylus. The ruined **theatre**, almost hidden in an olive grove, stands on a hillside above the landlocked bay. The outline of the diazoma and part of the stage-building are still visible. The city also had an odeum of which little remains. Part of the Roman aqueduct, which supplied Bargylia with water, is visible on the hillside to the NW of the castle.

In spring the site is carpeted with wild flowers and during the year the bay and salt flats are home to innumerable marsh birds. However, interest in Bargylia is not limited to nature-lovers. It will also attract those spirits who enjoy the melancholy contemplation of cities abandoned and forgotten. 'A monument of antiquity is never seen with indifference...No circumstance so forcibly marks the desolation of a spot once inhabited, as the prevalence of Nature over it'. (Thomas Whately).

Another interesting **excursion** from Güllük is to the site of the ancient city of **Ceramus**. Return to Peçin Kale and take a secondary road to c 40km **Ören**, the nearest village to the site. There are some good fish restaurants in Ören. The *Yiltur Pansiyon* is clean and comfortable.

Very little is known about the history of Ceramus. Its name means pottery or tile in Greek, and statues dated to the 6C BC, found here, show some Greek influence. Ceramus was a member of the Delian and Chrysaoric leagues. Later it was joined, uncomfortably, for a time in a sympolity with a neighbouring city, which may have been Stratoniceia. It also had an uneasy relationship with Rhodes. The city issued its own coins from the 2C BC to the 3C AD.

According to Bean, the ruins of Ceramus have suffered badly at the hands of vandals and, as a result, many of the remains recorded by earlier visitors have disappeared. There are the ruins of an **early Hellenistic polygonal wall** on the mountainside. In the **necropolis**, which is outside the wall, are several sarcophagi and a number of Carian tombs. There are the badly damaged remains of two **temples**, one of which was probably dedicated to Zeus Chrysaoreus. The head of an **archaic kouros** found in this temple is now in the İzmir Archaeological Museum. The walls of the second temple had a number of **decorative shields** which carried inscriptions commemorating, in rather flowery terms, its priests and their families.

From Güllük continue to c 38km **BODRUM**. The road, which follows the coastline for much of the way, offers tantalising glimpses of secluded bays, each fringed with a line of clean white sand. Finally, it descends to Bodrum through a landscape of pines interspersed with clumps of maquis which fills the air with its heady perfume during the summer months.

Bodrum means 'subterranean vault' or 'dungeon' in Turkish. It probably derives its name from the ruined Mausoleum of Halicarnassus. During recent years this small town has become one of the most popular resorts in

SW Turkey. Most of the development has taken place on the outskirts, allowing the narrow, winding streets of the old quarter to retain much of their charm, at least out of the holiday season.

There is much to see in Bodrum. In addition to the site of the Mausoleum, one of the Seven Wonders of the Ancient World, there is the Crusader castle of St Peter which now houses one of the finest museums in Turkey. In October the Bodrum Cup Race attracts yachts from many countries.

Bodrum

Accommodation, Information and Restaurants. Bodrum has a wide range of accommodation. There are two five-star, five four-star, 46 three-star and many two-star hotels, several holiday villages and a large number of pensions in or around the town. The comfortable and welcoming four-star *Azka Hotel* in Bardakçı Köyü is recommended. Budget travellers may like to try the centrally situated *Alias Pansiyon*. The **Tourist Information Office** is at 12 Eylül Meyd.

Bodrum is a gourmet's paradise. The fish is excellent. Among the town's many good restaurants are the chic *Pierre Loti*, the *Hades Restaurant* (do not be put off by the name), the *Hey Yavrum Hey* and, for a change of cuisine, the *Sandal* which serves Chinese and Thai food. A pleasant evening may be spent in the *Sapa Restaurant* near the top of the hill. Meals are served in the garden of this former, old private residence.

Bodrum has an agreeable climate. Temperatures range from 30°C in July and August to c 7°C in February. Even in the warmest months the high temperatures are modified by a cooling breeze from the sea. During January, February and part of March there is a good deal of rain, but it is seldom cold. Spring and autumn are the best times of the year to visit Bodrum. There are fewer visitors and prices are lower. In spring the countryside is carpeted with wild flowers and in the autumn citrus fruit is in season. Bodrum's tangerines are famous.

In summer there is a lively night-life, when the many bars, tavernas and discos offer everything from pop and jazz to Turkish folk music.

Transport. In spite of the fact that Bodrum is near the end of a peninsula, it has very good transport links. Bus services from the nearest airports at İzmir and Dalaman take five and three hours respectively. If you prefer a more leisurely method of travel, take one of the regular sailings from İstanbul operated by Turkish Maritime Lines.

Aquatic Activities. The yacht marina to the NW of the castle provides a comprehensive range of facilities. It attracts an international clientele and is used not only by visiting yachtsmen but by boat owners who make Bodrum their permanent headquarters.

There are excellent opportunities for aquatic sports, including sailing, fishing, wind surfing and water-skiing. The clear waters of the Aegean will prove irresistible to those who enjoy exploring the depths. One of best places for underwater swimming is **Adaboğazı**. Around this island the bottom is visible to a depth of 30m.

In the past Bodrum was an important boat-building centre and the characteristically-shaped craft produced in its yards were a familiar sight in most Aegean ports. Today they are still made, but for use as pleasure craft rather than cargo vessels. Visitors are welcomed in the boatyards, which are sited to the W of the harbour, providing they behave sensibly and do not interrupt the work.

Excursions. During the holiday season there is a daily boat service to the Greek island of **Cos**. The journey, for which passports are required, takes c two hours in each direction. Boats leave the W harbour at regular intervals for the excellent beaches at **Bardakçi, Gümbet** and **Karaincir**. Because of pollution it is not advisable to bathe near the town where, in any case, the beaches are small, stony and weed covered. For information about the service to Cos, boat-trips to the Datça peninsula and Cnidus and road and boat excursions around Bodrum apply to one of the travel agencies. Karya Tour at Karantina Cad. 13 near the castle can make reservations and issue tickets.

History. According to Herodotus and Strabo, **Halicarnassus** was founded by Dorians from Troezen in the eastern Peloponnese c 1000 BC. To judge by names found on inscriptions in the city, the newcomers appear to have established themselves without much difficulty, marrying with the native Carians and producing a mixed population. After some time the settlement came under the influence of its northern Ionian neighbours to such an extent that it was expelled from the Dorian Hexapolis, a grouping of six cities—Cos, Lindus, Camirus and Ialysus on Rhodes, Cnidus and Halicarnassus—which met from time to time near Cnidus during the festival of Triopian Apollo.

After the Persians had conquered Lydia and overrun the Greek cities on the Aegean, Halicarnassus was governed on their behalf by Carian dynasts. Artemisia the Elder was, perhaps, the best-known. In 480 BC she fought on the side of Persia. Commanding a ship at the battle of Salamis, the vigour of her attack attracted the attention and won the approval of Xerxes. After the defeat of the Persians, Halicarnassus became a member of the Delian league, contributing the modest sum of $1\frac{2}{3}$ talents annually.

Following the promulgation of the King's Peace in 386 BC, Caria came once more under the rule of the Persians. It was governed for them by a satrap named Hyssaldomus. His son, Hecatomnus, was the founder of a dynasty bearing his name that remained in power for more than 50 years. The Hecatomnids imported Greek intellectuals and craftsmen—masons, fortification experts, die-engravers and lapicides—but the extent to which they adopted Greek ways, e.g. by giving their children Greek names and speaking Greek instead of Carian, is not known with any degree of certainty.

Perhaps the most able of the Hecatomnids was Mausolus, who ruled between 377 and 353 BC. He managed to increase his personal authority and that of his family without putting his friendship with the Persians at risk. Having improved the defences of Caria, he turned his attention to its cities which he ornamented with fine buildings. In his new capital Halicarnassus, which was protected by an elaborate defensive system c 5.5km long, he built himself a luxurious palace whose walls were sheathed in Proconnesian marble. Dying at a comparatively young age he was commemorated by a magnificent monument, the Mausoleum, which perpetuates his name. Probably started during his lifetime, this was completed by his sister-wife, Artemisia the Younger, and other members of his family c 350 BC. The extent of Artemesia's affection for her brother-husband may be judged by the fact that every day until her death she drank wine mixed with some of his ashes.

Like Artemisia the Elder, she also distinguished herself in battle, inflicting a resounding defeat on the Rhodians who had made the mistake of thinking that a mere woman could not defend her territory. She captured their city and, to their shame and mortification, had a monument erected there to commemorate her victory. As custom prevented the Rhodians from removing the monument, they erected a building around it to conceal it from public view.

Artemisia was succeeded by Idrieus and Ada and, later, by their younger brother Pixodarus, who, until his death, ruled jointly with the Persian satrap, Orontobates. When Alexander attempted to take the city in 334 BC, he was resisted by the Persians who were aided by the Rhodian mercenary, Memnon. After the city's capture by the Macedonians, Alexander restored power to Ada, who had been exiled by Pixodarus to Alinda.

During the confused period that followed the death of Alexander, Halicarnassus shared the same fate as the other cities in Caria. At different times it was ruled by the Ptolemies, the Seleucids, the Macedonians and the Rhodians. After the establishment of Roman rule, it became an important city in the new Province of Asia. Impoverished by the extortions of the the infamous Verres, it suffered also from the attentions of the tyrannicides Brutus and Cassius. The city's fortunes were restored under the empire, when several temples, including one dedicated to Mars, were erected.

During the Byzantine period Halicarnassus was an episcopal see under the Metropolitan of Aphrodisias. Taken by the Turks in the 11C, it was later recaptured by a Christian army. It was known as Mesy during the First Crusade (1096–99). In the middle of the 13C it was taken by the Menteşe Turks, but, after the defeat of Beyazit I at the battle of Ankara in 1402, was occupied once more by the Knights of St John of Malta. Using material from the Mausoleum, which apparently had collapsed in an earthquake, they refortified the Castle of St Peter (built in 1402) between 1494 and 1522. The architect was a German, Henry Schlegelholt. The Knights occupied Bodrum until 1523. Then, after the capture of Rhodes by Süleyman the Magnificent, they withdrew to Malta. Bodrum became part of the Ottoman Empire.

The centuries that followed were equally stormy. In 1770 Bodrum was bombarded by ships of the Russian fleet sent by Catherine the Great to support a Greek rebellion against Ottoman rule. During the first World War the French attempted, unsuccessfully, to land an expeditionary force. In 1919 the town was occupied briefly by the Italians. After they had been compelled to withdraw by nationalist forces revitalised by Atatürk's leadership, Bodrum was restored to Turkish rule.

Halicarnassus was the birthplace of two historians—Herodotus, the 'father of history' (484–420 BC) and Dionysius (died 8 BC). Writing in the Ionic dialect, with admixtures of Dorian and Attic, Herodotus chronicled the epic struggle between Greece and Persia, its antecedents and aftermath. A great traveller, he visited many countries including Egypt, Babylonia, and Scythia. His history is full of entertaining stories and contains a wealth of general information about places and personages. Dionysius is remembered principally for his history of Rome from the city's mythological foundation to the middle of the 3C BC. Part of this work has been preserved.

Halicarnassus was also the home of the elegiac poet Heracleitus (fl. early 3C BC). Callimachus of Alexandria mourned the death of his 'Halicarnassian friend' in a celebrated poem:

'Someone spoke of your death, Herakleitos. It brought me
Tears, and I remembered how often together
We ran the sun down with talk...' (trs. Peter Jay)

Of the works of Heracleitus only one epigram remains. This was written in memory of Aretemias of Cnidus, who died in childbirth and who speaks from beyond the grave:

'I left one twin to guide my husband's old age,
and took the other to remind me of him...' (trs. Edwin Morgan)

About 18km W of Bodrum is the village of **Turgut Reis**, named after a celebrated corsair who, according to a popular tradition, was born there. Turgut Reis, also known as Dragut, was the scourge of European shipping in the Mediterranean during the mid 16C. Promised the governorship of Tripoli by Süleyman the Magnificent, if he could take it from the Knights of St John of Malta he laid siege to the city and captured it. Turgut Reis then led his forces against Malta where, during an unsuccessful assault on the citadel, he was killed in 1565. His bones lie in Tripoli, but his native village, in addition to bearing his name, has erected a statue in memory of him.

On a windy hill behind the village of Gümbet, 2.5km to the W of Bodrum, is the resting place of one of Turkey's most interesting modern writers, Cevat Şakir Kabaa-

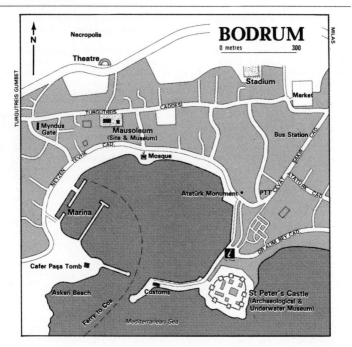

ğaçlı. Better known as the Fisherman of Halicarnassus, he wrote a number of delightful books about the lives of the fishermen and sponge-divers of Bodrum. In these he set out his understanding of the monuments of the past which surrounded him and of the philosophy that inspired them. Unfortunately, his books are available only in Turkish.

The most striking monument in Bodrum is the **Castle of St Peter**. Sited on a rocky promontory E of the main harbour, it occupies an area of c 180m by 185m. Access to the keep is by seven massive gates. A short ramp behind the police station in the harbour square leads to the first gate. An inscription in Greek placed there on the orders of Jacques Gatineau, Captain of the Castle in 1512, warns spies that they will be punished.

The castle's occupation by Christian armies is commemorated by almost 250 coats of arms. Inside the first gate there are several examples including the arms of Guy de Blanchefort, Grandmaster of the Order of St John and, in the centre of the group, those of Jacques Gatineau. To the left of the ramp is the N moat which is used sometimes for displays and theatrical performances. The building to the right is an **art gallery**. Under the trees to the left are a number of antiquities including altars and sarcophagi from Halicarnassus and the surrounding area.

The gate at the top of a flight of steps bears the arms of Cardinal Pierre d'Aubusson, Grandmaster from 1476–1503. He came from Rhodes on several occasions to visit the front line garrison of St Peter. To the right are the arms of an English nobleman, Thomas Dowcra, warden of the castle from 1498–99. He was a Turcopolier, a cavalry soldier who had adopted the arms and strategy of his Turkish opponents. The third gate, which is in a good state of preservation, bears the arms of Grandmaster Philibert de Naillac (1396–1421). After penetrating two more gates, also with coats of

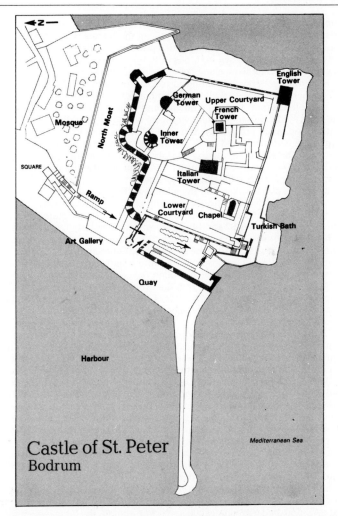

Castle of St. Peter
Bodrum

arms, you reach a short corridor decorated with representations of the Virgin and Child, St Peter, St Catherine and St Mary Magdalene. This leads to the sixth gate which bears an inscription in Latin invoking God's protection on the garrison: 'O Lord, protect us in our sleep, save us when we wake. Without your protection, nobody can keep us from harm'. Beyond lies a vaulted entrance, built above one of the 14 cisterns which provided water to the garrison. This finally admits to the lower courtyard of the castle.

The museum directorate has taken full advantage of the castle's magnificent setting and fine buildings to present antiquities from the Prehistoric, Carian, Hellenistic, Roman, Byzantine, Medieval and Turkish periods in a most interesting manner.

Within the castle walls there is a representative collection of trees and plants from the Bodrum peninsula. Underneath the ancient battlements, peacocks strut and display among oleanders, laurels, olives, myrtles and plane trees. In summer the still air between the towers is heavy with the scent of roses. Beside a crumbling wall a pile of shell-encrusted amphorae, lately rescued from the sea bed, lies in the purple shade of a battalion of tall carnations. Overhead, clouds of white doves wheel and glide between the high pinnacles before coming to rest in groves of pine, pomegranate and mulberry. Their voices fill the air with a gentle threnody.

In sheltered corners the violet flowers and orange fruits of the mandrake hide. This mildly poisonous plant was used during the Middle Ages in love philtres, and, more prosaically, as a pain killer. Because its root resembled a mannikin it was believed to cry out. Hence: 'And shrieks like mandrakes torn out of the earth, That living mortals hearing them, run mad' (Romeo and Juliet). Dogs were used to grub it up. In an unflattering description in Henry IV Part 2, Justice Shallow is described as 'the very genius of famine; yet lecherous as a monkey and the whores called him—mandrake'. Later, John Donne fantasized erotically 'get with child a mandrake root'.

On the right of the entrance is the **chapel**. This fine Gothic building, constructed between 1402 and 1437 from ancient materials, including some of the characteristic green stone from the Mausoleum, was restored by Spanish knights in 1519. After the arrival of the Ottomans in 1523, a minaret was added and the chapel was turned into a mosque. The building was badly damaged when the French shelled the castle in 1915.

The chapel now houses finds from the Bronze Age. These include pithoi which date from c 2500 BC; a number of Mycenaean objects—amphorae, cups, incense burners and perfume bottles found in a necropolis in Ortakent; and a quantity of artefacts from the wrecks of a number of ships. One, lost off Cape Gelidonya near Finike c 1200 BC, was a Syrian trader bringing a cargo of copper ingots from Cyprus. Another, discovered at Şeytan Deresi near Çatalburun in Gökova Bay, was lost in the 16C BC. It contained pithoi, amphorae and craters of local manufacture. A third, lost near Ulu Burun to the E of Kaş in the 14C or early 13C BC, had a rich cargo which included gold medallions, ostrich eggs, a gold cup, a tiny gold scarab of Nefertiti, and copper and tin ingots. Recovered by Turkish and American archaeologists, they form the core of Bodrum's **Museum of Underwater Archaeology**.

S of the chapel is a 19C **hamam** which was built when the castle was a prison. When restored this will house an ethnographic collection. By the side of the chapel a path lined with 2C and 1C BC cinerary urns, which are ornamented with erotes, bulls' heads, garlands and representations of the head of Medusa, leads up to an open air display of amphorae.

The building to the right is also devoted to underwater archaeology. It houses two ships which foundered near Yassiada near Turgut Reis. One, lost c AD 350, had more than 1000 amphorae aboard, the other, which sank c AD 641, contained gold coins bearing the head of the Emperor Heraclius (610–641), lamps, carpenter's tools, cooking pots and a fine bronze steelyard. A model explains the methods used by the archaeologists to survey wrecks and recover objects from them. To the N is the **serpent's tower**, named after the relief carved on the wall to the left of the lower entrance. This has another collection of amphorae. Further E is the **German tower** built between 1437–1440. This will house an exhibition of objects connected with the Knights of St John. Adjoining the tower is a collection of stone anchors recovered from the sea. Some have restored wooden shafts.

A gallery on the other side of the courtyard houses a restored 11C AD Byzantine ship found at Serçe Limanı near Marmaris. This contained a large quantity of glass and a number of iron weapons. Some of the glass is displayed in the nearby **Glass Gallery**. To prevent damage to the ship by the atmosphere, the gallery is open only for limited periods—normally 10.00–11.00 and 14.00–16.00. Twenty persons are admitted at one time.

The **Italian Tower**, completed in 1436, is to the S at a higher level. It has three exhibition rooms. The lowest is devoted to a display of coins and jewellery. Note particularly the coins issued by the Hecatomnid dynasty, including a rare example from the period of Hecatomnus. The middle floor contains objects from the Classical period. These include a fine 4C BC statute of Hecate; bronze and terracotta representations of deities; statuettes of women water-carriers and priests from Theangela; and a number of red figure vases. There is also a fine 4C BC female head from Cnidus which bears traces of the paint which covered it at one time.

On the top floor there are objects from the Hellenistic period. The most important are the bronze statues of a boy and of the goddess Isis, the protectress of sailors, which were found in a wreck lying on the sea-bed at a depth of 84m off the NW coast of the Bodrum peninsula. The distended stomach of the boy, who has negroid features, suggests that he probably suffered from malaria. Also noteworthy is a Roman copy of the famous statue from Cnidus of Aphrodite Euploia, Aphrodite of Fair Voyages, by Praxiteles which was the subject of an ancient scandal (see Cnidus below).

The **French Tower** is to the E. The lower floor has a number of finds from the medieval period. The most interesting are objects from the wreck of an early 11C Byzantine or Fatimid vessel discovered near Bozukkale, the ancient Loryma, c 40km from Marmaris. These include amphorae, Islamic glass and pottery, a steelyard ornamented with pigs' heads, daggers, spear-heads, chess and backgammon pieces, gold coins of the Fatimid Caliph Ebu El-Mansur El-Hakim bi Emru Ilah (996–1021) and Byzantine copper coins bearing the head of Basil II Bulgaroctonus, Basil the Bulgar Slayer (976–1025). On the upper floor are objects from the 11C to the 6C BC. The most interesting are: a 9C BC terracotta sarcophagus, which contained two skeletons, discovered by Professor Akurgal at Göçebel; a kantharos bearing a snake design from Dirmil; archaic kouroi, and a protogeometric crater with a rare representation of a ship.

The **English Tower**, sometimes called the Lion tower because of the sculpture of a lion on the W wall, is in the SE corner of the castle. Today its dungeons are used as storerooms; the middle floor serves as a workshop for the preservation of glass artefacts. The top floor, the banqueting hall of the knights, has been restored in the medieval style.

Over the entrance to the banqueting hall are the arms of King Henry IV of England (1399–1413). (The tower was built during his reign.) Inside the banners of the Grand Masters and of their Turkish opponents, including Dragut, sway gently in the candle-lit gloom. The muted strains of lutes fill the incense-laden air. Pages in medieval costume proffer goblets of wine.

Spare a thought for those English knights who made the long journey from their native land to this remote castle in southern Turkey more than five centuries ago. Some were filled with a fervent desire to serve God, while others had baser aims—the pursuit of fame or the acquisition of riches. The names of some of these men, which they carved on the window ledges of the tower in moments of idleness, constitute the sole memorial to their faith, their vanity and their greed.

Do not leave the castle without seeing the latest exhibit, the sarcophagus and remains of Queen Ada, the sister of Mausolus. Deposed by her brother, Pixodarus, Ada took refuge in Alinda. She was restored to her throne by Alexander the Great.

In 1989 Turkish archaeologists found a tomb, which had not been robbed, near Bodrum. Inside the sarcophagus there was the skeleton of a woman aged about 40 who had borne two children and who had been well nourished. Pottery found in the tomb enabled them to date the burial to between 360 BC and 325 BC. From a cast of the skull, Dr Richard Neave of Manchester University Medical School and Dr John Prag of Manchester University Musem, recreated the features of the dead woman. They used a pathological technique, sometimes employed by the police, to restore the flesh areas on skeletal remains. The result of their efforts bears a remark-able resemblance to a bust of Ada which is now in the British Museum.

Only eight are admitted to the exhibition at one time. It is in two parts. The ante-room is in the form of an andron similar to those built by Mausolus and his brother Idrieus at Labraynda. Charts outline the history of the Hecatomnids and a video shows how Ada's features were recreated by the British experts. In the room beyond is the sarcophagus of the dead queen, her skeleton arranged in the position in which it was found. Cabinets around the walls contain the grave goods: a gold crown, necklaces, gold bracelets, gold rings, a magnificent gold wreath of myrtle leaves, flowers and berries, and Greek pottery drinking cups. Then, in a stunning *coup de théâtre*, a model of the queen with her restored features has been placed in an alcove at the end of the room. Clad in a peplos and wearing some of her jewellery, Ada, serene, regal, aloof presides over her own obsequies.

Outside the castle is a two-storey *han* built by Hacı Molla in 1769. Now a restaurant, the upper floor served as a hotel until comparatively recently. Note the inscription carved above the entrance.

To the W of the harbour was **Salmacis**, a suburb of Halicarnassus, which enjoyed a certain measure of independence. It had a rather unenviable reputation. The water of one of its fountains had an unusual property. It was said that it robbed men of their virility. Strabo indignantly questions the veracity of this story. According to him effeminacy is caused by riches and wanton living! Because of erosion and changes in ground-level the fountain is now under the sea. Careful observation will reveal its waters bubbling up near the light at the harbour entrance.

Not far away are the ruins of the **Myndus gate**. Here, according to Arrian, a foolish sortie was made by some of the Persian garrison during Alexan-der's siege. It is possible to trace much of the ancient city wall which ran, first to the N, then E over Göktepe, the hill behind the theatre. On the summit of Göktepe there is a levelled space. This may mark the position of the temple of Mars mentioned by the Augustan architect, Vitruvius.

The remains of the **Mausoleum of Halicarnassus** are to the NW of the castle. Take the street that runs N from the harbour mosque to the T-junc-tion. The entrance is a short distance on the left.

As at the temple of Artemis at Ephesus, it requires a considerable effort to imagine what the Mausoleum of Halicarnassus looked like. Many visitors are disappointed. One of the Seven Wonders of the Ancient World, which is believed to have covered an area 38m by 32m and was c 45m high, little more than foundations and a few architectural fragments remain.

Years of painstaking research and inspired detective-work by a team of Danish archaeologists have made it possible to reconstruct the general appearance of the monument. The mausoleum was surrounded by a peribolos measuring c 242m by 105.5m. It had a solid base, on which rested a four-sided colonnade of 9 by 11 columns. Above the colonnade there was a 24-step pyramid on which—according to some authorities—there was a quadriga probably designed by Pytheos bearing a giant statue of Mausolus. There were reliefs of animal hunts, of scenes of sacrifice, of battles between Greek and Persian warriors, Lapiths and Centaurs, Greeks and Amazons on the base. Between the columns of the peristyle there were huge portrait statues of members of the Hecatomnid dynasty. These are believed to be the work of Bryaxis,

Scopas, Leochares and Timotheus, the best sculptors of the time. Two of the statues, the so called Mausolus and Artemisia, and part of the frieze of the Amazons and Greeks are in the British Museum.

According to Geoffrey Wayell the monument tried to combine features from three very different architectural styles—Lycian, Greek and Egyptian. A high rectangular podium is frequently found in Lycian tombs, the peristyle is Ionic Greek in character and the stepped pyramid roof suggests Egyptian influence. The combination could be read as a statement of the supremacy of Caria over the others.

An object of admiration and wonder in antiquity, the mausoleum is known to have existed in an undamaged state as late as the 12C when it was described by Bishop Eustathius. However, in 1494 the Knights of St John found it in ruins, destroyed, perhaps by an earthquake. They removed much of the cut stone and burned most of the marble statuary and friezes to make lime to refortify the Castle of St Peter. The distinctive green granite of the mausoleum may still be seen in various places in the fortress. Parts of the friezes of the battles between the Greeks and the Amazons and the Lapiths and the Centaurs were built into the castle wall.

In 1522, requiring more stone to strengthen the walls of the castle, the knights returned to the mausoleum. Burrowing into the base they discovered the burial chamber. An account published in 1581 by Claude Guichard tells how they were about to open the tomb when the evening curfew was sounded. Next morning they found that thieves had entered the chamber during the night and removed most of its precious contents.

In 1846 Lord Stratford de Redcliffe, British Ambassador to the Porte, obtained the Sultan's permission to send to England the 13 blocks of the Amazon frieze which the knights had used to decorate the castle. Eleven years later Charles Newton searched for and found the site of the mausoleum. There he uncovered a number of sculptures, including the statues which he believed to be of Mausolus and Artemisia, and the head and forepart of one of the horses from the quadriga. Having received the Sultan's firman, he sent these and a number of other sculptures to the British Museum where, with the frieze despatched by Lord Stratford de Redcliffe, they are now displayed. Only one panel of the frieze, which shows a Greek warrior attacking an Amazon, and a number of architectural fragments remain in Bodrum. During his search for the mausoleum, Newton uncovered some fine Roman mosaics in the ruins of a 4C AD villa. These are also in the British Museum.

The modern study of the mausoleum commenced with the Danish archaeological mission which, under the direction of Professor Christian Jeppesen, began working in Bodrum in 1966.

Begin by examining the plans and models prepared by the archaeologists. These are in a small antiquarium on the eastern side of the site. The explanatory texts are in Turkish and English. In the adjoining area there are a number of fragments of the frieze found in the castle, and some architectural remains recovered during the course of the excavations. Part of the wall, which enclosed the temenos, may also be seen here.

Descending into the great depression, which marks the position of the mausoleum, you will see on the S side a staircase which belonged to an earlier burial. A door to the right of the stairs leads to a tomb which is believed to date from 5C BC. This may be the tomb of Artemisia I who fought on the Persian side at Salamis. Note the niches in the walls where offerings to the dead were placed. The channels in the floor were used to drain away any water that gathered in the sub-structure.

The funeral chamber of Mausolus was located near the foot of the main stairs. It was closed by a huge green stone which survives. Note the marks made by tomb robbers who attempted, in vain, to gain entrance. Behind the stone the Danes found the bones of sheep or goats, a calf and an ox, chickens, doves, a goose and some eggs. According to Wayell these food offerings to the deceased were more a Near Eastern than Greek practice.

Why did Mausolus and Artemisia build this huge and expensive monument? Was it an expression of uncontrolled pride, a pious memorial or didit have some symbolic meaning? In Lucian of Samosata's *Dialogues of the Dead*, the 2C AD writer and satirist makes Diogenes ask, 'Why are you so proud and why do you expect to be honoured more than the rest of us?' 'Because I was handsome and tall and victorius in war. But most of all, because I have lying over me in Halicarnassus a gigantic monument such as no other dead person has, adorned in the finest way with statues of horses and men carved most realistically from the best quality marble...', Mausolus replies.

The **Theatre of Halicarnassus** is most easily reached by following the main road above the town. Constructed during the reign of Mausolus, it was modified during the Roman period. Although only the section below the diazoma remains, the capacity of the building has been estimated as 13,000. Some of the seats in the lower section, which was divided by 12 stairs, bear the names of regular patrons. A rectangular altar in the orchestra, which was larger than a semicircle, was dedicated to Dionysus. Between the cavea, which was supported by retaining walls, and the stage-building there were two parodoi. When the theatre was modified in the 3C AD for wild-beast shows and gladiatorial contests, barriers were erected to protect the audience. During the Byzantine period the stage-building, most of which has disappeared, was converted into a residence.

Near the summit of Göktepe, there are many **Hellenistic and Roman rock-cut tombs**. The dense undergrowth and rough terrain make it difficult to reach them. In some there are traces of frescoes. Most have suffered from being used as shelters by shepherds. Their walls have been blackened by fires and the façades damaged by vandalism and neglect.

Among the many **excursions** that may be made by boat from Bodrum is the long but pleasant voyage along the coast to **Ören** which is near the site of ancient Ceramus (p 262).

A shorter boat trip will take you to **Karaada**, Black Island, the ancient Arconessus, which is to the SE of Bodrum. A brisk climb from the landing point will bring you to the summit of the island where there are the remains of a small temple. The views towards Cos and the mainland are particularly fine.

It is a somewhat difficult journey by land to the ancient sites of **Syangela-Theangela** which are c 12km to the E of Bodrum near the villages of Alazeytin and Etrim. Of interest mainly to specialists, they contain some Lelegian remains.

At the western end of the Bodrum peninsula, near the village of **Gümüslük**, are the scanty remains of the city of Myndus. Host to rebel Aristonicus, c 131 BC, its harbour sheltered the ships of the tyrannicide Cassius after the murder of Julius Caesar in 44 BC. The city, which was sparsely populated under the Hecatomnids, issued its own coinage during the Hellenistic and Imperial Roman periods. It produced a very poor quality wine which when mixed with brine, as was customary, caused a bad hangover and prolonged flatulence, but was nevertheless considered to be good for the stomach.

The site of ancient Pedasa is at **Gökçeler**, c 8km to the N of Bodrum. It takes an hour to walk there but you will rewarded by some interesting ruins including chamber graves. Because of its successful resistance to the Persians, Pedasa acquired a reputation for producing tough fighting men. It was also prosperous. Its contribution to the Delian League was assessed at two talents, when Halicarnassus paid only $1\frac{2}{3}$.

17

Bodrum to Aydın

Total distance c 161km. Bodrum—c 60km Peçin Kale 32km Eskihisar/Stra-
toniceia—5km Yatağan—(c 18km Lagina)—(c 6km Gerga)—c 29km Çine
(c 8km Alabanda)—(c 25km Alinda)—(c 20km Amyzon)—c 35km Aydın.

Leave Bodrum (see Route 16) on Road 330 and return to c 60km Peçin Kale.
Continue in the direction of Yatağan and Muğla. Shortly after the junction
the road begins a steady climb along the flank of the Akdağ. Below the
road the ground falls steeply to deep valleys which shelter a few lonely
steadings. Above, pine woods clothe the slopes that lead to the highest
peaks. By the roadside and in clearings between the trees the local people
place rows of the traditional blue-painted beehives. This is an area which
produce çambalı, pine honey, a delicacy much appreciated in Turkey.

After the long drive from Bodrum, many travellers will be glad to stop at
a strategically-located rest area among the pine trees a short distance
before the village of **Eskihisar**. There are two good restaurants in Yatağan,
you may lunch here in the small restaurant or enjoy an alfresco meal in the
picnic-area.

The site of the ancient city of **STRATONICEIA** is after the village of
Eskihisar, and perilously close to a large and rapidly expanding quarry. As
a consequence, it has been necessary to undertake rescue archaeology.

History. The city of Stratoniceia was created in the early 3C BC, when the Seleucid
kings of Syria began to extend their rule over large areas of Asia Minor. It appears to
have replaced an earlier Carian foundation which, with the country around it, was
called Chrysaoris or Idrias.

At the age of 60, Seleucus I Nicator (321–281 BC), king of Syria, remarried. His new
bride, chosen largely for reasons of state, was Stratonice the daughter of Demetrius
the Besieger, ruler of Cyprus and of a number of Aegean and Phoenician cities.
Sometime after the wedding, his son Antiochus conceived a violent passion for his
stepmother and, feeling that his situation was hopeless, went into a decline. In due
course Seleucus learned the cause of the young man's illness and, although Stratonice
had already borne him a child, he decided to give her to his son. From that time onward
Antiochus ruled jointly with his father. It is not recorded whether Stratonice's second
marriage was a happy one, but she gave Antiochus three children. The new Carian
city, which had many fine buildings, was named after her.

In c 201 BC it appears to have been occupied for a time by Philip V of Macedon, but
it was later returned to the control of Rhodes, into whose hands it had passed from the
Seleucids. Stratoniceia supported Rome against Mithridates VI Eupator of Pontus in
88 BC and, after its capture by him, paid dearly for its fidelity. Later it was compensated
for its suffering and losses by the Romans. In 39 BC Labienus, an associate of the
tyrannicides Brutus and Cassius, led an army of barbarian Parthians into Asia Minor.
They caused much destruction in Caria. Having failed to take Stratoniceia, Labienus
attacked the shrines of Lagina and Panamara which were in Stratoniceian territory.
He failed to capture Panamara—it was said his army was repulsed through the
intervention of Zeus Panamaros—but he sacked the temple of Hecate at Lagina.

During the Imperial period Stratoniceia prospered. Augustus provided financial
assistance for the restoration of the temple of Hecate at Lagina and Hadrian ornamented the city with a number of fine buildings. Stratoniceia continued to be occupied
during the Byzantine era. Its bishop was subject to the Metropolitan of Aphrodosias.

The site of Stratoniceia was visited by Richard Chandler in the autumn of 1764. He
was well received by the inhabitants of Eskihisar. He found the remains of the theatre
and a number of altars and tombs and recorded several inscriptions.

The principal deity of Stratoniceia was Zeus Chrysaoreus, Zeus of the Golden Sword, an epithet which Homer and Pindar applied also to Apollo and a number of other gods. It was at the temple of Zeus that delegates from the cities in the Chrysaoric League met at regular intervals for their deliberations and to offer sacrifice. Membership of the league, which was first mentioned in 267 BC, was open to all Carians. The site of the temple of Zeus Chrysaoreus is believed to lie 4km to the E of Eskihisar village near the main road from Muğla to Aydın.

The large building of white stone in the centre of the village was the city's **bouleuterion**. Access to the interior of this structure, which has been dated to the Roman period, was provided by two staircases, one on each side. It was very similar to the bouleuteria of Priene and Miletus. The seats were arranged in a rectangular shape. Inscriptions found here offer thanks to Helios Zeus Serapis for preservation from the dangers of war and the perils of the sea and record a reassuring answer from the oracle of Zeus Panamaros concerning the possibility of an invasion by barbarian tribes, probably the Goths, in the 3C AD. Note the gate on the W side of the building.

The position of the city's **agora**, may be to the W or to the N of the bouleuterion. To the NW there is an elaborately ornamented structure which has been identified as the city's **gymnasium**. Excavation has revealed a beautiful exedra with two rows of rooms on the S side and two rooms on each side of the exedra. The S and N walls of the gymnasium are standing.

Sections of the wall which protected Stratoniceia climb up the hill to the S, cross on top to the E and descend to the N. The main gate was on the N side. Just inside the gate there is a single unfluted Corinthian column. A rectangular fortress, constructed of massive stone blocks, overlooked a ravine on the NE side of the city. This was repaired and extended during the Byzantine era.

Stratoniceia's **theatre**, which could seat 10,000, was to the S of the city at the foot of the acropolis-hill. Access to the seats was provided by a number of stairs. Because of earthquake damage it is impossible to say how many. There was a single diazoma. Unfortunately, only the foundations of the stage-building are preserved. The left parodos, which descended into the orchestra, has been discovered.

In a level space on the slope of the acropolis above the theatre the ruins of a small **Ionic temple**, dedicated to the imperial cult, were discovered by the archaeologists.

Artefacts found at Stratoniceia and in the surrounding countryside are kept in a small **antiquarium** in the village. They include a Mycenaean cup decorated with parallel red stripes. This suggests that the site was occupied as early as the 12C BC. There are also a number of tombstones and inscriptions, most of which date from the Roman period.

At Eskihisar the pine woods come to an end and the road to 5km Yatağan enters an uninteresting upland plateau which is covered in thorny scrub and scarred by the great, ugly pit of the quarry.

A short distance before Yatağan a turning on the left leads to c 18km **Lagina** which is located near the village of **Turgut**. The site may also be reached from the Aydın road.

The shrine at Lagina was dedicated to Hecate, one of the strangest and most sinister of the non-Olympian deities. Perhaps of Carian origin, she could grant success in business, victory in battle, eloquence in debate, or withhold these things. In time Hecate came to be regarded as the ruler of the dead and custodian of the key to the gate of Hades. She became, too, a deity associated with witchcraft and sorcery. Simaetha, a young Greek woman, invokes Selene, the Moon Goddess, and Hecate when preparing a love philtre for Delphis, a young athlete who has begun to neglect her.

'Shine brightly, Moon; I will softly chant to you, Goddess, and to Hecate in the Underworld—the dogs shiver before her when she comes over the graves of the dead and the dark blood. Hail, grim Hecate, and stay with me to the end; make these drugs as powerful as those of Circe and Medea and the golden-haired Perimede'. (Theocritus *Idylls* 2).

The temple at Lagina is one of the few shrines dedicated to Hecate. A moon goddess, she was usually worshipped under the cover of darkness at crossroads or road junctions. This may account for the location of her shrine at Lagina, as the ancient roads probably followed the same routes as their modern counterparts. Cake, cheese, fish and, sometimes, dogs were sacrificed in her honour. Representations of Hecate frequently took the form of three conjoined female figures—as in the statue in the museum at Bodrum—or as a female body with three heads.

The earliest known inscription referring to Hecate of Lagina dates from about the middle of the 2C BC, but it is likely that the goddess was worshipped here long before that time. After the defeat of Mithridates (see above), the Senate issued a decree which guaranteed the shrine from profanation, and a new festival entitled Hecatesia-Romaea was instituted at Lagina. According to Strabo this attracted large numbers of visitors each year. Evidence of Rome's continued interest in the cult is provided by the handsome contribution which Augustus made to the repair of the temple after its sack by Labienus and his Parthians in 40 BC. It would appear that the cult of Hecate continued to be practised at Lagina as late as the 3C AD. Presumably it ceased sometime after the issue of the edicts of Theodosius in AD 381 and 385 which put an end to most pagan practices in the Roman Empire.

Traces of the ancient paved way c 9.5km long, which stretched from Stratoniceia to Lagina, may still be seen. The site at Lagina is now very overgrown, so take a guide from Turgut. Village children, anxious to practise their English, are often willing to help.

The temenos of the temple of Hecate measured c 150m by 134m. It was enclosed on three sides by a Doric stoa. On the S side there were steps, which may have doubled as seats for spectators and initiates. On the E side of the steps there was a massive propylon. The jambs and lintel of this structure are still standing. The **Temple of Hecate**, which was towards the centre of the temenos, was a Corinthian pseudodipteros of 8 by 11 columns. On the E side a large pronaos with two columns in antis provided access to the cella. There was no opisthodomus. A partial investigation of the site at the end of the 19C yielded substantial sections of a frieze showing Hecate at the birth of Zeus, Greeks and Amazons, a gigantomachy and a number of other subjects. These are now in the İstanbul Archaeological Museum. All that remains at Lagina is a confused mass of broken columns and architectural fragments.

A short distance to the E of the temple are the remains of a structure which has been tentatively identified as an **altar**. A full excavation of the site would probably reveal traces of the buildings occupied by the priests, their assistants and the temple servants who lived inside the temenos.

The second sanctuary of Stratoniceia, that of **Zeus Panamaros**, lies c 11km to the SE of Eskihisar, near the village of **Bağyaka**. Apart from the remains of the peribolos on a hilltop and a stretch of the paved road that joined Panamara and Stratoniceia, little remains. The temple of Zeus Panamaros has not been found. Panamara is likely to be of interest mainly to specialists.

Yatağan is a dusty, unattractive town which matches perfectly the desolate and uninviting landscape. Few will be tempted to linger here. Whatever importance the town possesses, it owes to its position at the junction of the Aydın–Muğla road (550) with the route to Milas and Bodrum (330) and its proximity to a number of industrial establishments.

Leave Yatağan by Road 550 in the direction of Aydın. After a few kilometres the landscape changes dramatically. You enter a gorge which follows the course of the **Çine Çayı**, the ancient river Marsyas.

This beautiful stretch of wild, savage countryside was the setting for a legendary contest between the satyr Marsyas and Apollo. Marsyas, the son of Hyagnis and Olympus, was a follower of Cybele, the Great Mother. One day, while wandering by the river that later bore his name, he found a flute which Athena had made from the bones of a deer. This had been discarded by the goddess who was angered by the ugly way her cheeks puffed out when she played it. Marsyas ignored a prohibition placed by Athena on the use of the flute, and was delighted by the music which it made. Then, filled with a foolish pride, he had the temerity to challenge Apollo, the god of music, to a contest. Apollo accepted the challenge on condition that the winner could select the punishment to be imposed on the loser. The first contest ended in a draw. Then Apollo suggested that they play the instruments—flute and cithara—upside down. Marsyas lost and the god punished him savagely. He tied Marsyas to a pine or to plane tree (the accounts differ) and flayed him alive.

The woodland gods, his brother satyrs, the nymphs and Olympus, his son and pupil mourned for Marsyas. The earth wept for him and from these tears a spring was created. This grew into the clearest river in Caria and was named after the dead satyr. The story of the contest between Marsyas and Apollo is told in Ovid's *Metamorphoses* VI 382ff. It was a subject much favoured by Classical and Renaissance artists. There is a fine Hellenistic statue of the bound Marsyas in the İstanbul Archaeological Museum. Dating from the second half of the 3C BC, this was found in Tarsus.

At a point where the arches of an ancient **bridge** rise from the tumbling waters of the river Marsyas c 10km to the N of Yatağan, make a **detour** to **Gerga**, one of the more interesting of the smaller sites in Caria. The route is through fairly rough country, so wear stout shoes and carry a stick. The site is not easy to find so take a guide from Eskiçine or Çine.

The first signs of the settlement are a number of inscribed slabs bearing the word 'Gergas' or 'Gergakome', i.e. 'village of Gerga'. The Greek letters of the inscriptions vary in height from c 0.5m to c 1m.

Few other traces of Greek influence have been found in Gerga. Archaeologists, who have examined the ruins, believe that this was mainly, if not entirely, a Carian settlement. Despite the archaic appearance of some of the statues and the rough workmanship of the stone structures, it is believed that nothing here dates from before the Roman Imperial period.

Among the most important remains are dwelling houses, a temple or temple-tomb, two monumental stelae, a number of statues, and some open-fronted structures. The **temple**, which is an excellent state of preservation, still retains its roof. 'Gergas' is inscribed in Greek letters on a massive slab over the entrance. The **stelae**, which are c 3.35m high and pyramidal in shape, also have the word 'Gergas' on them. Note the colossal **headless statue** lying on the ground to the SW of the temple.

Some archaeologists believe that the settlement was a sanctuary dedicated to a Carian deity named Gergas and that the open-fronted structures were tombs containing the bones of the priests and of local dignitaries. Bean disagrees. He suggests that the open-fronted structures were fountainhouses or cisterns which the almost waterless state of the site made necessary. Perhaps a future examination of Gerga will solve the mystery and also provide an explanation for the presence on the site of the many slabs inscribed with its name.

A short distance from the bridge over the Marsyas river, c 10km N of Yatağan, Road 550 climbs to a height of c 400m at the Gökbel Pass before descending into a broad upland plain. This has two main centres, Eskiçine and Çine. Until the beginning of the century the area was governed from Eskiçine. Today the *kaymakam* is in **Çine**, c 9km to the N.

A passable road leads W from the centre of Çine to the site of the ancient city of **ALABANDA**. This is partly covered by the village of Araphisar.

History. According to Strabo, Alabanda was located at the foot of adjoining hills which looked like an ass carrying two panniers. He quotes the ancient wit, Apollonius Malacus, who described the place as 'an ass laden with panniers of scorpions'. The area was reputed to swarm with these unpleasant creatures.

According to tradition the city was called Alabanda after a mythical hero whose name was derived from a combination of two Carian words, 'ala', horse and 'banda', victory. The youth Alabandus was given this name by his royal father to celebrate a great victory won by the Alabandian cavalry.

Towards the end of the 3C BC Alabanda was known as Antiocheia of the Chrysaori-ans as a gesture of gratitude to the Seleucid king, Antiochus III, who was credited with preserving 'the democracy and peace of the city'. Besieged and captured by the Macedonian, Philip V c 201 BC, it reverted to its old name after the Seleucid domination in Asia Minor was broken at the Battle of Magnesia in 190 BC. With the rest of Caria it then came under the rule of Rhodes. However, it appears that Alabanda enjoyed a considerable degree of freedom under the Rhodians whose control appears to have been largely nominal.

In about 40 BC Alabanda was occupied by Labienus (see above), who placed a garrison in the city. When the inhabitants rebelled against his rule and put his soldiers to the sword, he punished them severely. They were fined and the temples were robbed of their treasures. The city's fortunes improved in the Roman Imperial period. There was a temple dedicated to Apollo Isotimus and the Theoi Sebastoi, the Divine Emperors. Alabanda became a conventus, a centre for the administration of justice. It also gained a reputation for luxurious living. According to Strabo, striking in a censorious vein, it was a city of 'people who live in luxury and debauchery'. As evidence he said it contained 'many girls who play the harp'!

Alabanda had few claims to fame. It was the home of two orators, the brothers Menecles and Hierocles, who were admired by Cicero. In the area around the city gemstones, resembling garnets, and an unusual red-brown marble were found.

Little is known about the city's later history. It continued to issue its own coinage until c AD 250. During the Byzantine era, Alabanda's bishop came under the jurisdiction Metropolitan of Stavropolis (Aphrodisias).

There are few visible traces of Alabanda's greatness and, alas, none of the debauchery mentioned by Strabo. The most striking building is at the N end just inside the line of the city walls. This has been identified as the **bouleuterion**. The S wall of this structure, which stands to a height of c 9m, was pierced by four doors. Traces of the semicircular seating may be found inside. In all four walls there is a horizontal row of square holes whose exact purpose is not known. They appear to be a late addition to the building.

A large level area to the S of the bouleuterion, which measures c 110 by 73m, has been identified as the **agora**. Of the colonnade which once surrounded it, no trace remains.

The site of the **Temple of Apollo Isotimus**, one of the principal deities of Alabanda, was a short distance to the SE of the agora. The title, which means 'equal in honour', may refer to the god's standing in relation to Zeus Chrysaoreus or to the Theoi Sebastoi during the Roman Imperial period. There is some speculation that Apollo Isotimus may have been a Carian deity who was Hellenised. Little remains of the temple. When it was excavated at the beginning of the century, sections of a decorative frieze showing a battle between the Greeks and Amazons were discovered. An Ionic pseudo-dipteros with 13 by 8 columns, it has been dated to c 200 BC.

A tumbled mound of stones to the W of the temple, believed to mark the position of a baths complex, awaits exploration. The site of a second **temple**, dated also to c 200 BC, was discovered on the slopes of the hill to the S of the city. Resting on a man-made terrace, this Doric structure of 11 by 6 columns had a deep pronaos, a cella and no opisthodomus. As the entrance was on the W side, it is believed to been dedicated, like the similarly oriented structure at Magnesia on the Maeander, to Artemis.

The ruins of the **theatre** are at the base of Alabanda's other hill. Apart from a section of the retaining walls of the cavea, very little remains of this structure. The passages, which provided access to the interior, have been closed with stones in modern times. There are a few traces of the stage-building and of the proscenium. The cavea is greater than a semicircle which suggests that the original building dated from the Hellenistic period.

On the western outskirts of the city, there is a large **necropolis**. The stone sarcophagi, simple in design, are closed with massive granite lids. Unusually, each states the occupation of the deceased—doctor, architect, schoolmaster, lamplighter, seller of pheasants.

About 6km to the N of Çine, a turning on the left leads to the village of 25km **Karpuzlu**, i.e. the place of watermelons. There the ruins of an ancient city, which has been identified as **ALINDA**, have been found.

History. Alinda made a dramatic appearance in the history of Caria towards the end of the 4C BC. When Ada, the sister of Mausolus of Halicarnassus (see Bodrum) was deposed by her younger brother Pixodarus c 340 BC, she left Halicarnassus and took up residence in Alinda. In the safety of this mountain stronghold she awaited an opportunity to recover her lost kingdom. When, in 334 BC, Alexander the Great, campaigning to remove the Persian threat from Greece and from the Greek cities in Asia Minor, marched into Caria at the head of his victorious army, this opportunity arrived. Ada left her fortress-city and went to meet the youthful conqueror. Offering to surrender Alinda to Alexander, she told him of the wrongs which she had suffered from her kinsmen, and promised to help him to conquer Caria.

A firm friendship was quickly established between them. Ada offered to adopt him as her son and with motherly concern sent choice food to tempt his appetite and then skilled cooks to prepare special meals. Alexander, touched by the recital of Ada's misfortunes and the regal manner with which she had borne them, returned Alinda to her control. He also allowed her to call him her son. The food and the cooks were gracefully refused. His preparation for breakfast was, he said, a night march and for lunch a frugal breakfast.

After Alexander had taken Halicarnassus and put the Persians and their allies to flight, he left Ada to capture the two headlands where remnants of the defenders held out. When this had been accomplished he confirmed her sovereignty over Caria. It has been suggested that, perhaps as an expression of gratitude, Alinda was renamed Alexandria-by-Latmus. If this hypothesis is correct, the city resumed its original name sometime in the following century.

During the years that followed Ada's reign there seems to have been a marked increase in Greek influence in Caria. This is evidenced by the reported presence of a statue of Aphrodite by the celebrated Athenian sculptor Praxiteles in a shrine dedicated to Adonis in Alexandria-by-Latmus. There is also a reference in an inscription, which may refer to Alinda, to an administrative section of the citizenry named after Erechtheus, a legendary king of Athens, .

Very little is known about the history of Alinda before or after the celebrated encounter between Alexander and Ada. It was probably one of the places which were fortified by Mausolus when he was consolidating his rule in Caria. Alinda issued its own coinage from about the beginning of the 2C BC to the 3C AD. It was a member of the Chrysaoric league. During the period when Caria was under the control of the Seleucids, Antiochus III, recognising the city's strategic importance, placed a garrison here. After the adoption of Christianity Alinda had its own bishop who came under the jurisdiction of the Metropolitan of Stavropolis (Aphrodisias).

One of the first travellers from W Europe to visit Alinda was Richard Chandler. He investigated the ruins of the ancient city in the spring of 1765. Making his way here from Heracleia under Latmus, he camped ovenight by a stream where he was 'serenaded in a disagreeable manner; frogs croaking, as it were in chorus; owls hooting; jackals in troops howling; and the village dogs barking'. Perhaps his disturbed slumbers account for the lacklustre description of Alinda in his journal. Mistaking it for Alabanda, he lists, almost without comment, the principal ruins: aqueduct, market building, theatre, tower, cisterns, necropolis and city walls. In later years the site was visited by Charles Fellows, who identified it correctly on the basis of coins discovered here. Curiously, there is a complete absence of inscriptions in Alinda. Perhaps they await discovery and will be revealed, when the site is given the systematic survey and examination which it deserves.

The most striking of Alinda's ruins is the **Hellenistic market building** which is reached by a short but fairly stiff climb from the village. This well-pre-served structure, c 99m long, had three storeys. Access to the bottom storey was provided by 12 large doors which open from a narrow terrace, part natural, part artificial. The interior was divided laterally into two sections. In the front there was a line of shops of varying sizes and behind them a series of dimly-lit storerooms. The middle storey, which was divided by a line of columns in the centre, may also have been used as storage space for the shops below and on the third storeys. Apart from some architectural fragments, little remains of the third storey which led directly to the agora.

Alinda's **agora**, which was c 30m square, was surrounded by a colonnade of which only traces remain. Olive trees have rooted themselves among the shattered columns and they mark the line of the wall which separated the agora from the buildings on the terrace above.

A short distance to the E are the ruins of a substantial building which has not been identified. In view of its location it was almost certainly connected in some way with the administration of the city.

On the hillside are the ruins of the **theatre**. This Graeco-Roman building, of which a substantial part remains standing, had a diameter of 65m. The original structure is believed to date from the beginning of the 2C BC. The Roman modifications probably took place during the reign of Augustus. Two arched entrances led to the single diazoma which divided the 35 rows of seats. Note the fine Hellenistic masonry of the supporting walls of the cavea. The ruined stage-building is almost completely buried. There is a fine view from the vaulted gallery at the top of the cavea.

Continue up the hill to the well-preserved remains of a two-storey **Hellenistic tower** constructed of ashlar masonry. Near the tower is the entrance to a tunnel which, according to the villagers, provided a link with the theatre where its supposed exit is pointed out to visitors. On the summit of the hill there are traces of a large **semicircular structure** which some believe was a nymphaeum. A more likely explanation is that it was an exedra where the citizens of Alinda sat while enjoying the evening air.

NW in a second **acropolis** surrounded by stout ashlar walls, are the remains of many private houses. The presence of six large cisterns suggests that it may also have been used as a place of refuge in times of danger.

In the valley below the acropolis there is a substantial stretch of the city's **aqueduct**. Four arches and a section of wall, pierced by an opening for the passage of vehicles, support the covered water-channel.

Around Alinda there was a large **necropolis**. Although there are several undecorated sarcophagi, most of the burials were in Carian-type graves cut from horizontal rock-surfaces and covered with closely-fitting stone lids. Unlike the graves in Alabanda on which the professions of the deceased were recorded, the tombs of Alinda bear no inscriptions.

Adventurous travellers may like to extend their tour to 20km **Gafarlar**, the nearest village to the site of the ancient city of **Amyzon**. According to Bean the road from

Karpuzlu to Gafarlar was one of the worst he ever encountered. It has improved but little and should only be attempted only by four-wheel drive vehicles.

Amyzon may also be reached from the N. Take the road to 10km Koçarlı which leaves the E87 on the left c 10km to the W of Aydın, and continue to Gafarlar which is c 16km to the S. This route also needs careful driving. Because the terrain is difficult and the site remote, engage a guide at Koçarlı or Gafarlar. Allow at least half a day for the excursion and take a picnic lunch.

Very little is known about the history of Amyzon and its ruins are not particularly striking. Its principal attraction is the wild beauty of its remote mountain location. Little visited and relatively unknown, it will appeal to those who like to contemplate ancient ruins undisturbed by coach parties or souvenir-vendors.

Strabo has a throwaway reference to Amyzon. He includes it in a group of Carian places which he categorises as 'dependencies' of minor importance, adding 'there is less to be said' (about them). According to inscriptions found at the site, the city supported the Ptolemies and the Seleucids in turn. In 203 BC, while under Syrian control, Antiochus III confirmed the right of asylum claimed by a temple in Amyzon dedicated to Artemis and Apollo. During the troubled period that marked the end of the Roman Empire and the beginning of the Byzantine period the city's temple-terrace was transformed into a fortified area. After the arrival of Christianity in Caria Amyzon became an episcopal see.

The scant remains of the 4C **Temple of Artemis and Apollo**, constructed in the Doric style, rest on a terrace which was approached by ceremonial stairs. Within the temenos there was accommodation for the priests and temple servants. Bean reports the discovery of an inscription which at some time had been placed upside down in the wall of the building. This listed the names of the officials of the temple.

Almost hidden by dense vegetation at the extreme end of the terrace are the ruins of another structure which may have been a small theatre or an odeum. On the S of the site just within the 4C BC **city walls**, stretches of which stand to a height of c 6m, are several large **underground rooms**. These were probably used for the storage of cereals. It is not known how Amyzon supplied its citizens with water. So far no trace of an aqueduct or cisterns has been found.

From Çine to c 35km Aydın Road 550 runs for some time parallel to the Marsyas, the Çine Çayı, until finally that river turns away to the NW and flows into the Büyük Menderes, the ancient Maeander. About 9km before its junction with the E87 the road crosses the torpid, sluggish Menderes and soon afterwards enters the leafy suburbs of Aydın.

18

Aydın to Pamukkale and Denizli

Total distance 153km. Aydın—29km Sultanhisar—(2km Nysa)—(71km Geyre/Aphrodisias)—98km Denizli—(20km Colossae)—(c 3km Laodiceia ad Lycum)—20km Pammukale/Hierapolis.

AYDIN, the administrative centre of the province of the same name, is a pleasant, bustling town whose wide tree-lined boulevards climb steeply from the busy E87. Near an important road junction, it is also on the railway line which links İzmir with Denizli. The *otogar* is at the foot of the hill, just off the E87. Aydın is a good centre for exploring the Maeander Valley.

Accommodation and Information. The four-star *Turtay Hotel* on the Aydın road, c 3km from the city centre, is recommended. There are also two two-stars hotels in the town.

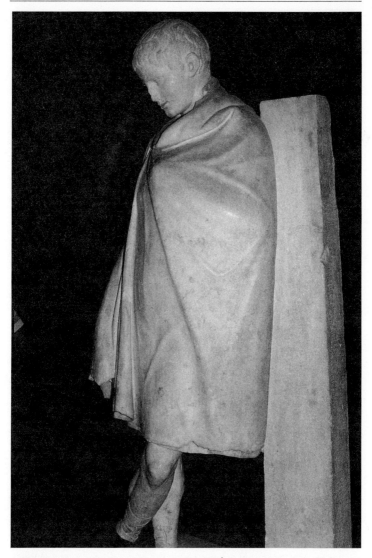

The Ephebe of Tralles (Aydın), now in the İstanbul Archaeological Museum

There is a good restaurant at the railway station. The **Tourist Information Office** is in Yeni Dörtyol Mevkii.

History. Aydın occupies the site of the ancient city of Tralles which, according to Strabo, was founded by Argive colonists and the Trallians, a barbarian tribe from Thrace, after whom it was named. The city was built on a trapezium-shaped plateau which had good natural defences. After the Peloponnesian War, when Sparta was endeavouring to fill the place formerly occupied by Athens in Asia Minor, a Spartan army tried, unsuccessfully, to take Tralles from the Persians. In 334 BC when Alexander arrived in Ephesus, delegations from Magnesia on the Maeander and Tralles came to offer submission. Antigonus, one of the Diadochoi, held Tralles from 313 until 301, when it came under the rule of the Seleucids. After their defeat at the battle of Magnesia ad Sipylum in 190 BC, Tralles passed to Pergamum. The elaborate palace of brick, which Attalus II (160–138 BC) built here, was later occupied by the priest of Zeus. Between 133 BC and 129 BC the city supported the Pergamene pretender, Aristonicus, against the Romans and, after his defeat, its citizens paid for their bad judgment by having the right to mint their own coins taken away from them.

Tralles was a conventus for some time under the republic, but eventually that honour was transferred to Ephesus. During the Mithridatic wars, according to Strabo, the sons of Cratippus ruled in Tralles. Tyrants, they were responsible for ordering the murder of many Roman residents. When Tralles was badly damaged by an earthquake in 27 BC Augustus provided generous aid for its reconstruction. In gratitude its citizens called it Caesarea, a name it retained for some time.

Strabo described Tralles as a wealthy city, adding that some of its citizens held 'the chief places in the Province [of Asia], being called Asiarchs'. A cultural centre of some importance, it was the home of a number of famous orators and teachers. Among those singled out by Strabo are Pythodorus, who moved here from Nysa because of Tralles' greater fame, and the orators Dionysocles and Damasus. The latter had the curious sobriquet of Scombrus (tuna-fish). Tralles was also the birthplace of Anthemius, the 6C architect and author of a number of mathematical treatises. With Isidorus of Miletus he designed the great church of Haghia Sophia in Constantinople. The stele of Seikilos, which dates from c 100 BC, was found at Tralles. This is an interesting example of the Greek system of musical notation which used letters to indicate the notes.

The principal deity of Tralles was Zeus Larisaeus, who was worshipped at a shrine c 5km to the N of the city on the slopes of Mt Messogis. The office of chief priest was not always entirely free from risk. In Strabo's time Menodorus, who held that position, was deposed through the machinations of a rival and murdered.

During the Roman Imperial period Tralles was made a neocorate by Caracalla. The city's coins showed a cuirassed emperor inside the imperial temple and the temple of Zeus. With imperial permission, games based on the great contests of Classical Greece were held in various cities of the Province of Asia. Those at Tralles were named after the athletic festivals of Delphi and Olympia.

Sometime after the conversion of Constantine, the inhabitants of Caria adopted Christianity and, in due course, Tralles became an episcopal see. After the defeat of the Byzantine army at the battle of Manzikert in 1071, the Selçuk Turks swept across Anatolia. By the end of the 12C they had captured most of the cities in Caria, including Tralles. For a number of years the city formed part of the sultanate of Konya. Retaken by Manuel I Comnenus (1143–80), it remained in Byzantine hands until 1282, when it was successfully invested by the Menteşe Turks. At that time it was renamed Aydın which means light, clear, or enlightened. In 1403 it was captured by Mehmet I and became part of the Ottoman Empire.

Today there are few traces of Aydın's past. The site of Tralles is part of a military zone and it is necessary to obtain a permit to visit it. Applications should be addressed to the Tourist Information Office or the Vilayet. Excavations carried out there by Turkish archaeologists at the beginning of the century revealed the remains of a stadium, a theatre, an agora and a gymnasium. In the theatre there was a tunnel c 2.5m deep under the orchestra. This permitted actors playing the parts of demons and chthonic gods to make dramatic entrances and exits.

Only a few **column stumps**, a section of the **wall** and **three tall arches**, the so-called Üç Göz, of the 3C AD gymnasium remain. The arches, which may be seen clearly from the E87 on the western approaches to the town, were constructed of a mixture of brick and stone covered with stucco.

Many of the objects found at the site of Tralles were taken to İstanbul and are now in the Archaeological Museum. Perhaps the finest is the so-called **Ephebe of Tralles**. This, a marble statue 1.48m tall of a boy wrapped in a thick mantle, is believed to date from the late 1C BC or early 1C AD. The sculptor has chosen to show his subject immediately after exercise or after a contest. In an attitude of exhaustion and dejection, with downcast gaze, he leans gracefully against a pillar. His swollen ears and battered nose suggest that he was either a boxer or a wrestler. This powerful and moving work of the early Roman Imperial period has too much humanity and immediacy to be anything but the representation of a real person.

Built into the gateway of Aydın's prison are two towers which formed part of a Byzantine fortress. In the town there are two Islamic monuments of particular interest. The **Ramazan Paşa Camii** and the **Bey Camii** were both constructed in the 16C. The latter incorporates a good deal of material taken from the buildings of Tralles.

Aydın's **museum** is a short distance W of the town centre. It has a fine collection of objects from Tralles and the surrounding area. In a pleasant garden, half-hidden by flowering shrubs, there are architectural fragments, sarcophagi, stelae and statues, most of which date from the Roman period. Inside, the exhibits, arranged in chronological order, include prehistoric bowls and platters, flint and obsidian tools, primitive cult statues, stone axe heads and arrows. Hittite culture is represented by gold crowns and diadems, jewellery and ceramics. From the Greek, Byzantine and Roman eras there are statues, reliefs, busts, coins, terracotta, bronze and marble figurines, lamps, glass objects and vases. Note in particular a fine statue of Nike, busts of Athena and of the Emperor Marcus Aurelius.

In the ethnographical section most of the objects date from the 19C and the early 20C. Collected in the Aydın area, they include embroidered garments, napkins, bed covers, silver jewellery, carpets and kilims.

The busy E87, on its way from Aydın to Denizli, follows the upper reaches of the Maeander river. On the left are the foothills of the Aydın Dağları, the ancient Mt Messogis, which have been tortured into grotesque shapes by thousands of years of erosion. Riven by deep torrents which overflow in the winter, they are arid, brown and dry, the nesting-place of scorpions, during the scorching days of summer. The road follows an ancient trade route which brought the products of eastern Anatolia and Mesopotamia to the Aegean ports, from where they were shipped to Greece and Rome. It passes through a rich and fertile area that is justly famed for the quality of its fruit. The grapes, peaches, oranges, lemons, and figs from the farms and orchards of the Maeander valley find a ready sale in the market places of Turkey.

At 29km Sultanhisar there is a good road to the ruins of (2km) **NYSA AD MAEANDRUM**. Soft drinks only are available on the site. If you intend to explore the ravine and tunnel, take a pocket lamp. Three hours should be enough for a visit and a picnic in the shade of one of the many olive trees.

History. Strabo (63 BC–AD 25), who studied rhetoric and grammar here under Aristodemus and presumably was well-informed about Nysa's history, says that it was an amalgamation of three cities. These were established by the brothers, Athymbrus, Athymbradus, and Hydrelus, who came to Caria from Sparta. The united city was known as Athymbra. The geographer's statement is supported by inscriptions which show that as late as the 3C BC the inhabitants were referred to as Athymbrians, a name which is also used in letters to the city from the Seleucid Antiochus I Soter. According to a late chronicle the city was renamed Nysa in honour of his wife. However, this account has not met with general acceptance. Modern historians agree only that the city began to be called Nysa some time towards the beginning of the 2C BC.

Nysa's fame as an educational centre drew pupils from all over Asia Minor. Aristodemus, a follower of the Stoic philosopher Panaetius, was one of the many teachers, who opened a school here. The city had in its territory the **Plutonium**, a shrine dedicated to Pluto, the god of the underworld, and to Kore, his consort. Near the Plutonium was the Charonium, a famous centre of healing. This attracted large numbers of sick people, who flocked to Nysa in the hope of obtaining a miraculous cure.

To judge by the visible ruins, Nysa seems to have flourished during the Roman Imperial period. It issued its own coinage from the beginning of the 1C AD to the middle of the 3C AD. After the adoption of Christianity, it became an episcopal see. Bishops from Nysa attended the Councils of Ephesus and Constantinople. Later, somewhat overshadowed by Tralles, and increasingly menaced by Arab raids and the advancing Turks, it was abandoned. The inhabitants moved down from the mountain and settled in the area now occupied by Sultanhisar. During the late Byzantine period Nysa had the same general history as the other cities of Caria.

One of the first Western European visitors to Nysa was Richard Chandler who came here in the late summer of 1765. He found the theatre, which at that time had most of its seats intact, and he explored the ravine below the amphitheatre. Later Nysa was visited by Leake, Fellows and Hamilton. The first scientific examination of the site was carried out by German archaeologists at the beginning of this century.

In recent years further work on the ruins of the city has been done through local initiative aided by the government. Nysa is little visited, by-passed by the tourist buses on their way to Aphrodisias and Hierapolis (Pamukkale). In an effort to change this regrettable situation the International Nysa Culture and Arts Festival is held here each year in May.

The road from Sultanhisar ends in a large car-park in front of the theatre. In ancient times this area, a square or piazza supported by vaults, was used for ceremonial purposes.

The well-preserved cavea of the **Roman theatre**, slightly larger than a semicircle, had 23 rows of seats below and 26 above the single diazoma. Spectators entered through vomitoria at each side and reached their seats by stairs. The orchestra had a diameter of 27m. The stage-building has some fine reliefs of Dionysiac revels.

Strabo has left an interesting description of the city as it was in his time. It is possible to gauge the accuracy of his observation by going to the highest level of the theatre. According to the geographer, a deep ravine with a stream at its base lay to the S. This divided the city into two parts. At one point the ravine was spanned by a bridge, at another covered by an amphitheatre. On the W side of the ravine was the gymnasium of the ephebes and on the E side the city's agora and the bouleuterion. Away to the S is the plain of the Maeander with its farms, orchards and busy road.

From the E side of the theatre a path descends steeply into the **ravine**. During the dry season it is possible to walk through a **Roman tunnel** which carried the waters of the mountain stream away from the city centre. The tunnel, c 150m long, was covered by barrel vaulting, which supported the piazza in front of the theatre. To the S of the tunnel are the scanty ruins of the **bridge** joining the two parts of the city which is mentioned by Strabo. Of the **amphitheatre** even less than the bridge remains standing. This huge structure, c 44m by 192m, which had 30 rows of seats, rested on vaulted supports over the stream. To permit the staging of naval battles water was drawn up from the stream and used to flood the arena.

W of the ravine a large rectangle, 70m by 165m, marks the site of a later version of the **gymnasium** described by Strabo. When this structure was enlarged in the 3C AD it was surrounded by a stoa, all traces of which disappeared a long time ago. A short distance to the N of the gymnasium are the substantial remains of the **library**. This building, which dates from the 2C AD, had two or possibly three storeys and a reading room measuring c 13.5 by 15m. To prevent the manuscripts and scrolls from being affected by damp, there was an air space between the niches in which they were stored and the outer walls. It is to be hoped that one day this library, the most important in Anatolia after the library of Celsus at Ephesus, will be

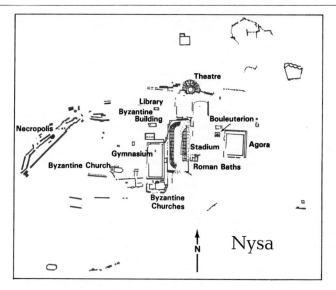

restored. S and W of the gymnasium there are the ruins of two **Byzantine churches** which are believed to occupy the sites of Roman temples.

In the **necropolis**, on the western edge of the city, the dead were placed in barrel-vaulted chambers arranged in tiers to make a continuous structure. A number of sarcophagi have been discovered in the chambers. The **Sacred Way**, which joined Nysa to the Plutonium and the Charonium started in the necropolis. As the bridges, which carried the ancient road across the ravines, no longer exist it is not possible to follow this route now.

The ruins of Nysa's well-preserved **bouleuterion** lie to the E of the ravine. This building, which has been dated to the 2C AD, is a Roman version of the Gerontikon or house of the elders mentioned by Strabo. Inside the rectangular structure 12 rows of limestone seats, divided by five stairs and arranged in a semicircle, faced the speakers' rostrum. The walls of rough masonry were concealed by decorative marble slabs.

A short distance to the S of the bouleuterion, enclosed by the remains of a portico, are some **mosaics** and an **ornamental basin**. To the NE a scattering of olive trees and a few architectural fragments mark the site of the city's **agora**. In its final form the agora, which was enlarged during the Roman Imperial period, measured 105m by 89m. It was surrounded by a colonnade, Doric on the N and W, Ionic on the S and E.

Climb the hill behind the theatre for the fine view and to examine the large square cistern from which Nysa obtained its water-supply.

To visit the site of the **Plutonium** and the **Charonium**, return to Sultanhisar and take the E87 in the direction of Aydın. At the village of 5km Çifte-kahveler continue to the hamlet of Salavatlı and ask for directions.

According to Strabo, the Plutonium, the shrine dedicated to Pluto and Kore, was enclosed in a richly-ornamented sacred precinct. The healing-centre known as the Charonium was in a natural cave above the shrine. The sick, who lodged in the nearby village, were sometimes placed by the priests inside the cave where they remained 'in quiet, like animals in their lurking-holes, without food for many days'. Patients were cured by following the treatment prescribed by the gods which was revealed to them or sometimes to the priests in dreams. Only the priests and the sick were allowed to enter the Charonium. For all others it was a dangerous and forbidden place.

At about noon on the day of an annual festival a sacrifice was made at the Charonium. Boys and young men from Nysa, nude and anointed with oil, led a bull to the cave. The animal entered the sacred precinct, advanced a short distance, and then, abruptly keeling over, died. Presumably it was asphyxiated by noxious vapours.

The site of the Plutonium lies to the E of the depression which carries in its depths the waters of the Sarısu, the Yellow Stream. From the few architectural fragments which remain, the archaeologists have suggested a very tentative reconstruction of the temple. It would appear that this unusual structure, which opened on the N side, was surrounded by a colonnade of 6 by 12 columns. The arrangement of the interior was also uncommon. For reasons that are not clear it seems to have been divided by parallel walls into long narrow corridor-like sections.

No certain traces of the Charonium have been found. Bean suggests that the natural cave, mentioned by Strabo, may have been in the ravine above the source of the Sarısu. It could have collapsed in the course of time. His theory is supported to some extent by the high concentration of sulphur in the Sarısu, over whose waters its nauseous smell sometimes hangs. Sulphur was almost certainly the principal curative agent used in the Charonium.

Return to Sultanhisar and continue E in the direction of Denizli. On the right side of the road the sluggish Maeander winds lazily westwards towards the sea. The river flows through the lush, green landscape which it has created, its reed-clothed banks sometimes approaching, sometimes drawing away from the highway. The eroded peaks of the Aydın Dağları become increasingly strange and bizarre and contrast violently with the pastoral calm of the river valley.

To reach Aphrodisias take a dolmuş from 13km Nazilli to 50km **Geyre**, the nearest village to the site, or travel to 40km Karacasu and from there take a bus, dolmuş or taxi to 10km Geyre.

There are organised tours from İzmir and Kuşadası to Aphrodisias during the holiday season, but they suffer from a number of disadvantages—a very early start, a long coach-ride and a comparatively short stay at the site.

Motorists should leave the E87 by a turning on the right-hand side of the road c 15km E of Nazilli signposted to Karacasu, Geyre and Aphrodisias. Left of the road, just after it crosses the Maeander, a low hill marks the site of **Antiocheia ad Maeandrum**, which has never been excavated.

In recent years the site of the ancient city of **APHRODISIAS**, which was located in a valley watered by a tributary of the Maeander, has excited worldwide interest because of the spectacular discoveries made there by an international team of archaeologists working under the direction of the late Professor Kenan Erim of New York University. They have brought to light the substantial remains of a theatre, an odeum, temples, baths, streets and public squares, a building that may have been a bishop's palace, several churches, and a Sebasteion with its propylon, porticoes and processional way. In addition, they have recovered from these structures a large number of statues of outstanding beauty, the work of local sculptors. Two substantial corpora of inscriptions, which throw an interesting light on the history of the city and on the life of its citizens, have been published. Most of the finds are in a well-arranged museum at the site; a few have been transferred to İstanbul's Archaeological Museum. Note that not all the buildings and sculptures described below are always open to visitors.

Until the archaeologists began their excavations much of Aphrodisias was hidden under the houses and fields of Geyre, a village which preserves in its name a memory of the ancient province of Caria. In 1956 Geyre was damaged in an earthquake and the villagers were rehoused 2km to the W.

Between Karacasu and modern Geyre there are several restaurants. These are often full with coach parties during the holiday season, so bring a picnic meal. Accommodation is available at the Chez Mestan Pansiyon and at the Aphrodisias Hotel. During the summer months drinks are sold at the site.

Unlike Ephesus, Pergamum and Side, Aphrodisias has been preserved from the excesses of commercialism. Visitors are unlikely to be harassed by vendors of postcards and souvenirs and peddlers of fake antiquities.

There is ample parking-space near the museum which is near the entrance to the site. Allow at least three hours for a tour of the ruins, which are spread over quite a wide area, and one hour for the museum which should be visited last.

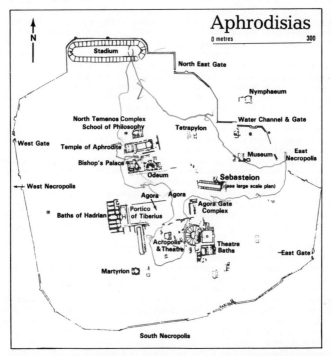

History. Excavation of the *hüyüks* in the centre of the city have revealed traces of occupation dating back to c 5800 BC. Finds include a number of small violin-shaped idols of marble and stone from the Bronze Age (c 2900–1200 BC). It would seem that from very early times there was a fertility cult at Aphrodisias which probably sprang from the desire of the early farmers in the river valley, to placate the Megale Meter and so ensure rich harvests and fruitful animals.

According to Stephanus, writing in the 6C AD, the settlement was at first called Ninoe after Ninus, the legendary founder of the Assyrian Empire. He was credited with having conquered most of western Anatolia. There is archaeological evidence to show that this foundation-legend was current earlier. Figures on a relief from the end of the 3C AD found in the city are captioned as Ninus and his consort, Semiramis. An interesting connection has been suggested between Ninus and Nin, the Akkadian goddess of love and war, who was better known by the Semitic name of Ishtar. It is not impossible that the Assyrians established a shrine dedicated to Ishtar at Aphrodisias and that in time she adopted further characteristics and took on the duties of the Great Mother who had long been worshipped here. Later Ishtar became Aphrodite.

'Behind the figure of Aphrodite there clearly stands the ancient Semitic goddess of love, Ishtar-Astarte, divine consort of the king, queen of heaven, and hetaera in one.' (Burkert *Greek Religion'*.)

The development of Aphrodisias was probably assisted by its position on the borders of Caria, Lydia and Phrygia and its proximity to the great E–W and N–S trade routes. However, for many centuries it appears to have been no more than a shrine, albeit an important one, dedicated to the goddess of love and war, Ishtar-Aphrodite. No doubt the settlement around the shrine housed the priests, their attendants and the servants of the goddess. By the 2C BC it was certainly known as Aphrodisias, but no description of it as a city has come to light before the second half of the century and then it was coupled with its neighbour Plarasa, with which it was joined in a sympolity. Note Plarasa has been identified with the unexcavated site of Bingeç S of Karacasu.

There was a dramatic change in the fortunes of Aphrodisias under Roman rule. During the horrors of the war against Mithridates VI Eupator (120–63 BC), king of Pontus, when more than 80,000 Romans were slaughtered in the province of Asia, Aphrodisias gave unstinted support to the Roman cause. Its citizens, declaring that life without the shield of Roman power would be impossible, voted to muster an army to assist the Romans in Caria. Such loyalty did not go unrewarded.

In 85 BC, after he had defeated Mithridates, the dictator Sulla sent gifts to the shrine of Aphrodite. These included a double axe, a traditional symbol of power in Caria, and a gold crown. Later Julius Caesar, whose family claimed Venus (Aphrodite) as an ancestress, had a gold statue of Eros dedicated at her shrine in Aphrodisias. He also granted the temple certain rights of asylum. Sacked by Labienus and his Parthians in 40 BC, the city was assisted in its recovery by Octavian who arranged that Aphrodisias became an ally of Rome and received the status of a free city. This meant in effect that it was removed from the control of the governor of the Roman Province of Asia. When, as Augustus, Octavian had assumed the supreme power, he continued to display a warm interest in the welfare of Aphrodisias and of its citizens and this benevolent attitude was continued by many of his successors.

Under the empire Aphrodisias was an important intellectual and cultural centre. Its schools attracted students not only from Asia Minor but from other parts of the Roman Empire. Towards the end of the 1C AD Xenocrates, the author of several treatises on medicine, taught here. At about the same time Chariton, the author of the oldest Greek novel, *Chaereas and Callirhoe*, writing his romantic story of star-crossed lovers proudly included a reference to his native city. 'I, Chariton of Aphrodisias, clerk to the rhetor Athenagoras will relate the love affair...'.

Aphrodisias was close to a quarry which produced fine pale white marble capable of taking a high polish. A school of sculpture, which acquired widespread fame in antiquity, grew and developed here. The work of sculptors from Aphrodisias reached Rome and other great centres of the empire. Fine examples have been found as far away as Leptis Magna in N Africa on an arch which was erected in honour of Septimius Severus and in a basilica built by him at the beginning of the 3C AD. Two centaurs from Hadrian's Villa at Tivoli have been identified as the creation of craftsmen from Aphrodisias, while a handsome relief of Antinous, that emperor's Bithynian lover, discovered at Lanuvium near Rome, was signed by Antoninianus of Aphrodisias.

Christianity made some progress in the city before the edict of Milan in AD 313 put an end to persecution. Two Aphrodisian martyrs, either under Decius or Diocletian, are recorded. A bishop from Aphrodisias attended the Council of Nicaea in AD 325. However, pagan influence continued for a very long time. In AD 391 Theodosius I banned paganism. This ban was repeated and extended by several of his successors, but there is evidence that in Aphrodisias sacrifice to the ancient gods continued for at least another century. Even in the 6C missionaries were still converting pagans in this area, but the prosperity and influence of the Christians is indicated by the conversion of the temple of Aphrodite into a Christian church.

Christianity's problems were not limited to conflicts with paganism. Heterodox Christian beliefs flourished in Aphrodisias and at the beginning of the 6C its bishop was removed from his see for his stubborn adherence to the Monophysite heresy. At the end of that century or the beginning of the next, in an attempt to break away from its pagan associations, Aphrodisias was renamed Stavropolis, the City of the Cross. Later it was simply known as Caria, a name recalled by its corrupt form Geyre.

Apparently in the middle of the 4C a wall was constructed for the first time around the city. About AD 350 Aphrodisias was badly damaged by an earthquake which devastated much of Caria and the neighbouring provinces. The 7C was marked by further calamities—Persian incursions into Anatolia and another disastrous earthquake. This time the city was too impoverished to repair the damage and many buildings were left in ruins. A citadel was constructed around the *hüyük* behind the theatre to provide the inhabitants with a place of refuge in times of danger.

At the end of the 12C the city was captured by the Selçuk Turks. Changing hands several times during the following century, its inhabitants were dispersed by its Turkish rulers c 1279 and the site was abandoned. Some time later farmers returned to the area and established the small village of Geyre among the ruins of the shattered buildings.

One of the first travellers from Western Europe to visit Aphrodisias was the British botanist William Sherard who explored the site in 1705. He was mainly interested in the inscriptions. W.R. Hamilton came to Aphrodisias in 1803. He was followed nine years later by members of the Society of Dilettanti under the leadership of William Gell. Their discoveries were published in *Ionian Antiquities* between 1821 and 1915. Charles Texier, who examined the ruins in 1835, wrote of his visit in *Description de l'Asie Mineure*, published in 1849. The first excavations were conducted by a French engineer Paul Gaudin in 1904. In 1937 an Italian team discovered a beautifully carved frieze from the Ionic portico dedicated to Tiberius in the Agora. This is now in the garden of the Archaeological Museum at İzmir. Professor Erim, who started at the site in 1961, continued to add to our knowledge of the city until his untimely death in 1990. His work is being continued by Professor R.R.R. Smith and his colleagues.

The approach to Aphrodisias is marked by ruined tombs in the large ancient cemeteries on the right of the road and by sections of the city wall built of white marble blocks. Sarcophagi found here are in the museum.

Entrance is from the car-park on the E side of the wall which surrounded the city. Aphrodisias appears to have relied for protection on the sacred character of its shrine until about the middle of the 4C AD. At that time work on a **fortification wall**, roughly circular in shape and extending for c 3.5km, was begun. This was reinforced by towers and had four main gates, one at each point of the compass. Litter-louts were not unknown in Aphrodisias, as built into the NE wall is a re-used stone with the following inscription: 'Whoever throws rubbish here shall incur the curse of the 318 fathers', i.e. the bishops, who took part in the Council of Nicaea (AD 325).

At the beginning of the 5C this wall may have been strengthened with building-material taken from earlier structures damaged by earthquakes and other disasters. The patchwork is particularly noticeable on the N side where inscribed bases from statues and carved stone blocks have been built into the fortification. The wall seems to have been maintained until the late 6C early 7C when the citizens withdrew for safety to the Acropolis.

One of the most recent and most exciting of the discoveries at Aphrodisias has been made in an area a short distance to the SW of the museum. Here are the ruins of the **Sebasteion**. This complex, which has been dated to the first half of the 1C AD, was dedicated to Aphrodite, with, no doubt, Augustus and certainly Tiberius and Livia. Gaius, Claudius, and Nero and other members of the Julio-Claudian family were also honoured here subsequently. Throughout the eastern Roman provinces, to regard the emperor as a divinity was a step which placed him in an understandable and acceptable context. In Aphrodisias the Sebasteion served this purpose.

Menander, his brother Eusebes and Eusebes' wife donated the N portico and the propylon. Tiberius Claudius Diogenes dedicated the S portico and the temple, which had been promised by his father Diogenes and his uncle Attalus and his uncle's wife Attalis Aphion.

The Sebasteion consisted of **twin parallel porticoes** 80m long which flanked a paved area 14m wide. At the E end a flight of steps led up to a large Corinthian-style temple. The W end was closed by a propylon which was built at an oblique angle to the porticoes. The propylon was ornamented with a statue of Aphrodite as first mother of the imperial family together with statues of other members of that family and of their legendary ancestors. The aim of the architect and his patrons was to lead worshippers along a processional avenue, whose decorative sculpture glorified Augustus and his Julio-Claudian successors especially for their military successes, to the temple where sacrifices were offered to them and to Aphrodite.

The porticoes, 12m high, were divided horizontally into three sections and within each section vertically by half-columns, Doric at the bottom, Ionic in the middle and Corinthian at the top. Between the columns in the middle and top sections were **deeply-carved reliefs**.

On the S portico these were representations of mythological scenes and of members of the imperial family in heroic poses. Among the most striking were representations of the Three Graces, Bellerophon and Pegasus, Leda and the Swan, Achilles and Penthesilea, Nero conquering Armenia (this relief was later defaced), a victorious Claudius about to despatch a prostrate Britannia, and a nude, youthful Augustus holding a cornucopia and an oar, symbols of his dominion over land and sea.

There are fewer reliefs extant from the N portico as this was severely damaged by the earthquake at the beginning of the 7C and material from it was used to fortify the theatre area. From inscriptions we know that they were of the peoples conquered by Augustus—Egyptians, Dacians, Thracian and Gallic tribes—together with some other works. From the latter a fine representation of the youthful Nero being crowned by his mother in the guise of Tyche remains. Even after the lapse of centuries the sculptures which decorated the Sebasteion are a vivid demonstration of the skill of the Aphrodisian artists who created them.

The dedication of the porticoes and their associated buildings to Aphrodite and the imperial family placed the Julio-Claudians firmly in the context of traditional Greek religious beliefs and accepted Greek culture.

During the 4C the rooms on the ground floor of the porticoes were probably used for a short period as shops. At about the same time the statues and reliefs of the more obvious pagan deities were mutilated.

To the S of the Sebasteion lie the substantial remains of a large structure which has been identified as a **2C propylon**. Originally it was believed that this led to the agora, which was located a short distance to the W, and as a consequence it was described at one time as the agora gate on plans.

Recent surveys of the area and an examination of statuary and the architectural fragments found here have produced a revised view. Archaeologists are now of the opinion that the monumental gate may have provided access from the agora to another building or complex, also dating from the 2C AD, whose remains lie in the unexcavated area to the E.

Sometime in the 5C the propylon was converted into a **nymphaeum**, probably in an attempt to contain the flood waters which, after the earthquakes of the mid 4C, caused many problems in this part of the city. Among the sculptures recovered from the structure are a massive, headless Antoninus Pius and the statue of a pensive togaed youth. There are also a number of friezes showing mythological subjects e.g. centaurs at a banquet and a

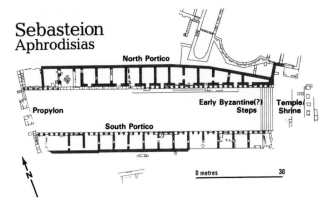

Sebasteion
Aphrodisias

North Portico

Propylon

Early Byzantine(?) Steps

Temple/ Shrine

South Portico

0 metres   30

gigantomachy, which were taken from another building to decorate the nymphaeum. A similar re-use of ornamental sculpture occurred at the Library of Celsus at Ephesus.

Immediately to the S is the **hüyük**, which Gaudin and the early archaeologists believed to be the city's acropolis. On the E side there is a large rectangular open space, the so-called **tetrastoon** which has been dated by finds to the reign of Julian (360–363). As its name suggests, this consisted of a paved area surrounded on all four sides by stoas. There was a circular fountain in the centre. The tetrastoon was a meeting-place and it facilitated access to the theatre and the small shops in it. Among the sculptures discovered in the tetrastoon are a sensitive representation of a sad-faced adolescent, reworked as a 4C prince from an earlier 1C statue, and the striking statue of grim, tight-lipped Flavius Palmatus, a late 5C governor of Caria and acting vicar of Asiana.

The well-preserved **Theatre of Aphrodisias** had an estimated seating capacity of 8000. Its horse-shoe shaped cavea had two, possibly three, diazomata. Of its seats, which were divided into 11 cunei, 27 rows remain. According to an inscription, the stage-building was constructed at the expense of a late 1C BC notable, Iulius Zoilos. A former slave, he played an active part in the affairs of the city at that time. Various factors have permitted the date of the construction to be narrowed down to the period between 39 BC and 27 BC. There were six vaulted chambers behind the stage. Names on the doorframes suggest that these were the dressing rooms used by some of the more important performers.

Originally constructed in the late Hellenistic period, the theatre was modified considerably during the second half of the 2C AD. By removing some of the lower rows of seats, dropping the level of the orchestra and erecting protective barriers and a parapet, it became possible to use it for gladiatorial contests and wild-beast shows. At the same time proedriai and a loge were added. Because of these alterations it was necessary to raise and widen the stage as had been done in the theatre at Priene (see above). Wild beasts were kept in secure cells underneath the stage before being released into the arena.

In the northern parodos the wall of the stage-building and the adjoining analemma are covered with inscriptions, letters and decrees which date from the period of the late Republic through to the middle of the 3C AD.

Recently published, they provide a unique record of the relationship between a loyal provincial centre and Rome. There is the text of a decree setting out the rights and privileges conferred on Aphrodisias by the Senate together with letters to the city from a number of emperors including Trajan, Hadrian, and Septimius Severus.

Among the mass of statuary discovered in or near the remains of the stage-building there are two pieces of particular interest: a 1C AD **relief bust of Aphrodite** and a more than life-size statue of a youth. The goddess, who gazes serenely at her worshippers, is portrayed wearing a polos. Suspended from an elaborate pectoral a crescent moon rests between her swelling breasts. According to an inscription on the base, the **youth** is a personification of the *demos*, the people of Aphrodisias.

During the Byzantine period small chapel-like rooms were constructed at each end of the stage-corridor. In one of these a fragmentary 6C fresco depicting the Archangel Michael was found.

It would appear that the theatre was so badly damaged by the earthquake at the beginning of the 7C that the reduced population was unable or unwilling to repair it. Because of the unsettled nature of the times the inhabitants turned their energies instead to making a fortress on the 'acropolis'. This they did by constructing a wall, complete with watch-towers, around the lower slopes. No attempt was made to rescue the stage-building from the debris, but a number of rough shelters were improvised among the tumbled masonry of the remainder of the structure.

The summit of the hill behind the theatre is easily reached from the top row of seats. Like the tells of Mesopotamia, the *hüyük* is an artificial mound composed of the remains of many successive levels of occupation. It is one of the oldest human settlements in Anatolia, the earliest finds have been dated to c 5800 BC. The archaeologists have established that as early as the fifth millennium BC the people, who lived here, were receiving goods from many distant sources, eg they used obsidian tools made in the islands of the Aegean. Excavations have produced pottery, gold and silver jewellery, tools, weapons, and primitive idols.

S of the tetrastoon there was a long hall which formed part of the **theatre baths complex**. This was unroofed except at the N end, where there was a small chamber paved with black and white marble which may have contained the statue of an emperor. Two pilasters, which flanked the entrance to the chamber, were carved in typical Aphrodisian style with an elaborate pattern of erotes, birds, and animals placed against an intricate background of foliage. The central paved area was flanked by colonnades, their blue-grey marble Corinthian columns separating it from the offices and shops which lined its sides.

Behind the hall lie the ruins of a large structure, the **theatre baths**. Note especially the enormous caldarium whose walls were 10m high. In the substantial remains of this chamber, now minus its roof, there are four arched niches, two of which lead to other parts of the complex. A large circular room contained two contiguous bathing pools.

Leave the theatre baths and continue towards the site of the agora which lies to the NW of the acropolis. To the S are the remains of a large **basilica** which is believed to date from the second half of the 1C AD. This structure, which was c 100m long, had the typical form, i.e. two aisles flanking a central nave. In the 3C the building appears to have assumed a new importance. This may have resulted from the establishment of the united province of Caria-Phrygia which had been created apparently in the reign of Decius (249–251). At about that time a number of reliefs of various mythological subjects were placed in the spaces between the columns on the eastern side. One of these shows Ninus, the legendary founder of Aphrodisias, and his wife, Semiramis (see above).

Another find in this area was the text of two decrees issued by Diocletian in AD 301. One revalued the silver currency, the other set out the maximum prices for a variety of goods and services including most foods, wood, metals, cloth, wooden and metal goods, shoes, drugs and transport.

Behind the palaestra and peristyle court, which were partially cleared by Gaudin at the beginning of the century, lie the substantial ruins of the **Baths of Hadrian**. This complex, dated by a dedicatory inscription, contained a large central hall, the caldarium, which was flanked on each side by parallel rectangular chambers. The ruins of a tepidarium and of a sudatorium were discovered among the chambers on the N side. An interesting inscription, found by Gaudin, warns bathers against leaving valuables with their clothes. The baths remained in use well into the Christian period. An inscription by a Christian cloakroom attendant has also been found.

Among the debris of the baths the archaeologists found **three fine marble heads**. One, which has been dated to the 2C, is believed to portray a priestess of Aphrodite. She wears an elaborate diadem which is decorated with a pattern of six-pointed stars. (A similar star appears on the relief of the goddess which was discovered in the theatre. See above.) The other two heads were representations of Apollo and Aphrodite.

A line of standing columns to the N and E of the baths marks the position of the great **double agora** of Aphrodisias. The N section, which was surrounded by a Doric portico, measured 205m by 120m. The S section, the **Portico of Tiberius**, which was in the Ionic style, measured 212m by 70m. This had a number of small rooms suitable for use as offices, shops, workshops and latrines. The enormous statue of a female deity and the damaged figure of a galloping horse were recovered here.

To the N, beyond a screen of poplar trees, are the extensive ruins of a building, which, after the mid 3C AD, is believed to have housed an official of some importance, perhaps the governor of the province of Caria-Phrygia and later of Caria or of the late Roman province. Subsequently it may have served as the **palace** of the bishop of Aphrodisias and Caria. The principal feature of this structure was an 'audience chamber' which had three large apses, a common characteristic of the residences of important officials.

Some of the blue-grey marble columns unearthed in the peristyle court, which provided access to the audience chamber, have been re-erected. Note the small bathroom and latrine on the S side of the S apse, proof that this was not purely a public building. On the N of the peristyle court, at a slightly higher level, there was a long narrow hall with an apse at its E end.

The discovery of a lead seal in the ruins, which mentions the 'Metropolitan Bishop of Caria', and the proximity of the building to the principal church in the city (the former temple of Aphrodite) suggest that it became an episcopal palace during the Byzantine era. In addition parts of two frescoes, one portraying Nike, the other the Three Graces, found here had been covered over with a rough coating of plaster. Perhaps they were considered unsuitable for the residence of a cleric.

One of the most beautiful and best-preserved buildings in Aphrodisias is to the E of the bishop's palace. This is the **odeum**, where concerts, theatrical productions requiring only small casts, lectures, discussions and political gatherings were held. The city council also met here. Built towards the end of 1C AD or the beginning of the 2C AD, it had, in its original state, a seating capacity of c 1700. Badly damaged by the 4C earthquake, the odeum became subject to flooding because of the disturbance of the water-table.

It also appears to have lost its roof about then, so leaving audiences and councillors alike exposed to the fury of the elements.

The cavea retains nine rows of its seats. These are divided into five cunei. Some of the seats carry rough inscriptions probably reserving them for particular groups, e.g. young men, Jews, partisans of the Blue Faction. Note the carved lion heads at the end of some of the rows. The orchestra floor was covered with a fine opus sectile design whose pattern was made up of segments of blue and white marble and red slate. The stage was decorated with statues placed in naiskoi. Some of those discovered by the archaeologists are of seated writers or philosophers, others have been identified as representations of local prominenti. There are a number of amusing graffiti on the walls of a passage at the back of the stage. One, perhaps the work of a bored performer awaiting his turn, is the spirited depiction of a horseman. The stage was separated from the agora by a portico with a double row of columns, Ionic on the outside, Corinthian on the inside.

It would appear that the odeum replaced an earlier building which may have been a gymnasium. Nearby are the remains of a **1C heroon**. A simple sarcophagus decorated with garlands rested on a circular dais supported by three steps. Adjacent was a round altar, ornamented with wreaths of flowers intertwined with bunches of fruit and the finely-carved figures of lively, carefree erotes. The tomb was robbed in antiquity. As burial within the city was a very high honour, it may be assumed that the deceased had performed some outstanding service to Aphrodisias and had been held in high esteem by his fellow citizens.

The discovery of a large quantity of marble chippings in this area led the archaeologists to the site of one of the many workshops which produced the sculpture that had made Aphrodisias famous. Among the discarded and unfinished works found here were an exquisite **statue of a young Hercules** which conveys admirably the gaucherie and uncertainty of adolescence, a blue and white marble representation of the rape of Europa and a particularly fine head of a bearded philosopher.

A short distance to the N are the ruins of the **Temple of Aphrodite**. We owe much of our understanding of this building to the skill and patience of Professor Erim and his colleagues, who had the not inconsiderable task of tracing its structural history through the disturbance of the site caused by earlier archaeologists and the extensive alterations made by the Byzantine architects, when they converted it into a church.

The temple, a pseudo-dipteros in the Ionic style with 8 by 13 columns, was begun in the 1C BC and continued in the 1C AD. Some of the columns bear inscriptions recording the fact that they were the gifts of individual citizens to the goddess and to the *demos* of Aphrodisias. Of the 40 columns which decorated the structure only 14 are still standing. The temple had a pronaos and cella. There was no opisthodomus.

It is clear that Aphrodite and the fertility deity, which preceded her, were worshipped in this place long before the construction of the temple. Excavations have revealed traces of much older structures, possibly treasuries, some of which date from the 7C BC. Fragments of terracotta statues of the goddess, dated to the 6C BC, have also been found on the site. When the pronaos of the temple was being constructed, the builders cut through a roughly-executed black and white Hellenistic mosaic depicting animals within a border. This is believed to belong to one of the earlier buildings.

During the reign of Hadrian (AD 117–138) the temple was enclosed on all four sides by elaborate porticoes, consisting of colonnades of Corinthian columns in front of walls with niches. Towards the middle of the 5C the temple was converted into a Christian basilica, probably dedicated to one or more of the archangels. The cult statue of the goddess and all traces of her worship were removed. A striking reminder of this dramatic change in the religious beliefs and practises of the Aphrodisians was provided by the discovery in the area to the S of the temenos of parts of a huge **marble statue of Aphrodite**. After the head and arms of the goddess had been crudely hacked off, the battered torso was built into a Byzantine wall. However, despite this apalling act of vandalism, enough remains to demonstrate the majesty and numinous quality which this work of art once possessed.

The reconstruction of the temple involved not only the destruction of the pronaos and cella, which contained the cult statue, but also the removal of the columns from the E and W ends. These were added to the existing columns on the long sides of the building. An apse was constructed at the E end and material from the Hadrianic peribolos was used to erect a narthex and an exonarthex. To complete the transformation of the temple into a church, an atrium and baptistery were added to the W end.

The alterations inside the basilica included the construction of an iconostasis in front of the sanctuary and of a synthronon. On the walls of a covered corridor behind the synthronon the archaeologists discovered the remains of 10C and 11C frescoes. These depicted Christ in Glory, the Blessed Virgin Mary and a number of the saints. Christian worship in the temple/church, which was repaired after the earthquake in the 7C and again in the 11C, ceased finally in the late 12C, when it fell into the hands of the Turcoman and Selçuk tribesmen, who overran western Anatolia at that time.

A short distance to the N of the peribolos of the temple of Aphrodite are the remains of the so-called **school of philosophy**. Access to the 3C structure was by way of a marble-paved courtyard on the E side. This was surrounded by columns of the local blue-grey marble and had a square pool in the centre. On the W side of the building there was another large courtyard which had an apse built into one wall. A third courtyard to the S and a number of rooms completed the structure.

Aphrodisias was the home of a number of noted philosophers, among them Alexander and Asklepiodotos. This fact coupled with the appearance and lay-out of the rooms in the complex, which are similar to those found in a number of schools of philosophy in various parts of the Greek world, suggested its name and use to the archaeologists. The building appears to have been occupied to a late date.

From the school of philosphy a path leads N to the **stadium** which was c 350m from the temple. This has been surveyed and soundings have been taken in various parts of the structure, but no further work has been done. One of the best-preserved Graeco-Roman stadia in Asia Minor, it was constructed during the 1C or 2C AD. Rounded at its E and W ends, it measures 262m by 59m. Its 30 rows of seats had an estimated capacity of 30,000. Special arrangements were made for the comfort of the spectators. The lines of seats on the long sides bulge slightly in the centre to ensure that everyone had an uninterrupted view and it would appear that there were loges for the more important officials and distinguished visitors in the centre of each side. Inscriptions on some of the seats indicate that they were reserved for particular groups, e.g. ephebes and certain craftsmen.

With the approval of the emperor many cities in the Roman province of Asia promoted games and competitions based on those held at Greek centres. At Aphrodisias they were modelled on Delphi's Pythian Games. In addition to the athletic events, which included foot-races, boxing, pancration and wrestling, there were music and drama competitions, exhibitions of oratory and competitive productions of tragedies and comedies. Prizes were modest, often no more than a wreath of laurel leaves, but as a rule the victor was rewarded in other ways by his patrons and followers.

A wall was built across the E end and a number of other changes were made in that part of the structure in the 7C. It is likely that the altered area was used for circus performances.

Later, when the city was menaced by threats of invasion and attack, the stadium was incorporated into its defensive system. The long N section became part of the fortifications and the access tunnels under the W end were closed off by walls.

On leaving the stadium walk in a SE direction towards the entrance to the site. A short distance to the E of the temple of Aphrodite are the remains of a magnificent **Tetrapylon**. This structure of four rows of four columns appears to have marked the junction of a N–S street with, perhaps, a processional way to the temple. Note the variation in the decoration of the column shafts of the tetrapylon. Those on the W are smooth, while some of the others have spiral markings. Fragments of the pediment reliefs recovered from the ruins portray chubby erotes hunting wild animals and figures of Nike emerging from a tangle of acanthus leaves.

Apart from those works left in situ, those being restored in the workshops, and those transferred to the İstanbul Archaeological Museum, the statues and architectural remains discovered by Professor Erim and his team are displayed in a well-arranged **museum** at the site. Financed jointly by the Turkish government and the National Geographic Society of America, this was opened in July 1979. An hour spent examining its exhibits makes a fitting conclusion to your visit to Aphrodisias, one of the most beautiful and exciting archaeological sites in Turkey.

If you have your own transport, continue to Denizli by way of 35km **Tavas**. This picturesque route is shorter, 69km as against 104km, than that via Karacasu and the E87. There are also bus and dolmuş services via Tavas, but they are relatively infrequent and may involve a number of changes.

A dazzling white scar on the brown slope of the mountain to the NE of Denizli marks the position of the great travertine basins of Pamukkale.

Denizli is the principal town and seat of the governor of the province of the same name. An important market centre, it is linked by train to İzmir and İstanbul and is well-served by inter-city buses.

The *otogar* is in the town centre, the airport is at Çardak, c 60km to the E on the road to Dinar.

The principal **Tourist Information Office** is at Atatürk Cad., No. 8, Kat. 2, Daire No. 4. There is also an office at the railway station in İstasyon Cad. on the W side of the town.

According to Ibn Battuta, Ladhiq (Denizli) was 'a most important town, with seven cathedral mosques'. He enthused over the 'matchless cotton fabrics with gold embroidered edges' made here. Most of the workers were Greek women. The large number of Greeks in Denizli paid a poll tax to the sultan. Greek men wore tall peaked red or white hats, the women capacious turbans, to distinguish them from the Turks.

When Charles Texier visited Denizli in the mid 19C, it was a quiet provincial backwater. The town was surrounded by beautiful gardens, oases of rest and pleasure where prosperous citizens whiled away the long, hot summers. Abandoning their houses, they took their repose in leafy bowers, enjoying the excellent fruit and garden produce for which the region was famous. According to Texier travellers arriving in Denizli found it quite deserted. Even the fortified area, '*la Cassaba, n'est plus habitée que par les chiens errants*'. (*Asie Mineure*, Paris, 1862.)

Denizli has one four-star, three three-star, 12 two-star, and four one-star hotels. The four-star *Grand Hotel Keskin* in İstasyon Cad. is recommended.

Frequent bus and dolmuş services leave the *otogar* during the daytime for 20km Pamukkale. In the evening or at night you will have to take a taxi.

As well as Hierapolis (Pamukkale) there are two sites in the neighbourhood of Denizli which are of particular interest to Christians: Colossae and Laodiceia ad Lycum. The remains of **Colossae** are c 20km to the E of Denizli. Take the Dinar road for c 8km to the point where it passes the ruins of a 13C Selçuk Ak Han on the left. There turn right towards **Honaz**. The ruins of Colossae are c 5km before the village.

History. The -ss in its name, relic of a pre-Greek language, suggests that Colossae was a settlement of considerable antiquity. The earliest reference to the city is found in accounts of Xerxes' invasion of Anatolia in 480 BC. When Cyrus set out on his ill-fated expedition to seize the throne of Persia from his brother, the newly-crowned Artaxerxes II, in the spring of 401 BC, Colossae was a large and prosperous place. Like neighbouring Laodiceia, it was a producer of fine wool which, according to Pliny the Elder, was dyed a purple 'colossinus'. As Laodiceia increased her share of the trade, so Colossae declined. By the time of Augustus it was a place of minor importance.

Christianity was brought to Colossae by Epaphras, the friend and companion of St Paul who was imprisoned with the apostle either in Caesarea or in Rome. Although it is unlikely that St Paul ever visited the city, it is clear that he took a deep interest in the growth and development of its Christian community. In his letter to the Colossians he warns its members of the dangers posed by paganism. In particular they are advised to beware of the activities of those who 'try to enter into some vision of their own'. (Colossians 2:18.) This is taken to refer to the adherents of the many mystery religions which flourished in the cities of the Roman Empire at that time.

Damaged by earthquakes, its trade taken away by Laodiceia, the ruin of Colossae was completed by the incursions first of the Arabs and later of the Turks. At about the beginning of the 9C the city was abandoned, the remaining inhabitants removing themselves and their possessions to nearby Chonae (Honaz).

Colossae was built on the S bank of the river Lycus at the head of a gorge. Today little remains of its ancient buildings. At the top of the low acropolis there are the scanty ruins of a **defensive wall**. Near the W edge is a large deep stone-lined pit. It is not known what purpose this served. The outline of Colossae's small **theatre** may be traced on the E side of the acropolis. The city's **necropolis** was on the N bank of the Lycus. Tombs, covered with flat slabs, were let into the ground. A church dedicated to St. Michael, one of the most important Christian shrines in Asia, was probably located in this area.

The **Ak Han**, which dates from the 13C, has a large square courtyard partially surrounded by arches and a covered hall. According to an inscription over the door of the hall, it was completed in 1253 by Karasungar during the reign of Sultan Kaykavus. The rest was finished a year later.

LAODICEIA AD LYCUM is nearer to Denizli than Colossae. A left turning c 3km from the town on the road to Pamukkale leads to the site. Little visited today except by those interested in its Christian connections—it is one of the Seven Cities of Asia mentioned in the Book of Revelation—Laodiceia has suffered from neglect and spoliation. Much of its worked stone was removed for building purposes and, unfortunately, little is being done to preserve its remaining structures from further damage.

History. Laodiceia was a Hellenistic foundation which may have replaced an earlier settlement called Diospolis. According to one tradition the city was established by the Syrian king, Antiochus I Soter (280–261 BC) in honour of his sister Laodice. However, it seems more likely that it was the foundation of his successor Antiochus II Theos (261–246 BC), who named it after his wife. If the latter hypothesis is correct, it would fix the date of Laodiceia's establishment between 261 and 253, the year in which Antiochus II divorced Laodice.

The location was carefully chosen at the junction of two important trade routes, one N–S between Lydia and Pamphylia and another E–W between the Euphrates and the

Aegean. It was c 1.5km from the Lycus, which flows into the Maeander, and it had an assured water-supply from two streams, the Asopus and the Caprus.

Little is known of the early history of Laodiceia. In 188 BC it came under the rule of Pergamum. In 129 BC it passed to Rome becoming part of Province of Asia. When Mithridates VI Eupator, king of Pontus, invaded in 88–85 BC it provided a refuge for a Roman general, but under coercion surrendered him. In 50 BC Cicero, governor of Cilicia, spent some months in Laodiceia administering justice and attempting to redress some of the wrongs perpetrated by his predecessor, Appius Claudius.

It suffered in the civil war that followed the assassination of Julius Caesar and again when Labienus invaded Asia Minor in 40 BC, but during the imperial period Laodiceia prospered. After the earthquake of AD 60 it was able to repair the damage sustained by its public buildings without assistance from the imperial treasury. It is probable that much of the city's wealth came from wool and from the cloth made from it. Laodicean wool was very soft, of a fine texture and deep black. According to Vitruvius it owed its distinctive colour to the presence of certain minerals in the sheep's drinking water.

According to Galen Laodiceia was for a time the sole source of an important medicine called *nard* (spikenard?). Strabo mentions another link with healing. There was, he said, a temple in the neighbourhood of Laodiceia dedicated to the youthful Anatolian moon-god Men, who was often associated with death and rebirth. He continues: 'In my own time a great school of medicine has been established [there]. A market was also held there under the protection of the god'.

However, the principal deity worshipped in the city was Laodicean Zeus or Zeus Aseis. It has been suggested that Aseis may be related to the Arabic word, *aziz* which means powerful. This may indicate a Syrian influence on the cult as among Laodiceia's cosmopolitan population there were many of Syrian origin. There was also a large and prosperous Jewish community whose members had freedom of worship.

Christianity was introduced into Laodiceia by Epaphras of Colossae (see above). It seems likely that the rapid spread of the new faith in the city was assisted by the presence of the Jewish community. However, there were also some who hesitated, as evidenced by John's forthright comment in Revelation 3. 15–17: 'I know all your ways; you are neither hot nor cold. But because you are lukewarm, neither hot nor cold, I will spit you out of my mouth'. During the Byzantine period Laodiceia was an episcopal see and in the 4C an important Church Council was held here.

Badly damaged by an earthquake towards the end of the 5C, Laodiceia never recovered. It was ruled by the Byzantines until the Selçuk and Turcoman invaders swept them away towards the end of the 12C. For some time afterwards the city, known as **Ladik** by its new rulers, continued to be inhabited, but eventually the site was abandoned and the remnants of its population moved to Denizli.

Laodiceia occupied the slopes and level ground on a low hill between the Asopus and Caprus. On the SW approaches to the city there are traces of the **aqueduct** which brought water 8km from a spring in Denizli. Fed into a large tank outside the city walls, it was delivered under pressure to a **water-tower** on the S slope of the hill. The remains of this are still visible.

Near the water-tower are the ruins of the **stadium** which was erected in honour of Vespasian in AD 79. This was 347m long and, like the stadium at Aphrodisias, had rounded ends. According to an inscription it was used for athletics and gladiatorial contests. Only a few rows of seats remain.

To the E of the stadium are the substantial ruins of a building that has been identified variously as a **gymnasium** or a **bath**. This was dedicated to Hadrian and his wife Sabina. Because of its unusual shape and its proximity to the water-tower, Bean's view that it was a bath is now generally accepted.

About 100m to the N are the insignificant remains of an **odeum**. Only a few rows of seats remain. As was often the case, it is probable that the building was also used as a bouleuterion.

Almost in the centre of the plateau are the ruins of a structure, which was built as a **nymphaeum** probably during the reign of Caracalla (211–217), but which was changed several times. In its original form it consisted of a large square basin surrounded by a colonnade on two sides, with two semicircular fountains to the S and E. It was ornamented with statues, including a life-size figure of Isis, and decorative friezes. Note the **inscribed base** of a statue of the consul Anicius Asper, one of the city's benefactors.

During one of the many alterations the square basin was removed and a small chamber built in its place. The structure was then used by the Christian community of Laodiceia for some purpose which, so far, has not been determined. The nymphaeum was excavated by French Canadian archaeologists between 1961–63 when the statue of Isis was discovered.

To the N of the nymphaeum a few stones mark the site of an **Ionic temple**. Beyond, at the crest of the N slope of the hill, are the remains of Laodiceia's two theatres. The **larger theatre** on the right, which faces towards the NE, is reasonably well preserved. Some of the seats and a part of the stage-building are still visible. The **smaller theatre**, which looks towards the NW, retains part of its cavea only.

Laodiceia's fortifications were pierced by gates on the E, N and NW sides. The E gate, the **Syrian gate**, is the best preserved. Note the remains of a **Roman bridge** over the river Asopus below the (NW) Ephesus gate.

As was the custom, burials took place outside the city. Sarcophagi have been found by the sides of the ancient roads which passed through the Syrian and Ephesian gates. It was outside the Syrian gate that the sophist Antonius Poleman (fl. reigns of Trajan and Hadrian) was buried. Tortured by gout, he had himself shut up in the tomb of his ancestors at the age of 65. It is reputed that he cried out as the tomb was being closed, 'Make fast, make fast, let the sun never see me reduced to silence'.

From Laodiceia return to the main road for c 17km Pamukkale.

Just after the small village which nestles at the base of the cliff the road from Denizli begins to climb up to **PAMUKKALE**. Neither the exaggerated prose of travel brochures nor its overexposure on posters are able to diminish the magnificence of Pamukkale. Fortunately, the scale and grandeur of this unique geological formation save it from being spoiled by the misguided commercial exploitation which it has suffered in recent years. It rarely fails to impress.

For countless millennia a spring located somewhere on the plateau, possibly in the neighbourhood of the ancient theatre, has been pouring out streams of hot mineral water. These have plunged down the mountain-side creating in the process enormous circular basins which are fringed with stalactites and surrounded by a huge area of smooth, dazzling, white calcareous rock—hence the Turkish name Pamukkale, Cotton Castle.

The description of Richard Chandler, who visited Pamukkale in the late summer of 1765, has seldom been bettered.

Our tent stood on a green dry spot beneath the cliff. The view before us was so marvellous, that the description of it, to bear even faint resemblance, ought to appear romantic. The vast slope, which at a distance we had taken for chalk, was now beheld with wonder, it seeming an immense frozen cascade, the surface wavy, as of water at once fixed, or in its headlong course suddenly petrified. Round about us were many high, bare, stony ridges; and close by our tent one with a wide basis, and a slender rill of water, clear, soft and warm, running in a small channel on the top. A woman was washing linen in it, with a child at her back; and beyond were cabins of the Turcomans, standing distinct, much neater than any we had seen; each with poultry feeding, and a fence of reeds in front.

By 1939 little had changed. George Bean, who came to Pamukkale that year, describes how 'the white cliffs, the ancient buildings, and the tombs stood deserted, and the sacred pool lay inviting the occasional visitor to a free and solitary bathe'.

Today the sacred pool is enclosed in the grounds of a motel! A modern, highly artificial resort has been created. This has several motels, a museum, a post-office and a clutter of mean shops peddling tawdry souvenirs. The motels concentrate almost entirely on coach parties which fill most of their rooms during the holiday season. Perhaps because most visitors stay for only one night, some motels fail to reach the standard usually obtained in Turkey. In return for high prices travellers get indifferent service and badly-cooked meals from surly, ill-trained staff.

Some of the best accommodation in Pamukkale is in the village at the base of the cliff where there are a number of modest, inexpensive pensions. The number of rooms in the village is limited and demand almost always exceeds supply. If you wish to stay here make an early reservation.

Maladies treated by bathing in or drinking the mineral waters of Pamukkale are kidney and heart disease and ailments of the digestive system. It is very pleasant to lie submerged for hours, especially in the autumn or spring, when there is a gentle nip in the air. The water is only slightly below blood heat and during cold weather a small cloud of steam marks the position of each pool. A leisurely bathe produces a delightful feeling of relaxation and well-being and is an excellent restorative after a strenuous day visiting the scattered remains of Hierapolis. Unfortunately, it leaves a whitish crust on the hair and skin which is difficult to remove.

Try the different pools by purchasing day-passes for a small sum from the motels which have enclosed them. The most impressive is the so-called sacred pool in the grounds of the Pamukkale Moteli, where you swim among submerged Roman columns. There is also a public swimming bath filled from the underground springs. This is clean and cheap, but during the holiday season it is usually very crowded. Its facilities and surroundings also have a distinctly municipal public-utility character and appearance.

History. It is almost certain that the unique appearance and curative properties of Pamukkale's springs attracted settlers from very early times. Herodotus (c 484–420 BC) writes about a city called Cydrara in this area and later there are references to a settlement named Hydrela (ὑδηλός, watery, moist). **Hierapolis**, which is first mentioned in 183 BC in connection with Apollonis, the mother of the Pergamene king Eumenes II Soter (197–160 BC), is believed to derive its name from Hiera, the wife of Telephus. When the Greeks made their first expedition against Troy, she led the women of Mysia against them and was killed by Nireus. The Pergamene dynasty claimed her as one of their ancestors. However, it is not absolutely certain that the city was founded by Eumenes or by one of his predecessors. A number of inscriptions from the 2C and 3C AD contain names like Antiochidos, Seleucidos and Attalidos, which suggests that it may have been a Seleucid foundation perhaps taken over by the Attalids, after the defeat of the Seleucid Antiochus III at the battle of Magnesia ad Sipylum in 190 BC.

With its neighbours Hierapolis became part of the Roman Province of Asia in 129 BC. Apart from the fact that it was devastated by serious earthquakes in AD 17 and AD 60, very little is known about the city's subsequent history. It was a prosperous trading centre producing a number of manufactured products. Inscriptions found here mention coppersmiths and nail-makers and, like neighbouring Laodiceia, Hierapolis had a flourishing wool industry. It also supplied a special kind of marble, whose unique colouring was believed to have been produced by the seepage of mineral water.

Antipater, a philosopher and rhetorician who became tutor to Caracalla and Geta was born here. There were contests and festivals in Hierapolis during the Imperial period. In addition to games based on Pythian and Olympic models, there was a special local celebration, the 'games of the Chrysorrhoas', the golden stream. According to Bean this was a fast-flowing rivulet to the N of the city not far from the necropolis.

Hierapolis seems to have enjoyed a considerable degree of imperial favour. It received help from Nero to repair earthquake damage in AD 60. Hadrian visited in AD 129, Caracalla in AD 215 and Valens in AD 370. Coins of the Claudian era show a temple dedicated to the imperial race, 'genei Sebaston'. In AD 221 Hierapolis was

Travertine basins at Pamukkale

granted the coveted title of Neocorus by the invert and degenerate, Elagabalus (218–222). This was a valuable status symbol. It permitted the city to erect a temple in honour of the emperor and to celebrate imperial festivals at regular intervals. Elagabalus appears on the city's coins of this period offering sacrifice.

As well as Roman emperors the Olympian gods, frequently merged with their Anatolian equivalents, were worshipped in Hierapolis. Thus, Apollo, the city's principal deity, was associated with a local sun-god Lairbenus and Leto, his mother, with Cybele. Poseidon the earth-shaker was feared and placated by its citizens. Offerings were made also to Pluto, the god of the underworld, in a dangerous and sinister cavern located near the temple of Apollo. In view of this religiosity it is not surprising that on some occasions the city's associations with the legendary Hiera were ignored and its name Hierapolis (ἱερα πόλις) was simply taken to mean 'the holy city'. Interestingly, it was also called Hieropolis, 'city of temples', on its coinage as late as the end of the 1C BC.

Like Laodiceia and Colossae, Hierapolis adopted Christianity at an early date. The presence of a sizeable Jewish community probably assisted the spread of the new faith. Hierapolis is mentioned in Paul's epistle to the Colossians:

'Your own fellow-countryman Epaphras sends you his greeting, a servant of Jesus Christ who ever remembers you anxiously in his prayers, hoping that you will stand firm in the perfect achievement of all that is God's will for you; I can vouch for him as one who is greatly concerned over you, and those others at Laodiceia and Hierapolis'. (Colossians: 4, 12 and 13.)

Epictetus was a contemporary of Epaphras. Born a slave in Hierapolis, Epictetus became a Stoic philosopher. Perhaps influenced by the early Christians he wrote about the perfect missionary whose bed is the ground, whose covering is the sky, and who must love those who do him injury.

The apostle Philip is believed to have lived in Hierapolis and to have been martyred here. According to an ancient tradition he was nailed upside down to a tree and stoned to death in AD 80. The remains of a martyrion erected in his honour are on the side of a hill to the N of the city. Another resident of Hierapolis was a disciple of St John named Papias. He was the author of a work, now lost, called *The Sayings of Jesus.*

Justinian (527–565), who instructed John the monophysite bishop of Ephesus in 542 to stamp out paganism, gave Hierapolis the status of a metropolitan see. John's authority extended over the provinces of Caria, Asia, Phrygia and Lydia, so it is unlikely that he ignored Hierapolis. This city so full of reminders of the old gods almost certainly engaged his attention. With his assistant priests and deacons John laboured mightily for several years destroying temples and shrines, demolishing pagan altars and cutting down sacred groves. Then, having made 80,000 converts , he erected 98 churches and 12 monasteries to serve their needs. (John of Ephesus, Vitae Sanctorum Orientalium, XL, XLIII, XLVII. Vide A.H.M. Jones *The Later Roman Empire*, vol. 2.)

Little is known about the history of Hierapolis during the middle and late Byzantine period. No doubt it suffered, like its neighbours, from the incursions of the Arabs, Turcoman and Selçuk raiders. Towards the end of the 12C the city passed permanently into Turkish hands. Shortly after its capture, when the people of nearby Laodiceia moved to Denizli, it, too, was abandoned. The 18C traveller Richard Chandler found only a small Turcoman village at the foot of the cliff. The first scientific examination of the site was made by a German team at the end of the 19C. Italian archaeologists, who began to excavate Hierapolis in 1957, continue with their work.

As the distances between some of the ruins is considerable and a certain amount of climbing is required, allow at least four hours for Hierapolis. Enjoy an alfresco meal on the hillside above the city or in the small picnic area in the copse near the ruined N baths. All the visible remains date from the Roman and Byzantine periods. Nothing earlier seems to have survived.

Behind the museum are the not inconsiderable remains of a 6C **basilica**. This was probably the cathedral of Hierapolis which may have been erected to mark the elevation of the see to episcopal status. The vaulted structure has a large central nave with a semicircular apse and two side aisles. There is a small chapel or baptistery at one end. To the E of the basilica is a section of the **colonnaded street** which ran through the centre of the city roughly in a N–S direction. To the W is the so-called **sacred pool**. Enclosed in the grounds of the Pamukkale Motel, this has a Roman foundation and a number of submerged columns. According to Bean it is believed to have been called, appropriately, Thermodon.

On the right of the road leading to the theatre are the remains of the restored 4C AD **nymphaeum**. A large basin, enclosed by walls on three sides, was approached by steps from the street. There are five niches, three on the back wall, one on each of the side walls, above a broad ledge. Below each niche is a semicircular recess. Water, from a resevoir to the E of the city, poured into the basin from the central niche. The whole structure was elaborately ornamented.

The ruins of the SW facing **Temple of Apollo** lie slightly to the right of the nymphaeum. The Italian archaeologists believe that, while the foundations were laid during the late Hellenistic period, the existing remains of the upper structure date from the 3C AD. The building, which measures c 18m by 13.5m, rests on a shelf of natural rock at the rear. The front, which was supported by an artificial platform c 2m high, was approached by a broad staircase. Behind the pronaos, which was preceded by a row on unfluted columns, lay the cella. There was no opisthodomus.

During the excavation, work was impeded considerably by noxious gas which seeped from the foundations. It was found that this gas originated in the **Plutonium** which lies to the right of the temple and is joined to it by a section of pavement. It appears that the gas was also a problem in ancient

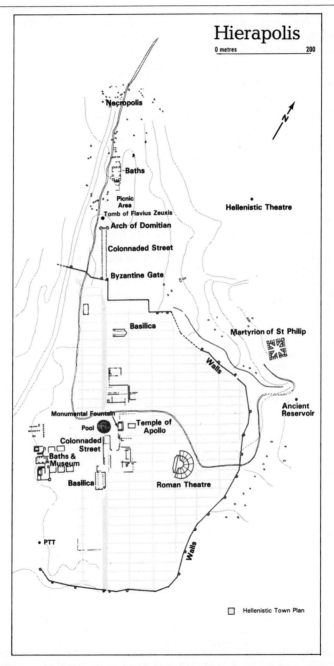

Hierapolis

0 metres   200

Necropolis

Baths

Picnic Area

Tomb of Flavius Zeuxis

Arch of Domitian

Colonnaded Street

Byzantine Gate

Hellenistic Theatre

Basilica

Martyrion of St Philip

Walls

Monumental Fountain

Pool

Temple of Apollo

Colonnaded Street

Baths & Museum

Basilica

Roman Theatre

Ancient Reservoir

PTT

Walls

☐ Hellenistic Town Plan

times, as a number of vents were placed in the substructure to allow it to escape. These are clearly visible on the left side of the platform.

According to Strabo a narrow entrance in the hillside provided access to the Plutonium, a sanctuary dedicated to Pluto, the god of the underworld. In front of the cleft there was a paved area c 4.5m sq which was enclosed by a handrail. The poisonous vapour, visible as a thick mist on the floor of the enclosure, was capable of killing animals as large as a bull. Only the Galli, voluntary castrati, the priests of Cybele, seemed to be unaffected by it. Strabo was not sure whether their invulnerability was shared by 'all who are maimed in this way, whether it resulted from divine intervention or some special physical attributes'.

By the 2C AD the Plutonium appears to have become a tourist attraction. When the historian Dio Cassius (fl. AD 180–229) visited it, he discovered that an auditorium had been built over the enclosure filled with the deadly vapour. Having tested its lethal properties on birds, he remarked also on the apparent immunity enjoyed by eunuchs. In the 5C AD a doctor, Asclepiodotus, penetrated some distance into the chamber. Winding his cloak over his face to conserve a supply of fresh air, he continued to the point where his way was barred by a channel of deep water.

Today three shallow steps lead down into a small dark, paved chamber c 2.75m sq. Waves of noxious vapour rise from a fast-running stream half-hidden in a deep natural cutting c 1m wide at the back of the chamber. The vapour acts like tear-gas, making the eyes water and producing a state of temporary incapacity. For the protection of visitors the entrance to the Plutonium is now closed by an iron grill and the authorities have placed a warning notice there. Fortunately, the disgusting practice mentioned by Bean, of testing the lethal properties of the gas on birds and small animals appears to have ceased.

A 6C house, in the area between the temple and the theatre, has opus sectile paving, wall paintings and a second order of Ionic columns.

Behind the temple and slightly higher up the hillside are the well preserved remains of a late **theatre**. Though slightly larger than a semicircle, it is not Greek, but dates from the 2C AD. It was restored during the reign of Septimius Severus (193–211). An inscription on the stage-building records its dedication and there is a decorative frieze showing the emperor and his family in procession with the gods. Two vomitoria provided access to the cavea which has a diameter of 91m. There was a single diazoma. Note the loge for distinguished spectators in the centre of the cavea. In the middle of the wall of the diazoma there is an inscription which hails Hierapolis as 'foremost land of broad Asia, mistress of the nymphs, adorned with streams of water and all beauty'.

The elaborately ornamented stage-building was c 3.70m high. A number of the reliefs used to decorate it have been left in position, others are in the museum. The frieze from the hyposcaenium was recovered almost intact. This shows the birth of Dionysus, the god of drama and of wine, and his triumphant progress through Asia. The god is in a car drawn by leopards. He has an entourage of capering, ithyphallic satyrs, sileni, bacchantes, a lusty Pan and a well-endowed Priapus. There are also portrayals of a procession and sacrifice at the temple of Artemis and of the punishment inflicted on Niobe and her children by Apollo and his sister, Artemis.

Another inscription states that in the middle of the 4C the stage-building was in urgent need of repair. The necessary work was put in hand on the orders of Constantius (337–361) who was in Hierapolis on 4 July 343. Alterations were also made to the orchestra and the surrounding area at that time, so that it could be filled with water for aquatic displays.

Return to the road and continue up the hill for c 250m. An unmarked turning on the left leads by a rough track across the mountainside to a large

water-storage tank and to the **Martyrion of the Apostle Philip**. The martyrion, which has been excavated and restored, dates from the beginning of the 5C. Approached from the SE by a broad flight of steps, it is a square building with nine small rooms on each outer face. These in turn enclose a central area made up of six rectangular rooms, formed by two crosses placed at an angle to each other, outside a large octagonal chamber. Openings in the centre of the four sides of the building lead directly to the octagon which contained a synthronon. As no trace of an altar or of a tomb has been found, it is believed the martyrion was used for processions and the preaching of panegyrics on the saint's day. The hole in the floor of the synthronon probably marks the position of a lectern. Note the crosses over the arches in the octagon. The small rooms on the outside of the building may have been used to house pilgrims.

From the martyrion continue along the hillside in a NW direction for c 150m to the site of a **theatre** which is believed to date from the Hellenistic period. En route you pass a number of tombs and sarcophagi, all of which have been robbed. Only the outline of the cavea and a few rows of seats remain to mark the position of the theatre. From the upper level of the cavea there is a splendid view over the whole site. The buildings on the plain immediately below the theatre date from the Byzantine period.

Walk downhill from the theatre to the grove where the picnic area is sited. This has rustic tables, seats and barbecue pits. The enormous arches on the right-hand side of the road belong to the **NW baths** which were erected towards the end of the 2C or the beginning of the 3C. The baths were converted into a church in the 5C.

During the Hellenistic and Roman periods burials were not usually permitted inside city boundaries. At Hierapolis some graves have been found outside the Byzantine walls on the SE side, but the city's **main necropolis** was a short distance beyond the NW baths. Perhaps the largest cemetery in Asia Minor, it contains tombs dating from the Hellenistic era to the early Christian period. For c 2km they are on both sides of the road—sarcophagi, in groups or singly, each resting on a low base; house and temple-tombs elaborately ornamented; and circular tumuli surmounted by phallic symbols. The tumuli are not unlike those found in Etruria.

Many of the tombs bear inscriptions and more than 300 of these have been transcribed and published. In addition to information about the deceased, some of the epitaphs prescribe measures to be taken against overcrowding in the cemetery and the protection of graves from desecration or damage. Most content themselves by setting out the fines to be paid by a transgressor, but one quoted by Bean invoked a comprehensive curse against the offender. Having expressed the wish that his life should be without joy or children, it continues 'may he find no land to tread nor sea to sail, but childless and destitute, crippled by every form of affliction let him perish, and after death may he meet the wrath and vengeance of the gods below. And the same curses on those who fail to prosecute him'.

At Hierapolis the tombs were surrounded by gardens which were maintained by guilds established for this purpose. These organisations were also charged with the duty of placing wreaths on the tombs on those days each year which had been nominated by the deceased or his family.

Some of the larger monuments had exedrae, which permitted the citizens of Hierapolis to enjoy the melancholy pleasure of meditating on the transient nature of human life and earthly happiness. They could contemplate the approach of their own inevitable dissolution, while seated in beautiful surroundings and in close proximity to the bones of their ancestors.

A **triple arch** marks the N end of the great colonnaded street which bisected the centre of Hierapolis. Constructed of the local travertine and flanked by two round towers, the arch was dedicated, c AD 83, to Domitian (81–96) by Julius Frontius, Proconsul of Asia. Like the better-preserved Hadrianic arch at Antalya, it had an upper storey, now lost.

A short distance to the right of the Domitian arch is the fine **tomb** of a merchant of Hierapolis, Flavius Zeuxis. Restored by the archaeologists, this had a marble door carved to resemble wood, a Doric frieze ornamented with rosettes and pilasters at the corners. According to an inscription Flavius Zeuxis was a traveller of some note. He claimed to have made 72 journeys by sea to Italy.

The **colonnaded street**, once the commercial centre of the city, has long been abandoned to colonies of torpid, sun-worshipping lizards. On warm days they form decorative patterns on the confused mass of stone blocks and architectural fragments which mark its position. The street is also the lair of youthful shepherds and village boys who, armed with quantities of fake antiquities and fake coins, lie here in ambush for gullible visitors.

From the arch of Domitian return by the modern road to the centre of the site. The **agora** had an area of c 280m x 180m. It was bounded on three sides by stoas, on the fourth by a marble basilica. It is the largest uncovered agora in the Roman world.

Most of the objects found in Hierapolis are in the **museum** which is housed in a **2C AD baths** to the right of the car-park. The restored bath complex had a large palaestra in addition to the usual caldarium, tepidarium, frigidarium, etc. There were also rooms reserved for the worship of the emperor and for other religious and civic ceremonies.

The exhibits, which are well-arranged and clearly labelled, fill several large rooms. They include funerary stelae, a terracotta coffin, a statue of Isis, heads and torsos of Marsyas and Eros, Asclepius, Dionysus and Tyche; sarcophagi, architectural fragments; pins, lamps, medical instruments, jewellery, and coins from the Hellenistic, Roman and Byzantine periods.

From Pamukkale you have a choice of routes. You may return to Yatağan via Denizli and Aydın and continue by Route 20 to Muğla and Marmaris. Or you may follow Route 19 from Denizli to Beyşehir.

19

Denizli to Beyşehir

Total distance (excluding deviations) 505km. Denizli—51km Bozkurt—6km Çardak—56km Dinar—57km Burdur—(15km Kuruçay-Höyügü)—(11km Hacılar)—(45km Tefenni)—36km Çeltik—18km Ağlasun—(7km Sagalassos)—59km İsparta—(28km Kovada Milli Parkı)—36km Eğridir—(Barla)—(29km Aksu)—c 29km Ertokuş Ham—65km Yalvaç—(c 5km Antiocheia in Pisidia)—(42km Akşehir)—(27km İshaklı Han—21km Çay)—(6km Kızıldağ Milli Parkı)—(50km Kubad Abad)—c 72km Eflatunpınarı—20km Beyşehir—(10km Fassılar).

Leave Denizli by the E24. After c 5km a turning on the left leads to Pamukkale and after a further 9km a minor road on the right goes to Colossae. (These places are described in Route 18.) After Bozkurt is Çardak, where Denizli's airport is located, you pass the sterile waters of **Acigöl**. On the shores of the lake, which are coated with a crust of salt, tractors trace a series of convoluted, abstract patterns. The peaks and barren slopes of Söğüt Dağı to the S are reflected in the still, poisonous blue waters. A scene of menacing beauty it evokes memories of Holman Hunt's 'The Scapegoat'.

In ancient times **Dinar** was called Apameia Cibotus. It was built by Antiochus I Soter (280–261 BC) in honour of his mother Apama. After his defeat by the Romans at Mt Sipylus near Magnesia in 190 BC, Antiochus III the Great signed the treaty of Apameia here in 188. Under its terms he ceded all his lands E of Mt Taurus and paid a fine of 15,000 Euboic talents.

According to Strabo (64 BC–AD 25), Apameia was a great emporium, an entrepôt for Greek and Italian merchandise. Today Dinar is a quiet country town. Poplar lined roads lead to the old fashioned *otogar* where cloth-capped farmers and their wives sit with their large, shapeless bundles and wait patiently for the bus or dolmuş which will take them home.

From Dinar Road 650 leads S to (57km) Burdur and, eventually, to Antalya. For the last 10km to Burdur you are not far from Burdur Gölü and the sparkling waters of the lake provide welcome relief from the brown and umber which have dominated this route so far.

Apart from its museum **Burdur** has little for the visitor. It is a good centre for visiting the ancient sites in the area and has one hotel on the Ministry of Tourism list, the one-star *Burdur Oteli*, Gazi Cad. The **Tourist Information Office** is at Cumhuriyet Meydanı, Kültür Sarayı, Kat 2.

A Hittite settlement has been confirmed in this area, and it is believed that the Arzawa royal family originated here. During the Classical period Burdur Gölü was known as Lake Ascania. Bean identified an ancient Hellenistic site called Lysinia on its N bank. All that remains are some walls and a number of rock tombs.

Burdur's **Ulu Cami** was built by Dündar Bey in the 14C. Ibn Battuta, who visited Burdur in the mid 14C, described it as 'a small place with many orchards and streams, and a strong fortress on a hilltop'. He and his companions were well received by the *Akhıya* Brotherhood whose members prepared a lavish banquet in their honour. Beyazit I brought the town under the Ottoman rule in 1391.

The **museum** occupies two rooms in the Ottoman *Bulgurlu Medrese*. Roman statues from Kremna near Bucak are displayed in the first room. They include marble figures of Athena, Aphrodite, Hygeia, Hercules, Dionysus, Asclepius and a bronze Apollo. The objects in the second room are arranged in chronological order. There are Neolithic figurines and pottery from Hacılar; Chalcolithic stone axes, idols and discs; Phrygian pottery; Hellenistic lekythoi and aryballoi; Roman perfume bottles, terracotta figurines, tear bottles, lamps, mirrors, gold, silver and bronze ornaments and jewellery; Byzantine lamps and ceramics; coins from various cities and Phoenician glassware.

In the garden there are statues of Asclepius and Hercules (headless), sarcophagi, grave stelae, dedicatory reliefs to various gods of the region, including Kakasbos (see below), and Roman architectural fragments. The collection of inscriptions is of outstanding historical importance. In the museum's stores ethnographic objects are kept . Some old Ottoman houses restored by the museum authorities are open to the public.

A minor road leads SW through a picturesque stretch of country to Hacılar. This passes near **Kuruçay-Höyüğü**, a prehistoric mound which Professor Refik Duru of İstanbul began to excavate in 1978. The lowest level dates from the Neolithic Age, 5500–5200 BC. The original walls and foundations of the buildings have been left in situ.

The prehistoric site of **Hacılar** is about 1.5km from the modern village. Excavations by Professor James Mellaart were made here between 1957 and 1960 under the auspices of the British Institute of Archaeology at Ankara. He uncovered nine building levels. Burials were discovered in eight of them. In the lowest, dating from the seventh millennium BC, houses made of mud brick were found. During the Early Neolithic Period the people of the settlement were engaged in agriculture, made pottery and had domesticated dogs. The oldest known statuettes of the Anatolian Mother Goddess were found at Hacılar. Dated to the sixth millennium BC, some, now in the Anatolian Civilisations Museum in Ankara, have bloated bodies, staring eyes and massive legs. During the Chalcolithic period the settlement was surrounded by fortifications, the single room houses had plastered walls and ceilings, the inhabitants made pottery by hand and had learned to weave fabrics. Small, nude steatopygous type, reclining figures of the Mother Goddess found in this layer are in the Ankara Museum.

If possible, go to the village of **Tefenni**. At **Kaya Kabartmaları** there are **rock reliefs** of the south Anatolian rider god Kakasbos. Often shown carrying a huge club, he is sometimes identified with Hercules.

From Burdur continue to Çeltiki and here take Road 685 through a picturesque stretch of country to Ağlasun. From this town a new road leads to the site of ancient **SAGALASSOS**, the largest city of Pisidia.

After five years of surveys carried out by an Anglo-Belgian team of archaeologists under the auspices of the British Institute of Archaeology at Ankara, excavations directed by Profesor Marc Waelkens of the Catholic University of Leuven were started here in 1990. Sagalassos was built on the southern slopes of Akdağ at a height of between 1460m and 1560m above sea level. Because of the difficult terrain, streets tended to follow the natural contours. Extensive terracing emphasises the irregular nature of the site. The city may never have been completely fortified. It relied on its postion for defence. In the late Roman period defensive walls linked the public buildings and the inhabitants could shelter in the civic centre, abandoning the residential quarter to the enemy. Although most of the monuments visible are from the Roman period, it is possible to gain a very good impression of Hellenistic Sagalassos when it was perhaps the most advanced city of Pisidia.

The first references to Sagalassos date from 333 BC, when Alexander the Great captured it after a difficult battle. The defenders were, according to Arrian, 'the boldest warriors of a warlike tribe'. The Macedonians lost 20 men and Cleandrus, the commander of the archers. Sagalassos, like the rest of Pisidia, remained largely independent of Hellenistic kings, but was forced to pay a tribute of 50 silver talents and large quantities of wheat and barley to the Roman consul Manlius Vulso, during his Anatolian expedition of 189 BC. Writing in the 1C BC, Livy described Sagalassos as being very fertile and famous for its fruit and a glance from the site down to the rich vegetation in the valley around Ağlasun confirms the accuracy of his judgement. After the arrival of Christianity, it became an episcopal see and there was a Christian community here until the 10C.

For part of the way from Ağlasun a modern highway covers a Roman road which was flanked by a number of Roman heroa. Traces of houses were also found, perhaps the winter quarters of the Sagalassians. The upper city is the oldest part of Sagalassos. One of the highest in the Roman Empire, it was exposed to the rigours of winter. Here are the ruins of a **Hellenistic heroon**, which was decorated on three sides with a frieze of dancers (now stored in the village). Below and to the W of the heroon there are the ruins of a **Doric temple in antis** which is believed to date from the late Hellenistic period. It was probably dedicated to the south Anatolian rider god Kakasbos. Figurines of a god on horseback, wearing a Phrygian cap and carrying a round shield and a sword, spear or club were found in the spoil. The late Hellenistic **bouleuterion** was below the temple and to the W of the **upper**

agora. The agora's 2C AD monuments have been restored. To the SE of the agora there was a Roman **macellum** dedicated to the emperor Commodus (180–192) and and his wife Crispina.

Just to the N of the **lower agora** was the **odeum** with an estimated capacity of 2000–3000. This was partly masked by a Hadrianic **nymphaeum**. There was a **temple** dedicated to Apollo Clarius and the Theoi Sebastoi and patris on the W side of the lower agora. This was rebuilt by a local family during the reign of Augustus as an Ionic peripteros. It was dismantled during the 5C and rebuilt as a basilica with a narthex, three entrances on the W side, and an apse on the E.

To the E of the lower agora there was a Roman **baths complex**, one of the largest in southern Asia Minor. It measured 80m E/W and 55m N/S. Because of the steep slope it had three storeys. There was an exercise area 12.8m wide on the E side of the building.

A **street**, colonnaded in parts, 280m long and 9m wide connected the lower agora with the southern gateway. The difference in levels of c 25m between the northern and southern ends was overcome by building it in three sections which were connected by monumental stairways. The northern section probably dates from the 1C BC.

To the E of the N/S street a **temple** dedicated to Antoninus Pius and the Patrioi Theoi (the Gods of the city) occupied a level stretch of ground. This was a Corinthian peripteros with six by eleven columns. Measuring 26.8m by 13.8m, it had an unusually deep pronaos (8m) and a short cella (9.3m).

On the NE of the city there are well-preserved remains of the 2C AD **Roman theatre**. Most of the seats and a large part of stage building are still standing. To the W of the theatre are a **late Hellenistic nymphaeum** and the remains of a **library**, buuilt under Trajan (98–117) and apparently restored during the reign of Julian (360–63). Both have been uncovered by the Belgian excavators. A **potters' quarter** occupied an area of c 15,000 sq m to the E of the theatre. Ten kilns, workshops, moulds and dumps containing thousands of rejected pots have been found. They date from the Late Hellenistic period to the early 6C AD. Sagalassos must have been a major production centre of pottery for the home and export markets.

As was customary, burials took place outside the city. Tombs have been found on the NW side and there were necropolises on the N and W.

Sagalassos is a romantic place redolent of history. Go there when mist covers the desecrated tombs on the hillside and sheep huddle for shelter among the tumbled stones of the theatre's vomitoria. Walk alone through the deserted streets and listen. The mist blurs reality, eliminates time. Are those muffled sounds the soft murmur of ancient voices, are those distant cries the echoes of long forgotten battles?

From Ağlasun continue on Road 685 to **İsparta**. In the gardens of İsparta grow the roses from which Turkey's most famous perfume is produced. İsparta is a good centre for visiting an interesting part of Pisidia. Railway enthusiasts will enjoy the steam train which puffs its unhurried way to Eğridir. (There is some doubt about the continued operation of this service. Enquire at the Tourist Office about the current position.)

Accommodation and Information. İsparta has four hotels on the Ministry of Tourism list: the four-star *Büyük İsparta Oteli*, Kaymak Kapı Mey. (recommended); the *Bolat Oteli*, Demirel Bul. 87 (recommended); the *Artan Oteli*, Cengiz Topel Cad. 12B and the *Mustantkı* Sok, 128 (both two-star); and the one-star *Erkoç Oteli*, Demirel Bul. 71. The **Tourist Information Office** is in the Hükümet Konağı, Kat 2.

History. İsparta appears to have been a town of no great importance until the invasions of the Persians and Arabs and the wars between Byzantium and the Turks reduced its neighbours to penury. During the 12C and 13C it was the premier episcopal see in Pisidia. Taken by the Turks in 1203, it became, towards the middle of that century, the capital of a minor principality centred on the Pisidian lakes. It was governed by the Hamid Oğulları until 1381 when the ruler disposed of it to the Ottomans.

Apart from the **castle** of the Hamitoğlu, which is in a ruinous condition, there are no buildings of interest in the town. The **museum** has a collection of objects from nearby ancient sites and of ethnographic material from the İsparta region. Note particularly the fine statue of a river god which was found at a sanctuary outside the Zindan Mağarası near Aksu to the E of Eğridir in 1977. The sanctuary overlooked the source of the ancient Eurymedon river, the Köprü İrmağı which reaches the Mediterranean near Aspendus. The statue, which is believed to date from the reign of Antoninus Pius c AD 150, is made of fine crystalline marble. It is of a clean-shaven young man who holds a cornucopia in his left hand. A cloak draped over his left shoulder leaves the right side of his torso bare. The statue has suffered some damage to the head and right arm. An inscription on the base states: 'The city set up the statue for the manifest god Eurymedon at its own expense; Attalus, son, grandson and great grandson of Attalus, was the supervisor'. The city was probably Tymbriada and the Attalus mentioned a member of the civic aristocracy. (A fuller account of the discovery of the sanctuary and the statue by Durmuş Kaya of İsparta Museum appears in *Anatolian Studies Vol. XXXV.*)

The **Kovada National Park** offers forest walks, water sports, fishing, climbing and camping. The season is from May to September. During the summer months Yürük people live in goat-hair tents near the lake, guarding their flocks which graze the *yayla.*

A short drive through some interesting country brings you to the pretty lakeside town of **Eğridir**, ancient Prostanna. The town's modern name is probably related to the Greek word Akroterion which means a precipitous mountain or a promontory. As Eğridir means 'it is bent', the inhabitants prefer to call the town Eğirdir, which means 'she is spinning', and adduce a legend about a king, his dead son and his wife to support their choice.

Today Eğridir earns its living from tourism and from a food freezing plant processing fruit and gourmet foods such as frogs' legs and snails which find a ready market in Europe. It is also a training centre for commandos, the élite troops of the Turkish army.

Accommodation and Information. There are two three-star hotels on the Ministry of Tourism list: the *Canan Oteli*, Yeşilada Mah, 15 and the lakeside *Eğirdir Oteli*, Kuzey Sahil Yolu (recommended), and also the *Çolak Pansiyon*, İplikçiler Pazarı. The **Tourist Information Office** is at 1 Sahil Yolu 13.

History. The earliest traces of occupation including the site of Prostanna itself are on Davras Dağı which towers more than 2600m above the lake. This is a military zone. During the Byzantine period Prostanna was abandoned and a settlement, which has developed into the present town, was established on the southern shore of the lake. After its conquest by the Turks, with İsparta, it was ruled by the Hamid Oğulları dynasty. In the 14C Ibn Battuta described it as 'a great and populous town with fine bazaars...(by) a lake with sweet water'. Like İsparta it came under Ottoman rule in 1381. The centuries that followed were marked by a steady decline.

Eğridir's **Ulu Cami** dates from the 15C. The nearby Selçuk *medrese*, which dates from the late 13C or early 14C, has been restored and its cells turned into smart shops. It was constructed of materials taken from the early 13C Eğridir Han. Note the re-used Byzantine capitals on some of the columns of the porticoes. Little remains of the **castle** except its imposing walls.

Thursday is market day in Eğridir. Country people bring their produce to town. Bargains are struck and sales made in the crowded market place. In the autumn this is the place to buy Eğridir's famous apples.

The town is connected by a causeway to two islands, **Can Ada** and **Yeşilada**. According to the 18C French traveller Paul Lucas, Yeşilada was inhabited exclusively by Christians. There are some fine old houses and a church, which was closed after the departure of the Greeks in the 1920s.

Excursions. You can make boat trips on the lake and to villages like Barla on its western shore. **Barla** is to be identified with Parlais, a colony established by Augustus to control the rebellious Pisidians. Parlais coins were inscribed IUL. AUG. COL. PARLAIS. Pottery sherds have been found in the cemetery and there are architectural fragments in the walls flanking a modern road, which runs through it, and built into the W side of the mosque. Note the fine Selçuk minaret ornamented with glazed tiles. Visits to ancient **Prostanna** are also possible. As the site is near the army base, it may be necessary to obtain a permit. Enquire at the Tourist Office about this and about boat trips.

At **Aksu**, formerly Anamas, there is a small Roman bridge. The shrine outside the nearby Zindan Mağarası was associated with the worship of the water god of the ancient Eurymedon river. A statue of the god, which was found here, is now in the İsparta Museum (see above). Inscribed and decorated stones were also discovered around the cave. The 13C Selçuk **Yılanoğlu Camii** in the town is worth a visit.

The road from Eğridir follows the eastern shore of the lake for c 40km. A short distance before the early 13C Selçuk **Ertokuş han**, which was on the caravan route between Denizli and Konya, the road turns inland. Pause here for a last look at the beautiful Eğridir Gölü. An ornamental portal provides access to the Han's courtyard which measures c 18m by 27m. There are vaulted rooms on each side.

Continue for c 10km to the junction with a minor road on the left which is signposted **Yalvaç**. This town supposedly derives its name from Yalvaç, a leader of the Oğuz Turks, who captured it after the battle of Manzikert in 1071. Sited on a windswept steppe at the base of the Sultan Dağları, Yalvaç is visited mainly because of its proximity to the site of the ancient city of Antiocheia in Pisidia. Apart from the mosque, which is built almost entirely of material taken from ancient buildings, and a small museum there is little to detain the visitor in Yalvaç.

The ruins of **Antiocheia in Pisidia** are on the mountain slope to the NE of Yalvaç on the road to the village of Hisarardı. The ancient city was probably founded by Antiochus I Soter (280–261), with settlers from Magnesia ad Maeandrum. Antiochus, who had conceived a mad passion for his stepmother, Stratonice, married her with his father's permission. He acquired the sobriquet Soter, Saviour, after he had defeated the Celts in battle by using armed Bactrian elephants against them, but later died fighting the invaders. The treaty of Apameia ended Seleucid rule in western Anatolia in 188 BC and, with other territories, in 39 BC Antiocheia was given by the Romans to Amyntas, the ruler of Galatia. It reverted to Roman rule after his death in 25 BC, was settled with army veterans and renamed Colonia Caesarea Antiocheia.

SS Paul and Barnabas visited Antiocheia and Paul preached in the synagogue drawing a large crowd of Jews and Gentiles. This infuriated some members of the regular congregation and they persuaded the rulers of the city to have the apostles expelled. (Acts, 13 and 14).

Antiocheia suffered badly during the 7C and 8C from attacks by Arab raiders. After the battle of Manzikert it came under the rule of the Oğuz Turks.

Excavations were conducted at Antiocheia between 1912 and 1929 by archaeologists from the University of Michigan. There is a useful plan at the site which shows the location of the principal monuments. The first remains on the road from Yalvač are those of a **triple-arched gateway**, probably of the late 2C AD. The main feature of the site is the acropolis (in fact the centre of the Roman colony) where there was once a monumental triumphal Corinthian-style **triple arch** which probably dates from c AD 50. Apart from one relief of a Victory figure, little can now be seen. A copy, in Latin, of the Res Gestae of Augustus was found here in 1912. (See also: Ankara, Temple of Augustus.)

A double **portico** with Ionic columns below and Doric above provided access to the so-called **Augustus Platea** which is enclosed on the eastern side by a steep, semi-circular rock wall. Here was sited a **temple** which was dedicated to the Imperial cult. A stone stairway led to a tetrastyle porch and the temple stood towards the rear of a large platform. Much of the decorated entablature from the temple carved in hard, fine-grained limestone can be seen around the rock-cut foundations. It includes one Corinthian column capital and two friezes, one with bulls' heads. The high-quality workmanship can be dated between AD 25–50.

On the N side of the so-called **Tiberia Platea** there are the ruins of some shops. The games inscribed on the pavement introduce a human note. Near the platea are the remains of two **Byzantine basilicas**. Outside the city there are substantial sections of an aqueduct. Remains of a **nymphaeum** and a **bath house** are at the N end of the city. The marble seats of the ruined **theatre** were carted away to Yalvaç during the last century, but the cavea can be made out on the slope of the hill.

Before leaving Yalvaç spend a little time in the **museum**. In the first room there are objects from Antiocheia and a chronological display of ceramics, stonework and glassware dating from c 2500 BC to the 4C AD. Note particularly the Roman statues, busts and figurines from the area around the ancient city. The second room has an ethnographic display and in the third room there are paintings by Turkish artists, Ottoman manuscripts and inscriptions. In the garden and museum colonnades Roman and Byzantine sarcophagi, reliefs, grave stelae, architectural fragments and amphorae are displayed.

Other finds from Antiocheia are in the museums of Afyon, Konya and the Archaeological Museum in İstanbul. The latter has a fine 2C AD statue of a local woman, Cornelia Antonia, and a head of Lucius Verus (AD 161–9). This emperor, who had a reputation for pleasure-seeking and who enjoyed gladiatorial games, conducted a successful campaign against the Parthians between 162 and 166. There is also a 2C AD **votive stele to Men** which bears a four-line Latin inscription.

From Yalvaç return to the road junction and continue through a picturesque stretch of country to **Akşehir**, the ancient Philomelium. Frederick Barbarossa passed through this town with his army in 1190 en route, not to the liberation of Jerusalem as he hoped, but to his untimely death in the Göksu river near Silifke.

After his defeat by Tamerlane, near Ankara, in 1402, Beyazit I was brought here where he died on 9 March 1403. According to Gibbon, Beyazit was well treated by his conqueror, who 'mingled with just reproaches a soothing pity for his rank and misfortune'. Quoting the Persian historian Şerefeddin Ali, he relates how Tamerlane met Beyazit at the door of his tent and, seating him by his side, greeted him as the 'champion of the Moslems'.

Nasreddin Hoca, the early 15C wise fool about whom a corpus of amusing, often bawdy, anecdotes has accumulated, lived here for 50 years. One of the stories, which is still told with gusto in Anatolia, records his reply to a trick question posed by Tamerlane. The emperor asked the sage to divide five eggs fairly among three persons—Tamerlane, one of his wives and himself. Without hesitation Nasreddin Hoca replied, 'Here is one for you, your majesty, and since you have two below your waist, that makes a total of three eggs for you. This one is mine, and that makes three for me too. And the other three are for your wife, for she has none below the waist'.

Charles Eliot, writing at the beginning of the century, describes the tomb of Nasreddin Hoca as a small domed building partly open at the sides. Under the dome hung the huge green turban, as large as an umbrella, which the sage had worn. At his request a small opening was left in the masonry covering his grave so that he could look out at the world of men. A joker to the end, the tomb gives the date of his death as 1366 AH i.e. AD 1950. Today the *türbe* of Nasreddin Hoca is one of the Islamic monuments which attract many Turkish and foreign visitors to the town.

Ulu Cami, with its five aisles and a *mihrab* dome, has suffered from restoration. An inscription records its repair by Alaeddin Keykubad at the beginning of the 13C. The date 1213 appears on the minaret. The **Taş Medrese**, built by the Selçuk vizier Sahip Ata in 1250, is a three-*eyvan* building with a *mescid* open to the façade. The brick minaret has two balconies. It now houses a **Museum of Stonework**. In the courtyard there are inscribed stones, grave stelae and architectural fragments from the Roman, Byzantine, Selçuk and Ottoman periods. Noteworthy are the Selçuk grave stones and the large fragment of a Sidamara-type sarcophagus.

In a pine grove on the hillside is the **Seyid Mahmud Hayrani Kümbet** which was completed in 1409. Like the tomb of Mevlana in Konya this has a fluted drum supporting a conical roof, a reminder of the tents used by the nomadic Turks. Note the cruciform plan of the interior.

If not pressed for time, you may like to visit the ruined **İşaklı Han**, which is 27km to the NW of Akşehir, and the town of Çay which is 21km farther on. The *han*, which was built by Sahip Ata in 1249, follows the classical plan with the kiosk *mescid* in the courtyard. At **Çay**, the **Taş Medrese** has an interesting lion motif on the portal and elaborate mosaic ornamentation inside. The ruined **Çay Han** was built by Oğul Bey bin Mehmed in 1279 for Ebul Mücahit bin Yakup. Note the relief of a lion rampant with a dragon's tail and the big triangles on the portal which is in the form of a niche with a half dome.

From Akşehir return S to the junction for Yalvaç and continue on Road 695 in a SE direction towards Beyşehir. After c 15km a turning on the right offers a choice. Nature lovers may be tempted by the road which goes S straight to 6km **Kızıldağ Milli Parkı**. From May to October there are facilities for camping and picnicking among the cedar trees. Lovers of the antique may opt for the road to Yenişarbademli, which will take them to 50km **Kubad Abad**, the site of Alaeddin Keykubad's fortified summer palace.

Keykubad's choice of this site for his summer palace was not accidental, as places overlooking a large stretch of water were favoured by early Turkish rulers. The archaeologists have laid bare substantial remains of the building which dates from c AD 1230. Its walls, lapped by the waters of the lake, were covered with painted stucco and beautiful tiles, some of which were made nearby. In the harem and private apartments the star-shaped and cruciform tiles bore representations of animals real and mythical: lions, dragons, single- and double-headed eagles, sphinxes, sirens and gryphons. Many were made by the underglaze technique which had black painted motifs under a turquoise glaze. Fine examples of the tiles from Kubad Abad are in the Çinli Kösk in İstanbul and of the tiles and painted stucco in the Ceramics Museum in Konya.

Diagonally across the lake from Kubad Abad is Eflatunpınar. From Akşehir Road 695, never far from the eastern shore of Beyşehir Gölü, passes through a particularly pleasant stretch of country. About 37km to the SE of Şarkikaraağa, look for a signposted turning on the left. **Eflatunpınarı** means the Spring of Plato. It is one of the many place names in Anatolia which mention the philosopher. In Turkish folk history he was regarded as both a wise man and a miracle worker.

This Hittite monument is not carved from a rock face but composed of huge blocks of masonry. It stands in a natural pool formed by a spring which was enlarged during the Hittite period by a dam and sluice. In the lower centre of the monument there are two seated figures. These may be Hattic deities. The male figure on the left with the conical head dress the sun god Estan, and the female on the right with the halo-like hair style the sun goddess Wurusemu. They are flanked by genii. Two of these support a huge winged sun symbol. A suggested reconstruction after Mellaart places two colossal copies of the deities below, on top of the platform. One of these may be the enormous statue which was found abandoned at Fassılar, c 10km SE of Beyşehir. It is known that springs played an important part in the Hittite religious ceremonies, and Eflatunpınarı may be an elaborate version of the many sacred springs which have not survived.

Gertrude Bell, who visited Eflatunpınarı in 1907, captured the numinous quality of the place. 'It was very hot and still; clouds of butterflies drifted across the path and there was no other living thing except a stork or two in the marshy ground and here and there a herd of buffaloes with a shepherd boy asleep beside them... a heavy thunderstorm gathered and crept along the low hills to the east and up into the middle of the sky... the clouds broke upon us in thunder and lightning and I saw the four Hittite kings, carved in massive stone, against a background of all the fury of the storm'.

From Eflatunpınarı return to Road 695 and continue to **Beyşehir** which occupies a pleasant position on the southern shore of Beyşehir Gölü. There are no hotels on the Ministry of Tourism list nor a Tourist Information Office in this small town, but it is only 92km from Konya where accommodation is usually available. (For Konya, see Route 31.)

Beyşehir was established by Keykubad I (1219–36) as a staging post on the trade route which linked Alanya and Antalya with Konya, the capital of his kingdom. In Classical times it was known as Mistea, a small Pisidian city which continued into Roman and late Roman times, on the shore of the ancient lake Koralis. Apart from some Islamic buildings, it has few reminders of the past. The Selçuk citadel and fortifications no longer exist.

The **Eşrefoğlu Camii**, which was completed in 1299, is one of the most refined examples of the Selçuk 'forest mosques'. Its roof rests on wooden consoles supported by 48 wooden pillars, the section over the nave being raised slightly like a gable. There is a brick dome over the *mihrab*. The spacious interior is divided into seven aisles. Note the high stone portal, the dark turquoise tiled *mihrab* and the fine wooden *mimber*. The *kümbet* of the founder has some delicate tiled mosaics on the inside of the dome.

The museum is in the rebuilt **Selçuk bedesten**, opposite the mosque.

At (10km) **Fassılar**, a colossal stele was found in the stadium of an Roman city. Now in the garden of the Museum of Anatolian Civilisations at Ankara, this may have been intended for the Hittite monument at Eflatunpınarı.

20

Yatağan to Marmaris

Total distance 75km. Yatağan—22km Muğla—30km Gökova İskele—
Idyma—(Şehir Ada/Cedreae)—30km Marmaris—(20km Hisarönü)—(7km
Amos)—(c 41km Bozburun).

From Yatağan Road 550 passes through a rather dull and uninteresting
stretch of countryside to 22km Muğla. If you wish to bypass Muğla, take
the right-hand fork immediately before the town.

Muğla, ancient Mobolla, is the provincial capital and the marketing and
trading centre for the region. There are two three-star star hotels in Muğla,
the *Petek Hotel* and *Özalp Hotel*, and a number of pensions. The **Tourist
Information Office** is in Cumhuriyet Meydanı, Belediye Atapark Sitesi.

Mobolla was for some time during the 2C BC under Rhodian rule. There
are the remains of buildings from this period on a hill behind the town. To
the SW were the cities of Pisye (modern Pisiköy) and Thera. At Pisiköy there
are traces of the acropolis and a few scattered stones. The remains of Thera
are equally scanty. In 333 BC it was occupied briefly by the Persian
Orontobates who succeeded the Hecatomnids as ruler of Caria.

After the first Turkish invaders had consolidated their hold on Caria in
the 14C, Muğla was much favoured by the Menteşe emirs. A reminder of
their rule is provided by **Ulu Camii** which was built by İbrahim Bey in 1344.
There are a number of interesting Ottoman houses in the old quarter.

Beyond the outskirts of Muğla, the road begins a steady climb through
low hills covered with thorny scrub. This uninspiring landscape is no
preparation for the splendid view, presented without warning, from the
crest of the Çiçeklibeli Pass. Almost 800m below the 'flower-decked' pass
is the fertile plain at the head of Gökova Körfezi, the ancient Gulf of
Ceramus. As the road descends you get tantalising glimpses of the glittering waters of the gulf, of its islands and sheltered bays. To the S an avenue
of eucalyptus trees marks the turning for Marmaris, while away to the E is
the great lake at Köyceğiz. A restaurant-café on a terrace below the crest
of the hill is an excellent place to admire this magnificent panorama.

History. From a very early period the cities of Rhodes possessed territory—the **Rhodian
Peraea**—in this part of Caria. After the formation of a unified Rhodian state in 408 BC,
the Carian territory was ruled from the island and its people were granted Rhodian
citizenship. Confined at first to the Loryma peninsula to the SW of Marmaris, in the
course of time the Rhodian Peraea extended as far N as Stratoniceia and as far E as
Caunus. Later it was reduced considerably in size, but the influence of Rhodes
continued to be felt in SW Caria as late as the 2C AD.

The remains scattered along the hillside belong to ancient **Idyma**. One of
the earliest references to this city dates from the beginning of the 5C BC,
when it was a member of the Delian League. It came under the rule of
Rhodes sometime before 200 BC.

Clearly visible from the road is a substantial section of the wall of the
acropolis. In the centre of the fortified area are the remains of a building
which had several rooms. Lower down the hill are the ruins of a **medieval
fortress** and a number of **rock-cut tombs**. Two of these, constructed in the
form of Ionic temples, are believed to date from the 4C BC.

A turning to the right at the foot of the hill leads to the small village of **Gökova İskele**. This is a pleasant place for a picnic or a meal in one of the small restaurants that look out over the gulf.

A short distance across the gulf is **Şehir Ada**, where there are the ruins of ancient **Cedreae**, which derives its name from the Greek word for cedar. Although a Carian foundation, Cedreae was also a member of the Delian League. During the Peloponnesian War it paid dearly for its support of Athens. Besieged and captured in 405 BC by the Spartans under Lysander, its unfortunate inhabitants were sold as slaves. Later Cedreae came under the domination of Rhodes.

You can reach the island by boat from Gökova İskele or from the villages of Gelibolu or Taşbükü on the opposite side of the gulf. In addition to the remains of substantial fortifications, complete with towers, there are traces of a **Doric temple** dedicated to Apollo and the considerable ruins of a medium-size **theatre**. All are buried in dense vegetation. According to inscriptions three athletic festivals were held in Cedreae. The city's **necropolis** on the mainland has a number of sarcophagi and vaulted tombs.

At the bottom of the hill the road divides. One branch goes E along the plain to Köyceğiz, Dalaman and Fethiye, the other S to Marmaris. The road to 30km Marmaris starts as a splendid straight avenue, 2km long, of tall, umbrageous eucalyptus trees. It then passes into the pine woods, where the famous *çambalı*, pine honey, is produced. Following a winding, convoluted course through shaded gorges, it rises gradually to the Çetibeli Pass, before descending from 550m to sea-level at Marmaris. Near Çetibeli village is the pleasant Çağlayan Pınarbaşı Restaurant.

The pine-clad hills, which encircle **MARMARİS** and its long fiord-like harbour, are a refreshing change from the coarse, brown maquis which predominates in the SE Mediterranean.

In recent years the yacht-marina has brought the rich and famous from Turkey and abroad to Marmaris. Unfortunately, its popularity is reflected in the prices charged by many of the hotels, restaurants and shops. There have been reports of the unfriendly attitude adopted by some of the town's youths towards foreign visitors, a sad result of over-exposure to tourism.

Information, Accommodation, Transport. The current Ministry of Tourism booklet lists two five-star hotels, 16 three-star, 28 two-star, and five one-star hotels in and around the town. In addition there are four holiday villages and many pensions. The *Yavuz Oteli* and the *Begonya* Hotel (a converted Ottoman mansion), both three-stars, are recommended. The **Tourist Information Office** at İskele Meyd. 92.

Many of the hotels, which cater almost exclusively for foreign visitors, are some distance from the centre. Some provide a free minibus service to and from the town, but in many cases it is necessary to use taxis. The slow, but not uncomfortable, tractor-drawn trailers offer a useful alternative.

As parking is not permitted on the Kordon, if you stay in the town centre you may have to leave your car some distance from the hotel. Enquire at the Tourist Information Office about transport and parking arrangements before making a hotel reservation. There are many good restaurants near the marina.

There are yacht cruises, yacht-charters, and day trips to **Datça**, **Cnidus**, the beaches on the **Loryma peninsula** and the islands.

Tickets for the c 3-hour boat-journey to Rhodes (passport required) are available from travel agents. It is advisable to book well in advance.

There are frequent bus services to İzmir (c 6 hours) and Fethiye (c 2 hours), and dolmuş services to Muğla, Bodrum, Köyceğiz and Datça.

Passengers arriving at Dalaman airport may be able to make the c 100km journey to Marmaris by one of the special minibuses meeting the charter flights. (Enquire about transport arrangements from the airport to Marmaris, when buying your air ticket.) Otherwise they can travel by regular bus or dolmuş from Dalaman village.

History. Marmaris occupies the site of ancient **Physcus** a deme that was attached to the city of Lindus. Although little is known about the early history of Physcus, it was under Rhodian rule by the latter part of the 4C BC.

In 1522 the forces of Süleyman the Magnificent were assembled in Marmaris for the successful assault which he mounted against Rhodes. According to a contemporary account a Turkish fleet of 700 ships, manned by 40,000 sailors and carrying 20,000 auxiliaries, sailed from İstanbul to Marmaris. There it was joined by an army of 140,000, which, with Süleyman at its head, had marched overland from the capital. Further reinforcements of ships and men were provided by the buccaneer-adventurer Cortoğlu. The great harbour of Marmaris was able to accommodate this vast force without difficulty, as it was able later to shelter the fleet of Nelson. In 1798 the British ships sailed from here to Egypt, where at the battle of Aboukir they defeated the French, earning for their commander the title of Baron Nelson of the Nile.

The scanty remains of Physcus, first recorded by C.T. Newton in the mid 19C, are on Asar Tepe, a hill c 1.5km to the N of Marmaris. Only the ruins of some **Classical and Hellenistic fortifications** are visible.

The picturesque **castle** near the yacht-marina dates from c 1522. Restored and refurbished, it is now the town's ethnographic museum. There are a few pieces of sculpture and some inscriptions of interest in the playground of the high school. These include a **relief of a youth** with a horse, a headless **marble lion** and a **marble female head** from the Roman period.

To the E of the town, in **Atatürk Parkı**, there is a grove of the rare **oriental sweet gum tree**. Not unlike a small plane tree, this has star shaped leaves interspersed with hanging bunches of round fruit.

There are a number of minor ancient sites on the **Loryma peninsula** to the S of Marmaris. Because of their attractive locations they attract large numbers of visitors. Many can be reached by road. However, it is more pleasant and a good deal less tiring to visit them during a leisurely boat-trip along the coast. Allow a day so that there is time for a bathe and a picnic meal at one of the fine beaches. Boat-trips around Marmaris are reasonably priced. Enquire at a travel agency or book directly with the boat operator.

Near the mouth of the great harbour, about one hour's boat-journey from the town or 7km by road, is the site of **Amos**. There are the remains of a Hellenistic wall, 3.5m high in places. Note the towers and gate on the N side. There are the foundations of a small **temple in antis** and of a moderately well-preserved **theatre**. Sections of the seating and parts of the supporting walls of the **cavea** remain standing. There are also traces of the stage-building. The principal deity of Amos was Apollo Samnaios.

The ancient city of **Loryma**, at the tip of the peninsula, can only be reached by boat. On a slender promontory, dominating the sheltered harbour of Bozukkale, there are the ruins of an impressive, elongated fort. An ashlar wall 2.5m wide, strengthened by nine towers on the long sides and by one at each of the narrow ends, enclosed an area measuring c 320m by 27.5m. Zeus Atabyrius, a Rhodian deity, was worshipped in Loryma.

The harbour of Loryma provided a sheltered base for the Athenian fleet during the Peloponnesian War. Conon, the Athenian commander, spent some time here before the sea-battle near Cnidus in 394 BC (see below) which effectively ended Spartan influence in this part of Caria. Almost a century later, when the Diadochoi fought over Alexander's empire, Demetrius, the son of Antigonus the One-eyed, assembled here part of the force, which he employed against Rhodes, the ally of Ptolemy. Despite the use of 40,000 soldiers, 200 warships, 170 transports, 30,000 labourers and an array of catapults and siege-engines, he was unable to capture the city. After a year's siege he was forced reluctantly to agree terms with the Rhodians and withdraw.

After the strait between the Greek island of **Symi** and the mainland, continue to **Bozburun** which is at the head of a deep, sheltered inlet. There is also a rough road to c 41km Bozburun, via Amos, from Marmaris. Near the village of **Saranda** (ancient deme of **Thyssanus**) inscriptions referring to rites connected with the worship of Zeus and Hera have been found.

Further to the N at the end of the Hisarönü Körfezi, near the village of **Hisarönü**, is the site of **Bybassus**. (This may also be reached by a minor road which is on the left of the Datça road c 17km from Marmaris.) Apart from traces of Hellenistic walls on the side of the acropolis, little remains of the ancient settlement. The fort on the top dates from the Middle Ages.

Bean reports the discovery of a **shrine** on the ridge of Evren Dağı, 274m above the plain to the S of Hisarönü. This was dedicated to a minor goddess called Hemithea. Traces of a 4C BC Ionic temple with Doric accretions have been found here. Surrounded by a colonnade of 11 by 6 columns, this had a **pronaos** and **cella** only. Hemithea was a goddess of healing, frequently invoked in cases of difficult childbirth. For about two centuries a festival called the Castabeia was held here in her honour.

21

Marmaris to Cnidus

Total distance c 108km. Marmaris—c 70km Datça—(c 4.5km Datça İskele)—c 38km Cnidus.

A daily service by dolmuş and minibus links Marmaris to 70km Datça. If you wish to continue to Cnidus, hire a taxi in the village or, if you arrive early enough, take one of the boats which, during the holiday season, operate from Datça İskele. If you are not staying overnight in Datça, check the departure time of the last service back to Marmaris, as sometimes this leaves in the afternoon.

Shortly after leaving Marmaris (see Route 20) the road enters the Reşadiye peninsula at its narrowest point near the little village of **Bencik**. Only c 800m wide, and no more than 15m high, this part of the peninsula is known in Turkish as Balıkaşıran, 'the place where the fish jump over'. Historians believe that it was here the inhabitants of Cnidus, faced with the threat of a Persian invasion in the middle of the 6C BC, tried to separate the peninsula from the mainland by cutting a channel through the isthmus.

From Bencik the road follows a tortuous course through pine woods, now clinging to the high, steep sides of the peninsula's backbone, now descending to the sea. Before reaching Datça it passes through a number of isolated forest-clearings where stacks of timber and the neat houses of the foresters are the only signs of man's presence in this wild, beautiful country.

The picturesque village of **Datça** attracts visitors who like its quiet, relaxed atmosphere—a pleasant contrast to the frenetic activity of Marmaris and Bodrum in the holiday season. Datça İskele, c 4.5km to the S, is the village's harbour. This is a popular port-of-call for yachts.

The village has two three-star hotels, one two-star hotel, a holiday village and several pensions. The **Tourist Information Office** is in the Hükümet Binaı. There is no accommodation at Cnidus.

The most pleasant way to go to Datça and Cnidus is by boat from Marmaris. Apart from enjoying a leisurely cruise, you will avoid a tiring road-journey, have more time at Cnidus and can swim and picnic en route. During the season there is also a boat-service between Bodrum and Cnidus. The voyage can take between three and five hours—it depends on the weather and the size of the boat. If the *meltem*, the NW wind, is blowing, this crossing may be uncomfortable for all but the most hardened sailors.

If you have not brought a picnic, lunch at one of several restaurants in Datça or ancient **CNIDUS**. The fish dishes are particularly good.

History. According to one ancient account, Cnidus was founded by Dorians from the Peloponnese in the early part of the first millennium BC, shortly after the end of the Trojan War. However, it is also claimed that a group of colonists from Argos led by Triopas, a hero of uncertain lineage, formed the nucleus of the first settlement. Triopas is commemorated by a shrine dedicated to Apollo, which it is believed was in Cnidian territory near Palamut Bükü, a bay between Datça and the promontory of Deveboynu. The original site of Cnidus was near the village of Datça.

Largely because rough terrain made communication with the hinterland difficult, Cnidian expansion was by sea. By the mid 6C BC the city had set up a number of colonies—first on the N coast of Sicily then on the nearby island of Lipari. It was also an active participant in the Greek trading post established in Egypt in the 7C BC at Naucratis near the mouth of the Nile. The success of the colonisation and commercial enterprises undertaken by Cnidus may be gauged by the splendid offerings which the city deposited in its treasury at Delphi.

Following their victory over the Lydians in 546 BC the Persians occupied, one by one, the Greek cities on the Aegean mainland. In a desperate attempt to keep the invaders from their doors, the Cnidians tried to isolate their peninsula from the mainland by cutting a deep channel at its narrowest point—probably near the village of Bencik. Many of those engaged in this desperate venture were seriously injured on the face or in the eyes by flying splinters of rock. Dismayed by these unlucky portents the Cnidians sought the advice of the oracle of Delphi. The reply can hardly have been welcome. The god told them to abandon their plan, adding that if Zeus had wanted to make their land an island, he would have done so. The Cnidians accepted the advice and surrendered their city to the Persian general Harpagus.

After the invasions of Greece by Darius and Xerxes had been defeated at the battles of Marathon, Salamis and Plataea, the Delian League was established c 478 BC to limit Persian expansion. Most Greek cities and towns on the Asian mainland enrolled in the League and were obliged to make an annual contribution to its funds. Cnidus was assessed for a sum which varied between two and five talents. The Athenian admiral Cimon based his fleet of 200 ships at Cnidus in 468 BC. From here his forces went on to defeat the Persians decisively at the battle of the Eurymedon river c 467 (see Aspendus). In 412 BC Cnidus transferred its allegiance briefly to Sparta. However, after the victory of the Athenian Conon at a naval battle near Cnidus in 394 BC put an end to Spartan influence in the area, it returned to the Athenian fold. Following the signing of the King's Peace in 386 BC, Cnidus came once more under Persian rule. Liberated by Alexander the Great in 334 BC, like its neighbours its possession was disputed by the Diadochoi after his death.

About 360 BC the Cnidians moved their city from near Datça to Tekir at the tip of the peninsula. This apparently inexplicable change of location from a relatively fertile stretch of land to the barren and almost waterless area at Cape Crio, the modern Deveboynu, was made for sound commercial reasons. When the *meltem*, the strong NW wind, blows, ships sailing from the S are unable to round the cape. Obliged to shelter for days at a time in the fine new harbour, which the Cnidians constructed at the cape, the crews contributed substantially to the city's revenues.

By the end of the 4C BC Cnidus, like its neighbour Cos, had established a medical school which produced a number of well-known practitioners. Their care was not limited to the citizens of Cnidus. They travelled widely. Ctesias (fl. early 4C), one of a family of Cnidian doctors, earned the gratitude of the Persian Artaxerxes II, when he cured the Great King of a severe battle-wound. While at the royal court Ctesias collected information for the *Persika*, his entertaining, if somewhat inaccurate,

23-volume history of Persia. Fragments of this work and of his *Indika*, a book about India, together with synopses in the *Bibliotheke* of Photius, the 9C AD Patriarch of Constantinople, give some idea of their style and quality.

Eudoxus of Cnidus (408–335 BC) was a philosopher, astronomer and mathematician. Some of his work on the doubling of the cube, the volume of spheres, and conic sections was incorporated in Euclid's *Elements*. Credited with the discovery of the star Canopus, Eudoxus formulated a number of theories to explain the movement of the stars and the planets.

About 279 BC Sostratus of Cnidus designed and constructed the Pharos, the great lighthouse of Alexandria. One of the Seven Wonders of the Ancient World, the Pharos was commissioned by Ptolemy I Soter and completed during the reign of his son Ptolemy II Philadelphus (282–246 BC).

When Lieutenant Spratt visited Datça in the middle of the 19C, he commented on the olive groves and fruit orchards in the fertile area around the village. To some extent the presence of these trees represented a continuing tradition, as in ancient times Cnidus was well-known as the source of a number of gourmet products. Its vinegar was comparable to the best produced in Egypt and it was renowned for a type of cabbage known as 'briny'. Best of all was Cnidian wine which was believed to improve the blood and ease the movement of the bowels. Even when drunk in immoderate quantities it produced no ill effects. On the contrary it soothed an upset digestion.

Down to the middle of the 2C BC, while Cnidus was under the rule of Rhodes, it continued to prosper. Thereafter the city's fortunes entered a downward spiral, though it managed to retain some importance. During the Imperial period Cnidus was declared a 'free' city and after the adoption of Christianity it became an episcopal see.

Not much is known about the last days of Cnidus. Its exposed position must have made it very vulnerable to attacks from the sea. At first the raiders were common pirates in search of booty. Later came the Arab corsairs, who terrorised the coastal cities of the eastern Mediterranean from the 7C onwards and caused many to be abandoned. Sometime in the late Byzantine era the last inhabitants of Cnidus moved away and the city was abandoned to the fox and jackal and largely forgotten.

One of the first travellers from Western Europe to visit Cnidus was James Caulfield, fourth Viscount Charlemont. To remove him for a time from the perils and pleasures of mid-18C Dublin's dissolute society, this rich and handsome youth was despatched by his mother on a grand tour of Greece and Turkey. On Sunday 9 November 1749 Charlemont's ship, like many before it, was delayed by contrary winds near Cape Crio (Develoyna). Remembering that here was the 'favoured seat of that universally adored divinity',

Quae Cnidon
Fulgentesque tenet Cycladas et Paphon
Junctis visit oloribus.

('Who holds Cnidos and the gleaming Cyclades, and visits Paphos with yoked swans'. Horace, *Odes*, 3,18, 13-15), Charlemont had himself rowed ashore to ancient Cnidus.

The young man was impressed by the ruins of the city, particularly by the fine theatre of white marble. He noted in his diary that the seats were 'hollowed in, or shaped into a concave form, for the greater convenience of sitting'. Higher up the hill, at the ruins of a magnificent temple of Parian marble, he speculated that this might be the building which had housed Praxitele's masterpiece, the famous nude statue of Venus.

Not only was the city favourably placed for trade, but Charlemont thought its position must 'have greatly contributed to the delight, as it certainly did to the wealth of the inhabitants, who in their parties of pleasure could every day vary their visits to innumerable great and polished nations'. Venus, he concluded, could 'not have chosen any habitation more worthy of Loves and Graces'.

Little more than a half-century later, while conducting a survey of the southern Turkish coast for the Admiralty during the years 1811 and 1812, Captain Beaufort landed briefly on Cape Crio. In *Karamania* he wrote:

On each side of the isthmus, there is an artificial harbour; the small one has a narrow entrance between high piers, and was evidently the closed basin for trieremes, which he [Strabo] mentions. The southern and largest port is formed by two transverse moles; these noble works were carried into the sea at the depth of nearly a hundred feet; one of them is almost perfect, the other, which is more exposed to the southwest swell, can only be seen under water.

One of Beaufort's sketch plans of Cnidus shows the location of the city's two theatres and of the moles in the S harbour. The remains of both moles now lie under the clear waters of the bay, where they constitute a dangerous obstacle for modern vessels.

William Gell visited Cnidus on behalf of the Society of Dilettanti in 1812. An account of his travels and discoveries is contained in *Ionian Antiquities* (Vol. I 1821, Vol. II 1840). In 1857 Charles T. Newton conducted some excavations at Cnidus. The fine statue of Demeter and the colossal marble lion, which he discovered in the city, are now in the British Museum. The exploration of Cnidus has been continued in this century by American archaeologists from Long Island University under the direction of Miss Iris Love. They began a systematic examination of the site in 1967.

It is clear that the old city of Cnidus near Datça was not abandoned when the bulk of the population moved to the new settlement at the tip of Cape Crio. However, apart from the ruins of its fortifications, little remains of the earlier foundation. The city's **acropolis** was on a promontory c 1.5km from Datça İskele. No buildings remain standing inside the walls, but evidence of occupation over a long period is provided by the large quantity of pottery sherds recovered by the archaeologists. These date from the 7–2C BC. It would seem that at some point the old city of Cnidus was renamed Stadia. This usage continued during the Byzantine period and is echoed in the name of the modern village of Datça.

A road linked Stadia to Triopium where the members of the Dorian Hexapolis (see above) held a festival in honour of Apollo. In addition to the usual athletic and musical competitions horse-races formed part of the celebrations. After Agasicles, a competitor from Halicarnassus, broke with tradition by keeping his prize, a bronze tripod, instead of dedicating it to Apollo and leaving it in the sanctuary of the god, his city was expelled from the league. That left Cnidus as the only mainland member of the renamed Dorian Pentapolis. The site of Triopium is believed to be near the village of Kumyer which lies behind Palamut Bay.

New Cnidus fell into two well-defined sections, one on the mainland, the other on the island to the S. Most of the public buildings were located on the mainland, while private houses occupied the greater part of the terraces on the island. Cnidus was laid out on the gridiron plan, popularised by Hippodamus of Miletus. This had streets crossing at right-angles. In many places the gradient was so steep that, as in Priene, flights of steps had to be constructed. The Cnidians built an artificial causeway, pierced by a channel, between the island and the mainland. This was flanked by the naval harbour, Strabo's 'harbour of the triremes' on the N, and by the larger commercial harbour on the S. It was in the S harbour that vessels waited for the fair wind which would allow them to continue their voyages.

During the course of centuries the channel in the causeway became filled with silt, so creating the narrow isthmus which now joins the former island to the mainland. Parts of the area to the S of the isthmus are closed to visitors for security reasons.

To the W of the city wall, not far from the modern lighthouse, there is a fine **Roman tomb**. Entrance to the burial chamber is through a vestibule. Note the fine black-and-white mosaic on the floor. In the chamber, which has an apse at the rear and niches in the side walls, archaeologists found the remains of three sarcophagi.

There are the ruins of a number of private houses on the island terraces which faced the commercial harbour and the mainland. Near the S mole are the remains of an ancient **lighthouse**.

Visible on the isthmus are traces of the ancient **bridge abutment**. The agora of Cnidus was located at the the foot of the hill to the N of the harbour of the triremes. In the Byzantine period two large churches were built here.

It is a stiff climb up the steep hillside to the N of the harbour of the triremes to the site of the 4C BC **Temple of Aphrodite Euploia**, Aphrodite of the fair voyages. This was identified partly from the descriptions in ancient writers and partly from the discovery of a large quantity of erotic and pornographic pottery in the area around the ruins. A circular structure surrounded by 18 Doric columns, which supported a cupola, it rested on a stepped base. The altar, on which sacrifices were made, faced the main entrance, which was in the customary position, on the E side of the building.

The temple contained a famous **statue of Aphrodite** by the Athenian sculptor Praxiteles (active c 370–330 BC). About 360 BC his studio contained two representations of the goddess. One, which was clothed, was purchased by the Coans, the other, which portrayed Aphrodite *in naturalibus*, was chosen by the citizens of Cnidus to be the principal ornament of their city. Believed to be the first monumental free-standing statue of a woman, the Aphrodite of Cnidus became the standard against which all subsequent representations of feminine beauty were measured. Subjected to profound critical appreciation and prurient voyeurism in equal measure, it was, according to Pliny, one of the great tourist attractions of the ancient world. Many travelled specially to Cnidus from afar to see it. Some, having seen it, wished to possess it. Nicomedes, king of Bithynia wanted the statue so badly that, in exchange, he offered to pay all the city's outstanding debts.

The best surviving description of the temple and of the statue of Aphrodite Euploia is contained in a dialogue known as the Erotes or Love Affairs. Sometimes ascribed to the 2C AD satirist and philosopher Lucian of Samosata (c AD 117–180), it was probably written by a later admirer and imitator. The Pseudo-Lucian, as many contemporary and earlier aesthetes had done, came by ship to Cnidus to see Praxiteles' masterpiece. Before going to the temple he played the part of the diligent tourist. Accompanied by two friends, who were according to him skilled in the art of love, he visited the the principal sights of the city. Having sauntered through the portico of Sostratus, he examined the goods offered for sale and found 'no little amusement in the wanton products of the potters, for I remembered I was in Aphrodite's city'.

There follows an interesting account of how some worshippers paid their respects to Aphrodite. Approaching the temple from the E, they entered a garden, whose shaded alleys were lined with bay trees, planes, cypresses and sweet-smelling myrtle, a plant beloved of the goddess. They passed the entrances to secluded bowers closed by screens of ivy, that symbol of true love, and vines heavy with bunches of grapes. 'For Aphrodite is more delightful when accompanied by Dionysus and the gifts of each are sweeter if blended together.' Then, after they had offered sacrifice and admired the famous statue, they made their way to one of the quiet alcoves scattered throughout the garden there to celebrate the rites of love to ἀφροδισιάζειν.

According to Pliny the statue of Aphrodite was so placed that it could be examined from all sides. This is confirmed by the Pseudo-Lucian. Having inspected it with great care, he concluded that the back view was as beautiful as the front. Noticing a small dark patch on the inside of one thigh, he asked the temple guardian if this were due to some flaw in the marble. It was, she told him, the result of an ancient scandalous occurrence. A young man became so infatuated with this representation of Aphrodite that he spent every day in the temple contemplating its beauty. Carried away by the strength of his unnatural love, he contrived one evening to secrete himself in the sanctuary and to spend the night alone with the statue. Next morning the result of his illicit passion was all too clearly visible. The youth, perhaps overcome by remorse for his sacrilegious act, jumped from a high cliff into the sea, but the stain remained as a permanent reminder of his sin.

The American archaeologists have discovered a plinth, which they believe supported the statue of Aphrodite Euploia. An imperfectly preserved inscription found nearby bears the letters PRAX and others, which have been teased out to spell out the name of the goddess. Of the statue itself no trace has been found. The cult of Aphrodite incurred the wrath of early Christian moralists like Clement of Alexandria, who railed against the licentiousness which surrounded it. As a result the temples of this goddess, born of the foam that sprang from the 'lecherous member' of Ouranos, as Clement described it, suffered greatly. It is unlikely that her temple at Cnidus, with its garden of love and statue, escaped the general orgy of destruction of pagan shrines which followed the adoption of Christianity.

Some idea of the power and beauty of the Aphrodite of Cnidus may be gained from the city's coins. In addition, a few copies or variants of Praxiteles' masterpiece, produced for the delectation of wealthy admirers, have survived. They are now in Munich in the Glyptothek (the so-called Venus Pudica), in New York's Metropolitan Museum and in Rome in the Museo Vaticano and the Museo Capitolino.

To the E and S of the temple of Aphrodite are the substantial remains of a **monumental building**. So far it has not been possible to establish the purpose for which this was constructed. On a lower terrace a confused heap of architectural fragments marks the position of a small marble Hadrianic **temple** which was recorded by members of the Society of Dilettanti. Seven steps on the E side of this Corinthian-style building led up to to the pronaos. Entrance was through a façade ornamented with four columns. The sides had six engaged half-columns, while a section of the pediment was decorated with a handsome relief of shields.

To the W are the foundations of a **temple**, which, according to an inscription, was dedicated to Apollo Karneios, a manifestation of that deity much honoured by the Spartans. Pausanias suggests that the punning epithet Karneios was derived from κράνειαι, the cornel trees sacred to Apollo which grew on Mt Ida near Troy and which were cut down to make the Wooden Horse. A festival, the Κάρνεια, was established by the Spartans to propitiate the angry god. In this part of the city the archaeologists found an unusual **sun-dial** which showed the seasons as well as the hours.

S of the temple are the ruins of a massive **Doric stoa** which was c 113m long and c 16m wide. Some authorities identify this with the *Pensilis Ambulatio*, the famous hanging walk which Sostratus (see above), built for his native city.

Just to the N of the commercial harbour are the substantial remains of the **lower theatre** of Cnidus. Constructed during the Hellenistic period, it was modified later. The stage-building, including an elaborate scaenae frons, dates from the Roman era. The theatre, which had 35 rows of seats separated by two diazomata, had an estimated seating-capacity of 8000. Many of the seats are in good condition though the orchestra is largely covered with coarse herbage. Of the **odeum/bouleuterion** of Cnidus, which was a short distance to the E of the theatre, little is visible today.

If you have enough time and energy climb the steep slope that rises from the bouleuterion to the **shrine of Demeter and Kore**. Here, under the lowering crags of the acropolis, volcanic action has created a smooth cliff face, c 18m high and 98m long, in which three niches for statues or offerings were carved. Below the cliff an artificial terrace 76m long and 46m wide is supported on three sides by polygonal walls. The shrine, constructed c 330 BC through the generosity of a pious benefactor, was a comparatively small structure. It contained the cult statues of Demeter, Kore and a number of other deities associated with the growth and cultivation of corn.

The majestic **Demeter of Cnidus**, now in the British Museum, was found here towards the middle of the 19C by C.T. Newton and taken back to England by him. The head and body of this impressive work of art were carved from separate blocks of Parian marble. It is the product of an unknown Athenian sculptor who was active in the middle of the 4C BC.

A short distance to the E are the scant remains of a large **theatre**. Early in the 19C this was robbed of its stone which was sent to Egypt. There it was used to construct a residence for the upstart Albanian militia officer Mehmet Ali (1769–1849), who ruled that country from 1805 to 1848.

The best-preserved section of the fortifications of Cnidus is on the E side of the acropolis. The city walls, which enclosed two-thirds of the island and an area c 1.6km by 800m on the mainland, were constructed of regular ashlar. Strengthened at intervals by towers, they had three gates, two on the N and one on the E side of the city.

To the S of the city on a cliff high above the sea was the so-called **lion monument** of Cnidus. Dated to the 2C or 3C BC, this was composed of a sandstone base 12m square which was covered with marble and ornamented with Doric half-columns. This was surmounted by a stepped pyramid crowned with the marble statue of a recumbent lion. In the base was a circular chamber c 5m in diameter which was surrounded by 12 alcoves. In view of its size—it was 19m high—and prominent location, it is believed that the monument was a communal tomb erected to honour the dead of an important naval victory. The **statue of the lion** found at the site by C.T. Newton was brought to England by him aboard HMS *Supply* in 1858. It is now in the British Museum, near the Demeter of Cnidus.

Some distance to the E of the city is an extensive **necropolis**. It contains a large number of tombs of many different kinds.

22

Marmaris to Fethiye

Total distance 146km. Marmaris—62km Köyceğiz—14km Akçakavak—(7km Dalyan/Caunus)—24km Dalaman—42km Fethiye.

There are frequent bus and dolmuş services from Marmaris to 62km **Köyceğiz**, a picturesque village a short distance to the S of Road 400.

Take Road 400 N to the plain of Gökova. At the end of the avenue of eucalyptus trees turn right and continue in an easterly direction. On the left are the craggy slopes of Boğa Dağ, the Bull Mountain, which give way to the bleak and forbidding peaks of Ali Dağ as you approach Köyceğiz.

The turning on the right to the village, offers no hint of the splendour that lies at the end of the main street. Just beyond a small, well-maintained public park stretches the great expanse of **Köyceğiz Gölü**. This enormous freshwater lake is particularly entrancing when seen in the soft light of early evening. The lake is alive with wild life. Look out for egrets and herons, pygmy cormorants and storks. Migrating ibis and spoonbills pause here on their long journeys.

Köyceğiz village will be appreciated most by those who subscribe to the philosophy of *dolce far niente*. The best time to come here is late spring or early autumn. Then candlelit dinner on the terrace of the well-run Özay Oteli, a few metres from the lake's edge, is an experience to be savoured at the time, and remembered later with pleasure.

Information and Accommodation. The **Tourist Information Office** is at Atatürk Kordonu, No. 1. Köyceğiz has one five-star, one four-star, two two-star hotels and several pensions. The two-star *Özay Oteli* is recommended. There are a few pensions

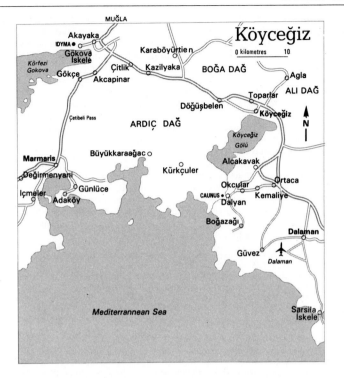

at Dalyan. The rather spartan *Keramos* is probably the best of the bunch. For fresh fish, usually sea bass or mullet, try the friendly *Çınaraltı restaurant* in Köyceğiz.

Although action has reduced the numbers of mosquitoes, they have not been eliminated completely. Use one of the modern repellent creams. The hotels provide sprays and other devices which keep bedrooms free of mosquitoes and other insects.

An interesting whole-day **excursion** may be made to the site of ancient **CAUNUS**. Take a taxi or dolmuş to Dalyan, where you can lunch near the river and continue by boat to Caunus. This excursion can be extended down the river to the sea.

During the holiday season there are boat-trips to Dalyan and Caunus—details of the cost and frequency from the Tourist Information Office.

Take the new road to Dalyan or Road 400 to just beyond the village of 14km **Akçakavak**. A signpost on the right marks the turning to 7km Dalyan. This minor road has a good surface, but is narrow and has many sharp bends. It carries a considerable amount of local traffic so be prepared for encounters with tractors, farm-machines and straying livestock.

Sleepy **Dalyan** achieved a degree of international fame when Turkish and foreign conservationists campaigned against proposed tourist developments which would have disturbed its unique environment and would have had an adverse effect on the breeding-ground of *Caretta caretta*, the loggerhead turtle, on the seashore S of the village. The Turkish Government accepted their arguments. The beach has been made a protected area and is closed to visitors between 20.00 and 08.00 from June to September, the months when the eggs are laid and the young turtles hatch.

The ponds and ditches near the river are full of *Rana ridibunda*, stripe-necked terrapins, marsh frogs and non-poisonous water snakes like the dice snake, *Natrix tessallata*. Somnolent tortoises congregate on the banks and vivid blue flashes marks the darting flight of kingfishers. In spring green and blue damsel flies, *Agrion sp.*, add their colours to the scene.

Behind the main street the Dalyan river flows deep and fast between its reed-lined banks. Here the boats leave for their trips downstream to Caunus and beyond. Here, too, is an excellent restaurant, the *Denizatı*, the Sea Horse, where friendly waiters serve good food and wine at very reasonable prices. Fish-lovers will want to try the fresh bass and mullet.

Across the river a group of Carian temple-tombs, clearly visible from the tables on the restaurant's outdoor terrace, are a silent reminder of the transient nature of human pleasures.

During the season boats take parties of up to 25 persons to **CAUNUS** and to the beach at intervals during the day. The tariff is fixed by an association to which all the boat-operators belong. Out of season you will have to agree a price with the boatman of your choice. If a visit to the rock-tombs is included, allow at least three to four hours for the excursion, and a further two hours for journeys that continue to the sea.

History. Sherds found at Caunus suggest that a settlement of some kind existed here as early as the 9C BC. A work of the 5C BC, the *Periplus* i.e. the Account of a Sailing Voyage, attributed to the Pseudo-Scylax, states that Caunus was a Carian foundation. There is no evidence that the Greeks ever established a settlement here. When the Carian cities were hellenised, it became fashionable to trace their foundation to a deity, demi-god or hero. Possibly to keep up with this trend and to explain the very un-Greek name of their city, which may be of Hittite or Lelegian origin, the Caunians 'discovered' an eponymous founder.

Caunus, according to Ovid (*Metamorphoses IX 431ff*) and a number of other ancient writers, was the son of Miletus and, consequently, the grandson of Apollo. One account states that he fled to Caria to escape from the incestuous advances of his twin sister Byblis. 'Not as a sister loves a brother did she love Caunus'. Another version suggests that Caunus was the guilty party and that he went into voluntary exile, as he was unable to control his unlawful desires. These stories may account for the expression 'a Caunian love', which was frequently used to describe an unhappy romance.

Worship of Caunus was not limited to his own city. A trilingual inscription found at Xanthus in Lycia refers to the establishment there of a cult in honour of the 'King' (Basileus), a deified version of Caunus. There is some evidence that this deity continued to be honoured into Roman times.

As, according to the legendary accounts, Miletus had been expelled from Crete by Minos, the Caunians believed that their ancestors too had come from that island. This is not accepted by Herodotus, who held that the Caunians were of Anatolian origin. However, both their customs and language marked them as being different from their nearest neighbours, the Carians. They adapted the Carian script, by the addition of a number of special characters, to meet the requirements of their own language. Neither Carian nor its Caunian variant has yet given up its secrets.

When c 540 BC the Persian Harpagus invaded Caria and Lycia, Caunus and Xanthus were among the few cities to offer any resistance. According to Herodotus, they shared a close relationship. This may explain the shrine in Xanthus dedicated to Caunus.

Perhaps because of fear of Persian reprisals the Caunians did not at first join the revolt of the Ionian cities which took place in 500 BC. After the defeat of the allies at the battle of Lade in 494 BC and later near the river Marsyas, Persian rule was re-established over the city. It did not last long. The expeditions of Darius and Xerxes against Athens and her allies came to grief at Marathon (490 BC), Salamis (480 BC) and Plataea (479 BC), and a defensive organisation, the Delian League, in 478–477 BC was formed to curb Persian expansionism. Caunus became a member of the League, its contribution being fixed at half a talent. This was later raised to ten talents. However, it is not certain that either sum was ever paid.

Cross the river Dalyan to visit ancient Caunus

The victory of the Athenian admiral-general Cimon at the battle of the Eurymedon river near Aspendus c 467 BC provided a further check to the Persians. However, after the defeat of Athens in 404 BC at the end of the Peloponnesian War, the victors, the Spartans, proved to be inept rulers. Very quickly they lost control of the League and its members, as a result Persian rule was soon re-established, a fact formally acknowledged by the King's Peace in 387 BC.

Caunus became part of the satrapy of Caria which was governed by Hecatomnos and his successors. The Hecatomnid dynasty rapidly developed a considerable degree of independence from Persia, particularly under Mausolus, the son of Hecatomnos. Evidence of Mausolus' interest in Caunus is provided by the discovery in the city of statue-bases bearing his and his father's name. The long walls surrounding the city suggest that he had grandiose plans for its development.

The decisive victories of Alexander the Great over the Persians at the battles of the Granicus in 334 BC and Issus in the following year heralded a period of comparative freedom for Caunus. Like Caria, the city probably came under the rule of Ada, the last of Hecatomnids, until 323 BC, when Alexander's successors, the Diadochoi, began a prolonged and unseemly struggle for the division of his empire. Caunus, like its neighbours, was caught up in the imbroglio. Antigonus, Ptolemy, Lysimachus and their descendants all ruled the city at different times.

Towards the beginning of the 2C BC Caunus was purchased from the Ptolemies by Rhodes for 200 talents. However, in 167 BC the Caunians, with the help of their neighbours, succeeded in throwing off the Rhodian yoke. Despite protests from Rhodes, Rome gave the city its freedom. This it retained until 129 BC, when it was incorporated in the newly-formed Roman Province of Asia.

In 88 BC Caunus made a fatal error. It supported Mithridates against Rome. As in Ephesus and a number of other cities in the province, there was a ruthless and bloody massacre of Roman citizens in Caunus. After the defeat of Mithridates, the Romans punished Caunus in 85 BC by returning it to Rhodian rule. With some interruptions this state of affairs continued well into the 1C AD.

Although Caunus appears to have been a wealthy city—it was famous for its exports of salt and slaves—it had few claims to fame and produced few citizens of note. Because it was reputed to be an unhealthy place, not many foreigners chose to live here. Furthermore, the dour, unattractive character given to its people by many of the ancient commentators can hardly have attracted immigrants.

In ancient times the unhealthy appearance of the Caunians was attributed in part to their addiction to fruit which was believed by many physicians, including Galen, to be a dangerous food. However, there seems little doubt that malaria was the real cause of the city's health problems. The marshes, which extended around Caunus then, as now, provided an ideal breeding-ground for mosquitoes.

Among the many jokes made about the health of Caunus and of its citizens, perhaps the most amusing is attributed to the 4C BC citharist and wit, Stratonicus. Noting the greenish cast of their complexions, he remarked that in Caunus he understood for the first time Homer's statement: 'as are the leaves of the trees, so are the generations of men'. When the Caunians protested, he replied tartly, 'How could I possibly call your city unhealthy, when every day dead men may be seen walking its streets!'.

Though the site of Caunus was known from the middle of the 19C, it attracted few scholars until George Bean made a series of exploratory visits here between 1946 and 1952. Since 1967 Turkish archaeologists, under the direction of Professor Baki Öğün and Associate Professor Ümit Serdaroğlu, have conducted surveys and excavations. During the same period the rock-tombs at Dalyan have been studied by Paavo Roos of the University of Lund.

The rock-tombs at Dalyan are not always included in the excursion to Caunus. If you wish to see them, tell the boatman before embarking. An additional payment may required. Allow c 30 minutes for the visit, which requires a crossing of the swift Dalyan river, and a scramble up a slippery mud-bank and the rocky slope below the cliff-face. Here there are large colonies of the mining bee, *Eucera sp.* In spring there are clouds of yellow butterflies, *Gonepteryx cleopatra*, and large tortoise shells.

There are two kinds of rock-tombs at Dalyan— simple chambers hollowed from the cliff in the lower row and more elaborate temple-tombs higher up. Most are believed to date from the middle of the 4C BC, a time when the Hecatomnid dynasty ruled Caria. Some see the use of Greek architectural forms in the service of the ancient, indigenous tradition of rock-burial as an interesting example of Hellenic influence.

Most of the tombs have two or more Ionic columns in antis. Some are surrounded by a passageway, others have an empty space above the roof which may be flat or barrel-vaulted. Inside there are usually three benches on which the bodies of the dead were laid. Finds in the tombs have shown that they were used and reused down to the Roman period. All those excavated had suffered at some time from the hands of tomb-robbers. Many

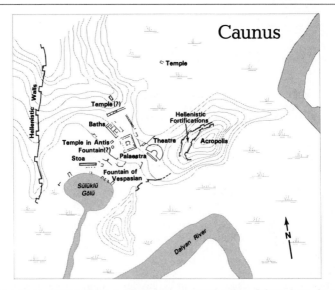

have been damaged by earthquakes or weathering. Others have been destroyed deliberately by human action e.g. to make lime. A number have been partially demolished by ignorant treasure-hunters, who believed, mistakenly, that they contained valuable grave goods. Today some of the tombs are used by the local farmers to shelter animals.

Note the large **unfinished tomb** in the upper row. The roof, pediment and frieze were completed, as were the tops of four capitals. Below the rock-surface was smoothed, but no further work was undertaken.

A short distance to the W of the principal group of rock-tombs are a number of Carian-style burials. The graves are cavities cut from the rock and covered with stone lids. Nearby are niches in which the mourners left offerings for the dead.

From Dalyan the river swings around in a wide arc to the S before it turns again towards the site of Caunus. The boat passes through the modern fish-trap which has replaced an older installation located near the village. It enters a narrow channel. This is fringed by swaying banks of tall, golden reeds which reflect, distort and magnify the sound of the engine, turning it into a rhythmic, hypnotic beat.

From the landing-stage at Caunus a wooden causeway stretches across a marsh to firm ground. From here it is a short walk to the site. The city is c 5km from the sea, separated from it by a vast expanse of fen, the result of centuries of activity by the Dalyan river.

The **acropolis** of Caunus was to the SE of the city on a steep hill which was once surrounded on three sides by the sea. The great harbour to the NE is now a marshy plain, while **Sülüklü Gölü**, the Lake of the Leeches, is believed to mark the site of the W harbour. According to Strabo, this could be closed in times of danger by a chain. On the summit of the 152m-high acropolis-hill are the ruins of a **Hellenistic fortified area** which is sur-rounded by a fine ashlar wall measuring 39m by 20m. The lower fortifications date from the Middle Ages or later.

To the NW and N of the city is one of the best preserved **defensive walls** in Anatolia. Around 8m high and strengthened with towers, it resembles the defences of Iasus and Heracleia under Latmus. Enclosing a vast area, which never appears to have been used productively, it ends abruptly at a cliff overlooking the village of Dalyan. The N stretch is believed to have been constructed by Mausolus. The NW section is later, probably dating from the Hellenistic period.

Near Sülüklü Gölü are the remains of a 1C AD Roman **nymphaeum**. Sometimes called the 'fountain of Vespasian' because an inscribed slab bearing that emperor's name was found in the street nearby, the nymphaeum has been restored by Turkish archaeologists. On its S wall there is the text of an interesting decree on customs dues. To encourage foreign traders to make greater use of Caunus a number of citizens donated 60,000 denarii to the city's treasury. Certain remissions of duty were offered, e.g. slaves, for which Caunus was famous, could be exported tax free.

To the N of the nymphaeum there was a two-storey, **Hellenistic stoa**, 94m long and 6.30m wide, which faced the harbour. This was ornamented with statues and had exedrae. Among the statue-bases discovered here one bore the name of Mausolus, another that of Hecatomnos.

On a raised terrace to the NE are the ruins of a **mysterious building** which some believe was a fountain, others a bathing pool. Dated to the late Hellenistic period, it was encircled—except on the E—by flat-fluted columns on a narrow stylobate. Entrance was on the E by way of a three-stepped, semicircular exedra. Slots in the columns suggest that the space between them was closed by a grille. Inside the building a low plastered wall, surmounted by unfluted columns, surrounded a shallow pool. In the centre of the pool lay a circular, flat, purple stone. This building is the subject of speculation and discussion.

Behind are the remains of a small **late Hellenistic Doric-style temple in antis**. Traces of stucco were found on the sandstone triglyphs and metopes.

Higher up the slope are the substantial remains of a **Roman bath** with a large palaestra to the E. After the arrival of Christianity an imposing church with three aisles and an apse was erected in the centre of the palaestra. There are plans to restore the bath and use it to display finds from the site and house the archeologists during the excavation season.

To the N are the ruins of a **late structure**. Sometimes described as a temple, Bean suggests a library. The ridge near this building overlooks a large stretch of the Dalyan river and the marshy ground marking the position of the NE harbour.

Perhaps the most imposing ruin in Caunus is the **theatre**. Constructed in the Greek style, the cavea is greater than a semicircle. It has a diameter of c 76m. Supported on the N by substantial walls, on the S it rests against the hillside. The single diazoma, with 18 rows of seats below and 16 above, is divided by stairs into nine cunei. Note the two arched entrances on the N side of the structure which, with two parodoi, provided access to the cavea. The stage-building measured c 38m by 8.5m. From the top row of seats there is a fine view W over the city towards Sülüklü Gölü.

The chatter of rock nuthatches, which nest in the theatre's walls, fill the air. Lizards, basking in the sun, retreat if you approach too closely.

Take the steep path which leads upwards from the rear of the theatre to the acropolis. Apart from the **medieval and Hellenistic fortifications**, there are no traces of human occupation on the hill. However, the magnificent view from its 152m summit over the site, the Dalyan river and the surrounding countryside is ample reward for the effort required by the climb.

Among the flowers which brighten the site are *Acanthus spinosa, Campanula tomentosa* and yellow henbane, *Hyoscamus aureus*.

From Caunus and Dalyan return to Road 400 and continue in an E direction towards Fethiye. Just after Ortaca the road crosses the broad, gravel-strewn bed of the **Dalaman Çayı**, the ancient Indus. According to Pliny this river, which rises c 100km away in the hills of NW Lycia not far from the site of Cibyra, had more than 60 tributaries and was fed by many torrents.

A short distance from **Dalaman** village is the busy airport which has done much to open up SW Turkey to holidaymakers. During the season there are frequent direct services from Gatwick and from a number of European cities. There are also flights to İstanbul, İzmir and Antalya.

About 5km to the S of Dalaman, on the coast, are the remains of a medieval settlement identified by George Bean as **Prepia**, a city mentioned in an Italian *portolano*. This may have succeeded an earlier foundation named Pisilis. In addition to the substantial ruins of a church, a reservoir and the extensive medieval fortifications there are traces of occupation from the Hellenistic and Roman periods, possibly from Pisilis. Nearby, on the island of **Baba Adası** is a **pyramidal structure** which is believed to have been a lighthouse or a beacon.

Between Dalaman and Fethiye there are a number of sites of minor interest. About 4km beyond the village on the right-hand side of the road are traces of a settlement which has been identified as that of ancient **Calynda**, one time a place of some importance. A ship and crew from Calynda fought on the side of Xerxes at the battle of Salamis (480 BC). This had the misfortune to be sunk with the loss of all hands by another vessel from the Persian fleet which was commanded by Artemisia, the ruler of Halicarnassus. Apart from the remains of some Hellenistic fortifications, there is little to be seen at the site.

Road 400, climbing steeply from the plain of Dalaman, passes through the pine-clad hills that signal the approach of Rugged Lycia. From the heights of the **Göcek Geç** the road descends in a series of sharp curves which provide occasional glimpses of the island-studded **Gulf of Fethiye**. On the left, high above the road, there is a cluster of square tombs cut into the steep hillside. Not unlike those at Pinara (see Route 23), they belonged to the ancient city of **Daedala**. A fortified acropolis, the broken walls of private houses, a number of rock-tombs (some Lycian in style), and sarcophagi may be reached with some difficulty. With the pigeon-hole tombs they are the only surviving traces of a settlement, which at one time formed part of the Rhodian Peraea and which, according to Strabo, marked the frontier between Caria and Lycia.

At Göcek, half-hidden in the pine woods, there are camp sites, a yacht marina, shops and market stalls. Excellent meals are served in the *Göcek* restaurant near the pier. The Club Marina has all the facilities and services required by even the most demanding yachtsman. Göcek is an ideal base for excursions to the islands on the W side of the Gulf of Fethiye. On the largest island, **Tersane Adası**, Dockyard Island, there are the remains of an ancient look-out post and of an elaborately-decorated tomb.

On the mainland a small fortified acropolis, a cistern, and temple tombs are believed to belong to the city of **Crya** which was mentioned by Pliny and was shown on a 1C BC pilot's guide to the Mediterranean. Farther S, near the tip of the peninsula, was **Lydae**. According to Bean the ruins, all of which date from the Roman and Byzantine periods, include two moderately-well preserved mausolea, a fort, and some architectural fragments.

From Göçek, Road 400 follows the curve of the bay, the Glaucus Sinus, to the holiday resort of Fethiye. This is the gateway to Lycia, land of a fiercely independent people and of a strikingly different civilisation.

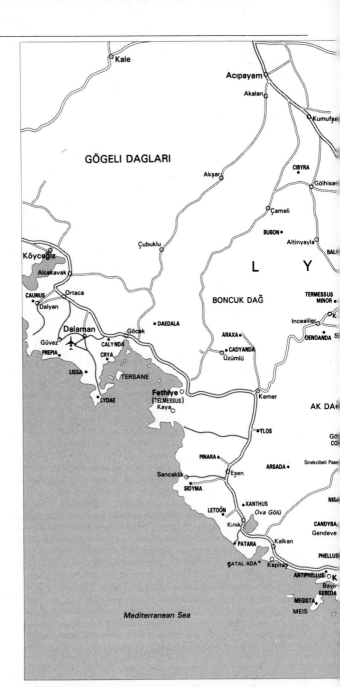

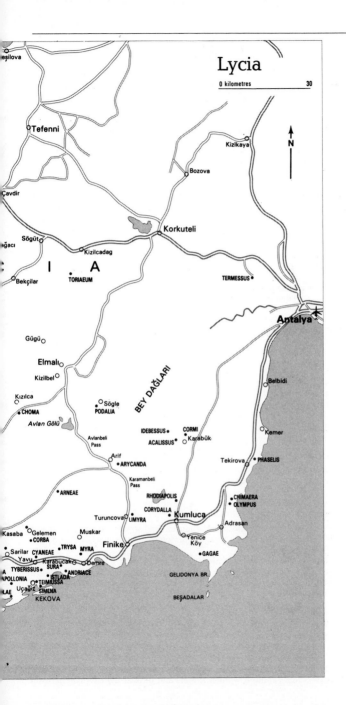

eşilova

Lycia

0 kilometres 30

N

Tefenni

Kızıkaya

Bozova

Çavdir

Söğüt
ağacı
Kızılcadag

Korkuteli

L   I   A

Bekçilar
TORIAEUM

TERMESSUS ●

Antalya

Güğü ○

Belbidi

Elmalı ○

Kızılbel ○

Kızılca

Sögle
CHOMA
PODALIA

BEY DAĞLARI

Avlan Gölü

Kemer

Avlanbeli
Pass

IDEBESSUS ●   CORMI
ACALISSUS ●   ● Karabük

Arif
ARYCANDA

Tekirova ● PHASELIS

Karamanbeli
Pass

ARNEAE ●

RHODIAPOLIS ●
CORYDALLA ●

● CHIMAERA
● OLYMPUS

Turuncova ● LIMYRA   Kumluca

Adrasan

Kasaba   ○ Gelemen   Muskar
● CORBA

Yenice
Köy

Sarilar ● CYANEAE ● TRYSA MYRA
Yavu ○ Karabucak ○   Finike ○
TYBERISSUS ●   SURA ● Demre   ● GAGAE
APOLLONIA   ● ANDRIACE
● ISTLADA
● TEIMIUSSA   GELIDONYA BR.
LAE   Uçağız ● SIMENA
KEKOVA   BEŞADALAR

23

Fethiye to Kaş

Total distance 109km. Fethiye—(c 15km Ölü Deniz)—(c 40km Kaya)—c 22km Kemer—(c 40km Oenoanda)—(c 4km Termessus Minor)—(c 17km Balbura)—(c 8km Bubon)—(c 25km Toriaeum)—(c 12km Cibyra)—(c 7km Tlos)—(c 7km Pinara)—(c 10km Sidyma)—c 41km Kınık—(c 4km Letoön)—(c 0.5km Xanthus)—(c 6km Patara)—c 16km Kalkan—c 27km Kaş.

FETHİYE, ancient Telmessus, is a pleasant town that straggles around a large sheltered bay. In 1957 it was almost completely destroyed by the earthquake which devastated SW Turkey. Most of its buildings have been erected since that time. As part of the reconstruction a promenade was built along the sea front. This is flanked by gardens where there are several small restaurants and tea houses. Fethiye is a popular tourist resort and a good centre for visiting the many ancient sites in western Lycia.

Information and Accommodation. Fethiye and (15km) Ölü Deniz have two four-star, five three-star, 14 two-star and two one-star hotels, many pensions and holiday villages. Recommended are the *Hotel Kemal* and the *Dedeoğlu Hotel*, both two-star, and the four-star *Aries Club Hotel* at Çaliş Mevkii which is c 4km from the town centre. Good value is offered by the *Mer Pansiyon* which provides excellent accommodation at budget prices. Occupying a wonderful position at the entrance to Fethiye harbour is the *Letonnia Holiday Village*. This has two kinds of accommodation, 'hotel' and the less expensive 'club' rooms.

The *Meğri* and *Rafet* restaurants serve good food at reasonable prices. Both vegetarians and meat-eaters are catered for at the *Rainbow Restaurant* which is c 6km from the town on the road to Ölü Deniz.

The **Tourist Information Office** is in İskele Meyd. near the yacht harbour and the Dedeoğlu hotel.

Fethiye is blessed with a pleasant climate. It is seldom too warm in summer and its winters are mild and relatively dry. As in most places in this part of Turkey, the heaviest rainfall occurs in January and February. There are good **beaches** at Çalisburnu, Belçelpiz and at Ölü Deniz where a small fee is sometimes payable.

There are frequent bus and dolmuş services from the *otogar* and dolmuş station which are on eastern side of the town. All the buses travelling along the coast road of Lycia call at Fethiye. The dolmuş services go to villages in the surrounding area.

Yacht charters, diving expeditions etc are organised by Cağa Tour, Fevzi Çakmak Cad., Körfez Apt. 9/1/14 amongst others.

History. The early history of **Telmessus**, the ancient city which occupied the site of present-day Fethiye, is somewhat obscure. The presence of the 'ss' in its name suggests that it was a pre-Greek foundation.

According to legend Lycia was colonised by Sarpedon after his expulsion by his brother, Minos, from Crete. However, it is likely that the earliest inhabitants were Anatolians who later married with Greek and Cretan colonists, but, interestingly, in antiquity the bay of Fethiye was known as the Bay of Glaucus, the Glaucus Sinus, after the companion and friend of Sarpedon.

Originally Telmessus was not considered to be part of Lycia. In a 5C BC list of the cities paying tribute to the Delian League, Telmessus is separated from those in Lycia. In the 4C BC Pericles of Limyra led the forces of the Lycian League against Telmessus and captured it. In 334 BC Alexander was well received by the Telmessians. However, Nearchus the Cretan, who ruled on behalf of Alexander, was obliged to resort to a trick to recover Telmessus from a man called Antipatrides who had occupied it. He asked if he could leave some captured women singers and boys in the city. The garrison

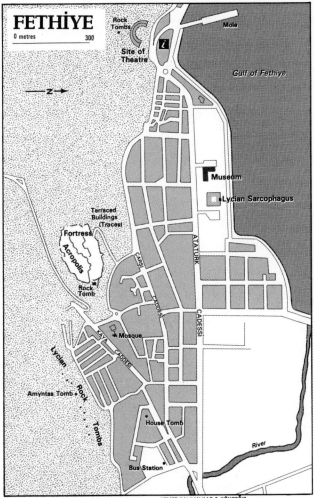

FETHİYE

0 metres   300

Rock Tombs

Mole

Site of Theatre

Gulf of Fethiye

N

Museum

Lycian Sarcophagus

Terraced Buildings (Traces)

Fortress

Acropolis

ATATÜRK

CARSI CADDESI

CADDESSI

Rock Tomb

Mosque

Lycian Rock Tombs

CADDESSI

Amyntas Tomb

House Tomb

River

Bus Station

KEMER,KALKAN,KAŞ & KÖYCEĞİZ

agreed, unaware that the boys carried daggers in their flute cases. Once inside the acropolis they produced the weapons and the city was seized by their escort.

After being ruled for some time by the Ptolemies, Telmessus passed to the kings of Pergamum. Later it became part of the Roman Province of Asia. In AD 451 Telmessus was represented at the Council of Chalcedon. During the following centuries it was pillaged by marauding Arabs and its importance decreased considerably. Under Byzantine rule it changed its name briefly to Anastasiopolis in honour of Anastasius II. In the 9C it became known as **Makri**.

Apart from its famous rock-tombs, little remains of the ancient city. An 18C traveller mentions a large Roman theatre, and in the early part of the 19C Fellows and Spratt saw it on the W side of the town near the sea shore. By 1881 most of this structure had been destroyed. Its stones were used for the construction of barracks in İstanbul. There appears to have been a smaller theatre on the W side of the acropolis.

Access to the **acropolis** is by a steep road from the yacht marina. This becomes a pleasant path which passes through the dusty streets of a small village. From here it is a scramble by a rough track to the top. On the summit are the remains of a **medieval castle**, believed to have been built by the Knights of St John at the beginning of the 15C. On the E side of the acropolis there are two small rock-tombs.

The most important remains of Telmessus are the rock-tombs on the E side of the town. The finest, the **Tomb of Amyntas**, which dates from the 4C BC, can be seen from most parts of Fethiye. One of a group cut into the rock-face above the road to Kemer, it is an easy walk from Atatürk Cad. by Çarşı Cad. and Kaya Cad.

The tomb of Amyntas takes the form of an Ionic temple with two Ionic columns framed by projecting anta or antae. Each is decorated with three rosettes. The pediment has three acroteria, two of which have been damaged. Below the pediment there is a dentil frieze. The left pilaster bears an inscription in Greek letters, 'Amyntas son of Hermapios'. Nothing is known about Amyntas. Four steps lead up to the entrance. Over the door Charles Texier, the 19C traveller, has left a record of his visit. Entrance was effected originally by a sliding stone slab on the bottom right-hand side. This was broken in ancient times by tomb robbers. The chamber has three stone *klinai* on which the dead were laid. To the left of the tomb of Amyntas there are more rock-tombs. Some have two or three storeys, others resemble pigeon holes like those at Pinara.

Fethiye also has some **Lycian sarcophagus tombs**. The finest is near the sub-prefecture in Atatürk Cad. Sarcophagus tombs of this type reflect Lycian domestic architecture. Houses were generally constructed of wood, so the stone tombs have imitation mortice joints and beams and are covered by pointed arches. This gives them the appearance of upturned boats with the ridged keel uppermost. The tomb near the sub-prefecture has an elaborate relief of warriors.

Fethiye's **museum**, off Atatürk Cad., has an interesting collection of pottery dating from the 8C to the 6C BC, Hellenistic terracotta statuettes, marble busts and bronze artefacts from the Roman period. The most important exhibit is the **Letoön Trilingual**, an inscription in Greek, Lycian and Aramaic which records the establishment of a religious cult. It has helped with work on the Lycian language. A room is devoted to ethnography. The garden contains architectural fragments, Roman funerary stelae and the cover of Lycian sarcophagus ornamented with a warrior frieze.

There are frequent services to 15km **Ölü Deniz**, the 'Dead Sea', a sheltered lagoon of great beauty. It has a fine beach and facilities for sailing, windsurfing and fishing. Meals are available from a number of small restaurants. There is a two-star hotel, the *Merih*, a few pensions and several camping sites near the beach.

On the island of **Gemiler** there are the ruins of five churches, an early Byzantine monastery and a necropolis. Some traces of wall paintings and a few fragmentary mosaics remain in the churches. Note the submerged foundations of ancient port facilities near the landing stage.

The ghost town of **Kaya** is c 8km S of Fethiye. Kaya had a Greek population of about 3000 until 1923, when there was a general exchange of Turks and Greeks. Then the town was virtually abandoned. The houses and the church were closed and locked. Today the presence of the few Turkish families, who cultivate their gardens and graze their cattle here, tends only to emphasise the pervading atmosphere of melancholy.

NE of Fethiye there are four interesting sites—Oenoanda, Balbura, Bubon, and Cibyra—which are not often visited. To reach them take Road 400 to c 22km **Kemer** and then turn N on the old road to **Korkuteli**. Note, minibuses and dolmuş services to the villages near the sites operate at irregular intervals and at inconvenient times.

From Kemer continue for c 35km to the village of İncealiler. From there a track leads to the site of **Oenoanda**. The city has not been excavated, but during recent years it has been surveyed by British archaeologists.

History. Little is known about the history of Oenoanda. A long inscription dated to the 2C AD, summarising the Epicurean philosophy, has been found here. This covers a wide range of subjects—chance, the nature of dreams, the creation of the world. It was the gift of a citizen of Oenoanda, named Diogenes, who, in his old age, presented it to the city 'for the salvation of men, present and future'. Of the complete text, estimated to have been 100m long, only a part has been found so far. The search for the remainder is unlikely to be easy, as in later times the inscription was broken up and parts were used to strengthen the city walls. Remains of other Hellenistic structures have been found in Oenoanda and it is known to have been a member of a tetrapolis, headed by its neighbour, Cibyra, in the 2C BC. It was probably influenced by the Lycian cities to the S and even by faraway Termessus. The city flourished under the Romans, reaching its period of greatest affluence during the 2C and 3C, when its architecture showed signs of being affected by the style of Aphrodisias. Towards the end of the 3C it suffered a temporary decline, but its fortunes revived again under the Byzantines.

On a hill, which slopes to the S, the principal buildings, enclosed by walls, include a number of unidentified structures and the agora. To the N, on the highest point, is the **theatre**. This had a diameter of c 30.5m, no diazoma and an unusually large orchestra. Portions of the proscenium described by Lieutenant Spratt as being 'very perfect' are still visible. The S part of the **city wall** was Hellenistic. It stands to a height of c 10m. Two towers and two postern gates, one ruined, remain. The section on the NW is, apart from a stretch which may be Hellenistic, of re-used material and is of later date. A small building N of the walls has been identified as a **temple**. On the NE of the city outside the line of the existing walls, a large flat area may have been the site of Diogenes' inscription. Blocks from it have been found here, inside, outside and built into the wall.

To the W of the site there are several **Carian-type tombs**, cut from the rock and covered with separate lids. Note the carving on a rock face of a figure in an aedicule. Nearby are a pair of open hands, symbols, according to Bean, of a violent or unnatural death. There are also a number of free-standing sarcophagi, surmounted by the carving of a recumbent lion. On the S slope of the hill to the W of the aqueduct there are the ruins of the particularly fine **2C AD marble tomb** of Licinnia Flavilla. A long inscription traces the genealogy of the local family back to the legendary founder of Cibyra, the Spartan, Cleander. A study, undertaken by the late Alan Hall, suggests that at one time there were further sections of the inscription, which perhaps dealt with branches of the family in Cibrya and Greece, on the W wall of the tomb.

About 14km N Oenoanda the road divides. To get to Balbura, Bubon and Cibyra take the left-hand fork signposted Gölhisar. About 5km after the junction, a side road to the right leads to the site of **Balbura**. Apart from the fact that it belonged to the tetrapolis, nothing is known about its history. The site has been surveyed, but not excavated. Material found on the surface suggest that Balbura did not exist before the 2C BC.

Set in a valley watered by a tributary of the Eşen Çayı, the ruins are dominated by an **acropolis** on a fortified hill. The summit is c 1500m above sea level. Artefacts discovered on the acropolis date from the 2–1C BC to the 5–7C AD. Below the acropolis, on the SW slope, there is an unusually small **theatre**, most of whose cavea is taken up with a large mass of unworked rock which greatly reduced the seating capacity. About 500m to the S, on the opposite hillside, there is a 48m long, **narrow platform** resting on arches. A few rudimentary seats on one side suggest that it may have been used not for theatrical performances but for public meetings.

It would appear that the public buildings and private houses moved from the hill to the plain during the Roman period. The agora, the principal street, a Severan gateway, a bath-gymnasium, a large basilical church and a temple dedicated to Nemesis have been identified in the lower city. Detailed studies of three buildings, the temple of Nemesis, and the exedrae of Meleager and of Onesimus, have been published. According to an inscription, Onesimus was a public slave. Public slaves served the community in a variety of ways—as town criers, executioners, street sweepers, policemen and firemen. They were also accountants and minor civil servants. In the cemeteries there are many sarcophagi with a carved recumbent lion on the lid (see Oenoanda).

Return to the main road and continue for c 8km to **Altınyayla**, where the ruins of **Bubon** are. A member of the tetrapolis, Bubon, under its leader Moagetes, is known to have invaded the territory of its neighbour, Araxa, in the 2C BC. Araxa appealed to Cibyra and managed to obtain a satisfactory settlement. However, sometime later Moagetes raided Araxa again and this time the Araxians appealed to the Lycian League. Although neither city belonged to the league, they appear to have accepted its arbitration. Diodorus Siculus mentions a ruler of Bubon c 145 BC named Molkestes. He was murdered by his brother, who replaced him as tyrant. Some authorities believe that Molkestes may be the same as Moagetes.

An inscription found by Bean at Bubon shows that the fortunes of the city had improved by the 2C AD. At that time it was a member of the Lycian League. The inscription, a copy of a letter from the Emperor Commodus (180–192), commended the Bubonians for ridding the area of brigands. It also confirmed a decision of the league to raise the number of the city's votes from two to three, the maximum permitted. This placed Bubon on the same level as Xanthus, Pinara, Patara, Tlos, Myra and Olympus.

Spratt described the ruins at Bubon—a small theatre, some terraces strewn with scattered fragments, and a walled acropolis—as disappointing. A century later Bean found that there had been a lot of unauthorised digging by villagers searching for buried treasure and that all traces of the ancient remains had disappeared.

A track leads NE from Bubon and Balbura to c 25km **Toriaeum** which is near the modern village of **Kozağaçı**. Not far from the village there are many **Hellenistic rock-carvings** of human figures cut in relief into the cliffs and rocky projections. Higher up, in a little valley, there is a small **sanctuary** dedicated to Mases, a local equestrian deity. The village may also be reached by a left-hand turn on the road S from Çavdır.

Cibyra is c 12km to the N of Bubon, near the modern town of **Gölhisar**.

History. According to Strabo, the first settlers in Cibyra came from Lydia. Later they were displaced by Pisidians, who transferred the city to a more easily defended position. Towards the end of the 2C BC the Roman consul, Manlius Vulso, came to N Lycia in pursuit of the Galatians who had supported Antiochus III. He took the opportunity to raise money from the cities he visited. At Cibyra he managed to extract 100 talents and 10,000 bushels of grain from its unwilling ruler. Later Cibyra, with Bubon, Balbura and Oenoanda formed a tetrapolis. Cibyra, as head, had two votes, the others one each. The city grew in importance and wealth and developed a formidable army. According to Strabo (13.4.17) it could put 30,000 foot soldiers and 2000 horses in the field.

The tetrapolis continued to function until 82 BC, when it was abolished by the Romans. Bubon and Balbura were transferred to Lycia, Cibyra remained in the Roman Province of Asia. It continued to prosper, becoming the seat of the provincial governor. Strabo states that the city was famous for the skill of its ironworkers. Perhaps because of its geographical situation, it became a place where many different races met. Pisidian and Solymian, as well as Greek and Lydian were spoken here. In AD 23, Cibyra was destroyed by an earthquake, but rebuilt soon afterwards with aid received from the Emperor Tiberius.

The site of Cibyra has not been excavated or given a detailed survey, so it is not possible to identify all the buildings which remain. The approach from the E is by way of a street lined with tombs. To the left of a ruined arch, there are the extensive remains of the **stadium**. This had a triple-arched entrance on the N, seats on the E and W sides and was rounded on the S. In the centre of the city there was a group of buildings which remain unidentified. Behind them, to the W, are the theatre and a small odeum. The **theatre** had one diazoma and c 50 rows of seats of which some are still visible. Access to the **odeum**, which is S of the theatre, was through five arched and two rectangular doors. Some of the seats remain.

If you are not in a hurry, return to Fethiye by a picturesque route which will take you through Çavdır, Korkuteli, Elmalı, Kaş and Kalkan.

Leave Fethiye on Road 400 in the direction of c 22km **Kemer**. About 10km from Kemer there is a signpost on the left for (7km) ancient **TLOS**. This is near the village of **Asar Kale**. Simple meals are available near the site.

The Tomb of Bellerophon at Tlos

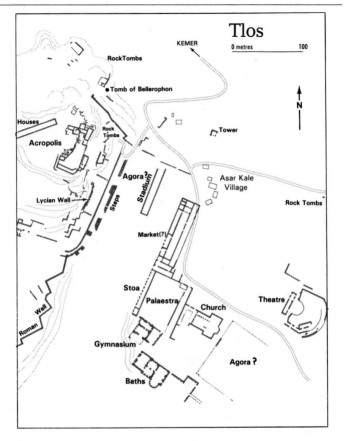

The **acropolis** which dominates the N end of the Xanthus valley, can be seen from a considerable distance. Most of the ruins on the summit date from the Ottoman period; the residence and barracks of a local 19C brigand, Kanlı Ali Ağa, occupying the highest ground.

History. The discovery of a bronze hatchet, dating from the second millennium BC, proves that Tlos was occupied from a very early date. In Lycian it was known as Tlawa or Tlave, and references in Hittite records from the 14C BC to Dalawa are taken to refer to Tlos. Very little is known about the history of the city. Its oldest monuments date from the 5C BC. Coins from the 4C BC bearing the name of Tlos in Lycian have been found. In the 2C BC, as the possessor of three votes, it was one of the six most important cities in the Lycian League. In the 2C AD it was the recipient of a grant of 60,000 denarii from the magnate Opramoas of Rhodiapolis. This was used mainly for the construction of the theatre. In Byzantine times Tlos was a bishopric. It was represented at the Council of Chalcedon in AD 415.

William James Müller (1812–45), the English artist who visited Lycia in 1843, spent ten days sketching at Tlos. Of all the places that he visited in Turkey, this relatively remote site seems to have made the greatest impression on him. In a letter to a friend he rhapsodises about the magnificent scenery in this part of Lycia: '...such mountains and valleys, such a distance, melting away and uniting with the sky! There lay the Taurus [sic] more like some faint sound, some distant recollection of a past event'.

Müller left the site with much regret. 'Tlos!', he wrote, 'I like your scenery, your melancholy tombs, your grand acropolis, your running streams and noble trees, your little Turkish children (my little coin-finders). I like them all'.

On the E side of the acropolis there are the remains of a Lycian wall, a substantial section of Roman wall and two important groups of Lycian tombs on the E and N sides.

The open space between the bottom of the acropolis and the village of Kale Asar may mark the position of the **agora** (see also below). Near the base of the hill are traces of the **stadium**, whose seats were partly supported and protected by a Roman wall. The double line of stones in the centre was probably part of the *spina*, around which chariots were raced. The long building on the E side has been described variously as a basilica or a market house. Beyond this is the palaestra and beyond the palaestra, the **baths**. One of the rooms of the baths, known as 'Yedi Kapı', the Seven Doors, offers a splendid view over the Xanthus valley. For the theatre, return to the modern road. On the right are the remains of a Byzantine basilica. Some believe that the agora of Tlos was sited in the large open area to the SE.

The **theatre**, very overgrown and difficult to examine, was built in the middle of the 2C AD with a large donation from Opramoas of Rhodiapolis and smaller sums from the priest of Dionysus and from private citizens. It had one diazoma. Many of the highly decorated stone blocks from the stage-building remain.

To the N of the village there is a well-preserved **Roman tower** and several sarcophagi. To visit the rock tombs of Tlos, cross the small stream and, passing the side of the stadium, go to the steep N face of the acropolis, then follow a narrow goat-path high above the stream. The so-called **Tomb of Bellerophon** is a temple-type tomb with pilasters between the antae. There are three carved doors. Note the elaborate decoration on the centre door. Entrance was through the side doors, which were raised above the ground on stone blocks. Each was carved with the figure of a horse. The carving, which gives the tomb its name and which is believed to represent Bellerophon mounted on Pegasus, is on the left wall of the porch. When Fellows came here in the early 19C, there were still traces of paint on the saddlecloth. Above the left door is the figure of a lion or leopard. The funeral chamber on the left-hand side has a niche for offerings and four *klinai* on which the dead were placed. One *kline*, presumably for the most important corpse, has a stone pillow. The chamber on the right-hand side is smaller and has places for three bodies only. There is no inscription, so it is not known for whom the tomb was built. From the tomb descend to the valley floor and, crossing the stream once more, return to Road 400.

You enter a delightful stretch of country. This is at its best in springtime, when multicoloured anemones carpet the ground and the pale flowers of the asphodel mourn the dead in the pine groves that crowd around the road.

Look for a signpost on the right to ancient **PINARA**. In **Minare**, the nearest village to the site, there is a small restaurant. If you wish to go direct to the site, take the signposted side road just outside Minare. Continue for c 2km to a large grassy space which serves as a car-park and picnic area. From here on you must proceed on foot.

History. Like many of the Lycian cities not much is known about the early history of Pinara. According to a 4C BC account the people of Xanthus were forced by overpopulation to establish a new city on a peak that curves out from Mt Cragus. They called it Pinara, after the Lycian word for 'round'. There is a reference in Homer to a Lycian archer called Pandarus who may be the same Pandarus honoured in later times in Pinara (Strabo, *Geography*, 14.3.5). The city enters history properly in 334 BC, when

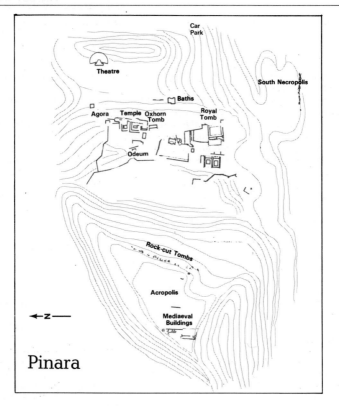

Pinara

it surrendered to Alexander the Great. However, there is no doubt about its importance before that time. It had three votes in the Lycian League. After the death of Alexander his empire was divided among the Diadochoi and Pinara came under the rule of Pergamum. When Attalus III bequeathed his kingdom to Rome in 133 BC Pinara became a Roman city. In the 2C AD, like Tlos and some other Lycian cities, it received a substantial gift of money from Opramoas of Rhodiapolis. In Roman times it enjoyed a considerable degree of prosperity and, although badly damaged by earthquakes in AD 141 and AD 240, was inhabited until the 9C.

In November 1843 William James Müller (1812–45), the English artist (see Xanthus), spent nine days exploring and sketching the ruins of Pinara. Eventually, the exceptionally bad weather—wind, rain and violent thunderstorm—forced him to return to his base at Xanthus.

The great red cliff, which rises to a height of c 500m, never fails to impress visitors. The summit may be reached, with some difficulty, by a path that starts on the S side. Presumably to protect its inhabitants, the earliest settlement was located on the top, but little of that remains to be seen today. The buildings in the SW area are thought to date from the Middle Ages, when the inhabitants retreated once more to the acropolis for safety. Their most astounding creation, the hundreds of **caves** hollowed out from the cliff's E face, are accessible only to experienced climbers. It is generally believed that these were rock-tombs, but some suggest that they could have been used for food storage.

In more settled times the city was moved to a smaller hill to the E of the cliff. This is overgrown and difficult to explore. There is a small theatre or odeum on the NW side and on the NE and S a number of interesting rock-tombs. One of these, the so-called **royal tomb** has relief carvings on the lintel and inside the porch. Those on the lintel show horses and people, while inside there are representations of fortified Lycian cities, possibly Xanthus and Telmessus. Note in particular the depiction of Lycian ogival tombs. Because of its rich decoration and the fact that it has a single *kline* it is thought to have been the last resting place of a prince or king. To the N there is another rock-tomb decorated with a pointed arch surmounted by ox-horns. Both tombs have been damaged by shepherds who have used them as shelters. The walls have been blackened by their fires and some of the important architectural features have been chipped and broken.

Pinara's **agora** is believed to have been to the N of the smaller hill, but little remains. Between its presumed site and the theatre there are the ruins of a large **temple**. The **theatre**, which was cleared recently, was constructed in the Greek form. It was larger than a semicircle. It had no diazoma and its 27 rows of seats were divided into nine cunei. A substantial part of the stage-building remains.

Return to Road 400 for **SIDYMA**, perhaps the least well known of the Lycian cities. It is not easy to reach. After Eşen and c 3km before the turning for Gölbent, turn right along a valley for 1km until the road divides. There take the left fork. The road is really a succession of rough tracks which for 6km cling to the side of the mountain and skirt frighteningly deep ravines. Covered with loose gravel, they are very narrow in parts and have many unfenced drops.

History. Sidyma's name suggests that it was of considerable antiquity. Its early history is shrouded in mystery. A coin of the Lycian League from the 2C BC, bearing the inscription 'Lukion Si', is believed to refer to Sidyma, but it is not until the 1C BC that the city appears in written records. Under the Romans and Byzantines Sidyma enjoyed a considerable degree of prosperity. Possibly its fame in later years came from its connection with the Eastern Emperor Marcian (AD 450–457). There is a story that Marcian, an ordinary soldier, taking part in a campaign against the Persians, fell ill and stayed for some time in Sidyma where he was nursed by two brothers. One day after his health had been restored he went hunting with his benefactors. While resting from the noon-day heat the youths were astonished to see that their former patient was being shaded from the sun's rays by a huge eagle. Assuming that this was a portent of greatness to come, they asked him later what he would do for them if he became emperor. Marcian promised that he would make them fathers of their city. When, unexpectedly, he succeeded Theodosius II as Eastern Emperor, he remembered his promise and gave the young men important positions in Lycia.

The village of **Dodurga**, which is 600m above seal level, covers the centre of the ancient city. Unfortunately, this has resulted in some damage to the ruins, which fall into two distinct groups: those on the acropolis which is to the N of the village and those at its base around the village. The extant wall and towers on the acropolis are Byzantine. The theatre, of which only a few very damaged rows exist, is also a late building. In the centre of Dodurga there are a few **columns** of a stoa built in the time of the Emperor Claudius (AD 41–54). There are also the scant remains of a small temple dedicated to the Roman emperors. The village mosque has been constructed from material taken from Sidyma. An inscription on the rear wall lists some of the pagan gods: Athena, Apollo, Artemis and Zeus.

Sidyma's **necropolis** is to the E of the village. Many of the tombs, nearly all of which date from the Roman period, are in gardens or in fields near modern houses. One, built in the form of a temple, has a roof decorated with well-preserved carvings of human heads and rosettes. Nearby are the remains of a large structure which was constructed mainly with material taken from other buildings. Note the door on the N side, with its ornamentation of rosettes and lions' heads. Not far away is a fine **double tomb**, which was occupied by two members of the same family, both named Aristodemus. A recent survey of Sidyma has produced a new Claudian inscription.

For **THE LETOÖN** (4km) take a right-hand turn from road 400 c 1km before **Kınık**. Apart from the signpost on the main road, there are few directions to the site, which is near the village of **Bozoluk**.

History. One of the most evocative ancient descriptions of the Letoön is provided by Ovid (Book VI of the Metamorphoses). He writes of 'an ancient altar black with the fires of many sacrifices, surrounded with shivering reeds'. This was the shrine dedicated to Leto and to her children, Apollo and Artemis, the principal deities of Lycia.

Several legends relate their connection with the Letoön. Leto, pregnant by Zeus, was harried by his jealous wife, Hera, who did not want the children to be born. Eventually, Leto gave birth on the island of Delos and then brought her children to Lycia, as she wished to wash them in the river Xanthus. Some boorish shepherds tried to stop her from doing this, but wolves came to her assistance and drove the churls away. As a punishment Leto turned the shepherds into frogs. She also changed the name of the country from Termilis to Lycia, after the Greek word for wolf, λύκος.

It has been suggested that the name Leto is derived from the Lycian word *lada*, woman. This would indicate a non-Greek origin for the cult and there is some evidence that a spring at the site was linked with the worship of the Mother Goddess and the Nymphs before the 7C BC. A stele inscribed in Greek, Lycian, and Aramaic has been found near one of the temples at the Letoön. This records the creation by the satrap, Pixodarus, the brother of Mausolus of Halicarnassus, of a cult devoted to the worship of two gods. These were the Carian deities Basileus Kaunios and Arkesimas; about the latter nothing is known. Those who offended against the provisions of the decree were threatened with the wrath of Leto, Apollo, Artemis and the Nymphs. This confirms the association of Leto with the Nymphs as early as the 4C BC and shows that even then the Letoön was a place where important religious texts were displayed.

Later the Letoön became the place of assembly of the Lycian League. Representatives of foreign countries came here and Lycian national festivals were celebrated here. Some believe that it was at the Letoön that Alexander the Great received the famous prophecy concerning the destruction of the Persian Empire recounted by Plutarch: 'In Lycia, near the city of Xanthus, there is a spring which it is said, gushed from the ground without apparent cause and, overflowing, threw up from its depths a tablet of bronze covered in archaic characters. There it was read that the Persian Empire would end, destroyed by the Greeks. Encouraged by this prophecy, Alexander proceeded to clear the coastline of Persians as far as Cilicia and Phoenicia'.

Divine intervention of another kind took place at the Letoön when in 88 BC Mithridates VI Eupator, the king of Pontus, besieged Patara. To make siege-engines he began to cut down trees in a grove sacred to Leto. Warned in a dream of his sacrilege, he desisted. The Letoön was occupied well into the Christian era when a church was erected here. It would appear that the last temple was not demolished until the 7C, when the site was abandoned at the time of the Arab raids.

Interest in the Letoön was revived in the 19C by the accounts of Fellows, Spratt and Forbes of their travels in Lycia. However, for many years it was little visited because of malaria and the generally unhealthy conditions in the area. Bean examined the site in 1946 and French archaeologists began to excavate here in 1962. They have uncovered three temples, a nymphaeum and two porticoes. In 1984 a number of interesting inscriptions were discovered. One laid down the conditions to be observed by anyone entering the sanctuary. According to M. Christian Le Roy visitors to the shrine were required to dress simply in tunics and plain shoes. The wearing of rich jewellery, especially brooches and rings, was forbidden, as were elaborate hairstyles and the πέτασος, a broad-brimmed felt hat. They had to be unarmed. Those not offering a sacrifice were not permitted to spend the night in the portico of the shrine. These ordinances, previously unknown among religious laws, are of great interest to historians of the sanctuary. The work of the French archaeologists continues.

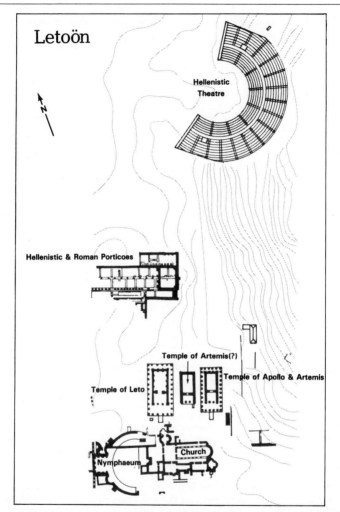

The site of the Letoön is compact and it is possible to see everything in about two hours. There are no refreshment facilities, so bring a picnic lunch. From the car-park, make your way to the ruins of **three temples**. Little exists above ground level. According to an inscription found in the cella, the first and largest (30.25m by 15.75m) was dedicated to Leto. Built in the Ionic style, it was a peripteros of 11 columns by 6. It had a deep pronaos and engaged half columns on the cella walls. It has been dated to the 3C BC. Recent excavations have revealed a pavement 4m below the level of the stylobate. An active spring was found at the foot of a stairway leading up from the pavement. Votive terracotta figurines dating from the 6C to the 1C BC were found in the spring, thus linking it with the cult of Leto and the Nymphs. It was customary for worshippers to place a statuette in the water as an offering to the goddess.

The centre temple, the smallest (18.20m by 8.70m) and the oldest (4C BC), was also in the Ionic style, but without a colonnade. The cella had a mysterious structure, partly composed of rough stone blocks and partly of a natural rocky outcrop at its N end.

A small monument bearing an inscription for Julia Sebaste, daughter of the emperor Titus, has been found c 200m to the SE. Finds at a 1C AD burial included statuettes of Tyche and of an ephebe.

The third temple (27.90m by 15.07m), which dates from the Hellenistic period, was in the Doric order. This was built over an earlier Lycian structure. It was also a peripteros of 11 by 6 columns and it had engaged half-columns on the cella walls. The fine mosaic on the floor depicting a lyre, a bow and quiver suggests that it was dedicated to Apollo and Artemis. (Ask the *bekçi* to brush away the protective covering of sand.) It was near this temple that the stele with the trilingual inscription concerning the cult of Basileus Kaunios and Arkesimas was found. All three temples opened towards the S.

SW of the temples is the **nymphaeum**, which replaced an earlier Hellenistic building. It is composed of two parts from different periods. On the E there is a rectangular basin lined with marble between retaining walls c 16m apart. This leads to a semicircular construction 27m in diameter with a depth of 4m. Some of this part may date from the Hellenistic period. Beyond the semicircular basin, and linked to it, is a room, flanked by two exedrae which had several niches for statues. The principal niche on the W side bears a dedication to Hadrian, which has been dated to about AD 130. Later a church (c 4C) was built over part of the E section of the nymphaeum. This was destroyed during the Arab invasions of the 7C.

Turning to the N you come to the partially-excavated porticoes. A **Doric portico** of the Hellenistic period enclosed the N and W sides of the temple area. This was altered considerably in Roman times, when, during the reign of Claudius, a second portico in the Ionic style was built inside the Doric construction. It had columns of brick resting on stone bases. On the N the new double portico was enclosed by a wall and here the archaeologists made an exciting discovery. They found 15,000 fragments from ten broken and burnt marble statues. Five of the statues, which date from the 2C BC, have been painstakingly reconstructed and are now in the Antalya Museum. Beneath the porticoes are the remains of earlier shrines. These have been dated to the 4C, 5C, and 6C BC. Fragments of archaic pottery from the 6C BC have also been found here, clear evidence that the site was occupied at an early date.

Much of the Letoön is below the water-table and as a result for most of the year part of the porticoes and the nymphaeum is flooded. While this adds considerably to the problems encountered by the archaeologists, it provides an agreeable environment for the many tortoises and frogs that thrive here. The latter keep up a noisy chorus, reminding us of the comment Ovid made about the metamorphosed shepherds: 'Even now, as of old [they] exercise their foul tongues in quarrel, and all shameless, though they may be under the water try to utter maledictions'.

The Hellenistic **theatre** is about 100m NE of the porticoes. Partly cut out of the hillside and greater than a semicircle, it has one diazoma. Apart from the loss of its stage-buildings, it is in good condition. Access to the cavea is by two vaulted passages. On the outer face of the NE passage there are masks of, among others, Silenus, Dionysus, a satyr and a girl.

It is worthwhile making a short visit to the site of ancient **Pydnae**. Instead of turning right to return to Kınık, take the left fork and continue on a good road for about 10km. Just before the beach you will see Pydnae on the hillside. This is one of the best-preserved **Hellenistic fortresses** of the region. A ring-wall with several towers encloses the ruins of a **Byzantine church**. There are some restaurants near the beach.

Return to Road 400 and continue for c 2km to Kınık. A modern bridge carries the road over the Xanthus river, the Eşen Çayı. There are restaurants in Kınık, but a picnic on the site of Xanthus—c 500m from the village centre—is more enjoyable. Refreshments are not available at the site.

Allow about four hours for a reasonably detailed examination of Xanthus. Wear stout shoes and thornproof clothing, especially if you intend to explore the more overgrown areas, e.g. the Hellenistic and Roman residential quarter and the upper acropolis.

XANTHUS is probably the most interesting of all the Lycian cities. Its situation on the great cliff, which rises steeply from the Xanthus river, makes its ruins visible from a considerable distance.

History. The earliest written reference to Xanthus, which was always considered to be the greatest of the Lycian cities, it is in the *Iliad*. Sarpedon, one of the heroes who fought on the side of the Trojans, speaks of their good fortune to Glaucus, his friend and asks: 'Cousin, why do the Lycians pay us semi-divine honours? Why do we get the most honourable seats at banquets, the finest cuts of meat, the fullest goblets, and the great estates of orchard and wheatland beside the River Xanthus?'.

Xanthus was twice razed to the ground and its inhabitants slaughtered. Around 540 BC the Persians under their general, Harpagus, attempted to conquer the western part of Asia Minor. Advancing along the river valley, they besieged the city. Seeing that resistance was useless, the inhabitants put their wives, children, slaves and property in the acropolis and set fire to it. Herodotus describes what happened next. 'Then the warriors of Xanthus made their final attack on the Persians, their voices raised in oaths of war, until every last man from Xanthus was killed.' The city later re-established by a number of Xanthian families (c 80 according to Herodotus), who happened to be absent at the time of the siege. Evidence that it soon regained its former status is provided by the fine monuments erected in the 5C. In 334 BC Xanthus, with Pinara, Patara and about 30 smaller Lycian cities surrendered to Alexander the Great.

After Alexander's death Xanthus was for some time under the rule of the Ptolemies who captured it from Antigonus. In 197 BC it acquired the status of a free city under the nominal control of Antiochus III of Syria. However, Lycia was awarded to the Rhodians after the defeat of Antiochus at the battle of Magnesia ad Sipylum in 190 BC and for a number of years its inhabitants fought bitterly for their freedom. In 167 BC the Roman Senate abolished the rule of Rhodes and Lycia became free once more. Early in the 2C BC an attempt was made to set up a tyranny in Xanthus. This was suppressed by the Lycian League.

The city's second ordeal took place in 42 BC. The tyrannicide Brutus came to Lycia to raise money for his struggle against Antony and Octavian. The cities of the Lycian League refused to contribute, were engaged by the Roman forces and defeated. Xanthus was besieged by the Romans and a furious battle ensued. The Xanthians showed great bravery, but finally the city fell to the enemy. The defenders then slaughtered their families, put their belongings on pyres and threw themselves on the flames. Only about 150 were captured by the Romans. However, Xanthus rose again from its ashes. As a city of the Roman province of Asia it prospered, had many fine buildings and continued to enjoy its place as the premier city of Lycia. Under Byzantine rule the fortifications were repaired and a monastery built on the upper acropolis. It was the seat of a bishop, who came under the jurisdiction of the Metropolitan of Myra.

In the 19C interest in Xanthus was revived in Western Europe by the exploration and writings of Sir Charles Fellows and by the sculptures transported back to England. When these were displayed for the first time in the British Museum they caused a sensation. Visitors flocked to admire the magnificent Nereid Tomb, the tomb of Payava and the reliefs from the Harpy tomb. The latter still stands in the Lycian acropolis, but, sadly, the reliefs on it are plaster casts of the originals supplied by the British Museum!

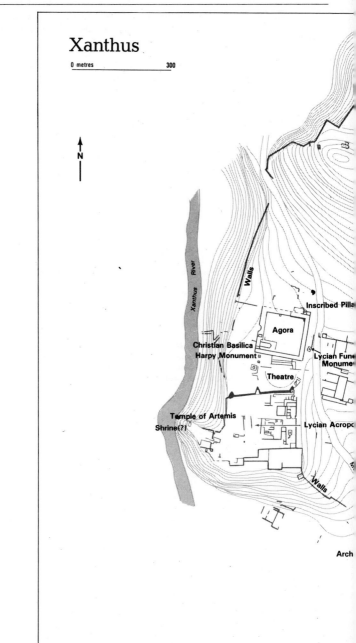

Xanthus

0 metres   300

N

Xanthus River

Walls

Inscribed Pilla

Agora

Christian Basilica
Harpy Monument

Lycian Fune
Monume

Theatre

Temple of Artemis
Shrine(?)

Lycian Acrop

Walls

Arch

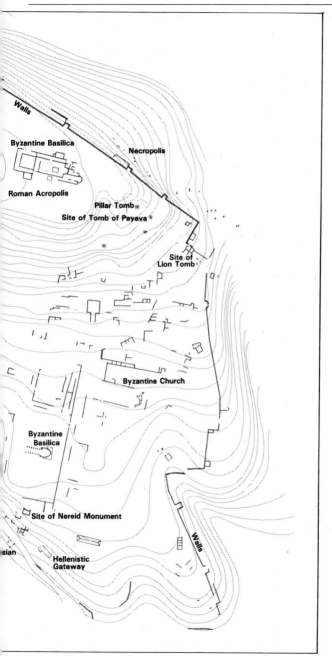

William James Müller (1812–45), the Bristol born painter, visited Turkey at the invitation of Sir Charles Fellows in 1843. After an agreeable stay in Smyrna (İzmir), he made his way S to Lycia.

Camping at Xanthus, Müller spent his days sketching the ruins of the ancient city, returning only at sunset for a simple meal and the escape provided by his tent against the 'malarious miasma' which pervaded the river valley. During the course of his stay he also produced dozens of sketches illustrating the lives of the villagers and of the Yürük. His Turkish neighbours were friendly and hospitable, though somewhat suspicious of his artistic skills, perhaps because of their religious beliefs. Hoping to break down their prejudices and interest them in portraiture, he made a sketch of a local youth and gave it to them as a present. His mortification may be imagined when they stoned the drawing before his face. A number of his drawings, together with his larger oil paintings, are in the Tate Gallery and in the art galleries of Bristol and Birmingham.

On the left, about half-way up the road from Kınık, are the ruins of a **Hellenistic gateway** which bears an inscription commemorating the consecration of the city in 197 BC by Antiochus III to the gods of Lycia. Just beyond is the well-preserved 1C AD **Arch of Vespasian** and traces of the ancient roadway that linked Xanthus with Patara and the Letoön. On the high bank on the right are the few sad remains of the **Nereid Monument** (?4C BC). Only the base and a few architectural fragments remain. The friezes and statues were taken to London in 1841–42 by Charles Fellows and are now in Room 7 of the British Museum. A reconstruction, based on the discoveries of the French archaeologists, has been made of the east façade of the tomb in the museum. It was probably the tomb of the Lycian dynast Arbinas and dates from between 390 and 80 BC. The sculptures were the work of two workshops, one Lycian and one Greek.

The Nereid tomb is of particular interest, as it was the only major tomb in Xanthus in a Greek architectural style. Constructed in the form of an Ionic temple on a high podium, it gets its name from the statues of the female figures placed between the columns. These have been identified variously as the Aurai, the Breezes or the Nereids, the daughters of Nereus, a sea god associated with the Aegean. The tomb was richly decorated with friezes showing battles between Greeks and barbarians, the siege of a city and hunting scenes. The seated male and female figures on the E pediment probably represent the Arbinas and his consort.

At the top of the hill, on the left, are the **Lycian acropolis**, the **Roman theatre**, and the **Roman agora**. The wall around the Lycian acropolis was built at different periods. The section on the E side, constructed from polygonal masonry, dates from the 4C BC, while that on the SW is Hellenistic. Note the massive free-standing house-tomb between the agora and the road.

The NE corner of the agora is dominated by the so-called **Inscribed Pillar**. This is in fact a normal pillar tomb erected for a Xanthian dignitary towards the end of the 5C BC. It gets its name from the inscription in Greek and Lycian which covers its four sides. The inscription appears to recount the life and exploits of a prince called Kerei. As Lycian is little understood most of our information about Kerei comes from the 12 lines of verse in Greek on the N side. According to this he was the son of Harpagus (not to be confused with the Persian general of the same name), a great wrestler in his youth, the conqueror of many cities and a champion who killed seven Arcadian foot soldiers in one day. The reliefs depicting his exploits, which are believed to have taken place during the Peloponnesian War, are now in the İstanbul Archaeological Museum. The Lycian inscription runs to 250 lines, the longest discovered so far. It is particularly interesting, as the text

The Rock and Pillar Tombs at Xanthus

on the W and part of the N side is written in a form of the language that is found in only one other place—on a tomb in ancient Antiphellus (Kaş).

On the W side of the agora there are two more tombs, a Lycian sarcophagus set on upright slabs, and the so-called Harpy Tomb. The **Lycian sarcophagus** poses a puzzle for archaeologists, as the burial found in its base can be dated by accompanying pottery to the Hellenistic period (3C BC). However, it also contained an archaic slab depicting wrestlers, now in the İstanbul Archaeological Museum, which dates from the 6C BC. Presumably the sarcophagus on the top must also be Hellenistic unless it, too, was also brought from another location and re-used.

The marble slabs which once decorated the top of the so-called **Harpy Tomb** (early 5C BC), which stands 7.6m high, were taken to London by Fellows and are now in Room 5 of the British Museum. They have been replaced with plaster casts of the originals. The winged figures at the N and S sides were originally identified as the harpies who stole the daughters of King Pandareus to make them slaves of the Furies. However, it is now believed that they represent the Sirens who carried the souls of the dead to Hades. The seated figures receiving offerings may be members of the deceased's family or deities. Artemis has been suggested for the E side, Aphrodite and Hera for the W. During the Byzantine era there was a small church near the Harpy Tomb and there is some evidence that the tomb itself was occupied for a time by a Christian hermit.

S of the forum is the **Roman theatre** (mid 2C AD). This was built with the help of a donation of 30,000 denarii from Opramoas of Rhodiapolis. The theatre, which has two parodoi, was so constructed that it did not obscure the Harpy Tomb or the Sarcophagus Tomb. Part of the stage-building remains. At some time several rows of seats were removed from the lower part to turn it into an amphitheatre, while others from the top were later incorporated into the Byzantine wall which lies behind. The terracotta pipes at the top levels on the W side brought water to the houses on the acropolis. On the E side of the theatre, near the road, are the remains of a **Lycian pillar tomb** which dates from the 4C BC. Presumably this was moved and placed in its present position when the theatre was built.

The **Lycian acropolis** is sited on the flat-topped hill behind the theatre, high above the Xanthus river. Geometric pottery found here dates the earliest occupation of Xanthus to the 8C BC, the time of Homer. As the acropolis contains the remains of a number of buildings from widely differing periods, and is very overgrown, it is not easy to understand.

In the NE corner there was a **Byzantine church and monastery**. There are the foundations of a building in the SE corner which, it is believed, was the palace of the earliest rulers of Xanthus. This was destroyed when the city was captured by the Persian, Harpagus, c 540 BC. To the W there are traces of a temple dedicated to Artemis, while on the cliff above the river there was another house or shrine richly decorated with friezes. Sculptures from this and from two other buildings on the acropolis were later incorporated in a Byzantine wall added to the back of the theatre to form a new line of defence. Removed by Fellows they are now in Room 5 of the British Museum. The friezes, an interesting blend of Greek and Persian subject-matter and style, depict satyrs stalking wild animals, fighting cocks with attendant hens, a procession of warriors and a banqueting scene. In the same room are the gables from two ogival Lycian tombs, each of which has a pair of sphinxes facing the false door of the tomb.

Cross the road and continue for about 200m to the site of the **late agora**. This was also the residential area of the Hellenistic and Roman cities. Now densely covered with undergrowth, it is difficult to explore.

The only building of importance uncovered here is a large **Byzantine basilica**. Excavation, begun by French archaeologists in 1970, continues. According to Professor Henri Metzger, the basilica was abandoned towards the end of the early Christian era, but was redecorated and brought into use again in the middle Byzantine period. A part of the mosaic floor survives in the W section of the building. At the E end there was a semicircular apse with a raised synthronon. Three doors in the narthex provided access to the nave and the side aisles. In size and decoration the building bears comparison with churches in the larger Byzantine cities.

A smaller Byzantine church, largely hidden by the undergrowth, has not yet been excavated. Apart from the vestiges of the retaining walls and a striking view of the Dumanlı mountains to the E there is little to see in this part of the site. The level space of the agora still fulfils a useful purpose. It serves as a football pitch for the youth of Kınık!

Walking diagonally across the hillside towards the N you soon reach the site of the **Tomb of Payava**. All that remains is the base. The tomb was taken to London by Fellows and is now in Room 10 of the British Museum. It is a typical Lycian tomb decorated with reliefs in the Greek style. These show various warlike exploits and peacetime occupations of the deceased. An inscription in Lycian is believed to mean 'Payava built this monument'.

At the eastern side of the Hellenistic and Roman acropolis there is a striking group of **rock-tombs** dominated by a **pillar tomb**. One of the rock-tombs, constructed in the Greek style, has an inscription in Lycian.

The climb to the top of the **Roman acropolis** is not difficult but, apart from a fine view of the whole site and an opportunity to examine the ruins of a

well-preserved **early Byzantine monastery**, there is little to justify the effort.
The monastery is believed to occupy the site of a Roman temple. Some care
is necessary, as the whole of the acropolis is covered with tangled undergrowth and there are many loose blocks of stone.

Descending from the acropolis, you reach the Hellenistic walls. In an
angle are the remains of the late 7C early 6C **lion tomb**, so called from a
sculpture which shows a lion attacking a bull. The reliefs from this tomb
are now in Room 3 of the British Museum. To the N and E of the Hellenistic
walls there are many **rock-tombs** and **sarcophagi** scattered over a wide
area. On leaving the necropolis turn left under the Roman acropolis and,
passing the theatre and the Lycian acropolis, return to Kınık.

Take Road 400 from Kınık in the direction of Kalkan and Kaş. About 8km
beyond the village, a sign on the right points to c 6km **PATARA**. This road,
narrow and twisting in parts, has a reasonably good surface.

Patara has one of the **finest beaches** on the Lycian coast. The swimming is excellent
and the conditions are usually good for surfing and windsurfing. The beach of fine
sand is sufficiently large to be uncrowded. It stretches for more than 18km. There are
two restaurants near the car-park and the beach, the *Patara* and the *Harabe*. Both offer
an excellent selection of *meze* and also serve *mantı*, a Turkish version of ravioli.

If you are seduced by the numinous character of Patara, want to enjoy its delights at
leisure, wander among the holm oaks and ruined buildings or laze on the beach, you
have a choice of several good pensions and the *Apollon Motel*.

Spring is the best time of the year to visit Patara. Then the site is carpeted with wild
flowers. *Anemone coronaria* and asphodel, the flower of the Elysian Fields, soften the
lines of the ancient walls and brighten its abandoned buildings.

History. There are many legends about the foundation of Patara. According to Strabo
it was named after Patarus, the son of Apollo and a nymph named Lycia, the daughter
of Xanthus. This may refer to the fact that Patara had a famous oracle of Apollo. It was
believed that the god spent the winter here, and the summer on the island of Delos.
Although little is known with certainty about the prophecies made in Patara, its oracle
had an importance which rivalled that of Delphi. Fish were used for divination at
nearby Sura, but there is no precise information about the methods employed at Patara.
There is a suggestion in Herodotus (1.182) that predictions were based on the dreams
of the priestess of the god. After a period of quiescence in the 1C AD, the oracle revived
during the reign of Antoninus Pius (138–161), when Opramoas of Rhodiapolis made a
generous donation to the shrine. Nothing is known about its later history. Presumably
it was suppressed, when effect was given to Theodosius' law of AD 385 against oracles.
Neither the temple of Apollo nor the shrine of his oracle at Patara has been found.

Pottery found at Patara has been dated to the 5C BC. However attractive the fanciful
legends of Strabo and other ancient historians and geographers may be, it would seem
that the city was a Lycian foundation. Its Lycian name, Pttara, has been found on coins
and insciptions. It is probable that it owed its development to two factors, the presence
of an oracle—at first of a Lycian god and later of Apollo—and the fact that it had one
of the best harbours on this part of the Lycian coast.

Patara enters written history in 333 BC, when, with Xanthus and other Lycian cities,
it surrendered to Alexander the Great. In the wars of succession that followed his death
its port attracted the attention of Antigonus and Demetrius and it was occupied by
each in turn. Ruled by the Ptolemies during the 3C BC, it took on the name Arsinoe
briefly in honour of the formidable wife of Ptolemy II. In 196 BC Patara, Xanthus and
several other Lycian cities were captured by Antiochus III of Syria. After some years
of rule by the Seleucids, Lycia passed into the control of Rhodes, the ally of Rome in
the war against Syria. In 167 BC it was finally granted its freedom by the Romans.

During the following century little is known about Patara. A period of peace and
development, it was marked by the revival of the Lycian League. Proof of the
importance of Patara is provided by the fact that, with Xanthus, Pinara and Tlos, it had
three votes, the maximum, in the League's Assembly. In 88 BC war came once more
to Lycia and Patara was besieged by Mithridates IV Eupator, king of Pontus. He cut
some of the trees in the sacred grove at the Letoön to provide battering rams and

ballistae. In 42 BC the city was again invested, this time by Brutus and Cassius who had come to Lycia in search of funds for their struggle against Antony and Octavian. After resisting the Romans for some time, Patara surrendered and consequently was treated more leniently than Xanthus. There was no massacre or enslavement. Brutus was content with the confiscation of the city's public and private wealth. Eighty years later when Lycia was attached to Pamphylia and annexed by the Romans (AD 43), Patara's importance increased rather than diminished. The Lycian League continued to be active, at least in internal affairs, and its official documents were deposited at Patara. The governor of the joint province of Lycia-Pamphylia resided here.

Patara figures in early Christian history. When SS Paul and Luke went from Miletus to Jerusalem, during their third missionary journey, they stopped here and changed ships. 'When at last (we) put out to sea, we made a straight course, sailing to Cos, and next day to Rhodes, and thence to Patara. There, finding a ship crossing to Phoenice, we went on board and set sail'. (Acts 21:1–2.) It seems likely that the Christian Church was established in Patara in apostolic times or very soon afterwards. St Nicholas of Myra was born at Patara (c 300) and spent his youth here. Patara was represented at the Council of Nicaea in AD 325 by Bishop Eudemus.

Patara continued to be of some importance until the Middle Ages. Pilgrims to the Holy Land used it as port of call. However, the harbour gradually silted up, it began to decline and finally it was abandoned completely and virtually forgotten.

Interest in Patara was revived in the 19C, when Fellows and his companions explored the Xanthus valley and the surrounding countryside. From here in 1842 the treasures of the city of Xanthus—the Nereid Monument, the tomb of Payava, the friezes from the Harpy Tomb—were loaded on to HMS *Beacon* by Lieutenant Spratt and brought to England. Before Fellows and Spratt came to Patara, Francis Beaufort, captain of HMS *Frederikssteen*, surveyed the southern coast of Turkey for the Admiralty in 1811–12. The description of 19C Patara in his book *Karamania* shows that little has changed in the last 182 years:

> Patara had formerly a harbour; the situation is still apparent, but at present it is a swamp, choked up with sand and bushes, and all communication with the sea cut off by a straight beach, through which there is no opening...Patara is now uninhabited; but a few solitary peasants were found tending the cattle that wandered about the plain.

The entrance to Patara is marked by a magnificent **Roman triple-arched gateway** of c AD 100 which is in a fine state of preservation. This was erected during the period of office of Mettius Modestus, a governor of Lycia and Pamphylia. The arches were ornamented on each façade with busts of the governor and of his family. The consoles on which the busts stood still bear the original inscriptions. On the N side an inscription states that the gateway was built by 'the People of Patara, metropolis of the Lycian nation'.

Near the gateway there are many well-preserved **Roman sarcophagi**. Some believe that the small hill to the SW may be the site of the temple of Apollo which so far has eluded discovery. A giant head of the god found there lends some support to this belief.

The ruins S of the hill mark the position of a **baths complex**, whose plan has not been determined. To the S and E of these baths are the scanty remains of a basilica. On the W side of the site a small **acropolis** overlooks the ancient harbour. This is surrounded by walls constructed during the Hellenistic and Byzantine periods. A survey of the masonry of the acropolis fortifications has been carried out recently. At the base of the walls, on the E side, there is a small, richly-decorated **temple in antis apteros**, i.e. without a row of columns, built in the Corinthian style. This dates from the 2C AD. Although sometimes called the temple of Apollo, it is generally accepted that it is too small to be the building mentioned by the ancient writers. Access to the temple, the interior of which is filled with undergrowth, is difficult in wet weather as the surrounding area is marshy.

To the S, beyond the temple, are the extensive remains of **Roman baths** which measured 105 by 48m. According to an inscription found here, they

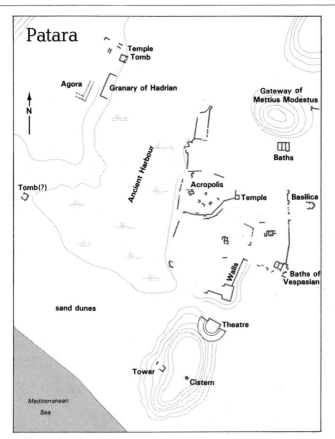

Patara

Temple Tomb

Agora   Granary of Hadrian

Gateway of Mettius Modestus

N↑

Ancient Harbour

Baths

Tomb(?)

Acropolis   Temple   Basilica

Walls

Baths of Vespasian

sand dunes

Theatre

Tower   Cistern

Mediterranean Sea

were built by Vespasian (AD 69–79). The walls had an elaborate decoration of marble or bronze sheets. Holes used to fix these are still visible.

The **theatre** of Patara is to the SW of the baths of Vespasian, at the foot of a small hill. It has a single diazoma. Entry to the cavea, which was divided into eight cunei, is by vaulted passageways. Now largely covered with sand, it is a melancholy place. Beaufort described it as:

> somewhat more than a semi-circle, whose external diameter is about two hundred feet; it contains thirty-four rows of marble seats, few of which have been disturbed; but the superior preservation of the proscenium distinguishes it from most ancient theatres which are extant, and would render it well worthy of more minute architectural detail. At the eastern entrance there is a long and very perfect inscription, recording the building of the theatre, by Q. Velius Titianus: and its dedication by his daughter Velia Procla, in the fourth consulate of the Emperor Antoninus Pius.

In fact, the inscription refers to certain alterations and additions to the proscenium, stage and auditorium made in AD 147. The theatre is much older than the 2C AD, as another inscription concerning repairs made to the structure during the reign of Tiberius (AD 14–37) makes clear.

From the rear of the theatre it is an easy climb to the top of the hill from where there is a striking view of the ancient city and the surrounding area.

To the N lie the theatre, the baths of Vespasian, the Corinthian-style temple, the Byzantine acropolis, the ancient harbour, the granary of Hadrian, the arch of Mettius Modestus and the ruined sarcophagi of the necropolis. To the S and W a fine beach stretches away into the distance. This is bordered by high sand dunes, the barrier which cut Patara off from the open sea and brought about its decline and abandonment.

On top of the hill there are some interesting remains, the stylobate of the **Temple of Athena** and a curious structure which has aroused much interest and controversy. This is a **circular pit** about 10m in diameter and the same in depth, partly cut from the natural rock, partly constructed from masonry. In the centre there is a stone pillar which rises about 2m above ground. A staircase cut into the rock provides rather precarious access to the bottom. Many theories have been put forward to explain the purpose of the structure. Although not positioned on the very summit of the hill, some are certain that it was a lighthouse, while others have decided that it marks the site of the oracle of Apollo. Beaufort appears to have originated the latter theory. However, most now agree that it was a cistern for water storage and that it dates from the time before aqueducts were constructed in Patara.

To visit the granary of Hadrian and the necropolis, go down the W side of the theatre hill and, crossing the sand dunes, skirt the edge of the fen that marks the site of the ancient harbour. There is no fixed path, so take care not to stray on to the marsh. In places the undergrowth is difficult to penetrate.

During one of his visits to Patara, Bean found the base of a large building projecting from the sand at the W edge of the ancient harbour at the point where one turns N towards the granary. This, he concluded, was the **lighthouse** which had been built, probably on a mole, at the entrance to the harbour. The **granary**, which, according to an inscription in Latin on the façade, was erected during the reign of Hadrian (117–138), is similar in size and construction to that at Andriace. It measures c 65m by 32m and was divided into eight single-storey rectangular rooms. Apart from being roofless, it is in a very good state of preservation. The façade had two storeys and was ornamented with busts placed on pedestals above the doors. The interior, which is very overgrown, appears to have had a single storey.

A short distance N of the granary are the remains of an elaborate free-standing Corinthian style **pseudo-peripteral temple-tomb**. Its presence and other tombs and sarcophagi nearby suggests that one of the necropolises of the city was located here.

In Roman times Patara was supplied with water by two aqueducts. Their remains are near the Letoön and in the hills above Kalkan.

Return to Road 400, turn right and continue in the direction of c 10km Kalkan. On the left there is a large marsh, the **Ova Gölü**. A century ago leeches were collected here and shipped from Kaş to Europe where doctors used them to bleed their patients. The road, shaded by pines, now climbs steeply, winding and twisting to the summit. The plain of Xanthus is far below. On the other side of the ridge the descent is equally steep. Flanked by olive groves, the road cuts a red scar across a mountain side pockmarked with scattered clumps of vegetation. After c 2km a sign indicates an abrupt right-hand turn to the pretty village of Kalkan.

Like Kaş, its close neighbour, **KALKAN** is built near the foot of a steep mountain. Its white houses sit at the northern end of a fiord whose mouth is protected by Çatal Ada. Kalkan is one of several places on the Lycian coast which has adapted itself with considerable success to the needs of tourism. In spite of a plethora of boutiques, hotels and pensions it has managed to retain much of the character and atmosphere of a Turkish fishing village. Among its smart shops, there are bakers, butchers, general stores, tailors, drapers, shoemakers and handicraft merchants who cater as much for the local people as for the tourists.

There are frequent bus and dolmuş services to Fethiye and Antalya.

Kalkan has one five-star, two three-star, one two-star hotel and many pensions. Recommended are the five-star *Hotel Patara Prince* and the *Akim Pansiyon*, the *Kalkan Han Pansiyon* and *Paşa's Inn Pansiyon*. Restaurants offer a wide choice and, of course, excellent fresh fish.

By the harbour there is a mobile health unit with ambulances and specialist facilities. The Yacht Club has showers, a self-service laundry and a restaurant—everything spray-soaked, fashion-conscious sailors need.

There are few good beaches near the village. The beach on the W, beyond the quarry, is by tradition reserved for ladies. To the E the shore is pebbly, subject to frequent rockfalls, and too near the village to be free from pollution. Take a boat to one of the more distant beaches, or a dolmuş to the small, but shadeless, strand at Kapitaş, 6km on the road to Kaş.

This is a resort which attracts those who want a conventional break in the sun and those who need a base from which to explore the ancient sites of western Lycia, particularly Xanthus, the Letoön and Patara. It is also a good centre for walking. To the E there are some attractive valleys, which are barely visible from the road. Spring, autumn and early winter are the best times to visit Kalkan. In summer the heat is overpowering, accommodation is strained to its limits and prices are at their highest. Spring comes early to Kalkan. At the beginning of March the winter rains are ending, wild flowers transform the surrounding countryside, there are few tourists, and hotels and pensions offer rooms at attractive rates.

The road to 27km Kaş follows the coastline. Narrow and with many bends, it is well surfaced. Care should be taken, especially on corners, as sheep and goats frequently stray on to the carriageway. At c 6km **Kapıtaş** there is a bridge over a small gorge. Here, steps lead down to a pebble and sandy beach. There is little shade and no refreshments, so bring a beach umbrella and a picnic lunch. A marble tablet on the cliff wall commemorates four workmen who were killed during the construction of the road.

The approach to Kaş is signalled by a peninsula which stretches S, like a long accusatory finger, towards the Greek island of **Meis** (sometimes called Kastellorizo). This peninsula separates the town from the NW harbour, Bucak Limanı, which was formerly called Vathy.

KAŞ, which means 'eyebrow' in Turkish, straggles picturesquely over the lower slopes of a 500m high cliff that rises abruptly from the sea. During recent years it has become increasingly popular with Turks and foreigners attracted by its situation, excellent climate and restful atmosphere.

Information, Accommodation, Transport. Although quite a few hotels and pensions have been erected in recent years, planning laws protect Kaş from over-development.

The **Tourist Information Office** is at Cumhuriyet Meydanı No. 6. The *otogar* is not far from the town centre.

Kaş has one three-star, three two-star, and one one-star hotel and many pensions. The three-star *Ekici Oteli*, the two-star *Mimosa Hotel*, and the *Limyra Pansiyon* are recommended. At the end of the peninsula to the W of the town is the *Hotel Sunset Club*. About 4.5km from the town centre, this has rooms and apartments which sleep up to five guests, and a swimming pool.

The long established *Eriş Restaurant*, which once was part of a church, and its larger neighbour, the *Mercan*, offer good, well cooked food at very reasonable prices. Try one of the many *lokantalar* in crowded, noisy *Çukurbağlı Sokak* on the northern side of Cumhuriyet Meydanı. Kaş has a fairly lively night life. Blasts of rock and pop from the discos behind the Mercan continue to disturb the peace almost to the dawn. For a quieter evening try the *Country Café* which is furnished like a house in Anatolia. Here you recline on cushions and sip your *rakı* like a latter day *paşa*.

The Cumhuriyet Meydanı is the centre of the town's social life. Here visitors and locals meet in the cafés for aperitifs, to chat and exchange news, to play backgammon, or just to plan tomorrow's programme.

The **post office** and **banks** are in a street to the right of Cumhuriyet Meydanı.

Down by the harbour there is a comfortable, well furnished **journalists' club** which serves drinks and light refreshments. This is open to non-journalists, but members of the profession get a discount on production of their business cards. Its pleasant lounge has a large open fire, a welcome amenity during cool spring and autumn evenings.

Excursions by boat. During the season you can make the 40-minute crossing to the Greek island of **Meis**. Seats may be booked from boat owners or from an agency in the town. As Meis is not an official entry point to Greece, visitors may be refused permission to land. If allowed to disembark, their stay is usually limited to a few hours. Passports are required. The skipper or agency will obtain the necessary customs and emigration clearances from the Turkish authorities. The skipper will also negotiate with the Greek port officials about landing on Meis. Note the Lycian rock tombs at the back of the port, proof of ancient links between the mainland and the island.

Another popular excursion is to the **Mavi Mağara**, the Blue Grotto, between Kalkan and Kaş. It is possible to combine this with a visit to the beach at Kapıtaş.

There are also excursions to the island of **Kekova**, famous for its submerged harbour, and to the sites of **Aperlae**, **Simena** and **Teimiussa**. The best beaches are most easily reached by boat. Bathing near Kaş is not recommended. The beaches are small, stony and are not always very clean. The sea near the rocky outcrops on the E and W sides of the town and on the peninsula is deep, rough and often polluted.

History. In ancient times Kaş was known as Antiphellus in Greek, Habesos in Lycian. It was the port of the city of Phellus, which is believed to have been sited in the mountainous area behind the town. Originally Phellus, which means stony land, was the more important foundation. Antiphellus had several disadvantages: it was vulnerable to attack from land and sea and the lack of level ground prevented expansion. Excavations have revealed that in the 4C BC it consisted of a few buildings near the harbour and some rock-tombs. A century later the situation had changed. Antiphellus had become a busy port, probably for the export of timber from the hinterland, while the star of Phellus had begun to wane. In Roman times Antiphellus was one of the major trading cities of Lycia. According to Pliny it was famous for its sponges.

There are few visible reminders of the past in Kaş: a Hellenistic theatre, some fragments of wall and a few Lycian tombs. Much was lost comparatively recently. In the 19C Charles Texier found several buildings including a basilica and a circular Byzantine church near the theatre. These have vanished completely. In 1842 Lieutenant Spratt noted that there were more than a hundred sarcophagi in Kaş. Most of these have disappeared, broken up for the sake of the stone slabs that formed their sides and bottoms. Only the rounded lids, useless for building purposes, remain.

For the **Hellenistic theatre**, take Hastane Cad. which starts near the mosque on the W side of the town. A short distance along on the left are the remains of a small **temple** which dates from the 1C BC. It is not known to whom it was dedicated. Just before the theatre, there is a section of the **Hellenistic sea wall** on the left.

The theatre, surrounded by ancient olive trees, is to the right of the road. Greater than a semicircle, it has 26 rows of seats, no parodoi and no diazoma. It would seem that there was no permanent stage-building either. The low curved wall in front is modern. The retaining wall of the cavea, constructed from huge stone blocks which vary considerably in size and shape, is best seen on the W side of the theatre. Continue to the top row for a splendid view of the sea and of the distant island of Meis. In early evening, when daylight begins to fade, the lights of the little island's port glow like jewels against the velvet of the gathering dark.

About 100m behind the theatre, on top of the hill, there is a very fine rock-cut tomb. This, the so-called **Doric Tomb**, dates from the 4C BC. It consists of a single chamber measuring 5m by 5m. There are traces of decoration on the outside. The tomb was closed by a sliding door. At the back, the *kline* on which the body was placed is decorated with a striking frieze of tiny female figures performing a ritual dance. Holding hands, they move in a stately measure which causes their skirts to billow outwards in graceful folds. Sadly, the tomb has been used as a shelter for animals and is fouled and odorous, its walls and floor blackened by fires.

Continue across the hill to the Bucak Limanı. From here it is just a few minutes' walk to the town centre. On the great cliff that dominates Kaş there are several **Lycian rock-tombs**. Access is by a narrow path which snakes through some private gardens and then climbs the hillside at an angle. It appears that one of the tombs was used twice, as it has two inscriptions from different periods, one in Lycian, the second in Latin.

Of greater interest is the so-called **Lion Tomb**. This is in a small street off the NE corner of Cumhuriyet Meydanı. The top part of the monument is one of the finest examples extant of a Lycian ogival sarcophagus. The lifting bosses on the cover are carved in the form of lions' heads resting on their forepaws, hence its name. On the top of the gable-end two figures are carved in shallow relief. The sarcophagus rests on a stone base and beneath this there is another burial chamber. Both chambers were broken into and robbed in antiquity. On the side of the lower chamber there is a long inscription in an unusual form of the Lycian language. This resembles the inscription on the Inscribed Pillar in the agora at Xanthus. Although not deciphered, it is presumed to be an epitaph, perhaps in poetical form.

On the harbour mole there is another ogival Lycian sarcophagus and there are several examples to the E of the town.

Excursion to Aperlae, Kekova, Kale (Simena), and Teimiussa

A popular day excursion from Kaş is the boat trip to Kekova and to the sites of the ancient cities of Aperlae, Teimiussa and Simena. During the holiday season boats leave from the harbour mole at about 9.00 and return at 18.00. Passing the island of Meis on the right you enter a narrow bay. At the head of the bay are the ruins of the city of **Aperlae**, a Lycian foundation. During the Roman period the leader of a sympolity, which included Apollonia, Isinda and Simena, Aperlae was never very important. No trace of a temple or theatre has been found here. As the boat approaches the shore it passes over the remains of the ancient harbour buildings. On the W side there was a quay, capable of berthing several ships.

The fortifications of Aperlae date from two distinct periods. The walls of the later city, which stretch down from the acropolis, appear to have been built to protect the harbour area. Note the gate on the E side which is now partly submerged. Between the inner and outer walls there are several ogival sarcophagi. The inner wall of the city was constructed of ashlar. This has been repaired in several places. On the W side there are three well-preserved gates. The main entrance, which had defensive towers on each side, was on the S wall. The acropolis of Aperlae, which is enclosed by the inner wall, is covered with undergrowth and is not easy to explore.

From Aperlae the boat usually goes to the island of **Kekova**. During the Hellenistic period there was a considerable increase in maritime trade between the cities of Lycia and other parts of the Greek world. Unfortunately, this was paralleled by a marked increase in piracy. As a result islands like Kekova were fortified and became both refuges in times of danger and advance warning posts for the cities on the mainland. They served the same purpose during the 7C AD Arab raids.

As it skirts the shoreline the boat glides over the remains of buildings, stairs and pavements which are clearly visible under the water. Usually there is time for a swim and a picnic at a small beach on the N side of the island. Prominent here are the remains of an **apsidal construction**, which some believe to be part of a Byzantine church, while others are of the opinion that it was a small boatyard. Its local name, 'Tersane', supports the second hypothesis. If you swim near the underwater ruins beware of the spiny sea urchins. Skin-diving is forbidden near the submerged buildings. **There are severe penalties for transgressing this rule and for removing any antiquities found in the sea or on land.** There are the remains of a number of buildings on the island, but these are almost hidden by the dense and thorny undergrowth and are not easy to find or investigate.

Near Kekova there are several islets whose shaved and sculptured outlines betray the fact that they were used as sources of stone by ancient builders. On the mainland the village of **Kale** (the castle) covers the site of the city of **Simena**. Kale has a few pensions which provide basic accommodation, and there are restaurants down by the harbour.

Left of the landing-stage there are some **partly submerged ruins**. The remains of a Roman **baths complex** of c AD 79 are on the shore nearby. According to an inscription this was dedicated by the city of Aperlae to the Emperor Titus. The ascent to the medieval **castle** is by a steep, narrow path which winds between houses and through gardens. It passes two **sarcophagi**, one dedicated to Mentor, the son of Idagrus; the other has a small exedra. The last part of the ascent is over a section of very slippery rock which should be negotiated with care. Below the ramparts there is a small rock-cut **theatre**. This could accommodate about 300 spectators in its seven rows of seats. The view from the theatre across the bay to the island of Kekova and down to the village of Kale is magnificent. Equally striking is the vista from the ramparts of the castle northwards to Üçağiz and the site of Teimiussa. On the way down to the landing-stage, a path on the left leads to the **necropolis** of Simena. This has several **ogival sarcophagi** and some **rock-cut tombs**, one of which bears an inscription in Lycian.

Üçağiz, like its Greek name Tristomo, means 'the three mouths'. This refers to the channel to the village and the two openings E and W of Kekova island. The village has a number of small restaurants and some pensions.

Most visitors go to Üçağiz by boat, but it can also be reached by land. Take a right-hand turn c 20km from Kaş on the way to Demre on to a minor road. This is passable as far as the village of Sıçak (c 9km), by most vehicles, but it deteriorates rapidly thereafter. Improvements are envisaged.

Sıçak is the site of the ancient settlement of **Apollonia**, a place not mentioned by ancient writers. It has been identified by inscriptions found on the spot. These mention 'Aperlites from Apollonia' and there are dedications made by the 'People of Apollonia' to Augustus and Tiberius. However, the settlement existed long before Roman times. Proof of this is provided by the presence of several Lycian pillar tombs and a Lycian rock-tomb with an inscription in Greek. 'Apollonia' is a Greek word, the Lycian name of the settlement is not known. It was built on a hill about 90m above the village of Sıçak. In addition to the tombs there are the remains of the city walls, traces of the theatre and a number of cisterns.

The site of **Teimiussa** is a short distance to the E of the village of Üçağiz. Like Apollonia it has been identified from an inscription. It was a small

The castle and village of Kale near Kaş

settlement, without walls or public buildings. The remains extant are almost all tombs. Many of these lie in a marshy area half hidden by clumps of reeds. Near the shore there are **two rock-cut tombs**. The tomb on the right bears a relief of a nude youth and has the Lycian name 'Kluwanimi', by the side of the decorated entrance. Beyond this tomb there is a jumbled mass of ogival sarcophagi from the Hellenistic and Roman periods. Many bear inscriptions in Greek, stating that their occupants were citizens of Cyaneae or Myra, proof of Teimiussa's dependence on one or both of these cities. To the E of the site there is a small rock-cut **landing-stage**, surrounded by desecrated tombs. One, which is placed c 2m above ground level, may be approached through a natural cleft in the rock.

Excursion to Comba and Choma

From Kaş take Road 400 to Demre (see Route 24). After c 11km branch left on to the road signposted Elmalı via c 12km Kasaba. This excursion, which crosses the Kohu Dağ by two passes, Karaovabeli Geç (1080m) and Sinekçibeli Geç (1545m), should not be attempted during bad weather.

The village of c 25km **Gömbe**, situated near the southern end of the Elmalı plain, preserves in its name a memory of the ancient city of **Comba**. The site of Comba is on a hilltop to the SW of the village. The few pathetic remains of the city hardly justify the exertion required by the climb.

Little is known about Comba. It had a Council and an Assembly and during the Byzantine period was an episcopal see. Its main claim to fame is that it was the cult centre of the Twelve Gods of Lycia. More than 20 carvings commemorating these hunting deities have been found in various places, including about eight in the neighbourhood of Gömbe. One is in the Antalya Museum. The carvings, which are remarkably similar, date from the 3C AD. The site of the city of Choma, near the village of **Hacımusalar**, is on a *hüyük* about 8km from Gombe. This has been identified by inscriptions dating from the Roman Imperial period. There are few visible remains. About 5km NW of Choma, near **Kızılca** there are two **Lycian rock-cut tombs**. One bears an inscription in the Lycian language, which mentions Pericles, the 4C BC dynast of Limyra.

After c 5km you reach the junction with road 635 which links Finike on the S coast of Lycia with 6km Elmalı (see Route 25).

24

Kaş to Demre (Myra)

Total distance c 48km. Kaş—c 23km Yavu—(c 3km Cyaneae)—(c 2.5km Tyberissus)—(c 4km Istlada)—(c 12km Trysa)—(c 0.5km Sura)—c 14km Demre/Myra.

Road 400 climbs through a series of bends to the plateau above Kaş. From the summit there are views to the Greek island of Meis and west to Kalkan. After c 11km a turning on the left leads via Elmalı and Korkuteli to Antalya (see Route 25). At c 20km a side road on the right goes to Apollonia and Üçağiz (see Route 23).

At this point the road enters a wild, picturesque and inhospitable land. Here the rocky bones of Lycia protrude through a thin covering of soil and only the tough, thorny maquis flourishes. In antiquity, there were several small cities and settlements between Kaş and Demre. Abandoned long ago and forgotten, except by archaeologists, their ruined fortifications, silent theatres and desecrated tombs bear mute witness to past glories. Lycian, Hellenistic and Roman ruins abound, but only a few tiny cultivated fields and scattered olive groves and the sight of an occasional shepherd and his flock testify to the continuing presence of man in this part of Lycia.

The village of c 23km **Yavu** is sited between a 200m high bluff and a plain which slopes gently towards the sea at Kekova. This is the starting point for a visit to the ancient city of **CYANEAE**. In the village centre a side-road is signposted 3km to the site. However, a more interesting, if somewhat more difficult, route starts from behind the village. This climbs at an angle until it reaches the base of the bluff at its eastern end. Allow about one hour for the ascent. Take a guide as the path is overgrown in parts and difficult to follow and there are cisterns partially concealed by vegetation inside the acropolis—a danger to the unwary and uninformed.

Cyaneae has been identified by inscriptions found on the spot. Its name may be derived from Κυάνεος, dark blue, the colour of lapis lazuli (the English words 'cyan', 'cyanic' and 'cyanide' are from the same Greek root) or from the city's unknown Lycian name.

History. Although mentioned by Pliny and other ancient writers, little is known about the history of Cyaneae. During the reign of Antoninus Pius (AD 138–161) the Lyciarch, Jason of Cyaneae, was involved in a dispute concerning certain honours that had been voted to him. The dispute was submitted to the emperor who found in his favour. Jason, like his contemporary Opramoas of Rhodiapolis, was famous for his benefactions. The territory of Cyaneae extended as far S as Kekova and is mentioned in a number of inscriptions found in other places. Originally a Lycian foundation, most of the extant remains date from the Roman period. Although an episcopal see and a city of some importance, its fortunes began to decline and Cyaneae was finally abandoned in the 10C. A large-scale survey of the city and its territory has been started by archaeologists.

Near the base of the bluff there are the vestiges of an **ancient path** which has steps cut into the rock at intervals. This will take you past an interesting group of **early tombs**. One of these appears at first sight to be a typical ogival sarcophagus with decorated lifting bosses in the form of lions' heads. However, the lid and body are made from a single piece of stone and an opening on the W side was made for the admission of the corpse.

The **acropolis** of Cyaneae is enclosed by walls on three sides, the fourth, the S side, is protected by the precipice. There are the remains of a baths complex, a library and several cisterns. However, it is not easy to find these buildings as the whole area is covered with thick, tangled undergrowth. Detailed exploration of the acropolis is almost impossible.

Cyaneae is reputed to have more sarcophagi than any other Lycian city. A fine example stands outside the entrance to Antalya's Archaeological Museum. Apart from those on the southern slope, there is a great concentration W of the acropolis where an avenue, which stretches almost to the theatre, is lined on both sides with tombs. Most date from the Roman period. Many of the sarcophagi are decorated with reliefs and bear inscriptions.

Apart from the almost complete disappearance of the stage-building and some damage to the retaining wall of the cavea, the **theatre** is in a good state of preservation. It has a single diazoma with five cunei below and nine above the division. Most of the original seats remain. Some of the rows have holes for wooden posts which were probably used to support the velum, an awning, which protected the spectators from the elements.

On the way back to the village the path passes underneath an interesting **rock-tomb** which has several unusual features. Built in the form of an Ionic temple, it has a single pillar, flanked by pilasters, in the centre of the entrance. A sarcophagus was placed on top of the pediment in a deep recess cut into the rock. According to an inscription above the lintel, Perpenenis, for whom the tomb was built, was buried with his wife in the sarcophagus, members of his family were placed in the upper and lower chambers.

Cyaneae, which is little visited, has an atmosphere of brooding melancholy, partly derived from its isolated position, partly from its neglected state. The effort required to climb to the top is more than repaid by the view at sunset of the serried ranks of tombs along the street of the dead. An image of the windswept theatre, empty except for a few agile goats that browse daintily on herbage growing through the broken seats, lingers in the memory. Cyaneae arouses feelings of profound melancholy. The shade of Villon mutters—'*mais où sont les neiges d'antan...*'

S of Yavu there are two settlements of minor importance—**Tyberissus** and **Istlada**. The former is on a hilltop about 400m above sea-level. It has a number of tombs dating from the Hellenistic and Roman periods and a small church built over a Doric temple dedicated to Apollo. The latter has the remains of some stone houses and a number of sarcophagi. Both have been identified by inscriptions.

A turning on the left c 6km from Yavu leads to c 12km **Trysa**, another site which has been identified by inscriptions. Nothing is known of its history. It may have been the fortified stronghold of a local chieftain. Sited on a small hill near the village of **Gölbaşı**, Trysa's remains are some of the oldest in Lycia, dating from the 5C BC. Most are in a very poor state of preservation. Apart from fragments of a pillar tomb and a small ruined temple there is the usual complement of ogival sarcophagi one of which is ornamented with reliefs and decorative bosses. However, Trysa's most remarkable feature is the

4C BC **heroon** located towards the NE of the acropolis. A wall 3m high surrounds the square enclosure containing the sarcophagus of a deified hero and his family. This wall was covered with a frieze in two bands representing various mythological subjects: the life of Theseus; incidents in the *Iliad* and the *Odyssey*; the battles of the Centaurs and Lapiths and the siege of a town. The frieze is no longer in Trysa or indeed in Turkey. It was removed to Vienna and is now in the Kunsthistorisches Museum.

Road 400 continues through another tract of wild country, first clinging to the side of the mountain, then turning through a series of lazy bends to descend at last to the fertile plain of Demre. From the top of the hill the surroundings of Demre present a startling appearance. A mosaic of plastic and glass-covered greenhouses, separated by the vivid green tesserae of orange groves, covers a huge area from the foot of the mountain to the sea.

On a curve towards the bottom of the hill an isolated cluster of houses, near a dewpond, marks the nearest point on the main road to Sura. There are no sign posts to the site which is due W over the fields. Take a guide as there is no clearly defined path. A guide will also keep at bay the aggressive sheepdogs which guard the farms and livestock near the site.

SURA, like Patara, probably owed its importance to its oracle of Apollo. However, unlike Patara it never developed a political dimension. It remained a religious centre and a dependency of Myra. This is reflected both in its size and in the type of buildings found here.

History. Most of the references to Sura in the works of ancient writers concern the unusual method of divination used by the oracle. These excited a great deal of interest. Pliny stated that fish, summoned 'three times on the pipe' to give augury, were thrown pieces of meat. If they took the meat, that was a good sign, if they pushed it away with their tails, a bad sign. A more detailed description is provided by the author of *Lycia*, the Hellenistic writer Polycharmus.

> When they come to the sea, where is the grove of Apollo by the shore, on which is the whirlpool on the sand, the clients present themselves holding two wooden spits, on each of which are ten pieces of roast meat. The priest takes his seat in silence by the grove, while the client throws the spits into the whirlpool and watches what happens. After the spits are thrown in, the pool fills with sea-water, and a multitude of fish appear as if by magic, and of a size to cause alarm. The prophet announces the species of the fish and the client accordingly receives his answer from the priest.

> According to the geographer Artemidorus of Ephesus (fl. c 100 BC), large fish appeared in a whirlpool of freshwater and those who came to consult the oracle threw pieces of meat, barley and wheat cakes to them. The three accounts, which may refer to practices employed at different times, differ on one point only—whether the predictions were based on the type of fish in the pool or on the way they reacted to the offerings.

No information is available about the later history of the oracle of Sura. We do not know if, like Patara, it suffered a period of decline and revival in the 1C and 2C AD. There is no record of when the last prophetic utterance was made. It is possible that the influence of St Nicholas of Myra and of the Christian community of that city had some effect by the middle of the 4C, a time when Christian shrines began to appear in the great temple of Apollo at Didyma. It is probable that the edict of Theodosius in 385 abolishing all oracles gave the cult at Sura the *coup de grâce*. Perhaps it was at this time that the triumph of Christianity over paganism at Sura was confirmed by the erection of a small church near the site of the temple of Apollo.

The few remains of ancient Sura are in two parts. At the W end of the plain there are the ruins of the tiny acropolis, the so-called house of the priests, two watch-towers, part of the walls and a number of tombs. Down by the ancient harbour, now silted up and overgrown, are the ruins of the temple of Apollo, the sacred spring and the walls of a small church.

Approaching the site from the main road the first building encountered is a **watch-tower**. This structure, which is in a good state of preservation,

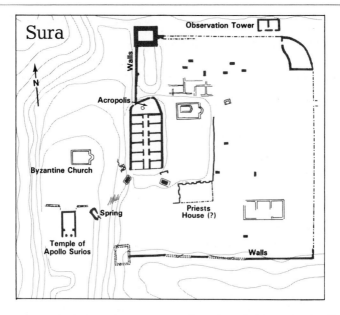

lies just outside the line of the ancient walls to the NE of the acropolis. The agora and residential area, which date from a late period of occupation, are between this tower and the acropolis. Sura's **acropolis** occupies a rocky spur c 10m high, near the extreme W edge of the plain at the point where it slopes steeply towards the harbour. It has a keep, some parts of which date from the 5C BC, divided into 12 small cell-like chambers, six on each side of a narrow passage. The junction of the W and N **walls** of the fortified area is marked by a square **watch-tower**. At the S end of the acropolis there is an interesting group of **tombs**. Below and to the left of a typical Lycian rock-tomb a large burial chamber has been constructed by the side of the hill. Resting on the flat roof of this structure is a tall **pillar tomb** with an ogival lid. Apparently this monument, dating from the 4C BC, was intended for family burial, the owner being placed in the pillar tomb and members of his family in the chamber underneath.

The site of the so-called **House of the Priests**, which some authorities believe formed part of a larger sacred area, lies to the SW of this group of tombs. All that remains is a terrace c 15m by c 9m which has been cut from the rock. Sockets for roof beams on the N wall 8m above the ground suggest that the structure had a wooden roof. On the N and W walls **tablets**, carved in relief, list the names of the priests of Apollo Surius.

Access to the harbour was by way of a rock-cut stairway which descended from the plateau at a point about 50m W of the house of the priests. Traces of the stairway remain. Today the lower part of the site is a marsh, passable only in summer. The stream that rises in the **sacred spring** meanders lazily for c 1.5km to the sea. The **temple of Apollo** is a small building, c 14m by c 7m, constructed in the Doric style. A temple in antis, built during the late Hellenistic period, it stood on or near the ancient harbour. The sacred spring is a few metres from the temple, near the bottom of the stairway. The small **Byzantine church** is a short distance to the N.

Some visitors are tempted to walk the few kilometres that separate Sura from Andriace. However, the route through the marsh and along the shoreline is difficult, uncomfortable and, in certain circumstances, **it may be dangerous**.

Return to the main road and continue in an easterly direction towards Demre. The road divides at the bottom of the hill. The left fork goes to Demre, the right to Andriace. At the crossroads there are the remains of a **Roman temple tomb**. This has suffered extensive damage on the W side, but otherwise is in a good state of preservation. Neither the date of its construction nor the name of its occupant is known. Built entirely of closely fitting masonry, it stands to a height of c 13m. Access to the interior is from the N side by an elaborate, tall doorway, flanked on the left by a Corinthian pilaster. The matching pilaster on the right has disappeared. Entrances on the S side, closed by stone slabs, led to two underground burial chambers. On the E and W walls there are *klinai* which may have been used for additional sarcophagi. Note the large false arches on the E and S walls and the carved lion heads on the *sima*.

From the Roman tomb, a road flanked by citrus groves and greenhouses leads to c 2.5km **Demre**, a pleasant, undistinguished country town, important only as a marketing centre for fruit and vegetables and of interest to visitors because of its proximity to the site of ancient Myra.

Information and Accommodation. There are several pensions in Demre. Finike and Kaş have a range of accommodation. Demre has frequent bus and dolmuş services to places on Road 400 from the *otogar*. Restaurants in the centre of the town provide simple meals. The post office is 150m to the E of the main square.

About 1.5km to the S of the town there is a long beach of gravel and sand. The best bathing is at **Andriace** c 2.5km to the SW. Andriace has a restaurant, but no hotel or pension. During the season there are daily boat excursions from Andriace to Kekova. For the ruins of the ancient city of Myra, 1.5km N of Demre, follow the signposts.

History. Although the earliest written references to Myra date from the 1C BC, Lycian inscriptions and monuments suggest that there was a settlement here at least as early as the 5C BC. During the 3C BC an elaborate system of watch-towers, stretching from Sura in the W to the E edge of the Demre plain, was constructed. In the 2C BC Myra was one of the six most important cities in the Lycian League. It issued federal coins, and was entitled to three votes, the maximum permitted, in the League's Assembly. According to an ancient tradition the city's name was derived from the Greek word for myrrh. This belief persisted into Byzantine times. Constantine VII, Porphyrogenitus, (913–959) described Myra as 'thrice blessed, myrrh-breathing city of the Lycians, where the mighty Nicolaus, servant of God, spouts forth myrrh in accordance with the city's name'. There is no evidence that myrrh was ever produced in Myra. As in the case of Patara, 'Myra' is almost certainly the original, or derived from the original, unknown Lycian name of the city.

In 42 BC, after he had captured Xanthus, Brutus sent an officer, Lentulus Spinther, to obtain money from Myra. The Myrans were unwilling to pay and Spinther had to force his way through the chain that closed the entrance to the harbour at Andriace. The city then reluctantly agreed to his demands. A year before his tragic death near Antioch in AD 19 Germanicus, the adopted son of the Emperor Tiberius, accompanied by his wife Agrippina, paid a visit to Myra. This was commemorated by the erection of statues at Andriace in their honour.

According to the Acts of the Apostles, when St Paul was a prisoner being taken to Rome in AD 60, his ship called at Myra: 'Then, setting sail, we coasted under the lee of Cyprus, to avoid contrary winds, but made a straight course over the open sea that lies off Cilicia and Pamphylia, and so reached Lystra (Myra) in Lycia. There the centurion found a boat from Alexandria which was sailing for Italy, and put us on board'. This was the voyage which, dogged by gales and contrary winds, ended in shipwreck off the coast of Malta.

Lycian rock-tombs at the site of Myra

In the 2C AD Myra benefited considerably from the generosity of Opramoas of Rhodiapolis and Jason of Cyaneae. (At about the same time it acquired the status of a metropolis.) Their gifts were used for the renovation and decoration of public buildings. With the spread of Christianity throughout the Roman Empire, Myra abandoned paganism. In the 4C it acquired new and widespread fame because of the miracles performed by its bishop, St Nicholas. The city reached its apogee during the reign of Theodosius II (408–450) when he made it the provincial capital of Lycia. Myra began to decline in the 7C. It suffered greatly from the Arab raids. In AD 809 it was occupied for some time by Harun al Rashid and in 1034 it was attacked once again from the sea by the Arabs. Finally, exhausted by warfare, threatened by earthquakes and impoverished by the silting of the river Myrus, most of its inhabitants moved away.

In the 19C the accounts of Fellows and Texier of their travels in Lycia did much to revive interest in Myra. When Beaufort came to Andriace in 1811 he described Myra as a small village situated on a plain well-stocked with cattle. This plain was 'partly cultivated; it also displayed some symptoms of commerce, in the heaps of billet wood and deal plank, which lay on the beach ready for embarkation'. Cockerell, who visited Myra a year later, sketched the ruins of the city and of the theatre, which were better preserved than at present. He was treated churlishly by the local inhabitants whom he described as being more than ordinarily jealous and ferocious. Newton describes how not far from Myra pirates attacked a boat which was sailing from Rhodes to Finike. Luckily, the 400 passengers only had their money taken from them. The previous day the same pirates boarded and sank a small boat from Simi and murdered all the crew.

A century later, when Freya Stark was in Myra, difficulty of access had replaced danger. Travel to and from Antalya was usually done by sea. A coast road was something people talked and dreamed about.

The remains of **MYRA** naturally fall into three distinct zones. The first, on the SW, includes the theatre, the so-called sea necropolis and the area occupied by the agora. The second, on the N, covers the acropolis, its buildings and its walls. The third, on the SE, encompasses the river necropolis and the channel which supplied Myra with water.

The **theatre** of Myra, destroyed by the earthquake that devastated the city in AD 141, was restored shortly afterwards through the generosity of Opramoas of Rhodiapolis. Some time later it was modified so that it could be used as an arena for gladiatorial games. There are six rows of seats above and 29 below the single diazoma. Holes indicate the places where a velum was erected to shelter spectators from the elements. The cavea, whose centre rests against the rock face, is supported at the sides by vaulted passages. These contain the stairs by which the spectators entered the auditorium. The two-storey passage on the W is flanked by a number of small rooms. An inscription in one states that it was used by a trader called Gelasius. The wide diazoma is backed by a 2m-high wall in whose centre, near the stairs leading to the upper rows, there is a representation of Tyche, goddess of fortune, and an inscription which reads: 'Fortune of the city, be ever victorious, with good luck'. Note the graffiti on the diazoma—these may indicate the reserved seats of regular patrons.

A substantial part of the stage-building remains. The façade facing the cavea was richly ornamented with theatrical masks and representations of mythological scenes and personages. These included Zeus' rape of Ganymede, and Medea and her children.

The so-called **sea necropolis** is on the cliff-face behind and to the NW and NE of the theatre. It contains a remarkable group of rock-tombs, several with richly-decorated façades. Most are of the familiar house type which are believed to copy the dwellings of the Lycians. Some have stylised representations of the wooden beams used as roof-supports in Lycian houses. A few have reliefs that still bear traces of colour. Inscriptions, where they exist, are usually in Lycian.

A **tomb** at ground level, at the base of the cliff, has a sculpture on the pediment which shows a critical moment in a conflict between two warriors. The figure on the left appears to be fleeing, but he is being restrained by his oppponent who has placed his hand on his shield.

A narrow goat track leads to a group of **three tombs** c 10m above ground level. One of these is decorated with an elaborate relief which dates from the middle of the 4C BC. In the centre panel a male figure, perhaps the deceased, is shown reclining on a couch, flanked on the right by a seated female figure and on the left by a musician and by a young slave carrying a bowl. On the extreme left there are three male figures. One in armour, is receiving his helmet from a page. The other two, nude, well-muscled youths, gaze dreamily into the distance.

The **agora** was probably to the E of the theatre. This part of the city has not been excavated. On the left of the road leading from Myra to Demre there are the **remains of a brick building** which dates from the late Roman period. This is described variously as a basilica or a baths complex. Several interesting inscriptions have been found here. One sets out the regulations applying to a ferry service operated during the Roman period between Andriace and Limyra. Unauthorised operators were obliged to pay a heavy fine to the city. The other inscription details the payments to be made to the Lycian League from import duties collected by Myra.

Coins issued by Myra show that the city's main deity was Artemis Eleutheria, Bountiful Artemis, a manifestation of Cybele the ancient mother goddess of Anatolia. Like the fecund Ephesian Artemis, she was usually decorated with a profusion of fertility objects which have been variously described as breasts, eggs, or bull's testes. After the earthquake of 141, her temple was restored by Opramoas of Rhodiapolis. Probably sited near the theatre and the agora, it has not been discovered so far.

The **acropolis** is reached from the plain by an ancient path. The outer walls were constructed during the Byzantine period. The inner Lycian walls are of polygonal masonry and date from the 5C BC. The central area contained a watch-tower and cisterns. Near the S gate there is the base of a small Roman temple. Apart from the view, largely spoiled by the plastic greenhouses, there is little to justify the climb.

The **river necropolis**, visited less often than the ruins on the W side of the site, contains several fine tombs including one, the Painted Tomb, which is of outstanding interest. Follow a rough path parallel to the cliff-face in a easterly direction. This passes a group of tombs, on the SW side of the cliff which can only be reached with difficulty. Just beyond the point where the acropolis projects into the plain, take a path across some fields to the cliff base. The tombs should be seen in the morning, when the architectural details and ornamentation are illuminated by the sun.

The **Painted Tomb** is one of the most remarkable in Lycia. When visited by Charles Fellows in the 19C, its reliefs still bore traces of yellow, red, blue and purple paint. Today—apart from some red and blue in the background to a reclining male figure—these have disappeared. Access to the tomb is by rather precarious stone steps which lead to a narrow platform. The tomb has *klinai* on which sarcophagi were placed. Around the outside and in the porch there are life-sized figures carved in relief. Inside the porch on the left a reclining man holds a wine-cup and on the right a seated woman is flanked by two children, one of whom is nude. On the left, outside the porch, where the rock has been smoothed, there is a magisterial male figure dressed in outdoor clothes and holding a staff. He is balanced on the right by a woman accompanied by a female child, who is holding her hand. The reliefs are believed to relate to the indoor and outdoor lives of those who were buried here. An element of mystery is introduced by the presence of three other figures, separated by an angle in the rock-face from the main group. A veiled woman carries a box in her hands which she extends towards a youth facing her. He stands in a relaxed pose with legs crossed, resting on a staff, and offers her a flower. Behind him a child grips the youth's cloak timidly. How these figures relate to the main group, if at all, is not known.

Bean mentions another tomb higher up on the cliff-face. This had a pediment decorated with a relief showing a lion attacking a bull. On the entrance porch there was a frieze with figures, which he believed to be dancers, on either side of a lion's head. Freya Stark, however, suggests that the figures represented Artemis of Thera, 'who stands on her double fish-tail between lion heads, and holds her long locks with upraised arms under a high crown'. Unfortunately this tomb has been damaged, apparently by a rock fall, and now scarcely merits the effort needed to reach it.

Myra received its water from a source high up in the plateau c 20km inland. It reached the city through an open channel, part of which may be seen to the N of the river necropolis.

The **Church of St Nicholas** is on the W side of Demre, about 150m from the main square. In a small garden to the left of the entrance, there is a rather incongruous statue of the saint in the persona of Santa Claus complete with a sack of presents and a mob of children.

Apart from the fact that he was born in Patara c 300 and later became bishop of Myra, little is known with certainty about the life of St Nicholas. The son of wealthy parents, he is said to have travelled to Palestine and Egypt in his youth. To judge by the number of stories told about him, Nicholas appears to have exercised considerable influence on the early and medieval church. In the 6C a basilica was erected in his honour in Constantinople and by the late Middle Ages 400 churches had been dedicated to him in England alone. He became the patron saint of Greece, Russia, children, prisoners, sailors and travellers. A life of the saint, embellished with legends, was written by Simon Metaphrastes in the 10C. It was Nicholas. An early biographer recounts his suffering during the persecutions of Diocletian:

> the divine Nicholas was seized by the magistrates, tortured, then chained and thrown into prison with many other Christians. But when ... Constantine ... assumed the imperial diadem ... the prisoners were released from their bonds and with them the illustrious Nicholas, who when he was set at liberty returned to Myra.

There is a tradition that he took part in the Council of Nicaea in 325 where, infuriated by the obstinacy of the heretic Arius, he slapped the face of that turbulent cleric with such vigour that his bones rattled!

It became a tradition in eastern Mediterranean countries for mariners to wish each other a safe voyage with the expression: 'May St Nicholas hold the tiller'. He saved Myra from starvation by commandeering a quantity of grain from ships that had called at Andriace on their way from Egypt to Byzantium. Miraculously, the cargo was found to be undiminished when the ships arrived at their final destination.

Two stories explain why Nicholas came to be the patron saint of children. In a time of famine a butcher lured three youths to his house. While they slept he killed them, cut up their bodies and placed them in a barrel of salt, intending to sell the flesh for food. The saint, told by an angel of this dreadful occurrence, hastened to the butcher's house and restored the boys to life. On another occasion Nicholas heard that the three daughters of a merchant, who had fallen on hard times, were about to take up a life of prostitution as they had no marriage dowries. The saint saved them from sin by throwing three bags of gold into the merchant's garden during the night, so enabling the girls to get married.

St Nicholas is usually shown wearing the vestments of a bishop. The three children whom he restored to life are in a tub at his feet, and there are three golden balls on a book, or three bags of money, or three loaves near him. Sometimes he is shown with a ship or anchor or rebuking the tempest as in the painting by Bicci di Lorenzo (1373–1452) in the Ashmolean Museums, Oxford.

An unsuccessful attempt was made to destroy the saint's tomb in the 9C during the occupation of Myra by the Arabs, but the body of St Nicholas remained, undisturbed, for more than 700 years. In 1087 a group of Italian merchants, ignoring the protests of the monks, broke open the sarcophagus. Inside they found the saint's bones covered in myrrh. They transported them to Bari and placed them in a shrine in the cathedral. Shortly afterwards the Venetians also claimed to have the body of the saint, stating that they had removed it from Myra at the time of the First Crusade. Today the only relics of St Nicholas in his native land are a few sad bones—and these are of doubtful authenticity—which are believed to come from the church at Myra. They are in a casket in the Antalya Museum.

While it is possible that a church existed on the site from the 3C or 4C, the present building has suffered many alterations and extensions. It was probably damaged by the earthquake of 529 and subsequently repaired at the same time as Myra's other buildings with help received from the Emperor Justinian. It is unlikely that it remained unscathed during the period of the first Arab invasions. After the attack in 1034, it was restored by Constantine IX in 1043. A walled monastery was founded nearby at about the same time.

By the middle of the 19C the church was in a very dilapidated condition. Two attempts by Russian interests to restore it were only partially success-ful. While it is difficult to distinguish between alterations and repairs made at different periods, the bell tower and upper storey are clearly relatively modern constructions. The church is used for religious purposes on one day every year—6 December, the feast day of St Nicholas. The Divine Liturgy of the Greek Orthodox Church is celebrated by the Metropolitan of Myra who is now resident in İstanbul. This is followed by a ecumenical service in which Orthodox Catholic and Protestant clergy take part. The Cardinal Archbishop of Bari is represented at these celebrations. The International St Nicholas Symposium is held at Demre in early December.

Access to the church is by a ramp which descends steeply to c 5m below road level. It has three side aisles. Two of these are on the S side and have chapels at the E end. The central nave is covered by a groined vault and it has a synthronon with a covered passage in the apse. The stone altar is surrounded by four broken pillars. From one of the rooms beyond the N aisle stairs ascend to the upper storey. The cloisters on the N side, though in a good state of repair, are being damaged by water. The narthex and exonarthex at the W end are well preserved. There are fine marble pavements in the church.

The sarcophagus believed to be that of St Nicholas is in the S aisle, between two pillars and behind a broken marble screen. It is surmounted by a damaged lid, which presumably came from another tomb as it has the effigies of a man and woman on it.

The road to (c 2.5km) **Andriace** from Demre is flanked on the right by the ancient river Androkos which enters the sea at Andriace. On the far bank there are many **sarcophagi**, the **ruins of a water mill** and of several large buildings dating from the Roman period. The ruined **aqueduct**, which brought water from Demre, is also to the N of the road. The modern harbour has become silted up and is shallow for a considerable distance from the shore. The beach, a mixture of sand and mud, is clean. The best bathing is on the W side. Where the Androkos flows into the sea, there is a good restaurant. There are no hotels or pensions in Andriace. It is a pleasant, unpretentious place popular with Turkish and foreign visitors.

History. There is some doubt as to whether Andriace was an independent Lycian city from the time of its foundation or just the port of Myra. Archaeological evidence shows that from Hellenistic times (4C BC) it formed an important part of Myra's defensive system which stretched from Sura on the W, to Andriace on the S, and to the edge of the plain on the E. The earliest written reference to Andriace is found in accounts of the campaign of Antiochus III of Syria in 197 BC, when he attempted to capture the Aegean cities from the Ptolemies. In 42 BC Lentulus Sphinter broke the chains at the entrance to the harbour and, proceeding to Myra, extracted money from its unwilling citizens to support Brutus' struggle against Octavian and Antony.

In AD 18 statues were erected in Andriace to commemorate the visit of Germanicus, the successful and popular Roman general, and of his wife, the elder Agrippina. Both met with tragic ends. Germanicus died in mysterious circumstances near Antioch a year after his stay in Andriace. He was probably poisoned with the connivance of Tiberius. Agrippina, his formidable widow, was arrested and banished to the island of Pandataria where she starved herself to death.

A century later Trajan, on his way to make war on the Parthians, surveyed the port facilities. Evidence of Andriace's later importance is provided by an inscription on the granary wall which records the use of weights and measures, based on standards sent from Byzantium, for Myra and Arneae.

The most important monument extant is the **Granary of Hadrian**. This is reached by turning left c 200m before the beach into a small clearing. The granary is a further 250m to the SE. To avoid the worst of the undergrowth and an area which is often marshy in spring and late autumn, walk to the base of the hill and there turn E.

This granary, like that at Patara and others in the Eastern Roman Empire, played an important part in the economy. It was used to store grain, which had been grown locally or imported from other countries in the Eastern Mediterranean, before it was sent to Rome, allocated to the army or otherwise distributed by the administration. Constructed during the reign

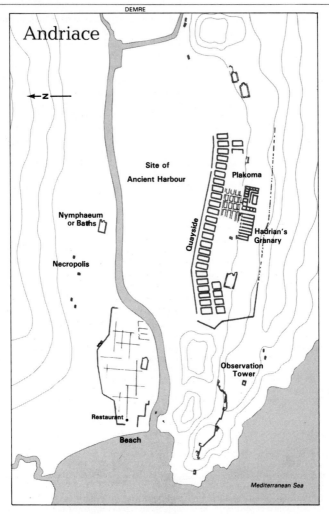

DEMRE

Andriace

←N—

Site of
Ancient Harbour

Nymphaeum
or Baths

Necropolis

Plakoma

Quayside

Hadrian's
Granary

Restaurant

Observation
Tower

Beach

Mediterranean Sea

of Hadrian (117–138), it measures 65m by 32m and has eight rooms. Six are
of equal size while two, on the W, are smaller. The rooms, entered by doors
on the N side, have dividing walls and a back wall constructed of polygonal
masonry. Internal communicating doors are near the entrances.

The façade of large, closely fitting square blocks, is flanked by two rooms
for the supervisors. On the W side, part of the pediment remains. When
Beaufort visited Andriace in 1811, the inscription was still complete: HORREA
IMP. CAESARIS DIVI TRAIANI PARTHICI F. DIVI, NERVAE NEPOTIS TRAIANI HADRIANI
AUGUSTI COS. III. Over the main door there are two busts. The male figure is
Hadrian. The identity of the female figure is disputed. It may be Hadrian's
wife Sabina or Faustina the Elder, the wife of Antoninus Pius. There is a
small relief on the front wall near the second door from the W. This shows

Serapis standing and Isis reclining on a couch with a griffin between them. According to the inscription, this was erected by an official of the granary called Herakleon, in obedience to instructions received in a dream.

Beaufort reports the ruins of a small temple, constructed from very white marble, on the hill to the S of the port. This may be the building which modern scholars believe was a watch-tower. Across the river Androkos, at a point level with the granary, there are the substantial remains of a construction sometimes described as a **nymphaeum**. However, as Andriace is known to have had mineral springs it is more likely to have been a baths complex. To the W of the granary, a **building with an apse** may have been a temple or a civil basilica. The so-called **plakoma** or market area, which was surrounded by a colonnade, is to the E of the granary. In the centre there is a **large cistern** enclosed by a double vault. Between the plakoma and the harbour lay the residential quarter where remains of houses 8–10m long and streets 3m wide may be seen. Further N is the quay which was once lined with warehouses. Beyond the quay, the ancient harbour of Andriace is now a reedy fen which has been abandoned to the frogs and the marsh birds.

Arneae, c 24km NW of Demre by a difficult road, is one of the most beautiful and isolated sites in Lycia. Inside the defensive wall there are Lycian rock-tombs, two ruined churches, sarcophagi and houses.

25

Demre to Antalya

A. Via Limyra, Elmalı and Termessus

Total distance c 209km. Demre—c 27km Finike—c 6km Turunçova—(c 4km Limyra)—c 20km Arif—(c 1km Arycanda)—c 32km Elmalı—c 54km Korkuteli—(c 9km Termessus)—(c 1km Evdır Hanı)—c 70km Antalya.

Road 400 from Demre to Finike follows a winding course along the coast. It passes a number of small, clean beaches, but few of these have adequate parking spaces. On the eastern edge of the Demre plain a large lake, well stocked with fish, is home to flocks of sea birds. Apart from a narrow channel, often closed by fishermen's nets, the lake is separated from the open sea by an enormous sand-bar. The lakeside restaurant has a good reputation, especially for its fish dishes!

Finike, a small sea port which is beginning to attract tourists, has several modest hotels and pensions. Near the harbour there are some excellent fish restaurants. Try the *Petek Restaurant*. In the marina there are shops, a snack bar, and all the facilities required by yachtsmen. Finike is a useful base for visiting Demre, ancient Limyra, and Arycanda, and for leisurely boat trips along the Lycian coast.

To reach **LIMYRA** take Road 635 from Finike for c 6km to the village of **Turunçova**, and continue E for c 4km. Park near the ancient theatre. Alternatively, take a bus from Finike to Turunçova and walk to the site.

History. Limyra may have been settled as early as the 5C BC. Known in Lycian as Zemu(ri), the city reached its apogee in the 4C BC, when its ruler, the dynast Pericles, made it the capital of Lycia. Pericles had successfully resisted the attempts of Mausolus to conquer Lycia and at the Battle of Issus in 333 BC Alexander the Great finally lifted the shadow of Persia from Asia Minor. Following the death of Alexander in 323 BC, Limyra and the rest of Lycia came under the domination of the Diadochoi. Ruled at various times by the Macedonians, the Ptolemies and the Seleucids and for a brief and stormy period by the Rhodians, it was made a free territory by Rome in 167 BC.

In February AD 4, 19-year-old Gaius Caesar died in Limyra on his way home to Rome from Armenia where he had carried out an important commission for the emperor. Grandson and adopted heir of Augustus, Gaius attended the Senate at 15, was made a priest and proclaimed *princeps iuventutis* and was destined to become a consul at 20. He was commemorated at Limyra by a magnificent funeral monument, decorated with reliefs which glorified his achievements.

When in AD 43 Lycia was joined with Pamphylia to form the new Roman Province of Asia, Limyra prospered. Partially destroyed by the earthquake of 141, the city's public buildings, including the theatre, were restored with the aid of generous donations from Opramoas of Rhodiapolis. Like Sura, Limyra had a fish oracle. According to Pliny, if the fish took the food offered to them, it was a good omen. The city's principal deity was Zeus, whose thunderbolt appeared on the coinage.

During the early Byzantine period Limyra's importance was little diminished. It became the seat of a bishop. However, from the 7C to the 9C it suffered grievously from raids by Arab pirates and finally, like Demre, most of its inhabitants moved away and the city was largely abandoned.

In the 19C the first European visitors to Limyra were from Britain. Cockerell and Beaufort came in 1811 and they were followed in 1838 by Fellows, who copied some of the inscriptions in the necropolis. Later, Spratt and Forbes explored the acropolis. In recent years German archaeologists under the direction of Dr Jürgen Borckhardt have been excavating the site.

On the left of the road from Turunçova there is a fine **two-storey tomb** in a citrus grove. Nearby, another tomb, dated to the 5C BC, has an interesting relief around the door. These and some rock-tombs were in the western necropolis. On the right of the road are the remains of the Roman and Byzantine walls which, unfortunately, are being raided continually for building stone. To the S, the marshy ground makes it very difficult to examine the ruined **cenotaph of Gaius Caesar**, the remains of an **episcopal palace**, and of a richly ornamented **Byzantine church** which may have been Limyra's cathedral.

Limyra's **theatre** had a single diazoma, backed by a wall c 1.6m high. There are several openings into a covered passageway. A velum protected the audience from the sun and inclement weather. Sockets for the poles may be seen in the upper rows of seats. The unusually large orchestra is flanked by two vaulted entrances. Of the stage-building only a few blocks of stone remain. A gift of about 20,000 denarii from Opramoas helped to repair the earthquake damage which the stage had suffered 50 years earlier in AD 141. Comparison of the architectural decoration with the theatres at Hierapolis, Perge and Olympos suggest a late 2C AD date for Limyra's theatre.

On the NW hillside the archaeologists found 4C BC terracotta figurines and a Roman altar of Artemis Pergaia in terraced houses which date from the 4C BC but continued to be occupied during the Hellenistic period.

Behind the theatre there is a group of **rock-tombs**, many of which are elaborately decorated. To the E of these there is a remarkable free-standing ogival **sarcophagus** on a tall base which dates from the 4C BC. An inscription in Lycian states that it was the tomb of Xatabura, who may have been related to Pericles, the founder of the Lycian League. It has a number of fine reliefs. On the N there is a chariot with an armed warrior; on the S

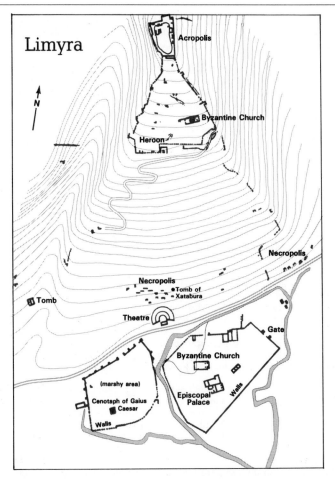

a funeral feast and sacrifice and on W the judgment of Xatabura after death. He is shown as a nude youth, standing between the seated, elderly judges. He holds his clothes in his left hand and gazes unwaveringly towards the land of the dead.

Studies have been made of the grave of Chuwata (c 360 BC) in Necropolis II. The warrior frieze on this tomb has been compared to the decoration on the short side of the Alexander Sarcophagus in the İstanbul Archaeological Museum which shows Macedonians fighting Persians.

On the W side of the city a **tholos** has been found. This has columns surrounding a circular cella built on a Lycian podium c 15m square and 10m high. Fragments of two statues c 2.3m tall have been identified as representations of Ptolemy II Philadelphus (285–246) and his consort Arsinoe II. These and a Celtic shield on a balustrade between the columns suggest that the tholos was dedicated to the cult of Ptolemy in gratitude for assistance received from him during the raids mounted by Celtic tribes from

Galatia in the early 3C BC. During the Roman period the tholos was linked to the southern harbour area by a colonnaded street c 8m wide.

Sondages at the so-called Lycian Gate near the northern Byzantine wall have produced red figure Attic and black glaze pottery of the 5C BC and 7C BC Samian hydriai and proto-geometric and geometric sherds.

A visit to the heroon and acropolis on the top of **Tocak Dağ**, which towers to the N of the site, is recommended. The ascent is best made in the early morning. By the path from the back of the village, it should take c 40 minutes. The earliest evidence of occupation found in the acropolis dates from the 4C BC. Today, little more than traces of the defensive wall remain.

Below the acropolis, to the SE, are the ruins of a **Byzantine church** which was built on the site of a Serapeion. The church measured 23m by 15m. Later a small chapel was constructed here.

The **heroon** or mausoleum, which was probably constructed for Pericles, is S of the crest on an artificial terrace measuring 19m x 18m. Examination of its remains suggest that it resembled the Nereid tomb at Xanthus. A lower burial chamber supported a small temple. This had four caryatids in the front and four in the back. The Limyra caryatids, heavier and less graceful than those in the Erectheum at Athens, wear bracelets crowned with lion heads, a decoration often found in Persian art, and carry funerary libation vessels in their hands. The sides of the upper chamber were decorated with a long frieze showing the hero, in a chariot, leading a motley band of soldiers who wear Persian, Greek or Lycian clothing. A further Persian motif may be found in the acroterion which decorated the pediment. Now in the Antalya Museum, this shows Perseus, from whom the Persians claimed descent, hurrying away in triumph with the severed head of Medusa. Apart from its magnificently commanding position on Tocak Dağ, the interest and importance of the Limyra heroon comes from its intriguing blend of Persian and Greek elements and for the light it throws on Lycia's central position between two great cultural influences.

From Finike Road 635 to Elmalı at first runs parallel with the Yaşgöz Çayı, the ancient Arycandus. Narrow in parts, this road has a good surface and is usually very busy with lorries bringing timber from the interior.

At Turunçova turn right for Limyra. The road now begins to climb through a pine-clothed gorge until it reaches Karamanbeyli Geçidi (1290m). This is the land of the *tahtacılar*, the taciturn woodcutters.

For **Arycanda** follow Road 635 as far as the village of c 20km **Arif** where there are restaurants with fresh trout on the menu. The site is c 30 minutes' walk from the main road. Arycanda is one of the most beautiful places in Turkey. It has been compared, not unfavourably, with Delphi in Greece.

History. The '-anda' in Arycanda suggests that the city was of considerable antiquity. Many pre-Greek settlements have '-ss' or '-anda' in their names. However, nothing is known of its history before the 5C BC. Coins found at Arycanda bear the name of Pericles of Limyra. It is probable that, like much of Lycia, it was under Persian domination until the arrival of Alexander the Great in 334 BC. Subsequently, the city was ruled at different times by the Ptolemies and the Seleucid kings of Syria. The Arycandans, sybaritic and profligate by temperament, lived well beyond their means. As a result they sided with Antiochus III in 197 BC against the Ptolemies in the hope of paying off their debts. During the 2C BC Arycanda became part of the Lycian League and issued its own coins. In c 188 BC it was briefly under the control of Rhodes and finally, in AD 43, it became part of the Roman province of Lycia-Pamphylia.

From Byzantine sources it is known that Arycanda had its own bishop and that it changed its name to **Acalanda**. During this period the city was moved to a new site which continued to be occupied until the 11C.

Arycanda was built on a series of terraces cut into the hillside. For a number of years excavations have been conducted here by Professor Cevdet Bayburtluoğlu. The **acropolis** is to the right of a track from the main road. Steps lead up to the gateway. Inside the defensive wall are the remains of a small building which is believed to be a **heroon**. The so-called *yazıtlı ev* or house of inscriptions to the W has been identified as a small 4C AD **bath house** built mainly from re-used material including a number of 2C AD inscriptions. There was a small square **caldarium** with an apse at the S end adjoining a **tepidarium** and a larger **frigidarium** on an E/W axis.

A short distance to the N there are the substantial remains of a large **Byzantine basilica**. This has a well-preserved synthronon and some fine floor mosaics. There are several temple tombs in the eastern necropolis. A number of these have been restored. One, the **heroon of Naltepe**, has been reconstructed. A small Corinthian style **temple tomb** appears to have been adapted for Christian worship. On the S wall of the pronaos there is a cross and the inscription 'Jesus Christ is victorious'. Byzantine houses with mosaic floors and stucco decorated walls were found in this area.

The **agora** to the N, which had a colonnade on three sides, is to the left of the path. In the centre a tree, surrounded by a ruined wall, is believed to mark the site of a small temple. As only a few shops were found in this part of the city, it is assumed that the agora was used mainly for meetings and debates and that the city's commercial quarter was situated elsewhere.

The N colonnade of the agora, which is 75m long and 8m wide, has five archways, three of which provide access to a small **odeum**. The centre arch was decorated with a sculpture of Hadrian, those on either side with representations of deities. Above the odeum, to the NE, there is a fine **theatre**. Dated to the 2C AD, it was constructed in the Greek manner, i.e. larger than a semicircle. There is no diazoma. The 20 rows of seats are divided into seven cunei. The well preserved Doric style stage-building dates from the Roman period.

Access to the **stadium**, which is at the highest level of the site, is by a stairway behind the theatre. Supported by a massive retaining wall, the stadium is c 100m long. Its seating was on the N side only. W of the stadium there was another **baths complex** which was used in the 3C, 4C and 6C AD. The circular E section is reminiscent of the baths of Tlos. NW of the baths an area has been identified as a **palaestra**. Arycanda's **bouleuterion**, also to the W of the stadium, is approached by a long stoa. Excavation has revealed much of the structure including the seats cut from the rock. Below the retaining wall there was a **villa** which had fine mosaic floors in the atrium and other rooms.

Return to Arif and continue N on Road 635. After crossing the Bey Dağları, you descend from the Avlanbeli Geçidi (1090m) through pleasant mountain pastures to the rather featureless Elmalı plain. This lunar landscape, which has been produced by the draining of a number of large lakes, finally gives way to the orchards which give Elmalı, 'Apple Town', its name.

Surrounded by fruit trees, **Elmalı** straggles up the side of Elmalı Dağ, the mountain which towers over the town and surrounding countryside.

Elmalı is the principal marketing and shopping centre for central Lycia. It has a number of small restaurants and one or two rather basic hotels. From the *otogar* buses depart at regular intervals to Finike and Antalya and there are frequent dolmuş services to surrounding villages. A festival of wrestling is held here each year in the first week in September.

Apart from a fine 15C mosque, **Ömerpaşa Camii**, in the centre of the town, Elmalı has few buildings of interest. However, it has become well known in recent years to students of ancient history. American archaeologists, working with Professor Machteld Mellink, have made a number of exciting discoveries in the surrounding area. At **Karataş-Semayük** they have found nearly 500 tombs and a fortified house dating from the Early Bronze Age (c 3000–2000 BC). Most of the burials were in pithoi, large pottery jars, placed with their openings to the E. An examination of the skeletons has shown that inhabitants of the site were well built and well nourished, but there was some evidence of arthritis and malaria and, in a few cases, of leprosy. Some of the pithoi and grave-goods—ear-studs, brush handles, bronze pins and spearheads—together with an imaginative reconstruction of a pithos-burial, can be seen in the Antalya Archaeological Museum.

The archaeologists also found two painted tomb-chambers in tumuli, one at **Kızılbel**, c 4km to the SW, near the lake of Elmalı, the other at **Karaburun**, 7km to the NE, on the Korkuteli road. Because of the blend of Greek, Lycian, and Persian influences which they display, these tombs are of great importance. Both were robbed in antiquity.

The painting in the **Kızılbel tomb**, which dates from c 525 BC, shows the departure of a warrior, a banquet, and a number of mythological subjects including Gorgons and the birth of Pegasus. Executed in the East Greek style, the painting is in shades of black, white and red on a light background. A study by Paschinger remarks on similarities between it and paintings in the Etruscan cemeteries of Tarquinia and Caere. Both may trace their origin to early 6C BC Ionic models. The grave furniture included a table and a *kline* made of stone. The skeletal remains suggest that the occupant was a well-built, active man aged about 50.

The tomb at **Karaburun**, which has been dated to c 470 BC, was decorated in a Graeco-Persian style. The paintings show the owner reclining on a couch. Elaborately dressed in a green himation and wearing a diadem, he beckons imperiously to two servants clad in Persian-style garments. Behind him stands his wife holding an alabastron and a fillet. There is also the depiction of a battle, of a funeral-procession with a wheeled throne, and of a funeral-cart and attendants. An examination of the bones indicated that the occupant of the tomb was a little older than 50 at the time of death, tall and of strong build. If the dating of the tomb is correct, the person buried here could have taken part on the Persian side in the campaign against Athens and her allies in southern Anatolia. This ended with Cimon's resounding victory at the battle of the Eurymedon river in 467 BC.

Because of the fragility of the paintings, it is necessary to preserve an even temperature in the tombs. They are not open to the public.

Road 635 to c 54km Korkuteli crosses the N end of the bare and featureless Elmalı plain. At the small town of **Korkuteli** it leaves this lunar landscape so lacking in appeal and joins Road 350. This begins to descend to Antalya, and almost immediately the scenery changes dramatically. Wooded mountain slopes replace the arid plateau and on the lush roadside verges sheep and goats graze under the watchful gaze of their youthful guardians.

About 20km from Korkuteli there is an ancient ashlar wall. Too far away to be part of the defences of Termessus, it may have been a customs and control point where the Termessians exacted tolls from passing travellers. There was a gateway on the old route. About 5km farther on a signpost on the right indicates 9km **TERMESSUS**.

Admission tickets to the site, which forms part of the Termessus National Park, are sold in buildings on the right of the entrance. There is an informative display about the protected flora and fauna of the park. Refreshments are available and there is a spacious, well-maintained picnic area. Wear strong shoes and thornproof clothing, as the terrain is rough and very overgrown in places. A stout stick will come in handy on the climb to the summit.

A further 9km on a new road will bring you to the parking area. From here the city, which is 500m farther on and 200m higher up, is reached by a very rough path. Like Olympus and Phaselis, much of the site is covered with a tangled mass of vegetation. It requires patience and determination to locate and examine some of the ruins. The charm of Termessus comes from its setting. High on a mountain side, more than 1000m above the Pamphylian plain, its serenity is delightful.

History. The people of Termessus were neither Greeks nor Lycians. They were Pisidians, a race which occupied the mountainous area N of Pamphylia. According to Strabo they called themselves the Solymi, after Mt Solymus, the modern Güllük Dağ, which towered over Termessus. Confusingly, the word Termessus, by which their city came to be known, is linked with Termilae, a name sometimes used for the Lycians.

From the beginning the Termessians had a reputation for being warlike and aggressive, and they were frequently in conflict with neighbouring cities. On one occasion they were brave or foolhardy enough to take on all 30 cities of the Lycian League. Because of the remote and inhospitable location of Termessus, where olives were the only food-crop, it is probable that they were driven to banditry from time to time to supplement the meagre return from their lands. Certainly, their strategic position enabled them to control—and interfere with—trade between the coast and the interior and it seems likely that in later times they levied a tax on passing travellers. They were not intimidated by the army of Alexander the Great and he was obliged to raise the siege on their city in 333 BC. Even under the Romans they enjoyed a considerable degree of freedom. However, they cannot have been entirely without the capacity to make friends, as they founded a colony at Oenoanda, sometimes known as Termessus Minor, c 80km to the W. This colony would have have been difficult to defend, so its inhabitants must have been on reasonably good terms with their neighbours.

Although the date of the foundation of Termessus is not known, the Solymi are mentioned in Book VI of the *Iliad*. So the city probably existed as early as the 8C BC. Homer tells the story of Bellerophon, who was falsely accused of seduction by the wife of the Argive king, Proetus. The young man was sent by Proetus to his father-in-law, Iobates, king of Lycia with a sealed message requesting that he be put to death. Iobates was unwilling to do the deed himself, so he set Bellerophon a series of tasks, which he believed to be impossible. First he ordered the youth to destroy the Chimaera. Having successfully disposed of that terrible monster, Bellerophon was then told to subdue the warlike Solymi. Pegasus carried him over the heads of this savage tribe, far above the reach of their arrows, and he rained down rocks on them until they and their allies, the Amazons, retreated in disorder. Then he returned to Iobates who, tired of the game, gave Bellerophon his daughter in marriage and accepted him as his heir.

Termessus is next mentioned in the campaign conducted by Alexander the Great in Lycia and Pamphylia in 333 BC. Having conquered Perge and Aspendus, Alexander marched N to Phrygia. His route took him near Termessus, which Arrian described:

'the town stands on a lofty and precipitous height, and the road which leads past it is an inconvenient one, because a ridge runs right down to it from the town above, breaking off short with the road at the bottom, while opposite to it, on the other side, the ground rises again in an equally steep ascent. The two cliffs make a sort of natural gateway on the road, so that quite a small force can, by holding the high ground, prevent an enemy from getting through. And this is precisely what the Telmessians [sic] did'.

Alexander did not attempt to force his way through the valley immediately. He made camp and waited for night-fall. When most of the Termessians had returned to their homes, he attacked the small force remaining and overcame it easily. He then took up his position under the city walls. There he was joined by representatives from the Pisidian city of Selge, enemies of the Termessians. They were unable to persuade Alexander to continue with his siege of the city. It is likely that he was discouraged by the formidable natural and artificial defences of Termessus. He returned to Perge and marched N, by way of Sagalassus, to Phrygia. Thus, with Sillyum, Termessus shares the distinction of having successfully stood out against Alexander and his army.

The Diadochoi fought over Alexander's empire. Termessus supported Alcetas against Antigonus Monophthalmos, who was trying to bring Asia under his rule. When Alcetas was defeated in 319 BC, he sought refuge in Termessus. Antigonus came to the city and demanded that his enemy be handed over to him. The Termessian elders were inclined to accede to this request, but they were fiercely opposed by the young men of the city. According to the historian, Diodorus, to resolve the matter to their satisfaction the elders suggested the following stratagem to Antigonus. He should withdraw his forces and, while the young men were harrying his rearguard, they would hand Alcetas over. Alcetas learned of the plot and, not wishing to fall into the hands of Antigonus, killed himself. The elders delivered his corpse to Antigonus, who subjected it to many indignities and, when it was beginning to decay, marched away, leaving it unburied. The young men, full of rage at the deception practised on them, decided at first to raze Termessus to the ground and take to a life of brigandage. Finally, they limited themselves to attacking the lands occupied by Antigonus and to recovering the body of their friend. This they buried in a splendid tomb, which archaeologists believe they have identified on the NW side of the city.

According to an inscription, the bellicose Termessians were at war with the Lycian League c 200 BC and just 11 years later with the neighbouring city of Isinda. When Attalus II of Pergamum attempted to subdue Selge c 158 BC, it is very likely that he was supported by the Termessians, the Selgians' ancient enemies. Attalus was unsuccessful and, anxious to consolidate his position in Pamphylia, founded the new port of Attaleia, the modern city of Antalya. He also caused a magnificent portico, which bore his name, to be erected in Termessus, perhaps to express his gratitude.

As a reward for its support during the Mithridatic War, Termessus was accorded a considerable degree of freedom by the Romans. During Imperial times the city issued coins which did not bear an effigy of the current emperor, but which carried the word, 'Autonomous' on them. In the early Byzantine period, Termessus retained some importance, becoming the seat of a bishop. However, the city appears to have been abandoned in the 5C, possibly because of the remoteness of its location.

The descriptive signs to the principal ruins in Termessus are not mentioned in the text, as they are often defaced, destroyed, or reversed by vandals.

On the ascent to the car-park look out for a number of ruins: first a watch-tower, then traces of the so-called 2C AD **King Street**, and finally the base of a **great gateway** which provided a ceremonial entrance to the area around the city. To the right of the car-park the handsome **propylon of Hadrian** leads to a ruined **Ionic peripteros** which has a cella 8m wide. The portal, with a finely carved lintel, is surrounded by a mass of architectural fragments which, perhaps, will be used one day to reconstruct this building. A path to the left leads to the **N necropolis** which contains a number of decorated tombs, including one with a fine lion relief.

Return to the car-park and take a path which ascends steeply. For part of the way this follows **King Street**, the 2C paved road that led to the city centre. Across the valley, to the right, there are several rock-tombs. These may be reached by a rough track that descends from the agora.

The **outer wall** has a fine **look-out tower** above and to the right of the path. The inner side of the **gateway** had an interesting **dice-oracle**. This consisted of a series of set answers, each of which was linked to a specified throw of the dice. The following is an example quoted by Bean:

44466 24 Cronos the Child-Eater
Three fours and two sixes. This is the god's advice:
Stay at home and go not elsewhere,
Lest the destructive Beast and avenging Fury come upon you;
For I see that the business is neither safe nor secure.

In the later Roman Empire, when superstition and credulity were rife, methods of divination like this dice-oracle and the tomb-oracle of Olympus, however fallible, enjoyed wide popularity.

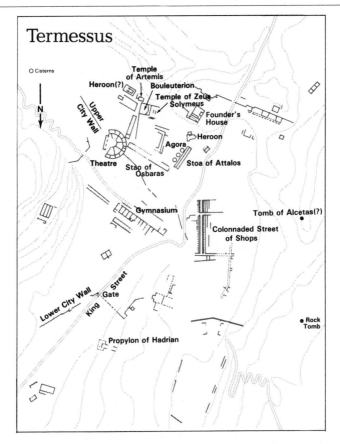

From the gateway, it is possible to see, high on the mountain-side to the left, the ruins of an **aqueduct** which brought the city some of its water.

Steps lead to the **inner fortification wall**. On the left there are the extensive remains of a large **gymnasium** which is smothered by undergrowth. A path here leads to the **necropolis** where shattered sarcophagi lie half buried in the thorny maquis. Just beyond is the site of the **agora**, all of whose buildings were wrecked by earthquakes and damaged by the unchecked growth of the luxuriant vegetation. This was bounded on the NW by a two-storey **stoa** composed of Doric columns. According to an inscription, this stoa was dedicated by Attalus II, King of Pergamum (160–139 BC). On the NE, there was a **matching stoa**, constructed during the Roman period by a rich citizen named Osbaras. Underneath the paved surface of the agora, on the NW side, there are five large **cisterns**. These were used to store rain water, so supplementing supplies from other sources within the walls and brought in by the aqueduct. Now open and unprotected, they have an average depth of 8m, so approach them with caution.

In the SW corner of the agora a large, natural rocky-outcrop was converted into a monumental tomb for some Termessian dignitary. His name and the date of the construction of the **heroon** are not known. The inscriptions carved in large letters on the back wall are believed to relate to two people who wished to be buried with or near him. Stairs lead to a platform 6m sq. The tomb, which was covered by a slab, was in the rear wall. On the W side of the rocky-outcrop there are three niches, where, perhaps, offerings to the dead man were placed.

You now come to the well-preserved **Hellenistic theatre**. Facing the twin peaks of Mt Solymus, it occupies a position of incomparable beauty SE of the agora. Constructed in the Greek style, it has a single diazoma with eight rows of seats above and 16 below. The cavea could seat more than 4000 spectators. Until alterations during the Roman period extended the cavea on the right-hand side as far as the stage-building, so providing extra seating, it had two parodoi. The right-hand parodos was then replaced by a covered passage. Entrance to the cavea below the diazoma was by stairs which led from a large door in the back wall. Access to the seats above the diazoma must have been by doors in the retaining wall, which have disappeared. The stage-building, which dates from c 2C AD, was backed by a long, narrow room. This had five doors and was faced by free-standing columns whose pedestals remain. Below the stage level five smaller openings, c 1m high, were used to admit animals into the orchestra area, when the theatre was used for wild-beast shows.

S of the theatre, steps lead down to a small **temple**. This stood on a podium which rested on a terrace cut into the hillside. Usually, temples of the Olympian gods had their entrances on the E side, and as access to this building was by a flight of steps on the W, it was probably dedicated to a hero or deified mortal. It is very overgrown and difficult to investigate.

W of this temple there are the substantial remains of a building which has been dated to the 1C BC. This may have been the **bouleuterion** of Termessus or, as some authorities believe, an **odeum**, where musical recitals and poetry performances were given. The upper part of the outer walls, which stand to a height of 10m, are decorated with narrow Doric pilasters. The presence of windows on the S and E sides suggest that is was roofed. In the interior, which is filled with broken masonry and vegetation, there are the remains of several rows of seats and traces of polychrome marble which was probably used to decorate the walls. Inscriptions cut into the N wall between the pilasters record the names of victors in various sporting events—wrestling, foot-races, horse-races. These probably took place in the city's small, gymnasium, which was sited to the SE of the agora.

S of the odeum there are the foundations of an **Ionic temple**. Reliefs of the sacrifice of Iphigenia and a dedication found there show that this was dedicated to Artemis.

To the N there is a smaller temple, also dedicated to Artemis, which has been dated to the beginning of the 3C AD. An inscription records that this building and the cult-statue were donated by Aurelia Armasta and her husband. NW of the odeum there are the substantial remains of a small **temple** dedicated to Zeus Solymeus. Only the walls, which stand to a height of 5m, and a bench on which statues were placed, remain. The principal temple of Zeus Solymeus has not yet been discovered. Fragments of reliefs showing Zeus and other deities, found by Austrian archaeologists towards the end of the 19C, suggest that it was somewhere W of this small shrine.

Due W of this temple there are the ruins of the so-called **Founder's House**. This gets its name from a rough inscription on the door which describes a man called Besas as a 'founder' of the city. The term probably means, as in the case of the founders of Perge, someone who contributed substantially to the public good, perhaps by the construction of public buildings. The house, which appears to follow the usual Roman pattern, is now in a very dilapidated condition and is choked with vegetation.

W of the agora the path divides. The left-hand fork leads to a group of rock-tombs on the W cliff-face. On the left of this path there is a spring of fresh water, as refreshing and welcome to the modern visitor as it must have been to the Termessians. E of the path, covered in undergrowth, the inscribed bases of several statues mark the site of a street of shops.

A scramble of about 150m through thick vegetation will bring you to a **rock-tomb** at the base of the cliff. Dated to the end of the 4C BC, some believe that Alcetas (see above) was buried here. On the left-hand wall, framed by a rough arch, there is a splendid life-like relief of a mounted soldier. He is shown at the moment when he reins in his mount. His cloak billows out behind him and his horse, balanced on its hind legs with front legs raised, is still pulling against the bit. Clad in a corselet, right hand lifted to throw a spear, he rides without a saddle, gripping the horses' flanks with his knees. It is a pose reminiscent of some of the heroic representations of Alexander the Great, e.g the small bronze in the Museo Archaeologico, Naples. Unfortunately, the relief has suffered some damage, partly from natural causes, partly from the destructive activity of treasure hunters. The rider's head, which was probably helmeted, has been defaced and the hindquarters of the horse are missing. Below the relief there is the carving of a crested helmet, a pair of greaves, a round shield and a sword.

On the right-hand side of the tomb there is a badly damaged sarcophagus in the form of a *kline*. This has legs ornamented with palmettes. To the left of the sarcophagus there is an *ostothek*. This had a false door carved on the front. To the right of the sarcophagus, offerings to the spirit of the deceased were placed in three containers, two of which have carvings. A low table in front was used for the same purpose. On the wall behind the sarcophagus, a trellis set between columns is carved in low-relief. This is surmounted by an eagle in flight carrying a snake in its claws.

You can return to the car-park by a very rough path which descends from the tomb of Alcetas. This passes several other rock-tombs of lesser interest. However, hardy spirits will almost certainly wish to return to the agora and take the path from behind the theatre to the **upper necropolis**. Here there are a large number of **tombs** dating from the 1C to the 3C AD. Most are sarcophagi, but some were constructed in the form of small funerary temples. Elaborately decorated with portraits of the deceased, with garlands or with the motif of crossed spears surmounted by a shield, which occurs so often in Termessus, they are scattered through the undergrowth in macabre, apocalyptic confusion. Gaping open, resting at strange angles, they resemble a Last Judgement by Bosch or Breughel. Their inscriptions, in addition to stating the names of the owners, frequently carry a curse against tomb-robbers and specify the penalty for such a desecration—usually a substantial fine payable to the temple of Zeus Solymeus.

A short walk upwards will bring you to a hut used by the forest fire-watchers. There is a magnificent view over the Termessus National Park, the ancient city and part of the plain of Pamphylia. If you are lucky, you may see some of the shy mountain goats which live on the higher slopes.

Leave the National Park turn right for Antalya. After c 5km a narrow road on the left leads to **Evdir Hanı**, a well-preserved Selçuk caravanserai built by İzzeddin Keykavus between 1214 and 1218. Note the fine decoration on the beautifully proportioned doorway which is flanked by two niches.

Between the road and the caravanserai there are the scattered ruins of a more ancient settlement. When the site was visited by Lieutenant Spratt in 1842, he saw several hundred **sarcophagi**. Unfortunately, only a few have survived. Not far from the road there are the remains of a small, richly ornamented **temple**, where George Bean found two architectural fragments decorated with representations of strange demonic creatures.

There are questions about the name of this site. Bean suggests that in the 5C it was called **Eudocias**, after Eudoxia, wife of the Emperor Theodosius II and that it was ruled by Termessus. He further proposes that in earlier times it may have been called **Anydrus**, which means waterless, an attractive hypothesis as the site is crossed by a number of channels which bring water from some distance to irrigate it.

Returning to Road 350, continue c 7km to the junction with Road 650 from Burdur and turn right for c 11km Antalya. You descend to the plain through a series of curves and enter the city by a wide boulevard. The whitewashed **cisterns** in the central reservation date from the Ottoman period.

B. Via Olympus and Phaselis

Total distance 119km. Finike—c 21km Kumluca—(c 2km Corydalla)—(c 3km Rhodiapolis)—(c 10km Idebessus)—(c 4km Gagae)—(c 9km Olympus)—c 45km Tekirova—(c 2km Phaselis)—c 8km Kemer—45km Antalya.

Return to Finike and take Road 400 to 21km Kumluca. The site of **Corydalla** is c 2km W of the town, near the village of **Hacıveliler**. Apart from a few scattered blocks of stone and the shape of the theatre on a hill to the S, there are no visible remains. In the mid 19C Spratt reported the existence of extensive ruins which included an aqueduct and the theatre. The site has been illegally stripped of all usable building material. Bean saw a stream of lorries carrying material away. In the walls of many of the houses in Kumluca and the neighbouring villages there are inscribed stones. One house in Kumluca has a Greek and Lycian text built into it.

The spoliation of Corydalla did not rest with the removal of the stones. A valuable Byzantine treasure of church plate found here some years ago was divided. Part of it remained in Turkey and can be seen in the Antalya Museum. The rest turned up in the United States of America.

Kumluca is a small, dusty town totally lacking in charm. Its only interest is to the visitor-sleuth, who may enjoy looking for traces of ancient Corydalla in its modern buildings.

Rhodiapolis, 3km N of Kumluca, may be reached from the villages of Hacıveliler or Seyköy. The road to the site is rough and it is advisable to use a four-wheel drive vehicle. Take a guide from one of the villages.

History. Although the name Rhodiapolis means 'city of the Rhodians' and E of Kumluca the ancient settlements are much less Lycian in character, it has been suggested that this city was named after Rhode, daughter of the legendary Mopsus. Whatever its origins, Rhodiapolis was certainly accepted as a full member of the Lycian League. This is proved conclusively by its coins.

The city's main claim to fame is that it was the home in the 2C AD of Opramoas. An important official in the Lycian League, who lived during the reign of Antoninus Pius (138–161), his generous benefactions to the cities of Lycia made him famous, not only in his own province but throughout the Roman Empire.

The ruins of Rhodiapolis are scattered through a pine forest and have suffered much from illegal excavation. In the middle of the city there is a well-preserved small **theatre**. Greater than a semi-circle, it has two unenclosed parodoi and no diazoma. Part of the stage-building still exists. S of the theatre are the remains of the **tomb of Opramoas**. This building, c 8m by 7m, bore copies of letters from the emperor and provincial governors which recorded the honours received by Opramoas and his many gifts to Rhodiapolis and to other Lycian cities. Unfortunately, it has been badly damaged and the inscriptions lie on the ground in a state of disorder and neglect. W of the theatre are the ruins of a **Byzantine church**. On top of the hill there is a **Hellenistic tower** which was altered at a later period. There are several cisterns and traces of an aqueduct. Lycian sarcophagi are scattered on the hillside below the city and there are several rock-tombs.

Idebessus is c 10km N of Kumluca. It can also be reached from **Hacıveliler** with a four-wheel drive vehicle. Go first to the dam at Alağir and then to the village of Yenikişla.

The city is c 900m above sea-level on a ridge which forms part of the Bey Dağları. With Acalissus and Cormi it formed a sympolity which belonged to the Lycian League. Although Idebessus and Acalissus have the pre-Greek '-ss' in their names no Lycian rock-tombs or inscriptions have been found in either. Acalissus, the head of the sympolity, received a donation from Opramoas and issued coins during the reign of the ill-fated Gordian III (238–244) who was assassinated by Philip the Arab.

There is a small, badly-damaged theatre which had a capacity of c 600. There are the ruins of baths and of a Byzantine basilica. The city does not appear to have had a necropolis, but there is a profusion of late **ogival tombs** scattered among the civic buildings. Many are decorated with reliefs which show cupids carrying garlands, or playing with animals. There are also representations of wild-beast fights.

According to Bean the ruins of nearby **Acalissus** and **Cormi** are fewer and less interesting than those of Idebessus. They are difficult to reach. Inscriptions include one relating to the first Mithidratic War (88–84 BC) and another apparently to the defeat of the pirate Zencites in 78 BC by Servilius Vatia, Roman governor of Cilicia.

Return to Kumluca and continue on Road 400 in the direction of Antalya. At c 16km from Kumluca take a side road on the right to **Yenice** for ancient **Gagae**. The ruins are c 4km from the village on a hilltop, c 200m high, near the sea-shore.

First mentioned in the 4C BC, Gagae was probably a Rhodian foundation. According to a legend a ship from Rhodes, having survived a severe storm, made a landfall here and the crew, overwhelmed with joy and relief at their escape, cried out 'ga, ga', the Doric form of 'ge', earth or land. In antiquity, Gagae was famous for a mineral, *lapis gagates* or jet. No trace of this is found here now.

Spratt saw many ruins at Gagae in the 19C and in 1960 Bean found the remains of a small **theatre** built into the NW side of the hill. This has now disappeared. Some scattered blocks of stone and the remains of a wall and tower on top of the hill survive. The ruins of Gagae, like those at Corydalla, have been plundered to provide building material for modern houses.

Here Road 400 begins its ascent of the mountain spur that terminates in Cape Chelidonia, the ancient *Promontorium Sacrum* which was believed to mark the boundary between the Phoenician and Greek seas.

At the summit the road enters the **Beydağları Sahil Milli Parkı**, the Bey Mountains Coastal National Park, home of the *tahtacılar*, wood-cutters.

About 23km from Kumluca a sign to the right points to 9km **OLYMPUS**. Until recently it was difficult to get to this site and, once there, to explore it properly. However, the authorities have improved the access road and have cleared away much of the scrub from the principal monuments.

There is no accommodation at Olympus, but there is now a small restaurant on the shore. Olympus has become a popular destination for boat trips from Antalya, so you may have to share it with beach parties. The peace and tranquillity provided by its former relative inaccessibility have, alas, gone forever. The mosquitoes from the marshes still thrive!

History. Olympus is believed to be a pre-Greek word for mountain. More than 20 peaks bore that name and in many cases gave it to an adjacent town or city.

Originally, neither Olympus nor its larger neighbour, Phaselis, formed part of Lycia. No Lycian tombs or inscriptions in the Lycian language have been found in either city. Olympus may have been founded during the Hellenistic period, but it is first mentioned in the 2C BC, as a member of the Lycian League. Towards the beginning of the 1C BC, when Phaselis had withdrawn from the League, Olympus represented E Lycia and had three votes, the maximum number, in the League's Assembly. Shortly afterwards, it and much of the adjacent coastline came under the control of pirates. According to Plutarch the pirates introduced the worship of Mithras to this area, practising the rites in secret on Mt Olympus. Mithras, a deity of Indo-Persian origin, was a god of light and creation. Restricted to men, his cult was popular with soldiers who helped to spread it far and wide through the Roman Empire.

Until defeated in 78 BC by Servilius Vatia, the Roman governor of Cilicia, the pirate chief, Zenicetes, made Olympus his headquarters. Servilius declared Olympus and nearby Phaselis to be public property which could be sold or let to anyone interested and this state of affairs probably continued until Imperial times. A further outbreak of piracy was ended by Pompey the Great, when he defeated the Cilician raiders at the battle of Coracesium, now Alanya, in 67 BC.

When Lycia was joined with Pamphylia and brought into the Roman Empire in AD 43 the fortunes of Olympus revived. It became once again an important member of the Lycian League. Opramoas of Rhodiapolis made the city a generous gift which was used for the restoration of many public buildings. There are records of the solemn celebrations held for the god Hephaestus, the principal deity of Olympus. An inscription in honour of Hadrian suggests that he may have visited the city c 130. During the reign of Diocletian (284–305), Methodius, the city's bishop was martyred. Renewed attacks by pirates in the 3C started a decline which was never completely arrested. In the 5C the bishops of Olympus attended the councils of Ephesus and Constantinople. During the later Byzantine Empire Olympus lost much of its importance. There was a brief revival in the 11C and 12C, when it was used as a trading post by the Venetians and Genoese, but it appears to have been abandoned finally sometime in the 15C, when the Ottoman navy established its mastery over the eastern Mediterranean.

Because of the rapid-growing, luxuriant vegetation Olympus is not easy to explore even now. Its attraction is due as much to the beauty of its situation as to the importance of its ruins. These are on both sides of a river which dries to a trickle in the summer. On the right there is an extensive **necropolis**. The tombs, of a kind not common in Lycia, consist of vaulted chambers cut into the rock which are closed with a vertical slab. In the western section, two of them bear, in addition to the usual epitaph, some curious inscriptions. According to Bean these were letter-oracles. There are 24 lines of advice, each of which is preceded by a different letter of the alphabet; a device which permitted enquirers to consult the spirits of their ancestors.

To the E of the necropolis, on the side of the hill, are the remains of the **theatre** which dates from the Roman period. The seats have vanished and, like most of the buildings, it is covered with tangled growth. One fine entrance arch remains. NE of the theatre the ruins of a **Byzantine basilica** and of several unidentified buildings, believed to be Roman, protrude from a spinney. The S bank of the river is marked by a fine stretch of **polygonal wall** which has been dated to the early Hellenistic period. Some believe that this was built to canalise the river, but the more widely accepted opinion is that it formed part of the harbour. The quay, 5m wide, is backed by a 3m-high wall, which terminates in a crudely constructed building

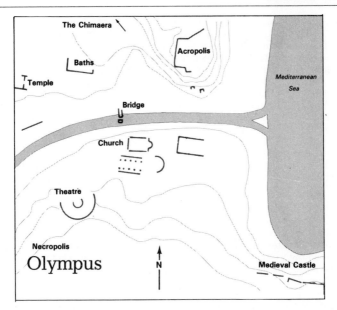

which may have been a warehouse. The entrance to the river is now closed by a sand-bank. Note the two fine, decorated **sarcophagi** near the beach.

The stream can be crossed easily near the remains of an ancient bridge. The **acropolis** is N of the river on a steep hill to the right, near the river-mouth. A splendid view of the whole area from the summit makes the climb worthwhile. The main part of the city lay to the NW. Apart from a **Roman baths complex** which has some fine geometric mosaics, and the decorated portal of a substantial building, little remains to be seen. The **portal** which is within a few metres of a marsh, once an ancient lake, is probably the most remarkable monument in Olympus. Approximately 5m high, it is believed to be the entrance to an **Ionic-style temple in antis**, dating from the late Antonine period or early part of the reign of Marcus Aurelius. The lintel and uprights, which are decorated on one side only, are flanked by a fine ashlar wall. Nearby there is the base of a statue dedicated c 172 to the Marcus Aurelius. Several large column-drums and parts of the architrave lie on the ground. As there is no room between the existing ruins and the lake for a building of this size, the decoration of the portal and the statue-base appeared, curiously, to be on the inside of the structure. This puzzle has now been resolved. It is believed that the portal marks the entrance to the **cella** of the temple.

The Turkish name for Olympus is *Yanartaş*, 'burning stone'. This refers to a natural phenomenon, known in antiquity as the **Chimaera**, on the mountainside to the N of the city. Transport is available to the base of the mountain. From here it is an undemanding 30 minute walk to the flames.

On the slope c 250m above sea-level, perpetual flames flicker and burn in a grey, rocky area. Probably produced by methane gas, they cannot be extinguished with water. If covered with soil, a flame will disappear for a few minutes, only to rekindle itself close by. At night the ghostly lights are clearly visible far out to sea. It not surprising that the ancients believed this phenomenon to be of supernatural origin. They called it the Chimaera after the fire-breathing beast which, according to legend, terrorised ancient Lycia. This composite creature had a lion's head and front, a goat's middle and a snake at the back. Bellerophon was set the task of killing it by Iobates, king of Lycia. He dropped lead into its mouth. This melted and choked it. Hephaestus, the god of fire, was worshipped at Olympus and the ruins of his shrine may be seen nearby. The site of the flame was linked to the city by a paved Roman road.

The first substantial buildings were erected here during the Christian period. There are the remains of a **Byzantine basilica** whose walls bear some traces of fresco.

Speculation that there might be petrol here provoked some investigations. These do not seem to have produced any positive results.

On the beach, there is a pierced rock, *Deliktaş* in Turkish, which has a tunnel wide enough for a man to pass through. This was used as late as the 19C as part of a pathway along the shore.

Return to Road 400 and continue in the direction of Antalya. You pass through the wild, dramatic scenery of the National Park. After c 21km look out for a turning on the right to 2km **PHASELIS**.

There are toilets, a small museum and parking for coaches in a clearing among the trees. Light refreshments and admission tickets to the site are sold here. Private cars may drive 1km farther to a parking place near the ancient aqueduct.

Professor Cevdet Bayburtluoğlu and his colleagues have excavated recently in the large 3C AD bath house, the theatre baths and the Hadrianic agora. Conservation measures have been taken on the stage building of the theatre and restoration work has been carried out on the gate built to commemorate the visit of Hadrian to the city in AD 131.

History. According to legend, Phaselis was founded by a group of colonists from Rhodes c 690 BC. The ground on which the city was built was owned by a shepherd named Cylabras. Lacius, the leader of the colonists, offered to purchase the site for a quantity of corn or some dried fish. Cylabras took the fish. His choice was commemorated by the practice of using dried salted fish as a sacrificial offering. Hence the expression 'a Phaselitan sacrifice', meaning an inexpensive oblation.

An extensive survey, begun in 1968 by German archaeologists, has revealed no trace of pre-Greek occupation. This tends to support the foundation legend. The deserted state of the site and the fact that, apart from Olympus, it has the only good harbours on this part of the coast could have attracted Rhodian colonists. The hinterland had vast quantities of timber, an eagerly sought commodity, and the city was well placed for trading with most ports in the eastern Mediterranean. The business acumen of the Phaselitans was demonstrated as early as the 6C BC, when the city combined with eight other Greek cities in Asia Minor to found the colony of Naucratis in the Nile Delta. In the 4C BC this same acumen was denounced by Demosthenes, who categorised the Phaselitans as dishonest. Pride in their commercial activities is evidenced by coins issued in the 5C BC which show the prow of a ship on one side and the stern on the reverse. By that time Phaselis was under Persian domination. Clearly, the city did not find the yoke a heavy one, as when the Athenian, Cimon, came to liberate the Lycian cities c 467 BC, the Phaselitans threw in their lot with the Persians. The city was besieged and they suffered grievously. Eventually, through the good offices of their friends, the Chians, they came to terms with Cimon. Plutarch relates that the Chians 'shot leaflets, attached to arrows, over the walls to tell the inhabitants what was happening'; eventually they brought the parties to terms. The Phaselitans agreed to pay ten talents and accompany Cimon on his campaign against the barbarians.

Following the defeat of the Persians by Cimon and the Athenians at the battle of the Eurymedon river (see Aspendus), Phaselis and other Lycian cities were enrolled in the Delian League. The city's wealth and importance at this time may be judged from the fact that, while the annual contribution from Ephesus to the League was six talents, the levy on Phaselis varied between three and six talents. It was paid regularly.

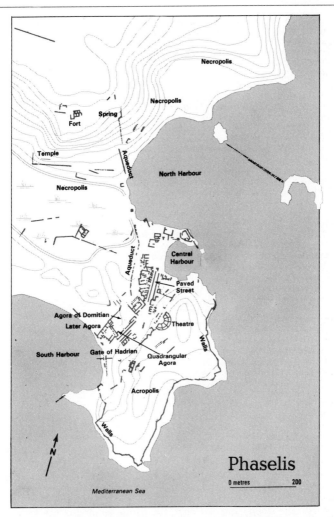

At the beginning of the 4C BC the Persian rule was restored and Lycia and Phaselis were placed under the control of Mausolus, satrap of Caria. The Lycians, led by the dynast Pericles of Limyra, raised the standard of revolt. However, the Phaselitans, who did not always agree with their Lycian neighbours, sided with Mausolus. Their independent status at this time is proved by the existence of a treaty between them and Mausolus which both parties signed as equals.

In 333 BC Alexander came to Phaselis. He was welcomed by the Phaselitans. They offered him the customary gold crown and opened the gates. In return Alexander helped them in a campaign against the Pisidians, who had been ravaging Phaselitan territory. After the death of Alexander, Phaselis sided with Antigonus Monophthalmos, but with the rest of Lycia soon came under Ptolemaic rule. In 197 BC Lycia, and presumably Phaselis, was occupied by Antiochus III of Syria. Following his defeat by the Romans in 190 BC Lycia was awarded to their allies, the Rhodians. Rhodian rule was bitterly resisted and, finally, in 167 BC Rome gave Lycia her freedom.

The Lycian League was revived. Phaselis became a full member and issued federal coins. At the beginning of the 1C BC the city and Olympus were occupied by Cilician pirates. After the campaigns of Servilius Vatia in 78 BC and Pompey in 67 BC had eliminated the pirate threat, Phaselis began to recover. However, progress was so slow that in 48 BC the Roman poet, Lucan, could call the city 'little' Phaselis.

In AD 43 Claudius created the province of Lycia-Pamphylia. Like most cities Phaselis appears to have enjoyed a prosperous, relatively uneventful existence. It was visited by Hadrian in AD 131, an event commemorated by the erection of statues and a ceremonial gateway. Because of his generous benefactions, Opramoas of Rhodiapolis became a citizen of Phaselis. This was a somewhat doubtful privilege, as the Phaselitans were alleged to have sold citizenship to anyone prepared to pay 100 drachme for it. The city was also notorious for a hairstyle called 'sisoe' which Christians found particularly offensive, probably because it was forbidden in the Bible. 'Ye shall not make a 'sisoe' of the hair of your heads'. (Leviticus, 19,27.), ie 'There must be no tonsuring of heads' (Knox). Phaselis had a reputation for being unhealthy. Livy describes a fever, which may have been malaria, that broke out among Rhodian sailors. This he attributes to unpleasant smells found here. These may have come from the swamp near the N fortress, home to swarms of mosquitoes. Aelian, writing c 200, says that the city had to be abandoned, presumably temporarily, because of a plague of wasps.

Phaselis was an episcopal see. Its bishop attended the Council of Chalcedon in 451. Having suffered greatly from Arab raids in the 7C AD, the city's prosperity revived in the 8C, when its fortifications were renewed and many new buildings were erected. In 1158 it was captured from the Byzantines by the Selçuk Turks. With the growth in importance of the ports of Antalya and Alanya, it declined as a trading centre until it was finally abandoned sometime in the early 13C.

Phaselis was visited in 1811 by Beaufort during his survey of the S coast of Turkey for the Admiralty. Most of the ruins which he saw are still visible. He found a sarcophagus which had escaped the attention of the tomb robbers. This had been concealed 'by a thick covering of earth, which the surf had lately removed, and exposed one end to view. Elated with the discovery, we eagerly proceeded to explore its contents: while the necessary implements were collecting, our imagination was on the stretch; and urns, or coins, or ancient weapons were, at least, expected to reward our labour. At length the tools arrived; the ponderous lid was removed; and the bones of a single skeleton were discovered, and nothing more. These were strong and firm, and did not undergo any immediate change from exposure to the air; the skeleton was of the middle size, and was placed with the face up, and the head to the northward'.

Having listed the principal ruins and transcribed a number of inscriptions, Beaufort affirms that everything was put back where it had been found or placed in a position calculated to aid its preservation. 'A practice', he adds, 'which we constantly adopted, for the benefit of future travellers'. What an example for those who came after him.

Visitors to Phaselis often confess themselves deeply moved by the beauty of its situation between the mountains and the sea. The sight of fragments of ancient buildings protruding from the lush undergrowth produces a mood of gentle melancholy. Bean found it had 'a charm beyond most others'. The sleepy summer heat, the gentle lapping of the waves, the distant hazy mountains, the utter solitude of the ancient city, combine to produce an effect not easily effaced.

To the left of the track, from the main road, is the northern fortified area. This is enclosed by a Hellenistic wall which is well preserved in its SW corner. Here, on the slope, there is the foundation of a **temple** or **monumental tomb**. A part of the **necropolis** lies below the W side of the hill. On the E side of the plateau a ramp leads to a **fortified area** 150m long and 25–50m wide. The 3C BC N wall of this structure, which is now 3m high, has the remains of a tower and three arrow slits. The fortified area dominated the city and protected a spring, now dry, which was near the base of the ramp. Water was carried from here in a **clay conduit** supported first by a solid wall and then by arches. This skirts the W side of the N harbour and ends near the rear of the quadrangular agora.

To the right of the track there is an extensive swampy area, which according to Strabo was once a lake. The swamp is now separated from the N harbour by an area of sand dunes and scrub c 150m wide. The **N harbour,** which appears to have been used mainly as a roadstead, is protected from the NE by a line of rocks which extends for 300m into the sea. An **artificial breakwater** 4m wide was constructed on top of this natural feature. The **largest section of the city's necropolis** is around the shore of the N harbour. There are a number of interesting **sarcophagi** and other tombs dating from the Roman and Byzantine periods here.

The central harbour of Phaselis, which was used for small and medium-sized ships, is c 100m to the SE. Facing E, it was protected on the N and NE by a wall which extended outwards over a breakwater and terminated in a tower. The 18m-wide harbour entrance between this and another tower on the S could be closed in time of danger. In the SW corner of the harbour **one of the bollards**, which projected horizontally from the ashlar facing of the quay wall, may still be seen. Behind the quay there were a number of warehouses on the hillside.

Archaic pottery sherds found on the **acropolis**, which lies to the S of the central harbour, suggest that the earliest occupation was here. Fortified on the seaward side, this is now covered with undergrowth through which the ruins of several buildings, tentatively identified as houses and a church, are visible. Because of the cool sea breezes and its distance from the noisome smells of the marsh, the SW tip of the acropolis peninsula was one of the most desirable areas of the city. It is known that public buildings and later, in Byzantine times, churches and private houses were constructed here on a series of terraces. No trace of the temple of Athena Polias where, according to Pausanias, the spear of Achilles was kept, has been found in Phaselis. It may have been on the acropolis. The discovery of a stone dated to the 5C BC, bearing the name of the goddess, which had been built into the wall of the stage-building of the theatre in late Roman or Byzantine times supports this theory. However, until the scrub has been cleared and the area investigated properly, the exact location of the temple must remain a matter of speculation.

A broad, **paved street** c 22m wide, flanked by steps and sidewalks, passed through the city centre and linked the S and central harbours. It was made up of two sections which met at an obtuse angle in front of the theatre. At the NE end of this street, near the central harbour, there was a long, narrow **two-storey building**, probably used for business purposes. Behind this, an elaborate **baths complex** still has traces of its mosaic pavements. Excavations have revealed well-preserved heating and ventilation systems.

To the SW, a wall of ashlar masonry marks the site of the **quadrangular agora**, which was probably the administrative centre of the city. This can be dated to 131 by a dedicatory inscription to Hadrian on the door lintel. Statue bases on either side of the entrance bear inscriptions commemorating some of the city's benefactors. Among these was Opramoas of Rhodiapolis. In Byzantine times a small **basilica** was constructed in the NW part of this agora.

To the SW is the **agora of Domitian**. Dated to c 93, this is an area c 60m by 40m with rooms on the SW and SE sides only. Beyond is a **late agora**, opening on to the S harbour, constructed of materials salvaged from other buildings. This has been dated to late Imperial or Byzantine times.

The **theatre** of Phaselis, believed to date from the 2C AD, faces the quadrangular agora from the E side of the street. Its cavea was cut out of the acropolis hill. Several rows of seats and substantial parts of the stage building remain. Conservation work has been undertaken on the stage building. Three monumental doors provided access to the stage area. This was c 2.5m above ground level and was probably constructed of wood. Below the stage four small doors opening on to the orchestra were used to admit animals into the arena when the theatre was used for wild-beast fights. The holes in the orchestra floor have been made by illegal treasure-hunters. It is probable that this building replaced an earlier Hellenistic theatre. At some point, perhaps during the Byzantine period, the wall of the stage building was incorporated in the acropolis fortifications.

At the southern end of the main street is the restored ceremonial **marble gateway**, erected to commemorate the visit of Hadrian to Phaselis in AD 131. The **S harbour**, the largest of the three, lies outside the fortifications. Here the bigger ships were loaded and unloaded by lighters or at the quayside. The harbour was protected from the weather on the SE by a breakwater which extended for c 100m from the acropolis promontory. It is not known with certainty when this breakwater and the other harbour structures at Phaselis were built. They probably date from the middle of the 2C AD, when Antoninus Pius and Hadrian promoted the construction and improvement of harbours in Asia Minor.

Little is visible of the western part of the ancient city. It is covered under sand dunes and dense vegetation. On the NW side of the marsh, to the left of the route back to main road, there is a stretch of c 300m of the **paved way** that linked Olympus and Phaselis. This is flanked by tombs.

Road 400 from Phaselis to c 45km Antalya follows the coastline closely, passing one sand-rimmed beach after another. Here, pine-clad mountain ridges tumble down to great jagged promontories that hurl themselves into the sea. River beds, foaming torrents in winter, arid nests of scorpions in summer, are dramatic punctuation marks in the landscape. This is a magical mysterious place.

On the western outskirts of **Kemer** the *Iberotel Kiris World*, the *Salima Tatil Köyü* and the *Ramada Renaissance Resort* are full of sun-starved northern Europeans. At Kemer, which has been developed with the aid of a World Bank loan, there are hotels, a modern marina, shops selling fashionable, expensive goods and several holiday villages. The four-star *Otem Hotel*, staffed by students from the Tourism school, near the marina commends itself.

The landscape between here and Antalya is, softer, gentler. Orange and lemon groves line the road. **Beldibi** is a smaller version of Kemer. It has a pebbly beach, hotels, holiday villages and a camping-place. Antalya is signalled by its commercial harbour on the right side of the road. Beyond the huge sweep of **Konyaaltı beach** stretches away in a great curve towards the city.

Road 400, the link between the coastal towns and villages of eastern Lycia and Antalya, was not completed until comparatively recently. The rugged terrain which lies between Finike and Antalya raised construction problems that could only be solved by the skills and machinery available to modern civil engineers. Before its completion, travel to and from the regional capital was usually by sea.

The absence of a route through eastern Lycia reminds one of an interesting historical puzzle. When, in 333 BC, Alexander the Great decided to march from Phaselis to the cities of Pamphylia, he had to get his army through a wild and trackless stretch of country. Arrian claims that he succeeded with the help of the gods. Sending some of his men over the high passes 'a long and difficult journey', he led the rest of his army along the sea-shore that lies between Phaselis and the approaches to Antalya. According to the historian, this was a venture that could only be attempted when the wind blew from the N. With a S wind, the route along the shore was impassable. As Alexander left Phaselis, there was a strong wind from the S. However, trusting in the gods and in his own destiny, he set out at the head of his men. Zeus was kind to him. Arrian writes: 'the wind turned to the N and made the passage quick and easy'. But his account has been questioned by more than one authority. Bean, who discussed the matter with local fishermen, was told that contrary to Arrian's version of events the wind makes little difference to the level of the sea, but that a N wind makes it rough. Bean accepts Strabo's version, with minor modifications. According to the geographer Alexander took his troops along the beach where the sea-level permitted and where the water was too high he made a diversion inland.

An attempt to follow the shore-line was made by Freya Stark in 1954, while she was researching *Alexander's Path* in Lycia and Pamphylia. She found that she could wade for part of the way, but that there were stretches of deep water where she was obliged to swim. It is unlikely that the mystery will ever be solved, as the physical configuration of the coast has almost certainly changed during the last 2000 years.

26

Antalya

ANTALYA, capital of the province of the same name, is a modern city which has become an important tourist destination in recent years. It is magnificently sited on the Gulf of Antalya. Adjacent to the Yat Limanı is the old quarter of the city. This is being restored and developed with considerable imagination. Antalya's main shopping centre is on Cumhuriyet Cad. and Atatürk Cad. The city park, which has spectacular views of the Gulf and of the Bey Dağları, is just off Otuz Ağustos Cad. About 1km to the W of the city is Konyaaltı Plajı, a clean but rather stony beach.

The industrial port is on the road W to Kemer. The city's main industries are tourism, the processing of sesame and sunflower seeds and of cotton. Antalya is also an important sale and distribution centre for a range of agricultural and horticultural produce including citrus fruit, olives, sugar beet and salad vegetables. The main grain crops of the region are wheat and barley. Antalya has very hot dry summers, when the temperature sometimes reaches 40°C. Winters are warm and wet, with the heaviest rainfall in January. Frosts are almost unknown and snow is found only on the peaks of the Taurus Mountains and the Bey Dağları.

Information and Accommodation. The **Tourist Information Office** is in Cumhuriyet Cad. It is open Monday to Saturday and also on Sunday during the holiday season.

Antalya has six five-star hotels, *Antalya Dedeman Oteli, Club Sera Oteli, Falez Oteli, Talya Oteli, Ofo Oteli, Sheraton Oteli*, and numerous hostelries in the other star categories, together with a multitude of relatively inexpensive pensions and several special category establishments. Recommended for their style, comfort, good restaurants, excellent service and location are the *Aspen Oteli*, Kılıç Aslan Mah., Kaleiçi and the nearby *Marina Oteli*, Mermerli Sok., No.15, Kaleiçi. Both are graded as 'special category'. They are tastefully converted old houses a few minutes' walk from the Yat Limanı and the shopping centre. There is a superfluity of hotels at **Lara Beach**, formerly a quiet seaside location, which is c 12km from the city centre.

Restaurants. Eating out is one of the pleasures of a stay in Antalya. The big hotels serve both Turkish and international cuisine and there are some excellent restaurants in the city, many of them near the Yat Limanı. Recommended are the *Hisar Restaurant*, which occupies a number of vaulted rooms and terraces of the old fortifications, and the *Sirri*, Üzun Çarşı. If you want to eat Chinese food in Turkey, try *Yesterday's* in the old town.

Post Office. The central post office is in Anafartalar Cad.

Banks. Branches of the principal Turkish banks may be found in the city centre in Cumhuriyet Cad., Ali Çetinkaya Cad. and Atatürk Cad.

Transport. Antalya's airport is c 8km to the E, just off the E24. It has connections via İstanbul with many European destinations. There are direct charter flights during the holiday season, frequent domestic flights, and services to North Cyprus and to some Middle East countries. A coach from the Turkish Airlines Cargo Terminal in Cumhuriyet Cad. takes passengers to the airport. For service times, enquire at the THY office.

The *otogar* is in Kâzim Özalp Cad. There are frequent services to Alanya (2 hours), Perge (½ hour), Aspendus (1 hour), Side via Manavgat (90 minutes), Ankara, (10 hours), Adana (11 hours), Konya (7 hours), Demre (4 hours), Kaş (5 hours), Fethiye (8 hours), and many other destinations in Turkey. Tickets may be purchased at the *otogar* and from the town offices of the various bus companies.

From the Dolmuş Garage, which is off Ali Çetinkaya Cad., minibuses provide a cheap and rapid transport service in the city and to many of the nearby towns and villages.

Antalya's **museum**, which has a large and well-displayed collection of archaeological and ethnographical objects, is at the western end of the city near Konyaaltı Beach.

History. Founded in the 2C BC by Attalus II (160–139 BC), king of Pergamum, and named **Attaleia** in his honour, modern Antalya has kept few relics of its ancient past. About 158 BC Attalus attempted to subdue the rebellious city of Selge, which was nominally part of the kingdom of Pergamum, and although he failed in his attempt, he managed to conquer a large part of Pamphylia. As Side, the only port of any importance in Pamphylia was under the protection of Rome, he was obliged to found a new city, Attaleia, to get an outlet to the Mediterranean.

His nephew and successor, Attalus III, (138–133 BC) bequeathed his kingdom to Rome in 133 BC, but the bequest did not include Pamphylia, Rough Cilicia and Lycia. Because of its wild and rugged nature and the abundance of small, safe anchorages, Rough Cilicia had long been a haven for pirates who preyed on shipping in the Eastern Mediterranean. Eventually, their activities spread and reached such proportions that Rome was obliged to take action. After a naval expedition against the pirates had only achieved a limited success, Pamphylia, with some surrounding territory, was annexed by the Romans. Direct rule brought few benefits to the inhabitants of the province. A succession of venal, grasping governors enriched themselves at the expense of their subjects and the pirates continued their depredations almost without check. It was not until 67 BC that a campaign conducted by Pompey put an end to their activities. In AD 130 Hadrian came to Antalya. His visit was commemorated by the erection of a ceremonial arch which still stands. St Paul visited nearby Perge, but little is known of the early history of Christianity in Antalya. It did not have its own bishop until the 11C.

During the Crusades Antalya was an important staging post for soldiers and the transport of their supplies to the Holy Land. Briefly occupied by the Selçuk Turks in the 12C and then returned to Byzantine rule, it was reconquered by Giyasettin Keyhusrev in 1206. During the reign of Yıldırım Beyazit it became part of the Ottoman Empire. It remained an Ottoman provincial sub-division until World War I. Then, as part of the spoils of war, it was ceded to Italy in 1918. In 1921 it was liberated by the Turkish army and became a provincial capital of the Turkish Republic.

Travellers. The Arab traveller Ibn Battuta visited Antalya in the mid 14C and found it 'a most beautiful city... It covers an immense area and though of vast bulk is one of the most attractive towns to be seen anywhere, besides being exceedingly populous and well laid out. Each section of the inhabitants lives in a separate quarter. The Christian merchants live in a quarter of the town known as the Mina [the Port], and are surrounded by a wall, the gates of which are shut upon them from without at night and during the Friday service. The Greeks, who were its former inhabitants, live by themselves in another quarter, the Jews in another, and the king and his court and mamluks in another, each of these quarters being walled off likewise. The rest of the Muslims live in the main city. Round the whole town and all the quarters mentioned there is another great wall. The town contains many orchards and

The Yivli Minare, the Fluted Minaret, the symbol of Antalya

produces fine fruits, including an admirable kind of apricot, called by them Qamar ad-Din, which has a sweet almond in its kernel. This fruit is dried and exported to Egypt, where it is regarded as a great luxury'.

In the 14C Antalya it was the most important port in southern Anatolia, particularly for trade with Cyprus and Egypt. Perhaps that is why the lemon is still called 'Adaliya' in Egypt.

In 1671 the Turkish traveller Evliya Çelebi visited Antalya. In his *Book of Travels* he says the city was 4400m long and enclosed by a wall surmounted by 80 towers and pierced by four great gates. The citadel inside the walls was divided into four districts. A further 22 gates gave access to these districts and to the thousand houses which they contained. The streets were paved.

> Each house has an open-ended verandah built on four high posts where the family sleeps. The cloth market is in the outer suburb. This suburb contains twenty Moslem and four Greek enclaves. It has one hundred and ninety houses, two hundred shops and more than two hundred fountains whose water comes from the Düden river. The harbour can accommodate two hundred ships and is protected from the eight winds. The weather in the city is very hot.

About 150 years later Francis Beaufort, captain of the frigate *Frederickssteen* made a survey of the coast of southern Turkey for the British Admiralty in 1811 and 1812. In *Karamania* he describes Antalya (Adalia) as follows:

> Adalia is beautifully situated round a small harbour; the streets appear to rise behind each other like the seats of a theatre; and on the level summit of the hill, the city is enclosed by a ditch, a double wall, and a series of square towers, about fifty yards asunder. The gardens round the town are beautiful; the trees are loaded with fruit; every kind of vegetation seemed to be exuberant; and the inhabitants spoke of their corn grounds as more than commonly productive.

Freya Stark visited the city in the 1950s and in *Alexander's Path* she enthuses on the view over the bay to the Lycian hills.

> In early spring the Bay of Antalya lies under a mist slightly raised above the surface of the water and filled with sunlight, until the warmth of day sucks it up. I would watch it from a slanting little breakfast shop that overhangs the harbour. ... roofs and the tops of trees push out from hidden gardens; and beyond them a caique might have been moving out from Antalya with the dawn: she would leave a curved trail, marked by the current, as wavering and edgeless as the seasonal pathways made by the feet of flocks; and beyond her and the misty bay, the Chelidonian peninsula spread its tented blue festoons from peak to peak.

The **Atatürk memorial** in a square off Cumhuriyet Cad. is in the centre of the city. The **Vilayet**, the administrative headquarters of the province, is across the road. From the square there is a splendid view of Antalya, of the gulf and, far to the W, of the Bey Dağları. On the left and a little below Cumhuriyet Cad. is the **Yivli Minare**, the Fluted Minaret. This structure, regarded as the symbol of Antalya, was built in 1230 during the reign of Sultan Aladdin Keykubad. Originally attached to a mosque converted from a Byzantine church, the minaret rests on a square stone base. Made of brick, it has eight fluted sections, hence its name. It is decorated with dark blue tiles. Those on the base bear the words 'Allah' and 'Muhammet'. The minaret is 38m high. The first mosque was destroyed in the 14C and replaced by the present building. This has six cupolas supported by columns capped with ancient Ionic and Corinthian capitals. It was constructed by Mehmet Bey, who also built the *türbe* with the pyramidal roof near the mosque to house the body of his eldest son who died in 1377. The building adjoining the *türbe* is an 18C *tekke* which was occupied by Mevlevi dervishes.

To the right of the clock-tower at Kalekapısı is the 18C **Tekeli Mehmet Pasha Camii**. It has three cupolas over the central area.

Return to Cumhuriyet Cad. and continue for c 100m before turning right into Atatürk Cad. A short distance along on the right is **Hadrian's Gate**, built to commemorate the emperor's visit to Antalya in AD 130. Constructed of marble, it has three arches with coffered ceilings decorated with rosettes. Four Corinthian columns with granite shafts stand in front of each of the piers. It has been imaginatively restored. The gate bore the following dedication: ΑΥΤΟΚΡΑΤΟΡΙ ΚΑΙΣΑΡΙ (ΤΡΑΙΑΝΩ) ΑΔΡΙΑΝΩ. A part of this inscription is in the Ashmolean Museum at Oxford. Hadrian's Gate is flanked by

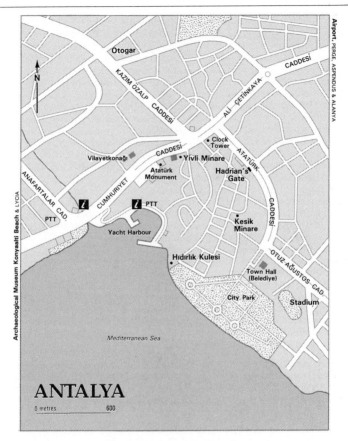

ANTALYA

0 metres   600

towers which are thought to date from the 2C BC when the city was founded.

Behind Hadrian's Gate is a maze of small streets which makes up the old quarter. Here, the overhanging wooden balconies of old, dilapidated houses lean companionably towards each other like ancient gossips exchanging the latest scandal. Sometimes, through a gap in a crumbling wall you glimpse an overgrown garden where a few neglected orange trees produce shrivelled, bitter fruit. Children play happily in narrow lanes which are little disturbed by traffic. Derelict houses are being painstakingly reconstructed in the old style and modern houses are not permitted.

Follow the slope down towards the harbour to the **Kesik Minare Camii**, the Truncated Minaret Mosque. In the 5C a church was built here, on the site of Roman temple, in honour of the Blessed Virgin Mary. It was converted into a mosque in the 13C by Şehzade Korkut, the son of Beyazit II. During the reconstruction a *mihrab* of cut stone was added. The mosque acquired its name after a fire in 1851 damaged the minaret. At present the building is in a ruinous condition. The column capitals, the decorated slabs between the windows of the apse and some floral carving are of the finest quality.

Bear left near the mosque for the **Karaalioğlu Parkı**, the city's principal park. The large building near the entrance is the **Belediye**. During the sweltering days of summer the palm-lined avenues provide a pleasant refuge from the heat. In the late afternoon and evening its tea gardens and belvedere are favourite rendezvous for visitors and residents. The cliff-top promenade offers a splendid view of the Gulf of Antalya and of the Bey Dağları of Lycia in the far distance.

The **Hıdırlık Kulesi**, a Roman building of the 2C AD, is 13.45m high, a round tower on a massive square base. Described at different times as a lighthouse, a fort and a tomb, its shape and the presence of a carving of fasces, a bundle of rods, the symbol of a Roman magistrate, tend to support the last hypothesis. It was probably the burial place of a local dignitary.

From the Hıdırlık Kulesi continue to the **Yat Limanı**, the yacht harbour. Where the road branches, just beyond the office of the Ministry of Tourism, take the left fork by the mosque. On the S side of the harbour there is a pleasant café which overlooks a tiny private beach. Steps lead down to the breakwater and the quay. You may also reach the harbour by following the road that runs parallel to the ancient city walls and passes the Aspen and Marina hotels. Turn left at the first main junction.

Near the fishing boats and pleasure craft is the very distinctive **Iskele Camii**, the Harbour Mosque. This building of cut stone has been restored recently. Access to the interior is by a wooden staircase.

The harbour area has been developed under the guidance of the Ministry of Tourism in an attractive manner. Some of the best restaurants in Antalya are here. There are also cafés, a post office, a bank, a barber, souvenir shops, a luxury hotel and a small open-air theatre. To dine by candlelight in the Hisar Restaurant within the city walls or in one of the *lokantas* that lie in their shadow is a memorable experience.

To visit **Antalya Museum**, take a dolmuş marked Meteoroloji, Bahçeli or Liman (Harbour) from the stop across the road from Kalekapısı. Alternatively, it is a pleasant 20-minute walk along Cumhuriyet Cad. and Konyaltı Bulv. The museum is on the right-hand side of the road, just after the Piri Reis Cad. junction.

Antalya Museum is open every day except Monday from 8.00 to 12.00 and from 13.30 to 17.00. There is a small bar which offers light refreshments.

Room 1, the Children's Museum, is the only one of its kind in Turkey. It is intended to interest children in history by relating the objects in the museum to everyday life. Examples of ancient pottery and scripts, demonstrations of crafts, posters and explanatory texts are used for this purpose.

Room 2 deals with the prehistory of the Antalya region. Artefacts from the Palaeolithic (to 8000), Neolithic (8000–5500), and Chalcolithic (5500–3000) Periods, Early Bronze (3000–2000) and Middle-Late Bronze (2000–1200) Ages are shown here. Many of the objects come from from the **Karain Cave** which is 30km NW of Antalya. First excavated by Prof. Dr I. Kılıç Kökten in 1946, only a part has been explored so far. Cases in this room contain hand axes, flint scrapers, bone awls, burins, and daggers and spear heads made from antlers. Fragments of the skull of a Neanderthal child, the skulls and skeletons of Homo Sapiens and the teeth and bones of extinct animals from the Palaeolithic age are on display. There is a fine example of mobiliary art, the head of a bison or of Elephantus Meridionalis carved in stone. From the Burdur area there is a female fertility figurine of the Chalcolithic period. Bronze Age grave goods from Karataş-Semayük/ Elmalı include ear-studs, brush handles, bronze pins and spearheads. At the end of the room there is the reconstruction of an Early Bronze Age **pithos burial** from Karataş-Semayük and a number of decorated pots and pithoi.

Joining Rooms 2 and 3 is the **Corridor of Short Inscriptions**. Two of the stelae here are of particular interest. One is from Perge the other from Aspendus. The **stele from Perge**, which dates from the 5C BC, is dedicated to Artemis of Perge under her ancient name. 'Klemutas son of L'Faramus of the tribe Wasir Fotas has dedicated this monument to Pergaean goddess Wanassa Preiia Goddess of Perge [as the result of an] order [received in a] dream'. The **stele from Aspendus**, which dates from the 3C BC, is important as it shows that there was also a temple dedicated to Artemis in that city. It demonstrates the remarkable degree of independence enjoyed by Aspendus during the period of Ptolemaic domination.The stele records the grant of citizenship to foreigners—Pamphylians, Lycians, Cretans, Greeks and Pisidians—living in the city.

Room 3 houses a magnificent display of Phrygian artefacts discovered in 1986 in tumuli at Çağıltemeller near the village of Bayındır in the Elmalı plain. These date from the late 8C or early 7C BC. The tumuli, which were made of wood covered on the top and sides with stone rubble, had collapsed under the pressure. Among the objects found were two bronze protomes; a bronze ceremonial symbol consisting of a ring with three groups of phallic knobs; bronze and silver cauldrons and ladles; bronze and silver omphalos bowls; pins, fibulae, earrings and a belt of electrum, silver, bronze and gold; silver appliqué plates; ivory furniture inlay, and a dagger, spearhead and arrowheads of iron. In Tumulus D the archaeologists found an exquisite **ivory statue** of a standing female figure with two children. They also discovered a **silver figurine** of a priest. Wearing a tall headdress, severe in mien, he stands with folded hands.

The next room contains small works of art. Note the fine **calyx crater** with representations of Dionysus, maenads, and a dancing satyr. A 5C **column crater** from the necropolis of Aspendus shows three *komasts* (revellers) dancing vigorously, while holding drinking cups. On the reverse, three youths are depicted arming themselves. A black figure lekythos from Yeniliman, Antalya shows three armed horsemen on a beige background. A black figure kylix is ornamented with pastoral scenes. On the right-hand wall, there are cases containing figurines from the Mycenaean period; a remarkable **terracotta head** believed to come from Cyprus and some vases from the Classical period. Note particularly a vase showing a boy with a hoop and cock. (Compare this with ARV 355,69 in the Ashmolean Museum, Oxford.) There are also some cases of jewellery—headbands, earrings, necklaces, an ivory comb, pins and a decorated bronze mirror. These date from the 4C BC to the 6C AD. Finally, a collection of Classical and Hellenistic lekythoi dating from the 5C to the 3C BC.

In **Room 4** are some of the major treasures of the museum. This is the so-called **'Gallery of the Gods'**. Here are displayed **statues** discovered in Perge dating from the 2C AD. They include a resting Mercury, the Egyptian trinity of Serapis, Isis and Harpocrates, Artemis, Athene, Apollo, Hygeia, Tyche, Aphrodite, a pensive Dioscuros, Aphrodite and Nemesis. Appropriately, the pantheon is dominated by a fine statue of Zeus.

Room 5 is devoted to small works of art and to objects recovered from the sea. Note in particular the 2C **bronze statue of Apollo** from Seleucia, the **bearded Priapus** from Aspendus, the **bronze head of Attis** from Perge and the bronze statuette of Hercules from Pogla (Çomaklı). On the end wall there is a display of amphorae, stone and metal objects and pottery found on the seabed. These date from the 3C to the 14C AD. Near the entrance to Room 6 there is a fine **Marsyas**, a headless Athena, and a fragment from a pillar bearing a **relief of Artemis Pergaea**. The latter, which was found in the theatre of Perge, dates from the 2C AD and shows the goddess in the form of a baetyl, a sacred stone. At the top there is the head of Artemis, crowned with a *polos*, above a crescent moon. Below are three scenes of ritual cults. On the right-hand side there is another bust of Artemis and below this the figure of Eros armed with a sword.

Room 6 is dominated by the magnificent statue of a **female dancer**. Behind her, in characteristic pose, are the **Three Graces**. Although Room 6 is known as the 'Room of the Emperors' because it contains fine statues of Trajan, Hadrian, and Septimius Severus found at Perge, perhaps its most interesting exhibit is the statue of a woman—**Plancia Magna**. A dominating figure in 2C AD Perge, she was priestess of Artemis and of the Mother of the Gods and demiourgis. A generous donor, she presented a number of statues depicting various members of the Roman imperial house to Perge c AD 120. Two of the 'founders' of Perge are described on statue bases found in that city as the father and brother of Plancia Magna! Note also the statues of **Julia Domna**, wife of Septimius Severus and mother of Caracalla and Geta, and of Sabina, the wife of Hadrian.

Room 7 contains some fine sarcophagi from Perge. Just inside there is the striking 3C **columnar Sidamara style sarcophagus** of Domitias-Filiskas from the eastern necropolis. A sarcophagus dated to the 2C AD is decorated with reliefs showing the **labours of Hercules**. A so-called medallion sarcophagus has sides decorated with winged figures supporting the head of Medusa. Along one wall there are a number of decorated cinerary chests. Along another there are fragments from sarcophagi, one of which depicts a scene from the *Iliad*. At the rear of the room there is a strange primitive votive stele dedicated to the **Twelve Gods of Lycia** from Comba near Kaş. This shows 12 armed figures on the upper row with 12 stylised dogs below. Dated to the 3C AD, it is one of many similar carvings of these hunting deities found in Lycia. The inscription reads, 'to Artemis, to the Twelve Gods and their father'.

Room 8, a long narrow room to the left, contains **icons** from churches in Antalya. All date from the 19C and early 20C. In the case on the left-hand wall there is a series on the life of Christ—Nativity, Presentation in the Temple, Circumcision, Teaching the Doctors, Healing the Blind Man, Speaking with the Samaritan Woman, Transfiguration, Triumphant Entry into Jerusalem, Last Supper, Washing the Feet of His Disciples, Carrying the Cross, Crucifixion and Resurrection. Other icons depict the Blessed Virgin and the Christ Child, the Evangelists, St John the Baptist, and St Nicholas of Myra. There is also a small **reliquary** containing some of the bones of St Nicholas (see Demre, Route 24). Note the part of the 6C silver treasure of Corydalla (modern Kumluca). This includes a number of ornate silver dishes decorated with crosses. A part of this hoard is in the USA.

In **Room 9** there are some fine, if rather damaged, **mosaics** from Seleucia and Xanthus. On one from Seleucia there are portrait heads of Solon, Thucydides, Lycurgus, Herodotus, Hesiod and Demosthenes with Homer's name is in the centre. Another mosaic, also from Seleucia, shows Orpheus surrounded by wild animals. On a mosaic from Xanthus there is a representation of Thetis bathing her child, Achilles, in the river Styx to make him invulnerable. Another is decorated with portraits of Eirene, goddess of peace, and Euprepeia, goddess of propriety. On the right-hand wall there is a large **2C disc** decorated with a relief of Artemis Pergaea and signs of the Zodiac, from Perge. Note particularly the **statue from the Letoön**, near Xanthus, which has been painstakingly reconstructed from hundreds of fragments. This once formed part of a shrine dedicated to Leto and her children, Artemis and Apollo, which was damaged in ancient times by fire.

Nearby is a **6C ambon** of Proconnesian marble decorated with a relief of the Angel Gabriel. The assured nature of the treatment suggests that it made either on Proconnesus or in Constantinople. Note the Arabic inscription 'Allah' in the roundel on the bottom left, proof of later re-use. On the wall there are two interesting fragments of unknown provenance: one of a male head; the other the arm from a colossal bronze statue. In front of these is a large **slab marked out as a gaming board**. This was found in the main street in Perge.

The museum's collection of **coins** is in **Room 10**. This is a representative selection from Lycia, Pisidia and Pamphylia from the Classical, Hellenistic, Roman, Byzantine, Selçuk and Ottoman periods. Note the fine late Hellenistic **silver tetradrachm** from Side with a helmeted Athena and on the reverse a standing Nike holding a laurel wreath, a pomegranate and the letters AR.

Rooms 11 to 13 are devoted to the museum's **ethnograhical collection**: in 11 there are some very fine examples of Selçuk and Ottoman porcelain; Room 12 has a selection of antique weapons and materials connected with the Yürük people, regional dresses and embroidery, fragments of old manuscripts, musical instruments, objects from the Abdal Musa Tekkesı and carpets; in Room 13 and the passage to the entrance hall there are some reconstructions of old Antalya houses. Note particularly the fine **ceiling** in the room immediately before the exit.

A door to the left of the ticket desk in the entrance hall leads to the museum garden where there are tables under a pergola. Tea and soft drinks may be obtained from the bar on the left. There is a public telephone.

By the door is a fragment with a rearing male goat and bunches of grapes which, perhaps, formed part of a Bacchic group. Nearby there are some theatre masks and a headless male figure. The fine **statue of Euphrosyne**, one of the Three Graces, lacks its head. From Side there is a **sarcophagus** elaborately decorated with cupids and garlands and a **sun dial** from Perge. In the garden is a **relief** of an enthroned Tyche holding a cult representation of Artemis in her right hand and a cornucopia in her left. The goddess is flanked by male priests leading sacrificial animals. All the sculptures date from the 2C AD.

Inscriptions and architectural fragments are often overlooked or ignored, even by the most enthusiastic museum visitors. There are several interesting examples in the colonnade of Antalya Museum. They include the touching, if rather fulsome, epitaph to an athlete named Miletus (Inv. 202):

> 'Behold the beautiful Miletus, great in the stadium, eight times victor who was like beautiful Adonis, son of Kinyras, at the hunt, or like beautiful young Hyakinthos killed by a discus. Now fate has carried me off in a gladitorial contest and put my body in the beloved Pamphylian soil. My tombstone was put here by my most noble friend Odyssesus in memory and friendship'.

Then there is the self-satisfied memorial to one Drungarius Stephanus (Inv. 35). This Byzantine period (909–910) inscription asks:

> 'O noble offspring of the brilliant city of Attalus, pray for Drungarious Stephanus (who built this splendid work) exactly like his industrious turn of mind, strong, admirable, enjoyable, in such good time, so that he will be forgiven his sins and escape eternal condemnation'.

The nature of Stephanus's 'splendid work' is not recorded!

Also in the colonnade there is a 2C AD **architectural fragment** from Perge which has a striking depiction of Bacchus and his attendants. The god is shown in a roundel in the centre seated on the back of a goat, a bunch of grapes to the right of his head. In a lozenge on his left there is a hairy, ithyphallic Pan. He is balanced by a similarly well-endowed, precocious looking young Bacchus or cupid on the right.

The antiquities in the garden have been arranged with taste and imagination, and when seen against the striking panorama of the Bay of Antalya and the violet-hued mountains of Lycia provide an aesthetically satisfying end to your visit to the museum.

Antalya to Bucak

Antalya—(c 19km Eudocias?)—(c 20 km Evdir Hanı)—(c 30km Karain Cave)—c 35km Kirkgöz Hanı—(c 50km Ariassos)—(c 67km Susuz Han)—c 77km Bucak—(c 81km İncir Hanı)—(c 83km Cremna)—(c 110km unnamed Pisidian city).

This excursion will take you from the green, fertile lowlands of Pamphylia to the mountainous country around Bucak. The scenery en route, especially during the climb through the Çubuk mountain gorge, is spectacular.

For a description of the putative site of Eudocias, and of Evdir Hanı, see Route 25A.

A signpost on the left points to the **Karain Cave** which is c 6km from the main road. Between 1946 and 1973, Turkish archaeologists found evidence of occupation dating from the Palaeolithic Period (30,000–10,000 BC) to Classical times. Finds included tools and weapons of flint and bone and part of the skull of a Neanderthal child. Many of these may be seen in the Antalya Museum. Evidence of a cult site was found near the entrance. Investigations recommenced in 1985. If you wish to explore the interior of the cave, bring a torch.

A yellow sign points E from the main road to an **ancient road** which ran from Pamphylia to Pisidia through the Doşeme Gorge. This is one of the most important and best preserved stretches of Roman road in Turkey. At the foot of the gorge are a **fortress**, a **way-station**, and a **bath house**. It is possible to distinguish an early Roman paved road suitable for vehicles, and the better-preserved **Byzantine road** which has steps and could be used by foot travellers and pack animals. A climb of 5km up the road, known to the Hellenistic historian Polybius as the climax, i.e. the ladder, leads to another **settlement** which includes a **Hellenistic watch tower**, a **gateway** over the road, many houses, churches and tombs. A **milestone** of AD 6 shows that this was part of the ancient **Via Seseute** which linked the S coast with Pisidian Antioch (see below). It was certainly the route followed by St Paul on his first journey to the interior of Asia Minor.

The **Kirkgöz Hanı**, which is near the road just before the Çubuk gorge, dates from the early 13C. Rougher in finish than the Evdir Hanı, it has one large room at the rear, measuring 45.7m by 10.6m, which is pierced by six arches. Strongly fortified, its rectangular towers make this *han* look more like a military outpost than a rest house for merchants.

The site of the ancient city of **ARIASSOS** is c 1km to the left of the main road just N of the Çubuk Boğazı. The access road is clearly signposted. The city was built at the bottom, and on the terraced sides, of a steep v-shaped valley. Much of the site is covered with thorny scrub.

Ariassos was visited in 1885 by an Austrian expedition which identified it wrongly as Cretopolis. The correct identification was made by French epigraphists in 1892. The earliest written reference to Ariassos is in a list of 13 Pisidian cities prepared by the geographer Artemidorus of Ephesus (fl. c 100 BC) where it is called Aarassus. (Strabo's *Geography* XII.7.2). There are later references in the mid 2C AD *Geography* of Claudios Ptolemaeus of Alexandria and in Byzantine ecclesiastical lists. Coins of Ariassos from the Hellenistic period to the mid 3C AD have been discovered locally. Inscriptions found at the site date mainly from the Roman imperial period.

During 1988 and 1989 a survey, sponsored by the British Institute of Archaeology at Ankara and the British Academy, was conducted at Ariassos by a team directed by Dr Stephen Mitchell. A plan of the site, prepared by Sabri Aydal of Antalya Museum, shows the original, Hellenistic civic centre on the W shoulder of the hill slope and the main Roman buildings on the SE side of the city. The Hellenistic fortifications were traced and the cemeteries of the N and SW necropolises were also examined. The survey provided a good deal of valuable information about urban settlements in Pisidia which could not be obtained from other sources.

The most striking structure in Ariassos, the well-preserved c 12m high **Roman arch** at the NE end of the valley, has been dated to between AD 220 and 240. Consoles on this rather austere monument once supported statues. The main street of the city stretched from the arch in a SW direction to the **Roman forum** which has been largely obscured by a ruined **Christian basilica**. This measured 23.4m long and 14.4m wide, had two aisles and a central nave, a narthex at the W end and a three-step dais in the apse at the E. The room at the SW corner was probably a **Baptistery**. Beyond the Forum the street continued to the **baths** and an adjoining **gymnasium**. A number of inscriptions found here included texts on the bases of statues of Caracalla, dated to c AD 214–5, and of Diotimos, son of Samos, who had been gymnasiarch in Ariassos between 236–42. According to another inscription, Diotimos promised to donate a piece of land to the city, the revenues from which would pay for the oil used by athletes in the gymnasium. All that remains of the **nymphaeum** at the SW end of the valley, which balanced the arch at the NE, is a semicircular apse. Water brought by an aqueduct in the hills was stored in two sets of public cisterns which probably supplied the baths and later the baptistery of the basilica.

The Hellenistic public buildings were at the W end around a small paved agora. In the **bouleuterion** on the N side, a rectangular building measuring c 18m by 14m, nine or ten rows of seats surrounded a small orchestra. Facing the bouleuterion was a small **prostyle temple** and to the SW there was a square building which may have been the **prytaneion**.

About 25 well-constructed **heroa** were found in cemeteries on the E, S and SW sides of the city. Three of the most striking are at the W end of the site, by the street from the valley to the Hellenistic civic centre. There are also many sarcophagi and lidded cists carved from the local hard limestone.

A section of the ancient road, which linked Ariassos with Termessus, and the aqueduct, which brought water from a source c 4km to the S, were also covered by the survey. A Bronze Age hand axe and some fragments of Islamic glazed pottery found by the archaeologists suggest earlier and later periods of occupation of the site.

About 5km N of Ariassos the main road passes the village of Boğazköy. On a hill slope E of the village are the remains of a small ancient city which has been identified, by an inscription, as ancient **Panemoteichos**.

A turning to the right c 10km to the S of Bucak leads to the classical-style Selçuk **Susuz Han** which is believed to date from c 1246. Unfortunately, this fine, well preserved building has attracted the attention of thieves, and is now locked. The key may be obtained from the *bekçi* in the nearby village.

The outer walls have **massive towers** of different designs built into them. An ornamented, **recessed portal** provides access to the interior. This is lit by small, round arched windows and five openings in the central dome which is clearly visible from the outside. The 26m square hall, has a principal aisle flanked by five side aisles. The pits in the floor were dug by thieves.

Continue to **Bucak**. Of little interest in itself, this town is a good centre for visiting sites and monuments in the surrounding area. About 1km to the N a turning on the left leads to **İncir Hanı**. This was built c 1238 by Gıyaseddin Keyhüsrev II (1236–46) in the style of the Sultan Han on the Konya–Aksaray road. It belongs to the series of *hans*—Evdir, Kırkgöz, Susuz—which linked Antalya with the interior. The entrance is set in an arched niche almost 2m deep. **Columns** crowned by acanthus capitals, topped by curious **lion reliefs**, support the arch. Inside, only the foundations of the W wall of the courtyard remain. The han is now isolated and deserted. Its halls, once filled with traders and their merchandise, are empty caverns. The last caravan left a long time ago. On the crumbling walls fig trees, which give the *han* its name, grow unchecked and in summer only the buzzing of flies feeding on rotting fruit breaks the heavy silence.

The site of ancient **Cremna** is c 10km to the N of Bucak near the village of Çamlık. Like Ariassos, Cremna was listed by Claudius Ptolemaeus of Alexandria as one of the cities of Pisidia. Excavations were begun in the 1970s by archaeologists from İstanbul University led by Professor Jale İnan. More recently it was surveyed by a team directed by Dr Stephen Mitchell.

Cremna was built on a high plateau which overlooks the valley of the Aksu river, the ancient Cestrus. It enjoys one of the most spectacular situations of any Pisidian city and is worth visiting for this reason alone! As it needed fortification on the W only—the other sides were protected by steep cliffs—it attracted settlers from early times. A collection of coins minted in Cremna during the 1C BC, now in Burdur Archaeological Museum, testify to its occupation in the late Hellenistic period. According to Strabo, Cremna, one of several places previously impregnable, was captured by Amyntas the king of Galatia (d. BC 25). After it had been retaken by the Romans, Augustus established a colony here and strengthened the W wall by rebuilding the 12 towers. In the late 3C, when Asia Minor was subjected to raids by the Goths and the Persians, the curtain walls between the towers were reconstructed with spoil from civic buildings under the Roman emperor Probus. About AD 270 Cremna was seized by a brigand named Lydius who held out against a Roman siege for a considerable time. During the recent survey large stones used by the defenders to roll on the enemy, artillery, missiles and a Latin dedication to the emperor Probus erected by the praeses of Lycia and Pamphylia in his headquarters, were found on the site. These and other finds are in the Burdur Museum. The siege mound raised by the Romans—a prominent bank of reddish soil towards the N end of the W wall—was identified by the surveying team.

To the E of the city wall there was a large **residential area**. A substantial rebuilding of Cremna, begun during the reign of Hadrian, continued to the end of the 2C AD. The **colonnaded street**, c 230m long, to the S of the residential area, dates from this period. To the N of the **main forum** a **monumental stairway** led to a two-storey **propylon** whose design and decoration resembled the Library of Celsus at Ephesus. To the S of the forum there are the substantial ruins of a **bath house**. A **theatre** overlooking the agora, was sited to the E. A short distance to the NE was the **Doric agora**, which was shaped like the Greek letter Pi. This originally dated from the Hellenistic period, but was remodelled in Roman times. Finally, on the SE side of the city commanding a magnificent view of the Aksu Valley are the foundations of a second theatre which was never completed.

About 25km to the SE of Bucak, a short drive from the town of Kocailler will bring you to the scant remains of an unnamed Pisidian city, a site mainly of interest to specialists. There are many tombs, and heroa, a well-preserved Hellenistic theatre, a (?) rock-cut sanctuary with a damaged relief, a massive cistern, the city's agora and perhaps a market. The fortifications command an impressive view of the mountainous country-side and deep valleys which lead down to Pamphylia.

At Bucak you have a choice: you can either return to Antalya or continue N to (10km) Çeltikçi and join Route 19 for an exploration of the area around the Pisidian lakes.

27

Antalya to Side

Total distance c 66km. Antalya—16km Aksu—(c 2km Perge)—(c 8km Sillyum)—c 28km Serik—(c 15km Aspendus)—(c 43km Selge)—c 26km Manavgat—(c 8km Lymbe)—c 7km Side.

Perge and Aspendus are easily reached by bus or dolmuş from Antalya. There are direct services to Side and via Manavgat. Private transport is recommended for Sillyum. The alternative is a long walk from the E24. For Selge private transport—preferably a four-wheeled drive vehicle—is necessary.

The E24 is a well-surfaced, busy road. It crosses the fertile Pamphylian plain, which is ringed on the N by the Taurus mountains, returning to the sea only as it approaches Alanya. About 6km from Antalya, a turning on the right leads to the airport.

At the village of **Aksu** look for a signpost on the left to 2km **PERGE**. The site is c 4km W of the Aksu Çayı, the ancient river Cestrus.

History. Legend states that Perge was founded after the Trojan War by Greek settlers led by the seers Calchas and Mopsus. Calchas was the prophet who advised Agamemnon to sacrifice Iphigenia to placate Artemis. Legend also relates that he remained in Asia Minor after the capture of Troy and continued to practice divination, until defeated in a contest of prophecy by Mopsus. The persistence of the belief that Calchas and Mopsus were connected with the foundation of Perge is demonstrated by the discovery here in 1953 of inscriptions on two 2C AD statue bases. They honour 'The founder Calchas of Argos, son of Thestor' and 'The founder Mopsus of Delphi, son of Apollo'.

A bronze tablet found at Boğazköy in 1986 contains the cuneifrom text of a treaty between the Hittite king Tudhaliyas IV (1250–20 BC) and a king called Kurunta who ruled over Tarhuntassa. The western boundary of that city was the river Kaştraja (Cestrus) and the city of Parha (Perge). Perge enters history properly with the arrival in Lycia of Alexander the Great in 333 BC. He was welcomed by its citizens, who provided him with guides for his journey from Phaselis to Pamphylia. After the death of Alexander, his empire was divided amongst his generals and Pamphylia was ruled at different times by the Ptolemaic and Seleucid dynasties. In 188 BC the Seleucids were expelled by the Romans. They exacted a tribute from the inhabitants and gave the territory to Eumenes II, King of Pergamum. In the 1C BC the Romans became increasingly concerned about the activity of Cilician pirates and set out to crush them. Then to maintain their presence, they set up the province of Cilicia. The Roman governors of the new province and their subordinates were corrupt and venal. Verres, who was later prosecuted by Cicero for extortion, robbed the temples of Aspendus and Perge of their statues and votive offerings. In AD 43 Pamphylia was joined with Lycia by Claudius and formally incorporated in the Roman Empire. Under the empire Perge prospered. It was during this period that many of the city's finest buildings, whose remains are still visible, were constructed. Perge was twice a *neocorus*, during the reigns of Valerian (253–60) and Gallienus (253–68).

Perge was the birthplace of the mathematician Apollonius (fl. 250–220 BC) and Varus, the 2C AD philosopher, who was sometimes called the Stork because of his prominent beak-like nose. Apollonius studied at Alexandria. Known for his work on conic sections, he was the author of several mathematical treatises, seven of which survive. These were used by the astronomers, Ptolemy of Alexander and Kepler, when formulating their theories on the motion of the planets.

Perge was visited by SS Paul and Barnabas on their first journey. 'After this Paul and his companions took ship from Paphos and made for Perge in Pamphylia; here John left them, and went back to Jerusalem. They passed on from Perge, and reached Pisidian Antioch, where they went and took their seats in the synagogue on the sabbath day'. (Acts 13, 13 and 14.) 'They preached the word of the Lord in Perge, and went down to Attalia, taking ship there for Antioch'. (Acts 14, 24.) It is probable that from the earliest times the city was an important centre for the diffusion of Christianity in Pamphylia. Perge was represented at the Council of Nicaea in 325 by the Metropolitan Callinicus and at the Council of Ephesus in 431 by one of his successors. The flourishing state of the church during the early Byzantine period is evidenced by the presence of two large basilicas. Later, weakened by persistent Arab attacks, Perge began to decline and sometime after the 7C most of the inhabitants moved away. However, there are reports of a small Christian community here as late as 1400.

Pamphylia came under the Selçuk Turks in 1078 and the Ottomans in 1392. Little is known about Perge's history from the 14C to the 17C. In 1671 it was visited by Evliya Çelebi. He called it 'the Castle of Teke Hisarı. It was, he wrote, 'a small rectangular castle situated on a mound...Behind, there is a fairly high hill. It has no moat. There are no guards, no soldiers, commandant, or any important official. The place is inhabited only by seventy or eighty households of the Turcoman tribe. They migrate to the summer pastures in July...the district is prosperous and the region fertile'.

Perge was rediscovered by European travellers in the 19C. It was visited by Walpole, Fellows, Forbes, Texier, Lanckoronski and others. Fellows describes the pleasures, and dangers, of his sojourn here in 1840:

> I pitched my tent amidst the ruins of Perge; near me was a small encampment of shepherds, who had brought their cattle to pasture amidst the ruins. The first object that strikes the traveller on arriving here is the extreme beauty of the situation of the ancient town, lying between and upon the sides of two hills, with an extensive valley in front, watered by the river Cestrus, and backed by the mountains of the Taurus. The howling and barking of the jackals and wolves around my tent lasted until daybreak.

Early colonists looked for a sea-girt peninsula, as at Side, or a flat-topped hill, which could be fortified. Perge, Aspendus and Sillyum are examples of cities built on an acropolis. In time these settlements spread out into the surrounding plain, only to retreat back to the citadel in times of danger.

Approaching the site from Aksu you pass a low hill to the right. Excavations have revealed the foundations of a small **Doric prostyle temple**, the only sacred structure so far discovered in Perge. Some architectural fragments in the Ionic style found nearby suggest that the great temple of Artemis Pergaea may have been located here. This would accord with Strabo's description: 'Then one comes to the Cestrus river; and, sailing sixty stadia up this river, one comes to Perge, a city; and near Perge, on a lofty site, to the temple of Artemis Pergaea, where a general festival is celebrated every year'. (*Geography* 14.3. 10-4.2.) He is supported by Polemon, the 2C AD Stoic philosopher and geographer. In a work, preserved in Arabic, he writes: 'Imagine me a city known as Perge. Here, outside the city, there is a temple of wonderful size, beauty and construction known as the temple of Artemis'. Up to the present, all efforts to locate the temple have failed.

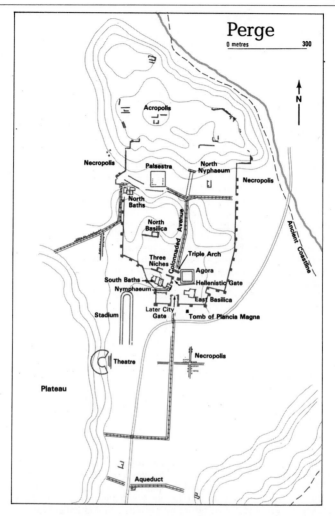

Perge

0 metres 300

N

Acropolis

Necropolis

Palaestra

North
Nyphaeum

Necropolis

North
Baths

North
Basilica

Colonnaded Avenue

Ancient Coastline

Triple Arch

Three
Niches

Agora

South Baths

Hellenistic Gate

Nymphaeum

East Basilica

Later City
Gate

Tomb of Plancia Magna

Stadium

Theatre

Necropolis

Plateau

Aqueduct

Artemis Pergaea, originally the Anatolian deity Vanassa Preiia, Queen of
Perge, later became identified with the Greek goddess of hunting, archery
and the moon. She was worshipped in the form of a baetyl, a block of stone,
possibly a meteorite, crowned with a female bust. There is a fine representation of the deity in this form in the Antalya Museum. She was also so
depicted on Pergean coins from the the 2C BC onwards.

Admission tickets are on sale in a kiosk near the Graeco-Roman theatre.
One ticket admits to the theatre, stadium and the rest of the site.

Excavations have been conducted at Perge by Turkish archaeologists
over a period of years, first by A. Müfit Mansel and latterly by Jale İnan
and H. Abbasoğlu. The **theatre** has been cleared of debris and partly
restored. Built against the hillside, it had a capacity of 14,000. Constructed

in the Greek style, it was modified during the Roman period. Its cavea, greater than a semicircle, is separated from the stage-building by two parodoi. There is a single diazoma, with 26 stairs above and 13 below. Level with the diazoma there are two vomitoria, which gave access to the cavea from the hillside. At the top of the cavea there is a covered gallery where patrons could stroll during the intervals and shelter from the elements. A parapet to protect the audience during gladiatorial games or wild beast shows separates the orchestra from the cavea.

The stage-building was ornamented with reliefs in Proconnesian marble. These show the river-god Cestrus, and the life of Dionysus: his birth from the thigh of Zeus, his transportation by Hermes to Mt Nysa where he was bathed by the nymphs, his voyage over the sea and his apotheosis. A damaged section probably shows the slaying of Pentheus. Pan and Ariadne figure in many of the reliefs. Other sculptures include a centauro- and gigantomachy frieze from the pulpitum and free-standing statues of Dionysus and of an armed emperor, Hadrian or Antoninus Pius. The archaeologists also unearthed huge statues of Hercules and, perhaps, Hermes, an archaizing sphinx and a number of composite capitals with human figures.

A late addition is the **nymphaeum** which had five niches for fountains. This was built against the outer wall of the stage-building.

From the covered gallery at the top of the theatre you can see the city's layout. Perge was enclosed by **walls** on the E, W and S sides. On the N it was protected by the acropolis. The walls on the E and W sides date from the 3C BC. The wall on the S was built in the 4C AD, when the city was extended outside its earlier boundaries.

NE of the theatre is one of the finest existing examples of a **Roman Stadium**. Constructed during the 2C AD, it had a capacity of 12,000. At the open S end there was an arch. All traces of this have disappeared. The N end is rounded. On the E, under the seats, there are 30 rooms, 20 of which were used as shops. According to Bean some of these had the name of the owner or the owner's trade on the wall. The other rooms led to the arena.

A track leads round the N end of the stadium to the car-park and the main entrance to the ancient city. At the ticket kiosk booklets, postcards and, sometimes, soft drinks may be purchased. There is no restaurant.

Immediately to the right of the late gate there are the remains of the **tomb of Plancia Magna**. A benefactress of distinction, she is mentioned in several inscriptions found in the city. About AD 120 she caused a number of statues of members of the imperial house to be erected in Perge. These, and her statue, are in the Antalya Museum. She was a priestess of Artemis and of the Mother of the Gods and held the high civic office of demiourgis. She belonged to a distinguished local family which had estates in Galatia and probably in Pamphylia. Her father and brother, M. Plancius Varus and C. Plancius Varus, are listed with Calchas, Mopsus and others as founders of the city. However, the association of their names with those of the mythical founding fathers probably meant no more than that they had contributed generously to the erection of public buildings in Perge. M. Plancius Varus was proconsul of Bithynia-Pontus during the reign of Vespasian.

The original pavement at the later city gate has been exposed and excavation has started on the **Byzantine basilica** on the inner, right side of the gate. To the left are the remains of a **nymphaeum** which was dedicated to Artemis Pergaea, the Emperor Septimius Severus (193–211) and his family. Farther to the N a magnificent Corinthian **propylon** of the same period, elaborately decorated with reliefs of Eros, Pan, Dionysus, Medusa, etc., led to the S baths complex. Nearby, in one of three niches was the statue of Plancia Magna. The **S baths**, which are believed to date from the

This statue of Harpocrates, which once decorated the Frigidarium at Perge, can now be seen in the museum at Antalya

reign of Hadrian, have now been completely exposed. The basins, floors and walls were lined with marble. Statues of Augustus, Trajan and Hermes, which decorated the rooms, are now in the Antalya Museum. Recent excavations have produced figures or heads of the muses and the head of a statue of Harpocrates. The torso had been found earlier.

Twin towers, similar to those found at Sillyum and Side, mark Perge's **Hellenistic gate**. Erected in the 3C BC, this formed part of the city's original defensive system. In the 2C AD, through the generosity of Plancia Magna, a horseshoe-shaped court and an ornamental triple arch were added on the N side of the gate towers. The court was embellished with statues in niches and on a ledge near the ground. The bases of nine of the statues from the ledge were discovered during excavations in 1954–56 and have been replaced in their original positions. These honoured Perge's founders: Riksos, Labos, Calchas, Machaon, Leonteus, Minyas, Mopsus and M. Plancius Varus and C. Plancius Varus, the father and brother of Plancia Magna.

To the right, beyond the Hellenistic gate, is the 4C AD **agora**. A square with sides 75m long, it had shops under a surrounding stoa. In the centre there are the substantial remains of a small circular **temple**, 13.5m in diameter. This may have been dedicated to Hermes, the patron of merchants. It was surmounted by a dome supported by 16 marble pillars. A similar building has been found in Side.

Perge was divided into four by two main arteries. One ran N–S for c 200m from a nymphaeum at the base of the acropolis through the Hellenistic and later gates. The other, which linked the E and W gates, crossed it at right-angles. These **colonnaded streets**, 20m wide, provided the Pergeans with shelter from the weather and a place where they could stroll, shop, meet their friends and gossip. **Water-channels**, which ran down the centre, gently cooled the air. Two shops have been excavated beside the colonnaded street. One belonged to someone called Polydeukos. The excavators found doctor's instruments here.

By the side of the N–S street there are a number of marble columns which have small reliefs near the top. One shows a Grecian Artemis carrying a bow and arrows and a torch. Another has a relief of Apollo; a third a male togaed figure pouring a libation. In this area a **carved slab**, marked out for an unknown game, was found. It is now in the Antalya Museum.

Almost hidden in the dense undergrowth to the left of the N–S street are the ruins of the **episcopal basilica** (5C). It faced E, with a narthex on the W. A large part of the apse remains standing.

At the junction of the two main streets an **arch**, facing E–W and dating from the 2C AD, is being restored. This was erected in honour of Artemis Pergaea and Apollo by Demetrios Apollonios. According to the inscription, he was a citizen of some importance—demiourgus, priest of Artemis and gymnasiarch. A deep sounding through the foundations of the arch has produced fine and coarse Roman pottery, some bearing stamped monograms, a small quantity of good quality glass and more than 550 coins.

The water channels in the two main streets were supplied by a **nymphaeum** at the base of the acropolis. The statue of a river god, probably Cestrus, placed in a central niche, dominated a large basin from which the water flowed. The Hadrianic nymphaeum was ornamented with reliefs.

W of the nymphaeum there are the substantial remains of a building measuring c 76m by 76m which has not yet been excavated. Identified as a **palaestra** by an inscription, it was dedicated to the Emperor Claudius (AD 41–54) by C. Julius Cornutus. The wall overlooking the street, which is pierced by several windows, is well preserved.

W of the palaestra, on the left side, in an area heavily overgrown, are the ruins of **Roman baths**, dating from the 3C AD. A courtyard surrounded by columns provided access to a number of parallel chambers.

In 1946 several sarcophagi were found in a **necropolis** outside the W gate. They are now in the Antalya Museum.

Two paths, which start near the nymphaeum, provide the only way up to the **acropolis**. This is a plateau of c 2500 sq m, 60m above the level of the plain. It was occupied by the first inhabitants of Perge and again during late Roman and Byzantine times. The visible remains date from the late period. On the S side of the hill a gateway, now destroyed, provided access to the acropolis, but there appear to have been no other fortifications. Near the site of the gateway is a large **vaulted cistern**, 13.5 sq m.

If not closed for excavation, leave the site by the E gate. By taking this route back to the car-park and to Aksu you will be able to examine the **Hellenistic city wall** which is in a good state of preservation.

For **SILLYUM** continue on the E24 in the direction of Alanya for c 15km. Look out for a signposted turning on the left, across the road from a petrol station. For c 8km follow the secondary road. At each junction take the main turning and keep heading towards the acropolis which is always clearly visible. There are two villages near Sillyum, **Yanköy** to the N and **Asar Köyü** to the SW. The ascent is made from Asar Köyü.

At Asar Köyü it is advisable to take a guide who will not only keep the village dogs at bay, but will help you to avoid the many deep, **unmarked and unprotected cisterns** on the summit. These constitute a real danger, particularly to children, who should never be allowed to wander off on their own. The climb to the top, which is more than 200m above sea-level, involves a certain amount of scrambling. There is little shade on the path and, in summer, temperatures can be very high.

Although Sillyum is clearly visible from the E24, it is somewhat neglected and does not attract many visitors. However, no student of history should miss an opportunity to explore this great brooding plateau on the Pamphylian plain between the Taurus Mountains and the sea. Anyone who has ever visited it will want to go back again and again. It has a magic which is particularly apparent at sunset, when the crumbling ruins are silhouetted against the sky, as the light fades and dies.

Allow at least three hours for your visit to Sillyum. If you wish to make a detailed study of the site, you may be able to find accommodation in Asar Köyü or Yanköy. The nearest restaurants are in Serik and Antalya, so bring a picnic lunch.

The summit of the acropolis is covered with pottery sherds, pieces of glass and fragments of carved stone from many periods. These should not be taken from Sillyum, as their loss could hinder archaeological investigation. One of the unfortunate results of tourism is an increase in illegal digging and in the production of fake antiquities. It is an offence to buy, sell or be in possession of antiquities without permission. Contravention of this law carries very severe penalties.

History. Apart from a brief reference in the *Periplus*, i.e. the Voyage of the 4C BC Pseudo-Scylax along the coast of Asia Minor, nothing is known with certainty about Sillyum before the arrival of Alexander the Great in 333 BC. If ancient legends are to be believed, it was founded, like the other cities in Pamphylia, c 1184 BC during the migrations that followed the Trojan War. A statue base found here, inscribed with the name of Mopsus, suggests that, like the Pergaeans, the inhabitants of Sillyum honoured that ancient seer and may have believed that their city was established by him. Certainly the security offered by the plateau, which may be scaled only on the SW, must have attracted settlers from the earliest times.

Sillyum and Termessus were the only cities in this part of Anatolia which did not surrender to or were not captured by Alexander. Arrian describes what happened:

'Alexander left a party of men to occupy Side and then proceeded to Syllium [sic], a fortified town garrisoned by mercenaries and native troops. He was unable, however, to take this place by assault, without regular siege operations, and this fact, combined with a report which he had received during his march, determined him to return to Aspendus'.

The report told him that the inhabitants of Aspendus had reneged on the agreement which they had made with his envoys, and were fortifying their city. Alexander's swift and unexpected arrival terrified the Aspendians and they asked for fresh terms. These were granted, but he chastised them by imposing harsher conditions and by taking hostages. He then returned to Perge, apparently ignoring Sillyum on the way.

Sillyum's history probably differed little from that of its neighbours during the centuries that followed. The first coins bearing its name date from the 3C BC. It was mentioned by Strabo (64 BC–AD 24), who lists it as one of the cities of Pamphylia. Sillyum was, he said, 40 stades (i.e. c 7km) from the sea. Between AD 786 and 869 it was joined with Perge to form a metropolitan bishopric. On the *Tabula Peutingeriana*, a map copied in the 13C from a 3C or 4C original, the city was shown as being on the main road from Pergamum to Side. With Alanya, Aspendus and Antalya, Sillyum was occupied during the Selçuk period, when it became known as Yanköy Hisarı.

Leave the village of Asar Köyü by the path which climbs gently at first. You pass on the left the scanty remains of a large **stadium** which was c 178m long, exclusive of the seating. The seats on the W side were supported by a vaulted gallery, on the E they rested on slope. The city's **Hellenistic lower gate**, like those of Perge and Side, consisted of a court and two fortified towers. To the left of the gate is the site of a **gymnasium** which later became the **bishop's palace**. It is now used as a sheepfold.

The acropolis is reached from the SW. On the other sides the cliffs rise sheer from the plain. Access was by two ramps. A large stretch of the well-preserved **lower ramp**, which carries a road c 5m wide, is supported by **massive buttresses**. Above and to the right there are two substantial bastions. The **necropolis**, which was in use from the 3C BC to the 6C AD, was below the ramp, to the left of the road. Most of the graves date from the Roman period. To the SW of the necropolis is a roofless, but otherwise well-preserved **tower** which formed part of the later fortifications.

The **upper city gate** was at the point where the two ramps met. To the SW of the gate are three interesting buildings. The most striking is a large **Byzantine structure**, whose upper storey is pierced by several arched windows. To the S of this is a long narrow **Hellenistic building** which may have been a public hall or part of a gymnasium. Look for the slots and holes which were used to close the wooden shutters on its windows.

To the E is a **smaller Hellenistic building** which has on the door jamb an interesting **inscription** dating from c 200 BC. Its 37 lines of text form the longest extant example of the Pamphylian language. This was a dialect of Greek, which used the Greek alphabet, and was not unlike the variants of Greek spoken in Perge and Aspendus. It continued to be used up to the 1C AD, when it appears to have been replaced, on coins and in inscriptions at least, by a Greek dialect in general use. Unlike the language spoken at Side, which has not yet been deciphered, some words and phrases of the Sillyum inscription can be read, but its precise meaning is not known. Decipherment has not been aided by the loss of a substantial section of the text, from a square hole cut in the door jamb.

To the S of these buildings a large part of the cliff has fallen away into the plain, taking with it most of a small **theatre**. Only the top rows of seats remain. To the E of the theatre there was an **odeum**, but it, too, has disappeared. Great care should be taken on this part of the acropolis, as the cliff-edge is unsafe and there are landslides from time to time.

E of the site of the odeum there are the remains of some **Hellenistic private houses** and of a small **Hellenistic temple**. The houses, partly of masonry and partly carved from the living rock, rested on terraces connected by steps. Three walls of the temple, which measured 11m by 7.5m,

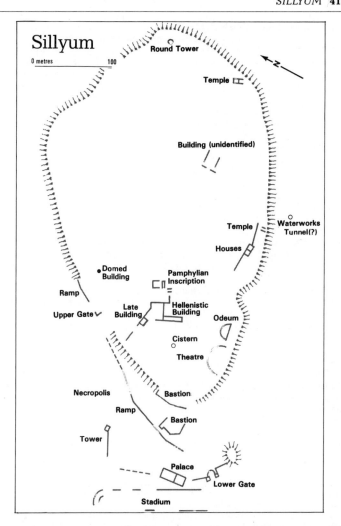

Sillyum

0 metres   100

Round Tower

Temple

Building (unidentified)

Temple

Waterworks Tunnel(?)

Houses

Domed Building

Pamphylian Inscription

Ramp

Upper Gate

Late Building

Hellenistic Building

Odeum

Cistern

Theatre

Necropolis

Bastion

Ramp

Bastion

Tower

Palace

Lower Gate

Stadium

remain. Masonry from the fourth, the S wall, lies at the bottom of the cliff. Just beyond the temple, gratings in the path mark the site of a large **cistern**.

The path, which continues around the cliff-top, offers an excellent view of the Pamphylian plain and of the Taurus Mountains to the N. Apart from a marshy area E of the acropolis, which probably marks the site of Lake Capria mentioned by Strabo (*Geography* 14.4.2), the plain is very fertile. In summer its many villages, surrounded by olive groves and orchards, are separated by the white squares of the cotton fields.

Near the eastern edge of the plateau are the ruins of a much repaired **temple** and a **watch-tower**. In the central and NW areas there are many deep, cigar-shaped **cisterns** which were lined with plaster to prevent seepage. They are often covered with vegetation and are very dangerous.

Sheep and other animals, which have fallen into them, have died from starvation. **These areas should be approached with caution and only in the company of a local guide**. The **domed building** to the E of the upper city gate may have been used as a mosque during the Selçuk period.

In addition to the path used for the ascent, there are two other, more difficult routes back to Asar Köyü. One, to the W of the theatre, descends steeply to the area near the lower gate, while the other circles the northern ramp to reach the village by way of the tower, the stadium and the gymnasium. They are not recommended.

About 300m NE of the lower city gate, at a point on the slope almost directly underneath the Hellenistic houses and temple, there is an ancient underground **water channel**. An outer chamber leads to a tunnel c 0.5m wide and c 25m long. This ends in three small rooms linked by narrow passages. Intrepid explorers who wish to examine this construction should be of slim build, should carry a light and should not suffer from claustrophobia. They should also be prepared for possible close encounters with snakes or scorpions or both! According to Bean there is a late inscription in the outer chamber—an invocation for the salvation of the emperor.

Return to the E24 and continue in the direction of Alanya. After c 13km a turning on the left leads to **Serik**. This has supermarkets, banks, a post office, chemists, shops and small restaurants offering simple meals. The E24 passes through the southern part of the town.

Belek, c 8km to the S of Serik, has three five-star and three four-star hotels, and three holiday villages. It is a useful centre for visiting historical sites and other places of interest in the area.

A signpost on the left, c 4km E of Serik, indicates the road to the site of ancient **ASPENDUS**. This is near the modern village of 5km **Belkis**. Not far from the junction with the main road there is a fine 13C **Selçuk bridge** over the Köprüçay, the ancient Eurymedon. Still used, this replaced a 2C Roman bridge, whose ruins may be seen in the river-bed a few metres to the N. A tentative reconstruction of the 5m wide Roman bridge, whose central span was 9m above the water, shows that large sea-going ships could have passed underneath it on their way to the docks of Aspendus. In relation to its Selçuk successor it was a veritable giant.

History. Although no archaeological evidence has been found which would indicate that Pamphylia was ever occupied by the Hittites, coins minted in Aspendus between the 6C and 4C BC give the name of the city as **Estwediiys**, which some link with Prince Azitawaddi, who is mentioned in a Neo-Hittite text unearthed at Karatepe. He founded a Cilician city in the 9C or 8C BC. The more generally accepted theory is that Aspendus, like Perge and Sillyum, was colonised during the migrations which followed the Trojan War c 1184 BC. As the name Aspendus is not Greek, but Anatolian, it is likely that the newcomers did not found the city, but merely took over an existing settlement. The ancient writers have conflicting stories. Dionysius Periegetes (probably 2C AD) in *De situ orbis habitabilis*, a recapitulation of the views of the late 3C BC Eratosthenes, says the legendary Mopsus was one of the city's founders, while the geographer Pomponius Mela (fl. c AD 43) in *De Chorographia* states that Aspendus was colonised by the Argives.

During the 6C BC Pamphylia was occupied briefly by Croesus, the King of Lydia. When he was defeated in 546 BC by Cyrus, it came under Persian rule. Pamphylian soldiers fought with Xerxes against the Greeks, but they were not considered very reliable allies. Following the battles of Salamis and Plataea, the Aegean coast came under the control of the Athenians, but Pamphylia, Lycia and Cilicia were still occupied by the Persians. In 467 BC the Athenians sent Cimon at the head of an expeditionary force to this part of Anatolia. Having persuaded the cities of Lycia to support the Greek cause, he came to Aspendus, where Xerxes had gathered a great army. With his ships Cimon attacked the Persians at the mouth of the Eurymedon. The battle, which raged

The fine 13C Selçuk bridge over the Köprüçay near Aspendus

all day, ended in an Athenian victory. This first victory was followed by another. As night fell, Cimon dressed some of his men in the clothes of captured Persians, and, putting them on Persian ships, landed them near the mouth of the river. Deceived and confused by the stratagem, the Persians were routed for the second time. While Cimon's unique double victory earned him a splendid monument in Athens, it had a less welcome result for Aspendus and the other cities of Pamphylia. They were enrolled, more or less compulsorily, in the Delian League, an organisation created to counter the Persian threat. It is doubtful if the Aspendians ever paid their annual dues.

In 404 BC, at the end of the Peloponnesian War, control of the Athenian Empire passed to Sparta. The Athenians, in an attempt to recoup some of the losses incurred during the war, sent an expedition to Asia Minor in 389 BC under the command of Thrasybulus to gather money. To avoid trouble the Aspendians paid up. However, the expedition ended disastrously, as the people of Aspendus, incensed by the bad behaviour of the Athenian soldiers, who had destroyed some of their crops, murdered Thrasybulus in his tent.

The Spartans proved to be ineffective rulers and by 386 BC the Asian cities were once more under the control of the Persians. They appointed satraps, who collected the taxes, but otherwise allowed the cities to manage their own affairs. Aspendus issued coins during this period. However, the flame of revolt still flickered and Aspendus and the other the Pamphylian cities, with their governing satraps, rose against the Persians in 365 BC. Defeated by superior forces, they remained under Persian domination until the arrival of Alexander the Great in 333 BC.

Welcomed by Perge, Alexander marched towards Aspendus. He was met on the way by envoys. They offered to surrender the city, but asked him not to leave a garrison there. Alexander agreed to their request on condition that Aspendus paid him 50 talents and provided him with the horses which they had been sending as tribute to the Persian king. The envoys accepted his terms and Alexander went on to Side and thence to Sillyum. While conducting the siege of Sillyum, he was incensed to hear that the people of Aspendus had refused to honour the terms which he had agreed with their envoys and that they were fortifying the city. Arrian describes what happened.

Alexander, as soon as he reached the town, led his men inside the outer wall—now defenceless—and took up his quarters in the deserted town. The shock of Alexander's presence and the sight of his army surrounding them were too much for the people of the town: they sent their spokesmen to him and begged to be allowed their original terms. Alexander, however, in spite of the fact that the position of Aspendus was obviously a strong one and he was not prepared for a protracted siege refused the request.

In addition to the horses, he demanded 100 talents and the surrender of some of the city's leading men as hostages. Aspendus was also to accept a governor appointed by him, to pay an annual tribute to Macedon and to submit its claim to some disputed land to an enquiry.

Anxious to deny Pamphylia and its ports to the Persians, Alexander left the province in the hands of his friend, the fleet-commander, Nearchus. After Alexander's death in 323 BC Pamphylia was ruled by Antigonus Monopthalmos until 301 BC. From then to c 187 BC it came, at different times, under the control of the Seleucid kings of Syria and Ptolemaic kings of Egypt. It then passed to the kings of Pergamum. When Attalus III, the last king of Pergamum, bequeathed his kingdom to the Romans, in 133 BC, they formed the Aegean area into the Province of Asia. However, they were not interested in Lycia, Pamphylia and Cilicia and only became involved in this region, when pirates began to interfere with shipping. For the Pamphylians this proved to be a mixed blessing. The consul, Manlius Vulso, extracted 50 talents from Aspendus as protection money. Worse was to follow. When a new Roman province, which included Pamphylia, was created, its rulers and their subordinates were rapacious and corrupt. Verres, assistant to the infamous governor Dolabella who was accused and convicted of theft, was indicted by Cicero in the following terms:

You are aware, gentlemen, that Aspendus is an old and famous town in Pamphylia, full of fine statuary. I shall not allege that from this town this or that a particular statue was removed. My charge is that Verres did not leave one single statue behind; that from temples and public places alike, with the whole of Aspendus looking on, they were all openly loaded on wagons and carted away. Yes, even the famous Harpist of Aspendus, about whom you have often heard the saying that is proverbial among the Greeks that 'he made his music inside'—him too he carried off.

Under the rule of the Roman emperors Pamphylia's fortunes improved. In AD 43 it was joined with Lycia to form a new province. However, its cities continued to enjoy a considerable degree of autonomy. Aspendus and several others issued their own coins. Under the Pax Romana the city prospered. Most of the buildings visible today were constructed at that time. In the 3C AD the city became a *neocous*.

Aspendus produced few citizens of note. One, the Pythagorean philosopher Diodorus, affected the unorthodox habits of the Cynics and became notorious for his dirty and unkempt appearance.

Apollonius of Tyana (c AD 4–97), a Neo-Pythagorean who claimed to have healed the sick and raised the dead, averted a dangerous crisis when he visited Aspendus sometime during the reign of Tiberius (AD 14–37). He found the chief magistrate, who had not been able to persuade the corn-merchants to release grain which they wanted to sell abroad, clinging to the statue of Tiberius in an effort to avoid being burned to death by an angry crowd of starving citizens. Apollonius decided to intervene. He wrote his judgement on a tablet: 'Apollonius, to the corn-merchants of Aspendus. The earth in her justice is the mother of all, but you in your injustice have made her mother to yourselves alone, and if you do not stop I will not even let you remain upon her'. Terrified, the corn-merchants released the grain and the people of Aspendus were saved from starvation.

Aspendus maintained its importance under the Byzantines, though, unlike Perge and Side, it did not have its own bishop. It came under the Metropolitan of Side. Like most cities in Pamphylia and Lycia it suffered considerably during the 7C from raids by the Arabs. In the 13C it was ruled by the Selçuk Turks. During this period the stage-building of the theatre was restored and converted into a palace. From the 15C to the 18C, when it was abandoned, the city was governed by the Ottomans.

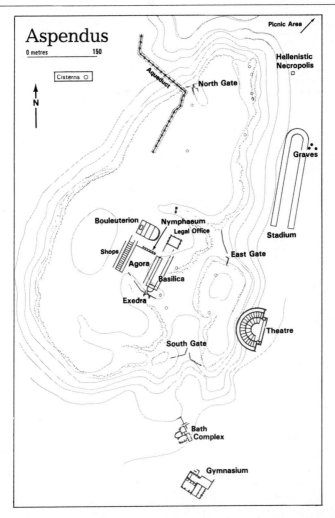

Aspendus

0 metres 150

Cisterns ○

N

Aqueduct

North Gate

Picnic Area

Hellenistic
Necropolis

Graves

Stadium

Bouleuterion

Nymphaeum

Legal Office

Shops

Agora

Basilica

East Gate

Exedra

Theatre

South Gate

Bath
Complex

Gymnasium

As you approach the site, the substantial remains of a 3C AD **Roman baths complex** are on the right. The foundations and upper walls were made of shaped blocks of the local pudding stone, while the vaults were of brick. Note the terracotta pipes running through the dividing walls.

Approximately 50m SE of the baths are the ruins of the 3C AD **gymnasium**. The main entrance on the S led to the palaestra. Behind this there was a long, narrow rectangular hall used for ceremonial purposes. On the E wall there were statues of the emperor and local dignitaries.

The ruins of Aspendus are widely scattered. To visit the theatre, the aqueduct and the acropolis demands at least a half-day. Refreshments are not available at the site, but there is a restaurant, the *Belkis*, in the village. Converted from an old mill, it offers a variety of Turkish dishes. It is much favoured by coach parties, as are the nearby Aspendos Jewellery and Bazaar 24 which has a wide range of carpets and kilims.

If you have brought your own food, you may picnic in a pleasantly-shaded park which borders the river c 2km NE of the site. This has benches, tables and facilities for a barbecue. Take the road that leads N from the car-park by the theatre and then follow the river up stream for a short distance.

The toilet and a wash room are near the car park. Admission tickets, postcards and booklets are sold just inside the entrance to the theatre.

In the right-hand parodos wall panels provide summary information about the theatre and its history. There is no museum at Aspendus, but many of the antiquities found here are in the Antalya Museum.

Aspendus has the most perfectly preserved **theatre** in the Roman world. Designed by the architect Zeno during the reign of Marcus Aurelius (AD 161–180), it was presented to the city by two brothers, Curtius Crispinus and Curtius Auspicatus. Their Greek and Latin dedication of the building to 'the gods of the country and to the Imperial House', though partially obscured by arches erected during the Selçuk period, may be seen over the entrances to the stage-building.

Constructed from pudding-stone, its seats, floors and wall-panels were of marble. The stage-building, which stands to its original height, has five doors and four rows of windows of different sizes. *Vela* were supported by poles held by stone corbels above and below the top row of windows. Vaulted parodoi, on each side of the stage-building, and two doors on the hillside, now closed, provided access to the cavea. Today visitors enter by the central door which faces the car-park.

Apart from some damage, now repaired, to the staircases on the extreme left and right of the cavea and to the vaulted gallery at the top, and the loss of decoration on the interior wall of the stage-building, the theatre is virtually as it was when first built. The semicircular cavea extends on both sides to the stage-building. Its 40 rows of marble seats are divided into cunei by 10 staircases below the single diazoma and 21 above. Over each parodos, an area reserved for the city magistrates and other dignitaries may be reached by stairs from the stage-building. Behind the highest row of seats a vaulted gallery offered protection during inclement weather. The smaller covered passage behind the diazoma and under the upper seats is a constructional feature and was not used by the audience. Several seats, including one near the upper gallery, have the names of individual spectators carved on them—perhaps a form of advance booking. The estimated capacity of the theatre is 15,000, though in recent years more than 40,000 have been squeezed in to see Turkish wrestling and song contests.

The inside of the stage-building was elaborately ornamented with about 40 free-standing columns in two rows, Ionic below, Corinthian above. These flanked a series of niches, each of which held a statue. Today only those parts of the decoration, which were attached to the wall remain. In the centre of the large pediment, which had two pairs of columns on each side, there is a **statue of Dionysus** surrounded by floral scrolls. It is believed that the name of the village of Belkis is derived from this figure which the local people called Bal Kız, the Honey Girl. An alternative explanation is that it comes from Belkis, the name of the Queen of Sheba in the Koran. She has been associated in the popular imagination with a number of ancient sites in Turkey. Five doors led to the wooden stage which stood c 1.5m above the ground and projected c 7m from the stage-building. Smaller doors below the level of the stage were used to admit animals, when the theatre was used for wild-beast shows.

Unlike the Greeks, who concentrated on 'looking' in the theatre (the word *theatron* is derived from θεαομαι, to view), the Romans emphasised the importance of 'hearing', hence 'auditorium'. So, in Aspendus they placed a wooden sounding-board in sloping grooves on the high side walls of the stage-building to improve the acoustics.

The **zigzag patterns** on the walls of the stage-building date from the 13C, when it was used as a palace by the Selçuk Turks. The Antalya Museum has a number of fine tiles showing birds surrounded by floral patterns, which were used by the Selçuks to decorate the theatre structure.

Leave the theatre, turn left and walk for c 100m around the base of the acropolis to the **S gate**, the principal entrance to the city. It is in a ravine which divides the acropolis into two unequal parts. Where the path divides, take the left fork to a plateau c 60m above sea-level covering c 20 hectares. No excavations have been conducted but surveys suggest that the ruins date from the 2C and 3C AD. Almost the whole of the plateau is covered with vegetation, which makes examination of the remains very difficult.

Where the path reaches the summit there are the substantial remains of an **exedra**, believed to have been used by orators and philosophers to address the populace. The semicircular structure, crowned by a dome faces the street. Constructed of dressed stone covered with marble slabs, it has five niches which once held statues.

The large open space N of this building is the **agora**. It was bounded on the E by a basilica, on the N by the bouleuterion and nymphaeum and on the W by shops. Care should be taken to avoid cisterns which are concealed by the vegetation.

The **shops** form a row of buildings 70m long, fronted by a stoa. Their dividing walls, constructed of dressed pudding-stone, are pierced with holes for the beams which supported the upper storeys.

Only the foundations of the **basilica** remain. This building, constructed in the 3C AD, was used originally as a hall of justice and an administrative centre. About 105m long and 27m wide, it was eminently suitable for conversion into a church in Byzantine times. The aisles were separated from the nave by rows of columns; some of the bases remain. Towards the S end, where it passes over the ravine, the basilica is supported by an arch. Its foundations were made of cut pudding-stone; the upper walls were of stone and brick. When it became a church, an apse was added to the S end. At the same time the vaulted area under the foundations was turned into a cistern.

At the N end of the basilica three archways provided access to a **square building** devoted to legal affairs. Its massive walls 2m thick, which stand to a height of c 17m, are supported on the E and W by substantial buttresses. The lower sections are of cut pudding-stone; the masonry-fill above is from later restorations. Entrance was by an arched doorway on the N. Inside, in the centre of both the E and the W walls there is a large niche, flanked by two smaller ones. A statue of Hadrian and another of an unknown woman, which were found nearby, probably came from this building. They are now in the Antalya Museum.

To the left of the basilica is the late 2C—early 3C AD **nymphaeum**, one of the most substantial buildings on the acropolis. Constructed of cut blocks of pudding-stone, it was 32.5m long, 15m high and 2m wide. The S wall had two rows of five niches, each covered by a semicircular dome. In the lower row the central niche served as a doorway. The others were blocked up. Between the niches free-standing pairs of Corinthian columns supported a marble entablature, parts of which still remain. The rest of the rich decoration of marble slabs has disappeared.

Water from the aqueduct was delivered to the nymphaeum by a double channel which was at the same level as the central niche. It flowed into a marble basin in the front of the structure. During the hot, dusty days of summer, the nymphaeum, which was both decorative and practical, must have been greatly appreciated by the people of Aspendus.

A rectangular building to the N of the nymphaeum has been identified by some as the **bouleuterion** and by others as the **odeum** of Aspendus. As in many Roman cities, it probably fulfilled both functions; performances of music alternating with meetings of the Council. Rounded on the E side, it is 38.5m long and 30m wide. Like the annex to the basilica devoted to legal affairs, it was built of worked blocks of pudding-stone. There is evidence of repairs carried out at a late date. On the W, in front of the entrance, there was an **altar** and a **bema**. Holes in the walls indicate that the seats and roof were made of wood. It, too, dates from the late 2C–early 3C AD.

Fight your way through the scrub to the point near the N gate, where the aqueduct enters the city. There are the remains of a number of buildings in this area, but they have not been identified. An alternative route back is by the NE edge of the plateau, where there are several cisterns. The **Hellenistic necropolis** was on the slope below. Most of the stelae found here bear the name of the deceased and of his father. Decoration was confined to a simple pediment with acroteria at the corners and rosettes in the centre. There are several examples in the Antalya Museum.

About 20m N of the bouleuterion a path descends to the site of the E gate. The remains of the **stadium** are 100m N of this point. Constructed in the form of an elongated U, open on the S, the stadium was 215m long and 30m wide. Most of the W section has collapsed and is partly buried. The best-preserved part is on the NE corner. The limestone seats are supported by walls and vaults of pudding stone. No trace of the main entrance remains. It was probably constructed of wood. Spectators could also enter the stadium from the vaults, some of which may have been used as shops.

The **Roman necropolis** was to the N and E of the stadium. A number of rock-tombs, which contained sarcophagi, may still be seen.

Apart from the theatre, the most interesting monument in Aspendus is the **aqueduct**. This brought water from the Isaurian Mountains in the N, a tremendous feat of engineering. The extant portion stretches for almost 1km over a former marsh and ends a short distance inside the N gate of the city. A 2C AD inscription, which almost certainly refers to the aqueduct, states that Tiberius Claudius Italicus donated the substantial amount of two million denarii to bring water to Aspendus. Better-preserved than similar aqueducts in the Roman Campagna or in France, it was constructed mainly of cut blocks of pudding-stone with some rubble infill. The remaining section consists of an arched structure 880m long and 15m high, which carried the limestone water pipes, and two pressure towers. The pipe-sections, many of which were used later to construct the Selçuk bridge below Aspendus, were joined by a flange and socket arrangement. On top of the towers, which are 3m sq and more than 30m high, an open chamber allowed the air to escape from the conduit, so reducing friction on the water-flow. The towers also permitted the aqueduct to change pressure when the water arrived in the city.

To get to the N tower, which is 3km from the city, take the road from the car-park as far as the irrigation canal and then turn S along a rough track. For the daring, a staircase provides access to the water-channel. The S tower is 100m NW of the acropolis in an area called Camili. It may be reached by following a track, which starts S of the city, for c 1km.

The **oldest necropolis** in Aspendus, with burials from the Classical period (5C BC), is in the foot-hills NW of the city. Grave goods and red-figure vases have been found in the tombs. These include a fine Attic crater which shows three nude komasts on one side and three youths arming themselves on the other. This is now in the Antalya Museum.

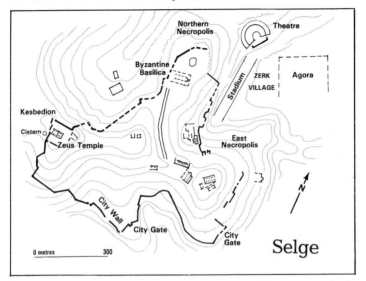

Return to the E24 and continue for c 5km in the direction of Alanya. To reach Selge, take the road on the left signposted Köprülükanyon Millipark and 23km Beşkonak.

SELGE is not the easiest site in Pamphylia to visit. As far as Beşkonak the road is reasonably good. From there to Zerk/Altınkaya, which occupies the site of the ancient city, there is a rough track. Allow a day for the visit and take a picnic, water, and some warm clothes. Selge is c 900m above sea-level and can be considerably cooler than the coast.

The road to Beşkonak passes through a pleasant wooded landscape, sometimes approaching, sometimes drawing away from the Eurymedon river. About 5km N of Beşkonak a restaurant and coffee house provide a welcome excuse for refreshments before attempting the climb to Zerk. Where the road forks just beyond the restaurant take the left-hand track, signposted Altınkaya. This leads to a **Roman bridge** over a deep gorge. Across the bridge, turn right on to a minor road that climbs to **Zerk**.

The mountain landscape is beautiful. Deep gorges clothed in cypress and cedar recede into the distance in delicate shades of blue. Olive, maple, carob and judas trees crowd the road and only gradually give way to oaks, as the track climbs ever higher. Occasionally the bright green of *Styrax officinalis* may be glimpsed through the darker foliage. The Selgians valued this shrub so highly that it appeared on their coins. According to Strabo an aromatic gum which it exuded was much in demand in ancient times. It was, and still is, used in the manufacture of incense and perfume.

Freya Stark went to Zerk in 1954. Then it had 'fifteen cottages or so scattered among prostrate columns under a Roman theatre in a hollow. It was shallow as a saucer and the ploughed fields filled it, and small pinnacles surrounded it, where temples had stood on easy slopes. Beyond them, the high peaks rose. Some in light and some in shadow, they had the cold pink mountain glow upon them'.

Because of an inadequate water-supply, Zerk was, she found, a poor village. The aqueduct and its terracotta pipes, which had enabled Selge to support a population of 20,000 had long ago fallen into ruin. The people of the modern village were obliged to rely on the meagre rainfall and melted snow to grow their crops.

History. Although generally considered to be a city of Pisidia, Selge was frequently at war with its Pisidian neighbours and looked to Pamphylia for its allies and its models. As early as the 5C BC, it appears to have had a monetary agreement with Aspendus and coins from that period give its name as **Estlegiys**, which is not unlike **Estwediiys**, the ancient name of Aspendus. Both words are Anatolian in origin. This suggests that Selge was not founded by Greek immigrants. In Hellenistic times, when it became fashionable to discover Greek ancestry, the Selgians claimed that their city was first settled by Calchas and his followers and later by the Spartans.

In 333 BC, while Alexander the Great was trying to capture Termessus by siege, the Selgians sent him offers of friendship. It is possible that they were motivated by dislike for the Termessians, as it seems unlikely that Alexander would ever have invaded their remote mountainous stronghold. When Alexander raised the siege of Termessus and abandoned his plan to go to Phrygia by that route, he marched N by way of the Pisidian stronghold of Sagalassus.

Polybius (c 200–118 BC) tells an interesting story of how Selge was saved from destruction c 220 BC by the vigilance and prompt action of a goatherd. The city was being besieged by the army of Garsyeris, a general of Syrian origin. He entered into protracted negotiations with the Selgians, who nominated one of their number, Logbasis, to speak for them. Unfortunately, Logbasis was a traitor and he hatched a plan with Garsyeris to surrender the city to him and to his master, Achaeus, the disloyal uncle of Antiochus III (223–187). However, the goatherd, seeing part of the enemy army advance towards the Kesbedion hill while another detachment moved towards the main gate, gave the alarm. The Selgians rushed to the house of Logbasis and put him and all his family to death. Then, sallying forth, they drove the enemy back and killed 700 of them. Achaeus lifted the siege and the Selgians made peace with him.

Perhaps because of its inaccessibility, the Romans took little interest in Selge and the city was able to maintain its independence. For a time it came under the rule of the Galatians, when Antony c 36 BC gave it to their king, Amyntas. Later, with the cities of Pisidia, Selge was incorporated in the Roman Empire. Like their neighbours on the coast, the Selgians prospered. In addition to the aromatic styrax gum, they produced an unguent made from the iris. Surprisingly, in view of the altitude, they were also famous for the quality of the olives grown in their lands.

In Byzantine times Selge retained its status. It was the seat of a bishop, who ranked after Side and before Aspendus. It continued to produce coins up to the end of the 3C AD. Little is known about its history subsequently. Presumably it began to decline when the irrigation system fell into disrepair and its inhabitants moved down to more temperate regions. Selge was rediscovered by travellers from Western Europe in the middle of the 19C, when it was visited by Schönborn and Daniell.

There are plans for a survey and excavation of Selge. At present the remains are sparse and visitors come here mainly for the beauty of its situation and for its atmosphere. Many feel the emotions experienced by Daniell in 1842:

'I came suddenly in view of a theatre magnificently situated, a stadium, a row of Ionic columns standing, and a square below, which must have been the Agora, though now a corn-field. Standing myself upon a large square platform of ancient pavement, with a beautiful foreground, I think in all my life I never saw such a mountain view'.

Selge's most striking monument is its **theatre** which lies to the NW of Zerk. Partly cut from the natural rock, partly constructed from masonry, it had a capacity of almost 10,000. Like most theatres built in the Greek style, the cavea is greater than a semicircle and, as at Aspendus, it is joined to the stage-building. There are 15 rows of seats above its single diazoma and 30 below. These were divided into cunei by 12 staircases. The stage-building, which is in ruins, had the customary five doors facing the audience.

On a hill to the NW of the theatre there are the remains of three **tombs**. About 100m to the SE there is the poorly-preserved **stadium**. The seats on one side were supported by the hill, on the other they rested on arches.

Selge's **agora**, on the hill to the S, was a paved area of c 45 sq m, open on the S and surrounded by buildings on the N, W and E sides. There are the ruins of a Byzantine church nearby. The city's main **necropolis** was on the E side of this hill. Many of the tombs have an unusual kind of decoration. Two small circles towards the top of a larger circle produce the appearance of a human face.

About 150m to the W there was a stoa 110m long. On the hill to the S there are the ruins of part of the **defensive walls** which extended for more than 3km around the city. The **main gate**, where perhaps the Selgians repulsed the attack of Achaeus, is in this stretch of wall.

To the N of the wall, on the Kesbedion, are the remains of two **temples**. One was probably dedicated to Zeus. An inscription found nearby suggests that the other was dedicated to Artemis. To the W of the temples there is a large **cistern** 21m in diameter and c 7.5m deep. This was filled by rain water and water carried by a channel from the hills to the NW of the city.

Many inscriptions have been found in Selge. A number bear the triskele, the three-legged symbol which also appeared on the coins of Aspendus. This represented the sun rising, at its zenith, and setting, and symbolised the constant renewal of life.

Return to the E24 and continue to c 23km **Manavgat**, a pleasant market town on the Manavgat Çayı, the ancient river Melas. There are frequent dolmuş services to Side. The *Develi restaurant* in the town centre has a good reputation.

W of Manavgat look for a signpost on the left to 4km **Manavgat Şelalesi**, Manavgat Falls, a beauty-spot favoured by Turkish and foreign gourmets. Here, under the pine trees, you may enjoy an excellent meal of freshly-grilled trout washed down by a local white wine.

Approximately 3km farther on is Şıhlar. From here it is an easy hour's walk to an ancient site which, until recently, was believed to be that of Seleuceia in Pamphylia. En route you will see the remains of the aqueduct which brought water from the Dumanlı source in Roman times.

The discovery here of a bilingual text in Greek and Sidetan, something which archaeologists and epigraphists would not expect to find in a new Hellenistic foundation, has thrown doubt on the earlier identification. It is now suggested that this was not Seleuceia in Pamphylia, but possibly the city of **Lyrbe**. Seleuceia was probably on the coast, perhaps where the Peri Çayı flows into the sea between Side and the mouth of the Köprüçay.

The city, built on a steep hill, was inaccessible except from the S. The approach is by way of a narrow depression. Just beyond this, to the left, a refreshing spring issues from a cave where there are traces of ancient masonry.

There are the ruins of a baths complex and an agora with a market hall and bouleuterion. A fine mosaic, showing Orpheus charming the animals, was found in the market hall.

There was a small, well-preserved temple to the N of the agora. The city's necropolis, which was on the W slope of the hill, has a number of tombs of worked stone.

About 3km W of Manavgat, by a petrol station, is the signposted turning to 4km **SIDE**.

Transport, Accommodation and Information. Many long-distance buses call at Side. There is a frequent dolmuş service from Manavgat. Side's *otogar* is some distance outside the town.

Side has four five-star, four four-star, three three-star, two two-star and one one-star hotels, three holiday villages and many pensions inspected by the Ministry of Tourism. There are other hotels and pensions not on the list and several campsites.

The five-star *Asteria Oteli* and the two-star *Cennet hotel* are recommended. The Cennet, one of the longest established hotel in Side, has extensive, well maintained gardens and is 15 minutes along the beach from the museum and the theatre.

There are several good restaurants. The *Cansin* has been praised for the extent of its wine list and the quality and range of its *mezes*.

Side is well equipped for sea sports. There is excellent bathing.

The **Tourist Information Office** is at Side Yolu Üzeri c 1km before the village.

Side is overdeveloped. Originally a small fishing village settled by Turkish immigrants from Crete at the end of the 19C, it has been subjected to uncoordinated and unrestricted growth which has destroyed much of its character. The main street, made hideous by a rash of boutiques and souvenir shops, has become indistinguishable from dozens of similar tourist traps scattered along the Mediterranean littoral. To find something of Side's former character look in the quieter side-streets, in the peaceful, ancient ruins and in the beautiful garden of the museum.

Much of ancient Side has been excavated by Turkish archaeologists. The late Professor Arif Müfit Mansel directed operations between 1947–67. Professor Jale İnan took over from Professor Mansel. The fruits of their labours are in the museum.

History. Early settlers in southern Anatolia looked for sites which could be defended easily. In Perge, Sillyum and Aspendus they built on an acropolis which they fortified. This served as a refuge in times of danger. In Side, they found a narrow peninsula, which could be protected on its landward and seaward sides by walls and whose harbour offered both a convenient point of supply and an escape route.

According to Arrian and Strabo, Side was a colony of the Aeolian city of Cyme which was located N of İzmir. After they had landed, Arrian claims, the colonists forgot their Greek and began to speak an incomprehensible language unrelated to those used in other cities in Pamphylia. This picturesque story may contain a kernel of truth. The settlers from Cyme were not strong enough to impose Greek on the indigenous inhabitants, but were obliged to accept the Anatolian language spoken here before their arrival.

Evidence of Side's unusual language is provided by its name, which means pomegranate and is of Anatolian origin, by coins dating from the 6C BC, and by three 3C BC inscriptions found here. So far the language has not been deciphered, but scholars are hopeful that they will be able to read it one day. Two of the inscriptions in Side's museum, are bilinguals, carrying the text in Sidetan and Greek. This unique language appears to have fallen into disuse after the conquest of Asia Minor by Alexander the Great c 333 BC. Greek became the common language of the new empire.

Unlike other Pamphylian cities which were colonised after the Trojan War, it would appear that the settlers from Cyme came to Side around the 7C BC. What little is known of its early history is derived from the general history of Pamphylia. In the 6C BC the whole area was under the domination of the kings of Lydia until they were defeated by the Persians. Nothing is known about Side during the period of Persian rule. Unlike Aspendus and Sillyum, Side welcomed Alexander, and like them was fought over by his successors. Until 218 BC Pamphylia was ruled by the Ptolemies of Egypt, then it came under the control of the Seleucid kings of Syria. Side supported the Seleucids against the rebel Achaeus and against the Rhodians in 190 BC.

Side appears to have avoided falling under the rule of Pergamum, and enjoyed a substantial degree of independence in the middle of the 2C BC. It entered a period of growth and prosperity, becoming one of the most important trading cities in the Eastern Mediterranean and a centre of culture and learning. Its citizens had a bad reputation. When asked to name the most unscrupulous people, the wit Stratonicus replied 'In Pamphylia the men of Phaselis, in the whole world the men of Side'.

According to Strabo, Side was deeply involved with the pirates, allowing them to sell their prisoners in the city and to repair their ships in the harbour. Two campaigns in the 1C BC to remove the threat posed by piracy from Cilicia and Pamphylia brought Side under Roman control. Again the city flourished. During the 2C and 3C AD, when it was the seat of the governor, many fine buildings, whose ruins may be seen today, were constructed. The arrival of hostile Isaurian tribes from the N in the 3C brought the first check to this period of prosperity. However, the Sidetans repaired the city's defences and during the reign of Julian (361–363) successfully resisted a siege.

The 5C and 6C were marked by another period of growth. The city walls were extended to enclose a larger area. Side again was an important commercial centre. The seat of a metropolitan bishop, it was famed for its learning. The Arab raids from the 7C onwards put an end to this, its last period of importance. No Byzantine buildings later than the 9C and 10C survive and excavations have revealed the burnt remains of houses destroyed at that time. It would appear that the city's destruction was completed by a number of earthquakes in the 12C. Idrisi, an Arab geographer (fl. c 1150), calls Side 'burnt Antalya' because the inhabitants abandoned the city and moved themselves and their belongings to Antalya. For this reason it was also known sometimes as Eski Antalya, Old Antalya. Pamphylia was captured by the Selçuk Turks in 1148 and by the Ottomans in 1442, but no traces of their occupation have been found here. Until it was rediscovered by Beaufort, Daniell and Fellows and other European travellers the 19C, the city disappeared from historical records.

The pleasures and the dangers experienced by these early travellers are summed up in an account by Fellows of an evening spent in the neighbourhood of Side.

'[I] am now sitting in my tent, surrounded by camels, goats, and cows, the care of the inhabitants of a few tents near me; their fires are blazing, and these, with the light of a full moon, and the various rustic noises of the shepherd's pipe, camels' tinkling bells, frogs croaking, nightingales singing in the trees, and owls hooting from the ruins, and now and then a burst of alarm from all the watch-dogs at the approach of jackals or wolves, give a peculiar effect to the scene; while the open sea before, and the splendid mountains behind, render the scene as picturesque as it is wildly interesting'.

There are few springs or wells in Side, so in Roman times water was brought a distance of 32km to the city from the Dumanlı source of the Melas river. This required an elaborate series of tunnels and channels cut through the rock and, on the lower level, an **aqueduct** supported on arches. Unfortunately, many of the rock-cut galleries, which were fitted with vents to admit air and light are now submerged under the waters of the Oymapınar Dam. However, much of the aqueduct remains and a long stretch may be seen from the approach road to Side. Constructed from shaped blocks of sandstone and pudding-stone, the aqueduct entered the city 150m N of the main gate and terminated near the inner gate, close to the theatre. There the water was stored in large cisterns near the baths, now the museum, and then distributed throughout the city by stone and terracotta pipes. During the period of decline in the 3C, this water-supply system fell into disrepair. It was restored during the reign of Diocletian (284–305) through the generosity of a citizen, one Bryonianus Lollianus, and of a number of wealthy foreigners. When during the 11C Side entered its last period of decay, the system could not be maintained and wells were sunk in various parts of the city by the remaining inhabitants.

The 2C AD **nymphaeum** was probably supplied by the aqueduct. Outside the city walls this faced the main gate. Like the nymphaeum at Aspendus, it consisted of a rectangular wall with projecting wings. Two of the original three storeys remain. The lower storey had three semicircular niches, surmounted by half-domes, which faced a large basin. The whole structure was covered with marble and decorated with statues and reliefs of mythological scenes. Fragments of this decoration lie in front of the nymphaeum on an area once paved with marble slabs.

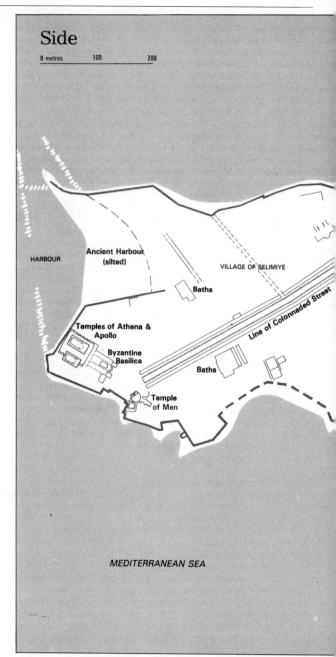

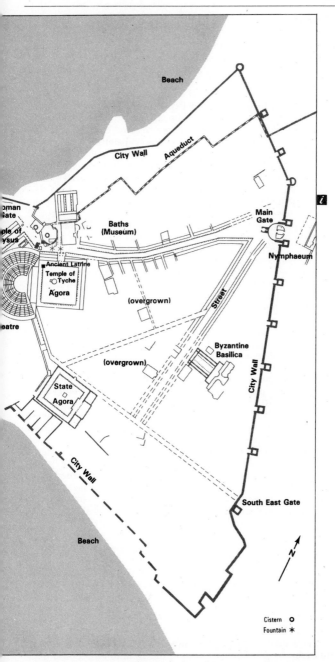

Beach

City Wall

Aqueduct

Roman
Gate

ele of
ysus

Baths
(Museum)

Ancient Latrine
Temple of
Tyche
Agora

(overgrown)

Street

Main
Gate

Nymphaeum

eatre

(overgrown)

Byzantine
Basilica

City Wall

State
Agora

City Wall

Beach

South East Gate

N

Cistern   O
Fountain ✷

Side's **necropolis** lay outside the city wall in an area now covered by cultivated land. Many of the fine sarcophagi and ostotheks (cinerary urns) found here are in the museum. A short distance to the W of the city there are the ruins of a **temple tomb** which dates from the 2C AD.

The **principal gate**, which faced the nymphaeum, was damaged when the modern road was constructed. In layout it resembled the city gates at Perge and Sillyum. An outer court, flanked by two towers on the city wall, led through a gateway to an inner semicircular court. From here, a second gate led to one of the principal streets of the city. During a period of peace c AD 200 the original Hellenistic structure was altered considerably. The wall of the court was covered with marble slabs and statues were placed in seven niches. Some of the statues from this are in the museum.

Side was surrounded by a **wall** of shaped, pudding-stone blocks erected during the Hellenistic period. Most of the eastern section is covered by sand and the wall on the S, which faced the sea, has largely disappeared. The best-preserved section is near the main gate on the landward side. On the inner surface there were three storeys. The bottom storey, partly furnished with arches and pillars, served to support the upper storeys. In the middle storey there were small rooms, fitted with openings for the discharge of missiles. The top storey had a parapet and look-out points which commanded the landward approaches. The defences were further strengthened by towers placed at irregular intervals. Bean has drawn attention to a curious construction feature for which there is no entirely satisfactory explanation. On the inner side of the wall there is a gap of c 7.5m between the towers. Was this perhaps bridged by planking?

As Side has not been completely excavated, it is not possible to say whether it was laid out in accordance with a formal plan or whether it followed the contours of the land. The modern road covers the colonnaded street which ran from the main gate to the city centre. The area to the right of this street was known as the Quarter of the Great Gate.

On the left lay the **Quarter of the Great Guild**. A visit to this area, now heavily overgrown and partly buried under sand dunes, will not deter those who are prepared to put up with a little discomfort. They will be rewarded by an opportunity to examine the substantial remains of a **Byzantine basilica** and of the **episcopal palace**. These buildings were located near the junction of two streets which joined the main and E gates.

The basilica dates from the 5C. To the left of the apse there was a large baptistery, divided into three sections. Three steps led down to the baptismal font which was in the central section. The basilica was attached to the palace on the SE side by a building which is believed to have been a martyrion. Some of the walls of the palace remain. It had a small private chapel with three rows of seats in the apse. Side's ecclesiastical quarter was completed by a large walled garden to the NE of the palace.

A rough path leads from the basilica to the **E gate**. Constructed during the Hellenistic period of shaped blocks of pudding-stone, this opened on to a rectangular courtyard. More than 10,000 cubic m of sand were cleared by the archaeologists to reveal some fine **Byzantine mosaics** and **reliefs**. Professor Mansel believed that the reliefs, which depict arms and weapons, probably commemorated a victory by the Sidetans over a Pergamene army in the 2C BC. They are now in the museum.

Continue in a southerly direction to the line of Side's sea-wall and then turn right towards the town. A short walk over the sand dunes will bring you to the inner walls of the city and the site of the **state agora**, a large open space surrounded by a colonnade. During the Byzantine period a giant cross stood on a two-level platform in the centre. An elaborately ornamented **three-room building** filled its E end. The middle room had a timber roof and its walls were covered with sheets of marble. It was decorated, on two levels, with copies of well-known Classical Greek statues. These were placed in semicircular domed niches or rested on bases that projected from the wall. Many of the statues were found during the excavations and are now in the museum. One, a headless **representation of Nemesis**, is in its original position, a niche in the SE corner. The room on the S side, which was restored by the Byzantines and decorated with a geometric mosaic design, may have been used as a library.

From here a short walk towards the modern road will bring you to Side's **main agora**, the commercial and social centre of the city. The slave market described by Strabo was probably held here. Covering an area c 91 by 94m, it was surrounded on four sides by stoas. The path passes the inner walls of the city which were constructed in the 4C, during the period of the barbarian invasions, from material salvaged from earlier buildings. This is evidenced by the many **column drums** which project from the hastily-built fortification. Note, too, that the back of the stage-building of the theatre was incorporated in these late defences.

In the centre of the agora are the ruins of a 2C AD building which was identified by Professor Mansel as a **Temple of Tyche**, the goddess of fortune. This was a circular cella, resting on a base, surrounded by 12 Corinthian columns and covered by a 12-sided pyramidal roof. Beaufort, who visited Side in 1811–12, saw three of the carved slabs which made up the ceiling of the temple, 'a series of figures that represent some of the signs of the zodiac; Pisces, Aries, Taurus, Gemini and Cancer, were placed in due succession; but the next was a swan, and then the naked figure of a young man'. Unfortunately, all have disappeared.

Behind the stoas were some of the city's shops. The largest were on the NE side. On the NW, on either side of the entrance, there was a double row. Some faced outwards to the street, others inwards to the agora. A number of columns, surmounted by Corinthian capitals, which lined the N side of the stoa, have been re-erected. On the SW, in addition to shops, which may have sold refreshments to theatre patrons, rooms admitted to the theatre from the stoa. A fine **public toilet** in the western corner of the agora, near the theatre, catered for other bodily needs. Lined with marble panels, it had 24 seats positioned over a water-channel.

On the right-hand side of the road the museum occupies a restored 5C AD baths complex. To the left of the entrance are the ruins of a **triple basin fountain**. This was ornamented with statues placed between the basins. A head of Hermes from one of these statues is in the museum.

The road passes under a **Roman monumental arch** which may have been surmounted by the quadriga that gave its name to this area of the city. When the inner defensive wall was constructed in the 4C, the arch became the main entrance to the city. For security reasons it was filled in with material taken from other buildings, and a small gate, surmounted by a relieving arch, was placed in its centre. This later addition was dismantled some years ago, as it was in danger of collapsing.

To the left of the arch there is a **nymphaeum**. This has a central niche flanked by two pedestals which supported statues. In front there was a basin fed by a pipe from the niche. According to its inscription this structure was erected in AD 74 in honour of the Emperors Titus and Vespasian. It was converted into a nymphaeum and moved to its present position in the 4C AD, at about the time the inner wall was constructed. Archaeologists restored it to its present state in 1962.

The road bends sharply under the arch, making it a hazardous place for pedestrians and motorists alike. To the right a path leads down to the beach. On the left there are the scant remains of a **temple**. Because of its proximity to the theatre it was probably dedicated to Dionysus. The small pseudo-peripteral structure, constructed of limestone on a base measuring 7.25 by 17.50m, was built during the Hellenistic period and repaired during the Roman era. Access was provided by steps on the N side. There were four Corinthian columns of red granite in front of the cella.

Side's **theatre** is one of the finest in Turkey. Apart from the stage-building and the orchestra, which have suffered considerable damage, it is in a very good state of repair. Archaeologists are clearing and restoring the damaged areas. Constructed during the 2C AD, its shape, greater than a semicircle, makes it almost certain that it replaced an earlier Hellenistic theatre. As the slope was not sufficiently great, the upper part of the auditorium had to be supported by an artificial structure which stands to a height of c 14m. (Originally it was c 2.5m higher). In the lower storey there is a vaulted corridor, pierced by vaulted openings. There was a parodos at each end of this corridor. The openings lead to an inner corridor, which in turn leads to the single diazoma, or to rooms, used perhaps as shops or storerooms. There were 29 rows of seats below the diazoma and 22 above. The lower section was divided into 11 and the upper section into 24 cunei. The seats in the lower section were reached from the diazoma. However, there was no direct access from the diazoma to the upper section. Interior staircases led to the top of the building from which patrons descended to their seats. The existing stairs in the upper section are modern.

Estimates of the theatre's capacity vary. Beaufort worked out the following: 'Now supposing that the antients sat as we do, with the legs pendent, and not crossed under them like the modern Greeks and Turks (as Dr Chandler seems to have thought), and therefore taking eighteen inches as sufficient for each person to occupy, this theatre would contain 13,370 persons, when regularly seated; but, in crowded exhibitions, many could sit on the flights of small steps, or could stand on the upper platform, and at the back of the broad Diazomatos these may be estimated at 1,870 more, and would together make the enormous aggregate of 15,240 spectators'.

The **stage-building**, like that of Aspendus, was constructed in the Graeco-Roman style. It had three storeys ornamented with Ionic, Composite and Corinthian columns and reached a height of c 21m. The central and upper storeys, which formed the background to the stage, were elaborately decorated with statues, niches and friezes. Unfortunately, most of these have been damaged, some by natural causes, some by human action. A number at the back of the stage are believed to have been mutilated by the Christians, when two small chapels were erected in the theatre and the building was used for worship.

In the later Roman period theatres were often used for wild animal fights, for gladiatorial games and for the staging of naval battles (naumachiae). To enable these to take place at Side, a wall c 2m high was constructed around the orchestra to protect the spectators.

Limited excavations in the theatre area have produced bronze and glass objects. The archaeologists also found two coin hoards. These contained 107 bronze coins of Theodosius I, Arcadius and Honorius (AD 379–423) and 443 coins of Licinus (AD 308–24).

To the right of the theatre is the car-park. Only cars with a special authorisation are allowed in the village. Side's main street follows the line of the ancient colonnaded way which led from the main gate to the harbour. To avoid the modern street's succession of boutiques, restaurants and souvenir shops, take the lane on the left around the side of the theatre. At the road junction, the left fork goes to a sandy beach that extends for several kilometres to the E. The right fork will bring you to the southern part of Side where the temples of Men, Athena and Apollo are located.

At the end of the ancient colonnaded street there was a semicircular building which has been identified as the **Temple of Men**. He was an Anatolian moon god often linked with Attis. Like Attis, Men was usually depicted as a handsome youth wearing a Phrygian cap. Among the many sites consecrated to his worship there was one near Antalya, where mysteries involving a sacred marriage were celebrated. Men's symbols were the pine cone, the peacock and, significantly, the pomegranate. The temple of Men at Side was raised on a base 2m high. Unlike shrines dedicated to the Greek gods, which faced E, access was by a flight of steps on the W side. The temple has been dated to the end of the 2C AD.

There were **temples**, dated to the 2C AD and dedicated to **Athena** and to **Apollo**, near the ancient harbour of Side. Each, a peripteros in the Corinthian style, had 11 columns on the sides and six on the front and on the back. The entrance to the pronaos was flanked by two columns. There was no opisthodomus. The columns of the W façade of the temple of Apollo supported an architrave and a frieze of Medusa heads and actors' masks. In Byzantine times the construction of a basilica completed the destruction of the temples which were probably in a ruinous condition. The archaeologists are currently engaged in the restoration of both buildings. Several columns of the Apollo temple have been re-erected.

Inscriptions found in Side refer to priests of Zeus, Poseidon, Serapis and Aphrodite and the city boasted that it was six times a *neocorus*. No traces of temples dedicated to these gods or to the worship of the emperors have been discovered so far.

There are substantial remains of the **Byzantine basilica**, dating from the 5C, which was built to the E of the temples. Its large forecourt occupied part of the eastern temple's platform. The division between the nave and the aisles was by two rows of 12 columns constructed from material salvaged from Roman buildings. The apse had a synthronon reached by six marble steps, and sacristies on either side. Later a martyrion was added to the S side. In the 9C or 10C a smaller church was constructed in the centre of the basilica. The buildings remained largely intact until the 19C, when much of the marble used to decorate them was burned to make lime.

The first **harbour** of Side was constructed during the Hellenistic period on the SE side of the peninsula. It extended as far as the harbour baths which are now some distance from the sea. Surrounded by a quay built of pudding-stone and protected from the SW gales, it played a large part in the city's prosperity. However, it had to be cleared of accumulated silt so frequently that in antiquity any recurring, expensive and difficult task was likened to the dredging of Side's harbour. By the 5C AD it had become so shallow that it was decided to abandon it and build a new harbour to the NE. This is still used by the local fishermen.

Side's **museum** occupies a restored 5C AD baths complex across the road from the commercial agora. The entrance is by a narrow, colonnaded street which led originally to the sea wall. On the left there is a kiosk, where tea and cold drinks, postcards, replicas, etc., are sold. The street continues to what was originally a courtyard and is now a pleasant shaded garden, where sarcophagi, cinerary urns and fragments of antique sculpture lie half-hidden among a profusion of flowering shrubs. Constructed during the last period of Side's prosperity, the rectangular building follows the usual plan of a Roman bath. Restored through the initiative of Professor Mansel, it contains many of the antiquities discovered by him and his colleagues.

The original entrance was by two arched doorways, which led from the courtyard to the **frigidarium**. Originally roofed, the floor here is paved with re-used marble slabs, many bearing inscriptions. A large **semicircular basin** on the NE side was filled with cold water. Bathers descended into the basin, which was covered by a dome and lined with marble, by a flight of steps on the left. At the back there are niches for statues. On the left is the narrow channel which delivered water from the aqueduct.

Along the wall facing the basin are the **reliefs** depicting arms which were found at the city's eastern gate (see above). These are believed to commemorate a victory by the Sidetans over an army from Pergamum in the 2C BC. In the centre of the room are two Roman altars which were later hollowed out and turned into well-heads. Nearby is a late **Hittite column base**, dated to the 7C BC, which was discovered near the site of the temples of Apollo and Athena.

A narrow doorway leads to the **sudatorium**, the hottest room in the baths, which was built over a furnace. Now circular in shape, it was originally square. The four niches in the corners contain a selection of small objects found in Side. Note in particular the fine **terracotta head**.

Continue into the **caldarium**, a rectangular room, which originally had basins at its N and S ends only. Later one large and two small basins were added on the E side. Facing the entrance is a beautifully sculpted and composed representation of the **Three Graces**. In the centre of the room is a **statue of Hercules**, holding the golden apples of the Hesperides. The niches above the basin to the left of the entrance contain Roman copies of Hellenistic statues of a woman and a girl. Along the side of the basin are a number of Roman amphorae, which were recovered from the sea. To the left of the semicircular basins there is a **relief of Ixion**, King of Thessaly, who was condemned by Zeus to spend eternity bound to a rotating fiery wheel because of his attempted seduction of Hera. Nearby is a **statue of the river-god, Melas**, the modern Manavgat Çayı. A short 2C BC **inscription in the Sidetan language** (see above), found near the E gate, is displayed near the central semicircular basin. In the basin at the S side of the room there are parts of a 2C AD sarcophagus. The niche in the centre has a headless **Nike**, the goddess of victory, found in the library of the state agora, flanked by representations of **Dionysus** and **Apollo**.

In the **tepedarium** there is a fine **statue of Hygeia**, the daughter of Asclepius, the god of healing. Note the snake, twined around her arms, which came to be associated with the care and nursing of the sick. An almost complete **statue of Apollo**, dating from the 2C AD, is flanked by a head of Apollo and a head of Hermes. The head of Apollo is a Roman copy of the famous Hellenistic original known as the Kassel Apollo. The **head of Hermes**, who is depicted as a sullen, pensive youth, was discovered in the triple-basin nymphaeum near the museum. It was identified as a result of some interesting detective work. Archaeologists believe that in the 3C AD, when Side had become impoverished, a statue of Hermes was taken from another site in the city, the wings were removed from its head and in its new persona of Apollo erected in the nymphaeum.

There follows a series of incomplete statues which date from the Roman period. In a niche on the S side of the room are two **3C AD sphinxes** which were found in the orchestra of the theatre. In the corner is a damaged statue of Demeter. An interesting composite statue of a **Roman emperor** stands in a niche nearby. The head and torso belong to different periods. The body has been dated by the decoration on the armour to the 2C AD, while the head, which is much smaller in proportion, dates from the 4C AD. As in the case of the Hermes' head, it was changed in antiquity. The hair and beard were removed to create a better representation of the later emperor.

In the centre of the room, there is a Roman 2C AD copy of the famous 5C BC **discus thrower** of Myron (fl. 480–40 BC) and **headless statues of Hermes** and **Ares**, the god of war. Hermes was the guardian of merchants and so no doubt was very popular in a trading city like Side. A well-preserved **statue of Hermes**, also found in the area of the triple-basin fountain, stands in a corner of the room. He is shown as a nude, muscular adolescent, carrying a purse in his right hand. He is partly supported on his left by a herm: a plinth, which slopes gradually towards its base, decorated with a bearded head and phallus. Between two sarcophagi in the centre of the room, there is an altar, ornamented with a bust and two small male figures. All date from the 2C AD. The **first sarcophagus**, from the W necropolis, is decorated with a frieze of children playing musical instruments and making preparations for a sacrifice. On the back two griffins confront each other. On top there is a headless reclining male figure. The **second sarcophagus**, from the E necropolis, has a decoration on the sides of charming, tipsy erotes, who support each other in a sensual, precocious embrace. The cover of this sarcophagus is shaped like a roof. One pediment has a representation of Medusa, the other a round shield.

The last room in the complex was probably the **apodyterium**. Now roofless, it serves as the entrance to the museum. There are **inscriptions** from various monuments in Side and a giant, **headless statue of Nike** which was found near the nymphaeum at the principal gate to the city.

Amongst the antiquities in the garden there are two fine **sarcophagi**. On one, two erotes support a garland which has a column crater in the centre. On the other side there is an inscription inside a *tabula ansata*. One of the pediments has a damaged Medusa head. Along the wall there are some architectural fragments from a building near the necropolis. These have representations of **Selene**, the moon goddess, and **Helios**, the sun god. Among the Corinthian and Ionic capitals, cinerary urns and damaged reliefs, there is an interesting **triangular altar**, with a relief showing a humped bull and a bay tree. This was found in the harbour area, near the temples of Apollo and Athena. By the wall on the N side of the garden a **relief** from the great baths shows a procession of sea-creatures bearing gifts to the wedding of Poseidon and Amphitrite.

28

Side to Alanya

Total distance c 61km. Side—c 7km Manavgat—(c 9km Alarahan)—c 34km Şarapsa Hanı—c 20km Alanya.

After Manavgat the coastal plain begins to narrow. The Taurus Mountains draw near the E24 which now crosses a stretch of very fertile but rather dull countryside. After c 10km Road 695 departs on the left for a spectacular and sinuous journey through the mountains and over the Irmasan Geç (1525m) to 175km **Beyşehir**. There it joins with Road 330 to Konya. About

10km further a secondary road on the left leads to 9km Alarahan where there are tea houses and a picnic area on the banks of the Alara Çayı.

Alarahan is a 13C inn, one of a number on the road from Konya to Alanya. These *hans* were constructed by the sultans to provide travellers and merchants with secure and comfortable overnight resting places. They could store their goods in safety, stable their animals, prepare their meals, enjoy a bath, and pray in the small mosque.

Alarahan crouches under a protective hillside near the remains of an ancient bridge. You will need a torch to explore the well-preserved interior. At the ornamented entrance there is a small **mosque** and quarters for the porter/guard. The central chamber is surrounded by a number of rooms which were occupied by the travellers. Note the stone brackets, carved in the form of lions' heads, which supported lamps.

At the head of the valley are the ruins of a 13C castle, **Alarakale**. Follow the road to its end. Then, cross the vegetable gardens and make your way along a precarious path that skirts the river's edge. From here a low-roofed tunnel leads upwards for c 100m to the outer courtyard. Again a lamp is necessary, as there is little light in the passage. Its sides and roof are rough and have many rocky protuberances. The rudimentary steps are covered with loose stones. This tunnel will not commend itself to those affected by claustrophobia or worried about snakes or scorpions.

From the outer court there is a splendid view over the valley. Worn steps lead to the dizzy heights of the second court and thence to the top of the castle. Above the ruins of the residential quarters there is a *hamam* with traces of decoration on its domes. Other buildings—a ruined palace, servants' quarters, a mosque—are hard to reach and contain little of interest.

Return to the E24 which approaches the sea once more. It passes sandy beaches—some with a clutch of hotels and restaurants, others untouched and undeveloped. The landscape changes dramatically. The mountains approach the seashore. You are leaving Pamphylia and entering Cilicia where banana plantations among the citrus groves provide an exotic touch.

There are the ruins of an ancient city, perhaps Annesis, on both sides of the road just before c 15km **Şarapsa Hanı**. This Selçuk inn, on the left of the E24, was constructed by Sultan Giyaseddin Keyhusrev II (1236–46) and, like Alarahan, was a staging post between Konya and Alanya. In an excellent state of preservation, it measures 70m by 15m. There was a small **mosque** at the E end. Until recently examination of the building had to be limited to the exterior, as farmers used it as a store and kept it locked. The latest news is that 'progress' has caught up with Şarapsa Hanı and that it has become a discotheque!

About 5km before Alanya there is a small, well-kept rest area on a promontory to the right of the road. This has pleasantly shaded paths, tables, benches, and barbecue pits. No refreshments are available. There is a small gravelly beach on one side and the place is sufficiently far from Alanya to be free from pollution. Parking space is limited. As the rest area is on a very busy road, take care when entering and leaving.

The headland above **ALANYA** can be seen from a considerable distance. Crowned by a Selçuk fortress, it projects into the Mediterranean like a Turkish Gibraltar. Alanya may be divided into two areas: the older and more interesting part under the fortress, and the brash, ribbon-development on the E24.

Alanya is one of the most popular tourist resorts on Turkey's Mediterranean coast. This is something of a mixed blessing. The rash of new, rather characterless hotels along the shore-line to the E and W of the town add

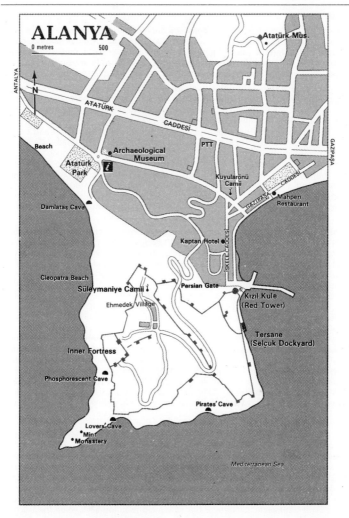

little to its charm. Fortunately, the old quarter still retains some of the original atmosphere and character of a Turkish town. This, coupled with its splendid situation and magnificent climate, combine to make it an attractive and interesting place to visit.

Information and Accommodation. The **Tourist Information Office** is near the museum and the W beach.

There are two five-star and five four-star hotels which have been inspected by the Ministry of Tourism, together with a large number of establishments in the other categories. There are also pensions and holiday villages. The comfortable and friendly three-star *Kaptan Hotel* at İskele Cad. 62 and the *Alanya Divan Hotel* (a converted old house) near the museum are recommended.

Restaurants offer everything from pizza and Chinese food to juicy steaks and traditional Turkish cuisine. Try the *Yönen* and the *Mahperi* which serve excellent fish dishes. Ask for them to be served with *tarator* (hazelnut) sauce. Both restaurants have terraces overlooking the sea and dinner here on a summer night, under the floodlit battlements of the Selçuk fortress, makes a very pleasant end to the day.

Most Turkish banks have branches in Alanya. The main post office is in Atatürk Cad.

Transport. Alanya's *otogar* is on the W of the town, c 150m off the E24. Many companies operating long-distance buses provide a free service from the *otogar* to their offices in the town centre. Some will also pick up passengers from and take them to the principal hotels. There are taxis for hire at the *otogar* and in the town.

Travel agencies arrange **day trips** to places like Side, Aspendus and Perge and longer excursions farther afield. There are **boat trips** to the Lovers' Cave, Pirates' Cave and Phosphorescent Cave. Damlataş Cave, on the W side of the town, is much visited by asthma and rheumatism sufferers. There are facilities for visiting yachts in the harbour area. Boutiques and shops in the old quarter offer the usual range of leather clothes, ceramics, and souvenirs and these may also be purchased in the new Damlataş shopping centre.

Alanya's principal beach is on the W side of the promontory, but there is also reasonably good bathing on the eastern outskirts of the town.

History. The site of Alanya was occupied in ancient times by the city of **Coracesium**. Apart from a brief reference in the mid 4C BC *Periplus*, attributed to the geographer known as the Pseudo-Scylax, when Cilicia was ruled by the Persians, nothing is known about Alanya's early history. Its commanding and easily-defensible position almost certainly attracted settlers from the earliest times. Remains of a Hellenistic wall can be seen under the Selçuk fortifications above the town. About 197 BC Coracesium was besieged by Antiochus III of Syria. Later the city became the haunt of pirates. One of them, Diodotus Tryphon, belied his name, which is derived from τρύφή, effeminate or wanton, by wresting it from Antiochus VII. Eventually the activities of the pirates, forced the Romans to intervene. Pompey defeated them in 67 BC in a sea-battle off Coracesium and removed this menace from the Eastern Mediterranean for a considerable time. Later Coracesium and the surrounding area were given to Cleopatra by Antony. This was a valuable gift, as timber from the hinterland, a scarce commodity in Egypt, was used by the Egyptians to build their warships.

Coracesium appears to have had an uneventful life under the Romans. Apart from a few artefacts in the museum, there are no remains from that period in the town. Coracesium was probably visited by Trajan, who died in nearby Gazipaşa in August AD 117. During the Byzantine period the city, an episcopal see under Side, changed its name to Kalonoros, which means 'beautiful mountain' and variants of this continued to be used in Greek and Italian *portolanos* (pilot manuals) long after it had fallen to the Turks.

Following the victory of the Selçuk Turks at the battle of Manzikert in 1071, Kalonoros was occupied by the Armenians, who ceded it to the Selçuk Sultan Alaeddin Keykubad I c 1221. He called the city **Alaiye**, which means 'city of Ala', a name derived from Alaeddin. He also constructed the citadel and its protective walls and a number of other buildings which still survive. Under Keykubad, Alaiye became an important cultural and commercial centre and this continued until the 13C, when the Selçuks were ousted by the Karamanid dynasties. Finally, in 1471 the city was captured by an Ottoman army led by the Grand Vizier of Mehmet the Conqueror.

Alaiye was visited by Ibn Battuta in the middle of the 14C. 'It is inhabited', he wrote, 'by Turkmens, and is visited by the merchants of Cairo, Alexandria and Syria. The district is well-wooded, and wood is exported from there to Alexandria and Damietta, whence it is carried to other cities of Egypt'. Three centuries later Evliya Çelebi found that, although it had lost some of its former grandeur, Aläiye still had many imposing buildings.

One of the first European visitors in modern times was Captain Francis Beaufort, who surveyed the southern coastline of Turkey in 1811/12 for the Admiralty. He received a somewhat mixed reception. A party from his ship, on its way to visit the fortress, was stoned by some boys. Beaufort complained to the Turkish authorities and the culprits were bastinadoed. The city, which he identified correctly as the ancient Coracesium, was in a very run-down condition: 'Its present importance is not great, though capital of a Pashalik: the streets and houses are miserable; there are but few moskes, and they are very mean; there were no signs of commerce; nor can the population exceeded fifteen hundred, or two thousand at the utmost'.

Alanya: the Kızıl Kule, the Red Tower, dates from 1226

One of the most striking monument in Alanya is the **Kızıl Kule**, the Red Tower, which is at the harbour end of İskele Cad. One of the first buildings to be constructed by Sultan Keykubad, it dates from 1226. This simple octagonal structure more than 30m high was designed by a Syrian architect from Aleppo. The parapet has openings from which arrows could be shot and missiles dropped on besiegers. The tower protected the harbour and the lower reaches of the fortifications. It has five floors, each divided into eight sections. The central core is a huge cistern in which sufficient water was stored to sustain the garrison for a long period. Restored in 1951–53, it now houses a collection of ethnographical objects. There is a small admission charge. A flight of steps leads up to the entrance on the S side. The objects on display include a nomad's tent, a loom, kilims, embroidered garments, and some fine examples of wood-carving. The parapet at the top of the tower is reached by open, unprotected, vertiginous stairs. From here there is a magnificent view of the harbour and the town.

To the left of the Kızıl Kule a path leads to the lower fortification walls. Follow a narrow cat-walk for c 200m to the **tersane**, the only remaining Selçuk dockyard in Turkey. In places the walls are broken and it is necessary to descend to ground level. The *tersane* has five vaulted chambers each measuring c 43m by 7.5m. All open directly on the sea. An embrasure provides access to the beach, from where you can enter the building. The two small rooms near the entrance on the N side probably served as stores or offices. To the S of the *tersane* is a large tower, the **tophane** or arsenal. Weapons and ammunition were stored here.

Near the Kızıl Kule a narrow lane, which leads S along the promontory, provides access to the many houses which cling to the precipitous hillside. In ancient times Alanya possessed only one well. This was located near the Red Tower. The inhabitants' needs were met by huge cisterns which stored rain water. Of the 400 that once existed a number are still in use.

From the centre of the old quarter of Alanya a steep unshaded road snakes upwards for c 3km to the great **fortress** constructed by Keykubad on the summit of the promontory. In the early morning it is an undemanding 40 minutes' walk from the town. Taxis may be hired for the single or return journey. There is also an infrequent dolmuş service. If you decide to ride up to the fortress, walk back down. You will be rewarded by a series of fine views of Alanya and the surrounding countryside. Below you a vast stretch of the Cilician coastline, dotted with picturesque villages, banana plantations and citrus groves, recedes into the distance.

About half-way to the top the road passes under a modern arch by the side of a fine **double gate**. For defensive purposes this gate was so constructed that the entrance and exit are at right angles to each other. Inscriptions in Persian date the gate to 1226–31. It was constructed at a point on the lower fortifications which stretch from the Red Tower to the N fortress at Ehmedek. Here the wall needed to be at its strongest and the defences were reinforced by towers, a second wall and a fosse.

In a corner of the fortifications between the outer and inner parts of the citadel is the small 11C Byzantine chapel known as **Arap Evliyası**, the church of the Arab Saint or of the Black Saint. Built on the remains of a Hellenistic tower measuring 6m by 6m, it was carefully preserved and turned into a mosque after the capture of Alanya by the Selçuks.

The road curves upwards towards the İç Kale, the Inner Fortress. Here several courses of ashlar masonry of the Hellenistic wall are visible. The Selçuk fortifications were built on this. If you are not in a hurry, visit **Ehmedek**, the N part of the fortress. This was also a residential area during the Selçuk and early Ottoman periods. Today it is a charming village surrounded by orange groves and olive trees. Turn right at the curve into a narrow lane. Inside the fortified area there is a paved court with cisterns. Stairs lead to three ruined towers which formed part of the Hellenistic defences. A short distance to the S is the **Süleymaniye Mosque**, a plain box-like building with a much repaired minaret. This was built in the 16C on the site of a Selçuk mosque erected during the reign of Alaeddin Keykubad I. Beyond the mosque a **17C han** has been converted into the *Bedesten Hotel*. It retains the traditional shape—a rectangular courtyard surrounded by simply-appointed guest rooms. Nearby there is an early 13C building, known as the **Akşebe Türbesi**, which houses the tomb of a holy man much honoured by local people. Note the rags, votive offering from the faithful, on the trees and bushes around the *türbe*.

A path from Ehmedek ascends to the **İç Kale**. This can also be reached by the road which bypasses Ehmedek. In the parking place in front of the entrance, admission tickets and postcards are sold. Teahouses offer refreshments and a chance to catch your breath. Before entering the İç Kale you may like to examine—from a distance—some ruined structures on the promontory, the **Cılvarda Burnu**, which extends southwards into the sea for c 300m. The nearest is a **tower** which formed part of the ancient defensive system, the second a ruin known as the **Darphane**, the mint, and the third a small **11C Byzantine monastery**. The monastery may be reached, with some difficulty, from the sea, but the other structures are inaccessible to all but the most experienced rock climbers.

Avoiding the importunate vendors of hand-knitted and crocheted table mats who thrust their beautiful products under your nose, enter the Iç Kale. The original entrance was on the E side and it had the customary right-angled bend to delay attackers. Note the painted lozenge decoration high up on the wall inside the modern entrance. The walls enclose a large open space c 180m long, with buildings on all but the W side, where the cliffs drop sheer into the sea.

One of the most striking structures is the small 11C **Byzantine church** dedicated to St George. Sited near the eastern gate, this was built on the ruined apse of a much larger, older church. The dome, with its alternating windows and blind niches, rests on a high drum. Note the faint traces of frescoes on the pendentives, the side walls and the dome. Like the chapel of Arap Evliyası it was converted into a mosque by the Selçuks.

The **vaulted galleries** may have served as barracks. There are several large **cisterns** in the centre, near the modern toilet and washroom.

A platform overlooking a sheer, vertiginous drop into the sea on the W side is known as **Adam Atacağı**, i.e. the place where men are thrown. According to a tradition, condemned prisoners were executed by being helped over the edge. A cynic observed that any who survived the drop were allowed to go free! Another account states that the condemned were given three stones. If they succeeded in pitching one of these into the waves, they were pardoned. If not, they were pushed abruptly into the void—and the next life—by the executioners. In a less dangerous imitation of this gamble with death, modern visitors try to throw stones into the sea. Apparently, nobody has succeeded in doing so yet.

In spite of its violent history, the Iç Kale is now a place of peace and beauty. At sunset the views from the ramparts are spectacular. To the E the sea and the mountains are clothed in a purple, gauzy haze reminiscent of Shelley's Spirit of Night who 'walkd oe'r the western wave' at the approach of darkness. In the west the sun in a great crimson and golden blaze sets behind the high peaks of the Taurus Mountains.

The cave of **Damlataş** on the W side of Alanya is a place of treatment for non-allergic asthma and rheumatism. Its beneficial properties are attributed to high humidity (between 90 and 100 per cent), high temperature (22–23°C), the presence of an unusually high level of carbon dioxide, and to naturally occurring ionisation and radioactivity.

Alanya's **museum**, one of the most attractive in southern Turkey, is near the Tourist Information Office, the Damlataş cave, and the new shopping centre. The collection is displayed in the garden and in two large rooms. One room contains the archaeological exhibits, the other the ethnographical collection. Some of the objects are labelled in English.

In the garden there are some fine ostotheks (cinerary urns), damaged Roman statuary, cannon-balls and Islamic tombstones. The corridor to the first room has a heterogeneous collection from the Hatti and Urartian civilisations, coins from Coracesium, Side, Antalya, etc., ornamented cinerary urns from Alanya, amphorae, and Hellenistic vases. In the large room to the right there are some fine examples of Roman glass, statuettes of stone, some exquisite **terracottas**, stelae, bronzes, anchors, amphorae and pottery recovered from the sea. Note particularly the small 2C AD **bronze statue of Hercules**. He is nude, holds the skin of the Nemean lion in his left hand and a cudgel in his right. A **floor mosaic** from Syedra has a representation of the Three Graces bordered by a hunting scene. There is a **gold treasure** recovered from a tomb at Anamurium and bronze and terracotta lamps from the same site.

The ethnographical collection has carpets, kilims, weapons, Selçuk tiles, manuscripts and inscriptions, coins and clothing. There is also a reconstructed 19C room from a local house.

Alanya is the only place in Turkey where bananas are grown. They are small, sweet and have a distinctive flavour. In season look out for them in the open air market and in fruit and vegetable shops.

29

Alanya to Anamur

Total distance c 108km. Alanya—(c 10km Laertes)—c 22km Syedra—c 13km Iotape—c 9km Gazipaşa—(c 2km Selinus)—(c 3km Antiochia ad Cragum)—c 34km Kalediran—c 30km Anamur (c 6km Anemurium).

In ancient times Alanya (see Route 28) was often referred to as 'the gateway to Cilicia'. This province, once the home of bandits, pirates and brigands, was divided into Cilicia Tracheia, Rough Cilicia, and Cilicia Campestris, Smooth Cilicia. Cilicia Tracheia, the western part of the province, was wild, craggy, and heavily forested and had few settlements of any size. Cilicia Campestris was the large fertile plain watered by the rivers Seyhan and Ceyhan and had cities like Tarsus and Adana. Today little has changed in Rugged Cilicia. The towns are still small and depend largely on fishing and forestry, though tourism is beginning to make an impact.

The road from Alanya to Anamur, a major engineering feat, passes through beautiful scenery. For much of the way it clings to the mountainside and offers spectacular views of the rocky shoreline far below. Motorists may have problems with the narrow carriageway and many sharp bends. Overtaking is rarely easy. The heavy traffic includes slow-moving and heavily-laden vehicles, so care, patience and skill are called for.

Between Alanya and 44km Gazipaşa there are the ruins of four ancient cities: Laertes, Syedra, Iotape and Selinus. They have been surveyed, but have not been excavated. The sites are very overgrown and, with the exception of Iotape, are not particularly easy to reach. They are visited infrequently. This is a pity. Their commanding and beautiful situations and the romantic melancholy of their ruins should attract more of those travellers who are not deterred by a little physical effort and minor discomfort.

Syedra, Iotape, and Selinus are mentioned by geographers of the Classical and Byzantine periods and are listed in the ancient itineraries. Little is known of their individual histories. It is probable they shared the fate of their larger and better-known neighbours. After the arrival of Christianity in Rough Cilicia three of them became episcopal sees. Syedra came under the Metropolitan of Pamphylia, Iotape and Selinus under the Metropolitan of Seleucia. In the 12C and 13C they formed part of the Cilician Kingdom of Lesser Armenia. Later abandoned, they were not resettled when the population of the area increased in recent times.

For much of the way to Gazipaşa the E24 runs near the sea. As far as the turn-off for 25km Belen, there are good, clean beaches of shingle and sand. Banana plantations and citrus groves fill every patch of arable land.

For **Laertes**, turn left c 20km from Alanya in the direction of Mahmutlar. As the site is not easy to find, take a guide. From Mahmutlar follow a road, suitable for four-wheel drive vehicles only, for c 10km in the direction of Hadım Yolu, Eunuch Road. There is no clearly-defined path to the site. A certain amount of scrambling through thick undergrowth over rocky slopes is required. The splendid view over the ancient city and southwards to the sea compensates for the energy expended in getting there.

Laertes main claim to fame is that it was the birthplace and home of Diogenes Laertius (fl. early 3C AD). He was the author of the *Lives and Opinions of Eminent Philosophers*, a work, in ten books, particularly valuable for the information it contains on Epicurus. Diogenes Laertius preserved the epigram of Callimachus on the death of his friend Heracleitus of Halicarnassus (see Bodrum).

Laertes is built on the slopes of Cebelireş, the highest mountain in the region, on a large terraced area. On the N edge there is an underground construction, the so-called '**house of seven doors**', which is believed to have been dedicated to the chthonic gods. Below are the remains of the theatre and a number of cisterns. Beyond the agora and near the terrace, are the ruins of a large building which appears to have been used as a palace and a house at different times.

About 2km farther on are the ruins of ancient **Syedra**. The city was in two parts: one near the modern road, the other some considerable distance away (c 90 minute walk) on the mountain-side. The name Syedra is commemorated by the Sedre Çayı to the E. The city issued coins during the period from Tiberius (AD 14–37) to Gallienus (253–268).

Turn left from the E24 to the **upper city**. Cross a rocky slope covered with thorny scrub. There are several buildings on a large terrace which is flanked by the remains of the fortifications. In one there are three chambers whose walls stand to a height of 10m. Nearby is a house which has traces of wall paintings. A fine mosaic depicting the Three Graces and a hunting scene from Syedra is now in the Alanya Museum.

In the **lower city** there are the remains of a **baths complex** on a hillside 100m W of the road. In the **necropolis** to the E there are many tombs, some of a type found also at Iotape and Selinus. Most are in a ruinous condition. One barrel-vaulted structure with six niches, has traces of fresco on the interior walls. The niches are surrounded with a stucco-like decoration of concrete. There are splendid views.

About 35km from Alanya the E24 passes through the centre of **Iotape**. Founded by Antiochus IV Epiphanes (175–164 BC), it was named after his wife, Iotape Philadelphus. Identified by inscriptions found here, Iotape issued coins from the period of Trajan (AD 98–117) to Valerian (253–260).

Built around a small inlet, the first settlement was almost certainly on the peninsula which overlooks the sea and landward approaches to the city. Later this became the site of the **acropolis**. Apart from a fine temple-tomb (now destroyed), which is believed to have dated from the late Hellenistic period, no pre-Roman remains have been found in Iotape.

Although the site is overgrown, it is possible to examine many of the buildings in the city centre which faced the acropolis. This residential area was bounded on the N by a ravine, on the S by the sea and on the E by the necropolis. Among the buildings here were a **church**, dedicated to Hagios Georgios Stratelates, and two large barrel-vaulted structures. In the necropolis, to the NE of the E24, most of the tombs are in a poor condition. Nearby are the ruins of a **small medieval church** which has traces of frescoes of the Nativity, a number of unidentified saints and some other subjects.

Gazipaşa was formerly known as Selinty, a corruption of Selinus, its old name. This sprawling, dusty, overgrown village, 44km from Alanya, is a market and administrative centre. Buses stop at a restaurant in the centre.

On the western outskirts a road on the right leads to **Selinus**. The ancient city was built on and around a steep headland which towers over the surrounding area. On the summit there was a castle, probably constructed by the Byzantines, but repaired and extended by their Turkish successors. In the early 19C Selinus was visited by Captain Francis Beaufort during the course of a survey of the S Turkish coast which he made for the Admirality. He seems to have been quite taken by Selinus. He writes in *Karamania*:

'The evening was clear and this spot [the castle] afforded a beautiful prospect. We could trace the coast that had been already explored, to an immense distance; the plain, with its winding rivers and ruins, was spread out like a map at our feet; and behind all, a prodigious ridge of mountains, whose black sides, having already lost the evening sun, formed a singular contrast with their snowy tops. We had a distinct view of the island of Cyprus rising from the southern horizon, though not less than seventy miles distant'.

According to Livy, Selinus was captured by Antiochus III in 197 BC. It was probably fortified by Antiochus IV Epiphanes (175–164 BC), when he founded Iotape and Antiochia ad Cragum to protect traders from the pirates and bandits who plagued Cilicia at that time. Evidence that Selinus was occupied during the late Hellenistic period is provided by the remains of a temple tomb, similar to one at Iotape. The city issued coins during the reign of Antiochus IV and under the Romans from Trajan (AD 98–117) to Philip the Arab (244–249). Trajan, exhausted by the rigours of the Parthian campaign, died here in August AD 117. Selinus was known as **Trajanopolis** for sometime thereafter.

Although much of Selinus has been carried away by the river, some ruins described by Beaufort may still be seen. There are a few hundred metres of the **aqueduct** and a **large vaulted Roman structure** which some romantics believe was Trajan's first tomb. On the side of the hill there are the ruins of a structure which was probably a **baths complex**, and of a number of **tombs**. Unlike those in neighbouring cities, many tombs have inscriptions, usually on the lintel. The area has also yielded a large number of cinerary urns, decorated with garlands, masks and bulls or rams' heads.

Near the river there is the outline of an area 80m sq surrounded by a colonnade. A building nearby has been tentatively identified as a small **theatre** or an **odeum**. The line of the ancient **fortifications**, which ran from the castle to the river, may still be traced. The **castle**, surrounded by its protective walls and moats, and the **large church** nearby are not easy to reach, as there is no clearly defined path. The view from the summit is as striking as it was in Beaufort's day.

The E24 begins to climb steadily. Then, in a series of sharp curves, it snakes along the mountain-side far above the sea.

For **Antiochia-ad-Cragum**, look for a turning on the right c 20km after Gazipasa signposted **Güney**. The ruins are not outstanding. However, the beauty of their situation on the clifftop make the diversion worthwhile. To see everything requires about three hours and a good deal of walking. There are many places where one may picnic.

Founded by Antiochus IV Epiphanes (175–164 BC) at about the same time as Iotape, Antiochia issued coins from the time of Antoninus Pius (AD 138–161) to Valerian (253–260). In Byzantine times it was an episcopal see under the jurisdiction of the Metropolitan of Seleucia. Like its neighbours, it was part of the Cilician Kingdom of

Lesser Armenia in the 12C and 13C. In 1332 the Armenians offered the castle to the Knights Hospitallers, as they were no longer able to defend it and it became known as Antiocheta in Rufine (Papal Bull of John XXII) or Antichia Parva.

The ruins of Antiochia are in three distinct areas: the city centre and main necropolis, the W necropolis and the citadel. Güney is built over part of the main necropolis, and little remains to be seen. Note the **two monumental tombs** of a type found also in Iotape and Selinus, and the carved stones from buildings in the ancient city in the walls of some modern houses.

On a terrace to the N of the village there is a large **barrel-vaulted structure** supported by massive buttresses. To the E of this there was a colonnade which led to a terraced area bounded by a ravine. To the N of the colonnade are the ruins of a **triconchos** with a W facing entrance measuring c 8m by 6.5m. Across the ravine is a **baths complex**.

The **western necropolis** is on a small peninsula. As well as a number of fine tombs, there are a well-preserved **medieval chapel** with traces of fresco in a niche on the SW corner, and two cisterns. The **tombs**, which are all located on the S part of the peninsula, date from the Roman period.

The **medieval citadel** is encircled by two walls and is fortified with round and angular towers. At the entrance there is a small **chapel** built into the outer wall. In the central court are another **chapel**, a **tower** and the ruins of an unidentified building. A further group of three small chapels is sited to the W of the citadel.

At 34km from Gazipaşa the E24 reaches sea-level at **Kaledıran**, whose name commemorates ancient **Charadrus**. Described by Strabo as a fortified harbour 'on a rough coast, called Platanistes', it is a sleepy village circled by banana groves and dominated by the ruins of an ancient fortress.

After Kaledıran the road rises again and for a further c 30km continues its tortuous way eastwards, until it descends at last through pine forests to the plain of Anamur.

Silifke and Anamur are the only towns of any size in Rugged Cilicia. **Anamur** derives its name from ἄνεμος, the Greek word for wind. Appropriately, it is a breezy place where dust devils rise without warning. There is little to see in Anamur, but it is surrounded by places of interest: the medieval castle, Mamure Kalesi; a number of caves and grottoes; and the ruins of the ancient city of Anemurium. A museum, long-promised, has been opened in İskele. Most of the finds from Anemurium have been placed here. There are a few in the Antalya and Alanya museums.

Information, Transport and Accommodation. The **Tourist Information Office**, post office, banks and shops are in the main street. There are several restaurants near the main square. Dolmuş services leave from the town-centre.

Many private houses in Anamur provide simple, clean, cheap accommodation. Ask at the *otogar* or Tourist Information Office for details. In summer select a room that has effective mosquito-screens on the windows, as the marshes around Anamur produce a a particularly vicious breed of mosquitoes. One two-star and one one-star hotel are listed in the Ministry of Tourism booklet. There are several pensions. The comfortable, air-conditioned *Hotel Hermes* is on the coast at İskele, 3km to the S. This, the two-star *Anahan Oteli*, the small *Karan Motel* and the *Star Sonarex Motel* are recommended. The motels are c 7km to the E and are within walking distance of Mamure Kalesi. The Karan Motel has its own private beach and a small restaurant. The Star Sonarex Motel has a reputation for good cooking. Long-distance buses stop near the motels and there is a somewhat infrequent dolmuş service to and from Anamur.

Ancient **ANEMURIUM**, c 6km to the SW, is reached by taking the Alanya road for c 4km and by turning left on to a minor road. The most southerly city in Anatolia, Anemurium has been surveyed and partly excavated by archaeologists from the universities of Toronto and British Columbia. Restoration, where undertaken, has been limited to preventing further deterioration of the better-preserved structures.

There is a good beach at Anemurium and the sea is free from pollution. There are no cafés or restaurants but many spots where one may picnic.

History. Because of its favourable situation, Anemurium almost certainly attracted settlers from the earliest times. Sheltered from the prevailing SW winds, only 65km from Cyprus, it must have benefited also from its proximity to the large fertile plain to the E. Although there are references to Anemurium by ancient writers as early as the 4C BC, the visible ruins date from the late Roman, the Byzantine and the medieval periods.

According to Livy, Antiochus III passed near the city in 197 BC on his way to the siege and capture of Selinus. When Anemurium was attacked by tribes from the interior in AD 52, the last Commagene king, Antiochus IV, who ruled the Cilician coastal area at that time, came to the rescue. Anemurium issued coins during his reign and in the Roman Imperial period from Titus (AD 79–81) to Valerian (253–260). It was during the early Roman period, the 1C and 2C AD, that Anemurium, described by Professor Russell, who has directed the excavations at Anemurium since 1971, as a 'modest market centre in a relatively isolated corner of the ancient world', reached its apogee. This prosperity was ended abruptly c AD 260, when Cilicia was invaded by the Persians. Although their stay was comparatively short, further raids by Isaurian tribes from the interior continued to disturb the peace of the city. This necessitated the construction of a new defensive system which was completed in the late 4C.

Sometime after the arrival of Christianity in Cilicia, Anemurium became an episcopal see under the Metropolitan of Seleucia. Emphasis switched from the construction of public buildings to churches and several were erected. During the 5C and 6C Anemurium's bishops took part in a number of church councils. Like their neighbours in Isauria, the Anemurians were Monophysites. The Monophysite heresy troubled orthodox Christianity for several centuries and is still accepted by the Coptic, Armenian and Ethiopian churches. This denies the humanity of Christ, teaching that He has one nature, the divine, only.

During the early Byzantine era Anemurium had a further period of quiet prosperity. This ended suddenly c 580. The city was devastated by an earthquake from which it never recovered entirely. The situation was made worse by a further Persian invasion between 610–630 and the arrival of the Arabs in Cyprus in 650. Frequent attacks by the Arabs caused Anemurium to be abandoned finally in the middle of the 7C. Its population moved to a safer and less vulnerable area. Part of the site was re-occupied in the 12C and 13C, when Cilicia was part of the kingdom of Armenia. However, the successors of the Armenians, the Selçuk Karamanoğlu, appear to have ignored Anemurium. They concentrated their attention on the plain to the E, where they constructed Mamure Kalesi. Anemurium became a forgotten city, unknown and neglected until Beaufort and other 19C travellers visited it and wrote about its ruins.

The buildings of Anemurium were constructed from limestone rubble which was probably covered with marble inlay and stucco. This decorative veneer disappeared a long time ago, so that even in bright sunshine the ruins have a strange, grey, ghostly appearance. The site is large and widely spread. For a small consideration the *bekçi* will be your guide. He will also open the tombs which have the best-preserved mosaics and frescoes.

You approach Anemurium through an extensive necropolis which was in use for many centuries. The tombs range from simple barrel-vaulted chambers to large two-storey constructions. A good deal of information has been gleaned about the Anemurians and their way of life from the decoration and furnishing.

Beaufort was impressed by the necropolis:

> We hastened to examine a wide field of ruins outside the walls, which had appeared from the top of the cape like the remains of a large city. It was indeed a city, but a city of tombs, a true Necropolis. The contrast between the slight and perishable

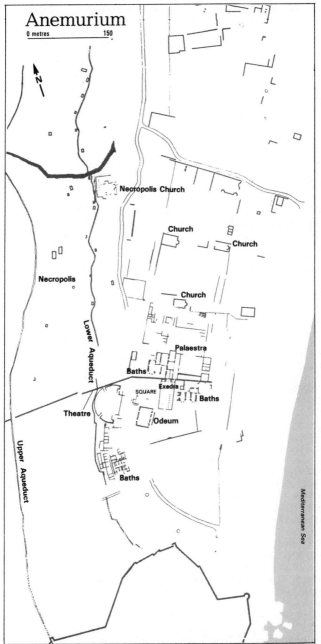

Anemurium

0 metres   150

N

Necropolis Church

Church

Church

Church

Necropolis

Lower Aqueduct

Palaestra

Baths

Exedra

SQUARE

Baths

Theatre

Odeum

Upper Aqueduct

Baths

Mediterranean Sea

materials with which the habitations of the living were constructed, and the care and skill which the antients employed to render durable the abodes of the dead, is more than ordinarily impressed upon the mind at this place; for though all the tombs have been long since opened and ransacked, the walls are still sound; whereas of their dwellings not one continues in existence.

Most tombs were divided into two parts, an inner chamber where the dead were laid, and an ante-room used by relatives and friends, when they came to pray and make offerings to the deceased. Many of the ante-rooms had mosaic pavements and their walls were decorated with geometric patterns or pictures of flowers, birds, animals and sometimes erotes. A **tomb**, which is a short distance from the lower aqueduct, has a vault painted with representations of the four seasons. Hermes in his role as Psychopompus, the conductor of souls, is depicted on one of the walls. The Anemurians appear to have adopted a very philosophical attitude towards death. Professor Russell describes a tomb which has a fresco of the deceased couple and the laconic inscription, ὁ Βίος ταυτα, 'That's life'.

On the northern edge of the necropolis are the ruins of **church A II.1**. According to an inscription recording the gifts of Flavius Valerius, a protector, this was built in the late 4C on the remains of a Roman building. In the following century it was replaced by a larger structure in basilical form. Cathecumens, who were not admitted to the main part of the church until they had been baptised, were able to follow the services from an extension to the N aisle which had a baptistery at its E end. Like the earlier church, the basilica was decorated with **mosaics**. On the floor in front of the apse there is a roughly-executed representation of a leopard and kid flanking a palm tree, accompanied by a quotation from Isaiah 11.6: 'And a little child will lead them and the leopard will lie down with the kid'. There was an earlier floor underneath the mosaic.

Anemurium had two aqueducts—stone-lined channels cut into the hillside and carried on arches over small ravines. The upper aqueduct supplied the citadel.

To the left of the road, just outside the city walls, are the ruins of a large 3C AD **baths complex**. This rested on a platform facing a **palaestra**. The total area was c 1000 sq m. The palaestra, whose surface was covered with **geometric mosaics**, was surrounded by colonnades on three sides. The baths, which tried to emulate the bath complexes in other cities of the Roman province of Asia, betrayed their provincial ethos by the homely exhortation, 'Have a good bath', at the entrance, and, 'You have had a good bath', at the exit! To the N of the colonnade was a **triconchos** with apses on the N, E and S walls and an entrance on the W side.

In Byzantine times, when the city fortunes were in decline, a shortage of wood for heating and water-supply problems produced a drastic change in the baths and palaestra. The palaestra was turned into a **market** and a number of small, poorly-constructed **houses** were built on its N side. The great halls of the baths were used for trades like flour milling, lime burning, and as potteries. Smaller baths, more in keeping with Anemurium's straitened circumstances, were built in other parts of the city.

The **theatre** was on the S side of the city wall. Partly cut out of the hillside, its cavea, 60m in diameter, may still be distinguished. All the seats have disappeared. Beaufort surmised that these and other building material were taken to Cyprus, 'where art and commerce flourished long after this coast had become the prey of a succession of ruffian conquerors'.

Below the road are the ruins of a building which has been identified as an **odeum** or **bouleuterion**. This is 30m long by 20m wide and still has six rows of seats. It was probably roofed.

The best-preserved building in Anemurium—another large **baths complex**—was begun in the 3C AD. A covered stairs, with 30 steps, leads up to the entrance on the N side. Most of the vaults are intact. Fragments of decoration and mosaics from various periods have been found here.

Many of the floors in the private houses in Anemurium were decorated with **mosaics**. These include a **winged Victory** bearing a palm-branch, a representation of **Hermes**, and another of **Thetis** surrounded by sea creatures. Ask the *Bekçi* to remove the sand which protects them.

If you are not in a hurry, climb up to the **citadel** for the sake of the view from this the southernmost point of Anatolia. You should be able to see Cyprus on a clear day. The citadel was surrounded by a wall which was fortified with towers and had angled recesses. Most of the enclosed area was not inhabited. On the summit there are some ruins from the medieval period. Note in particular a **small church** and a **tower** at the intersection of the upper aqueduct and the defensive wall.

A popular **excursion** from Anamur is to **Köşekbükü Mağarası**. These caves, which are c 15km from the town, are reached via **Kalın Ören** where there are the unexcavated ruins of a Byzantine city. Leave by a street on the left just before the post office and then continue on the main road through a pleasant forested area.

As there is no fixed rate for the journey by taxi to the caves, agree this with the driver before departure. There is a small café near the caves, where light refreshments are sold. The caves have a constant temperature of 27°C. They are believed to benefit asthmatics and infertile women.

30

Anamur to Silifke

Total distance c 121km. Anamur—c 7km Mamure Kalesi—(c 1.5km Softa Kalesi)—c 50km Aydıncık—c 51km Boğsak—15km Taşucu—8km Silifke.

The road between Softa Kalesi and Taşucu—an outstanding engineering feat—progresses in a series of sharp curves over vertiginous drops. It demands very careful driving. The main E–W road, it is always busy and is used by heavily-laden and, sometimes very slow-moving, lorries.

On leaving Anamur (see Route 29) you cross a broad plain, returning to the coastline once more at c 7km **Mamure Kalesi**. This striking building, on the right hand side of the road, is one of the finest medieval castles in southern Turkey. Its crenellated walls strengthened by towers—dodecagonal, square, octagonal, and round—stand to their original height. Surrounded by a shallow moat, which is half-filled with the silt and detritus of centuries, the castle still dominates the eastern sea and land approaches to Anamur.

History. A fortress of some kind has stood here since the 3C AD. An earlier building, enlarged and extended by the Byzantines and the rulers of the Cilician kingdom of Armenia, was reduced almost to the ground by the Selçuk sultan, Alaeddin Keykubad when he built the present castle in the 13C. An inscription over the principal entrance, now walled up, on the W side of the building, refers to this refoundation. The castle was later occupied by the Karamanoğlu dynasty, whose members made further alterations to the structure. In the 16C Mamure Kalesi was captured by the Ottomans. It remained in use until the last days of the empire.

When visited by Beaufort in 1811–12 the castle was in a semi-ruinous condition. Substantial repairs and restorations were made to it in the middle of the 19C. Beaufort received a cordial welcome from the *Bey*, Abdul Muim, who ruled the area, and was allowed to make a detailed examination of the castle. The *Bey*, accompanied by some of his retainers, came down to the shore and spent several hours observing Beaufort's ship with the aid of a pocket telescope. However, fearing the long sea swell, he could not be tempted to board HMS *Frederikssteen*.

Mamure Kalesi's era of martial splendour finished long ago. Today the castle echoes, not to the sounds of battle, but to the cries of the amorous frogs which populate the moat. Boys play football in the great court and girls from the nearby village, weaving graceful patterns in the air with their spindles, watch over grazing cattle. In this bucolic setting only the thunder of the waves against the great sea-walls remind one of the battles, assaults and sieges that marked Mamure Kalesi's turbulent past.

Admission tickets are sold at the modern entrance on the E side of the castle. You will need a torch to explore the towers and storerooms. There are no refreshment facilities or toilets in the castle. Tea, coffee and soft drinks are available in nearby coffee-houses. The *Karan Motel* and the *Star Sonarex Motel* are c 1km to the E. There is a good, clean, uncrowded beach near the castle.

A passage, whose bends and curves were designed to aid the defence, leads to the **towers** on the E side. These give a fine view over the surrounding land- and seascape. The **principal court** is divided by a partially-demolished wall. Near the centre there is a much restored **mosque**. Beyond, to the W, were the quarters of the castle's commander. It is possible to walk around the greater part of the ramparts, but care should be taken on the W side which is in a ruinous condition. The large **vaulted chambers** under the ramparts were used as storerooms or arsenals.

Across the road there are the ruins of **Ottoman baths**. These are very overgrown and, if one believes local gossip, infested with snakes.

Approximately 1km to the E of the Karan Motel there is a **picnic area** among the pine trees to the right of the road. Nearby is a small, clean beach of coarse sand and pebbles.

On the summit of a rocky pinnacle, c 10km from Mamure Kalesi, are the ruins of **Softa Kalesi**, the 'Castle of the Fanatics'. The stronghold of bandits, it was replaced with a guard-post by the Romans during their drive to suppress brigandage in Cilicia. The structure visible today was constructed by the Byzantines and restored and extended later by the Armenians and the Turks. The castle is not easy to reach. Within its walls there is little to see apart from a number of cisterns and the ruins of medieval baths.

An inscription from the reign of Ptolemy II Philadelphus and Arsinoe II (285–246 BC) has been found at Softa Kalesi. This provided information about a 3C BC **Ptolemaic settlement** here and about Ptolemaic interest in this part of southern Anatolia. The area occupied by the settlement previously belonged to the small city of **Nagidus** which was on the peninsula of Boz Yazı.

For c 40km the E24 continues its spectacular course high above the sea. It descends to the pretty little village of **Aydıncık**, the site of the Samian colony of **Celendris**, founded in the 5C BC. Its ruins are near the village. Recent excavations here have laid bare a fine 4C **church mosaic** in *opus sectile* and a number of **tombs**. These include a distinctive local type which were built to a square plan with a high podium, corner columns and a steep, pyramidal roof. In 5C and 4C BC **rock tombs** in the W cemetery the archaeologists found Attic white ground and red figure lekyhthoi. In 1974 a hoard of 65 gold coins was discovered at Celendris. These included octadrachms of Arsinoe II and octadrachms or tetradrachms of Ptolemy II and Arsinoe II. The latest dated from 261–60 BC. The hoard was probably buried during the Second Syrian War of 261–56.

Aydıncık is a pleasant place to break your journey. There are several restaurants which specialise in fish, notably *Le Pécheur* and *Arsinoe*, on the seashore. There are also secluded corners on the beach where you could picnic. Basic accommodation is available at budget prices.

Between Aydıncık and c 66km Taşucu the E24 crosses the base of Cape Cavaliere, now called Ovacık Burnu, and then, entering a relatively fertile area, continues to the eastern part of Rugged Cilicia.

The hamlet of **Boğsak**, on the northern shore of a crescent-shaped bay, is an enticing alternative to Taşucu which is c 15km to the E. It has a motel within a few metres of the sandy beach and some inexpensive restaurants. As there are relatively few long-distance buses and local dolmuş services on this stretch of the E24, Boğsak will be of interest mainly to those who have their own transport.

Offshore is **Provençal Island**, so called because it was occupied in the 12C and 13C by the Provençal division of the Knights' Hospitallers of St John. The Knights were divided into eight groups, of which the first was known as the Langue de Provence. After the fall of Jerusalem in 1290, they moved to Cyprus and also took possession of Rhodes and of a number of castles on the coast of Asia Minor. These served as advanced posts on the fringes of Muslim territory and also provided refuges for escaped Christian slaves. Provençal Island, which has high cliffs on the seaward side, is covered with the ruins of houses, churches and cemeteries. On its summit there are the remains of a citadel. There are no springs, but a number of ruined cisterns have been found.

On the promontory to the E of Boğsak is the 14C Turkish castle of **Liman Kalesi**. From here the E24 follows the coastline closely, passing the ruins of two small **medieval churches**. There are several good beaches within a few metres of the road, but not many safe parking places.

Taşucu, the port of Silifke, is a nondescript, characterless, semi-industrialised place. It has a number of modern hotels and expensive restaurants on a strip development which runs parallel to the main road. There is a daytime ferryboat service to Girne, Kyrenia, in the Turkish Federated Republic of Northern Cyprus. Details of fares and timetables may be obtained from the Tourist Information Offices in Silifke and Mersin.

SİLİFKE is a sprawling town built along the banks of the Göksu, the ancient Calycadnus. From early times there was a settlement here at the junction of the road along the southern coastline and a road over the Taurus Mountains to the centre of Anatolia.

Information and Accommodation. The **Tourist Information Office**, on the N side of the bridge at the corner of Atatürk Cad., is one of the most efficient in Turkey. The staff deal very capably with enquiries in a variety of languages. They have produced useful booklets about Silifke and its environs in English, French and German.

There are courses in Turkish for foreigners in Silifke and an international music and folklore festival in May; details may be obtained from the Tourist Information Office.

Silifke has a number of modest hotels and pensions, but many visitors prefer to stay by the sea at **Taşucu**, 8km to the W, or at c 15km **Susanoğlu** and c 27km **Kızkalesi** to the E. Reserve accommodation well in advance, particularly during summer.

There are several inexpensive restaurants in Silifke. The *Piknik* in İnönü Cad. in the town centre and the *Babaoğlu* near the *otogar* are recommended.

The post office is on the S bank of the Göksu. Nearby, in the town's main shopping area there are branches of the principal Turkish banks.

Transport. There is a frequent bus-service between Silifke and Taşucu from a stop near the post office. Long-distance buses and dolmuş services from the *otogar* call at Susanoğlu and Kızkalesi.

History. Silifke, the ancient **Seleucia ad Calycadnum**, is named after its founder, Seleucus I Nicator (321–280 BC), one of the diadochoi and first king of the Seleucid dynasty of Syria. Anxious to emphasise the family connection with his new kingdom, he was a prodigal creator of cities named after himself and his relatives. In *Syriaca* the Roman historian Appianus of Alexandria (fl. c AD 160) states that Seleucus founded 16 Antiochs named after his father, Antiochus, five Laodiceas named after his mother, four cities in honour of his wives and nine which bore his own name.

Seleucia ad Calycadnum replaced an earlier Greek settlement founded in the 7C BC. What little is known of its history has been gleaned from events in Cilicia. It enjoyed a period of prosperity under the Romans. From the earliest days of Christianity it was associated with the new religion. St Thecla found sanctuary here.

Later the city came under the control of the Isaurians, a wild tribe from the mountainous interior, which later provided two emperors, Zeno (474–491) and Leo III (717–741). Although raided frequently by Arab pirates from Cyprus, it continued to be an important embarkation point for Christian pilgrims on their way to the Holy Land.

In the 12C Silifke was the scene of an event which had a dramatic effect on the Third Crusade. The Emperor Frederick Barbarossa, who had set out from Germany in May 1189 at the head of a great army to liberate the Holy Land from the Saracens, drowned near Silifke on 10 June 1190 in the swift, deep waters of the river Saleph, now the Göksu. The are conflicting stories about the way in which he met his death. Some accounts state that the day was warm and that the emperor was swimming in the river, when suddenly he cried out for help and disappeared. Although his knights rushed to the rescue, when they brought him to the bank he was dead. Other chroniclers suggest that he may have fallen from his horse into the water. A man in his late sixties, he was unable to swim to safety because of the weight of his armour. Whatever the cause, the untimely death of Barbarossa had disastrous consequences for the great enterprise which he had undertaken. A part of the army, which had left Germany so proudly a year before, managed to struggle home. A few soldiers went on to the Holy Land. The rest perished from plague or were slaughtered by the Turks.

After a brief period under the kings of Lesser Armenia, Silifke passed into the hands of the Selçuk Turks. In turn they were dispossessed by the Karamanoğlu. Finally, in 1471 the city and its fortress were captured for the Ottomans by Gedik Ahmet Paşa.

During the centuries that followed, Silifke declined in importance. By the 19C it had only a handful of inhabitants. Recent years have been marked by a revival in its fortunes brought about by the growth of trade, agriculture and, latterly, by tourism.

Silifke's **museum** is on the outskirts of the town on the road to Taşucu. On the ground floor there is a fine collection of **Persian and Byzantine coins** found in the area. Note, in particular, the **daric** struck during the reign of Darius. There is also an interesting display of **statues**, most of which date from the Roman period. Upstairs is exhibited the **Gülnar hoard**, 5215 mainly Ptolemaic silver coins minted during the 4C and 3C BC (see Gülnar). There are several small bronzes, which were found in the town near the temple of Zeus, and a number of statuettes dating from the 3C and 4C BC.

The museum also has a large ethnographical collection. Statues and sarcophagi are displayed in the garden. These include the headless, but otherwise almost complete, statue of a Roman emperor or general discovered behind the temple of Zeus.

Little of Silifke's past remains. The bridge across the Göksu, erected by L. Octavius Memor in honour of Vespasian and Titus and Domitian in AD 77–78, was replaced by the present structure at the end of the 19C.

In İnönü Cad. are the ruins of the impressive 2C AD **temple of Zeus**. This was a peripteros with 8 by 14 columns in the Corinthian style. The one fluted column still standing now supports a stork's nest each spring. The area S of the temple is still being excavated. Some fine **mosaic pavements**

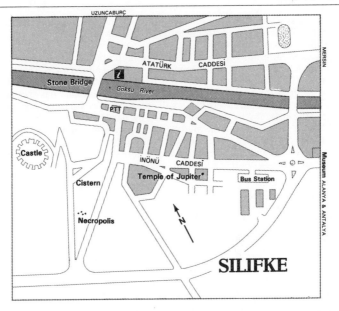

UZUNCABURÇ

ATATÜRK CADDESİ

Stone Bridge

Goksu River

PTT

MERSIN

Castle

İNÖNÜ CADDESİ

Cistern

Temple of Jupiter°

Bus Station

Necropolis

N

Museum ALANYA & ANTALYA

SILIFKE

depicting the Four Seasons and other subjects are covered with sand for
their protection. A Roman statue found here is in the garden of the museum.

Silifke's **Ulu Cami** dates from the Selçuk period. The roof is supported by
three arches. A dome covers the area in front of the *mihrab*. The *mihrab*
and the entrance are the oldest parts of the building.

The hill above the town was almost certainly fortified from the earliest
times. The Byzantines constructed a fortress here in the 7C during the Arab
raids. The present structure dates from the 12C. Occupied in turn by the
Armenians and the Crusaders, it was captured by the Karamanoğlu by
trickery towards the end of the 13C. Disguising themselves as Christian
merchants, they infiltrated the keep and overcame the defenders. At the
end of the 15C it fell to the Ottomans.

It is an easy walk from the town to the **castle** which is c 180m above
sea-level. Surrounded by a double wall, entrance was by a huge gateway
which had a right-angled bend to impede attackers equipped with siege-
engines. This was further strengthened by the addition of an iron door in
the 15C. Covering an area c 345m by 95m the castle is in a ruinous
condition. Take care when walking in or over the vaulted chambers and in
exploring the ramparts. The great breach in the E wall, which provides
access today, was made during the Ottoman attack in the 15C.

There are excellent views over Silifke and the surrounding countryside
from the ramparts. Restaurants near the castle offer simple dishes.

At the foot of the castle, a short distance to the SE, is a large Byzantine
cistern which supplied the upper part of the town with water. Known
popularly as *Tekirambarı*, the 'striped granary', it is 46m long, 23m wide
and 12m high. The courageous descend into its depths by a spiral staircase.

Silifke's **necropolis** was by the side of the road from Silifke to Mut and
Konya. Many of the tombs and tombstones have inscriptions and reliefs.
More elaborate funerary monuments are in the hills around the town.

The most interesting way to **Ayatekla** is by the ancient **pilgrims' road** from the S of the town. Partly cut through the rock, this climbs gradually to the hill of c 1km **Meryemlik**.

The most striking feature at Meryemlik is the huge ruined apse of the **basilica** which was built by the Emperor Zeno the Isaurian c 476. The **grotto** where St Thecla lived is a few metres to the N. If locked, the key may be obtained from the *bekçi* who lives in the village. The basilica was excavated a few years ago. There were two small chapels, which had altars, on either side of the apse. On the W there was a narrow narthex and on the S a gallery. The walls were lined with marble, the floors were of mosaic and the building was covered with a wooden roof.

Scattered around the summit of the hill are the scant remains of many other structures—churches, hostels, cisterns and monasteries.

St Thecla was a friend and follower of St Paul. Born in Iconium, the modern Konya, she was imprisoned and tortured for her faith. Fleeing to Silifke, she built a grotto at Meryemlik. Because of the many cures attributed to her, Thecla's fame spread rapidly and contributed to the growth of Christianity in the area. Some accounts state that she lived to a ripe old age, others that she was slain by marauders. She was buried in the grotto where she had lived and prayed.

Her life is told in the apocryphal *Acts of Paul and Thecla* which was written in the 2C. Described as a member of a noble family, she is said to have broken off her engagement and, dressed as a youth, to have attached herself to St Paul. Lions, sent to devour her in the arena, lay at her feet and, when her torturers attempted to burn her to death, the fire could not be lit. St Thecla's feast day is 23 September.

SW, not far from the town of **Gülnar**, is **Meydancık Kale**. This is a pleasant 75km drive from Silifke. The castle is at the village of **Emir Hacı**, c 9km to the S of Gülnar. French archaeologists working here since 1970 have discovered remains from the Hittite occupation (second millennium BC) to the Byzantine era. Because of its strategic position Meydancık Kale controlled the trade routes between the sea and the mountains and access to the timber resources of the interior. The earliest occupation of the fortress, which is on a hill linked to the plateau by a ridge, has been dated by a cartouche found here to the time of the Hittite king, Muwattali (c 1300 BC). There are several stelae and orthostats, much eroded, from that era. Artefacts from many periods have been found in the spoil-heap at the base of the cliff.

According to an inscription discovered on the site, the Aramaic name of the settlement was KRS. This has been identified with Kirşi or Kurşu which, according to the Neo-Babylonian chronicle of the campaign of Neriglissar in 557–56 BC, was the original home of the Cilician royal dynasty of Appuasu king of Pirindu.

Near the road are the ruins of a **Persian palace** which may have been occupied by the satrap appointed by the Great King as ruler of Cilicia. Reliefs and inscriptions in Aramaic suggest that it dates from the Achaemenid period (6C BC). On one relief there is the introductory formula of a law promulgated by one of the three Persian kings called Artaxerxes. An early use of architectural caryatids occurs in a 6C BC built tomb found on the E side of the site. This bears some resemblence to the royal tombs of Tamassos in Cyprus. Still awaiting the archaeologists' spade are the ruins of a Hellenistic city which covers almost the whole surface of the plateau.

Meas of Aspendus dedicated a gymnasium here in honour of Ptolemy III Eurgetes (246–222 BC), Berenice III, and their children. Meas played an important part in the establishment of Arsinoe (see above). On the acropolis a huge hoard of 5215 mainly Ptolemaic silver coins issued between 330–220

BC was found hidden in a public building which may have been the treasury of a Lagid garrison. The coins are now in the Silifke museum.

The remains from the period of Byzantine occupation are numerous, but less interesting than those from earlier times.

Nearer to Silifke is the place where, it is is believed, Frederick Barbarossa drowned (see above and Route 31). This is c 7km from the town, on the road to Konya. A plaque commemorates this tragic event.

31

Silifke to Konya

Total distance c 252km. Silifke—c 7km Barbarossa Memorial—c 76km Mut—(c 2km Alahan)—c 70km Karaman—(c 12km Canhasan)—(c 38km Binbir Kilise)—(c 26km Çatalhöyük)—c 109km Konya.

Road 715 from Silifke to Konya is one of the most interesting and most beautiful in Turkey. In geographic terms it takes you from the fertile plains by the Mediterranean, over the high passes of the Taurus Mountains, to the wide, featureless steppe of Central Anatolia. Historically, it is a journey through ancient Karamania, that microcosm of Turkish history. The Neolithic inhabitants of Canhasan and Çatalhöyük, the Byzantines, the Crusaders, the Karamanids, the Selçuk and Ottoman Turks, all have left their settlements and monuments scattered across its landscape. Karamania is a palimpsest from which the history of many cultures may be read.

The route starts under the high battlements of Silifke's medieval castle (see above). At first it follows the course of the Göksu river. Then in the depths of a stony gorge it begins a steady climb through the pine woods that clothe the southern slopes of the Taurus range.

About 7km from Silifke in a car-park on the right-hand side of the road a simple plaque records, in Turkish, that on 10 June 1190, somewhere near this place, the Emperor Frederick Barbarossa was drowned in the Saleph river, now the Göksu Çayı.

Frederick's followers were demoralised. 'At this point and at this sad news', one wrote, 'our pen is stilled, and our story finished.' His body, pickled in a vat of vinegar, was taken to Antioch where it was buried in the cathedral. The German knights carried a few of his bones to the Holy Land which he had sworn to liberate and which he was destined never to see.

From the oppressive Göksu gorge, bounded by sheer cliffs and jagged peaks, Road 715 emerges at last into an upland valley, whose austere aspect presages the arid steppes that lie beyond. At 76km **Mut**, the ancient Claudiopolis, is the first sizeable town on this road. A coffee-house, pleasantly shaded by a cluster of huge plane trees, provides an excellent excuse for a stop. From one of its tables the traveller may survey, under the tolerant gaze of its regular clients, the leisurely daily life of the town.

Founded towards the middle of the 1C AD by Marcus Aurelius Polemo, high priest of nearby Olba, Mut's principal monuments are two **türbeler** and the 14C Karamanid Lal Ağa Camii. The mid 14C **Hocendi türbe** has a high pyramidal roof over a squat polygonal chamber. The slim, graceful minaret of the **Lal Ağa Camii** adjoins a monumental entrance porch. The domed prayer room is flanked by two aisle-like recesses. Mut's romantic, decayed **fortress**, with ruined walls and imposing keep, was built by the Byzantines and enlarged and extended by the Karamanids in the 14C.

From Mut, Road 715 continues towards Konya, its many curves taxing the concentration and skill of even the most experienced drivers. A signpost on the right-hand side, near a small coffee-house, c 20km N of Mut, points to 2km **Alahan**. Here, perched on a rocky shelf high over the Göksu, are the ruins of an interesting **Byzantine monastery**. This was first investigated in 1961 by Michael Gough, at that time Director of the British Institute of Archaeology at Ankara. His wife, Mary Gough, has published *Alahan. An Early Christian Monastery in Southern Turkey*, a description of the architecture and the finds made in the monastery.

The monastery had two churches. The **Church of the Evangelists** (end of the 5C), has suffered a considerable amount of damage. Originally this building had three naves separated by rows of Corinthian columns, but it was modified later. Note the carving over the main door, the symbols of the Four Evangelists, and representations of the triumph of the angels Gabriel and Michael over Mithraism and the worship of Cybele.

Beyond the ruins of the **baptistery** is the so-called **East church**, which is in a better state of preservation. Dated to the beginning of the 6C, this was also constructed in basilical form. Note the fine sculptures adorning the doors leading from the narthex to the interior and the slender pillars which supported the roof. The refectory, kitchens, and the monks' cells, which were cut out of the soft rock, are well preserved.

After Alahan the road reaches its highest point (1610m) at the Sertavul Geç and descends by stages into the great steppe of central Anatolia. In this wild and forlorn land often the only sign of life is provided by an occasional flock of sheep or goats. The grazing animals are watched over by a patriarchal shepherd, a lonely hierarch in a tent-like cloak, whose acolytes, fierce, vigilant guard-dogs circle the flock ceaselessly.

Karaman, at c 48km, is a pleasant oasis of green which provides a welcome relief from the monotonous grey and brown colours of the steppe. Formerly the Byzantine fortress of Laranda, it was founded in the 4C BC. It has a single hotel on the Ministry of Tourism list, the one-star *Nas Oteli*, İsmetpaşa Cad. No.2. The **Tourist Information Office** is in Eski Buğday Pazarı, Şimşek Apt. C Blok Kat 2, No.39.

From early times its commanding position allowed Karaman to control trade between the coast and the interior. It fell to the Selçuk Turks after the battle of Manzikert in 1071, but shortly after was taken by the Danishmendids. Subsequently, it was held by the Selçuks, the Crusaders, the Armenians, the Selçuks again and the Karamanids. Frederick Barbarossa occupied it briefly on his way S to the Mediterranean and his death. The town's name is derived from the Karamanids. They founded an emirate which dominated this part of Anatolia—Karamania—for almost 250 years.

Most of Karaman's monuments date from the emirate. The **Yunus Emre Camii**, which was constructed c 1349, is named after a famous peasant poet. It claims to contain his remains. A line written by Yunus Emre, 'I love you, so the hand of death can never touch me', is still quoted frequently.

Around the **fortress**, which was built in the 12C by the Selçuks and restored by the Karamanids c 1356, there are a number of mosques, tombs and religious buildings. Visit the late 14C **Hatuniye Medresesi**, the early 15C **İbrahim Bey İmareti** and the late 14C **Ak Tekke**. The latter housed a community of Mevlevi dervishes until the order was abolished in 1925. Here are the simply furnished cells where the dervishes lived a life of prayer and contemplation. In the precincts of the tekke there are the tombs of several members of the family of Jalal ad-Din ar-Rumi, the founder of the Mevlevi order.

Karaman's small **museum** is to the S of the Hatuniye Medrese. This has artefacts found in the town and in sites in the surrounding countryside including Canhasan. There are objects from the prehistoric, Roman, Byzantine, Selçuk and Karamanid periods and also an interesting ethnographic collection.

About 13km to the NE of Karaman is the Chalcolithic site of **Canhasan**. Excavations between 1961 and 1970 revealed traces of occupation dating from the end of the sixth millennium BC.

A strong resemblance has been noted between some of the pottery from Canhasan and that found in certain layers of Yümüktepe near Mersin. Both have distinctive reddish brown geometric patterns. As Canhasan was near the route which linked Central Anatolia with the Mediterranean at Çukurova, some believe that the pottery found here may have been brought from Yümüktepe.

Apart from the thick mud-brick walls of the rectangular or square houses, which stand to a height of c 3m in places, little remains at the site. Most of the objects found here are now in the Museum of Anatolian Civilisations in Ankara and in Karaman's museum. In addition to bulbous polychrome and monotone pots, these include stone and clay figures of the Anatolian Mother Goddess, a necklace of stone beads and sea shells, millstones, and some fragmentary wall-paintings.

A difficult, but worthwhile, **excursion** is to **Binbir Kilise**, the Thousand and One Churches, a monastic site on the lower slopes of Kara Dağ near the hamlet of Maden Şehir, c 38km to the N of Karaman. From Maden Şehir, which is reached via 18km Kılbasan and c 10km Dınek, a very rough track leads to the remote valley where the churches are located.

The earliest occupation of the site, first investigated by Gertrude Bell and Sir William Ramsey in 1905, dates from the 4C BC. This was a small, unfortified settlement at the foot of a steep hill. It was established during the Hellenistic period. Occupied during Roman and Byzantine times, it was abandoned by most of its inhabitants towards the end of the 7C AD, when bands of marauding Arabs swept over southern Anatolia. By the 5C and 6C some monasteries had been established here and in the middle of the 9C, after the power of the Arabs had been curbed, the area was re-occupied. A feverish bout of church building commenced. Most of the churches and monastic foundations in the valley were erected during the next 200 years. Today only the shells survive. Some of the walls have traces of frescoes. Architecturally the churches resembled the Syrian African basilicas. Because there was little wood, they had stone domes. There were galleries above the aisles and the apses had double-arched windows. If you wish to make a complete tour of all the extant buildings and to ascend 2270m high Kara Dağ hire a guide in Maden Şehir. There are the remains of a 9C monastery and a cave containing Hittite inscriptions on the summit.

Road 715 continues for c 60km to a signposted turning on the right which leads to 13km Çumra. To get to c 20km Çatalhöyük, cross the railway line which skirts the NE side of the village.

ÇATALHÖYÜK is undoubtedly the most important Neolithic site in Turkey. Discovered by James Mellaart in 1958, excavations were conducted here by him under the aegis of the British Institute of Archaeology in Ankara between 1961 and 1963 and again in 1965. The settlement, which is 900m above sea-level, consisted of a double-mound measuring 275m by

450m and 17m high. Ten successive levels of occupation were found at Çatalhöyük. Objects from the lowest level have been dated to 6500 BC.

The archaeologists were intrigued to discover the first signs of a planned urban development. The settlement's mud-brick dwellings were built in carefully laid-out blocks. Most of the houses had two rooms and large, airy, well-lit inner courts. Entrance was by ladders through openings in the roof. The inner walls of the rooms were plastered and elaborately decorated with scenes of hunting and religious ceremonies. The depiction of musicians, dancing girls and acrobats gives some indication of the amusements favoured by the site's Neolithic inhabitants.

Some of the paintings show the bodies of the dead being torn by vultures. It is thought that the bones were collected, covered with a straw mat and buried under the seats which were placed against the walls of the houses. Remains discovered by the archaeologists were in the Hocker position ie like a foetus in the womb. Grave goods include wooden cups, stone hatchets and straw baskets.

The presence of many carvings and reliefs of bulls' heads attests to the antiquity of this symbol of male generative power which appears repeatedly in Anatolia. Stone and terracotta statuettes of a grotesquely gravid Mother Goddess were found in large numbers. Sometimes she appears alone, sometimes in the company of other female deities or she is attended by sacred leopards. Weapons included stone maces, clubs, and clay balls to be used in slings. Tools, seeds and animal bones from deer, boar, sheep and goats and extinct wild cattle provide valuable information about the food and agricultural practices of the people who lived here.

Little remains at the site of Çatalhöyük. It will appeal mainly to specialists. Objects found here are in the Museum of Anatolian Civilisations at Ankara.

From the junction for Çumra it is an unremarkable 60km journey to **KONYA** (population 438,859). Continue straight across the steppe to the southern suburbs and enter Konya by the long sweep of Karaman Cad.

Ibn Battuta (1304–69) visited Konya c 1333. He wrote: 'It is a large town with fine buildings and has many streams and fruit-gardens. The streets are exceedingly broad, and the bazaars admirably planned, with each craft in a bazaar of its own. It is said that this city was built by Alexander'.

Today Konya is a bustling, noisy town, filled with chaotic, undisciplined traffic, a place where buses and lorries compete—not always successfully—with carts drawn by lively, high-stepping horses. There are still reminders of that green oasis which so delighted Ibn Battuta and earlier visitors. Its fine Selçuk buildings refresh the eyes and revive the spirits of travellers exhausted by weary hours crossing the great Anatolian plain.

Industrial development has encircled Konya with a belt of hideous buildings. The grey concrete factories lining the great boulevards which carry traffic to the centre are a poor introduction to a town of such historic importance. But one can see this juxtaposition of beauty and ugliness as being in character. Konya is a place of extremes. In summer the temperature may rise to 38°C and the sun is blotted by duststorms. During the winter icy winds bring snow from the frozen steppes.

Undoubtedly, Konya's greatest attraction is its association with the mystic **Jalal ad-Din ar-Rumi**, better known as **Mevlana**. Throughout the year, but especially between 9 and 17 December when the Festival of the Dancing Dervishes is held, pilgrims flock to Konya to visit the Mevlana Tekke, where the sage is buried, and to attend performances of the *Sema*.

Information, Accommodation, Transport. Konya has three three-star, six two-star, and three one-star registered with the Ministry of Tourism. Recommended are three-star

Balıkçılar Oteli, Dergah Oteli, and the refurbished *Selçuk Oteli*. As accommodation in the town is limited and often difficult to obtain, it is advisable to make reservations in advance, especially during the period of the Mevlana festival. Restaurants which have excited favourable comment include: *Sema*, which offers vegetarian dishes; *Damak*; *Şifa Lokantasi*; and *Hanedan Restoran*. The **Tourist Information Office** is at Mevlana Cad. 21. Tickets for the Mevlana Festival are sold at the Municipal Information Office which is on the other side of the boulevard.

There are frequent bus services to Ankara, İstanbul, İzmir, to cities on the Mediterranean coast, and to eastern Turkey. The non-stop luxury bus services to Ankara are recommended. A morning train to İstanbul has first class coaches and a dining car. There is no direct train service to Ankara. Konya has no airport.

History. Ibn Battuta was misinformed (see above). Long before the time of Alexander there were people living on the site of Alaeddin Parkı, which is in the centre of the modern town. A limited excavation conducted here has revealed traces of occupation from the Chalcolithic period (third millennium BC). The settlement came under the control of the Hittites and from them it passed to the Phrygians who believed that it was the first place to be settled after the great flood. According to the Greeks the city got its name, εἰκών, Latin, Icon hence Iconium, from an icon or image of Perseus holding the Gorgon's head which stood before the main gate.

The Phrygians were followed by the Lydians and the Persians. After Alexander broke the Persians at the battles of the Granicus and Issus, Iconium and the surrounding territory became part of his empire. After his death it fell into the hands of Lysimachus, one of his ablest generals. Subsequently, possession of the city was disputed by the Seleucids and the Attalids. When Attalus III died in 133 BC, he bequeathed his kingdom, including Iconium, to Rome. The city appears to have prospered under its new masters. During the Imperial period, perhaps in an attempt to curry favour, it changed its name twice—first, in AD 41, to Claudiconium in honour of Claudius and later to Colonia Aelia Hadriana Augusta Iconiensium as a compliment to Hadrian.

According to the Acts of the Apostles, Iconium was visited by SS Paul and Barnabas. They preached in the synagogue and their message attracted the attention of many Jews and gentiles. However, some dissident Jews spoke against them and the city was divided about the new faith. When Paul and his companions heard that their adversaries were plotting to stone them, they fled to Lystra and Derbe for safety.

The apocryphal *Acts of Paul and Thecla* contain some additional material about the apostle's stay in Iconium. A catechumen named Thecla, who lived here, pestered St Paul to baptise her. For some reason this request caused an outcry and both were brought before the tribunal. Paul was condemned to be beaten and exiled from the city and it was ordered that Thecla should suffer death by burning. However, an opportune shower put out the fire and saved her life. Nothing daunted by this narrow escape, Thecla dressed herself as a boy and followed Paul to Antioch. There she came to the attention of the authorities once more and was sentenced, this time to be thrown to the lions. She managed to escape this punishment also and, perhaps having learned her lesson at last, withdrew to Seleucia, modern Silifke. There she lived out the remainder of her days in a convent which she had founded (see Silifke). It has been suggested that Thecla's persistence, which caused Paul so much trouble, may have generated the apostle's alleged anti-feminist bias.

Byzantine Iconium was an episcopal see. Like most of south and central Anatolia the city suffered badly from Arab raids from the 7C to the 9C. First attacked by the Selçuks in 1069, the city was taken by them a century later. As the capital of the Sultanate of Rum it enjoyed a period of great prosperity under Selçuk rule and was enriched with many splendid buildings. Apart from two brief periods when it came under the control of the Crusaders—Barbarossa stopped there briefly in 1190—it remained in Selçuk hands until their defeat by the Mongols at the battle of Kösedağ in 1242. From the Mongols it passed to the Karamanid dynasty. They were the rulers of the city when Ibn Battuta visited it c 1333. Konya was captured by Mehmet II in 1467.

Konya requires at least one day. Start in the centre of the town at Alaeddin Parki. On the NE side of the park, is **Alaeddin Camii**, the largest of the town's Selçuk mosques. This is a complicated, rambling structure which was begun c 1150 and completed 70 years later. The entrance on the E side

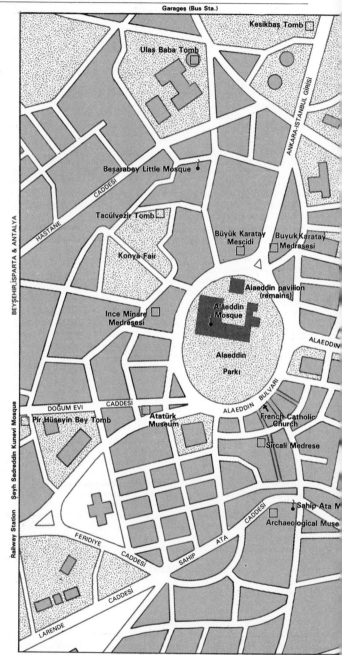

Garageş (Bus Sta.)

Kesikbaş Tomb

Ulaş Baba Tomb

ANKARA-ISTANBUL GIRISI

Beşarabey Little Mosque

CADDESI

HASTANE

BEYŞEHIR,ISPARTA & ANTALYA

Tacülvezir Tomb

Büyük Karatay
Mescidi

Buyuk Karatay
Medresesi

Konya Fair

Alaeddin pavilion
(remains)

Ince Minare
Medresesi

Alaeddin
Mosque

ALAEDDIN

Alaeddin
Parkı

ALAEDDIN BULVARI

ALAEDDIN

DOĞUM EVI

CADDESI

Pir Hüseyin Bey Tomb

Atatürk
Museum

French Catholic
Church

Sircali Medrese

Şeyh Sadreddin Kunevi Mosque

Sahip Ata M

Railway Station

Archaeological Muse

FERIDIYE

CADDESI

SAHIP

ATA

CADDESI

CADDESI

LARENDE

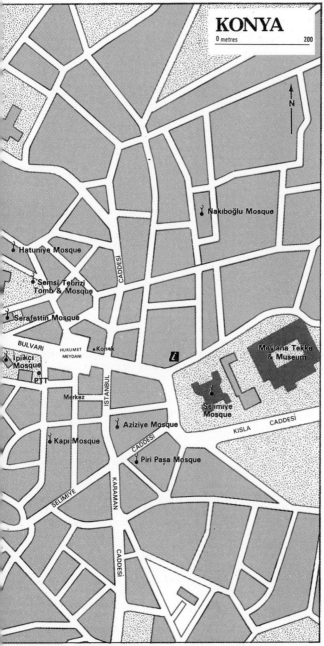

KONYA

0 metres   200

Nakıboğlu Mosque

Hatuniye Mosque

Şemsi Tebrizi
Tomb & Mosque

Şerafettin Mosque

BULVARI

HUKUMET
MEYDANI

Konak

İplikçi
Mosque

PTT

Merkez

Aziziye Mosque

Kapı Mosque

Piri Paşa Mosque

İSTANBUL CADDESİ

CADDESİ

KARAMAN

SELIMIYE

Mevlana Tekke
& Museum

Selimiye
Mosque

KISLA CADDESİ

CADDESİ

leads to a large rectangular prayer hall built by Sultan Alaeddin Keykubad I (1219–36). It has a flat timbered roof supported by 42 antique columns with Roman and Byzantine capitals. The domed area beyond the hall was started by Mesud I (1116–56) and completed by his son Kılıç Arslan II (1156–88). Note the beautifully-carved ebony *mimber* (c 1155), one of the finest examples of Selçuk art. To the W is a hall divided into four irregularly-shaped aisles. This is believed to have been completed during the reign of Keykavus I (1210–19). To the N is an octagonal *türbe* built by Alaeddin Keykubad. The decagonal *türbe* beside it contains the tomb of Kılıç Arslan II. It also holds the remains of seven other sultans, including Keyhusrev III (1264–83), the last Selçuk ruler of the Sultanate of Rum.

A tower forming part of the defensive wall, which surrounded the area now occupied by the park, is to the N of the mosque. This, the so-called **Alaeddin Köşkü**, Alaeddin's Kiosk, was used as a royal residence during the last years of Selçuk rule. It is protected by a modern concrete roof.

Cross the road to the **Büyük Karatay Medresesi** which is named after its founder, Celaleddin Karatay. This remarkable court official of Greek origin held high office under two sultans and was appointed regent when the stability and very existence of the sultanate was threatened by Mongol invaders. The *medrese*, which was completed c 1251, was repaired in 1955 and now houses a magnificent collection of tiles. Particularly rich in specimens of the fine glazed faience which was used to decorate the interiors of buildings during the Selçuk era, it covers all periods from the 13C to the 18C. Note particularly the wall-tiles from a palace built by Alaeddin Keykubad I on the W shore of Beysehir Lake at Kubab-Abab. These have representations of people and animals on brilliantly-coloured glazed tiles shaped like stars, octagons, squares, crosses and other forms.

The doorway of the *medrese* has intricately carved designs and inlays of blue and white marble. Above the entrance there is an inscription in Cufic script of some of the sayings of the Prophet. The dome of the principal chamber is covered with a pattern of blue and gold tiles which represents a firmament resplendent with the sun and stars. Below the dome is an inscription in Cufic of a verse from the Koran. On the pendentives are, also in Cufic, the names of Abu-Bekr, Omar, Othman and Ali, the first four caliphs of Islam. The *türbe* of Celaleddin Karatay opens off the central chamber.

According to the constitution of the *medrese*, students had to be selected from one of the four Sünni divisions of Islam and the scholar and his assistant from the Hanefi division. Another rule stated that study should be held every day except Tuesday and Friday.

On the W side of the park is the **İnce Minare Medresesi**, the Medrese of the Slender Minaret. The minaret, which is covered with an elaborate design of blue and red tiles, was badly damaged by lightning in 1901 and is less than half its original height. With its adjoining mosque, now in ruins, it was the gift of one of the most prolific builders of his day, the Emir Sahip Ata Fahrettin Ali. It was completed c 1267 to the design of an architect named Keluk, son of Abdullah. Repaired in 1956, the *medrese* has been re-opened as a museum of stone and wood carving.

A highly decorated entrance leads to a court containing inscriptions and gravestones of the Selçuk and Karamanid periods from the Konya region. In the principal room there are a number of reliefs from the castle built by Alaeddin Keykubad I in 1221. These include representations of lions, an elephant, fish, a rhinoceros, human beings and mythical beasts—dragons, a two headed eagle, and a harpy. In addition to windows and doors from the Selçuk period there are finely-carved pieces of Ottoman furniture.

On the S side of the park take the Ressam Sami Sokağı to the **Sırçalı Medrese**. This, the so-called Glazed Medrese, was founded by Badr al-Din Muslih in 1242. Rescued from its semi-ruinous condition it was re-opened in 1960 as a museum of tombstones from the Selçuk, Karamanid and Ottoman periods. In an alley nearby there is an interesting example of Karamanid architecture, the **Hasbey Darülhafızı** which dates from 1421. Here students were taught to memorise the Koran.

Farther along Ressam Sami Sokağı is the **Sahip Ata Foundation**. The gift of Sahip Ata Fahrettin Ali, who founded the Ince Minare Medresesi, it comprises a *mescid*, a *türbe*, and a *hamam*. Completed in 1258, it was also the work of the architect Keluk. The *türbe*, which is decorated with mosaic tiles, contains the sarcopahgi of the founder, his daughter, sons, and grandsons. A passage leads to a vaulted burial chamber under the *türbe*.

Konya's **Archaeological Museum** has a rich collection of objects from the Prehistoric Age to the end of the Byzantine period. All were found in Konya or in the surrounding countryside. They are displayed in the courtyard, garden and in a number of pavilions. In the garden and first pavilion there are statues, grave stelae, sarcophagi, inscriptions, altars and architectural fragments from the Classical, Roman and Byzantine periods. In most cases the provenance of the exhibits is not known.

The second pavilion contains the museum's greatest treasure, a 3C AD **sarcophagus in the Sidamara style**. This was found in 1958 near the village of Yunuslar, ancient Tiberiapolis. Finely-carved reliefs on the sides show the twelve labours of Hercules. He is shown fighting the Nemean lion, killing the Hydra of Lerna, capturing the Erymanthian boar, killing the Cerynitian Hind, removing the Stymphalian birds, obtaining the Amazon's girdle, cleansing the Augean stables, capturing the Cretan bull, seizing the mares of Diomedes, taking the cattle of Geryon, bringing Cerberus from Hades, and stealing the Golden Apples of the Hesperides. On one of the short sides of the sarcophagus there is a representation of the deceased. Other exhibits from ancient Isauria and Lycaonia in this pavilion include incriptions, statues, and a large collection of objects in bronze and marble.

The third pavilion is devoted to the Prehistoric, Hittite and Phrygian periods. These include pottery, stone and metal objects, seals, jewellery, and statuettes, mainly from Canhasan and Çatalhöyük.

Return to the park and take the third street on the right, Alaeddin Bulv. At Hükümet Meyd. is the 12C **Iplikçi Camii**, a much restored mosque. Left of its attractively-carved *mihrab* there are some traces of 13C mosaic.

The large mosque on the other side of the square is the **Şerafettin Camii** which also has received much attention from restorers. Just before Mevlana Cad. a warren of small streets on the right leads to Konya's **bazaar**. At the W end of the bazaar is the **Azizye Camii**, notable for the extravagant, almost Rococo, style of its architecture and decoration.

At the end of Mevlana Bulv., in front of Mevlana Tekke, is the **Selimiye Camii** which dates from the reign of Selim II the Sot (1566–74).

The **Mevlana Tekke** is, without a doubt, the most important monument in Konya. It contains the tombs of the mystic philosopher and theologian, Jalal ad-Din ar-Rumi, who is better known as Mevlana (Lord in Arabic) and of his father Bahaeddin Veled. Perhaps the most important Islamic shrine in Turkey, it brings thousands of pilgrims to Konya each year.

Mevlana was born in Balkh, Bakhtri in Persian, the capital of the ancient Greek kingdom of Bactria, Afghanistan c 1207. His father was a distinguished teacher who, because of his great learning, had been honoured with the title of Sultan, ül-Ulema, Lord of Scholars. Balkh had been exposed to many different cultural and religious influences. Before the advent of Islam, the Zoroastrian Magi, the Hellenistic philosophers of the Seleucids, Christian missionaries and Buddhist sages had all left their mark on the city. It has been suggested that this heady mixture of beliefs may have produced an atmosphere of speculation and enquiry in Balkh. If so, that may explain Mevlana's spiritual and intellectual development.

Many legends and stories were told about the young Mevlana. One day, while playing with other children, he disappeared into the sky. When he returned 'greatly altered in complexion' he talked about a 'legion of beings clothed in green mantles', who had shown him many strange and mysterious things of a celestial nature. Possibly because of the threat offered by the approaching Mongol armies, Bahaeddin decided to take his family away from Balkh. They went first to Nishapur, then to Baghdad, Kufa, Mecca, Medina, Jerusalem, Damascus and Aleppo. After spending some time there Bahaeddin felt drawn to Anatolia. His little caravan journeyed to Malatya, Erzincan, Sivas, Kayseri, Niğde and finally to Karaman in 1221. They stayed there for seven years and there Mevlana was married in 1225.

Alaeddin Keykubad, the ruler of Konya, learning that the famous teacher Bahaeddin Veled from Balkh was in Karaman, implored him to come to Konya. Bahaeddin finally acceded to the sultan's request in 1228 and he taught in Konya until his death in 1231. Mevlana took his father's place and quickly established a reputation for scholarship. His speciality was canonical jurisprudence, but he had an extensive knowledge of all branches of philosophy and was well-read in Greek Classical authors.

An event of great importance occurred in November 1244. Riding his donkey home from the *medrese* in the company of a group of admiring students Mevlana was accosted by a ragged dervish who proceeded to ask him a number of searching questions. This was the man known in Persian as Shams Tabrizi, Sun of Tabriz, or Şems in Turkish. Şems and Mevlana quickly became close friends and spent days and weeks closeted together in philosophical discussion. Mevlana abandoned his teaching and appeared rarely in public. This caused jealousy and anger among his students and friends who began to put it about that he had been bewitched by an evil sorcerer. Perhaps in response to this pressure, in February 1246 Şems disappeared as suddenly and as mysteriously as he had appeared.

Mevlana was heartbroken at the loss of his friend. When he discovered after many enquiries that Şems was in Damascus, he begged him to return to Konya. Şems did so eventually and the two men resumed their friendship and their discussions. To draw him more into his family, Mevalana gave his adopted daughter, Kimya Hatun, to Şems in marriage. However, before long fresh plots were hatched against Şems and this time Mevlana's younger son, Alaeddin Çelebi, was induced to join the conspirators. One dark night in December 1247 Şems disappeared and was never seen again. It is probable that he was murdered by his enemies. Mevlana could not be comforted. He tried to come to terms with his grief by writing poetry about Şems. 'Oh my soul's essence, how did you hide yourself from me?' Hoping that Şems had returned to Damascus, Mevlana searched for him there, but the two sages never met again.

With the help of other companions Mevlana continued his philosophical speculations. The Sufic seed planted by Şems germinated and flourished with their help and encouragement. One of his friends, Çelebi Hüsamettin, inspired Mevlana to write his greatest work, the *Mesnevi*. This collection of more than 25,000 poems fills six volumes. As an exposition of his philosophy it had a great effect on his followers. It was studied in schools established specially for that purpose.

In 1273 Mevlana's health began to fail. In December of that year a great cold settled on Konya and he began to sink rapidly. To his weeping friends and followers Mevlana spoke constantly of the longing which he felt for his forthcoming union with God. He called his approaching death '*şeb-i-arus*', the night of union. Mevlana died on 17 December 1273. He was held in such esteem that members of all races and creeds mourned his passing. Jews, Christians and pagans walked with their Islamic brothers in his funeral procession which took a whole day to pass through Konya. Mevlana was buried near his father and a *türbe* was erected to shelter their sarcophagi.

The followers of the mystic philosopher decided to continue to study his teaching and they appointed Çelebi Hüsamettin as his successor. When he died, Mevlana's son, Sultan Veled, became head of the order. It was Veled who was mainly responsible for formulating and popularising his father's teachings. Soon other *tekkes* were established, first in various parts of Anatolia then as far away as Egypt. In time the Mehlevi

Mevlevi Devishes perform the 'sema' at Konya on 17 December each year

order acquired royal recognition, so that when a new sultan came to the throne, he received the sword of state from the Çelebi Efendi, the head of the Mehlevis.

In 1925, when the Islamic mystic orders were abolished by the Government of the Turkish Republic, the Mevlevi lost their convents and numbers declined. However, in recent years public performances of the *sema* have recommenced. Held in December each year on the anniversary of Mevlana's death, they attract large attendances.

After the supression of the Mevlevi the Mevlana Tekke was turned into a museum. Originally the site, which it occupies, was a garden given to Mevlana's father as a gift by Alaeddin Keykubad I. Bahaeddin Veled was buried here and later Mevlana was laid to rest by his side. At first a simple *türbe* housed the two sarcophagi. In 1397 the striking cylindrical spire, divided into 16 sections, was constructed by Emir Alaeddin Ali. Some of the original turquoise-coloured tiles, which covered it, remain.

In front of the *türbe* there is a spacious courtyard with a *şadirvan* in the centre. On the left side are rooms built by Murat III in 1584 to house the dervishes. A number of these have been refurbished to show them as they were, when occupied by members of the community. In others a collection of Selçuk, Karamanid and Ottoman fabrics and carpets is displayed. These include the late 13C/early 14C carpets from the Eşrefoğlu mosque in Beyşehir, the so-called Konya carpets. These are the earliest examples of Islamic carpet making. On the S side of the courtyard are the kitchens, where food for the dervishes and their guests was prepared. The fountain to the right of the entrance was known as **Şebi Arus**, the Night of Union, in memory of Mevlana's death. Each year on 17 December, after the members of the *tekke* had eaten their evening meal, they performed the *sema* around this pool. The four *türbeler* at the extreme right date from the 16C and contain the sarcophagi of various Karamanid and Ottoman high officials of state.

Over the door to the mausoleum the following is written in Persian:

This station is the Mecca of all dervishes.
What is lacking in them is here completed
Whoever came here unfulfilled was here made whole.

In the ante-room the dervishes read passages from the Koran. It now contains examples of the work of some well-known Ottoman calligraphers. These include Mustafa Rakım, Izzet, Mahmud Celaleddin and Hamid. A **door of walnut** covered with silver plaques, which was presented to the tekke by Hasan Paşa in 1559, leads to the main chamber of the *tekke*, the *Huzuri-i Pir*, the Presence of the Saint. The **tombs** of Mevlana and of his son, Sultan Veled, are under the green dome. They are covered with a richly-embroidered tapestry presented by Sultan Abdulhamid II in 1894. The silver lattice-work **grill** surrounding Mevlana's tomb was given to the tekke by Mahmud Paşa, Governor of Maraş, in 1597. The plaque fixed to it is inscribed with a poem in Turkish by the celebrated poet Mani. Below the grill is the **silver threshold**, where the dervishes made their obeisances to their founder. On the E side is the **tomb** of Bahaeddin Veled; on the W the tombs of Mevlana's wife and children and some of his descendants. On a dais there are six tombs arranged in two rows of three. Here were laid to rest the Horasan Erkekler, the Horosan Men, dervishes from Balkh, who came with Bahaeddin Veled and his family to Konya.

There are some early manuscripts of the Mesnevi, the *Divan* by Sultan Veled and other early writings. The famous **April Cup**, a beautiful bronze bowl, decorated with damascene figures and ornamented in gold and silver, is also kept here. This was given by the Mongol Sultan Ebu Said Bahadir Han to the *tekke* in 1333. The bowl was used to collect the spring rain which was believed to have curative properties. Prayers were said over it, the tip of Mevlana's turban was placed in it, and then it was offered to the pilgrims.

On the N of the *tekke* are two large domed chambers. One of these, which served as a *mescid*, a small mosque, now contains a collection of beauti-fully-illuminated **Korans**. Note especially a tiny version of the sacred book which is decorated with exquisitely-executed miniature ornamentation. In the area between the *mescid* and the *semahane* there are two carved **walnut lecterns** from the Selçuk period.

The other chamber was the *semahane*, the room where the dervishes performed the *sema*. Dating from the reign of Süleyman the Magnificent (1520–66), this now houses a selection of the instruments used to accompany the dance—the *ney*, reed flute, *rebab*, a stringed instrument similar to a violin, *tef*, hand drum and *tambur*, lute. Some of **Mevlana's garments** are also kept here.

The dervishes no longer dance in the *semahane*. The *sema* is now held in a high school gymnasium in another part of Konya. Presented as an exhibition of folklore, for some it is nothing more. However, others find it a moving religious experience. The dervishes who take part in the *sema* today live in the world. They are bus mechanics, teachers, schoolboys. They are no longer obliged to submit to the extended novitiate and strict discipline of the past. Yet, when they dance, the air becomes charged with a feeling of great spirituality and the spectators forget the bleak setting in which the *sema* is being held, are no longer conscious of the icy temperature and discomfort of the unheated arena.

For the *sema* the dervish wears a white jacket over a long white skirt, the *tennure*, which represents his burial garment. These are covered by a voluminous black cloak, the *hurka*, which represents his tomb. On his head is a conical brown felt hat, the *sikke*, representing his tombstone. Around his waist is a long girdle of cloth and on his feet are high slippers of soft, pliable leather. The sheik's costume differs from that of the dervishes in that his *sikke* is encircled by a black band.

The ceremony begins with a prayer and a *sura* from the Koran. This is followed by a plaintive melody on the *ney*. Before beginning their dance, the dervishes bow to the sheik and kiss his hand. Then, letting fall their black cloaks to symbolise their escape from the tomb and their readiness to dance for God, they begin to turn slowly. Each dervish raises his right arm above his head with the palm facing upwards, while turning his left hand downwards. This indicates his willingness to receive God's grace and blessing and to pass it on to mankind. Then, as the dancers begin to move faster and faster and their garments billow outwards, the hall appears to be full of large white flowers opening in the sunlight. Mevlana believed that the sema enabled his followers to reach out and touch the Infinite. He did not restrict his teaching to the dervishes. The way of enlightenment was to be open to everyone. He wrote:

Come, come again, and again...
Come, be you unbeliever, idolator or fire
worshipper...
Our hearth is not the threshold of despair
Even if you have broken your vow of
repentance a hundred times
Come again.'

32

Silifke to Uzuncaburç

Total distance c 32km. Silifke—7km Demircili/İmbriogon—c 25km Uzun-caburç—(4km Ura).

One of the most interesting excursions from Silifke (see Route 30) is to Demircili, Uzuncaburç—the ancient city of Olba/Diocaesarea—and Ura, three villages high up in the foothills of the Taurus Mountains. Allow a full day for this excursion. There are no restaurants in the villages, but there are plenty of places for a picnic en route and at the sites. You may be invited to eat with one of the village families or with the Yürük people.

If you do not have your own transport, you can get to the villages by dolmuş. They leave—usually early in the morning—from Atatürk Square, near the bridge over the Göksu. There is also a bus at about midday from the same place. This returns to Silifke the next day. As a rule, it is not difficult to find overnight accommodation in the villages.

From the N bank of the Göksu take the Mara (Kırobası) road which is well-surfaced, if rather narrow. This climbs steadily. Entering a forest of pine and laurel it makes its sinous way to 7km **Demircili**.

This village, built over the ancient settlement of **İmbriogon**, has six well-preserved Roman mausolea. Near the school is the **Lower Mauso-leum**. This measures 5.3m by 4.25m by 6.25m. The two central columns and the architrave have collapsed. Two columns attached to the side walls are surmounted by Corinthian capitals. The burial chamber is empty. On the wall at the back is a console which may have supported a statue of the deceased. The mausoleum's pediment has a circular relief, much eroded. There are a several rock-cut graves in front of the mausoleum.

Across the road there are more remains. A 5m-long column lies on the ground. By its side is the Corinthian capital which once crowned it. To the

W there are two empty sarcophagi on a stone base. The lids lie on the ground nearby, where they were left by the tomb-robbers. To the NE is the **Three-Storey Mausoleum**. Its W wall still stands. A door on the S side led to a dark underground chamber and another on the W to the upper storey.

About 500m to the N there are two more **mausolea**. The **tomb on the left** measures 5m by 6m by 6m. Supported in the front by stone blocks, its handsome Corinthian columns lead the eye upwards to a frieze of acanthus leaves and a cornice ornamented with geometric designs.

The **tomb on the right**, which has two storeys, measures 4m by 4m by 7.5m. It is the only mausoleum in Demircili where sarcophagi were found in place. The lower chamber, which is carved from the rock, is fronted by four Ionic columns 2.3m high. The entrance to the chamber, on the right-hand side, is blocked with fallen masonry. The upper floor has four fluted columns in the Corinthian style which support a pediment decorated with a damaged relief. Inside there were three sarcophagi, 1m by 2m by 1m, arranged along the side walls. The lid of the **sarcophagus on the left** is decorated with a lion couchant carved in high relief. The **sarcophagus in the centre** has an inscription picked out in red and a male head flanked by two female figures on the front and two lions facing each other on the lid. The **sarcophagus on the right** has been largely destroyed. Only the base and a few fragments of the lid remain. In view of the size of the sarcophagi, they must have been placed in the burial chamber before the tomb was completed. Two **consoles**, which may have supported busts of the deceased, are fixed to the side walls.

The **Upper Mausoleum** of Demircili, located on the right-hand side of the road near the outskirts of the village, measures 4.5m by 4m by 7.5m and has two storeys. The lower storey is carved from the rock and is fronted by four Ionic columns c 2.6m high. The entrance to the empty burial chamber is c 1m back from the columns. Behind four Corinthian columns an arched entrance 2.75m high provided access to the upper burial chamber, also empty. Fragments of the pediment lie on the ground in front of the tomb.

The sixth **mausoleum**, which betrays some orientalising influences, is some distance to the E of the village. Apart from damage to the SW corner and S face, it is in a good state of preservation. Measuring 4m by 4m by 8.5m, it has a pyramid-shaped roof which was probably surmounted by a statue of the deceased. There is no trace of a burial inside.

On leaving Demircili, continue for c 21km to Kırağıbucağı. The road to c 4km **UZUNCABURÇ** is signposted to the right.

If you require accommodation in Uzuncaburç, ask the *Bekçi* at the site, one of the school teachers or the proprietor of the village *kahve*. You might also try the *Burç Pansiyon* near the temple of Tyche. In addition to tea and coffee the *kahve* has soft drinks and some of the specialities of the region: *kenger kahvesi*, coffee made from the fruit of the acanthus, and *pekmez*, boiled, concentrated grape juice.

There are some local handicrafts—rugs (*çul*), saddle-bags, *meşe külü* soap made from oak ash—and fine needlework. Uzuncaburç has a population of 3000. Surrounded by rich pastures, where the *yürük* graze their herds in the summer, it is an important farming and agricultural centre.

More than 1000m above sea-level and far from the debilitating heat and the crowded resorts on the coast, Uzuncaburç is an exhilarating place in the summer. You will explore **Olba/Diocaesarea** with zest and energy.

History. After the death of Alexander in 323 BC, control of Rugged Cilicia was disputed by the Seleucids and the Ptolemies. By 300 BC Seleucus I Nicator (321–280 BC) appears to have consolidated his hold on the area. At about that time he founded the city of Seleucia ad Calycadnum, modern Silifke, and built the temple of Zeus at Olba.

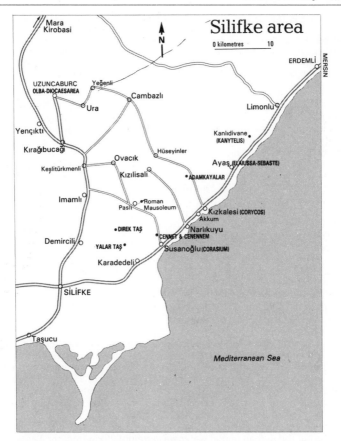

Mara
Kirobasi

Silifke area

↑
N

0 kilometres   10

ERDEMLİ   MERSİN

UZUNCABURC
OLBA-DIOCAESAREA   Yeğenli

Cambazlı

Ura   Limonlu

Yençıktı   Kanlıdivane
(KANYTELIS)

Kırağıbucağı   Hüseyinler

Ovacık   Ayaş (ELAIUSSA-SEBASTE)

Keşlitürkmenli   Kızılisalı   •ADAMKAYALAR

Imamlı   Roman
Paslı   Mausoleum   Kızkalesi (CORYCOS)
Akkum
Narlıkuyu
•DIREK TAŞ   CENNET & CENENNEM

Demircili   YALAR TAŞ •   Susanoğlu (CORASIUM)

Karadedeli

SİLİFKE

Taşucu

Mediterranean Sea

According to Strabo, Olba was founded by Ajax, the son of Teucer. (Teucer was the half-brother of the more famous Ajax of the Iliad. He married Eune, daughter of king Cyprus, eponym of the island.) The priests of the temple of Zeus at Olba became the rulers of this part of Cilicia. Most of them were called Teucer or Ajax (Strabo 14.5. 10).

Certainly, Olba was governed by a dynasty of priest-kings, called the Teukrides, towards the end of the 3C and beginning of the 2C BC. It is not known when or under what circumstances this dynasty was established, but it appears to have had more than a local importance. The discovery of a dedicatory inscription to Zeus Olbios on a fortified Hellenistic tower at Elaeusa/Sebaste suggests that the rule of the Teukrides extended at one time as far as the coast. They suffered a period of temporary eclipse between 150 BC and 50 BC, possibly as the result of a revolt or an invasion, but had recovered power by AD 17. Apparently they were not regarded as posing a threat to Roman authority as they continued to rule when Cilicia came under the control of the Romans in the early part of the 1C. Marcus Aurelius Polemo, a high priest of Olba, who united and led the Isaurian tribes, founded the city of Claudiopolis, the modern town of Mut, c AD 50. Olba changed its name during the reign of Vespasian (AD 69–79) to Diocaesarea and was so known from then onwards. During the Byzantine period its temples were preserved by being turned into churches. Later Olba/Diocaesarea entered a period of decline from which it never recovered. For centuries it remained an obscure, almost forgotten village in the foothills of the Taurus Mountains.

Interest in Olba/Diocaesarea was revived by the publication of Victor Langlois's *Voyage dans la Cilicie et dans les montagnes du Taurus* in 1861. In 1890 the area was visited by an English scholar, Thomas Bent, and later by the Austrians, Rudolf, Heberdey and Wilhelm. Important research by Herzfeld at the beginning of this century is contained in *Monumenta Asiae Minoris Antiqua*. In 1925 Keil and Wilhelm of the American Society for Archaeological Research in Asia Minor surveyed the ruins of the city and published their findings.

Apart from a striking **Hellenistic pyramid-roofed tomb** on the southern approaches of Uzuncaburç, the ruins of Olba/Diocaesarea occupy a compact area near the modern village. The tomb, which is on the summit of a hill c 1200m above sea-level, measures 5m by 5m by 16m. Constructed from stone blocks without mortar, it has a plain architrave 10m from the ground. This is surmounted by a frieze bearing metopes and triglyphs in the Doric style. The pyramid-shaped roof supported a platform on which a statue of the deceased was placed. Entrance to the burial chamber was by way of a cleverly concealed door which, unfortunately, was discovered by tomb robbers. There is no sarcophagus. Inhumation took place under the stone floor. For safety reasons entrance to the tomb is forbidden.

There was a **colonnaded street** S of the centre of the modern village. This continued the line of the ancient paved road linking Corycus (now Kızkalesi), Ura and Olba with Seleucia. Five limestone columns, crowned with Corinthian capitals, part of a Roman **monumental arch** which spanned this street, remain in place. Half-way up the columns, which are 6.75m high and 1m in diameter, there are **consoles** on which statues were placed. This regrettable practice, which may have originated in the Middle East, breaks the line of the column in an unpleasant, abrupt way. Other examples are at Pompeiopolis.

To the left of the street are the ruins of a **Roman theatre**. According to an inscription found here, the theatre was built during the joint reign of Marcus Aurelius (161–180) and Lucius Verus (161–169). Access from the street was by a vomitorium. The cavea, which had a capacity of 2500, was supported at the back by a stone wall. No trace of the stage-building remains.

Opposite are the remains of a **Roman nymphaeum** which was linked to the city's water supply system. Note the channels through which the water flowed into the basin.

During the Roman period water was brought 20km from the Lamas river through channels and tunnels cut into the rock. This ancient system, supplemented by the winter's rain and snow stored in ancient cisterns, still provides Uzuncaburç and a number of other villages with fresh water.

The imposing ruins of the **Temple of Zeus Olbius** are on the left-hand side of the street in the centre of a vegetable garden. This was a peripteros of 6 by 12 columns of the Corinthian order which measured c 40m by 21m. It is in a good state of preservation. In 1958 the stylobate and crepidoma were cleared of debris. Founded by Seleucus I Nicator (321–281) towards the beginning of the 3C BC, it has the distinction of being the earliest known Corinthian temple in Asia Minor. Of the 30 standing columns four still have their capitals. Each column is c 10m high and has a diameter of 1.5m. Most of the architrave has disappeared.

When the temple was turned into a church, an apse (now removed) was added to the E end, and the columns, on three sides, were pared to permit the construction of walls and doorways. At the same time the ceiling was removed and replaced by a wooden roof. The inside faces of the columns show that the building was seriously damaged by fire at some time.

In the temenos there are a number of reliefs, a sarcophagus, and some architectural fragments. Note the **defensive wall** on the street-side of the

Uzuncaburç
(Olba/Diocaesarea)

sanctuary which protected the temple and its treasures from marauders and thieves. To the S of the temple are the ruins of a building which may have been a gymnasium. It is believed to date from the Roman period.

Return to the street and walk towards the W end of the site. The ruins of the **Roman Temple of Tyche** are here.

Tyche, the Greek goddess of chance or fortune, was the daughter of Oceanus or Zeus and Tethys. She is not mentioned in the Homeric poems, but became very popular during the Hellenistic period when she was first given the status of a goddess. Every city had its Tyche. She was usually shown crowned with towers as befitted the guardian of the city and was sometimes blind. During the Roman period Tyche was often equated with the ancient Latin deity Fortuna.

The temple of Tyche had an interesting plan. The square cella containing the cult-statue of the goddess was c 34m behind a row of six columns surmounted by Corinthian capitals which supported an architrave. Five of the columns survive. Each has a shaft made from a single piece of imported granite and is 5.5m high and 0.65m in diameter. According to an **inscription** on the architrave, the temple was the gift of one Oppius and of his wife, Kyria. It has been dated, by the inscription and the style of the Corinthian capitals, to the end of the 1C AD.

To the right of the temple of Tyche a short colonnaded street (only the bases of the columns remain) leads to the **NW gate**. This well-preserved, late Roman structure, which was joined to the city's defensive wall, is 31.5m long, 12m at its highest point, and 1.15m wide. There are four **consoles**, two on the inner and two on the outer face of the wall near the central arch. According to an **inscription** to the right of the arch, the gate was constructed during the reign of the Eastern Roman Emperor Arcadius (395–408) and of the Western Roman Emperor Honorius (395–423). These young and unskilled rulers, the sons of Theodosius the Great, were dominated by their regents. They reigned at a time of insecurity and uncertainty. The Eastern Empire was under threat from the Ostrogoths and the Huns and many of its cities erected walls for protection against them.

The **necropolis** is in a valley N of the village. Follow the road from the coffee-house past the bust of Atatürk and the secondary school. There were interments during the Hellenistic, Roman and Byzantine periods. These included individual burials in sarcophagi, graves carved from the rock, and family mausolea in caves which have several tombs. Most of the sarcophagi are similar in style. A number bear inscriptions in Greek. During the Byzantine period a mortuary church was erected here.

Return to the village centre and walk a short distance to the E. The **Hellenistic tower**, which gives the village its modern name—Uzuncaburç means high tower— is 12.5m by 15.5m by c 22.5m. Apparently constructed as a watch-tower and for defensive purposes, it has five storeys. Its importance to the inhabitants of Olba/Diocaesarea may be judged from the fact that it appeared on its coins. Like some of the other buildings it bears traces of damage by fire and was heavily restored at various perods. An **inscription in Greek** on the S side, near the entrance, appears to refer to some repair or refurbishment in the latter part of the 3C AD.

The tower is in urgent need of repair and restoration. Some of the walls bulge ominously. **Because of its dangerous state, entry is strictly forbidden.**

Note the ingenious **device** near the tower which was used to control the flow and pressure of the water brought from the Lamas river and to direct it to various parts of the city.

During the Byzantine period, when the temple of Zeus was converted into a Christian basilica, a number of other churches were built in Olba/Diocaesarea. The ruins of two of these lie to the S of the theatre, while in the area of the Hellenistic tower there are the remains of the **Stephanos church**.

For **Ura** follow the road from the left of the theatre in a SE direction for 4km. Built on the slope of a hill, whose summit is 1100m above sea-level, Ura may have been a dependency of Olba/Diocaesarea or the original site of the city.

Apart from some architectural fragments near the school, a Roman nymphaeum and a theatre at the base of the hill, the remaining ruins are on the hillside. These include houses, cisterns, watch-towers, churches, an aqueduct and the necropolis. Ura was occupied during the Roman and Byzantine periods.

The road to **Yeğenli** village cuts through another **necropolis**. By the signpost there are two fine sarcophagi decorated with garlands and a representation of Eros.

33

Silifke to Mersin

Total distance c 72km. Silifke—7km Karadedli—5km Susanoğlu—(17km Türkmenuşağı Paslı)—5km Narlikuyu—(c 2km Cennet and Cehennem)—3km Akkum—(c 7km Adamkayalar)—(12km Cambazlı)—5km Kizkalesi—3km Ayaş—(c 4km Kanlıdivane)—14km Erdemli—23km Mezitli (2km Viranşehir/Soli/Pompeiopolis)—11km Mersin.

Note. All distances are approximate.

E of Silifke (see Route 30) the E24 crosses the rather featureless plain at the delta of the Göksu river. **Karadedli** is a new village inhabited by *yürük* people who have abandoned their nomadic life. An agricultural centre it is well-known for its woven rugs and saddle-bags produced in traditional patterns and styles. There is a ruined **Byzantine church** near the village.

After 5km the road returns to the sea at the pretty village of **Susanoğlu**. A considerable amount of development is taking place here. There are two good hotels, four-star *Altınorfoz* and two-star *Tolya*, several pensions and restaurants. Susanoğlu is a pleasant place for a few relaxing days on the beach; it is also a good centre for visiting the ancient sites around Silifke.

Near the village are the ruins of ancient **Corasium**, founded c AD 375 by Flavius Uranius, Governor of Isauria. There are the substantial remains of fortifications, churches, and baths, also a number of stelae and two necropolises. The remains date from the beginning of the 5C AD to the 8C AD.

About 17km N of Susanoğlu, near the village of **Paslı**, there is an interesting 2C Roman **temple-tomb**. The village has no restaurant but there are several places en route where it is possible to picnic. The Serin family, which lives near the tomb, is well-known for the welcome it extends to visitors. It is not unusual to be invited to share a meal with them. During the summer months the family moves to their *yayla* in the mountains.

The road from the coast climbs steadily, first through olive-groves and then through plantations of pine. It demands careful driving. Continue through Türkmenuşağı to Paslı. As the tomb is not easy to find, ask a member of the Serin family to take you to it. He will also keep the fierce guard-dogs, which protect the villagers' herds at bay!.

The tomb, which was built near the ancient paved road linking Corycus with Seleucia, is in an excellent state of preservation. It has four double columns surmounted by a decorated pediment. Consoles, which may have supported statues, project from the columns. In the burial chamber there were two sarcophagi, both of which have been destroyed. The names of those buried in the tomb are not known.

On the left-hand outer wall there is the relief of a large, **erect phallus**. Local tradition, which equates virility with courage and majesty, has given the building its popular name, the **Tomb of the Great King**. It is also called the **Priapus Tomb**.

Priapus, a god of Phrygian origin, enjoyed great popularity during the Hellenistic and Roman periods. The son of Aphrodite and Dionysus or perhaps of Aphrodite and Zeus, he was endowed with a phallus as large as the rest of his body. The worship of Priapus spread from Lampsacus on the Hellespont to the whole of the ancient world. The donkey, an animal notorious for its unbridled lust, was sacrificed in his honour. As the god of fertility and growth, his garlanded ithyphallic image watched over fields and gardens. He was also credited with the ability to ward off the evil eye and to neutralise the spells of the envious. In literature he was honoured especially by the Bucolic Poets. Moschus, who lived in Syracuse c 150 BC, wrote: 'Your sudden end, sweet Bion, was matter of weeping even unto Apollo; the Satyrs did lament you, and every Priapus made you his moan in sable garb'. The Romans, too, honoured him. The *Carmina Priapea*, a collection of 80 lively, witty, mildly obscene poems which dates from the 1C AD, celebrates the exploits of this popular god. Even after Christianity had triumphed and most pagan practices had been suppressed, Priapus was not forgotten in Asia Minor. With Pan and the Satyrs he continued to preside over 'country matters'.

To the right of the tomb there is a deep, uncovered **cistern**, 5m wide, 20m long and 8m deep. Nearby are two large **cylindrical stones** used for crushing olives and a **carved slab** bearing a brief inscription in Greek.

After Susanoğlu the road follows the coastline, passing on the way a number of small bays which offer excellent swimming. At 5km **Narlikuyu**, the Well of the Pomegranate, there are several good, if rather expensive, restaurants. Their speciality is fish, which is served grilled, fried or baked with *buğulama*, a mouth-watering vegetable sauce. Try the *lakoz*, grey mullet, steaks or the fried *barbunya*, red mullet.

In a small building at the entrance to the village, the **Kızlar Hamamı** or **Bath of the Maidens**, there is a 4C AD Roman **mosaic** of the *Charites*. Better known as the Three Graces, Euphrosyne, Aglaia and Thalia, they were minor goddesses usually associated with Aphrodite. First mentioned in Homeric times, they personified beauty, gentleness and friendship. Depicted in the usual manner as seductive, nude female figures, in this mosaic they are surrounded by fluttering doves and partridges. According to an inscription, the mosaic came from the bath of Poimenius, who claims to have been the friend of emperors and was governor of the Sacred Islands i.e. the Princes' Islands in the Sea of Marmara.

At Narlikuyu a subterranean river empties into the bay and pushes the salt water back. At sunset cowherds bring their animals down to the shore to slake their thirst in the sea, a sight which never fails to astonish visitors. The river is the **Cennet Deresi** from **Cennet**, Paradise, which is a short distance inland. Its water, much colder than the sea, can give the unsuspecting bather an unpleasant shock.

According to Strabo, the **Corycian Cave** where the monster Typhon imprisoned Zeus, was in this part of Cilicia. The cave has been identified with the gigantic hollow known as **Cennet**, Paradise, which is c 2km inland from Narlikuyu.

Typhon, a chthonic deity, was the fruit of the incestuous union of Tartarus with his mother Gaia or he was produced from two eggs which Chronus coated with his own semen and gave to Hera. The accounts vary. Typhon was half man, half animal. He was higher than the mountains and his head touched the stars. He had a hundred serpentine heads which roared like a bull, barked like a dog and spoke the language of the gods. Having disputed control of the world unsuccessfully with Zeus, he was buried under Mt Etna. According to Hesiod, Typhon was confined in the depths of the underworld with the Titans, where he fathered harmful winds like the typhoon which is named after him. Some accounts identify him with Seth who killed Osiris. Before his defeat by Zeus, he mated with Echidna, a coupling which produced the Chimaera, the Sphinx, the Sow of Crommyon, the Nemean Lion and the eagle that tormented Prometheus. Typhon is usually portrayed as a many-headed snake-like creature. The early Christians identified him with the devil, a belief later adopted by the Muslims.

Cennet is a chasm 200m long and 70m deep. Because of the effort required, it is best explored in the cool of early morning or late afternoon. If you have not brought a pocket-torch, you may hire a lamp near the entrance. More than 450 steps lead down to a small grassy plateau. At the far end there is an exquisite 5C **Byzantine church** dedicated to the the Blessed Virgin. This had an apse flanked by two domed sacristies and was probably covered with a pitched wooden roof. The apse and side walls were decorated with some fine frescoes. Unfortunately, these have been almost completely obliterated by the graffiti of mindless vandals. Unless the authorities take action to protect the frescoes a precious piece of history will be lost forever.

To visit the area below the church you will need a lamp. A rudimentary path leads downwards for c 200m to a huge cavern. This was believed to be a place where Typhon imprisoned Zeus. At the rear, a river, the Cennet Deresi, the Stream of Paradise, disappears through a gap with a thunderous roar. It reappears in the sea at Narlikuyu 2km away (see above).

The bushes by the path at Cennet are covered with rags, the votive offerings of modern pilgrims.

Cehennem, Hell, is c 75m to the E of Cennet. Precipitous cliffs line the sides of this 120m deep sinkage. The descent to the bottom can only be made by experienced rock-climbers. You may walk down to Paradise, but to get into Hell requires expertise! Still regarded as one of the gates of the underworld, the bushes here are also festooned with scraps of cloth.

A road from the left of the car-park leads to **Dilek Mağarası**, the Cave of Wishes, which is also part of the Corycian Cave group. It is being developed as a health centre. Asthma sufferers come here in search of a cure.

To the NE of the cave there is a **Hellenistic peribolos** which encloses a 5C church. It is probable that the pagan sanctuary, which dates from the 3C or 2C BC, was dedicated to Zeus Corycius.

From Narlikuyu to 5km Kızkalesi the road passes a number of small, clean beaches. One of the most attractive of these is at 4km **Akkum**, where there are several good pensions and an excellent restaurant *Mola 33*.

Between Akkum and Kızkalesi a rough track on the left leads 8km to **Adamkayalar**, the Cliff of Men, one of the most interesting sites in Cilicia.

The track climbs into the hills, offering magnificent views of a coastline littered with the ruins of ancient cities. Away to the right, on higher ground, are the ruins of a 1C building, which may have formed part of an early Christian settlement, and a perfectly-preserved Roman tomb.

Look for a sign on the left. From the track continue on foot for c 1km on a route marked by red stripes. Adamkayalar is a large **Roman necropolis** of the 1C AD. The **tombs**, cut from a terraced rock-face, have reliefs of the deceased. Some are shown reclining on couches, others are depicted as armed warriors. A few are accompanied by their wives. A male figure holds a battle axe, another a lance and a bird, a third a bunch of grapes. Two have inscriptions. The reliefs, executed with a touching naivety, may be of the rulers and important citizens of a small, nearby town, or of Roman citizens in Asia Minor.

Continue N by way of Hüseyinler to c 12km **Cambazlı** where there are the ruins of a **Byzantine church**. There is an alternative route back to the coast via Keşlitürkmenli, Demircili and Silifke.

Time was when **Kızkalesi** was a small quiet resort, known only to Turkish holidaymakers and a few foreign visitors. An explosion of hotel building has done little to increase its attractiveness. However, the fine sandy beaches, castles, and an ancient city which will satisfy the most fanatical lover of ruins, are still there. Recommended are the well-run, welcoming two-star *Yaka Otel*, and the three-star *Club Barbarossa*. There are also some small, clean pensions.

At Kızkalesi there are two of those fairytale **castles** that hang like jewels from the southern Turkish coastline. One is at the end of a narrow promontory, the other on a rocky islet c 150m out to sea. Kızkalesi, means the Maiden's Castle. It got its name from the oft-repeated legend about the princess who was kept in isolation in a castle for her own safety. The prophecy that she would meet an untimely death from a snake bite was fulfilled when one day a basket of figs containing a hidden viper was brought to her bed chamber by an unwitting servant.

The real history of the Corycian castles is scarcely less dramatic than the legend. An Armenian inscription on the island castle records the fact that they were constructed in the 12C, when this area was part of the Cilician Kingdom of Armenia. Originally connected by a causeway or jetty, the castles were built to protect the city and port of Corycus.

History. After the defeat of the Byzantine army by the Selçuk Turks at the battle of Manzikert in 1071 many Armenians settled in Cilicia. About 1080 two nobles, Ruben and Oshin, established dynasties in the Taurus Mountains. Their successors increased the territory controlled by them, largely at the expense of the Byzantines, so that by 1132 Sis, Anavarza, Adana and Tarsus were under Rubenid control. In 1199 Leo II the Great (1187–1219), the friend and ally of Frederick Barbarossa was crowned in Tarsus in the presence of the Papal Legate, Cardinal Conrad von Wittelsbach.

Under Leo, the Cilician Kingdom of Armenia came under western influence. In close contact with Crusader families, it developed trading links with the Venetians and Genoese. The Armenian language was strongly affected by French. Control of the kingdom passed from the Rubenids to one of the descendants of Oshin, Hethum I (1226–69). He and his successors allied themselves with the Mongols against the Mamelukes of Egypt who were beginning to pose a threat in the Levant. In the 14C the kingdom went to a member of the Lusignan dynasty of Cyprus, but by then the end was near. The Mamelukes continued their advance. By 1359 Adana, Tarsus and most of the Cilician plain was in their hands. The Corycian castles fell to Peter I of Cyprus in 1361. The capital, Sis, and the king, Leo VI were captured by the Mamelukes in 1375. Ransomed, Leo VI died in exile in Paris in 1393 and was buried in St Denis, where his monument may be seen. The title King of Armenia went to the Cypriot James I. Through one of his descendants it passed to the House of Savoy. However, by this time Armenia had ceased to exist as a separate state.

The **land castle** was constructed largely of material from the ancient city of Corycus. The walls contain many broken columns, some of which are laid in regular courses. One tower has a complete **Roman door** which may have come from a tomb. It was protected by a **moat** connected to the sea by a rock-cut channel 10m deep, and by a double wall flanked by towers. Reservoirs provided an adequate water supply.

Access to the interior is from the sandy beach on the W side. A breach leads through the first defensive wall to an area that is very overgrown and filled with debris. By proceeding carefully it is possible to reach a gate which led to the **causeway** linking the two castles. Continue along the ramparts to the E where a ruined tower affords a fine view of the sea, the interior of the castle and the surrounding countryside. Three **churches** inside the castle have traces of faded frescoes on their walls.

There can be few sights more romantic than Kızkalesi's **sea castle**. Mirrored in the calm waters of the harbour at sunset, it is easy to see it as Keats' enchanted castle which had,

> Charm'd magic casements, opening on the foam
> Of perilous seas, in faery lands forlorn.

Remote and unreal, it floats between sea and sky, nearer to the world of abandoned, love-lorn maidens than that of the warring factions of Crusaders, Armenians and Mamelukes who fought for its possession.

Visitors go to the outer castle by boats which leave from the beach to the W of the land castle at frequent intervals. The trip takes 20 minutes.

The walls, which are in a better state of preservation than those of the land castle, are 3m thick and 8m high. Roughly triangular in shape it has towers at each corner 20m high, with five turrets in between. Entry is by a door at the E end, the keystone of which is decorated with a finely-carved cross. Above the door there are two inscriptions in Armenian which give the date of the castle's construction as AD 1151, i.e. during the reign of Hetoum I. A stone stairs leads to one of the towers, from where you get a splendid view of the whole structure. You can make a circuit of the ramparts which have been repaired recently in part. Note the **reservoirs** hollowed from the rock and the ruins of a small **church** in the centre of the keep.

Across the road from the land castle are the ruins of **Corycus**. Here ruined tombs, baths, churches and private houses are scattered over the hillside. For the most part they are covered in tangled vegetation which makes detailed examination difficult. Many of the tombs are decorated with reliefs. According to the inscriptions people of all occupations were buried here—cobblers, goldsmiths, fruiterers, shipbuilders, weavers and mid-wives. Note the crude 4C AD **carving of an armed warrior**. Headless now, he stands stiffly, legs apart, his left hand resting lightly on his sword-hilt.

Archaeologists have found **Graeco-Persian reliefs** on a monument from Corycus. These are believed to show a scene of ritual *hommage* to the dead conducted in an oriental manner with two women riding side-saddle. Two further blocks from the same monument, which has been dated to the last quarter of the 4C BC, are in the museums of Silifke and Adana.

Many visitors have noted the profusion of ancient ruins on the coastline between Corycus and Ayaş. Beaufort wrote:

> the shore presents a continued scene of ruins, all of which being white, and relieved by the dark wooded hills behind them, give to the country an appearance of splendour and populousness, that serves only, on nearer approach, to heighten the contrast with its real poverty and degradation.

At **Ayaş**, 3km to the E of Kızkalesi, you will find the extensive ruins of the city of **Elaeusa/Sebaste**. There is a coffee-house on the right of the E24 where you may park. Dolmuş and long-distance bus services stop here.

History. Some identify Elaeusa with **Vilusa**, a town mentioned in Hittite records of c 1400 BC. The first definite proof of the city's existence is provided by a late 2C or early 1C BC tetradrachm. This gives the city's name and bears a representation of a female deity holding a rudder, perhaps a reference to Elaeusa's importance as a port.

When Pompey cleared the pirates from Cilicia in 67 BC, many of its inhabitants were settled in other parts of the Roman dominions. Some were sent as far away as southern Italy. Virgil recalls this resettlement:

> Beneath the towers of a Calabrian town,
> Where dark Galaesus waters yellow fields,
> I once beheld an old Cilician
> Who owned a paltry patch of unclaimed land...

In the 1C BC the area around Elaeusa was controlled by Tarcondimotus Philantonius, a dynast from eastern Cilicia. Later, c 20 BC, it was given by Augustus to Archelaus I of Cappadocia. To express his gratitude he renamed the city Sebaste, the Greek for Augustus. According to Strabo, Archelaus built a palace here. He may also have enlarged the city, as on his coins he describes himself as a builder. In AD 38 Sebaste came under the control of Antiochus I of Commagene and of his wife, Iotape.

Sebaste was an episcopal see in the province of Cilicia Prima. Its bishop attended the Council of Chalcedon in AD 451. Little is known of the city's subsequent history under the Byzantines and the Turks.

Elaeusa's original settlement was on an island, which in the course of time was joined through silting to the mainland. The N end of the peninsula thus formed has been separated from the rest of the city by the modern road. The island site, which is very overgrown, is reached from the beach to the E of the coffee-house. There are the remains of a **Byzantine basilica**.

The most interesting monument in Elaeusa/Sebaste is the **Roman temple** which was built on the S end of a headland at the SW side of the bay. To the NW there was a terrace 100m wide, while on the E several smaller terraces supported a number of **tombs** and **heroa**. The temple was a peripteros with 6 by 12 columns in the Corinthian order. The stylobate, 17.6m by 32.9m, is paved with stone slabs. Only five of the columns now stand higher than their bases. With the Temple of Zeus Olbius at Uzuncaburç it ranks as one of the best-preserved classical temples in Cilicia.

In the late 5C a small **church**, measuring 11.35m by 7.30m, was built inside the temple. This was frequently done, partly to save construction costs and partly to affirm Christianity's victory. A crudely-executed **mosaic** in the apse, depicting birds and animals in a setting of paradise, is reminiscent of earlier mosaics of Orpheus charming the animals.

The city's **necropolis** was to the N of the modern road. Terraces here support row after row of **heroa**, while the road to an inland site at Çatı Ören is lined with sarcophagi.

About 3.5km E of Ayaş a road on the left leads to 4km **KANLIDİVANE**, perhaps the strangest site in Cilicia. Known in ancient times as **Kanytelis** or **Neapolis**, it has not been excavated and much of that which has been said and written about it is based on folklore and conjecture.

To appreciate fully the eerie atmosphere of Kanlıdivane, go there at twilight, when the shadows lengthen in the necropolis and the great cliffs of the central chasm are stained scarlet. Then you will understand the meaning of its Turkish name. Kanlıdivane means 'the crazy place of blood'. It is said that condemned criminals were thrown into the chasm, there to be devoured by wild animals.

There are no refreshment facilities at Kanlıdivane. It is little visited even during the holiday season. There are, however, several places where you may picnic—if you are not put off by the surroundings.

History. Kanlıdivane, probably founded during the Hellenistic period, was almost certainly a dependency of Olba. The ruins visible today are almost all Roman and Byzantine. The Byzantine town is believed to date from the reign of Theodosius II (408–450). Sufficiently far away from the coast to be unaffected by the Arab raids, it appears to have enjoyed a long period of prosperity. After the capture of the Cilician coastal area by the Selçuk Turks, at the beginning of the 13C, Kanlıdivane entered a decline from which it never recovered. It was virtually forgotten until the accounts of 19C travellers, like Victor Langlois, brought it once more to the notice of scholars.

The **Hellenistic tower**, 15m by 9.25m by 17m high, guarded the approaches to the city. According to inscriptions on the seventh and ninth corner stones it was dedicated to Olban Zeus c 200 BC by a priest named Teucros. Further proof of its links with Olba is provided by the carving of a *triskele* above the entrance. Some authorities, however, maintain that it was constructed during the Roman period. It certainly antedates the Byzantine era, when it was repaired and reinforced. To the left of the tower are the remains of a large Byzantine **church**. Like all the churches at Kanlıdivane, it was a basilica. Its walls, which stand to c 10m, have well-preserved doorways.

On the S wall of the chasm there is an interesting **relief** which is believed to date from the 3C BC, the period of Olban domination. The relief, sited in a recess, measures c 4m by 2m and is executed in a naive, childish style. It is surmounted by an inscription in Greek letters which is partly worn away. There are six figures, two male and four female. Their identity is not known; they may be members of the Olban priestly dynasty. Seated on a tribune at the right-hand side there is the figure of an old man wearing a toga. He holds his right hand across his breast; by his side is a female figure. To the left there are four younger persons, a man wearing a toga, and three females. The female figures are also shown with their right hands across their breasts. This relief is faced by another on the NW wall of the chasm. Set somewhat lower down, it shows the standing figure of an **armed warrior** dressed in a Roman tunic with his left on his sword.

To the left of the path, which encircles the chasm, there is a small Muslim cemetery which is still in use. Beyond the cemetery are the ruins of a **church** and of buildings which are believed to have been occupied by a monastic community. Note in particular the fine vaulted **cistern**. To the right of the path, on a terrace overlooking the chasm, are the remains of a **small temple**. The path terminates in a plateau occupied by a large **church** which is in a good state of repair. The apse, choir and the lower part of the doorway remain. Note the inscription above the entrance. This states that the church was built by somebody named Papylos. To the N of the church are the ruins of a **temple-tomb** which, like most funerary monuments in the area, has been robbed. There are fine views of the city's ruins and of the great pit in its centre from this plateau.

To the E, half-hidden by a tangled mass of vegetation, there are the remains of many buildings, including a number of churches. Some of these ruins are now used as shelters by nomadic shepherds who graze their flocks near the site. Care should be taken in exploring this area, as it contains several cisterns partly or entirely covered by the dense undergrowth.

Kanlıdivane is surrounded by ancient cemeteries. **Tombs**, many dating from the Roman period, are scattered across the hillsides. A number bear representations of the deceased: soldiers in armour; men reclining on couches; women in graceful poses. There are several good examples on the approach road from the S. All have been robbed, and most are partly covered by the thorny scrub which makes it difficult to examine them.

A short distance after the turning for Kanlıdivane at the village of Limonlu, the E24 crosses the **Lamas Çayi**, the ancient **Lamus** river. This river was regarded by Strabo as the boundary between Rugged and Smooth Cilicia. Just beyond the river, on the left-hand side of the road, are the remains of the aqueducts which brought water from the Taurus Mountains to Kanytelis/Neapolis, Elaeusa/Sebaste and Corycus.

In the Middle Ages the Lamus separated two warring worlds. According to Gibbon, Christian and Muslim prisoners were exchanged here in the 9C. When they reached their own lines, the Arabs cried out '*Allah Akbar*'; the Christians countered with a lusty chant of '*Kyrie Eleison*'.

At this point the foothills of the Taurus Mountains give way to the great plain which extends eastwards to Adana and beyond. Lacking the variety and the ancient ruins which make the journey across Pamphylia and Rough Cilicia so interesting, Smooth Cilicia, Cilicia Campestris, does not tempt the traveller to linger. In summer a sea of green rice fields, relieved only by the white squares of the cotton plantations, it swelters under a fierce and unrelenting sun. In winter, swept by cold winds from the Taurus Mountains, it is equally uninviting.

Between the Lamas river and Mersin the E24 carries a good deal of commercial traffic and follows a relatively straight course across the plain. At 14km **Erdemli**, the only town of any size before Mersin, there is a camping site, **Erdemli Çamlığı**, set among pine trees on the right. Open all the year round this has a small *lokanta*, electricity and running water.

At 23km is the village of Mezitli. A turning on the right leads to 2km **Viranşehir**, ancient **Soli** or **Pompeiopolis**.

Viranşehir is a small resort much favoured by the people of Mersin. Near the rather uninviting beach of grey sand and mud, there are several motels and camping places. Because of its proximity to the city, the sea may not be free from pollution.

History. Founded by the Rhodians c 700 BC, Soli was one of the oldest settlements in Rugged Cilicia. The orthodox Stoic philosopher Chrysippus (c 280–207 BC) was born here. In 83 BC the Armenian king Tigranes the Great (94–55 BC) captured the city during the campaign that won him the Syrian monarchy. His kingdom then extended from the Euphrates to the sea. Tigranes moved the inhabitants of Soli to his capital, Tigranocerta, on the Tigris. After Pompey had defeated and routed the Cilician pirates at the battle of Coracesium (modern Alanya) in 67 BC, he turned his attention to Tigranes who offered his submission. Pompey built a new city at Soli, and as an expression of gratitude its citizens named his foundation Pompeiopolis.

In antiquity the people of Soli were reputed to speak such an incorrect form of Greek that the word σολοικισμός was coined from the name of their city to describe it. The English word solecism is derived from this. An unsupported tradition relates that Alexander the Great was so angered by the failure of Soli to preserve the purity of the Greek language that he imposed heavy penalties on its citizens. However, according to Arrian, its citizens were fined, not for bad grammar, but for their support of the Persian cause.

Soli/Pompeiopolis, which is believed to have had a population of 250,000 at one time, was almost completely destroyed by an earthquake in the 6C AD, hence its Turkish name Viranşehir, Ruined City. The most imposing monument from the past is the line of **37 columns** on the right of the road which leads to the sea. These columns, some of whose capitals are ornamented with human figures and mythological animals, formed part of a colonnaded street c 450m long and 10m wide constructed in the 2C or 3C AD. Each column has a console which supported a bronze statue.

Beaufort was impressed by this colonnade as an architectural feature, though critical of the workmanship and design. In *Karamania*, he wrote: 'the taste of the architect seems to have been as corrupt as the execution ... the design of the foliage differs in capitals of the same order; and between the volutes of some, are placed the human bust, or figures of animals and other meretricious ornaments'.

Around the colonnade there are the ruins of several unidentified buildings and a number of cisterns. In Beaufort's time Soli had the remains of its theatre, city walls, aqueduct and a prodigal scattering of tombs. There was also 'a beautiful harbour, or basin, with parallel sides, and circular ends; it is', he wrote, 'entirely artificial, being formed by surrounding walls, or moles, which are fifty feet in thickness, and seven in height'. Traces of the mole exist. Soli has not been surveyed or excavated.

From Metzitli to 11km Mersin the E24 is lined with apartments, restaurants and hotels.

34

Mersin (İçel) to Adana

Total distance 67km. Mersin—29km Tarsus—38km Adana (c 50km Karataş/Megarsus).

The history of **MERSİN (İçel)** can be traced back to the Hittites. However, the city has kept few traces of its past and most visitors use it as a base for excursions to places of interest in the surrounding countryside or as a staging-post on journeys in SE Turkey.

When Beaufort sailed along the southern Turkish coast in 1811–12, Mersin was a hamlet of a few miserable huts. Today it has a population of more than half a million and is Turkey's largest port on the Mediterranean. An important trading centre, it now handles much of the produce of the great fertile plain of Çukurova. Linked by the E24 with the cities on the western Mediterranean littoral and with Adana and other large centres to the E, it also has good communications with central Anatolia through the Cilician Gates. There is a night ferry service to **Gazimağusa** (Famagusta) in Northern Cyprus and frequent services to other Mediterranean ports.

The city has been well planned. It has wide boulevards and on the seafront there are attractive formal gardens full of exotic plants. There are good hotels and restaurants. However, despite strenuous efforts to turn it into a tourist centre, Mersin's future appears to be linked firmly with commerce. The plumes of smoke that float across the city from the industrial area to the E, disfiguring the azure sky, are vivid reminders of that fact.

Information and Accommodation. The **Tourist Information Office** is in Yeni Mah., İnönü Bul., Liman Girişi. According to the Ministry of Tourism list the city has one five-star, three four-star, two three-star, and eleven two-star hotels. The *Ramada*, the *Hilton* and the *Mersin Oteli* are recommended.

Post Office and Banks. Mersin's main post office is near the Mersin Oteli in Gümrük Meyd. Branches of the principal Turkish banks are to be found throughout the city.

Transport. Mersin is linked by train to 29km Tarsus and 67km Adana. Adana is on the Turkish Railways network. The nearest airport is at Adana, from where there are frequent internal flights by Turkish Airlines. City buses, including those to Mezitli and Viranşehir, and dolmuş services for destinations in the city and environs leave from stops near the Tourist Information Office. Long-distance buses depart from the new *otogar* on the northern outskirts of the city.

Museums. There are plans to establish a museum in the city. Some artefacts from Mersin are displayed in the Adana Archaeological Museum.

The earliest signs of occupation have been found in a mound, **Yümüktepe**. This is easily reached by bus from the city centre. A site for the specialist, it is now largely covered by a run-down municipal park. Excavations made by Professor Garstang of the University of Liverpool have revealed 23 levels of occupation. The earliest dates from c 6300 BC, the latest from the Selçuk period (16C). Sherds and earthenware link it with Çatalhöyük and Can-hasan and with the N Syrian sites of Byblos and Ras Shamara. Many of the objects found here are in the Adana Archaeological Museum.

East of Mersin there is a substantial increase in traffic on the E24. Having passed through an unattractive stretch of landscape, pockmarked by ugly industrial development, it is with some relief that the traveller turns off the main road to 29km Tarsus.

Although **TARSUS** has kept few reminders of its long and turbulent history, the Ottoman houses, rambling streets and flower-filled gardens produce an effect which is difficult to resist. Tarsus wears its ravaged features with a charming air of insouciance that disarms and stifles criticism. However sceptical one feels, there is an urge to believe that on an autumn day in 41 BC Cleopatra came through this crumbling gateway to meet Mark Antony and that St Paul once quenched his thirst at that unremarkable well.

History. The origins of Tarsus are lost in legend. According to an Islamic tradition it was established by Seth, the son of Adam. Excavations prove that it existed during the Early Bronze Age (between 3000 and 2500 BC). A fortified settlement c 2500 BC, it was then the capital of a minor kingdom. Its position on the coast S of the Cilician Gates enabled it to control trade from Syria and Egypt to places to the S and E, and to central Anatolia. Imported artefacts testify to its status on this trade route.

Greek settlers from Argos, attracted no doubt by its commercial reputation, founded a colony at Tarsus in the 12C BC. Captured by the Assyrians towards the end of the 8C BC, it revolted and was razed to the ground by Sennacherib (705–681 BC) in 696 BC. Xenophon came here in 400 BC during the course of his famous and unsuccessful expedition to put Cyrus on the throne of Persia. He describes it as being a rich and powerful city which was governed by a king named Synnesis.

Alexander came to Tarsus in 333 BC and fell seriously ill, because, according to the ancient historians, he had bathed in the icy waters of the Cydnus. It is possible, however, that he contracted a fever in the malaria-ridden plains around the city. After the death of Alexander, Tarsus came under the control of Seleucus Nicator, king of Syria (c 321–281 BC). By the 2C BC Tarsus was an important centre of learning and it had a large Jewish community. The city was occupied for a time by Tigranes the Great (94–55 BC) and it attracted the attention of the pirates who had begun to prey on the coastal trade. After Pompey put an end to piracy in 67 BC, Tarsus and the rest of Cilicia came under Roman rule. Cicero, who was one of the first Roman governors of Cilicia, lived here from 51–50 BC. Julius Caesar visited the city in 47 BC.

In 41 BC Tarsus was the scene of one of the most romantic encounters of antiquity. Cleopatra, queen of Egypt, came to the city to meet Mark Antony, the 'triple pillar of the world' whom she 'transformed into strumpet's fool'. Shakespeare, drawing on the account in Plutarch, describes her arrival:

> The barge she sat in, like a burnish'd throne,
> Burn'd on the water: the poop was beaten gold,
> Purple the sails, and so perfumed that
> The winds were love-sick with them; ...
> ...For her own person,
> It beggar'd all description: she did lie
> In her pavilion, cloth of gold, of tissue,
> O'er picturing that Venus where we see
> The fancy outwork nature; on each side her
> Stood pretty dimpled boys, like smiling Cupids, ...

About 46 years later Saul, the future St Paul, was born in Tarsus. A Jew he was also a Roman citizen. After his dramatic conversion on the road to Damascus he was obliged to flee from that city and Jerusalem, and he returned for a time to his native city. Though it is not recorded in the Bible, it seems likely that he visited Tarsus also during his missionary journeys to Galatia and Phrygia. Paul's pride in his native city is reflected in his statement to the Roman Commandant in Jerusalem. 'I am a Jew, a Tarsian from Cilicia, a citizen of no mean city'. Tarsus became an important Christian centre and three of the great councils of the church were held here in 431, 435 and 1177.

After a period of prosperity under the Byzantines, the fortunes of Tarsus suffered a reverse in 641, when it was sacked by the Arabs. During the centuries that followed the city had many rulers. The Arabs held it until it was recaptured by Nicephorus Phocas in 965. In 1087 it was taken by the Selçuk Turks. Ten years later during the First Crusade it was recaptured by Christian forces under Baldwin and Tancred, who placed a Byzantine garrison here. From 1132–1375 Tarsus was part of the Cilician kingdom of Armenia. In 1199 Leo II was crowned here by the Papal Legate, Cardinal Conrad von Wittelsbach. Pillaged twice by the Arabs towards the end of the 13C, it was taken by the Mamelukes in 1359. Finally, in 1515 it came under Ottoman rule.

When Beaufort came to Tarsus in 1812, he received a cool welcome from the governor and his officers were rudely treated by the populace. It was then a city of several thousand inhabitants and had a number of 'respectable looking moskes' and well-stocked bazaars. However, apart from the governor's residence, Beaufort thought its houses small and wretched.

At the entrance to the city there is the **Kancık Kapışı**, the Gate of the Bitch. This is also known as Cleopatra's Gate or St Paul's Gate, though it has no known links with either. It was probably a portal in the ancient city-walls which gave access to the harbour.

Not far from the Kancık Kapışı is Tarsus American College, a a co-educational Turkish junior and senior high school established in 1888. Under the grounds lie the foundations of a 1C AD Roman hippodrome.

Near the vegetable market in the city centre is an ancient spring which romantics call **St Paul's Well**. The guardian will assure you that the saint often drank here and that its waters have remarkable curative properties. About 1m below ground level, it is surrounded by Roman paving. There are plans to excavate the area and restore the well to its original state.

Also in the city centre are the ruins of a Roman building which may have been a bath. By the side of this building is **Kilise Cami** which was built over a 14C Armenian church dedicated to St Peter. According to an Islamic legend, the prophet Daniel is buried under a stream which flows close to the nearby **Makam Cami**.

The **museum** of Tarsus, Tahakhane Mah., 155 Sok., No. 1, is housed in the **Kulat Paşa Medrese**, built in 1570. Each cell is devoted to a particular period. In the courtyard there is a fine **Roman sarcophagus**, decorated with erotes and garlands. In the apse there is an **Assyrian or late Hittite stele** with representations of the sun-god and moon-goddess in roundels and a male figure between two lions. Nearby is a **Urartian urn**. Note also the beautifully carved **mihrab** which dates from c 1600. Against the left-hand wall is a mysterious **graffito** which depicts a figure of indeterminate sex partially encircled by a snake. By popular tradition this is called the King of the Snakes, but its subject, period and provenance are unknown.

In the ethnographical collection are Ottoman illuminated Korans, hamam shoes, silver head-covers and silver belts and buckles. Note the Ottoman gravestones, many of which are elaborately carved.

The museum has a fine collection of Greek, Roman and Byzantine coins and some interesting jewellery including a 2C AD **gold diadem** found in Tarsus and Roman rings and bracelets.

Ulu Cami was built in the 16C on the site of the Cathedral of St Paul. Following the customary plan of mosques of that time, it is rectangular in shape, with a length three times its width. Inside are the tombs of the Caliph Mamoun, of Seth son of Noah, and of Lokman Hekim. (The tomb of Seth may have been an early Christian shrine.) Near Ulu Cami is **Kırk Kaşik**, a covered market which dates from the same period as the mosque. It has been restored recently.

Outside the medieval city walls, to the E, there is a remarkable construction called **Donuktaş**, the Frozen Stones. It is hidden in a maze of tiny streets and is not easy to find without the help of a guide. Popular tradition asserts that it was the tomb of the Assyrian Sardanapalus who perished at the siege of Nineveh in 612 BC. In fact, it is believed to be the core-wall of a **2C AD Roman temple** which has lost the marble slabs that once covered it. It was probably a large peripteral temple with 10 by 21 columns on a three-stepped crepidoma which measured 49 by 102m with architraves of Proconnesian marble. It has been tentatively identified with the neocorus erected during the reign of Commodus (AD 180–92). Recent excavations have produced a number of small finds including some Roman lamps.

To the NW of the city is **Gözlükule**, a tumulus, which has been excavated by the University of Princeton. It has revealed remains that date from the Bronze Age to the 16C AD. These include baths and a portico from the Hellenistic period and part of a Roman theatre. From the top of the tumulus there is a fine view of the plain that stretches S from Tarsus to the sea. This was once covered by the lake called Rhegma which Strabo said formed the harbour of Tarsus, where Cleopatra disembarked from her golden barge.

As part of a scheme to prevent flooding of the city, the emperor Justinian (527–565), had a **bridge** constructed on the Tarsus river, the ancient Cydnus. Repaired and restored during the Ottoman period, it is still in use.

A pleasant **excursion** may be made up the valley of the Cydnus and to a eucalyptus forest on the outskirts of the town. The banks of the river, which here descends in a series of rapids, are favourite places for summer picnics. The eucalyptus forest abounds in game, especially wild boar. All the animals are protected by law and may not be hunted.

Between Tarsus and 38km Adana the E24 passes through an area, formerly dependent on agriculture, which is rapidly becoming industrialised. As it approaches Adana, traffic density increases. Everything from slow-moving bullock-carts to heavily laden lorries may be encountered.

A wide boulevard leads to the centre of Turkey's fourth largest city, **ADANA**, which has a population of almost one million. A provincial capital, it derives its wealth from the agricultural produce of the Çukurova Plain and from its strategic position at the junction of the main E–W highway and the route through the Cilician Gates to central Anatolia. Pleasantly laid-out along the banks of the Seyhan river, the ancient Sarus, the city is surrounded by gardens and citrus groves which give it a pleasant feeling of *rus in urbe*.

Information and Accommodation. The **Tourist Information Office** is at Atatürk Cad. 13. The Ministry of Tourism lists two five-star, three four-star, one three-star, and five two-star hotels together with a number of more modest establishments. Recommended are the five-star *Büyük Sürmeli Oteli* and the four-star *Inci Oteli*. There are a several inexpensive pensions which offer varying degrees of comfort and service. Apart from the hotel restaurants, there are others, particularly in the area near Ulu Cami, which specialise in regional dishes like the spicy Adana Kebab.

Post Office and Banks. Adana's principal post office is near the Kemeraltı mosque in the city centre. There are branches of the main Turkish banks.

Transport. Adana has good road, rail, and air connections. There are long-distance bus services by the E24 to Alanya and Antalya, via Gaziantep to eastern Turkey, by the E5 S to Antayka and N, via the Cilician Gates, to Ankara. There are comfortable, long-distance trains, including a night sleeper to Ankara. THY provides connections with all the principal Turkish cities and, via İstanbul, with destinations abroad.

History. The origins of Adana are shrouded in legend. Its name may be derived from Adanos, son of Uranus, who is credited with having founded the city c 1000 BC. It has been tentatively identified with **Danunas**, the city of the Hittite king Asitawadda, which is mentioned on an inscription found at Karatepe, 125km to the NE.

From early times there was a colony of Greek traders and it had important commercial relations with countries in the Middle East. According to the Bible (I Kings 10.28), Solomon imported horses from the plain of Coa (Çukurova). Conquered by the Assyrian Sargon II c 712 BC, it and the surrounding area came under Persian control.

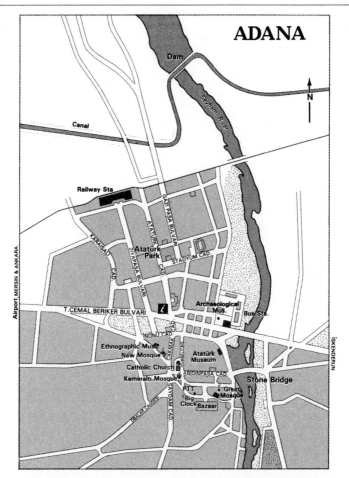

Until the Hellenistic period, Adana was overshadowed by its larger and more important neighbour, Tarsus. It enjoyed a period of prosperity under the Seleucid Antiochus IV Epiphanes (175–164 BC), who renamed it Antiocheia on the Sarus. When Cilicia came under Roman rule in the 1C BC the strategic and economic importance of Adana's location was recognised. During the reign of Hadrian (117–138) a stone bridge, which is still used, was constructed over the Sarus (Seyhan) river.

During the centuries that followed, Adana changed hands frequently. Like its neighbours it was conquered by the Arabs and became part of a chain of fortified outposts on the frontier with Byzantium. In the 11C the city came, successively, under the rule of the Selçuks and the Armenians. It fell into the hands of the Mamelukes in the 14C, when they overran the Cilician Kingdom of Armenia. Finally, in 1515, during the reign of Selim I, Adana was captured by the Ottoman Turks.

Adana's **Archaeological Museum**, in Fuzuli Cad. near the Seyhan River, has a fine collection of artefacts most of which were found in the city and surrounding countryside. Unfortunately, only a few bear labels giving dates, and provenance. Apart from a short leaflet in somewhat fractured English, there is no published information about the collection.

In the garden there is a collection of architectural fragments, stelae and funerary monuments from various periods. In the entrance hall is the so-called **Achilles sarcophagus** from Tarsus which dates from the 2C AD. The long sides are decorated with scenes from the *Iliad*: the dead Hector, Priam before Achilles, Hermes and Briseis, the dead Patroclus. At the ends there are representations of a sphinx and of a griffin. A 4C BC **anthropoid sarcophagus,** which was found at Soli, came originally from Sidon in Phoenicia. This takes the form of a figure of indeterminate sex with long hair. Three Roman **cinerary urns** from near Adana contain human remains. On the wall to the right there is a large **broken statue** from Kadirli which is believed to represent a Roman senator.

Just inside the door of the room to the right are two **lead coffins** which date from c 1400. One has the representation of a seven-branched candle-stick on the inside. Note the large sections of **Roman and Byzantine mosaics** from Adana on the wall nearby. A fine **Hittite stele** from Maraş shows a male figure standing on a bull's back holding an axe. In the centre of the room there is a large **bronze statue** of a Roman senator which was found in the sea at Karataş. This has been skilfully restored by Turkish archae-ologists. On the end wall is a 2C AD **mosaic** from Adana showing two erotes, one fighting an animal, the other holding a bow. The two large **bronze bowls** are Roman, as is the substantial fragment of a **statue of Bes**. On the landing upstairs there are late period funerary stelae and cases of **Roman glass**. Note also the fine **female head** with an oriental-type headdress.

Apart from a large **mosaic** from Adana, which may depict Orpheus, the rooms on the first floor are devoted to a display of ceramics, terracottas, bronzes and coins. Among the Roman bronzes there are two fine **figurines of Mithras**, one wearing a curious cloak. There are also busts of Ares, Zeus, Apollo, Aphrodite, Tyche and Pan. A **bronze Hittite figure** is fitted with a detachable gold mask. Objects found in 1972 at Anazarbus in a 2C or 3C AD sarcophagus include a marble bust, glass rod, bone needle, glass bottles and glass hairpins, gold earrings and a ring, and a pottery lamp. Among the jewellery there is an **iron seal ring** which has a red agate engraved with a representation of Augustus. There is a large selection of **gold grave goods**, including a circlet of leaves which was placed on the head of the corpse, and a crown. Among a fine display of seals from many periods and locations note the interesting group of **Hittite seals** from Tarsus.

The **Ethnographical Museum** in the city centre, near the Adana Hotel, is housed in a former church. In addition to the usual collection of costumes, household objects, jewellery, musical instruments, carpets and kilims, there is an excellent reconstruction of a **nomads' tent**. Note also the fine display of copies of the Koran and of traditional embroidery.

When Atatürk visited Adana in 1923 and 1925, he stayed in the former palace of Suphi Paşa. This building, located near the Seyhan, has been turned into a **museum** to commemorate his visits.

Adana's most striking reminder of the past is the **Taş Köprü**, the Stone Bridge, which spans the river Seyhan, the ancient Sarus. An inscription in Museum suggests that it was constructed by an engineer named Auxentius in the reign of Hadrian. Akurgal, however, proposes that it may have been built by the Auxentius, the *comes et mechanicus* who was known as a constructor of bridges in Rome c AD 384. The bridge was restored by Justinian in the 6C, by the Caliph Memoun, the son of Haroun-al-Rashid, in the 9C, and several times under Ottoman rule. Until the beginning of this century a toll had to be paid by those who used it.

Secured in the past by strong gates at either end, the Taş Köpru is 300m long and 13m high. Three of its 21 arches have been filled in. At one time the Seyhan was navigable as far as the bridge. However, the water-level of the river has been lowered by the construction of two dams upstream. A pleasant evening walk, particularly during the fierce heat of Adana's summer, is from Taş Köpru to the lower dam, a distance of c 1.5km.

Adana has a rich heritage of Islamic buildings. In the centre of the city, at the back of of Abidin Paşa Cad., is the 16C **Ulu Camii**. Constructed by members of the Ramazan family in a style found frequently in northern Syria, the outside is decorated with black and white marble. The *mihrab* is surrounded by a band of the same marble and ornamented with ceramic tiles from Kütahya and İznik. In a park nearby is the tomb of the well-known Turkish poet **Ziya Paşa**. To the rear of Ulu Camii is the small 15C **Akça Mesçidi**. Two fine old houses are the late 15C **Harem Dairesi** and **Selamlik Dairesi**. They were built by Halil Bey, a distinguished member of the Ramazan family. Much loved by the people of Adana is the late Ottoman period **clock tower**. Built of brick, its stark, simple lines are reminiscent of the medieval watch-towers of San Gimignano.

You can get to an **artificial lake** created by the upper dam on the Seyhan river by the road to c 10km **Çıraklı** and c 35km **Çatalan**. Here there are facilities for boating and a number of pleasant picnic sites.

To the S of the city, Road 815 crosses a fertile, if monotonous, plain to reach the sea at 50km **Karataş**. This has been identified as the site of **Megarsus** which was visited by Alexander in 333 BC. Here, according to Arrian, he sacrificed to the 'local Athene'.

On the outskirts of the village are the remains of ancient walls and baths, while a short distance from the shore there are some submerged ruins. A fine bronze statue, believed to be a representation of a Roman senator, was found in the sea off Karataş. It is now in the Adana Archaeological Museum.

About 2km to the E of Karataş there is a pleasant camping site in a small wood. The modern village has few attractions. The surrounding coastline is dull. The beaches are muddy and not very clean. Interest in this part of Cilicia springs from its historical associations. Alexander came to Megarsus at a critical moment in his campaign against the Persians and it was from here that he went on to his decisive encounter with Darius at Issus.

The site of ancient **Mallus** is a short distance inland on the Pyramus river, the modern Ceyhan Nehri. Here Alexander sacrificed to the ghost of the seer and demi-god Amphilochus, who was, according to Strabo, the son of Alcmaeon and Manto. With his half-brother Mopsus, also a famous sooth-sayer, he established a dream oracle at Mallus. Later they quarrelled over who should rule the place and, engaging in single combat, each fell by the other's hand. They were buried at Megarsus but their enmity continued after death. The tombs of the soothsayers were so placed that one could not be seen from the other! (Strabo, *Geography* 14.5.16).

Alexander settled some local political problems at Mallus. As he claimed descent from the Argive Heracleidae and as Mallus was a colony of Argos, Alexander also remitted the tribute which the town paid to Darius. Today nothing remains of this ancient settlement. All its stones were carted away to be used in the construction of the modern village of Kızıltahta.

35

Excursions from Adana

A. Yılan Kalesi, Anavarza (Anazarbus), Kadirli and Karatape

Total distance c 169km. Adana—E24/E5 c 25km—(c 3km Yakapınar, formerly Misis, ancient Mopsuetia)—(c 10km Sirkeli)—(c 3km Yılan Kalesi)—(c 3km Ceyhan)—(c 4km Anavarza/Anazarbus)—c 12km Çukurköprü—c 15km Kadirli/Flaviopolis—c 21km Karatepe—c 18km Bodrum/Hierapolis Castabala—c 3km Toprakkale—c 75km Adana.

This excursion will take you to some of the Hittite, Roman, Crusader and Armenian sites around Adana. It is aimed at visitors who have their own transport. While the route can be covered in one day, a fuller, more rewarding examination of the sites requires at least two days. As accommodation outside Adana is not easy to find, it is suggested that you use the city as a base. There are restaurants at Ceyhan and Kadirli and light refreshments may be obtainable at or near the other sites. However, there are many places on the route where it is possible to picnic. All of these sites can be reached by some form of public transport. However, this will certainly be at the cost of much wasted time as connections between the various towns and villages are neither frequent nor reliable.

Leave Adana by the E24/E5 in the direction of Ceyhan. After c 25km turn right to 38km **Yakapınar**, formerly known as **Misis**. In ancient times it was called **Mopsuestia** because of a tradition that it was founded by Mopsus.

History. According to legend Mopsus fled with a group of followers from Troy after its capture by the Greeks. In addition to Mallus and Mopsuestia, he is credited with having established a number of other cities in Asia Minor. An interesting link with this belief is provided by an inscription at Karatepe (c 60km to the NE). This states that the Hittite king Azitawadda, who reigned in the late 9C or early 8C BC, claimed descent from Mopsus. The presence of Hittites in the area around Mopsuestia is proved by the discovery of a 13C BC relief of King Muwattalli at nearby Sirkeli.

After the death of Alexander, Mopsuestia became part of the Seleucid kingdom of Syria and, to flatter its conquerors, called itself for a time Seleucia. Later, when it passed into the hands of the Romans, it reverted to its old name. However, the Mopseustians were always ready to change when it was to their advantage. During the reign of Hadrian (117–138), the town took his name. Not surprisingly, under the *Pax Romana* it enjoyed a period of considerable affluence. It was an episcopal see.

In the 7C and 8C, when the Arabs ravaged Cilicia, Mopsuestia suffered badly. During the centuries that followed, it shared the fate of its neighbours. At different times it was ruled by the Byzantines, Arabs, Armenians, Crusaders, Mamelukes and Turks. The Crusaders called it Mamistra. Under its walls the bloody, fratricidal encounter between Baldwin and Tancred, which so disgraced the First Crusade, took place in 1097. Because of the Roman bridge over the Pyramus (Ceyhan Nehri) at Mamistra and its importance as a stronghold on the route to Syria, possession of the city was frequently disputed by the various Christian factions and by the Muslims. About 1134 it was captured by the Armenian Leo I, but retaken shortly afterwards by the Byzantines under John Comnenus. In 1158 Manuel I Comnenus received the submission of Reginald de Chatillon, who had ravaged Cyprus, at Mamistra. From 1173 onwards, after Mleh's victory over the Byzantines, it was again in Armenian hands. Despite all the turmoil, the city was an important trading post until the late 14C. Genoese and other European merchants established depots here and bartered for goods brought overland by caravan from the Far East. With the rest of Cilicia, Mamistra came under Ottoman rule in 1515, when it was captured by Selim the Grim (1512–20).

There are few traces of the past at Yakapınar. When Victor Langlois visited Cilicia in 1852 and 1853, the **Roman bridge** over the Pyramus had a *cippus* commemorating a soldier of the XVI legion, who had served in Cilicia, Lycia and Palestine. The bridge, which was repaired by Justinian (527–565), was damaged by a flood in 1717 and again after the battle of Beylan in 1832.

There are also the ruins of a **theatre**, of a **temple of Apollo**, and of a Graeco-Roman **aqueduct**. A fine 4C **mosaic** shows Noah's Ark surrounded by a decorative border of animals. Found some years ago in an orange grove near the village, this probably ornamented the floor of a Byzantine basilica. For conservation reasons it is not open to the public. Although Mamistra was a Byzantine episcopal see and the Venetians had a church here, no other Christian buildings have been found so far.

The Ottoman period is represented by a *caravanserai* and a small mosque near the bridge.

For the Hittite relief at 10km **Sirkeli**, take the old road from Yakapınar to Ceyhan. The **relief**, which shows King Muwattalli (c 1315–1282 BC), is on a rock by the Ceyhan Nehri. Muwattalli defeated Rameses II at the battle of Kadesh (1285 BC) and made the Hittite Empire into a formidable power which rivalled Egypt. It is known that he moved from Hattusa to a new capital called Dattassa, which so far has not been discovered. Because of the relief, some believe that Dattassa may have been located here.

From Yakapınar return to the E24 and continue in the direction of Ceyhan. After c 8km you will see **YİLAN KALESI** on the southern skyline. At c 12km turn right and continue for c 3km to a parking place just below the castle.

The medieval name of this castle is not known. It has not been possible to link either its Turkish name, which means the Castle of the Snake, or its Kurdish name Shah Meran, King of Snakes, with any of those in the baronial lists or those mentioned in medieval chronicles. In popular mythology it was believed to be the home of a tyrant with magical powers, a medieval Typhon, part-man and part-snake. Serpents came at his bidding and he used them to enforce his will. He was slain at Tarsus where he had gone to kidnap the daughter of the king of that city. Another legend states that the castle was never captured, but that it had to be abandoned as it was infested with snakes. Both stories probably originate from the relief over the main gateway. This shows a majestic seated figure holding sceptre-like objects which resemble snakes.

Yılan Kalesi is sited strategically on a ridge which dominates both the road between Adana and the Armenian capital Sis, modern Kozan, and a wide stretch of the Pyramus river. Its design and structure suggest that it was built by the Armenian Crown Prince Leo, later Leo III (1270–89), sometime before his capture by the Arabs in 1266. A rough path leads upwards from the car park to the outer fortifications. From here the going is difficult, as to get to the castle's only entrance it is necessary to clamber over a confused mass of huge boulders. Reaching up for hand-holds out of sight, one remembers the castle's name with some misgivings. However, there appear to be few snakes now in Yılan Kalesi. As a rule, the only reptiles visible are the sun-loving lizards which gaze fearlessly at visitors and wait until the last moment before disappearing into cracks in the ancient masonry.

The **gatehouse** is guarded by two projecting towers. Facing the **relief** over the entrance (see above) is another of a rampant lion. The belief that the castle was built by a prince and not a king is based on the fact that the seated figure and the lion are not crowned.

To assist the defenders, access to the interior was by a passage at right angles to the gateway. This opens on to a large **courtyard** which was probably used to shelter the local inhabitants in times of danger. A **cistern**, which still bears traces of its waterproof coating, ensured the water supply of the defenders. Around the ramparts there are several **vaulted chambers** which may have served as storerooms or quarters for the garrison. There are the remains of a small **chapel** and the more substantial lodgings of the castle's commander. From the walls there are fine views S over the Pyramus river, the modern Ceyhan Nehri, and N to the distant Taurus Mountains.

In the late evening, when the towers and ramparts of Yılan Kalesi turn red in the light of the setting sun, and the shadows, gather at its feet, this castle becomes both a symbol and a reminder of the turbulent history of the Cilician Kingdom of Armenia. After the Mamelukes had defeated the Armenians and captured Crown Prince Leo in 1266, they roamed, unchecked, pillaging and ravaging the cities and towns of the plain. The chronicler laments: 'Sis [the capital] and its chief church were given to the flames, the tombs of the kings and princes violated, and their bones torn from this last resting place, burned, and scattered to the winds...'.

Continue towards 5km Ceyhan which is reached by a turning on the right. **Ceyhan**, with a population of c 60,000, is a bustling market town.

If you do not wish to visit Ceyhan, take a left turn on to Road 817, signposted Kozan and Kadirli. After c 23km turn right on to a minor road which leads to the village of c 4km **ANAVARZA**. The great **fortress of ANAZARBUS** is on a limestone escarpment which measures 4.5km N–S and rises to a height of 200m. An area much subject to earthquakes—it suffered a particularly severe shock in 1945—it also has a very capricious climate.

History. The history of Anazarbus has been pieced together from a variety of sources. Coins, inscriptions and an examination of its ancient remains have all helped to produce a picture of its past. Some identify the city with a place called Kundu which revolted in the mid 7C BC against Assyria. However, the first hard evidence is provided by coins which have been dated to the 1C BC. Research by the British archaeologist Michael Gough suggests that the city's name, which is not Greek, may be derived from the Persian *nabarza* which means unconquered and is an adjective frequently applied to Mithras. The name Anazarbus was probably first applied to the escarpment and the buildings on it and later to the lower city.

Two inscriptions found here support the theory that it formed part of the realm of Tarcondimotus, who c 52 BC ruled a large part of the Cilician plain from nearby Hieropolis Castabala. In 19 BC Tarcondimotus II Philopator renamed it Anazarbus Caesarea or Caesarea by Anazarbus as a sign of gratitude to Augustus, who had restored his kingdom to him. A marble head, now in the Adana Museum, has been identified recently as a portrait of Tarcondimotus II. The city probably came under direct Roman rule during the reign of Claudius (41–54 AD).

By the reign of Domitian (81–96 AD) the office of demiurge existed in Anazarbus. In 207 it began to call itself a metropolis and from then on appears to have had equal status with Tarsus. A commemorative coin was issued in 221, when it enjoyed the dubious honour of having the notorious and dissolute Emperor Elagabalus as one of its two demiurges.

Little is known about the city during the late Roman and Byzantine periods. It became the principal city of Cilicia Secunda during the reign of Theodosius II (408–450). Twice in the following century it suffered severe earthquake damage and changed its name, first to Justinopolis and then to Justinianopolis, perhaps as a mark of gratitude for imperial assistance.

When the Arab raids began, the city's isolated position on the frontier of Byzantine territory made it particularly vulnerable. From the late 8C to the late 10C it was in Arab

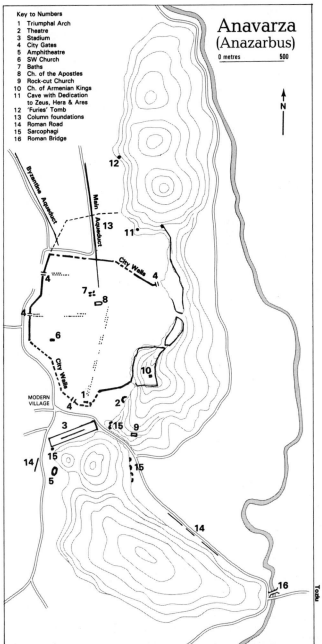

Key to Numbers
1 Triumphal Arch
2 Theatre
3 Stadium
4 City Gates
5 Amphitheatre
6 SW Church
7 Baths
8 Ch. of the Apostles
9 Rock-cut Church
10 Ch. of Armenian Kings
11 Cave with Dedication
   to Zeus, Hera & Ares
12 'Furies' Tomb
13 Column foundations
14 Roman Road
15 Sarcophagi
16 Roman Bridge

Anavarza
(Anazarbus)

0 metres   500

N

Byzantine Aqueduct

Main Aqueduct

City Walls

City Walls

MODERN
VILLAGE

Tozlu

hands. During this period the fortifications of Ayn Zarba, as it had become known, were improved twice; first by Haroun al Rashid in 796 and then by the Hamdanids from Syria in the 10C. After a brief period of re-occupation by the Byzantines, it passed to the Armenians and Toros I made it his capital in 1100. It retained that status for almost a century, but when the centre of power moved first to Tarsus and then to Sis, Anazarbus began to decline. When the Mamelukes finally swept away the Cilician Kingdom of Armenia in 1375, the city was abandoned and was never re-occupied.

A number of antiquities found in the city are kept in the courtyard of the *bekçi's* house which is in the centre of the modern village of Anavarza. These include some fine **mosaics**, one of which shows Thetis with dolphins, late Roman **sarcophagi** and **funerary stelae**. The *bekçi*, who has a fund of information about the site, will sometimes entertain visitors with his comments on the collection. He will also indicate the best and safest way to get to the summit of the escarpment. Anyone wishing to visit the castle should take a guide, as parts of the enceinte are in a dangerous condition.

The remains in the lower city fall into three main sections—those to the right of the dirt road which passes through the artificial cleft in the escarpment, those on the W slope of the escarpment, and those in the large area enclosed by the walls.

The most striking ruin to the right of this road is the **stadium** which measures 410m by 64m. At the principal entrance on the SW there are a few damaged cornice blocks and part of a pilaster. On the SE side spectators sat in two stands cut from the rock-face. Above the top level of seats, holes cut into the rock probably held beams which supported *vela*. The *spina* in the centre of the track is well preserved. There is no trace of the seating on the NW side. Wooden stands may have been used there. A very worn inscription on the front of the SW stand has been dated to the 3C or 4C AD.

Above the stadium and to the S are sarcophagi and a number of rock-tombs. About 100m to the SW, part of the **ancient road** to Mopsuestia may be seen. To ensure that it was not flooded during the winter, this was built on a causeway. Traces of an **amphitheatre** lie c 150m to the E of the road. As far as can be judged from the small part remaining, this was an elliptical structure measuring c 60m by 80m which backed on to the rockface. When the amphitheatre was used for wild beast shows, the animals were probably brought into the arena through an underground passage on the W side which is now largely filled with debris.

The **artificial cleft**, 250m long and 4–5m wide, dividing the escarpment, may date from the late Roman or early Byzantine period. The road, which passes through it, probably connected Anazarbus with Flaviopolis, modern Kadirli, and Hieropolis Castabala. It was carried by a Roman bridge, now ruined, over the the Sumbas Çayı, c 1.5km to the E. In the cleft there are several 4C **tombs** and **sarcophagi** cut from the rock-face. There is also an **inscription** which quotes the opening words of the 46th psalm, 'God is our refuge and stronghold'. This probably relates to the earthquakes which devastated Anazarbus so often, as it continues, 'sovereign aid He has brought us in the hour of peril. Not for us to be afraid, though earth should tumble about us, and the hills be carried away into the depths of the sea'—a moving reflection of the strong faith of the Christians of Anazarbus.

N of the cleft are the remains of the **theatre** which is in a ruinous condition. It had a diameter of c 60m. On the S side where the retaining wall of the cavea was supported by concrete piers that reduce in height. On the N it was built into the hill. At each side of the cavea there was a covered parodos. Most of the scaena has disappeared. Because of its poor state of preservation, it is impossible to determine the seating arrangement or capacity.

Above the theatre there are several **sarcophagi** and two interesting **reliefs**. One, which was first described by J.T. Bent in 1890, shows four nude athletes in a palaestra. One youth is doing a handstand with the help of a companion. Their exercises are presided over by a clothed figure, presumably the gymnasiarch, who holds a wreath and a palm branch. The other shows a winged deity, who stands on the back of a dolphin while holding a funerary inscription above his head.

Continue around the base of the escarpment to a stretch of the city wall which is well-preserved. About 250m to the N of this is the **cave** where Bent discovered a dedication made in AD 153 by the priestess Regina to the gods of the city, Zeus, Hera Gamelia and Ares. The inscription is on the the upper surface of the S wall of the outer part of the cave. Access to the cave, which is c 30m above ground-level, is not easy. Be careful on the descent.

At the bottom of the escarpment, c 500km N of this cave, is the **rock-tomb of the two eunuchs**, the so-called Furies' Tomb. The eunuchs were the servants of Queen Julia the Younger, sister of Philopator, who died in AD 17. An inscription over the tomb has been partly erased. It appears to invoke a curse on anyone who disturbs the burial.

To the W are the substantial remains of the principal **aqueduct** which is believed to date from the time of Domitian. This brought water from the upper reaches of the Sumbas river. S of the aqueduct, towards the centre of the area enclosed by the walls, are the ruins of a church and of a baths complex. The **church**, dedicated to the Apostles, was an early Byzantine basilica. The **baths**, which were also constructed during the Byzantine period, measured c 40m by 25m. About half of the area was taken up by the vaulted frigidarium on the W, the remainder being divided between the tepidarium in the SE and the calidarium in the NE corner of the complex.

From here walk S for c 700m to the substantial remains of a **triumphal arch** which is believed to date from the time of Septimius Severus (193–211). This measures c 30m by 9m. The height of the central arch is c 10.5m and that of the side arches 7m. It was constructed of concrete faced with ashlar and, on the upper part, tufa. Elaborately decorated with columns and pilasters of the Corinthian order, the three arches are linked by an internal vaulted corridor.

If you have the time and the energy to go to the castle, return to the theatre. From here rock-cut steps lead up to the first enceinte. This is an easy climb and well worth the effort. There is a splendid view from the ridge over the walled lower city and the surrounding countryside.

The fortified area stretches for c 700m along the escarpment. It is divided into three sections: the first enceinte, where the garrison was quartered and where the city's inhabitants took refuge in time of danger; a three-storeyed tower, and the second enceinte.

Entrance to the **first enceinte** is by a gateway at the W end of the S wall. This is believed to date from the 8C AD, when Anazarbus was occupied by the Arabs under Haroun al-Raschid. The stretch of wall to the E of the gate, which has four **defensive towers**, was constructed by the Armenians. Access to the semicircular towers is provided by doors raised c 1m above the ground. Their dusty interiors are dimly lit by arrow slits. Wooden beams, which have disappeared, supported an upper floor. Towards the SE corner of the wall there was a **primitive toilet**.

Flights of steps lead to the battlements where there is a parapet 1m wide protected by a curtain wall. Most of the E defensive wall, which is in a ruinous condition, dates from the Byzantine period. The W side of the enceinte was never walled as, sloping at a steep angle, it soon becomes a cliff that drops sheer to the plain.

In the SE corner of the first enceinte are the ruins of the **Church of the Armenian Kings**. This building, measuring 13m by 9.6m, had a central nave flanked by two aisles. There were three narrow windows at the E end, three on N wall and one on the W and S.

Around the top of the wall there was inscription in Armenian, part of which was still intact when Victor Langlois visited the castle in the mid 19C. Much of this has fallen down and suffered damage in the intervening period. Among prayers 'for the health of my children; in memory of my parents' he found a **memorial** to an unknown nephew of Leo I named Ochin and another, dating from 1188, which mentions Rupen III. This was the Rupen who, according to the chroniclers, went to Antioch, towards the end of his life, 'for orgies with evil women', but instead was seized and imprisoned there by Bohemond III. Presumably chastened by this experience, he gave the throne to his younger brother Leo and retired to a monastery near Sis in 1187, where he died within the year.

The interior of the church was covered with **frescoes**. Langlois comments on the well-preserved representations of saints of the Armenian church which he saw there. Unfortunately, these have suffered much damage from the weather and some have been defaced deliberately. It is still just possible to make out the the the figure of **Christ Pantocrator** on the dome.

To the NE of the church is the outline of a small **Byzantine chapel**. Gough reports having found an empty burial vault to the SW.

N of the first enceinte, the escarpment narrows dramatically. A wide gap, which presumably was spanned by a bridge, separated it from a three-storyed **Armenian tower**. The gap is not easy to cross and many abandon their tour at this point. According to an inscription in Armenian, the tower was erected in 1188, just after Rupen's brother, Leo II, came to the throne.

Access to the **second enceinte** is no easier. It is separated from the tower by a gap c 4m wide, whose base has been shaped artificially so that it slopes to the precipice on the W and the cliff on the E. Great care should be taken in crossing it.

The oldest buildings in the castle are in the second enceinte. Many have been damaged, perhaps by earthquakes, during the course of the centuries and it is difficult to determine their purpose. There are several **cisterns**, the ruins of a **small Armenian chapel**, a **postern** and **vaulted passages**.

Gough describes a **long, narrow room** 12m by 7m on the W side of the second enceinte. This has a blackened patch on the ceiling, the only place in the castle with evidence of artificial lighting. The room also has a large window on the W wall with a terrifying view. 'Its sill is at the same level as the present floor. The cliff overhangs slightly at this point, and there is nothing to be seen between it [the window] and the plain, except the eagles below, circling about their nests in the rock'.

On returning to the main road continue N to c 12km Çukurköprü. There turn right for c 15km **Kadirli**, the ancient **Flaviopolis**. One of the few visible remains of this city's past is **Ala Camii**, a former Christian basilica, built on the foundations of a Roman temple which was later turned into the mosque. It has been deconsecrated. Ask for directions.

Leave Kadirli by the Andın road. Take a right-hand turn signposted to c 21km Karatepe. Careful driving is required as this road is very narrow in parts and has many bends. Climbing steadily for most of the way, it reveals pleasant vistas of the surrounding countryside.

KARATEPE is on a slight, pine-clad eminence that projects into a modern artificial lake produced by the construction of a dam on the Ceyhan Nehri. Its situation and lay-out make it one of the most attractive sites in Cilicia.

Near the entrance there is a small tourist pavilion where refreshments may be bought. There are plans to provide camping facilities.

Excavations have been conducted for almost 30 years at Karatepe by Professors Bossert, Alkım and Çambel. The site has been turned into an open-air museum. The finds are displayed where they were discovered. Because they have not been published, photography is not allowed. Cameras must be left with the *bekçi* at the entrance.

History. The Hittites, a people of Indo-European origin, conquered a large area of central Anatolia towards the beginning of the second millennium BC. Hattusas, modern Boğazköy, on the Halys river was their capital. Towards 1640 BC they extended their influence to southern Anatolia and northern Syria. This brought them into conflict with the Egyptians, whom they defeated at the battle of Kadesh in 1285 BC.

The first phase of Hittite civilisation came to a comparatively sudden end towards 1200 BC. Its downfall is usually attributed to an onslaught mounted by a mysterious race which the Egyptians called the Sea People. They are blamed not only for the destruction of the Hittite Empire and the reduction of Egyptian influence in the Middle East, but for the overthrow of the Mycenaeans and the creation of widespread chaos throughout the Eastern Mediterranean.

Hittite influence did not end. A number of petty kingdoms, whose rulers had Hittite names, sprang up in Syria and in the Taurus Mountains. One, located in Cilicia, had an interesting link with Greek legends. According to a text of the 8C BC Asitawada, the ruler of Neo-Hittite Karatepe, described himself as belonging to the 'House of Mps'. This Mps is usually taken to be Mopsus, the legendary founder of Mopsuestia and a number of other cities in Asia Minor. The orthostats, described below, display signs of Greek influence and some of the inscriptions on them refer to a people called Danuna and Danauna. They may have been the Danaoi mentioned by Homer, who took the side of the Achaeans in the Trojan War. This theory is supported to some extent by the discovery by Myres in 1903 in Troy I of fragments of pottery, which he described as Anatolian. Similar pottery has been found at Karatepe.

About 500 years after the fall of their empire, the extinction of the Hittites as a political force was completed. One by one the Neo-Hittite kingdoms were overthrown by the Assyrians and their peoples merged with other races.

A path leads upwards through the pine woods to the gate of the **palace**. This was surrounded by a defensive wall c 1km in circumference which was pierced by gateways guarded by lions and sphinxes. Karatepe was the summer palace of King Asitawada and there are a number of **orthostats** which illustrate, in a delightful way, the relaxed atmosphere of his court. The king is portrayed at dinner. Holding a meat patty in his left hand, he leans forward to take a loaf of bread from a bowl. Two attendants gently fan the air to cool him. More food, including roast hare and other meats, fruit and drink, is being brought from the kitchens. On the lower part of the slab servants lead an ox and a lamb to the palace where they will be slaughtered for the feast. During the meal musicians with lyres play for the king's entertainment.

Daily life at the court of Asitawadda is shown in a number of naturalistic tableaux. A monkey crouches half-hidden under the king's table, bears perform a shambling dance, the grotesque god Bes carries two monkeys on his shoulders, birds of prey peck at a dead hare, warriors display their weapons, and a mother leans forward protectively to suckle her child.

A path to the right leads across the promontory to the **lower gate** of the palace. Like the principal entrance this is also protected by lions and sphinxes. The orthostats here carry a number of **inscriptions in hieroglyphic Hittite** on the right-hand side and in **old Phoenician** on the left. This has enabled the archaeologists to decipher the Hittite texts. Note the particularly fine **representation of a ship**. From the lower gate take the path above the lake by the ancient walls back to the entrance.

A large part of the enjoyment derived from a visit to Karatepe comes from the beauty of the surroundings and from the imaginative way in which the archaeologists have displayed their finds.

Domuztepe is about 5km to the NE. In addition to remains contemporaneous with those of 8C Karatepe, it has two layers of occupation dated to c 9C BC. These show traces of destruction by fire. A 7C BC gateway is decorated with sculptures taken from a much earlier building. The site appears to have been occupied also during the Hellenistic and Roman periods.

From Karatepe take the first turning on the left along a rough track for c 10km. At the main road, turn right and continue for c 15km to the dam at Çevdetiye Köyü. Follow the track, which runs parallel with the canal for c 5km, and then turn right on to the main road. On the left, a short distance before Toprakkale Köyü, are the ruins of **Hierapolis Castabala**, known today as **Bodrum**.

History. The 1C AD Roman historian Curtius states that Alexander joined forces with Parmenion at Hierapolis Castabala in 333 BC. However, it seems more likely that they met on the southern part of Castabala territory and that Parmenion visited the city during his exploratory patrols in the northern passes of the Cilician plain. After they had marched S towards Issus, Darius followed them with his army. Freya Stark, paraphrasing Curtius, provides an imaginative description of the exotic spectacle.

> The fire altars were carried across the pass and the young men in red cloaks marched before him [Darius]; and those who led the chariot and the horses of the sun; and the twelve nations; and the Immortals with their apples, in sleeved tunics and gold; and the King's relatives that surrounded his high car; and the thirty thousand footmen and the four hundred horses; and the six hundred mules and three hundred camels with money; and the chariots of the mother and wife, the women and children behind'.

Three hundred years later, Castabala was an insignificant principality in Cilicia which achieved brief fame in 31 BC, when its king, Tarcondimotus, was killed at the battle of Actium opposing Octavian. Augustus appears to have borne no grudge as he later confirmed Tarcondimotus II as its ruler. However, the dynasty did not prosper. It appears to have died out in the early 1C AD.

The ruins of Castabala have not been excavated and in summer they are partly hidden in fields of golden corn. A ragged **colonnade**, some of the standing columns still crowned with their Corinthian capitals and bearing the same unsightly brackets found at Pompeiopolis and Olba, straddles the plain at the foot of the acropolis. From a later period there are the **walls** and **choirs** of churches. On the right-hand side of the road are the remains of the **theatre** and a **baths complex**.

It has not been possible to identify positively the **castle** of Castabala—a successor to the fortress which witnessed the passage of Darius's army—with any of those which appear on the list of Cilician barons compiled in AD 1198. It may have been constructed by the Armenians in the 13C or, as others claim, by the Knights of St John to guard the route through Syria to the Holy Land. Separated from the nearby hill by a gap 5m wide made in ancient times, its ruined towers and broken walls, home of countless sun-worshipping lizards, are rarely visited today. However, its peaceful appearance belies a violent history. It may have been here that Stephen, brother of Thoros II, was boiled alive by the Greek garrison in AD 1164.

Toprakkale is c 3km to the S. Constructed of volcanic rock, it sits menacingly on a low hill at the point where two of Southern Turkey's busiest roads, the E24 and the E5, separate. In the Middle Ages, **Til Hamdoun**, as it was known, was one of the most important castles in Cilicia, as its situation allowed it to control the traffic through Maraş and Antep to the E and down through Alexandretta (İskenderun) and Antioch (Antakya) to the S. On a clear day it is possible to see Anazarbus and even Sis from Toprakkale.

Like all the castles and cities in the area, it changed hands frequently. In 1151 it was occupied by the Armenians under Thoros II. In 1158 it was captured by the Byzantines under Manuel Comnenus. In 1185 it was delivered to the son of the Crusader Tancred, Boehmond of Antioch, as part of the ransom of Rupen (see above). Later it was regained by the Armenians under Leo II. He had established good relations with the Hospitallers (the Knights of St John of Jerusalem) and placed the castle in their hands. In 1266 it came under the control of the Mamelukes, but was recaptured by the Armenians. In 1337 it was surrendered by Leo V to the Mamelukes and from then onwards it appears to have been abandoned.

Take care when visiting Toprakkale. Parts of the ruins, particularly the roofs of the vaulted chambers, are in an unsafe condition. There are also many deep cisterns.

Toprakkale was protected by a double enceinte c 100m by 70m. Constructed by the Byzantines, it was rebuilt by Armenian masons for the Hospitallers. Modelled on Krak des Chevaliers in Syria, it was almost impregnable. The inner bailey had ingenious defences. Its garrison could deliver a concentrated and highly directional stream of arrows from the inner and outer enceintes. Specially constructed embrasures in the curtain walls, and later in the towers and battlements, were often shaped at the base to increase the archer's field of fire. On the W there was a large thinly-walled enclosure. Added at a late period, this may have been used as temporary quarters for refugees or reinforcements to the garrison.

Access to the castle is by a minor road signposted in the village. From the car-park walk up a track towards a doorway on the N side. There, a great gap in the wall leads first to a large vaulted chamber and then to a central courtyard which is much overgrown. In this area there are several **cisterns** which are partially covered by vegetation.

From the courtyard mount the **battlements**. On the SW, in an area protected by the inner and outer defences, the commander of the castle had his quarters. Underneath the battlements large vaulted rooms, which could be entered from the inner ward, provided lodgings for the garrison and were also used as storerooms and arsenals.

From Toprakkale, return to 75km Adana (see Route 34) by the E24/E5.

B. Kozan

Round trip c 162km. Adana—c 35km Ceyhan road junction—c 46km Kozan/Sis.

To visit **KOZAN**, ancient **SIS**, capital of the Cilician Kingdom of Armenia, leave Adana by the E24/E5 and continue to the turning for **Ceyhan**. Here take Road 817, signposted Kadirli and Kozan, and at c 29km Çukurköprü turn left to 17km Kozan (see also Route 35A).

The great fortress, constructed by Leo II (1187–1219), still dominates the town. Built on a long ridge that projects from the Taurus Mountains into the Cilician plain, it controlled an important trade and communications route from the coast to the interior.

History. The Armenians were not the first to appreciate the strategic value of Sis. A Byzantine stronghold in the 9C, it was captured by the Abassids who enlarged it and improved its defences. During his great campaign against the Arabs, the town and castle were recaptured by Nicephorus Phocas in 962. Occupied by the Armenians for the first time under Thoros I (1102–29), Sis was retaken by John Comnenus. In 1114 a great earthquake centred on Maraş did considerable damage to the cities of Cilicia, including Sis. The town later fell to the Armenians again and was capital of Armenia from 1162 until 1375. It had its share of violence and drama. In 1225 Philip, son of Bohemond IV of Antioch and king for three years only, was first imprisoned and then poisoned here. In 1309 heretics, who refused to 'accept water in the chalice and other religious innovations', were brutally punished by Oshin in Sis.

The last days of the Armenian capital were, perhaps, its most dramatic. Leo VI and his wife, Margaret of Soissons, were crowned in Sis on 14 September 1374. Leo's reign was brief. Mameluke forces, encouraged by a traitorous Armenian called Achot, who had become a Muslim in Egypt, were soon camped outside the walls. A contemporary chronicler voices the despair felt by many in the Levant when the lower town was sacked: 'Who can recount the tragedy that my eyes witnessed, for I saw the bright sun, the stars and the moon fall down'. In the castle the defenders were weakened by a shortage of supplies and the fear of approaching famine. Traitors attempted to seize the king, but he made a dramatic escape by rope down into the castle moat. However, further resistance was fruitless and Leo capitulated. News of the victory produced great rejoicing in Cairo. The drums beat without ceasing for three days.

Leo and his family were taken in chains to Egypt, but later were ransomed. Then for many years, like an unwelcome ghost, he haunted the courts of Europe in a hopeless quest for help. Leo, the last king of the Cilician Kingdom of Armenia, died in Paris in 1393. He was buried in St Denis, where his monument may still be seen.

Having sacked the town, the Mamelukes dismantled the castle. As time passed it fell into ruin and many of its stones were taken to build a new town.

Sis was visited in the mid 19C by Langlois and at the beginning of the 20C by Lohmann. In 1901, in the Armenian church, Lohmann saw the throne of Leo II which was ornamented with the carving of a double eagle. It has disappeared.

Apart from the ruined **castle**, there are few reminders of the past in Kozan. Stretching for c 900m along a narrow ridge high above the town, the design of the castle was adapted to the shape of the escarpment. Where the cliffs are low, walls and towers crowned with continuous rows of machicolations were constructed. Otherwise the builders relied on the protection provided by natural features. As it is surrounded by steep rocky slopes where siege engines could only be used with difficulty, its walls are slimmer than those of contemporary Crusader castles in more vulnerable positions.

Access to the castle is by a narrow path on the E side. On the right, to the N of the entrance, a spacious court now heavily overgrown, provided shelter for the townspeople in time of danger. Near the W wall there is a large, vaulted **underground cistern**. Smothered by undergrowth are the ruined quarters of the garrison.

To the S of the entrance two gates lead, by way of narrow corridors, to the inner keep of the castle where the **royal apartments** were sited. These terminate in a strongly fortified tower which fills the whole width of the escarpment and drops sheer to a deep rock-cut moat. The southern enceinte is separated from the rest of the castle by this moat.

Even in its ruined state the castle of Sis is one of the most striking medieval buildings in Cilicia. Sadly, it attracts few visitors.

If you have time—and fortitude—you may like to extend your excursion by c 20km to **Fehratlı**, where there are the ruins of a small **Roman sanctuary** and an unusual **Assyrian relief**. The relief is believed to depict Shalmaneser III (858–824 BC) who led several expeditions against Babylonia, Anatolia and Syria. He is shown, arms raised, facing religious symbols.

36

Adana to İskenderun

Total distance c 124km. Adan—75km Toprakkale—c 7km Epiphania—
19km Dörtyol—4km Yakacık/Baiae—9km Saraseki—10km İskenderun
(c 32km Ulucınar).

Leave Adana (see Route 34) by the E5 and continue for c 75km to Toprakkale, where the roads divide. Take the right-hand turn which is signposted
Dörtyol, İskenderun and Antakya.

For thousands of years the strip of land between the Amanus Mountains
and the sea has been an important trade route linking Anatolia with Syria
and the S. It has also seen the passage of the armies of many conquerors.
In 333 BC Persian might and Greek valour met here in a battle that made
a significant change to world history. Thirteen centuries later Tancred led
his band of Crusaders through the Amanus Gates and the Pillars of Jonah
to Syria, the Lebanon and Palestine in the first of many vain, idealistic and
blood-stained attempts to liberate the holy places of Christendom.

After c 7km, where a turning on the left leads to **Yeşilkent**, a few ruined
walls and the broken arches of an aqueduct on the right-hand side of the
road mark the site of **Epiphania**. This city was founded c 175 BC by one of
the strangest of the Seleucid kings, Antiochus IV Epiphanes (175–164),
sometimes known as Antiochus the Mad.

After spending 12 years as a hostage in Rome, he succeeded his brother Seleucus IV
Philopator. Shortly after his return to Syria, Antiochus embarked on a series of military
adventures which met with varying degrees of success. In an attempt to unite his
Greek, Macedonian and Syrian subjects he declared himself to be Theos Epiphanes,
'God made Manifest'. His critics called him Antiochus Epimanes, Antiochus the Mad.
His efforts to establish the worship of the Greek gods in Jerusalem provoked a
successful revolt led by Mattathias and his sons, the Maccabees.

The sleepy town of 19km **Dörtyol** is the nearest place to the site of one of
the great battles of the ancient world.

Here, on the **Plain of Issus**, Alexander the Great and Darius, King of Persia, had their
fateful encounter on a winter's day in 333 BC. The location of the battlefield has not
been identified with certainty. It is known that the Persians had drawn up their army
on the steep banks of a river, which most modern historians believe to have been the
Payas. However, during the intervening centuries the three rivers, which cross the
plain at this point, have almost certainly changed their courses and may have
deepened their beds. Consequently, it is very likely that both the configuration and
height of their banks are different today.

Alexander marched S along the coast as far as the Pillars of Jonah in search of Darius,
who had been camped at Sochoi on the other side of the Amanus Mountains. However,
the king had left this encampment and had marched his army N. When he discovered
that Alexander had gone to the S, Darius followed him and took up a position behind
him on the Plain of Issus. Alexander was informed by his scouts of the Persians' new
location. So, early on a cold November morning, after a dreadful night of gales and
rain during which he offered sacrifice to Thetis, the mother of his great hero, Achilles,
he turned his army around and marched N to meet the king.

Darius, accompanied by his family and his courtiers, had an army of 30,000 cavalry,
60,000 Cardaces, the equivalent of the Greek epheboi, and 10,000 Greek mercenaries.
Alexander faced this formidable force with fewer than 35,000 men. He and the
Companions were on the right near the mountains. In the centre there were Foot

Companions and Shield Bearers and the left flank by the sea was covered by Parmenion and the cavalry.

The battle was confused and bloody. Its turning point was a daring charge by Alexander and the Companions against the centre of the Persian army, where the king was directing the battle. Darius panicked. Then he fled in his chariot followed by part of his host. According to Arrian 'he led the race for safety'. This point in the battle is depicted in the famous mosaic in the Museo Archeologico in Naples.

The king kept to his chariot until, as Arrian relates, 'he was forced to abandon it when ravines and other obstructions barred his way; then, dropping his shield and stripping off his candys—and even leaving his bow in the war chariot—he leapt upon a horse and rode for his life. Darkness soon closed in; and that alone saved him from from falling into the hands of Alexander, who, while daylight held, relentlessly pressed the pursuit; but when there was no longer light enough to see what he was coming to, he turned back—but not without taking possession of Darius' chariot together with his shield, mantle and bow'. He also took more valuable booty. In Darius' headquarters he found the king's wife, his infant son, his mother and his sisters. Alexander treated them with the courtesy due to their rank.

According to Callisthenes, the Greek historian who accompanied Alexander on his campaigns, the Persian casualties at Issus were 110,000 dead against a loss of 302 Macedonians. The great army of Darius was scattered to the winds. Some of his soldiers had fled with him, others had gone N into Cappadocia, others again to Egypt and Cyprus. The way to the S was open for Alexander.

Today the Plain of Issus is a pleasant, fertile area of orchards and citrus groves. Bounded on the E by the green slopes and deep ravines of the Amanus Mountains and by a low, bleak coastline on the W, it is bisected by the narrow, busy E5 which pursues its charmless way southwards.

At 4km **Yakacık**, formerly Payas, ruined columns mark the site of the Seleucid city of **Baiae**. A small **fort** overlooking the sea was constructed by Ibrahim Khan-Zadek in the time of Süleyman II and restored in the 19C. Olive groves shelter a **16C mosque** and **bedesten**. The charm of the site is greatly reduced by its proximity to a large modern industrial complex.

About 9km to the S is **Saraseki**. Here were the the **Pillars of Jonah**, a pass which guarded the approaches to Syria. It was here that Alexander came in his search for Darius.

A **tower**, which may have been part of a Seleucid customs post, is popularly known as **Baba Yunus**, Father Jonah, as it is believed that Jonah was delivered from the belly of the whale on a nearby beach. There are also the ruins of a **castle** which some have identified with the medieval Castrum Puellarum or Castle of Godfrey of Lortet. Apart from a ruined tower by the entrance which may be Frankish, the visible remains date from the Ottoman period.

About 10km from Yakacık is the modern city of **İSKENDERUN**, formerly **Alexandretta**. This is a busy commercial and trading town with a fine harbour. Sheltered by the verdant slopes by Mt Amanus, Kizil Dağ, it has a pleasant, cosmopolitan air. İskenderun is an agreeable place to spend a few restful days. It has several good hotels and some interesting restaurants along the seafront. However, apart from its name—İskender is the Turkish for Alexander—the city has few links with its ancient past.

Information and Accommodation. The **Tourist Information Office** is at Atatürk Bulv. No. 99/B. The Ministry of Tourism lists five two-star and two one-star hotels. There are several pensions. At 32km Uluçinar (Arsuz) there is the very comfortable, friendly, well run three-star *Arsuz Oteli*. This and the two-star *Bahadırlı Oteli*, Pr. Muammer Aksoy Cad. No.31 are recommended. The banks and post office are in the business centre.

History. To celebrate his triumph, Alexander dedicated altars to Zeus, Athena and Heracles on the banks of the river Payas. He further commanded that a city, Alexandria ad Issum, be founded to commemorate his great victory over the Persians.

Under the Seleucids, and later the Romans, the city enjoyed a modest degree of prosperity. Two factors limited its expansion. As a port it could not compete with Seleuceia Pieria, which was nearer to Antioch, and because of its proximity to marshy ground and the absence of cleansing winds, it had an unhealthy climate.

Captured by the Arabs in the 7C, it was ruled by a Selçuk vassal in 1097 at the time of the First Crusade. At different times it was under Frankish, Byzantine, Armenian and Arab control. In the 16C it became part of the Ottoman Empire.

According to Langlois, Alexandretta had developed a considerable commercial importance by the mid 19C, despite its dangerous climate. It was the port of Aleppo and had attracted a number of European consular and shipping agents. Apart from the ruins of a castle built by Ibn Aly Daoud, during the caliphate of Vasik, the city had no ancient remains.

Occupied by French and British troops towards the end of World War I, it later became the Sancak of Alexandretta, a special administrative region. In 1939, with the rest of the Hatay province, it was returned to Turkey.

A pleasant **excursion** from İskenderun is to 32km **Uluçınar**. There are frequent dolmuş services from the centre of İskenderun. Take the E5 in the direction of Antakya and then turn right on to Road 817 which runs close to the seashore. Bathing here is not recommended. The beaches are pebbly and the sea is not always free from pollution.

Uluçınar, now a sleepy little village, occupies the site of the city of **Rhosus** or Rhosopolis, built by the Seleucids c 300 BC. It is briefly mentioned by Strabo. In Byzantine times an episcopal see, there are a few traces of its past on a hill to the SE.

A rough track, not suitable for cars, will take you S to **Hınzır Burnu**, where there are the ruins of a **Crusader fortress** which belonged to the La Roche family. Attacked by Saladin in 1188, it was later occupied by the Templars who held it until 1267, when they were ousted by the Mamelukes.

The attraction of Uluçınar lies more in its delightful situation and relaxed atmosphere than its historical associations. To stand on the bridge over the small river and watch the fishermen land their catch, to swim from the clean beach of the Arsuz Hotel, to enjoy an excellent meal on the terrace within a few metres of the sea, these must be sufficient reward for even the most demanding traveller.

37

İskenderun to Antakya

Total distance 57km. İskenderun—13km Belen—(c 4km Bağras/Baghras)—44km Antakya.

There are frequent coach services from İskenderun to Antakya. The journey takes about two hours. If not pressed for time, stop at 13km **Belen** for lunch at the *Kurtoğlu Restaurant* or to drink the waters at the spa. From Belen the road climbs to the Topbogazi Geç (1750m), the ancient **Pylae Syriae**, the Syrian Gates. The pass was of great strategic importance, as all traffic between Alexandretta and Antioch had to pass through it.

About 20km from Belen a turning to the right leads to the 4km **Castle of Bağras**, formerly Baghras. This is on a hillside at the end of a narrow valley. It controlled the old road from Alexandretta and Belen to Antioch.

Strabo, Pliny and Ptolemy refer to a settlement in this area called *Pagrai* or *Pagras* and in the 5C AD there was a σταθμός, quarters for soldiers, here. After the Arab conquest in the 7C AD the first stronghold was constructed at Baghras. It was used to mount attacks against the Byzantines and to prevent counter incursions.

Demolished by Tancred during the First Crusade, Baghras was fought over fiercely in 1156 by the prince of Antioch and the Templars on one side and Thoros, ruler of the Cilician Kingdom of Armenia on the other. Known to the Crusaders as Gaston or Gastrim, the castle was a keypoint in the Templars' defensive system. Captured by Saladin in 1188, its possession was disputed subsequently by the Templars, the Armenians and the Arabs. After the destruction of the Cicilian Kingdom of Armenia in the 14C, it remained in Arab hands until it was captured by the Ottomans at the beginning of the 16C.

The castle occupies an area c 120m by 100m. It was surrounded by a double enceinte. Entrance was by a gate-tower on the NE corner which overlooked the precipitous N slope of the hill. Inside a ramp led to a complex of rooms and buildings on several levels. These were dominated by a **large pentagonal structure** (possibly a stable) and a **chapel**. The garrison's water supply was ensured by a large **cistern** under the chapel and an **aqueduct** which entered the keep in the SW corner. In spite of earthquake damage and the removal in modern times of large quantities of worked stone for building purposes, the ruins of Baghras are substantial. It merits a visit.

From Bakras the E5, passing Amikgölü on the left, continues across the plain to 30km **ANTAKYA,** the ancient Antiocheia ad Orontem, better known as **Antioch**.

Antakya, with a population of more than 100,000, is a pleasant, compact city, reminiscent of a French town in the foothills of the Alps. This may be due to its wide boulevards and steep-banked river and, of course, some lingering traces of the inter-war French mandate. It also has something Arabic in its appearance.

Information and Accommodation. The **Tourist Information Office** is at Vali Ürgen Alanı, No. 47. The Ministry of Tourism lists two three-star, one two-star, and three one-star hotels in and around the city. The *Büyük Antakya Oteli* and *Atahan Hotel* in the city, and the *Hotel Çağlayan* and the *Hidro* at Harbiye are recommended.

The **banks** are on the right bank of the river. The main **post office** and the **Hatay Museum** are near the bridge in the same part of the town.

History. Founded by Seleucus I Nicator (321–281) c 300 BC and named after his father, Antioch's first inhabitants were a mixture of local people and Graeco-Macedonian settlers. Many of the latter, including more than 5000 Macedonian and Athenian ex-soldiers, came from the nearby city of Antigonea, the short-lived creation of Antigonous I Monophthalmos (382–301 BC). The new city became the capital of an empire which at the time of the death of Seleucus extended from Macedonia to the borders of India.

Called Tetrapolis by Strabo because of its division into four self-contained areas, its great wealth attracted artists from many countries. Eutychides of Sicyon, the pupil of Lysippus, made a famous bronze statue of Tyche, the Goddess of Fortune and the Protector of Cities, for Antioch. This statue is known only from a heavily-restored Roman copy in the Vatican Museum and from coins where the goddess was shown seated on Mt Sipylus, wearing a turreted crown which represented the city's fortifications. She held the palm of victory in her right hand, rested a foot on the river-god Orontes, while Seleucus I and Antiochus I placed a wreath on her head.

Because it was on the Silk Road, the city popularised this material. Surrounded by wealth and luxury the inhabitants of Antioch soon adopted such a sybaritic, self-indulgent life-style that it acquired a scabrous reputation for licence and decadence. This persisted into Roman times. The 2C AD Roman poet, Juvenal, described the Orontes as 'the stream that wanton Syria laves' (*Satire* III. 66).

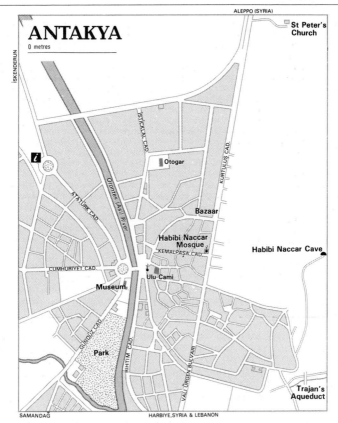

ANTAKYA

0 metres

ALEPPO (SYRIA)

St Peter's Church

İSKENDERUN

Orontes (ASI) River

ATATÜRK CAD.

İSTİCKLAL CAD.

Otogar

KURTULUS CAD.

Bazaar

Habibi Naccar Mosque

KEMALPAŞA CAD.

Habibi Naccar Cave

CUMHURIYET CAD.

Ulu Cami

Museum

GÜNDÜZ CAD.

RIHTIM CAD.

VALİ ÜRGEN BULVARI

Park

Trajan's Aqueduct

SAMANDAĞ

HARBİYE, SYRIA & LEBANON

The Seleucid Empire was ended by the invasion of Tigranes the Great (94–56 BC) in 83 BC. In 64 BC Antioch was created capital of the Roman province of Syria by Pompey and under the Pax Romana its wealth and power increased. Only Rome and Alexandria surpassed it in importance.

The brave and able Germanicus died here from poison in AD 19. It is believed he was murdered by Piso with the connivance and approval of hs uncle, Tiberius.

Among the foreigners in Antioch there was a large community of Jews. Their numbers were greatly increased during the reign of Antiochus IV Epiphanes (175–164), when the troubles in Judaea forced many to take refuge in Syria. Accustomed to living among unbelievers, some used the Septuagint, the Greek translation of the Bible, in their synagogues. Jewish beliefs permeated non-Jewish society and, as a result, many gentiles in Antioch were familiar with Jewish ethical and spiritual values. It is hardly surprising, therefore, that Christianity soon made many converts. As they included both Jews and Gentiles, the concept of a universal church whose members called themselves Christians began in Antioch. St Peter lived for a time here and SS Paul and Barnabas used the city as a missionary centre. Under Diocletian the Christians of Antioch suffered grievously. Many of their churches were destroyed by the pagans.

Later the city was not only an important centre for the diffusion of orthodox Christianity but also of heresy. Arius and Eusebius, who promoted the heretical doctrine that Christ is not co-substantial with the Father, were educated and, according to some historians, infected with their unorthodox beliefs here. Condemned by the

Council of Nicaea in 325, Arianism continued to trouble the Church until the end of the 4C. However, Antioch was also the city of Ignatius, famous for his expositive letters on Christian doctrine to Polycarp and it was the birthplace c 345 of St John Chrysostom, the great Patriarch of Constantinople.

Under the Byzantines Antioch continued to prosper. Filled with beautiful buildings and a centre of intellectual ferment, it challenged both new and old Rome. In the 6C it suffered two devastating blows. It was badly damaged by an earthquake, which killed more than 200,000 of its inhabitants, and later it was taken by the Persians who sacked and burned it. Rebuilt by Justinian, it was taken again by the Persians and then by the Arabs, who had overrun Syria.

Antioch remained in Arab hands until 969, when the Byzantine Nicephorus II Phocas recaptured it. In 1084 new conquerors, the Selçuks, appeared. The Crusaders under Boehmund took it in 1098 and made it the capital of the principality of Antioch. The city remained in Christian hands until 1268, when a Mameluke army under Baibars razed it to the ground.

Antioch never recovered from this blow. In 1516 it was captured by the Ottomans under Selim II the Sot. The centuries that followed were marked by decay and decline. It became little more than a village inhabited by a few hundred people, who lived in a cluster of miserable huts surrounded by the ruins of ancient splendour.

Ruled briefly by the Egyptian Mehmet Ali from 1831–40 it came under French jurisdiction after World War I. In 1939, as the result of a plebiscite, with the Sancak of Alexandretta, Antakya was returned to Turkey.

Apart from the city walls, a Roman aqueduct, some mysterious reliefs and the Church of St Peter, few traces of ancient Antioch remain. The best impression of its past glories may be obtained from the wonderful collection of late Roman and Byzantine mosaics in the **Archaeological Museum**. Allow at least two hours for your visit.

Entry hall. Two statues of Venus. One found at Mağaracık near Samandağı, dating from the 1C AD, shows the goddess seated on a rock with her left hand resting on an amphora. The other from Antioch, is a **crouching Venus**, of the 1C or 2C AD. This is a Roman copy of a Greek original.

Room 1. Mosaics from Daphne: **Narcissus by a stream** (2C AD); the **Four Seasons** (2C AD) includes the Calydonian boar hunt, Paris and Helen, **Hippolytus and Phaedra**; the **Bird Mosaic** (5C AD); personification of Ge, Pegasus and the Nymphs (3C AD); the Triumph of Dionysus 2C AD; the Handing over of Chryseis; a ceremony of Isis. Mosaics from Antioch: **personification of Soteria** (Salvation) (5C AD), **Iphigenia in Aulis** (3C AD) and the Judgement of Paris (2C AD). Statues and statuettes: a Roman faun; Hygeia (3C AD) and Fortuna (2C AD).

Room 2. Mosaics from Daphne: a **theatre scene; Narcissus and Echo**; and the **Buffet Mosaic** which shows the rape of Ganymede by Zeus in the guise of an eagle. All 3C AD.

Room 3. Mosaic from Daphne: **Oceanus and Thetis** (4C AD). Mosaics from Antioch: the priapic **happy hunchback** and the **negro fisherman**; the infant **Hercules strangling serpents** and the **attack on the evil eye**. All 2C AD.

Room 4. Mosaics from Antioch: Oceanus and Thetis (2C AD); the **jugglers** (4C AD); the **drunken Dionysus**. Mosaics from Tarsus: **Zeus and Ganymede**; Dionysiac subject; **Orpheus charming the beasts**. All 3C AD. Mosaics from Daphne: **Satyr and Hermaphrodite; Apollo and Daphne**. Both (3C AD). Statues: Hades, Roman; relief head of Thetis (4C AD). Both from Kapısuyu.

Hall. Mosaics from Daphne: summer; the sundial. Both 4C AD. Mosaic from Antioch: **Dionysus** (2C AD).

Room 5. On the wall at the entrance: four **funeral stelae** in the style of Palmyra. All 3C AD. In this room are displayed Mitanni, Assyrian, Hittite and Post-Hittite artefacts found in four mounds in the Amik plain. They include altars, idols, and reliefs dating from the 15C to the 7C BC.

Orpheus charming the beasts, a mosaic from Antioch now in the Archaeological Museum at Antakya

Room 6. Small objects found near Antioch. These date from the Palaeolitic age to the Islamic era. Note especially the Roman bronzes, including one of **Tyche** and a number of small statues and busts, including the fine **head of an ephebe**, found at İskenderun. There is also a collection of coins dating from the 5C BC to the Ottoman period.

Portico and garden. A number of Roman sarcophagi from various locations; mosaics from Daphne, İskenderun and Seleuceia Pieria.

Antakya's main thoroughfare, the Kurtuluş Cad., follows the line of a magnificent colonnaded street that divided the centre of ancient Antioch. Traces of this were discovered during the course of excavations made in the 1930s. Approximately 10m wide and 4km from N to S it had ceremonial arches at either end and a large circular forum in the centre. After the city was almost completely destroyed by earthquakes in the 6C, this great artery was partially rebuilt by Justinian.

In the Kurtuluş Cad. is the **Mosque of Habib Neccar**. Originally a Crusader church, it was converted into a mosque after the city was captured by the Muslims. The minaret was added in the 17C. It contains a number of interesting tombs.

The ruins of a **Roman aqueduct** built in the reign of Trajan (98–117) are near the city hospital. It is known today as the Memikli bridge.

To visit the **Church of St Peter**, cross the Orontes, the Asi, and turn left along Rıhtım Cad. Continue on Road 420 towards Reyhanlı and Aleppo for c 2km. Turn right to the church which is in a grotto in the rocky hillside.

The Christians of Antioch, fearful of persecution, met here in secret for prayer and worship. It is known that St Peter was in the city between AD 47 and 54, and according to an ancient tradition he preached and taught here. The present façade dates from the period in the 11C and 12C when Antioch was in Christian hands. The mosaic floors, which have suffered some damage, are much older, dating from the 4C or 5C. On the left side of the apse there is an opening which is now partially blocked. According to legend this was used by the congregation as an emergency exit in times of danger. A pious tradition claims that the water, which flows from a fissure in the wall, is blessed and has curative properties.

Mass is celebrated in the church on 29 June, the feast day of SS Peter and Paul, and at a number of other times during the year. There are small Catholic and Syrian Orthodox communities in the city.

About 200m to the NW of the church there is a mysterious **relief**. This is reached by scrambling up the hillside on the left to a small artificial terrace. The relief, cut into the cliff face, is of a veiled person, who gazes steadily and menacingly over the city. Nothing is known with certainty about either the subject or the date of the relief. An account in a 6C chronicle dates it to the reign of Antiochus IV Epiphanes (175–164 BC), the king who claimed to be Theos Epiphanes, God made Manifest. It may represent Charon, who ferried the dead across the Styx to Hades and perhaps was carved at a time when Antioch was being ravaged by plague. The smaller draped figure nearby may depict the king.

To visit the **fortifications**, continue on Road 420 in the direction of Aleppo for c 5km. Turn right on to a side road which winds sinuously up the E slope of Mt Sipylus for c 10km. The earliest surviving portions of the walls date from the time of Theodosius (AD 378–395), but they were repaired, enlarged and extended many times during the succeeding centuries. Access to the section, which ran along the crest of the mountain, is made difficult by dense vegetation. However, a splendid view of Antakya and the Orontes valley may be obtained from a modern viewing platform.

A **castle**, which formed part of the fortifications, was constructed by Nicephorus Phocas c 969. Refurbished by Basil II in the 11C, it remained largely untouched until the 19C. Then, during the occupation of Antakya by the Egyptians, it was stripped of its much of cut stone. This was used both by the invaders and the local people to construct new buildings.

To visit 22km **Açana Höyük**, formerly known as Alalakh, continue on road 420 towards Reyhanlı. Excavations conducted here between 1937–48 have revealed 17 separate levels of occupation dating from the Chalcolithic period, c 4500 BC to c 1200 BC.

Remains of two palaces were found in the tell which was the site of the capital of the kingdom of Mukish. One dating from c 1785 BC, was constructed by the Hittite Yarim-Lim, the other built by Nigme-Pa, dates from the 15C BC. Possession of the city was contested on several occasions by the Egyptians and it was sacked by Ramesses II in 1285.

Some **objects found in the tell** are now in the Archaeological Museum in Antakya. They include two idols carved from basalt, one male, one female; a 15C BC basalt altar; a 15C BC dolomite ram's head and a 13C BC fresco from a Hittite palace.

38

Excursions from Antakya

A. Yayladağı, via Harbiye, Cursat and Çatbaşı

Total distance c 40km. Antakya—9km Harbiye—(c 3km Cursat—(c 2km Şenköy/Çatbaşı)—31km Yayladağı.

For Çatbaşı and Yayladağı it is advisable to take guides from the villages. Before going to Yayladağı, check with the Tourist Information Office in Antakya about any restrictions on visiting the frontier area.

HARBİYE, a picturesque village in the hills 9km S of Antakya, occupies the site of ancient **DAPHNE**. Take Road 825 in the direction of Yayladağı. There are frequent dolmuş services from the city centre.

In summer the citizens of Antakya go to Daphne frequently to enjoy its cool breezes, wander through the laurel groves and escape from the stifling heat of the city.

The *Hidro Hotel* at Harbiye has an atmosphere of comfortable informality—and unpredicable French-style plumbing. Its restaurant overlooks a huge fish tank.

History. The importance of Daphne in ancient times may be gauged from the fact that the great city of Antioch was sometimes called Epidaphne i.e. near Daphne. Many legends were attached by imaginative Antiochians to this beautiful gorge with its cascades and its shady groves of laurel and brooding cypress trees. Here, it was said, the youth Cyparissus accidentally killed his pet stag and, grieving over its body, was turned by Apollo into a cypress, the tree of mourning and weeping. Here, too, it was said Paris delivered his fateful judgement. In the groves of Daphne he gave the golden apple to Aphrodite and set in train the events that led to the Trojan War.

Perhaps the best known legend concerns Apollo's pursuit of the nymph Daphne, the daughter of the river god Peneus. Seized by him on the banks of her father's river, she prayed for deliverance. Peneus turned her into a laurel tree which took root on the river bank. From then on the laurel was called *Daphne* in memory of the nymph. Apollo, saddened by his loss, decorated his lyre with a wreath taken from the tree and, as god of music, decreed that thenceforth prize-winning musicians should be crowned with laurel. (See the painting ascribed to the 15C Florentine artists Antonio and Piero del Pollaiuolo in the National Gallery in London.)

Apollo's infatuation with Daphne was commemorated in a temple erected here in his honour by Seleucus I. This contained a famous statue of the god, the Apollo Citharoedos, by the celebrated Athenian sculptor, Bryaxis. This has been lost and is known only from coins and from Roman copies in Florence and Naples. Other members of the Olympian pantheon, Artemis, Aphrodite and Zeus also had their sanctuaries in Daphne. Antiochus IV Epiphanes, who ordered the construction of the temple of Zeus here, instituted the Olympic Games of Antioch and built a stadium for them. Not only athletic events took place, there were also contests for plays, music and poetry.

The Romans displayed a similar enthusiasm for this suburb of Antioch. Indeed it became so notorious that for a time it was declared off-limits for the Roman army! In addition to theatres and fine public buildings, they built luxurious villas and created elaborate gardens amongst the laurel groves.

With the arrival of Christianity the fortunes of Daphne began to decline. Apart from a short period during the reign of Julian the Apostate (361–363), when paganism enjoyed a temporary revival, ancient rituals were allowed to lapse and temples everywhere fell into decay. In Daphne the temple of Apollo was destroyed by fire, an incident for which the Christians were blamed by Julian. The devastation produced by the Persians in the 6C, the Arab raids in the 7C and their subsequent occupation of Antioch and the surrounding countryside reduced Daphne to the status of an impoverished village. It never recovered its former glory.

There are no visible remains of Daphne's past. All the great buildings have disappeared and of the formal gardens there is no trace. The gorge is once more a wild and untamed place. Water cascades through natural channels and laurels and cypresses grow where their seeds have fallen. It is a wilderness, but beautiful, evocative and numinous as it was in the days of the Seleucids and the Romans.

Continue S on Road 825 in the direction of Yayladağı. After c 8km a turning to the right leads to the ruined **Castle of Cursat**, Qalat az Zaw. Built on a narrow plateau protected by deep river valleys this fortress fulfilled the same function as Bağras to the N. It defended the southern approaches to Antioch. Fought over by many armies and factions, it was captured, after a long siege, by the Mamelukes in 1275. As access to the castle is difficult, allow at least two hours for your visit.

About 10km to the S of Cursat a track to the left leads to the village of **Senköy**. From here, with the help of a guide, it is possible to visit the **reliefs** of **Karabar** located near **Çatbaşı**. Dating from the 8C BC, when the area was under Assyrian rule, one shows a bearded god imparting his blessing, the other a suppliant and a god surrounded by symbols of divinity.

A further 13km will bring you to **Yayladağı**, the last Turkish village before the border with Syria. Nearby is Djebel Akra (1759m), the ancient Mt Cassius. Regarded as sacred from the earliest times—the Hittites had a sanctuary on the summit—it was the site of the temple of Zeus Cassius. Seleucus I Nicator (321–281) sacrificed there before deciding on the site of Seleuceia Pieria, the port of Antioch.

No trace of the temple remains. Excavations suggest that it may lie under the foundations of the ruined **Monastery of St Barlaam** which dates from the 5C. If you wish to climb the mountain, employ a guide and obtain any permits necessary from the local and civil military authorities. Initial enquiries should be made to the Tourist Information Office in Antakya.

B. Seleuceia Pieria

Total distance c 32km. Antakya—28km Samandağ—c 4km Çevlik/ Seleuceia Pieria—Al Mina.

Samandağ is a small seaside resort to the N of the mouth of the Orontes. Surrounded by olive groves and plantations of fig trees, it is also close to the remains of Seleuceia Pieria and Al Mina.

On a mountain peak to the left of the road, c 20km from Antakya, are the ruins of two **churches** which were built in honour of St Simeon Stylites the Younger (521–592). Imitating the better-known St Simeon Stylites the Elder (fl. 390), Simeon the Younger, while still a child, embraced a life of prayer and fasting and ascended a column where he spent the rest of his life. Pillar saints, like the two Simeons, played an important part in the history of the early Church. Great crowds came to hear them preach and both the civil and ecclesiastical authorities were much influenced by their views.

The ruins of **Seleuceia Pieria** are c 4km to the N of Samnadağ, near the village of **Çevlik**.

History. Seleuceia Pieria was founded by Seleucus I Nicator (311–281) in 300 BC as the port of his new capital Antioch. According to legend, he chose the site while sacrificing to Zeus on Mt Cassius. An eagle snatched part of the sacrificial victim and carried it N to the place where the new town was built.

A prosperous trading centre under the Seleucids, it continued to flourish when Antioch became the capital of the Roman province of Syria. Goods were shipped from here to Rome and other parts in the empire. SS Paul and Barnabas sailed from Seleuceia to Cyprus c 47–49 on their first missionary journey (Acts 13–14).

The port, badly damaged by the earthquake which devastated Antioch in 526, began to decline under the Byzantines. This state of affairs continued after the Arab conquest of Syria in the mid 7C, when it became known as Soueidiyeh. On 19 March 1148 Louis VII of France, one of the leaders of the Second Crusade, who had sailed from Attaleia (Antalya) with part of his army, arrived at Seleucia or St Simeon, as it was known to the Crusaders. Here he was greeted warmly by Raymond, prince of Antioch.

After the sack of Antioch by the Mamelukes in 1268, Seleuceia seems to have been abandoned. There are no further references to it by the chroniclers.

Now Seleuceia Pieria, like Harbiye, is visited more for the beauty of its setting and for its historical associations than for its ruins. Apart from an impressive **underground water-channel**, few traces of its past remain. The town was built partly on a rocky promontory which projects from the foothills of Musa Dağı and partly on a small plain at its foot. The port was created by the enlargement of a natural basin which had been formed by a fast-flowing stream. To prevent flooding, a dam and an artificial water-course were commenced during the reigns of Vespasian (69–79) and Titus (79–81) and completed in the 2C under the Antonines. The river was diverted into an underground channel c 1400m long, whose construction is commemorated by **two inscriptions** carved on its walls. A formidable engineering achievement, the work was done by legionaries, sailors and prisoners from Judea.

In an area called Beşikli Cave there are several **rock-tombs**, some of which bear low reliefs. In the upper part of Seleuceia there are the insignificant remains of a gateway and of two temples, one of which, constructed in the Doric style, was dedicated to Zeus. The acropolis was surrounded by walls dating from the Hellenistic period.

In 1936–37 Sir Leonard Woolley excavated **Al Mina** at the mouth of the Orontes river. This had been inhabited from before the 9C BC to the end of the 4C BC. On the basis of pottery which he found here Woolley distinguished ten separate levels of occupation. From the archaeological evidence it is clear that Al Mina was an important emporium where both Greek and Syrian traders lived and worked side by side. Their homes and warehouses have been laid bare. The principal product traded by the Greeks appears to have been pottery. It is not clear what they obtained in exchange—some authorities suggest metals, perhaps iron and copper.

Trading posts like Al Mina did more than facilitate the exchange of goods. They were channels through which ideas, skills, and artistic influences flowed. It is probable that the adoption of orientalising motifs like the palmette, lotus and sphinx by Greek potters may be traced to emporia like Al Mina. In turn there is evidence that local pottery was affected by Greek taste and style.

It is possible that the Greeks acquired their alphabet through contacts provided by Al Mina. Herodotus states (Book 5. 58) that they learned writing from the Phoenicians, a suggestion supported by their word for the letters of the alphabet, φοινίκεια, Phoenician things. Some of the oldest Greek inscriptions have been found in Euboea and the Euboeans were probably the first Greek traders to come to Al Mina. Their pottery has been discovered in levels IX and VIII (late 9C BC) of the site. Some of the later Greek pottery found here has graffiti in Aramaic.

Al Mina declined in importance towards the end of the 4C BC. It is not clear whether this was due to the activities of Ptolemy Soter I or commercial competition from the new port of Seleuceia Pieria which was just 7km to the N. Woolley suggests that the population of Al Mina and Sabouni may have been removed by force to the new city by Seleucus.

The fortunes of Al Mina enjoyed a brief revival during the Crusades, but later the settlement was neglected and sank into obscurity once more. Recent visitors report few traces of the buildings laid bare by Woolley during the course of his excavations. It now requires a considerable effort of imagination to visualise them in their original state. However, the excellent display of artefacts from Al Mina in the Ashmolean Museum, Oxford, is a lasting reminder of the discoveries made by the archaeologist and his colleagues in this remote site in SE Turkey nearly 60 years ago.

39

Adana to Şanlı Urfa

Total distance 345km. Adana—E24/E5 75km Toprakkale—E5 13km Osmaniye—56km Nurdağı—(c 70km Kahraman Maraş)—(15km Zincirli—10km İslahiye—10km Tilmen Höyük—27km Yesemek)—17km Sakçagöz—48km Gaziantep (10km Dülük)—(90km Gavur Kalesi—124km Hisar—131km Elif—135km Hasanoğlu)—38km Nizip (30km Cerabalus—Carchemish) (15km Zeugma\Belkis)—9km Birecik—89km Şanlı Urfa—(18km Sultantepe—48km Eski Sumatar—48km Harran.

The journey from Adana to Toprakkale on the E24/E5 is described in Route 35A. At Toprakkale there is a major road junction where the E5 turns S to Antakya. This route continues in an easterly direction on the E24 sign-posted to Gaziantep and Şanlı Urfa.

After c 13km you arrive at the pretty little town of **Osmaniye** which has developed largely because it is on the railway line which links SE Turkey with Ankara. At 18km to the E of the town a turning on the left leads to the village of (15km) **Haruniye** where there is a late 8C fortress constructed during the reign of the Abbasside Caliph Haroun al Raschid.

The E24 now begins to climb steadily until it reaches a height of 1150m at the **Nurdağı Pass**. It then makes a leisurely descent to a wide, intensively cultivated, fertile plain only to rise once more. There are magnificent views of an ochre-coloured tableland where an occasional tree offers welcome shelter to wandering goatherds and their flocks. Away to the E and S the jagged peaks of **Kara Dağı** and **Kartal Dağı** are dramatic exclamation marks on the skyline.

At c 56km from Osmaniye the E24 crosses Road 825 at Nurdağı. To the N this leads to (48km) **Kahraman Maraş**, while the southern fork goes to Antakya by way of (23km) İslahiye and (28km) Hassa.

The epithet Kahraman (hero) was added to the city's name to honour the resistance of its citizens to foreign occupation after the First World War. Maraş is famous for the quality of its ice cream.

History. Capital of a Neo-Hittite state in 8C BC, Maraş was occupied by the Assyrians, Arabs, Byzantines, Armenians, Crusaders, Selçuks and Mameluks. It was taken by the Ottomans in 1515.

The **citadel**, established by the Byzantines, was enlarged and rebuilt during the Ottoman period. The interior is now laid out as a park. The **Archaeological Museum**, which is sited in the citadel, has an interesting collection of artefacts from the prehistoric era, Hittite ceramics and reliefs, Roman ceramics, figurines and grave stelae and ethnographic material from Maraş and the surrounding area. **Ulu Cami** and **Taş Medrese** date from the end of the 15C. There is also an interesting 17C **bedesten**.

From Maraş return to road E24 and continue to Gaziantep.

Excavations carried out by Garstang between 1908 and 1911 and continued in 1949 by Waechter at mounds near (17km) **Sakçagöz** have revealed traces of occupation dating to the fifth and fourth millennia BC.

GAZİANTEP (population 485,000) on the Sacır Suyu, is the sixth largest city in Turkey. Its name is probably derived from the Arabic word '*Ayntab*', which means 'good spring'. At an average height of 870m above sea level, its summers are hot and dry and its winters warm and rainy. It is famous for handicrafts in copper and nacre, and for the pistachio nuts which are grown in the surrounding countryside.

Information and Accommodation. The **Tourist Information Office** is at Atatürk Bul. 38A. The *Hotel Kaleli*, Hürriyet Cad. 68 is recommended. There are two other hotels, *Mimar* and *Alfim*, in the same street.

Transport. Frequent coach services from the *otogar* on the NW side of the city link Gaziantep with İstanbul, Ankara, İzmir, Antalya and other cities. Dolmuş and minibuses serve places in the surrounding area. The railway station is just to the NE of the *otogar*. The Toros Ekpres, with two classes and sleeping berths, provides a comfortable service to Adana, Ankara, İstanbul.

History. The earliest traces of occupation in Gaziantep are from the middle of the fourth millennium BC. Pottery fragments found in the artificial mound in the centre of the city are believed to date from the period 3800 to 3500 BC.

Always an important trading emporium on the caravan routes which linked Caucasia and the Arabian peninsula with the Mediterranean and the Aegean, the city acquired fresh importance during the Neo-Hittite period in the first millennium BC. It was at the centre of a group of city states sited at Carchemish, Sakçagöz and Zincirli. In the late 8C BC it became part of the Assyrian Empire.

Its possession was fiercely contested by the Byzantines and the Arabs for many years. Occupied in the 11C AD by the Selçuk Turks, it was ruled by the Counts of Edessa (Urfa) for a time. It fell to Saladin, was ravaged by the Mongols and came under the control of the Mamelukes. In the 16C the city was taken by Selim I, the Grim, and became part of the Ottoman Empire. Later, overshadowed by its powerful neighbour Aleppo, its fortunes and importance declined.

In 1921 the honorific 'Gazi' was added to Antep's name by a decree of the Turkish Grand National Assembly. This was in recognition of the stand which its inhabitants had taken against French occupying forces. Incensed by the death of a twelve-year-old boy, Mehmet Kamil, who was murdered while trying to protect his mother from the unwelcome attentions of French soldiers, the people rose up against the invaders. More than 7000 citizens perished in the subsequent fighting and the city was badly damaged. However, the French were obliged to sue for peace.

Gaziantep is best visited on foot. In the centre are the **Boyacı** and **Şirvani mosques**. Note the intricate carving on the minarets. A number of the city's old *hans* have been preserved. The fine courtyard of the **İcioğlu Han** is often used as a fruit market.

In the **Museum of Independence** documents, weapons and photographs illustrate the city's struggle in 1921 against foreign invaders. The museum was established in 1981 on the 100th anniversary of Atatürk's birth and 59th anniversary of the liberation of Gaziantep.

The **Hasan Süzer Ethnographical Museum** in Hanifoğlu Cad. occupies a fine house which had fallen into a very dilapidated state. It has been carefully restored and refurbished by Mr Süzer.

The house has three storeys and a cellar. The courtyard or *hayat* is paved with coloured stones. The two-storey building on the left of the *hayat* was occupied by the servants. In the cellar of the main building there are two large rooms with different floor levels. They contain storage jars for olive oil and grape molasses, and a large hand loom. The well which provided water for the household is also located here. On the ground floor are the kitchen, a bathroom and a furnace for heating the bathwater. To the right is the Tandır Room. The name Tandır refers to a heating system peculiar to the Gaziantep area. It consisted of a buried stone furnace topped by a seat which was covered with a padded quilt. Note the elaborate tiled fountain on the first floor. Three rooms overlook the *hayat*—a 'bride's room', a living room and the *selamlık* where male guests were received. The family's private quarters, including the harem, were on the second floor. On the floor above there is a large well-lit room where members of the family, soothed by the cooing of doves from the nearby pigeon loft, enjoyed periods of tranquil contemplation. Throughout the house there are carpets, furniture and domestic objects from the Gaziantep area. Figures wearing regional costumes complete the illusion of a visit to the town house of a prosperous Ottoman family.

For the **castle** turn right into İstasyon Cad. This rests partly on a rocky spur, partly on an artificial mound of considerable antiquity. In the 11C and 12C AD the Selçuk Turks restored and enlarged the original Justinian foundation. The defenders were protected by a moat and fortified gate.

Gaziantep's **Archaeological Museum** is just beyond the municipal stadium on the N side of the city. This houses a fine collection of objects which are well-displayed and labelled. There is a guidebook in English.

Among the objects of particular interest are: from the third millennium BC a decorated vase from E Anatolia; pottery vessels from Belkis and Gedikli Höyük; terracotta models of open and covered domestic chariots and of a **war chariot** from the Gaziantep region; terracotta idols from Tilmen Höyük and Gaziantep; a late third millennium BC **bronze statuette** of a bull from Anez village, Kilis; cylinder seals from the second and first millennia BC found at Oylum village, Kilis and Gaziantep; a bronze statuette of a god from the mid second millennium BC found at Fevzipaşa; a striking **bronze statuette of a charioteer** from Sakçagöz; 8C BC **grave stelae** from İslahiye; an 8C BC basalt slab bearing a representation of the Hurrian weather god Teshub also from İslahiye; a **gate lion** and a **gate sphinx** from Zincirli; Urartian bronze belts, harness, fibulae, bells, statuettes and votive plaques from the Van region.

Note the fine limestone **head of Antiochus I** of Commagene from Kahta, 1C BC, and a **stele from Sofraz** showing a royal personage being greeted by a deity, perhaps Helios. The latter resembles the stele at Arsameia on Nymphaios where Antiochus I of Commagene is shown greeting Mithra-Helios and two rock carvings of similar scenes c 14km N of Adıyaman. These were known as *dexiosis* scenes—offering the right hand.

There are some 3C AD **grave stelae from Palmyra**; a striking **statue of Tyche**, goddess of chance from Tahtalı village, Kilis; bronze statuettes of Mercury and of a Lar, a household god, both Roman period from Gaziantep region; Roman period **mosaics** including one of a pensive girl holding a pen to her lips (c.f. the wall painting of Paquio Proculo and his wife from Pompeii

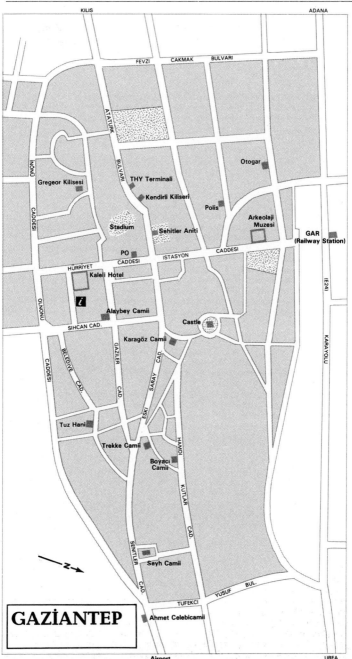

KILIS
ADANA

FEVZI ÇAKMAK BULVARI

ATATÜRK BULVARI

İNÖNÜ CADDESI

Otogar

Gregeor Kilisesi

THY Terminali

Kendirli Kiliseri

Polis

Stadium

Arkeolaji Muzesi

GAR (Railway Station)

Sehitler Aniti

PO

CADDESI

ISTASYON CADDESI

HÜRRIYET

Kaleli Hotel

İNÖNÜ CADDESI

i

Alaybey Camii

SIHCAN CAD.

Castle

BELEDIYE CAD.

GAZILER CAD.

Karagöz Camii

ESKİ SARAY CAD.

(E24) KARAYOLU

Tuz Hani

Trekke Camii

Boyacı Camii

HAMDI

KUTLAR CAD.

SENTLER CAD.

Sayh Camii

GAZİANTEP

YUSUF BUL.

TUFEKCI

Ahmet Celebicamii

Airport
URFA

now in the Museo Archaeologico, Naples), of a cock fight, of a deer, of a lion and of a bear, all from Akdeğirmen, Yavuzeli; decorated glassware of various periods; Hellenistic and late Roman **gold diadems** and **earrings** from the Gaziantep area; coins found at Kuşakkaya and Zeugma (Belkis); Ottoman period kilims, carpets, costumes, weapons and furniture from the Gaziantep region.

There are several places around Gaziantep which can only be reached conveniently by private transport. Although a litle off the beaten track they merit a detour.

About 15km S of Nurdağı, to the left of Road 825 to İslahiye and Antakya, is the site of **Zincirli** or Sam'al which, archaeologists believe, was founded in the 14C BC. Beneath the foothills of Mt Amanus, Zincirli commanded the trade routes which go N to the Halys and E to the Euphrates.

Zincirli was particularly rich in sculpture which ranged in style from the Hittite to the Aramaean and Assyrian. Examples are preserved in the museums of İstanbul, Berlin and Gaziantep.

İslahiye may have been the city of Nikopolis which Alexander the Great founded to celebrate his victory over Darius at the battle of Issus in 333 BC.

Tilmen Höyük is c 10km due E of İslahiye. Turkish archaeologists, working here between 1958 and 1960, discovered the remains of a palace which they dated to c 1700 BC. Note the basalt basin which served as a shower or shallow bath, in the E part of the palace. This, and its 3.35m drainage channel, were cut from a single block of stone. There are the substantial remains of a paved street.

About 27km to the SE of İslahiye at **Yesemek** is one of the oldest quarries in Anatolia. This was the site of a sculpture workshop from the 13C to the late 8C BC. Scattered across a gentle slope there are more than 300 statues and stelae. Their subjects—wild animals, sphinxes, mountain gods, mythical creatures, war chariots—are in various stages of completion. They lie on the hillside just as the ancient sculptors and stone cutters left them. Sculptures from Yesemek have been found as far away as Syria. Those discovered at Zincirli came from here.

At **Dülük**, 10km to the NW of Gaziantep, there is a camping and picnic site. Important material from the Palaeolithic Age has been discovered in the Dülük Caves. Known as Dabigu in the Assyrian period and Doliche during the Hellenistic and Roman periods, Dülük was an important religious centre from the earliest times. The worship of Jupiter Dolichenus, whose images have been found throughout the Roman Empire from Africa to Britain, originated here. The god, who is described in an inscription from a 2C AD shrine on the Aventine in Rome as 'Jupiter, the Best and Greatest, Dolichenus, the Eternal', is usually shown holding a labrys and a thunderbolt. There are a few rock tombs at Dülük, but no trace of the temple dedicated to the god remains.

Leave Gaziantep by the E90 in the direction signposted Şanlı Urfa. At first the road passes through a landscape of bare rounded hills with only the occasional splash of green to relieve the monotony. Then come the olive groves and pistachio orchards where the trees, standing in straight lines, emulate soldiers on parade. At the dusty town of Nizip a minor road leads S to the site of ancient **Carchemish**. This is near the village of (30km) Cerablus. Because of its proximity to the Syrian border you may require a permit to visit Carchemish. Enquire at the local police station.

History. The earliest references to Carchemish date from c 1750 BC. They are on cuneiform tablets found at Tell Hariri, the ancient Mari, which is on the Middle Euphrates to the S. The city's strategic position on the Euphrates (Fırat in Turkish) invited the attention of both the Egyptian and Hittite empires. During the reign of Suppiluliumas I (1375–35), who extended the frontier of his realm to the Lebanon, it came under Hittite rule. Carchemish was the centre of worship of the goddess Kubaba, the prototype of Cybele. In an Akkadian document she is described as 'the Lady Kubaba, mistress of the land of Carchemish'. Out of respect for her the invaders spared the temples and buildings on the citadel. Pillage was confined to the lower city. Suppiluliumas placed his son Piyassili on the throne of Carchemish. He adopted the

Hurrian name of Sarri-kusuh, as did most of his successors. When the enfeebled Hittite Empire fell to the onslaughts of the Sea People, Carchemish did not escape. It was captured and destroyed c 1190 BC. Because of its value as a trading centre on the Euphrates, however, it was soon restored and became the dominant member of a new confederation of small states in that area. Its rulers even adopted the old Hittite title of Great King. The Neo-Hittite state of Carchemish continued until 717 BC when it was conquered by Sargon II and incorporated in the Assyrian Empire. A century later a new power was in the ascendant in Mesopotamia. The Babylonians and the Medes destroyed Harran, the last bastion of the Assyrian Empire, and in 609 BC a Babylonian army defeated the Egyptians at Carchemish. During the late Hellenistic and the Roman periods there was a trading settlement known as Europos by the river to the N of the site of the ancient city.

The first exploration of Carchemish was made by a British Museum expedition in 1879. This produced several inscriptions and monuments. A second expedition organised by the museum between 1911 and 1914 was led by Leonard Woolley. T.E. Lawrence was one of his assistants. They found a number of orthostats with fine relief sculptures on a broad, open terrace. These showed deities, kings, priests and warriors and had accompanying inscriptions in the Luwian language. Decipherment of the inscriptions, which were written in Hittite pictographs, is almost complete. Unfortunately, many of the orthostats were wantonly destroyed during the troubles of 1920. Others were stolen and sold abroad. Those saved are now in the Archaeological Museum in Ankara. They include a 9C BC basalt statue pedestal flanked by lions; an orthostat relief of King Araras with his wife and children from the second half of the 8C BC; part of 9C BC relief showing the goddess Kubaba; reliefs of a sphinx and of a battle scene, and a hieroglyphic inscription with a representation of King Katuvas, all from the 9C BC.

Carchemish was built on and below a hill on the W bank of the Euphrates. It was in two parts. The lower city was protected by a wall which had a gate on the S and W side. The upper city, built on the hill overlooking the river, contained the acropolis and, at its foot, the royal palace. A terrace or processional way lined with orthostats led to the palace. Access to the upper city from the lower city was by gates in an inner defensive wall. Apart from the meagre ruins of a Roman temple on the summit of the hill and a few scatterd stones there is not much to see on the site.

A 15km journey by a dirt road from Nizip will bring you to the site of the ancient city of **Zeugma**, also known as Belkis. Strategically situated on a curve of the Euphrates, this was an important crossing point from the earliest times. Thucydides (5C BC) uses the word 'zeugma' in his histories to describe a bridge of boats. According to Pausanias, writing in the 2C AD, the god Dionysus bridged the Euphrates for the first time here: 'the city in the place where the Euphrates was spanned was named the Span (Zeugma), and in our own day they still have the cable there on which he spanned the river, plaited with vine branches and ivy branches'. There are a few sections of the wall of the citadel which crowned the hill above the city. Important finds from the Hellenistic and Roman periods, including a fine mosaic showing the Wedding of Dionysus and Ariadne, when Zeugma enjoyed considerable prosperity, have been found.

Zeugma is in the reservoir area of the Birecik dam of the GAP project. Rescue excavation has started.

History. It seems likely that there was a settlement at Zeugma from the Bronze Age, c 3000 to 2000 BC. Some believe that the first substantial foundation here was created in the 4C BC by Seleucus I Nikator. The road, which linked Antioch, the western Seleucid capital, with Seleucia on the Tigris, the eastern capital, passed through Zeugma. It was a regular staging post on the caravan route between the Far East and Antioch. Zeugma was given to Antiochus I of Commagene in 64 BC. Although he had good relations with Rome and had assumed the *toga praetexta* in 59 BC, Antiochus also had close links with Parthia, Rome's rival and enemy. In 53 BC an event occurred not far from Zeugma which may have affected his foreign policy. Crassus, the Roman general and member of the First Triumvirate, crossed the Euphrates at the head of a large army and marched to Carrhae (Harran). There the Romans were defeated utterly by the Parthians and shortly after the battle Crassus was slain during the course of a discussion with the Parthian general.

Roman legions, including *Legio X Fretensis* and *Legio IV Scythica* were stationed at Zeugma between the 1C and 4C AD and eventually the legionary camp became part of the city. Like soldiers everywhere the legionaries have left traces of their presence. Carved into the rock face of Ehnes quarry is a representation of the **insignia** of Legio IV. Tunnels in the cliff face high above the Euphrates formed part of the road system linking Cappadocia with Syria which was built by the Roman army. Among the many memorials commemorating soldiers who died at Zeugma is one to Septimius Longinus *miles* of the *Legio I adiutrix pia fidelis*.

In AD 49 Abgar, king of Edessa, came to Zeugma to greet Mihrdad, 'an inexperienced youth who identified the acme of fortune with dissipation' (Tacitus: *Annals*).

Despite the presence of the legions, Zeugma fell to Shapur I in AD 256 when the Persians defeated a Roman army of 60,000, ravaged Cappadocia and Syria and captured Antioch on the Orontes. The repercussions of this disaster on Zeugma were considerable. Its fortunes declined and the population was greatly reduced. A garrison in the acropolis continued to control the river crossing during the Byzantine period, but with the arrival of the Crusaders at Birecik even this activity ceased.

One of the few later references to Zeugma is attributed to Joshua the Stylite. He relates how credulous Jews and Christians in Zeugma were taken in by a magical egg which was laid there by a goose in March AD 504. This, it was alleged, bore an inscription in Greek script which said, 'The Greeks shall conquer (the Persians)'!

Excursions. On the Euphrates, N of Zeugma, are Gavur Kalesi, Hasanoğlu, Elif and Hisar. For Gavur Kalesi take Road 850 from Gaziantep to (65km) Yavuzeli and then follow a minor road in an easterly direction for a further 25km to Kasaba. For the other places continue on Road 850 from Yavuzeli to (26km) Araban. There take a side road first in an easterly, then in a southerly, direction to (33km) Hisar, (40km) Elif and (44km) Hasanoğlu.

Gavur Kalesi or **Rum Kalesi**—the names mean the Castle of the Infidels or the Castle of the Byzantines—is perched like a swallow's nest high above the Euphrates where the river is joined by a tributary known in ancient times as the Marsyas. Its strategic position attracted the Assyrians, Romans, Byzantines, Arabs and Turks. With an almost sheer drop on three sides, Rum Kalesi was not easy to capture. Connected to the river by a tunnel and steps, its water supply was ensured by a deep cistern. The castle probably owes its name to the fact that it remained in Christian hands until the end of 13C. There is a tradition that St John the Apostle was buried here.

At **Hasanoğlu**, **Elif** and **Hisar** there are three monumental Roman tombs dating from the late 2C or early 3C AD. Very similar in construction, but in varying states of preservation, they stand by the side of a military road which here follows the course of the river. At Hisar a door in the 2m high square base provides access to the burial chamber. At the corners of the platform above the base engaged pilasters support a pyramidal roof. The tops of the pilasters and a cube at the apex of the pyramid bear an acanthus design. The roof of the tomb at Elif is missing. There are large arches and a door above the base.

From Nizip continue on the E90 to (9km) **Birecik**. The town's ancient name, Birtha, is believed to be derived from the Armenian word for castle. Birecik is at the point where the Euphrates becomes navigable and was almost certainly fortified from very early times. The town is built on the left bank of the river. Although its tourist facilities are somewhat spartan in character, it is worth spending a few hours in Birecik exploring the castle or walking by the sluggish, green waters of the Euphrates. A rare species of bird, the **bald ibis**, nests here.

After Birecik the E24 traverses a bare, dun-coloured plain where there is little to attract the eye of the traveller or to hold his attention. Only an isolated village with its huddle of flat-roofed houses or the occasional tractor-drawn trailer carrying a family to work in the fields testifies to the presence of man in this desolate area. A long line of telegraph poles marches away to the horizon marking the monotonous passage of the kilometres on a journey that seems interminable. The road, black, sinuous and empty stretches as far as the eye can see and serves only to emphasise the traveller's sense of loneliness and isolation.

Arrival at (89km) **ŞANLI URFA** from the W is sudden and unexpected. Abruptly, the barren landscape gives way to gardens and orchards and beyond them are the terraced rows of houses, the mosques with their tall minarets, and the public buildings of the city. The road from the *otogar* to the centre of Urfa passes through a large, picturesque **cemetery**. You enter the abode of the living by way of the city of the dead.

Information and Acommodation. The **Tourist Information Office** is in Yusufpaşa Mah. Asfalt Cad. 4. The *Harran Hotel*, Atatürk Bul. and *Koran Hotel*, İpek Yolu are recommended.

Transport. There are frequent coach services from Urfa's *otogar* to Ankara, İstanbul and other cities in Turkey. THT provides regular flights to Ankara. The THY office is at Atatürk Bulv. 5/A.

History. It seems likely that there was a settlement at Urfa as early as the beginning of the second millennium BC. It had a good, if somewhat capricious, water supply from the NW. This came from a river called Daisan in Syriac, Scirtos in Greek, names which mean the 'leaping (river)'—it was liable to overflow suddenly during the winter rains or when the snow melted on the mountains during the spring. There were disastrous floods in AD 201, 303, 413 and in 515, when 30,000 died, one third of the population. The author of the so-called anonymous chronicle, *Anonymi auctoris chronicon ad annum Christi 1234 pertineus*, has left a vivid account of a flood in AD 835. 'It came at night when people were sleeping. The waters raged and rose outside the wall. When the wall was unable to resist the force of the water the wall was broken and the water entered the town and filled the streets and houses. About 3000 people were drowned in their houses, and many buildings were destroyed and collapsed. The water broke through the east side of the wall and went out'.

The earliest foundation was called Ursu, a name mentioned in Sumerian, Akkadian and Hittite cuneiform texts. Later it seems to have been part of a kingdom known to the Assyrians as Hanigalbat which was conquered by Suppiluliumas I c 1370. After the collapse of the Hittite Empire, it came under the rule of Carchemish. Following the death of Alexander the satrapy of Babylon and the territory known as Syria passed into the hands of Seleucus. He assumed the title Seleucus I Nicator in 306 BC and became the founder and first king of the Seleucid dynasty. Seleucus re-established the settlement and named it, perhaps for sentimental reasons, Edessa after the ancient capital of the Macedonians. Following the decline of the Seleucid dynasty Edessa came under the rule of a local princeling named Aryu c 132 BC. The dynasty which he founded lasted until AD 242. In that year the last king, Abgar X, and his wife retired to Rome. Thereafter, Edessa was administered by a Roman governor and two *strategoi*.

Edessa had a long, complicated and sometimes ambiguous relationship with Rome. Abgar II (68–53 BC) was blamed by Plutarch for bringing about the defeat of Crassus and the destruction of his army by the Parthians in 53 BC. He alleges that Abgar persuaded the Romans to come down from the mountains and march across the desert. Once they were in the wilderness the king slipped quietly away and left Crassus and his soldiers to their fate. At the beginning of the 1C AD Abgar V Ukkama, the Black, welcomed Mihrad, Rome's candidate for the throne of Parthia, to Edessa. After detaining the youth for months in the city and entertaining him lavishly, Abgar and Mihrad's other allies abandoned him in the mountains where he was captured by the Parthian king. After suffering hideous torture and mutilation, the unfortunate Mihrad was put to death. When Trajan came to Edessa in AD 114, Abjar VII sought to win favour by offering costly presents and by allowing his son to perform a 'barbaric dance' for the emperor's entertainment. The stratagem was successful. Abgar regained his throne and his handsome son became one of the emperor's favourites.

In AD 260 Valerian crossed the Euphrates to attack the Sassanian Shapur I who was besieging Edessa. However, the Romans were defeated in a 'great battle between Harran and Edessa' and Valerian was captured. He spent the remainder of his life as prisoner of the Persians.

At the beginning of the 3C most of the inhabitants of Edessa were pagans; by the end of that century Christianity had established a firm hold in the city. Abgar VIII, the Great (177–212) is believed to have been the first Christian king of Edessa, but the city had earlier links with Christianity. According to Eusebius, Abgar toparch of Edessa wrote to Jesus asking to be cured of a disease which was 'beyond human power to heal'. In his reply Jesus said that He would send a disciple to heal Abgar. The disciple Thaddaeus came to Edessa after the Resurrection and cured the king.

Christianity took many forms in Edessa. In addition to the Arians, there were Melkites, Jacobites, Nestorians and more obscure sects like the Borborians, who were accused of shameful practices, and the followers of one Adelphus of Ephesus who taught that sin could be defeated by the power of prayer. The Letter of Jesus appears to have belonged to the Jacobites, while the Melkites had a Portrait of Jesus which, it was claimed, had been painted by Hannan, Abgar's emissary, who was also an artist.

At the beginning of the 6C Edessa was besieged and captured by Chosroes II Aparvez, but was retaken by a Byzantine army under Heraclius in AD 628. Heraclius spent some time in Edessa overhauling the city's administration and curbing the influence of the rich property owners. He attempted in vain to reconcile the theological differences of the Monophysite and Orthodox branches of the church. His proposed solution of the theological problem was blocked by Sophronius the newly-elected, Orthodox patriarch of Jerusalem and his overtures to the Monophysite clergy of Edessa were rebuffed. The writer of the Anonymous Chronicle of 1234 tells the story. 'One day when he (Heraclius) went down to take communion in the great church, Isaiah, the (Monophysite) metropolitan of the city confronted him...saying 'If you do not anathematize in writing the synod of Chalcedon and the Tome of Leo (Pope Leo I), I will not give you communion!' Whereupon the king, inflamed with anger, expelled the bishop from the church and handed him over to the Chalcedonians...'.

In 1098 Baldwin I of Boulogne was invited by Thoros, the ruler of Edessa, to become his adopted son and co-ruler. This he did in a rather unusual ceremony: 'Thoros and Baldwin both stripped to the waist, whereupon together they donned a gargantuan shirt, and within its privacy they rubbed their bare breasts together. This, however, was not the end of the matter, for having performed the ritual with Thoros, Baldwin was expected to repeat the ceremony with his wife: a procedure which, one would have thought, must have had some embarrassing aspects'. According to Arab chroniclers, when this unusual ceremony was reported to the Muslim army it provoked much ribald mirth, as the adopted son was no child but a great hairy man. Thoros was not popular with his subjects and in a short time Baldwin was able to get rid of him and become sole ruler of the County of Edessa, an entity which, with one brief interruption, existed for half a century.

In 1146 the city fell to Nur ed-Din of Aleppo who took a savage revenge on the inhabitants for their resistance. It was razed to the ground, the churches were desecrated and the inhabitants massacred or sold into slavery. Subsequently Edessa was occupied by Saladin, the Selçuks, the Mongols and the Mamelukes. In 1516 it was captured by Selim I, the Grim, but did not become part of the Ottoman empire until 1637. It was occupied, briefly, by Mohammed Ali in 1837 and by the French at the end of the First World War.

The **citadel** at Urfa occupies an area of c 80–120m by 400m. Protected on the S by a deep moat, it had two defensive walls. The inner wall was strengthened by 25 towers. The two standing columns with Corinthian capitals on the mount are believed to date from the end of the 2C or beginning of the 3C AD. The eastern column bears a dedication in Syriac to Queen Shalmath, who may have been the wife of Abgar the Great. The other columns, similar in design, but not in size, may have formed part of

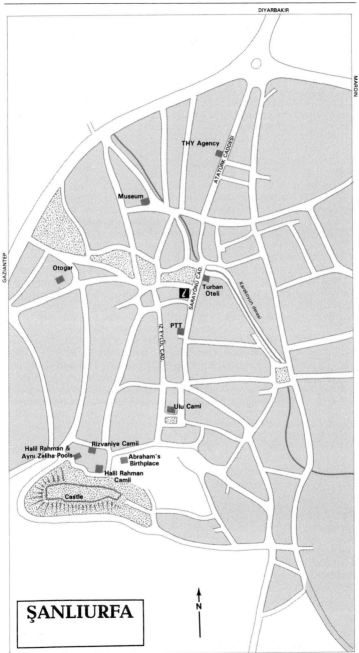

DIYARBAKIR

MARDIN

GAZIANTEP

THY Agency

ATATÜRK CADDESI

Museum

Otogar

SARAYÖNÜ CAD.

Turban
Oteli

Karakoyun deresi

PTT

12 EYLÜL CAD.

Ulu Cami

Rizvaniye Camii

Halil Rahman &
Aynı Zeliha Pools

Abraham's
Birthplace

Halil Rahman
Camii

Castle

ŞANLIURFA

N

a colonnade and probably stood to the N of a group of buildings. The citadel mount is sometimes called the Throne of Nimrod. According to a popular legend the wicked Nimrod used the columns as a sling to throw Abraham (İbrahim) from the mount. Where the prophet fell springs burst from the ground to form Birket İbrahim, the Pool of Abraham.

Archaeologists found a fine mosaic, which is believed to date to the 3C AD, in a tomb to the S of the citadel. This shows an noble Edessan family. It is now in the city's museum.

Birket İbrahim, c 30 by 150m, is full of carp which are regarded as sacred. There are several small restaurants and cafés by the pool. At weekends and holidays these are crowded with visitors and local people who come to stroll, relax and feed the fish. **Halil Rahman Cami** nearby may occupy the site of the Jacobite church dedicated to the Mother of God. To the S is **Birket Zulha**, the Pool of Zulha. Some say this commemorates Zulaika, Potiphar's wife or the mother of Nimrod whom the Muslims call Sulkha.

To the E is **Makam İbrahim Camii** where, according to legend, the child Abraham was hidden from Nimrod. This was built on the site of the Cathedral Church of the Saviour which was later called the Old Church or the Church of Qona. (Bishop Qona occupied the see of Edessa c AD 313.)

The late 12C **Ulu Cami** in the centre of the city may be built on the site of a church dedicated to St Stephen which itself had replaced a synagogue. The octagonal minaret bears an inscription of Saladin dated AD 1191.

The **Museum** is in the Place of the Martyrs. An extension houses the material found during rescue operations in the area of the Lower Euphrates Dam Project. Many of the exhibits are labelled in English. There is a small *kahve* in the garden where you can take refreshments surrounded by stelae, funerary monuments and other reminders of the past.

Among the objects on display are a **cylinder seal** and a violin-shaped idol both dated to the third millennium BC from the necropolis of Titris; a **stele** from Harran with a **cuneiform inscription** relating to Nabonidus, the last king of Babylon; a fragmentary tablet with a reference to the temple of Sin (the moon god) of Harran; mosaics with representations of animals and the **family portrait mosaic**, the **funerary couch mosaic** and the **tripod mosaic**, all of which bear inscriptions in Syriac and date from the 2C and 3C AD.

In Urfa's **covered bazaar** shops sell everything from food, clothing, household utensils to radios and television sets. Its narrow lanes, lit by stray beams of dusty sunlight, are filled with noisy shoppers, who poke at the merchandise and launch a barrage of critical comments about its price, quality and value. A friendly, noisy, bustling place full of interesting smells where mules and donkeys laden with fresh country produce have priority over pedestrians, Urfa's bazaar should not be missed.

S of Urfa are Harran, Sultantepe and Sumatar Harabesi. Harran is served irregularly by public transport. For Sumatar Harabesi you will need a four-wheel drive and a guide.

Leave Urfa by Road 885 in the direction of Akçakale. After c 15km take a left turn on to a stabilised side road and continue for 3km to the *hüyük* of **Sultantepe**. During the 8C and 7C BC there was a substantial Assyrian settlement here which was protected by a rampart. In addition to the remains of a temple, which may have been dedicated to Sin, the moon god of Harran, excavations in the 1950s revealed **artefacts in ivory**, a **stele** bearing the symbols of Sin and a large number of **tablets** written in Assyrian and Sumerian. The tablets were found in a private house, which the archaeologists called Qurdi Negal, after a person who is mentioned frequently in the texts. Perhaps belonging to a school of scribes, they cover many subjects—magic, mathematics, medicine, astrology, prayers and curses. Some tell the story of the Creation and the Flood, while others relate the adventures of the hero Gilgamesh.

Based on a Sumerian king of c 2850 BC, the mythical **Gilgamesh** was one third man and two thirds god. Until Gilgamesh civilised him, his companion, Enkidu, lived with animals in the wild. Together the heroes conquered giants, averted famine and killed the Bull of Heaven. The gods, angered by the latter exploit, punished Enkidu by giving him a fatal illness and he went to Irkalla, the place of no return. Gilgamesh tried to bring his friend back to life, but failed and joined Enkidu voluntarily in Irkalla. The tablets cease abruptly two years after the capture of Nineveh by the Medes and the Babylonians in 612 BC, an event which brought the Assyrian Empire to an end. Some are now kept in the Anatolian Civilizations Museum in Ankara.

To visit Sumatar Harabesi follow the rough road around the mound and continue in an easterly direction. Crossing an irrigation ditch c 30cm deep en route, you arrive at the village of (28km) Sumatar. Here take a guide as the track for the last 20km of the journey to the site is poorly marked.

At **Sumatar Harabesi** a number of *wadis* meet. Blessed with wells of sweet water it is used by nomadic shepherds who bring their flocks here. At the centre of the site there is a natural mound c 50m high. To the W and N of this mound, at a distance of between 400m and 800m, are eight ruined buildings perched on small hills. Inscriptions found at Sumatar Harabesi and other places in the neighbourhood suggest that it was a sanctuary of the mysterious Sabians.

There is a reference to '**Sabians**' in the Koran, where they are linked with Jews, Christians and those who believe in one God and in the Last Judgement and who live righteous lives. In the 9C AD the inhabitants of Harran found it expedient to claim membership of this sect. The Sabians worshipped Helios (the sun), Sin (the moon), Saturn (Qronos), Jupiter (Bel), Mars (Ares), Venus (Balti) and Mercury (Nabuq). These deities were in turn ruled by a supreme god who remained remote and aloof from the affairs of men. Facing the north, the Sabians prayed at sunrise, noon and sunset. Their holy book was called Hanphe. Each day of the week was dedicated to one of the seven planets. Each planet had a temple built in a different style of architecture. The temple of the sun was square, his day was Sunday; the temple of Mars was oblong, his day was Tuesday and so on through the week. The buildings at Sumatar Harabesi conform to the descriptions of those used by later planet-worshippers. One is square, one cylinder-shaped, a third cylindrical on a quadrilateral base. In addition, an inscription in Syriac by the side of a relief on the central mound mentions Sin, the moon god. 'Sila made (this) image to Sin the deity for the life of Tiridates...'. This dedication has been dated to the mid 2C AD and there are others at the site from the same period. Each of the subsidiary buildings had a subterranean chamber whose entrance faced the central mound where the supreme deity, Marilaha, was worshipped.

Most of the existing information about the Sabians was written by Jewish, Christian and Muslim chroniclers who were not particularly well disposed towards them. The discourse, 'On the Fall of Idols', by the late 5C Mono-physite bishop Jacob of Serug, which is often quoted by modern commentators, accuses the Sabians of practising human sacrifice and hints at orgiastic rites. Segal drily suggests that some allowance should be made for poetic hyperbole in Jacob's dissertation.

From Sumatar Harabesi return to the main road and continue S in the direction of Akçakale. At present the flat, featureless plain to the SE of Urfa is not very fertile and is sparsely populated. It lacks water. However, the Turkish government has undertaken a vast irrigation scheme which will improve both the appearance and economy of the region. The East Anatolia Project (GAP) will bring water from the Atatürk Dam near Adıyaman through two underground pipes c 8m in diameter and 100km long. More than 1.5 million acres will be irrigated. The drift of peasants from the land will be stemmed and crops like cotton will be produced regularly and in quantity.

At c 38km from Urfa turn left for 10km **HARRAN**. It is difficult to believe that this small settlement on the edge of the desert was once a major economic, religious and cultural centre. Harran, the name means 'crossroads' has been occupied since at least 2000 BC. It was an important trading posts on the road which linked Amida (Diyarbakır) with the great cities in S and SW Syria.

History. One of the earliest references to Harran has been found in the records of Mari, a city on the middle Euphrates. It concerns a treaty ratified in the temple of Sin c 2000 BC. Genesis XI, 12 states that Terah took Abraham his son, and Lot the wife of Haran, his grandson and Sarai his daughter-in-law from Ur of the Chaldees to the land of Canaan and that on the way they dwelt in Harran. Biblical scholars have dated this event to the 19C BC. The temple of Sin was restored by Shalmaneser III in the 9C BC, by Ashurbanipal in the 7C and in the last days of the Babylonian empire by Nabonidus. Esarhaddon (681–669) visited the temple on his way to Egypt and was told by the god that he would be victorious. His campaign took him to Memphis and Thebes and he won the loyalty of some of the petty princes of the Delta.

In May 53 BC an army under the command of Crassus, the triumvir and consul, was defeated utterly at the battle of Carrhae, as Harran was called during the Roman period. For more than a century Carrhae, Edessa and the surrounding area were under Parthian rule. In AD 217 the dissolute and cruel emperor Caracalla was murdered while on his way to the temple of Sin at Harran where he intended to invoke the blessing of the god on his forthcoming campaign against the Parthians. He had incurred the enmity of a soldier named Martialis whom he had refused to promote to the rank of centurion. Martialis and two military tribunes in the Praetorian Guard were suborned by Macrinus, the Praetorian Prefect, and they agreed to kill the emperor for a price. A sudden bout of diarrhoea caused Caracalla to retire behind the bushes which lined the road. After a few moments Martialis told the other members of the escort that the emperor had called him and he rushed behind the screen of bushes. There he found Caracalla crouching and unable to defend himself. Martialis stabbed him with his dagger. Badly wounded, Caracalla cried out for help and some of the German guards rushed to his aid. They, seeing Martialis with the bloody dagger in his hand, pursued and killed him. However, in the ensuing confusion the tribunes were able to hack Caracalla to death. Macrinus succeeded Caracalla as emperor, but after a disastrous campaign against the Parthians, he and his son were killed by his own soldiers. The legions elected the bizarre pathic Elagabalus as emperor in his place.

Julian the Apostate came to Harran in AD 363. According to Ammianus he offered sacrifice to the moon god in accordance with a rubric favoured by the local people. Paganism in Harran suffered a severe blow in AD 382 during the reign of Theodosius, when the temple of Sin was pulled down. Though the city's defences were strengthened in the 6C at the orders of Justinian, Harran fell to the Arabs in AD 639.

About two centuries later the Caliph Abdallah al-Ma'mun visited Harran. Approached by a group of pagans he asked them, 'to which tolerated community do you belong?' 'We are Harranians', they answered. Ma'mun then asked if they were Christians, Jews or Zoroastrians and if they had a revealed book and a prophet. Not receiving a satisfactory answer, he said, 'in that case you are pagans...you are not a tolerated community'. 'But we pay the poll tax', they protested. In desperation, the pagans consulted a Muslim lawyer. He suggested they call themselves Sabians, as Jews, Christians and Sabians are mentioned in the Koran. Some of the pagans accepted his advice and abandoned their distinctive dress—a kind of loose frock coat—and cut off their long hair.

The Sabians of Harran worshipped Shamal, Lord of the Jinn, the moon god Mars, and other deities. Women had equality with men. Procreation was the sole purpose of marriage. They were monogamous. Marriage between close relatives was not permitted. Divorce was allowed if evidence of unfaithfulness could be produced. Contact with lepers and those suffering from contagious diseases was to be avoided. Circumcision was not practised. There were many dietary restrictions. The meat of pigs, dogs, camels, fish, pigeons and chickens was forbidden. They could not eat lentils, cabbage, cauliflower or kidney beans. Wine was allowed and they enjoyed drinking it. There was a festival to celebrate the new vintage and libations were poured to the dead.

In 1104 an army of 3000 knights and 7000 foot soldiers under the command of Baldwin and Tancred laid siege to Harran. The Harranians offered unconditional surrender, but this was refused by Baldwin. The Muslim army then regrouped and attacked. The Crusaders were routed and Baldwin was taken prisoner. This defeat had the effect of limiting Christian influence to Palestine and the E shore of the Mediterranean.

In the 12C Harran was taken, first by Nur-ed Din, and then by Saladin. In 1260 it was destroyed by the Mongols under Hulagu. Greatly reduced in size and influence, it came under Ottoman rule in 1637 during the reign of Murad IV.

What happened to the Sabians of Harran? Some opine that the Mandaeans, who live in the marshes of the lower Euphrates and Tigris, are descended from them. Their language is not unlike the Syriac spoken at Harran. However, while there are some similarities between their beliefs and practices and those of the Sabians, it seems unlikely that a firm connection between the two sects can be proved conclusively.

Allow at least three hours for a visit to Harran. In the summer go early as there is little shade at the site. Take a picnic. As Harran is near the Syrian frontier, there may be restrictions on taking photographs. Enquire at the Tourist Information Office in Urfa. Some men and most women in Harran and the surrounding area will almost certainly not want to be photographed. To avoid giving offence, ask permission before taking pictures of adults. Usually, there is no problem about photographing children.

Recent excavations and surveys by Turkish archaeologists have provided much information about Harran's past. The area around the 11C **citadel** in the SE part of the city has been cleared. Only three of the original four towers still stand. Erected before the Arab conquest, it was strengthened by the Fatimids and later by the Crusaders. According to a 14C chronicle it occupies the site of a Sabian temple dedicated to the moon god.

In the *hüyük* the discovery of a brick and a tablet with cuneiform inscriptions, which mention Nabonidus and the temple of Sin (see above), have convinced the archaeologists that they are near the site of this building. Other finds include a second millennium female idol in the Syrian style, silver and bronze bracelets, rings, bronze coins and a bone musical pipe. Architectural remains of the 12C and 13C AD were also laid bare. The houses, rectangular and square, had courtyards with deep wells. The streets were very narrow.

The site of **Ulu Cami**, which measured 104m by 107m, has been cleared. Drawings and studies were made of the minaret, şadirvan, mihrab and the pavilions at the E and N with a view to restoration. Sited to the NE of the *hüyük*, this is the oldest mosque in Turkey. It was built by Caliph Merman II (AD 744–750) during his sojourn in Harran. The mosque was restored by Saladin in the late 12C.

There are remains of the 4km long defensive wall and of the seven gates of Harran. The **Aleppo Gate** on the W side, which bears an inscription with the name of Saladin and the date AH 588 (AD 1192), is the most complete.

The **beehive-shaped houses** are in the SE corner of the village. Perfectly adapted to the climate, they are warm in winter and cool in summer. There are no restaurants in Harran, but the hospitable villagers often invite visitors to take refreshments in their houses. Children, curious about the strange ways of foreigners, follow visitors around. Some, anxious to show off their excellent knowledge of English and other languages, offer to be guides.

From Harran return to Urfa.

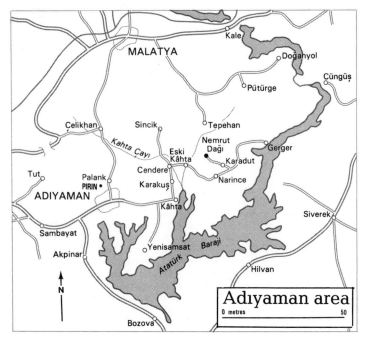

40

Şanlı Urfa to Adıyaman and Nemrut Dağı

Total distance 106km. Şanlı Urfa—36km Bozova—c 5km Atatürk Baraj—70km Adıyaman (35km Kahta—10km Karakuş—9km Cendere—7km Eski Kahta—21km Narince—24km Nemrut Dağı).

Leave Şanli Urfa by road E99/885 signposted Hilvan, Siverek and Diyarbakır. At a crossroads 9km to the N of Urfa take the left fork and continue in the direction of Kızlar and Bozova. You pass through a bare, rather uninteresting landscape where the occasional clump of trees in a *wadi* indicates the presence of water. After 27km a turning on the right leads to

Bozova. Shortly after, power lines and industrial buildings indicate that you are near the **Atatürk Baraj**. At the time of writing it is possible, with permission, to visit the dam. Enquire at the Tourist Information Office in Urfa. Overnight accommodation, for which there is a small charge, is often available in the official guest house at the site.

The rock-filled Atatürk High Dam, one of the largest in the world, is an awe-inspiring sight. When completed it will be 180m high and 84.5 million cubic metres of rock and clay will have been used for the body fill. The lake will contain 48.5 million cubic metres of water. The capacity of the power plant is 2400MW and the annual electricity output will be 8.900 million kwh. Water will be taken by two huge concrete tunnels at the rate of 164 cubic metres per second per tunnel to irrigate the Şanlı Urfa—Harran and Mardin—Ceylanpınar plains. The GAP Project, of which the dam forms part, is designed to increase agricultural production and power supplies for a projected population growth of 80 million. It will create employment and improve the health, education and transport services for the people of the region.

Submerged beneath the lake is the village of **Samsat**, formerly Samosata, capital of the ancient Commagene kingdom. The inhabitants have been rehoused in Yenisamsat (New Samsat) which is 25km to the S of Kahta.

History. Samosata was founded by the eponymous Samos I c 130 BC. In the 8C BC this area formed part of the Neo-Hittite kingdom of Kummukhi which extended as far S as the Euphrates. Heavily forested and well-watered, Samosata was described as 'a city fortified by nature...surrounded by an exceedingly fertile, though small, territory'. (Strabo. *Geography* Vol. VII.) Criss-crossed by trade routes, it possessed valuable iron mines. The phrase often used to describe it was '*ubi ferrum nascitur*', the land where iron grows. Jupiter Dolichenus (see Dülük above) was the most important deity. The Commagene kingdom was subjected to Greek and Iranian influences and, as a result, displayed some elements of the culture and religion of both.

The marriage of Mithridates I Kallinikos of Commagene to Laodike, the daughter of the Seleucid Antiochus VIII, improved relations between the two kingdoms. During the reign of their son Antiochus I (69–34) Commagene reached its apogee. Antiochus built the *hierothesion* on the top of Nemrut Dağı (see below) where he was buried. His successors, Mithridates II and Mithridates III, were weak and ineffectual rulers and in AD 72 Commagene came under direct Roman rule. Samsat enjoyed a certain degree of importance during the 7C to 10C AD when it was under Arab control. By the time of its disappearance under the waters of the lake it was a quiet country village.

Born here was Lucian the Sophist (c AD 117–180), the author of the amusing *Satirical Sketches*. Because of his lack of respect for all religions, including Christianity, he was vilified by Christian writers. In a 10C biography he is called Lucian the Blasphemer, the Slanderer, the Atheist and the failed barrister who turned to literature. His biographer claims that he was torn to pieces by mad dogs 'because he had been so rabid against the truth', and affirms that this was an adequate punishment for his misdemeanours in this life. In the next he is promised the eternal fire of hell in the company of Satan. A second, Lucian, was a distinguished scriptural scholar. He set up a school of exegesis in Antioch, so is usually known as St Lucian of Antioch. He was martyred in Nicomedia in AD 312.

Very little remained of Samosata's past—the walls of its ruined, hill-top castle and part of the aqueduct built during the reign of Septimius Severus c AD 200. A survey was made and rescue archaeology took place.

Continue in a NW direction for c 60km to the junction with Road 360. There turn right for the short 10km drive to **Adıyaman**.

Adıyaman, one of the main centres for visits to Nemrut Dağı, Karakuş, and Eski Kahta, is plagued by touts who hang around the bus station and prey on unwary travellers. They offer accommodation and tours at what appear to be advantageous prices but their dubious offers are best ignored.

Information and Accommodation. The **Tourist Information Office** is at Atatürk Bul. 184. The *Serdaroğlu Oteli* at Turgutreis Cad. 20. is recommended.

Adıyaman was founded in the 7C AD. Known as Hisn Mansur, it was occupied between the 7C and 10C by the Omayyads of Damascus and the Abbasids of Baghdad. In the 13C the Selçuk Turks were succeeded by the Mongols who destroyed the town and ravaged the surrounding countryside. In the 14C the area was ruled by the Mamelukes. Hisn Mansur became part of the Ottoman Empire in the early 16C. However, tribal conflicts continued to trouble the area and large tracts were depopulated. Records of the time paint a gloomy picture of misery and despair.

Ulu Cami, near the bazaar, replaced Eski Cami (the Old Mosque) which was torn down in the mid 19C. The **Çarsı** or **Abdulgani Camii** dates from 1557. Located in the market, it was restored in the 17C and again in 1957. The **Eski Saray Mosque** in the W part of the town was built by Ibrahim Bey in 1638—see the inscription over the portal. It also has been renovated. Only the E and S faces are original. Note the very fine *mihrab*. A **Syrian Orthodox church** in the town centre is looked after by a Christian family.

On an artificial mound in the centre are the remains of Adıyaman's **citadel**. This is sometimes called Hisn Mansur citadel after Ebu Caferil Mansur, the Omayyad general who repaired it in the late 7C or early 8C. A *han*, which may be Selçuk in origin, is still used for the sale of livestock. Its stalls for cattle and horses are usually occupied and are filled with characteristic smells. The walls and upper floors have been much patched and repaired.

By making an early start from Adıyaman it is possible to visit the most important sites—**Karakuş, Cendere, Yeni Kale, Eski Kale** (Arsameia on the Nymphaios) and **Nemrut Dağı**—in one day. Refreshments are available at Cendere and near Eski Kale. Even in summer it can be very cold on the summit of Nemrut Dağı (2150m), so take warm clothing.

A separate excursion is recommended to places of secondary importance around Adıyaman like Pirin, Göksü Köprüsü and Sesönk.

Leave Adıyaman by Road 360 for (35km) **Kahta**. You pass through a of countryside of carefully tended orchards and areas of intense cultivation. Kahta is a dusty, unimpressive little town which owes its importance entirely to its proximity to Nemrut Dağı. Those who want to see the sunrise from the summit, often stay here. There are two motels, *Nemrut Tur Moteli* and *Zeus Moteli*, and the *Kommagene Pansiyon* in the (Yeni) Kahta area.

From Kahta take a minor road signposted Sincik and continue to 10km **Karakuş** where there is a **tumulus** and several **columns**. According to an inscription on one of the columns the tumulus was constructed by Mithridates as the resting place of three female members of the royal family.

> This is the hierothesion of Isias, whom Great King Mithridates…thought worthy of this last honour, she being his own mother. But first the girl Antiochis lay here, sister of the king by the same mother. She was the most beautiful of women; her life was short, and long will be her honours in the long time (to come). Both of these, as you see, are here, and after them the granddaughter of Isias, Aka, daughter of Antiochis. This is a memorial by the king of her life along with theirs'. At first it was believed that the king referred to was Mithridates I Kallinikos (c 100–c 70 BC), the father of Antiochus I Theos (c 70–36 BC). However, another inscription was found recently on a column just below a *dexiosis* relief which includes a female figure. This mentions Laodice, the daughter of Antiochus I who became queen of Parthia. It would seem that the monument was erected by Mithridates II (c 36–20 BC), the son and successor of Antiochus I.

Three pairs of columns, each crowned by a sculpted figure, once stood on the NE, NW and S sides of the tumulus. Today only **four columns** remain.

Funerary columns at Karakuş

One is surmounted by an eagle, now headless. This carving, which represented Zeus, has given the site its Turkish name. Karakuş means Black Bird. Note the much weathered **statue of a lion** on the ground near the tumulus.

In 1967 archaeologists found the burial chamber in the tumulus, but grave robbers had been there before them, possibly in ancient times. The chamber was empty.

From Karakuş continue for 9km to the Roman bridge at **Cendere**. Here the landscape opens out dramatically. To the right is the broad, stony bed of the Cendere Suyu, the ancient Chabinas. In summer and autumn the river dwindles to a number of narrow streams which meander lazily between sun-bleached boulders and accumulated debris brought down by the winter floods. To the E of Cendere are the foothills of Eski Kahta and beyond them, away in the distance, the great bare cone of Nemrut Dağı. The bridge, c 118m long, was built between AD 198 and 200 by the XVI Legio Flavia Firma which was based at Samosata. They used material taken from Karakuş. A single graceful arch of c 35m carries the road high above the water. Originally there were four tall columns, two at either end of the bridge. Three remain. Inscriptions on the columns and the parapet state that the bridge was built at the request of four cities in Commagene in honour of the emperor Septimius Severus (AD 193–211), his wife, Julia Domna, and their sons, Geta and Caracalla. When Caracalla became emperor, he had Geta murdered (AD 212). The column bearing Geta's name was removed from the bridge. (For the death of Caracalla, see Harran.) The bridge, which is in regular use, will probably be submerged when a dam on the Kahta Çayı has been completed.

At Cendere there are fine views of the *wadi* which gives the place its name (Cendere means 'narrow gorge' in Turkish), of the river valley and the bridge. Photographers will be entranced. It is possible to explore the gorge and caves on the N side. There are tea houses by the bridge.

From Cendere the road turns E and rises gently as it moves away from the river. The louring bulk of Yeni Kale, the New Castle, is visible before you reach the village of **Eski Kahta**. At the end of the dusty street, between the flat roofed houses, is the village school. Ask there for the *bekçi* who will conduct you around the castle.

Yeni Kale is believed to have replaced an earlier fortress which was destroyed in the 13C. Inscriptions over the entrance state that the existing building was constructed by the Mameluke sultans Kalaun (1279–90), Eşref Halil (1290–93) and Nasır Muhammed (1293–1341). Protected by massive walls, its inner keep soars almost 300m above the village. A huge portal provides access to the lower part of the castle. Here are **dungeons**, a large **underground chamber** which may have been the castle's dining hall, the **harem** and a **mosque**. In the upper part a narrow, twisting corridor leads to an isolated fortified spur where supplies were received from traders. A vertiginous set of steps leads down to the castle's **water gate**. Note the well-preserved lock-up and the pigeon loft with perches for 32 birds. Carrier pigeons were used here perhaps as early as the 12C. There are fine views from the walls of the inner keep.

On leaving Yeni Kale the road enters a **picturesque gorge** and crosses the Kahta Çayı by a well-preserved **Selçuk bridge**. Here turn left on to a narrow track which leads to the car-park. You continue on foot. A zigzag path follows an **ancient processional way** up the very steep slope.

Eski Kale was known in Commagene times as **Arsameia on the Nymphaios**. It was the *hierothesion* of Mithridates I Kallinikos (c 100–c 70 BC), who made a dynastic alliance with the Seleucid princess, Laodice Thea Philadelphos, the daughter of Antiochus VIII Grypus (Eagle Nose). The marriage linked the Commagene kings with the Seleucid and Ptolemaic dynasties. To mark such an important event Mithridates took his father-in-law's surname 'Kallinikos' which means 'gloriously victorious'. When Tigranes the Great of Armenia (c 94–c 56 BC) laid claim to the Seleucid throne and occupied Syria, to safeguard his line of communications he brought the Commagene kingdom under his control. Its rulers then became subordinate to the 'King of Kings' as Tigranes styled himself. After the defeat of Tigranes by Lucullus in 69 BC, Antiochus I Theos, the son and successor of Mithridates, sought and secured the friendship of Rome. With minor interruptions this relationship continued for a century and a half.

View from Nemrut Dağı, with the head of Antiochus I in the foreground

Part of a c 5m high **stele**, which had a *dexiosis* scene of Antiochus I greeting Mithra-Helios, has been re-erected. Sculptures which place the king on an equal footing with the gods are a frequently-repeated feature in Commagene art. The relief, which has been damaged and weathered, shows the god wearing a Phrygian cap. At the second stopping place there is another **stele** with a *dexiosis* scene of Mithridates and Hercules. The king is wearing the *kitaris*, an adaptation of the Armenian tiara, and is dressed in his robes of state. In contrast, the muscular figure of Hercules is completely nude. He carries two of his customary symbols—a club and the skin of the Nemean lion. Behind the stele a **long inscription** in Greek states that the *hierothesion* was created by Antiochus I in honour of his father, Mithridates. It gives Antiochus all his titles—the Righteous, Theos (God), Epiphanes, Romanophile, Hellenophile—and stresses his royal pedigree as son of King Mithridates and Queen Laodice, daughter of Antiochus of Syria. The inscription, the longest Greek text discovered in Turkey, covers the walls around the entrance to a **deep tunnel** which extends for c 170m into the mountain. The purpose of the tunnel is not known. It was probably used for religious ceremonies connected with the *hierothesion*.

A path leads from the stele to the summit of the mountain where several fine pattern **mosaics** dating from the 2C BC were found. Some of these have been moved to the Anatolian Civilisations Museum in Ankara. Others have been covered over to protect them from damage. On one mosaic successive bands of stylised battlements, pyramids, stepped ziggurats, wave-like curlicues and a maeander pattern enclose the centre area. There are the foundations of several large buildings and a number of architectural fragments and sculptures. According to Dörner, the German archaeologist who found the site and excavated it, Mithridate's mausoleum and the buildings associated with it stood on the mountain top. Today, only a few column bases remain on the site.

Return to the stele of Mithridates and Hercules and follow the processional way to the W end of the site. Here 14 steps lead down into a lofty **chamber** c 10m by 10m. Cut out of the rock, this may have been used for the worship of Mithra. His temples were usually in man-made or natural caves.

In the late afternoon the reliefs and inscriptions are clearly outlined by the westering sun. This is the best time for photography.

From Eski Kahta continue around the S side of the mountain towards **NEMRUT DAĞI**. There are several small restaurants en route which serve well-prepared, simple meals. From time to time you pass through mountain villages where mean houses crouch by the side of the pot-holed streets. As you approach the summit the road ascends at an ever steeper angle and the landscape becomes more wild and desolate. The last few kilometres of the road, paved with irregularly-shaped slabs of basalt, turn through a series of steep, unprotected bends which will terrify all but the most seasoned travellers. There is a small rest house and café near the car-park at the base of the summit. Here you may obtain tea and soft drinks and change into warmer clothes before climbing the last 500m to the sanctuary.

The Commagene Antiochus I Theos, the ruler of a relatively unimportant but wealthy kingdom in Central Anatolia, built this magnificent funerary monument on the summit of the highest mountain in his realm. A self-styled god (Theos), he had two desires—to be buried 'close to the celestial throne' and to leave visible proof of his royal descent from Alexander the Great and the Achaemenids of Persia. The Commagene kingdom had been subjected to both Greek and Persian influences so it is not surprising that it produced a fusion of two religious beliefs and two cultural traditions. In a long inscription Antiochus set out his wishes for the celebrations to be made on his birthday and on the anniversary of his coronation. The text specified what prayers were to be said, what food was to be given to the participants, even what music was to be played. He begged 'the paternal gods of the land of Persia and of Macedonia, in this way the family of the Commagenes' to look with favour on those who obeyed his commands. On anyone who disobeyed him he called 'the inexorable anger of all the spirits' and wished that all the gods would 'strike him, and his race, with all chastisements'.

Forgotten for almost 2000 years, the *hierothesion* was rediscovered by a German engineer, Karl Sester, in 1881. His report caused considerable interest and the site was visited by Osman Hamdi Bey, the director of the İstanbul Museum in 1883. In 1984 German archaeologists under the direction of F.K. Dörner began to survey and restore the monuments. So far the burial chamber of Antiochus has not been found. The cone-shaped tumulus is 150m in diameter and 50m high. There were three terraces in the sanctuary—on the E, N and W sides. The remains of the sculptures, which once decorated all three, give some idea of the size and grandeur of Antiochus' magnificent folly.

Follow the path of large, rough stones which ascends at an acute angle from the back of the rest house to the **E terrace**. In deep shade during the afternoon this terrace is intensely cold and it requires considerable stamina and determination to linger over its extraordinary monuments. As it faced the dawn, the E terrace was probably the most important part of the sanctuary. In its centre there was a fire altar. A line of **seated figures** looked towards the sunrise. Apart from the heads which have been thrown to the ground, they are in a good state of preservation. **Antiochus** is seated next to the Commagene **goddess of plenty** who is easily distinguished by the cornucopia in her arms. The large figure in the centre is **Zeus-Ahurmazda**.

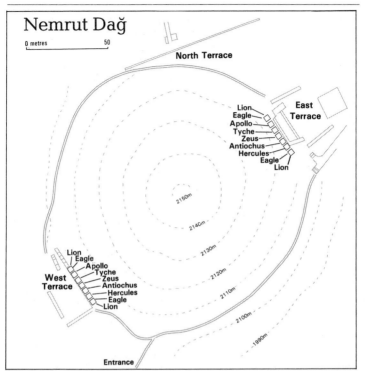

Nemrut Dağ

0 metres   50

North Terrace

East Terrace

Lion
Eagle
Apollo
Tyche
Zeus
Antiochus
Hercules
Eagle
Lion

2150m
2140m
2130m
2120m
2110m
2100m
1990m

West Terrace

Lion
Eagle
Apollo
Tyche
Zeus
Antiochus
Hercules
Eagle
Lion

Entrance

Next to him is **Apollo-Mithra-Helios**. Then comes another syncretic deity, **Ares-Artagenes-Hercules** distinguished by his club. The **orthostats**, which once lined the N and the S sides of the terrace, have been badly damaged. They traced the royal ancestry of Antiochus—through his mother, Laodice, and the Seleucids to Alexander the Great on the S and through his father, Mithridates, to the Achaemenids on the N.

The processional way continues from the E to the **N terrace**, which is in a ruinous condition. The **W terrace**, which is lower than its E counterpart, had another **line of statues** of the same deities. Here the bodies have been mutilated. The heads, which have escaped damage, have been re-erected. A youthful **Antiochus** wears a tall, flattened hat which reveals his ears. Underneath a broad band there is another decorated with star-like rosettes. By his side is the menacing, beaked head of an **eagle**. **Mithra-Helios**, also beardless, wears an elaborate cap with a pattern of rays at the top. There is a bearded **Hercules** and another head which is believed to be that of **Zeus-Ahurmazda**. The **female head** with an elaborate decoration of fruit and ears of corn is the Commagene goddess of plenty. The **orthostat reliefs** on the W terrace are well-preserved. In *dexiosis* scenes are **Antiochus** and a naked **Hercules** with his club, **Apollo-Mithra** crowned with the sun's rays, **Zeus-Ahurmazda** and the **Commagene goddess**. A **relief of a lion** has a pattern of stars on and around its body, while a crescent moon hangs like a pendant torque below its head. This appears to be a horoscope. According to an inscription the three celestial bodies above the animal's back represent Jupiter, Mercury and Mars, a conjunction of the planets which is believed to have taken place on 7 July 62 BC. The significance of this date is not known. On the S side of the terrace there are some fragmentary orthostats which show the **Achaemenid ancestors** of Antiochus.

From the W terrace there is a magnificent view. In good weather you will be able to see the Atatürk Dam. It is a good position for photographers.

Perhaps the best time of the year to visit Nemrut Dağı is early October, as then the loneliness and isolation of this bizarre funerary monument are very apparent. There are few visitors and the first flakes of snow on the summit herald blizzards that will soon isolate the mountain sanctuary completely. Abandoned by man, only the wild animals and birds that shelter among its ruined stones keep company with the spirit of Antiochus during the long, dark months of winter.

To return to Adıyaman turn right at Narince and, a short distance afterwards, pick up the main Diyarbakir–Adıyaman road.

There are several less well-known sites near Adıyaman—Pirin, Haydaran, Sesönk, Arsameia on Euphrates and Süpürgüç. For most of them you will need your own transport, preferably a vehicle with four-wheel drive.

Pirin, known in ancient times as Perre, is c 5km to the NE of Adıyaman on the way to Kuyucak. Take a minor road on the left, just outside the town. There is no yellow sign. There are the substantial remains of an aqueduct, a fountain which is still in use, and a large Roman necropolis. Many of the 200 tombs are in natural caves. Others are in grottoes whose walls still bear the chisel marks of the stone masons who made them. Usually there are two or three *klinai* in each tomb.

From Pirin continue to c 12km **Haydaran**. Near Haydaran there is an interesting **rock carving**. Take a guide from the village. The relief is c 2m from the ground on a rocky outcrop. It resembles the *dexiosis* reliefs of Antiochus and Mithra found in other places near Adıyaman.

On the way back to Adıyaman there is a **prehistoric cave** on the side of a river valley below the road. You will need a guide. **The descent is difficult and, in places, not without danger.** Inside the cave are the reliefs of two animals. One is almost completely obscured by soot from fires made by the wandering shepherds.

To the SW of Adıyaman are Sesönk and Süpürgüç, two places which are not easy to reach. For Sesönk leave Adıyaman by Road 360 in the direction of Gölbaşşı. At Sambayat turn left and continue to Kızilin. Note the **Roman bridge** over the Göksü river on the outskirts of Kızilin. The arches on both banks of the river still stand, but the central span has disappeared. This bridge and one on the Karasu were on a Roman military road constructed W of the Euphrates during the reign of Septimius Severus (AD 193–211). The **tumulus** at **Sesönk**, is on the W bank of the river. About 115m in diameter, its top has been flattened and is only c 6m high. It is believed to be the burial place of Mithridates II (c 36–20 BC) and of his consort. A grave chamber for three persons was discovered by tomb robbers in 1984.

About 15km to the SW of Sesönk there is a **Neo-Hittite relief** at **Süpürgüç**. On a stony hillside near the junction of the Karasu river with the Euphrates, it shows a guardian deity standing on the back of a stag. He holds a bow in his left hand and flourishes a sword in his right. A sun-disk with out-stretched wings hovers above his head. The relief has been dated to c 950 BC. Nearby is a **Roman bridge** over the Karasu river. It is similar to the Göksü bridge (see above) but is in a better state of preservation.

Picturesque **Arsameia on the Euphrates** is near the town of **Gerger** c 65km to the NE of Adıyaman. Take the road from Kahta to Narince and continuing for c 10km to where a rough track on the right is dominated by a ruined castle. Note the archaic relief, c 4.5m by c 3m, cut into the living rock. According to an inscription, it represents Samos (c 130–100), the royal grandfather of Antiochus I. Samos is portrayed like a participant in a *dexiosis* scene.

41

Adıyaman to Diyarbakır

Total distance 221km. Adıyaman—75km Bozova—45km Hilvan—28km Siverek—23km Karacadağ—50km Diyarbakır.

Leave Adıyaman by Road 360 signposted Gölbaşı and after c 10km turn S in the direction of Bozova and Şanlı Urfa. This part of the journey is described in Route 40. At a major road junction c 9km N of Urfa turn left on to the E99 signposted Hilvan, Siverek and Diyarbakır.

At first you pass through fertile, cultivated areas, but these become more and more infrequent. At **Siverek** there was a Byzantine fortress to defend the W approaches to Diyarbakır. The last part of the journey is over a barren plain strewn with large lumps of basalt, the petrified debris of Karacadağ (1957m), an extinct volcano.

DİYARBAKIR, ancient Amida, is a city which reveals itself gradually to the visitor. There has been a large expansion on the W side outside the walls. The *otogar*, the museum, the railway station and a number of hotels are in this area. Entrance to the walled city is by the Mardin, Dicle Dağ, and Urfa Gates.

Information and Accommodation. The **Tourist Information Office** is in Vilayet Cad. In addition to the four-star *Demir Hotel* there are the *Kristal Hotel* and the *Turistik Hotel*, both two-star establishments. The Turistik Hotel, which is clean, comfortable and has a good restaurant, is recommended. If cost is not a consideration, stay at the *Kervansaray Hotel* near the Mardin Gate. The rooms of this restored *han* look out over the lush, green Esfel Bahçeleri and the Tigris which here makes a wide loop around the city. The *han* was constructed by Hüsrev Paşa, a 16C governor of the city, to house the guides who led the pilgrimages from Diyarbakır to Mecca.

Transport. There are frequent bus services from the *otogar* on the NW side of the city to Ankara, İstanbul and other cities. The *Anadolu Güney Ekpres* provides a rail connection to Ankara and the national rail network. There are daily flights by THY to Ankara and İstanbul from the airport which is located to the SW of the city.

Food. Food in Diyarbakır tends to be spicy. Try *kaburga*—ribs of lamb stuffed with rice pilaf, raisins, nuts, herbs and spices, then finish your meal with *mirra*, strong, unsweetened coffee served in small bowls. Diyarbakır is famous for its watermelons which can weigh as much as 60kg. They have been adopted as the city's symbol.

Climate. Diyarbakır has a typical SE Anatolia climate. The summers are very hot and dry, the winters cold and wet. Autumn and spring are the best seasons, but there are often cold winds in the evening.

Handicrafts. Jewellery, copperwork, carpets, kilims, *cicim* (embroidered flat weave carpets), saddlebags and silk are of excellent quality. Recommended is the *puşu*, a handwoven silk headscarf.

Museums. The **Archaeological and Ethnographic Museum** is just off Ziya Gökalp Bul. in Nevşehir. It houses more than 10,000 objects dating from the Neolithic Age to Ottoman times. All were found in the city or surrounding countryside. A basalt block, which shows persons in Assyrian dress, testifies to the antiquity of Diyarbakır's foundation. There is a fine collection of Roman funerary stelae, statues and architectural fragments, Artukid tiles, Ottoman weapons, objects from Dervish *tekkes* and coins from many periods.

The **Ziya Gökalp Museum** is in the walled city near Melek Ahmetpaşa Cad. It occupies the old two-storey house which belonged to the family of this writer and philosopher. The museum, which has an interesting collection of his books, manuscripts, photographs and memorabilia, was opened to the public in 1962.

The **Cahit Sitki Taranci Culture Museum** is in the house near Ulu Cami where this famous Turkish poet was born. Photographs, manuscripts and books provide a valuable record of his life and work.

Atatürk Köşkü, 2.5km to the S of Diyarbakır was presented to Atatürk by the city in 1934. This 19C house, constructed in an architectural style particular to Diyarbakır, contains photographs, documents and some of Atatürk's possessions. Its beautiful situation, with views towards the Tigris valley and the ancient city walls, makes it a popular place for walks and summer picnics.

History. Settlers were drawn to this high, level plateau of basalt strategically situated at a point where the Tigris becomes navigable. It may have been an Assyrian *karum* (trading post) on the road to Edessa, Maraş and Malatya. A broken stele in the museum, which was found within the city walls, shows figures in Assyrian dress.

The Romans called the city Amida and disputed its possession first with the Parthians and then with the Persians. A Roman army was defeated by the Persians under Narses in AD 298, but the terms of the subsequent peace treaty allowed Amida and the important frontier town of Nisibis (the modern Nusaybin) to remain under Roman rule. Constantine II (337–361) enclosed a part of the city 'with solid towers and walls and (equipped) it with a battery of defensive artillery'. In spite of this, Amida was captured by the Persian Sapor II in AD 359. The historian Ammianus Marcellinus, who was a serving Roman officer on the eastern frontier at that time, has left a vivid account of the siege. Returning from a scouting expedition against the advancing Persians, he was trapped for hours on a narrow path leading up from the river wedged uncomfortably against the body of a soldier whose head had been split open like a ripe melon. Entering Amida under cover of darkness, Ammianus found it full of peasants who had come in from the surrounding countryside to celebrate an annual fair. The narrow streets were crowded with frightened people, some wounded, some crying over their dead, some looking for their families. The city fell after a siege of 73 days, but was retaken by the Romans under Julian the Apostate in AD 363.

Julian was succeeded by the easy-going, youthful Jovian (AD 363–364) who, according to Ammianus, liked food, drink and sex. To extricate his army from Assyria, Jovian was obliged to surrender a number of Roman possessions to the Persians. These included the cities of Singara and Nisibis. The Christians of Nisibis were obliged to leave their city within three days. Many of them settled in Amida, doubling its population. Jovian died soon afterwards at Dadastana between Ancyra and Nicaea. His demise was attributed to acute indigestion produced either by the quantity of wine he had drunk or the quality of some mushrooms which he had consumed.

An inscription beginning 'Virtute Precipuis Invictis Imperatoribus Salvi(s) Valentiniano V(alente Et) Gratiano Perpetuis (?Ducibus)...' records the rebuilding of Amida during the reign of the 'grotesque, bandy-legged, pot-bellied, squinting' eastern emperor Valens (364–78). This was later placed on one of towers of the Dağ Kapısı, sometimes known as the Harput Kapısı.

In Amida Christianity took a variety of forms. There were Monophysites, Melkites, Jacobites and Nestorians, each with its own clergy and churches. Amida was represented at the Council of Constantinople in AD 381 by a Monophysite bishop.

After holding out for 97 days, Amida fell to a Persian army led by Kavadh II in AD 503. Incensed by this resistance, the Persians took a terrible revenge on the defenders, slaughtering more than 80,000 of them. The Persians herded the men into the amphitheatre where they died of hunger, but they fed the women 'because they used them to satisfy their lust and because they required them to grind and bake for them'.

The defences of Amida were reinforced during the reign of Justinian (527–565). However, it was taken by Chosroes II (591–628), but recaptured later by the Byzantines under Heraclius. With the defeat of the Byzantine army by the Arabs at the battle of the Yarmuk river in AD 636 a new power entered the scene. Amida was taken by the Arabs three years later. Given to the Beni Bakr tribe, the city acquired a new name,

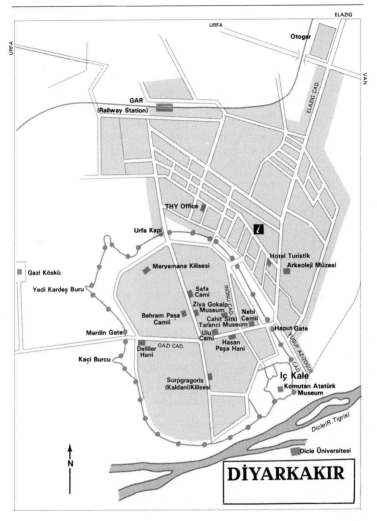

Diyarbakır, the Place of the Bakr. It was ruled by the Omayyad Caliphs of Damascus from AD 660–750, then by the Abbasid Caliphate of Baghdad. Attempts by the Byzantines to recapture the city in AD 856 and 957 failed, but it was occupied by them for a short period in AD 974.

In AD 990 a breakaway dynasty of local rulers repaired and reinforced the defences of Diayarbakır or Kara Amida, as it was sometimes called. They ruled the city until 1085 when it fell into the hands of the Selçuk Turks. Captured by the Mongols in AD 1259, it came under the control of the Turcoman Akkoyunlu clan in the 14C. Diayarbakır was taken by Selim I the Grim in AD 1515.

The City Wall. From the air the wall around Diyarbakır looks like a turbot. The İç Kale, the inner keep, on the NE forms the head of the fish and the stretch of wall between the Evli Beden Burcu and the Yedi Kardeş Burcu in the SE its tail. Apart from two short stretches, which were demolished in this century, the wall is intact. The original fortifications built by Constantine II in the 4C were rebuilt by the Selçuks in the 11C and restored by the Artukid Turcoman Emir al Malik al-Salih Mahmud in 1208. They are only indirectly related to the defences known to Ammianus. Constructed of massive blocks of black basalt the wall is 5.5km long, 12m high and between 3m and 5m wide. There are **four main gates**—the Dağ Kapısı (sometimes called the Harput Kapısı), Urfa Kapısı, Mardin Kapısı and Yenikapı (or Dicle Kapısı)—and 82 towers and bastions.

If you are careful and are not troubled by vertigo, you should be able to walk on top of the wall for the greater part of the circuit. Tracing the wall at ground level, inside or outside, is not easy or always very pleasant. Inside your progress is likely to be barred frequently by private property and outside, between the Urfa Kapısı and the Evli Beden Burcu, you will have to negotiate a rubbish dump. Try to see the Evli Beden Burcu and the Yedi Kardeş Burcu in the SE, the Mardin Kapısı and the Keçi Burcu in the S, the Urfa Kapısı in the W, the Dağ Kapısı in the N and the İç Kale in the NE.

The **Dağ Kapısı** is sometimes called the Harput Kapısı after the ancient city of that name near Elazığ. In medieval times it was known as Bab el-Armen, the Gate of the Armenians. Flanked by two projecting towers, it probably occupies the site of a Roman gate. Note the **relief** above the entrance of two lions passant and a bird with out-stretched wings. An inscription in Greek records the construction of a hospice for travellers by the deacon Appius in the 5C, another in Latin at the base of the left tower commemorates the reconstruction of Amida by Valens, Valentinian I and Gratian in the 4C (see above). The inscriptions in Arabic relate to various repairs and reconstructions effected to the gate.

On the ninth tower there is a **Selçuk relief** of a sphinx and an **inscription** recording the restoration of the tower in 1237. On the tenth tower note the much damaged **relief** of a male figure holding an axe.

The **Urfa Kapısı**, known in medieval times as Bab er-Rum, the Gate of the Romans, had three openings. Two were closed by the Artukid Sultan Muhammad in the 12C. The **keystone** of the arch over the entrance is ornamented with the relief of an eagle whose out-stretched wings shade the head of a bull. An **inscription** above the gate is flanked by two winged dragons. The ornamental iron leaves of the door probably date from the period of Artukid rule.

Just before the Evli Beden Burcu, where the wall turns to the SE, there is **Melikşah Burcu** with some damaged **Selçuk reliefs** of dragons. They flank an **inscription in Kufic script** which records a restoration of the tower in AD 1052. The upper part of the **Evli Beden Burcu** has been destroyed. It would appear this tower was originally erected by the Byzantines. However, the inscription in Kufic claims that it was constructed by the Artukid ruler, Melik Salih, in AD 1209. In fact he only restored and enlarged it. Note the **reliefs** of the two-headed eagle and the lions with human heads.

The SE corner of the wall was protected by the **Yedi Kardeş Burcu**, the Tower of the Seven Brothers. An **inscription in Kufic** flanked by two lions passant claims that this was also built by Melik Salih in 1208. The name of the architect is given as Yahya, son of İbrahim. However, it would seem that this two-storey tower with casemates was built on a Byzantine foundation. The next tower, the **Nur Burcu**, has many **Selçuk reliefs** and an **inscription** which states that it was completely reconstructed in AD 1088. From here the wall continues in a NE direction to the Mardin Kapısı.

According to **inscriptions** on the **Mardin Kapısı** it was restored by the Caliph Muktadir in AD 909. At some point two of the original openings

The walled city of Diyarbakır

were walled up. To ease the passage of traffic a part of the E archway has been removed. The gate overlooks the lush green fields of the **Esfel Bahçeler**, the Esfel Gardens.

This part of the wall is much favoured by *flâneurs*, resident and visiting, who make their way here each evening to watch the gathering shadows move slowly over the valley of the Tigris until at last they reach the city.

During the daytime the Mardin Kapısı is full of bustle and excitement. In summer small boys rush excitedly from one parapet to the other chasing huge, yellow hornets which they catch and imprison in plastic boxes. Then, proudly comparing and displaying their collections of trapped insects, they plunge their bare hands into the midst of the buzzing, angry mass and invite bemused spectators to do the same. On an open space inside the wall older boys play a game of football that seems to have no beginning or end. Overhead, clouds of pigeons whirl and wheel in unison before returning on the specially-constructed *güvercinlikler* (pigeon cotes) near the wall. The people of Diyarbakır are devoted to their pigeons. After all *koğa* (pigeon manure) produces the huge watermelons for which the city is famous, and, it is said, gives them their distinctive sweetness and flavour.

Families are busily tending their plots in the Esfel Gardens, tying, cutting, pruning and hoeing. A constant stream of horse-drawn carts, laden with produce for the city's markets, passes through the Mardin Gate. This is truly *rus in urbe*. According to a popular local legend God placed the Garden of Eden under the walls of Diyarbakır. Whether one believes that or not, it is impossible not to be moved by the beauty of the countryside here.

On the wall just beyond the Mardin Gate is the **Keçi Burcu**, the Tower of the Goat. This has a huge chamber with three large bays. An inscription states that the tower was erected between AD 1029 and 1037. Next comes the 11C **Fındık Burcu**, the Hazel-Nut Tower. A section of the wall, c 100m long, just before the next gate has been pulled down. The **Dicle Kapısı**, the Tigris Gate, is sometimes known as the Yeni Kapı, the New Gate. It may be about here that Ammianus managed to enter the city while it was under attack by the Persians.

The Dicle Kapısı is flanked on the N by the Kral Kızı Burcu. From here to the İç Kale, the Inner Fortress on the NE corner, the defences are lighter because of the protection afforded by natural features. The **İç Kale** rests on a *hüyük* c 40m high which was formed by the debris of earlier settlements. The present keep was constructed by Süleyman the Magnificent in 1527. An earlier 12C Artukid keep, built on Byzantine foundations, was much smaller. Excavations on the *hüyük* in 1961–62 produced pottery sherds and an interesting Artukid double-headed eagle. In the SE corner is a **mosque** built by the Artukids in 1160.

At this point the wall turns W and from here to the Dağ Kapısı it is on level ground. Consequently the fortifications are considerably stronger.

Entering the Dağ Kapısı you come to Diyarbakır's main N–S street, Gazi Caddesi. Almost certainly this follows the line of the *cardo maximus* of the Roman town. Just inside the gate on the right-hand side is the **Nebi** or **Peygamber Camii**, the Prophet's Mosque. It acquired its name from the many references to Mohammed on the minaret. The mosque was probably constructed during the Akkoyunlu period in the 15C. The minaret, which was moved to its present position in 1960, was built by a butcher, Hacı Hüseyin, in 1530 during the reign of Süleyman the Magnificent. Note the attractive façade of alternating black and white stone. It has a single dome.

At the end of İzzetpaşa Cad., to the right, is the İç Kale, the Inner Fortress of Diyarbakır (see above). In the wall which separates this from the city, there are 18 towers and two gates, the Saray Kapısı and the Dicle Kapısı (not to be confused with the gate of the same name on the outer wall).

Do not fail to visit the noisy, odorous, lively **bazaars** on both sides of the Gazi Cad. where small, dark shops are grouped according to their trades. The narrow lanes in between are full of pushing, jostling shoppers. They gesticulate, bargain and shout at each other in Turkish, Kurdish and Arabic. Heavily-laden donkeys, handcarts and barrows piled high with merchandise push their way through the throng.

About half-way along Gazi Cad. is Diyarbakır's most important building. **Ulu Cami** is one of the oldest mosques in Anatolia and one of the holy places of Islam. According to an ancient tradition it occupies the site of a 7C Christian church dedicated to St Thomas which had been built during the reign of Heraclius. In 770 Christians worshipped in one part of the building, Muslims in the other. According to the chronicler Matthew of Edessa (AD 962–1136) it was destroyed by an earthquake and fire in 1115. The mosque was rebuilt by the Selçuk sultan Melik Şah between 1091 and 1092. Above the round arch of the entrance to the courtyard there is an **inscription** and **two reliefs** showing a lion attacking a bull. In the large, rectangular courtyard there are two *şadırvan*. On the left is the raised prayer hall with the *mihrab* at the far end. The prayer hall is flanked on each side by three long, narrow aisles separated from each other by two rows of antique columns. Note the **ebony ceiling** over the central area and the decorative **Kufic inscription** inlaid with mother of pearl. Two later additions to the mosque complex are a small *mescid* and the **Mesidiye Medresesi** built by the Artukid emir Sökmen II (1198–1223). The *medrese*, one of the first religious colleges in Anatolia, is on two floors. Its *mihrab* is flanked on each side by a column which can move during earthquakes.

Leave Ulu Cami by a door on the W side of the courtyard. At the bottom of a narrow lane is the **Zinciriye Medresesi** which was also built during the reign of Sökmen II. It follows the traditional plan of early religious schools. An *eyvan* opens on to a central court which has study halls and student rooms on each side. The *medrese* housed Diyarbakır's archaeological collection before the completion of the new museum.

Near the *medrese* is **Cahit Sıtkı Tarancı Museum**. (For a description, see above.) A short distance to the W is **İskender Paşa Camii** which was built by one of the Ottoman governors of Diyarbakır in 1551 in alternating bands of black and white stone. Inside the mosque note the interesting decoration of enamelled faience. Slightly to the S is **Safa Camii** which may have been built by Uzun Hasan (1435–78), that redoubtable leader of the Turcoman Akkoyunlu who sought the aid of Venice in his struggle against the Ottomans. The mosque was restored in the 16C. It is said that herbs were mixed with the mortar used in the construction of the minaret and that they gave off a delicate fragrance for many years. Not far from the Urfa Gate is **Melek Ahmet Camii** which was built in 1591 at the behest of Melek Ahmet, governor of Diyarbakır. Note the faience decoration of the mihrab and the fine mosaics on the minaret.

On the way back to Gazi Cad. you pass the **Ziya Gökalp Museum** on the left (see above). On the other side of Gazi Cad. is the Hasan Paşa Hanı. This was built by the third governor of the city in 1572 in an interesting combination of basalt and limestone. Today it houses a carpet bazaar.

Near the E wall is **Fatih Paşa Camii**. It was built between 1516 and 1520 by Bıyıklı Mehmet Paşa, who captured Diyarbakır for Selim I and became the city's first governor. The *mihrab* and *mimber* are particularly fine. Note the use of Ottoman tiles. The founder's *türbe* is in the courtyard.

To the SW just off Yenikapı Cad. is the small **Keldani Kilise**, the Chaldaean Christian church. Christians of the Syrian rite, who are in communion with the Roman Catholic church, worship here.

To the S of Yenikapı Cad. is **Dört Ayaklı Minare**, the Four-Legged Minaret, and its associated mosque **Şeyh Mutahhar Camii** which was built by the Akkoyunlu rulers. The base of the minaret is composed of four columns carved from a single block of stone.

Return to Gazi Cad. In the SE part of the city is **Behram Paşa Camii**, the largest mosque in Diyarbakır. It was built in 1572 by the thirteenth governor of the city whose name it bears. This 'prince of provincial mosques' (Goodwin) is remarkable for the elegance of its proportions and beauty of its decoration. In the fine domed prayer hall there are tile panels which fit perfectly. In several shades of blue, relieved occasionally by red, on a white background, they must have been made specially for this building. Note the marble *mimber* with carved doors.

To the SW of the mosque and not far from the wall and Evli Beden Burcu is **Meryem Ana Kilise**, the Church of the Virgin Mary. Part of a large monastic foundation, it has been dated variously to the 3C, 6C and 7C. The church is used by the Syrian Orthodox community in Diyarbakır.

Syrian Orthodox Christians are sometimes known as Jacobites after the 6C Jacob Baradaeus or Jacob Burd'aya (the nickname Burd'aya means 'horse cloth' and referred to his cloak). Jacob, bishop of Edessa, founded new Monophysite churches in Syria, Mesopotamia and Anatolia. He claimed to have consecrated 27 bishops and 100,000 priests during his lifetime. The Monophysites refused to accept the decree of the Council of Chalcedon (AD 451) which stated that Christ had two natures—human and divine—united unconfusedly and unchangeably. The Monophysites taught that the person of Christ was formed by a union of two natures. Rome and Constantinople accepted Chalcedon. Antioch and Alexandria did not. The non-Chalcedonian churches are the Syrian Orthodox, the Copts, Armenians and Ethiopians.

Syrian Orthodox services are conducted in Aramaic, the language spoken by Jesus. The altar in Meryem Ana Kilise dates from the Byzantine period; there are several interesting icons. The church has been restored more than once.

A short distance to the NE of Mardin Kapısı is **Hüsrev Paşa Camii**. According to an inscription on the gate this was to have been a *medrese*.

Built by Hüsrev Paşa (1522–58) when he was governor of Diyarbakır, it has a black basalt, Selçuk-style minaret.

There are several places of interest to the NW of Diyarbakır but you will need your own transport.

Leave Diyarbakır by Road 885, signposted Elaziğ. After c 25km turn right on to a minor road which leads to Oyali, Kazkan and **Eğil** where there is an **Assyrian castle**. Dating from the first millennium BC, this occupies a magnificent position on an escarpment high above the Tigris. About 7m from the ground on the W facing slope of the castle's rock base there is an unusual **relief**. This shows the figure of a god holding a sword and an axe. It fills the left-hand side of the relief. Below the top of the frame, and level with his face, there are the symbols of several divinities. It would appear that there was a figure on the right which has been erased. The relief has been dated to the reign of Sargon II (722–705 BC), who deposed Shalmaneser V, the son and legitimate heir of Tiglath-pileser.

At one time passages cut into the rock led down to the Tigris from the fortress. These are now blocked, but the entrances can still be seen. On the banks of the river there are some Assyrian tombs.

From Eğil return to the main road and continue for c 16km in the direction of Ergani. Near the town is **Zülkifil Dağı**, the Mountain of Ezekiel. There is an ancient tradition that the prophet lived here and the mountain is sacred to both Christians and Muslims. There are the ruins of an early church.

At **Çayönü**, a short distance to the W of Ergani, there are the remains of a settlement which has been dated to the seventh millennium BC. Archaeologists believe that the people who lived here were making the transition from wandering hunters to settled farmers. In the village of Hilar, near Çayönü, are the **Hilar Mağaraları**, the Hilar Caves, one of the earliest human settlements in this area, with interesting reliefs.

42

Diyarbakır to Mardin

Total distance 94km. Road 950 Diyarbakır—(2km Tigris Bridge)—94km Mardin (c 21km Kızıltepe—(93km Viranşehir) (56km Nusaybin—c 24km Mor Augen—c 14km Akarsu) (59km Midyat) (72km Mor Gabriel) (102km Hasankeyf).

A new road from Diyarbakır to Mardin reduces travelling time between the two places to about an hour. For the **Tigris Bridge**, which is c 2km to the S of Diyarbakır, take the old Mardin road. You will be able to join the motor road a short distance below the bridge.

According to an inscription on the S parapet, the present bridge was built in AD 1065 during the rule of the Marwanid dynasty. This graceful ten-arch structure of black basalt is not the first bridge to span the Tigris at Diyarbakır. The Chronicle of 819, a Syriac text discovered in 1911 in the village of Beth Svirina in the Tur Abdin states that 'In the year 795 of the Greeks (AD 483/4) John Saoro of Qartmin Abbey was made bishop of Amida, where he built a large and splendid church dedicated to the Forty Martyrs of Sebaste and a bridge over the river Tigris outside the city'. It is likely that Metropolitan John did not build a new bridge but that he repaired an existing structure which had been erected during the Roman period. This work was probably done at the request of the Emperor Anastasius and with imperial funds. An unpublished inscription on one of the sides of the bridge, which is visible only when the waters of the Tigris are low, suggests that the foundations of John's bridge were incorporated in later reconstructions.

There is a fine view of the Mardin Gate and of the southern part of Diyarbakır's fortifications from the bridge. Unfortunately, a considerable quantity of unpleasant rubbish has been allowed to accumulate on the banks of the Tigris. Also, swarms of vicious mosquitoes infest the area. Use a strong insect repellent.

S of Diyarbakır you pass through a pleasant area of fields and orchards. On the S facing hillsides there are vineyards which produce dessert grapes.

MARDİN is built on the S slope of a steep escarpment crowned by an ancient citadel. The road touches the N edge of the escarpment and enters the town on the W side. To the left is a bastion, **Telhan Kalesi**, part of a defensive wall around the lower town which was linked to the citadel fortifications.

Sultan Kasim Medrese, Mardin

Information and Accommodation. The **Tourist Information Office** is at Meydanbaşı Cad., İl Halk Kütüphanesi. There are no hotels registered with the Ministry of Tourism. The restaurants in Mardin are rather basic, so it is advisable to bring a picnic lunch.

Museum. There is an interesting collection of artefacts including seals, pottery and inscribed tablets from the Assyrian city of **Girnavaz**, near Nusaybin, in Mardin's Archaeological and Ethnographic Museum. Note particularly the broad **ceramic bowl** decorated with ox heads between the handles and raised faces near the stem. The museum is housed in a disused Koranic school near the Sultan İsa medrese.

Climate. The summers are very hot and dry. The winters are cold.

Handicrafts. Gold jewellery made in Mardin is of excellent quality. The village of Söğütlü is a centre for the production of a unique type of 'Telkari', silver filigree. Fine woven goods from villages near Hasankeyf, Silopi and Cizre, are sold in Mardin.

In Mardin three cultures, Turkish, Arabic and Kurdish, and two religions, Islam and Christianity meet. The stone houses, which appear to have been scattered at random across the steep, rocky side of the escarpment, have been influenced by the architectural styles of nearby Iraq and Syria. Mardin is the centre of an important community of **Syrian Orthodox Christians**, the so-called Jacobites. The nearby monastery of Deir al-Zafaran, the Saffron Monastery, (see below) was for many years the official residence of the Jacobite Patriarch.

History. In ancient times the town was known as Marida. Its history dates back to the period of the early Assyrian Empire. Part of a stele recording a victory of Shamshi-Adad I (1813–1741 BC), who claimed to control 'the land between the Tigris and the Euphrates' and who founded a new dynasty in Assyria, was discovered in Mardin. Despite its strategic position it never achieved the importance enjoyed by its neighbours, Amida and Nisibis during the Roman and Byzantine periods. It was just a bordertown of Osroene, the area between the Khabur river and the great bend of the Euphrates. In AD 640 Mardin was taken by the Arabs. Mardin's fortress was large enough to shelter the whole population in time of danger and it resisted a number of attempts to retake it. Saladin tried unsuccessfully in 1183. The Mongols fared no better in 1259. When Tamerlane managed to take the citadel in 1394, he placed it under the control of his brother, İsa, who rebelled several times. It was not until 1401 that Tamerlane was able to bring him to heel. In 1408 Mardin came under the rule of the Karakoyunlu Turcoman clan, but 23 years later it was taken by their enemies, the Akkoyunlu. Captured by the Persians under Şah İsmaïl in 1508, the lower city was wrested from them by Selim I, the Grim, in 1516. The citadel fell to the Ottomans a year later. There were Kurdish revolts in 1832 and in 1840. In that year Mardin was occupied for a brief period by Mohammed Ali of Egypt.

Mardin is best visited on foot. The main street, which runs along the side of the escarpment, divides it neatly into upper and lower districts. The street is narrow and almost always crowded. As there are few places to park in the centre, leave your car at the W side of town. After c 500m a turning on the right will bring you to the **Latifiye Cami**. This was built in 1371 by the Artukid ruler, Melik Abdülatif. The **minaret**, erected in 1845, was the gift of an Egyptian governor, Muhammed Ziya Tayyer. Note the fine **trilobite arch** with stalactite ornamentation at the E entry.

Ulu Cami and its minaret were badly damaged during the rebellion of 1832 and rebuilt later. An **inscription** at the base of the minaret states that it was erected originally in 1176 on the orders of the Artukid ruler Melik Kubeddin. In the NE corner of the huge courtyard there are the remains of a **colonnade** which formerly lined all four sides. Note the building's finely-proportioned, **fluted dome**. The interior of the mosque is divided into three aisles by two rows of arched columns. The *mihrab* in the S wall is sur-mounted by a cupola.

Perhaps the most interesting building in Mardin is the Zincire or **Isa Bey Medresesı** which is reached by a flight of steps. Entrance to the two-storey Koranic school is by a magnificent portal approached by a double row of steps. Note the finely-carved **inscription** over the door. In addition to the school the complex has a **mosque** with a fluted dome, a **tomb** and **two courtyards**. The *medrese* was built on the orders of Melik Necmettin İsa ben Muzaffer Davut ben Elmelik Salih in 1385. Its harmonious design and beautiful stone carving combine to make it one of the best examples of Artukid craftsmanship. There are fine views of Mardin and of the plain to the S from the terrace of the *medrese*.

A winding path leads up the steep slope of the escarpment to the **citadel**. Over the entrance are **two lions passant in relief** and a worn **inscription** which contains the names of Osman Bahadır and his son Hamza Bahadır. Osman Bahadır was the founder of the Akkoyunlu dynasty, so this dates the inscription to sometime after 1431, the year in which the Akkoyunlu captured Mardin. A **rock-cut gallery** leads to the summit. Near the E side is a late 16C mosque. The W side of the plateau served as a place of refuge for the people of Mardin during times of danger. The best preserved part of the fortifications is on the S side. Part of the citadel is closed to the public.

Behind Ulu Cami is the **Kayseriye Bazaar** which was constructed between 1480 and 1500 by the Akkoyunlu Kasım Padişah. Full of tiny shops, which line the narrow lanes, this is a fascinating place. In dark interiors, lit only by the glowing light of furnaces, shadowy figures shape and torture metal into elaborate forms.

Sultan Kasım Medrese, the largest ancient structure in Mardin, is reached by a rough track from the main road. This *medrese* was also built by Kasım Padişah between 1469 and 1503 (the Akkoyunlu period). A staircase on the S side of the building leads to a vestibule just inside the entrance.

The courtyard has porticoes on the S, E and W sides, on the N there is an *eyvan*. Stairs on the E and W sides lead to the rooms occupied by the students. A corridor provides access to the **domed mosque**. The *medrese* is not now used and is usually locked, so you may have to confine your examination to the exterior.

The Syrian Orthodox monastery of **Deir-al-Zafaran**, the Saffron Monastery, is 7km to the SE of Mardin.

Syrian Orthodox Christians, sometimes called Jacobites after the 5C Monophysite bishop of Edessa, Jacob Burd'aya or Baradaeus (see above), rejected the ruling of the Council of Chalcedon (451) concerning the nature of Christ. The Council's decree, which was accepted by the sees of Rome and Constantinople, stated that the person of Christ had two natures, united unconfusedly and unchangeably. The Syrians, Copts and Armenians taught that the person of Christ was formed by a union of two natures and that He was 'one incarnate nature of God the Word'. As a result they became known as the Monophysites, a description which they have always rejected. It is estimated that there are about 42,000 Syrian Orthodox Christians in İstanbul and in the Tur Abdin area. There are also communities in N America, in India and in England. For many years the monastery of Deir-al-Zafaran was the official residence of the Patriarch of the Syrian Orthodox Church.

Perched high above the plain like an eagle's eyrie, the monastery's deep, hooded windows look broodingly over a green, intensively-cultivated land that stretches away to the Syrian border. Far in the distance is the 1500m high Jebel Sinjar. Its steep N slopes are often clearly visible from the monastery. According to the Chronicle of Michael the Syrian, Jacobite Patriarch of Antioch (1166–99), a monk of Kallinikos named Ananias was appointed bishop of Mardin in 793. Shortly afterwards he founded the Saffron Monastery. A Nestorian writer states that he bought 'a castle, built in hewn stone in Roman times'. However, John of Mardin (d.1165) believed there had been a monastic foundation here before the time of Ananias, although his researches produced no information about it. The location and structure of the existing building suggests that John's surmise was correct.

When the great door of Deir-al-Zafaran creaks open, it admits the visitor to a place where Christian worship has taken place for more than 1200 years. Although the number of monks has dwindled to two or three, the Syrian Orthodox liturgy is still celebrated daily in the great church of Ananias. A cloister, restored in the 19C, provides access to the monastic buildings. Stylistic evidence suggests that the Church of Ananias, a large rectangular structure with a pyramidal roof, dates from the 6C. Note the three radiating apses and the elaborately carved stone friezes and niches.

The prominent bell-tower was added later. In the Church of St Mary there is an ancient **octagonal baptismal font** cut from a single block of stone and a floor of marble tesserae. In the **Martyrion** the remains of Syrian Orthodox saints and patriarchs rest in **niches** in the wall. Ask to see the beautiful Syriac service books and bibles. Note the many carved crosses on the walls of the monastery building, both inside and out.

Steps lead to a terrace above the courtyard. Here are the rooms used by the Patriarch when he visits the monastery. (He now lives in Damascus.) On the walls of the reception room, which is dominated by a large throne, photographs show him meeting other religious leaders. There are several small rooms with splendid views which are available to more ordinary visitors. Although the monks make no charge for their hospitality, it is customary, whether one stays overnight or not, to make a donation to the monastery's funds.

On the cliffs to the N and E there are many caves, natural and artificial. Some were occupied by anchorites, others were chapels or were used as places of refuge by members of the community in times of war or persecution. According to the Chronicle of Amida of 569 the 'monastery of Notfo, Our Lady of the Water-Drop', on the cliff above Deir-al-Zafaran sheltered Monophysite bishops in times of danger. The anchorites, men who wished to be dead to the world and its temptations, chose to live in tombs or in places that resembled tombs. Like the founder of monasticism the Egyptian St Antony, they wished to confront the demons who were believed to congregate in the abodes of the dead.

The Yezidis. Some of the villages near Mardin are occupied, not by Muslims or by Christians, but by the Yezidis. Their beliefs include elements taken from the Jewish, Nestorian Christian, Islamic, Manichaean and Zoroastrian religions. They believe in one God whom they call Khuda. He is the supreme ruler, the creator of the universe and of man. Below Khuda there are seven angels who were given the task of creating the animals and plants. The principal angel, Azaziel rebelled against Khuda, but repented and was forgiven. Azaziel did not bring about Adam's fall from grace, but provided him with some practical advice on human biological functions. Those who recognise Azaziel will gain his protection. The name Azaziel is not often used by the Yezidis and his less flattering name Satan is forbidden. If used by non-believers in their presence, it can produce a violent reaction. Because the Yezidis honour Azaziel, they are incorrectly regarded as devil-worshippers. They call the principal angel Melek Taus, the Peacock Angel, and the main symbol of their faith is a bronze peacock.

Like members of other religions the Yezidis believe in justice, mercy, love, truth, right and wrong. They do not believe in sin, the devil and hell. Until the far distant Day of Judgement souls will transmigrate, sometimes occupying the bodies of animals, and in the process of metempsychosis will achieve spiritual purity. A connection of the Yezidis, suggested by some authorities, with the Umayyad Caliph Yezid I (c 645–683), has not been clearly established. The principal Yezidi saint is the 12C Sheik Adi ben Musafir. His tomb at ash-Shayk Adi to the N of Mosul in Iraq is their main religious centre and a place of annual pilgrimage. They have two sacred books, the Kitab-al-Jilwah, Book of Revelation, and the Meshaf Resh, the Black Book, which is attributed to Sheik Hasan, a descendant of Sheik Adi. The Black Book contains their account of the creation of the universe and of Adam and Eve. Total membership of the Yezidi religion is approximately 150,000. There are c 10,000 in Turkey and Germany. The remainder are in Iraq, Syria and the former Soviet Union.

Viranşehir is c 93km to the SW of Mardin. Take the road to 21km Kızıltepe and then turn right on the busy E24 signposted Şanlı Urfa. The little town of **Kızıltepe** in its stony, arid setting, was once the important trading post of Dunyasir on a route which linked Antakya and Adana with Mosul, Persia and the east. Only the magnificent 13C Artukid Ulu Cami and a few *türbe* bear witness to its past glories.

Viranşehir, its name means ruined city, occupies the site of the ancient Roman Constantina. All that remains of Constantina are its great basalt walls which enclosed a rectangular area c 600m by 500m. Strengthened by towers, the walls were restored in the 6C during the reign of Justinian. There were four gates, one on each side of the rectangle, protected by flanking bastions.

From Mardin take the road signposted Akıncı and continue to its junction with the E24 signposted Cizre. This stretch of the E24 passes through flat, arid country near the border with Syria. It is an area with few attractions, so travellers will not be tempted to linger. Do not take any photographs. **Nusaybin**, 56km from Mardin, is a frontier post on the border with Syria and is the last Turkish station on the railway line to Baghdad. Across the river Djada is the Syrian town of Al Qamichli.

History. There are references in Assyrian inscriptions to Nasibina dating from the beginning of the first millennium BC. At **Girnavaz**, c 5km upstream, archaeologists found traces of a much older settlement. Artefacts found here are in Mardin's Museum. At the junction of two important trade routes, Girnavaz has been dated to the beginning of the third millennium BC. Under the Seleucids in the 3C BC it was known as Antiocheia of Mygdonia and was the capital of a prosperous Parthian province. The city was fought over by the Romans, the Parthians and the Persians. Lucullus took it in 68 BC, but the Romans lost it 15 years later to the Parthians after the defeat of Crassus at Carrhae. In AD 115 Trajan took it during the course of an expedition to Ctesiphon. In AD 195 it became the capital of the Roman province of Mesopotamia.

The Sassanians laid siege to Nisibis, unsuccessfully, in 338, 346 and 350. There was an ancient tradition that Jacob, the first bishop of Nisibis (337–8) saved the city from a siege by his prayers. After the death of Julian the Apostate in 363, the new emperor Jovian (see above) concluded a very disadvantageous treaty with the Persians. He did so in order to be able to bring the Roman army back safely from Assyria. Jovian was obliged to surrender five of the Transtigritane satrapies with Nisibis, Singara, the castra Maurorum and 15 castellae. The loss of Nisibis and Singara was a bitter blow as they had belonged to the Roman Empire since the time of Septimius Severus (193–211).

In 640 Nisibis was taken by the Arabs. It flourished under their rule. In the 10C it was still prosperous, famous for its gardens and its white roses. Like many of its neighbours it was captured and destroyed by the Mongols in the middle of the 13C. In 1515 Nisibis was incorporated in the Ottoman Empire.

Apart from a ruined **Roman arch** and the 4C **Church of Mor Jacob** there are few reminders of the past in Nisibis. The church is a square structure with a narthex, two aisles, an apse and a pyramidal roof. Enlarged in 759, it was extensively restored in 1872. In the crypt is the **sarcophagus of St Jacob**. This has acroteria on the corners.

About 24km to the E of Nusaybin and near the village of Girmeli is the **Monastery of Mor Augen**. This is reached by a combination of careful driving and, at the end, a steep, testing climb. Mor Augen was once the home of several hundred monks, but they departed long ago. A Muslim family now lives in a modern house at the back of the monastic buildings. Established towards the end of the 4C or the beginning of the 5C, it was a Nestorian monastery until 1505 when it was taken over by monks of the Syrian Orthodox rite. According to an ancient tradition one of the duties of the community was to provide water for the travellers who passed along the great East to West trade route below the monastery. In the cloister there is a well from which clear, cold water is still drawn.

Entrance is by a door which was restored in the 19C. A small vaulted chamber leads to the **cloister**. Apart from a few arches on the S side, this is an 18C restoration. From the cloister an entrance on the left leads to the church. Note particularly the **capitals** in the choir which almost certainly came from the first (5C) **church**. There is a **burial chamber** off the N side of the cloister. To the E of the courtyard a small chapel is backed by a large chamber. There are splendid views of the steep mountainside and of the plain beyond from the monastery's terrace.

Just 3km to the E of Mor Augen is **Mor John the Arab**. This church has a narthex covered by a dome. Its single, vaulted nave is separated from the choir by a partition.

There is a secondary road which runs N from Nusaybin to Midyat, but it is not recommended. **It is not advisable to continue E to Cizre because of the current problems in that area**.

About 14km to the W of Nusaybin a road on the right leads to (17km) **Akarsu**. This village, sometimes known as İstilil, occupies the site of the town of Dara Anastasioupolis. Founded by the emperor Anastasius I (491–518), its construction was supervised by Thomas, bishop of Amida. The architects were Theodosius and Theodore, the sons of Shufnay, who, apparently had been trained in Constantinople. The city was built on three hills with the citadel at the summit of the highest. The emperor's intention was to construct a bastion which would inhibit further advances by the Persians. Although Dara's defences had been strengthened in the mid 6C by Justinian, it fell to the Arabs in 639. The Roman garrison suffered severe losses during the assault. Under Arab rule Dara entered a decline from which it never recovered.

The Tur Abdin. (Before visiting the Tur Abdin, check on the current position with the Tourist Information Office in Diyarbakır.) To the N and E of Midyat the Tigris encloses a high plateau of porous limestone. A part of this, known as the Tur Abdin, the Mountain of the Servant of God, has been inhabited by Syrian Orthodox Christians from about the 5C. The Byzantine emperors encouraged them to settle here in the hope that their presence would prevent further advances by the Persians into the SE part of the empire. At one time thousands of monks lived, worked and prayed in more than 80 monasteries in the Tur Abdin. They came under the jurisdiction of four bishops. There was also a large lay population. Although the Tur Abdin suffered during the time of the Crusades and later during the invasion of the Mongols, there was a big Christian community here until the troubled period which followed the First World War. Now there are six monasteries in the Tur Abdin and a Christian population of about 20,000.

From Mardin take the road signposted Yeşilli and Savur. At 10km Yeşilli turn right for Midyat. An hour's drive through pleasant countryside will bring you to (59km) **Midyat**. The town is in two parts, one occupied by Muslims, the other mainly by Syrian Orthodox Christians. In the Christian part there are several churches. The largest, **Mor Aznoyo**, formerly known as Mor Philoxenos has been reconstructed comparatively recently. The churches are usually locked but the priest or a member of his congregation will show visitors around. A donation to church funds will be appreciated.

From Midyat take the road signposted to Hasankeyf and Batman and after c 10km turn right in the direction of Dargeçit. Near the village of Salah is the 14C **Church of Mor Yakob**, Jacob the Recluse. This belonged to a monastery established sometime towards the end of the 4C. A vaulted narthex with elaborately ornamented pillars and lintel leads to the single nave. The pillars joining the semicircular arch, which provides access to the triple sanctuary, have a rich decoration of scrolls and birds.

Near the village of (5km) Bağlarbası is the **Church of Mor Kyriakos**. The choir screen has been dated to the 8C. However, the church, which also formed part of a monastery, is considerably older.

Crowning a hill c 5km to the SE and near the village of Altın taş, is the **Church of Mor Azaziel**. Structurally, this is very similar to Mor Kyriakos. Note the iconostasis, which has four columns topped with acanthus decorated capitals supporting an architrave, and the interesting moulding around the windows on the E wall.

Return to the Dargeçit road and continue for c 7km in a NE direction. A turning on the right leads to Anıtlı. On the outskirts of the village is the most beautiful church in the Tur Abdin, **El Hadra**, the Church of the Mother of God (late 7C or early 8C). Note the elegant blind arches on the exterior and the curious domed roof. The pillared central door from the narthex to the nave has a lintel decorated with scrolls, palmettes and acanthus leaves.

To visit the largest and most important church in the Tur Abdin, return to Midyat and take the road to the SE which is signposted Cizre. After c 25km a new minor road to the left will bring you, after 3km, to **Mor Gabriel** or **Qartmin Monastery**.

According to an ancient tradition the monastery was founded in 396/7 by the aged Samuel of Eshtin who fled from the land of the Persians and settled by a spring at Qartmin. He saved the life of Simeon, the son of one of the villagers, and the boy's grateful father gave him money to build a monastery. With the help of an angel, Samuel and Simeon, who had become his disciple, laid the first stones. It seems likely that the building material came from a former pagan shrine to the SSE of the monastery. After Samuel's death in 410, Simeon became the second abbot. The monastery flourished under his rule. When he died in 433 there were 400 monks. During the late 4C–early 5C Qartmin received valuable benefactions from imperial funds. 'The faithful kings Honorius and Arcadius sent gifts with much gold in the hands of Rumelius, the king's (Arcadius) chief eunuch, and they arrived at this place and set down in it wealth without end; and he (Rumelius) built a great vault to the south of the Temple of Mor Samuel; and they dug two great, deep pits, one to the north and one to the east of the Temple. Furthermore, they built a great dome to the south of the Temple and the great vault'. Further gifts followed in the 6C: 'When, therefore, king Anastasius heard of the fine reputation of the blessed men in this abbey, he sent much gold…' (Qartmin Trilogy). The monastery continued to be a place of learning for many centuries, producing chronicles, commentaries and lives of the saints. Today it has a resident bishop and a small community of monks and lay assistants. Accommodation for visitors is sometimes available in a modern extension to the monastery. It is necessary to apply in writing well in advance of the date of the visit.

To enter the conventual church, usually called the **Church of Gabriel** after a revered 7C bishop of Dara and abbot of Qartmin, it is necessary to descend a number of steps. Two large windows on either side of the door leading from the narthex to the nave permitted sinners, the sick and overflow congregations to see and take part in the services. For protection against raiders and to reduce heat loss during the winter the unglazed windows of the vaulted church are small and, as a result, the interior is quite dark. The **nave**, designed for monastic services, is set transversely to the narthex. Rectangular rooms flank the apse and in niches by the side of the sanctuary there are the **tombs of holy men** associated with the monastery. The weighty service books used by the monks are usually placed on top of these shrines. In the central part of the sanctuary there are **symbols of the Holy Eucharist in mosaic form**. On the vault three crosses are surrounded by leaves and bunches of grapes from vines growing in four large vases. Although the mosaics high up on the side walls are less complete, it is possible to make out **domed ciboria** on altars flanked by trees and columns. Two **chalices** and a round, segmented **loaf of bread** may be discerned in the mosaic on the S side. The background of all the mosaics is gold. Six coloured marbles—white, red, black, green, amber and purple—were used to make the well-preserved opus sectile pavement in the sanctuary. There are 19C paintings on the W wall.

From the conventual church take a long covered passage to the octagon known as the **Dome of Theodora**. This building with eight niches was probably a baptistery. It is believed to be the same age as the conventual church. Note the **Open Eye of God** at the apex. Farther along on the right were the monastery's kitchens. The passage ends in a small courtyard, on whose S side is the **Church of the Mother of God**. No longer used, this is believed to date from the reign of Theodosius II (408–50). The raised sanctuary is three steps higher than the nave. On the left is the bishop's **cathedra**, on the right a **lectern** for the Book of Propitiation from which prayers were read while incense was burned. A hole in the chamber on the S side of the sanctuary provides access to a cell which was probably occupied by a hermit. Beyond is an underground passage to a **cistern** known as the Pit of the Star which supplied the occupant of the cell with water. Note the **unusual cross** made up of six interlocking smaller crosses and the representation of a right hand with outspread fingers on the plaster of the late vault at the W end of the church.

On the N side of the courtyard is the **House of the Martyrs**. Although the first occupants may have been martyrs, it is likely that in later times the remains of bishops, abbots and patriarchs connected with the monastery were buried here. On the floor of the vaulted burial chambers there are **two ancient marble tombs**. A small hole in the sides permitted the faithful to touch the holy dust of those entombed within. Other burials were made in recesses between the arches which support the roof.

To the N of the House of the Martyrs is the **Dome of the Egyptians**. According to one account this contained the remains of 800 Egyptian princes who came to Qartmin as pilgrims 'bearing gifts of gold'. These royal visitors were so overcome by what they saw that they sold their possessions and became monks. A British Library manuscript dated 1484 gives a slightly different account. 'From the solitaries of the Egyptian desert—Skete and the Thebaid—of Abba Shenudin, there came to the abbey by divine revelation eight hundred perfect and godly men, who went to sleep and took their rest in the abbey'. The **Dome of the Departed** is a short distance to the W. Both buildings are octagonal inside and have domes resting on eight arches. However, their shape is concealed by a square outer structure and the domes have been covered with flat roofs.

From Mor Gabriel return to Mardin and take Road 955 signposted Gercüş to (102km) **Hasankeyf**. From Midyat to Hasankeyf the road passes through an interesting stretch of country. The descent from the high plateau of the Tur Abdin to the valley of the Tigris towards the end of the journey is quite spectacular.

History. Here, where the Tigris passes through a narrow defile, the Romans built a stronghold which they called Cepha. In Byzantine times a bishopric, it was an important outpost on the troubled frontier with Persia. When the Arabs came c 640, they changed its name from the Greek Kiphas to Hisn Kayfa which in the course of time evolved into Hasankeyf. The Artukids ruled Hasankeyf for more than a century and have left many reminders of their presence. An Arab chronicle states that the bridge over the Tigris, regarded as the finest in Anatolia, was repaired in 1116 by an Artukid emir, Fahreddin Kara Aslan. At the beginning of the 13C the Artukids were succeeded by the Ayyubids, the descendants of Saladin. Its capture by the Mongols in 1260 initiated a period of decline from which Hasankeyf never recovered. Mehmet I brought the town into the Ottoman Empire in 1416.

As you cross the modern bridge note the remains of its Artukid predecessor, **four sturdy arches** which still resist the swift-flowing Tigris. On an eminence to the right of the bridge the remains of a **convent** remind us of Hasankeyf's Christian past. The modern town is dominated by a tall red brick minaret.

A steep path leads up to the Artukid citadel. Passing through an imposing gate you enter an eerie, deserted city of broken walls and roofless buildings. On the very edge of the cliff is a **ruined palace** with a finely-decorated great hall. From the windows and battlements of this building you share with the diving and whirling swifts a breathtaking view of the river far below. Beyond the palace are the remains of private houses and of some public buildings. Note especially the **mosque**, with it large courtyard, and the two-domed *türbe*.

The cliff faces outside the town are pitted with **caves** which are used as stables or as storehouses. Some, near the citadel, provide agreeable shelter, cool in summmer and warm in winter, for modern troglodytes. Do not miss the fine 15C **Zeynel Bey Türbesi**, the cylinder-shaped tomb of an Ayyubid king. Decorated with patterns of blue-glazed bricks, it is crowned with an unusual onion-shaped dome.

From Hasankeyf it is possible to join Route 43 by continuing N through Batman to the Malabadi bridge, a distance of c 81km.

43

Diyarbakır to Tatvan

Total distance 255km. Diyarbakır E99/R965—(57km Lice)—70km Silvan—29km Malabadi Köprüsü—(21km Yanarsu)—(40km Siirt)—Baykan—57km Bitlis—26km Tatvan.

Leave Diyarbakır by the E99/Road 965. For the first 100km there is little to attract the eye or hold the attention of the traveller. If you have time, make a detour of c 55km to **Lice** where one of the sources of the Tigris is located and there are some Assyrian reliefs. About 25km from Diyarbakır turn left on to Road 950 which is signposted to Bingöl. Continue for 52km as far as a major road junction and there take the right-hand fork to (11km) Lice.

In the Fis Valley there are the ruins of the city of Dakyanus and, a brisk two hour walk away, a series of caves known as the **Eshab-Ül Kehf Mağaraları**, the Cave of the Seven Sleepers.

Not far from a bridge over the Sebenet Su look on the right-hand side of the road for a pool formed by the Tigris. Steps, which are believed to have been made by the Urartians in the 8C or 7C BC, lead up the steep mountainside to a narrow defile. Here, in a cave on the left, is a relief of Shalmaneser III (858–824) and a cuneiform inscription. Both are much damaged. The Assyrian king's visit to the source of the Tigris in 852 BC is recorded on a bronze strip which decorated the gate of a palace at Balawat in northern Iraq. (Exhibit WAA 124656 in Room 26 in the British Museum.) Workmen are shown cutting commemorative stelae on the rock face, animals are being dragged protestingly to sacrifice while courtiers holding torches explore the cave from which the river gushes forth.

On the cliff face near the pool there is a much older and better-preserved relief accompanied by an inscription in cuneiform. This is of the Assyrian Tiglath-Pileser I (1114–1076) who conducted a successful campaign in Anatolia. Nearby there is another relief of Shalmaneser III, but it can only be seen clearly when the lighting conditions are right.

From Lice return to Road E99 and continue to (70km) **Silvan**. Formerly known as Mayyafarikin, according to some authorities it occupies the site of Tigranocerta, the city founded by Tigranes I, who died c 56 BC.

The most important building in Silvan is **Ulu Cami** which was built by the Artukid emir Najm al-Din Alpi between 1152 and 1157. Much of the material used in its construction came from a Byzantine church. The **main door** is flanked by **pilasters** and surmounted by three elaborately carved circular arches. Above these there is a **carved roundel** with delicately cut, fan-shaped, stone traceries on each side, which rise to a peak beneath a deep, pointed arch.

From Silvan continue to the (29km) **Malabadi Köprüsü**. This fine bridge near the village of Malabadi was built by the Artukids in AD 1146. Bypassed by the modern road a few metres to the N, it was once an important link on the old trade route between Diyarbakır and Van. The approaches to the bridge rest on rounded arches. The delicately **curved central span** measures 35m. At each end there were rooms where travellers could refresh themselves before continuing their journeys. Mirrored in the still waters of the Batman Suyu, the Malabadi Köprüsü no longer echoes to the plodding feet of camels or to the urgent cries of their drivers. The beauty of its design and situation lifts the heart of the modern traveller.

Just after the bridge the road enters a more interesting stretch of country as it begins the slow ascent to the eastern Anatolian plateau. If you wish to visit 40km Siirt, take the signposted right-hand turn about 63km from the Malabadi Köprüsü. There have been disturbances in recent years in the wild, beautiful countryside around Siirt, so take advice before going there.

A turning on the right from the Siirt road will take you to (23km) **Yanarsu**, the site of the ancient Armenian city of Garzan. All that remains of this are the ruins of its citadel. At **Aydinlar** c 8km to the NW of Siirt is the tomb of İbrahim Hakkı. Situated near the borders with Iraq and Syria, the town of **Siirt** has had a long and turbulent history.

History. First settled by the Assyrians, it was later occupied by the Urartians and the Persians. For the Romans it was a strategic post on the marches with Persia. The Byzantines disputed its possession with the Arabs. The Abbasids were replaced by the Selçuks. At the beginning of the 16C İdris Bitlisi, acting on behalf of Sultan Selim I, evicted the Safavids of Iran from this part of Anatolia with the help of local Kurdish *beys* and made it part of the Ottoman Empire. The *beys* accepted Selim's suzerainty in return for being made hereditary governors of their territories.

Surrounded by lush green pastures with a circle of snow-capped mountains in the distance, Siirt is an interesting mixture of the old and the new. Down the narrow alleyways and in the quiet side streets there are many Arab-style tall, **mud-brick houses**. Siirt is famous for the fine, soft blankets made locally from goat hair. As well as **Ulu Cami**, which was built in 1229 by the Selçuk ruler Muciz ad-Din, the 8C Abassid **Cumhuriyet Camii** and the 11C Selçuk **Kavvam Hamamı** merit a visit. There is one two-star hotel in Siirt—the *Erdef Oteli*, in Cumhuriyet Cadddesi.

From Siirt return to the E99 and continue to (5km) **Baykan**. Here the road starts to follow the course of the Bitlis Suyu. It passes through wooded gorges where nature begins to imitate art. The strangely-shaped rock outcrops, stained red and green by minerals, that tower over the rushing stream would not be out of place in a landscape by Joachim Patenier. Here and there pockets of fertile land are assiduously cultivated and young shepherds lead their flocks to feed on the rich, green roadside verges.

According to a local legend **Bitlis** is named after Batlis, a general of Alexander the Great. Another account gives the honour to Bagoas, the young Iranian eunuch who became Alexander's confidant and favourite. Bitlis was taken by the Arab armies which swept up from northern Syria and Mesopotamia in AD 641. In the 11C it fell to the Selçuks and, like its neighbours, was ravaged by the Mongols in the 13C. Later it became an important stage on the trade route between Diyarbakır and Van. It was ruled by Kurdish *beys* until its incorporation into the Ottoman Empire.

Bitlis occupies a narrow valley dominated by bare rounded hills. A quiet backwater, the town comes to life on market day when the streets are filled with country people shouting the merits of their produce and bartering with the shopkeepers. The people are friendly and hospitable and are proud of their town's ancient buildings. A strong, light-coloured tobacco produced in the Bitlis region is much appreciated in Turkey.

The great walls and towers of the **Citadel** look down menacingly on the town's narrow streets. Access is from the W. Apart from the **outer fortifications** little remains. Originally a Byzantine foundation, it was enlarged and rebuilt many times. The much restored **Ulu Cami** was built by the Selçuks towards the end of the 11C. Note the curious **conical roof** over the *mihrab* and the domed roof of the free-standing minaret. There is a Koranic school in the **İlhasiye Şerefhan Medresesi**. It is worthwhile spending a little time near the river where the citadel may be seen to the best advantage. On the way down you pass some interesting stone houses.

As you leave Bitlis look to the right. The rock slabs on the cliff above the river look like giant organ pipes forged by Vulcan. The road climbs from here until it reaches the level of Van plateau, then for long stretches it is a causeway high above the fields. About 14km from Bilis, on the right-hand side, are the ruins of the **Pabsin Hanı**, one of the resting places on the trade route which linked Diyarbakır with Van. There are the remains of another *caravanserai*, **Aleman Hanı**, near the turning on the left to Elaziğ and Malatya (see Route 44). Before entering Tatvan pause for a moment to take in the beauty of the lake with (Van) Nemrut Dağı on the left and, if you are lucky, a glimpse of the great peak of Süphan Dağı away to the NE.

44

Tatvan to Malatya

Total distance 452km. Road 300 Tatvan—84km Muş—(5km Arak Vank—c 15km Surp Karapet—c 4km Surp Salah—c 30km Kayalıdere Kalesi)—110km Bingöl—88km Kovancılar—(8km Palu)—31km İçme—(25km Hazar Gölü)—35km Elaziğ—(6km Harput—c 25km Pertek)—(50km Keban—c 3km Habibursağı)—104km Malatya—(7km Arslantepe—12km Eski Malatya).

Leave Tatvan (see Route 45) by Road 300 signposted Muş and Bingöl. Just after the junction with the E99, you cross a bare plain bounded on the S by the Muş Güneyi Dağları. In the autumn, when the poplars by the roadside blaze like golden candles, great herds of cattle, sheep and goats browse on the stubble of wheat fields that stretch away into distance. Overhead, noisy flocks of crows wheel and spin menacingly, occasionally diving to snatch the grains missed by the farm animals. Children rush out from isolated houses to wave to the passing travellers, while their parents cut and stack wood in preparation for the cold days to come. The road runs parallel to the railway line which links İstanbul and Ankara with eastern Turkey. Sometimes a train trundles past, but usually the only competition to cars and buses is provided by village boys racing them on their wiry ponies.

The town of **Muş**, severely damaged by earthquakes in recent years, has lost most of its old buildings.

According to tradition it was founded in the 6C by Prince Mushegh Mamikonian, member of a family which ruled Armenia between 377 and 750. With the assistance of Haroun al-Raschid a rival family, the Bagratids, displaced the Mamikonians. The Abbasid Caliph hoped that the Armenians would counter the growing influence of the Byzantines in eastern and central Anatolia. In 1514 Selim I, the Grim, led a great army against the Safavids and their allies, the Kızılbaş, and on 23 August defeated them roundly at Çaldıran. The following year Selim consolidated his gains in central and eastern Anatolia, bringing many cities and towns, including Muş, into the Ottoman Empire. Occupied by the Russians during the First World War, they held it until 1917.

There are the ruins of the ancient **citadel**, **Ulu Cami**, **Alaeddin Paşa Camii** and **Hacı Şeref Camii** (both Selçuk), and **Arslanhanı**, a medieval *han*.

Approximately 5km to the SE of the town, near the village of Arak, there are the ruins of **Arak Vank**, an Armenian monastery dedicated to Lazarus. If you have time and a four-wheel drive vehicle, visit the sites of two other Armenian monasteries NW of Muş. After c 13km take a side road on the right signposted to Varto. A rough track leads to the site of **Surp Karapet** (5C), a church dedicated to John the Baptist built over a tomb in which it was believed he was buried. Most of the stones have been taken away for building purposes. Only the foundations and two vaults remain.

About 4km to the SE are the ruins of **Surp Salah**, a religious centre founded by the Apostle of the Armenians, Gregory the Illuminator, in the 4C. The Katholikos of the Armenian Church lived here.

Near the village of Tepeköy, on a hill above the Murat Nehri, are the ruins of **Kayalıdere Kalesi**, a Urartian fortress. The site was excavated in 1965 by a team from the British Institute of Archaeology at Ankara and the universities of London and Manchester under the direction of Seton Lloyd. They found a citadel at the top of the cliff. Inside were the foundations of a square tower temple with massive walls. A thick layer of ash suggests that the citadel was destroyed by fire.

Road 300 climbs to the **Buğları Geçidi** (1640m), then passes through a rocky landscape where, for long stretches, there is little vegetation. Even in the hillside cemeteries jagged boulders project from the bare soil between the graves.

After c 110km you arrive at **Bingöl**, whose name means 'a thousand lakes'. Like Muş, it has suffered greatly from earthquakes. There are the ruins of a **medieval fortress**, but no other ancient buildings. Bingöl is an excellent centre for walking holidays. The surrounding countryside is very attractive and there are many glacial lakes in the mountains to the N. It has one two-star hotel, *Büyük Bingöl Oteli*, in Genç Cad.

Road 300 begins a steady climb through wooded hills to **Kurucu Geçidi** (1800m). As it descends there are tantalising glimpses of the great lake which forms part of the Keban Dam project.

The ruins of **Eski Palu**, as yet unexplored, are to the SE near a steep hill surrounded on three sides by the Murat Nehri. A freestanding **cuneiform inscription** records the conquest of Malatya and some neighbouring territories by the Urartian king, Menua, c 800 BC. In thanksgiving for his victory Menua built a sanctuary to Khaldi, the principal god of the Urartians. The inscription invokes a curse against anyone who damages or destroys it: 'let the gods Khaldi, Teisheba (a storm god), Shivini (a sun god), wipe him out of the sight of the sun'.

From Palu return to the main road and continue for 31km to the site of **İçme**. Known as Arsamosata in Roman times, it was the most important city in the area and later a stopping place on the trade route which linked Malatya and Diyarbakır.

About 25km from İçme a turning on the left will take you over the 1280m **Koç Geçidi** to **Sivrice** on the **Hazar Gölü**. This slightly salt lake has an area of 50 km sq and a maximum depth of 90m. It is one of the sources of the Tigris. Encircled by brown, barren hills its waters abound with fish. Sample them at a small restaurant c 1km from Sivrice. There is a clean beach near the restaurant, but only the hardy swim in the lake before mid summer. It is 1220m above sea level.

A further 35km on the main road will bring you to **Elazığ**. This provincial capital, 1020m above sea level, was founded by Sultan Abdül Aziz (1861–76) and named in his honour Mamuret el-Aziz or Alaziz. This was changed to Elazığ after the establishment of the Turkish Republic. Elazığ replaced Harput which for many centuries was the principal town in the region.

There are two hotels inspected by the Tourism Ministry, *Beritan Oteli*, Hürriyet Cad. and *Büyuk Elazığ Oteli*, Harput Cad., both are graded two-star. The *otogar* is on the eastern outskirts, the railway station is on the S of the town. There are frequent flights to Ankara from the airport located at the NW of the town. The **Tourist Information Office** at Halk Kütüphanesi, İstasyon Cad. 25 is efficient and helpful.

Vineyards around Elazığ produce the dark red grapes called *öküzgözü* (ox-eye), from which Buzbağ wine is made, and the long white *keçik memesi* (goat teat) grapes. The town has an unusually large number of *pastahanler*, pastry shops, which are filled with delicious, fattening cakes and pastries. Elazığ is clean, modern and a little dull.

The **Archaeological and Ethnographic Museum**, on the campus of Fırat Üniversitesi, has a large collection of pottery, statuettes, stelae, mirrors, bronze objects, marble statues and architectural fragments and coins from the prehistoric era to the Byzantine period. The ethnographic material includes embroidery, kilims, carpets, household utensils and female dresses and ornaments from Elazığ and the surrounding area.

Objects found in rescue digs made between 1968 and 1974 at sites to be flooded by the Keban Dam project include a remarkable collection of Urartian ivories, jewellery and gold ornaments.

Ancient **Harput**, 1280m above sea level, is 6km to the NE of Elazığ. Badly damaged by earthquakes over the centuries, it was largely abandoned by its population after the establishment of Elazığ in the 19C.

History. The earliest finds at Harput date from the 16C BC. The Urartians, Romans and Byzantines, recognising its strategic importance, fortified the hill. Known to the Armenians as Khartabit, it was the Hisn Ziyad of the Arabs. In the 10C it was ruled by the Hamdanids, who occupied Mesopotamia and a large part of Syria. They were replaced by the Selçuks, who, in turn, were displaced by a *condottiere* named Philaretus. In 1090 it fell to Malik Şah, the son of Alp Arslan. After his capture by the Artukid Balak in 1122, Joscelyn de Courtney the Younger was imprisoned here. He was rescued in dramatic circumstances. Twenty Armenians from Edessa, disguised as peasants, broke into the citadel, seized weapons from the walls, killed the guards and set him free. From 1124 to 1230 it was ruled by the Artukids, then successively by Kadi Burhaneddin of Sivas, the Timurids and the Akkoyunlu. Uzun Hasan, the Akkoyunlu emir, married Katherine, daughter of the Lascarid emperor John IV (see İznik). Katherine and her daughters lived here from 1475 to 1485. In 1515 the town came under Ottoman rule, when Selim I, the Grim, took it from the Safavid Şah Ismail.

Ulu Cami, easily recognised by its distinctive red brick minaret, dates from 1166, the period of Artukid rule. It was restored by the Ottomans who placed the cylindrical cap on the minaret. The walls of the **citadel** look most impressive. However, nothing of interest remains of the inner structure. There are two Selçuk mosques, **Arapbaba Camii** and **Alaca Camii**. The **Alaca Mesçidi** was built during the 12C. The **Sara Hatun Camii** dates from the 15C when Harput was ruled by the Akkoyunlu. In the Alaca Camii there is a small collection of finds from Harput and the surrounding area. These include a Urartian inscription from Bağın, stelae and Roman inscriptions. Note the unusual Islamic tombstones which are shaped like rams.

The well-preserved, medieval castle of **Pertek** is c 25km to the NE of Elaziğ—as the crow flies. The road now lies under the waters of the Keban Dam lake. Until the new bridge has been completed, it is necessary to take a car ferry which operates intermittently. The castle, which was built c 1367, guarded an important road over the Murat river. In the nearby village there are an 18C han and a 17C mosque.

A road to the NW of Elaziğ, which passes the airport, leads to the village of Poyraz. Access to the **Keban Dam**, c 50km to the NW, is restricted—ask at the Tourist Information Office. Built by a Franco-Italian consortium, the dam is 650m long and 200m high. It has created an artificial lake of 75,000 ha which contains 34 million cubic metres of water. In addition to irrigating a vast area, generators produce 1240 mgW of electricity. The Keban Dam project is the first of a series designed to improve the living conditions of the people of SE Turkey. (See also Adıyaman—the GAP project.)

About 52km on the Malatya road take a track on the left to the village of **Kale**. At 3km **Habibursağı** German archaeologists found a Urartian cuneiform inscription in 1839 which records the victory of Sarduri II (c 760–30) over the king of Malatya. Sarduri boasts of his capture of many cities which he plundered and burned, of the gold, silver and bronze which he looted, and of the boys and unmarried girls whom he carried into captivity. King Khilaruada of Malatya was brought prisoner to Sarduri's capital, there humiliated and then consigned to oblivion by having his name changed.

Malatya, the provincial capital with a population of c 300,000, replaced ancient Melitene in the 19C. It has no ancient buildings, but is a good centre for visiting places like Milid (Aslantepe), and Melitene (Eski Malatya).

Malatya has one two-star hotel, *Malatya Büük Oteli*, Yeni Cami Karşıı, Zafer İşhanı and two one-star hotels, *Kent Oteli* and *Sinan Oteli*. The **Tourist Information Office** is in İnönü Cad., Tütünbank Üstü. The *otogar* is located in the centre of the city. THY operates frequent air services to Ankara.

Strabo mentioned the fruit trees of Melitene (see below) and Malatya is still famous for its apricots and its apples. Fresh in season, apricots are also sold dried and are included in the tempting cakes and sweetmeats produced by the local pastrycooks.

History. Malatya occupies a strategic position on the edge of the fertile Euphrates plain. After its conquest by Selim I in 1515, it was a favourite summer retreat of the Ottoman sultans, who built their pavilions on the bosky slopes of the Bey Dağı. It was then known as Aspuzu. In 1832 İbrahim, the son of Mehmet Ali, the rebel Albanian general who became ruler of Egypt, defeated an Ottoman army at Konya. He evicted the inhabitants of Melitene and used it as winter quarters for his troops. After his departure most of the refugees stayed on in Arspuzu. This started the decline of Melitene and the growth of Malatya.

Malatya's **museum** in the Municipal Park opened to the public in 1971. Its collection is divided into the following sections: **Chalcolithic Age. 5000–3000 BC**. Tools of stone and obsidian and clay pots from Aslantepe. **Early Bronze Age. 3000–2000 BC**. The contents of a grave and clay pots decorated with geometric motifs found under the floor of a house at Aslantepe. **Age of the Assyrian Trading Colonies. 1950–1650 BC**. Cuneiform cylinder and stamp seals, drinking bowls and statuettes from Aslantepe and Gelin-ciktepe. **Hittite Period 1650–700 BC**: earthenware pots, metal discs, rhy-tons, stone reliefs, a gold necklace, etc, from various sites. **Hellenistic 330–30 BC; Roman 30 BC–AD 395; Byzantine 395–1453 Periods**: bowls, statues, figurines, reliefs etc. **Selçuk and Ottoman Periods**: Selçuk ceramics from Aslantepe. Ottoman clothing, embroidery, ornaments in ivory, a mother of pearl inlaid candlestick base, medals and coins.

Aslantepe, the ancient Milid, is 7km to the NE of Malatya.

History. The earliest traces of occupation date from the first half of the fourth millennium BC. The earliest written references to Milid come from Bogazköy and are from the 18C BC. In the 14C BC its possession was disputed by the Hittites of Hattusas and the Hurrians of northern Mesopotamia. An important source of metals, it attracted the attention of the Assyrians and was obliged to pay tribute to Tiglath Pileser I in the 12C. From the 11C–9C BC it was the capital of the Neo-Hittite principality of Kammanu.The eclipse of Milid came c 657 BC when the Cimmerians, a savage tribe from S Russia, sacked the city. Its inhabitants fled and the ruins were abandoned.

There are traces of Milid's Hittite walls and gates. A colossal limestone statue of king Tarhunza (8C BC) and basalt orthostats (10C–8C BC), from the Neo-Hittite wall, are in the Anatolian Civilizations Museum in Ankara. The orthostats show a lion hunt and king Sulumeli making an offering to a deity. Tarhunza's hair style and sandals reflect Assyrian fashion.

Melitene, **Eski Malatya**, is c 12km to the NE of Malatya on the Sivas road.

History. 'Melitene is similar to Commagene, for ... it is planted with fruit-trees, the only country in all Cappadocia of which this is true, so that it produces not only the olive, but also the Monarite wine, which rivals the Greek wines... the Euphrates River flows between it and Commagene...neither the plain of the Cataonians nor the country Melitene has a city, but they have strongholds on the mountains' (Strabo). The Roman XII Legion, the Fulminata, established a camp here in AD 70.

When the Byzantines began to persecute the Paulicians during the reign of Michael III (842–867), the emir of Malatya gave the heretics shelter here and in Divriği. Large numbers of them were forcibly settled by the Byzantines in Thrace. The Paulicians had a special respect for the writings of St Paul, hence the name by which they were known. Although they called themselves Christians, their beliefs were a heady mixture of Gnosticism and Manichcaeism. Their spiritual descendants were the Bogomils, the Cathars and the Albigenses. Small groups of Paulicians existed in Armenia until comparatively recently.

Melitene was taken by the Ottomans in 1515 during the campaign by Selim I in eastern Anatolia. It was occupied briefly by the army of Mehmet Ali in 1838. The inhabitants were forced to move to Arspuzu (modern Malatya) and much damage was caused to Melitene by defences erected by the Egyptian soldiers. Many of the houses in Battalgazi, the small village which now occupies the site, are constructed of material from the ancient buildings.

W of the site there are two *türbe* and a small graveyard. Melitene was protected by a **moat** and a **double wall** fortified with polygonal and rectangular towers. On the E side a river, the Dermes Su, provided an additional line of defence. Entrance is on the S side through the best-preserved section of the fortifications. A large part of the enclosed area is now taken up by the gardens of the villagers.

Ulu Cami is a 13C Selçuk building which was altered in the 14C and 15C. Over the W entrance is the date 1247. Nothing remains of the earlier mosques on this site. The rectangular courtyard, 50m by 35m, is bordered on three sides by galleries. On the S, a deep *eyvan* leads to the prayer hall. Note the faience decoration on the rear wall.

To the N are the ruins of the 17C **Mustafa Paşa Hanı**, named after the ambitious grand vezir of Murad IV who was beheaded by the Janissaries in 1655. The *han* has a large rectangular courtyard surrounded by porticoes on three sides. On the S are the **rooms** used by the merchants and a well-preserved **large hall** divided by pillars into three sections.

From Melitene return to Malatya.

45

Tatvan to Van

Tatvan (population c 30,000). Although pleasantly sited on the western shoreline of Lake Van within easy reach of Bitlis, Nemrut Dağ, Ahlat and Adilcevaz, Tatvan does not attract many visitors. It has acquired a reputation for raffish seediness, which is not entirely undeserved. Accommodation scarcely meets acceptable standards and few attempts had been made to take advantage of the town's splendid situation.

The **Tourist Information Office** is at Sahil Mah. İşletme Cad.

Fair. Tatvan's summer fair is held on a permanent site near the lake. The industrial and agricultural exhibits and the amusement park draw large crowds.

Excursions. One of the most popular excursions from Tatvan is to Nemrut Dağı, Ahlat and Adilcevaz. By taxi it is possible to visit all three places in the course of one day. Bargain with the youths who tout for the taxi drivers.

During the holiday season there are occasional minibus excursions to Nemrut Dağı. These are relatively inexpensive, but allow limited time in the crater.

Only light refreshments are available at Nemrut, Ahlat and Adilcevaz.

A. Tatvan to Van (southern shore)

Total distance c 130km. Tatvan R300—c 8km (c 42km Hizan)—c 22km (c1km Reşadiye)—c 40km (c 10km Göründü) c 16km (c 2km Akhtamar) c 4km Gevaş—c 40km Van.

Leave Tatvan in the direction of Reşadiye and Gevaş. After following the shoreline for some time Road 300 turns inland and begins to climb steadily, passing through a pleasant, well-watered stretch of countryside.

There are many ruined churches and abandoned monastic settlements on the S side of Lake Van. Some of these are easily reached by a few minutes' drive on a dirt road, others require long treks on foot or on horseback through rough country and are difficult to locate without the help of a local guide.

They include **Hizan** (c 50km from Tavan) where a group of medieval monasteries and churches is used as cattle shelters or grainstores. Others are the 11C **Monastery of the Mother of God** (c 5km from Hizan), a 10C church also dedicated to Mary and the 11C **Convent of the Holy Cross** said to have been founded by St Gregory the Illuminator.

Church of the Holy Cross, Akhtamar island

Where the Road 300 turns away from the lake at c 30km from Tatvan, a minor road on the left leads to 1km **Reşadiye**, a delightful place for a picnic lunch. There are the remains of monastic settlements—the 10C **Convent of St John the Baptist** at Sorb, and the 10C lakeside church of the monastic settlement of **St George** at Goms. This is not easy to find. Ask for directions. For c 40km the road climbs, twists and bends, as it passes over the base of the aptly named Deveboynu Yarım Adası), the Camel's Neck peninsula.

A 10km deviation to Göründü will bring you to two well-preserved 10C churches, part of a monastic complex known as **Karmrak Vank**, founded by Gagik I Artsuni (see below). It is advisable to take a guide.

Boats carry visitors the 2km across to **Akhtamar**. Soft drinks are available on the island. There is a small restaurant near the embarkation point.

History. From the 6C onwards there was a small monastery on Akhtamar. During the troubled Dark Ages, the island was used as a place of refuge in times of danger by the people living on the S shore of Lake Van. In the early part of the 10C Gagik I Artsuni strengthened its defences and turned it into one of the principal administrative centres of his kingdom, building a magnificent palace on the W side of the island and a church dedicated to the Holy Cross on a small plateau facing the shore. For a time a monastery on Akhtamar was the official residence of the Armenian Patriarch. All traces of Gagik's palace and fortifications disappeared long ago, but the **Church of the Holy Cross**, a magnificent example of Armenian ecclesiastical architecture, remains.

The crossing takes about 20 minutes. From the landing stage on the E side of the island an easy climb through the ruined terraced gardens of the monastery brings you to the **Church of the Holy Cross**.

Constructed of beautifully cut and joined blocks of reddish-pink sandstone backed by an inner core of rubble, it is quite small, measuring only 14.8m long by 11.5m wide. The main entrance is on the W, with other entrances on the N and S. Its plan, dictated by the requirements of the Armenian liturgy, is that of a four leaf clover. The square central area is covered by a pyramidal roof resting on a tall drum. The raised sanctuary on the E is formed by an exedra. This is flanked by two niches. Until the last century, when it was destroyed to permit the construction of a bell tower, an **exterior stair** provided access to the **royal loge**, which was housed in the S exedra. The church is well lit by 24 windows, eight on the drum and 16 in the side walls.

The floor of the building is covered with fallen masonry. On the walls there are traces of **frescoes**. Although very faded, it is possible to make out some of the subjects. In the exedrae various gospel stories are depicted, while high up on the dome there is a representation of the creation of Adam and Eve, and of their temptation and expulsion from the Garden of Eden.

The principal glory of the church is outside. The walls are covered with **reliefs**, some merely decorative, others decorative and didactic. Below the roof there is a dynamic **frieze of dogs, hares, lions, gazelles, and foxes** engaged in a pursuit that has no beginning or end. Between the animals are **stylised birds** and **grinning human faces**. Above the windows of the drum end encircling its base there is an attractive, **abstract design**. Under the eaves of the church a second band of carving has lively representations of **human faces** and of the animals shown in the upper band with, in addition, snakes, bulls and panthers.

Just above the windows on the side walls there is another **circular frieze**, the so-called vine relief, which has animals, birds and human figures half concealed by vine leaves and bunches of grapes. Below this is the most important group of carvings. On the W wall **Gagik is shown presenting a model of his church to Christ**. They are flanked by seraphim with folded wings. On the S wall a smirking, self-confident **David** holds his sling ready to slay a lumbering, loutish **Goliath**. Also on the S there is a spirited depiction of **Jonah** about to be swallowed by a very strange whale. On the N side of the church there is a badly damaged relief of **Adam and Eve** standing on either side of the Tree of the Forbidden Fruit. The sculptor has given our First Parents heavy, lumpish bodies and their appearance has not been improved by the deliberate damage inflicted by vandals, who have chiseled away most of their faces. In between the principal subjects there are carvings of the saints, engraved crosses, reliefs of domestic animals and birds and hunting scenes. Note the particularly graphic representation of the spearing of a bear. A final band of palmettes and pine cones completes the outside decoration of the building.

Now a museum, the Church of the Holy Cross was used for worship until the First World War. Urgent action is needed to preserve the remaining frescoes and to clear the interior of the vegetation and accumulated rubbish, which spoil its appearance. A small levy on visitors would enable the work to be put in hand.

From the highest point of Akhtamar there is a splendid view over Lake Van and its S shore, which is overshadowed by the towering, snow-covered peaks of Çandır Dağı. If you swim from the small rocky bathing place near the landing stage, take care. It is said to be much favoured by scorpions.

Continue on Road 300 for c 4km to **Gevaş** where there is a large **Selçuk Cemetery**, which was used from the 14C to the 16C. The gravestones bear ornamental inscriptions in various Arabic scripts and, in some cases, geometric designs or plant motifs. These differ substantially from the decoration found on the Ahlat tombstones (see below).

The fine **kümbet** at Gevaş was constructed in 1358 for **Halime Hatun**, a Black Sheep Turcoman princess. It has a pyramidal roof and is decorated with shallow niches. Steps lead down to the **burial chamber**.

At the road junction c 6km from Gevaş, the right-hand fork (Road 975) goes to Gürpınar, Başkale and Hakkari. The left to c 40km Van, which follows the lakeside, is lined with small restaurants and bathing places.

B.   Tatvan to Van (northern shore)

Total distance c 210km. Tatvan R965—c 4.5km (c 15km Nemrut Dağı)—c 28km Ahlat—c 21km Adilcevaz (c 10km Kefkalesi)—c 64km Ercis—c 52km Timar—c 41km Van.

Leave Tatvan by Road 300, signposted Bitlis and Muş. Turn right on to Road 965 and continue for c 4.5km towards Ahlat. Take the rough, unsurfaced road on the left, signposted 15km Nemrut Dağı. Climbing steadily up the barren southern slope of the volcano, this offers fine views over the W part of Lake Van. On clear days the snow-rimmed crater of Nemrut's companion volcano, Süphan Dağı, may be glimpsed away to the NE. Yürük encampments on the mountainside should be approached with caution, as they are guarded by dogs which are trained to keep intruders at bay. Some Yürük allow photographs of their tents, menfolk and children, usually for a small consideration.

The highest point of **Nemrut Dağı**, which should not be confused with the mountain of the same name near Adıyaman (see Route 40), is 2935m above sea level. As a consequence, the road to the top and into the crater is sometimes closed by snow until early June. The contrast between the sombre browns of the arid exterior and the riotous colours of the lush vegetation in the interior is startling. During the summer grass and flowering plants cover all but the steep, shale slopes that ring the 7km jagged rim of the volcano. On the level floor of the crater flocks of sheep and goats and herds of cattle graze under the watchful eye of their guardians.

The road from the rim descends to the first of **three lakes**. Although the volcano has been quiescent since the mid 15C, evidence of continuing subterranean activity is provided by the high temperature of the water in this lake. Many of the boulders near the shore are covered with a thick white mineral deposit.

The **second, larger, lake**, is under the N rim of the volcano. A narrow band of vegetation near the water soon gives way to acres of barren scree. On a peninsula covered with fragrant maquis, there is a small *kahve*.

In a narrow creek Yürük women wash their clothes and spread them on the rocks to dry. Their menfolk stretch a net across the mouth of the creek. On one of my visits this held a large yellow-green snake, whose silent, desperate threshing served only to entangle it further in the mesh.

Nemrut's **third lake** is the largest. Here herds of cattle graze the meadows on the water's edge or, sometimes, stand placidly for hours in the shallows, while their nut-brown, youthful guardians, splash and frolic around them in a carefree explosion of bucolic high spirits.

Continue on Road 965, which follows the lake shore, to 28km Ahlat.

Ahlat had a chequered history. Taken by the Arabs in the 7C, it was occupied subsequently by the Byzantines, Selçuk Turks, Mongols, the White Sheep and Black Sheep Turcomans, and finally by the Ottomans in the 16C. Selim the Grim's (1512–20) castle was restored in 1536 by Süleyman the Magnificent.

A visit to Ahlat's *kümbetler*, Selçuk graveyard and museum requires a minimum of three hours.

The **kümbetler** are curious conical shaped mausolea, which are believed to resemble the tents used by the nomads of Central Asia. In accordance with Islamic law the bodies were buried under the floor of the underground chamber. The upper chamber served as a funerary chapel. Ahlat posseses a dozen of these striking tombs, all from the pre-Ottoman period.

Ulu Kümbet, the largest of the mausolea, is on the right-hand side of the road, not far from the lake. Sometimes also known as **Usta Şakir** this was built c 1273. A cylindrical structure resting on a square base, it is entered by a door on the E side.

The other *kümbetler* are scattered over a wide area to the left of the Road 965. Among the most interesting are: the **Erzen Hatun Kümbeti**, which was built for a Black Sheep Turcoman princess in 1396 (note the interesting inscription on the frieze), and the **Türbe of Sheik Necmeddin** (dating from 1222), which is located nearby; the **Bayındır Tübesi** built in 1492 for a White Sheep Turcoman emir, the grandson of Uzun Hasan, which is entered on the S side through a portico of squat columns and which has an adjoining *mescit*; the **Çifte Kümbetler**, two mausolea located side by side, which date from c 1281 and were built for Emir Huseyin Timur and Esentekin.

Beyond the *kümbetler* is a large Selçuk cemetery, which was in use from the 12C to 14C. Here highly decorated, moss-covered **tombstones** mark the burial places of long forgotten nobles and their families. **Inscriptions** in Arabic, Greek and Latin scripts are intertwined with stars, plants and mythical animals. Today, the stones, some of which are more than two metres high, lean drunkenly over the grass-covered mounds. The best time to visit the cemetery is at sunset. Then, long black shadows shroud the graves and the pervading sense of vanished glory is a melancholy reminder of the transient nature of power and of man's mortality.

In Ahlat's **museum** there is an interesting collection of Urartian pottery, weapons and jewellery, Roman glass, Byzantine and Selçuk coins and pottery, and Ottoman costumes. In the small garden there are fragments of sculpture from the Urartian to the Selçuk periods.

On the outskirts of the town are the substantial remains of the **Ottoman fortress** (see above). Covering an area of c 200m by 400m, this was protected by high walls strengthened by 13 towers. Behind the fortress there is a ruined **mosque**, which is now used as a store for garden tools.

On the road to c 21km Adilcevaz there are splendid views over the lake. **Adilcevaz**, overshadowed by the menacing shape of Süphan Dağı, is a pleasant place of running water and tree-shadowed streets. On a rocky spur near the lake are the ruins of a **Selçuk castle**. Little remains of the interior.

If you wish to visit the **Urartian fortress** known as Kefkalesi c 10km N of Adilcevaz, take a guide. The rough track is passable only in a four wheel drive vehicle. From the point where the track peters out there is a further half-hour walk over upland meadows to the site.

There are the ruins of a **palace** of more than 30 rooms with walls of brick resting on massive stone blocks, **fortifications** and a **citadel**. Some believe that Kefkalesi may be the ancient city of Qallania, which Sargon II of Assyria chose to ignore, because of its reputation for impregnability, during his celebrated campaign against Urartu in 714 BC.

An **inscription** found at Kefkalesi mentions the invasion of Phrygia by Rusa II (680–639 BC). Other discoveries include figurines of deities and a number of reliefs. A **relief-base** with inscription from the site is in the Anatolian Civilisations Museum in Ankara. Another relief of a king standing on a bull in Van museum, which was found near Adilcavaz's Selçuk castle, is believed to have come originally from Kefkalesi.

The ruins at the foot of the hill are of the **Monastery of the Miracles of Ardzgani**. The **cruciform church** has been dated to the late 8C or early 9C.

During the summer months there are expeditions from Adilcevaz to the summit of **Süphan Dağı** (4058m). Apparently, the climb, which takes several days, is not particularly strenuous and requires no great mountaineering skills. From Adilcevaz to c 64km Erciş the scenery is not particularly interesting. Birdwatchers may like to stop at 16km **Sodalı Gölü**, where several species of birds have been recorded.

At **Erciş** there is the restored **Kadem Hatun Paşa Türbesi**, which was built in 1458 to house the body of the mother of a Black Sheep Turcoman ruler. A pleasant town surrounded by poplar groves, Erciş dates from the early 19C, when the level of Lake Van rose dramatically and covered an earlier foundation. This is in a marshy area near the lake's edge.

At Erciş Road 965 joins Road 975 and continues near the lake through a rather uninteresting stretch of country to the Bendimaha river.

For the journey from the Bendimaha river to Van, see Route 47.

46

Van to Hakkari

Total distance c 196km Van—c 16km junction Gürpınar—R975—c 3km Çavuştepe—c 13km Zernek—c 16km Hoşap—c 16km Güzeldere Geçidi—48km Başkale—c 84km Hakkari.

The best time to visit Çavuştepe is early in the morning. There is little shade at the site and it can be very hot in this part of Anatolia from May through to September. There are no refreshments at Çavuştepe and the *kahve* at Hoşap serves drinks only.

Leave Van by the Gürpınar road. Passing the Şamiram Suyu on the right, this climbs to the Kurubas Geçidi (2260m). From the pass there is a fine view over the lake and the western approaches to Van. Excavations at **Tilki Tepe**, a short distance to the right of the road, suggest that it was occupied from the sixth millennium BC. Tilki Tepe was an important trading centre for obsidian. Found on the slopes of Süphan Dağı and Nemrut Dağı, this was used not only locally, but was exported widely.

At the junction with Road 975, c 24km from Van, turn left towards Başkale and Hakkari. At c 3km a signpost on the right points to the Urartian fortress of **Çavuştepe** on a long rocky ridge c 500m back from the road. Excavations have been conducted at Çavuştepe for more than 20 years by Professor Afif Erzen of İstanbul University.

Known to the Urartians as Sardurihinili, the City of Sarduri, the fortress, which occupies the western extremity of the Bol range, was built during the reign of Sardur II (764–735). Separated from the main part of the mountain by a deep man-made ditch, it was 850m long and about 80m above the level of the plain. A rough track built over one of the ancient access ramps leads to a low saddle between the upper and lower keep of the fortress.

On the upper keep, which lay to the E of the saddle, are the remains of a large **temple** and its associated buildings dedicated to Haldi, the principal deity of the Urartians. The temple, a square structure surrounded by a colonnade, was badly damaged, when the fortress was attacked by the Scythians in the 7C BC and by later occupants. Today only the bases of the columns remain. The large platform cut from the living rock probably served some religious purpose.

The lower keep, which occupied the W end of the ridge, covers a much larger area. The main entrance to this part of the fortress is known today as **Uç Kale**. In places, the stone walls of this structure, which supported fortifications of mud brick, remain to a height of 3m. Beyond Uç Kale there are the ruins of a number of workshops. Further to the W long corridors lead to the **palace store rooms**. Provisions for the king, his court and the garrison of the fortress were contained in the huge pithoi buried in the floor. One of these was filled with broken pottery labels. Others bore inscriptions in cuneiform, which provided information about their contents.

In the paved court of a small square **temple** there is a rectangular **stone altar** on which worshippers placed their offerings. By the side of the entrance a well-preserved **inscription** in Urartian cuneiform states that Sarduri II dedicated the temple to the god Irmushini. It goes on to explain how the king constructed canals to bring water from the Hoşap river to irrigate the plain and make it fertile. The inscription, which is on massive blocks of basalt, probably owes its preservation to the mud bricks which covered it after the destruction of the fortress. Note the circular **sacrificial stone**, where blood offerings were made to the god.

Many of the rooms of the three storey royal palace, which occupied the extreme W end of the ridge, were cut out of the rock. In addition to a large hall where the king received visiting dignitaries and the state and private royal apartments, there were servants' quarters, kitchens, store rooms, cisterns and a harem. The palace also had an efficient **water closet**, which had a closed drain leading to a septic tank.

A small bronze plaque in the British Museum, found at Toprakkale, shows a typical Urartian fortified palace. This had three storeys with windows at each level, a large central entrance and crenellated walls. It is likely that the palace at Çavuştepe resembled this building.

Among the objects found on the site are bronze helmets, weapons, rhytons, cuneiform inscriptions and sections of mosaic.

Before leaving Çavuştepe take a moment to admire the splendid view of the Gürpınar plain, which Sarduri II and his successors enjoyed. During late spring and early summmer—the best time to visit this part of Anatolia—it is a dazzling mosaic of wild flowers.

Continue in the direction of Hoşap and Başkale. At c 16km Zernek a large **reservoir** has been created by damming the Hoşap river. For several kilometres the road bends and twists in sympathy with the contours of the lake, whose grey-green waters are stained in places by dust blown down from its smooth, steep sides. It is a strange, eerie landscape, where a disused road without warning, plunges down the bank and disappears into the depths of the lake. Rich in wild life, it is not unusual to see a bird of prey sweep down in swift, silent flight on a roadside covert, then soar away a moment later with a screaming rabbit or hare dangling from its claws.

Hoşap Castle (16km) was built in 1643 by Sarı Süleyman Bey, a local war-lord and member of the Mahmudi tribe, who, it is safe to assume, grew rich from the taxes he exacted from passing traders. The road through Hoşap, an ancient trade route linking E Anatolia and NW Iran, follows the line of an older Urartian military highway. The Urartians were the first people to recognise the strategic importance of Hoşap and the first to build a fortress here. Sarı Süleyman's building rests on a 15C structure, which was built on some of the large stone blocks of the original Urartian structure.

The fine double-arched early 16C **bridge** near the entrance to the village was built by Zeynel Bey, another member of the semi-independent Mahmudis. This is decorated with alternate bands of cut stone and basalt and has a panel bearing an **inscription**.

Take the first turning on the left over a modern bridge and follow the unmade road to a small parking area in front of the castle entrance. The low squat door is set in a great arch ornamented with the leaf or tear design frequently found in eastern Anatolia. There is also a highly decorative inscription in Farsi. Very little light penetrates the high vaulted entrance tower, so take care. The large area in the centre is believed to have been an assembly and dining hall. Post holes mark the position of an upper floor, which has disappeared. There was a *selamlık, medrese* and several dungeons, all now in a very ruinous condition.

The **private apartments** of the ruler at the top level, included a **mosque** and a very compact **hamam**. From the towers and embrasures there are fine views over the village of Hoşap and the river valley. The walls of the highest tower are pierced by curious peep-holes, which Goodwin suggests, may have allowed the sentries to keep watch without being exposed to the fierce cold of the Anatolian winter.

The mud-brick curtain walls around the castle, stand to a considerable height, but have been so eroded that they appear rounded, softened, without substance, almost incorporeal.

From the river valley the road begins to climb to the 16km **Güzeldere Geçidi** (2730m). From here there is a breathtaking view of the plain far below. This stretches away into the distance, confined at last by the Hakkari Dağları whose snow-covered peaks rim the far horizon.

About 12km before Başkale an unmade road on the left leads to c 10km **Albayrak** where there are the ruins of a 12C church and monastery. Because of the proximity to the frontier, you need a permit to visit Albayrak.

48km **Başkale**, on the lower slopes of Başkale Dağı, claims to be the highest town in Turkey. A dusty little place, it comes to life when a bus arrives from Van or Hakkari.

Soon after Başkale the road enters the valley of the **Zap Suyu**, that tumultuous tributary of the Tigris. At first, lush green meadows bright with flowers flank the placid waters of the river. Then, as the valley narrows until there is barely room for the road and the river, the pace of the Zap increases. Towering cliffs, their scarred faces tortured and contorted by erosion, shut out the sunlight. Where subsidence has carried away a section of the road, the bus slows to a walking pace, as the driver edges cautiously past the gaping drop. There are no houses, no fields in this part of the Zap valley. Only the occasional narrow wooden bridge, swaying wildly over the boiling waters of the river, testifies to the presence of man.

Then the cliffs recede and the valley opens out once more. To the left are signposted Yüksekova and Iran. Just beyond a **ruined castle** there is an abandoned **Nestorian church** used as a cattle shelter. Then the road starts to climb once more. Leaving the river far below it passes under the shadow of Sümbül Dağı, Hyacinth Mountain, (3467m) to enter Hakkari.

Hakkari (population 20,650) is the smallest provincial capital in Turkey. An important trading centre for villages hidden away in the surrounding mountains, its greatest attraction for visitors is the beauty of its setting. At an altitude of 1650m the air is clear and free from pollution. During the summer months the daytime temperature hovers around a comfortable 25°C, but at night it can drop considerably below that figure.

Accommodation and Restaurants. There is only one hotel for tourists, the one star *Ümit Oteli*. Its management and staff are welcoming and attentive. Apart from breakfast the hotel does not serve meals. However, there are several restaurants in the town centre, which have a variety of good, inexpensive dishes on offer. The *kahve* in the square is the principal meeting place and the social centre of Hakkari.

Apart from the ruins of a small 17C *medrese* at the entrance to the town there are no buildings of historical interest in Hakkari. However, near Gevaruk Lake there are primitive drawings on a rock face and within easy walking distance of the town a number of disused **Nestorian churches**. Dating from the 14C and 15C these buildings were used for worship up to the end of the First World War. The Nestorian heresy was first propounded by Nestorius (d. c 451) a patriarch of Constantinople. He maintained that there were two distinct persons in Jesus, one human and one divine, and that Mary was not the mother of God, but the mother of the human Jesus only.

Hakkari is an excellent centre for walkers. For long walks and for visits to the Nestorian churches, take a guide. The **Tourist Information Office** in the town library can advise on routes.

During the spring and summer tulips, hollyhocks, primulas, buttercups, and huge poppies turn the fields around Hakkari into a riot of colour. The air is full of bird song and in the tangled coverts and copses hares, foxes, partridges even jackals may be glimpsed by the patient and alert observer. During the long hard winters other, less friendly animals approach the town. The local people tell of hair-raising encounters with the bears and wolves, which come down from the mountains at that time in search of food.

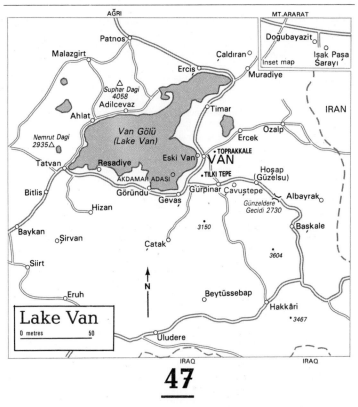

Lake Van
0 metres   50

47

Van to Doğubayazit

Total distance c 187km. Van R975—c 41km Timar—c 44km Muradiye
R975/E99—c 102km Doğubayazit.

VAN (estimated population 121,306) is one of the most important tourist
centres in eastern Anatolia. Built on a large fertile plain on the eastern shore
of Van Gölü, c 4km from the lake, it is untidy, uncoordinated, but not
unattractive. Away from the tourist shops, life proceeds at the leisurely pace
of an Anatolian village. Among the purveyors of seeds and agricultural
implements small shops still sell the highly decorated knitted woollen socks
and the minerals and spices that so delighted Williams 20 years ago. He
found four different kinds of salt on offer. I was only able to discover one.

Van is an important marketing centre for agricultural products, particularly skins, vegetables, fruit and grain. In antiquity the area was famous for
its horses. The tradition continues. Lively, high stepping stallions still
compete on equal terms with buses, lorries, dolmuşes, cars and bicycles on
the town's crowded streets.

Transport and Communications. There are regular bus services from the *otogar* to
Ankara and the principal cities of Anatolia. A courtesy minibus takes passengers from
the town offices of the bus companies to the *otogar*.

For an interesting experience try the Van Gölü Expresi, which takes almost two days to make the journey to İstanbul. There are also train services to Tabriz and Teheran.

Ferry boats leave Van several times a day for Tatvan. Though run primarily for the benefit of train passengers, others may use them. The journey takes about four hours. Smaller boats link Van with Gevaş, Reşadiye, Ahlat, Adilcevaz, and Erciş.

There are regular air services between Van and Ankara. The approach by air to Van is spectacular, affording splendid views of the lake, the deep crater of (Van) Nemrut Dağı (2935m) and the snow-capped cone of Süphan Dağı (4058m).

Information. The **Tourist Information Office** is at Cumhuriyet Cad. No. 127. The staff speak German and French and some of them a little English.

Accommodation. There is a wide range of accommodation in Van. One of the most comfortable hotels is the *Büyük Urartu*, Hastane Sok., 60. Conveniently sited near the main shopping area and the town offices of the bus companies, its rooms are large and quiet. It has a reasonably good restaurant and an excellent resident barber and a ladies' hairdresser. An up-to-date list of hotels and restaurants in Van, with prices, details of services available, etc, may be obtained from the Tourist Information Office.

Post Office and Banks. The main post office and branches of the principal Turkish banks are located in the town centre.

History. One of the earliest references to Van, under its ancient name Tushpa, is to be found in the reliefs from the great bronze gates of the country palace of Shalmaneser III, king of Assyria (858–824 BC). Discovered at Balawat near Nimrud in northern Iraq and now in the British Museum, these reliefs provide a lively account of Shalmaneser's campaigns against Urartu. Cities are shown being attacked, captured and looted and Shalmaneser boasts in one of the accompanying inscriptions 'I descended to the sea of the land of Nairi (Lake Van); the terrible weapons I washed in the sea'.

The Assyrians are shown feeding a large animal which appears to be emerging from the lake. Could this be one of the celebrated Van cats, which, it is claimed, enjoy swimming so much that they dive into the lake in search of a fresh fish dinner?

Sarduri I (840–830 BC), who is mentioned in the Balawat reliefs, is believed to be the king who united the Urartian people. A number of inscriptions recording the achievements of his reign have been found. One, written in Assyrian cuneiform, appears several times on gigantic blocks of limestone in Van castle.

Under Menua (810–786 BC) Urartu reached its apogee, becoming one of the most powerful states in W Asia. His kingdom extended as far as Erzurum and Erzincan in the N, Malatya in the W and beyond Lake Urmia in the SE. He was a great builder not only of castles and fortifications, temples and shrines, but of aqueducts, gardens and irrigation systems, so that the area around Tushpa was renowned for its fertility and the quality of its produce. Some scholars suggest that the description in the Bible of the Garden of Eden may be based on Tushpa at the time of Menua. This is only one of several intriguing connections between the Old Testament stories and Urartu—the Ark coming to rest on Mt Ararat (Ararat is a corruption of Urartu) and the drunkenness of Noah (the Urartians cultivated the vine and were famous winemakers).

During the reign of Menua a canal 51km long was built to bring water from the Gürpınar plain to Van. Now called Şamıram Su, it is still in use.

Menua was succeeded by Argishti I (786–764) and Sarduri II (764–735). Argishti's achievements are recorded in a long cuneiform inscription outside his tomb in Van castle. Sarduri's reign began well. He is generally credited with the construction of the castle of Çavuştepe (see Route 46).

Rusa I (735–714) succeeded Sarduri. During his reign Urartu was invaded by Sargon II. A detailed account of this campaign, made by Sargon in a report to the Assyrian god Ashur, is preserved in the Louvre. The Assyrians ravaged the area around Lake Van, destroying the farms and orchards and slaughtering the peasants. Although they did not capture the capital, they took the holy city of Musasir, which was located to the SW of Lake Urmia. Entering the temple of Haldi, the principal Urartian god, they stole its treasure, a total of 333,500 objects of gold and silver, and then set fire to the building. According to an Assyrian relief at Khorsabad the temple had a sloping roof with a triangular pediment and it was surrounded by a colonnade. This Urartian design, which was later adopted by the Greeks and the Romans, has been used by countless architects during the last two millennia.

Rusa's successor, Argishti II (714–685 BC), concentrated on repairing the damage inflicted by the Assyrians and in repelling the Cimmerians, a warlike people from the Crimea, who were becoming increasingly troublesome. Perhaps, the greatest achievement of his reign was the construction of the fortress of Altıntepe near Erzincan.

Rusa II (680–639 BC) was the last of the great Urartian kings, his long reign was marked by the construction of a number of fortresses on the periphery of his kingdom—at Teishebaina to the S of Erevan, at Kayalidere on the bank of the Murat Su near Muş and at Kefkalesi to the NE of Adilcevaz. He also built a new palace, which he called Rusahinili, the city of Rusa, on Toprakkale the ridge which overlooks the modern town of Van (see below).

Although Urartian bronzes have been discovered as far away as Italy, all knowledge of Urartu disappeared for almost 2500 years. Its rediscovery began in 1827, when a young German scholar, Friedrich Eduard Schulz, was commissioned by the French government to copy a number of inscriptions, which were cut into the steep side of the ancient citadel on Toprakkale.

Excavations conducted by German, Russian and Turkish archaeologists and the painstaking study of inscriptions by Guyard of Paris, Sayce of Oxford and their successors gradually revealed the history and cultural achievements of Urartu. Since 1960 Turkish archaeologists have been working in the area.

Towards the end of the 6C BC a large area of eastern Anatolia, which included Van, came under the control of a people that had migrated from SW Anatolia. Originally neighbours of the Cilicians (Herodotus The History, Book 5.49) the Armenians, after settling in their new country, appear to have absorbed their Urartian predecessors and ruled as Achaemenid satraps. In the 1C BC Tigranes I the Great (died after 56 BC) allied himself with Mithridates VI Eupator, king of Pontus, against Rome. However, after surrendering to Pompey in 66 BC Tigranes was permitted to retain his kingdom.

During the centuries that followed, Van continued to be one of the principal cities of eastern Anatolia, becoming in the 10C the capital of the Artsuni kingdom of Vaspurakan. In 1021 Prince Sennacherib-John, the last ruler of Vaspurakan, harassed by the advancing Turks and the weakened by the machinations of the Byzantines, ceded his kingdom to the Emperor Basil II. The Byzantines did not enjoy their newly-acquired territory for long, as after the battle of Manzikert in 1071 eastern Anatolia came under the rule of the Selçuk Turks.

By the early 14C Van and the surrounding area was controlled by the Black Sheep Turcomans. The city's fortunes waxed and waned. Stormed and sacked by Tamerlane, it later recovered its prosperity. Following Süleyman the Magnificent's successful campaign against the Iranian Safavids in 1534, eastern Anatolia was joined to the Ottoman Empire. The garrison of Van offered no resistance to the army of İbrahim Paşa and Süleyman accepted the submission of the Mahmudi tribe there. A period of peace and stability followed.

For 400 years Eski Van, the old city of Van, rested secure beneath the protective shadow of its castle. Occupied by the Russians during the First World War, it was utterly destroyed and the present town, which replaced it, was built on the site of a garden suburb of the old city.

Museum. Van's museum is near the Tourist Information Office. On the ground floor there is a well-displayed collection of 7C and 8C BC Urartian finds from Patnos, Toprakkale, Çavuştepe and Giyimli. These include fragments of murals, gold jewellery, childrens' toy pottery vessels, and bronze plaques and vessels. In a central domed chamber there is a small display of inscriptions. The upper floor has a representative ethnographic collection of costumes, 13C and 14C Cufic inscriptions, Byzantine, Sassanian, Selçuk and Ottoman coins and a number of objects from the old city of Van. In the garden there are sculptures, Urartian stelae with cuneiform inscriptions and a number of Ottoman canons.

Toprakkale is in a restricted area, so it is necessary to get permission to visit the ruins. Initial enquiries should be addressed to the Tourist Information Office. The view from the summit is wonderful. It is also a reminder of the saying heard by Lynch a century ago 'Van in this world and Paradise in the next'.

Toprakkale occupies the southern end of the Zızım ridge. There are only a few sad remains of the huge palace, which once crowned the summit. Many of the dependent buildings were constructed of mud brick. In ancient times this part of Tushpa was known as *Rusahinili* the city of Rusa. A short walk from the W side of the mound brings you to the highest point of the ridge. Here gigantic blocks of cut stone mark the site of a **temple**, which was probably dedicated to Haldi the principal deity of the Urartians. This building was destroyed by the Medes c 590 BC.

At the foot of a stepped rock-face a square shaped opening leads, by way of a winding stair, to a huge **underground chamber**, which has been laboriously chiselled out of the mountain. At one time believed to be an assembly hall, it is now generally accepted that this was a cistern. On the top of the mound there was a **storehouse** containing rows of large **pithoi** in which grain and oil were kept.

Toprakkale has suffered badly from neglect and from the depredations of treasure hunters. Parts of a great bronze throne found here were bought by Layard in 1877. They are now in the British Museum. Other finds are in the museums of Berlin, Leningrad and Paris. Mosaics from Toprakkale are in Van museum and in the Museum of Anatolian Civilisations in Ankara, while a fine basalt altar is in Istanbul's Museum of the Ancient Orient.

To the NE of Toprakkale is the great **Pool of Sıkhe**. Constructed by Rusa to supply his city with water, it has been repaired recently.

Van Gölü. Known to the ancients as Thopitis or Arsene (Strabo 7.229), Lake Van is the largest lake in Turkey. It has an area of 3574 sq km, is 119km across at its widest point and its surface is 1648m above sea-level. It has a volume of 607 cubic km and a maximum depth of 451m. Triangular in shape, the lake is surrounded by mountains; Süphan Dağı (4058m) on the N and Nemrut Dağı (2935m) on the NW are extinct volcanos. Fed by a number of rivers—notably by the Güzel Su and Mermit Çayı on the E and the Bendimahi and Oruç rivers on the N—it has no significant outflow. During the Pleistocene Era (10,000 to 2,000,000 years ago) an eruption of lava from Nemrut Dağı closed the Murat Valley and prevented the Zilan and Bendimahi rivers from joining the Murat, a tributary of the Euphrates. A rough balance is maintained in the lake between loss through evaporation and inflow from the rivers and precipitation. However, a survey conducted over a period of 30 years has shown that, during the spring, melted snow and increased rainfall can raise the level by as much as 50cm.

Lake Van is the largest soda lake in the world. Its water can not be drunk or used for irrigation, but it is much appreciated by swimmers as it produces a pleasant silky feeling on the skin. It is alleged to bleach the hair.

There are fish in Lake Van, notably the *darek*, a member of the carp family, which has adapted to the brackish water. These usually congregate where the rivers flow in, but have also been caught in deeper water.

There are several islands on Lake Van. The largest is Gadir on the N. Akhtamar on the S attracts most visitors because of its well-preserved church dedicated to the Holy Apostles. The steep rocky sides of Van's islands provide nesting places for the myriad screaming gulls, which are the lake's most prolific and visible form of life.

Van Kalesi. Not far from the eastern shore of the lake, Van Castle perches dramatically on a 2km long, narrow ridge. Protected by stout man-made fortifications on the N and 200m high cliffs on the S, it was described by Evliya Çelebi as looking like a kneeling camel.

A short, inexpensive taxi ride from the town, the castle may also be reached by an infrequent dolmuş service. Allow at least two hours for the visit, four, if you intend to explore **Eski Van**.

Just beyond a small Muslim cemetery, where a holy man is buried, a limestone platform marks the site of a **Urartian temple** constructed by King Menua c 800 BC. The inscription on a statue base in one of the temple alcoves names its royal founder.

Slightly to the W of the ridge there is a rectangular stone structure 47m long, 13m wide and 4m high. Known as **Sardur Burcu** (the tower of Sarduri) or sometimes Madır Burcu, this was built by Sarduri I (840–830 BC). Several of the huge stone blocks bear inscriptions in Assyrian cuneiform: 'This is the inscription of King Sarduri, son of the great king Lutipri, the powerful king who does not fear to fight, the amazing shepherd, the king who ruled the rebels. (I) am Sardur, son of Lutipri, the king of kings and the king who received tribute from all the kings. Sardur, son of Lutipri says I brought these stone blocks from the city of Alniunu. I built this wall'. Sarduri began the expansion of the Urartian kingdom, which was continued by his son, Ishpuini (830–810 BC). He pushed the eastern boundary of Urartu to the shores of Lake Urmia.

On reaching the top of the ridge turn to the S. Here on a small ledge is the entrance to the **tomb of King Argishti I** (786–764 BC). A large window-less chamber, surrounded by a number of smaller rooms, it was used during the Ottoman period for the storage of provisions and weapons. Around the entrance to the tomb a long, well-preserved cuneiform inscription records the principal events of Argishti's reign.

There are the ruins of **Turkish barracks** and of a mosque erected during the reign of Süleyman the Magnificent. Towards the centre, rock-cut steps lead to the **burial chambers of King Menua and King Sarduri I**. The door of Menua's tomb faces S, that of Sarduri opens to the E. Both tombs, robbed in antiquity, were used as stores and prisons by the Ottomans.

On the NE slope of the ridge two niches cut into the rock, known as **Analı Kız**, 'Mother and Maiden', because of their appearance, contain stelae recording the achievements of King Sarduri II. In front of the niches are a sacrificial altar and a channel down which the blood of the victims flowed. Local gossip says that animals are still sacrificed at the altar by superstitious people, who believe that their wishes will be granted if they do this! The ritual requires the participants to slide down the blood stained channel!

To reach the site of Old Van return to the *kahve* and then walk around the western edge of the ridge. Very little remains of the ancient city, which was extensively damaged during the First World War. Towards the end of the 19C Van was surrounded on three sides by a crenellated, battlemented wall, the fourth side being protected by the towering cliffs of the castle. It had four gates, which were closed at night and in time of danger. Mosques and churches catered for the spiritual needs of its mixed population of Muslims and Christians. The wealthy had splendid houses in a garden suburb 4km away, the area now occupied by the modern town.

At the bottom of the cliff towards the western end are the remains of **Ulu Cami**, which was constructed in the 15C by Kara Yusuf of the Black Sheep Turcomans. According to Goodwin this building displayed Iranian influences being 'eccentrically modelled on the south dome of the Friday mosque of Isfahan'. Part of the structure may have collapsed during the great earthquake of 1648 and, already a ruin in the 19C, it received further damage during the 1914–18 war. Today only some of its walls and its minaret remain standing.

Near the S gate is the **Hüsrev Paşa Camii**. Built c 1567 by Hüsrev Paşa, Governor of Van, it has a single dome and minaret. Badly damaged during the Great War, it has been restored.

Joined to the mosque is the **tomb of Hüsrev Paşa**, which was built between 1557–58. This has a conical roof and its windows and doors are ornamented with delicately-carved rosettes and palmettes. There are some interesting dervish symbols on the walls. The tomb has also been restored.

About 100m to the E is the **Kaya Çelebi Camii**. Built about the same time as the Hüsrev Paşa Camii, this elegant building has also been restored.

In the neglected, overgrown **Orta Kapı (Middle Gate) Cemetery** there are two fine late 18C tombs, the so-called İkiz Kümbetler.

There are other interesting sites in the area around Van, but some are not easy to reach and others are occasionally closed to visitors. They include the **Yedi Kilise Monastery**, the **Urartian fortresses** at Anzaf and the **Convents of Aparank**. The Yedi Kilise Monastery is c 20km to the E of Van on the side of Erek Dağı. The Anzaf Urartian fortresses are reached by leaving Van on Road 300 and continuing in the direction of Özalp for c 10km. A visit to Aparank requires time, a four-wheel drive vehicle, a guide and stamina—part of the journey has to be made on horse-back.

Leave Van by Road 975 in the direction of Muradiye. A short distance from the town the road abandons the lake for a stretch of unremarkable, uninspiring countryside. It is not until Timar that vistas of misty blue water and distant snow-capped peaks return once more to delight the eye. Where Road 975 crosses the Bendimaha Çayı take your last look at Lake Van, and begin the climb to Muradiye and the **Gönderme Geçidi** (1900m). Soon you enter a savage landscape where jagged rocky outcrops surround the occasional huddle of small houses or cluster of squat, brown Yürük tents. There is a pervading sense of loneliness and isolation.

After **Çaldiran** there is an abrupt change. The road enters a river valley, where, in spring and early summer, flowers cover the water meadows with brilliant patches of red, yellow and deep blue. Here you pass close to the Iranian border.

The final stretch of c 20km to the junction with the E80/Road 100, is over a narrow, rough track. This part of the route provides a stimulating and unusual driving experience.

On the last 8km of the route to Doğubayazit there are excellent views of Büyük Ara Dağı and of Ishak Paşa Sarayı on its lofty perch to the right.

48

Van to Erzurum

Total distance c 392km. Van R975—c 41km Timar—R280 c 52km Erciş—c47km Patnos—(c 36km Malazgirt) R965—c 40km Tutak—c 40km Ağrı E80/R100—c 34km Eleşkirt—c 58km Horasan—c 43km Pasinler—c 37km Erzurum.

The first part of this journey, from Van to the Bendimaha Çayı, is described in Route 47.

At the Bandimaha river, where Road 975 continues by way of Muradiye and Çaldıran to Doğubayazit, take the left fork on Road 280 to Erciş. (For a description of Erciş see Route 45.)

After leaving Erciş the road enters a featureless landscape dominated by the brooding shadow of Süphan Dağı on the far W horizon. In this desolate place only the telegraph poles marching endlessly into the distance testify to the presence of man, while the only movement to catch the eye is of dry, brown grasses bending before the never-ceasing wind. The green oasis of Erciş and the blue waters of Lake Van are far behind. Here the colours are drab and lifeless—shades of brown and ochre repeated interminably.

This stretch of Road 280 attracts little traffic and has a good surface. You reach Patnos quickly. There is nothing of interest here.

The ruins of a large Urartian walled city have been found at **Aznavurtepe** near Patnos. The fortifications extended downwards from the citadel, which was on a 300m high peak, and enclosed not only the residential and business quarters of the city, but also a large man-made **reservoir**. Substantial sections of the **fortifications** were uncovered and an **inscription** recording the achievements of the reign of King Menua (810—786 BC) were found on a temple wall.

Excavations at **Giriktepe** on the outskirts of Patnos have uncovered a **columned hall**, which is believed to have formed part of a well-appointed **country residence**. This appears to have been destroyed by fire. The bodies of a number of ladies wearing rich costumes and of several armed soldiers were found in rooms behind the hall, presumably victims of the conflagration.

A secondary road leads SW from Patnos to 36km **Malazgirt**, the ancient Manzikert, where in 1071 an important battle was fought. The Selçuk Turks under the command of Alp Arslan defeated a Byzantine army led by the experienced and courageous emperor Romanos IV Diogenes. This victory permitted the unhindered advance of the Selçuks into Anatolia.

History. On the morning of 19 August 1071 Alp Arslan, the brave and resourceful Selçuk leader, by pretending to withdraw his troops, tricked the Byzantine army into a narrow valley near Manzikert. Here the emperor was obliged to give battle, even though his forces had been seriously depleted by the defection during the night of some of his Turkish mercenaries and by the refusal of his Frankish troops to fight. Although superior in number, the Byzantines could not stand up to the fierce attacks of the Selçuks and soon broke and fled. The emperor's bodyguard abandoned him and he was captured and brought before Alp Arslan.

After a period of captivity Romanos IV was ransomed for one and half million dinars. In addition the Byzantines were obliged to release all Muslim prisoners, to agree to a 50 year truce and they had to promise to supply a substantial body of troops to the Selçuks, if at any time they were requested to do so. Neither protagonist survived the battle for long. Alp Arslan died from stab wounds inflicted by a Kwarazmian leader named Yusuf, whom he was judging. Romanos IV was blinded by his sucessor, Michael VII, and died in exile on the Princes Islands.

Historical associations and the remains of its 13C fortifications are the only inducements to visit the modern town of Malazgirt.

At Patnos Road 280 becomes Road 965 and deteriorates substantially. The journey to 40km Tutak is even more monotonous than that from Erciş to Patnos. The last section follows the winding valley of the Murat Nehri before descending at last to the plain at 40km Ağrı.

For Ağrı to Erzurum on E80/Road 100 see Routes 49 and 50.

49

Doğubayazit to Erzurum

Total Distance c 256km. Doğubayazit E23—c 58km Taşliçay—c 26km Ağrı—c 34km Eleşkirt—c 58km Horasan—E23—c 25km Köprüköy (Çobandede)—c 18km Pasinler—c 37km Erzurum.

Places betweem Horasan and Erzurum are described in Route 50.

Doğubayzit is the last town of any size before the Turco-Iranian border. Sited on a desolate plain 1800m above sea-level it is wreathed in dust clouds in summer and racked by icy winds in winter. A place of few attractions, it is just a convenient centre for visiting one of the strangest and most exotic buildings in Turkey, **İshak Paşa Sarayı**, and for exploring the bleak, fascinating, countryside around Mount Ararat, **Büyük Ara Dağı**.

Doğubayazit owed its importance in the past to its proximity to a trade route, which linked NW Iran with the Black Sea port of Trabzon. It suffered severely during the 19C wars with Russia and during the first World War, when it came under Russian rule again. More recently it became a staging post for the long-distance lorries which carry goods to and from Iran.

Accommodation. Doğubayazit has a number of hotels. Recommended is the three-star *Sim-Er Hotel*. A few kilometres from the town centre on the Iran Transit Yolu, surrounded by an an untidy, overgrown garden whose vivid green provides welcome relief from the monotonous brown and umber plain, it sprawls at the base of a red-gold cliff. The windows look on to the great peak of Büyük Ara Dağı and its smaller neighbour, Küçük Ara Dağı. The hotel provides a courtesy minibus service to Doğubayazit, where taxis and the occasional dolmuş take visitors to İshak Paşa Sarayı.

Transport and Excursions. There are regular buses from Doğubayazit to Ağrı and Erzurum and infrequent minibus services by way of Çaldıran and Muradiye to Van.

Travel agencies in Doğubayazit offer interesting tours of the surrounding countryside. A typical half-day excursion will take you to the border post on the Turco-Iranian frontier, to a crater made by a giant meteorite, to some of the hill villages and, on the return journey, allow enough time for a brief visit to İshak Paşa Sarayı. There are expeditions for experienced climbers on Mount Ararat. Permits are required.

Banks and Shops. In the centre of Doğubayazit there are branches of most of the Turkish banks and shops which supply a surprisingly wide variety of goods.

Mount Ararat consists of two peaks, Büyük Ara Dağı (5165m) and Küçük Ara Dağı (3925m), joined by an 11km long ridge. Evidence of the volcanic formation of both mountains is provided by the extensive cracks and fissures on their sides. During the summer months the grass-covered slopes above 1500m provide good pasturage for sheep. Among the more unusual products of the area is 'Kermes' a red dye produced from aphides which congregate in springtime on the roots of a plant growing on the lower slopes of the mountain.

Büyük Ara Dağı and Küçük Ara Dağı have an inhospitable climate with sudden mists and snow storms. Other dangers include rock falls and the presence of large numbers of scorpions, venomous snakes and wolves. During the harsh winter months the wolves, driven by the cold and lack of food, hunt in packs on the plain.

According to an ancient tradition Ararat is the mountain on which Noah's Ark rested. In recent years a number of expeditions have been organised with the avowed intention of finding the Ark and so proving the veracity of the tradition.

Travellers have always been drawn to these mountains. In the 14C *Sir John Mandeville's Travels* there is the following account of Ararat and its association with the biblical story: 'From the city of Erzeroum go men to an hill that is clept Sabissocolle. And there beside is another hill that men clepe Ararat, but the Jews clepe it Taneez, where Noah's ship rested, and is yet upon the mountain. And men may see it afar in clear weather. And that mountain is well a seven mile high...ne never man (went up there) save a monk that, by the grace of God, brought one of the planks down, that yet is in the minster at the foot of the mountain'.

This may have been the relic venerated in a monastery dedicated to St Jacob, who was believed to have made several unsuccessful attempts to reach the summit. This monastery and a nearby village were destroyed by a great landslide produced by the earthquake of 1840. Several expeditions have reached the summit and sightings of the ark continue to be reported in the more sensational newspapers.

İshak Paşa Sarayı at Doğubayazit

For **İshak Paşa Sarayı** take a taxi or dolmuş from Doğubayazit. The 7km journey is by a narrow winding road with a good surface which climbs steadily from the plain. Near the parking area there is a *kahve* which sells tea and soft drinks. As the visit to the palace, the mosque and the hill fortress requires a minimum of three hours, bring a picnic lunch.

History. İshak Paşa Sarayı was built towards the end of the 18C by a powerful local family, the Çildiroğlu, who were the *de facto* rulers of a substantial part of eastern Anatolia. Very little is known about them. According to some accounts they were Georgians. Others say they were Armenians, yet others that they were Kurds. Their palace dominated the ancient Silk Route and its occupants grew rich from the tribute which they exacted from the caravans passing beneath its walls.

Although it takes its name from Ishak Paşa, who was Vezir in 1789, the palace was probably begun by his father and completed by his son, Mahmut Paşa.

Though its design is traditional, the building has been constructed in a variety of styles with Georgian and Selçuk predominating. The name of the architect is not known. Goodwin surmises that it may have been designed by İshak Pasha himself with the help of skilled craftsmen. Whoever was responsible, it is clear that he gave considerable thought to the comfort of its occupants. To combat the extreme cold of the eastern Anatolian winters every room was provided with a fireplace and, in addition, there was a hot air central heating system.

İshak Paşa Sarayı has an area of 7600m sq and is built on a narrow spur, which juts out from the mountainside. Terraced on the E and W sides, it rises high above the plain, a magnificent anachronism which commemorates the ambition and taste of a cultivated, rich family of robber barons.

Entrance is through a magnificent **portal** ornamented in the Selçuk style. According to a local tradition this was once closed by gold-plated doors which were stolen by the Russians when they had a garrison here. A large **outer courtyard** furnished with stables and outbuildings, one of which contained the furnace for the central heating system, leads to an **inner court**. On the N side of this is the *selamlık*, the men's apartments. A narrow passage provides access to a number of small rooms, one of which is believed to have been the library, and to the **mosque**. This retains its roof and is in a good state of repair. Note the **womens' gallery** supported by columns, the **original lamp chains** and the traces of **painted decoration** on the interior of the dome. The *mimber* is reached by a stairs in the wall at the side of the *mihrab*.

From the mosque return to the inner court. In the NW corner is the *türbe* of the ruler and his wife. Constructed in the Selçuk style, this has steep stairs leading down to the burial chamber. The structures at the side of the *türbe*, which resemble dog kennels, are **ventilators** for the tomb. To the S of the *türbe* is the elaborate entrance, ornamented with lions in the Persian and Selçuk style, to the harem. A hall decorated with patterns formed from basalt and sandstone leads to the apartments of the harem. These have a magnificent view across the plain to Ararat. To the S of the hall is the palace's **large kitchen** with its huge fireplace and openings to permit the heat and smoke to escape in the dome.

Among other conveniences was the **master's water closet**. According to Williams its position and appointments are proof of the ruler's megalomania and contempt for his subjects. 'This has an open window, high up in the sheer wall which overlooks village and road. Squatting there, face towards the window and the western spur of Ararat, İshak Pasha must have felt that he was doing it on the world'.

A short walk up the old Silk Road will bring you to the **mosque** built by Selim I the Grim. This plain building rests on a huge platform that projects agressively from the side of the mountain. The stone-capped **minaret** rises from a base that is lower than the main structure. The interior, which can be glimpsed through the windows, appears to be smaller than the palace mosque, but is of similar design. The door is firmly locked and, sadly, the building bears all the signs of neglect and abandonment.

Above the mosque are the ruins of an ancient **fortress**, which was founded by the Urartians and renovated by the Byzantines and the Selçuk and Ottoman Turks. There is an interesting **relief** and a **cuneiform inscription** dating from the Urartian period. Access to the relief and the fortress is made difficult by the angle of the slope and the fine scree, with which it is covered. A gallery in the upper part of the fortress provides a splendid view of the palace and the wild and desolate valley beyond.

Leaving Doğubayazit by the E23 you pass through an unremarkable stretch of country, over the 2040m **Ipek Geçidi**, to reach the small town of 58km Taşliçay. From there it is a further 26km to the provincial capital of **Ağrı**. Formerly known as Karaköse, this is an important market centre and road junction. Although the town contains nothing of historical interest, even the most blasé traveller will be fascinated by the animated scenes at the *otogar*.

From Ağrı it is about 34km to Eleşkirt, another small market town. From here the road climbs steadily until it reaches the **Saç Geçidi**, 2315m, to descend slowly to c 58km Horasan, an important road junction. At Horasan it may be necessary to change buses for Erzurum. Places between Horasan and Erzurum are described in Route 50.

50

Erzurum to Kars and Ani

Total distance c 260km. Erzurum—E23—37km Pasinler—18km Köprüköy (Çobandede—25km Horasan—82km Sarıkamış—56km Kars—42km Ani.

Founded in remote antiquity, **ERZURUM** was for many centuries an important commercial centre on one of the trade routes, which linked Iran with Anatolia. Because of its strategic position a succession of invading armies fought bitterly for its possession. Among the reminders of the city's turbulent past are the graceful mosques and tombs of the Selçuks and the solid grey stone houses of the Russians, which are scattered among the city's tall new buildings.

Sited on a high, wind-swept plateau 1950m above sea-level, Erzurum is reputed to be one of the coldest places in Turkey during the winter months. Foraging wolves from the surrounding mountains are said to prowl through its suburbs at night in search of food.

Erzurum (estimated population 252,648) is the provincial capital of an area which produces wheat, barley, millet, sugar beet and garden produce in substantial quantities. Its boulevards are lined with modern buildings—replacements of those destroyed by earthquakes in this century. Its craftsmen are renowned for their work in gold, silver, copper, iron and leather. Erzurum's saddles are famous throughout Turkey. They also make jewellery from *oltutaş*, a type of jet found at Oltu, a small town c 100km to the N.

Erzurum's Atatürk University has faculties of medicine, dentistry, engineering and agriculture and a school of veterinary science at Kars.

Accommodation and Information. There are eight hotels on the Ministry of Tourism's list. The three-star *Büyük Erzurum Oteli* is recommended. The *Güzelyurt Restaurant*, Cumhuriyet Cad. 64, has an interesting menu. Try their *türlügüveç*, a meat and vegetable casserole. The **Tourist and Information Office** is in Cemal Gürsel Cad. on the W side of the city.

Transport. THY has daily flights to and from Ankara. There are frequent long-distance bus services from the *otogar* on the NW side of the city. Minibus services to Artvin and local destinations leave from various locations in the centre.

A train which connects İstanbul and Ankara with eastern Turkey involves a journey through time and space, which requires a certain degree of fortitude and a great deal of patience, but offers interesting encounters with the Turkish people and an unhurried examination of the landscape of central Anatolia.

Banks, Post Office and Museum. There are branches of the principal Turkish banks in the city centre. The main Post Office is in Cumhuriyet Cad. and the museum in Paşalar Cad.

Winter Sports. Erzurum is being developed as a winter sports resort. There is a fine new hotel on the slopes of Palandöken Dağ.

History. Excavations conducted near the city have revealed settlements dating from the Neolithic Age (4th millennium BC). Traces of occupation by the Hittites during the third millennium BC have also been found. To the Byzantines of the 5C AD the city was known as Theodosiopolis. The Armenians called it Karin. Its modern name, Erzurum, is probably derived from the Arabic Arzan ar-Rum or Arz ar-Rum, the land of the Romans, the term applied to the Byzantine Empire by the Selçuks.

From the 5C to the middle of the 7C AD Erzurum was occupied at various times by the Byzantines and the Persians. A synod held here in 623 attempted to establish the control of the Greek Orthodox over the Armenian Church. Little more than 20 years later the city was occupied for the first time by the Arabs. During the succeeding two centuries control of Erzurum passed from the Arabs to the Byzantines and back again. About 961 it became part of the Bagratid kingdom of Tayk, which reached from Erzurum to the Black Sea near Trabzon. Captured shortly after the Battle of Manzikert (1071) by the Selçuk Turks, it prospered greatly under their rule.

At the beginning of the 14C Erzurum was visited by Ibn Battuta. He describes it as 'a vast town...mostly in ruins as a result of a civil war between two Turkmen tribes'.

Another early 14C description of Erzurum is provided by the author of '*The Travels of Sir John Mandeville*': '...men go from Trebizond,' he writes, '...unto a city that is clept Erzeroum, that was wont to be a good city and a plenteous; but the Turks have greatly wasted it. There-about groweth no wine nor fruit, but little or else none. In this land is the earth more high than any other, and that maketh great cold'. In 1515 Erzurum was taken by Selim I (the Grim) during his campaign against the Safavids.

Evliya Çelebi, served here as a customs clerk from 1646 to 1648. It may have then that he heard the story of the Erzurum cat, which froze solid as it made its way across the rooftops one winter night only to revive miraculously the following spring.

Towards the end of the 17C Britain despatched a representative to Erzurum to look after her trading interests. Until superseded by the railway at the end of the 19C, great camel trains, bearing goods for Europe, passed through the city each year on their way over the mountains to the Black Sea port of Trabzon.

During the 19C wars between Russia and Turkey Erzurum was twice occupied by the Russians, in 1829 and 1878. It came under their control again between 1916 and 1918. Atatürk presided over the first Turkish National Congress which was held here in 1919. This led in due course to the foundation of the Turkish Republic.

Allow a day and a half for a visit to Erzurum.

In the garden and under the colonnade of the **museum** there are fragments of sculpture, stelae and inscriptions from various periods. The first room downstairs contains a heterogeneous collection of objects—stone axes, cutting instruments of obsidian, ceramics, ornaments and mosaics dating from the prehistoric era to the Byzantine period. In the corridor between the downstairs rooms Urartu and Selçuk works are displayed. The second room has an ethnographic collection from the Erzurum area. This includes weapons, ornamented bed linen, clothing, tobacco pouches, cigarette holders and household utensils. In a small room upstairs there are beautifully decorated books and some fine examples of calligraphy.

If you are interested in modern handicrafts, visit the **Halıcılık Enst.**, near the museum. Here young girls are taught carpet-weaving on handlooms.

The **Yakutiye Medresesi**, in a small garden off Cumhuriyet Cad., has been closed to the public for some time.

A covered *medrese*, this was built by Cemaleddin Yakut c 1310 during the reign of the Ilhanid Mongol ruler, Ölcetü. Its **entrance**, elaborately ornamented with stonework carved into geometric and floral designs, has palmette and lion reliefs on the side. The surviving **minaret** on the right, which has lost its crown, is decorated with an intricate pattern in brick and tile. The centre of the courtyard inside the *medrese* is covered by a square vault resting on four tall pillars. On either side there are six cells. One, on the right, has a stairs, which leads to the roof and to the top of the minaret. At the rear of the courtyard is an empty *türbe*. Presumably intended to be Yakut's last resting place, this does not appear to have been used. The *türbe* has a fine conical stone roof divided into arched panels.

The **Lala Mustafa Paşa Camii** dates from 1563. It was built by the fierce and ruthless conqueror of Cyprus, while he was governor of Erzurum. At one time attributed to Sinan, the mosque is now generally believed to be the work of local architects. The squat, rather ugly minaret with its alternating bands of red and grey stone, the use of vaults instead of semi-domes and the clumsy treatment of the NW exterior suggest a provincial hand. The fine stone *mihrab* and the delicately decorated tiles on the window frames are the most interesting features of the interior.

The **Rüstem Paşa Bedesten** is devoted to the manufacture and sale of *Oltutaş* jewellery. Usually set in silver the jet is carved into necklaces, earrings, pendants and *tesbih* (worry beads).

Return to Cumhuriyet Cad. and continue in an easterly direction towards one of Erzurum's great architectural glories, the **Çifte Minareli Medrese**. On the right-hand side of the road, just before the *medrese* and partially concealing it, is the simple, undecorated façade of **Ulu Cami**.

Built in 1179 by Melik Mehmet, grandson of Ali ibn Saltık the founder of the Saltıd rulers of Erzurum, Ulu Cami has been restored and is open once more for worship. One of the earliest of the Selçuk mosques, it retains the rectangular design of the *eyvan* hall, which they borrowed from the Sassanians. Entrance is directly from the street, but the open courtyard of its Persian prototypes, which the Selçuks abandoned because of the harsh climate of Anatolia, is remembered by a opening, now glazed, in the roof. Inside the lines of columns, which divide the structure into seven naves, and the dim lighting combine to produce a feeling of religious awe.

The **Çifte Minareli Medrese** was probably built c 1253 by Hüdavend Hatun, daughter of Sultan Alaeddin Keykubad. It takes its name from the twin minarets, which tower over the **great entrance portal**. Set in a stalactite surmounted recess, this is surrounded by bands of elaborately carved stonework. Note the relief of a **double-headed eagle** to the right of the door and on the left, high up on the façade, there is a **six-pointed star** and an **inscription**. The **fluted minarets**, decorated with turquoise blue tiles, are capped, but do not have **şerefes**. The interior courtyard, sadly overgrown, is flanked by cloisters and galleries on the E and W sides. The **cells**, which housed the students and later the collection of Erzurum's museum, are now empty. At the southern end is the **Hatuniye Türbesi**.

The lane to the right leads to a dusty open space where the **Uç Kümbetler** are located. Two of the mausolea are believed to date from the late 13C or early 14C. Their occupants have not been identified. The third, which sits on an octagonal base, is probably the tomb of Ali ibn Saltık, the founder of the Saltık dynasty, which ruled Erzurum from 1103 for about a century.

A narrow alley opposite Ulu Cami leads to the main entrance of the **Citadel**. There are no signposts. Ask for the 'Kale'.

Built during the reign of the emperor Theodosius II, the citadel's fortifications have been renewed many times. Occupying the highest part of the ancient city, here c 2000m above sea-level, it is mainly visited for the fine panorama it offers of Erzurum and its environs. Photographers will be particularly interested in the view of the Çifte Minareli Medrese. On the S there is an interesting 12C *mescid*. Constructed in the form of a *kümbet*, its *mihrab* is built into the citadel's wall. In the W corner is a Selçuk minaret, which was converted into a clock tower in the 19C. Among the ancient cannon and assorted military impedimenta in the citadel's central court a thoughtful municipality has scattered benches and tables, where weary visitors may take a brief rest from sightseeing or enjoy a quiet picnic.

Buses leave Erzurum's *otogar* at frequent intervals for Pasinler, Sarikamış and Kars. The journey to Kars takes about 5 hours. Leave the city by the Kars Kapı and take the E23 to Horasan, then Road 080 to Karakurt, Sarikamış, Selim and Kars. For a short distance outside Erzurum the E23 is a well-surfaced dual carriage way. Later it conforms to the usual pattern of alternating good and bad stretches.

From Erzurum the E23 climbs steadily, passing through a stretch of dull, uninteresting countryside before descending into the pleasant, green valley of the Aras Nehri, the ancient Araxes. The course of this river takes it from its source in the Bingöl Daglari, c 100km S of Erzurum, to the Caspian Sea, a distance of more than 1000km.

Pasinler, c 37km from Erzurum, a small spa town in a pretty setting, is of no great interest to the modern traveller. Here in 1400 Tamerlane received a deputation of Turcomen rulers, who begged him to restore the lands, which had been taken from them by Beyazit I.

Not far from Pasinler is a fortress known as **Hasan Kale**. Towering over the road, this Armenian structure was restored by Uzun Hasan (1433–1478), the ruler of the White Sheep Turcomans. Apart from some splendid views over the Aras valley, there is nothing in Hasan Kale, now a ruined shell, to detain the visitor.

About 18km from Pasinler is the village of **Köprüköy**, formerly Çobandede. On the outskirts a fine Ottoman Bridge more than 220m long spans the Aras. Believed by some to have been built by Sinan, this six-arched structure is closed to traffic.

The Aras runs parallel with the road to 25km **Horasan**. In this market town the roads divide. The E23 continues through Eleskirt, Agri and Dogubayazit to the Iranian border. Take the left-hand fork to Sarikamis and Kars.

After Horasan there is a marked change in the landscape. The road leaves the Aras river at 55km **Karakurt** and begins a steady climb through pleasant alpine pastures dotted with clumps of pine trees to 27km **Sarikamış**.

Once a favourite retreat of the Tsars of Russia, Sarikamış (2100m) has been developed as a winter sports' resort. The *Turislik Oteli* is recommended. With careful planning even visitors who travel by public transport can make day trips to Kars and Ani and stay overnight in the hotel.

Shortly after leaving the tree-clad slopes of Sarikamış the road descends to the great plain of Kars. Here during the warm days of eastern Turkey's brief summer large herds of horses roam at will. Feeding on the lush grass, they fix the passing traveller with a clear gaze, but the labouring engine of an ancient bus will send them galloping away into the distance.

About 10km from Kars look out for the ruined **Kümbet Kilise**. This 10C structure, which lies c 200m back from the road on the right-hand side, apparently formed part of an Armenian church. Amongst the damaged sculpture inside the building are the symbols of the Four Evangelists.

KARS (estimated population 70,400). The name Kars is believed to come from a Georgian word, '*kari*', which means gate. For centuries its rulers have controlled the valley of the Kars Çayı, one of the important gateways to Anatolia. Many armies have fought for its possession and some have left evidence of their presence.

Today, the provincial capital of a sparsely-populated region, Kars is a bleak, untidy place of litle charm. Most visitors only stay there long enough to get their permits for the ruined city of Ani (see below).

Accommodation and Information. None of the hotels in Kars can be recommended. The best hotel in the area is at Sarikamış. The **Tourist Information Office** is at Ordu Cad. No. 241.

Transport. There are regular bus services to Erzurum, Ankara and İstanbul and less frequently S to Doğubayazit. Turkish Railways operate a train service to Erzurum and points westward and provide a connection with c 87km Leninakan in Armenia. If you are staying at Sarikamış check the departure time of the last bus and last dolmuş from Kars, as even during the holiday season they leave in mid-afternoon.

History. Little is known about the early history of Kars, but it seems likely that it attracted settlers from the earliest times. In AD 961 the Bagratid kingdom of Kars was founded by Mushegh, the brother of Ashot III, the Merciful, (951–977) who had made Ani his capital. The Bagratid dynasty came into being in 806, when Ashot Bagratuni was recognised as prince of Armenia by the Abbasid Caliph Harun ar-Raschid. The Bagratids continued to rule until the mid 11C when, weakened by the attacks of the Byzantines and the Sekçuks, they disappear from history. In 1053 the Selçuks Turks attacked Kars and in 1064 the city was taken by Alp Arslan.

In 1205 Kars succumbed to a siege mounted by a Georgian army and became part of the kingdom of Georgia. Incorporated in the Ottoman Empire in 1514, it was fought over by the Turks and the Russians on more than one occasion in the centuries that followed. During the Crimean War (1854–56) Kars' joint Turkish-British garrison was forced to surrender after holding out for five months against a superior Russian force. Captured again by the Russians in 1877, the city remained in their hands until 1920, when it was returned to Turkish rule.

Church of the Holy Apostles. Built c 930 by the Bagratid king Abas I (928–951) this is located in a run down area not far from the Kars Çayı. A solid square building, with apse-like projections on each wall, supports a circular drum above which there is a tiled conical roof. There are roughly-executed carvings of the Twelve Apostles on the outside of the drum. After the Ottoman conquest the church was converted into a mosque. During the Russian occupation of Kars it became an Orthodox church. Later it was a store and it housed Kars' collection of antiquities until the opening of the new museum. It is now empty. Access to the interior, which contains little of interest, depends on one being able to find the caretaker.

Near the Church of the Holy Apostles is the *Taş Köprü*, a 15C stone bridge.

Kars lies under the menacing shape of the **citadel**, 'out of the plain a harsh and gloomy outline began to rise; square, squat, dark; stone walls ringing the stony hill; a fortress formidable enough to guard the most romantic frontier of the imagination' (Glazebrook). The citadel has endured many transformations. Constructed by the Armenians, restored by the Selçuks, it was strengthened by the Ottomans in the 15C and later by the Russian invaders. The garrison quarters and central keep were enclosed by a formidable double row of fortifications. The citadel is not open to the public.

The new **museum** on the eastern outskirts of the city has an small collection of archaeological finds from the surrounding area, notably from Ani, and a good ethnographic section, where clothes, household utensils, jewellery, carpets and kilims are displayed.

Kars is not a beautiful place. Apart from the citadel and the Church of the Holy Apostles there are few reminders of its ancient past. It has an air of transience and impermanence, often a characteristic of frontier settlements.

Apart from a few 19C Neo-Classical buildings, which were erected by the Russians, its architecture is unremarkable.

Before visiting **Ani**, which lies close to the frontier with Armenia, it is necessary to obtain a special permit from the Emniyet Müdürlüğü in Kars. This can be done through the Tourist Information Office. Cameras may now be taken to Ani.

The route from Kars to 47km Ani is signposted. There is an excellent new road to the site. Take a picnic.

In late summer cattle and sheep forage in the unfenced fields by the roadside. Tractor-drawn trailers laden with straw make slow and eratic progress to isolated hamlets. Peregrines and eagles quarter the great plain in search of their prey. Away to the E, in Armenia. a snow-capped peak is stark against the deep blue sky.

History. Ani occupied a high triangular plateau protected on the E by the deep valley of the Arpa Çayı, on the W by the ravine of the Alaca Çay and on the NE by a double line of fortifications erected by the Bagratid kings. There is some evidence that a settlement existed here as early as the second millennium BC and there are references to the castle of Ani dating from the 5C AD. However, the city's history really began in 806 when Ashot Bagratuni was chosen by the Abbasid Caliph Harun ar-Raschid to be prince of the Armenians. In 862 his descendant, Ashot I, son of Smbat the Confessor, was recognised by the Abbasids as Prince of Princes and in 885 he was crowned king of Armenia. Ashot received golden crowns from the Caliph and the Byzantine emperor as a sign of their approval. His successors were able to persuade their nobles to unite behind them and for almost two centuries they continued to extend and consolidate their power.

The Bagratid dynasty remained in favour with the Arabs. In 922 Ashot II (915–928) was given the title of 'Shahanshah', king of kings by the Caliph. After Ashot III (952–977), the Merciful, moved his capital to Ani in 961, he and his successors began to enrich it with fine buildings and beautiful churches. Ani's golden age came during the reign of Gagik I (989–1020). All the arts flourished and the population of the city almost reached 100,000, so that it rivalled Constantinople in fame and power and was known throughout Christendom. Its defences were not neglected. Gagik strengthened the fortifications on the NE side of the plateau. This period of greatness was not soon forgotten. In the early years of the 14C the author of 'The Travels of Sir John Mandeville' wrote of 'the city of Any in which were wont to be a thousand churches'.

The decline began during the reign of Gagik's successors—the easy-going John Smbat (1020–41) and Ashot IV, the Valiant (1020 19640). They divided the kingdom between them, John Smbat continuing to rule from Ani. He willed his share to the emperor Basil II and when he died childless in 1040 the Byzantines came to claim their inheritance. The Armenians resisted the invaders. In 1042 the boy king Gagik II (1042–45), John Smbat's nephew and successor, with the able assistance of Prince Vahram Pahlavuni, defeated the Byzantines. In a terrible battle beneath the walls of Ani more than 20,000 of their soldiers perished miserably. Unable to win by force of arms, the Byzantines resorted to trickery. Promising him safe conduct, they invited Gagik to come to Constantinople to sign a peace treaty. However, the emperor breaking the oath which he had sworn, treacherously seized the young king and imprisoned him. The Byzantines then occupied Ani. Their gain was short-lived. The Selçuk Turks, under Alp Arslan, took it from them in 1064. This marked the beginning of the end of Byzantine rule in Anatolia. Seven years later the Selçuks defeated them decisively at Manzikert and captured the emperor Romanus IV Diogenes.

In the 12C and early 13 C the Selçuks' domination of eastern Anatolia was broken by an alliance of Georgian and Armenian princes. New churches and monastic settlements were built in Ani and there was a revival of interest in the arts. The arrival of the Mongols in Anatolia in 1236 checked, but did not destroy, this brief renaissance. In 1319 Ani was devastated by a terrible earthquake and its demoralised inhabitants began to move away from the city. This exodus continued, accelerated, no doubt, by the atrocities of Tamerlane and his savage soldiers. No inscription later than the middle of the 14C has been found here. A dead city, its buildings and churches abandoned to the owl and the jackal, it passed into oblivion. The mystic poet Aristakes of Lastivert

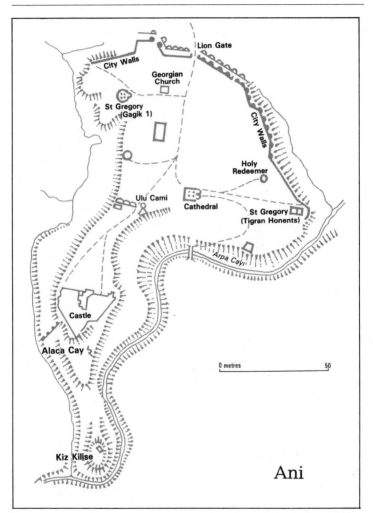

Ani

wrote movingly of the last days of Ani: 'The voices and the sermons of the priests are silent now. The chandeliers are extinguished now and the lamps are dimmed, the sweet fragrance of incence is gone, the altar of Our Lord is covered with dust and ashes....tell the mountains and the hills, the trees of the dense woodlands that they too may weep over our destruction'.

The great double wall, with its massive square and circular towers, was erected by the Bagratids to protect the vulnerable NE side of the city. Largely intact, it glows blood red in the sunlight. Entrance is through the **Arslan Kapısı**, the Lion Gate. This gets its name from the relief of a charging lion on the upper part of the inside wall. Beyond the gate is a large sloping plateau, which was once occupied by the city. Scattered among the rough grass and coarse vegetation are churches, towers, and mosques in various stages of dilapidation. From a distance many appear undamaged.

The Armenian city of Ani

Allow at least three hours for a visit to Ani. There is much to see and the area to be covered is large.

The path from the gate leads to the ruins of the so-called **Georgian Church**. Dedicated in 1218 this has a number of interesting reliefs depicting scenes from the life of the Virgin Mary.

About 100m to the right are the foundations of the **Church of St Gregory the Illuminator**. One of three in Ani dedicated to the saint, this circular church was constructed c 998 during the reign of Gagik I.

An Arascid prince, Gregory had been brought up as a Christian in Cappadocia. Returning to Armenia to convert his childhood friend, king Trdat III (AD 287–330), he was tortured and thrown into prison, as his father had brought about the assassination of Khosrov, Trdat's father. During his 13 years imprisonment he was kept alive by food brought to him by a pious widow. Released at last at the request of Trdat's sister, he cured the king of lycanthropy. Trdat became a Christian, proscribed paganism and set about enthusiastically smashing idols and closing their shrines. According to tradition these events took place in AD 301, so the Armenians claimed that their nation was the first to adopt Christianity as the state religion.

Do not miss the 11C **Church of the Holy Redeemer**, the great **Cathedral** and the **third church dedicated to St Gregory**. The latter is on the edge of the precipice above the Arpa Çayı and was built in the early 13C by a merchant, Tigran Honents. The interior is decorated with some wonderful frescoes.

51

Erzurum to Sivas

Total distance 448km. Erzurum—17km İlıca—26km Aşkale—38km Tercan—(83km Altıntepe)—18km Erzincan—(54km Kemah)—(76km Kelkit)—201km Zara—65km Sivas—(83km Kangal)—(95km Balıklı Kaplıca)—(174km Divriği).

This is a long journey which, ideally, should be broken at Erzincan. However, because of earthquake damage, there are no hotels in that town at present. It may be possible to stay with a Turkish family. Enquire at the Tourist Information Office about private accommodation.

Leave Erzurum by the E23. This crosses the Erzurum Ovası, a great grassy plain bounded on the S by the Palendöken Dağları, on the E by the Kargapazarı Dağları, and on the N by the Mescit Dağları. At (17km) İlıca there are mineral springs. Continue to (26km) Aşkale, a busy little town with a population of 15,500.

At Aşkale the road divides. The right fork will take you over the mountains, by way of Bayburt and Gümüşhane, to Trabzon (see Route 58). The E23 to Erzincan, soon begins a steady climb and enters a stretch of rugged country. Here a handful of olive trees, scattered among the contorted rock formations, fight for survival with the sparse, coarse vegetation. After c18km you pass through the Tercan Tüneli. Just beyond the tunnel there is a picnic area, with drinkable water, on the left side of the road.

In the autumn the poplars in valley of the Çat river are ablaze with colour. Shepherds and goatherds, guarding their flocks, acknowledge the passing traffic with a languid wave and then turn away to guide the grazing animals to fresh pastures. It is a scene from the Golden Age.

Just before the Tercan Barajı the river broadens, deepens and flows more slowly. In **Tercan** there are **two Selçuk monuments** which deserve more than a cursory examination. Ask for directions and for the *bekçi* who will open them for you. Mama Hatun, a Selçuk princess, who helped Saladin in his campaigns in this part of Anatolia, is buried in the *Mama Hatun Kümbet*. The architect was Ebul Nema bin Mufaddal from Ahlat. Constructed in 1182, it is in two parts: the prayer room with its *mihrab* is slightly above ground level; the sarcophagus of the princess is in the vault below.

The ground plan of the tomb is in the shape of a rosette formed by eight niches. The convex sections of the *türbe's* outer wall are separated by slender ribs which rise to the delicate, pointed roof. A circular outer wall with 11 niches on the inside, and an elaborately ornamented portal, surrounds the tomb. Just inside the door stairs lead to the top of the wall. On the left there is a *mihrab*. There are said to be resemblances between this *kümbet* and the 3C BC tombs of the Huns near Lake Aral.

A short distance to W is a well-preserved *han* of the 'concentrically planned' type. Similar *hans* are to be found at Alara between Antalya and Alanya and at Afşin (see above). Entrance to the *han* is through a richly decorated door. Inside there are lofty galleries and rather **unusual stabling arrangements**: camels were kept in the high-roofed stables, horses and mules in lower ones. Note the large kitchen.

Near the village the **late 12C bridge** is also named after Mama Hatun.

Shortly after leaving Tercan you enter a wide plain watered by the Fırat Nehri (the Euphrates). The landscape is particularly beautiful where a road leads S to Tunceli. There are many vineyards in this fertile and intensively cultivated countryside, particularly near the aptly named village of Üzümlü. Its name is derived from *üzüm*, the Turkish word for grape. Just before Erzincan a turning on the right leads to the site of ancient Altıntepe.

ERZİNCAN, a friendly, busy place, appears to be making a good recovery from the last earthquake which caused a great deal of damage. Unfortunately, its hotels have not yet been rebuilt. If you wish to stay overnight enquire at the **Tourist Information Office** in the Yeni Vilayet Binası where they may be able to arrange accommodation with a Turkish family. No buildings of historical interest remain in the city.

History. Apart from its name, Erek, little is known about the early history of Erzincan. Xenophon mentions the presence of Chaldaeans, i.e. worshippers of Khaldi, the supreme god of the Urartians, in this part of Anatolia (Anabasis IV 3 and V 5) and there are references to a golden statue of Anaïtis, a Urartian goddess sometimes equated with Artemis, in a temple in Erek. According to Strabo (*Geography*, 11.16) the followers of Anaïtis practised sacred prostitution… 'the most illustrious men… actually consecrate to her their daughters while maidens; and it is the custom for these first to be prostituted in the temple of the goddess for a long time and after this to be given in marriage; and no one disdains to live in wedlock with such a woman'. There is some uncertainty about the fate of the statue at Anaïtis. One account states that it was stolen sometime in the 1C BC by the wife of Tigranes, another that it was destroyed by St Gregory the Illuminator.

The city was sacked by the Mongols in 1235 and 1243. Towards the end of the 13C it was under the rule of the Akkoyunlu. After the defeat of Beyazit I at the battle of Çubuk near Ankara in July 1402, Erzincan and the rest of Anatolia were at the mercy of Tamerlane. The countryside was laid waste and thousands were slaughtered or sent into slavery. Beyazit died in captivity at Akşehir in 1403, Tamerlane two years later.

From 1916 to 1918 the city was occupied by the Russians. Twice in this century it was almost completely destroyed by earthquakes.

Altıntepe, the Golden Hill, an important Urartian site, is c 18km to the E of the city and 2km to the N of the Erzurum road. The site was first explored methodically by Turkish archaeologists between 1959–66, but artefacts had been found here in 1938 during the construction of the railway line from Sivas to Erzurum. The archaeologists discovered the remains of a **palace** and a **temple** which they dated to the end of the 8C or the beginning of the 7C BC, and a number of tombs. The palace and temple were in an area protected by a **double line of fortifications**. Salients and casemates protected the defenders manning the massive stone and brick walls. The **palace audience chamber** measured 44m by 25m. Its roof was supported by 18 columns. The walls, which were 3m thick, were decorated with elaborate designs of palmettes, winged sphinxes, animals and sacred trees. Bright colours were favoured—blue, beige, red, black, white and sometimes green were used. The paintings show strong Assyrian influence but this is modified by local taste in the choice of design and style.

The 15m square **temple** had walls c 4.5m thick. Built towards the end of the 8C BC, it stood in a temenos surrounded by colonnades. It was dedicated to Khaldi. The **base** of the cult statue is against the wall facing the entrance. Raised **stone benches** for the officiating hierophants are arranged around the walls. Sacrifices were made at an external altar near the entrance on the SE side of the building. Many votive offerings of a military nature—club handles, shields, helmets—were found in the temple. The building was destroyed sometime in the 7C, but the palace continued to be used until the early 6C, when, perhaps, the site was abandoned.

The **burial chambers**, outside the walls on the S side of the site, were constructed of large stone blocks. When complete they were covered over with soil. In each tomb there are several vaults. The grave goods include weapons, furniture and horse trappings. Their quality suggests that those buried here were persons of some importance, perhaps members of the nobility. Four **stelae** mark the place where offerings were made to the dead.

Finds from Altıntepe in the Anatolian Civilizations Museum in Ankara include a large bronze cauldron decorated with bulls' heads on the rim and a supporting bronze tripod, ivory statuettes of seated lions and of a winged demon, a gold relief of a sphinx, gold buttons and an ivory mask.

If you have time visit Kemah and Kelkit. **Kemah**, the ancient Kamakha, is 54km to the SE of Erzincan and has the ruins of a **Byzantine fortress**, the 13C **türbe of Sultan Melik**, the **Gazi türbe** and the **Gülalibey Cami**. To the SE, near Ovacık, is the **Munzur Vadisi National Park** which offers excellent walking by quiet trout streams. There are facilities for camping, picnicking and fishing. Near **Kelkit**, 76km to the N of Erzincan, are the scant remains of a ruined Roman fortress and aqueduct in ancient Sadak.

Zara, c 201km from Erzincan has two Islamic monuments which merit a visit, the **Çarşı Cami** and the **Şeyh Merzuban Türbesi**. Nearby is **Tödürga Lake**, a popular place for picnics. There are facilities for boating and fishing and a small café by the lake shore offers light refreshments.

SİVAS, capital of the province of the same name, has a population of 197,300. It has some of the most interesting Selçuk monuments in Anatolia. The kilims and carpets made here base their designs on a rich tradition of folklore and have a widespread reputation for quality and originality.

Accommodation and Information. The city has two hotels registered with the Ministry of Tourism, the two star *Köşk Oteli*, Atatürk Cad. 11, and the one star *Sultan Oteli* at Belediye Sok. 16. The **Tourist Information Office** is in the Hükümet Konağı, Kat. 4. There are frequent bus services from the *otogar* to İstanbul, Ankara and other cities. The Doğu Ekpres provides a rail connection with Ankara, İstanbul, Erzincan, Erzurum and Kars.

History. Sivas has had a long and chequered history. It was known to the Romans as Megalopolis which suggests that it was a place of some size and importance. In the 1C BC the triumvir, Gnaeus Pompeius Magnus, granted the city certain civic rights. During the reign of Augustus, it changed its name to Sebasteia. The emperor Licinius (AD 308–324), who was castigated by Eusebius for his treachery and cruelty, initiated a campaign of persecution against the Christians. Among those who suffered and died were the Forty Martyrs of Sebasteia. Members of the Legio XII Fulminata, they refused to abjure their faith and were forced to stand naked on the ice of a frozen lake. A warm bath was placed on the bank to tempt them to apostasise. Only one soldier weakened. His place was taken immediately by a member of the guard who was impressed by the faith and heroism of the young soldiers. On the morrow all but one, the youngest, were dead. His mother carried the dying boy in her arms and, when he too expired, placed his body with the others. The Forty Martyrs are still venerated by the Eastern Churches, but the Catholic Church suppressed the cult in 1969. Their martyrdom was the subject of many paintings including one by Pontormo which now hangs in the Uffizi Gallery in Florence.

Justinian restored the city's fortifications in the 6C, but these were not sufficiently strong to keep out the Persian Chosroes II in 575. In 712 it was sacked by the Arabs. An exchange of territory between the Byzantines and the Armenians brought 40,000 Armenians from near Lake Van to Sebasteia and the surrounding area where they established a new kingdom. After the battle of Manzikert in 1071, Sebasteia, like its neighbours, came under Selçuk rule and had its name changed to Sivas. From 1080 it was ruled by the Turcoman Danishmendids and later by the Selçuks under Kılıç Arslan. Sivas was captured by the Mongols in the 13C. A Mongol governor of the city, named Eretna, established a dynasty which ruled here until 1380 when it was supplanted by the vizier Kadi Burhaneddin. He was killed by the Akkoyunlu in 1386. Tamerlane attacked the city in 1400 and 1402. He slaughtered all the defenders, Muslims and Christians, and had the city's walls destroyed. For Sivas there followed a period of decline. During the Ottoman centuries it was just a stopping place on the trade route to Persia and Syria.

In 1919 the famous Sivas Congress under the presidency of Atatürk established the Society for the Defence of the Rights of Anatolia and Thrace. This gave the independence movement a national character.

Sivas is a relatively compact city and all the principal places of interest may be visited on foot in the course of a single day.

The **Çifte Minareli Medrese** was established in 1271 by the Mongol governor Şemseddin Mehmed Cüve as a school for the study of the Koran and the sayings of the Prophet. The architect is believed to have been Kölük Bin Abdullah. Today only a section of the E wall of the building remains standing. Two magnificent red brick minarets flank an elaborately decorated portal. Note the inscription below a deep niche formed of receding stalactites. The pilasters on each side of the entrance and the round buttresses at the corners are covered with a delicate lace-like tracery of abstract patterns.

Nearby is the **Bürüciye Medresesi**. According to an **inscription** over the entrance, this was founded in 1271 during the reign of Giyaseddin Keyhüsrev by a certain Hibetullah Burucerdioğlu Muzaffer from Iran. It now houses a museum in which objects from the Selçuk period are displayed. On the left of the entrance is the *türbe* of the founder and on the right a *mescid*. A touching inscription on the façade of the tomb reads, 'This is the tomb of Muzaffer of Bürücird, the humble servant and homeless stranger. May Allah forgive his sins'. The columns and some of the capitals on the N and S sides of the central courtyard are of Byzantine origin.

To the right of the Bürüciye Medresesi is the **Şifaiye Medresesi**. It was built in 1217 by the Selçuk Sultan Keykavus I as a hospital, medical school and mental asylum. The treatment of mental patients was in advance of its time. Music and hypnosis were frequently used by the doctors. The building was later turned into a *medrese*. The entrance, under a deep niche ornamented with stalactites, is surrounded by a finely carved stone border. From the entrance hall you enter a courtyard with colonnades on the right and left. In his will Keykavus requested that he be buried in the hospital which he had founded. His tomb is in a *türbe* whose walls are decorated with enamel bricks on the S side of the building.

The **Kale Camii** dates from the Ottoman period. It was built in 1580 by a governor of Sivas, Mahmut Paşa, during the reign of Murat III. Its sensitive design and fine materials combine to make it one of the most beautiful Ottoman mosques in Sivas.

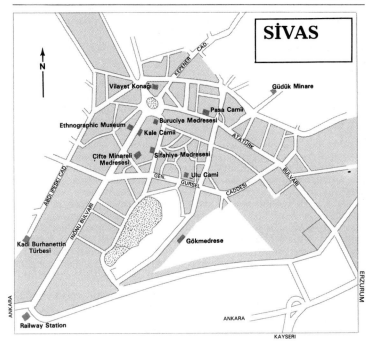

According to records in the Sivas Museum **Ulu Cami** was built by Kızıl
Arslan bin İbrahim in 1196 during the period of the Danishmendid emirate.
This rectangular building, measuring 45m by 31m, opens on to a large
courtyard of c 1670 sq m. The prayer hall is divided into 11 sections by ten
rows of columns. These support the pointed arches on which the roof joists
rest. Half way up the cylindrical brick minaret, which dates from the 13C,
there is an **inscription** in Cufic characters.

The so-called **Güdük Minare**—its name means the stumpy minaret—is
the *türbe* of Şeyh Hasan Bey, the son of Eretna (see above). His remains lie
in a black marble sarcophagus in the tomb chamber.

Gök in Turkish means the heavens, the sky, blue, sky-blue or beautiful
and the **Gök Medrese** gets its name from the exquisite blue enamel tiles
on its twin minarets. Built in 1271 by a Christian architect from Konya
named Kaloyan al-Qunewi, for Sahip Ata Fahreddin Ali, this is one of the
most remarkable Selçuk monumments in Anatolia. The elaborately decorated **entrance** is flanked by the **minarets** which project from the façade.
Their square bases are ornamented with carved abstract patterns. Beyond
the **great door** is a large courtyard with lecture and study rooms on two
floors on each side and a fountain on the left. Note the faience tiles in the
mescid. Some of the capitals of the columns in the porticoes are Byzantine.

The Sivas Congress (see above) took place in the large building near the
Atatürk memorial. This now houses the **Ethnographical Museum** which
has a display of costumes, household utensils, weapons etc from Sivas
province. On the first floor are the room where the Congress was held,
Atatürk's bedroom and the rooms allocated to members of his suite.

While in Sivas you can visit Kangal, Balıklı Çermik and Divriği, a round trip of c 350km. Take a picnic. Leave Sivas by the Malatya road. Just outside the city the **Eğri Köprü**, the twisted bridge, spans the Kızılı İrmak. Its name refers to the bend in the middle which offers maximum resistance to the pressure exerted by the waters of the river when it is in spate. Keeping the bold mass of the Tecer mountains to the S and E, continue through a stretch of rolling uplands and cross the **Yağdonduran Geçidi** (1750m). After c 72km take a left turn on to a minor road signposted Kangal and Divriği.

Kangal has given its name to a breed of dogs used for centuries by Turkish shepherds to defend their flocks from wolves and other wild animals. When working, the dogs usually wear an iron collar liberally sprinkled with long sharp spikes as a protection. In recent years they have become increasingly popular as guard dogs and, indeed, as domestic pets. The kennels around Kangal welcome visitors. Ask the Tourist Information Office in Sivas to make the necessary arrangements or enquire in the village.

From Kangal continue for a further 12km to **Balıklı Çermik**, a thermal establishment much favoured by suffers from eczema, psoriasis and other skin complaints. The treatment here is somewhat unusual. During each immersion in the 38°C water thousands of tiny fish and small snakes, which live in the baths, congregate in shoals around the patient and nibble happily at the affected parts. Apparently the treatment is very pleasant. Patients say that it resembles a delicate, soothing massage. It is claimed to be very effective. Many sufferers are cured.

From Balıklı Çermik continue for c 79km to **Divriği** which is hidden away in a deep valley watered by the Çaltı Çayı. At an altitude of c 1200m, it is often cut off for long periods in the winter. Divriği is visited mainly for the splendid monuments which were built towards the end of the 12C and the beginning of the 13C by its Mengücekid rulers.

History. Divriği has a long and turbulent history which caused some interesting resonances in the religious and social life of Western Europe. In the beginning it was Tephrike, an isolated outpost of the Byzantine Empire among the high peaks of the Tecer Dağları. In the 9C the Islamic ruler of Malatya allowed members of the Paulicians, a heretical Christian sect persecuted by the Byzantines, to settle here. With their Islamic protectors, they defended it enthusiastically against their persecutors. In 969 the Paulicians were subjected to ethnic cleansing by the Byzantines. They were transported to Thrace. In time their beliefs spread to Bulgaria where they were taken up by the priest Bogomil, the eponymous founder of Bogomilism. Soon Bosnia and Herzegovina were infected and the heresy spread to northern Italy, southern Germany and southern France. In Provence its followers were known as Cathars or Albigensians. The heresy was based on the Manichaean belief in two equally powerful principals, God and the Devil. Their adherents rejected every form of outward worship and all ecclesiastical authority. As a consequence they were regarded as a threat to established order and Church and State combined to suppress them.

After the battle of Manzikert, Divriği was ruled by the Mengücekids on behalf of the Selçuks. The Mengücekids erected the beautiful buildings that are the town's glory. They were dispossessed by the Mongols who were succeeded by the rulers of Sivas. In 1516 Divriği was taken by the Ottomans.

At the entrance to the town are the ruins of the **castle**. Founded by the Byzantines, this was restored and repaired several times. The present structure is believed to date from the 13C. The castle **mosque** was constructed in 1180 by Hasan bin Firuz from Merga for the Mengücek Seif ad Din Şahanşah. The central nave is covered by a barrel vault, the two side aisles by four domes. The portals are decorated with stylised designs of foliage and geometric forms in stone and plain and turquoise glazed brick.

Note the stepped second entrance on the right side. This is an early example of *mafils* (ruler's balcony) in Anatolian mosques.

At the foot of the hill is the **Sitte Melik Kümbet** (1196). This is an octagonal structure of cut stone surmounted by a pyramid-shaped roof. The geometric design on the façade is based on traditional ornamental patterns.

Divriği's **Ulu Cami** and **Şifahane**, which cover an area c 31m by 62m, were built on the orders of Ahmed Şah and his wife Melike Turan in 1228–29. The architect was Hurrem Şah from Ahlat. Entrance is by four portals elaborately decorated with the **Selçuk double-headed eagle**, falcons and floral and geometric designs reminiscent of Persian stucco and Armenian manuscripts. The mosque has a central nave flanked by two aisles. Note the *mihrab* niche which is surrounded by beautifully carved moulding. The dome in front is crowned, externally, by a pyramid-shaped cone. The very fine *mimber* of 1241 is the work of Ahmed bin İbrahim, a craftsman from Tiflis. The Şifahane (hospital) is of the four *eyvan medrese* type with a covered central courtyard. The cylindrical columns on the right and octagonal columns on the left are surmounted by large, unusual capitals. In the centre of the courtyard there is a pool under an oculus. There are two storeys above the entrance which is on the W side of the complex. The **inscription** over the portal gives the date of construction.

Also in Divriği is the **Kamereddin Kümbet**. This resembles the Sitte Melik Kümbet in design and construction.

52

Sivas to Ankara

Total distance 431km. Sivas—42km Yıldızeli—(c 39km Çiftlik Hanı)—(c 13km Horostepe)—(c 9km Tokat)—(10km Gümenek)—(c 47km Niksar)—(32km Pazar)—(c 13km Turhal)—(c 24km Zile)—(c 21km Masat Hüyük)—(c 104km Çınçınlı Sultan Hanı—(**Alişar** Hüyük)—(c 36km Kerkenes)—179km Yozgat—(38km Boğazkale)—(c 2.5km Yazılıkaya)—(36km Alacahöyük)—144km Kırıkkale—(c 23km Kalecik)—(c4km Hasanoğlan)—66km Ankara.

The journey from Sivas to Ankara is long and rather tedious. Fortunately, it is possible to do it in stages by making excursions to Tokat and Boğazkale, important Hittite and Pontic sites. A stopover of two days at each place is suggested. Tokat has several hotels and there are motels at Boğazkale and nearby Sungurlu.

Leave Sivas by the E23 signposted to Yıldızeli, Yozgat and Ankara. At (42km) **Yıldızeli**, a run-down village, there are the ruins of a large *caravanserai* built by the Mongols in the 15C. Continue over the **Çamlibel Geçidi** (1980m) to Tokat. On the northern side of the pass you enter a new world. The tree-lined valleys of the Pontus are in startling contrast to the bare, brown hills of central Anatolia. At c 39km, just to the N of Çamlibel, there are the remains of the **Çiftlik Hanı**. This was one of the *han*s on the trade route between Sivas and Amasya which were built by Mahperi Hatun, the mother of Keyhusrev II, at the beginning of the 13C. A further 13km is **Horos Tepesi**, the Cock Hill. The ruined **medieval castle** on the left side of the road is believed to be sited on a fortress constructed by the kings of

Pontus to defend their realm. There are several **rock tombs** nearby. At Keşik a similar rock tomb was used as a chapel by the Byzantines.

TOKAT, 9km, a provincial capital, on the banks of the Tokat Suyu, rests comfortably on the southern slopes of the Yaylacık Dağı. Like Sivas, Tokat is visited mainly for its fine Islamic buildings.

There are three hotels which have been inspected by the Tourism Ministry: the four-star *Tokat Oteli* in Demir Köprü Mey.; the *Plevne Oteli* in Gaziomanpaşa Bul. 83, and the *Turist Oteli* in Cumhuriyet Mey., both of which have one star. The **Tourist Information Office** is at Taşhan Turizm Sitesi 25. There are frequent coach services to Ankara, İstanbul and other cities.

Tokat's **museum** is housed in a Selçuk building, the **Gök Medrese**. Its large collection includes sarcophagi, ceramics, statues, grave stelae, glass, coins and architectural fragments from the Roman, Byzantine and Selçuk periods and axes, tekke objects, musical instruments, standards, clothing and embroidery from the Ottoman period.

History. Tokat grew up around the walls of the fortress of Dazimon which guarded the southern approaches to Comana Pontica c 9km to the NE. Strabo links that ancient city with its namesake in Cappadocia where the Anatolian mother goddess was also worshipped. Some believe that it was a Hittite foundation of the second millennium BC. At Comana Pontica the temple dedicated to the mother goddess was served by an aristocratic, hereditary priesthood. The high priest, who ranked next to the king, controlled the 6000 slaves who tilled the land and maintained the temple buildings. The cult statue of the goddess was believed to be the venerable image of Artemis which Orestes stole from the land of the Taurians with the assistance of his sister Iphigeneia (see Euriphides' *Iphigeneia in Tauris*). Strabo states that the people of Comana lived in luxury. So many women 'make gain from their persons', as he put it delicately, that Comana resembled Corinth, a city notorious for the number of its prostitutes. This gave rise to the proverb, 'Not for every man is the voyage to Corinth (necessary)'.

The orgiastic twice-yearly festivals of the goddess, who was called Ma in Pontus, were celebrated enthusiastically with a wild procession through the streets of the city. The temple servants bearing the statue of the goddess were followed by the hierophant, who wore a royal diadem, the temple prostitutes and a crowd of delirious, self-flagellating worshippers. The fortunes of Comana Pontica reached their apogee during the Roman period. After the conversion of the people of Pontus to Christianity, pagan worship was abolished and the city was deserted. Tokat took its place.

Of little importance under the Byzantines, Tokat fell into Turkish hands in the 11C. It was ruled first by the Danishmendids, then by the Selçuks under Kılıç Arslan II and his son Rükn ad Din. Captured and sacked by the Mongols in the second part of the 13C, it was governed by Eretna of Sivas and his successors. Tokat was looted by Uzun Hasan of the Akkoyunlu in 1471. Later in that century it came under Ottoman rule.

Tokat's **Gök Medrese** was built c 1270 by Mu'in al-Din Süleyman. The entrance door is surmounted by a deep niche ornamented with stalactites. This leads to the vestibule and, beyond, to a large courtyard which has porticoes on the W, N and E sides. On the S there is a deep *eyvan* surmounted by galleries. The rooms behind the porticoes, occupied by students until the early 19C, house a collection of antiquities. Some of the blue tiles which gave the building its name (*Gök* means sky or blue) survive.

In the SE corner of the *medrese* there is a room containing several sarcophagi. In one rest the bones of the founder, Mu'in al-Din Süleyman. He was Kılıç Arslan IV's *pervane*. This word may be translated as 'moth circling a candle' or 'protector', but Mu'in al-Din Süleyman was more the *éminence grise* who wielded real power. In 1264 he had the sultan strangled at a banquet and arranged to be appointed regent to the infant successor. Twelve years later he joined with the Mamelukes of Egypt in a plot to expel the Mongols from Anatolia and to make himself Sultan of Rum. After some initial successes the plot collapsed and the Mameluke army returned home.

In 1278 Mu'in al-Din Süleyman was captured and executed by the victorious Mongols. The moth was singed by the flame.

The **Hatuniye Camii and Medresesi** on the other side of the square were erected in 1485 by Beyazit II in honour of his mother, Gülbahar Hatun. A vaulted portico with reused classical columns leads to the domed prayer room of the mosque.

The **Voyvoda Hanı** was built in the early 17C, mainly for the use of Armenian merchants who had traded in Pontus for many centuries. The two-storey buildings of the *han* surround a rectangular courtyard.

In Sulu Sokağı there are the Ottoman **Ali Paşa Camii** which was built in 1573, and the early 15C **Paşa Hamami**. Ali Paşa, who may have been descended from Eretna, the founder of the Eretnid Turcoman dynasty, is buried in the garden of the mosque which bears his name. The bazaar in Sulu Sokağı is famous for its copperware. The early 13C **Yağıbasan Medrese**, now in ruins, was one of the first covered *medreses* to be built in Anatolia. The *eyvans* and students' rooms were arranged around a courtyard covered by a squinched central dome (see Niksar below).

To the N of the square are the **Halef Gazi Tekkesi** and the **Sümbül Baba Zaviyesi**, both late 13C dervish foundations. A little farther on are the ruins of the Mongol Emir Nureddin Şen Timur's *türbe* which dates from 1313. The road is carried over the Yeşil İrmak by a **Selçuk bridge** of 1250.

Tokat's **castle**, difficult of access, was built on a rocky eminence to the N of the town. Little remains on the western spur, but there are the ruins of some Ottoman buildings on the eastern crag.

Several Hittite and Pontic sites to the N and W of Tokat merit a visit. All may be reached by car in the course of a day. Take the road N signposted Niksar. At c 10km **Gümenek** there are the scant remains of **Comana Pontica** (see above).

Continue to 47km **Niksar**, the ancient Cabeira, a stronghold of the Pontic kings. That celebrated maverick, Mithridates VI Eupator (120–63 BC), built a palace, a zoo, a water mill and a deer park here. In 71 BC he was defeated near Cabeira by the Roman L. Licinus Lucullus in one of the most important battles of the Third Mithridatic War. According to Strabo, the cult centre of the god Men was established by Pharnaces I (c 185–169 BC) of Pontus at Cabeira. Like Comana Pontica this had many servants and a sacred territory whose fruit was always harvested by a priest.

In the 11C it was the principal city of the Danishmendid dynasty. Its founder, Melik Gazi, was buried here. There are the ruins of the **Yağıbasan Medrese** at Niksar. This type of *medrese* was introduced into Anatolia by the Danishmendids (see Tokat above).

Return to the outskirts of Tokat and take the road signposted Turhal. After c 26km turn left on to a minor road for (6km) **Pazar** where there is a very fine *caravanserai*, built by Hatun Hanı in 1238/9. This was one of a chain on the ancient trade route between Sivas and Amasya which passed to the W of Tokat. An elaborately decorated door in the façade, which bears an elegant design of geometric motifs, provides access to the spacious interior. The chamber to the left of the entrance was probably used for prayers. In addition to the vaulted rooms used by individual merchants there was a large hall divided into three sections. Not far from the *han* there is a **Selçuk bridge** over the Yeşil İrmak.

Continue on the main road to **Turhal**. This town, on the right bank of the Yeşil İrmak, was known as **Gaziura** in ancient times. According to Strabo it had been a royal residence of the Pontic kings, but was deserted in his time. There are the **ruins of a Pontic castle** on a crag above the town.

From Turhal turn S to (24km) **Zila**, the ancient Zela, whose origins date to the Hittite period. The temple dedicated to the god Anaïtis at Zela, like those at Comana Pontica and Cabeira, was served by a quasi-royal priesthood and maintained by an army of servants. In 47 BC Pharnaces, son of Mithridates VI Eupator, revolted against the Romans, but he was routed at a battle near Zela by Julius Caesar who reported his victory to the Senate in a famous laconic despatch: *'Veni, Vidi, Vici'*. A ruined **Pontic castle** overlooks the modern town.

From Zila take a minor road SW to (c 21km) **Maşat Hüyük**.

This important site, on the frontier of the Hittite Empire, was excavated in 1945 and 1973. In stratum III two wings of a large palace were found inside a protective enceinte. The palace occupied an area of c 79m by 100m, and had more than 40 rooms and a colonnaded courtyard measuring c 41m by 36m. The entrance was at first floor level. The rooms underneath were used for storage. There was also a second storey constructed of wood. The walls of the palace were covered with cream or red plaster. The only decoration was provided by a series of thin red lines. Apparently the building was the residence of a Hittite governor. Correspondence on clay tablets between him and the Hittite king at Hattusa, 115km to the W, gives the name of the palace as Tappiga. It was destroyed by fire c 1400 BC at the same time as the capital was attacked. In the mid 14C a new building (stratum II) was constructed on the NW corner of the site. This was destroyed c 1300 BC. In the last level of Hittite occupation (stratum I) evidence of direct contact with the Mycenaeans, in the form of a Mycenaean IIIB flask, was found. A part of the site was occupied in the 6C BC by the Phrygians, who used the foundations and stones of the Hittite palaces for the construction of their buildings, and later by the Scythians.

Return to Yıldızeli and continue W, in the direction of Yozgat. After c 98km a turning on the right leads to **Çınçınlı Sultan Hanı**, a ruined Selçuk *han* which was built c 1239.

At the junction 4km before Sorgun take the road S which is signposted to Boğazlıyan. Continue to c 28km **Alişar Hüyük**, a site excavated between 1927 and 1932 by archaeologists from the Oriental Institute of Chicago. Houses of an unfortified village found at the lowest level date from the fourth millennium BC. Pottery made without a wheel from the Early Bronze Age (c 2500 BC and later) was discovered in the next stratum. Traces of a looted and burned out Assyrian *karum*, of a kind common in Anatolia between 1950 and 1750 BC, were found on the site. During the Hittite period it may have been the royal winter residence called Ankuwa on various inscriptions. Sometime after the collapse of the Hittite empire in the 13C BC the site was fortified by the Phrygians.

A further 40km towards Yozgat a turning on the left leads to 15km **Kerkenes Dağı**. Here archaeologists have laid bare fortifications which have aroused some controversy. Some authorities maintain that they were erected by the Phrygians, others that they were built by the indigenous people as a defence against the Phrygians.

Founded in the mid 18C, **Yozgat** (25km) is a quiet market town which attracts few visitors.

It has one hotel, the two-star *Yılmaz Oteli* in Ankara Cad. The **Tourist Information Office** on the third floor of the Özel İdare Binası may be able to arrange private accommodation. All the long-distance coaches on the Ankara–Sivas route stop at Yozgat and there are bus and dolmuş services to places in the surrounding area, including Boğazkale.

Yozgat has two interesting mosques, the **Çapanoğlu Mustafa Paşa Camii** and the nearby **Süleyman Bey Camii**. In an early 19C town house, the **Nizamoğlu Sarayı**, there is a representative ethnographical collection. The rolling hills and lush green valleys of the **Çamlık National Park** are 5km to the S of Yozgat. This unspoiled stretch of countryside will appeal particularly to bird watchers and walkers. There are camping and picnicking facilities in the park between April and October.

BOĞAZKALE (formerly Boğazköy) is 37km N of Yozgat.

If you wish to stay overnight and have not reserved accommodation, go to one of Boğazkale's two motels. They are small, simple, inexpensive and friendly. The facilities are basic. The motel near the museum has a camping ground. If your stay coincides with a group, it can be noisy. An alternative to Boğazkale's motels is the grade two *Hitit Motel* in Sungurlu, 27km to the NW. This has quiet, carpeted rooms with private facilities, a garden, a swimming pool and a restaurant. There are taxis and a somewhat infrequent dolmuş service from Sungurlu to Boğazkale.

The site at Boğazkale is extensive and requires a great deal of walking, some of it over rough terrain. An unhurried exploration of it, Yazılıkaya and Alacahöyük requires at least one day. There are taxis which will take you around the site. Competition is keen, so get several quotations before reaching a decision. Bargaining is expected and will not be resented.

History. The earliest traces of man found at Boğazkale date from Palaeolithic times. However, the first substantial evidence of permanent occupation is from the third millennium BC. The site had many attractions for those early inhabitants—it could be fortified easily, there was an abundant supply of water, and the land to the N was very fertile. About 2000 BC the rocky plateau of Büyükkale and an area to the SW of the lower city terrace, plus the slope in between, formed part of a large settlement occupied by a people known to the archaeologists as the Hatti. Old Assyrian texts of c 1900 BC and a later Hittite document refer to this settlement as Hattus. The kings of Hattus lived on Büyükkale. On a terrace to the N of the site, occupied later by Hittite temple I, there was an Assyrian *karum* which traded for c 50 years. About 1720 BC it and the city of Hattus were destroyed by Anitta, the Hittite king of Kushar and Nesha. In a cuneiform text written in old Hittite, which was carefully preserved in the city's records, Anitta boasts of his victory over Pijusti, the last king of Hattus. He also cursed the place so that it would never be occupied again.

However, about 120 years later the kings of Kushar, a city which has not been identified, ignored the curse, made Hattus their capital and renamed it Hattusa. The first king of Hattusa called himself Hattusili i.e. the man from Hattusa. Apart from the fact that it had temples dedicated to Arinna the sun goddess and her daughter Mezulla, which were adorned with treasures brought back by Hattusili from his campaigns in N Syria and Mesopotamia, little is known about the early history of Hattusa. In the middle of the 16C BC King Hantili reinforced the fortifications of Hattusa. About 150 years later the city was attacked by a number of hostile neighbours. It was burned to the ground by the Kaskha people from the Pontus during the reign of Tudhaliya III (fl. c 1400 BC), but soon recovered. King Muwatalli (1305–1282) moved the capital to Kummanni, the modern Şar in Cappadocia. This period of exile to escape further invasion, ended during the reign of Muwatalli's son, Mursili III (1282–1276). He was deposed by his uncle Hattusili III. The palace at Hattusa was burned down, possibly during this period of internal struggle. Hattusili III concluded the first recorded peace treaty between sovereign states with Ramesses II of Egypt. Tudhaliya IV (1250–20), his successor, constructed new fortifications and buildings in the acropolis. By the end of his reign Hattusa was largely as we see it today.

The last known Hittite king was Suppiluliuma II. He was engaged in fierce battles with the so-called People of the Sea who also ravaged the Lebanon and Palestine. Hattusa was sacked and then torched. This destruction is marked by a thick stratum of burned material. The Hittite Empire finally collapsed sometime between 1200 and 1180 BC. Boğazkale was abandoned for about three centuries. From the 9C to the 6C BC the Phrygians occupied a part of the site. They restored the fortifications on the citadel and built a temple dedicated to Cybele. Archaeologists found her cult image in a niche in the city gate. This is now in the Anatolian Civilisations Museum in Ankara. In the 3C a Galatian tribe settled in the area. Their capital was c 21km to the SW at Tavium, now Büyük Nefesköy. Graves were found in a late Hellenistic cemetery in

Temple I. Roman remains were discovered here and on Büyükkale. There was a small Byzantine church at Mihraplıkaya. Only the apse and traces of the nave are left.

The small village of Boğazköy was established in the 18C. The first European visitors to the site were Charles Texier in 1834 and William J. Hamilton in 1835.

Boğazkale does not look very attractive. Scattered, in an apparently haphazard fashion, across a hilly landscape covered in brown, thorny scrub, are what appear to be dry-stone walls. They are the limestone foundations of the ancient buildings of Hattusa. The walls, which were made of clay bricks and wood disappeared a long time ago, and it is not always easy to distinguish man-made structures from natural rock formations. However, the scale and magnificence of the site soon erase initial unfavourable impressions and few travellers feel disappointed at the end of their visit. Archaeologists from the German Oriental Society and the German Archaeological Institute, who started work here in 1906, have laid bare the artefacts and buildings of the ancient city. They have found the palaces and temples, the statues and pottery, the archives of a long-forgotten people. They have brought the civilisation of the Hittites into the light of day.

Hattusa was protected by walls 6.5km in length. From the village drive to the site which is open daily until dusk. (Retain your ticket as it will admit you to the museum in the village.) From the ticket kiosk go to the Lion Gate which is near the highest point of the city.

The well-preserved **Lion Gate** gets its name from two carved lion torsos (late 14C–13C BC) which project from the outer side of the gate. Their open snarling mouths and threatening expressions were intended to deflect malefic influences. The left lion's head has been destroyed and the head on the right has lost its teeth. Note the characteristic Hittite treatment of the mane, whiskers and breast hair and the clumsy body which rests on stilt-like legs. There is a barely visible **inscription** in Hittite hieroglyphic script on the flank of one of the animals.

It is worthwhile walking the short distance from the Lion Gate to Yer Kapı as here the **city wall** is very well preserved. The fortification was in two distinct sections: a lower wall and above this a rampart strengthened by **rectangular towers** placed at irregular intervals. At the highest point of the city, 12m below the double walls, a **postern** admits to a corbelled passage some 71m long. Still open, this leads into Büyükkale. Some believe that it was intended to facilitate passage in and out of the city in times of peace and to permit the defenders to make surprise attacks against the enemy in wartime. Others contend that it function was religious, pointing out that the entrance was not disguised in any way and that the southern approach to the city was the most difficult one for a hostile force. The door at the city end of the postern has been destroyed, but the lower, **outer door** is well preserved. Note the **seat** at the E side for the doorkeeper.

Two flights of steps, equidistant from the tunnel opening, lead up a manmade embankment to the city walls. Above the postern and built into the main wall is **Yer Kapı. Two sphinxes** protected this gate and the important section of the wall near it. When discovered, the bodies of these mythological creatures were in a very damaged state. The core of one still remains standing.

From Yer Kapı continue around the wall to the **King's Gate**. A gently sloping ramp leads up to a rectangular platform in front of this gate which was protected by flanking towers. Note the **sockets** for the bolts and hinges and the slots for the bars which secured the massive double door. This was made of wood strengthened with metal plates. In 1907 a **limestone relief** of a male figure was found on the left, inner side of this gate. Believed to be the representation of a Hittite king, it gave the gate its name. The larger-than-life figure wears a short kilt. His pointed helmet with cheek flaps is decorated with horns. Facing right, he holds an axe in his right hand and carries a short sword or dagger in his belt. His left hand is clenched and raised in a gesture which has been variously interpreted as greeting, warning or worship. The 225cm high relief is now believed to be that of a warrior god whose function was to protect the gate and the people who used it. Dated to the 14C or 13C BC, it is in the Anatolian Civilizations Museum in Ankara. A much weathered cast replaces it at the site.

In the area enclosed by the city wall between the Lion Gate and the King's Gate the archaeologists have found a number of **temples**. For a bird's-eye view return to the Sphinx Gate. Below and to the right are the ruins of Temples III, II and V. To the left are Temples IV and VI. Temple VII is near Nişentepe. Other buildings found in this area may also have been cult centres. The quarters occupied by the priests and temple servants and those used of the royal family during the great religious festivals were probably located here. Temples II, III and V had propylaea which led to paved courtyards. Beyond the courtyard in II and III was the adyton where the cult statue was placed. In temple V the archaeologists found two adyta. Some of the adjoining rooms were used for the storage of the sacred vessels and other objects used by the priests. A number of the temples had stairs. It is not known if they led to an upper storey or to a flat roof.

At **Yenicekale** a Hittite architect displayed considerable skill in constructing a castle on top of this 30m high crag. Cut stone blocks were used to fill in gaps in the living rock. Unfortunately the only remaining traces of this graceful and inventive structure are its **foundations** and the **outer courtyard** on the S side. It is believed to date from the 13C BC.

The **Southern Fort** and Nişantepe may have formed part of the Büyükkale complex during the Hittite period. The 14C BC fort, built on a small plateau, has not yet been excavated. There are the ruins of a wall and of a gate on the NW side. Some believe that it may be a post-Hittite construction. On the eastern side of **Nişantepe** there is a badly defaced ten-line **Hittite inscription**. Only part of the first line on the top right hand corner can be read. This mentions the name of the last Hittite king, Suppiluliuma II, who ruled c 1200 BC (see above). A separate **cuneiform text** states that he had a statue of his father, Tudhaliya, placed in a specially constructed *hegur*, i.e. a building on top of a rock. Traces of a structure have been found on top of Nişantepe. Could it be that Suppiluliuma's *hegur* was here?

To the W of Nişantepe is **Sarıkale**, the Yellow Castle. This occupies a plateau which drops steeply on the N side. Part of the building may date from the Phrygian period, but the original construction is 14C or 13C Hittite. It may have been a dependency of the palace occupied by members of the royal family or by favoured courtiers. Further examination is required.

The main entrance to **Büyükkale** was at the SW corner of the acropolis, to the right of the modern road. First occupied by the Hatti (see above), the Hittite kings built their **citadel** and **royal residence** here. The trapezoidal site measures c 250m by 140m and is protected on the N and E sides by the 90m deep ravine of the Büyükkaya Deresi. Within a defensive outer wall the Hittites placed their buildings on raised terraces. A series of courtyards surrounded by tall structures and isolated from each other by stout doors led to the highest part in the citadel. This arrangement helped the garrison as attackers would face a separate battle for each part of the complex.

The visible ruins are those of the 13C BC citadel and palace. Earlier structures were examined and recorded by the archaeologists and then covered over to preserve them from damage. In the course of centuries the buildings were robbed of their fine cut stone blocks and only the foundations were left. There are some traces of the **mud-brick walls** and a few **stone bases** of the brick columns remain.

Steps have replaced the ramp which led up to the outer gate in the SW wall. This was flanked by protective towers. From here visitors passed over a pavement of red flagstones to the lower courtyard. This had buildings of two or more storeys on the SE and SW sides. Three of the buildings on the SW may have been used for religious purposes. Cult objects were found in one of them. A propylon ornamented with basalt lion sculptures provided access to the middle courtyard. According to an inscription the propylon was erected by king Tudhaliya IV (fl. 1250–1220 BC). A building on the S side of the courtyard was the **royal archive**. More than 3000 cuneiform tablets were found here. The largest Hittite building, 49m by 30m, on Büyükkale was on the W side. On the first floor the king held court and gave audiences. The pillared basement was probably a storeroom. At the extreme NE of the acropolis were the private apartments of the royal family. In the building just N of the audience chamber 2500 cuneiform texts were found. One of them records the **treaty** made by Hattusili III and Ramesses II of Egypt c 1270 BC. This made peace between the two countries after the indecisive battle of Kadesh on the Orontes river (c 1296). Written in Akkadian cuneiform, the diplomatic language of the time, copies of the tablet are in the Museum of the Ancient Orient in İstanbul and the Anatolian Civilisations Museum in Ankara.

A **gate** on the SE side of the acropolis, which gave direct access to the middle courtyard, was probably reserved for use by the king. In times of danger it could be sealed off by two strong doors.

It is not easy to visualise Büyükkale in its heyday. Weathering and spoliation have taken their toll. Many of the great stone blocks, which supported the terraces, now lie at the bottom of the hill. Additions and alterations made during the 7C and 6C Phrygian occupation, further confuse the picture. The hills have been denuded of trees.

The site of the **Great Temple** of Hattusa is a short distance to the NW of Büyükkale. This was dedicated to the Weather God, Teshub of Hatti, and the Sun Goddess, Hebut of Arinna. Inside the temenos were the temple, a large number of storerooms and the quarters of the priests and of the temple servants. The entrance to the temenos was on the SE side. A short distance to the S of the propylon there are the remains of a large stone basin. This has been broken into four pieces. On the short sides there are **stylised lions** in flat relief. It has been suggested that this was a lustral basin used by worshippers, but it has no drainage point. Note the three huge **thresholds** of the propylon and the **cubicles** on each side for the guards. At the point where the way to the temple turns right there was a large **limestone water basin** which had an outlet to the main sewer. Work on the temple began sometime in the 14C and it was completed in stages by c 1250 BC. It covers an area of 64m by 42m. An imposing portal on the SE led to a courtyard, 26m by 19m, which had a colonnade at one side. In the NE corner of the courtyard there was a square, single-room building whose purpose is not known. The adyton on the Sun Goddess was probably on the right, that of the Storm God on the left of the NE end of the sanctuary. Unusually for an oriental cult the statues of the deities were brightly lit. There were large windows in each cella. The base of one of the statues is in its original place.

There were c 80 storage rooms around the temple building. Because the ground slopes from S to N those on the N side had three floors while those on the other three sides had two. In many of the rooms there are huge pithoi which were used for the storage of liquids. Their capacity varied between

900 and 3000 litres. Some are free standing, others are buried in the ground. Note the decoration on the shoulders of the jars, the inscriptions which stated their capacity and the seal marks. Thousands of cuneiform tablets were found in three of the rooms on the NE side. Clay bullae used to seal packages were discovered in rooms on the NW side of the complex.

On the S side of the complex and separated from the main group of buildings is the so-called **House of Service**. The discovery of writing materials and a cuneiform text suggests that the temple offices and servants' living quarters were here. The text mentions 18 priests, 29 women musicians, 19 scribes for clay tablets, 33 scribes for wooden tablets, 35 soothsayers, 10 Hurrian singers.... The temple was destroyed c 1200 BC at the same time as the city. It was looted systematically and nothing of value was left in its ruins.

The site of the Assyrian **karum** (see above) is a short distance to the N of the temple, on the right side of the modern road. This was a subsidiary of the principal karum in Anatolia at Kanesh (Kültepe near Kayseri). Between c 1950 and 1750 BC these trading posts organised and controlled trade between the cities of Anatolia and Assyria. The Assyrian merchants purchased minerals—gold, silver and copper—and supplied woollen cloth, clothes and, perhaps, tin, a vital commodity for the Bronze Age people of Anatolia. They arranged the despatch of caravans and ensured their safety, operated a credit transfer system, fixed the prices of goods and arbitrated in disputes. All goods entering a *karum* paid tax to the local ruler. The Assyrian traders maintained friendly relations with their Anatolian neighbours and intermarriage was not uncommon.

Before leaving Boğazkale visit the museum which is outside the village on the road to Sungurlu. Your ticket to the site admits you. While the most important finds from Hattusa are in the Anatolian Civilisations Museum at Ankara, this small collection is not without interest. In the garden there are inscriptions and grave stelae from the Roman and Byzantine periods. Near the entrance are plans and information about the ancient city. The collection includes ceramics, statuettes, animal figurines, reliefs and bone and metal objects. All periods of Hattusa's history are represented. Note the small **stone head of a goddess** which has lost its inlaid eyes. There is also a room devoted to local crafts—carpets, kilims, embroidery etc.

The rock shrine of **YAZILIKAYA** is about 2km to the NE of Boğazkale village. The best times to see the reliefs are as follows: between 11.00 and 13.00 for the male deities, the early afternoon for the female deities in Chamber A and between 12.00 and 13.00 for the reliefs in Chamber B.

On the way to Yazılıkaya, just after the bridge over the Büyükkaya Deresi, you approach the base of **Büyükkaya**, a massive rocky peak. Its fortifications were linked to the city's defensive wall at a point near Ambarlıkaya, a lower spur on the other side of the river. The Hittites constructed a bridge and gallery which spanned the gorge, and, below these, a portcullis which was lowered in times of danger. This permitted the water, but not the enemy, to pass through. Note the three pairs of **vertical grooves** in the rock face which guided the portcullis down to the river bed. Near Ambarlıkaya minerals were smelted during the period when the Assyrian *karum* was active. Later it appears to have been the industrial area of the city.

The shrine at Yazılıkaya is believed to date from the reign of king Tudhaliya IV (1250–1220 BC). Its Turkish name means Inscribed Rock. It consists of a temple and two narrow ravines whose walls are covered with reliefs. Only the **foundations** remain. The mudbrick walls disappeared a long time ago. A detached gateway led, through the vestibule of the shrine, to a large courtyard. Here were a sacrificial altar and a free-standing lustral room. From the courtyard the worshippers passed into the sanctuary which was open to the sky. This has been designated **Chamber A** by the archaeologists. The rocky floor was smoothed and in part covered with flagstones. Offerings were placed in the **niches** under the reliefs and at the rear of the chamber there were piscinae for libations. There are **66 figures** on the walls of chamber A. All but one are of deities. On average, the reliefs are 80cm high. The left wall is given over mainly of **male deities**. Their rank may be gauged by the number of horns on their helmets. A minor god has one horn. A major god, like Teshub, has five. The male figures wear pointed hats or helmets, short belted kilts, earrings (sometimes) and boots with turned-up toes. A number sport long cloaks. Some are armed with a mace or scimitar. Most of the **female deities** are on the right side of the chamber. They are clothed in long trailing robes under a belted cloak. On their heads they wear a *polos*. Their long braided hair hangs down underneath.

The Hurrian people, who lived in eastern Anatolia, northern Syria and Mesopotamia, exerted a considerable influence on the Hittites. So perhaps it is not surprising that the deities who are named at Yazılıkaya have Hurrian and not Hittite names. Look for the **oval symbol** for 'god' above a raised hand. This is followed by the name of the deity which is sometimes in the form of an ideogram, sometimes in syllabic script.

On the left side there are the figures of 12 gods carrying scimitars. They are followed by two mountain gods. The next important group shows two bull-men supporting the hieroglyphic sign for the sky. The **Sun God** has a round cap, wears a long coat and carries an inverted shepherd's crook. Above his head is the sun disk. Next is winged **Kushuh**, the Moon God. A crescent moon pierces his pointed helmet. The following two figures are Kulitta and Ninatta, handmaids of Shaushga. They hold musical instruments. **Shaushga (Ishtar)**, the winged Goddess of War wears a pleated skirt. She is followed by Ea, the God of Water who holds a mace. The names of the next two gods are not known. The first is a God of Grain. He holds a sword and stands on two mountains. The second is a **Weather God**. He has a sword, mace and lance and also stands on two mountains. Then comes **Teshub**, the **Weather God**. He has a sword and mace and stands on two mountains shaped in the form of men. Behind him is the symbol of his divinity, a running bull wearing a pointed hat. Facing Teshub is his consort, **Hepatu**, the **Sun Goddess**. She stands on the back of a panther which, in turn, stands on mountains. Behind her is a bull with a pointed hat, her symbol of divinity. Next is a smaller figure, **Sharruma**, the son of Teshub and Hepatu. Like Hepatu, he stands on the back of a panther which rests on two mountain peaks. Behind him are the daughters of Hepatu standing on a twin-headed eagle. The next figure is of the goddess, **Hutilura**. On a block leaning against the wall is the figure of **Shaushga—Ishtar** in her personification of the Goddess of Love.

The relief of **Tudhaliya IV**, on a projection to the right of the entrance of the chamber, is always in the shade. It faces the procession of deities. The king wears priestly garments: a round hat, a long coat and a cape. Standing on two mountains, like the principal gods and goddesses, he holds an inverted shepherd's crook. His name is written over his raised right hand. The hieroglyphs for Great King are on the right and left of the figure and there is a winged solar disk above it. Archaeologists believe that a Spring Festival lasting several days, which signalled the beginning of the Hittite New Year, was celebrated in this sanctuary.

The narrow entrance to Chamber B is guarded by two mythological figures which have winged human bodies and lions' heads. Their paws are raised threatningly. A number of improvements were made to this natural enclosure. Niches were placed in the wall of the entrance passage for lamps and its floor was smoothed and covered with stone slabs. Walls were erected at the N end to cover faults in the rock face. The chamber, which was paved, is 20m long and 4m wide at the N end, 2m at the S. Two niches in the W wall and one in the E probably held funerary urns.

The reliefs in **Chamber B** are in a better state of preservation than those in Chamber A. On the W wall there is a lively representation of the **Twelve Gods** who appear to be jogging. As in the relief in Chamber A they carry scimitars. On the E wall there are two reliefs. The first, 3.39m high, is of a **strange figure** wearing the pointed hat of a god. His body takes the form of a sword plunged deeply into the rock. The hilt has lions' heads on each side and two lions hang down towards the blade. The second relief, which is in a niche 1.7m high and 1.4m wide, shows the god **Sharruma** holding king **Tudhaliya IV** in a protective embrace. Sharruma wears a pointed helmet decorated with six horns and a number of large disks, a kilt, boots with turned up toes and he has a sword in his belt. The figure of the king, which is much smaller, wears a royal cap and a long cloak. He has a sword and, as in the large relief in Chamber A, holds an inverted shepherd's crook.

Hittite texts mention the 'bronze swords of Nergal', the god of the underworld, and 'the twelve gods of the crossroads', deities which may have been associated with the afterlife. There are also references to rituals during which the priests fashioned images of the chthonic gods in the form of swords and stuck them in the ground. Accordingly, many archaeologists believe that Chamber B was the mortuary chapel of Tudhaliya IV. This view is supported by the discovery of burials in the nearby area.

There is some evidence that a large statue of the king stood at the N wall of the chamber near where his name appears. A stone base, which was being used as a washboard in a village near Yazılıkaya, may belong to this statue. All that remain of the figure, which it once supported, are **two slippered feet**. Judging by their size the statue must have stood c 3.5m high. Assuming that the view expressed above is correct, the question whether Chamber B was prepared as a funerary chapel by the king during his lifetime or whether it was created as an act of piety by one of his successors, Arnuwanda III or Suppiluliuma II will, no doubt, continue to exercise scholars for many years to come.

Chamber C, at the NE end of B, has been walled off. This has a small, winding stairs which leads outside the sanctuary. It was probably reserved for the use of the priests. A quantity of wood ash was found in this chamber.

From Boğazkale take the road N towards to Sungurlu. After c 14km turn right and continue for 28km to **ALACAHÖYÜK**. Sadly, this important site is bypassed by many visitors to Boğazkale and Yazılıkaya. At Alacahöyük excavations conducted by Turkish archaeologists in 1935–36 and 1962 revealed the tombs of 13 royal personages. Dating from the late third millennium BC they contained a rich hoard of grave goods. Most of these are in the Anatolian Civilisations Museum in Ankara. A small, representative selection is kept in the local village museum.

History. Alacahöyük was first occupied c 3500 BC. There is some suggestion that it was the site of Kushar or of Arinna which are often mentioned in Hittite texts, but whose locations are not known. The inhabitants, usually designated proto-Hittites or Hatti, were supplanted, perhaps violently, by the Hittites around 1700 BC when Hattus also taken by them (see above). Evidence of a conflagration has been found by the archaeologists. Between 1600 and 1200 BC Alacahöyük was somewhat overshadowed by its powerful Hittite neighbours at Hattusa. However, it also prospered and was protected by a defensive system in which there were at least two gates. After the fall of Hattusa, Alacahöyük was abandoned. There was a Phrygian settlement here for a short time in the first half of the first millennium BC. During the Roman period it was a small, unimportant village which continued to be inhabited into modern times.

About a third of Alacahöyük, which covers almost two hectares, has been excavated. Entrance is by the **Sphinx Gate** which dates from the 14C BC. The function of the two mythological creatures, which emerge menacingly from the great gateposts, was apotropaic. Their large wigs and long tresses suggest Egyptian influence. On the right hand gatepost there is the **relief** of a double-headed eagle with outstretched wings gripping a brace of hares or rabbits in its claws. The towers, which flanked the gateway, were ornamented with a unique group of **reliefs**. The andesite originals, now in the Anatolian Civilisations Museum in Ankara, have been replaced by copies. They show a group of worshippers before a deity, who may be the sun-goddess Arinna, goats being led to sacrifice by a priest, a musician and, behind him, acrobats with a ladder, a king and queen pouring a libation before the statue of a bull, which represents the weather god, and a procession of priests. A section of the frieze from the upper part of the gates is also in the Ankara museum. This is devoted entirely to hunting scenes.

Inside the gate a **courtyard** leads to a **small square**. Note the **sewer** which is in an excellent state of preservation. On the left is the **great pit** where the so-called royal tombs were discovered (see below). Here the path narrows and then opens out into a large rectangular space which was partially lined with porticoes. On the right is the palace area. Among the private apartments of the royal family and the administrative offices there is a **temple**. All these buildings date from the period of Hittite rule (1600–1200 BC). At the end of the open space a **tunnel** leads to a **postern** outside the walls. Armed with a torch you can explore the tunnel in dry weather and admire its cyclopean masonry.

From here return to the tall wooden tower which dominates the site. A path leads down into the depression made by the Turkish archaeologists when they excavated the area containing the proto-Hittite tombs. Evidently the resting places of noble or royal personages these date from the late third millennium BC. Crowded together in an area c 30m square there were 13 tombs at c 7m below the surface. On average each tomb measured 4m by 8m and was 0.75m deep. The body was laid in a corner, on its side in a contracted position facing in a southerly direction. Men were buried with their weapons, while women had their toiletries and ornaments. On the S side of the pit were placed a number of copper solar discs and metal statuettes of stags and bulls. These appear to have had some religious significance. Domestic utensils, presumably for use in the afterlife, were also found in the pits. The tombs were covered with wooden beams and a layer of earth. The heads and feet of beasts, which perhaps had been consumed at the funeral feast, were laid by the grave markers. The tombs have been covered with a layer of concrete to protect them and on some wooden beams have been placed to simulate their original appearance. Most of the grave goods are now in the Anatolian Civilisations Museum in Ankara. Similar grave goods have been found in tombs of a slightly later period nearer the Black Sea littoral and in the Kuban basin in Russia. The objects found in Russia have been ascribed to the Kurgan peoples. Accordingly, it has been suggested that Alacahöyük may have marked the southernmost extension of this foreign culture in Anatolia and that the persons buried here may have been non-Hattic speaking immigrants.

Spend a little time in the museum. In the garden there are **Roman and Byzantine stelae**, a **basalt lion** and the lower part of a large statue found near the Sphinx Gate. Inside are weapons from the Royal Tombs, bronze artefacts and vases from the Hittite period,

Phrygian ceramics and **terracotta reliefs** from nearby Pazarlı. There are also copies of the standards now in Ankara.

From Alacahöyük return to Yozgat and continue towards Ankara, or take the faster route via Sungurlu which joins the E23 c 24km to the E of Kırıkkale. A turning on the right just to W of Kırıkkale leads N to (23km) **Kalecik**. This has been identified variously with the station of **Acitoriciacum** on the Tabula Peutingeriana between Ankyra and Amasya and the city of **Malos** which is mentioned in the Acts of St Theodosius of Ancyra. In the 11C an important fortress on the border between the Byzantine Empire and the Danishmendid sultanate, it guarded a ford on the Halys river (now the Kızılırmak). Little remains of the fortress which has been robbed of its cut stone by the villagers over the centuries.

A turning on the right 24km farther on will take you to (4km) **Hasanoğlan** where a very beautiful electrum and bronze statuette of a female fertility goddess was found. It is now in the Anatolian Civilisations Museum in Ankara. There are some very weathered 1C AD **rock reliefs** a 15 minute walk from the village. These are believed to have been made by the descendants of Celtic tribes who settled here in the 3C BC.

From Hasanoğlan return to the E23 and continue to (29km) Ankara.

53

Ankara

Like Janus, **ANKARA** has two faces. It is the capital of Turkey and as such has all the trappings of a modern metropolis—a president's palace, a parliament building, government offices, foreign embassies, the headquarters of important national enterprises, luxurious hotels and gourmet restaurants, smart shops and, dominating all of these, the imposing mausoleum of Atatürk, the Father of the Turks. Joined to this glittering city are the remains of Ancyra, an Anatolian city which traces its history back to a mid 8C BC Phrygian settlement. In workshops in its quiet streets ancient crafts are still practised and weekly markets bring country people to sell their produce and bargain for factory-made goods.

Information. The main **Tourist Information Office** is at Gazi Mustafa Kemal Bulvarı, No. 121, Tandoğan and Esenboğa Hava Limanı (the Airport). There is a freephone (in Ankara only) tourist information service on 900447090.

Accommodation. Almost 60 hotels in Ankara are on the Ministry of Tourism's approved list, from the luxurious five-star *Hilton* and *Sheraton* down to more simple, and less expensive, accommodation. Recommended are the very comfortable *Omni Residence*, Tahran Cad., No. 5 and the friendly two-star *Melodi Oteli*, Karanfil Sok., No. 10, Kizilay.

Post Office and Banks. The main Post Office in Kızılay is open 24 hours a day. There are many subsidiary offices scattered throughout the city. All of the Turkish banks have offices in Ankara. Most have branches in the different districts.

Climate. Ankara has a continental climate. The summers are long and pleasantly warm with cool nights. The winters are cold with snow and rain. The city suffers badly from smog. Temperatures range from -1°C in January to 23°C in July and August.

Embassies. The British Embassy is in Çankaya, Şehit Ersan Cad., No:46/A. The United States Embassy is in Kavaklidere, Atatürk Bul., No.110. The Australian Embassy is in Gaziomanpaşa, Nenehatun Cad., No:83. The Canadian Embassy is at Nenehatun Cad., No. 75.

Transport. Ankara is at the centre of Turkey's transport system. Most long distance buses arrive at and depart from the crowded, noisy, chaotic **otogar** in Ulus. Two companies, Varan and Ulusoy, have their own modern, clean and very comfortable terminals on the outskirts of the city. The **railway station** and the **THY town terminal** are near the *otogar*.

Ankara's airport is **Esenboğa**, c 33km to the NE of the city. There is an inexpensive coach service between the airport and the THY Town Terminal.

City buses are frequent, cheap and often very crowded. Two lines, which visitors will find useful, are No. 8, which runs from Ulus to Çankaya, and No. 63, which runs from Ulus to Anıt Kabir.

Taxis, which are metered, provided a fast and more comfortable ride than the buses. At the time of writing, most journeys inside the city limits cost between £1.50 and £2.00. The driver will expect a tip.

Churches. **Mass** is celebrated in the **Vatican Embassy Church**, Italian Embassy, Atatürk Bul., 118 Kavaklidere and in the **Church of the French Embassy**, Kardeşler Sok., 8, Ulus, on Sundays and religious holidays.

There are **Anglican services** in the British Embassy **Church of St Nicholas**, Şehit Erşan Cad., 46/A on Sundays and religious holidays. Bring your passport as the church is in the Embassy grounds.

On special occasions and religious days there are services in the **Jewish Synagogue**, Birlik Sok., 8, Samanpazarı.

Hospitals. The **American Hospital** is in Balgat Amerikan Tesisleri.

The British Institute of Archaeology at Ankara, 24 Tahran Cad., Kavaklidere (near the Hilton Hotel) is always pleased to meet members who are visiting, or who live in, Turkey. The Institute, which publishes 'Anatolian Studies' (free to members) annually, has an excellent reference library and its staff is extremely well-informed on the archaeology and early history of Anatolia. It depends to a large extent for support on the subscriptions of its world-wide membership and on voluntary contributions. To join, write to: The London Secretary, B.I.A.A., c/o The British Academy, 20–21 Cornwall Terrace, London NW1 4QP.

Museums. No visitor to Ankara should miss the Museum of Anatolian Civilisations which is located near the Citadel. Other museums of interest are the Ethnographic Museum, Talat Paşa Cad.; the Painting and Sculpture Museum, near the Ethnographic Museum; the Museum of Liberation, near Ulus Square; the Museum of the Republic, Cumhuriyet Bul.; the Railway Museum, Ankara Railway Station.

Shopping. Atatürk Bulavarı is the Bond Street of Ankara. In its modern stores there are impressive displays of expensive clothes, jewellery and leather goods. **Karum**, a shopping mall near the Sheraton Hotel, has a mixture of expensive and middle-price boutiques. It also has some good fast food restaurants.

In the Street of the Copperworkers, Bakırcılar Çarşısı, in Ulus not only copper products but jewellery, carpets, antiques and fabrics embroidered with traditional designs are sold. Near the main entrance to the Citadel there is an open-air market for nuts, dried fruit and spices of all kinds.

History. Evidence of human occupation has been discovered in Neolithic tumuli (8000–5500 BC) in the countryside around Ankara. Although no evidence has been found, it is believed that there was a Hittite city here. The Phrygians occupied the area c 1200 BC and from grave goods found in tumuli near Anıt Kabir would appear to have established an important settlement between 750 and 500 BC. Ancyra was a staging post on the Royal Road which linked Susa and Sardis. Alexander the Great came here from Gordion in 333 BC and received a delegation of Paphlagonians who accepted his rule. After the death of Alexander, it came under Seleucid rule.

Between 278 and 277 BC marauding armies of Celts arrived in western Anatolia. After their defeat by Attalus I in 228 BC, they established petty kingdoms in Greater Phrygia. Adopting many of the ways of their Greek-speaking neighbours, they formed

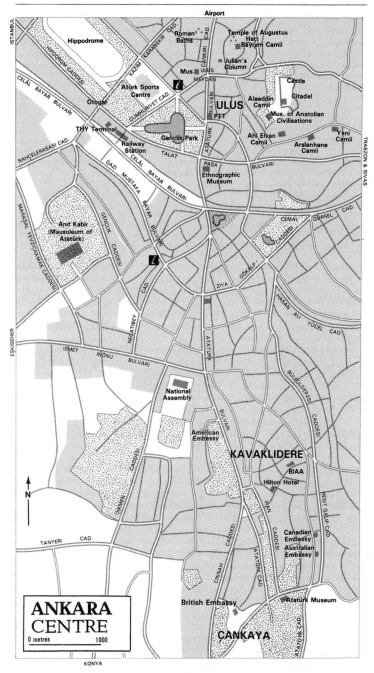

Airport

ISTANBUL

Hippodrome

Roman
Baths

Temple of Augustus
Hacı
Bayram Camii

KAZIM KARABEKIR CAD.

ÇANKIRI CAD.

Julian's
Column

HIPODROM CADDESI

CELAL BAYAR BULVARI

Mus.
ULUS
MEYDAN

Atürk Sports
Centre

CUMHURIYET CAD.

Castle

Citadel

Alaeddin
Camii

Ötogar

ULUS

PTT

Mus. of Anatolian
Civilisations

THY Terminal

Railway
Station

Gençlik Park

Yeni
Camii

Ahi Elvan
Camii

Arslanhane
Camii

ATATÜRK BULVARI

BAHCELERASASI CAD.

TALAT

PASA

TRABZON & SIVAS

GAZI MUSTAFA BAYAR BULVARI

İÇELAL BAYAR BULVARI

BULVARI

Ethnographic
Museum

CEMAL

GÜRSEL CAD.

MARASAL FEVZİÇAKMAK CADDESI

Anıt Kabir
(Mausoleum of
Atatürk)

GENÇLIK CADDESI

CADDESI

GÖKALP

ZIYA

HASAN ALI YÜCEL CAD.

ESKISEHIR

NEGATIBEY CAD.

ATATÜRK

ISMET INÖNÜ BULVARI

National
Assembly

CADDESI

American
Embassy

BULVARI

BÜLBÜLDERESI CADDESI

KAVAKLIDERE

BIAA

Hilton Hotel

DIKMEN CADDESI

IRAN CADDESI

FESIT GALIP CAD.

TANYERI CAD.

N

Canadian
Embassy
Australian
Embassy

CINNAH CADDESI

ATATÜRK CAD.

British Embassy

Atatürk Museum

ATATÜRK CAD.

ÇANKAYA

ANKARA
CENTRE
0 metres   1000

KONYA

a loose confederation of tribes. According to Strabo the fortress Ancyra belonged to the tribe called the Tectosages. Traces of this building have been found in the foundations of the Citadel. The Celts appear to have established good relations with the Romans. In 74 BC Deiotaris, who had brought all the Celtic tribes under his rule, received Julius Caesar. Galatia was annexed by Augustus in 24 BC. Ancyra was renamed Sebaste Tectosagum and became the capital of the province. Of the many fine buildings erected by the Romans, one, the **Temple of Augustus**, remains.

St Paul visited Ancyra in AD 50 and subsequently wrote his celebrated Epistle to the Galatians. However, strong pagan influences remained, as the people of the city welcomed Julian the Apostate in 362. Valens was proclaimed emperor here in 364.

Ancyra prospered under Byzantine rule. However, in the early 7C it was attacked by the Persians and in the 7C and 8C by the Arabs. Later assailants included the Paulicians, the Turks and the Crusaders. After Manzikert it came under Selçuk control. It was ruled at different times by the Danishmendid, the Eretnids and the Mongols. It first came under Ottoman rule in 1354. In 1402 Tamerlane defeated Beyazit to the W of Ankara, but he did not invest the city. It was taken by Mehmet I in 1414 and from then onwards remained under Ottoman control. During the centuries that followed Ancyra declined in importance. In 1893 the railway link with Istanbul brought some revival in its fortunes. The first meeting of the Grand National Assembly was held here in 1920 and in 1923 Atatürk made it the capital of the new republic of Turkey. Under his guidance European architects and planners designed and created a new city, whose population has increased from 30,000 to almost three million.

Anıt Kabir, the marble mausoleum of Kemal Atatürk, founder of the Turkish Republic, is on the summit of Anıttepe. Completed in 1953, it dominates the city. The building, an impressive fusion of ancient and modern architectural styles, houses an important collection of Atatürk memorabilia and has a photographic exhibition of important events in his life and in the formative years of the republic. There is a *son et lumière* display each evening during the summer.

Mustafa Kemal Atatürk was born in Salonika in 1881. He led the Turkish movement from 1909 and was a General in World War I. After the collapse of Ottoman power he founded the Turkish National Party. The Allies were occupying Constantinople, so he set up government in Ankara. He expelled the Greeks from Anatolia, abolished the sultanate and gained recognition of the republic from the European powers. He instituted widespread reforms and pursued an ambitious and successful campaign to modernise Turkey. He was president of the Turkish Republic from 1923–38.

From Anıt Kabir go to Atatürk Bulvarı and continue N towards Ulus Meydanı. A short distance to the right of the junction with Talat Paşa Bul. is the **Ethnographical Museum**. In ten halls, this houses a collection of folk art and artefacts from various parts of Anatolia. Do not miss the fine **carved door** from the Alaeddin Camii in the citadel, the **throne of Keyhüsrev III** from the Kızıl Bey Camii, and the **sarcophagus of Ahi Şerafettin**.

To the left of a striking **equestrian statue of Atatürk**, the work of the Italian sculptor Canonica, in **Ulus Meydanı**, is the Old Parliament Building, now the **Museum of Liberation**. Here, and in the nearby **Museum of the Republic**, displays of photographs and historical objects are used imaginatively to record the early history of the republic.

Behind the square, in Hükümet Meydanı, is the so-called **Column of Julian the Apostate**. There is no evidence to support the popular belief that this was erected to commemorate Julian's visit to Ancyra in 362. The Ottomans called it Belkiz Minaresi, the Minaret of Belkis Queen of Sheba, and that name is still used by some of the local people. The slender 14.5m column, surmounted by a Corinthian capital, frequently provides a precarious resting place for a large, untidy storks' nest.

From Hükümet Meydanı make your way uphill to the **Hacı Bayram Camii**. This mosque, which was built in 1427 and extensively restored in the 18C, occupies one side of a large open space. Hacı Bayramı Veli founded the Bayram dervishes and his *türbe* by the side of the mosque has long been a popular place of pilgrimage. The people of Ankara come to pray here on important family occasions—to celebrate a marriage or a birth, or to mourn the loss of a loved one. The square has become a popular meeting place. During the long summer evenings old men sit here enjoying the last of the sun while children play noisy games around their feet.

At the back of the mosque are the substantial remains of the **Temple of Augustus**. Built between 29 and 25 BC, on the site of a Hellenistic shrine dedicated to two Anatolian deities, Cybele the Mother Goddess and Men the moon god, it was a provincial temple of the cult of Rome and Augustus (a Sebasteion). Some believe that this earlier dedication may account for the fact that it opened on the W, where traces of an **altar** have been found. It was restored in the middle of the 2C AD as an Ionic pseudo-dipteros.

When the temple was converted into a church during the early Byzantine period, a number of structural alterations were made. Three small windows were opened high up on the N wall of the cella, the wall dividing the opisthodomus from the cella was removed and an apse was added to the E end. The church ceased to be used sometime after the city was taken by the Turks and it fell into ruin. Much of its cut stone was appropriated by the builders of the Hacı Bayram Camii.

The temple's great claim to fame is that it has the *Monumentum Ancyranum*, an inscription in Greek and Latin which records the achievements, the *Res Gestae* of Augustus. This was read to the Senate after the death of the emperor and inscribed on bronze tablets which were placed outside his mausoleum. Copies were sent to the principal provincial cities for display on the temples dedicated to him. No manuscript of the text exists. The copy in Ankara, which is the most complete, was rediscovered in 1555. More recently, fragmentary copies have been found in Pisidia at Antiocheia and Apollonia.

The Latin text was inscribed on the antae of the pronaos. It begins, RERUM GESTARUM DIVI AUGUSTI... (The achievement of the Divine Augustus...). The Greek text is in horizontal bands on the outside wall. The account is divided into four parts. The first records the military achievements of Augustus between 44 and 28 BC. The second is concerned with domestic administration and public affairs, e.g. the bestowal of titles and honours, triumphs and thanksgivings. The third deals with financial matters like pensions and gratuities to old soldiers, funds for public works, road construction, distribution of grain to the citizens of Rome, the provision of games and gladiatorial shows. The fourth is concerned with the emperor's political and diplomatic achievements. He boasts, rather chillingly, that he had 'captured about 30,000 slaves who had escaped from their masters (and that he had) handed them over to their masters for punishment'. Those slaves whose owners could not be traced were, according to the historian Dio Cassius, impaled.

There is also a reference in the *Res Gestae* to the census which he ordered in the twentieth year of his reign and which caused Mary and Joseph to go to Bethlehem to be enrolled.

There are plans in hand to protect the inscription from further damage by weathering and vandalism. The site may be closed to the public while this work is carried out.

From the Temple of Augustus return to Çankırı Cad. The remains of the **Roman baths**, which date from the reign of Caracalla (AD 211–17), are on the right-hand side of the road. Once covered with sheets of marble and ornamented with statues, the baths were used until the 6C AD. You enter the complex by the **palaestra** where young athletes exercised under the critical or appreciative eyes of their elders. Access to the baths was by the **frigidaria** where there was an unheated pool and dressing rooms. Beyond were a series of **tepidaria**, hot rooms, and the steam bath, the **calidarium**. The pool in the frigidarium is well preserved and there are many broken pieces of sculpture and architectural fragments in the palaestra.

The **Anatolian Civilisations Museum** is not far from the Roman baths, at the top of a steep hill. The museum is a treasure house of finds from the Palaeolithic Era to the Greek and Roman periods. The following is a brief description of the most important exhibits. There is a detailed, illustrated guide in English on sale in the museum.

The museum is made up of two buildings, the **Mahmut Paşa Bedesteni** and the **Kurşunlu Han**. The *bedesten* was built in 1464–71 by Mahmut Paşa, the grand vizier of Mehmet the Conqueror, to store valuable goods. The *han* was constructed by Mehmet Paşa who succeeded Mahmut Paşa as vizier. It provided funds for the soup kitchen which he had built in Üsküdar, İstanbul to feed the poor. The *bedesten* now houses the exhibits and the administrative offices, library, study rooms and a conference hall; the laboratory and workshops are in the *han*.

In the museum garden there are statues, stelae and architectural frage-ments from various places in Turkey. One of the most remarkable objects is the 7.4m high **statue from Fasilar** near Beyşehir which is believed to date from the Middle Bronze Age. Kurt Bittel is of the opinion that it was a victory monument destined by the Hittite king, Tudhaliya IV (1250–20 BC), for the cult centre of Eflatunpınar (see Route 19).

The exhibits in the museum are arranged in chronological order. Facing the sales desk is a section devoted to the **Palaeolithic Period**, c 30,000–8000 BC. The finest exhibits here come from the **Karain Cave**, 30km NW of Antalya. They include stone tools, hand axes, arrowheads, scrapers, orna-ments, needles and awls.

In the W hall there are exhibits from the **Neolithic Age**, 8000–5500 BC. These include the **reconstruction of a cult room** from Çatal Höyük, 6800–5700 BC, 52km SE of Konya, with frescoes of hunting scenes, an erupting volcano (possibly Hasan Dağı), and representations of leopards, deer, wild pigs, lions, bears and other animals. There are also **steatopygous statuettes** of the Mother Goddess, including one which shows her giving birth.

The next section has exhibits from the **Chalcolithic Period**, 5500–3000 BC. These include some fine **painted pottery** from Canhasan, Hacılar, Beycesultan, Alişar and Alacahüyük. Note the **painted bowl** from Hacılar with the representation of a four-fingered hand.

You now come to a large area devoted to the **Early Bronze Age**, 3000–2000 BC. The most striking exhibits here are from the royal tombs at **Alacahüyük**, 212km NE of Ankara. Dating from the second half of the third millennium BC, they include **bronze statuettes of stags**, ceremonial stand-ards in bronze and silver, a **twin idol** in gold, the stylised figure of a woman with golden breasts and golden boots, bracelets and necklaces, a golden mace head, **gold diadems**, a gold hair ornament, a **gold belt buckle**, a gold belt, a gold pin, pitchers, vessels and cups in gold, a gold and bronze hammer axe, a gold and bronze dagger and baked clay pots and pitchers. It is believed that the standards were fixed to staffs or mounted on a canopy or on the funeral bier. Some are simple metal discs with pendants, others bear the figures of stags. Note also the beautiful third millennium BC **silver statuette** of a female deity which was found at Hasanoğlan, c 38km to the

NE of Ankara. Her face, neck and breasts are covered with gold plate and thin gold bands are crossed under her high, pubescent breasts.

Next are exhibits from the **Assyrian Colonies Period**, 1950–1750 BC. From Kültepe near Kayseri, the principal Assyrian *karum* in Anatolia, there are decorated pots, some with human features, an **ivory statuette** of a nude female goddess, **envelopes of baked clay**, seals, bronze spools, a steatite figurine mould and the **bronze dagger** of King Anitta of Kaniş.

The last section on the S side of the museum has exhibits from the **Old Hittite and Imperial Hittite Periods**, 1750–1200 BC. There are flasks, kantharoi, rhyta in the form of bulls, ceremonial vessels, the famous **İnandık vase** with its decorative frieze of singers, musicians, priests, revellers and a couple busily engaged in sodomy, statuettes of gods and goddesses, a gold signet ring and **cuneiform baked clay tablets**. Note especially the **copy of the treaty** signed by the Hittites and the Egyptians after the Battle of Kadesh (1286 BC).

The large Hittite sculptures are exhibited in the centre hall. From the **Imperial Period**, 1400–1200 BC, there are the **relief of a warrior god** from Boğazkale and the **andesite orthostats** from the Sphinx Gate at Alaca-höyük. These show goats being taken to sacrifice, a king and queen pouring a libation, acrobats, and priests in procession.

From the **Neo-Hittite Period**, 1200–700 BC, there are a **Gate Lion**, a giant statue of king Tarhunza, and **orthostat reliefs** of king Sulumeli offering sacrifice, and of a lion hunt, all from Aslantepe–Malatya; from Carchemish a **statue base** with lions, and **basalt reliefs** of king Aras and his family, soldiers, officers, a battle chariot etc. Note the fine **fragmentary relief**, also from Carchemish, showing the head of the goddess Kubaba.

Return to the E side of the museum, to the section devoted to the **Phrygians**, 1200–700 BC. Most of the exhibits come from the tombs of the kings at Gordion. They include **inlaid tables**, bronze fibulae, decorated pottery, a **bronze situla** with a ram's head at its base, rhyta, pitchers and a **miniature bronze quadriga**.

Next is a section displaying objects from the **Urartian Kingdom**, 900–600 BC. Note the magnificent 7C **bronze cauldron**, with bulls' heads on the rim, from Altıntepe. This rests on a bronze stand with cloven feet. Similar cauldrons were exported from Urartu to Phrygia, Greece and Italy. There are also fine **ivory statuettes** of a winged demon and of lions, a section of **wall painting** from Altıntepe, bronze votive plaques, belts, helmets and shields, gold seals and buttons and an interesting **relief** from Adilcevaz-Kefkalesi of two winged gods standing on the backs of lions.

The last section has exhibits from the 7C to the 20C. These include a late 6C marble portrait head of a ruler, the column and capital of a mid 5C Greek funerary stele, a late Hellenistic marble **female portrait head**, a red-figure 5C crater and a **red figure pelike**, a **Hellenistic amphora** with a hunting scene (note the oriental dress of the hunter), **Roman bronze statuettes** of Zeus, Venus and Hercules, a Hadrianic bronze male head, a portrait bust of Trajan, Roman and Byzantine jewellery, Roman decorated glassware, Roman coins of Ankara and Galatia, some with the temple of Augustus, coins from the Selçuk and Ottoman periods and from the Turkish Republic.

Finally, in an alcove on the right there is one of the most striking exhibits in the museum, a **limestone statue of Cybele** flanked by dwarf musicians. Dating from the mid 6C BC, this was found at Boğazkale. The goddess is crowned with a polos. She holds a bird in her left hand. Her clothing shows Greek influence and she has the archaic, enigmatic smile of a Greek kore.

Before going to the citadel, you may like to visit three mosques near the museum. To the S is the **Ahi Elvan Camii** which was established in the late

13C. This was the mosque of the Ahi brotherhood, a craft guild which had close associations with the dervish sect. The present building dates from the early 15C, when it was restored. Its flat wooden ceiling is supported by 12 columns topped by Roman or Byzantine capitals. The finely carved walnut *mimber* dates from the period of the mosque's restoration.

Nearby is the **Arslanhane Camii** which was built in the late 13C. This Selçuk mosque has been little changed since its repair in 1289 by the brothers Hüsammedin and Hasan. The ornate *mimber* and the *mihrab* with its decoration of tiled mosaic and stucco are, perhaps, its finest features. The roof is supported by 24 wooden columns. It has a clearly defined raised nave and four side aisles. Material taken from Roman and Byzantine structures was re-used by the builders, particularly in the base of the minaret. Adjoining the mosque is the *türbe* of its founder, Ahi Şerafettin. He was buried here c 1292. The tomb with its distinctive octagonal drum and conical roof was restored recently. The finely carved wooden sarcophagus has been moved to the Ethnographic Museum.

A short distance to the E, on Ulucanlar Cad., is the 16C **Yeni Cami** which was designed by Sinan. Built of red porphry, this is the largest Ottoman mosque in Ankara. Note the *mimber* and *mihrab* of white marble.

The main part of the fortifications of Ankara's **citadel** dates from the reign of the emperor Heraclius (AD 610–41). It was probably completed after he had defeated the Persians c 627. With a length of c 1.2km, this has 40 polygonal shaped towers. The outer wall, which is lower down the hill on the W and S sides, has a total length of c 1.6km. Originally it had 18 towers; 15 are still standing. This outer wall, which is made up largely of material taken from older structures, was the work of Michael II (820–29). The fortifications were repaired several times by the Selçuks and the Ottomans who erected or restored the **Ak Kale** at the eastern end of the keep.

The **Hisar Kapısı** provides access to the area protected by the lower wall. This is largely occupied by ancient houses in various stages of picturesque dilapidation. To get to the keep you pass through **Parmak Kapısı**, a double gate at an angle flanked by towers. Built into the curtain wall between the towers are several ancient altars and a number of badly damaged statues of Priapus, the fertility god. You are now in an Ottoman village where rickety wooden houses and a few shops line the narrow, twisting alleyways. One or two of the old *konaks*, restored and re-opened as restaurants, have become fashionable rendezvous.

Not far from the Parmak gate is the **Alaeddin Camii**. This Selçuk mosque, built c 1178 during the reign of Kılıçarslan II, was restored by the Ottomans. Note the finely carved 12C *mimber*. The mosque's elaborately ornamented door is now in the Ethnographic Museum. An inscription of 1361 in the mosque mentions Orhan Gazi who captured Ancyra in 1354.

For a panoramic view of eastern Ankara from the ramparts take the narrow street to the right of the mosque. There is a good view of the centre of the city from the garden and belvedere below Ak Kale. From here you can also see *gecekondu* which cling precariously to the steeply sloping sides of some of the hills around the city. Looking as though they are about to collapse or slide down into the deep canyons which score the hillsides, these illegal squatters' houses were erected during the night—hence their name—to take advantage of a loophole in the law. Often without water, electricity or sewage, they are a danger to those who live in them.

55

Ankara to Nevşehir and Cappadocia

Total distance 261km. Ankara 33km Elmadağ—33km Kırıkkale—107km
Kirşehir—(18km Kesikköprü)—45km Hacıbektaş—24km Gülşehir—3km
Açık Sarayı—16km Nevşehir—(8km Üçhisar)—(2km Avcılar)—(3km
Çavusin)—(7.5km Zelve)—(20km Sarıhan)—(15km Avanos)—(20km
Özkonak)—(13km Göreme)—(4km Ortahisar)—(5km Ürgüp)—(5km Mus-
tafapaşa)—(4km Damsa)—(5km Cemilköy)—(8km Şahineffendi)—(14km
Güzelöz)—(14km Soğanlı)—(33km Derinkuyu)—(17km Göllü Dağ)—
(34km İhlara)—(15km Güzelyürt)—(9km Kaymaklı).

Leave Ankara by the E23 in the direction of Yozgat and Sivas. **Elmadağ**,
33km from the capital, is a popular winter sports resort which offers good
skiing on the slopes of Elmadağ mountain (1955m). Accommodation is
available in the *Turban Elmadağ Dağ Evi* and in chalets. The resort has a
snack bar, a discotheque and a restaurant which serves à la carte meals.

Continue for 33km to the industrial centre of Kırıkkale (700m). Here turn
S on to Road 765 signposted Keskin and Kirşehir. At first this road runs
parallel to the Kızılırmak river then rises steadily to 1140m at Akpınar. It
joins Road 260 c 23km before Kirşehir. Capital of the province of the same
name, **Kirşehir** is believed to occupy the site of Justianopolis Mokyssos
which is named after Justinian I. He granted it city status c AD 536. Kirşehir
had acquired its present name by the early 14C when it was mentioned in
a treaty between an emir of Karaman and the Ottoman sultan. Between the
14C and the 18C it was an important centre of the *Ahi*. They were urban
guilds of unmarried young men recruited largely from the artisan and
merchant classes which exercised considerable influence in local affairs.
Their members often filled important posts in the administration. Many of
them became provincial governors. The Ahi of Kirşehir were tanners.

There are several interesting Islamic monuments in Kirşehir. The **Caca-
bey Camii**, established in the 13C by a Selçuk sultan of Konya as an
observatory, was later turned into a mosque. Note the different types of
stone used in the portal. The *kümbet* on the façade and the minaret, which
is a late addition, are decorated with tiles. The 13C **Alaettin Camii**, the **Aşik
Paşa Veli Turbesi** (tomb of a 13C poet and historian), the **Melik Gazi
Kümbet** and the **Ahi Avran Türbesi**, where the founder of the Ahi brotherhood is buried, merit a visit. The Melik Gazi Kümbet dates from AD 1228
when the Mengücekids were under Selçuk rule. There are certain similarities between the roof connections to the lower chamber of this *kümbet* and
one of the *kümbets* at Divrigi.

About 18km to the S of Kirşehir on the road to Ortaköy there are the
remains of a *han* which was built in 1268 on the orders of the vizier
Nureddin Cebrail bin Caca Béy. **Kesikköprü Hanı**, the Broken Bridge Han,
gets its name from a ruined bridge over the nearby Kızılırmak river. The
han's finely decorated entry and the vault of its great central hall are well
preserved. The mosque was on the ground floor to the left of the entrance.

Return to Kirşehir and continue to (45km) **Hacıbektaş**, the putative birthplace of the founder of the Bektaşi order of dervishes.

The doctrines of the Bektaşi were a synthesis of orthodox Islamic, Shiite and Christian beliefs. They venerated a trinity of God, Muhammed and Ali, made offerings of bread and wine at initiation ceremonies and required their teachers to be celibate. Members of the order were introduced gradually to its secrets. Hacı Bektaş Veli, the founder of the order, converted Tatar communities to Islam and arranged for them to be given grants of land in return for undertaking military service. Some authorities claim that he was involved in the establishment of the Janissaries, that elite army corps formed of youths taken from Christian countries in the Ottoman Empire. Certainly the Bektaşi dervishes were chaplains to the Janissaries and in that capacity were responsible for the conversion of Albania to Islam. They had many links with villagers and the rural poor. Liberal in outlook, they later acquired a certain reputation for loose living. Women were allowed to attend their services unveiled. The Bektaşi and the Janissaries were suppressed in 1826.

The *tekke* of the order is in a small, carefully-tended garden. There are **three courtyards**. In the first, Üçler Çeşmesi (the three fountains) there are baths and the laundry of the *tekke*. You pass from there to the second courtyard where, in the soup kitchen, food was prepared and served to the poor. Note the huge black cauldron, the Kara Kazan, which was considered holy by the sect. The Janissaries used similar cauldrons, not only to prepare their food, but, on occasions, to express their dissatisfaction with the sultan when they banged loudly on the base and sides. On the right is the **Lion Fountain**. The marble lion was brought from Egypt. On the left are the guest house, the cellar and the chapter house where new members of the *tekke* were initiated, confessions were heard, lots were drawn and the Bektaşi ceremony of *Cem Ayini* took place. The inscription on the door dates from AD 1326. In one of the rooms are the 12 *Makam Postu* (12 Authorities Hide) and the **Bektaşi throne**. A **portrait of Hacı Bektaş** shows him holding a stag and caressing the head of a lion. In other rooms there are objects from the Bronze Age and the Hittite, Phrygian and Hellenistic periods which were found in Hacıbektaş-Sulucakarahüyük.

In the beautifully decorated *türbe* there are two tombs separated by a silken banner. The larger is that of Hacı Bektaş, the smaller that of his successor. Note the collection of huge axes. The rags tied to the trees outside the *türbe* are a reminder of the time when the nomadic Turks were animists and their shamans marked holy places in this way.

Continue in the direction of Nevşehir to (24km) Gülşehir, formerly known as Arabsun and Zoropassos. Here you enter the fantastic, convoluted, corrugated landscape of Cappadocia. Seyit Mehmet Paşa, also known as Karavezir (the Black Vizier), built a mosque, library, hamam and several fountains here.

About 1.5km to the S is the cruciform **Karşı Kilise** which was in use until 1922. The frescoes in this church have suffered considerably from the hands of vandals who, in a pathetic attempt to be remembered, have scratched their names on the walls. In the upper part of the church the paintings, blackened by centuries of candle smoke and incense, are dated by an inscription to 25 April 1212, i.e. to the reign of the Lascarid emperor Theodore I (1204–22). He ruled from Nicaea during the period of the Latin occupation of Constantinople. Note in particular the lady donor in the scene of the Last Judgement. Nimbed, she stands with her hands on the heads of two children. Only the names Maria and Eirene are legible.

About 3km to the S of Gülşehir is **Açık Sarayı** with its striking façade of blind arches cut out of the rock face. This large monastic complex is on several levels. It has three churches, cells, a kitchen and a refectory dug out of the soft tufa. The decoration consists mainly of crosses but inside the door of the first church there is an unusual motif. Two bulls, which have adopted an aggressive stance, appear to be about to charge.

In the village of Gökçetoprak, formerly Sivasa, which is about 30km to the SW of Gülşehir, there is a **relief of Zeus** on a rocky outcrop. The 10C **underground city of Yeraktı Şehir** is at Ovaören, 5km farther on. Nearby, there is a **Hittite inscription** cut into the rock face.

NEVŞEHİR is c 16km to the S of Açık Sarayı. Capital of the province of the same name, it is an excellent centre for visiting Cappadocia.

Accommodation and Information. The town has nine hotels inspected by the Ministry of Tourism. These range from the luxurious, four-star *Nevşehir Dedeman Oteli* to more modest establishments. The three-star *Orsan Kapadokya Oteli* on the E side of the town near the museum is clean, comfortable, and well run. From the *otogar* at the western end of Atatürk Bul., buses depart to Ankara, İstanbul and other cities at frequent intervals. There are also three mini-bus stations for local services.

The **Tourist Information Office** is in the centre of Atatürk Bul., Hastane Yanı, near the junction with Lale Cad. Its well-informed, helpful, multilingual staff provide an excellent service.

Nevşehir's Archaeological and Ethnographic Museum, on the E side of the town, is housed in the İmaret building which was built by Sadrazam Damat İbrahim Paşa at the beginning of the 18C. In the garden there are Byzantine water jars, **grave stelae**, altars, **inscriptions** and architectural fragments from various periods. **Room I** is devoted to miniatures of palace life, books, manuscripts, writing sets, 18C clothing and photographs of architectural works. In **Room II** there are prehistoric axes, earthenware dishes, **Hittite pottery**, **Phrygian fibulae** and other ornaments and artefacts from the Roman period. Note the mother of pearl pictures of Jesus. **Room III** has the ethnographic collection. There are porcelain, tiles, dishes, Ottoman period clothing, kitchen utensils, jewellery, bows, arrows and other weapons.

Nevşehir means New City. Although the site was occupied by the Hittites, the Phrygians, Alexander the Great, the Romans, the Byzantines and the Selçuks there are few ancient buildings. In earlier times it was known as Nisa and Soranos. The Ottomans called it Muşkara. This name was changed in the 18C to Nevşehir. Today it sprawls untidily across a steep hillside. On the summit the Selçuks built a **fortress** which was later restored and enlarged by the Ottomans.

In 1726 the **Kurşunlu Camii** was established here by the Nevşehrli Vizier Damat İbrahim Paşa. The first Ottoman minister to cultivate good relations with Europe, he sent ambassadors to Vienna and Paris to sign treaties and trade agreements, to learn about European diplomacy and military strength. A master of palace intrigue, he managed the affairs of the Ottoman Empire with consummate skill. However, in September 1730 the Janissaries revolted against him and the sultan, Ahmet III, fearing for his own life, dismissed İbrahim and had him strangled. This brought to an end the so-called Tulip Period of Ottoman history.

Because of its roof covering the Kurşunlu Camii is sometimes called the Lead Mosque. Attached to it were a finely decorated library, a hospital and a Koranic School. Nevşehir's 13C **Kaya Camii** also merits a visit.

Cappadocia

Bounded by Aksaray in the W, Kayseri in the E and Niğde in the S, Cappadocia may be visited from Nevşehir, Avanos or Ürgüp. All three towns have excellent hotel accommodation. For visitors without their own transport there are inexpensive tours operated by local travel agencies. There are also taxis which may be hired by the day. It is advisable to agree the price with the driver before setting out. Bargaining is not frowned on. Many of the places may also be reached by public transport, but this method of travel requires time, patience, a study of the bus schedules and a good deal of careful planning.

Spring and autumn are the best seasons for visiting Cappadocia. The summers are hot and enervating. During the holiday months popular places like Göreme, Derinkuyu and Kaymakli are crowded with visitors and there are long queues for the churches and underground cities.

In the main centres there are some reasonably good restaurants. A picnic in a quiet corner of one of the valleys is an attractive alternative. Take a bottle or two of the excellent Cappadocian wine. There are strict penalties about litter. This should always be placed in the containers marked *Çöp*.

History. Cappadocia's strange, lunar landscape has been carved out of a plateau formed from lava and mud which poured out in remote geological time from two volcanoes, Erciyas Dağı (3917m) to the S of Kayseri and Hasan Dağı (3268m) between Niğde and Aksaray. Eons of erosion have shaped the resulting tufa into fantastic forms. In some places a layer of basalt, which is less affected by weathering, covered the softer rock. This juxtaposition of materials has produced capped columns, towers, and pyramids and the cone-shaped peaks known as *peribacalar*.

The oldest traces of human occupation in Cappadocia have been found on the slopes of Avla Dağ c 9km to the SE of Ürgüp. There archaeologists discovered pottery and obsidian tools which they dated to the Neolithic period. Acemhöyük, 34km to the S of Aksaray, has been identified with the city of Purushanda or Purushattum which was destroyed by barbarian hordes c 2230 BC. Excavations at the site have produced ceramics, bronze vessels and ivories. These are now in Ankara. Assyrian traders had an important *karum* at Kanesh near Kayseri c 1900 BC. In the village of Mamasun, which is also near Aksaray, there is an inscription dating from c 1200 BC. Traces of Hittite occupation have been found at Acemhöyük, Niğde, Acigöl and at a number of other places in Cappadocia. Remains from the Neo-Hittite period have been discovered at Kemerhisar, 5km from Bor, and at Niğde.

The earliest known reference to Cappadocia is by the 5C BC historian Herodotus. He says the Greeks called its people Syrians and that it lay between Phrygia and Cilicia. From the mid 6C BC to 334 BC Cappadocia was one of the Persian satrapies in Anatolia. Its people appear to have been greatly influenced by the religion of their rulers, merging some of its dogmas with beliefs inherited from their Hittite ancestors. Later, to this syncretic faith were added the gods of the Graeco-Roman pantheon. Strabo, writing in the 1C AD, mentions the existence of a great temple dedicated to Zeus at Venasa.

After the death of Alexander the Great in 323 BC, Cappadocia was awarded to his Chief of Secretariat, Eumenes of Cardia. Six years later Eumenes was betrayed by his Macedonian soldiers to Antigonus the One-Eyed who had him executed. Cappadocia was ruled by a native dynasty until AD 17, when Tiberius made it a Roman province.

Christianity came early to Cappadocia. There is a reference in 1 Peter 1:1-2 to God's scattered people in Pontus, Galatia, Cappadocia, Asia and Bithynia. St Paul passed through Cappadocia on his way to Ancyra. He was held prisoner for a time in Caesarea (Kayseri). There is a record of a bishop named Alexander from Cappadocia visiting Jerusalem c AD 200. In the 4C the area produced three saints who are honoured by both the Eastern and the Western Churches. St Basil the Great, who was born in Caesarea, saved Cappadocia from the errors of the Arians and the Macedonians. His friend, St Gregory Nazianen, is surnamed 'the Divine', ὁ Θεόλογος, by the Greek

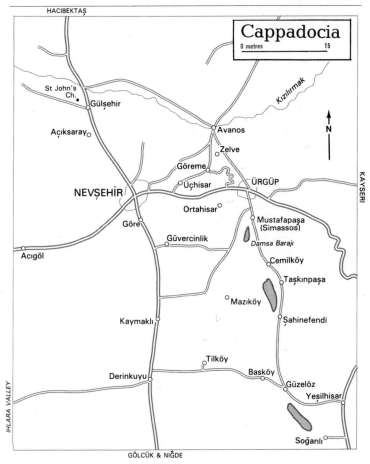

Orthodox Church because of the profundity of his writings. St Gregory of Nysa, a younger brother of St Basil the Great, was a doughty fighter against the Arian heresy and a theologian of considerable distinction.

It seems likely that Cappadocian monasticism developed from the anchorites of the Early Church who sought refuge from the distractions of the world in wild, remote places. They devoted their lives to prayer, penance and fasting, often living in man-made or natural caves. The austere landscape and difficult climate of Cappadocia provided them with a perfect habitat. There may have been troglodytes, like those described by Xenophon in Anabasis 4.5.25, living here already.

In time the anchorites found it convenient to gather in loosely-formed groups which were so constituted that they could still live largely separate lives. That changed in the mid 4C when St Basil the Great (see above) drew up his rule for monastic settlements and founded a community of monks on the river Iris (the modern Yeşilirmak) in Pontus

In the 7C and 8C when the Arabs began to raid central Anatolia, the monastic communities went underground. Churches and living quarters were cut out of the soft tufa. Members of the local Christian communities joined the monks and further rooms were made to accommodate them. Eventually there were several subterranean cities, with storage places for food and ventilator shafts, in the area. These provided a safe refuge in times of danger.

As many of the churches and some of the underground cities have no lighting or are badly lit, take a torch. The earliest Cappadocian churches were ornamented mainly with representations of the cross, a potent symbol for a people frequently under attack by hostile Islamic forces. After the resolution of the iconoclastic controversy which lasted from 726 to 843, their walls and ceilings were covered with frescoes portraying the life of Christ and the saints. In addition to the Deisis, the Descent of the Holy Spirit and the Resurrection, SS Barbara, Catherine, George and Christopher are frequently depicted. Imperial personages are also featured. St Helena discovering the Holy Cross and idealised portraits of Constantine figure prominently. The churches were made as though they were free-standing buildings of stone or brick in the open air. The simplest have a rectangular, vaulted nave with an apse covered by a projecting arch, but there are many variations. There are churches with two naves, pillared side aisles, a triple apse and a dome. The columns and vaults are, of course, only structural symbols. The columns support nothing and the vaults do not rest on walls. Many of the churches have elaborately ornamented façades.

For the most part, the monasteries were abandoned after the arrival of the Turks in Anatolia and they were occupied by the local people. However, some of the churches continued to be used until 1923 when there was an exchange of populations between Turkey and Greece and the Christians left the area.

In 1907 a young Jesuit priest, Fr Guillaume de Jerphanion, came to Cappadocia. He began a study of the rockcut churches and their paintings which lasted more than 30 years. His findings are contained in a massive work, *Une nouvelle province de l'art byzantin: Les églises rupestres de Cappadoce* (five volumes published in Paris between 1925 and 1942). Jerphanion's lead was followed by other scholars and the importance of the churches was recognised. Today many have been designated archaeological monuments and are carefully maintained and preserved.

Unfortunately, in a number of churches the frescoes have been defaced, because the depiction of the human form is anathema to strict Muslims. The faces or sometimes just the eyes have been obliterated, as it was believed that this action 'killed' the painted subject. Some of the Greeks, who lived in Cappadocia until the 1920s, were also not without blame. Superstitious members of that community believed that illness could be cured by treating the patient with a potion made from a powdered sacred painting mixed with water. Modern vandals who scratch their initials on the walls have added to the process of destruction. This practice is now strictly forbidden and offenders are punished severely by the authorities.

It is estimated that there are more than 600 rock-cut churches in Cappadocia. Their Turkish names are usually based on architectural style or decoration, e.g. the Apple Church, the Buckle Church. In addition, there are thousands of underground rooms which were used by the monks and by lay people as living quarters and for the storage of foodstuffs. The most important and most accessible are described below.

From Nevşehir follow the road signposted Ürgüp for c 5km and then take take a turning on the left to (3km) **Üçhisar**. This village is dominated by the ruins of a medieval castle which crowns a cliff pockmarked with caves. The breathtaking view from the castle covers a vast area between Nevşehir, Avanos, Ürgüp and Ortahisar. Deep ravines and gulleys, rock outcrops shaped by the weather into cones, pyramids and towers of every shape and size form a bizarre landscape reminiscent of a Bosch or Brueghel painting. In the village many of the houses have façades ornamented with scallop-shaped carvings and consoles. A hotel cut from the rock has wine on tap in its rooms. In addition to carpet-making and marble carving Üçhisar has a flourishing jewellery industry which uses turquoise-coloured apatite.

From Üçhisar continue to **Avcılar**. In the centre of this village there is a **Roman tomb** near the top of a huge pointed cone. Two broken Doric columns hang suspended from the roof of the recessed entrance. The base on which they once rested has disappeared.

Near the village, which was formerly called Göremeköy, a priapic profusion of *peribacalar* introduces a defiant note of pagan sensuality into this landscape redolent of prayer and asceticism. Like giant, rampant phalli, they thrust their great shafts urgently into the air.

Continue to **Çavuşin**, a village now abandoned because of earthquakes and frequent rock falls. The **Church of St John**, believed to date from the 5C, is probably the oldest Christian building in Cappadocia. It was decorated with paintings from the Pre-Iconoclastic period. Only the apse, with its flanking stone seats, remains. The imposing entrance collapsed some years ago. A little way outside the village is a church which local people call **Güvercinlik**, the Dovecote. An iron ladder leads up to the recessed doorway. Note the faded frescoes above and to the right of the entrance. This church dates from the 10C and may have been made to commemorate the visit of emperor Nicephorus II Phocas (963–9), the so-called White Death of the Saracens, to his native Cappadocia. Born into an aristocratic family, Nicephorus was an ascetic, happiest in the company of holy men. Betrayed by his wife and her handsome lover, the emperor's former friend John Tzimisces, he was murdered in his bed on the night of 10–11 December 969. There is a portrait of Nicephorus in the church.

At **Zelve** (4km) there is a huge amphitheatre where three canyons meet in the Valley of the Monks (Paşabağı). Near the entrance to the valley is the Cone of St Simeon, an outcrop of tufa surmounted by three squat, mushroom-shaped pinnacles. At ground level a **chapel** has been cut out of the rock. This has some interesting, but very damaged, frescoes (10C). They depict incidents in the life of St Simeon Stylites the Elder (c 390–459). He lived for 37 years on a platform 90cm wide at the top of a 20m high pillar (see Route 38B). The saint is shown with his mother, healing a woman who had swallowed a snake, taming a dragon, and being called to a life of prayer and asceticism. Above the chapel there is an **anchorite's cell**.

There are clusters of single, double and triple-headed *peribacalar* each crowned with a neat black cap, among the vines and orchards of Paşabağı. More grotesque than those at Avcılar, they crowd the landscape like giant phalli from a nightmare painting by Dali.

The rock face at Zelve is honeycombed with caves and there are about ten churches dating from the 9C and 10C. There are also three churches from the Pre-Iconoclastic period. Much of the decoration in these buildings is symbolic. Grapes represent the Blood of Christ which is received by the congregation at the celebration of the Eucharist. Fish symbolise the faithful who were often called pisciculi and who became members of the church by being baptised in the piscina (literally the fishpond). Jesus called the Apostles Fishers of Men, and the letters of the Greek word for fish, ἰχθύς, were used by the early Christians to form the phrase, Iesous Christos Theou Huios Soter, Jesus Christ, Son of God, Saviour. A cross in a circle flanked by fish stood for mankind attracted to the doctrines of Christ. These, and other symbols, are to be found in the **Üzümlü Kilise**, the Church of the Grapes, and in the **Geyikli Kilise**, the Church of the Deer.

The caves were used as dwellings from the earliest times and there is evidence of human occupation in many of them e.g. storage bins and stone wheels used for grinding grain. During the Islamic period a *mescid*, fronted by a four-columned minaret, was hewn from the tufa. Zelve is sited in one of the oldest geological regions in Cappadocia and has been much affected by erosion. It was inhabited until in 1950. The rock-cut walls of the houses had weakened and were dangerous and its inhabitants moved to another location where they established the village of Yeni Zelve, New Zelve.

From Zelve return to the main road and continue in a northerly direction to (6km) Avanos. Just before the entrance to the town look for a minor road on the right which is signposted to **Sarıhan**. This 13C Selçuk *han*, on the left bank of the Kızılırmak, was probably built by İzzeddin Keykavus. It was one of the stopping places on the old caravan route from Kayseri to Aksaray and Konya. Above the dilapidated entrance on the E side there was a *mescid*. The courtyard is flanked by a domed arcade on the left and a number of chambers on the right. The central pillared hall is reached through a splendid doorway. On one of the pillars there is a painting in black of mounted soldiers. Plans are in hand to restore the *han* which has been plundered for many years by local people in search of building material. The beautiful yellow stone, which gives the *han* its name, is seen to best advantage at sunrise and sunset.

Avanos has been identified with ancient Venasa where, according to Strabo, there was a temple dedicated to Zeus. A prosperous establishment, the temple had almost 3000 servants. Its fertile sacred lands produced an annual income of 15 talents for the priest. He was appointed for life and ranked second to the priest of Comana (see above).

Information. This small town has two three-star and two two-star hotels inspected by the Ministry of Tourism. The **Tourist Information Office** is in Kenan Evran Cad., Heykel Yanı. Avanos has a tradition of pottery-making which dates back to Roman times. It is also famous for its fine carpets. In recent years tourism has become an important industry.

The town is built along the banks of the Kızılırmak, the ancient River Halys. This is the longest river in Anatolia. From its source to the E of Sivas it flows westward as far as Kırıkkale before turning N in a great arc to the Black Sea. Its waters are coloured by Cappadocia's rich deposits of clay, hence Kızılırmak, the Red River. The clay, taken from pits by the river bank, is used by the potters of Avanos to make cups, plates, beakers and jugs which are decorated with traditional designs. Visitors, encouraged by generous quantities of Cappadocian wine, have been known to try their hands at the potter's wheel.

From Avanos take the Kayseri road. After c 12km a signpost on the left points to 7km **Özkonak**. A little off the beaten track, this underground complex is usually less crowded than Derinkuyu and Kaymaklı (see below) which are better known. Largely unexplored, it is estimated that this city could house more than 60,000 souls. The entrance, which is protected by an overhang of tufa, leads to the part open to the public. Hollowed out from the tufa are four large halls, a number of rooms, several graves, air channels and niches which may have been used for storage. Note the large round stones with which the troglodytes blocked the entrances in times of danger.

From Özkonak return to Avanos and continue in a southerly direction for 9km to the **Open Air Museum of Göreme**. Near the entrance to the museum there are souvenir shops, a refreshments stand, a bank, parking facilities for cars and coaches and a kiosk where admission tickets are sold.

Göreme was known in ancient times as Korama. The first references to it are in the early 7C *Acts of St Hieron*. This 3C saint was a native of Matianoi, modern Maçan. Captured by Roman soldiers in the vineyard where he worked, he managed to escape and hid 'in a mighty cavern in the flank of a hill, which had been carved out of the rock with great skill'. He was martyred during the reign of Diocletian.

Göreme is an amphitheatre of ample proportions surrounded by steep cliffs leading to a pleasant, verdant valley. Apart from small openings, which served as doors, windows and air vents, there are few clues to the existence of the churches and monastic settlements. The Oxford geographer, H.F. Tozer, who visited Göreme in 1907 described it as 'one sepult monastic dwelling-place—a Byzantine Pompeii'. He was puzzled by the difficult access to many of the caves and suggested that their inhabitants must have used scaffolding or movable ladders. The lack of outward show and relative inaccessibility of some of the living quarters was surely deliberate, a protective device against hostile invaders.

A short distance outside the museum area is the **Tokalı Kilise**, the Church of the Buckle. Its Turkish name is probably derived from a buckle-like ornament on the central arch in the so-called New Church. Usually locked, the Buckle Church will be opened on request and the lights will be switched on by the *bekçi*. One of the largest and most interesting churches in Göreme, the Tokalı Kilise, has a Mesopotamian type, vaulted transverse nave with three apses (the New Church) which is preceded by a porch and a narthex. The narthex is formed from an earlier structure, which for convenience is called the Old Church. The walls and vaults of the narthex and nave are decorated with frescoes which date from the reign of Nicephorus Phocas II (963–69). Many of the paintings, which are executed in an attractive style, have a distinctive blue background. The figures are lively and animated. They depict the life of Christ from the Annunciation to the Ascension. On the lower part of the N wall of the narthex there are representations of a number of saints including Catherine, Helena and Theodore. In the New Church a large painting of the Crucifixion fills the wall of the main apse. SS Basil, Ephraim, Simeon Stylites, the Forty Martyrs of Sebaste and other saints, bishops, priests and monks of the Early Church are also depicted. An inscription in the N apse names one of one of the artists, who worked in the church, and his patron. 'The bema was decorated by Nicephorus at the expense of Leon, son of Constantine. You who read, pray for them to the Lord. Amen'.

Near the Buckle Church there are **chapels** dedicated to St Eustace, the Theotokos, Mary the Mother of God and to the Prophet Daniel. St Eustace was a Roman officer martyred c 118 during the reign of Hadrian. A pious legend relates that he was converted to Christianity when a white stag, which he was hunting, turned to confront him. The animal had a crucifix between its antlers. The paintings in the chapel date from the 11C. There are many representations of the legend of St Eustace in French cathedrals of the 13C. In the chapel of the Theotokos there are fine frescoes depicting Christ Pantocrator, Christ the Creator of All Things, Mary with her arms raised in prayer and realistic representations of five named saints each holding a martyr's palm. There are also scenes from the life of Christ. Note the elaborate *trompe l'oeil* decoration under some of the paintings. Unfortunately, many of the frescoes in this chapel have been damaged by erosion.

Just inside the door of the **Daniel Chapel**, on the right, there is a vivid depiction of the prophet in the lions' den. The two majestic equestrian figures are believed to date from after the triumph of the iconodules.

Just inside the museum area is the **Elmalı Kilise**, the Apple Church. A narrow passage leads to a small inner court and from there a short corridor provides access to the church. This has an inscribed cross plan. Four columns surround the central domed bay. This, in turn, is flanked by eight smaller bays which are also domed. The predominant colour in the paintings, which date from the 11C, is a warm yellow. Decoration from the Iconoclastic period may be seen in places where the later paintings have disappeared. In the central dome there is a representation, partly damaged at the top, of Christ Pantocrator. The main apse, which has a fresco of the Deisis, was closed by an iconostasis. The walls are decorated with scenes from the Life of Christ. The lower parts have suffered a good deal of damage. Among the saints depicted are Barbara, Sergius, Bacchus, Anicetus, Photinus and Demetrius. The church probably derives its name from the object held in Christ's hand. Formerly believed to be an apple, this is now thought to be a symbolic globe representing the world.

Towards the back of the outcrop which houses the Apple Church is the small, cruciform **Church of St Barbara**. According to a 10C legend, ascribed to Metaphrastes, Barbara was shut up in a tower and killed by her father because of her Christian faith. He was punished by being struck by lightning. Barbara's martyrdom was believed to have taken place in Nicomedia, modern İzmit, during the rule of Maximinus Thrax. In fact she probably never existed. Her cult was suppressed in 1969. She was the patron saint of architects, artillery men, stonemasons and grave diggers.

The church of St Barbara is decorated with crudely drawn designs in red ochre, which have been dated to the 11C. In some cases they were painted directly on to the rock, in others on to a very thin coat of plaster. A cross over the right hand aisle is surrounded with rough drawings of what look like *peribacalar*. There is a polychrome representation of St Barbara on the N wall. To the left of the entrance there is a Deisis and in the apse a painting of Christ Pantocrator. The equestrian figures, which face each other, are SS George and Theodore Tyro. Theodore was a recruit—hence his sobriquet—in the Roman army who was burned to death for setting fire to the temple of Cybele at Amasia. The esoteric symbols on the walls have given rise to much speculation. The strange beetle-like creature was believed by some to represent the devil. However, they have been identified recently as Byzantine military standards and insignia. The work, perhaps, of soldiers who became monks, they would be entirely appropriate in the company of the soldier saints, George and Theodore.

Continuing across the valley you come next to the **Yılanlı Kilise**, the Church of the Serpent. This double-celled church is entered through a long barrel-vaulted atrium. The paintings on its walls are enclosed in frames like icons. Among the figures represented are Constantine the Great and his mother, St Helena. They are holding the True Cross. When Helena was 80 years old she had a vision of the True Cross which had been lost after the Crucifixion. She went to Jerusalem and found three crosses buried in the temple of Venus. In turn these were placed on the body of a dead youth. When touched by the True Cross, he was restored to life.

To the left of Helena and Constantine stands St Onuphrius, his hands raised in a dismissive gesture. He was a 5C hermit who spent 70 years in the desert of Upper Egypt. Onuphrius was the patron saint of weavers, as he often shown covered only by his own abundant hair and a loin cloth of leaves. An apocryphal version of his life relates that originally he was a beautiful, lecherous girl who repented of her sins and asked God to rescue her from the lust of men. Her prayer was answered and she was turned into an ugly old man. Here the saint is depicted as a white bearded man with wrinkled breasts. A carefully positioned cactus hides his pudenda.

The church gets its Turkish name from a representation of SS George and Theodore. On horseback, they harass the devil who has taken on the form of a monstrous serpent. At the S end of the nave there is a much damaged painting of Christ. The small figure on the left is probably the donor who paid for the excavation of the church and its decoration.

Passing the refectory and its associated rooms on the slope to your right, you come to the **Karanlık Kilise**, the Dark Church, so called because it has only one small window. Armed with a torch, mount the narrow winding stairway. This leads to the atrium, a large part of which has fallen away. You enter a cross-vaulted cruciform church which has a central dome with four pillars. The iconostasis has been badly damaged. The paintings in the Dark Church betray a degree of sophistication lacking in some of the other churches in Göreme. The figures are animated and lifelike and there is a sense of movement in the depiction of important scenes from the life of Christ. These are not in chronological order. Among the most interesting are the betrayal of Christ by a youthful Judas who, surprisingly, has a halo; the Christ Pantocrator who raises his hand in blessing; the Nativity with a watchful Mary and the heads of the cow and donkey which warmed the infant with their breath; the Crucifixion, and a very well preserved Last Supper. Note the large fish in the centre of the table. There is an extensive use of blue, an expensive pigment made from lapis lazuli, in the backgrounds of the frescoes.

Two of the donors appear in the painting of the Blessing of the Apostles in the narthex vault. Genethlios and John are prostrate before theSaviour. John was described as *entalmatikos*, an entrepreneur. Two other donors, Nikephoros, a priest, and Bassianos, a layman, are portrayed in the Deisis painting in the central apse.

This was a monastic church. Nearby there is a refectory whose table and benches have been cut from the rock. The seat at the top of the table was for the father abbot. Above the refectory are the cells used by the monks.

Next is the **Çarıklı Kilise**, the Church of the Sandal. This crucifrom church, which is reached by an iron stairway, gets its name from sandal marks on the floor. The only illumination comes through the doorway. The frescoes here are similar in style and execution to those in the Dark Church. Unfortunately, many have been defaced with graffiti. On the central dome is a representation of Christ Pantocrator surrounded by the archangels Michael, Uriel, Raphael and Gabriel. In the central apse there is a Deisis. The N apse has portraits of SS Blaise, Gregory Nazianen, Basil, John Chrysostom, Nicholas and Hypatius.The Virgin and Child are depicted in the S apse. There are representations of some royal personages including Constantine, Helena and Eudocia. The donors of the church, Theognostos, Leo and Michael, are portrayed on the W wall of the W bay.

On the way to the exit you pass the ruins of the **Convent**. The first and second floors were taken up by the kitchen, refectory, nuns' parlour and storerooms. The **chapel**, with 11C frescoes, is on the third floor. The doors on the fourth and fifth floors were secured by great circular stones which could be rolled into place in times of danger.

In a gorge between Göreme Open Air Museum and Göreme village stands **El Nazar Church**. This two-storey T-shaped church, cut from a conic, rocky outcrop, has some of the oldest wall paintings in Göreme. Done in a simple linear style those that remain depict Christ between two angels, portraits of the saints and incidents from their lives. They date from the 11C.

On a slope nearby is the **Saklı Kilise**, the Hidden Church. After being covered for centuries with silt it was discovered in 1957. The church has a narthex, a nave divided by three arches, and three apses. The12C frescoes portray incidents from the lives of Christ and of Mary—from the Nativity to the Crucifixion and the Dormition. They were painted directly on the walls with broad, vigorous strokes. The predominant colour is red. St John the

Baptist in the desert inhabits a typical Göreme landscape with *peribacalar,* fruit trees and sparse vegetation. Note the exaggerated anatomical detail in the figure of Christ on the cross. The paintings on the lower part of the walls have suffered considerable water damage. Those on the upper part are in reasonably good condition, but the faces of many of the figures appear to have been damaged deliberately.

Ortahisar (4km) seems to huddle for protection under a huge, irregularly shaped, rocky mass which contains a castle and is pierced with caves. The splendid view from the top more than compensates for the stiff climb up a very narrow path. There are two churches of interest in the village, the **Harim (Private) Church** and the **Sarica (Yellow) Church**. Both are decorated with scenes from the Old and New Testaments. Note particularly the fresco of the Annunciation in the Sarica Church.

If you have time, visit the monastic complex at Firkatan, the lavishly decorated Armenian monastery in the Halaşdere valley and the four churches in the Balkan Deresi valley. All are within easy reach of Ortahisar. Take a guide. In the Balkan Deresi valley the frescoes in the cruciform Chapel I, of which only a part of the central dome and the S arm survive, portray scenes from the life of St Basil. The long captions, which accompany them, are taken from the text of Pseudo-Amphilochios. The earliest paintings here date from the 6C. Unfortunately, they are all in a very poor state of preservation.

Caves on the outskirts of Ortahisar are used to store oranges and lemons from southern Turkey, and locally grown apples and potatoes. 5km from Ortahisar, **Ürgüp**, like Nevşehir and Avanos, is a popular centre for visiting Cappadocia. It has two four-star hotels, one three-star hotel, a one-star hotel and two M1 motels inspected by the Ministry of Tourism. The *Perissia Oteli* (four-star) and the *Yeni Yükseller Oteli* (three-star) are recommended. The **Tourist Information Office** is at Kayseri Cad. No. 37.

The town's small museum has an interesting display of objects from Ürgüp and the surrounding area. These include ceramics from the Prehistoric period and figurines, lamps, stelae, statues, ornaments, ceramics, and metal and glass objects from the Hittite, Phrygian, Hellenistic, Roman and Byzantine periods. Note the **black figure kylix** with hunters and bird-like creatures and the **lekythos** with a banqueting scene. The ethnographical section exhibits tapestries, jewellery, costumes, manuscripts and weapons.

Ürgüp's shops have carpets, pottery, jewellery and souvenirs of all kinds. Not to be missed is the locally produced wine which has a heady, unusual bouquet. The town has some fine old houses. Several have been restored with loving care, others, alas, have been allowed to fall into ruin.

From Ürgüp take the road S to 5km **Mustafapaşa**. Before the exchange of populations in 1920–23 this town was occupied mainly by Greeks and was known as Sinassos. Because of its commerce with İstanbul, Sinassos prospered and its citizens built themselves fine stone houses with wrought iron balconies and elaborately ornamented façades.

Near the town is the **Church of the Holy Apostles**, sometimes known as the Church of Pentecost. This archaic period (c 850–950) building has two parallel naves. Note the **niches** along the walls formed by the arcades on piers. It is decorated with frescoes which are typical of the time. The figures are short and stocky, the faces are rather pudgy and have pursed lips. The painting of the bodies emphasises the mass and volume of the human form. Folds in the clothing form repetitive patterns.

About 200m from the town centre a **locked church** is surrounded by a large, neglected cemetery. Among the tumbled gravestones there is a **well** which, according to the local people, has healing properties. Sick children are brought here to drink and bathe in its water. The bushes around the well are festooned with pieces of cloth, ex voto offerings placed here by those who hope for a cure.

The **Church of St Basil**, c 1km from the town, is poised on the edge of a deep, wild ravine. Steps lead down to the entrance of this square building which has been carved from the rock. Four large columns support the ceiling. **Inscriptions** date the relief ornamentation to the mid 8C. There are spectacular views from the windows of the church across, and down into, the ravine. A **19C church** in the town centre is being restored.

In the village of **Damsa**, 4km to the S, there are some interesting Islamic buildings—a mosque, two *türbe* and a ruined Selçuk *medrese*. There are also the ruins of several churches. The nearby **Damsa Lake** is a favourite place for picnics and barbecues.

From Damsa continue to (5km) Cemil. In a lonely valley 2km to the S of the village is the well-preserved **Monastery of Ayios Archangelos**. Surrounded by trees and rocky outcrops, this eerie place attracts few visitors. Care should be taken in approaching the monastery, as there is an unprotected drop of c 6m from an opening in the wall down to the dusty floor. All of the buildings are very dark. To examine them properly you will need a powerful torch. The **geometrical wall paintings**, much blackened by smoke, in the church dedicated to St Stephen may date from the Iconoclastic period. The figurative frescoes in the St Michael church are from the 13C and 14C. In the refectory, divided into two sections by an arcade, has a massive stone table.

The road to **Şahinefendi** passes through a pleasant river valley shaded by poplars. Formerly known as Suveş and Sebastos this village has a church dedicated to the Forty Martyrs of Sebaste. It has been dated to 1216 in the reign of the Lascarid emperor Theodore (see above). There are two parallel naves ornamented with frescoes. The work of a painter called Etios, they are rather uninspired copies of the more accomplished wall paintings in the Göreme churches. Those concerned with the decoration of the church appear to have had a rather limited knowledge of the Scriptures. A passage ascribed to Solomon is from Zechariah. These late works have been described as the products of a hybrid art derived from Armenian, Islamic and Latin models.

Continue S for 14km to **Güzelöz**, the former Mavrucan. Here at the end of a wooded valley is a late (1223) triconch church dedicated to St George. Among its paintings there is a striking representation of the Last Judgement. Unfortunately, all of the frescoes in this church are badly damaged.

The **Soğanlı Valley** is one of the most attractive places in central Anatolia. From Güzelöz, go first to (9km) Yeşilhisar and there take the signposted right-hand turn to the village of (5km) Soğanlı. Quiet and unspoiled, the valley has been spared the excessive commercialisation that mars some of the better known centres in Cappadocia. It deserves at least a day of quiet, leisurely exploration. Wide enough to permit the construction of roads and paths, its monasteries and churches are hollowed out, not from the cliff face, but from outcrops of rock between the river and the steep, barren slopes of the mesa. A plan in the centre of the village shows the location of the principal churches. All are within easy walking distance. An additional incentive, if one were needed, to linger in Soğanlı is provided by a small family-run restaurant which serves good, simple food. The people of the valley are dignified, friendly and helpful and, a refreshing change from other places in Cappadocia, do not badger visitors to buy souvenirs.

It is estimated that there were about 150 churches in the valley. However, many have been filled in, others have been turned into dovecotes or materials taken from them have been used to build houses, as in the case of the Akkilise near the entrance to the village. The cliff face is pockmarked with caves, natural and artificial. Dovecotes are outlined in white.

The **Geyikli Kilise**, the Church of the Deer, is at the point where the two branches of the valley meet. It derives its name from a fresco near the door which depicts the legend of St Eustace (see also Göreme). The saint, with lowered lance, is in close pursuit of a deer, unaware that Christ has taken on the form of this animal. Eustace rides his horse at speed through a rocky landscape only to find that his prey has stopped and turned to face him. Between its horns there is a crucifix. An inscription reads, 'Plakides, why are you chasing me? I turned myself into a beast for you, and now you hunt me'. The church, which dates from the Middle Byzantine Period (c 1020–1130), has two parallel naves. One is in a ruinous state. The frescoes are not in a very good condition. The donor, John Skepides, a protospatharios and consul-strategos, belonged to a Cappadocian family well-known for its interest in painting and generous patronage.

The Transitional Phase (c 950–1020) **Church of St Barbara**, sometimes known as the Tahtalı Kilise (the Wooden Church), was excavated from a prominent rocky outcrop. It has two parallel naves, each with an apse. One of the naves has wall paintings which, according to an inscription, date from the reigns of Constantine VIII and Basil II (1006–21). The paintings are in a poor condition. Note the striking depiction of Christ's Descent into Hell. With a comforting gesture, he releases the souls of the faithful who have awaited his coming since the fall of Adam.

A narrow path above the stream leads to the **Kubbeli Kilise**, the Domed Church, which is also known as the Belli Kilise. It is the only rock-cut church in Cappadocia which had the top of the tufa cone shaped into a dome. Painted in polychrome shades, this is not unlike the domes of Armenian churches and some authorities believe that it may have been the work of Armenian Christians fleeing from Arab persecution. There are three chapels connected by spiral staircases. The paintings in the first chapel date from the Archaic Period (c 850–950). Note the excellent view of the valley from the windows of the largest chapel. A look-out here would be able to alert the monastic community of approaching danger. There are some well-preserved graves in the lower chapel.

Across the valley from the Kubbeli Kilise is the **Yılanlı Kilise**, the Snake Church, sometimes called the Canavar Kilise. It derives its name from a fresco of St George killing the Dragon. The approach to the church is through a courtyard lined with the cells, refectory and kitchen of the monastery. The rectangular church has two parallel, barrel-vaulted naves and a crypt. The frescoes in the N nave have been destroyed. Those in the S nave are believed to date from the 15C or 16C. They include a huge Last Judgement which was painted at a time when monasticism in the Soğanlı Valley was beginning to come to an end. On the dome there is a representation of Christ Pantocrator surrounded by saints. The cryptic painting in the ruined narthex of nude women suckling snakes may be an oblique reference to the temptation of Eve in the Garden of Eden by Satan who came to her in the form of a serpent.

The **Karabaş Kilise**, the Dark Church, gets its name from the darkened haloes around the heads of the saints, the effect of oxidation.Carved from the tufa c 900, it has four parallel naves. As in the Church of the Holy Apostles at Sinassos the walls have deep niches formed by arcades on piers. The paintings, some of which are almost completely obliterated by graffiti, have been dated by an inscription to 1060–61 in the Middle Byzantine

Period (c 1020–1130). Note especially those showing the Birth of Jesus, the Washing of the Infant Jesus and his Circumcision.

One of the donors, Michael Skepides, a protospatharios during the reign of Emperor Constantine X Dukas (1059–67), and his family are depicted in frescoes in the principal nave. Michael is standing, proud and erect. He holds a lance in his right hand. His left rests lightly on the hilt of his sword. John Skepides, another member of this family of Cappadocian landowners and soldiers, contributed to the cost of decorating the Geyikli Kilise.

From the Soğanlı Valley return to Guzelöz and there take the road signposted to (21km) Derinkuyu. En route, you come first to Başköy and then to the pretty little village of Tilköy which is spread across a steep hillside. The **Underground City of Derinkuyu** attracts some of the largest crowds in Cappadocia. During the holiday months its low, narrow, cramped passageways are filled with sweating tourists pushing and shoving in a desperate attempt to examine yet another rock-cut room or, more often, to escape to the surface and fresh air. If you are tall, suffer from claustrophobia or have any condition which makes it difficult for you to bend, a visit to the underground city may be more of a penance than a pleasure.

Derinkuyu is an untidy, rather dirty village. In marked contrast to places like Avanos or Soğanlı, its inhabitants appear to take little pride in its appearance and make few attempts to keep it clean. A **church** in the village centre, which was converted into a mosque in 1949, has some frescoes on the dome of Christ, Mary, the Angels and the Apostles. The other **church** in the village, which has a separate belfry, dates from the 19C. Its walls, fine door and the lower part of the pillars in the nave are disfigured with moronic scribbles. A half-hearted attempt has been made to clean up the interior. On the central dome there is a fresco of Christ Pantocrator. Fortunately, this is far enough from the ground to escape the disfiguration and defilement inflicted by vandals on the other wall paintings.

It is estimated that there are between 18 and 20 floors in the underground city of Derinkuyu. All are connected by a steep, narrow passage. At present eight floors may be visited by the public. Rooms open to the left and right of the passage at each level. The first and second levels were given over to the communal kitchens, store rooms, bedrooms, refectories and toilets. The stalls for the animals were here also. On the lowest level, adjoining a **cruciform chapel**, which has a narthex and an apse, is a **large room** which may have been used for meetings.

So far 36 underground cities have been discovered in Cappadocia. Some believe that the upper levels were excavated by the Hittites and that in the 6C and 7C these were enlarged and extended by Christian communities. The underground city of Derinkuyu is estimated to have a capacity of 20,000. Despite the fact that it and the other 35 have a reasonably pleasant temperature of c 16°C and are free from insect pests, it is difficult to believe that large numbers of people could have lived in them permanently. There is no natural light and,although they have airshafts and wells and bins for the storage of food, surely only the most grave danger could persuade people to live in such an unhealthy environment.

There is a theory that the underground cities were used mainly for storage purposes, rather like the subterranean caves at Ortahisar where citrus fruit is kept fresh for several months. However, this does not explain why it was necessary to excavate so many different types and sizes of rooms.

About 17km to the SW of Derinkuyu, on the summit of **Göllü Dağ** (2143m), there are the ruins of a late Hittite city which was destroyed by fire in the 8C BC. Inside a defensive wall, which had four gates, are the remains of several buildings separated by narrow lanes.The principal structure, which occupied the highest point, was probably a palace. This was guarded by statues of sphinxes and double-headed lions. Ceramics decorated with animal figures discovered during excavations by Turkish archaeologists are divided between the museums of Kayseri and Niğde. The lions from the palace are in Kayseri Museum. The ascent to the city takes some time and is not easy. It is essential to have a guide.

From Derinkuyu continue in a W direction to the beautiful valley of **Ihlara**. Formerly known as Peristrema, this has some of the most interesting rock cut churches in Cappadocia. Summer is the best season to visit Ihlara. Then the Melendiz Dere, which has gouged the valley out of the soft tufa, is at its lowest. Wading back and forth across the stream to visit the churches, which line both banks, is easy and pleasant. In spring and autumn the river is often in spate after heavy rain and it floods the lower paths making it impossible to visit a number of the churches.

From the outskirts of Ihlara village there is an excellent view of the valley. Photographers will be tempted. Adjoining the car-park there is a small hotel which serves meals and light refreshments. Several hundred steps descend in stages c 150m to the valley floor. Note that there is no lift to ease the tiring return to the village.

There are about 60 churches, monasteries and hermits' cells in the valley. No matter how limited your time try to see the half-dozen between Ihlara and Belisırma. If you are not in a hurry, continue your exploration downstream—to Yaprak Hisar and beyond. There is no better way to spend a summer's day. Soothed by the sound of the wind in the trees and by the soft voice of the stream you will be dazzled by the abundant flora and fauna and amazed at the vistas in this Arcadian landscape.

Almost at the bottom of the steps is the cruciform **Ağaç Altı Kilisesi**, the Church under the Tree. This has two small aisles and an apse. In the dome there is a striking representation of Christ in a mandorla being carried up to heaven by four angels. The style is primitive. The faces are orange and white, the eyes unfocused and empty. The ornamental decoration has echoes of Muslim and Coptic art. Other subjects include the Dormition, the Adoration of the Magi, the Flight into Egypt and Daniel in the Lions' Den.

In the valley turn right and walk upstream to the **Pürenli Seki Kilisesi**, the Church with the Terrace. This has two parallel naves. In the N nave there are paintings, partly damaged, in the Cappadocian style, of the Last Judgement, the Annunciation, the Visitation, the Journey to Bethlehem, Christ's Entry to Jerusalem, the Wedding Feast at Cana, the Nativity, the Crucifixion and the Entombment.

The **Kokar Kilise** is a single-aisled basilica. In the nave there are paintings of various episodes from the life of Christ arranged in chronological order. These include the Annunciation, the Visitation, the Adoration of the Magi, the Flight into Egypt and the Wedding Feast at Cana. There is also a Deisis. The hand in the huge cross surrounded by abstract decoration in the centre of the barrel roofed nave represents the Trinity. The little figure behind Judas in the scene of the Last Supper is the demon Selephouze. Many of the figures in the lower registers have had their eyes, in some cases their faces, obliterated by religious fanatics.

Now return to the steps and walk downstream. The **Sümbüllü Kilisesi**, the Hyacinth Church, is part of a two-storey monastery. It has a domed single nave with later additions. The façade, with its arched doorways between pillars, suggests a Persian influence. The wall paintings, which have suffered damage from water seepage, are of exceptional quality. On the central dome is the Christ Pantocrator. There are representations of the Annunciation and the Dormition and of saints including Sergius and Bacchus, George, Theodore, Barbara, Nicholas and Catherine and of the angels Michael and Gabriel.

Traces of paintings remain in the 11C **Karagedik Kilisesi**, the Church of the Black Collar. This was dedicated to St Hermolaos, an aged priest of Nicomedia who converted the imperial physician St Pantaleon and was martyred with him. The church was badly damaged by an earth fall. Its paintings appear to tell the story of St George.

The **Kirk Dam Altı Kilisesi**, the Church of the Forty Roofs, is a one aisled basilica. Because of its dedication, it is sometimes known as the Church of St George. An **inscription** records the dedication and the names of the donors, Basil Giagoupes and the lady Thamar, and mentions 'his high Majesty, the most noble and great Sultan Masud' and the emperor Andronikos II Palaeologos. This dates the church to between 1283 and 1295. Basil is described as an emir and wears a kaftan and turban, indications that he was an official of the Selçuk sultanate. The paintings, which are executed in a delicate style, are of various episodes in the life of Christ and of the saints.

Among the saints portrayed are Marina and George. St Marina was martyred in Antioch during the reign of Diocletian (284–305). In the painting, which is not in a very good condition, she is shown gripping the hair of a small, nude, male demon. According to a popular legend, she reacted to his fiendish temptations by tearing out handfuls of his beard, beating him over the head with a mallet and blinding him in one eye. Vanquished by these assaults, the demon, who says his name is Beelzebub, complains ruefully 'I have tempted many saints in my time, and now I am defeated by this young maiden of Christ, Marina'. It is the only representation of the story in Cappadocia.

The **Bahattin Samanlığı Kilisesi**, the Church of Bahattin's Straw Loft, is a single-aisled basilica with apse of the Archaic Phase (c 850–950). There are stylistic similarities between the paintings in this church and those in the Church of Holy Apostles at Sinassos (see above). In subdued colours, they portray scenes from the life of Christ.

A little farther downstream near the bridge to Belisırma is the **Direkli Kilise**, the Pillared Church. This cross-in-square church has three apses. The paintings are mainly of saints and martyrs. They can be dated by an **inscription** to the reigns of Basil II, the Bulgar Slayer, (976–1025) and Constantine VIII (1025–28).

A short distance N of Belisırma is the **Ala Kilise**, the Spotted Church. This cross-in-square church has a fine façade which, like that of the Sümbüllü Kilisesi (see above), betrays some Persian influence. It has a nave and two aisles. The poorly preserved paintings from the Middle Byzantine Phase (c 1020–1130) have some stylistic affinity with those in Göreme.

Upstream from Belisırma is the **Yilanli Kilisesi**, the Church of the Serpents. It is easy to miss the entrance which is partially concealed by fallen rocks. This cruciform church has a fine horseshoe-shaped apse. The paintings in the narthex are in a better state of preservation than those in the main body of the church. There is a striking representation of Christ the Judge. Flanked by angels, he is seated in a mandorla. Below him are the Forty Martyrs of Sebaste in long oriental robes and the Twenty-Four Elders of the Apocalypse.

In the lowest section there is a scene of the Weighing of the Souls by the devil and frightening paintings of the torments of Hell which St Basil described so vividly: 'Those ... set on the left hand shall be enveloped in the fire of Gehenna and everlasting darkness'. A monster with three heads and the body of a serpent devours some of the damned. This is one of the paintings which gives the church its Turkish name. The heads of the wicked protrude from the waters of Tartarus and rise out of the Rivers of Fire and of Tar. Naked women are being assaulted by snakes. One, possibly an adultress, is enveloped in the coils of eight snakes. Serpents gnaw at the breasts of a woman who abandoned her children. Others guilty of disobedience and calumny are attacked on the ear and the mouth.

In addition to scenes from the life of Christ there are paintings of various saints, Old Testament figures, and angels. These include SS Anne, Zachary, John the Baptist, Nicholas, John Chrysostom, Mary the Egyptian, Stephen and Gamaliel, Elias, David and Gabriel. In an arcosolium there is a Deisis; in the apse Christ in Glory and Mary with the Apostles. To the S of the sanctuary there are paintings of SS Helena and Constantine and of the Dormition. St Zosimus is shown giving holy communion to St Mary the Egyptian and officiating at her funeral. In the nave one of the Forty Martyrs of Sebaste, unable to bear the freezing waters of the lake, is shown entering the bathhouse and apostatising. A guard strips off his clothes and takes the place of the apostate, so keeping the number of martyrs at 40. As in the case of the temptation of St Marina in the Kirk Dam Altı Kilisesi (see above) the devil complains, 'Woe is me. I am defeated by these saints'. Note the unusual representation of Christ in the W arm. He is not on a throne, but sits cross-legged in the oriental manner.

To the S of the Yilanli Kilisesi is one of the largest monastic complexes in Cappadocia. This is **Karanlık Kale**, the Dark Fort.Two entrances are cut into the steep rock face. One leads by way of a narrow passage to the church, the other to rooms in the monastery. The decoration is sober, a pattern of inscribed crosses on the ceiling of the passage to the church.

From the monastery make your way back to the steps and commence the steep ascent to the village.

St Gregory Nazianzen (329–389) is believed to have been born near **Güzelyurt** in the ancient village of Arianzos. Closely associated with St Basil, he is called 'ὁ θεόλογος' by Orthodox Christians because of his theological writings. The ancient Byzantine, cruciform church at the foot of a cliff riddled with cave houses was dedicated to St Gregory. It is now a mosque.

From Güzelyurt return to Derinkuyu and follow the Nevşehir road for 10km to **Kaymaklı**, where there is another **subterranean city**. Stalls selling cheap souvenirs crowd around the ticket booth and the entrance. The plan of Kaymakli differs from that of Derinkuyu. It is a rabbit warren of rooms and stores cut from the rock on eight levels. The passageways are very narrow and the ceilings often very low, factors which make a visit somewhat exhausting. Visit Kaymaklı early in the morning before the coach parties arrive, and to take a guide. The room complexes tend to be grouped around airshafts. There is a **church** with two apses. No wall paintings have been found in the city.

The road back to Nevşhir crosses a plain. Watching the passing traffic, a youthful shepherd shelters in his cloak against the wind. Watchful dogs tirelessly circle the sheep as they feed on the thin stubble. Only the raucous cries of the crows and magpies break the silence. Far across the plain the louring peak of snow-clad Erycis, a stark reminder to the traveller of Cappadocia's violent birth pangs, points an accusing finger into the darkening sky.

55

Excursions from Nevşehir to Aksaray Kayseri and Niğde

Nevşehir—22km Acıgöl—(7km Tatlarin)—13km Alay Hanı—28km Öresin Hanı—c 10km Ağzi Kara Hanı—c 8km Aksaray—(12km Akhisar)—(c 30km Helvadere)—(48km Sultanhanı).

Nevşehir—110km Kayseri—(4km Çifte Kümbet)—(24km Gezi)—(23km Kültepe)—(44km Karatay Hanı)—(27km Sultanhanı).

Kayseri—(9km Talas)—(46km Tomarza)—52km Develi or 87km via Incesu)—(15kmFiraktin)—(29km Taşı/Bakirdağı)—(8km İmamkulu)—(15km Hanyeri/Gezbeli).

Nevşehir—100km Misli—(c 4km Eski Gümüş)—30km Niğde—(14km Bor)—(19km Kemerhisar).

Nevşehir is a good centre for excursions to Aksaray, Kayseri and Niğde. The journey time in each case is about an hour. Buses depart at regular intervals from the *otogar*.

A. Nevşehir to Aksaray

Total distance (excluding deviations) c 70km.

Leave Nevşehir by the Konya road. Just before **Acıgöl** there is a **crater lake** on the left. It is believed that Acıgöl is built on the site of Topada. A late 9C BC ruler of Topada named Tutwatis has left an **inscription** in hieroglyphs.

If you not been sated by your visits to the underground cities of Derinkuyu and Kaymaklı, make a short diversion to (7km) **Tatlarin**. This is one of the most recently discovered troglodytic complexes. Ask in the village for the *bekçi* who will gladly take you to the small section open to the public. At the end of your visit it would be appropriate to offer him a gratuity for his services.

The city extends E and W for several kilometres under a steep-sided mesa. It will take many years to explore it fully, to record its contents and to preserve them. Conservation experts from Ankara are currently working on the paintings in many of the rooms. A tunnel descends steeply to a large chamber with blackened walls which may have been a communal kitchen.Nearby there is a room which could have been used for worship. Graves have been found in the floor of a room to the right. The smaller excavations were for the bodies of children and infants. Here smoke-blackened frescoes on the walls are being cleaned. A large hole marks the place from where a fresco was stolen. It is believed that the city was occupied during Byzantine times.

Regrettably, those rooms near the surface, which are not protected by railings, are being used as unofficial toilets.

The red marks high up on the right mark the position of the villagers' dovecotes. Man-made circular excavations and some natural caves on the other side of the valley were used until recently as dwellings. Animals were kept on the lower floors. The villagers claim that their small mosque was designed by Sinan.

Return to Acıgöl and continue 13km to **Alay Hanı**, the earliest example of a Sultan Han. This was built by Kılıçarslan II (1156–92). Its access gate leads to a heavily ornamented portal. Only the ruins of the late 13C Selçuk **Öresin Hanı** remain. They are on the right side of the road c 28km from Alay Hanı. The third, and most remarkable *han* on this stretch of the **Uzun Yol**, the great caravan route which linked Konya the Selçuk capital with Persia and the Orient, is the **Ağzi Kara Hanı**, completed in 1237 by Hoca Mesut. The **portal** is not centred. **Geometric motifs** are used extensively in the ornamentation. It was designed in the classical style. In the courtyard there is a kiosk *mescid*. Note the elaborately decorated oculus.

Approximately 2km after the Ağzi Kara Hanı a road to the left leads to 7km **Mamasun**. Here is the Greek cross plan **Köy Esesi Kilisesi**, the Church behind the Village. This has some interesting late 10C frescoes of Christ in Majesty with the Four Beasts of the Apocalypse, the Twelve Apostles and the archangels Gabriel and Michael. The village is named after St Mamas, a shepherd of Caesarea (modern Kayseri) who was martyred c 275 during the reign of Aurelian. He is greatly venerated by the Eastern Church. His remains are kept in the village mosque as there is a Muslim belief that he converted to Islam.

Return to the main road and continue to **Aksaray**. To the S of the town are the Melendiz mountains and the twin peaks of Büyük Hasandağ (3628m) and Küçük Hasandağ (3069m). Aksaray has some interesting Islamic monuments.

There is a motel inspected by the Tourism Ministry, the Orhan Ağaçlı Tur Tes, on the Ankara–Adana road. The **Tourist Information Office** is at Ankara Cad. Dinçer Apt, No. 2/2.

History. Because the Romans called this place Garsaura, some identify it with the ancient city of Kursaura. In a tradition current c 1400, Kursaura is one of 17 cities which formed a coalition c 2200 BC against Naram-Sin, the king of Akkad. In Byzantine times the town was known as Coloneia Archelais. Captured and sacked by the Selçuks in the 11C, it was rebuilt by Kılıçarslan II (1156–88). Two centuries later it was taken by the Mongols. In the 14C Aksaray was ruled by the Karamanids. After the capture of Constantinople by the Ottomans in 1453 some of its inhabitants were forced to move to the new capital. To keep alive the memory of their native city they called the area in İstanbul where they were settled, Aksaray, a name which is still in use.

Aksaray's **Ulu Cami** was built by the Selçuks. However, it has been altered extensively and little of the original structure remains. The *mimber* is from the foundation period. Note the attractive brickwork of the **Kızıl Minare**. The castle, which dominates the town, dates from the period of Selçuk rule. There are two Koranic schools. The Karamanids built the **Zinciriye Medrese** c 1345. The Selçuk **İbrahim Kadiroğlu Medresesi** was restored in the 15C by the Ottomans.

In the village of **Akhisar**, 12km to the SE, there are the ruins of the **Çanlı Kilisesi**, the Church of the Bell. This late 10C or early 11C church has three apses and a two storey narthex. Most of the frescoes, which once decorated it, have disappeared. There were also several **rock cut monasteries** here. The **ruined castle** on the cliff top dates from the Byzantine period. At **Helvadere**, c 30km, farther on there are the ruins of two early churches which formed part of a large monastic complex·now called Viranşehir.

One of the most striking of the *han*s on the Uzun Yol is **Sultanhanı** 48km to the SW of Aksaray on the Konya road. A day's caravan journey from Aksaray, this was designed and built in 1229 by the architect Muhammed bin Havlan el Dımışki for Sultan Alaeddin Keykubad I. Occupying an area of 4500 sq m, it is in two parts. Entry is by a huge gate ornamented with stalactite niches. In the centre of the courtyard there is an elegantly decorated *mescid* which rests on four piers. Under the arches on the left side were the rooms occupied by the merchants and their servants, shops and a *hamam*. The animals were stabled in a large, vaulted hall divided into five sections at the far end of the courtyard. The defences of the *han* were strengthened by a series of turrets on the outside walls. It is in a very good state of repair.

B. Nevşehir to Kayseri

Total distance (excluding deviations) c 110km.

The road to Kayseri passes through Ortahisar, Üçhisar and Ürgüp. For a description of these places see Route 54.

KAYSERİ occupies a strategic position on a broad, flat plain dominated by Mt Erciyes. In ancient times trade routes from the Aegean, Mediterranean and Black Sea met here. The trading tradition continues. Today the emporia of Kayseri are filled with carpets and kilims. Its persuasive salesmen have the reputation, perhaps not entirely undeserved, of being shrewd to the point of sharpness. *Caveat emptor*. With the development of interest in Cappadocia the town has become an important tourist centre.

Acoommodation and Information. Nine hotels in Kayseri have been inspected by the Ministry of Tourism. One has three stars, six have two stars, and two have one star each. Recommended are the three-star *Hotel Almer* and the two-star *Hotel Hattat*. The **Tourist Information Office** is in Sahabiye Mah., Yıldırım Cad. No.1. Buses leave for destinations all over Turkey from the *otogar* on the W side of the town. There are train services to Ankara and İstanbul and flights by THT to Ankara.

History. A hypogeum dating from the late Hellenistic or early Roman period has been found in the centre of Kayseri. Originally called Mazarca, it was the capital of the independent kingdom of Cappadocia. In 36 BC Cappadocia was awarded to Archelaus, the son of the high priest of Comana, by Antony—largely because of the charms of his mother, Glaphyra. When Archelaus, died in Rome in AD 17, Cappadocia became a Roman province and the name of its capital was changed to Caesarea in honour of Tiberius Caesar (AD 14–37).

The people of Caesarea accepted Christianity enthusiastically. They destroyed the principal temples dedicated to Zeus and Apollo. Then, during the reign of Julian the Apostate (361–63), they pulled down the temple of Fortuna, the last pagan shrine in their city. From the time of Diocletian (284–305) Caesarea was an important manufacturing centre of heavy cavalry armour (*clibanariae*). The capital of Cappadocia Prima, it was renamed Eusebia in honour of Eusebius who was bishop of Caesarea between c 315 and 340. He was the author of a number of important works including the Ecclesiastical History, Praeparatio Evangelica, Chronica and a Life of Constantine the Great. St Basil, a later occupant of the see, formulated a Rule for monastic life which has been adopted by the Eastern Church. He won the gratitude of his fellow citizens by persuading the corn merchants to release supplies of grain during a period of famine and set up so many charitable institutions that they added a new quarter to the city. At the beginning of the 5C, according to the letters of St John Chrysostom, Caesarea lived in constant fear of attack by marauding bands of Isaurians who burned the surrounding villages.

When the Arab incursions began in the 7C the city suffered grievously. It was occupied in 1087 by a Turcoman horde. In the second half of the 11C Armenian refugees from Ani, accompanied by their king, Gagik II, came to Caesarea. It fell to the Selçuks and in 1174 Kılıçarslan II made it the second city of his kingdom. It was besieged by the Crusaders in 1097, but remained under Selçuk rule until 1243, when it was sacked by the Mongols. In 1335 Eretna, the Mongol governor, seized power and founded the Eretnid dynasty which ruled over Kayseri, Aksaray, Sivas and Amasya for 45 years. The Eretnids were succeeded by Kadi Burhaneddin, a former chief vizier of the principality. In 1397 the city was captured by Beyazit I. After the battle of Ankara in 1402 it came under the rule of the Karamanids—probably with the tacit approval of Tamerlane. In 1419 Kayseri was occupied by the Mamelukes and almost a century later was taken by Selim I, the Grim.

The **citadel** occupies an area of 822m by 183m. Built by the emperor Justinian in the 6C, it was reconstructed by the Selçuks between 1210 and 1226 and restored several times during the Ottoman period. The walls, fortified by 19 towers, are c 3m thick. The huge blocks of dark volcanic rock used in its construction give the building a particularly sinister appearance. Entrance is through a gate on the S side. The *mescid* in the courtyard was erected by Mehmet II Fatih in 1466 on the site of an earlier prayer house.

The **Huant Medresesi** and the nearby **Honat Hatun Camii** date from the early 13C. With their associated *hamam*, *çeşme* and *türbe* they form part of the first complex of this kind built by the Selçuks. It was established by Mahperi Huant Hatun, the Greek wife of Sultan Alaeddin Keykubad I. Her marble tomb is in a corner of the *medrese*. Kayseri's Ethnographical Museum is now housed here. The customary exhibiton of costumes, household utensils, tools and weapons is enlivened by the presence of a **yürük tent** furnished with a representative selection of the goods and chattels used by Turkey's nomadic people.

To get to Ulu Cami return to the citadel and then walk S in the direction of the sombre, late 18C Ottoman Vizir Hanı. Kayseri's **Ulu Cami** was probably built by a vizier of the Danishmendids, Mehmet Gazim, in 1136. It was altered extensively during the reign of Keyhüsrev I (1192–1210).

The **Hatuniye Medresesi** and the **Melek Gazi Medresesi**, which are just S of Ulu Cami, were built in 1431–32. Note the extensive re-use of materials taken from other buildings in the Hatuniye Medresesi.

The **Kurşunlu Cami**, the Lead Mosque, in the Atatürk Parkı was built in 1585 at the behest of Kızıl Ahmet Paşa, scion of an ancient Selçuk family. It is claimed that the mosque was designed by Sinan.

On the NW corner of Cumhuriyet Meydanı is the **Sahibiye Medresesi** which was established in 1268 by Sahip Ata Fahrettin Ali, vizier of the Selçuk sultan Keyhüsrev III. Note the magnificent **entrance portal** with its fine stalactite ornamentation. To the N of the *medrese* there is a well-preserved late Hellenistic or early Roman **hypogeum**.

The **Çifte Medrese** contained a hospital and a medical school. The medical school was established in 1206 by sultan Keyhüsrev I (1192–1210), the hospital by his sister, Gevher Nesibe. Both structures have an arcaded courtyard and *eyvans*. The pyramid shaped *kümbet* with dome squinches at the rear of the *medrese* probably houses the remains of Gevher Nesibe. A short distance to the N is the ruined 13C **Haci Kılıç Camii**.

Perhaps the most striking of Kayseri's many mausolea is the **Döner Kümbet** which is believed to date from c 1276. This gets its name from a supposed resemblance to a turning spit. An **inscription** over the entrance states that it was erected for a Selçuk princess named Şah Cihan Hatun. On the outside there are 12 blank arches crowned by a conical roof. Its elaborate decoration includes the double-headed eagle of the Selçuks, a griffin and winged leopards.

Two survivors from the period of Eretnid rule in Kayseri are the 14C **Köşk Medrese** and the **Sirçali Kümbet**. Both are located near the museum. The *medrese* is a small building with a *kümbet* in the centre of its arcaded courtyard. It high, blank outer walls with their crenellations give it the appearance of a stronghold. It was built in 1339 by Eretna for his wife Suli Paşa. It is believed that they are both buried in the *kümbet*.

Kayseri's **Archaeological Museum** has an attractively displayed collection of artefacts, arranged chronologically, from the town and its environs. These include stone and bone objects and ceramics from the Prehistoric Period, **inscribed tablets** from Kültepe, **statues** from Kulu, stelae and inscriptions, Phrygian, Roman and Byzantine **ceramics**, glass, metal objects and statuettes. In the garden there are the lion sculptures from Gölludağ, sarcophagi, statues and architectural fragments.

Visit Kültepe which is 21km outside the town on the Sivas road. En route look out for the **Cifte Kümbet**, an octagonal tomb on a raised base. This Selçuk monument is on the right-hand side of the road about 4km from Kayseri. It was built in 1243 to house the remains of Princess al-Malika al-Adilya, one of the wives of Keykubad I. The pyramid-shaped roof has disappeared revealing the dome which covered the interior.

After a further 12km a road to the right leads to **Gesi**, the ancient Nea Kassiane. The ruins of the **Armenian monastery of Surb Karapet** are by the side of this secondary road. At Üsgübi look for the foundations of a pre-9C church dedicated to Mary, the Mother of God.

Before the archaeologists began their investigations, the hüyük of **Kültepe**, ancient **Kanesh**, was the largest artificial mound in Turkey. It was more than 500m in diameter and was c 19m high. The Assyrian *karum* (see below) at its foot covered an area measuring c 1000m by 690m.

Archaeologists have found traces of two very destructive fires at Kültepe (the Hill of Ashes). Five layers of occupation were discovered—Roman, Phrygian, Hittite, Bronze and Chalcolithic. The earliest finds date from the fourth millennium BC, but this walled city enjoyed its period of greatest importance in the second millennium BC when it was inhabited by the indigenous people of Anatolia. According to a late Hittite text the Akkadian king, Naram Sin (c 2320–2284 BC) was opposed by a coalition of 17 states, one of which was ruled by Zipani, king of Kanesh. An Assyrian trading post, a *karum*, was established outside the walls c 1950 BC. The city and the *karum* were destroyed by fire c 1850 BC. However, the *karum* was rebuilt and it flourished for a further 50 years. About 1780 BC Assyrian trade with Anatolia ceased completely, perhaps because of political and ethnic changes in Mesopotamia. After the departure of the Assyrians Kanesh declined. Its decay was hastened by a period of internecine strife. Sometime between 1200 and 1180 BC the city was burned down again. However, the site continued to be occupied well into the Roman period.

The archaeologists have laid bare the ruins of the king's palace (19C BC), which covered an area of c 3000 sq m, and a number of workshops and storerooms. They found a large quantity of obsidian, fashioned and ready for use, which may have been intended for threshing sledges. They uncovered partly buried jars which were for the storage of grain and liquids. In addition to ceramics from the Proto-Hattian to the Roman periods, they unearthed a number of alabaster idols and a large quantity of clay tablets and the cylinder seals used on them. A square building with towers on the corners was probably a temple. The thin layer of ash over the ruins came from the burned wooden superstructure of the buildings. Sometime after this period of violence megaron-type buildings were erected in the city. These, in turn, were burned down c 1200 BC. Traces of a Phrygian defensive wall c 6m thick, which had been erected on the remains of the earlier Hittite fortifications, were also uncovered.

The *karum* operated like a chamber of commerce. It organised the caravans of black donkeys which carried merchandise to and from Assyria. Their route was by way of Elbistan, Maraş, Sincerli, Gaziantep, Birecik, Harran and Habura. Well paid caravan leaders were responsible for the transportation and delivery of the goods. The *karum* sent metals, mainly copper, to Assyria and imported lead, cloth and garments. It arranged payments and had a tribunal which fixed prices and resolved disputes. Any serious matter, which could not be settled locally, was referred to the king of Assyria.

Although all goods passing through the the trading post paid a tax to the lord of Kanesh, the ruba'um, the traders enjoyed a considerable degree of independence. They had little direct contact with the ruler, dealing mainly with his officials who had the right to make the first choice from the merchandise.

In the *karum* the shops, offices, warehouses and living quarters were packed tightly together inside a stout defensive wall. The houses were of mud brick resting on foundations of uncut stone and were supported with wooden beams. Some had an inner courtyard with rooms opening from it. In others the courtyard was reached by a corridor. In those houses, which had two storeys, the upper floor was used as living quarters and for the transaction of business. On the lower floor were workrooms, stores and, sometimes, the large ovens used to bake the clay tablets.

Because the merchants were obliged to leave in haste, they abandoned many of their personal possessions including vessels of Cappadocian and Hittite ware. Many of these were theriomorphic, fashioned in the form of lions' or bulls' heads or mythical animals. In the kitchens there were horseshoe shaped terracotta hearths, braziers like the *mangals* of the Ottomans and domed ovens with the cooking pots still in place.

Members of the family were not forgotten in death. They were buried, in terracotta coffins or in cists lined with stone, under the floors of the houses. With them were placed elaborate funeral gifts—animal statuettes, weapons, figurines of the gods and domestic utensils fashioned from gold, silver and bronze.

The Assyrians left detailed records of their commercial dealings with firms and individual merchants. From these it is possible to build up a shadowy picture of life in Anatolia in the 19C BC. The tablets, which measured no more than 7.5cm, were written in Akkadian, the old commercial language of Mesopotamia. Names found on them indicate that the traders married with the local people, maintained friendly relations with them, respecting their customs and the gods of Anatolia.

The *karum* at Kanesh was the most important Assyrian trading post in Anatolia, acting as headquarters for others which covered not only the interior but extended to the Aegean and Mediterranean coasts.

The small museum includes clay tablets, seals and ceramics. There are also sketches and photographs of the excavations. The most important objects from Kültepe are in the Anatolian Civilisations Museum at Ankara.

A short distance to the N of Kültepe a turning on the right will take you to (44km) **Karatay Hanı**. This was completed during the reign of Gıyaseddin Keyhüsrev II (1236–46). After many years of neglect, it was restored in 1964. In addition to the rooms for the travellers there were a *mescid, türbe, hamam,* kitchen, dining room, safe deposit and ample stabling for the animals. This *han* is noted for its fine stonework. Note especially the **water spouts on the roof** which have been carved into human and animal forms.

Return to the main road and continue for c 27km to **Sultanhanı**. This should not be confused with the han of the same name on the road from Kayseri to Aksaray which it resembles in design. It has also been carefully restored.

The pleasant suburb of **Talas**, 9km to the SE of Kayseri, occupies the site of the Roman Flaviana. Once the metropolitans of Kayseri lived here. Now it is the favoured retreat of wealthy local families. The only reminders of Talas's past are two **rock-cut chapels** and an **underground church**. From here continue for 46km to **Tomarza** where there are several rock-cut churches and monasteries. Tomarza's fine Latin cross church of the Panagia was wantonly destroyed in the recent past.

A picturesque, if rather difficult, drive S from Kayseri will take you to 52km **Develi**, a town of little interest, but an excellent starting point for excursions to four important, but little-visited, Hittite bas-reliefs. Take a picnic lunch.

If you feel daunted by the prospect of tackling the direct route, which passes between Erciyes Dağı and Koç Dağı, you can go to Develi via İncesu. This will add 35km in each direction to your journey. Leave Kayseri by the Tarsus road and continue for c 52km to a major crossroads and there bear left.

Develi, the ancient Everek, climbs the southern slope of Erciyes Dağı. On a hillock above the town are the ruins of a medieval castle. Develi's only other buildings of interest are a 13C *türbe*, a 19C mosque and a ruined church dedicated to SS Cosmas and Damian.

The first and perhaps the most important of the four sites is at **Firaktin** on a signposted route c 18km to the SE of Develi. Firaktin has been identified with the Dastarcum, mentioned by Strabo in *Geography* 12.2.5., whose temple dedicated to Apollo was honoured throughout Cappadocia. The **relief**, which is on the far bank of the Yenice-ırmak, the ancient Carmalas River, shows a male martial figure making an offering to a water god. According to an **inscription**, the warrior, who has a pointed hat like that worn by the god, is king Hattusilis I (1650–20). On the right side of the relief queen Puduhepa sacrifices to the goddess Hepa.

The second relief is near the village of **Taşçı** or Bakırdağı, 36km SE of Develi. Sited also on the opposite bank of the Yeniceırmak river, it has been partially obscured by silt. Because the carving is quite shallow, try to see it around midday when sunlight outlines three praying figures and an inscription in hieroglyphs. A cartouche of king Hattusilis III dates the relief to between 1275 and 1250.

About 8km after Taşçı a minor road on the left leads to **İmamkulu**. On a slope c 275m to the right of the road there is an elaborate **relief** which is believed to date from the reign of king Tudhaliya IV (1250–20). In the centre a weather god stands in a chariot pulled by bulls. Below the chariot are three mountain gods supported by creatures which have human bodies and bird-like heads. The female figure on the right, who opens her clothes invitingly, is probably Ishtar, the goddess of love. On the left side of the relief a warrior armed with a bow marches forward purposefully.

The **fourth relief** is at the village of **Hanyeri**, sometimes called Gezbeli, c 29km from Taşçı. It faces E and is most clearly visible just after sunrise. Measuring 3.34m by 1.8m, it shows a royal figure carrying a lance and a bow. He is worshipping a bull which rests on two mountain gods. There is an accompanying **inscription** in hieroglyphs. The relief is believed to date from the 13C BC.

C. Nevşehir to Niğde

Total distance (excluding deviations) c 134km.

Leave Nevşehir by the road to Kaymaklı and Derinkuyu,places described in Route 54. In **Misli**, the ancient Musilia, there are many troglodytic dwellings. Until the exchange of populations in the 1920s this village was inhabited exclusively by Greeks. Exempted from taxes by the Ottoman government, they were subject to the bishop of Niğde. Very conservative in outlook, the villagers did not marry outside their own community. In the nearby village of Hasanköy a 19C church dedicated to St Makrina has been turned into a mosque. St Makrina was the paternal grandmother of SS Basil and Gregory of Nysa. A pupil of St Gregory Thaumaturgus, Makrina and her husband were obliged to hide for seven years near the Black Sea during the persecutions of Diocletian.

From Misli continue S towards (34km) Niğde. About 5km before the town a signposted turning on the left leads to the village of **Eski Gümüş** where one of the most remarkable **rock-cut monasteries** in Cappadocia is located. Used as a stable until recently, its frescoes are well preserved.

The inconspicuous entrance to the complex is cut from the soft tufa. The parapet above the door was part of the monastery's defensive system—from it boiling oil or molten lead could be poured on the heads of attackers. A narrow passage from the entrance leads to a square courtyard open to the sky. This provided light and air for the church and the rooms of the monastery. It may also have served as a cloister. The walls, which are c 14m high, have arched niches and holes for beams near the top. This suggests that the courtyard had galleries or a wooden awning around the sides.

The opening on the left of the end wall led to an exonarthex which was never completed. The opening on the right is the entrance to the vaulted narthex where there is a wall painting of Mary and the Christ Child flanked by the Archangels Gabriel and Michael. Inside the cross-in-square church four massive plaster covered columns reach up from octagonal bases to the high dome. A corridor in the NE corner leads to the apsed mortuary chapel. In a recess in the N wall there are two sarcophagi.

The walls of the church were carefully smoothed and plastered before they were painted. On the left side there are frescoes of the Annunciation and the Nativity. On the dome of the central apse there is a Christ Pantocrator. Other paintings are of Mary, the Archangel Michael, the Apostles, the Evangelists, and the Doctors of the Church. Two distinct styles of painting have been distinguished by the experts in this church. The figures in the frescoes from the earlier period (11C) are bold and striking and must have struck fear into the hearts of the faithful. Below stern brows the staring eyes of the saints fix themselves unwaveringly on the viewer and their narrow lips tighten as though preparing to consign unrepentant sinners to eternal darkness and torment without end.

A metal staircase leads to the upper storey. Note the unusual **decorative frieze** which enlivens the walls of a monk's cell above the narthex. The subjects of the rather crude drawings are from Aesop's fables—the story of the Wolf and the Lamb, the story of the Man and the Ungrateful Snake, and the story of the Eagle and the Flighted Arrow are among those illustrated. In the refectory there are a rock-cut table and benches. It is believed that the monastic complex of Eski Gümüş is linked to an underground city which, as yet, remains unexplored.

Groves of nodding poplars shield **NIGDE**, a quiet provincial backwater richly endowed with Islamic buildings, from the passing traffic.

Information. There are eight hotels in the town. None are on the Ministry of Tourism list. The **Tourist Information Office** is at İstiklal Cad., Vakıf İşhanı No.1/D.

History. Niğde has been identified by some with a Hittite city called Nakita. Tin, a metal much in demand in ancient times, has been found in the neighbourhood. Overshadowed, perhaps, by nearby Tyana, little is known about Niğde during the Roman and Byzantine periods. In the 11C the city was taken by the Selçuks. Later its possession was disputed by the Mongols and the Karamanoğlu. The first mention of its present name is in a document of AD 1188.

When Ibn Battuta visited Niğde in 1333, he found the greater part in ruins. There were three bridges over the Kara Su, which he describes erroneously as a 'great river'. Hydraulic wheels, inside and outside the city boundaries, drew up water for its gardens, which produced fruit in abundance. He comments favourably on his comfortable lodgings which were provided by Akhy Djarouk, the young commandant of the city.

Eretna, the former Mongol governor of Sivas, took Niğde in 1335. Apart from a brief period in 1393 when it was in the hands of Kadı Burhaneddin, the city was ruled by the Karamanoğlu until 1467. In that year it was captured from them by the Ottomans.

The **citadel** crowns a rocky spur in the town centre. It is believed that this was built c 1230 during the reign of sultan Alaeddin Keykubad. Its massive octagonal tower is almost certainly Ottoman, dating from c 1470.

S of the citadel is the **Alaeddin Camii** constructed at the behest of the eponymous Alaeddin Keykubad in 1223. According to an **inscription** it was built by Beşare bin Abdullah. The architects were Sıddık and Gazi bin Mahmud. It has three aisles separated by two lines of four columns. The area in front of the *mihrab* is covered by three domes, of different sizes, placed side by side. Entrance is by a richly decorated **portal** on the E side. The squat cylindrical minaret rests on an ornamented octagonal base.

At the bottom of the hill is the 17C **bedesten**. About 90m long, this has a pointed tunnel vault and houses a large number of shops.

The **Sungur Bey Camii** is at the S end of the bedesten. This was built by a Mongol ruler during the first part of the 14C. Entrance is via a finely ornamented portal on the N side. A considerable number of changes were made to the interior of the mosque after a disastrous fire in the 18C.

On the S side of the town is the **Ak Medrese**, a Koranic school established in 1409 by Alaeddin Ali Bey at a time when Niğde was ruled by the Karamanoğlu dynasty. Unusually, there are two storeys. The central courtyard has porticoes on three sides and an *eyvan* on the S. Note the high **stalactite ornamented portal** and the double windows with ogee arches on the upper storey.

On the NW side of the town, behind a lycée, there are three tombs. The finest of these, the **Hudavent Hatun Türbesi**, was built in 1312 for Hudavent Hatun, the daughter of Sultan Rukeddin Kılıçarslan IV (1246–1264). The princess was interred here in 1331.

The *kümbet* rests on an octagonal base. On the bas-reliefs above the burial chamber, which is lit by three windows, there are representations of a lion, birds with human faces etc. The *türbe* nearest the *lycée* dates from the first part of the 14C. The third tomb was built in 1324.

Niğde's **Archaeological and Ethnographic Museum** merits a visit. In the ethnographic section there is the usual display of costumes, household utensils, weapons, tools, musical instruments and furniture. Note the **hair tent** in the exedra. This belonged to a Türkmen tribe from the Niğde area. The **9C or 10C mummy**, which attracts the attention of most visitors, is of a 15-year-old girl. It was found in the Ihlara Valley.

In the archaeological section the most important objects are the **neolithic and chalcolithic pots** from the excavations at Kösk (see below). Their decoration is reminiscent of the wall paintings found at Çatal Hüyük. There is also material from Acemhöyük and a number of Neo-Hittite stelae from Keşlik. You can not fail to see the huge **Phrygian funerary pithos** which stands 1.45m tall and has a capacity of c 850 litres. From the Roman and Byzantine periods there are figurines, stelae, tear flasks, lamps, pottery and jewellery. There is a fine display of gold, silver and bronze coins from the Hellenistic to the Ottoman period. Note especially the collection of **coins of the Cappadocian kings**.

At c 12km from Niğde on the road S to Ulukişla and Tarsus there is a **Roman ornamental basin**. This was fed from a spring on top of the hill at **Köşk** and linked to the aqueduct at Kemerhisar. At Köşk Turkish archaeologists have found the first known examples of Neolithic decorated pottery, also some objects of bone and obsidian. These are in Niğde's museum.

From here go first to Bor and then to (5km) Kemerhisar. Near this village, on a site once occupied by the Hittite city of Tuwanuwa, are the ruins of ancient **Tyana**. A fertile oasis, Tyana was important because of its position on the trade route which went from Ancyra to the Mediterranean by way of the Cilician Gates. The site continued to be occupied into the Neo-Hittite period (c 1200–700). There is a fine representation of Warpalawas, a king who ruled Tyana c 740 BC, on a rock-cut relief at İvriz near Ereğli. He is shown in an attitude of prayer before the Hittite god Tarhunzas.

The Neo-Hittites were succeeded by the Phrygians. They dominated central Anatolia until c 680 when their power was broken by the Cimmerians from southern Russia.

According to Strabo the city was called Eusebeia near the Taurus. It was built 'upon a mound of Semiramis', the 9C BC wife of Ninus and co-founder of Nineveh, and was beautifully fortified. For the most part its territory was fertile and level'.

Tyana's most famous son was Apollonius, a peripatetic Neo-Pythagorean philosopher who was credited with supernatural powers. According to his followers he performed many miracles, healing the sick and raising the dead before ascending into heaven. He was born into a wealthy family early in the 1C AD and died sometime during the reign of Nerva (96–98). His life was written by the sophist Philostratus c AD 220 at the behest of the Syrian empress Julia Domna, wife of Septimius Severus. She accompanied her son Caracalla on his visit to Cappadocia in AD 215. During their stay in Tyana Carcalla ordered a shrine to be erected in the city in honour of Apollonius. He made it a Roman colony at the same time.

Philostratus claims that Apollonius, while living in Ephesus, had a vision of the murder of Domitian in Rome. When he was a very old man—some say 80, some 90, some 100—it was said that he had 'the perfect use and enjoyment of his body, and with more charm than he had in his youth…descriptions…are more lyrical about him as an old man than the accounts used to be of Alcibiades as a young one'. There are various stories about his end. He was said to have died at Ephesus in the care of two maid servants. Others asserted that his apotheosis occurred in Lindos where he went into the temple of Athena and vanished. The most extraordinary account states that he visited the shrine of Dictynna (Artemis) in Crete at night. This was guarded by fierce dogs, but instead of attacking him they came to greet him. Arrested as a magician and robber, Apollonius freed himself around midnight and, calling the priests to witness the event, ran to the main doors of the shrine which opened magically, then closed behind him. From within the shrine the voices of maidens were heard singing, 'Proceed from earth! Proceed to heaven! Proceed!'.

Comparisons were first made between Apollonius and Christ during the persecution of the Christians under Diocletian. Hierocles, governor of Bithynia, wrote an anti-Christian tract, The Lover of Truth, which claimed that Apollonius was the equal of Christ. The tract no longer exists,but parts of are quoted in a magisterial rebuttal prepared by Bishop Eusebius of Caesarea. Apollonius thus became an important figure in the struggle between a dying paganism and nascent Christianity. The matter continued to trouble the church well into the 4C and 5C. St Augustine (AD 354–430), in his refutation of the comparison, took it very seriously.

During the Roman and Byzantine periods Tyana was an important fortress on the Cappadocian frontier. In AD 709 it was besieged by the Arabs. After a long and exhausting siege, the badly-led defenders were obliged to surrender to the superior enemy force. In 806 Harun al Raschid, at the head of a large army, invaded Byzantine territory and captured Tyana. It was abandoned, probably because of repeated Arab attacks, sometime in the 11C, Bor and Niğde taking its place .

French archaeologists have been working on the site of Tyana for some time.

56

Ankara to Afyon, including Gordion

Total distance (excluding diversions and excursions) 256km. Ankara—
75km Polatlı—(40km Haymana-Gavurkalesi)—(29km Gordion)—42km
Sivrihisar—(16km Pessinus)—122km Afyon—(12km Ayazin)—(12km
Aslantaş)—(11km Kümbet)—(12km Midasşehri)—(29km Seyitgazi)—
(c 32km Aslankaya).

Leave Ankara by the E23 in the direction of Sivrihisar. This motor road takes
you through an unremarkable stretch of country where a monotonous
succession of rounded hills, covered with a thin layer of umber vegetation,
bear the scars of centuries of erosion.

At the small town of Polatlı turn left for (40km) **Haymana**. In ancient times
this was known as Therma because of its hot mineral spring. There are no
visible traces of Therma, but some of its cut stone has been re-used in the
buildings of the modern town.

A short distance to the SE is **Gavurkalesi**, the Fortress of the Infidels, a
13C BC Hittite cult centre devoted to the dead. A **terraced processional
road** leads to a plateau masuring c 36.5m square. This was protected by
cyclopean walls. Just below the summit there are two rock-cut reliefs. One
shows Kubaba (Cybele) on the left and two male deities, probably the
Weather God Teshub and his son Sharma, on the right. The second relief,
which is badly damaged, depicts a cult scene. The male gods wear conical
hats, carry swords and have shoes with upturned points. They are walking
towards the seated figure of Kubaba which has almost been completely
effaced. At the rear of the plateau there is a burial chamber measuring c 4m
by 3m. This may have an ossuary, but whatever it contained was stolen a
long time ago.

Gordion

About 17km to the W of Polatlı a turning on the right leads to the village of
Yassıhöyük. Here in a bleak, upland landscape are the ruins of the ancient
city of **GORDION**. This was the capital of the Phrygian Empire, the city of
king Midas who was cursed with the legendary golden touch. Here Alexander the Great cut the Gordian Knot. Archaeologists from the University
of Pennsylvania, who have been working at Gordion since 1950, have
discovered the tomb of a Phrygian king and laid bare 18 successive layers
of occupation which extend from the Bronze Age through the Hittite,
Phrygian, Persian, Greek and Roman periods.

History. The earliest traces of occupation date from the middle of the third millennium
BC. Sometime in the second millennium the Hittites occupied the site. The American
archaeologists have uncovered a large cemetery which dates from that period. Neo-
Hittite rule of the area was ended by the Phrygians, a horse-rearing, military aristocracy. From c 1200 BC onward these invaders came in succesive waves from Thrace
and Macedonia and, apart from the Aegean coast, occupied the whole of Anatolia
between the Assyrian frontier and the Sea of Marmara. It seems likely that they formed
a loose confederation of tribes rather than a centrally ruled kingdom. According to an
ancient tradition they were related to the royal house of Priam, as Hecuba was said to
be the daughter of the River Sangarius. Their principal deity was the epicene Cybele-
Agdistis. (See the entries for Pessinus and Midas Şehri below.) They are credited with
having introduced the worship of the Kabeiroi to Miletus and other Greek cities on

the Aegean coast. The records of the Assyrian king Sargon II (722–05) mention a people called the Mushki, who have been identified with the Phrygians. The Mushki were defeated in battle by the Assyrians and their king was slain. They were obliged to pay a tribute to the victors, but their kingdom was not occupied.

The Phrygians settled in Gordion in the mid 9C BC and made it their capital a century later. Adopting many of the customs and practices of their Hittite predecessors, they buried their dead in the former Hittite cemetery. Painted tiles from one of their cities, now in Ankara, show Phrygian soldiers. Their accoutrements differ from anything seen before in Anatolia. They carry round shields and wear plumed helmets.

According to a legend the eponymous Gordius, his wife and son Midas, arrived at the city in a peasant's cart at a time when the Phrygians were in a state of unrest. They appointed Gordius king immediately, as an oracle had predicted that a humble cart would bring them a ruler who would put an end to civil disorder. Gordius dedicated his cart and the yoke to which the oxen had been fastened to Zeus and placed them in a temple on the acropolis. Later, another oracle foretold that the person who could undo the knot of cornel bark, which fastened the pole to the yoke to the cart, would rule over Asia. Many unsuccessful attempts were made before Alexander the Great cut through it with his sword in the winter of 334/333.

Successive rulers were called, alternately, Gordius and Midas. Ovid in the *Metamorphoses* tells how the Midas entertained Silenus, the grotesque companion of Dionysus, in his palace. In return the king was given a wish. He asked that everything he touched be turned into gold. When he discovered that this applied also to his food and that he was in danger of dying of starvation, he asked to have the gift taken away. He was told to bathe in the Pactolus and, as result, ever since the sands of this river have been rich in gold. According to another story he captured Silenus in his garden and learned the satyr's wisdom by means of a trick. He made him drunk by putting wine in the spring. It is believed Silenus told him that man's best fortune was not to be born or, if born, to die in the shortest possible time. Apollo gave Midas asses' ears because he chose Marysas as winner of the musical contest between the god and the satyr. Ashamed, the king concealed them beneath a special head covering. His barber, becoming privy to the secret, wanted to tell it out loud. But, afraid of Midas's anger, he whispered into a hole in the ground. However, the reeds which grew from the hole revealed the king's shameful deformity. Whenever the wind blew through them, they murmured, 'King Midas has asses' ears. King Midas has asses' ears'.

Gordion was sited at a point where a much used trade route crossed the river Sangarius, the modern Sakarya Nerhi. Later this became the Royal Road of the Persians which went from Sardis to Susa. Built on the ruins of the Hittite city, 8C BC Gordion had substantial defences. Entrance was through a fortified gateway in a great wall which surrounded the city. However, this was unable to save it from capture in 684 by the Cimmerians, fierce barbarians from the Tauric Chersonesus and Asiatic Sarmatia. A smaller city or military outpost, which was probably under Lydian suzerainty from c 650, was built on Kücük Höyük to the SE. Sometime after the defeat of the Lydians by the Persians in 546, the victors laid a thick layer of clay over the site of the old Gordion and built a new city there. This lasted until c 400, when it was badly damaged by an earthquake, and rebuilt.

During the Hellenistic period Celtic tribes from the Danube basin invaded Anatolia. About 277 they were settled, with calamitous effects on their neighbours, in an area around the Sangarius river by Nicomedes I of Bithynia as a reward for having helped him to consolidate his position and extend his kingdom. In 189 the Romans, during the course of a campaign against the Celts, arrived in Gordion and rased it to the ground. According to Strabo, it continued as an unimportant village for some time after. In 116, with most of Phrygia, it became part of the Roman Province of Asia.

The Phrygian inventions of the frieze and embroidery are commemorated in the Latin words Phrygium and Phrygio (embroiderer). They were also credited with having invented several musical instruments eg the flute, triangle, syrinx, aulos (double clarinet), lyre and cymbals. More fancifully, Midas is credited with having 'discovered' roses! Their alphabet, which was derived from Phoenician, may be the parent of early Greek scripts.

Gordion appeals mainly to specialists, but no visitor can fail to be impressed by the 80 great *hüyüks* which tower over its ruins.

The **Phrygian Gate** at the W side of the acropolis was approached by a ramp 6m wide. This was so angled that hostile forces advancing towards it would have their unprotected left flank exposed to the defenders. At the top of the ramp there was a terrace. Traces of 8C Persian restoration are visible in the well-preserved gate. The entrance, which is flanked by towers, was 9m wide and c 22m long. Inside are the remains of walls made of coloured stone which formed part of an earlier portal. Giant pithoi, which were used for the storage of grain, oil and wine, were found here.

The royal palace and its associated buildings concerned with the religious and secular administration of the city were inside a **fortified enclosure**. Here the archaeologists have laid bare the ruins of four megara. The floor of the **second megaron** from the gate is covered with a very early mosaic which is in a good state of preservation. This is formed from red, white and blue pebbles arranged in geometric patterns. The second megaron is believed to have been the king's palace. It had a central nave separated from two aisles by rows of posts. Holes for posts high up on three of the walls of the inner room suggest that it had a gallery on these sides.

Megaron four may have been the temple dedicated to Cybele or Zeus in which Gordion's cart was placed.

The Phrygian necropolis is dominated by the huge mass of the **Royal Tomb**. This 60m high tumulus has a diameter of 300m. It was erected before the Cimmerian invasion when the power of the kings of Gordion reached its greatest height. The archaeologists had to overcome many difficulties before they reached the burial chamber which was undisturbed. It measures 6.2m by 5.15m and was roofed with a great dome of clay on which rubble had been placed.

The body lay on the remains of a huge wooden bed which had collapsed. It was that of a man aged about 60, c 1.59m tall. He was resting on his back, his head turned to the E, his hands by his sides. He was covered with two garments fastened with fibulae and wore buskins. Among the grave goods there were nine three-legged wooden tables, three stools, two inlaid screens, 169 bronze vessels and 165 fibulae. There were no weapons and, surprisingly, no gold or silver jewellery. Three bronze cauldrons, Urartian in style, were almost certainly imports. Inscriptions were found on wax panels below the rims of some of the bronze bowls. The grave goods date the burial to between 750 and 725 BC.

Nearby is the so-called **Prince's Tomb**. This contained the body of a child aged about five. Touchingly, bowls of food had been placed under the bed on which the corpse rested. The boy had his toys—miniature wooden animals and pottery vessels in animal shapes.

The common people of Gordion lived outside the fortified acropolis on the plain below and perhaps on the tumulus known as **Küçük Hüyük**, the Small Tumulus. Its citadel, which was destroyed by fire in the middle of the 6C BC, was buried underneath the tumulus. Evidence of a siege was found, perhaps an assault of Cyrus the Great, as he marched against Sardis. The tumulus is believed to have contained the bodies of those slain in the battle.

Before leaving the site it is worthwhile spending a little time in the **museum**. Built in the shape of a megaron, it has objects from the Bronze Age, the Hittite, Phrygian and Hellenistic periods. They include pitchers, bowls, cups, ladles, fibulae and arrow heads. Note the stone, bronze and silver figurines of birds which are believed to be votive offerings made to Kubaba-Cybele. The finest objects are in the Anatolian Civilisations Museum in Ankara.

Return to the E23 and continue for 42km to **Sivrihisar**. This town, the ancient Justinianpolis, crouches beneath a crag crowned with the ruins of a Byzantine fortress. This was erected by Justinian to protect the western approaches to Ancyra.

Ulu Cami dates from the mid 13C. Parallel to the *mihrab* wall are six aisles separated by more than 60 wooden pillars. The upper sections of some of the capitals are painted and have interesting carvings. According to an **inscription** the *mimber* of 1244 was made by Hasan bin Mehmed. Another **inscription** mentions repairs carried out to the mosque in 1274–75 by Emir Mikail bin Abdullah, the regent of Gıyaseddin Keyhüsrev III.

A turning to the SE leads to the village of (16km) Balhisar and the ancient city of **Pessinus**. This was an important centre of the cult of the mother goddess Cybele and of Attis. It seems likely that when the Phrygians arrived in Anatolia towards the beginning of the first millennium BC there was a already a shrine of Cybele here and that the invaders soon established good relations with its powerful, conservative, land-owning priesthood. Cybele has been identified with the ancient Anatolian mother goddess, Kubaba, whose name is a 'stammer-word' i.e. one in which the last syllable is repeated as in 'Mama' and 'Papa'. Known as Mater Kubile or Agdistis to the Phrygians, she was Cybele to the Greeks, and the Bona Dea of the Romans. Her shrines were often on mountains and were usually associated with springs of fresh water. (Agdistis, which means 'She of the Rock', is derived from the Phrygian word Agdos, a rock.)

There are many legends about Cybele and Attis. One claims that Attis was the grandson of Zeus. The king of the gods made unwelcome advances to Mount Agdus and was repulsed. As a result some of his seed fell on the mountain and in time a wild, androgynous creature called Agdistis was produced. To tame him the gods put wine in the well from which he usually drank. While he was in a drunken stupor Dionysus tied the monster's genitals to tree, so that when he woke up and tried to escape he castrated himself. From his blood a tree grew and the fruit of this fell into the lap of a king's daughter, Nana. She became pregnant and produced a son, Attis, who grew up to be a handsome and very desirable young shepherd.

Another account state that Agdistis fell in love with Attis and trained him to become a successful hunter. When Attis decided to marry, Agdistis came to the wedding in a rage and upset the proceedings. The bride killed herself and Attis roamed the countryside in a mad frenzy. Overcome by grief he emasculated himself and died. Agdistis was stricken with remorse and he persuaded Zeus to preserve the body of of his beloved in an incorrupt state.

In the *Fasti*, Ovid tells of Cybele's love for the handsome shepherd boy. When Attis falls in love with a beautiful nymph, Cybele is torn with jealousy and kills her rival. As a result Attis goes mad and cuts off with a sharp stone those parts of his body which have caused his infidelity.

In a very moving poem Catullus describes how Attis, having 'lopped of the load of his loins with a sharp flint' regrets his wasted manhood. The common theme of all the legends about Cybele and Attis is the castration of the young god, so it is not surprising that during an annual spring festival prospective priests of the cult followed his example. This extreme sacrifice was made in the belief that it would bring Attis back to life. The priests were named Galli after their symbol, the cock. They dressed in an extravagant fashion, had their hair waved like women and were usually heavily made up. Followed by a retinue of enthusiastic followers they begged for alms and told fortunes. According to Vermaseren, in the West the head of the Galli was the Archigallus, the 'Arch Cock'. Many Romans were quite unable to understand how men could mutilate themselves in the way and the ridicule sometimes heaped on Attis was applied with greater force to his followers.

Nevertheless, the Romans greatly honoured the Baitylos, a black meteor which represented Cybele at Pessinus. A prophecy in the Sybilline Books said that it should be brought to Rome. This was done in 205 BC with the assistance of Attalus I of Pergamum, and placed in a special temple on the Capitoline Hill. When a Roman army marched into Galatia in 188 BC, the priests of Cybele came to meet it. They assured the commander, the proconsul Manlius Volso, that he would be victorious. He was.

Pessinus was ruled for a time by the kings of Pergamum. According to Strabo they built the sanctuary and ornamented the temple with porticos of white marble. Later it was occupied by a tribe of Celts who made the place their capital. Although they adopted many of the ways and customs of the indigenous people they continued to speak their own language, as well as Greek, into the Byzantine period. In Strabo's time the power of the priesthood had been substantially reduced, though the temple of the Great Mother continued to be honoured. The invasion of the Goths in the mid 3C AD and the edict of Theodosius I (379–395), which prohibited pagan cults, brought an end to Pessinus's prosperity and eventually the place was abandoned.

In 1967 Belgian archaeologists discovered the remains of a **Temple of Cybele** which formed part of the shrine of the goddess. The cella measured c 8m by 8m. Note the **bath**, which was probably used for lustral rites. Near the temple there was a flight of 24 steps which served as seats for those who had come to take part in or to witness the ceremonies held in the temple. Facing the steps are the **ruins of a long Ionic portico**. Dating from the 1C AD, this was destroyed, probably by the Goths, in the mid 3C.

From Pessinus return to the E23 and continue in the direction of Afyon. After c 38km a turning on the right will take you to the ruins of Byzantine **Amorium**, the city from which the Amorian dynasty (820–867) sprang. The most important fortress in the Anatolian *theme*, Amorium resisted an attempt by Muawija, the Arab governor of Syria, to capture it in 647, but it fell to Maslama, the caliph's brother, in 717. In 838 it was taken again, as a result of treason, after an 11 day siege by an Arab army led by the Caliph Mutasim. The garrison was slain and the people of the city enslaved. Mutasim took some of the senior officers to Samarra, where he tried to convert them to Islam. However, they steadfastly refused to apostasise and after seven years in captivity were executed. They are honoured by the Eastern Church as the Forty-Two Martyrs of Amorium. At the site there are the remains of the city walls and of a number of buildings. No excavations have been made here so far.

From Amorium continue to **Afyon**. This town has another more sinister name redolent of past sins—Afyonkarahisar, the Black Fortress of Opium. The poppies, from which the drug is produced, are now grown under strict supervision and most of the fields where they once flowered, are devoted to the innocuous sunflower.

Afyon occupies a strategic position in NW Anatolia. Roads from Ankara, Konya, Antalya, İzmir and İstanbul by way of Bursa meet here, linking it with the Aegean, Marmara and Mediterranean seas.

Accommodation and Information. Afyon is a good centre for visiting historic sites in Phrygia. It boasts a motel graded M2, the *Güzelköy Turistik Tesisleri* on the Afyon–İzmir road, and two hotels, *Ece Oteli* and *Oruçoğlu Oteli*, which have two stars each. The Oruçoğlu is recommended. The **Tourist Information Office** is Dumlupınar Mah., Ordu Bulv., No. 22, first floor. The town has three museums.

History. In view of its position it is not surprising that Afyon has attracted settlers from the earliest times. The Hittite fortress of Chapanuva was probably sited here and there is evidence of occupation by the Phrygians.

That flamboyant soldier, politician, playboy, friend and pupil of Socrates, Alcibiades, was murdered here in 404 BC.

Rome inherited the city from Pergamum. Later the Byzantines built a fortress here. The Selçuks, who took it towards the end of the 12C, left a legacy of fine buildings. Afyon came under Ottoman rule in 1428.

Ulu Cami, a Selçuk wooden building, was erected in 1272 by Hasan Nusretüddin. It has a central nave flanked by aisles and a low ceiling supported by 40 wooden columns. Traces of brushwork are visible on some of the carved stalactite capitals. Note the fine **old wooden houses** in the area near the mosque.

Other monuments of interest are the **Kuyulu Camii**, the Mosque of the Well, whose minaret is ornamented with glazed tiles, and the **Kubbeli Mescid**, the Domed Mescid, which was built in 1330.

Climb up the 225m to the top of the great black crag which overlooks the town. Here are the remains of a **fortress** which was founded by the Hittites about the middle of second millennium BC and restored and enlarged by the Phrygians, the Byzantines and the Turks. It had deep **cisterns** for water, **residential quarters** and a *mescid*. The citadel was protected by strong walls strengthened with towers.

The **Archaeological Museum** has nine exhibition rooms, a library, a laboratory, a conference hall, administration offices and store rooms. The objects on display date from the Neolithic Era to the Byzantine period and come from Afyon and places in the provinces of Burdur, Kütahya, Uşak, and İsparta as well as from excavations at Kusura, Yazılıkaya and Hacilar. **Room 1**. Bas-reliefs, statuettes and urns from the Byzantine period. **Room 2**. Roman statues and stelae. **Room 3**. Prehistoric weapons, idols and ceramics. **Room 4**. Kusura-type prehistoric ceramics. **Room 5**. Various objects from the Phrygian period. **Room 6**. Coins and medallions. **Room 7**. Terracotta figurines and glass. **Room 8**. Lamps and other objects from the Roman period. **Room 9**. Roman statues and sarcophagi and Islamic objects.

In the garden there are Roman and Byzantine sarcophagi, Roman statues, altars, grave stones, plinths, Greek and Latin inscriptions, bas-reliefs, a Roman price list, the Synnada sarcophagus, and various architectural fragments.

Afyon's **Ethnographic Museum** is housed in an old Islamic building, the **Gedik Ahmed Paşa Medrese**. This was designed and built by the architect Ayas for an Ottoman minister, Gedik Ahmed Paşa, in 1477. In the museum are weapons, clothing, embroidery, tapestries, a lectern, books and copper dishes from Afyon and the surrounding area.

After the Great Assault, on 27 August 1922 the Turkish army established its headquarters in the Afyon Municipality building. Here Atatürk spent the night of 28 August. The room to the right of the entrance has been designated the Victory Room and in it are kept the table and armchairs used by Atatürk, together with furnishings of the period, maps used during the Great Assault, photographs, pictures and documents.

The principal religious monuments of the Phrygians are located in the hilly, wooded countryside to the N of Afyon. Here in Phrygia Epictetus, Little Phrygia, where the Sangarius, the Rhyndacus, the Tembris and the Parthenius rise, rivers sacred in myth and religion, are the City of the Mother, of Cybele, and the cult shrines of Aslantaş and Aslankaya.

By using your own transport you can visit these places in the course of a single day. However, an early start and much patience are required as neither the roads nor the sites are always well signposted. Cars can be hired in Afyon and taxis are also available here. Before setting out in a taxi it is advisable to get several quotations and agree the fare for the return trip. Bargaining is acceptable, indeed expected. There are few restaurants in the area, so take a picnic lunch.

Leave Afyon by the road N to İhsaniye and after c 20km take the right-hand fork at Gazlıgöl to (12km) **Ayazin**. Here there is a large, well-preserved, early church which has been cut out of the rock. The protruding apse, with its three lozenge shaped windows, is clearly visible from the path leading up from the village. In the columned interior there are two transepts under a high dome and a separate baptistery at the rear. Note the finely carved decoration of the windows, pillars and doors. Around the church there are many caves, often elaborately ornamented, which also have been carved from the soft tufa.

From Ayazin go back to (5km) Kunduzlu and there turn right for (7km) **Aslantaş**, the Lions' Stone. As its name indicates, this large Phrygian tomb had two ornamental, tutelary lions. The burial chamber is c 7m wide and c 11m high. Nearby there are other rock-cut monuments, often elaborately carved. The most important are **Yılantaş**, where the guardian lion sculpture has been overturned, and **Mal Taş**, whose façade resembles that of the cult chamber at Midas Şehri.

Return to the main road and after c 6km turn right to (5km) **Kümbet**, a picturesquely sited village with a number of interesting monuments. These include the **Tomb of Solon**, a Roman rock cut tomb with a fine pediment relief of two lions on either side of an urn, the so-called rock throne with its decorative canopy, and a Selçuk *türbe* made of re-used materials.

From Kümbet it just 12km to **Midasşehri**, Midas City. This place was given its name by a 19C British traveller, Captain Leake, who believed that part of an inscription in Phrygian on the façade of its most impressive monument referred to King Midas. In ancient times it was called Metropolis, the City of the Mother (Cybele). A fragmentary torso of Agdistis (see above) was found on the site.

The earliest traces of occupation date from the 8C BC. It would appear that the city was deserted sometime in the 6C and re-occupied about 100 years later. It was finally abandoned in the 3C AD.

Below the ancient city, on a NW facing cliff, is the monument dubbed by Leake the Tomb of Midas. Modern archaeologists have established that this was a **shrine** dedicated to Cybele. The façade of an imaginary building, carved from the smooth surface of the cliff, is c 18m high. It is decorated with an elaborate maze like pattern of flat geometric shapes and crowned by an ornamental pediment. There are several Phrygian inscriptions on the façade. It was one of these, which mentions Mida, another name for Cybele, that was misread by Leake. There was probably a cult statue of the goddess in the door-shaped niche. A **subterranean chamber** beneath the monument is reached by a long passage. The monument, which has been dated to the last part of the 8C BC, gives some idea of the appearance of Phrygian houses of that period.

The city was in two parts. The acropolis, which measures c 800m by 135m, was surrounded by a massive wall strengthened with towers. It was approached by a ramp on the S side and a flight of steps on E. Note the very eroded **Neo-Hittite reliefs** by the side of the ramp. On the acropolis there are the remains of rooms connected with the worship of the gods, rock tombs and stone altars. One of the altars has a small platform on which the statue of a deity rested. The worship of Cybele often took place near rocks. A vaulted **staircase** leads to a **cavern** where a well, which provided fresh water for those living on the acropolis, may have been used also for ritual purification. Farther to the W is **Küçük Yazılıkaya**, the Small Inscribed Rock, which was never finished.

The villages of Yazılıkaya and nearby **Gökbahçe** are inhabited by Circassians who were settled here in the 19C. There is an interesting **Phrygian relief** on the rock face high above the village of Gökbahçe.

From Gökbaçe continue N to (29km) **Seyitgazi**. This town is believed by authorities to occupy the site of ancient Prymnessus. It is named after Seyit Battal Gazi, an 8C Arab army commander who perished at the siege of Afyon. According to a popular legend, he had fallen in love with a Byzantine princess who pined away after his death and was buried with him. The place of their interment in a Christian monastery was revealed in a dream to the mother of Sultan Alaeddin Keykubad I. She arranged for a *türbe* to be built over their remains. In time this became a place of pilgrimage and Hacı Bektaş founded a dervish *tekke* here. Selim I (1512–20) added a mosque and an *imaret* and enlarged and enriched the *türbe* of the warrior and his beloved. To symbolise his greatness, the sarcophagus of Battal is c 8m long. Beside it is the normal-sized tomb of his princess. In front of the mosque there is a large Byzantine church. From the nearby monks' day room there is a fine view over the surrounding countryside.

From Seyitgazi return to Gazigöl. There turn right for İhsaniye and continue to (12km) Döger, where there is ruined *han*, and follow the signs to the last site on this excursion, **Aslankaya**, Lion Rock.

On the outskirts of Döger there are the remains of a **shrine of Cybele** which has been badly damaged by bungling, illegal treasure hunters. A little farther on is Aslankaya. This is cut into the smooth face of an isolated tufa peak. The **relief**, which is c 9.5m high, shows Cybele, guarded by two large lions, in a gate-shaped niche. Above the lintel of the niche are **representations of two sphinxes**. This monument is believed to have been made sometime between 900 and 600 BC.

From Aslankaya return to Afyon, where you may join Route 13.

57

Erzurum to Hopa

Total distance c 250km. Erzurum R950—c 18km Dumlu—c 36km Tortum—c 24km Bağbaşı—c 6km Uzundere—c 8km (c 7km Vank)—c 24km Işhan)—(c 64km Penek)c 10km Dörtkilise)—(c 18km Parhal)—c 25km (c 10km Yusufeli)—c 59km Artvin—(c 5km Kafkasör Tatil Köyü)—(c 5km Hamamlı)—(c 11km Ardanuç)—(c 24km Yeni Rabat)—c 38km Borçka—c 37km Hopa.

Transport. There is a daily minibus service between Erzurum and Artvin. The journey, including brief stops for refreshments, takes about four hours.

Shortly after leaving Erzurum, the road crosses the northern part of the **Erzurum Ovası**, a broad grassy plain which is carpeted with wild flowers in the spring. It then enters the valley of the **Tortum Çayı**. Reminiscent of the Zap (see Route 46), the Tortum is, however, less wild. Its gorges have more vegetation and the umber-coloured mountains that define and determine its boundaries are not so intimidating. Frail bridges with slatted wooden walkways and rope hand-rails provide a precarious link with tiny hamlets hidden away in the remote valleys.

A signpost on the left, c 24km beyond Tortum, points to the village of 8km Bağbaşı, formerly known as **Haho**, where one of the many ruined Georgian churches is located. This formed part of a monastic foundation consisting of a 9C chapel built by David I and a 10C church dedicated to the Mother of God. The church was converted into a mosque, still in use, when the people in this area converted to Islam in the 17C.

The scenery takes on a distinctly Swiss character at the pretty little village of **Uzundere**. Here, wooden houses with steeply-pitched roofs and balconies full of flowers perch high over the dark green waters of the river.

An unmarked road on the left just before Tortum Gölü leads to the site of the **Monastery of Vank**. All that remains is the huge 10C basilical church which was dedicated to the Deisis. Now roofless and used as a store and volley ball court, the building contains a number of fine sculptures and a narrow band of **11C frescoes**.

Despite its appearance, **Tortum Gölü** is not an artific[...] 10km long lake was formed by a landslip, which damme[...] several centuries ago.

As it approaches the lake, the road climbs steeply until i[...] height. Drivers negotiate a succession of sharp curves wi[...] ....., averting their eyes from the crumbling, unfenced edge of the road and the long drop to the emerald waters of the lake.

There is a brief descent to a narrow, bare promontory which stands like a dramatic exclamation mark on the straight, monotonous shoreline. A hawk pivots on one wing high above the still waters of the lake and then drops like a stone on its prey. The bus moves on. An unending procession of cloud shadows cross the arid, treeless slopes of a distant mountain. At the crossroads near the confluence of the Tortum and Oltu rivers, take the right-hand fork and follow the road signposted Olur for c 4km. A narrow, unmade track on the left, which cuts a deep scar into the hillside, leads to c 5km İşhan and one of the most beautiful of the Georgian churches.

İşhan is a verdant oasis on a sheltered plateau high above the Oltu river. At the entrance to the village the dome of the ruined **11C church** floats into view. Dedicated to the Mother of God, it stands surrounded by fruit trees on a level greensward in the centre of the tiny settlement. There are **traces of paint** on the outside walls and a few **badly faded frescoes** of angels in the interior. Note the **windows** ornamented with fine carvings and the **inscriptions in Georgian** on the S wall and over the doorway of an adjoining building which may have been the bishop's residence. The church has lost its roof, but the 42m high **central dome** remains, a graceful airy miracle resting on four slender pillars.

The green at İşhan is an excellent place for a picnic. There is a small fountain, which supplies clean drinking water, and it is not unusual for the hospitable villagers to bring gifts of fresh fruit to their guests—mulberries, peaches, pears, apples or figs, according to the time of year.

Return to Road 060, turn left and continue in the direction of Akşar and Göle, if you wish to visit an interesting group of churches near the 64km village of **Penek**. Otherwise turn right, return to the junction with Road 950. After c 8km a turning to the left leads to 10km Yusufeli.

Using **Yusufeli** as a centre, it is possible to visit two of the more remote Georgian churches. For **Dörtkilise**, follow the İspir road S from Yusufeli for c 8km. At the point where it reaches a ruined castle, turn right and continue for a further 2km. Although Dörtkilise means Four Churches, only one remains standing. This 10C basilica, which retains part of its roof, has some very damaged frescoes in the interior. For **Parhal church** take the road N to 18km Sarıgöl. The walls of this 10C basilica, which is in a good state of repair, also has some damaged paintings.

For the remaining 59km to Artvin Road 950 follows the valley of the Çoruh Nehri which is reputed to be the fastest flowing river in Turkey.

Great rose-coloured cliffs form a narrow gorge in which there is just enough room for the road and the foam-flecked river. Riding the Çoruh rapids is a favourite sport of daredevil Turkish boys and bands of excited youths may sometimes be glimpsed clinging to makeshift rafts that toss and spin alarmingly in the current which bears them rapidly downstream. White-water rafting is now being developed for tourists.

The occasional rickety wooden bridge, neat pile of logs awaiting transport or lonely cluster of wooden houses are the only other signs of man's presence in this area.

Near Artvin the gorge opens out, revealing high tree covered mountains with a scattering of farmsteads on the lower slopes. The river, too, spreads itself among wide gravel beds, but deceptively maintains its momentum.

tors to Artvin are frequently regaled with tales about foolish swimmers and careless fishermen, who were either unaware of the danger or who ignored local advice and disappeared for ever in the Çoruh's muddy waters.

Crossing the river near the ancient castle, which has guarded this route to the sea for many centuries, the bus begins its slow climb the 2km to the town centre.

ARTVIN, estimated population 20,000, altitude 500m, is a picturesque town which straggles untidily up a steep hillside. Surrounded by forests of conifers, beech, chestnut, hornbeam and oak, it is an important agricultural centre. Wheat and barley are the main grain crops, while olives, pomegranates and mulberries are grown in the sheltered valleys. The area is also famous for its honey, including the intoxicating variety, *deli bal*, produced from the flowers of the azalea and rhododendron (see below).

Apart from its 15C castle, which is not open to the public, Artvin has no buildings of historical interest. However, it is beginning to attract an increasing number of visitors who use it as a centre for visiting the Georgian churches in the surrounding area or for walking and climbing.

Accommodation At present Artvin has only one hotel, the two-star *Karahan*. Located in the main street, this can be noisy and its restaurant menu is somewhat limited. *Kafkasör Tatil Köyü* is an attractive alternative . This holiday village is 5km, 15 minutes by taxi, from the town centre. Delightfully sited in an area of virgin forest, the village has 90 beds in 22 chalets. Each chalet has a kitchen, toilet, shower, telephone, hot water and electricity. There is a small café.

Tourist Information Office. There is a small, but very active and helpful, Tourist Information Office in the municipal building at the rear of the Karahan hotel.

Transport. There are bus and minibus services to Erzurum and Hopa. Some of the services leave from the town centre, others from the bus station or from a stop on the main road near the bridge over the Çoruh.

Festival. During the last week of June Artvin's Folklore Festival is held at Kafkasör Tatil Köyü. In addition to child wrestlers, dancing, bagpipe music and jugglers there are the famous, bloodless bull wrestling contests.

Excursions. Many of the Georgian churches are easily reached from Artvin by taxi or private transport. In some cases there are bus and dolmuş connections with the villages where they are located.

The wild beauty of its setting adds to the enjoyment of a visit to the **Georgian church of Hamamlı**. Take Road 965 from Artvin for 10km in the direction of Şavşat. A rough track on the left climbs rapidly away from the valley of the Berta Suyu and after many sharp bends eventually reaches c 5km Hamamlı. The small 10C church, half-hidden by fruit trees, is surrounded by the village houses. Now a mosque, it is in a good state of preservation. The *imam*, who is well informed about the history of the building, welcomes visitors. There are traces of paintings on the lime-washed ceiling and walls of the interior. Outside, high up on the S wall, look for an **inscription** and **carvings of the Star of David and of the Angels Gabriel and Michael**. These are partly obscured by the *imam*'s house, which has been built against the side of the church. In the **crypt** there are the substantial remains of life size **wall paintings** of the Four Evangelists. Only the faces have been damaged.

On the way back to the main road it is worth pausing briefly to admire the magnificent view over the valley of the Berta Suyu. The stabilised surface of the track calls for very careful driving and negotiating the unfenced edge, particularly in the face of oncoming traffic, will test the nerves of even the most phlegmatic and experienced motorists.

View over the valley of the Çoruh Nehri near Artvin

If you have time, continue to the little town of Ardanuç. Return to Road 965 and take the first right hand turn. Then follow the valley of the Köprüler Dere for c 11km. **Ardanuç**, once a place of some importance on a hazardous mountain trade route between Kars and Artvin, was ruled by the Bagratids until the beginning of the 11C. All that remains of its past glories are the **ruined outer walls** and **defensive towers** of a **great fortress**. These rest precariously on a crumbling cliff above a deep gorge.

The ruins of the church, which formed part of the 10C **Monastery of Yeni Rabat**, are located c 24km to the E of Ardanuç. This was one of the first monasteries founded by St Gregory the Illuminator. Two of the fine manuscripts produced in this monastery, the **9C Gospel of Scribe Michael** and **10C Gospel of Scribe Grigol**, are now in the Tbilisi museum.

Botanists and hill walkers will enjoy exploring the Parmak Dağı and Kaçkar Dağları which lie to the SW of Artvin. The slopes of these mountains are covered with dense clumps of azaleas and rhododendrons including *Rhododendron luteum*, formerly *Azalea pontica*. According to Pliny the pungent, sweet-smelling yellow flowers of this shrub are the source of the honey which the Turks call *deli bal*, crazy honey.

Perhaps the earliest description of the alarming effects of crazy honey on those who consume it is contained in Xenophon's *Anabasis* (IV, 8):

there were great numbers of bee hives in these parts, and all the soldiers who ate the honey went off their heads and suffered from vomiting and diarrhoea and were unable to stand upright. Those who had only eaten a little behaved as though they were drunk, and those who had eaten a lot were like mad people. Some actually died. So there were numbers of them lying on the ground, as though after a defeat, and there was a general state of despondency. However, they were all alive on the next day, and came to themselves at about the same hour as they had eaten the honey the day before. On the third and fourth days they were able to get up, and felt just as if they had been taking medicine.

According to Strabo, the honey had a similar effect on Pompey's soldiers, against whom it was used as a military weapon. The Heptacometae, who lived in the Pontus,

cut down three maniples of Pompey's army when they were passing through the mountainous country; for they mixed bowls of the crazing honey…and placed them in the roads, and then, when the soldiers drank the mixture and lost their senses, they attacked them and easily disposed of them.

This wild and barbarous race, sometimes known as the Mossynoeci, had a reputation for odd behaviour. Xenophon relates how boys from selected, wealthy Mossynoecian families were force-fed on boiled chestnuts until they were almost square in shape. They were then tattooed all over, back and front, with bright floral designs before being sold or offered as gifts.

The Mossynoecians did everything in reverse. They had sexual congress and performed other private acts in public, but when alone, behaved as though they were in the company of their friends, talking and laughing and executing little dance steps. Perhaps their strange behaviour may be attributed to over indulgence in *deli bal*. Modern visitors to the Pontic Mountains would be well advised to avoid this alarming substance. Apparently, it still produces the symptoms of severe drunkness i.e. temporary loss of balance, vomiting and disturbing hallucinations. A number of people require treatment each year in the hospital at Trabzon for conditions produced by crazy honey.

On leaving Artvin Road 010 follows the course of the Çoruh Nehri closely as far as Borçka. The hills pull back to form a broad open, airy valley. The riverbed widens too, so that in some places during the summer months the Çoruh is hidden by large mounds of gravel which surround and hem it in. It becomes a vast playground and recreation area. At a safe distance from the main stream children splash happily through shallow lagoons in vain pursuit of the shoals of tiny fish that live in the tepid water. Families picnic on the banks of polished white stones thrown up by the winter floods, while above the dried-up channels fishermen build little shanties of driftwood.

Although its width is reduced substantially during the summer, the speed of the Çoruh does not change. It still pursues its mad rush to consummate its union with the Black Sea.

At 38km **Borçka** buses and minibuses stop briefly in a large open space near the river. Borçka, a shabby, nondescript place, has the air of two-dimensional unreality and impermanence of a stage set which sometimes marks frontier towns. Within the town limits the Çoruh makes an abrupt right-hand turn and, flowing away to the NE, crosses into Georgia where at last it loses itself in the sea at Batum.

From Borçka Road 010 makes slow, snakelike progress up the S slope of the Pontic Mountains. Fringed by vegetation that becomes more dense, more lush, as it climbs, at last the road reaches Cankurtaran Gec. (690m). Once over the pass it swings round in a vast semicircle, which affords a magnificent view of the thickly-wooded N slopes of the mountains, before beginning the descent to Hopa. Soon the first tea plantation comes into view. Then increasingly the hillsides are covered with the squat green bushes, which contribute so much to the prosperity of this part of Turkey.

The principal, indeed the only, attraction of **Hopa** is the Black Sea. The sight on stormy days of great waves crashing against the boulders and black stones of its pebbly beaches or of the azure mirror that stretches away to an apparently illimitable horizon on windless mornings makes a welcome change from the eye-aching contemplation of the barren mountains and arid steppes of eastern Anatolia.

In ancient times Hopa was called Apsyrtus after the unfortunate son of Aeetes, king of Colchis. Aeetes' daughter, the witch Medea, having helped Jason to steal the Golden Fleece fled with him and the Argonauts from her father's wrath. To distract the pursuers she killed her little brother Apsyrtus, dismembering his body and scattered the infant's limbs over the sea. Her grisly stratagem succeeded. Aeetes abandoned the pursuit and, having collected the remains of his child, buried them on the seashore. In later ages visitors to the town were shown the tomb.

Modern Hopa is little more than a long promenade which follows the shoreline for c 2km. It ends in mud, boulders and potholes near the commercial harbour where a new road to Kemalpaşa and the frontier town of Sarp is being constructed.

Its two hotels, the *Papila* and the *Cihan*, main restaurant, tea-garden, cinema and official buildings are all on or near this promenade. Here the townspeople take their evening stroll, the older men in dark clothes, the youngsters in jeans. The women's dress bridges two cultures. Some wear clothes that would be unremarkable in Ankara or London, while others favour the picturesque traditional red shawls.

The bus terminal—there is no *otogar*—is at the W end of the town where the shops are located.

Hopa, on the same latitude as the Roman Campagna, is hot in summer. It is also very humid. Many days are warm and overcast, an admirable climate for growing tea, but not for attracting visitors. Apart from a few decaying 19C houses, the town has no buildings of historical or architectural interest. For most travellers Hopa is no more than a mildly interesting overnight stop on a tour of the Black Sea coast and eastern Anatolia.

The journey over the mountains from Artvin to Hopa is short, c 75km, and takes only two hours. However, the environmental, social, economic and cultural differences between the two places are considerable. The inhabitants of Hopa and the surrounding countryside claim to be a mixture of Laz, Hamsi and Georgian. Like most of the Black Sea people they have a well-deserved reputation for hard work and, despite the many jokes about the Laz, for intelligence. Like all Turks they are kind, hospitable and welcoming to strangers. If you spend a few days in Hopa, you may be invited to visit one of the tea plantations or tea-processing factories.

58

Trabzon to Erzurum

Total distance 307km (excluding deviations). Trabzon—24km Maçka—52km Torul—25km Gümüşhane—(20km Kösedağı Pass)—(39km Yağmurdere)—5km Kale—54km Bayburt—19km Maden—72km Aşkale—56km Erzurum.

Visitors who wish to go inland to Erzurum by a spectacular route are recommended to make this journey. For much of the way it follows the old silk road over the Pontic Mountains, climbing at times to almost 2500m above sea level. Although the distance covered is little more than 300km, it takes about six hours by bus. Because of landfalls and subsidence, sections of the road need almost constant maintenance.

If you have your own transport ensure that it is in a good state of repair. Take sufficient petrol for the full distance. The surface on parts of the route is stabilised and not tarmacadam. There are very steep ascents and even steeper descents, unfenced, vertiginous drops, often on bends, and extreme weather conditions at certain times of the year. However, there is little traffic and one breathtaking view after another.

Leave Trabzon by the E390. This runs through the valley of the Maçka Deresi keeping close to the river for several kilometres. The landscape is lush and soaked, acid green from the frequent heavy rains. **Maçka**, the ancient Dikaisimon, is now a sleepy little place. During the Byzantine period it was the administrative centre of the district of Matzouka. Caravans from the Black Sea made their first overnight stop here.

The road begins to climb and soon enters an area of pine forests interspersed with cropped alpine meadows. Isolated timber houses crouch for protection in natural hollows. Each is flanked by woodpiles, fuel for the bitterly cold winters. As you approach the Zigana Tunnel, houses become fewer. Often the only signs of human activity are provided by the engineers who are engaged in a never ending battle with the elements to keep the road open. Sections of the old trade route are visible, but in many places it has been covered by artificial screes, a by-product of the wide new highway.

At the **Zigana Tunnel** (2010m) stop for a moment. Turn, look back and make your adieux to the Black Sea before continuing inland. It may have been here that Xenophon and the Ten Thousand cried aloud with joy: Θάλασσα, Θάλασσα, the Sea, the Sea, knowing that their long route march from Cunaxa was coming to an end at last.

Shortly after passing through the tunnel you arrive in **Torul** where buses make a brief stop in the dusty little square. This was the ancient Ardasa. It is dominated by the gaunt remains of a ruined castle which held out against the soldiers of Mehmet II in 1461. They took the town on their way to Trebizond, but the garrison of the castle did not surrender to the Ottomans until 1479–80. Today the silence of Torul is disturbed only by an infrequent long-distance bus and its chattering passengers or by a farmer bringing produce to town in a tractor-drawn trailer. From a muddy, half-covered stream at one side of the square comes a sweet, pungent smell that lingers in the nostrils. It is best not to look too closely for its source.

For much of the way from Torul to Gümüşhane the road follows the upper reaches of the **Harşit Çayı**. Here the river is lined with tall poplars, which blaze with colour in the autumn, and the hedgerows are full of the twisted skeins of old man's beard. The gardens of apple, pear, apricot, pomegranate and peach trees contribute to the wealth of valley's inhabitants. Rising, curving, descending the road arrives at last at Gümüşhane. This area is full of half-forgotten monuments. Just before the town look out for the yellow signs to two of them, **Olucak Monastery** and **Canca Castle** with their fresco-decorated chapels.

In Turkish **Gümüşhane** means the Silver Han and this echoes the place's 19C Greek name, **Argyropolis**, Silver City. Both refer to the silver mines near the town which were exploited from ancient times to the 19C and were known to Marco Polo. During the late Byzantine period this was an important ecclesiastical, administrative and commercial centre. When the Danishmendid Turks captured it towards the end of the 11C, they struck their first coins in metal mined here. According to Ibn Battuta it was a populous town much visited by merchants from Syria and Iraq.

The present town was built after the troubles which disturbed Turkey during the First World War and in the early 1920s. It is now a quiet, provincial backwater. Most of the buildings are painted in pleasing shades of green. Unfortunately, the harmonious colour scheme is spoiled by the ugly corrugated iron roofs which disfigure some of them.

Gümüşhane is famous for the scarves and shawls ornamented with silver threads made here. Many of the women wear the black silk *chador*.

Allow some time for a visit to the old town, **Eski Gümüşhane**. Wander through its streets, peopled only by ghosts from the past. Visit the ruined *hamams*, sturdy stone-built houses and mosques. Examine the interesting **Byzantine frescoes** on the walls of some of the secularised churches.

About 16km from Gümüşhane, Road 885 on the right leads towards Erzincan. After c 20km it climbs to the 1910m high **Kösedağ Geç**. where one of the decisive battles in Turkish history was fought. Here, on 26 June 1242, the Mongols defeated a Selçuk army, ending their rule in Anatolia.

A further 4km from this turning a roughly paved road on the left will take you to 39km **Yağmurdere**. After crossing the 2280m high **Kostandağı Geç**., you arrive at a beautiful, remote *yayla* settlement which is perched on a narrow ledge high above a tributary of the Kara Dere. Its charming, hospitable inhabitants are delighted to welcome the few foreign visitors who make their way there.

Return to the E390 and continue to the village of **Kale**, the Byzantine **Mesochaldia**. Crowning a 250m high rocky spur on the left side of the road are the ruins of the fortress which gives the place its name. Constructed originally by the Byzantines, this was rebuilt and strengthened by the Grand Comneni.

Shortly after Kale the road passes through a narrow canyon bounded by high rocky walls. It then climbs to the 1875m high **Vau Dağı Geç**. before descending to the plain. This is bounded by the bare, rounded mountains which are a typical feature of the eastern Anatolian high plateau.

Bayburt, the ancient Paipertes, was a garrison town on the upper Çoruh. It is believed to have been founded by the Scythians and was ruled at various times by the Byzantines, the Bagratids and Turkish clans. Apart from its well preserved **medieval fortress**, only the early 13C **Ulu Cami**, built by a local Saltukid ruler, the **Yakutiye Cami**, endowed by a Mongol governor in 1315, and two *Kümbetler* need detain the visitor. In the 16C and 17C Bayburt appears on the list of Anatolian towns from which Christian children were taken under the Ottoman system of *devşirme*.

At almost 1500m above a sea level, Bayburt is a cold, windswept place. Its climate appears to have affected the inhabitants who are, in the main, dour and reserved. The gaiety and spontaneity of the Black Sea peoples is regarded with suspicion here. Bayburt women, hidden in dun coloured, shapeless body bags, promenade and shop in the market. The height of male fashion appears to be a fierce, bristling moustache.

From Bayburt the road follows the valley of the Masat Çayı, a tributary of the Çoruh, to 19km Maden. It then begins the slow, tortuous ascent of the 2425m high **Kop Geç.** This pass is notorious for its sudden, savage blizzards and many caravans froze to death on it. The road passes through a wild, desolate landscape, where patches of thin vegetation struggle for existence. There is no shelter anywhere. A monument marks the highest point of the pass and from it there is a magnificent view over the mountain-encircled plain which stretches from Aşkale to Erzurum.

From the pass the road descends through a series of tight bends to 72km **Aşkale**. This town and the last part of the journey to Erzurum are described in Route 51.

59

Hopa to Trabzon

Total distance c 151km. (excluding diversions). Hopa—c 11km Arhavi—c 16km Fındıklı—c 16km Ardeşen—(c 20km Çamlıhemşin)—c 9km Pazar—c 19km Çayelı—c 16km Rize—c 18km Of—(c 50km Uzungöl)—c 14km Sürmene—c 6km Araklı—c 12km Arsin—c 6km Yomra—c 12km Trabzon—(c 54km Sumela Monastery).

.Although there are good bus and minibus services between Hopa and Trabzon, it is advisable to make reservations a day or two in advance of the date of travel. Departures are from the W end of the town. The journey takes between three and four hours, depending on the amount of traffic and on delays caused by road repairs.

Leave Hopa by Road 010, the road which follows the Black Sea coastline from Turkey's border with Georgia. There is a scattering of houses, but little sign of planned development, on the way to Arhavi. On the left-hand side of the road trees and bushes entwined with tangled vines, the result of the abundant rainfall, form a dense cover on the hillsides and fill the valleys and ravines. On the right a low wall separates the road from the sea. Small beaches, edged with the distinctive black boulders and coarse dark pebbles of the Black Sea, repeat themselves monotonously.

Between Arhavi and Rize there is a succession of small towns, whose prosperity depends largely on tea. The cultivation of tea in Turkey was suggested by a botanist, Ali Rıza Erten, in 1919 and the first serious experiments were conducted in 1924 with plants and seeds brought from Batum in the USSR. Large plantations were established in 1939 and the first crop of tea was picked in the following year. The warm, humid conditions found in the Black Sea area are ideal for this crop. The soil is rich in nutrients and it retains water, which the plants need.

At **Fındıklı** a different crop, the hazel nut, *fındık* in Turkish, predominates. Every level piece of ground near the town has its stand of hazel trees.

Ardeşen, Pazar and Çayelı are small, pleasant coastal resorts, where a stop can be made for refreshments. Apart from their picturesque locations they have little to offer.

If you have time, make an excursion from Ardeşen or Pazar to **Çamlıhemşin**, a typical Kaçkar mountain village. The people here are Hemşinli and speak their own dialect of Turkish. Enjoy the hospitality and good food of the Hoşdere Lokantası whose balcony juts out precariously over the foaming waters of the Fırtına river. Buy some of the woollen socks made in the village and the silk scarves which are a feature of Hemşin attire. If you want to explore the mountains, find a local guide. Visit the picturesque ruins of **Zil Kale**, the Castle of the Bells or Cymbals, and the beautiful crater lakes hidden among the higher peaks.

The territory of the Grand Comneni extended E as far as **Çayeli**, the ancient Mavpari. Its name is derived from çay, the Turkish for tea.

Rize, population 50,156, is the capital of the province of the same name. It is an attractive town built on two wooded hills which shelter a crescent-shaped bay. Apart from the ruined fortress, built by Justinian and restored by the Grand Comneni, and a 16C mosque, **Islam Paşa Camii**, built during the reign of Selim I the Grim (1512–20), there are no buildings of historical interest in Rize.

Information. There is one hotel on the Ministry of Tourism list, the two-star *Keleş* at Palandöken Cad., No. 2–53020. The **Tourist Information Office** is in Belediye Karşısı.

History. Inhabited at first by indigenous tribes, Rize and the surrounding countryside eventually became part of the Hittite Empire. In the 7C and 6C BC the economic and cultural horizons of the area were extended, when some of the Ionian cities established colonies on the Black Sea coast, notably at Sinop (Sinope), Samsun (Amisus) and Trabzon (Trapezus). Strongly fortified by the Byzantines during the reign of Justinian I (527–565), the settlement became known as Rhisos, from which its modern name may be derived. After the capture and occupation of Constantinople by the Crusaders in 1204 Alexius and David Comnenus, grandsons of Andronicus I, founded the Byzantine Empire of Trebizond. Rize was part of that empire until the surrender of its capital to Mehmet the Conqueror in 1464 brought the rule of the Grand Comneni to an end.

A town of some importance during the Ottoman period, Rize was ruled by the provincial governor of Trabzon. Occupied by the Russians on 21 February 1916, it was liberated on 2 March 1918 by Turkish forces.

Rize was made a provincial capital in 1924. Its Governor administers an area of 3920 sq km (population 378,760). In addition to tea, the province produces maize, fruit, hemp, hazelnuts and mulberries. It is well-known for cattle rearing and for the production of a special kind of honey from **Ballıköy Anzer**. Because of its medicinal properties this enjoys a wide popularity in Turkey. In recent years the growth of the tea industry has brought increased prosperity to the province.

Steps have been taken to encourage the artificial rearing of trout in Rize province and there are substantial landings by the Black Sea fishing boats of anchovies, red mullet, mackerel, turbot, tuna, and sea-bass.

Continue from Rize on Road 010 in the direction of Trabzon. Just after **Of**, the ancient Ophis, a road leads inland along the valley of the Solaki Deres to c 26km **Uzungöl**. Here there is a 250-year-old covered bridge. According to the proud villagers it is the only one of its kind in Turkey.

At **Sürmene** there is a remarkable Ottoman house. This was built c 1800 by the Yakupoğlu family, who bore the title of Derebeyler, Lords of the (Gürçay) Valley. The three-storey structure, which is surmounted by a projecting roof resting on great wooden beams, is now a museum.

Road 010 remains in the narrow, humid coastal plain. It passes through three small towns, **Araklı**, **Arsin** and **Yomra**. Each has a small harbour protected by a rough stone breakwater. Arakli, the most picturesque of the three, was the birthplace of the ill-fated Byzantine emperor Heraclonas and it took its ancient name, Heracleia, from him.

TRABZON, population 155,960, formerly Trebizond and in ancient times Trapezus, is a busy, modern provincial capital. Under the canopy of low, grey cloud, which frequently covers the city, its buildings appear sombre and uninviting. Visitors reared on stories of the peacock brilliance of the Comneni and expecting to find the remains of their glittering palaces will be disappointed. The few remaining traces of the city's long and distinguished past have to be sought out with diligence. The towers of Trebizond, Rose Macaulay's 'fabled city', disappeared a long time ago.

Information and Accommodation. The **Tourist Information Office** is in Atatürk Alanı, Park Köşesi. The two-star *Usta Hotel* at Telegrafhane Sok. 1, just off Atatürk Alanı, is recommended. Clean, comfortable and quiet, it has its own restaurant. This hotel is very well managed and has an attentive and helpful staff.

There is quite a wide choice of eating places in Trabzon. One of the best is the *Trapezus Taverna Restaurant*.

Transport. There are frequent bus and dolmuş services from the *otogar* on the E side of the city to Samsun, Sinop, Rize and Hopa, and long-distance buses to İstanbul, Ankara and other cities.

A weekly ferry boat to İstanbul calls at Samsun and Sinop. The journey takes one and a half days. Cabins are available. Book well in advance.

THY operates daily flights to Ankara and İstanbul.

Post Office and Banks. The principal post office and branches of the main Turkish banks are in the city centre.

Museums. Trabzon's **Atatürk Museum**, located in the Soğuksu district of the city, contains a collection of memoribilia including the text of a speech, which the founder of modern Turkey made when he visited the city on 15 September 1924.

In the grounds of **Haghia Sophia** there is a small collection of Roman, Byzantine and Ottoman stelae and fragments of sculpture.

Excursions. Tours to Haghia Sophia, the Atatürk Museum, Sumela Monastery and other places of interest around Trabzon are organised by **Saktur Tourism and Travel Agency**, Gazipaşa Cad., 21A. There are frequent dolmuş services to Haghia Sophia from Atatürk Alanı.

History. Trapezus was founded by settlers from the Milesian colony of Sinope, modern Sinop, towards the end of the 7C BC. They were followed by emigrants from Trapezus in Arcadia, who gave the foundation its name. In addition to seeking new land for cultivation, it seems likely that the settlers were also engaged in trading in metals with northern Anatolia and the Caucasus. Some authorities maintain that it was through Trapezus and Sinope that Urartian bronzes reached the Greek world, so helping to produce the so-called orientalising period (c 720–550 BC) in Greek art.

In the summer of 400 BC, a few days after their unnerving encounter experience with *deli bal*, crazy honey (see Artvin), Xenophon and his Ten Thousand reached Trapezus. They stayed for about 30 days, camping in the Colchian villages. According to Xenophon (*Anabasis* IV, 8) they spent most of their time ravaging the countryside, an action unlikely to endear them to their hosts. Relations with the colonists of Trapezus were better. They gave the mercenaries presents of oxen, barley and wine.

Because of its geographical location Trapezus was better-suited than either Sinope or Amisus to be the terminus of the long trade route from Persia and eastern Anatolia to the Black Sea. Although occupied by Mithridates and later by a Roman army under Lucullus, the city came through the Mithridatic Wars (88–63 BC) largely unscathed.

Hadrian (AD 117–138) visited Trapezus in 129 and adorned it with many buildings and ordered the construction of a large harbour. The city continued to prosper under his successors. Captured and sacked by the Goths c AD 260, it was rebuilt during the reign of Diocletian. Justinian the Great (527–565) had its fortifications extended and improved. In the 11C Trapezus successfully repulsed the attacks of the Selçuks.

The early 14C author of *The Travels of Sir John Mandeville* describes it as a 'good city' where St Athanasius, bishop of Alexandria, who wrote the psalm *Quicunque vult* was buried 'upon the gate of the city'. It was governed by Guido 'of the lineage of the emperors of Constantinople', but subject to the rule of the Tartars.

Shortly before the capture of Constantinople by the Crusaders in 1204 the Grand Comneni Alexius and David, grandsons of that unhappy emperor, Andronicus I, who was torn to pieces by an enraged mob in Constantinople in 1185, founded the Empire of Trebizond. Reared to manhood by their Georgian royal cousins, they captured the city in April 1204. Then, marching westward along the coast they took Sinope, and brought Paphlogonia and the Heraclea Pontica under their control.

The 19 emperors and three empresses of their royal house ruled over a long narrow strip of land, 7000 square miles in area, which stretched along the eastern shoreline of the Black Sea. Renowned for their great physical beauty they lived in surroundings of unparalleled splendour. Cardinal Bessarion, who was born in Trebizond and who lived through the last days of this Byzantine outpost, has left a detailed account of the wonders of the royal palace. He describes the myriad ante-chambers and wind-towers, the magnificent state apartments, whose walls blazed with brilliant frescoes and mosaics, and the great balcony with a pyramid-shaped roof where the emperor gave audience to ambassadors and issued instructions to the officials of his court.

However, in time the strength of the dynasty was sapped by internal rivalries, which produced plots and counter-plots. Emperors perished, an ex-empress was strangled, a usurper poisoned. Trebizond acquired an unmatched reputation for decadence and intrigue. It was rumoured that every form of vice was practiced by members of the imperial court.

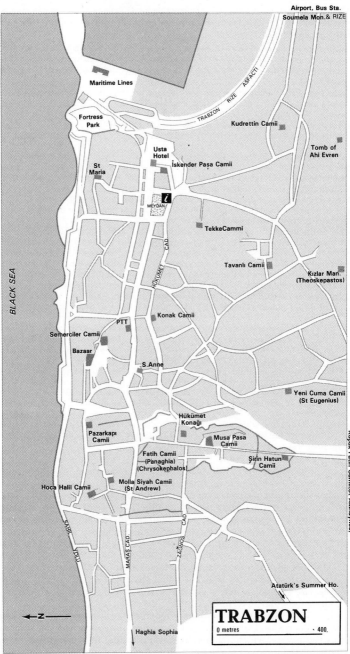

Airport, Bus Sta.
Soumela Mon.& RIZE

Maritime Lines

TRABZON RIZE ASFACTI

Fortress
Park

Kudrettin Camii

Usta
Hotel

Tomb of
Ahi Evren

İskender Paşa Camii

St
Maria

MEYDAN

HÜKÜMET CAD.

TekkeCammi

Tavanlı Camii

Kızlar Man.
(Theoskepastos)

BLACK SEA

Konak Camii

PTT

Semerciler Camii

Bazaar

S.Anne

Yeni Cuma Camii
(St Eugenius)

Hükümet
Konağı

Pazarkapı
Camii

Musa Pasa
Camii

Fatih Camii
(Panaghia)
(Chrysokephalos)

Şirin Hatun
Camii

Molla Siyah Camii
(St Andrew)

Hoca Halil Camii

Küçük Fatih Camii(St Akindynos)

SABIL YOLU

MARAŞ CAD.

ZAGNOS CAD.

Atatürk's Summer Ho.

← Z ──

Haghia Sophia

TRABZON

0 metres   400.

The judgement of historians on the Grand Comneni has been harsh, but it is unlikely that the rulers of Trebizond were more cruel or more debauched than their Georgian, Byzantine or Ottoman counterparts. According to Pereira,

'Their main interest seems to have been the pursuit of beauty, and their tastes were catholic: a church or a palace, a dancing-girl or a page-boy, all found favour in their eyes provided they were beautiful; they loved music and literature; and they wore splendid clothes'.

The end of the empire came very swiftly. Mehmet the Conqueror, who had taken Constantinople in 1453, assembled a great army in Bursa in 1461 and marched E across Anatolia. Stopping briefly to invest Sinop, which was surrendered to him without a struggle by the Muslim rulers who had seized it from the Comneni, he reached Trebizond in the incredibly short time of 18 days. At the same time his fleet of 200 ships anchored off the coast. Although some historians suggest that the city was treacherously handed over to the enemy by the Imperial Treasurer, George Amiroutzes, it seems likely that David, the last emperor of Trebizond, recognised that defeat was inevitable. He was treated generously by his conqueror. He and his family, including his handsome, sexually ambivalent nephew Alexios, were given a safe conduct to lands in the Struma Valley in the Balkans and a pension of 300,000 pieces of silver. His subjects were not so fortunate. One third were sold into slavery, one third sent to İstanbul, the rest were allowed to stay in Trebizond.

David did not live long after the destruction of his empire. A letter from his niece, who was married to Uzun Hasan, the White Sheep Emir, was intercepted and shown to the Sultan by Amiroutzes. This contained an innocent request to her uncle to send one of his sons to Uzun Hasan's court. Although David was almost certainly not guilty of any intrigue, Mehmet decided to take no risks. The ex-emperor and all his sons, except a child aged three, were brought to İstanbul. There they were beheaded.

Trabzon had important links with the Ottoman court. Before he became sultan, Beyazit II was governor of the city. His son and successor, Selim I, held the same position. Selim's son, Süleyman the Magnificent, was born in Trabzon.

Under Ottoman rule the city continued to be a major centre of commerce. Until the construction of the railway line between Ankara and Erzurum, caravans of camels, travelling over the perilous mountain trade route, continued to bring their precious loads of silks and spices from Persia and beyond.

The Russians occupied the city from 1916 to 1918. Since the collapse of the Soviet Union, they have returned in large numbers to trade in the so-called Russian Bazar. In recent years there has been a considerable increase in industrial development in Trabzon and its port facilities have been expanded appropriately.

Atatürk Alanı is a pleasant, tree-shaded square in the city centre, where local people gather to drink tea, play cards or waste an hour in idle conversation.

The **Church of St Anne**, the oldest extant Byzantine monument in Trabzon, is a short walk from Atatürk Alanı along Maraş Cad. to a point where this street begins to approach the NE wall of the citadel. The church is a few metres up a narrow street on the left side. In its present form it dates from the reign of the Byzantine emperor Basil I (867–86). It is a small stone building of considerable presence, stands in the corner of a tiny square surrounded by modern structures of extreme mediocrity. The central nave and side aisles in its plain, undecorated interior are separated by Ionic columns taken from a more ancient building. Over the door, which is usually locked, there is a much **damaged relief and inscription** which records its restoration in 884. The relief shows an armed soldier and an angel. The church, which was a mortuary chapel for senior clerics and courtiers in the late 14C and early 15C, was used until 1923.

From Maraş Cad. walk S to Hükumet Cad., sometimes known as Uzun Yol, the Long Street, and continue in a westerly direction. The road crosses the deep ravine, which divides the ancient citadel from the E side of the city. Today a large part of the ravine is taken up by an exotic garden filled

Haghia Sophia at Trabzon

with plants, flowers, shrubs and trees, a delightful oasis of green surrounded, but not submerged, by Trabzon's busy traffic.

Within the walls of the citadel the striking Neo-Classical building on the left side of the street is the former **Vilayet Konağı**. Alas, this fine structure is showing signs of neglect and is falling into disrepair.

Facing the Vilayet in the centre of a small square is **Fatih Camii**, sometimes known as Ortahisar Camii. This is the former cathedral of Trebizond, the **Panagia Chrysokephalos**, the Golden-Headed Virgin, so called because of the gilded copper plates which covered the dome.

Tradition ascribed the foundation of the original building to Constantine (306–37), but the existing structure dates from the late 10C. The dome was added in the 13C. The coronations of most of the Grand Comneni took place here and they were buried here. After the surrender of Trebizond to Mehmet in 1461 the church was converted into a mosque. A portal flanked by two antique columns was added and the staircase, which provided access to the S gallery, was removed to permit the construction of the *mihrab*. The wall paintings and mosaics in the apse have been covered with plaster and a wooden floor installed over the opus sectile pavement. Note the fine *sebil* and *Şadirvan* in the courtyard.

In a small, shady garden just outside the W wall of the citadel is the most important Ottoman building in Trabzon, the **Gülbaharhatun Camii**, the Mosque of the Spring Rose. This is named after Ayşe Hatun, wife of Beyazit II and mother of Selim I, the Grim. Born Princess Maria, a member of the Comneni, she was famed for her kindness and charity. The mosque was built in 1512 by Selim in her memory and she lies at rest in a magnificent *türbe* nearby.

A short distance to the N of Gülbaharhatun Camii is the dilapidated **Nakip Camii**. Before the conquest this was a church dedicated to St Andrew the Apostle. According to an ancient tradition, he brought Christianity to Trebizond. Constructed of materials taken from an older structure, this building is believed to date from the 10C or 11C.

From Nakip Camii return to the citadel. On the left there is a substantial section of the ancient walls in a good state of repair. Note the **inscription in Greek** near the top of the wall and the elegant **Ottoman fountain** at the point where the fortifications are breached by Uzun Yol.

İçkale Cad. climbs steeply from Fatih Camii to the remains of the ancient **citadel of the Comneni**. At the top of the street take a turning on the right into a narrow lane. To reach the ruins it is necessary to pass in front of a number of houses and walk through neat kitchen gardens under the incurious gaze of the owners, who clearly are not unaccustomed to visitors.

At the end of the last century, when Lynch made a plan of the citadel, a good deal of the palace and its defences remained. Today it requires a great effort of the imagination to relate the overgrown, shattered walls, the rooms filled with rampant vegetation and shaded by tall fig-trees with Cardinal Bessarion's description of the palace. However, one has only to look down from the broken window embrasures on to the haphazard huddle of modern houses that covers the sides and bottom of the W ravine to see how it still dominates the city, even its ruined condition. Rose Macaulay conjures up a vision of

> the Comnenus emperors sitting on their golden thrones, and the Byzantine courtiers and clergymen talking to one another, intriguing, arranging murders, discussing the Trinity, in which they took such an immense interest, talking of the barbarians who were threatening the Empire and later, after Constantinople had fallen, and Trebizond was the Empire, debating how to hold it, how much tribute should be paid to the Turks, how best to form an anti-Turk union, whose eyes should be put out, what envoys should be sent to Rome. [...Eheu Fugaces.]

Clearly visible from the citadel on the eastern skyline is **Yeni Cuma Camii**, the New Friday Mosque, whose name commemorates the fact that Mehmet II gave thanks here on the first Friday after the city had capitulated to him. It had been a monastic church dedicated to St Eugenius, the patron saint of Trebizond, who was martyred during the reign of Diocletian (284–305). It seems probable that there was a Christian shrine on the site from the earliest times. The existing building, which is believed to date from the middle of the 14C, replaced an ancient basilica. This had been badly damaged by fire. During the reconstruction the dome was added. After its conversion into a mosque a porch was built on the N side of the building and a fine sculptured *mihrab* constructed in the S wall.

Haghia Sophia occupies a raised, levelled area a short distance from the seashore, the site of a temple erected by Hadrian (117–38) in honour of Apollo. Originally the conventual church of a monastery, which has disappeared, it was a basilica. This was transformed, probably during the reign of Manuel I (1238–63), into a cross-in-square building with an enormous central dome on a high drum. At the W end a porch leads to the narthex which stretches the width of the building. This has a small chapel above. The columns and capitals in the porches on the N, W and S sides were taken from other buildings. The oldest dates from the 5C. At the E end, the central apse is flanked by two smaller apses; that on the S served as the diaconicon or vestry, while the N apse was the prothesis where the Communion

Elements and the Blessed Sacrament were kept. The central dome is supported by four magnificent columns of Proconnesian marble. Note the magnificent Opus Alexandrinum floor under the dome which combines mosaic and Opus Sectile in a pattern of interlacing bands.

A much-damaged **frieze** on the outside of the S porch, which displays Syrian, Georgian and Armenian influences, tells the story of Adam and Eve. On the right side Adam is shown resting on the ground, while the Serpent tempts Eve. On the left Adam takes the forbidden fruit from Eve. The keystone has the heraldic symbol of the Comneni—an eagle.

After the fall of Trebizond, Haghia Sophia, like many of the churches in the city, became a mosque and its wonderful frescoes were covered with plaster. Later the building was used as a store and then as a hospital. When in 1957 Professor Talbot Rice and his colleagues began their work on the restoration and preservation of the wall paintings, it was in a very bad state of repair. The laborious work of conservation was completed in 1963 and the restored building re-opened as a museum.

The principal paintings remaining are as follows. Over the door to the narthex: *the Agony in the Garden, the Last Supper* and *the Washing of the Apostles' Feet*. Over the main door of the narthex: *an Angel with the veil of St Veronica*, in the central vault *Angels and the Four Evangelists*, on the vault of the S bay *the Wedding Feast at Cana, the Healing of the Paralysed Man* and *SS Bacchus and Sergius*, on the side wall *the Casting out of an Evil Spirit*, in the N bay *Christ calming the storm, walking on the water and curing St Peter's mother-in-law*.

In the W porch *the Blessed in Paradise, the Suffering of the Damned* and the *the Last Judgement*. Inside the church on the central dome *Christ Pantocrator*, on the drum *the Apostles and the Prophets*, on the pendentives *St Mark and the Baptism of Christ, St. Luke and the Nativity, St Matthew and the Crucifixion, St John and the Harrowing of Hell*. The inscription is from Psalm 101, verses 19 and 20 which begins, 'Out of the heavens did the Lord behold the earth'.

In the main apse *the Annunciation and the Visitation, the Miraculous Draught of Fishes, Doubting Thomas*, the *Virgin and Child* and the *The Ascension of Christ into Heaven*. An unpaved area in the S apse is said to mark the grave of Manuel I.

The foundations outside the N porch of Haghia Sophia belong to a smaller, earlier church. The 20m high **bell tower** on the W edge of the garden was completed in 1443 shortly before the capture of the city by the Turks. This also contains a number of **frescoes**. However, they are of poor quality, evidence of the decline in artistic standards during the last days of the Trapezuntine Empire.

In the garden, along the S wall, there is a small collection of Byzantine and Ottoman **funerary monuments**. The trees and flowering shrubs zealously tended by the gardeners help to place this beautiful church in a worthy setting, but unfortunately do not altogether hide the mean buildings which in recent years have been erected in the surrounding streets.

Excursions from Trabzon. To the S of the city, high up on **Boztepe**, there are the ruins of the **Monastery of Panagia Theoskepastos** which was founded c 1340 by the Empress Eirene. This is sometimes known as the Kızlar Manastırı. Here are substantial remains of a church which has a number of damaged wall paintings, a dormitory, refectory and bell tower. The monastery was in use until 1923. The original church was in a cave which is believed to have been a shrine of the Persian sun god Mithras in pre-Christian times. Hence Boztepe's ancient name, Mount Mithrion.

About 1km further on is **Kamakli Manastırı**. Now a farm, this housed a community of Armenian monks until 1923. In adddition to the stone church, which dates from 1431, and the belfry, there is a small chapel. Note the fine **17C wall paintings** which include a frightening depiction of hell and the torments of the damned. Fortunately, they have been preserved from the weather, from religious fanatics who would have covered them with limewash and from vandals who would have defaced them with graffiti, and are in an excellent state of preservation.

Signposts point the way to **Atatürk Köşkü**. This is a delightful 19C pavilion c 4km from the centre of the city. Set in a well-tended garden, it contains an interesting collection of memorabilia connected with the founder of modern Turkey.

Few visitors will want to leave Trabzon without going to **Sumela Monastery**. Resting precariously on a rocky ledge c 300m above a rockbound torrent, this striking monastic complex is 54km to the S of the city. During the holiday season there are daily excursions from Trabzon.

Leave the city by E390, the Erzurum road, and continue as far as 28km Maçka. (Trabzon to Maçka is described in Route 58.) At Maçka there are several restaurants which serve simple meals. Recommended are the *köfte*. A route from Maçka to 20km Sumela is well-signposted. The newly-made road passes through a densely forested valley by the side of a mountain stream. At the car park there is a restaurant and post office.

Stout shoes are necessary for the 30-minute walk to the monastery. Although the path ascends only 300m, because of its meandering course the actual distance covered is about 1km.

History. According to an ancient tradition Sumela Monastery was established c 386 by two monks from Athens, Barnabas and Sophronius. In a dream Barnabas was told by the Blessed Virgin to found a monastery in her honour in the Pontus. He and his companion were guided by a famous icon, the Panayia Atheniotissa, which it was believed had been painted by St Luke, to a cave sited near a spring high up on Mount Mela. The monastic settlement was known as Panagia tou Melas, Our Lady of the Black Mountain. In time this became Soumelas or Sumela in the Pontic Greek dialect.

After their death in 412—it is said they expired on the same day—Barnabas and Sophronius were revered as saints. Soon pilgrims began to flock to the monastery. Honoured by Justinian (527–565), who had the body of Barnabas enclosed in a silver reliquary, Sumela endured many changes of fortune during the centuries that followed. Looted and burned in the middle of the 7C, it was rebuilt soon afterwards and the monks returned to resume their life of prayer.

Until the establishment by the Grand Comneni of the Trapezuntine Empire at the beginning of the 13C, it is likely that Sumela retained its original simple form. Near the sacred spring a rock chapel housed the icon of the Panayia and the monks lived in wooden huts, which projected dangerously from the mountain side. During the reign of Alexius III of Trebizond (1349–90) the monastery was rebuilt once more and given endowments of land in the surrounding countryside. About this time it added an icon known as the Rose-Complexioned Mother of God and a relic of the True Cross to its extensive collection of sacred treasures.

After the surrender of Trebizond to Fatih Mehmet II (1451–81) in 1461, the sultan placed the monastery under his protection, guaranteeing its rights and privileges. This guarantee was honoured by his successors, some of whom made rich gifts to the foundation. Sultan Selim I (1512–20), the son of Ayşe Hatun, wife of Beyazit II, gave the monastery a magnificent pair of silver candlesticks, perhaps in memory of his mother, who was born Princess Maria of the Comneni.

In the middle of the 19C the monastery acquired its present appearance. The wooden living quarters of the monks were removed and replaced by the existing buildings. To help the pilgrims, many of them Muslim, who flocked to the monastery each year on the 15 August, the Feast of the Assumption of Mary, a new road and an aqueduct were constructed. A library was also built to house the monastery's valuable collection of books and manuscripts.

Sumela continued to be occupied by a small community of monks until 1916, when they were obliged to abandon it in the face of advancing Russian troops. The monks returned a short time afterwards, but finally left during the exchange of populations between Turkey and Greece which took place in 1923.

A new Sumela monastery was built in Greece and pilgrims go there each year on the Feast of the Assumption to honour the ancient icon of the Panayia. Sumela's other ancient treasures were scattered widely. One icon went to Oxford, another to New York. The Rose-Complexioned Mother of God icon is in Dublin and most of the manuscripts and some of the books are in İstanbul.

After the monks had departed, the monastery was left to the mercy of the elements. For a while it became the haunt of criminals and suffered from neglect and deliberate damage. Great destruction was caused by a fire in 1930. Twenty years later the first visitors began to arrive at the monastery. Unfortunately, some were ignorant vandals who commemorated their visit by scratching their names and other graffiti on the walls, causing irreparable damage to the ancient paintings in the process.

In 1961 Sumela came under the control of the Turkish Government's Forestry Service. Its officers have cleared most of the buildings of debris and they ensure, as far as their limited numbers permit, that modern visitors behave properly and do no damage to the monastery or to its artistic treasures.

A fortunate few see Sumela bathed in sunshine. However, on most days the mountain is shrouded in mist and one's first glimpse of the monastery is often from the path which leads up from the car park.

Having passed the ruins of the 19C aqueduct, walk down a few steps to a small courtyard. From here a long staircase leads to the inner court of the monastery and to the ruins of the **library**, an ornamental **fountain** and a small **cave church**. In a chapel on the NE side of the court there are **wall paintings** which may date from the reign of Alexius III.

The **principal church** of the monastery, which was dedicated to the Assumption of the Virgin Mary, is in two parts one formed from a natural cave, the other constructed in the shape of an extended apse. On the exterior walls there is an enormous painting of the **Last Judgement**, while on the narthex there are scenes from the Life of Christ and rather badly damaged representations of the Temptation of Adam and Eve. On the outer wall of the apse a **cycle of paintings** is devoted to the Life of the Virgin. All of these date from the beginning of the 18C. Inside the church the most interesting paintings are from the early 15C. These depict some of the Grand Comneni, Andronicus III (1330–32), Alexius III (1338–90) and Manuel III (1390–1412). On the ceiling, aureoles surround striking representations of Christ Pantocrator and of the Virgin Mary.

The remaining part of the monastery contains dormitories, a refectory and storerooms. All are in a sad state of dilapidation.

60

Trabzon to Sinop

Total distance (excluding diversions) c 492km. Trabzon—c 17km Akçaabat—c 31km Vakfıkebir—c 8km Eynesil—c 12km Görele—c 14km Tirebolu—c 12km Esbiye—(Giresun Adası)—c 26km Giresun—(103km Şebinkarahisar)—45km Ordu—c 16km Perşembe—c 32km Bolaman—c 6km Fatsa—c 21km Ünye—(c 5km Castle of Çaleoğlu)—c 31km Terme—c 21km Çarşamba—c 34km Samsun—(c 127km Amasya)—(49km Merzifon)—(35km Yedikuğular Cenneti)—(c 65km Borabay Gölü)—(2km Aynılı Mağara)—54km Bafra—77km Gerze—35km Sinop.

Leave Trabzon by the Sahil Yolu in the direction signposted Samsun and Sinop. Shortly after passing under the ancient walls of Haghia Sophia this joins the road which links the cities and towns of the Black Sea littoral.

Because it carries much heavy traffic and sections are frequently under repair, delays can be expected and progress is likely to be slow. On large stretches the surface is pitted and uneven. Be on the lookout for cattle, sheep and goats which elude their diminutive guardians from time to time and stray on to the road.

For much of the way to Samsum the road is no more than a few metres from the sea. It passes through a number of towns which occupy the sites of Milesian trading posts, some of which were founded as early as the 8C BC. Today they are centres for marketing the produce of the surrounding countryside and also serve as home ports for Black Sea inshore fishing boats. A number of towns, particularly from Giresun westwards, have begun to attract tourists and have built small hotels and restaurants. Eating out is not expensive here. The fish is particularly good. Try the *hamsi* (fresh anchovies), *palamut* (short-finned tuna) and *istavrit* (horse mackerel). Most visitors are Turkish. For foreigners the area is largely a terra incognita.

The small port of **Akçaabat** is c 17km from Trabzon. Formerly called Hermonassa, it was, according to Strabo, a moderate-sized settlement in the 1C BC. It later became known as Platana, perhaps because it had so many plane trees. Its two-star *Sumela Oteli*, İnönü Cad., is on the Ministry of Tourism list.

There are two interesting churches in Akçaabat. The 13C **Church of St Michael**, in the W part of the town, has a single nave, a semicircular apse and walls ornamented with small blind arches. The church is now a dwelling. On the walls of another church, which is dedicated to the Incorporeal Saints, there are some fragmentary paintings including a fine representation of the Deisis. Alas, this church has been turned into a farm-building. There are some fine traditional style houses in Orta Mahalle. Note particularly those in Dutlu Cad.

On Tuesday of each week the women from the mountain villages, wearing their colourful *peştemal*, come to Akçaabat to sell their produce at the Womens' Market. Between 18 and 20 July large numbers of the best *horon* dancers gather in the town for the Hıdırnebi Festival. Sometimes as many as 500 men and women dance together to the lively, foot-tapping music of the Black Sea people.

About 11km from Akçaabat are the ruins of a **13C castle** built by the Comneni of Trebizond. Only the walls remain.

At the tip of the promontory is **Fener Burnu**. As an apotropaic gesture, the Ionian traders, who sailed beneath the cape's threatening cliffs, called it Hieron, the Holy Place. Near the village of Vakfıkebir, c 31km from Akçaabat, was the ancient settlement of Liviopolis. The *Vakfıkebir Oteli* gets two stars from the Ministry of Tourism.

Tonya, c 25km to the S of Vakfıkebir, is inhabited by Greek-speaking Muslims, descendants, perhaps, of the subjects of the Grand Comneni. The Tonyalı have acquired a fearsome reputation for violence. Apparently the two principal families in the village have been engaged in a bloody vendetta for many years. To strangers they are friendly, warm-hearted, open, kind and welcoming. Tonya is famous for its butter and cheese.

On the third weekend in July the **Kadırga Festival** is held on a mountain top c 25km from Tonya. Three days of wild, exciting revelry replace the meetings which in former days settled boundary disputes about the *yaylas*.

Rounding another promontory, Kale Burnu, the road reaches 8km **Eynesil**, the site of ancient Coryalla. There are the ruins of a **Byzantine fortress** at the entrance to the town. A further 12km brings you to Görele. From here a minor road leads inland to **Kuşkö**, Bird Village. Its inhabitants are experts in the unique whistle-language which people in this part of the Pontus use to communicate with their neighbours in distant villages.

From Görele to **Tirebolu** the road passes through one of the most beautiful parts of the route. On the left thickly wooded hills, pierced by lush green valleys, lead to the high peaks of the Pontic Mountains. On the right there are tantalising glimpses of small bays and of a blue sea that stretches to the far horizon.

Near the mouth of the Harşit Çayı, c 5km before Tirebolu, are the ruins of **Kara Burnu Kale**, while inland is **Petroma Kale**, a romantic ruin perched high on a rocky spur above the tumbling waters of the river.

The port of **Tirebolu** has a sheltered position on a crescent-shaped bay. It occupies the site of ancient Tripolis, which was built on three promontaries, and was concerned formerly with the export of silver mined in the hinterland. The Genoese had an important trading centre here in the Middle Ages. The western promontory was protected by an Ottoman fort, **Çuruk Kale**. The impressive fort on the eastern promontory, **Kastro**, was probably constructed by the Grand Comneni. It is one of the largest on the Black Sea littoral.

Just after (12km) Esbiye you pass Ulu Burnu, the ancient Zephryion Akrotirion or Promontory of the West Wind where there are the remains of **two medieval forts**. **Giresun Adası**, lies just off the coast c 4km to the E of the town. This tiny island was the ancient Aretias or Areonisis, where Antiope, queen of the Amazons, consecrated an altar to Ares (Mars).

On the 20 May, the feast day of a Muslim holy man named Hıdırellez, a curious ceremony takes place here. Pilgrims from Giresun and the surrounding area stand in a circle around a large black rock at the eastern end of the island and, while inserting pebbles in crevices in the rock, make wishes for good fortune, the restoration of health or the birth of a child. The ceremony at Giresun Adası is evidently a very old one, as in the *Argonautica*, Apollonius Rhodius says that there was a black stone in the temple of Ares on the island when the Argonauts offered sacrifice there. The ruins on the islet are of a **10C Byzantine monastery**.

The modern town of **Giresun** occupies the site of the ancient Sinopean colony of Cerasus.

Accommodation and Information, Giresun has three hotels inspected by the Ministry of Tourism, the three-star *Kit-Tur*, Arifbey Cad., No.2; and the *Çarıkça Oteli*, Osmanağa Cad., No.6 and the *Giresun Oteli*, Atatürk Bul. No.103, both of which have two stars. The **Tourist Information Office** is in Şeyh Keramettin Mah., H. Avni Öğütcü Sok., No.11, Özel İdare İşhanı, Kat. 2 (second floor).

History. In 183 BC Pharnaces I, king of Pontus, captured Sinope and made it his capital. Soon after he took Cerasus and renamed it Pharnaceia. The city was taken by Lucullus in 71 BC during the Third Mithridatic War and again by Pompey in 64 BC. There is a tradition, unsupported by factual evidence, that Lucullus introduced the cherry tree to Europe from here. This may have arisen from a confusion between the Latin for cherry, *cerasus* (Greek, Κέρασος), and the name of the town. Possession of Cerasus was disputed by the Byzantines and the Selçuks. It was part of the Eastern Byzantine Empire of Trebizond from 1204 until 1461 when it was taken by the Ottomans.

Cerasus was built on a long volcanic spur that projects into the sea on the W side of the modern town. There are substantial remains of the **citadel**, its walls and gates. In the lower town the Greek Orthodox church has been converted into a rather uninspiring museum. A Turkish leader killed during the battle for Giresun in 1461 is buried in the **Seyyid Vakkas Türbesi** which bears his name. The **Gedik Kaya fortress** on the E side of the harbour was built by Alexius III Comnenus (1349–90) to defend Giresun against attacks from the direction of Şebinkarahisar in the Pontic Mountains to the S.

If you are not in a hurry, make the worthwhile, if difficult, excursion to little-visited **Şebinkarahisar**. The three-hour journey of 103km will take you through wild mountain scenery, over the 2260m **Eğribel Geç** and down into a huge horseshoe-shaped valley. Şebinkarahisar is at the N end of this valley on a pretty, tree-clad plateau.

An important military stronghold of the Pontic kings, it was razed to the ground by Pompey. After the defeat of Mithridates, the Romans established a settlement here which, with a singular lack of imagination, they called Colonia. Apart from its strategic importance, the place had extensive deposits of alum which was much in demand by cloth manufacturers.

The town maintained its position, largely unchanged, during the Byzantine and Ottoman periods, only to meet with a series of disasters in this century. The fortress founded during the reign of Justinian was badly damaged during fighting in 1915 between the Turkish and Armenian communities and Taşanlar, a 17C covered market, and the 15C Fatih Camii were destroyed by the earthquake of 1939.

Near the town there are several **Greek churches** and a **monastery** which rivals Sumela near Trabzon for its size and the beauty of its setting. Alas, all have been desecrated by bigots and ravaged by treasure hunters. The four-storey monastery, which the local people call Meryemana, was founded in the 5C and re-established in the 19C by the Armenians who dedicated it to St Philip. It is in a great cave at the top of a steep cliff. Only the apse of the church remains, the rest of the monastery, more than 40 rooms, is filled with overturned stones, the spoil of vandalism.

Şebinkarahisar is markedly different in character to the towns on the coast. Its people, though polite and welcoming to strangers, are quiet and reserved, apparently content that their beautiful town should remain a forgotten backwater. Enter Şebinkarahisar and you step into another age: this is Turkey's Shangri-La.

Hazel nuts, which are grown in vast quantities along this part of the Black Sea coast, are sold all over the world for use in confectionery and cakes. July and August are the months to sample the new season's crop.

From Giresun to (45km) **Ordu** the road never strays very far from the sea. Ordu is built on the site of ancient Cotyora, a colony of Sinope.

There are two hotels inspected by the Ministry of Tourism, the three-star *Belde Oteli*, Kirazlimanı Mah., 52100 and the two-star *Turist Otel*, Atatürk Bul. No. 134–52100. There is also a grade two motel, *Denizcan Motel*, Güzelyalı Mah. The **Tourist Information Office** is in the Vilayet Binası, A Blok, Kat (Floor) 1. There is good bathing from the beach to the E of the town.

Founded by colonists from Sinope in the 8C BC, Cotyora appears to have developed into a thriving settlement. In 401 BC it was less than welcoming to Xenophon and the Ten Thousand. He was obliged to use force to get quarters for his sick soldiers. In the 1C AD Strabo calls it Cytorus in error. There are no later references to the city.

Apart from the **Paşaoğlu Mansion**, an elegant 19C Ottoman town house, there is little to detain the visitor in Ordu. The **18C Armenian church** on the W side of the town, used for a time as a prison, is now a forlorn, abandoned shell.

From Ordu to Fatsa the road follows the coast around a great cape which projects for almost 14km into the Black Sea. On the E is **Çam Burnu**. On the W at **Yasun Burnu** there was a temple dedicated to Jason (Yasun in Turkish) who braved the turbulent waters around the cape on his voyage to Colchis in search of the Golden Fleece. In Christian times the temple was replaced by a church where prayers were said for the safety of mariners.

The landscape between Perşembe and Bolaman is entrancing. The road climbs, descends then winds around a series of secluded bays. When the sun shines, and it does so more frequently here than on the eastern Black Sea coast, the sea becomes a deep azure and the trees on the slender, finger-shaped peninsulas glow with a thousand shades of green.

Small boats ride at anchor in **Bolaman** harbour. In the calm light of evening images of the façades of old Ottoman houses and of the accusatory white finger of a minaret are reflected in the calm waters. The name Bolaman commemorates brave and honest Polemon of Laodiceia who was deemed worthy of a kingdom first by Antony and later by Augustus and who, in time, became Polemon I of Pontus and the Bosporus and the husband of Pythodoris of Amasra.

During the late 18C and early 19C Bolaman was the seat of the Haznerdaroğlu family. They cocked a snook at the Ottoman government and, rather grandly, called themselves Governors of Trabzon. They lived in a **strange building** overlooking the harbour which had a Byzantine base topped by an 18C wooden superstructure. Part of this was pulled down about 30 years ago. A resident caretaker looks after the rest.

About 6km to the W of Bolaman is **Fatsa**, the ancient Phadisane. In Bolaman and Fatsa most of the inhabitants are Shiite Muslims. The ministry-rated second category *Dolunay Motel* is near Fatsa.

On both sides of **Ünye**, 21km to the west, there is a variety of accommodation from campsites with rather basic facilities to small, unpretentious hotels. The single-star *Kumsal Oteli*, Gölevi Köyü, is on the Ministry of Tourism list. Ünye's crescent shaped beach, pleasant promenade and slightly louche reputation attract week end visitors from nearby Samsun.

Ünye occupies the site of ancient Oinaion which had links with the Empire of Trebizond. Andronicus I Comnenus, the grandfather of Alexius and David Comnenus, the founders of the eastern Byzantine Empire which embraced Pontus and Paphlagonia, held the castle of Oinaion before becoming emperor in Constantinople in 1183. Alexius and David took Oinaion and it was held by their successors until 1461 when Mehmet the Conqueror took Trebizond and ended the rule of the Grand Comneni.

About 5km to the S of the town on the road to Niksar is the ruined medieval **Castle of Çaleoğlu**. The presence of an unusual **rock tomb** near the entrance suggests that the site was fortified by the Pontic kings or by the Romans. The pediment was decorated with a sculptured eagle with outspread wings.

About 12km to the W of Ünye the road enters the Çarşamba Ovası, the Çarşamba Plain. This fertile delta of the Yeşil Irmak is largely devoted to the growing of tobacco. Criss-crossed with canals, dotted with isolated coppices, it is farmed intensively by a hardy race which still has time to fish and hunt its lonely reaches. The Simenlik Gölü at its eastern end teems with fish, especially grey mullet, and there are many species of birds, including wild duck. Few foreigners visit the delta. Those who do are assured of a warm and friendly welcome.

In ancient times this was believed to be the land of the Amazons, those mythical fearless female fighters who cauterized their right breasts so that they could shoot with the bow or throw the spear with greater ease. (Their name comes from the Greek words α (no) and μαζός (breast)—those without breasts.) The Amazons could not bear the company of men and shunned marriage. According to Strabo, to beget children they mated with their neighbours, the Gagarians, during two months of each year. They coupled on a mountain side at night with any man who happened by and so were ἀφανή, unseen. The Amazons kept the female children and sent the males to the Gagarians who reared them. The town of **Terme** preserves a memory of their capital city, Themiscyra, and Terme Suyu of the ancient river Thermodon which runs near it.

From Terme to Çarşamba and Samsun the road has been raised above the plain to preserve it from flooding. It is straight, fast and well- surfaced and, apart from straying animals, presents no hazards.

SAMSUN is a busy port and an important emporium with good road, rail and air connections. An international trade fair is held here each year in July. At the centre of one of the largest tobacco growing regions in Turkey, its air is permanently scented by the aromatic outpourings of the Tekel factory which produces most of Turkey's cigarettes.

Accommodation and Information. Samsun has five hotels on the Ministry of Tourism's list. The four-star *Turban Büyük Samsun Oteli*, Atatürk Bul., is recommended. Samsun's **Tourist Information Office** is in 19 Mayıs Mah., Talimhane Cad., No. 6.

History. Despite the fact that Samsun has a long history the city has very few ancient monuments. Its large, protected harbour attracted colonists in the middle of the 6C BC. Ionian Greeks settled here on the level top of a large hill to the W of the modern city. In the 5C BC there was a further influx of colonists, this time from Athens, under the leadership of Athenocles. Homesick perhaps, they changed the name of the place from Amisus to Piraeus. However, the colony soon reverted to its old name and, establishing good trade links with the peoples of the interior, it flourished.

Mithridates VI Eupator, ornamented the city with many temples and extended it. During the Third Mithridatic War Amisus was burned to the ground by the Roman general Lucullus. Later, regretting his action, he had it rebuilt. Captured by Pharnaces, the son of Mithridates, it was liberated by Caesar after he had defeated Pharnaces at Zela. Following this victory Caesar sent his famous laconic message to the Senate, '*Veni, Vidi, Vici*'.

Subsequently the city had many rulers. In AD 863 it was taken by the Byzantines from Omar, the emir of Melitene. It was captured by the Selçuks c 1194 and from then until its annexation by the Ottomans in 1425, it was held at various times and for various periods by the Comneni of Trebizond, the Mongols and the Isfendiyarid of Kastamonu. The Genoese, who had established a trading centre here, set fire to the city before leaving it to the Ottomans.

Until the railway came in the mid 19C, Samsun was made up of two small villages, one inhabited by Greeks, the other by Turks. With better means of transportation, the local tobacco trade revived, the place prospered and a population of less than 5000 grew to 40,000 at the beginning of the 20C. About 200,000 people live in the city now.

On 19 May 1919 Atatürk landed at Samsun and launched the movement which ultimately led to the formation of the Turkish Republic. This event is commemorated by a splendid equestrian monument in the main square.

At Kara Samsun, c 3km to the W of the city, is the ancient **acropolis**, now a military area, where the first settlement was established. There are a few broken column shafts, ruined walls, filled cisterns and a number of funerary monuments. One of the rock tombs on the hillside was used as a **chapel** during the Byzantine period.

Samsun's oldest mosque, **Pazar Camii**, was built by the Ilkhanid Mongols in the 13C. The oldest Ottoman mosque dates from 1503. The former **Mintika Palace Hotel**, where Atatürk stayed for a week in May 1916, has been converted into the May 19 Museum. Here are Atatürk's bedroom, study and conference room. There is a small collection of ancient artefacts found in Samsun on the first floor. Another museum devoted to Atatürk is at the entrance to the Samsun Fair. Housed in a new building are memorabilia and a photographic exhibition of his life and achievements.

Before continuing your journey westward, visit Amasya which lies c 127km to the S. Leave Samsun by Road 795 signposted to Havza, Suluova and Amasya. This climbs steadily until it reaches a height of 940m at **Karadağ Geç** c 16km beyond Kavak. About 11km after Havza, Road 795 turns right to Merzifon and Çorum. The left fork, the E80, leads to (39km) Amasya.

The geographer Strabo was born in **AMASYA**, the ancient Amaseia, c 64 BC. 'My city', he wrote, 'is situated in a large deep valley through which flows the river Iris'. He describes with pride how human foresight and an admirable situation combined to make it a perfect combination of city and fortress. Today the river is called the Yeşilırmak and Amasya is no longer fortified, but its setting is still one of the most beautiful in central Anatolia.

Amasya is famous for the quality of its fruit, especially apples, cherries and peaches. Among the many local food specialities are *keşek*, a meat stew cooked overnight in a clay pot; okra with meat; beef or mutton cooked with okra and lemon juice, *haşhaşlı çörek*, dough sticks containing ground poppy seeds; *hasuda*, a jelly made from rose water, starch and sugar served with ground walnuts, and *kuşburnu*, marmalade made from wild rose hips.

Accommodation and Information. Amasya has one hotel on the Tourism Ministry's list, the two-star *Turban Amasya Oteli*, Helkis Mah. This is close both to the river and the railway line. There are two well-run pensions which offer good value and are recommended. The *İlk Pansiyon* in Gümüşlü Mah., Hitit Sok. 1, has been carefully restored by architect Ali Kamil Yalçin and is furnished in the style of a 19C provincial mansion. The *Yuvam Pension* is owned and run by İlker Esin Yener of Atatürk Cad., No. 24--25. He organises musical evenings for the entertainment of his guests. Although only five minutes' walk from the main street, the balcony of his pension overlooks a small orchard where nightingales sing during the long balmy evenings.

Excellent meals are available at Amasya's *Şehir Klübü*, the City Club, whose clientele is drawn largely from the ranks of business men and officials. Visitors receive a warm welcome.

Amasya's **Tourist Information Office** is located in a new building in Mehmetpaşa Mah., Mustafa Kemal Bulv., No. 27, not far from the *otogar*.

History. The first settlement was established on the summit of a precipitous peak which here dominates a narrow part of the river valley. It probably antedates the arrival of Alexander the Great in Asia Minor. After the death of Antigonus, Mithridates proclaimed himself king of Pontus, made Amaseia his capital and founded a dynasty which lasted for almost 300 years.

During the Third Mithridatic War Pompey captured the city and razed it to the ground. Later rebuilt, under the Romans Amaseia was a provincial capital. After the arrival of Christianity it became an episcopal see. Bishop Eulalios of Amaseia attended the Council of Nicaea in 325. The fortress, enlarged and strengthened by the Byzantines, fell to the Arabs in 712, but was recaptured by the Byzantines during the reign of Leo the Isaurian (717–41). The last Bagratid king of Armenia, Gagik II (1042–45) received a grant of lands from the Byzantine emperor Constantine IX in eastern Cappadocia and made Amaseia his capital.

After the battle of Manzikert in 1071 the Turks took Amaseia and renamed it Amasya. The Danishmendid clan established a powerful emirate here. In 1133 John II Comnenus failed to capture the citadel and had to be content with pillaging the lands of the Danishmendid. Later Amasya came under the rule of Kılıç Arslan and his successors. Taken by the Mongols in the 13C, it became part of the possessions of the Eretnids and of Kadı Burhaneddin, the emir of Sivas. In 1392 it was taken by Beyazit I for the Ottomans. During the centuries that followed Amasya was greatly favoured by several Ottoman sultans who chose to live here. They made it a centre of culture and learning that was frequently compared with Baghdad. Later the town fell into a decline which was compounded by earthquake damage in the 18C, 19C and 20C and a disastrous fire in 1915. It has never quite recovered from these catastrophes and today seems to have accepted the rôle of quiet provincial capital.

Strabo, the Geographer, was born c 64 BC into a distinguished local family which at first supported the Pontic king Mithridates VI in his struggle against Rome, but which later changed sides and adopted the Roman cause. Strabo studied at Nysa and later in Rome where he lived for a number of years. He travelled from the Black Sea to Ethiopia and from Armenia to Etruria. In AD 24 he visited Egypt with his friend Aelius Gallus, the governor of that country. It seems likely that he spent some time studying mathematics and astronomy in Alexandria. Strabo wrote his *Historical Memoranda*, a 47-book work of which only fragments survive. His *Geography* in 17 books, which draws heavily on the work of earlier Greek geographers, was designed for the use of members of the government and higher civil servants. In addition to the detailed practical information it is peppered with anecdotes and legends and describes the antiquities and customs of the lands which it covers. Strabo, whose name rather unflatteringly means 'squint-eyed', died c AD 21.

Amasya is not a large town and is easily visited on foot. It can be divided conveniently into three sections—the old town, the Hellenistic tombs and the citadel on the N side of the river, and the areas to the W and E of the Atatürk monument on the S side. The N and S parts are linked by five bridges spaced at fairly regular intervals.

The houses in the old town lean out over the Yeşilırmak and are mirrored in its placid waters. In ancient times this area was protected by the city walls, which fronting the river, ascended the steep slope of the cliff to the fortress on the summit.

A late 19C Ottoman house built by Hasan Talat Efendi, Abdul Aziz's Minister of Finance, the **Hazaranlar Konağı**, is now the town's ethnographical museum. A well in the courtyard supplied the mansion with fresh water. Much of the family's cooking was done in the outdoor oven.

Nearby is the **Bülbül Hatun Camii**, the Lady Nightingale Mosque. This was built c 1510 by the wife of Beyazit II who was governor of Amasya before he became sultan in 1481.

Follow the signposts up some steep steps to the **Kızlar Sarayı**, the Palace of the Virgins. This occupies the site of the residence of the Pontic kings. All traces of the earlier building have disappeared. The modern name probably refers to the harem of a later Selçuk or Ottoman structure.

About a dozen **Hellenistic tombs** have been cut out of the cliff face. A rocky path from the Kızlar Sarayı leads up to three of them. Wear shoes which have a good grip, as the surface of the path has been polished smooth by the feet of countless generations and there is a dangerous unfenced drop on the left. Some of the kings of Pontus were buried in these tombs. According to an **inscription**, the aggressive and ambitious Pharnaces I (185–169 BC) was was laid to rest in one them. He is remembered for taking Sinope, so giving Pontus an outlet on the Black Sea, and for founding another city on the coast which he named after himself (see Sinop and Giresun). An interior passage joins two of the tombs. During the Byzantine period the last tomb was used a chapel.

On the right of the road which leads up to the citadel is the octagonal **Kapı Ağası Medresesi**. Established in 1488 by Hüseyin Ağa, Beyazit II's Chief White Eunuch, each side of the octagon has three rooms which open on to a central courtyard. Note the highly **decorative portal** on the NW side. The *dershane* is on the S. The *medrese* is now a Koranic School.

A short distance to the NE of the Turban Amasya hotel an unmade road, signposted Kale, leads to the **citadel**. This road has many hairpin bends in its 2km length, but is negotiable with careful driving. Built originally by the Pontic kings, the citadel was occupied successively by the Romans, Byzantines, Danishmendid, Selçuks, Mongols and Ottomans and many of these enlarged, extended and strengthened its fortifications. Apart from **two Hellenistic towers** the **walls** still standing date from the Byzantine, Selçuk and Ottoman periods. There is a splendid view of Amasya, the river and the surrounding countryside from near the flagpole which marks the highest point in the citadel.

On the western edge of the town, not far from the river, is the **Yörgüç Paşa Külliyesi**. This was built in 1428 at the behest of Yörgüç Paşa, a vizier and tutor of Mehmet I. In this Bursa style mosque the tomb of the founder is one of three in a chamber to the right of the entrance. The *tabhane* and *medrese* are in the courtyard of the *külliye*.

On the right-hand side of the road are the **Torumtay Türbesi** and the **Gökmedrese Camii**. In the *türbe*, which dates from 1278, the emir Şerefettin Torumtay is buried under a black marble slab. A former slave of Keykubad II who became governor of Amasya, he had the Gökmedrese

Amasya: the houses in the old part of town lean out over the Yeşilmırmak

Camii built in 1266. Note the pointed, stalactite-ornamented **portal** on the N side of the building and the **two windows** with ornamented voussoirs which light a part of the *medrese*. The three aisles of the prayer hall are separated by two rows of piers and covered by five domes. There is a partly ruined *türbe* on the E side of the mosque.

A short distance to the E are the **Sadgeldi Türbe** which was built in 1381, and the Danishmendid **Emir Halifat Gazi Türbesi** which dates from 1145.

Amasya's **Archaeological Museum** is housed in a fine new building set in a pleasant garden. The collection includes ceramics, glass, bronze objects, statuettes, coins, ornaments, jewellery and stelae from the Bronze Age to the Byzantine period. Note particularly a small Hittite statue of a goddess, **Phrygian oinochoe** and rhyta, **Roman gold jewellery** from Kulistepe, Byzantine crosses, candlesticks and crosses, and the hoard of medieval coins found in the Gümüşlü area of the town.

In the ethnographic section there are Selçuk and Ottoman household vessels, books, apparel, weapons, carpets, lecterns, grave stones and coins. In the garden grave stelae and architectural fragments from the Hellenistic, Roman, Byzantine, Selçuk and Ottoman periods crowd the green lawn. The building at the back of the lawn is the 14C **Türbe of Sultan Ruknuddin Mesud I** who ruled from 1116 to 1156. In it are displayed the pathetic, shrivelled mummies of six Ilkhanid Mongol nobles.

In a side street on the other side of the road are the **Şehzade Türbesi** which Beyazit I (1389–1402) built to house the body of his son Osman, and the **Şehzadeler Türbesi** which was constructed by Mehmet I in 1410 as a last resting place for four princes. Beyazit was defeated by Tamerlane at the battle of Çubuk near Ankara in 1402 and died in captivity nine months later. After his death one of his sons, Mehmet Çelebi, held Amasya.

The **Sultan Beyazit Külliyesi**, which dates from 1486, is the largest Islamic structure in Amasya. Near the river and pleasantly shaded by trees, it was constructed by Prince Ahmet, the eldest son of Beyazit II. Heir to the throne and governor of Amasya, Ahmet was killed by his younger brother Selim who disputed the succession after the death of their father. The entrance to the mosque is by an arched portico on the side of the building which faces the river. The **portico** is covered by domes supported by ancient columns. In the prayer hall note the marble *mihrab* and *mimber* and the faience decoration on the inside arches of the windows. The library has about 20,000 books and some fine manuscripts of the Koran. In the *külliye* there are a *medrese* and an *imaret* which is still used. The decoration on the two slender minarets is different.

On the right side of the street, which leads to the post office, is the **bedesten**, a rectangular covered market. This was built by Hüseyin Ağa.

In a side street on the other side of the road is the **Taşhan** which was designed by Mehmet Kalfa and built by him in 1758 for Rahtuvan Hacı Mehmet Paşa, governor of Amasya at that time. Part of the two-storey rectangular building is now in ruins.

Just behind the Taşhan is the mid 13C Selçuk **Burmalı Minare Camii**, the Spiral Minaret Mosque. According to an **inscription** at the entrance, this was built on the orders of the vizier Farruh and his brother the Treasurer Yusuf. They are buried nearby in an octagonal *türbe*. On the left side is a classical octagonal Selçuk dome and on the right the spiral ornamented minaret which gives the mosque its name.

On the slope above the Burmalı Minare Camii is the **Fethiye Camii**. This was formerly a Byzantine church. According to an **inscription** it was founded by Helena, the daughter of Caesar Phocas. The building was badly damaged by fire in 1915. The minaret is an early 19C addition.

In the centre of the Meydan is the **Atatürk Anıtı**, the Atatürk Memorial. Just to the S of the memorial is the Pir Mehmet Çelebi Camii. The early 14C Gümüşluzade Camii on the E side of the Meydan has suffered from the hands of the restorers.

On the river side promenade the **Tourist Information kiosk** dispenses useful leaflets in several languages about Amasya. About 70m from the kiosk, on the other side of the road, is the İlk Pansiyon.

There are plans to restore the classic Selçuk building known as the **Bimarhane** which is on the other side of the road. This mental hospital was established by the Ilkhanid Mongol sultan Ölceytü in 1308 in honour of his wife Yıldız Hatun. It is the only remaining Ilhanid monument in Amasya. Parts of the top and the left side of the highly ornamented **portal** have been damaged. Note the **keystone** which is carved in the form of a squatting human figure. Patients were treated in the rooms on the E and W sides of the enclosed courtyard.

Visit the Bimarhane in the evening when the first stars begin to appear in the eastern sky. The massive door protests as you push it open, then slams shut behind you. Cut off from the reassuring sounds of the street by the asylum's massive walls, stand alone in the central courtyard. The still, heavy air seems to fill with the anguished cries and senseless babble of long dead patients and shadows flit through the darkening rooms. Then, the beating wings of a night bird break the spell and, hastening to the door, you leave this eerie place to its sad memories.

The **Mehmet Paşa Camii** dates from 1486. According to an **inscription** at the entrance, it was built on the orders of Mehmet Paşa who was tutor and regent of Şehzade Mehmet, son of Beyazit II, when the youth was governor of Amasya. The mosque was part of a complex set in a small garden. A *hamam*, a *türbe* and the mosque remain. The fine entrance has six bays. Note the *mimber* which is elaborately decorated in the arabesque style.

Just to the S of the **Kuş Köprüsü**, the Bird Bridge, is the **Beyazit Paşa Camii**. This, and the adjoining **misafirhane**, were constructed on the orders of Mehmet I's vizier, Beyazit Paşa, in 1419. Entrance is by an elegant, **domed porch** which is supported by six matching columns. Some of the windows in the prayer hall have sheets of delicately coloured glass.

It would be a pity to make a hurried visit to Amasya. To enjoy the beauty of its setting and savour its many pleasures you need at least two days.

Amasya is a good centre for visiting places like **Merzifon**, 49km to the NW, where there are three interesting Ottoman mosques. One was built by Kara Mustafa Paşa who brought an Ottoman army to the gates of Vienna in 1683. The curative waters at *Terziköy* were known to the Romans and they still attract visitors seeking cures for rheumatism, digestive and urinary problems and gynaecological infections.

About 35km to the NW of Amasya, near Suluova, is the romantically named **Yedikuğular Cenneti**, Seven Swans Nature Reserve, where, in addition to swans there are various species of wild duck and birds of prey including eagles and falcons.

Borabay Gölü is a crater lake surrounded by pine and cedar forests c 65km to the E of Amasya. It is popular with fishermen and the surrounding countryside attracts hikers and campers during the summer months.

Just 2km to the N of the town, by the side of the Yeşilırmak, is **Aynalı Mağara**, a rock-cut tomb with **Greek inscriptions**. This has an interesting façade with pilasters and a window.

From Amasya return to Samsun and continue to (54km) **Bafra**. Almost in the centre of the **Bafra Ovası**, an alluvial plain formed by the waters of the Kızılırmak, Bafra is another important centre for the tobacco industry. The town has a 13C *hamam*, a 15C *külliye* and an 18C mosque, **Büyük Cami**. This was built on the orders of Ayşe Hatun, the wife of Köprülü Mehmet Paşa. There are two 15C *türbe* on the outskirts of the town.

The road from Bafra to Gerze and Sinop passes through one of the most attractive stretches of country in the Black Sea littoral. It pursues a sinuous course, frequently descending to the sea then climbing the softly rounded hills. From the summits there are tantalising glimpses of distant capes and great, deep fiords. Here the land is very fertile and in summer a soft breeze caresses the fields of golden grain by the roadside.

The picturesque village of **Gerze**, sited at the end of a narrow peninsula, claims descent from a settlement of the Gasgali who, it is said, occupied the site c 1400 BC. Later the place attracted the attention of Greek settlers and the kings of Pontus, and was ruled, successively, by the Romans, Byzantines, Selçuks and Ottomans. Much of Gerze is new, as a great fire in 1956 destroyed many of the old buildings. Among the few relics of the past that remain are the **Kök Hamamı**, the **Esma Zade Paşa Camii** and the **Çeçe Sultan Türbesi**.

Accommodation and Information. Gerze's *Hotel Ermiş*, which overlooks the harbour, has 72 beds. There is also a small, very attractive, inexpensive pension in the centre of the village near the Belediye.

The **Gerze Culture and Arts Festival** is held each year during the third week in July. Then the village, en fête, welcomes international folk groups, holds sporting events and elects a beauty queen. The festivities continue non-stop day and night. Neither the villagers nor the visitors have much opportunity for sleep. Among the more unusual events is a public circumcision of boys from Gerze and surrounding area. Distracted by circus clowns and other entertainers, they take their first step to manhood. 'It is', as the festival programme states, 'an occasion which they will never forget'.

From Gerze to (35km) Sinop the road turns inland briefly before returning to the coast. It passes through a stretch of countryside which is reminiscent of England. Cattle graze in fields bounded by tangled hedgerows which in autumn produce a rich crop of blackberries. Shortly before Sinop, a turning on the left leads to Kastamonu and Safranbolu (see Route 62).

SİNOP is built on a narrow neck of land which opens out into a great cape, the İnce Burnu. This is the most northerly point in Anatolia. Sinop's pleasant climate and agreeable cafés life attract large numbers of visitors, foreign and Turkish. A new hotel is being built to cater for them.

Accommodation. At present the town has one hotel, the two-star *Melia Kasım Oteli*, Gazi Cad., No. 5, on the Ministry of Tourism list. It is a popular venue for weddings and other events which are celebrated with characteristic Turkish brio.

Recommended is the *Karaküm Tatil Köyü* which is c 2km to the W of Sinop. A quieter and more restful place, this hotel has a good restaurant and its own private beach.

There are several good **restaurants** in Sinop, many with tables overlooking the fishing harbour. *Uzun Mehmet Lokantası* is recommended. Try the fish dishes.

The principal **Tourist Information Office** is in the Hükümet Konaği. There is also a kiosk at İskele Meydanı where multilingual staff dispense advice and information.

Transport. Sinop is a port of call for the boats of Türkiye Denizcilik İşletmeleri which ply between İstanbul and Trabzon.

Buses from Sinop go E to Samsun, SW to Kastamonu, and to İstanbul and Ankara. Services on the coastal road S to Abana, İnebolu, Amasra and beyond are not very satisfactory (see Route 61).

History. The earliest traces of human occupation found near Sinop, date from the Chalcolithic Period c 4500 BC. There were small settlements in the area during the Early Bronze Age, 3000–2700 BC, and the Early Hittite period, 1800 BC, but no traces of occupation from the Imperial Hittite period have been discovered.

During the mid 8C BC colonists from Miletus established a trading post and naval station here and called it Sinope. According to a legend, Sinope was the daughter of a river god. Zeus desired the nymph and offered to grant her any wish. She asked him to be allowed to keep her virginity.

With Trapezus (Trabzon) Sinope may have been one of the points through which bronzes from Urartu and Armenia passed to the Greek world. It became a city of some importance. Raided by the Cimmerians c 690 BC, it was occupied by them for a time. Freed and rebuilt, it founded daughter colonies at Cotyora (Ordu), Cerasus (Giresun) and Trapezus. It also established control over three strips of coastal land. The first extended eastward from Sinope to the Halys river (the Kızılırmak), the second was from Cape Jason (Yasun Burnu) to Cotyora and Cerasus, and the third was around Trapezus.

In 399 BC the Sinopeans, apprehensive about the intentions of Xenophon and his Ten Thousand, provided the mercenaries with ships for their journey home and, to emphasise their friendship, gave them gifts, 4000 bushels of barley meal and 1500 jars of wine. Sinope maintained its independence until 375 BC when it came under the rule of Datames. He had been the satrap of Cappadocia, but had rebelled against his Persian overlords. After a few years Sinope regained its freedom, but recognised the authority of Persia. Quantities of Phrygian pottery found in graves near Sinop indicate that the city was in contact with the peoples of the interior. The arrival of Alexander the Great in Asia Minor in 333 BC encouraged the Paphlagonians to declare independence and Mithridates Ktistes brought many of the cities under his rule.

Mithridates III and his son Pharnaces I took Sinope and its dependencies in 183 BC and made it the capital of the kingdom of Pontus. Mithridates V Philopator, who succeeded to the throne in 169 BC embellished the city with many fine buildings and increased its power and prosperity. Mithridates the VI Eupator, that arch-enemy of the Romans, was born here in 135 BC. He built temples and the citadel and strengthened the fortifications. In 73 BC, a defeated man, his latest campaign against the Romans in ruins, he returned briefly to Sinope before seeking refuge with his son-in-law Tigranes, the king of Armenia. Their combined armies were defeated by the

Romans under Lucullus in two battles, in 69 and 68 BC. Lucullus took Sinope and five years later the city was formally annexed by Pompey.

During the Hellenistic period Sinope exported olives, olive oil and amphorae. Its coins showed the head of the nymph Sinope and on the reverse an eagle holding a dolphin in its claws, an eagle's head or the prow of a ship.

In 45 BC Sinope changed its name to Colonia Iulia Felix, accepted an influx of colonists from Nicaea (İznik), and continued to prosper and maintain its status under Roman hegemony. It issued coins with the letters C.I.F. or C.I.F.S., i.e. Colonia Iulia Felix Sinope, on them. In AD 110 Pliny the Younger, with the approval of the emperor Trajan, made a survey of the area around the city and had an aqueduct constructed to ensure that Sinope had an adequate supply of water.

During the Byzantine period Sinope declined somewhat in importance. In the first half of the 6C there was a brief revival during the reign of Justinian, when castles, aqueducts, bridges and churches were built. However, the wars with Persia put an end to any further development. Records indicate that Sinope was taken by the emir Karatekin in 1084 and formed into an emirate with Kastamonu and Çankırı. It was recaptured later by the Byzantines. When the Latins seized Constantinople in 1204, Sinope came under the rule of Emperor Alexius I Comnenus, of Trebizond. Genoese merchants established a trading centre here with the agreement of the Comneni.

In 1214 the city was taken by the Selçuks. Izzedin Keykavus I had the defences rebuilt and an inner fortress constructed. Sinope was retaken by Manuel I Comnenus of Trebizond in 1254 and held by him until 1265, when it fell again to the Selçuks. Administration of the city was given by them to the Pervane Oğulları. The most celebrated member of this clan was Gazi Çelebi who died in 1322.

In 1324 the city was taken by the Türkoman rulers of Kastamonu. About this time it was renamed Sinop. When Beyazit I took Kastamonu from the İsfendiyaroğulları, they moved to Sinop. The city remained in their hands until 1461, when Mehmet II Fatih brought the Black Sea area under Ottoman rule. They encouraged Sinop's shipbuilding industry, but the town entered a period of decline after the garrison was withdrawn.

In 1614 Sinop was attacked by a Cossack band of marauders and in November 1853 it was bombarded by Russian ships and badly damaged. This event precipitated the Crimean War. Atatürk came to Sinop on the ship Bandırma on 18 May 1919. As there was no road between Sinop and Samsun at that time, he continued his journey by sea.

Diogenes the Cynic (c 400–323 BC) was born in Sinope, but moved to Athens after either he or his father was accused of adulterating the coinage. Because of his uncouth manners and bizarre life style he was nicknamed the dog, Κύων in Greek, so his followers became known as the Κύνες, the cynics. Diogenes had a contempt for rules and the conventions of polite society. He slept in the open, satisfied his hunger with raw meat, and, according to Dio of Prusa, joked about his habit of practising self-abuse in public. Many stories are told about him. His reply to Alexander the Great's offer, 'Ask of me anything you like', was 'Stand aside, you're in my light'.

Legends have also accumulated around Gazi Çelebi who ruled Sinop from 1300 to 1322. These portray him as a brave and audacious man. According to Ibn Battuta, who stopped at Sinop on his way to the Crimea, Gazi Çelebi would swim underwater during sea battles and bore holes in the warships of his Greek opponents so that they sank without warning.

The oldest building in Sinop is the 2C BC Hellenistic **Temple of Serapis** in the museum garden. This rectangular structure, which measures 15m by 8.6m, was excavated by Professors Ekrem Akurgal and Ludwig Budde in 1951. An **inscription**, discovered in the 19C, suggests that it was dedicated to Serapis, but the archaeologists found figures of Dionysus, Hercules, Kore, and Isis as well as those of Serapis on the site. According to Tacitus the worship of Serapis started in Sinope and was introduced to Egypt by Ptolemy I Soter (367–283 BC).

The **museum** in Sinop occupies a fine, modern building. Previously the collection was housed in the *medrese* of Süleyman Pervane. In the museum's large garden there is an interesting display of grave stelae, sarcophagi, altars, milestones and mosaics from the Archaic, Hellenic, Hellenistic, Roman and Byzantine periods.

In addition, there are Selçuk and Ottoman tombstones under the portico and scattered under the trees, the ruins of the Temple of Serapis, the *türbe* of Aynalı Kadın and a monument to the Turkish sailors who perished during the Russian attack on Sinop in 1853.

In the **Ground Floor Gallery** there are objects found in the prehistoric levels of Kocagöz Tepesi and from a Bronze Age necropolis in the centre of Sinop. These include household vessels, implements used for weaving, bronze pins and weapons. There are also coins from the Hellenistic to the Ottoman periods. Note especially the **Gelincik Hoard**, gold coins minted by various Islamic rulers and by 13C Venice and Luxembourg.

In the **First Hall** (Classical Section) there are bronze objects, household utensils, painted bowls, glass vessels, ornaments, finds from the Serapis temple and marble sculptures from the Early Hittite, Late Phrygian, Hellenic, Hellenistic, Roman and Byzantine periods. These include a fine archaic funerary stele, a **terracotta mask** from the Serapis temple, a Hellenistic vase decorated with reliefs, Roman portrait busts, **Roman mosaics**, a statue of Dionysus and a **marble group of two lions** fighting over a stag.

The **Second Hall** houses an ethnographic collection of embroidered costumes, knitted and woven garments, ornaments, writing equipment, jewellery and weapons from Sinop and the surrounding area.

On the **First Floor** inner balcony there are carpets, manuscripts, prayer rugs, silk furnishings, handwritten Korans, an ivory inlaid lectern and examples of calligraphy.

The First Floor **hall** has a fine collection of 19C icons which are believed to come from churches in and around Sinop.

A short distance to the SE of the museum are the remains of **Balat**, a Byzantine palace. The **apse and walls** of a mid 17C church dedicated to the Dormition of the Virgin form the most striking part of this ruined structure.

To the W is **Seyit Bilal Camisi**, a Selçuk mosque. Note the elaborate decoration in enamelled faïence.

The **Alaattin Camisi** was built shortly after the capture of Sinop by the Selçks in 1214. It is a transverse building with three domes side by side in front of the *mihrab*. Architecturally it has close links with the Artukid mosques of SE Anatolia. It has been repaired several times—after the attack by the Comneni in 1254, by the Çandaroğulları and by the Ottomans. Unfortunately, the *mimber* was damaged when one of the domes collapsed.

Adjoining the Alaattin Camisi is the **Pervane Medresesi**. This was constructed by the Selçuk vizier Süleyman Pervane to commemorate the deliverance of Sinop from its enemies. Entrance is by a fine marble decorated portal. In the centre of the large courtyard there is a *şahdırvan*. The *eyvan* arch is còvered with marble. There are 16 rooms behind the mable columned arcades which line two sides of the courtyard.

Near the *otogar* is **Kumkapı**, one of Sinop's two surviving city gates. The other, **Lonca Kapıs**, is not far away. There are plans to close the prison, which is across the road from the *otogar*, and turn it into a tourist bazaar.

The largest and most complete section of the **ancient fortifications** is near the inner harbour. These terminate in a huge tower which was reinforced by the Genoese. Note the extensive re-use of ancient materials.

To the W of Sinop, on the left of the road to Karakum, are the ruins of **Riza Nur's library**. A little farther, on the right, is the 19C **Paşa Battery** which formed part of the coastal defence system. There are also the ruins of a lazaret on the costal road. Continue to the tip of the peninsula where the scenery is wild and beautiful. The road, which is stabilised and passable by ordinary vehicles, loops round and brings you back to the N side of the town. Unfortunately, the last section passes very near the insalubrious town rubbish dump. There are plans to move this to a more secluded place.

There is good swimming around Sinop. The sand and sea at Akliman, which is to the E of the town, are usually clean and free from the detritus which spoils so many beaches on the Black Sea coast. Nearby **Hamsaroz fiord** is a quiet, attractive area much favoured by walkers.

61

Sinop to İstanbul

Total distance c 806km. Sinop—45km Ayancık—35km Çatalzeytin—5km Cinolis—21km Abana—c 22km İnebolu—68km Cide—c 12km Gideros Mahallesi—15km Kurucaşile—29km Çakrazboz—16km Amasra—23km Bartın—66km Hisarönü—23km Zonguldak—62 or 74km Ereğli—13km Alaplı—c 92km Bolu. (For Bolu–İstanbul see Route 63.)

This picturesque route, which follows the coastline of ancient Paphlagonia closely for most of the way, may pose difficulties for travellers who do not have their own transport. At present there is no bus or dolmuş service from Sinop to İstanbul by this road, so if you decide to take it, make a virtue out of necessity and enjoy the frequent stopovers.

The splendid views en route are more than adequate compensation for any travel difficulties. Though the mountains are lower to the W of Sinop, they come down to the seashore and form one rock-bound, secluded bay after another. The many fine stretches of sandy beach are a strong temptation to stop and bathe and, on a sunny day, the misty, soft green of the tree-clad promontories and the deep blue of the sea will charm even the most blasé traveller.

There are no hotels or pensions registered with the Ministry of Tourism before Amasra and no Tourist Information Offices before Zonguldak. However, Turkish people often offer hospitality to foreign visitors. Enquire at the *otogar* on arrival or at one of the local schools.

Just to the N of Sinop on İnce Burnu is the site of ancient Armene. From Ayancık to Amasra you will seldom be out of sight of the sea.

Among the many relatively unknown sites along this stretch of the Black Sea coastline is **Cinolis** which was on the peninsula of Gınolu c 5km to the W of (35km) Çatalzeytin. This ancient city, which is mentioned by Strabo (*Geography* 12.3.10), was protected by substantial walls and had a monumental propylon which faced the isthmus. There are the foundations of the walls and of the propylon and large quantities of pottery sherds. On the eastern side of the peninsula is a sandy beach.

Continue to (21km) **Abana**. This may have been the Abonuteichus which Strabo describes as a small town (*Geography* 12.3.11). During the Antonine period Abonuteichus became an administrative centre through the efforts of a charlatan named Alexander.

About 22km to the W, **İnebolu** straddles the mouth of the İnebolu Çayı. Some believe that this was site of Abonuteichus.

About 68km to the W of İnebolu is **Cide**. This has been identified with the ancient city of Aigialos whose name means the seashore or the beach. There is a ruined Genoese tower on a hill near the town.

About 12km to the W of Cide is the little village of **Gideros Mahallesi**. This was the site of ancient Cytorum, an emporium of the Sinopeans according to Strabo. The best boxwood came from around Cytorum. There are the **ruins of a medieval castle**, but nothing of the ancient city remains. Gideros has a pretty little harbour which is almost completely landlocked.

The site of ancient Cromna is believed to be at or near the modern town of Kurucaşile. There are no visible remains.

A further 29km to the W is **Çakrazboz**. This may occupy the site of the city of the Erythrini, who were also called Erythini, the Reds, because of their colour. No trace of the ancient city remains.

From Çakrazboz it is 16km to **AMASRA**.

Accommodation is very limited in this pretty little town. Only the *Nur Aile Pansiyonu* appears on the Ministry of Tourism list. Travellers who have stayed at the *Paşa Kaptan Oteli*, speak highly of it, and there are also the *Huzur Pansiyon* and the *Belvü Palas*.

History. A colony named Sesamus was established on this site by Miletus in the 6C BC. However, there must have been a settlement here in the 9C BC or earlier as Homer refers in the Iliad (Book II. Line 853) to the Paphlagonians who came to Troy from their pleasant homesteads by the Parthenius River near Sesamus and who were led by the colourfully named Pylaemenes of the shaggy breast.

Strabo relates how Sesamus was absorbed in the 3C BC by Amastris, a new foundation named after the queen regent of Heracleia Pontica. Amastris was the niece of Darius III who was defeated by Alexander the Great at the battle of Issus in 333 BC. She was married first to Craterus, a Macedonian soldier who had earned Alexander's friendship by saving his life during a lion hunt in an animal park at Sidon, then to Dionysios, the tyrant of Heracleia Pontica. After the death of Dionysius she acted as regent for her young son. Apparently Amastris had learned Greek at Alexander's court and, abandoning her Persian ways, she promoted the amalgamation of several townships into the new city which was named after her. She gave this the style and appearance of an Ionian Greek foundation. Amastris and her city are commemorated in the name of the modern town.

In 288 BC Amastris was murdered by her ungrateful sons and the city came under the rule of Eumenes of Tieum, the brother of Philetaerus of Pergamum. Unable to defend the city, Eumenes surrendered it to Ariobarzanes, the king of Pontus. Amastris sided with Mithridates VI Eupator in his war against Rome. It was occupied by Lucullus who drove Mithridates from Pontus into exile in Armenia. After Pompey finally crushed Mithridates in 63 BC at Nicopolis, Pontus was divided and the area W of the Halys River, the modern Kızılırmak, which included Paphlagonia, became part of the Roman Province of Asia.

Pliny the Younger was appointed special commissioner to Bithynia-Pontus by Trajan c AD 110. He described Amastris as being well built and laid out, but he was disturbed by the stench from an open sewer which ran by the side of the main street. He asked the emperor's permission to have it covered over, as it was a 'disgusting eyesore' and a danger to the health of the citizens. Pliny was something of an expert on sewers, as from AD 104–106 he was Curator Alvei Tiberis et Riparum et Cloacarum Urbis, i.e. superintendent of the bed and banks of the Tiber and of the sewers of Rome. Trajan readily gave his permission.

Sacked by barbarians in the 9C, Amastris declined in importance, though the Byzantines still maintained a garrison there. In 1214 Theodore I Lascaris seized all the possessions, including Amastris, of David Comnenus W of Sinop. When the Byzantine empire began to disintegrate, the Genoese occupied Amastris and held it until it was taken by the Ottomans c 1460.

The site of the earliest settlement is probably under the town centre. Erosion of **Tekke Tepesi**, near the post office, has shown this to be a *hüyük*. **Pliny's sewer** is once more open to the elements, as the covering which he had installed was destroyed by a storm in 1930. There are few reminders of Hellenistic and Roman Amastris. Between the museum and the so-called bedesten are the remains of the vomitorium of the theatre. The rest of the structure has disappeared. The *bedesten* was probably a gymnasium. There were **two Roman necropolises**. One on the SE slope of the citadel overlooked the harbour; the other was high above the SW beach. In the museum there are some funerary stelae and small objects found in Amastris and the surrounding area.

The walls of the **citadel** were constructed by the Byzantines on earlier fortifications erected during the Hellenistic and Roman periods. Note particularly the walls on the S side which rest on a Hellenistic foundation. Substantial sections of the Byzantine walls remain at their full height, but they are not easy to see because of thick vegetation. The Genoese fortified the narrow entrance to the peninsula. Their **coats of arms** can be seen on various parts of the walls.

The **peninsula** is linked to the island by a **Roman bridge**. Three large buildings on the island may have been the barracks of the naval garrison. The **Fatih Camii** near the gate leading to the large harbour was a church until the time of the Ottoman conquest. Near the gate to the smaller harbour is the roofless **Kilise Mescidi**, originally the private chapel of the Christian garrison commander.

Do not hurry on the winding road to (16km) **Bartın**. At every bend there is a fresh view of Amasra and of the attractive coastline. Bartın, the ancient Parthenium, has some fine **wooden houses** from the Ottoman period. It was linked by a Roman road of the Claudian period to Amastris.

From Bartın continue to (66km) Hisarönü. The ancient city of Tieum was sited to the W of the mouth of the Filyos river. Strabo was dismissive of Tieum. Its only claim to fame, according to him, was that it was the birthplace of the eunuch Philetaerus who founded the Attalid dynasty in Pergamum. There are very few remains of the ancient city—a part of the vomitorium and a few rows of seats of the amphitheatre, the ruins of a large temple between the road and the railway line and a section of arched wall.

Zonguldak is at the centre of Turkey's coal-mining area. A clean and tidy place, the only visible signs of industry are on the outskirts of the town.

Accommodation and Information. There are three hotels inspected by the Ministry of Tourism—the two-star *Konak Oteli*, Nizam Cad. No.8, the one-star *Ay Oteli*, Gazipaşa Cad. No.61-67040 and the one-star *Otel 67*, Fevzipaşa Cad. No.1-67020. The **Tourist Information Office** is in the Hükümet Konağı, 5 Kat (5th Floor).

The road from Zonguldak follows a twisting, winding course as far as (45km) Neyran. Here it divides. By the coastal road it is 17km to Ereğli; the inland route is 12km longer. **Ereğli**, the ancient Heracleia Pontica, is an industrial town which has preserved few monuments from the past. It has the largest steel works in the Middle East.

Accommodation. One-star *Etaş Oteli*, Yurt Cad. No. 14, is on the Ministry's list.

History. Greeks from Megara and Tanagra in Boeotia founded Heracleia near Acherousias Point, the modern Baba Burnu, in the 6C BC. Soon the city became one of the most important Hellenic commercial and cultural centres on the Black Sea coast. Early legends associate it with the descent of Hercules into Hades. Acherousias is derived from Acheron, the river of the dead, and the ancients gave this name to the river which flows into the sea near Heracleia.

On the voyage to Colchis with the Argonauts Hercules was delayed at Gemlik by a fruitless search for his page and lover, Hylas. Jason and the Argonauts sailed away without Hercules and he followed them on foot. At Heracleia he descended into Hades where, after many adventures, he subdued Cerberus, the triple-headed, monstrous dog which guarded the dead. From the Underworld he brought back with him Acherois, white poplar bark, the only wood allowed in sacrifices to Olympian Zeus.

Xenophon (d. 355 BC) was well received by the people of Heracleia.They sent him gifts of barley meal, wine, oxen and sheep. He was shown the place on the Acherusian peninsula where Hercules descended into Hades.

Heracleia was ruled by a tyrant named Clearchus c 364–353 BC. Credited with liberating the serfs and erecting the first public library, he was murdered. The dynasty, which he founded, remained in power until 288 BC. His son Dionysios ruled over a group of cities that included Sesamos and Tieum. He was married to Amastris, the founder and ruler of Amastris.

Heracleia was an ally of Mithridates Eupator (c 120–63 BC) and came under his rule. It was razed to the ground by Cotta during the Third Mithridatic War. Strabo describes it as a city with good harbours. It established the colonies of Chersonesus and Calliata. A Roman colony established here was massacred by Adiatorix, the son of the tetrarch of the Galatians, before the Battle of Actium. Pliny the Younger received an inheritance to erect public buildings or establish games in honour of Trajan.

Heracleides Ponticus (c 390–310 BC) was born in Heracleia. He studied with Plato at the Academy in Athens, but later joined the school of Aristotle. His writings on mathematics, literary criticism, ethics, music, and physics were famed for their elegant style. All have been lost. Anticipating Copernicus, he taught that the earth revolved and the stars remained still and that at least some of the planets orbited the sun. Described as fat, he was wealthy and had a penchant for soft apparel.

Dionysius of Heracleia (c 330–250 BC) was a Stoic philosopher. He was a friend of Zeno of Citium in Cyprus, the founder of Stoicism, and of the poet Aratus of Soli in Cilicia. Dionysius abandoned Stoicism when he discovered that he could not support the pain caused by an eye disease. He went to the other extreme and became a hedonist. According to late sources he indulged in carnal pleasure in public. When he reached the age of 80, he deliberately starved himself to death.

The Byzantines built the citadel. In 1360 the town was taken by the Turks and was used by the Genoese as a trading post. Later it was incorporated in the Ottoman Empire. During the exchange of populations in 1922, its Greek inhabitants left.

Ereğli has few reminders of its ancient past. Much of the ancient stonework was taken in 1452 to build the fortress of Rumeli Hisarı in İstanbul. Occasionally fragments of ancient buildings are dug up and some houses in the old part of the town have re-used material in their walls. The **cave of Hercules** on the NE side of the town may be visited. The **castle** and far end of Baba Burnu are in a military area and are closed to the public.

From Ereğli westward there is a succession of sandy beaches which are largely patronised by people from İstanbul escaping from the city for the day or the weekend. At (13km) Alaplı, turn S over the mountains to (c 92km) Bolu and continue the journey to İstanbul by Route 63.

62

Sinop to Safranbolu

Total distance (excluding deviations) 251km. Sinop—60km Boyabat—(26km Durağan)—32km Hanönü—27km Taşköprü—(c 8km Kalekapı)—40km Kastamonu—43km Araç—49km Safranbolu.

Leave Sinop by Road 010 signposted Samsun and at a crossroads c 26km from the town take the right-hand fork to Boyabat amd Kastamonu. Near the coast the scenery is very English in character with neat well-tended fields, clumps of broom and coppices of beech and oak. Only the sight of an occasional olive tree indicates that you are far from England.

Soon the road begins to climb steadily through magnificent, tree-clothed hills that hint at the splendid scenery ahead. At 1370m labouring vehicles pause momentarily at Dranoz Geç. The descent on the other side of this pass is dramatic. The road was gouged out of the side of a mountain that has been pared and shaped by the elements. You skid around sharp bends on the friable surface and come perilously close to unfenced verges that drop away into deep ravines. Tiny hamlets of ancient lath and plaster houses appear without warning. Old women avert their gaze and children wave shyly from the shelter of doorways. On overcast days the road enters the cloud base and you travel through a clammy, eerie world, where only the noise of your vehicle breaks the silence.

At a solitary house by the roadside a group of mountain women have been waiting patiently for the bus and there is a brief pause while, bent under their heavy bundles, they clamber aboard. A young boy, who carries an ancient gun brigand-fashion across his back, remains behind. His deep blue eyes, under a shaven head, fix the bus and its passengers with a frank, open gaze. He is his own man in his own country.

The descent to Boyabat is gradual. An arid stretch of country, which has suffered much from erosion, gives place to a large plain where an attempt is being made to repair the neglect of centuries. The new forest, dedicated to Atatürk, is full of sturdy pine trees.

The country town of **Boyabat** is overlooked by a **Byzantine fortress** which is perched precariously on a rocky spur above a deep ravine. On market day the town bustles with life. Colourful stalls full of fine fruit and vegetables do steady business.

If you have time, visit some of the monumental tombs near Boyabat. **Ambarkayası**, c 5km to the E of Durağan and near the Gökırmak river, is cut from the rock face on a bare hillside. It has three columns, but no reliefs. Farther E is **Terelek Kaya** which has three columns and a number of reliefs. This is at the foot of the mountains, not far from the Kızılırmak River. Take a guide or ask for directions.

To the N of the village of Salar Köy, c 13km from Boyabat on the way to Kastamonu, is the columned, **rock-cut tomb** known locally as **Direklikaya**. This is located on the right-hand side of the road, high above the plain. Believed to date from 7C or 6C BC, it has **reliefs** of kneeling animals and on the pediment a hero, presumably the person buried here, is shown fighting a lion.

The road from Boyabat to Taşköprü via Hanönü crosses a rather uninteresting plateau which is bounded on the N by the serrated peaks of the Küre Dağları. The town of **Taşköprü**, the Stone Bridge, gets its name from the five-arched, 150m **long bridge** over the Gökırmak. It occupies the site of Roman Pompeiopolis, whose eponymous founder established a city here after he had defeated Mithridates Eupator in the Third Mithradatic War.

According to Strabo, there were some mines with a very bad reputation near Pompeiopolis. Their owners used slaves, usually condemned criminals, to recover the realgar ore. This disulphide of arsenic gives off deadly fumes and as a result the miners suffered a painful, if swift, death. The mines were unprofitable, Strabo concludes, as there were only about 200 workers and their numbers were constantly depleted by disease and the high mortality rate.

Nothing remains of the city founded by Pompey. Its acropolis was on the hill now called Zimbilli Tepe. The principal public and religious buildings and the houses of the wealthy crowded the summit and the slopes. From time to time architectural fragments are dug up and a floor mosaic was found in the town. This is now in the museum at Kastamonu. During the Byzantine period the city had its own diocesan bishop and for a short period it was an archepiscopal see.

About 20km to the W of Taşköprü on the road to Kastamonu a turning on the right leads to (c 8km) **Kalekapı**. This 7C BC rock-cut tomb has two columns and its façade is decorated with 4C reliefs of bulls, eagles and lions. Nearby, there is another tomb which is also ornamented with lion reliefs. It has no columns.

The town of **Kastamonu**, on the Gökırmak river, is believed to derive its name from Castra Comneni, the fortress of the Comneni. This patrician family from Thrace, which gave five emperors to Byzantium, owned extensive estates around Kastamonu in the 12C.

The town has no hotel on the Ministry of Tourism's list. The **Tourist Information Office** is at Cumhuriyet Cad. 22–23.

History. The site may have been occupied as early as the 14C BC. Rock tombs extant are believed to date from c 700 BC. It was an episcopal see during the Byzantine period. In the 11C the town was captured by the Selçuks. They were displaced by the Danishmendids. The Byzantines wrested Kastamonu from them at the beginning of the 12C and held it for almost a hundred years. Then came the Isfendiyaroğlu who took it with the connivance of the Mongols. Süleyman, the second ruler of the dynasty, captured almost all of Paphlagonia. Beyazit wrested the city from the İsfendiyaroğlu in 1392–93 and in turn the Ottomans were ousted in 1402 by Tamerlane. He razed Kastamonu to the ground. Rebuilt, the city came once more under the rule of the İsfendiyaroğlu. They held it until 1459, when they were replaced by the Ottomans.

During the 16C and 17C Kastamonu was one of many Anatolian towns from which large numbers of Christian youths were taken under the *devişirme* system for service in the Janissary corps or in the Ottoman administration.

The rock tombs carved from the Şehinşah Kayası near the Ismail Bey Camii and at the Endüstri Meslek Lisesi date from c 700 BC. The **castle** is a Byzantine construction on earlier foundations. Repaired by the Ottomans, it was badly damaged by an earthquake in 1943.

Kastamonu is rich in Islamic buildings. The **Atabey Camii** was part of a *külliye* which has disappeared. Built at the behest of Çobanoğlu Atabey c 1273, it is the town's oldest mosque. The founder is buried in the precincts. The **Yilanlı Darüşşafakası**—its name means the Snake Orphanage—was built c 1271. A fine Selçuk-style entrance leads to a small mosque which is still in use. There are several *türbe* in rooms on the ground floor.

The **İsmail Bey Camii** was built during the last days of İsfendiyaroğlu rule. It houses the founder's tomb and has a kitchen which dispenses food to the poor. Note the fine portal.

The **Karanlık Bedesten** is famed for its ropemaking. The **Yaküub Ağa Külliyesi** with its mosque, school and kitchen was built in 1547. The recently restored Selçuk **Hamam of Cemaleddin Firkenşah** dates from c 1262, and the **Ibni Neccar Camii** of 1353 has exquisite wood carving.

The exhibits in Kastamonu's **museum** are divided into five main sections. In the entrance hall and corridor there is a collection of weapons. These include 17C flintlock guns and pistols, bows, arrows, swords, pikes and shields. Atatürk memorabilia in the room on the right commemorate his visit to the town in 1925. Another room on the right has tools, lamps, statuettes, glass and ceramics from the Prehistoric Age and the Hellenistic, Roman and Byzantine periods. Note the **statues** of a satyr, **Eros**, **Artemis** and **Nike**. In the room at the end of the corridor there are Roman sarcophagi, mosaics, stelae, inscriptions and small architectural fragments.

The first floor is devoted to ethnography. Clothing, leather and metal artefacts, household utensils, embroidery and objects from tekkes are displayed here. In the library, which is not usually open to the public, there are manuscripts, inscriptions, archive material and a coin collection.

In the garden funerary inscriptions, large architectural fragments, statues of lions and bulls from the Roman period, Ottoman grave stones and storage jars are ranged among the trees and flowering shrubs.

The road from Kastamonu to Safranbolu pursues a winding course as far as (43km) Araç. For the remainder of the journey it never strays very far from the Araç Çayı. Travellers using public transport, may have to go to Karabük first and take a taxi from there to (5km) Safranbolu.

Safranbolu is built around a sinkhole which has been emptied of its mineral contents. It is visited mainly because of the many fine 19C provincial style houses in the old quarter. These are being restored with loving care by craftsmen and students working under the supervision of specialists from Zonguldak University. In time the town will be an open-air museum of this kind of architecture. Safranbolu's name is derived from a former industry, the production of saffron from the stigmas of the Autumnal Crocus. This was used for colouring and flavouring confectionery and liquors. The town's hazel-nut sweetmeats are delicious and deservedly famous.

Information. For an interesting experience stay at an old Turkish house, the *Havuzlu Konak*, Hacı Halil Mah., 1867700. This has been carefully restored and refurbished by the Turkish Touring and Automobile Association. It offers very comfortable accommodation in 35 rooms which are furnished in traditional style. An unusual feature is the huge tank full of water which takes up most of the space in the salon. In the evening the gentle trickle from the ornamental lions' heads into the pool, the flickering flames of wax candles reflected on its dark surface and the soft, half-heard cadences of distant music conjure up 'dreams that wave before the half-shut eye'. The Havuzlu Konak has a good restaurant.

The Uz Oteli, Misaki Milli Mah., Arpa Hacı Sok. 67700 has been given two stars by the Ministry of Tourism. Safranbolu's **Tourist Information Office** is at Arasta Çarşısı, No. 7.

At one time Safranbolu was composed of two towns. The Greeks lived on one side of the sinkhole, the Turks on the other. Contrary to the commonly held belief that the best houses in Anatolia were constructed by the Greeks and Armenians, the buildings in both parts of Safranbolu are very similar in style and finish. Many prosperous Muslim business men and farmers had their *konaks* here. A typical mansion rests on a stone basement with the rooms on the upper floors reaching out over the narrow lanes of the town or their private gardens.

There are many fine houses in Safranbolu and the best way to see them all is by strolling through the town's cobbled streets. Among the finest are the **Kaymakamlar Evi**, the **Karaosmanların Evi**, the **Paşacıoğlu Evi** and the **Hacıhüseyinlerin Evi**.

Pause for a moment to watch the craftsmen at work in the Arasta, talk to the student restorers of the old houses about their work and make a leisurely stop for refreshments in one of the town's many cafés. Then, for an overall impression of Safranbolu climb the hillock crowned with the burned shell of the Renaissance style Government House. Below you, the huddled red roofs, the white, vine covered walls and the vivid green orchards and gardens of the konaks are spread out in a colourful, confused, yet completely harmonious tapestry.

63

Safranbolu to İstanbul

Total distance (excluding deviations) 358km. Safranbolu—5km Karabük—
81km Gerede—49km Bolu—(35km Abant Gölü)—44km Düzce—(5km
Konuralp)—(30km Akçakoca)—8km Cumaova—(4km Adapazarı)—76km
İzmit—95km İstanbul.

It is a short journey from tranquil Safranbolu to the bustle of industrial
Karabük, an important production centre of iron and steel. Although
Karabük's great mills are all too visible, they do not overwhelm the town,
which is saved by its pleasant setting in the valley of the Soğanlı Çayı.

This route keeps close to the river valley as far as Eskipazar. Passing
through neat villages and near great logging camps, it joins the busy E–W
road, which links İstanbul with Samsun and the Black Sea coast, about
11km beyond Eskipazar. Here it turns right and continues for c 33km in a
westerly direction to Gerede. Shortly after Gerede it begins a steady climb
to the **Fakılar Geç.** (1050m), then makes a precipitous descent to Bolu.

The plateau on the E side of the Fakılar pass is a popular halt for
long-distance buses. There are several restaurants serving hot meals and
a number of well stocked shops. As this is a heavily forested area all kinds
of wood products, from garden furniture to book-ends, are sold. On a fine
day the view from the top of the pass is spectacular.

The road down the W side of the pass is lined with restaurants which
promise the traveller home cooked meals. Chefs from the **Bolu** area have
a high reputation in Turkey, so you are unlikely to be disappointed if you
stop and sample the fare.

Accommodation and Information. Bolu is the centre for activity holidays in the
surrounding mountains and as a result has several good hotels. These include the *Bolu
Termal Oteli*, Karacasu Köyü and the *Koru Oteli*, Ömerler Köyü, Bakırlı Mev., both
with three stars; the two-star *Yurdaer Oteli*, Belediye Meydanı; the one-star *Menekşe
Oteli*, İzzet Baysal Cad., 14200; and two Grade 2 motels, the *Çizmeci Moteli*, Kılıçarslan
Köyü Mevkii and the *Emniyet Moteli*, Aynlık Çeşmesi Mevkii. The *Koru Oteli*, in the
mountains outside Bolu, and the *Bolu Termal Oteli* are recommended. Bolu's **Tourist
Information Office** is at Eski İstanbul Cad., No. 2.

History. The provincial capital **Bolu** was known at different times in antiquity as
Bithynium, Claudiopolis, Hadriana and Honorias. According to Pausanias the first
foundation was made by Arcadians from Mantinea. However, traces of Hittite and
Phrygian settlements have been found which suggest a much earlier occupation of the
site. It was re-established by Prusias I (228–185 BC) as Bithynium. Strabo confined his
comments on Bithynium to country matters. It controlled, he wrote, the area around
Salon, a place where there was excellent pasturage for cattle and which produced,
what was presumably a well-known delicacy, Salonian cheese. A little later, Pliny the
Younger, Trajan's special commissioner in Bithynia, was worried about a possible
abuse of the emperor's generosity at Claudiopolis, as the place was then called, and
asked for the emperor's advice.

The handsome youth Antinous, first the constant companion and then the lover of
Hadrian, came from Bithynium. Not surprisingly, the emperor favoured the city,
causing many fine public buildings to be erected here. Envious courtiers told the youth
that Hadrian's life would be forfeit unless someone close to him died on his behalf.
Believing this lie, Antinous drowned himself in the Nile during a visit to Egypt with
the emperor in AD 130. Hadrian, overcome with grief, had the boy deified and
established temples devoted to his cult in all the major cities of the empire. He also

founded the city of Antinoopolis in his honour. One of the finest of the many statues of Antinous extant is in the Walker Art Gallery, Liverpool. Another may be seen in the Museo Archaeologico, Naples.

The town's modern name is a corruption of the Greek word Πόλις (Polis), a city.

There are no visible remains of the ancient cities which once stood here. Architectural fragments are recovered occasionally during building works.

Among Bolu's many Islamic monuments the most important is the **Ulu Cami** which was built during the reign of Beyazit I Yıldırım (1389–1403). Other buildings of interest are the **Orta Hamam**, the **Tabaklar Hamam** and the **Şemsi Paşa Camii**.

Just 35km from Bolu is **Abant Gölü**. This beautiful lake, c 1450m above sea level, is popular with visitors from İstanbul and Ankara. They come here in search of fresh air and good food. The lake's trout-filled waters attract many fishermen and in villages on the littoral locally-made, colourful basketwork is sold.

From Bolu continue westward to (44km) Düzce. If you have time, visit the site of ancient **Prusias ad Hypium**, the modern **Üskübü** and **Akçakoca**, which is believed to occupy the site of ancient Dia.

Üskübü, sometimes known as Konuralp after Osman Gazi's general who conquered this area, is 7km to the N of Düzce on the road to the Black Sea coast. The village covers part of the site of Prusias ad Hypium (Hypius is the modern river Melen) established by Prusias I of Bithynia (228–185 BC), the friend and ally of Hannibal. An earlier settlement here was called Kieros.

There are the substantial remains of the city's **Byzantine walls**. Note the way material from earlier structures has been re-used in them. The **gate** on the southern section is known as the Atkapı, because, until vandals destroyed it, it bore the relief of a horse. The skene of the 1C AD theatre has been badly damaged by a pathway cut through it. Sections of the cavea remain intact. About 200m from the theatre are the ruins of a **Roman aqueduct**. Beside the modern bridge are the remains of a 1C AD three-arch **Roman bridge**.

Some idea of the wealth Prusias ad Hypium may be gained from statues found here. Now in the İstanbul Archaeological Museum are a fine 4C AD statue of Tyche, the goddess of fortune, a statue of Sophocles from the Hellenistic period, and a statue of a seated woman, a 2C AD copy of a Hellenistic original.

There is a small museum where some of the artefacts discovered on the site are displayed.

From Üskübü continue to (31km) Akçakoca, a small seaside resort blessed with a beach of rather gritty sand. About 2km from the town there are the ruins of a Genoese castle.

Return to Düzce and continue westward by way of Cumaova in the direction of İzmit. After c 46km a turning on the right leads to (c 4km) **Adapazarı**, sometimes called **Sakarya**. The **Byzantine bridge** over the former course of the Sakarya (ancient Sangarios) river was built in AD 560 during the reign of the emperor Justinian I. Its 12 great arches now cross a dry river bed. The course of the Sakarya has changed. It now flows c 3km to the E of the bridge. There is nothing to detain you in Adapazarı, a modern industrial town lacking both distinction and interest.

From Justinian's bridge return to the main road and continue towards İzmit. Just S of the highway is **Sapanca Gölü**. In antiquity plans were made several times to connect this lake with the Gulf of Nicomedia, the modern İzmit Körfezi, so as to facilitate the movement of goods from the interior of Bithynia to the sea and vice versa. Pliny the

Younger recommended such a scheme to Trajan in the 2C AD. He drew the emperor's attention to the existence of a canal constructed by one of the Bithynian kings which, he surmised, might have been an earlier attempt to make this link. He asked Trajan for the services of a competent architect or engineer. The problem seems to have been the height of the lake above sea level. Pliny estimated this to be c 36.5m. Trajan sent him an expert and suggested that he apply to Calpurnius Macer, the legate of Lower Moesia, for an engineer. Presumably they reported that the construction and engineering difficulties were too great, as nothing was done.

The proposal was revived in an even more ambitious form in the 6C AD towards the end of the reign of Justinian. This suggested the diversion of the course of the Sangarios river so that it no longer flowed into the Black Sea but was directed to the lake and thence by the canal to the Gulf of Nicomedia. Nothing came of this scheme either, or of a later one made to Süleyman I in the 16C.

For a description of İzmit (Kocaeli) and the places between it and İstanbul, see Route 1.

Women making bread near Adıyaman

INDEX

The index lists all of the places described in the book, highlighting the most important cities, towns and sites in bold. Both ancient and modern place names are included. Significant historical figures, and other relevant subjects are also indexed.

ATLAS

Key to Route Maps

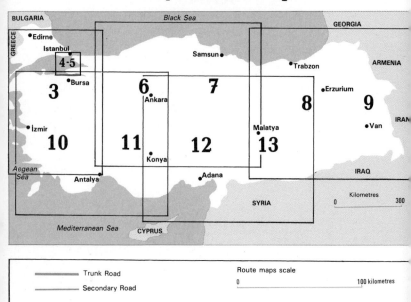

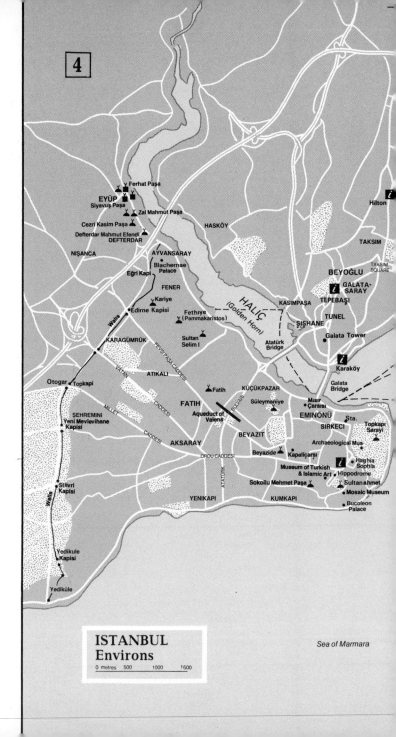

4

Ferhat Paşa
EYÜP
Siyavuş Paşa
Zal Mahmut Paşa
Cezri Kasim Paşa
Defterdar Mahmut Efendi
DEFTERDAR

HASKÖY

Hilton

TAKSIM

NIŞANCA

AYVANSARAY
Blachernae
Palace

BEYOĞLU

TAKSIM
SQUARE

Eğri Kapi

FENER

GALATA-
SARAY
TEPEBAŞI

Kariye

KASIMPAŞA

ŞIŞHANE

TUNEL

Edirne Kapisi

Fethiye
(Pammakaristos)

HALIÇ
(Golden Horn)

Galata Tower

Walls

KARAGÜMRÜK

Sultan
Selim I

Atatürk
Bridge

Karaköy

FEVSIPAŞA CADDESI

ATIKALI

VATAN

Galata
Bridge

Fatih

KÜÇÜKPAZAR

Misir
Çarşisi

Otogar Topkapi

CADDESI

FATIH

Süleymaniye

EMINÖNÜ

Sta.

ŞEHREMINI
Yeni Mevlevihane
Kapisi

MILLET

Aqueduct of
Valens

BULVAR

BEYAZIT

SIRKECI

Topkapi
Sarayi

Walls

CADDESI

AKSARAY

Beyazide

Kapaliçarşi

Archaeological Mus

ORDU CADDESI

ATATÜRK

Museum of Turkish
& Islamic Art

Haghia
Sophia
Hippodrome

Silivri
Kapisi

Sokollu Mehmet Paşa

Sultanahmet

YENIKAPI

KUMKAPI

Mosaic Museum

Bucoleon
Palace

Yedikule
Kapisi

Walls

Yediküle

ISTANBUL
Environs

0 metres   500   1000   1500

Sea of Marmara

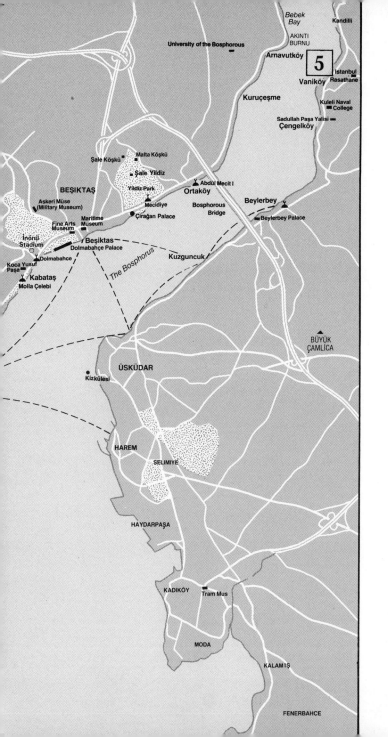

Bebek
Bay

Kandilli

AKINTI
BURNU

University of the Bosphorous

Arnavutköy

5

İstanbul
Rasathane

Vaniköy

Kuruçeşme

Kuleli Naval
College

Sadullah Paşa Yalisi

Çengelköy

Şale Köşkü

Malta Köşkü

Şale Yildiz

BEŞİKTAŞ

Yıldız Park

Askeri Müse
(Military Museum)

Abdül Mecit I

Ortaköy

Beylerbey

Fine Arts
Museum

Mecidiye

Maritime
Museum

Çirağan Palace

Bosphorous
Bridge

Beylerbey Palace

İnönü
Stadium

Beşiktas

Dolmabahçe Palace

Dolmabahçe

Koca Yusuf
Paşa

The Bosphorus

Kuzguncuk

Kabataş

Molla Çelebi

BÜYÜK
ÇAMLİCA

ÜSKÜDAR

Kizkülesi

HAREM

SELIMIYE

HAYDARPAŞA

KADIKÖY

Tram Mus

MODA

KALAMIŞ

FENERBAHCE

6

Black Sea

Abana
İnebolu
Cide
Küre
Kurucasile
Amasra
BARTIN
Azdavay
Seydiler
Hisarönü
Daday
ZONGULDAK
KASTAMONU
Safranbolu
Araç
İhsangazi
Ereğli • HEREKLEA
Devrek
Yenice
Karabük
P
A
P
H
L
Alaplı
Eskipazar
İlgaz
Tosya
Karasu
Akçakoca
Yığılca
Mengen
Çerkeş
Atkaracalar
Korgun
Söğütlü
Cumaova
Düzce
BOLU
Yeniçağa
Gerede
ÇANKIRI
SAKARYA
(Adapazarı)
Hendek
Fakılar Geçidi
1050
Akyazı
Çamlıdere
Kızılcahamam
Şabanözü
Geyve
Göynük
Mudurnu
Seben
Kıbrıscık
Güdül
Çubuk
Kalecik
aneli
Nallıhan
Beypazarı
HYNIA
Kazan
Elmadağ
Mihalgazi
ANKARA
KIRIKKAL
öğüt
Mihalıççık
üyük
Alpu
G
İnönü
ESKİŞEHİR
Beylikova
GORDION
İkizce
Karakeçili
Polatlı
Bala
Kaman
Mahmudiye
Günyüzü
Haymana
Seyitgazi
Sivrihisar
GAVURKALESİ
1829
Çifteler
OF
PESSINUS
Kulu
Evre
Şerefli-
İhsaniye
Emirdağ
Koçhisa
ntaş
MİDASSEHRİ
Tuz Gölü
A
AYAZIN
Yunak
Cihanbeyli
AFYON
Bolvadin
Akşehir
Gölü
Eskil
Sultanhan
Çay
Tuzlukçu
Sultandağı
Altınekin
Akşehir
Sarayönü
Obruk
Yalvaç
İlgın
Kadınhanı
Eğirdir
Gölü
Gelendost
LYCAONIA
Dinar
Senirkent
Uluborlu
PİSİDİA
11
KONYA
azkırı
Keçiberlu
Eğirdir
Aksu
Kızılören
Karapınar
ISPARTA
Beyşehir
Gölü

Black Sea

SINOP

Ayvancik
Catalzeytin
Erfelek
Gerze
Hanönü
Yakakent
Alaçam
Bafra
Taşköprü
Boyabat
Durağan
SAMSUN
Simenlik Gölü
Terme
Ünye
Perşembe
Saraydüzü
Kavak
Çarşamba
Ayvacık
Kumru
Gürgentepe
Aybastı
OR
Kargı
Vezirköprü
Havza
*Karadağ Geçidi 940
Lâdik
Taşova
Erbaa
Niksar
Mesudiye
Ke
Osmancık
Merzifon
Suluova
Gümüşhacıköy
İskilip
Mecitözü
AMASYA
COMANA PONTICA
Resadiye
Uğurludağ
ÇORUM
Turhal
MAHBERİ HATUN
TOKAT
Su
• ALACAHÜYÜK
Ortaköy
Pazar
Zile
*Kızılırıs Geçidi 1150
Sungurlu
Alaca
MASAT HÜYÜK
Çekerek
Sulusaray
SIFTLIK HANI
Artova
*Camlibel Geçidi 1646
Zara
Boğazkale
• YAZILIKAYA
Kadişehri
Hafik
Delice
CINCINLI SULTAN HAN
Yıldızeli
SİVAS
YOZGAT
Sorgun
Akdağmadeni
TUZLA HAN •
2262
• ALISAR
Ulaş
Yağdonduran Geçidi 1750
Yerköy
Sarıkaya
Akpınar
Çiçekdağı
Şarkışla
Kangal
KIRŞEHİR
Yenifakılı
Çayıralan
Özvatan
Bogazliyan
Sarıoğlan
Akkışla
Mucur
• KESİKKÖPRÜ HANI
Hacıbektaş
Bünyan
Pınarbaşı
Gürün
Dar
Ortaköy
Gülşehir
Avanos
KAYSERİ
NEVŞEHİR
Ürgüp
See separate map
Sarız
AKSARAY
IHLARA (PERISTREMA)
Acıgöl
Derinkuyu
Yeşilhisar
Develi
Tomarza
Elbistan
Nu
Güzelyurt
Gölcük
Bakırdağı
3253
Göksun
Gö
NİĞDE
Saimbeyli
12
Bor
• 2689
Çamardı
Feke
TYANA
Kermerhisar
MOUNTAINS
Ardırın
KAHRAMAN MARAŞ
Pazarcı
CILICIA

8

Black Sea

GEO

Sarp
Hopa
Borçka
Arhavi
Fındıklı
ARTVİN
Pazar
Ardeşen
Çayeli
Çamlıhemsin
Sarıgöl
RİZE
Kalkandere
Yusufeli
S
Hayrat
U
Of
Sürmene
Uzundere
TRABZON
Araklı
Görele
Vakfıkebir
Akçaabat
Yomra
Düzköy
Çaykara
Tirebolu
İspir
Pirazziz
GİRESUN
Şalpazarı
Tonya
OU
Keşap
SUMELA
T
Pazaryolu
Tortum
Dereli
Kürtün
N
Zigana Tunnel 2025
Yağmurdere
Dumlu
Torul
Kostandağı Geçidi 2010
Pasinler
Eğribel Geçidi 2200
O
GÜMÜŞHANE
Vaudağı Geçidi 1875
Aydıntepe
BAYBURT
P
Şebinkarahisar
Kösedağı Geçidi 1910
Maden
İlıca
ERZURUM
yulhisar
Şiran
Köse
Kop Geçidi 2305
şehri
Gölova
Kelkit
Aşkale
2652
MAMA HATUN TÜRBESİ
Tekman
Kızıldağ Geçidi 2190
Sakaltutan Geçidi 2160
Tercan
Refahiye
ALTINTEPE
Çat
ERZİNCAN
3078
Kemah
Pülümür
Karlıova
Varto
İliç
Ovacık
2305
Solhan
Divriği
Hozat
Buğlan Geçidi 1640
MUŞ
Kemaliye
TUNCELİ
Kurucu Geçidi 1800
BİNGÖL
Musgüreyi
Arapgir
Çemiskezek
Ağın
Pertek
Keban Barajı
ESKİ PALU
Kulp
Kovancılar
Sason
Hekimhan
Keban
ELAZIĞ
Arıcak
Lice
İçme
Hani
Hazro
Çatakköprü
Baskil
Koç Geçidi 1280
Dicle
(MALABAD
Yazıhan
Sivrice
Maden
Silvan
Beşiri
ARSLANTEPE
Kale
Doğanyol
Ergani
Eğil
BATMAN
Akçadağ
MALATYA
Cüngüş
Cermik
DİYARBAKIR
Bismil
Doğanşehir
Sınık
Gerger
Çelikhan
NEMRUT DAĞI
Çınar
Savur
ak
Tut
PİRİN
Kâhta
Siverek
Karacadağ
Mazıdağı
Yeşilli
Ömerli
aşı
ADIYAMAN
1957
MARDİN
Akarsu
Besni
Hilvan
SÜPÜRGÜÇ
See separate map
Kızıltepe
Araban
Bozova
Akziyaret
Viranşehir
zeli
HASANOĞLU
13
HİSAR
RUMKELESİ
ŞANLI URFA
SYRIA
KARAHÜYÜK
BELKIS/ZEUGMA
SULTANTEPE

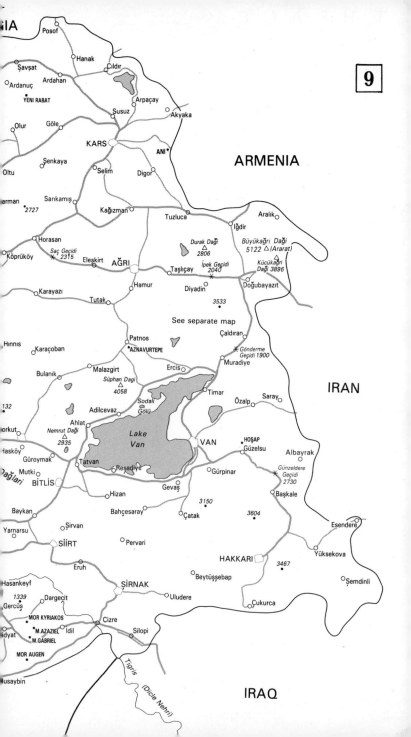

9

GIA

Posof

Hanak

Şavşat

Ardanuç
Ardahan
YENİ RABAT

Çıldır

Arpaçay

Susuz

Akyaka

Olur

Göle

KARS

ANI

ARMENIA

Şenkaya
Oltu

Selim

Digor

arman

Sarıkamış

2727

Kağızman

Tuzluca

Iğdır

Aralık

Horasan

Saç Geçidi
2315

Eleşkirt

AĞRI

Durak Dağı
2806

Taşlıçay

İpek Geçidi
2040

Büyükağrı Dağı
5122 (Ararat)

Küçükağrı
Dağı 3896

Köprüköy

Hamur

Diyadin

Doğubayazıt

Karayazı

Tutak

3533

See separate map

Çaldıran

Hınnıs

Karaçoban

Patnos

AZNAVURTEPE

Erciş

Muradiye

Gönderme
Geçidi 1900

IRAN

Bulanık

Malazgirt
Süphan Dağı
4058

Timar

Özalp

Saray

132

Adilcevaz

Sodalı
Gölü

orkut

Ahlat

Nemrut Dağı
2935

Lake
Van

VAN

HOŞAP
Güzelsu

Albayrak

Günzeldere
Geçidi
2730

Haskö

Güroymak

Mutki

Dağları

BİTLİS

Tatvan

Reşadiye

Gürpinar

Gevaş

Başkale

Baykan

Hizan

Bahçesaray

3150

Çatak

3604

Esendere

Yarnarsu

Şirvan

SİİRT

Pervari

HAKKARİ

3467

Yüksekova

Eruh

Beytüşşebap

Şemdinli

Hasankeyf

1339

Dargeçit

Gercüş

MOR KYRIAKOS

M.AZAZIEL

İdil

ŞIRNAK

Cizre

Uludere

Çukurca

idyat

M.GABRIEL

Silopi

MOR AUGEN

Tigris
(Dicle Nehri)

usaybin

IRAQ